Encyclopedia of
SOCIAL
PROBLEMS

Editorial Board

Encyclopedia of
SOCIAL
PROBLEMS

1

Vincent N. Parrillo

William Paterson University

Editor

Los Angeles • London • New Delhi • Singapore

A SAGE Reference Publication

For information:

SAGE Publications, Inc.
2455 Teller Road
Thousand Oaks, California 91320
E-mail: order@sagepub.com

SAGE Publications Ltd.
1 Oliver's Yard
55 City Road
London EC1Y 1SP
United Kingdom

SAGE Publications India Pvt. Ltd.
B 1/I 1 Mohan Cooperative Industrial Area
Mathura Road, New Delhi 110 044
India

SAGE Publications Asia-Pacific Pte. Ltd.
33 Pekin Street #02-01
Far East Square
Singapore 048763

Printed in the United States of America.

Library of Congress Cataloging-in-Publication Data

Encyclopedia of social problems/Vincent N. Parrillo, editor.
    p. cm.
"A SAGE Reference Publication."
Includes bibliographical references and index.
ISBN 978-1-4129-4165-5 (cloth)
  1. Social problems—Encyclopedias. I. Parrillo, Vincent N.

HN28.E55 2008
361.103—dc22   2008001214

This book is printed on acid-free paper.

08   09   10   11   12   10 9 8 7 6 5 4 3 2 1

Publisher:	Rolf A. Janke
Acquisitions Editor:	Benjamin Penner
Developmental Editor:	Yvette Pollastrini
Reference Systems Manager:	Leticia Gutierrez
Production Editor:	Tracy Buyan
Copy Editors:	Colleen Brennan, Pam Suwinsky
Typesetter:	C&M Digitals (P) Ltd.
Proofreaders:	Andrea Martin, Scott Oney
Indexer:	Sheila Bodell
Cover Designer:	Michelle Kenny
Marketing Manager:	Amberlyn Erzinger

Contents

List of Entries

Reader's Guide

The Reader's Guide can assist readers in locating entries on related topics. It classifies entries into 16 general topical categories: Aging and the Life Course; Community, Culture, and Change; Crime and Deviance; Economics and Work; Education; Family; Gender Inequality and Sexual Orientation; Health; Housing and Urbanization; Politics, Power, and War; Population and Environment; Poverty and Social Class; Race and Ethnic Relations; Social Movements; Social Theory; and Substance Abuse. Entries may be listed under more than one topic.

Aging and the Life Course

Activity Theory
Ageism
Anomie
Baby Boomers
Dependency Ratio
Disengagement Theory
Elderly Socioeconomic Status
Life Course
Population, Graying of
Pensions and Social Security
Retirement
Sandwich Generation
Stereotyping
Stratification, Age
Stressors
Suicide
Widowhood

Community, Culture, and Change

Communitarianism
Community
Cults
Cultural Capital
Cultural Diffusion
Cultural Imperialism

Cultural Lag
Cultural Relativism
Cultural Values
Culture of Dependency
Culture of Poverty
Culture Shock
Culture Wars
Cyberspace
Digital Divide
Faith-Based Social Initiatives
Focus Groups
Fundamentalism
Gambling
Gangsta Rap
Institutional Ethnography
Islam and Modernity
Latent Functions
Manifest Functions
Mass Media
Media
Norms
Obscenity
Prestige
Privacy
Role Conflict
Role Strain
Secularization
Social Change
Social Conflict

Social Disorganization
Social Institutions
Social Mobility
Social Networks
Subcultures
Values

Crime and Deviance

Abuse, Child Sexual
Abuse, Elderly
Abuse, Intimate Partner
Abuse, Sibling
Addiction
Alcoholism
Arson
Assault
Binge Drinking
Bullying
Capital Punishment
Child Abduction
Community Corrections
Community Crime Control
Community Service
Corporate Crime
Corruption
Crime
Crime, Fear of
Crime Rates

Economics and Work

About the Editor

 **Vincent N. Parrillo**, born and raised in Paterson, New Jersey, experienced multiculturalism early as the son of a second-generation Italian American father and Irish/German American mother. He grew up in an ethnically diverse neighborhood, developing friendships and teenage romances with second- and third-generation Dutch, German, Italian, and Polish Americans. As he grew older, he developed other friendships that frequently crossed racial and religious lines.

Dr. Parrillo came to the field of sociology after first completing a bachelor's degree in business management and a master's degree in English. After teaching high school English and then serving as a college administrator, he took his first sociology course when he began doctoral studies at Rutgers University. Inspired by a discipline that scientifically investigates social issues, he changed his major and completed his degree in sociology.

Leaving his administrative post but staying at William Paterson University, Dr. Parrillo has since taught sociology for more than 30 years. He has lectured throughout the United States, Canada, and Europe and has regularly conducted diversity leadership programs for the military and large corporations. His keynote address at a 2001 bilingual educators' conference was published in *Vital Speeches of the Day*, which normally contains only speeches by national political leaders and heads of corporations and organizations.

An internationally renowned expert on immigration and multiculturalism, Dr. Parrillo was a Fulbright Scholar in the Czech Republic and Scholar-in-Residence at the University of Pisa. He was the keynote speaker at international conferences in Belgium, Canada, Denmark, Germany, Italy, Poland, and Sweden. He is also a Fulbright Senior Specialist. Through the U.S. Information Agency, he met with government leaders, nongovernment agency leaders, law enforcement officials, and educators in more than a dozen countries as a consultant on immigration policy, hate crimes, and multicultural education. He has done on-air interviews with Radio Free Europe and Voice of America, appeared on national Canadian television, and been interviewed by numerous Canadian and European reporters.

Dr. Parrillo's ventures into U.S. media include writing, narrating, and producing two award-winning PBS documentaries, *Ellis Island: Gateway to America* and *Smokestacks and Steeples: A Portrait of Paterson*. Contacted by reporters across the nation for interviews on race and ethnic relations, he has been quoted in dozens of newspapers, including the *Chicago Sun-Times, Cincinnati Inquirer, Houston Chronicle, Hartford Courant, Omaha World-Herald, Orlando Sentinel,* and *Virginian Pilot*. He has also appeared on numerous U.S. radio and television programs.

Dr. Parrillo is also the author of *Strangers to These Shores* (9th ed., 2009), *Diversity in America* (3rd ed., 2008), *Understanding Race and Ethnic Relations* (3rd ed., 2008), *Contemporary Social Problems* (6th ed., 2005), *Cities and Urban Life* (4th ed. [with John Macionis], 2007), and *Rethinking Today's Minorities* (1991). His articles and book reviews have appeared in such journals as the *Social Science Journal, Sociological Forum, Social Forces, Journal of Comparative Family Studies, Journal of American Ethnic History, Encyclopedia of American Immigration*, and the *Encyclopedia of Sociology*. Several of his books and articles have been translated into other languages, including Chinese, Czech, Danish, German, Italian, Japanese, Polish, Romanian, and Swedish.

An active participant in various capacities throughout the years in the American Sociological Association (ASA) and Eastern Sociological Society (ESS), Dr. Parrillo was the ESS Robin M. Williams, Jr. Distinguished Lecturer for 2005–06 and is ESS vice president for 2008–09. He has been listed in *Who's Who in International Education, Outstanding Educators of America, American Men and Women of Science*, and *Who's Who in the East*. In 2004, he received the Award for Excellence in Scholarship from William Paterson University.

About the Associate Editors

Margaret L. Andersen is the Edward F. and Elizabeth Goodman Rosenberg Professor of Sociology at the University of Delaware, where she also holds joint appointments in women's studies and black American studies. She is the author of *On Land and on Sea: A Century of Women in the Rosenfeld Collection*; *Thinking About Women: Sociological Perspectives on Sex and Gender*; *Race, Class and Gender* (with Patricia Hill Collins); *Race and Ethnicity in the United States: The Changing Landscape* (with Elizabeth Higginbotham); *Sociology: Understanding a Diverse Society* (with Howard F. Taylor); and *Sociology: The Essentials* (with Howard Taylor). She is the 2008–09 vice president of the American Sociological Association (ASA). In 2006 she received the ASA's Jessie Bernard Award, given annually for a person whose work has expanded the horizons of sociology to include women. She has also received the Sociologists for Women in Society's Feminist Lecturer Award and the 2007–08 Robin M. Williams, Jr. Distinguished Lecturer Award from the Eastern Sociological Society (ESS), of which she is the former president. She has received two teaching awards from the University of Delaware.

Joel Best is professor of sociology and criminal justice at the University of Delaware. He is a past president of the Midwest Sociological Society and the Society for the Study of Social Problems, a former editor of *Social Problems*, and the current editor-in-chief of *Sociology Compass*. Much of his work concerns the sociology of social problems; his recent books include *Random Violence* (1999), *Damned Lies and Statistics* (2001), *Deviance: Career of a Concept* (2004), *More Damned Lies and Statistics* (2004), *Flavor of the Month: Why Smart People Fall for Fads* (2006), and *Social Problems* (2008). He has also edited several collections of original papers on social problems, including *Images of Issues* (2nd ed., 1995) and *How Claims Spread: Cross-National Diffusion of Social Problems* (2001). His current research concerns awards, prizes, and honors in American culture.

William Kornblum conducts research on urban social ecology and community studies. Among his publications are *At Sea in the City: New York from the Water's Edge*; *Blue Collar Community,* a study of the steel mill neighborhoods of South Chicago; *Growing Up Poor* and *Uptown Kids* (written with Terry Williams); and *West 42nd Street: The Bright Lights*, which during the 1980s became a guide to understanding the street life of lower Times Square. He has served as a social scientist for the U.S. Department of the Interior and worked on the development of national parks and environmental reserves in the nation's metropolitan regions. Kornblum received his undergraduate degree in biology from Cornell University (1961) and his PhD in sociology from the University of Chicago (1971). He taught physics and chemistry as a Peace Corps volunteer in Ivory Coast (1962–63) and was on the faculty at the University of Washington before he came to the Graduate Center of the City University of New York in 1973.

Claire M. Renzetti is professor of sociology at the University of Dayton. She is editor of the international, interdisciplinary journal *Violence Against Women*, coeditor of the *Encyclopedia of Interpersonal Violence* and of the Interpersonal Violence book series for Oxford University Press, and editor of the Gender, Crime and Law book series for Northeastern University Press/University Press of New England. She has authored or edited 16 books, including *Women, Men, and Society* and *Violent Betrayal,* as well as numerous book chapters and articles in professional journals. Her current research focuses on the violent victimization experiences of economically marginalized women living in public housing developments. Dr. Renzetti has held elected and appointed positions on the governing bodies of several national professional organizations, including the Society for the Study of Social Problems, the Eastern Sociological Society, and Alpha Kappa Delta, the sociological honors society.

Mary Romero is professor of justice studies and social inquiry at Arizona State University and affiliate research faculty of the North American Center for Transborder Studies. She is the author of *Maid in the U.S.A.* (1992, Tenth Anniversary Edition 2002) and coeditor of *Blackwell Companion to Social Inequalities* (2005), *Latino/a Popular Culture* (2002), *Women's Untold Stories*: *Breaking Silence, Talking Back, Voicing Complexity* (1999), *Challenging Fronteras: Structuring Latina and Latino Lives in the U.S.* (1997), and *Women and Work: Exploring Race, Ethnicity and Class* (1997). Her most recent articles are published in *Contemporary Justice Review, Critical Sociology, Law & Society Review, British Journal of Industrial Relations, Villanova Law Review*, and *Cleveland State Law Review*. She currently serves on the Law and Society Association Board of Trustees (Class of 2008) and the Council of the American Sociological Association.

Contributors

Marina A. Adler
University of Maryland, Baltimore County

Robert Agnew
Emory University

Scott Akins
Oregon State University

Richard Alba
University at Albany, State University of New York

Joseph L. Albini
Wayne State University

Mohsen S. Alizadeh
John Jay College of Criminal Justice

Faye Allard
University of Pennsylvania

Liana L. Allen
William Paterson University

Lynda J. Ames
State University of New York, Plattsburgh

Randall Amster
Prescott College

Margaret L. Andersen
University of Delaware

Robin Andersen
Fordham University

Elijah Anderson
Yale University

Tammy L. Anderson
University of Delaware

Giuliana Campanelli Andreopoulos
William Paterson University

Maboud Ansari
William Paterson University

Victor Argothy
University of Delaware

Elizabeth Mitchell Armstrong
Princeton University

Bruce A. Arrigo
University of North Carolina

Molefi Kete Asante
Temple University

John Asimakopoulos
City University of New York, Bronx

Matthew Christopher Atherton
California State University, San Marcos

Feona Attwood
Sheffield Hallam University

Laura Auf der Heide
University of Arizona

Ronet Bachman
University of Delaware

Sarah Bacon
Florida State University

Chris Baker
Walters State Community College

H. Kent Baker
American University

Nicholas W. Bakken
University of Delaware

James David Ballard
California State University, Northridge

John Barnshaw
University of Delaware

Eli Bartle
California State University, Northridge

Arnab K. Basu
College of William and Mary

M. P. Baumgartner
William Paterson University

Morton Beiser
University of Toronto

Mitch Berbrier
University of Alabama in Huntsville

Ellen Berrey
Northwestern University

Amy L. Best
George Mason University

Joel Best
University of Delaware

Richard Blonna
William Paterson University

Kathleen A. Bogle
LaSalle University

John Bongaarts
Population Council

Elizabeth Borland
College of New Jersey

Wilma Borrelli
The Graduate Center—City University of New York

Elizabeth Heger Boyle
University of Minnesota

Sara F. Bradley
Franklin College

Richard K. Brail
Rutgers University

Jennie E. Brand
University of Michigan

Francesca Bray
University of Edinburgh

Hank J. Brightman
Saint Peter's College

Thomas Brignall III
Fisk University

Ray Bromley
University at Albany, State University of New York

Alyson Brown
Edge Hill

Stephen E. Brown
East Tennessee State University

Michelle J. Budig
University of Massachusetts

Regina M. Bures
University of Florida

Marcos Burgos
Graduate Center, City University of New York

Gregory D. Busse
American University

Christine Byron
University of Manchester

Christine Caffrey
Miami University

Wendy Sellers Campbell
Winthrop University

Gail A. Caputo
Rutgers University

Erynn Masi de Casanova
Graduate Center, City University of New York

Matthew A. Cazessus
University of South Carolina

Karen Cerulo
Rutgers University

Christopher Chase-Dunn
University of California, Riverside

Madhabi Chatterji
Teachers College, Columbia University

Nancy H. Chau
Cornell University

Margaret I. Chelnik
William Paterson University

Katherine K. Chen
William Paterson University

Michael Cherbonneau
University of Missouri–Saint Louis

Steven M. Chermak
Michigan State University

Yen-Sheng Chiang
University of Washington

Felix O. Chima
Prairie View A&M University

Joyce N. Chinen
University of Hawaii–West Oahu

Carol A. Christensen
University of Queensland

Mark Christian
Miami University

Elizabeth Morrow Clark
West Texas A&M University

Roger S. Clark
Rutgers Law School

Rodney D. Coates
Miami University

Sheila D. Collins
William Paterson University

Peter Conrad
Brandeis University

Douglas Harbin Constance
Sam Houston State University

Randol Contreras
Towson University

Celia Cook-Huffman
Juniata College

Jill F. Cooper
University of California, Berkeley

Denise A. Copelton
State University of New York, Brockport

Martha Copp
East Tennessee State University

Bridget M. Costello
King's College

Gerry Cox
University of Wisconsin–La Crosse

Michael J. Coyle
Arizona State University

DeLois "Kijana" Crawford
Rochester Institute of Technology

Michael H. Crespin
University of Georgia

Angela D. Crews
Marshall University

Gordon A. Crews
Marshall University

Martha Crowley
North Carolina State University

Richard Culp
John Jay College of Criminal Justice

Kimberly Cunningham
The Graduate Center—City University of New York

William Curcio
Montclair State University

Harry F. Dahms
University of Tennessee

Alky A. Danikas
Saint Peter's College

Susan R. Dauria
Bloomsburg University

William S. Davidson II
Michigan State University

Joseph E. Davis
University of Virginia

Shannon N. Davis
George Mason University

Mathieu Deflem
University of South Carolina

David A. Deitch
University of California, San Diego

Marc JW de Jong
University of Southern California

William DeJong
Boston University

Richard A. Dello Buono
Society for the Study of Social Problems, Global Division

Rutledge M. Dennis
George Mason University

Nancy A. Denton
University at Albany, State University of New York

Manisha Desai
University of Illinois

Edwin Dickens
Saint Peter's College

Lisa Dilks
University of South Carolina

Rebecca G. Dirks
Northwest Center for Optimal Health

Roz Dixon
University of London, Birkbeck

Ashley Doane
University of Hartford

Mary Dodge
University of Colorado at Denver

Patrick Donnelly
University of Dayton

Christopher Donoghue
Kean University

Ronald G. Downey
Kansas State University

Heather Downs
University of Illinois at Urbana-Champaign

Joanna Dreby
Kent State University

Julia A. Rivera Drew
Brown University

Rhonda E. Dugan
California State University, Bakersfield

John P. J. Dussich
California State University, Fresno

Robert F. Duvall
National Council on Economic Education

Franck Düvell
University of Oxford

Bob Edwards
East Carolina University

Christine A. Eith
Towson University

Sharon Elise
California State University, San Marcos

H. Mark Ellis
William Paterson University

Leslie R. S. Elrod
University of Cincinnati

Felix Elwert
University of Wisconsin–Madison

Amon Emeka
University of Southern California

Rodney Engen
North Carolina State University

Richard N. Engstrom
Georgia State University

M. David Ermann
University of Delaware

Dula J. Espinosa
University of Houston at Clear Lake

Lorraine Evans
Bradley University

Louwanda Evans
Texas A&M University

Hugh Everman
Morehead State University

Jamie J. Fader
University of Pennsylvania

Christian Faltis
Arizona State University

Joe R. Feagin
Texas A&M University

Barbara Feldman
Montclair State University

Paula B. Fernández
William Paterson University

Alexandra Fidyk
National Louis University

Pierre Filion
University of Waterloo

Amy C. Finnegan
Boston College

Thomas L. Fleischner
Prescott College

Benjamin Fleury-Steiner
University of Delaware

Charley B. Flint
William Paterson University

LaNina Nicole Floyd
John Jay College of Criminal Justice

Kathryn J. Fox
University of Vermont

David M. Freeman
Colorado State University

Joshua D. Freilich
John Jay College of Criminal Justice

Samantha Friedman
University at Albany, State University of New York

Xuanning Fu
California State University, Fresno

Gennifer Furst
William Paterson University

John F. Galliher
University of Missouri

Maria L. Garase
Gannon University

Heather Gautney
Towson University

Gilbert Geis
University of California, Irvine

Naomi Gerstel
University of Massachusetts

Jen Gieseking
Graduate Center, City University of New York

Linda M. Glenn
Alden March Bioethics Institute

Julie L. Globokar
University of Illinois at Chicago

Doğan Göçmen
University of London

Erich Goode
University of Maryland at College Park

Edmund W. Gordon
Teachers College, Columbia University

Brian Gran
Case Western Reserve University

Renee D. Graphia
Rutgers University

Leslie Greenwald
RTI International

Karen Gregory
City University of New York

Heather M. Griffiths
Fayetteville State University

Peter Griswold
William Paterson University

Rachel N. Grob
Sarah Lawrence College

Janet A. Grossman
Medical University of South Carolina

Frank R. Gunter
Lehigh University

Mustafa E. Gurbuz
University of Connecticut

Barbara J. Guzzetti
Arizona State University

Martine Hackett
City University of New York Graduate Center

David Halle
University of California, Los Angeles

David Hall-Matthews
Leeds University

Leslie B. Hammer
Portland State University

Michael J. Handel
Northeastern University

Angelique Harris
California State University, Fullerton

Grant T. Harris
MHC Penetanguishene

Robert Harris
William Paterson University

Lana D. Harrison
University of Delaware

Elizabeth Hartung
California State University, Channel Islands

Steven H. Hatting
University of St. Thomas

L. Joseph Hebert
St. Ambrose University

Scott Heil
City University of New York

Tom Heinzen
William Paterson University

Sameer Hinduja
Florida Atlantic University

John P. Hoffmann
Brigham Young University

Donna Dea Holland
Indiana University–Purdue University Fort Wayne

Leslie Doty Hollingsworth
University of Michigan

Richard D. Holowczak
Baruch College

Evren Hosgor
Lancaster University

Daniel Howard
University of Delaware

Matthew W. Hughey
University of Virginia

Li-Ching Hung
Mississippi State University

John Iceland
University of Maryland

Emily S. Ihara
George Mason University

Leslie Irvine
University of Colorado

Jonathan Isler
University of Illinois–Springfield

Danielle M. Jackson
City University of New York

James B. Jacobs
New York University

Robert Jarvenpa
University at Albany, State University of New York

Rukmalie Jayakody
Pennsylvania State University

Patricia K. Jennings
California State University, East Bay

Vickie Jensen
California State University, Northridge

Colin Jerolmack
City University of New York

Jamie L. Johnson
Western Illinois University

John M. Johnson
Arizona State University

Hank Johnston
San Diego State University

Katherine Castiello Jones
University of Massachusetts

Paul Joseph
Tufts University

Diana M. Judd
William Paterson University

Jeffrey S. Juris
Arizona State University

Deborah Sawers Kaiser
Graduate Center, City University of New York

Philip R. Kavanaugh
University of Delaware

Alem Kebede
California State University, Bakersfield

Keumsil Kim Yoon
William Paterson University

Kenneth Kipnis
University of Hawaii at Manoa

James A. Kitts
Columbia University

Peter Kivisto
Augustana College

Halil Kiymaz
Rollins College

Gary Kleck
Florida State University

Gerald Kloby
County College of Morris

Neringa Klumbytė
University of Pittsburgh

Jennifer M. Koleser
William Paterson University

Rosalind Kopfstein
Western Connecticut State University

Kathleen Korgen
William Paterson University

William Kornblum
City University of New York

Roland Kostic
Uppsala University

Marilyn C. Krogh
Loyola University Chicago

Timothy Kubal
California State University, Fresno

Danielle C. Kuhl
Bowling Green State University

Basak Kus
University of California, Berkeley

Emily E. LaBeff
Midwestern State University

Peter R. Lamptey
Family Health International

William S. Lang
University of South Florida

James E. Lange
San Diego State University

Jooyoung Lee
University of California, Los Angeles

William H. Leggett
Middle Tennessee State University

Margaret Leigey
California State University, Chico

Leslie Leighninger
Arizona State University

Anthony Lemon
Oxford University

Hilary Levey
Princeton University

Amy Levin
California State University, Northridge

Jack Levin
Northeastern University

Antonia Levy
City University of New York

Dan A. Lewis
Northwestern University

Danielle Liautaud-Watkins
William Paterson University

Annulla Linders
University of Cincinnati

Joseph P. Linskey
Centenary College

Jay Livingston
Montclair State University

Kim A. Logio
St. Joseph's University

Ross D. London
Berkeley College

Jamie Longazel
University of Delaware

Vera Lopez
Arizona State University

Kathleen S. Lowney
Valdosta State University

David F. Luckenbill
Northern Illinois University

Paul C. Luken
University of West Georgia

Howard Lune
William Paterson University

Yingyi Ma
Syracuse University

Kara E. MacLeod
University of California, Berkeley

Emily H. Mahon
The Graduate Center—City University of New York

James H. Mahon
William Paterson University

Kristin M. Maiden
University of Delaware

Mark Major
William Paterson University

Siniša Malešević
National University of Ireland, Galway

Ray Maratea
University of Delaware

Eric Margolis
Arizona State University

Matthew D. Marr
University of California, Los Angeles

Brenda Marshall
Montclair State University

Douglas A. Marshall
University of South Alabama

Matthew P. Martens
University at Albany, State University of New York

Lauren Jade Martin
The Graduate Center—City University of New York

Rosanne Martorella
William Paterson University

Sanjay Marwah
Guilford College

Lorna Mason
Queens College

Pedro Mateu-Gelabert
Center for Drug Use and HIV Research

Ross L. Matsueda
University of Washington

Richard Matthew
University of California, Irvine

Donna Maurer
University of Maryland University College

Kenneth I. Mavor
Australian National University

Victoria Mayer
University of Wisconsin–Madison

Douglas C. Maynard
State University of New York, New Paltz

Mary Lou Mayo
Kean University

Lawrence E. Y. Mbogoni
William Paterson University

Kate McCarthy
California State University, Chico

Anne McCloskey
University of Illinois at Urbana-Champaign

Jack McDevitt
Northeastern University

Lauren McDonald
City University of New York

Stacy K. McGoldrick
California Polytechnic University, Pomona

Kimberly McKabe
Lynchburg College

Judith McKay
Nova Southeastern University

Shamla L. McLaurin
Virginia Polytechnic Institute and State University

Penelope A. McLorg
Indiana University–Purdue University Fort Wayne

Pamela McMullin-Messier
Kutztown University

DeMond S. Miller
Rowan University

Donald H. Miller
University of Washington

Kirk Miller
Northern Illinois University

Diana Mincyte
University of Illinois, Urbana

Luis Mirón
Florida International University

Philip Mirrer-Singer
New York attorney

Ronald L. Mize
Cornell University

Noelle J. Molé
Princeton University

Stephanie Moller
University of North Carolina at Charlotte

Brian A. Monahan
Iowa State University

Alan C. Monheit
University of Medicine and Dentistry of New Jersey

David L. Monk
California State University, Sacramento

Daniel Joseph Monti
Boston University

D. Chanele Moore
University of Delaware

Stephen J. Morse
University of Pennsylvania Law School

Clayton Mosher
Washington State University, Vancouver

Eric J. Moskowitz
Thomas Jefferson University

Jonathon Mote
University of Maryland

Kristine B. Mullendore
Grand Valley State University

Christopher W. Mullins
University of Northern Iowa

Sarah E. Murray
William Paterson University

Glenn W. Muschert
Miami University

Elizabeth Ehrhardt Mustaine
University of Central Florida

John P. Myers
Rowan University

Tina Nabatchi
Indiana University

David B. Nash
Jefferson Medical College

Balmurli Natrajan
William Paterson University

Frank Naughton
Kean University

Margaret B. Neal
Portland State University

Victor Nee
Cornell University

Melanie-Angela Neuilly
University of Idaho

Michelle L. Neumyer
William Paterson University

Robert Newby
Central Michigan University

Bridget Rose Nolan
University of Pennsylvania

Susan A. Nolan
Seton Hall University

Deirdre Oakley
Northern Illinois University

Richard E. Ocejo
The Graduate Center—City University of New York

Gabriel Maduka Okafor
William Paterson University

Louise Olsson
Uppsala University

Eyitayo Onifade
Michigan State University

Debra Osnowitz
Brandeis University

Laura L. O'Toole
Roanoke College

Graham C. Ousey
College of William & Mary

Thomas Y. Owusu
William Paterson University

Eugene R. Packer
New Jersey Center for Rehabilitation of Torture Victims

Alessandra Padula
Università degli Studi di L'Aquila (Italy)

Behnaz Pakizegi
William Paterson University

Alexandros Panayides
William Paterson University

Attasit Pankaew
Georgia State University

Richard R. Pardi
William Paterson University

Keumjae Park
William Paterson University

Vincent N. Parrillo
William Paterson University

Denise Lani Pascual
Indiana University–Purdue University

Gina Pazzaglia
Arizona State University

A. Fiona Pearson
Central Connecticut State University

Anthony A. Peguero
Miami University

David N. Pellow
University of California, San Diego

Rudolph G. Penner
Urban Institute

Jes Peters
Graduate Center, City University of New York

Stephen Pfohl
Boston College

Richard P. Phelps
Third Education Group

Nickie D. Phillips
St. Francis College

John W. Pickering
ie Limited, New Zealand

Judith Pintar
University of Illinois at Urbana-Champaign

Todd L. Pittinsky
Harvard University

Ann Marie Popp
Duquesne University

Rachel Porter
John Jay College of Criminal Justice

Blyden Potts
Shippensburg University

Srirupa Prasad
University of Missouri–Columbia

Michael Luis Principe
William Paterson University

Max Probst
*The Graduate Center—City
   University of New York*

Douglas W. Pryor
Towson University

James Michael Pulsifer
Presbyterian Church (USA)

Enrique S. Pumar
Catholic University of America

Stella R. Quah
National University of Singapore

Sara A. Quandt
Wake Forest University

Michael A. Quinn
Bentley College

Richard Race
Roehampton University

Lawrence E. Raffalovich
*University at Albany,
   State University of New York*

David R. Ragland
University of California, Berkeley

Raymond R. Rainville
St. Peter's College

Antonia Randolph
University of Delaware

Sachiko K. Reed
University of California, Santa Cruz

Michael Reisch
University of California, Berkeley

Claire M. Renzetti
University of Dayton

Jeanne B. Repetto
University of Florida

Harry M. Rhea
The Richard Stockton College of New Jersey

Marnie E. Rice
Mental Health Centre Penetanguishene

Lauren M. Rich
University of Chicago

Meghan Ashlin Rich
University of Scranton

Stephen C. Richards
University of Wisconsin, Oshkosh

Anthony L. Riley
American University

Blaine G. Robbins
University of Washington

Cynthia Robbins
University of Delaware

Gina Robertiello
Harvest Run Development

Paul Robertson
Oglala Lakota College

Myra Robinson
William Paterson University

Russell Rockwell
New York State Department of Health

Nestor Rodriguez
University of Houston

Garry L. Rolison
California State University, San Marcos

Michelle Ronda
Marymount Manhattan College

Jeff Rosen
Snap! VRS

Julie L. Rosenthal
William Paterson University

John K. Roth
Claremont McKenna College

Dawn L. Rothe
University of Northern Iowa

Barbara Katz Rothman
City University of New York

Daniel Colb Rothman
University at Albany, State University of New York

Nathan Rousseau
Jacksonville University

Janet M. Ruane
Montclair State University

David R. Rudy
Morehead State University

Scott Ryan
Florida State University

Vincent F. Sacco
Queen's University

Saskia Sassen
Columbia University

Theodore Sasson
Middlebury College

Arlene Holpp Scala
William Paterson University

Richard T. Schaefer
De Paul University

Enid Schatz
University of Missouri

Traci Schlesinger
DePaul University

Frederika E. Schmitt
Millersville University

Christopher Schneider
Arizona State University

Robert A. Schwartz
Baruch College

Gladys V. Scott
William Paterson University

Michael J. Sebetich
William Paterson University

Natasha Semmens
University of Sheffield

Roberta Senechal de la Roche
Washington and Lee University

Vincent Serravallo
Rochester Institute of Technology

Paul Shaker
Simon Fraser University

Stephen R. Shalom
William Paterson University

Matthew J. Sheridan
Georgian Court University

Vera Sheridan
Dublin City University

Richard Shorten
University of Oxford

Arthur Bennet Shostak
Drexel University

Matthew Silberman
Bucknell University

Stephen J. Sills
University of North Carolina at Greensboro

Roxane Cohen Silver
University of California, Irvine

Cynthia Simon
William Paterson University

Charles R. Simpson
State University of New York, Plattsburgh

Sita Nataraj Slavov
Occidental College

André P. Smith
University of Victoria

Cary Stacy Smith
Mississippi State University

Danielle Taana Smith
Rochester Institute of Technology

James F. Smith
University of North Carolina

Deirdre Mary Smythe
St. Mary's University

David A. Snow
University of California, Irvine

William H. Sousa
University of Nevada, Las Vegas

Joan Z. Spade
State University of New York, Brockport

T. Patrick Stablein
University of Connecticut

Walter Stafford
New York University

Karen M. Staller
University of Michigan

Peter J. Stein
University of North Carolina

Ronnie J. Steinberg
Vanderbilt University

Thomas G. Sticht
Independent Consultant

Amy L. Stone
Trinity University

Cheryl Stults
Brandeis University

Alicia E. Suarez
Pacific Lutheran University

Karen A. Swanson
William Paterson University

Paul A. Swanson
William Paterson University

Amanda Swygart-Hobaugh
Cornell College

Susanna Tardi
William Paterson University

Robert Edward Tarwacki, Sr.
John Jay College of Criminal Justice

Diane E. Taub
Indiana University–Purdue University Fort Wayne

Howard F. Taylor
Princeton University

Cheray T. W. Teeple
William Paterson University

Vaso Thomas
Bronx Community College

Michael J. Thompson
William Paterson University

Cindy Tidwell
Community Counseling Services

Amy Traver
State University of New York, Stony Brook

Linda A. Treiber
Kennesaw State University

James Tyner
Kent State University

Mark S. Umbreit
University of Minnesota

Sheldon Ungar
University of Toronto at Scarborough

Arnout van de Rijt
Cornell University

Sheryl L. Van Horne
Rutgers University

Mirellise Vazquez
Christian Children's Fund

Santiago R. Verón
Instituto de Clima y Agua, Argentina

Elena Vesselinov
University of South Carolina

Matt Vidal
University of Wisconsin–Madison

Maria de Lourdes Villar
William Paterson University

Charles M. ViVona
State University of New York, Old Westbury

Christina Voight
The Graduate Center—City University of New York

Thomas Volscho
University of Connecticut

Miryam Z. Wahrman
William Paterson University

Linda J. Waite
University of Chicago

Patricia Y. Warren
Florida State University

Bradley C. S. Watson
Saint Vincent College

Andrew J. Wefald
Kansas State University

Joyce Weil
Fordham University

Christopher Weiss
Columbia University

Michael Welch
Rutgers University

Sandy Welsh
University of Toronto

Mark D. Whitaker
University of Wisconsin–Madison

Dianne E. Whitney
Kansas State University

Jeffrey Whitney
InterRes (International Resources Associates)

K. A. S. Wickrama
Iowa State University

Judy R. Wilkerson
Florida Gulf Coast University

Rima Wilkes
University of British Columbia

Marion C. Willetts
Illinois State University

Marian R. Williams
Bowling Green State University

Loretta I. Winters
California State University, Northridge

Yvonne Chilik Wollenberg
William Paterson University

Mark Worrell
State University of New York, Cortland

Julia Wrigley
Graduate Center, City University of New York

Joel Yelin
Rowan University

Kersti Yllo
Wheaton College

Grace J. Yoo
San Francisco State University

Melissa Young-Spillers
Purdue University

Milan Zafirovski
University of North Texas

Orli Zaprir
University of Florida

Heather Zaykowski
University of Delaware

Wenquan Zhang
Texas A&M University

Tiantian Zheng
State University of New York, Cortland

Min Zhou
University of California, Los Angeles

Marcy Zipke
Providence College

Introduction

Social problems affect everyone. Some of us encounter problems of unequal treatment and opportunity virtually every day as a result of our race, religion, gender, or low income. Others experience problems in their lives from chemical dependency, family dissolution and disorganization, technological change, or declining neighborhoods. Crime and violence affect many people directly, while others live fearfully in their shadow, threatened further by the possibility of terrorism. And these are but a few of the social problems people face.

Because so many actual and potential problems confront us, it is often difficult to decide which ones affect us most severely. Is it the threat of death or injury during a terrorist attack? Is it the threat caused by industrial pollution that may poison us or destroy our physical environment? Or does quiet but viciously damaging gender, age, class, racial, or ethnic discrimination have the most far-reaching effect? Do the problems of cities affect us if we live in the suburbs? Do poorer nations' problems with overpopulation affect *our* quality of life? No consensus exists on which problem is most severe; in fact, some might argue it is none of the above but something else instead.

Developed societies are extremely complex entities. Any attempt, therefore, to examine the many social problems confronting such societies must encompass a wide scope of issues, ranging from those on a seemingly personal level (such as mental health and substance abuse) to those on a global scale (such as economics, environment, and pandemics). Moreover, the myriad of problems challenging both the social order and quality of life encompass so many areas of concern that only an interdisciplinary approach can offer a thorough approach in gaining sufficient understanding into their causes and consequences. This *Encyclopedia of Social Problems*, therefore, utilizes experts and scholars from *19 disciplines* in an effort to provide as comprehensive an approach as possible to this multifaceted field. These subject areas include anthropology, biology, business, chemistry, communications, criminal justice, demography, economics, education, environmental studies, geography, health, history, languages, political science, psychology, social work, sociology, and women's studies.

Although some social problems are fairly new (such as computer crimes and identity theft), others are centuries old (such as poverty and prostitution). Some social problems have been viewed differently from place to place and from one era to another (such as attitudes about poverty and prostitution), while others have almost always drawn societal disapproval (such as incest, although even here—such as in ancient Egypt and in the Hawaiian kingdom—its acceptance among the ruling class once existed). In fact, this last point brings to the forefront an important element about social problems: a social condition, whatever it may be, often does not become defined as a social problem until members of some powerful group perceive it as a problem affecting them in some way—perhaps as a threat to their well-being. A subjective component of moral outrage thus sparks social problem definitions.

Members of a social class tend to see reality from their class's point of view and form a set of moral and lifestyle definitions about themselves and others that is unique to their stratum. Thus what one group sees as important (such as welfare, social security, or tax loopholes), another may not consider valuable to society. People in positions of power tend to value stability, social order, and the preservation of the existing privilege structure. In contrast, people trying to gain power tend to be interested in new ideas, innovative policies, and challenges to the status quo. Sometimes age also influences these differences in perspective.

People in power typically are older and try to maintain the structure that nurtured them, while those beginning their careers see many ways to improve the system.

Another important factor that complicates our understanding of social problems is the fact that none of them exists in isolation from other social conditions and problems. Essentially, a high degree of interconnectivity exists between each social problem and mutually supportive social institutions. Successfully overcoming any single social problem requires examining and changing many others. For example, we can only eliminate (or at least reduce) poverty if we also do something about improving people's life chances through better education in our inner cities and rural communities; increasing job skill training and the jobs themselves; reducing gang activities, street crimes, and drug use; eliminating racism and other forms of prejudice; providing more affordable housing and child care for low-income families; and changing perceptions from blaming poverty on individual character flaws to a realization that almost all poverty results from societal factors that can be altered.

We must also recognize that many social problems persist because someone is profiting from them. Resistance to anti-pollution regulations, for example, is often rooted in producers' or workers' desires to avoid reducing profits or jobs. However, the benefits gained by resisting new policies need not be monetary ones. Many proposed solutions to social problems encounter resistance because they threaten to upset society's traditional authority structure. The resistance to women in upper management (the "glass ceiling") is a recent example. Furthermore, the threat does not have to be direct or powerful or even real to cause a reaction. People resist change if it upsets how they think things should be. Every society's power structure of vested interest groups justifies itself by an ideology that seems to explain why some members "deserve" more power or privilege. It may respond to any solution that contradicts the ideological structure by dismissing the plan as nonsensical or too radical unless the solution enjoys strong enough proof and support to overcome the ideology.

Helpful to our gaining a deeper understanding of the many social problems we face is the utilization of social theories to explain our empirical reality. Some theories are *macrosocial* in nature, employing the larger context of society in their approach, while others are *microsocial,* focusing on some aspect of everyday life, and still other theories are *mesosocial*, taking a middle ground between the two, making use of just one variable (such as differences in power between two competing groups) to understand a problem at the societal level. Just as close-up or wide-angle camera lenses enable us to focus on different aspects of the same reality, so too do the various social theories. Included in these encyclopedia pages, therefore, are entries on these theories, explaining their perspectives and foundations as well as their application in many of the other entries on various social problems.

This brief introduction to the field of social problems gives only an inkling of the topic. Within the pages to follow are hundreds of entries to offer the reader a fuller insight into the many and complex challenges to the human condition.

Rationale for the *Encyclopedia*

Despite the fact that social problems affect everyone and that they occur on so many levels in so many areas, until now, library reference shelves have lacked a current *Encyclopedia of Social Problems.* One may find reference works on many specific social issues (such as crime, education, environment, gender, and race), or on related elements (such as social class and social policy), but because social problems are so complex and interconnected, a real need exists for a single reference work that enables the reader to access information about all of these interconnected elements to gain more easily a complete insight and understanding.

Furthermore, most reference works about particular social issues or problems approach their subject from the area of expertise of their authors or editors. To illustrate, political scientists are likely to write about governmental policy, environmentalists about global warming, and criminologists about crime. Yet, as stated earlier, each of these and all other problem areas are interconnected with additional elements of society, and a multidisciplinary approach to even a single problem will better inform the reader. Thus, after completing a particular entry, the reader will find cross-references that will enable him or her to explore other dimensions of that topic within this *Encyclopedia.*

Also, a simple exposition of historical overviews and empirical data is not sufficient to comprehend the reality of our world. We further require a means to interpret and analyze that information, to gain perspectives into what is happening and why. Here, social theory provides the window into that understanding. No one theory can provide insights into all problems, and each problem can have more than one interpretation.

As mentioned earlier, the various social theories offer different lenses to view the same reality. Accordingly, this *Encyclopedia* applies theory, wherever applicable, within an entry or as a cross-reference to that entry's content.

To offer a systematic approach to such a vast and complex topic, the *Encyclopedia* adopts the following organization of social problem themes:

Aging and the Life Course

Community, Culture, and Change

Crime and Deviance

Economics and Work

Education

Family

Gender Inequality and Sexual Orientation

Health

Housing and Urbanization

Politics, Power, and War

Population and Environment

Poverty and Social Class

Race and Ethnic Relations

Social Movements

Social Theory

Substance Abuse

These topics provide the headings for the Reader's Guide, with all of the articles in the *Encyclopedia* appearing under one or more of these broad themes. As the list indicates, the scope of the *Encyclopedia* encompasses the major subject areas found in social problems textbooks and in current research. As such, it attempts to meet the needs of all who utilize this reference work.

Content and Organization

The *Encyclopedia* is composed of 632 articles arranged in alphabetical order and ranging in length from about 500 to 3,000 words. Although we believe that this reference work provides the most comprehensive coverage possible in its wide range of material, no encyclopedia can possibly include all of the

subfields and specific applications of social problems on individual, local, regional, national, and global levels. Nevertheless, we are confident that the reader investigating virtually any social problem will find in this reference work a rich treasure of information and insights.

Because so many of the topics discussed in the *Encyclopedia* relate to other topics, every article has cross-references to other entries in the *Encyclopedia.* In addition, a list of Further Readings accompanies each article. The Reader's Guide will also enable any user of the *Encyclopedia* to find many articles related to each of the broad themes appearing in this work.

Creation of the *Encyclopedia*

A systematic, step-by-step process led to the creation of the *Encyclopedia:*

1. After first developing a prospectus for this project, I identified some of the leading U.S. scholars in various social problem areas, whose highly respected research and leadership would bring much to this effort. I then invited their participation as associate editors and happily succeeded in that quest.

2. The associate editors and I began to develop a list of headword entries. We approached this task by examining all of the leading university texts in social problems to create an initial list of potential headwords. We also reviewed the Special Problems Divisions of the Society for the Study of Social Problems (SSSP), as well as the papers presented at SSSP meetings and/or published in its *Social Problems* journal in the past five years, to identify the subject areas of interest to educators and scholars. In addition, we conducted content computer searches of articles published within the past 5 years in other leading journals in all relevant fields. From these varied sources and through a series of brainstorming sessions, we refined and expanded the headword list until we were satisfied that we had a comprehensive list.

3. Armed with the final headword list, the editors collectively began to develop a list of potential contributors for each topic. The associate editors and I first assumed responsibility for certain topics in our areas of expertise. We next identified potential authors from our own network of professional colleagues as well as from the recently published articles and conference paper presenters identified in the previous step. This ever-widening search for the best scholars in the field

xliv   **Encyclopedia of Social Problems**

eventually resulted in our securing contributors from *18 countries:* Argentina, Australia, Canada, England, France, Germany, Greece, Hong Kong, India, Ireland, Italy, Kenya, New Zealand, Romania, Scotland, Singapore, Turkey, and throughout the United States, including Hawaii. This is truly an international effort in addition to an interdisciplinary one.

4. Each author received detailed submission guidelines and writing samples to illustrate the approach, format, style, substance, and level of intellectual rigor that we required. As general editor, I reviewed their submitted drafts for content accuracy and completeness, as well as grammar and style, and suggested revisions (sometimes several revisions) of virtually every article before assigning it final-draft status.

5. In different phases at the next level, Sage editors further reviewed the articles for clarity of expression, objectivity, and writing style to ensure that each entry was of the highest caliber in its content and presentation.

6. This lengthy process of selection, evaluation, constructive criticism, refinement, and review at multiple levels has resulted in not only an encyclopedia about which we are quite proud, but also one that the reader can confidently embrace.

Acknowledgments

This project began when Ben Penner, acquisitions editor for Sage Publications, approached me with the idea of developing a two-volume encyclopedia on social problems. He found in me a receptive audience. As with all sociologists, my teaching, public speaking, research, and writing focus in one way or another on some aspect of this broad subject matter. I am also the author of a social problems textbook that went through six editions. Moreover, I was attracted by the immense challenge of this endeavor, and I believed that such an inclusive reference work would fill an important void in this area by providing, in one work, the reliable information not just on a specific topic, but also on its related and/or interconnected topics. Thus, the idea of creating a major reference work that would be both comprehensive and comprehensible was too enticing a professional enterprise to refuse.

The associate editors—Margaret Andersen, Joel Best, William Kornblum, Claire Renzetti, and Mary Romero—were each important in the development of this *Encyclopedia.* They helped shape the content, suggested names of contributors, offered me encouragement at times when the project seemed overwhelming, and contributed articles as well. Certainly, the many hundreds of scholars and experts who contributed their expertise to the content of this reference work deserve much appreciation. Sharing with me the belief in this encyclopedia's importance to the field, they all took precious time away from their other demands to write for this publication, then willingly worked to improve the articles according to the editing suggestions.

From the moment of my accepting this project and onward throughout its planning, writing, and editing phases, I worked closely with Yvette Pollastrini, the developmental editor for the *Encyclopedia* at Sage. Yvette answered all my questions, or quickly found someone who could, and guided me through my own growth as general editor. With a sharp eye and a keen mind, she read every entry for substance and style and never hesitated to ask for clarification of passages that were too technical or too complex for the average reader. As we moved into production, Tracy Buyan, senior project editor and reference production supervisor at Sage, shepherded the *Encyclopedia* through that phase. I had worked with Tracy previously in the production of the second edition of my *Diversity in America* book for Sage, so I knew that I was in good hands, and indeed I was. In addition, Colleen Brennan and Pam Suwinsky were outstanding copy editors, going far beyond their normal responsibilities to suggest elements to add to enhance the content.

To all of these people, whether old or new friends or colleagues with whom I was delighted to have worked on this project, I owe a large debt of gratitude. However, I would be remiss if I did not especially thank the one person who lived the entire multiyear experience of creating the *Encyclopedia.* My wife, Beth, listened to my ongoing concerns as the project unfolded, was always understanding when work of the *Encyclopedia* consumed so many hours of my time, and provided the necessary support to sustain me through the difficult days.

Vincent N. Parrillo

ABILITY GROUPING

Ability grouping is the practice of teaching homogeneous groups of students, stratified by achievement or perceived ability. Among the various forms of ability grouping are within-class ability grouping, cross-grade grouping, and between-class ability grouping, also known as tracking. Several comprehensive research reviews have explored whether or not students benefit from ability grouping methods, with effects varying depending on the method of grouping examined. Within-class and cross-grade grouping share features that appear to benefit a broad range of students. The research shows between-class grouping to be of little value for most students, and researchers widely criticize this practice because, by definition, it creates groups of low achievers.

In cross-grade and within-class ability grouping, students identify with a heterogeneous class, although they are homogeneously grouped for instruction in only one or two subjects, usually reading, math, or both. Flexibility in grouping allows students to change groups based on changes in performance. In cross-grade grouping plans, students, assigned to heterogeneous classes for most of the day, regroup across grade levels for reading and sometimes other subjects. Within-class ability grouping involves teacher-assigned homogeneous groups for reading or math instruction, and evidence shows this produces gains in student achievement when compared with heterogeneous grouping or whole class instruction. Furthermore, because the teacher determines students' group placements, students have more opportunity to move up into higher groups as their skills and abilities improve.

Common forms of between-class grouping include multilevel classes, which split same-grade students into separate classes, usually high, middle, and low. Also included in between-class grouping are accelerated or enriched classes for high achievers and special or remedial classes for low achievers.

In various forms, between-class ability grouping has been a common school practice since the early 20th-century Industrial Revolution, when curricula were increasingly differentiated into vocational and academic tracks. During the 1960s, concern about U.S. students' standing in math and science compared with students abroad increased emphasis on special programs for the top achievers. At the same time, heightened concern about racial discrimination and segregation, poverty, and social inequity fostered the growth of programs aimed at leveling the playing field. A multitude of programs targeting specific categories of children emerged, including gifted education, compensatory education, special education, and bilingual programs. The existence of these programs strengthened convictions that standardized education could not best serve all children, and so schools grew more and more differentiated.

In theory, between-class ability grouping reduces homogeneity, allowing teachers to develop curricula more effectively according to the unique needs of their group. Whereas a teacher of low-achieving students might focus attention on specific skill remediation, repetition, and review, a teacher of high achievers might provide a more challenging curriculum and increased instructional pace. Research findings point to the benefits of accelerated classes for high-achieving students but show mixed results for average and low-achieving students, ranging from small positive gains to small negative losses in these students' achievement levels.

In the 1970s and 1980s, the effects of between-class grouping came under attack. Although created in the name of educational equality, stratified educational programs may have actually widened the achievement gap between more and less economically advantaged groups. Critics point to the disproportionate representation in low-track classes of children from lower socioeconomic groups, who tend to be predominantly Latin American and African American. Wealthier white students disproportionately populate high tracks. Lower-track students experience a curriculum far less rigorous than their high-achieving counterparts. Lower-achieving students in homogeneous groups lack the stimulation and academic behavior models provided by high achievers. Further exacerbating the problem, the act of categorizing students has a stigmatizing effect: Teachers tend to develop lowered expectations for children in lower tracks. Students in these groups may be denied opportunities to advance academically, and struggling learners consigned to lower tracks often remain there for life.

Efforts at detracking began in earnest in the late 1980s and early 1990s. For example, in 1990 the National Education Association recommended that schools abandon conventional tracking practices, stating that they lead to inequity in learning opportunities. In that same year, the Carnegie Corporation declared that the creation of heterogeneous classrooms was key to school environments that are democratic as well as academic. Courts around the nation ruled that the tracking system segregated students and restricted Latino/a and African American access to high-quality curricula. Despite the detracking movement, many schools continue to sort students based on perceived ability, with students of color disproportionately tracked into the lowest classes in racially mixed schools; racially segregated schools predominantly house either higher or lower tracks.

Objections to detracking come mostly from educators and parents of high-achieving students. Many worry that detracking results in the elimination of enriched and accelerated classes for the fastest learners and that the achievement level of such students falls when these classes are not available. Indeed, the argument for providing special classes for the most academically advanced students is currently regaining strength, with the recent emphasis on standardized testing. Results from research on the effects of accelerated classes on the gifted have been positive and significant.

Studied and debated for almost 100 years, ability grouping still elicits controversy. Flexible grouping based on ability in individual subjects can help struggling learners overcome their academic obstacles, allowing them to learn at an appropriate pace, and can challenge the fastest learners. However, tracking students from an early age leads them to very different life destinations and propagates the inequality and injustice that education is meant to help overcome.

Julie L. Rosenthal

See also Academic Standards; Education, Academic Performance; Educational Equity

Further Readings

Kulik, James A. and Chen-Lin C. Kulik. 1992. "Meta-Analytic Findings on Grouping Programs." *Gifted Child Quarterly* 36:73–77.

Loveless, Tom. 2003. *The Tracking and Ability Grouping Debate*. Washington, DC: Thomas B. Fordham Foundation. Retrieved October 31, 2006 (http://www.edexcellence.net/foundation/publication/publication.cfm?id=127).

Oakes, Jeannie. 2005. *Keeping Track: How Schools Structure Inequality.* New Haven, CT: Yale University Press.

Slavin, Robert E. 1987. "Ability Grouping and Student Achievement in Elementary Schools: A Best-Evidence Synthesis." *Review of Educational Research* 57:293–336.

ABORTION

Worldwide, some 46 million women have abortions every year. Of these abortions, only slightly more than half are legal, that is, take place under conditions that are medically safe and where neither the woman nor the provider is subject to criminal prosecution. According to the World Health Organization (WHO), about 13 percent of all pregnancy-related deaths, or 78,000, are linked to complications resulting from unsafe abortions.

In the United States, the legalization of abortion occurred in 1973 with the Supreme Court decision

Roe v. Wade. After an initial sharp increase in the number of abortions, the abortion rate steadily declined to approximately 21 abortions per 1,000 women age 15 to 44, which amounts to about 1.3 million abortions annually. This rate falls within the norm of developed nations but is higher than in most of Western Europe, where the Netherlands occupies the low end with an abortion rate of about 8 per 1,000 women. Contrary to popular belief, high abortion rates generally do not correlate with low birth rates. On the contrary, both abortion rates and birth rates are high when the rate of pregnancy is high.

The incidence of abortion is not the same across all social groups, however. Currently in the United States, poor women, women of color, and young women are more likely to have an abortion than women who are in a better position to either prevent an unwanted pregnancy or care for an unplanned child. About 6 in 10 women who have abortions are already mothers. The overwhelming number of abortions (90 percent) takes place within the first 12 weeks of gestation, and all but a very small portion take place at clinics wholly or partially devoted to providing abortion services. Only about 13 percent of all counties in the United States currently have at least one abortion provider.

The legalization in 1973 brought abortion to the forefront of the political and legal agendas where it remains, with supporters and opponents embroiled in conflicts over what kind of problem it is and what can and should be done about it. As a result of these conflicts, the legal status of abortion is a constantly shifting patchwork of national and state law and various judicial injunctions. Currently, in 2006, according to state-level information collected by the Alan Guttmacher Institute, 32 states have a counseling requirement; 24 states impose a waiting period on abortion-seeking women; 34 states require notification of the parents of minors who seek abortion; 31 states ban the abortion procedure called "partial-birth" (the legal status of some of these laws is currently uncertain, especially those that make no exception for the woman's health); 32 states allow for public funding of abortion only in cases of life endangerment, rape, or incest; 46 states give health care providers the right to refuse participation in abortion services; 13 states restrict insurance coverage of abortion; 13 states allow for the sale of "Choose Life" license plates; and finally, 16 states have laws against

various activities directed at abortion providers, including property damage or threats, intimidations, and harassment aimed at doctors, staff, and patients.

What Kind of Problem Is Abortion?

As a social problem, abortion in the United States, as elsewhere, is only marginally related to variations in the incidence of abortion. During the past century and a half, women's reproductive practices, including abortion, have attracted the attention of a wide range of social actors, including medical professionals, politicians, religious groups, legal experts, scientists, women's rights organizations, and various other groups and individuals taking an active interest in the issue. These various groups approach the issue of abortion from different vantage points, identify different aspects of abortion as problematic, pursue different understandings of the causes and consequences of abortion (for the women who have them as well as for society at large), and propose different kinds of solutions. As a result, abortion has long occupied a contentious position in the sociopolitical landscape, uneasily situated in the intersection of medicine, women's rights, and morality.

Abortion as a Medical Problem

Before the 19th century, abortion as a sociolegal problem was bundled together with other practices aimed at escaping the moral stain associated with illicit sexuality, including the concealment of birth, the abandonment of infants, and infanticide. From a legal perspective, however, abortion was punishable only after *quickening,* that is, after women start feeling fetal movements. During the 19th century, a number of factors coalesced to turn abortion into a problem primarily pursued by the medical profession. The 19th-century campaign to professionalize medicine was, in large part, waged as a war against competing health practitioners, including not only midwives, who hitherto had provided reproductive care to women, but also the rapidly expanding ranks of commercial abortion providers. Claiming professional expertise that nonlicensed practitioners lacked, the medical profession effectively medicalized women's reproductive lives, appropriated the service domain previously occupied by midwives, and removed the medically dubious quickening distinction that had enabled abortion providers to largely operate with legal impunity. The conclusion of this campaign was a drastically changed landscape in which all abortions became illegal except the ones performed by licensed physicians for the purpose of saving a woman's life (the so-called therapeutic exemption), and women's reproductive lives thus fell almost entirely under the purview of professional medicine. Accompanying this reorganization of the medical context surrounding abortion was a reinterpretation of abortion as a social problem. In short, the doctors argued that abortion was no longer a practice exclusive to the unmarried, no longer an act prompted by social desperation, and no longer a practice engaged in by those women who might be considered unsuitable as mothers. Instead, the doctors emphasized, abortion had turned into a fashionable practice among those upon whom the nation depended for its healthy reproduction, in both numerical and moral terms. In this sense, abortion became increasingly viewed as a moral gangrene of sorts, seducing (by its very availability) middle-class women into abandoning their higher purpose as mothers and moral guardians.

With this definition firmly in place, abortion fell out of the public spotlight and survived for the next several decades primarily as a clandestine and largely invisible practice that operated under the legal radar save for a few widely publicized scandals involving illegal abortion rings. When opposition against restrictive abortion regulations began to mount in the 1950s and 1960s, the impetus for reform was once again spearheaded by doctors and other professionals. Formulated as a set of reforms aimed at bringing the abortion law into greater conformity with modern medical and psychiatric standards, this pressure led to relatively uncontroversial legal reform in at least a dozen states years before *Roe v. Wade*. These laws expanded the grounds for legal abortion somewhat (rape, incest, mental and physical health), but the authority to make abortion decisions remained with the medical profession. This authority effectively ended when the Supreme Court ruled in *Roe v. Wade* that the abortion decision rested with the woman, not her doctor. Since then, the position of organized medicine toward abortion has been ambivalent, even as some of its members have long occupied vulnerable frontline positions in the abortion conflict as service providers.

Abortion as a Problem of Women's Rights

Abortion as a problem of women's rights also has deep historical roots, even if abortion itself was a latecomer to the bundle of issues that women's rights activists long pursued under the rubric of gender equality. The women's rights pioneers of the 19th century, without directly confronting pregnancy and birth, pushed for an expansion of women's social and political roles beyond the confines of the home, thus challenging the widespread assumption that motherhood was destiny and, therefore, that womanhood was incompatible with the rights, responsibilities, and opportunities associated with manhood and full citizenship. The call for "voluntary motherhood" during this time did not encompass a call for reproductive freedom in the modern sense. Instead, it was a response to the proliferation of illicit sexuality among men (expressed in prostitution and the spread of venereal diseases), which was perceived as a threat to the integrity of the family and women's place therein. In the early 20th century, the birth control movement more directly confronted women's efforts at controlling their own reproductive lives but did so without including abortion among the birth control practices they sought to make available to women. Nonetheless, the emphasis on planned parenthood placed reproductive control at the center of women's liberation as well as the well-being of the nation more generally. What the abortion rights movement added to these earlier movements was a reformulation of the foundation upon which women's reproductive agency rested: Whereas motherhood had been a powerful platform of earlier activists and a justification for expanded social and political influence, the abortion rights movement, precisely because it emphasized that motherhood was a choice rather than an inevitable conclusion of womanhood, helped sever the link between women's rights and women's roles as mothers.

When the movement gained political momentum during the 1960s, there was growing recognition that the prohibition against abortion not only was ineffective but also placed women at a distinct health disadvantage precisely because abortion was illegal and therefore often medically unsafe. While the medical solution to the problem of illegal abortion was a modest expansion of the grounds for legal abortion, advocates of women's rights offered a much more profound reinterpretation of abortion. Abortion, they argued, was not a medical problem to be solved by doctors once they were convinced that women really "needed" them, but instead a collective problem impacting all women. Abortion, in short, was part of a much larger problem of women's rights and, therefore, political at its very core. Hence, according to this movement, only if the abortion decision was placed in the hands of women could the problem ever be solved; that is, women needed full authority over the abortion decision *irrespective* of their reasons.

The tension around abortion as an unconstrained choice captures the fundamental disagreements over motherhood—and, by extension, gender roles—that have permeated the abortion conflict since the early 19th century. These disagreements, then as now, focus less on the extent to which women in fact have abortions than on the extent to which women's reasons for having abortions are justifiable or not.

Abortion as a Moral Problem

Abortion as a moral problem has roots in a traditional religious-based morality that, before the contemporary abortion conflict, constituted a blend of concerns for sexual morality and the sanctity of motherhood. Although the moral force of these concerns eroded somewhat as women's social status underwent an irrevocable transformation, traces still remain of these concerns in the tensions around the meanings of motherhood that permeate much of the abortion conflict. Thus the opposition to abortion, although currently mobilized most overtly around fetal life, captures an amalgam of larger social concerns that broaden the social base of the opposition movement from religious leaders who derive their position from a theological perspective to grassroots activists, many of whom are women, who find justification for their opposition in the circumstances of their own personal and political lives.

The contemporary movement against abortion emerged out of Catholic opposition to the reform movement of the late 1960s and early 1970s but has since expanded to include a range of religious congregations and groups with more or less strong ties to organized religion. Initially mobilized under the rubric of *Right to Life*, this opposition formulated its objection to abortion around the loss of human life and, once *Roe v. Wade* became the law of the land, mounted a vigorous campaign with a multi-institutional

focus aimed at (a) undermining public support for women's right to choose, (b) making it increasingly difficult for women to obtain abortion, and (c) once again outlawing abortion. The emphasis on fetal life, in conjunction with a vision of the abortion-seeking woman as freely choosing abortion, has contributed to the "clash of absolutes" that now defines much of the contemporary abortion conflict. In this view, which is quite specific to the U.S. case, abortion is wrong precisely because it involves the deliberate destruction of the most innocent of human lives by a woman who claims it is her right to do so. Thus, from the perspective of the pro-life movement, the relationship between the fetus and the woman sustaining it is potentially adversarial, and, accordingly, the ultimate solution to the problem lies not in efforts to reduce women's abortion needs but instead in prohibition and moral instruction.

Although *Roe v. Wade* still stands, its foundation has eroded, through the courts of law as well as the court of public opinion, by the many challenges launched by this opposition, even if the extreme end of the pro-life position—that abortion is tantamount to murder and hence always wrong—has attracted relatively few adherents among the public at large. Nevertheless, given the emphasis on fetal life, even the expansion of a right to abortion in cases of pregnancy that result from rape or incest is met with tension and ambivalence in some pro-life circles, where sympathy for a woman's suffering is outweighed by concerns for the fetus. When carrying a pregnancy to term would threaten a woman's life or health, the life of the fetus is pitted against the life and well-being of the mother. A similar tension, albeit with very different ingredients, accompanies violent protest tactics, especially the murder of abortion providers in the name of the pro-life cause. While most mainstream pro-life groups distance themselves from such extreme tactics, the moral dilemma they reveal—whose life is more important and why—is central to the definition of abortion as a social problem.

Annulla Linders

See also Contraception; Eugenics; Neo-Malthusians; Religion and Politics; Sex Education; Social Movements; Teenage Pregnancy and Parenting; Women's Rights Movement

Further Readings

Burns, Gene. 2005. *The Moral Veto: Framing Contraception, Abortion, and Cultural Pluralism in the United States.* New York: Cambridge University Press.

Ferree, Myra Marx, William Anthony Gamson, Jürgen Gerhards, and Dieter Rucht. 2002. *Shaping Abortion Discourse: Democracy and the Public Sphere in Germany and the United States.* New York: Cambridge University Press.

Ginsburg, Faye D. 1989. *Contested Lives: The Abortion Debate in an American Community.* Berkeley, CA: University of California Press.

Luker, Kristin. 1984. *Abortion and the Politics of Motherhood.* Berkeley, CA: University of California Press.

Mohr, James C. 1978. *Abortion in America.* New York: Oxford University Press.

Reagan, Leslie J. 1997. *When Abortion Was a Crime: Women, Medicine, and the Law in the United States, 1867–1973.* Berkeley, CA: University of California Press.

Staggenborg, Suzanne. 1991. *The Pro-choice Movement: Organization and Activism in the Abortion Conflict.* New York: Oxford University Press.

Tribe, Laurence H. 1990. *Abortion: The Clash of Absolutes.* New York: Norton.

ABUSE, CHILD

The term *child abuse* refers to the multiple ways in which children are victimized by the willful or negligent actions of adults. The abusive victimization of children includes three broad categories of harm: (1) caretaker neglect of children's health and well-being, (2) acts of physical violence by adults against children, and (3) sexual violations of young people's psychic and physical boundaries before "the age of consent" to sex, established by the cultural and legal norms of a given society.

Child abuse is commonly viewed today as a troubling social problem. It is combated by legal punishments, therapeutic interventions, and social reforms. But, from a historical perspective, it is important to recognize that for centuries Western societies ignored, and even authorized and defended, routine assaults by adults upon children. This was particularly the case for harm done to children by their "God given" or legal guardians. Indeed, until recently, according to the patriarchal precepts of ancient Roman law and the common law traditions of Britain and the United States, parents and legal guardians were granted almost limitless power over children placed under their authority. This meant that legal guardians had the right to impose any punishment deemed necessary for a child's upbringing. At the same time, children—even those targeted by severe acts of physical violence—had virtually no rights to protect them against harsh and excessive sanctions of abusive caretakers. As late as the early 19th century, despite a proliferation of all kinds of punishment against alleged social wrongdoings, there existed no formal laws aimed at stemming the caretaker abuse of children. During this time, a major North Carolina court ruled, in the case of *State v. Pendergrass,* that a parent's judgment concerning a child's "need for punishment" was presumed to be correct and that criminal liability was limited to cases resulting in "permanent injury."

Despite the "child saving" efforts of several generations of 19th- and early 20th-century reformers, the precarious legal position of children changed little until the early 1960s. Noteworthy among the relative failures of child reform efforts were the House of Refuge Movement, the Society for the Prevention of Cruelty to Children (an organization occasioned by the widely publicized 1875 case of "Mary Ellen," a 9-year-old girl viciously assaulted by her foster parents), and the early years of the juvenile court. Despite an abundance of pro-child rhetoric, these early attempts at "child saving" contributed more to strategies of "preventive penology" than to actually curtailing the abusive power of adults over children. As a strategy of social control, preventive penology sought to reduce crime and social unrest by removing delinquency-prone youths from corrupt urban environments and improper homes. Those removed from their homes were placed in public or privately funded child reformatories. Public intervention against abusive adults lagged by comparison. In truth, it was not until the early 1960s that laws were placed on the books against caretaker assaults upon children. These laws resulted from publicity surrounding the "discovery" of the so-called child battering syndrome by pediatric radiologists and their medical allies, pediatricians and child mental health specialists.

The historical "discovery" of child abuse by mid-20th-century pediatric radiologists is a complex and contradictory matter. It suggests as much about the power dynamics of organized medical interests as it does about social concerns for child welfare. Before child abuse was labeled as an illness by pediatric radiologists, numerous factors may have prevented physicians from both "seeing" and reporting child abuse. Of particular significance were (a) the lack of an available diagnostic category to guide physician judgments; (b) doctors' complicity with dominant cultural norms that paired parental power with images of benevolence, making it difficult for physicians to believe that parents could be responsible for deliberate injuries to their children; (c) fears of legal liability for violating physician–patient relations; and (d) reluctance on the part of the medical establishment to subordinate its clinical expertise to the power of police officers, lawyers, judges, and other agents of the criminal justice system.

Pediatric radiologists were less constrained than other medical professionals by such obstacles. Radiologists were research oriented and gained prominence by discovering new categories of pathology and disease. Unlike clinicians, they were less hampered in their observations of childhood injuries by a lack of existing diagnostic classifications. Removed from direct clinical contact with battered children and their parents, radiologists studied black-and-white X-rays. This made pediatric radiologists less susceptible to denials of parental responsibility rooted in normative or emotional identification with parents. Because their primary clients were doctor colleagues requesting their services, radiologists were also less afraid of betraying patient confidentiality. In addition, until "discovering" child battering, pediatric radiology represented a relatively low-ranking specialty within the medical profession. High-ranking medical specialties were characterized by hands-on life-or-death contact with patients. By engaging with the life-or-death exigencies of caretaker violence, while defining abuse as primarily an illness or syndrome in need of medical treatment, pediatric radiologists were able to move upward within the ranks of the medical profession without compromising medical control over an alleged form of sickness.

Beginning in 1946 with Dr. John Caffey's observations about the "unspecified origins" of various long bone fractures in children, over the next decade pediatric radiologists moved from speculations about the mysterious physiological basis of childhood bone and skeletal traumas to something more troubling. Caffey, like other doctors, had attributed injuries he observed in children to nebulous causes. But by 1957 he had become convinced that parental "misconduct and deliberate injury" lay behind the horrific bone fractures pictured on X-ray screens. Breaking a code of cultural silence concerning violent parental and caretaker behavior, Caffey and other pediatric radiologists joined with pediatricians and child psychiatrists in drawing attention to a new public health menace—*the child-battering syndrome.*

Public response to the medical "discovery" of child abuse was swift and far-reaching. Over the following 10 years, a multitude of professional conferences, newspaper and magazine articles, and sensational media reports directed attention to this new social problem. As a result, between 1962 and 1966 all 50 U.S. states passed laws aimed against caretaker violence. Many laws included mandatory reporting requirements for doctors, educators, and others in regular contact with children. Researchers also labored to survey the scope and causes of child battering. Although plagued by methodological problems concerning the reliability of reports and how to best measure degrees of abuse, studies estimated that more than 1.5 million U.S. children were seriously abused by adult caretakers each year. Data presented by the U.S. Department of Health and Human Services for 2004 indicate 3 million alleged and 872,000 confirmed incidents of serious abuse. This includes an estimated 1,490 deaths of children at the hands of caretakers.

Researchers have identified a number of factors that appear to increase the likelihood of a child being abused. It is important to recognize that what is known today about child abuse is, for the most part, based on relatively small samples of known offenders. As such, while providing a suggestive picture of conditions contributing to the likelihood of abuse, current knowledge remains tentative and awaits refinement. Moreover, while no single factor is viewed as causative by itself, one thing appears clear: There is little empirical support for the medicalized image of parental violence as a supposed disease or "syndrome." More important are sociological factors affecting the caretaker–child relationship. Of these, the most consistently recognized are (a) stressful social, economic, and emotional situations; (b) the relative powerlessness of the family unit involved (a factor that may lead disadvantaged adults to search for distorted forms of power in violent relations with children); and (c) the prevalence of powerful cultural norms legitimizing the authoritative use of violence as a means of childrearing.

Stress is particularly important in creating a social environment conducive to abuse. Stressful living situations also amplify the impact of other conditions associated with a higher likelihood of abuse. These include low family income; the presence of premature, unwanted, or handicapped children; families with four or more children; and families headed by single mothers employed in low-paying jobs outside the home. Other factors identified as amplifying the likelihood of abuse are the social isolation of abusive families, unrealistic parental expectations for a child's performance, a parent's own experience of having been abused as a child, and inconsistencies in caretaker approaches to discipline. Together, these factors combine with situations of stress, powerlessness, and cultural support for authoritarian childrearing in making caretaker violence against children more likely.

To combat the routine abuse of children by adults, it is necessary to go beyond existing legal and therapeutic efforts to punish or rehabilitate known offenders. It is important to also uproot deeply entrenched ways of living that amplify stress and reinforce social inequality and to lessen cultural support for violence as a solution to everyday feelings of frustration. Without realizing far-reaching social changes in these areas, it is likely that the tragedy of child abuse will continue to haunt society long into the future.

Stephen Pfohl

See also Abuse, Child Sexual

Further Readings

Caffey, John. 1957. "Traumatic Lesions in Growing Bones Other Than Fractures and Lesions." *British Journal of Radiology* 30(May):225–38.

Dailey, T. B. 1979. "Parental Power Breeds Violence against Children." *Sociological Focus* 12(October):311–22.

Gelles, Richard J. and Murray A. Straus. 1988. *Intimate Violence.* New York: Simon & Schuster.

Gil, David. 1970. *Violence against Children.* Cambridge, MA: Harvard University Press.

McCaghy, Charles H., Timothy A. Capron, J. Jamieson, and Sandra Harley Carey. 2006. "Assaults against Children and Spouses." Pp. 167–204 in *Deviant Behavior: Crime, Conflict and Interest Groups.* 7th ed. Boston: Pearson.

Pfohl, Stephen J. 1977. "The 'Discovery' of Child Abuse." *Social Problems* 24(3):310–23.

Straus, Murray A., Richard J. Gelles, and Suzanne K. Steinmetz. 1980. *Behind Closed Doors: Violence in the American Family.* Garden City, NY: Anchor Press.

U.S. Department of Health and Human Services, Administration of Children, Youth and Families. 2006. "Child Maltreatment 2004." Washington, DC: U.S. Government Printing Office.

ABUSE, CHILD SEXUAL

Child sexual abuse refers to adult sexual contact with children under the legal age of consent. Whereas caretaker neglect and physical violence against children became major social problems during the 1960s, the sexual violation of children by adults became a focus for public concern from the 1970s to the present. In large measure, this resulted from attention generated by feminist activists and scholars concerned with the psychic and physical well-being of young people reared within sexist or male-dominated social environments. Whereas some non-Western societies permit, or even foster, limited ritual sexual contact between adults and young people, in contemporary Western society nearly all forms of sexual interaction between adults and children are thought of as harmful to children, even when children are said to consent to acts of sex with adults. This is because children are materially, socially, and emotionally dependent upon adult caretakers and, as such, are viewed as never entirely free to choose sex with adults who hold power over them. Thus, in the United States and other Western countries, it is a violation of criminal law for adults to engage sexually with youth below the age of 16, with or without a child's consent.

Although illegal, adult sexual relations with children are not entirely uncommon. Data analyzed by the U.S. Department of Health and Human Services indicate that 10 percent of approximately 3 million cases of alleged child abuse reported in 2004 involved violations of a sexual nature. This figure rose to 16 percent of all reported cases of abuse when considering children ages 12 to 16. While the most damaging forms of child sexual abuse involve coercion and rape, statistically speaking, far more typical are nonviolent, noncoital sexual exchanges between a child and an adult known to the child. Three quarters of all known cases of child sexual abuse involve offenders who were friends or neighbors of a victim's families. Surveys of college students report even higher findings, with 11.3 percent of women and 4.1 percent of men reporting having had sex with an adult (18 years or older) while they were under age 13. When sexual abuse or "incest" takes place within the family, surveys indicate that about three quarters of the time the offender is an adult relative, while about one quarter of those surveyed report sexual contact with a father or stepfather. Unfortunately, much of what is known about childhood sexual abuse is based on small clinical studies and surveys of middle-class and mostly white college populations. There is also considerable variation in the estimated incidence of child sexual abuse, although most researchers agree that the vast majority of perpetrators are males and that young women are about 4 times more likely to be victimized than young men.

Many victims of child sexual abuse experience long-lasting bodily and emotional problems, including post-traumatic stress disorder, sleeplessness, depression, eating and anxiety disorders, and difficulties in later establishing meaningful adult sexual relations. Since the mid-1980s, concern with these problems has been amplified by sensational media coverage of father–daughter incest, as well as the sexual abuse of children by educators and coaches in schools and day care centers and by priests and ministers in churches. Dramatic cases of child abduction by strangers and equally dramatic, although often undocumented, reports of ritual and satanic abuse have also fueled public fears. Sometimes reports of abuse are shrouded in controversy. This is particularly the case with regard to "recovered memories" of traumatic sexual violations said to have occurred in the distant past. In such cases, awareness of abuse is said to be repressed until brought to consciousness by suggestive therapeutic techniques, such as hypnotic regression or trance-like imaging.

Although debates surrounding the use of suggestive clinical procedures have raised questions about the verifiable character of some therapeutically "recovered memories," what researchers do know about childhood sexual abuse challenges stereotypes about the prevalence of anonymous child molesters—"dirty old men" who seduce children away from playgrounds with promises of candy, money, or adventure. Although the dangers presented by such predatory pedophiles are real, the likelihood of a child being molested by a stranger pales in comparison with the chance of being sexually abused by a trusted authority figure, male parent, relative, neighbor, or close friend of the family.

What causes adults to impose themselves sexually upon children? In asking this question it is important to remember that there is neither a single profile of types of abuse nor of abusers. Research shows that the most common form of father/stepfather and daughter incest involves situations where an adult male becomes overly dependent on a child for emotional warmth or affection absent in adult world relations. A far smaller number of offenders manifest pedophiliac sexual desires for children, regardless of whether they are related to or emotionally invested in the child. But when considering the wider sexual molestation of children by caretakers, factors affecting other (nonsexual) forms of child abuse also appear relevant. Of particular concern, however, is the equation of sex with power in a society in which dominant forms of both sex and power are governed by the prerogatives of adult males over both women and children. In combination with gender norms that teach women and girls to be nurturing, while instructing men and boys to aggressively assert power, it is no surprise that rates of child sexual victimization remain alarmingly high. In addition, other stresses, such as relative powerlessness in other social realms, may lead adults into what researchers call isolating and "symbiotic" dependence upon their children for affection, warmth, and even sexual gratification. The eroticization of images of children in mass media and consumer society also may be a factor.

Effectively countering the sexual abuse of children will probably require society-wide efforts that reach beyond the targeting of offenders by the criminal justice and mental health systems. To combat the sexual exploitation of children by adults, it may be necessary to also dramatically alter dominant social norms pertaining to gender and sexuality and to reduce the relative powerlessness that adults—particularly adult men—may experience as a result of high levels of stress and social inequality. Without realizing such far-reaching social and cultural changes, it is likely that the sexual abuse of children will remain a social problem well into the future.

Stephen Pfohl

See also Abuse, Child

Further Readings

Danni, Kristin A. and Gary D. Hampe. 2000. "An Analysis of Predictors of Child Sex Offender Types Using Presentence Investigation Reports." *International Journal of Offender Therapy and Comparative Criminology* 44(August):490–504.

Finkelhor, David and Patricia Y. Hashima. 2001. "The Victimization of Children and Youth: A Comprehensive Overview." Pp. 49–78 in *Handbook of Youth and Justice,* edited by S. O. White. New York: Kluwer Academic/Plenum.

Herman, Judith. 1981. *Father-Daughter Incest.* Cambridge, MA: Harvard University Press.

McCaghy, Charles H., Timothy A. Capron, J. Jamieson, and Sandra Harley Carey. 2006. "Assaults against Children and Spouses." Pp. 167–204 in *Deviant Behavior: Crime, Conflict and Interest Groups.* 7th ed. Boston: Pearson.

Russell, Diana. 1984. *Sexual Exploitation: Rape, Child Sexual Abuse, and Workplace Harassment.* Beverly Hills, CA: Sage.

Tyler, Kimberly A., Dan R. Hoyt, and Les B. Whitbeck. 2000. "The Effects of Early Sexual Abuse on Later Sexual Victimization among Female Homeless and Runaway Adolescents." *Journal of Interpersonal Violence* 15(4):235–50.

U.S. Department of Health and Human Services, Administration of Children, Youth and Families. 2006. "Child Maltreatment 2004." Washington, DC: U.S. Government Printing Office.

ABUSE, ELDERLY

Awareness of elder abuse as a social problem has increased in recent years because of attention to the identification of those who are likely to be abused. As the elderly population in the United States and around the world increases, a greater number will be dependent on others for their care. By 2010 approximately 46.6 percent of the aged will be 75 years of age or over. Also by 2050, more than 55 percent of the aged are projected to be 75 years of age or older.

Definition and Classifications

Broadly defined, elder abuse is the adverse commission or omission of acts against an elderly person. Elder abuse can assume varied forms, including physical, psychological, financial, and sexual abuse as well as neglect.

Physical abuse is the nonaccidental infliction of physical force that results in body injury, pain, or impairment. Physical abuse acts include bruising, punching, restraining, sexually molesting, or force-feeding.

Psychological or emotional abuse is any willful conduct that causes mental or emotional anguish. Examples include verbal or nonverbal insults, intimidating, humiliating, isolating, or threatening harm.

Financial or material abuse refers to the unauthorized or improper exploitation of funds, property, assets, or any resources of an older person. Such acts include stealing money, changing will content, or cashing the elder's social security check.

Sexual abuse involves nonconsensual sexual or intimate contact or exposure of any kind with an older person. Family members, institutional employees, and friends can commit sexual abuse.

Neglect is the deliberate failure or refusal of a caretaker to fulfill his or her obligation to provide for the elder person's basic needs. Examples include denial of food, clothing, or health care items such as eyeglasses, hearing aids, or false teeth; abandoning the elderly for long periods; and preventing safe housing.

Self-abuse or self-neglect is abusive or neglectful behavior of an older person directed at himself or herself that compromises or threatens his or her health or safety. Self-abuse mostly results from the elder person's failure or inability to provide for his or her basic needs, despite being considered legally competent.

Sources of Elder Abuse

Major sources of elder abuse can be categorized as institutional, societal, and familial.

Institutional sources would be intentional or unintentional adverse actions and negative attitudes from professionals, such as workers in nursing homes, physicians, nurses, psychologists, and social workers. Institutional abuses are activities that are not in the best interest of the elderly.

Societal sources are thinking of old age in negative ways, stereotypes, discrimination, and ageism. Society has contributed to the transformation of aging from a natural process into a social problem. Elders can be, for example, targets of job discrimination when seeking employment and promotion.

Familial sources involve families and may be referred to as domestic elder abuse. Familial elder abuse results from increased levels of stress and frustration among caregivers. Caregivers with substance abuse problems and limited resources frequently face problems in caring for older members and have higher rates of abuse.

Felix O. Chima

See also Ageism; Domestic Violence; Family; Family, Dysfunctional; Family, Extended; Violence

Further Readings

Chima, Felix O. 1998. "Familial, Institutional, and Societal Sources of Elder Abuse: Perspective on Empowerment." *International Review of Modern Sociology* 28(1):103–16.
————. 2003. "Age Discrimination in the Workplace and Human Rights Implications." *Journal of Intergroup Relations* 30:3–19.
Tatara, Toshio. 1995. "Elder Abuse." *Encyclopedia of Social Work,* 19th ed., edited by R. L. Edwards. Atlanta, GA: NASW Press.
U.S. Census Bureau. 2007. "Statistical Abstract of the United States." Washington, DC: U.S. Government Printing Office.

ABUSE, INTIMATE PARTNER

Intimate partner violence (IPV), or abuse, generally refers to violence involving spouses, ex-spouses, and boyfriends or girlfriends and exes. Other phrases sometimes used include wife battering, wife abuse, intimate terrorism, and spousal violence. The Centers for Disease Control and Prevention define IPV as

> the intentional use of physical force with the potential for causing death, disability, injury, or harm. Physical violence includes, but is not limited to, scratching; pushing; shoving; throwing; grabbing; biting; choking; shaking; slapping; punching; burning; use of a weapon; and use of restraints or one's body, size, or strength against another person.

Estimates of Intimate Partner Violence

Because IPV is usually more private and hidden compared with other violence, its magnitude remains in dispute. The stigma often attached to intimate partner violence, fear of retaliation from the perpetrators, and numerous other safety concerns make estimating incidence rates difficult.

Fatal Violence: The Federal Bureau of Investigation (FBI) Supplementary Homicide Reports reveal that homicides between ex-spouses and boyfriends and girlfriends remained relatively stable from 1976 through 2005. During this same time, homicides between married couples significantly declined through 2001 but have remained relatively stable since then. Although the overall number of women and men murdered by their intimate partners decreased during the past few decades, this decrease was more significant for males killed by their intimate partners than for female victims. Overall, women are much more likely to be killed by their intimate partners than are men.

Nonfatal Violence: Relying on such reports as the FBI Uniform Crime Reports or the National Incident Based Reporting System (NIBRS) to estimate nonfatal incidence of IPV is problematic because a high percentage of victims never report these crimes to police. Typically, IPV researchers and policymakers rely on nationally representative surveys to monitor its magnitude. The National Crime Victimization Survey (NCVS), conducted by the Bureau of Justice Statistics, is the only ongoing survey that monitors IPV on an annual basis. To measure IPV incidents, the NCVS cues respondents to think of victimizations perpetrated by "a neighbor or friend, someone at work or school, or a family member," rather than specifically asking respondents about incidents perpetrated by intimate partners such as spouses, boyfriends, or girlfriends.

NCVS data indicate that, on average, females are assaulted by intimate partners at a rate of 6.4 per 1,000 every year compared with a rate of 1.1 for their male counterparts. This translates into more than 1 million females age 12 and older violently attacked by their intimate partners annually.

The National Violence Against Women and Men Survey (NVAWMS) asked respondents in 1995 about assaults they experienced as children and as adults, using specific screening questions about incidents of pushing, grabbing or shoving, pulling hair, slapping, hitting, and so forth. In addition to being asked about strangers or known offenders, respondents also were asked about victimizations perpetrated by all possible types of intimate or ex-intimate partners. The NVAWMS obtained higher annual rates of IPV than the NCVS: a rate of 13 per 1,000 women age 18 and over and a rate of 9 per 1,000 adult men. Significantly, this survey also examined how many women and men experienced violent attacks in their adult lives, with over 1 in 5 (22 percent) of women and 7.4 percent of men reporting an assault by an intimate partner. Similar to homicide victimization, then, both the

NCVS and the NVAWMS indicate that females are more likely than males to experience nonfatal IPV.

Several factors contributed to the higher incidence rates obtained by the NVAWMS compared with the NCVS, including behaviorally specific questions, specific relationship cues regarding intimate partners, and the noncrime context of the survey. Thus, the ways in which people are asked about their victimization experiences significantly impact the number of people reporting this violence. Regardless of estimates used, however, intimate partner violence is a significant problem. For all too many women, their partner poses a greater risk for serious harm and death than does the stranger on the street.

Ronet Bachman and Margaret Leigey

See also National Crime Victimization Survey; Uniform Crime Report; Violence

Further Readings

Bachman, Ronet. 2000. "A Comparison of Annual Incidence Rates and Contextual Characteristics of Intimate-Partner Violence against Women from the National Crime Victimization Survey (NCVS) and the National Violence Against Women Survey (NVAWS)." *Violence against Women* 6(8):839–67.

Catalano, Shannan. *Intimate Partner Violence in the United States.* Bureau of Justice Statistics. Retrieved December 3, 2007 (http://www.ojp.usdoj.gov/bjs/intimate/ipv.htm).

Centers for Disease Control and Prevention. 2006. "Understanding Intimate Partner Violence." Retrieved December 3, 2007 (http://www.cdc.gov/ncipc/dvp/ipv_factsheet.pdf).

Tjaden, Patricia and Nancy Thoennes. 1998. *Prevalence, Incidence, and Consequences of Violence against Women: Findings from the National Violence Against Women Survey.* NCJ 172837. Washington, DC: National Institute of Justice and Centers for Disease Control and Prevention.

ABUSE, SIBLING

Sibling abuse can be defined as inappropriate behavior among siblings related by marriage, blood, adoption, or living arrangement. This conduct constitutes any behaviors that are not considered age or developmentally appropriate. Sibling abuse usually falls in one of three categories: inappropriate sexual behavior or contact, acts of violence or aggression, or psychological maltreatment. These three forms of abuse are not mutually exclusive: Any combination of the three can be found in a sibling abusive relationship. The general assumption is that psychological maltreatment precedes other forms of abuse and often sets the stage for abuse to occur.

Sibling sexual abuse may be defined as a compulsive inappropriate sexual activity toward a sibling extending over a period of time. It may include, but is not limited to, sexual touching, fondling, indecent exposure, attempted penetration, intercourse, rape, sodomy, or any other inappropriate sexual contact. Physical abuse involves repeated acts of aggression toward a sibling that have a high potential for causing injury and are committed with the intention of inflicting harm. These acts could include, but are not limited to, such things as hitting, punching, slapping, or other, more serious life-threatening assaults or violence. Psychological maltreatment, more commonly known as emotional abuse, may involve, but is not restricted to, name-calling, intimidation, ridicule, destruction of property, teasing, rejecting, terrorizing, isolating, corrupting, or denying emotional responsiveness or any acts done with the intention of creating an atmosphere of humiliation.

Minimization of sibling abuse is common and a primary reason why so little is known about this phenomenon. Precursors to sibling abuse are often minimized as behaviors common to age, gender, or both. For example, with regard to sibling sexual abuse, sexual exploration is one of the main precursors to abuse. Likewise, parental unavailability is a widespread family systemic factor contributing to sibling abuse. When parental figures are emotionally or physically absent, there can be an increased motivation to offend. A common instance in which sibling abuse takes place is in situations where siblings are placed in the role of caretaker.

Sibling abuse, not unlike other forms of abuse, may have a significant impact on the victim's psychological health, stability, or both, for many years to come. Sibling abuse victims can experience various forms of mental health and interpersonal issues. Sibling abuse has the potential to increase both a victim's vulnerability to revictimization and an offender's tendency toward more offending behaviors in the future. Recognizing the common warning signs of sibling abuse can effectively help educators and health care practitioners identify abusive situations. Knowledge about the warning signs and behavior precursors to abuse will aid in prevention and treatment as well. Increasing the functionality of the family system by adhering to the mental, physical, and emotional needs of the children can create an atmosphere that fosters successful prevention of sibling abuse.

Shamla L. McLaurin

See also Abuse, Child; Abuse, Child Sexual; Family, Dysfunctional; Violence

Further Readings

Caffaro, John V. and Allison Conn-Caffaro. 1998. *Sibling Abuse Trauma: Assessment and Intervention Strategies for Children, Families, and Adults.* Binghamton, NY: Hawthorne.

Wiehe, Vernon R. 1997. *Sibling Abuse: Hidden Physical, Emotional, and Sexual Trauma.* 2nd ed. Thousand Oaks, CA: Sage.

ACADEMIC STANDARDS

Setting high academic standards is a key component in the drive to achieve educational equality today. However, academic standards cannot be separated from the environments in which they exist—in classrooms, schools, districts, and states and nationwide. One important factor in the call for academic standards is political pressure related to the position of the United States in the global society as well as the need to strengthen what the 1983 report *A Nation at Risk* called "the intellectual, moral, and spiritual strengths of our people which knit together the very fabric of our society." A review of the recent history of academic standards reforms is important in understanding how this movement relates to both assessment and standardized curriculum.

Among other reforms, *A Nation at Risk* called for "more rigorous and measurable standards." This early call for academic standards at both collegiate and precollegiate levels was linked to assessment as well as higher curricular expectations. Although the call for academic standards was nationwide, the efforts toward reform were focused within the schools themselves.

In 1994, Congress passed the Goals 2000: Educate America Act, further refining the demand to increase academic standards in U.S. schools. Among other things, Goals 2000 set specific, measurable academic standards, particularly in mathematics and science. Higher academic performance was to be achieved via the development of "voluntary national" content and performance standards. The act encouraged states to become more actively involved in setting performance standards (assessment) while defining content standards nationally. Needless to say, it was easier for states to develop performance standards than it was for diverse groups of individuals to agree on the content of material to be taught in schools. Only content standards for mathematics were established, and even those were debated vigorously.

In 2001, the No Child Left Behind educational reform effort called for increased accountability based upon "state standards in reading and mathematics." As with the two preceding reform efforts, it embedded academic standards in the curriculum, generating an even stronger reliance on assessment under the No Child Left Behind Act. State governments must establish criteria (standardized testing) that the federal government approves, with the explicit end result being either success or failure. Although No Child Left Behind is a national reform effort, the criteria for academic standards vary considerably across states. Thus, while this push toward academic standards is embedded in the curriculum, with a standardized test labeling the school as succeeding or failing, pressure for student success can translate into teaching to tests.

The call for higher academic standards changed over the years as various reform efforts shaped the criteria for setting the curriculum and assessment of academic standards. Colleges and universities, while encouraged to develop higher academic standards beginning with *A Nation at Risk,* have not yet had to conduct rigorous national assessments of curricula. The push for higher academic standards in elementary and secondary education, however, has moved beyond the classroom and schools and is currently embedded in state and national assessment.

Joan Z. Spade

See also Charter Schools; Education, Academic Performance; Education, Policy and Politics; Educational Equity; School Vouchers; Social Promotions

Further Readings

Goals 2000: Educate America Act. 1994. Washington, DC: House of Representatives.

National Commission on Excellence in Education. 1983. "A Nation at Risk: The Imperative for Educational Reform." Washington, DC: U.S. Department of Education.

No Child Left Behind Act of 2001. U.S. Department of Education. Retrieved January 30, 2008 (http://www.ed .gov/policy/elsec/leg/esea02/index.html).

ACCIDENTS, AUTOMOBILE

An automobile accident is defined as a crash that occurs between an automobile and another automobile, human, animal, or fixed object. Automobile accidents are also commonly called traffic collisions, traffic crashes, motor vehicle collisions, and motor vehicle crashes. Among the professionals who aim to reduce the number of traffic crashes and related injuries, use of the word *accident* is often debated as the term suggests that such events are unexpected and unpreventable.

Traffic crashes are a major public safety problem; overall, they are the leading cause of death by injury in the United States. The National Highway Traffic Safety Administration (NHTSA) reports that in 2005, there were almost 6.16 million police-reported crashes, 2.7 million injuries, and 43,443 deaths. Injuries that result from traffic crashes are the leading cause of death to individuals ages 1 through 34 and are the leading contributor to years of life lost due to premature death, surpassing heart disease, cancer, AIDS, and stroke. A 2000 NHTSA report estimated the cost of U.S. traffic crashes at over $230.6 billion annually.

Globally, traffic safety is a rising concern. The World Health Organization projects that by 2020, road traffic injuries and deaths will be the third most important contributor to global health problems, up from ninth in 2000. Eighty-five percent of the traffic deaths around the world occur to pedestrians, bicyclists, and motorcyclists in low- and middle-income countries. More than half of these fatalities occur among younger, able-bodied adults; the economic cost of these fatalities to these countries is estimated at $65 billion each year.

Who Is at Risk?

Some populations may be overrepresented in the crash data because of behaviors associated with greater risks or may be overrepresented in injury data because they are less protected in some way. Such vulnerable populations include children, teenagers, older adults, communities of color, and nonmotorized road users (pedestrians and bicyclists).

Child passenger safety seats are key to protecting infants and children from motor vehicle injury. Because of their size and level of physical development, children are extremely vulnerable to injury and fatality as unrestrained passengers. Infants and toddlers are 4 times more likely to be unrestrained with an unrestrained driver than with a restrained driver. Even with the increase in car and booster seat use, many child safety seats are not installed properly.

Per population, the crash involvement rate of teen drivers is higher than that of any other age group. Issues related to human development, personality, peer influence, driving experience, and demographics all contribute to risk. New research in brain development shows that development of the prefrontal cortex, responsible for executive decision making, is not complete until the early 20s. Graduated driver licensing shows promise in reducing the teen crash rate, as do laws targeting underage drinking and driving and enforcing restricted alcohol sales to minors.

Although injury and fatality rates decline dramatically after young adulthood, they begin to rise again in older adulthood. Older adults face more severe injury risk in traffic crashes and are more likely to die from injuries. Some skills (vision, cognition, and sensory motor skills) important for safe driving may decline with the aging process, although age is not a predictor of driving skills and not all older adults experience a decline in skills that affect safe driving. As a percentage of the population, older drivers are least likely to be involved in motor vehicle crashes. However, per mile driven, older drivers have a higher rate of crash involvement. This is an increasing problem, as older adults comprise the fastest-growing age group in the United States. The National Center for Injury Prevention and Control reports that by 2020, there will be more than 40 million older licensed drivers.

In addition to varying across age groups, collision involvement differs by ethnicity. Collision rates are higher among Latinos/as, African Americans, and Native Americans than among whites and Asians.

Safety belt compliance, higher rates of impaired driving, and higher rates of pedestrian injury and fatality have been found to occur disproportionately among communities of color. These racial disparities are partially correlated with lower socioeconomic status and may be partially due to the confluence of many factors, including language and culture barriers, mistrust of law enforcement, insufficient knowledge of relevant laws, and the increased likelihood of rural residence. Focus groups and other research have identified culturally appropriate and sensitive educational materials geared toward special populations. This will be integral in reducing racial disparities in traffic safety.

Pedestrians and bicyclists, in particular, face hazards on the streets. Pedestrian deaths account for just over 11 percent of the country's traffic fatalities. Walking or riding a bicycle reduces road congestion, air pollution, and global climate change and offers other health benefits. However, pedestrians and cyclists frequently encounter problems with a road infrastructure designed primarily for motor vehicles, thereby creating greater risks. Unfortunately, creating reliable estimates of pedestrian accident rates is impossible without adequate information about pedestrian exposure (e.g., how many people walk, how many miles people walk). Currently, no widespread systematic and accessible method exists to estimate pedestrian exposure.

Addressing the Problem

Many traffic crashes result from poor driver behavior. Driving while distracted, driving while under the influence, and speeding are among the leading driver behaviors contributing to traffic crashes. In recent years, alcohol involvement was a factor in about 40 percent of fatal motor vehicle crashes and driver inattention in at least 25 percent of police-reported crashes. In 2004, speeding was a contributing factor in 30 percent of fatal crashes.

Effective in reducing alcohol-related crashes are policies addressing drinking and driving, such as legal blood alcohol content limits set at .08 percent, license suspension laws, minimum drinking age laws, monitoring retail compliance with regard to sales to minors, vehicle impounding, and ignition interlock systems. Besides interventions to prevent crashes by targeting driving behavior, other efforts seek to reduce the effects of traffic crashes through safety devices. One of the most common devices, the seat belt, has a substantial effect on survivability in a crash. The NHTSA reported in 2004 that seat belts saved 15,434 lives. Rates of seat belt use vary among states but climbed between 1975 and 2004 in every state, most dramatically in states with laws requiring seat belt use.

At the national level, the NHTSA has led a sustained effort over the past few decades to reduce traffic crashes and subsequent injuries and death, resulting in greatly increased use of occupant restraints, decreased alcohol-related injuries and fatalities, and a reduction in the death rate per million miles traveled.

Need for a Systematic Approach

Expertise in transportation engineering, enforcement, city planning, public health, policy, and other relevant professions is critical to meeting the nation's complex traffic safety challenges. Reducing the toll that traffic injury takes on society requires a committed and comprehensive approach that covers education, engineering, enforcement, and environmental modifications. A critical element of injury prevention is to reach out to vulnerable populations by tailoring messages and programs to fit specific groups and their cultural norms, backgrounds, and experiences.

A systematic approach to traffic safety that addresses human behavior, vehicle design, and roadway design as interacting approaches to preventing traffic crashes and injury is needed. Cross-training and interdisciplinary work is central. For example, law enforcement must understand how data related to injuries and fatalities can inform formation and enforcement of traffic safety laws. Engineers must understand where and how injuries occur so that they can design roadways that are safe for drivers, passengers, pedestrians, and bicyclists. Planners must understand the traffic safety issues in land use decisions. Teachers and social service professionals need to know how alcohol and other drugs affect driving behavior.

One way of organizing the diverse approaches to traffic safety is in terms of the Haddon matrix, developed by William Haddon, the first director of the NHTSA. The matrix is a tool for describing opportunities for where and when to conduct traffic safety interventions. The Haddon matrix looks at injuries in terms of causal and contributing factors by examining the factors of the driver, the vehicle, and the highway, as well as time phases before a potential vehicle collision ("pre-crash"), during the vehicle collision ("crash"), and after the collision ("post-crash").

The value of the Haddon matrix is that each cell illustrates a different area in which to mount interventions to improve traffic safety. Intervention designs that apply to the pre-crash phase can reduce the number of collisions. Interventions that apply to the crash phase do not stop the crash, but they reduce the number or severity of injuries that occur as a result. Interventions that apply to the post-crash phase do not stop the initial crash or the injury from occurring, but they optimize the outcome for people with injuries.

Jill F. Cooper, Kara E. MacLeod,
and David R. Ragland

See also Drunk Driving; Traffic Congestion

Further Readings

AAA Foundation for Traffic Safety. 2001. "The Role of Driver Distraction in Traffic Crashes." Washington, DC: AAA Foundation for Traffic Safety. Retrieved December 4, 2007 (http://www.aaafoundation.org/pdf/distraction.pdf).

National Highway Traffic Safety Administration. 2002. "The Economic Impact of Motor Vehicle Crashes, 2000." Retrieved November 30, 2007 (http://www.nhtsa.dot.gov/staticfiles/DOT/NHTSA/Communication%20&%20Consumer%20Information/Articles/Associated%20Files/EconomicImpact2000.pdf).

———. 2004. "Traffic Safety Facts." Retrieved November 30, 2007 (http://www.trb.org/news/blurb_detail.asp?id=5838).

Pedestrian and Bicycle Information Center. 2006. "Pedestrian Crash Facts." Chapel Hill, NC: Pedestrian and Bicycle Information Center. Retrieved November 30, 2007 (http://www.walkinginfo.org/facts/facts.cfm).

ACCOMMODATION

See PLURALISM

ACCULTURATION

Acculturation remains a significant issue in a diverse society. It refers to the process of cultural exchanges as a result of continuous firsthand contact among cultural groups. The primary focus lies in the change occurring among minority group members, particularly immigrants, after adopting the cultural features of the majority group. Change may occur in beliefs, values, behavioral practices, languages, or all of these.

Perspectives

Historically, acculturation is conceptualized with a one-dimensional approach. That is to say, individuals must lose cultural traits of their own group to gain characteristics from other groups for adaptation. This approach fits into the larger picture of the straight line model of assimilation. This model maps the process of assimilation in a linear fashion wherein immigrants relinquish their own ethnic culture before taking on (presumably) more beneficial host cultural behaviors. In a series of stages, immigrants first predominantly retain their own ethnic cultures, and as contacts with host society increase, they enter a stage where aspects of the two cultures combine. Finally, the host culture overwhelms the ethnic culture, and immigrants come to full adoption of the host culture.

The unidimensional perspective on acculturation makes an important assumption that ethnic culture and host culture are mutually exclusive. However, contemporary theorists on acculturation challenge this assumption. Instead, these theorists view acculturation as multifaceted, such that ethnic culture and host culture exist on different dimensions. This perspective believes immigrants have the ability to retain some of their ethnic practices and, at the same time, adopt other aspects of the host society's culture.

Acculturation and Assimilation

Many observers often equated acculturation with assimilation in public discourse and in earlier assimilation theory until 1964, when Milton Gordon eliminated this confusion and provided a systematic dissection of the assimilation concept. In his conceptual scheme, acculturation is only one aspect of assimilation, sometimes called cultural assimilation, and it is the first step toward full assimilation. In his formulation, Gordon made a critical distinction between acculturation and what he called "structural assimilation," by which he meant the entry of members of a minority group into primary-group relationships with the majority group. The primary group relationship refers to institutions or associations such as social clubs and cliques. Because discrimination and avoidance responses often lead to exclusion of immigrants and even the second generation, structural assimilation is slower than acculturation. Whereas acculturation is an inevitable outcome resulting from continuous contact between ethnic and majority groups, structural assimilation is not, because it requires new members to move out of their own groups or associations into the equivalent associations of the host society, which may not necessarily happen.

Gordon and other assimilation theorists view acculturation as one-directional, meaning that members of an ethnic group adopt the culture of the majority group. This largely fits the reality of the old era of immigration where Anglo-American culture clearly constituted the societal mainstream. Now, as U.S. society becomes more diverse and the demographic proportion of the earlier majority group shrinks, the boundaries of group cultural differences often get blurred. For example, children of immigrant families typically acculturate to the dominant culture and the immigrant culture; therefore, both cultures become important elements of the children's development.

Measures for Acculturation

Language, often the largest initial barrier that immigrants encounter, is the first step and most widely assessed cultural practice associated with acculturation. In the U.S. context, English language use represents the first step toward successful adaptation. Language proficiency can enable immigrants to access the host society's institutions, such as the media; to make friends with members of the host society; and to find better employment opportunities. Retention of native languages is often seen as a key indicator of ethnic identity. Because of the functional and cultural significance of language, many scholars have used language alone as an index for acculturation.

The second major measure of acculturation is participation in cultural practices of both majority and minority groups, which include a wide spectrum ranging from pragmatic activities such as food preferences and modes of dress to pursuits such as religion and artistic inclination. The unidimensional perspective of acculturation holds that retaining traditional cultural practices such as food and dress may alienate immigrants from members of the mainstream, slow down the process of their adaptation to the host society, and ultimately prevent them from full assimilation into the host society. On the other hand, the multidimensional perspective of acculturation holds that immigrants are able to retain their cultural heritage and adopt cultural practices of the host society, and more important, they are encouraged to do so.

The third major measure of acculturation is ethnic identity, which refers to how members of an ethnic group relate to their own group as a subgroup of the larger society.

Ethnic identity is only meaningful in the context of a pluralistic society. In a racially or ethnically homogeneous society, ethnic identity is virtually meaningless. In light of the two perspectives on acculturation, two models emerge to conceptualize ethnic identity. One is a bipolar model, guided by a unidimensional perspective toward acculturation, assuming that ethnic identity and acculturation are in opposition to each other. That is, a weakening of ethnic identity is an inevitable outcome of acculturation. The alternative model views minority group members as having either strong or weak identifications with their own culture and that of the mainstream. Strong identification with both groups indicates biculturalism; identification with neither group suggests marginality. Strong identification with the ethnic group but weak attachment to the host society suggests separation or isolation of the ethnic group.

Acculturation and Psychological Outcome

Researchers on acculturation often concentrate on the consequences of acculturation, particularly, its potential impact on psychological functioning. Two views emerge predicting opposite outcomes of psychological well-being as a result of acculturation.

One school of thought argues that the more acculturated a member from a minority group is, the more psychological distress he or she suffers. This rationale draws from Émile Durkheim's social integration theory, in the sense that adopting the majority group's culture may remove the minority member from the ethnic community and isolate that person from an ethnic support base. The minority member may experience alienation that increases the possibility of psychological distress. Externally, a minority member who attempts to acculturate may encounter resistance and discrimination from the host society, which could exacerbate psychological distress. The result is that members of minority groups do not find acceptance by either their own ethnic group or the majority group. Thus they find themselves experiencing marginality and psychological distress.

The opposing view predicts higher self-esteem and less psychological distress among people who are more acculturated than those who are less acculturated. This view sees psychological harm in any conflict between host and native cultures. Therefore, acculturation should improve one's self-esteem and reduce psychological distress. When closely tied to the ethnic culture and exposed to conflicting practices, beliefs, and attitudes in the host society, a minority group member may feel confused, challenged, and lost about what he or she believes. In particular, if one is not equipped with strategies to achieve the goals valued by the host society, self-esteem will be damaged.

Empirical evidence exists to support both views. Both do agree that if minority members are not equipped with strategies to reconcile the cultural differences between the host society and their own group, they will experience acculturative stress that might lead to psychological distress.

Yingyi Ma

See also Assimilation; Ethnic Group; Ethnicity; Ethnocentrism; Multiculturalism; Pluralism

Further Readings

Alba, Richard and Victor Nee. 1997. "Rethinking Assimilation Theory for a New Era of Immigration." *International Migration Review* 31:826–74.

Berry, J. W. 1980. "Acculturation as Varieties of Adaptation." Pp. 9–26 in *Acculturation: Theory, Models, and Some New Findings,* edited by A. M. Padilla. Boulder, CO: Westview.

Gans, Herbert. 1997. "Toward a Reconciliation of 'Assimilation' and 'Pluralism': The Interplay of Acculturation and Ethnic Retention." *International Migration Review* 31:875–92.

Gordon, Milton M. 1964. *Assimilation in American Life.* New York: Oxford University Press.

Phinney, Jean. 1990. "Ethnic Identity in Adolescents and Adults: Review of Research." *Psychological Bulletin* 108:499–514.

ACID RAIN

Acid rain refers to both wet and dry deposition of atmospheric materials that contain high concentrations of nitric and sulfuric acid. The wet deposition can include fog, hail, sleet, or snow in addition to rain; the dry deposition is usually dust or smoke.

How Does Acid Rain Form?

Acid rain is a secondary air pollutant. It is not released directly into the air; rather, it forms as a result of the discharge of sulfur dioxide (SO_2) and nitrogen oxides (NO_x) into the atmosphere. In the atmosphere, SO_2 reacts with other chemicals, primarily water and oxygen, to form sulfuric acid (H_2SO_4); the nitrogen oxides react to form nitric acid (HNO_3). Once formed, prevailing winds can transport these compounds to distances as great as hundreds of miles, across state and national boundaries.

Although natural sources such as erupting volcanoes and decaying plant material can release these gases, most emissions result primarily from the combustion of fossil fuels. In the United States, approximately 67 percent of all the emitted SO_2 and 25 percent of the emitted NO_x come from electrical power plants that burn fossil fuels. Other sources for these gases are also primarily industrial in nature, including ore smelting, coal-fired generators, and combustion of fuel in motor vehicles.

How Is Acid Rain Measured?

All acids, including acid rain, are measured using the pH scale. The pH scale is based on the tendency of a substance to release hydrogen ions in solution; the more readily a substance releases hydrogen ions, the stronger an acid it is. The pH scale runs from a value of 0 for very strong acid (very weak base) to a high value of 14 for a very weak acid (very strong base). Calculating in powers of 10, water with a pH of 4 is 10 times more acidic than water with a pH of 5. Distilled water has a pH of 7, something rarely seen in nature, even with unpolluted rain. This is because naturally occurring carbon dioxide (CO_2) in the atmosphere dissolves into the rainwater, forming weak carbonic acid and lowering the pH to around 5.6. According to the U.S. Environmental Protection Agency (USEPA), as of 2000, the most acidic rain falling in the United States had a pH of approximately 4.3.

Where Is Acid Rain a Problem?

In the United States, acid rain is a problem primarily in the eastern half of the country, in parts of the Northeast and the northern Midwest. The lowest pH values—the result of heavy industrialization in

Pennsylvania, Ohio, and Illinois—are found in New York and central New England, as well as in Ontario, Quebec, and the Maritime Provinces in Canada. Except for some localized instances of slightly lower pH values, the problem is less pronounced in the southern and western parts of the United States.

A National Surface Water Survey conducted by USEPA in the mid-1980s investigated more than 1,000 lakes larger than 10 acres and many streams thought to be vulnerable to acidification. The survey found that many of these lakes and streams suffer from chronic acidity, with the water constantly maintaining a low pH. The survey found that of the lakes and streams surveyed, acid rain was the cause of acidity in 75 percent of the acidic lakes and 50 percent of the acidic streams. The survey identified the Adirondacks and Catskill Mountains in New York, the mid-Appalachian highlands along the East Coast, the northern Midwest, and mountainous areas of the West as areas where many of the surface waters are particularly sensitive to acidification.

Ongoing monitoring by the U.S. Geological Survey, as well as a study conducted by the Hubbard Brook Research Foundation, has found that conditions have not significantly improved. In the Northeast, where the soils have little ability to neutralize acids (known as buffering capacity), some lakes now have a pH of 5 or less, with a lowest reported pH of 4.2 in Little Echo Pond in Franklin, New York. The scope of the problem is even greater if lakes smaller than 10 acres are considered.

Eastern Canada has soil quite similar to that in the Adirondack Mountains, and its lakes are extremely vulnerable to chronic acidification. An estimated 14,000 lakes in that region are acidic, according to the Canadian government. Also susceptible to the effects of acid deposition are streams flowing over soils with little buffering capacity. The survey found that 580 streams in the Mid-Atlantic coastal plain are acidic. The highest concentration of acidic streams was found in the New Jersey Pinelands, where over 90 percent of the streams are acidic. In the Mid-Atlantic Highlands, more than 1,350 of the streams are acidic.

In addition to chronic acidification, there can be brief periods, known as episodic acidification, when pH drops because of heavy downpours of rain or runoff from snowmelt. Many lakes and streams in the United States and Canada are susceptible to this episodic effect. USEPA estimates that approximately 70 percent of lakes in the Adirondacks are at risk.

What Are the Effects of Acid Rain?

The environmental effects of acid rain are most clearly seen in surface water environments such as streams, lakes, and marshes. Acid rain falls directly on these aquatic habitats, and acidic runoff flows into them after falling on rural and urban areas. The impact can be disastrous. In the United States, many aquatic species are showing the deadly effects of prolonged exposure to acidic conditions, sometimes to such an extent that the overall populations of whole species are reduced and species that are more sensitive to low pH levels become extinct. All of these effects contribute to a reduction in the biodiversity of the affected systems. Some acid lakes no longer have fish in them.

Aquatic systems are not the only ones affected. Forest systems in Europe, North America, and Asia also show damage from acid rain, negatively affecting seedling production, tree density, and overall viability of the forests. The problem is particularly serious in high-altitude forests, where the trees are exposed to the acidic precipitation for longer periods. The most direct damage is to seedlings and to the tissues of adult trees. However, the higher acidity can leach nutrients from the soil and mobilize metals, such as aluminum, that are toxic to the plants. Furthermore, weakened trees can become vulnerable to insects and diseases.

In addition to damage done to the natural environment, acid rain also causes damage to non-natural objects. In many cities, acid precipitation is destroying numerous historic and contemporary buildings and works of art. Structures of limestone and marble—including the Parthenon, the Taj Mahal, the Washington Monument, and numerous medieval cathedrals throughout Europe—are most vulnerable because of their high reactivity with acids. Additionally, acid precipitation can corrode the steel in reinforced concrete, damaging buildings, bridges, and roads. The Council on Environmental Quality estimates that the economic losses in the United States amount to about $4.8 billion in direct costs every year.

What Can Be Done?

Because acid precipitation is a result of air pollution, the most effective strategy is to reduce emissions of the pollutants to the atmosphere. New technology has allowed factories to decrease amounts of SO_2 in smokestack emissions. However, emissions of NO_x

have increased over the same time period, suggesting the need for more stringent air pollution regulation.

Karen A. Swanson

See also Environment, Runoff and Eutrophication; Environment, Sewage Disposal; Water Organization; Water Quality; Water Resources

Further Readings

Environment Canada. 2002. "Acid Rain." Retrieved December 3, 2007 (http://www.ec.gc.ca/acidrain/).

Hubbard Brook Research Foundation. "Acid Rain." Retrieved December 3, 2007 (http://www.hubbard brookfoundation.org/article/view/12940/1/2076/).

U.S. Environmental Protection Agency. 2007. "Acid Rain." Retrieved December 3, 2007 (http://www.epa.gov/acidrain/).

U.S. Geological Survey. "Acid Deposition." Retrieved December 3, 2007 (http://www.usgs.gov/science/science.php?term=6).

ACTIVITY THEORY

Activity theory predicts that more frequent social interaction and engagement in society will lead people to attain greater life satisfaction, enhanced self-image, and positive adjustment in old age. By remaining active, elders retain the capability of enhancing both their physical and psychological well-being. According to many activity theorists, the interests of society tend to be antagonistic to those of the elderly. Ageism, or negative stereotypes based on one's age, is a barrier to a more integrated society between younger and older people. Institutionalized forms of exclusion based on age are also a formal means of discouraging the elderly from actively participating in society. These obstacles tend to induce withdrawal from society by people as they advance into old age. Activity theorists contend that by remaining active and resisting this tendency to enter isolation, older members of society can live happier and healthier lives.

Activity in old age can take place in multiple forms. Informal activity would be engagement with relatives, neighbors, friends, or other acquaintances, while formal activities involve established organizations, associations, or clubs. Studies show both types are associated with higher life satisfaction, although ailing health and disability preclude some of the elderly from frequent activity. Social support from both formal and informal sources also improves health outcomes and life chances. Activity theorists claim that these positive results from interactions with others occur because they allow older people to continue carrying out meaningful roles in society. In some cases they permit the continuation of roles carried out in middle age. For others, they enable the initiation of new roles that substitute for (or replace) those that are no longer viable. Most important, they facilitate role stability in the lives of the elderly. Activity theorists believe this is crucial because sudden change in the lifestyles of those in old age is disruptive and potentially harmful.

Critics of activity theory claim that socioeconomic characteristics tend to grant or inhibit entry into the types of associations that foster productive activity. For this reason, the relationship between activity and life satisfaction may be spurious, meaning that those with more education or those of a higher social class might be more active and more satisfied simply because of the elevated position they hold in society. Other criticisms center on the theory's premise that people must play productive roles in society to make their lives seem meaningful. As the distinction between a productive role and an unproductive role is open to interpretation, some argue that the quality of life among those who prefer a life of solitude and contemplation tends to be underestimated.

Christopher Donoghue

See also Ageism; Disengagement Theory; Life Course

Further Readings

Havighurst, Robert J. 1963. "Successful Aging." Pp. 299–320 in *Process of Aging: Social and Psychological Perspectives,* vol. 1, edited by R. Williams, C. Tibbits, and W. Donahue. New York: Atherton.

Litwin, Howard and Sharon Shiovitz-Ezra. 2006. "The Association between Activity and Well-being in Later Life: What Really Matters?" *Ageing & Society* 26:225–42.

ADDICTION

Drug addiction as a social phenomenon is a relatively recent construct. That is, despite the use of psychoactive drugs for thousands of years, drug use and abuse only became a social problem when the functioning of a member of a particular group or the activities of the group itself became impaired through another's drug-taking behavior. Thus, the construct of drug addiction evolved through the interconnectedness and impact that one person's behavior has on another. Although the word *addiction* finds its roots in the Latin *addictus,* meaning "to deliver" or "to devote," it was not until William Shakespeare modernized the word in *Henry V* that it took on a meaning similar to that of today. Still, Shakespeare's reference to addiction referred more to the king's predilections for theology than any drug use. Despite this evolution of the vernacular, the people of ancient Greece and Rome knew that many substances (e.g., opium) were capable of producing varying levels of dependence.

The rise of drug addiction as a significant global social problem began in the 17th century with the emergence of the opium trade between the Chinese and British Empires. Desperate to find a commodity to trade for Chinese tea, the British exported massive amounts of opium from India via the East India Trading Company. In the process, the British opium trade addicted a nation to the drug and eventually sparked two bloody wars, appropriately referred to as the Opium Wars. Trade also became the impetus for other notable drugs introduced to the masses. In fact, the trade of cocaine, tea and coffee (caffeine), and tobacco (nicotine) provided a considerable income for many countries with the ability to deliver these cash crops internationally. Thus, through global trade, many drug-naive populations were exposed to exotic mind-altering drugs.

Other significant changes during the Industrial Revolution also contributed to the global consumption of drugs. During the 19th century, more efficient drug delivery systems became available. For example, the invention of the hypodermic needle allowed for the delivery of morphine, a drug isolated from opium in 1805, in a manner other than by oral administration. Given the prevailing misconception during this era that drugs produced addiction only when administered through the mouth (as in the case of alcohol, nicotine, and snuff preparations of cocaine), the administration of drugs through a syringe lessened the population's anxiety about the addictive potential of newer drug derivatives that, in some cases, were much more potent. Further, industrialization and the ensuing mass production of drugs by a variety of pharmaceutical companies exposed individuals of limited economic means to substances that were once only available to the upper echelons of society. The

addictive potential of these drugs now knew neither geographical boundary nor social class, resulting in pandemics of drug abuse.

As drug use increased across the social spectrum during the 19th and 20th centuries, so did the opposition to drug taking. Analysts suggest that this change in society's perception of drug use rested on several key patterns prevalent during this time. For instance, as excessive drug use increased, so did other risk-taking behaviors. This phenomenon resulted in an increase in mortality rates for drug addicts. Second, the loss of productivity resulting from drug use affected not only the individual's ability to survive in an increasingly competitive world but also societal functioning, particularly in lost work hours, production, and sales. In addition, the association of drugs with certain minority groups shifted attitudes about their social acceptability. For example, during the expansion of the railways in the United States, a cheaper and more abundant immigrant Chinese labor force replaced domestic workers. Chinese immigrants also engaged in opium smoking, which by this time was a cultural practice. The job loss that resulted from the influx of Chinese immigrants sparked many prejudicial attitudes and discriminatory behaviors against this minority group. Merely through association, recreational drug use became a frowned-upon practice, only committed by members of an undesirable group. As such, the conditions were ripe for a significant shift in international and domestic drug policy during the early 20th century.

In response to the emerging threat of increased drug misuse, many governments worldwide reacted by enacting regulatory and prohibitive drug legislation. For example, in the United States, the Harrison Narcotics Act of 1914 levied a tax on narcotics. This tax was aimed at decreasing the open distribution and consumption of many drugs like cocaine and opium, even though taxes on other drugs (e.g., cigarettes and alcohol) provided considerable sources of revenue. Thus, in some respects governments relied on the drug trade for profit. Another example of legislation aimed at affecting the drug market was Prohibition (the Volstead Act of 1919). Rather than taxing alcohol, the purpose of Prohibition was to eliminate its consumption altogether. In retrospect, all this legislation accomplished was creation of a black market for alcohol and criminalization of a rather large population of individuals. In 1970, the Controlled Substance Act provided a more measured reaction to drug use. Although it severely restricted the use of many drugs, threatening large fines and prison time for those caught possessing or distributing drugs with abuse potential, it also allowed for many drugs to remain available within a medical setting.

A second response to increasing drug use was the proliferation of treatment options for the drug abuser. Notable psychiatrists like Sigmund Freud (despite being addicted to cocaine himself) and Carl Jung attempted to develop theories of, and treatments for, drug addiction. The U.S. government created the first prison farm/hospital in 1929 dedicated to the treatment of addiction. Bill Wilson devised the 12-step program for alcohol addiction in the 1930s, the significance of which was that drug misuse would be framed as a problem that was largely outside of the abuser's control, rather than a moral failing of the individual. Methadone maintenance emerged in the 1960s as a viable option to heroin detoxification programs. Other opiate substitution and antagonist programs remain active and effective today.

Educating the populace about the dangers of drug addiction was a third front in the battle against drug use and abuse. Films like *Reefer Madness* attempted to scare the public into discontinuance. Such efforts, however, were largely uncoordinated and not rooted in any cohesive domestic or international policy. Attempting to focus the nation on the dangers of drug use, President Richard Nixon formally declared a "War on Drugs" in 1971, a war that still continues.

One beneficial product from increased public awareness of drug addiction as a significant social problem was the increase in efforts to understand its causes and consequences. If scientists could understand both the behavioral and biological bases of drug addiction, then better treatments could be devised. U.S. Addiction Research Centers, founded in the 1930s, sought to develop such viable treatment options. In the 1970s, the divisions of the National Institutes of Health, namely, the National Institute on Drug Abuse and the National Institute on Alcohol Abuse and Alcoholism, took on this task. These institutes, in conjunction with many academic scientists, would provide the public with many groundbreaking discoveries about drug addiction.

Although the resulting research postulated multiple models of the etiology of drug addiction, people nonetheless use recreational drugs because they make them feel good (or, in some cases, different). Specifically, drugs produce a sense of euphoria by hijacking the natural reward structures within the brain (e.g., the ventral tegmentum, nucleus accumbens, and medial prefrontal cortex). Through the pharmacological action of drugs, these structures become active when they might otherwise lie relatively dormant. Recreational drugs, either directly or indirectly, increase the levels of the neurotransmitter dopamine within these brain regions. As dopamine levels increase, so does the sense of reward. Interestingly, these same neurophysiological systems are the ones thought to underlie the transitions from drug use to abuse, as neuroplasticity becomes associated with escalated and problem drug use. Not surprisingly, much research focusing on treating drug addiction attempts to devise new medications that either alter or block the action of recreational drugs at this level of the brain. In addition, other research efforts are also attempting to uncover why some individuals are more responsive than others to the effects of drugs within this system. Is the propensity to move from casual drug use to drug abuse a function of genetics, environment, or a combination of these factors? These questions, among others, continue to drive research efforts on addiction. Current understanding of addiction rests, in large part, on assessment of times past and the status of drug addiction in the present.

Gregory D. Busse and Anthony L. Riley

See also Cocaine and Crack; Culture of Dependency; Drug Abuse; Methadone; Organized Crime; Prohibition; Psychoactive Drugs, Misuse of; Twelve-Step Programs

Further Readings

Courtwright, David T. 2001. *Forces of Habit: Drugs and the Making of the Modern World.* Cambridge, MA: Harvard University Press.
Goldstein, Avram. 2001. *Addiction: From Biology to Drug Policy.* New York: Oxford University Press.
Hanes, W. Travis, III and Frank Sanello. 2002. *The Opium Wars: The Addiction of One Empire and the Corruption of Another.* Naperville, IL: Sourcebook.

ADOPTION

Few in the United States have not been touched by adoption—either as members of the adoption triad (biological parents, adoptive parents, and adopted persons) or being related to or having (had) an association with adoption involving others. *Adoption* is the legal and permanent placement of a child with an adult who is not the child's biological parent. Once an adoption is legally finalized, adopted children have all the rights accruing to biological children, including the right to inherit.

Characteristics

Adoption may involve stepchildren, biologically related children, previous foster children, and children who are strangers to (have never met) the adoptive parents. Adoptions may be *closed* (sharing no information between the biological parents and adoptive parents); *semi-open* (sharing limited information, such as medical history or pictures at certain occasions, between the biological parents and adoptive parents); or *open* (making provision for ongoing contact between the biological parents and adoptive parents, and possibly the adoptee). Adoptions may be *matched* (for similarity between adoptive parents and adopted person in such areas as race, religion, physical features, nationality, and ethnicity), *transracial* (historically involving U.S. Caucasian parents and African American, Hispanic, or Native American children), *international/intercountry* (historically involving U.S. Caucasian parents and children of countries other than the United States—generally developing countries or economically impoverished countries), or *transcultural* (involving differences between adopted parents and adoptee in any aspect of culture such as religious background, sexual orientation background, or ethnic background).

Incidence

Based on the 2000 census, an estimated 2.1 million adopted children live with U.S. householders. These children are distinguished from stepchildren (the biological children of the householder's spouse or partner).

While U.S. parents generally complete the largest number of international adoptions, these adoptions also occur among families in such countries as Canada, Denmark, England, France, Italy, Norway, and Sweden. In some countries, laws in force for religious reasons prohibit the adoption of children by foreigners, although in some cases foreigners may become guardians of a child who is subsequently adopted in the country of origin of the adoptive parents.

Historical Overview

Adoption originated in Rome for the purpose of providing an heir to families without a male heir. Even with legalized adoption for this purpose, the adopted child continued to reside with the biological family and maintained the usual relationship with, and rights accorded biological children of, the biological family as well as the inheritance rights and responsibilities associated with membership in the adoptive family.

During and shortly after the Great Depression of 1929, agencies transported street children of large cities like New York, whose parents were financially unable to care for them, to foster-care-like families, mostly in the Midwest—a period that, because of the method of transporting them, became known as the period of the orphan trains. Although the purpose was usually to provide care in exchange for work by the children, some families adopted these children.

Following the period of the orphan trains, the adoption of children born to unmarried mothers became prevalent. Increased social freedom of adolescents and young adults occurred at a time when effective methods of preventing or terminating unwanted pregnancies were not yet available. Accompanying this relaxing of social norms were substantially increased numbers of pregnancies among unwed women. Social stigma surrounding these pregnancies and prohibition of governmental assistance to unmarried mothers left many women little choice but to relinquish their children for adoption. A private social welfare system for placing the children with more advantaged, mostly Caucasian married couples ensued, and adoption became an avenue to family formation for married couples for whom infertility prevented biological births. Children born out-of-wedlock to minority group mothers, particularly African American children, were generally informally adopted and raised by the mother's extended family.

Adoptions of infants born to unmarried mothers were generally closed and birth certificates changed to reflect the child's birth to the adoptive parents. Children were matched with adoptive parents according to race, religion, and physical features—all aimed at increasing the likelihood that children would look as if they were the biological children of the adoptive parents. European children orphaned in World War II also became a source of adoption for U.S. couples. For the first time, however, some children were placed with adoptive families who could not be matched on physical features (as in the case of orphaned children from Japan). The ending of the Korean War and the placement of large numbers of Korean War orphans with U.S. families further restricted the possibility of matching children and adoptive parents.

Effect of Social Changes

Effective artificial birth control methods beginning in the 1960s, followed by a decrease in social stigma associated with unwed pregnancy and, finally, the legalization of abortion in 1973, substantially reduced the number of healthy, Caucasian infants available for adoption. Although some infants remained available through private, independent adoptions, numbers were much smaller and biological mothers had increased control over the selection or eligibility determination of adoptive parents. Costs associated with these adoptions increased.

Already accustomed to seeing international adoptees in their communities and supported by public policy changes, Caucasian couples began to embrace the adoption of Native American, Hispanic, and African American children. A number of federal, state, and private agency policies provided financial, medical, tax, and employment incentives for the adoption of children considered otherwise hard to place. (These children were frequently older, members of sibling groups, and troubled by behavioral or developmental disabilities.) Support for these transracial adoptions eventually reopened interest in the international adoption of children who were frequently much younger than children available for domestic adoption, leading to an increase in international adoptions. In addition, same-race adoptions by minority group parents were encouraged, along with support for adoption by single parents and parents with limited incomes and resources.

Trends and Future Directions

Controversy still surrounds the adoption of children. Adults who were products of closed adoptions frequently search for their biological parents and, in the case of adoptions that occurred in this country, with some success. These adults have also sought policy changes aimed at opening information between biological parents and adoptees. Birth mothers have organized to support each other in searching for their relinquished children, to call the public's attention to the circumstances surrounding their early decisions, and to effect laws more responsive to openness in adoption records. While open adoption is more common than previously, there is substantial variation in the structure and success of these arrangements.

For numerous reasons, adopted children more frequently than their nonadopted peers have behavioral problems and receive psychiatric treatment. Some adoptions disrupt (terminate before adoption finalization) or dissolve (terminate after the adoption finalization). Questions arise regarding the existence of loss and grief experiences associated with adoption; the effect of transracial, international, and transcultural adoption on the identity of adopted children; and whether, and under what circumstances, adoption is in the best interest of children. Design and sampling difficulties hinder the use of research in addressing these questions. At the same time, adoption continues to be a positive reality in many U.S. families, and adopted children are more likely to be economically advantaged, excel academically, and advance socially than their nonadopted counterparts.

New reproductive technologies, including in vitro fertilization and donor insemination, surrogacy, and embryo donation have increased alternatives to traditional adoption although they involve various ethical, legal, and social questions. Support for transracial adoptions reopened interest in the international adoption of children who are frequently much younger than children available for domestic adoption, leading to an increase in international adoptions.

Altruism or Commodification?

From its earliest practices, adoption has been recognized as an altruistic act—whether to provide a loving family to a child born to a young, unmarried mother; or to provide a life rich in social, economic, and educational resources and potential freedom from discrimination to impoverished biracial or minority group children who were often also victims of abuse or neglect; or to provide an alternative to abandonment, existence in the emotionally stark atmosphere of an orphanage, or even death, in the case of international adoptees. Some, however, call attention to the fact that in many cases, the adoption provides both a child and the opportunity to parent to individuals and couples who would otherwise be biologically unable to do so. These persons point to the extensive market that exists for adoptable children, particularly healthy infants, and to private adoption agencies and independent adoption facilitators as businesses that provide jobs and economic profit. Critics apply such terms as *colonialism* and *cultural imperialism* to international and transcultural adoptions.

Leslie Doty Hollingsworth

See also Adoption, Gay and Lesbian; Adoption, Transracial

Further Readings

Kreider, Rose M. 2003. *Adopted Children and Stepchildren: 2000.* Census Special Reports, CENSR-6RV. Washington, DC: U.S. Census Bureau. Retrieved December 3, 2007 (http://www.census.gov/prod/2003pubs/censr-6.pdf).

McGowan, B. G. 2005. "Historical Evolution of Child Welfare Services." Pp. 10–46 in *Child Welfare for the Twenty-first Century: A Handbook of Practices, Policies, and Programs,* edited by G. P. Mallon and P. M. Hess. New York: Columbia University Press.

U.S. Department of Health and Human Services, Administration for Children and Families, Administration on Children, Youth, and Families, Children's Bureau. 2006. "AFCARS Report: Preliminary FY 2005 Estimates as of September 2006." Retrieved December 18, 2006 (http://www.acf.hhs.gov/programs/cb/stats_research/afcars/tar/report13.htm).

U.S. Department of State, Bureau of Consular Affairs. "Immigrant Visas Issued to Orphans Coming to the U.S." Retrieved December 12, 2006 (http://www.travel.state.gov/family/adoption/stats/stats_451.html).

ADOPTION, GAY AND LESBIAN

Some people see the adoption of children by gay men or lesbians as a threat to the social fabric of society, whereas others view it as an appropriate placement resource for children awaiting an adoptive family. With more than 500,000 children in the nation's foster care system and 100,000 of them needing adoptive homes, the need for such homes has never been greater. As a result, this debate, which centers on the appropriateness of allowing children to be raised by gay men or lesbians, has received great attention in recent years, although it has been at the forefront of the cultural divide for several decades.

Gay and Lesbian Adoptive Parents

According to the 2000 U.S. Census, many thousands of same-sex couples live with adopted children. However, because data on gay or lesbian single persons who are also parenting adopted children were not also collected, this number is thought to be significantly under-reported, especially when one realizes that most states allowing gay or lesbian persons to adopt only allow single persons to do so. Parental sexual orientation is not systematically collected in the adoption process. As a result, although the actual number of new adoptions of children by gay or lesbian adoptive parents is unknown, best estimates place it at more than several hundred each year from international or domestic, private or public adoption sources.

Many who oppose adoptions by gay or lesbian persons argue that such adoptions are ill-advised at best and destructive at worst. They hold that adoption by gay and lesbian persons holds substantial risks for children. Little research purports to demonstrate these risks, and scholars widely condemn those few as misinterpreting and misrepresenting sociological research. Nonetheless, these studies have been the basis for many debunked myths about gay and lesbian parenting, including, for example, that children of gay parents are at risk for confusion about their sexual identities and more likely to become homosexual, or that their parents are more likely to sexually abuse these children.

Most studies indicate that parental homosexuality does not give rise to gender identity confusion, inappropriate behavior, psychopathology, or homosexual behavior in children. These studies further revealed that children of gay or lesbian parents were virtually indistinguishable from children of heterosexual single or divorced parents. In addition, research consistently notes the lack of a connection between homosexuality and child molestation. Studies point out that the offenders who select underage male victims either always did so or regressed from adult heterosexual relations. Research demonstrates that homosexuality and homosexual pedophilia are not synonymous and are, in fact, almost mutually exclusive. This is because the homosexual male is attracted to fundamentally masculine qualities, which are lacking in the prepubescent male.

The empirical literature on such adoptive family forms consistently illustrates that no significant differences exist between homosexual and heterosexual adoptive parents in their parenting success, or lack thereof. In fact, children appear to develop healthy bonds with their gay or lesbian parent(s).

Adoption Laws

Despite the removal of homosexuality from the American Psychological Association's list of mental disorders in 1974, Anita Bryant led a "Save Our Children" campaign in 1977 to repeal a gay rights ordinance in Dade County, Florida. The spin-off effect prompted Florida legislators to subsequently pass a law banning adoptions by gay and lesbian persons. The law is still in effect today and is the most restrictive in the nation, the only law specifically denying consideration of an adult as a potential adoptive parent specifically because of his or her sexual orientation.

In general, individual states outline who may and who may not adopt children, with relevant case law also setting the precedent. As such, it is often difficult to determine a particular state's position because many jurisdictions do not publish adoption decisions. Nevertheless, the laws and policies of four other states (Mississippi, Nebraska, Oklahoma, and Utah) have followed Florida's lead and currently prohibit or completely restrict gay or lesbian persons from adopting. Other states either allow such adoptions by statute or do not specifically ban them.

Professional and Organizational Policies

For 3 decades the American Psychiatric Association, the American Psychological Association, and the National Association of Social Workers have had official policy statements stating that an adoptive parent applicant's sexual orientation should not be a factor that automatically rules someone out for becoming an adoptive parent. More recently, the American Academy of Pediatrics released a policy statement endorsing not only adoptions by gay men and lesbians but also adoptions by same-sex couples, asserting that children who are born to, or adopted by, one member of a same-sex couple deserve the security of two legally recognized parents. The American Academy of Child and Adolescent Psychiatry and the American Psychoanalytic Association have taken similar positions.

In addition to major professional discipline-focused organizations, other entities have also supported such adoptive placements. The Child Welfare League of America, the nation's oldest and largest child advocacy group, explicitly asserts that lesbians and gay men seeking to adopt shall be judged by the same standards applied to heterosexuals. Also, the North American Council on Adoptable Children adopted a policy that children should not be denied a permanent family because of the sexual orientation of potential parents. Thus, virtually all major professional organizations in the mental health, child health, and child welfare fields take affirmative positions on allowing children to be adopted by gay or lesbian persons or couples.

Although the exact number of adopted children residing with parents who are gay or lesbian is unknown, both sides in this debate agree that many thousands of such family forms exist. To date, not one study of such adoptive families shows any negative outcome for any member of those families. In fact, quite the opposite is true. Nevertheless, this topic continues to polarize many around the concept of parenthood and what characteristics make a "good" parent.

Scott Ryan

See also Adoption; Sexual Orientation

Further Readings

Ryan, Scott, Laura Bedard, and Marc Gertz. 2004. "Florida's Gay Adoption Ban: What Do Floridians Think?" *Journal of Law and Public Policy* 15(2):261–83.

Ryan, Scott and S. Cash. 2004. "Adoptive Families Headed by Gay or Lesbian Parents: A Threat . . . or Hidden Resource?" *Journal of Law and Public Policy* 15(3):443–66.

Ryan, Scott, Sue Pearlmutter, and Victor Groza. 2004. "Coming out of the Closet: Opening Agencies to Gay Men and Lesbian Adoptive Parents." *Social Work* 49(1):85–96.

ADOPTION, TRANSRACIAL

Transracial adoption (also known as inter-racial adoption) refers to adoptions that occur across racial boundaries. At the level of biology, no adoption is transracial because race is a meaningless category;

however, because race is socially significant, transracial adoption remains a controversial method of family formation.

In the United States, much of this controversy centers on the two streams that feed transracial adoption. Adoption itself is one such stream: Why are children placed for adoption? Adoption solves the problem of infertility for so many people, yet it is not just a solution but also an indicator of a larger social problem, for its need results from forces and policies that push women into giving birth to babies that they cannot rear. Consequently, countries with good social services, readily available and culturally accepted contraception means, safe and legal abortion, and support for single mothers have the lowest adoption rates. For example, in 2005, only 48 domestic nonstepchild adoptions took place in Norway.

Racism is the other stream: More women of color than white women are forced to relinquish their children. This is best illustrated by the over-representation of children of color in the U.S. foster care system: In 2005, almost 60 percent of U.S. children served in foster care were minorities. One driving force for this is poverty, specifically a lack of access to contraception, abortion, and the resources to rear children. However, it is not just that people of color are more likely to be poor. Many still face the remnants of institutionalized discrimination and lack the resources to overcome the resultant disadvantages, and thus a much greater percentage are found living in poverty than is the case among whites. In fact, U.S. Census data indicate that, whereas approximately 8 percent of whites are poor, more than 20 percent of both the black and Hispanic communities are similarly impoverished. Consequently, race and poverty work together to push and pull children of color out of their families of origin and to limit the number of racially similar families able to absorb them. As such, children of color are disproportionately available for adoption, and white middle-class families disproportionately have the wherewithal to adopt.

This phenomenon also operates at the global level, with the children of greatest poverty disproportionately found among the darker children of the world. Among families formed by adoption that crosses any color line, it is almost always children of darker skin going to lighter-skinned parents. For example, in 2006, children of color represented approximately 80 percent of the "orphans" relinquished by the top five sending nations (China, Guatemala, Russia, South Korea, and Ethiopia, respectively) and adopted by (mostly white) U.S. families. Yet, unlike the domestic adoption of black children by white families, in most cases of international adoption, the children are perhaps less valued but not racially disvalued. In other words, while international adoptees are not white, they usually are not black either. Oftentimes, it is this almost-whiteness that makes international adoption, particularly the adoption of children from Asian nations, so appealing for American would-be adopters.

When navigating the streams and controversies of domestic transracial adoption, most Americans take one of three positions on these placements. The first position advocates for color blindness in adoption, meaning the random assignment of children available for adoption to potential adoptive parents. Given the current demographics of adoption, this position would result in some black families ending up with white children, more white families with black children, and some families accidentally "matched." The second position encourages moderate race matching in adoption, as long as a same-race match can be arranged in a timely manner. The third position promotes only race matching in adoption. Most often this position develops in response to the cultural and structural intricacies of racism, not out of ideologies of racial purity or separatism.

The most famous articulation of this third position can be found in the National Association of Black Social Workers (NABSW) 1972 statement against transracial adoption, which decreed that the history and existence of white racism require race matching for black children. According to the NABSW, these children need the support and socialization of black families just as much as the black community needs to maintain and sustain its children and families. Yet, in contrast to the whitening processes of international adoption, the transracial adoption of black children appears predicated on the children returning in adulthood to the black community. In fact, one of the definitions of success in these placements is the formation of an appropriate (i.e., black) racial identity. Significantly, data indicate that transracially adopted black children and adults tend to meet this measure; most do well psychologically and socially, and most develop strong identities as black Americans.

Research also indicates that white people raising black children in America, whether they have given birth to them or adopted them, need assistance from the black community. However, participating in, or even just being supportive of, transracial adoption inevitably puts one in an impossible situation. Placing a child or helping the family formed by transracial adoption implicitly supports the formation of such families. One issue is whether such actions encourage the removal of black children from the black community. The adoptive family and particularly the child do need support, but the circumstances creating such a situation also require attention and correction. In this way, transracial adoption is a Band-Aid resolution that calls out for a more satisfactory solution.

Barbara Katz Rothman and Amy Traver

See also Abortion; Adoption; Adoption, Gay and Lesbian; Biracial; Civil Rights; Contraception; Family; Family, Blended; Fertility; Foster Children, Aging Out; Intermarriage; Miscegenation; Multiracial Identity; Race

Further Readings

Fogg-Davis, Hawley. 2002. *The Ethics of Transracial Adoption.* Ithaca, NY: Cornell University Press.

Kennedy, Randall. 2003. *Interracial Intimacies: Sex, Marriage, Identity, and Adoption.* New York: Pantheon.

Rothman, Barbara Katz. 2005. *Weaving a Family: Untangling Race and Adoption.* Boston: Beacon Press.

Simon, Rita J. and Howard Altstein. 2000. *Adoption across Borders: Serving the Children in Transracial and Intercountry Adoptions.* Lanham, MD: Rowman & Littlefield.

Smith, Janet Farrell. 1996. "Analyzing Ethical Conflict in the Transracial Adoption Debate: Three Conflicts Involving Community." *Hypatia* 11(2):1–21.

AFFIRMATIVE ACTION

Affirmative action refers to programs designed to assist disadvantaged groups of people by giving them certain preferences. Affirmative action goes beyond banning negative treatment of members of specified disadvantaged groups to requiring some form of positive treatment in order to equalize opportunity.

In the United States, beneficiaries of affirmative action programs have included African Americans and women, as well as Latinos/as, Native Americans, and Asian and Pacific Islanders. In India, members of "scheduled castes" (the lower-status castes) are the beneficiaries. Preferential treatment is also afforded to women in the European Union, "visible minorities" in Canada, the Māori in New Zealand, and the Roma in eastern Europe. Some affirmative action programs involve small preferences (such as placing job advertisements in African American newspapers to encourage members of a previously excluded group to apply for a job), whereas others can be substantial (going as far as restricting a particular job to members of disadvantaged groups). A quota is when a job or a certain percentage of jobs is open only to members of the disadvantaged group. Not all affirmative action programs involve quotas, and, indeed, in the United States quotas are generally illegal in most situations. Even without quotas, however, affirmative action has been an extremely contentious issue, for what is at stake is the allocation of a society's scarce resources: jobs, university positions, government contracts, and so on.

Moral and Political Arguments

Some critics of affirmative action, of course, openly want to maintain the subordinate position of the disadvantaged group. But many critics condemn the discriminatory and unfair policies of the past that have harmed the disadvantaged group and call for the elimination of such policies. To this end, they favor vigorous enforcement of anti-discrimination laws, prohibiting discrimination in such areas as employment, housing, public accommodations, and educational institutions. What they do not support, however, are policies that give preferences to the disadvantaged. To give advantages to anyone—even the previously disadvantaged—departs from the important moral principle of equal treatment. In the past, jobs were allocated on the basis of race, gender, or some other morally impermissible characteristic, rather than merit. Now, according to this view, jobs should be given out on the basis of merit alone. Employers should be "color-blind" (or "race-blind") and "gender-blind": That is, they should act as if they do not know the race or gender of the applicants. Just as it was wrong to pay attention to people's race or gender in order to discriminate against them, so it is wrong to be "color-conscious" or "gender-conscious" in order to help them.

Critics of affirmative action point out that discriminating *in favor of* the previously disadvantaged necessarily entails discriminating *against* those from advantaged groups, a form of reverse discrimination that is morally unacceptable. This is especially so given that any particular member of a disadvantaged group may not have personally experienced discrimination, and any particular member of an advantaged group may never have engaged in any act of discrimination.

Supporters of affirmative action, on the other hand, argue that while a color- and gender-blind society is an ultimate ideal, in the short run color- and gender-conscious policies are necessary and justified for remedying past and present discrimination. There is no moral equivalence, in this view, between discrimination intended to keep down some oppressed groups and the discrimination intended to help provide equality—to level the playing field—for these victims of past societal discrimination.

Advocates note that various studies (using matched pairs of job applicants, interviews with employers, and other methodologies) reveal the persistence of discrimination, even after its legal prohibition. Antidiscrimination laws alone are insufficient to eliminate discrimination. How, for example, would an unsuccessful job applicant know that she has been the victim of discrimination unless she had access to the application files of her competitors? Moreover, according to affirmative action supporters, even if all discrimination ended, the harm caused by previous discrimination continues into the present. For example, much hiring occurs through word of mouth, personal connections, and referrals. Many colleges and universities give preferences to those whose parents attended the institution. All of these mechanisms reproduce in the present whatever employment or educational imbalances may have existed previously due to discrimination.

Supporters of affirmative action insist that they too value merit, but not the narrow meaning of merit as measured by standardized tests. If merit is correctly defined as being best able to help an organization achieve its goals, it will often be the case that color- or gender-conscious factors ought to be considered. For example, if the goal of a police department is to serve and protect its community, and if in a particular multiracial city with a history of racial tension the police department is all white because of previous discrimination, it may well be that a new black officer will better help the department serve the community

than would a white officer who scored slightly higher on some standardized test.

Many workplaces and educational institutions consider diversity a positive value, and therefore, according to advocates of affirmative action, favoring applicants who further the diversity of the workforce or student body involves no conflict with the principle of merit. For example, a college applicant from an under-represented minority group might be more qualified than someone with slightly better color-blind credentials when qualification is viewed as including the extent to which the applicant will help the college in its mission of exposing all its students to people from different backgrounds and giving them the experience of interacting with such people. Critics of affirmative action, on the other hand, argue that seeking out applicants with diverse *political* views would do more for the diversity of a student body than would granting preferences to racial or ethnic minorities.

Critics of affirmative action note that, to decide preferential treatment entitlement, it is necessary to determine the race or ethnicity of applicants. Sometimes the determination is straightforward, but given the prevalence of people with multiracial backgrounds and the ugly history of how racist societies judged which racial category people belonged to, critics charge that it is morally objectionable to assign racial labels to people. Yet without such labels, affirmative action would be impossible. In fact, true color blindness demands that the government not ask for or collect information that distinguishes people by race or ethnicity at all.

Supporters of affirmative action agree that categorizing people by race or ethnicity is morally awkward. However, they note that even minimal enforcement of anti-discrimination laws requires categorizing people. (How can we determine whether a landlord has been discriminating if we don't know the race of prospective renters?) In an ideal society, there would be no need to gather data on any morally irrelevant category. But when a society has a long history of oppressing certain groups, data broken down by group is necessary if we are to measure and judge our progress in overcoming that past oppression. When a society does not collect information on the differential circumstances of dominant groups and oppressed groups, such action may be a sign not of color blindness but of trying to hide ongoing mistreatment.

Considerable debate exists as to the appropriate beneficiaries of affirmative action. In the United States, supporters of affirmative action hoped that, by expanding the coverage to apply to many minority groups, they would broaden the political base favoring such programs. In practice, however, the wider coverage has diluted, in the minds of some, the moral argument in favor of a program intended to help the most obvious victims of governmental discrimination: African Americans and Native Americans. Some argue that the context matters. Thus, because Asian Americans and women are generally not under-represented among university student bodies, affirmative action admissions for them would now be inappropriate (though they should not be singled out for restrictions). On the other hand, among corporate executives or university faculties, blacks, Asians, Latinos, and women all faced exclusion in the past and remain under-represented today; therefore, in these areas all four groups ought to be beneficiaries of affirmative action.

Some argue that "class-based" affirmative action ought to replace race-based programs, both for reasons of equity (why is the son of a black doctor more deserving of university admissions than the son of a white coal miner?) and to avoid provoking a backlash from poor and working-class whites who might be natural political allies of poor blacks. Many supporters of race-based affirmative action support class-based preferences to supplement, but not supplant, race-based preferences. They note that programs intended to benefit the poor and the working class provoked a political backlash (e.g., "welfare" or equalization of education funding). More important, they argue that race-neutral criteria will still leave minorities—who have been the victims of both class and caste discrimination—under-represented.

Impact

Measuring the impact of affirmative action is difficult and controversial. Some critics argue that worldwide the record of affirmative action has been disastrous, even driving some societies to civil war (e.g., Sri Lanka), but given the history of ethnic and racial conflict in societies where affirmative action has been introduced, it is not simple to isolate cause and effect.

Most U.S. studies agree that affirmative action has redistributed jobs, college admissions, and government contracts from white males to minorities and females, though only to a small extent. A more substantial shift occurred in minority enrollments at elite colleges and universities and in graduate programs, law schools, and medical schools.

Critics claim that departure from the principle of merit led to positions being filled by less-qualified people, with a corresponding loss of quality and efficiency in the economy. Most studies found no evidence of weaker performance by women relative to men in those sectors of the economy with mandated affirmative action. And though substantial evidence exists that minorities have weaker credentials than whites, their actual performance is only modestly weaker. On the other hand, some counterbalancing benefits also occur, such as many minority doctors locating their practices in poor and underserved communities, leading to a gain in the nation's health care.

Opponents argue that affirmative action is harmful to its supposed beneficiaries by creating a "mismatch" between the skills of minority employees and students and the skills that their positions require. For example, one study found that affirmative action *reduced* the number of African American lawyers because minority students admitted through affirmative action did worse in law school (and then drop out or fail the bar exam) than they would have if they had gone to easier law schools where they had not received admissions preferences. Critics of this study challenge it on methodological grounds, finding that affirmative action actually increased the number of African American lawyers. Also contradicting the mismatch hypothesis is the fact that blacks who attend elite colleges and universities (where affirmative action is most prevalent) have higher graduation rates and greater future success than do those who attend less competitive institutions.

Another way in which affirmative action is said to harm beneficiaries is psychologically, on the grounds that those admitted into schools or jobs on the basis of preferences are likely to suffer in terms of self-esteem or ambition. Others view them as not really qualified, and worse yet, they may view themselves that way as well. Supporters of affirmative action reply that white men did not feel undeserving during the years of open discrimination, even though they earned their credentials in a contest where many of their competitors were severely handicapped. Although some minority individuals may wonder whether they got their position based on color-blind credentials or because of preferences, unemployment and lack of promotion are surely more serious blows to anyone's self-esteem. As for stigmatization, stereotyping the abilities of subordinated minorities and women long predated affirmative action. Limited survey data suggest that blacks (male and female) and white females at firms with affirmative action programs do not have any lower scores on various psychological variables than their peers at other firms and that blacks at affirmative action firms have more ambition than blacks at other firms.

History

In the United States, legislation was passed in the aftermath of the Civil War to affirmatively assist African Americans, but with the end of Reconstruction, race-conscious measures were enacted exclusively for the purpose of subordinating blacks. Much of the ensuing struggle for civil rights involved attempts to remove legal impediments to equal rights; these efforts culminated in the Civil Rights Act of 1964.

The first official use of the term *affirmative action* was in 1961, when President John F. Kennedy issued Executive Order 10925, requiring that federal contractors not only pledge nondiscrimination but also "take affirmative action to ensure" equal opportunity. In 1965, President Lyndon Johnson promulgated Executive Order 11246, establishing the Office of Federal Contract Compliance to enforce affirmative action requirements. In a speech at Howard University, Johnson explained the rationale for such programs: "You do not take a person who for years has been hobbled by chains, and liberate him, bring him up to the starting line, and then say, 'You are free to compete with all the others.'" In 1967, Executive Order 11246 was expanded to cover women. The 1969 "Philadelphia Plan" under President Richard Nixon required government contractors to set numerical goals for hiring minorities, particularly in the construction industry where blacks long experienced exclusion from labor unions.

Court challenges to affirmative action resulted in rulings that often left the question unsettled. In *Regents of the University of California v. Bakke* in 1978, a divided Supreme Court ruled that a medical school could not set aside a fixed number of seats for minority applicants, but it could use race or ethnicity as a plus factor in admissions. The next year, in *United Steelworkers v. Weber,* the Supreme Court allowed private companies to enact affirmative action programs for the purpose of overcoming traditional patterns of racial segregation. And in 1980, in *Fullilove v. Klutznick,* the Supreme Court upheld the setting aside of 10 percent of government public works funds for minority-owned businesses. A decade later, however, a more conservative court narrowed the scope of permissible affirmative action; while agreeing that strict color blindness was not required, the court—in *City of Richmond v. Croson* in 1989 and *Adarand Constructors v. Pena* in 1995—held that affirmative action programs must serve a compelling government interest and be narrowly tailored to meet that interest.

In 1996, voters in California passed Proposition 209, outlawing race-conscious programs in any state institution, thus ending affirmative action in the state's college and university system. At California's top universities, black enrollment declined from 6.6 percent in 1994 to 3.0 percent in 2004. In two cases decided in 2003, *Grutter v. Bollinger* and *Granz v. Bollinger,* the Supreme Court affirmed that race or ethnicity could be considered as one admissions factor among many others, provided that it was not done in a mechanical way.

Stephen R. Shalom

See also Civil Rights; Discrimination; Equal Protection; Jim Crow; Race-Blind Policies; Racism; Segregation; Sexism; Skills Mismatch

Further Readings

Anderson, Terry H. 2004. *The Pursuit of Fairness: A History of Affirmative Action.* New York: Oxford University Press.

Bowen, William G. and Derek Bok. 1998. *The Shape of the River: The Long-Term Consequences of Considering Race in College and University Admissions.* Princeton, NJ: Princeton University Press.

Boxill, Bernard R. 1992. *Blacks and Social Justice.* Rev. ed. Lanham, MD: Rowman & Littlefield.

Crosby, Faye J., Aarti Iyer, Susan Clayton, and Roberta A. Downing. 2003. "Affirmative Action: Psychological Data and the Policy Debates." *American Psychologist* 58(2):93–115.

Eastland, Terry. 1996. *Ending Affirmative Action: The Case for Colorblind Justice.* New York: Basic Books.

Ezorsky, Gertrude. 1991. *Racism and Justice: The Case for Affirmative Action.* Ithaca, NY: Cornell University Press.

Holzer, Harry J. and David Neumark. 2006. "Affirmative Action: What Do We Know?" *Journal of Policy Analysis and Management* 25(2):463–90.

Kahlenberg, Richard D. 1996. *The Remedy: Class, Race, and Affirmative Action.* New York: Basic Books.

Livingston, John C. 1979. *Fair Game? Inequality and Affirmative Action.* San Francisco: W. H. Freeman.

Thernstrom, Stephan and Abigail Thernstrom. 1997. *America in Black and White: One Nation, Indivisible.* New York: Simon & Schuster.

AFFIRMATIVE DEFENSE

The structure of criminal liability or guilt in Anglo-American law is straightforward. (The same structure of liability applies in general in civil suits, but this entry focuses on criminal law.) Crimes are defined by their criteria, which lawyers call the "elements." Most crimes require some prohibited action and an accompanying mental state (the *mens rea*). For example, one definition of murder is the intentional killing of a human being. The prohibited action is any type of killing conduct and the required mental state is intent, the purpose to kill. The State has enormous discretion concerning what behavior to criminalize and what the specific elements of crimes should be. The State (prosecution) must prove these elements beyond a reasonable doubt. Even if the prosecution is able to prove all the elements beyond a reasonable doubt, the defendant may nonetheless avoid criminal liability and be found not guilty (or less guilty) by establishing a defense. These defenses are termed *affirmative defenses* and, like the definitions of *crimes*, have definitional criteria. Affirmative defenses may be grouped into three categories: justifications, excuses, and policy defenses. The former two focus on the defendant's culpability or blameworthiness. The State creates the latter to serve goals other than adjudicating guilt. The State has enormous discretion concerning what affirmative defenses to establish, if any, and what their criteria should be. In the United States, it is in the State's discretion to allocate the burden of proof on affirmative defenses to either the prosecution or the defense.

Behavior that would otherwise be criminal is justified if it is right or at least permissible in the individual circumstances. For example, the intentional killing of another person is typically criminal homicide, but if someone kills in response to a wrongful and imminent threat of deadly harm, that person will be justified by the affirmative defense of self-defense.

Other traditional justifications include the defense of another, the defense of property, law enforcement, and the general justification of "necessity" or "balance of evils," which is often established to address cases in which the more specific justifications do not strictly apply. The defendant will be justified only if he or she actually believes that the justifying circumstances exist and that belief is reasonable. There is often substantial dispute about the criteria for a reasonable belief. A defendant found not guilty because his or her conduct was justified is freed outright from state control.

Criminal behavior is excused if the defendant was not criminally responsible at the time of the crime. For example, suppose someone intentionally kills because severe mental disorder produces a delusion that he or she is about to be killed. The individual is not justified because the belief is mistaken and unreasonable, but this person is sufficiently irrational to be considered nonresponsible, and the excuse of legal insanity applies. Other traditional excuses include infancy, which excuses from criminal responsibility juveniles below a certain age, and duress, which excuses an individual who is wrongfully threatened with death or serious bodily injury unless he or she commits a crime and a person of reasonable firmness would have yielded to the threat under the circumstances. A defendant who is excused may be subject to further state noncriminal control if the person remains dangerous. For example, a defendant who is found not guilty by reason of insanity may be civilly committed to a secure hospital if he or she remains dangerous and may be kept there until he or she is no longer mentally disordered or dangerous.

Considerable dispute exists about the rationale for the excusing affirmative defenses, but most depend on a finding that the defendant was not capable of rationality or that the defendant was compelled to act. Legal insanity is an example of the former; duress is an example of the latter. An important question is whether the law should establish new affirmative defenses of excuse for newly discovered variables, such as new mental syndromes or brain abnormalities that seem to play a causal role in criminal behavior. Advocates argue for such excuses, but causation alone is not an excusing condition. At most, such causes can support the existence or expansion of a genuine existing excuse, such as legal insanity.

Although the distinction between justifications and excuses can be stated clearly, it can be very blurry. For example, suppose a homicide defendant actually believed that he was in deadly danger, but he made a reasonable mistake and was not in danger at all. Has this person done the right thing, or was it wrong but he was not responsible? For another example, suppose the defendant kills for no justifying reason, but he would have been justified if he knew all the facts, such as that the victim had a hidden weapon and was about to kill the defendant wrongfully. Justification or excuse? On the one hand, the defendant's conduct was "objectively" justified, but, on the other, the defendant subjectively acted for a nonjustified reason.

Such questions divide criminal lawyers and raise important theoretical and practical issues about culpability. Justified and excused defendants are both found not guilty, but the former have done the right thing; the latter have done the wrong thing and, in some cases, may still be dangerous. The criminal law is a teacher that educates and guides citizens. It should therefore announce clearly what behavior is right or permissible and what is wrong and forbidden. Defendants also care about whether their conduct is justified or excused because any defendant would prefer to have his or her harmful conduct authoritatively labeled right, rather than wrong but excused, and justifications do not trigger state control.

Policy affirmative defenses do not negate the defendant's blameworthiness, but permit exoneration for other good reasons. The statute of limitations and diplomatic immunity, for example, bar conviction of a defendant who has undoubtedly committed a crime. The State concludes, respectively, that the defendant may not be able to defend himself adequately after a certain period of time, or that good international relations require that we not convict the diplomats of other nations residing in the United States.

Stephen J. Morse

See also Crime; Justice; Juvenile Justice System; Social Control

Further Readings

Dressler, Joshua. 2006. *Understanding Criminal Law.* 4th ed. Dayton, OH: Matthew Bender.

Greenawalt, Kent. 1984. "The Perplexing Borders of Justification and Excuse." *Columbia Law Review* 84:1897.

Morse, Stephen J. 1998. "Excusing and the New Excuse Defenses: A Legal and Conceptual Review." *Crime and Justice* 23:329–406.

———. 2002. "Uncontrollable Urges and Irrational People." *Virginia Law Review* 88:1025–78.

AFROCENTRICITY

Afrocentricity is a paradigm based on the idea that African people should reassert a sense of agency to achieve sanity. During the 1960s a group of African American intellectuals in the newly formed black studies departments at universities began to formulate novel ways of analyzing information. In some cases, these new ways were called looking at information from "a black perspective," as opposed to what had been considered the "white perspective" of most information in the American academy.

In the late 1970s Molefi Kete Asante began speaking of the need for an Afrocentric orientation to data and, in 1980, published a book, *Afrocentricity: The Theory of Social Change,* which launched the first full discussion of the concept. Although the word existed before Asante's book and many people, including Kwame Nkrumah in the 1960s, had used it, the intellectual idea did not have substance as a philosophical concept until 1980.

The Afrocentric paradigm is a revolutionary shift in thinking proposed as a *constructural* adjustment to black disorientation, decenteredness, and lack of agency. The Afrocentrist asks the question, "What would African people do if there were no white people?" In other words, what natural responses would occur in the relationships, attitudes toward the environment, kinship patterns, preferences for colors, type of religion, and historical referent points for African people if there had not been any intervention of colonialism or enslavement? Afrocentricity answers this question by asserting the central role of the African subject within the context of African history, thereby removing Europe from the center of the African reality. In this way, Afrocentricity becomes a revolutionary idea because it studies ideas, concepts, events, personalities, and political and economic processes from a standpoint of black people as subjects and not as objects, basing all knowledge on the authentic interrogation of *location*.

It thus becomes legitimate to ask, "Where is the sistah coming from?" or "Where is the brotha at?" "Are you down with overcoming oppression?" These are assessment and evaluative questions that allow the interrogator to accurately pinpoint the responder's location, whether it be a cultural or a psychological location. As a paradigm, Afrocentricity enthrones the centrality of the African, that is, black ideals and values, as expressed in the highest forms of African culture, and activates consciousness as a functional aspect of any revolutionary approach to phenomena. The cognitive and structural aspects of a paradigm are incomplete without the *functional* aspect. There is something more than knowing in the Afrocentric sense; there is also *doing*. Afrocentricity holds that all definitions are autobiographical.

One of the key assumptions of the Afrocentrist is that all relationships are based on centers and margins and the distances from either the center or the margin. When black people view themselves as centered and central in their own history, then they see themselves as agents, actors, and participants rather than as marginals on the periphery of political or economic experience. According to this paradigm, human beings have discovered that all phenomena are expressed in the fundamental categories of *space* and *time*. Furthermore, it is then understood that relationships develop and knowledge increases to the extent that we are able to appreciate the issues of space and time.

The Afrocentric scholar or practitioner knows that one way to express Afrocentricity is by *marking*. Whenever a person delineates a cultural boundary around a particular cultural space in human time, this is called marking. It might be done with the announcement of a certain symbol, the creation of a special bonding, or the citing of personal heroes of African history and culture. Beyond citing the revolutionary thinkers in history; that is, beyond Amilcar Cabral, Frantz Fanon, Malcolm X, and Nkrumah, black people must be prepared to act upon their interpretation of what is in their best interests, that is, in their interests as a historically oppressed population. This is the fundamental necessity for advancing the political process.

Afrocentricity is the substance of African regeneration because it is in line with what contemporary philosophers Haki Madhubuti and Maulana Karenga, among others, have articulated as in the best image and interest of African people. They ask, What is any better than operating and acting out of one's own collective interest? What is any greater than seeing the world through African eyes? What resonates more with people than understanding that Africans are central to their history, not someone else's? If Africans can, in the process of materializing their consciousness, claim space as agents of progressive change, then they can change their condition and change the world.

Afrocentricity maintains that one can claim this space only if one knows the general characteristics of Afrocentricity as well as the practical applications of the field.

Five General Characteristics of the Afrocentric Method

First, the Afrocentric method considers that no phenomenon can be apprehended adequately without locating it first. A *phenom* must be studied and analyzed in relationship to psychological time and space. It must always be located. This is the only way to investigate the complex interrelationships of science and art, design and execution, creation and maintenance, generation and tradition, and other areas bypassed by theory.

Second, the Afrocentric method considers phenomena to be diverse, dynamic, and in motion, and therefore it is necessary for a person to accurately note and record the location of phenomena even in the midst of fluctuations. This means that the investigator must know where he or she is standing in the process.

Third, the Afrocentric method is a form of cultural criticism that examines etymological uses of words and terms in order to know the source of an author's location. This allows for the intersection of ideas with actions and actions with ideas on the basis of what is pejorative and ineffective and what is creative and transformative at the political and economic levels.

Fourth, the Afrocentric method seeks to uncover the masks behind the rhetoric of power, privilege, and position to establish how principal myths create place. The method enthrones critical reflection that reveals the perception of monolithic power as nothing but the projection of a cadre of adventurers.

Fifth, the Afrocentric method locates the imaginative structure of a system of economics, bureau of politics, policy of government, and expression of cultural form in the attitude, direction, and language of the phenom, be it text, institution, personality, interaction, or event.

Analytic Afrocentricity

Analytic Afrocentricity is the application of the principles of the Afrocentric method to textual analysis. An Afrocentrist seeks to understand the principles of the Afrocentric method so that he or she may use them as a guide in analysis and discourse. It goes without saying that the Afrocentrist cannot function properly as a scientist or humanist if he or she does not adequately locate the phenom in time and space. This means that chronology is as important in some situations as location. The two aspects of analysis are central to any proper understanding of society, history, or personality.

Inasmuch as phenoms are active, dynamic, and diverse in society, the Afrocentric method requires the scientist to focus on accurate notations and recording of space and time. In fact, the best way to apprehend location of a text is to first determine where the researcher is located in time and space. Once the location and time of the researcher or author are known, it is fairly easy to establish the parameters for the phenom itself. The value of etymology, that is, the origin of terms and words, is in the proper identification and location of concepts. The Afrocentrist seeks to demonstrate clarity by exposing dislocations, disorientations, and decenteredness. One of the simplest ways of accessing textual clarity is through etymology.

Myths tie all relationships together, whether personal or conceptual. It is the Afrocentrist's task to determine to what extent the myths of society are represented as being central to, or marginal to, society. This means that any textual analysis must involve the concrete realities of lived experiences, thus making historical experiences a key element in analytical Afrocentricity. In examining attitude, direction, and language, the Afrocentrist is seeking to uncover the imagination of the author. What one seeks to do is to create an opportunity for the writer to show where he or she stands in relationship to the subject. Is the writer centered, or is the writer marginalized within his or her own story?

Afrocentric Philosophy

The philosophy of Afrocentricity as expounded by Molefi Kete Asante and Ama Mazama, central figures of the Temple School, is a way of answering all cultural, economic, political, and social questions related to African people from a centered position. Indeed,

Afrocentricity cannot be reconciled to any hegemonic or idealistic philosophy. It is opposed to radical individualism as expressed in the postmodern school. But it is also opposed to *spookism,* confusion, and superstition. As an example of the differences between the methods of Afrocentricity and postmodernism, consider the following question, "Why have Africans been shut out of global development?"

The postmodernist would begin by saying that there is no such thing as "Africans" because there are many different types of Africans and all Africans are not equal. The postmodernist would go on to say that if there were Africans and if the conditions were as described by the querist, then the answer would be that Africans had not fully developed their own capacities in relationship to the global economy and therefore they are outside of the normal development patterns of the world economy. On the other hand, the Afrocentrist does not question the fact that there is a collective sense of Africanity revealed in the common experiences of the African world. The Afrocentrist would look to the questions of location, control of the hegemonic global economy, marginalization, and power positions as keys to understanding the underdevelopment of African people.

Molefi Kete Asante

See also Race; Racism; Social Bond Theory; Social Constructionist Theory

Further Readings

Asante, Molefi Kete. 1998. *The Afrocentric Idea.* Philadelphia: Temple University Press.
Mazama, Ama, ed. 2003. *The Afrocentric Paradigm.* Trenton, NJ: Africa World.

Ageism

Ageism is a form of prejudice directed toward older members of a society. Like other forms of negative group stereotyping, ageism can vary in both its intensity and its effect on the targeted group. People who possess unflattering dispositions toward the elderly may not cause them direct harm if their feelings are unexpressed. When these sentiments are more severe or very commonly held by dominant groups, however, they may take institutionalized forms as in the case of discriminatory labor practices. Many sociologists believe that these practices are responsible for the subordination of the elderly in an age-stratified society.

Theories on Age Prejudice

Cognitive theorists believe that people develop mental images of what it means to be old that guide their understanding of the late stages of the life course. According to communication accommodation theory, these images tend to induce the young to expect certain behaviors from the old, and to act according to these expectations when they are in their presence. The communication predicament of aging model further predicts that these encounters between the young and the old will tend to result in the reinforcement of age-based stereotypes among both the old and the young. For example, as younger people attempt to assist older people with tasks that they are capable of handling on their own, both may experience frustration at the lack of perceived compatibility with one another. These frustrating experiences may then influence their expectations for future encounters, which can result in a self-fulfilling prophecy.

Elders may also be the targets of prejudice due to what social constructivists describe as a bias toward the young in a society's stock of knowledge about old age. The social constructivist perspective identifies ways in which people interpret old age through language, culture, and social behavior. The media are also actors in this process because they influence popular beliefs about old age by promoting age-based stereotypes in literature, film, and news reporting. The constructivist paradigm has been used to support the notion that elders in society make up a minority group that suffers from the control that younger people hold over the dissemination of legitimated knowledge.

Ageism in the Workplace

In 1967, the U.S. Congress enacted the Age Discrimination in Employment Act (ADEA), which prohibited discrimination against Americans over the age of 40 in hiring, promoting, compensating, or any other action that affects entry or favor in the workplace. The U.S. Equal Employment Opportunity Commission (EEOC) is responsible for the enforcement of this law as well as the Civil Rights Act of 1964,

Titles I and V of the Americans with Disabilities Act of 1990, and other laws that protect the equal rights of U.S. workers. As awareness of the ADEA grew in recent decades, the number of complaints increased. Some critics charge, however, that the commission does not prosecute enough cases to make a real difference in U.S. society. The EEOC settled over 14,000 age discrimination cases in 2005, totaling approximately $77 million in settlements.

These statistics cannot measure the full extent of age discrimination in the workplace, nor do they suggest that the system adequately addresses the problem. Most analysts believe that the number of actual cases is far higher than the number of complaints made to the EEOC. The trend of early retirement among the elderly may be an indirect sign that older Americans experience difficulty staying employed as they advance in age. Although full Social Security retirement benefits are only available to those who begin collecting at the age of 65 (plus a few months at present), many workers, especially men, are applying for reduced early retirement benefits in their early 60s. Even though the ADEA prohibits mandatory retirement policies for most jobs, many older workers face subtle disincentives from their employers to continue working beyond certain ages.

Are the Elderly a Minority Group?

Debate among sociologists on the subject of ageism often centers on the classification of the old as a minority group. Proponents for the application of the minority group paradigm contend that older members of society tend to be judged on the basis of overgeneralizations about their personalities, behavior, and health. Social scientific research reveals that many younger people believe that the elderly generally possess characteristics such as being stubborn, obstinate, and weak. Although normally false, these stereotypes may lead to group prejudice and discrimination against older people. Another common belief is that elders see themselves as members of a subculture in society, as evidenced by the leisure groups and political action organizations that recruit many elders. In fact, some people label such groups in political arenas as "greedy geezers" who seek to unfairly maximize their government pensions and benefits. Organizations such as the AARP, formerly known as the American Association of Retired Persons, represent the interests of elders in a formalized way, helping to improve their quality of life.

On the other hand, some insist that age cannot be used as a basis for a minority group, offering several arguments to support their position. Some contend that minority group status cannot depend on age because all people would enter into or out of it over the course of their lives. Also, because age is an arbitrary measure, the exact point at which one would become a member of the aged minority group is naturally subject to debate. In response to the claim that the aged are victims of prejudice, critics of the minority group paradigm have pointed out that many surveys also show that the young hold very positive images of the old in some important ways. For example, psychologists and communications theorists have found that despite the prevalence of negative aging stereotypes held by the young, they actually see many positive characteristics in the old, such as dependability, pride, loyalty, and patriotism. Finally, political science research shows that, despite high levels of voter turnout among the aged, most tend not to vote in a bloc, which some define as evidence that older people do not see themselves as members of a minority group.

Christopher Donoghue

See also Discrimination; Elderly Socioeconomic Status; Life Course; Minority Group; Stereotyping

Further Readings

Hummert, Mary Lee, Teri A. Garstka, Ellen Bouchard Ryan, and Jaye L. Bonnesan. 2004. "The Role of Age Stereotypes in Interpersonal Communication." Pp. 91–114 in *Handbook of Communication and Aging Research,* edited by J. F. Nussbaum and J. Coupland. Mahwah, NJ: Erlbaum.

Levin, Jack and William C. Levin. 1980. *Ageism: Prejudice and Discrimination against the Elderly.* Belmont, CA: Wadsworth.

Nelson, Todd D. 2004. *Ageism: Stereotyping and Prejudice against Older Persons.* Cambridge, MA: MIT Press.

Palmore, Erdman B. 1999. *Ageism: Negative and Positive.* New York: Springer.

Streib, Gordon F. 1965. "Are the Aged a Minority Group?" Pp. 35–46 in *Middle Age and Aging,* edited by B. L. Neugarten. Chicago: University of Chicago Press.

AID TO FAMILIES WITH DEPENDENT CHILDREN

From 1935 to 1996, Aid to Families with Dependent Children (AFDC) was the major government-funded means-tested public assistance program for low-income children and their caretakers. Its antecedents were states' mothers pension programs, which reflected the child-centered, "maternalist" philosophy of the Progressive Era.

Originally a relatively minor component of the Social Security Act targeted at poor widows and their children, AFDC was a federal–state cost-sharing partnership. States retained the authority to determine eligibility requirements and benefit levels and to administer the program. However, the program lacked specific safeguards against racial discrimination, particularly in determination of eligibility. It was not controversial until the size and racial composition of caseloads began to change in the 1950s.

In 1961, amendments to the Social Security Act created AFDC-UP, giving states the option of extending benefits to families with unemployed fathers and creating an extensive set of rehabilitation and prevention services. Five years later, other amendments emphasized work as an alternative to welfare, establishing the Work Incentive Program and allowing AFDC recipients to keep the first $30 in monthly earnings and one third of subsequent earnings without a cut in benefits. Although judicial decisions in the 1960s struck down "suitable home" and "man-in-the-house" provisions and states' residency requirements, efforts by advocates to establish a constitutional "right to welfare" through the courts failed. Proposals to establish a guaranteed annual income, such as the Family Assistance Plan of 1970, were defeated in Congress by an unusual coalition of conservatives and liberals.

The dramatic increase in welfare costs and caseloads in the 1960s led to calls for welfare reform. The proponents of reform, however, generally overlooked the small percentage of the federal budget (1 percent) that AFDC consumed, the low level and wide variation of benefits, and the percentage of Americans who received AFDC (about 5 percent). They also significantly overstated the extent of long-term dependency and welfare fraud and ignored the fact that about 70 percent of recipients were children.

Failure to reform AFDC in the 1970s led to further changes in 1981, restricting access to benefits and encouraging states to establish work incentive demonstration programs. Families with fathers absent due to military service and caretakers who participated in strikes were now ineligible. The definition of *dependent child* was narrowed; states could require employment searches at the time of application. An income limit of 150 percent of states' need standard was set and the sequence of the earned income disregards changed. States could also count previously excluded income sources available to some families.

Between 1970 and 1996, through benefit cuts and failure to keep pace with inflation, AFDC grants lost between 18 percent and 68 percent of their value. By 1995, states' maximum AFDC grants ranged from 8.6 percent to 46.1 percent of per capita income, and the combined benefits of AFDC and food stamps ranged from 41 percent to 85 percent of the federal poverty threshold.

Michael Reisch

See also Culture of Dependency; Culture of Poverty; Poverty; Temporary Assistance for Needy Families

Further Readings

Patterson, James. 2000. *America's Struggle against Poverty in the 20th Century.* Cambridge, MA: Harvard University Press.
Piven, Frances and Richard Cloward. 1993. *Regulating the Poor: The Functions of Public Welfare.* New York: Vintage.

ALCOHOLISM

Alcoholism is a type of substance addiction characterized by a preoccupation with alcohol and impaired control over alcohol consumption. Alcoholism is similar to illicit drug addiction in its association with physical and psychological dependence. However, as alcohol consumption is legal and socially accepted, problematic use often goes unrecognized and lacks the same social stigma as illicit drug use. Alcoholism falls into two separate but overlapping categories: dependence and abuse.

Alcohol abuse is more prevalent among youth and young adults and is characterized by binge drinking, often resulting in legal problems such as drunk-driving arrests or interpersonal problems such as failure to fulfill employment responsibilities. In this entry the chronic and degenerative form of alcoholism—dependence—is the primary focus. Characterizing alcohol dependence is long-term abuse and the degradation of health caused by sustained long-term use. Onset of dependence can be slow, often taking years. The major criteria for diagnosis are increasing tolerance to the effects of use, loss of control over consumption, unsuccessful attempts to control use, continued drinking despite negative consequences stemming from use, the experience of withdrawal symptoms (the shakes, nausea) when consumption ceases, and drinking alcohol to relieve such symptoms.

History

The alcohol temperance and prohibition movements of the late 19th and early 20th centuries had some moderate success in framing alcoholism as a moral and social problem. Shortly after the repeal of prohibition, the foundation of *Alcoholics Anonymous* and the *Yale Research Center* played a key role in changing the definition of alcoholism from that of a personal defect and moral weakness to one based on the "disease model" that is dominant today. The *American Medical Association* (AMA) officially recognized alcoholism as a nonpsychiatric disease in 1956. This acknowledgment was an important step in reducing the social stigma previously associated with alcoholism. The creation of the *National Institute on Alcohol Abuse and Alcoholism* (NIAAA) in 1971 and the passing of the Comprehensive Alcohol Abuse and Alcoholism Prevention, Treatment, and Rehabilitation Act in 1970 were instrumental in the increased proliferation of treatment and counseling services that began in the 1970s, as well as further reducing social stigma by protecting alcoholics from job discrimination.

Whereas the adoption of a disease model of alcoholism is generally viewed as a progressive development in medical science, it should also be viewed as a significant social and political accomplishment. By increasing the scope of institutions such as the AMA and giving rise to new government bureaucracies such as the NIAAA, the disease model laid the foundation for the birth of a multimillion-dollar "alcoholism industry" devoted to the scientific study and treatment of alcohol use.

Demographics

Among the U.S. working-age population, an estimated 24.5 million meet the criteria for alcohol dependence, and lifetime prevalence rates among adults are between 14 percent and 24 percent. Generally speaking, rates of alcoholism decline as age increases. With respect to sex, alcoholism is at least twice as prevalent in males as females. Alcoholism is somewhat more prevalent among those of lower socioeconomic status groups and those with lower levels of educational attainment. That is, as income and education level increase, the likelihood of alcoholism decreases. Finally, with regard to race, research consistently finds higher levels of alcoholism in whites than in blacks. Prevalence among Asians and Hispanics is generally lower than in whites, whereas Native Americans generally display higher levels of both dependency and general use than other racial or ethnic groups.

Causes

Reliably identifying the causes of alcoholism is challenging. Twin and adoption studies found evidence of a hereditary predisposition, but a genetic basis for alcoholism has not been consistently established. Other research suggests that a family history of alcoholism is largely dependent on race and ethnicity. For example, alcoholism among Native American families is twice as common as among white, black, and Hispanic families. However, such research is socially controversial and widely criticized. In addition to research elucidating genetic and biological correlations, numerous social variables are also linked to alcoholism. Factors such as family structure, peer networks and the reinforcement of alcohol use, and alcohol availability are key contributors. Additionally, cognitive factors such as increased stress or strain, combined with an inadequate ability to effectively cope with emotional distress and other problems, can play a role.

Associated Problems

The physical health risks resulting from alcoholism are numerous. Such risks include death from alcohol poisoning, heart disease, brain damage, nerve damage leading to impaired mobility, various types of liver problems, poor nutrition, severe and prolonged depression, insomnia, and sexual dysfunction. Withdrawal from sustained alcohol dependence is similar to withdrawal from heroin and is occasionally fatal. Symptoms can include nausea, severe headaches, seizures, the shakes, and hallucinations.

In terms of social health, alcohol is a major contributor to motor vehicle accidents, violence, and assaults, as well as such problems as drunk driving and public disorder. Alcoholism also correlates highly with homelessness, and research indicates that over half of the homeless population in the United States meets the criteria for alcoholism. With respect to violent crime, research consistently notes that the psychopharmacological effects of alcohol significantly increase the propensity toward aggressiveness and violent behavior, particularly among males. Research indicates that a substantial number of homicide and assault offenders are drunk at the time of their crimes. With respect to domestic violence and abuse, roughly two thirds of those who experienced violence by a partner reported that alcohol was a contributing factor. Among victims of spousal abuse specifically, roughly 75 percent of incidents involve an offender who had been drinking. Excessive alcohol use among offenders is also common in various acts of sexual assault, including rape.

Other research specifies a negative association between alcoholism and employment opportunities and wages for both males and females. Alcohol dependence also decreases the likelihood of full-time work and educational attainment. The broader social and economic costs of alcohol dependence are also substantial. The NIAAA estimates that the annual economic cost of alcoholism in the United States is approximately $150 billion. The cost includes health care for physical and mental problems related to alcoholism, abuse and addiction treatment services, and lost work potential and productivity.

Economists and other researchers strongly criticize the NIAAA cost estimates in the areas of medical care, social services, and lost productivity, asserting that estimates in the hundreds of billions of dollars are grossly overstated. Still, even using conservative estimates, alcoholism is one of the most widespread and costly substance abuse problems in the United States. With the exception of nicotine addiction, alcoholism is more costly to the United States than all drug problems combined.

Philip R. Kavanaugh

See also Addiction; Binge Drinking

Further Readings

Heien, David. 1996. "The External Costs of Alcohol Abuse." *Journal of Studies on Alcohol* 57:336–42.

National Institute on Alcohol Abuse and Alcoholism. 1998. "Drinking in the United States: Main Findings from the 1992 National Longitudinal Alcohol Epidemiologic Survey." Rockville, MD: NIAAA.

National Institute on Drug Abuse. 1997. "The Economic Costs of Alcohol and Drug Abuse in the United States, 1992." Rockville, MD: NIDA.

Schneider, Joseph W. 1978. "Deviant Drinking as a Disease: Alcoholism as a Social Accomplishment." *Social Problems* 25:361–72.

ALIENATION

Alienation is related to social problems both in substance and in terms of how we look at social problems. In the context of modern everyday language and "commonsense" perspectives and views, the term *alienation* frequently is employed to express a feeling of separation—ranging from one's experiences with others, work, nature, social environment, political process, and system, all the way to "the world as it is." Yet this feeling of being separated links concretely to the prevalence of myriad social problems (unemployment, drug abuse, poverty, mental illness, domestic violence, etc.). Understood in this latter sense, alienation can serve as a means to express and describe a certain type of experience and, more important, as a tool to address and dissect the nature of everyday life and to identify its origins and causes. Depending on how the concept is employed, momentous implications result for the orientation and purpose of social research and social scientists' perspectives on social problems.

At its most basic level, the concept served to verbalize the experience of individuals who were alienated, or "estranged," from their social environment. Though dating back to the ancient Romans, the modern use of the concept originated, above all, in the philosophy of G. W. F. Hegel and the early writings of Karl Marx. Hegel argued that it is not possible for enlightened individuals to identify fully with a society as a concrete sociohistoric reality. Throughout history, religions purported to offer a solution to individuals' experience of separation—solutions that had to be illusory, because religion as an institution is contingent on individuals being unable to grasp how the experience

of separation is a corollary of life in increasingly complex aggregates of human beings. Yet, Hegel argued, the modern age promises the reconciliation of individuals and society through the development of institutions that reflect the values of individuals as citizens and their ability to recognize that those values cannot be translated directly into social, political, and economic reality, but instead are implemented in a mediated fashion, through a dialectical process.

In Marx's critical theory, alienation served to capture the highly problematic condition of social life in the modern age. Marx's use of the term *alienation* went beyond that of Hegel, as he argued that individuals experience in "bourgeois society" an alienation from the product of their labor, from themselves, from nature, from each other, and from the species, which is thus a new form of alienation that is qualitatively different from the past history of human civilization. Though it is widely acknowledged that Marx's theoretical agenda began with his critique of alienation as a by-product of the economic processes that made possible the rise of bourgeois society—the price society must pay to make possible the continuous pursuit of prosperity—there is less awareness of the extent to which his entire critical project is built around his concern about alienation as a feature of modern social life. In his 1844 *Economic and Philosophical Manuscripts,* Marx famously laid the foundation for his later critique of political economy, in whose context he reformulated his earlier critique of alienation as the critique of "commodity fetishism."

Marx came to understand that, to grasp the nature of the link between the capitalist mode of production and alienation, as both a societal condition and a social mechanism, he had to develop the tools to identify the specific process that generated alienation and thus followed his step toward the systematic critique of political economy. In the process, he came to appreciate how successive generations of people internalize compounded levels of alienation, interpreting them as "natural" to human existence on Earth. Consequently, commodity fetishism is both a more theoretically sophisticated mode of capturing alienation and a means to capture a more subtle, historically later form of alienation—"alienation as second nature." If it was Marx's initial philosophical goal to conceive of strategies to overcome alienation, his later work turned around the realization that the capitalist mode of production undercuts opportunities to bring about desirable qualitative change. Marx's critiques of political economy, from *Grundrisse* to *Das Kapital,* thus should be read as a sustained explanation for why it is increasingly difficult to reconcile norms and facts in modern society, even though the latter postures as the kind of society that makes reconciliation more conceivable and realizable than any other.

Among the implications of perspectives on modern society through alienation is the realization that we are naturally positioned neither to recognize alienation as a by-product of the pursuit of prosperity nor to conceive of the detrimental impact it has on our ability to acknowledge and make explicit the dynamics that are at the core of modern society. These implications apply in particular with regard to the relationships between, first, science—especially social science—and society, and second, individual and society. If we are not able to recognize that modern society is constituted through sedimented layers of alienation, we interpret its concrete forms as expressions of human nature and the logic of social order, independently of the social forces that may actually generate alienation: the capitalist mode of production that creates the logic of a particular social order. While we must be concerned with whether the logic of social order in complex and contradictory societies can be conceived independently of alienation, in both cases, the challenge is recognizing the sway of alienation. If we assume that modern complex societies are not possible without alienation and conclude that there is no need to acknowledge the sway of alienation, we further amplify alienation. If we assume that our nature is what it is with or without alienation and that because without alienation we would not have become who we are, it is not necessary to acknowledge alienation as a crucial force, we not only neglect its actual power, but double it. We are *how* we are to a large extent because of alienation. As we try to grasp how we have been shaped by the prevalence of alienation, efforts to theorize truly alternative forms of social life become all the more daunting. Can social scientists escape the vicious cycle—and if so, how?

Despite frequent assertions that the theoretical preoccupation with alienation is outdated, the agenda posed by alienation remains central to the very possibility of social science. Many of the most problematic features of modern society—the exaggerated orientation toward economic considerations, the perpetuation of path-dependent developments without acknowledging how they limit our ability to confront the actual complexity and contradictory nature of modern society, and so forth—are not becoming less pronounced under conditions of globalization, but much more so.

If we were to eliminate the concept of alienation from the sociological vocabulary, we not only would deprive ourselves of one of the most powerful tools to scrutinize the flawed character of the modern world. By default, we also would assert that the current trajectory of sociohistorical change is as desirable as it is necessary. Thus we would support, de facto, the neoliberal conceit that pushing ahead as far and as fast as possible the process of globalization will bring "the end of poverty" and increasing control over social problems. Yet this conceit is contradicted by overwhelming empirical evidence indicating that economic inequality (along with forms of social, political, and cultural inequality) is increasing not just globally, but especially nationally around the globe. We also have at our disposal theoretically grounded explanations of why and how growing inequality, within the modern framework of purportedly self-regulating market economies and democratic nation-states, does not expand the ability of citizenries and institutions to tackle (not to mention *solve*) the myriad social problems but solidifies their "quasi-natural" character and air of inevitability. Holding on to, and sharpening further, the concept of alienation for analytical purposes neither implies, nor must it be based upon the expectation, that eliminating alienation is a realistic goal for the foreseeable future. At best, strategies directed at "overcoming" alienation may achieve some limited successes if they are not directed at radically transforming the current system of global transnational capitalism, as this system keeps driving its ability to immunize itself against scrutiny as well as collective action to ever greater heights. Rather, endeavors to overcome alienation as a determining factor in the lives of individuals, social groups, institutions, organizations, and nation-states must be directed at identifying and preparing the necessary preconditions for efforts to reduce the prevalence of alienation to be minimally successful. Basic income-related proposals, for instance, provide an example for endeavors that are directed at creating circumstances that allow for forms of action, solidarity, and organization that point beyond alienated conditions.

From Psychoanalysis to "Socioanalysis"

Individuals cannot actively overcome alienation, because it is an inherently social condition that is at the very core of modern society. Yet we may be able to take steps toward *recognizing* the power of alienation over our lives and existence. Because alienation first and foremost is manifest in concrete practices, relationships, and ways of thinking, altering each and all of those will be necessary first steps. Sociologists seek to help the rest of us conceive of, and to scrutinize rigorously, who and what we are as individuals, as a reflection and representation of specific, defining features of modern society—both in general and in particular. As long as individuals are oblivious to this fact, our lives—more than not—are reenactments of practices related to values which, in the interest of social stability and integration, we must regard as our very own, but which are, in fact, imprinted onto our selves as an integral part of the process of identity-formation, well before we become conscious of our own selves. The nature of the relationship between self and society is becoming increasingly problematic proportionately to the degree to which the configuration of modern society itself is becoming problematic. Compounded layers of alienation undermine our ability to recognize the intrinsic relationship between the growing potential for destruction that comes with the pursuit of prosperity. In analogy to psychoanalysis, sociology must embrace the possibility of and need for *socioanalysis* as one of its greatest yet unopened treasure troves. Socioanalysis in this sense involves therapeutically enabling the individual to recognize how, in addition to psychological limitations and barriers, there are societal limitations and barriers that both are built into and constitute our very selves as social beings. As long as these limitations and barriers are not recognizable as necessary preconditions for the possibility of social order and integration, individual efforts to achieve freedom and to engage in agency will be thwarted by the (socially imposed) imperative to interpret the disabling consequences of those limitations for individuals' efforts to construct meaningful life histories as "personal" and "psychological" in the language of mental illness rather than of "false consciousness." Whether sociologists in the future will make a truly constructive contribution to the lives of human beings and their efforts to overcome social problems indeed may depend on our ability and willingness to meet the challenge of circumscribing the thrust and purpose of socioanalysis, above and beyond the confines of what Freud erroneously ascribed to psychoanalysis, neglecting that many mental problems are expressions of the contradictions of the modern age.

Harry F. Dahms

See also Mental Depression; Socialism; Stressors

Further Readings

Dahms, Harry F. 2005. "Globalization or Hyper-alienation? Critiques of Traditional Marxism as Arguments for Basic Income." *Current Perspectives in Social Theory* 23:205–76.

———. 2006. "Does *Alienation* Have a Future? Recapturing the Core of Critical Theory." Pp. 23–46 in *The Evolution of Alienation: Trauma, Promise, and the Millennium,* edited by L. Langman and D. Kalekin-Fishman. Lanham, MD: Rowman & Littlefield.

Gabel, Joseph. 1975. *False Consciousness: An Essay on Reification.* Oxford, England: Blackwell.

Ludz, Peter Christian. 1973. "Alienation as a Concept in the Social Sciences." *Current Sociology* 21(1):5–39.

Marx, Karl. [1844] 1978. "Economic and Philosophical Manuscripts of 1844." Pp. 66–125 in *The Marx-Engels Reader,* edited by R. C. Tucker. New York: Norton.

Ollman, Bertell. 1976. *Alienation: Marx's Concept of Man in Capitalist Society.* 2nd ed. Cambridge, England: Cambridge University Press.

Sachs, Jeffrey. 2005. *The End of Poverty: Economic Possibilities for Our Time.* London: Penguin.

Schacht, Richard. 1994. *The Future of Alienation.* Urbana, IL: University of Illinois Press.

American Dream

For an immigrant, the American Dream is to achieve economic well-being and a good quality of life through hard work, entrepreneurship, and perseverance. It is the driving force behind most immigration, and its realization is the achievement dimension of the incorporation process. A main topic addressed in immigration literature is the high variance of intragenerational mobility. Why do some immigrants advance quickly while others remain at the bottom end of the economic ladder?

Essentially, incorporation along one dimension speeds up incorporation along another. For example, better command of the native tongue allows for better-paying jobs that involve day-to-day use of the native tongue, which in turn enhance language improvement. This mechanism, together with others, gives rise to two incorporation tracks: a fast and a stationary one. As a result, incorporation outcomes, particularly achievement, tend to be dichotomous.

Another mechanism is the one that causes growing income inequality in any capitalist system:

money accumulation. The returns on previous investments allow for subsequent larger investments with greater returns. This is, of course, true for any participant in a capitalist society, immigrant or native. For the special case of immigrants, accompanying this core mechanism is a host of additional mechanisms that further widen the gap between rich and poor.

When immigrants find better-paying jobs outside their ethnic economy, this is often through a referral by someone already participating in the mixed economy. Migrants with a friend outside the ethnic group more likely receive news about jobs outside the ethnic economy. Those who lack such a friend will more likely continue to work in the ethnic economy. Given that cross-ethnic friends are more likely to know about jobs in the mixed economy than co-ethnic friends, economic incorporation is contingent upon incorporation along the friendship dimension. Vice versa, some colleagues and their contacts—who most likely also work outside the ethnic economy—become friends. Incorporation in multiethnic friendship networks is therefore also contingent upon economic incorporation. The new friends will further enhance job opportunities. This spiraling process will increasingly distinguish economically a group of people with largely co-ethnic friends and co-ethnic colleagues and another with largely cross-ethnic friends and cross-ethnic colleagues.

Cross-ethnic contact facilitates language improvement, and, vice versa, cross-ethnic contacts more readily develop if one speaks the host language better. The former is true because conversations with those of a different ethnicity are more likely in the host language. Language skills then develop more rapidly if more contacts are cross-ethnic. Conversely, because a better command of the spoken language facilitates conversations, cross-ethnic contacts develop more rapidly with improved language skills. Those who barely speak the host language, by contrast, find it difficult to maintain such contacts and tend to lose even the few they may have. This feedback process causes a greater and greater divergence between those with both language skills and a network entrance into the mixed economy and those who are incorporated along neither dimension. The former's economic opportunities become better and better than the latter's.

Interaction breeds similarity and similarity breeds interaction. These tendencies are known as *influence* and *attraction*. Attraction is the tendency of people to interact with similar others more than with dissimilar others. Influence concerns the opposite causality and is the tendency of people to grow similar to interaction partners. Together these two pervasive tendencies produce the phenomenon of homophily. In the case of immigrants, those who interact with members of other ethnic groups more often acculturate faster, more readily adopting norms, values, and traditions widely shared across society and losing ethnic-specific norms, values, and traditions. Frequent cross-ethnic contact may erode ethnic traditions and encourage identification with those from another ethnicity, whereas continuous participation in co-ethnic friendship networks, colleagueship, and neighborhoods enhances ethnic solidarity. Conversely, the sharing of norms, values, and traditions eases interaction, decreasing social distance. In combination, they produce a dichotomy between those who, with increasing speed, drift away from their ethnic traditions and contacts and those who maintain strong bonds and cherish ethnic traditions.

Immigrants with higher incomes can more readily find housing outside the ethnic neighborhood. Economic incorporation thus facilitates spatial integration (the spatial assimilation hypothesis). These more affluent neighborhoods, in turn, are perhaps closer to better-paying jobs and have resources that facilitate economic advancement. Again, a spiral is present that, in combination with the previously described spirals, breaks up the immigrant population into those who incorporate along all dimensions and those who continue to cherish ethnic norms, values, and traditions; have friends in ethnic networks; work in the ethnic economy; reside in the ethnic neighborhood; and speak the host language poorly.

These polarizing mechanisms provide a simple theoretical account of polarization in immigrants' economic advancement. Thus, economic success, on the one hand, and incorporation along other dimensions (residential integration, native language improvement, acculturation), on the other hand, affect each other positively. At least three counteracting mechanisms weaken this correlation of economic success with noneconomic incorporation. First, dense and exclusive ethnic networks can function as a resource rather than as a restriction in immigrant economic advancement, as fellow ethnic group members, building on trust and friendship ties, provide startup funds for a business in the ethnic economy. Second, cross-ethnic contact may increase rather than decrease ethnic awareness, a phenomenon called *reactive ethnicity*. Third, critics of the spatial assimilation hypothesis say it neglects the ethnic barriers that, through discrimination and in-group favoritism, prevent income increases from automatically translating into neighborhood integration.

Arnout van de Rijt

See also Acculturation; Assimilation; Discrimination; Ethnic Group; Immigration; Inequality; Intergenerational Mobility; Labor Market; Mixed Economy; Norms; Segmented Assimilation; Social Capital; Social Networks; Values

Further Readings

Nee, Victor, Jimy Sanders, and Scott Sernau. 1994. "Job Transitions in an Immigrant Metropolis: Ethnic Boundaries and Mixed Economy." *American Sociological Review* 59:849–72.

Portes, Alejandro and J. Sensenbrenner. 1993. "Embeddedness and Immigration: Notes on the Social Determinants of Economic Action." *American Journal of Sociology* 98:1320–50.

Van Tubergen, Frank, Ineke Maas, and Henk Flap. 2004. "The Economic Incorporation of Immigrants in 18 Western Societies: Origin, Destination, and Community Effects." *American Sociological Review* 69:704–27.

AMERICANIZATION

The term *Americanization* generally refers to the assimilation of immigrants into U.S. society, a meaning now endowed with negative connotations. The unpopular interpretation rests on its association with the Americanization movement of the late 19th and early 20th centuries. This movement, particularly during and after World War I, advocated immediate and coercive assimilation through English language and citizenship programs to the dominant Anglo-Saxon culture, then considered by nativists to be superior. Thus, the Americanization movements became synonymous with forced assimilation, nationalism, and xenophobia.

Historically, several factors led to the escalation of nativist fears. First, specific circumstances in Europe, like the Irish famine and the change in British government policies, sent immigrants to the United States in exponentially increasing numbers. Between 1841 and 1860, over 1.7 million persons arrived. Second, the

discovery of gold in California in 1848 initiated yet another new immigration stream, that of the Chinese. By the early 1900s, technological improvements and increased trade made travel much more affordable, leading to an unprecedented increase in the number of immigrants from southern and eastern Europe. The lack of knowledge about the new groups, as well as their different appearance and customs, brought about heightened concerns among native whites, particularly on the eve of World War I.

Nativist sentiments and social movements like the Know-Nothing Movement, established in 1850 with the motto "America for Americans," defined a path for the first policy restrictions on immigration. In 1875, the U.S. government passed the first law directly restricting immigration by prohibiting the entrance of "convicts and prostitutes." A few years later, in 1882, the Chinese Exclusionary Act passed, after the urging of California voters who overwhelmingly agreed with their Republican senator, Aaron Sargent, that "Chinese immigrants are unwilling to conform to our institutions, to become permanent citizens of our country, to accept the rights and responsibilities of citizenship and have indicated no capacity to assimilate with our people."

On a larger national scale, the Immigration Restriction League, founded in 1894 by a group of Harvard College graduates, many of whom believed in eugenics and Anglo-Saxon superiority, became among the first groups to demand the establishment of an entrance literacy test for all immigrants. They considered people from southern and eastern Europe (Greeks, Italians, Slavs, and Jews) to be an inferior race. American Federation of Labor leaders, believing that a large flow of immigrant workers could jeopardize the labor movement, supported the literacy test, which passed as legislation in 1917. Nevertheless, it did not inhibit immigration much, as most immigrants from southern and eastern Europe were literate by then.

Parallel with the push for immigrant restrictions were attempts to "absorb" the immigrants. The absorption process built upon the melting pot idea, at the time associated with a "pressure-cooker" Americanization. The public schools offered classes in English language and citizenship to new immigrants, with evening classes sponsored by businessmen, who did not want immigration restrictions but feared a radicalized labor force, given the rise of Bolshevism and the "red scare." Private immigrant groups also offered educational programs that stressed the teaching of English and "civics" as the most secure road to Americanization. Creating further an atmosphere of urgency and necessity, the Americanization movement took upon itself to institute English language classes in factories. The first phase, starting in 1907 under the auspices of the YMCA, combined the process of naturalization with an industrial safety campaign. Employers supported this process, because it was essential that workers understand simple safety instructions to minimize work-related accidents. The second phase started in 1915 and became a central part of the "Americanization crusade."

One of the most influential persons in the militant phase of the Americanization movement was Frances Kellor, an "authority" on immigration and immigrant legislation, advising Roosevelt on immigrant matters. In 1914, Ms. Kellor became vice chair of the Committee on Immigrants in America and, a year later, editor of its journal, *Immigrants in America Review,* which was devoted to Americanization. In the *Yale Review* of 1919 she wrote, "Americanization is the science of racial relations in America, dealing with the assimilation and amalgamation of diverse races in equity into an integral part of the national life." This point of view was the apogee of the model of Anglo-conformity and the epitome of the Americanization movement, which, during and after World War I, called for the immediate "100 percent Americanization" of immigrants. Notably, most of these discussions of immigrant Americanization and assimilation excluded blacks as participants and as a topic in the debates. Consequently, Americanization became associated with racism, nationalism, and xenophobia.

Two additional historical processes solidified the unfavorable connotations of the term *Americanization*: the treatment of American Indians and the annexation of Puerto Rico. The process of naturalization for American Indians included destroying tribal organizations, repressing religious ceremonies, allowing only English in schools, and teaching about only white culture and history. The occupation of Puerto Rico was followed by discouraging Spanish cultural identification and traditions and enforcing the English language.

Whereas *Americanization* relates to a difficult history of coercion in the United States, the contemporary view of the adaptation, incorporation, and assimilation of immigrants into U.S. society is one of a voluntary process, through which immigrants make choices guided by rational strategies to improve their own lives. However, even the most sensitive approaches to immigrant incorporation cannot "save" the term *Americanization*. In more international interpretations, Americanization now means imposing U.S. culture, traditions, and the capitalist economic system on other countries around the world. It may thus be one rather daunting task to restore this term to a more lasting and positive meaning.

Elena Vesselinov

See also Acculturation; Assimilation; Cultural Imperialism; Cultural Relativism; Ethnicity; Ethnocentrism; Melting Pot; Multiculturalism; Nativism; Pluralism

Further Readings

Alba, Richard and Victor Nee. 2003. *Remaking the American Mainstream: Assimilation and Contemporary Immigration.* Cambridge, MA: Harvard University Press.

Downey, Harry. 1999. "From Americanization to Multiculturalism: Political Symbols and Struggles for Cultural Diversity in Twentieth-Century American Race Relations." *Sociological Perspectives* 42(2):249–78.

Glazer, Nathan. 1993. "Is Assimilation Dead?" *Annals of the American Academy of Political and Social Science* 530:122–36.

Gordon, Milton M. 1964. *Assimilation in American Life: The Role of Race, Religion and National Origin.* New York: Oxford University Press.

Heer, David. 1996. *Immigration in America's Future: Social Science Findings and Policy Debate.* Boulder, CO: Westview.

Korman, Gerd. 1965. "Americanization at the Factory Gate." *Industrial and Labor Relations Review* 18(3):397–419.

Parrillo, Vincent N. Forthcoming. *Strangers to These Shores.* 9th ed. Boston: Allyn & Bacon.

ANOMIE

Anomie refers to the improper operation or relative absence of normative regulation in an aggregate entity or environment, ranging from groups and communities to entire societies and the globe. Most conceptualizations of anomie stress normative breakdown, making this aspect critical to understanding any form of anomie. Its importance lies in the impacts and effects of inadequate regulation on individual, group, and societal pathologies. For these and other reasons, anomie has been an integral part of philosophical and social science debates about the nature of modern individuals and societies. Anomie-related research is thus prominent in multiple disciplines, including psychology, sociology, criminology, criminal justice, and political science.

Anomie varies by duration, intensity, source, and location. Some of its main types and typologies incorporating space and time elements include chronic, acute, simple, political, economic, institutional, cultural, social, and psychological anomie. Anomic conditions create unstable and uncertain environments where individuals face difficulties in coordination and cooperation and in determining whether or which formal and informal norms to follow. Generally, all types of anomie are consequential for the viability and predictability of social relationships, in the functioning of societal institutions and groups, and in producing crime and other pathological and deviant behavior. Although sometimes viewed in absolutist terms, anomie is a relative phenomenon with particular spatial and temporal referents.

The origin of anomie traces back to the notions in classical Greece of *anomia* and *anomus*, defined respectively as lawlessness and "without law." The use of anomie in Renaissance England debates about human nature, religion, and the law rested on these earlier Greek roots. The view of anomie in these debates was as a condition of society with a lack of, or a lack of compliance with, laws and as representing a situation that might emerge without a rational foundation of law.

Émile Durkheim (1858–1917) presented the most widely known historical use of anomie, borrowing the term from French philosopher Jean Marie Guyau (1854–88). Guyau advocated an individual-based notion of anomie, viewing it as a positive condition countering the dominance of religious dogma and morality. Although Durkheim's interpretation offered some positive features and a few similarities to Guyau's individual-level anomie, Durkheim's work is largely negative and emphasized social institutions and societal changes as responsible for anomie. Durkheim's activist side emphasized restoration and repair of society's normative systems using social institutions to counter any negative aspects of anomic conditions. Academically, Durkheim's applications of anomie exemplify early positivistic sociological methodologies.

Anomie, for Durkheim, is a moral judgment on the condition of society and the basis for normative prescriptions on needed changes, rather than a moral or psychological state of an individual. Sociological and social science conceptualizations of anomie differ specifically on this point with their psychological and philosophical counterparts. Most macro-sociological conceptions of anomie build upon the work of Durkheim in viewing societal conditions as having a reality independent and distinct from the mental and emotional characteristics and actions of individuals. Further, these conditions including anomie were external to individuals and constrained individual behavior. Durkheim saw modern individuals with natural egoistical desires but with inherently social attributes that required cultivation and regulation.

Some sociologists unduly emphasize the individualistic side of Durkheim's view of human nature to develop social control, bonding, and disorganization theories to examine individual-centered and institutionally mediated deviance. These interpretations of anomie are incompatible with Durkheim's societal and functional focus on the necessity of extra-individual organs to counter anomic tendencies accompanying modernization. High levels of controls and regulation were also problematic for Durkheim. Micro conceptualizations of anomie exclusively focus on the individual manifestations, origins, and effects of anomie as well as on its subjective aspects.

U.S. sociologist Robert K. Merton developed his conceptualization of anomie through extension of the macro-sociological tradition built by Durkheim. For Merton, anomie was a cultural imbalance between cultural goals and norms, with emphasis of promoted goals over approved means. A poorly integrated culture was one of the critical ingredients producing a nonrandom, but patterned, distribution of deviant behavior. Unlike Talcott Parsons and other functionalists bent on advocating social engineering of institutions to achieve regulation of individual goals to meet predetermined societal ends, Merton examined these ends and accompanying regulatory norms as empirical and contingent outcomes dependent on individual decisions and societal structures. When institutionalized expectations do not guide behavior and individuals do not use the prescribed norms, some individuals choose to use nonprescribed means attenuating the already imbalanced culture. For Merton, anomie becomes a more permanent fixture in society for these reasons.

In Merton's analysis, the organization of society and normal operation of societal institutions created the conditions of deviant behavior. Merton promoted the notion that nonconformity is rooted in society rather than in human nature and is a result of normal (not abnormal) conditions. Unlike Durkheim, Merton emphasized the distributional consequences of anomie in a stratified society, stressed the magnification and intensification of anomie through individual adaptations, and recognized the plurality of social controls and individual normative commitments that inhibited single-cause, general explanations of anomie and deviant behavior. Extensive debates about the broader application and testing of both Merton's and Durkheim's concepts of anomie and the labeling of both theorists as functionalists are responsible for the distortion of their theories and for misapplications and empirical testing of anomie at individual levels of analyses.

Anomie is not a unitary concept; it is subject to varying interpretations depending on the theories and partialities of the academic disciplines. The most prominent current application of anomie is in developmental contexts of societies undergoing dramatic transformations and adaptations to a globalizing world. While this is consistent with the macro-sociological tradition of anomie, anomie has emerged as a psychological concept requiring individualistic responses rather than as a social problem with societal implications and effects. Anomie as a cultural/societal phenomenon has little visibility to many segments of a society's population. Further, defining anomie as a truly societal problem is unlikely because those greatly impacted by anomie may not be aware of its sources and effects. Moreover, anomic arrangements are not necessarily incompatible with the structures of society.

Sanjay Marwah

See also Deviance; Norms; Role Conflict; Role Strain; Social Change; Social Disorganization

Further Readings

Adler, Freda and William S. Laufer. 1995. *The Legacy of Anomie Theory.* New Brunswick, NJ: Transaction.

Western, John, Bettina Gransow, and Peter M. Atteslander, eds. 1999. *Comparative Anomie Research: Hidden Barriers, Hidden Potential for Social Development.* Aldershot, England: Ashgate.

ANTI-DRUG ABUSE ACT OF 1986

The Anti-Drug Abuse Act of 1986 enacted mandatory minimum prison sentences designed to provide severe penalties for violations involving the possession or distribution of crack cocaine. Inspired by the hysteria surrounding the national crack and AIDS epidemics in the early 1980s, the Reagan administration reintroduced mandatory minimum sentencing laws, making them broader and more rigid than earlier drug laws. This act subsequently led to the Anti-Drug Abuse Act of 1988, which approved the death penalty for drug traffickers and gave the military the authority to pursue and apprehend those individuals smuggling drugs into the United States.

The act imposed severe penalties for high-profile drugs (i.e., crack cocaine): a prison sentence of 5 to 40 years for possession of the substance. These newly enacted laws ranked drug crimes among the most severely punished offenses in the United States. Sentencing guidelines adopted a 100:1 quantity ratio, treating 1 gram of crack cocaine the same as 100 grams of powdered cocaine. Also, new mandatory minimum sentences, without the possibility for probation or parole, were adopted for drug violations that involved even small amounts of crack cocaine. Conversely, individuals convicted of possession or distribution of considerably larger amounts of powder cocaine were not subject to mandatory minimum sentences. This disparity ended in December 2007, when the Supreme Court ruled that federal judges can impose sentences for crack cocaine users that are more in line with those for powder cocaine users. Because the majority of crack offenders are black, this decision eliminates an unintended racial bias embedded in the legislation.

As a part of the Reagan administration's War on Drugs, the Anti-Drug Abuse Act of 1986 led to substantial increases in the arrests of drug offenders and inadvertently targeted minority offenders for the possession and sale of crack cocaine. New legislation prevented judges from looking at the individual circumstances surrounding the offense when sentencing drug offenders and gave an unparalleled amount of power to federal prosecutors; these changes had devastating effects on minority defendants. Although one of the ultimate goals of the mandatory minimum sentencing legislation within the Anti-Drug Abuse Act was to target the foremost drug traffickers, it was actually the low-level contributors to the drug trade (i.e., street dealers, lookouts) who were most severely penalized. Recent data illustrate that roughly 70 percent of those prosecuted for crack offenses were only involved in this low-level activity within the drug trade.

Although the Anti-Drug Abuse Act was sparked by the crack epidemic, it was actually the death of Len Bias, a promising University of Maryland basketball prodigy, that quickly pushed the new laws through Congress. Bias died of a drug overdose subsequently following his selection in the National Basketball Association draft by the Boston Celtics, which instigated a sensational media campaign focused on the drug crack cocaine, which was erroneously believed to have killed him. Although it was later discovered that it was actually powder cocaine, not crack cocaine, that killed Bias, his death pressed the Anti-Drug Abuse Act of 1986 into legislation, making it one of the harshest and most controversial drug laws ever enacted.

Nicholas W. Bakken

See also Cocaine and Crack; Drug Abuse; Drug Abuse, Sports; Zero-Tolerance Policies

Further Readings

Angeli, David H. 1997. "A Second Look at Crack Cocaine Sentencing Policies: One More Try for Federal Equal Protection." *American Criminal Law Review* 34(3):1211–41.

Inciardi, James A. and Karen McElrath. 2001. *The American Drug Scene.* Los Angeles: Roxbury.

Musto, David. 1999. *The American Disease: Origins of Narcotic Control.* 3rd ed. New York: Oxford University Press.

Anti-Globalization Movement

The anti-globalization movement is a broad-based popular struggle involving workers, environmentalists, youths, peasants, the urban poor, indigenous people, and other actors across the developing and industrialized worlds striving for social and economic justice and greater democratic control over their daily lives. Activists come from diverse spheres, including nongovernmental organizations, political parties, trade unions, mass movements, informal networks and collectives, and revolutionary fronts. Moreover, anti-globalization activists combine diverse forms of action, including nonviolent civil disobedience, marches and rallies, public education, and lobbying. With this movement perhaps more aptly known as the global justice movement, participants do not oppose globalization per se, but rather corporate globalization, or the extension of corporate power around the world, undermining local communities, democracy, and the environment. The movement addresses the root causes of various social problems linked to free-market capitalism, including poverty, inequality, social dislocation, hunger, poor health, and ecological destruction.

Background

Over the past several decades national governments and multilateral institutions, such as the World Bank, International Monetary Fund (IMF), and World Trade Organization (WTO), have implemented free-market policies such as privatization, trade liberalization, deregulation, export-oriented production, and cuts in social spending and basic subsidies. These neoliberal measures have brought new regions into the global economy, while transforming social rights, such as health care and education, into commodities. Although some areas and groups have benefited, for many others the results have been disastrous, particularly in the Southern Hemisphere. During the 1990s, for example, the number of people living in poverty around the globe increased by 100 million, even as world income grew 2.5 percent per year, while more than 80 countries had per capita incomes lower than the previous decade.

Over the past 10 years, corporate globalization has faced increasing opposition. Building on previous IMF food riots, grassroots mobilizations against the World Bank, anti–free trade campaigns, radical ecology and squatter movements, anti-sweatshop activism, the Zapatistas, and solidarity struggles, anti-globalization activists have built broad-based networks for social and economic justice. The movement burst onto the public radar screen in Seattle, where 50,000 protesters shut down the WTO Summit on November 30, 1999. Counter-summit actions soon spread around the world, including blockades against the World Bank/IMF meetings in Prague in September 2000 and the Free Trade Area of the Americas Summit in Quebec City in April 2001. Protests reached an explosive crescendo with violent clashes in Gothenburg, Barcelona, and Genoa in summer 2001. Since then, activist focus has shifted toward world and regional social forums, as tens of thousands have converged at mass gatherings in cities such as Porto Alegre, Mumbai, Quito, Florence, Paris, and London to discuss alternatives to corporate globalization.

New Information and Communication Technologies

The anti-globalization movement is characterized by the innovative use of new information and communication technologies (ICTs) to organize actions, share information and resources, and plan and coordinate activities. Although activists primarily employ e-mail and electronic listservs, during mobilizations they also create temporary Web sites that provide contact lists, information, and resources; post calls to action and other documents; and house discussion forums and real-time chat rooms. Particular networks also have their own Web pages, where activists can post reflections, analyses, updates, links, and logistical information. Interactive Web sites offering multiple tools for coordination are increasingly popular, including open publishing projects such as Indymedia, which allow users to freely post news and information without editorial selection and control.

Local/Global Networks

The anti-globalization movement is primarily organized around flexible, decentralized networks, such as the former Direct Action Network in North America or Peoples Global Action at the transnational scale. Anti-globalization networks are locally rooted, yet *globally* connected. Local/global activist networking is facilitated by new ICTs, which allow for coordination and communication across vast distances among small, decentralized units. In contrast to traditional parties and unions, networked movements are spaces of convergence involving a multiplicity of organizations, collectives, and networks, each retaining its own identity and autonomy. Such grassroots forms of political participation are widely seen as an alternative mode of democratic practice. Anti-globalization

movements thus promote global democracy, even as they emphasize autonomy and local self-management.

Creative Direct Action

More radical anti-globalization activists have developed innovative forms of direct action protest. Found in different contexts, these activists use tactics to create theatrical images for mass media coverage, while the overall blockade strategy, where activists "swarm" their target from multiple directions, produces high-powered social drama. The performances staged by activists, including giant puppets and street theater, mobile carnivals (Reclaim the Streets), spectacular protest involving white outfits, protective shields, and padding (White Overalls), and militant attacks against the symbols of corporate capitalism (Black Bloc), are designed to capture mass media attention while expressing alternative political identities.

Lived Experience and Process

Finally, more grassroots sectors within the anti-globalization movement view social transformation as an ongoing collective process. Rather than focusing on messianic visions or an already established project, activists focus on day-to-day practices. The collaborative, interactive nature of the new ICTs is thus reflected in the rise of new political visions and forms of interaction. These combine elements of certain traditional ideologies, such as anarchism, an emphasis on internal democracy and autonomy (feminism and grassroots movements such as the Zapatistas have been particularly influential in this respect), and a commitment to openness, collaboration, and horizontal connections. Younger activists, in particular, emphasize direct democracy, grassroots participation, and personal interaction within daily social life. Meetings, protests, action camps, and other anti-globalization gatherings thus provide spaces for experiencing and experimenting with alternative ways of life.

Despite their numerous differences, anti-globalization activists from diverse political backgrounds are struggling to regain democratic control over their daily lives, wresting it back from transnational corporations and global financial elites. The anti-globalization movement points to a democratic deficit in the current global political and economic order as corporate globalization has disembedded the market from society.

What makes the anti-globalization movement unique is its capacity for coordinating across vast distances and high levels of diversity and difference, overcoming many of the political and geographic obstacles that have stymied past mass movements.

Jeffrey S. Juris

See also Countermovements; Social Conflict; Social Movements

Further Readings

Hardt, Michael and Antonio Negri. 2004. *Multitude: War and Democracy in the Age of Empire.* New York: Penguin.

Juris, Jeffrey S. 2004. "Networked Social Movements: Global Movements for Global Justice." Pp. 341–62 in *The Network Society: A Cross-Cultural Perspective,* edited by M. Castells. London: Edward Elgar.

Sen, Jai, Anita Anand, Arturo Escobar, and Peter Waterman. 2004. *The World Social Forum: Challenging Empires.* New Delhi: Viveka Foundation.

Starr, Amory. 2005. *Global Revolt: A Guide to the Movements against Globalization.* London: Zed.

ANTI-SEMITISM

Anti-Semitism is the active or passive, individual or collective, hatred of either empirically existing or purely mythological Jews, such that the signifier "Jew" functions as a representational substitute for social conduct or institutions deemed by the anti-Semite to be abnormal and pathological. Especially important is the manner in which "the Jew" stands in for excesses and deficiencies in social relations such that "Jews" embody a simultaneous "too much" and "not enough" logic. For example, Jews have been criticized for being simultaneously too egoistic and too altruistic or agents of both anomie (deregulation or normlessness) and fatalism (excessive regulation); in other words, "Jews" personify social imbalances.

Anti-Semitism may manifest itself in religious, political-economic, ethnoracial, and cultural terms and is typically correlated positively with psychological authoritarianism and political models such as fascism, Nazism, right-wing populism, nativism, and other movements that scapegoat a pernicious "other." It can find expression in reactions ranging from stereotypical insults at one end of the spectrum to

all-out genocide at the other. More than routine bias or simple prejudice, anti-Semitism is a demonizing ideology that attempts to explain events, crises, inequalities, exploitation, and villainy by exposing the malevolent intentions of Jews as the primary, visible or invisible, causal factor. The Jew, in other words, becomes the master key to unlock the mysteries of all social problems and can therefore shade off into a freestanding worldview. In Western political culture, references to "the Jew" are frequently veiled in populist and fundamentalist currents with codes such as "European bankers" or anti-Christian, international "money barons" in order to preserve a veneer of respectability.

As a social problem, anti-Semitism fluctuates in intensity, depending on changes in social organization and social dynamics. After the Holocaust, for example, anti-Semitism was inextricably associated with Nazism and, as such, was relegated to the fringes of society in the industrialized West, and, by the 1960s, anti-Semitism was believed to be, if not nearly extinct, then definitely on the list of endangered ideological species in the United States. Since the mid-1990s, however, anti-Semitism appears to be making a comeback in the United States, especially among minority groups that, in previous generations, were relatively immune to the abstract demonization of Jews. Also, through the Internet, many hate groups have found a way to maximize their anti-Semitic diatribes. Globally, levels of anti-Semitism may be at an all-time high, especially in the Middle East, where demonological anti-Semitism has reached hysterical proportions and Jews are fully identified with Israeli state policies. Any attempt to further explain anti-Semitism must, first, distinguish between concrete anti-Jewish bias and abstract demonization and, second, between premodern and modern forms of anti-Semitism.

Routine Bias and Demonization

Garden-variety recriminations ("My Jewish landlord is cheap") fall short of true anti-Semitism. It would be unsurprising to learn, for example, that some landlords are in fact cheap and that some cheap landlords are Jews. Accusations of this concrete and specific nature frequently intersect with routine prejudice and racism. One way in which anti-Semitism and other forms of simple prejudice do coincide is in their essentializing constructions of the other, such that, keeping with the above example, "cheapness" becomes identical with Jewishness itself—from *"This Jew is cheap"* to *"All* Jews are cheap." But anti-Semitism is not conceptually reducible to routine bias or prejudice. In simple racism or bigotry, we do not find paranoid fantasies pertaining to global domination, secret world governments, or the hidden hand of global finance and international communism. Anti-Semitism is capable of embodying any and all accusations and moves toward its pure form the closer it comes to expressing purely otherworldly and abstract conceptions.

Distinguishing between abstract and concrete forms of anti-Jewish animosity is in keeping with the main currents of critical social scientific and historical analysis over the past few generations that treat "the Jew" of anti-Semitic propaganda as a socially constructed object of hatred. Theodor W. Adorno, Maurice Samuel, Jean-Paul Sartre, Norman Cohn, Gavin Langmuir, David Norman Smith, and Stephen Wilson have all put forward authoritative, constructionist explanations that distinguish between concrete and demonological *Judenhass*. Abstract demonization came of age in medieval Europe and was expressed primarily in religious terms.

Premodern and Modern Anti-Semitism

Under the sway of Augustinian doctrines, European society conceived of itself as an organic whole, incorporated on the basis of God's free gift of grace and morally regulated through the Church. Those who did not recognize Christ's claim, it was thought, may have been evil, but, in Augustine's *Enchiridion,* evil represented only a wound or defect in the social body and, as such, was not substantively apart from good. This was important for Jews, because their not recognizing Christ's charisma led to their portrayal as defective but still human. As defective aliens within the body of Christian society, Jews were nonetheless important for their political-economic functions, especially as sources of loans, and for this reason they were subjects of alternating tolerance and persecution. The resulting arrangement between Jews and Christians was tense and often violent yet nothing like wholesale genocide in the modern sense. This situation began to change as early as the first Crusade in the 11th century and accelerated as the 14th century approached. Medieval anti-Semitism evolved in conjunction with the Black Plague, as the Catholic Church transformed itself into a cult of death and Christians persecuted

Jews for their expiatory value. The 14th century represented a decisive transformation in the way European anti-Semites thought about Jews: from defective humans to devils. This period also marked the beginning of what can be called a fully developed, abstract Christian anti-Semitism and ushered in the era of spasmodic genocide against Jews that lasted for approximately 500 years.

Modern European anti-Semitism spoke French and German in the final quarter of the 19th century, but even though France delivered the spectacle of the Dreyfus Affair, French anti-Semitism was deeply contradictory and in many ways derivative. Perhaps one could make a similar assessment in the case of Russia, which contributed the pathetic *Protocols of the Elders of Zion* and a wave of pogroms yet was riddled with deep internal contradictions and influenced by external sources. The French also lacked the deadly seriousness that marked the spirit of *Judenhass* that developed in Germany, where the reactionary Wilhelm Marr purportedly coined the term *anti-Semitism* during a period of profound, turbulent modernization and economic convulsions, most dramatically represented by the crash of 1873.

A crucial development in the German variety was the shift from a religiously oriented hatred toward, on the one hand, a pseudoscientific attack against Jews as an inferior racial category and, on the other, a class-based criticism of culture, capital, and liberalism. In short, Jews were no longer just "Christ-killers" or petty "loan sharks" but also biologically inferior though cunning masters of modern economic institutions sucking the lifeblood out of the Fatherland through the treachery of compound interest, political corruption, domination of administrative units, and international intrigue. Jews had been identified with capitalism before, but with the ascendancy of finance capital and speculation mania in the 1870s, the criticism of capital acquired new elements that would prove crucial in the 20th century. The key was the conservative Catholic formulation of two distinct species of capital: good, productive, Christian capital on the one hand and rapacious, parasitic, Jewish finance capital on the other. This spurious compartmentalization of capital was of paramount importance in the development of modern anti-Semitic propaganda and arguably functions today as the dominant theme among anti-Semites and as the basis for world domination conspiracies.

The consequences of organized anti-Semitism were nowhere more catastrophic than in Nazi

Germany, yet the United States represents a more instructive sociological laboratory in the study of anti-Jewish hatred. In colonial times anti-Semitism was virtually unknown, but successive waves of immigrants brought Old World prejudices. Anti-Semitism became an obvious social problem with the third wave of eastern European Jewish immigrants. Although elite snobbery existed, the greatest threat to Jews was posed by Catholic arrivals. During the Great Depression, demagogues such as Father Coughlin harangued against Jews with a Euro-Catholic style of fascist propaganda, yet the message resonated best with older Catholic males with low levels of education and weak ties to the Church, and lacking the oft-noted conditioning called "Americanization."

Mark Worrell

See also Americanization; Ethnocentrism; Prejudice; Racism; Religion and Conflict

Further Readings

Adorno, T. W., Else Frenkel-Brunswik, Daniel J. Levinson, and R. Nevitt Sanford. 1950. *The Authoritarian Personality.* New York: Norton.

Cohn, Norman. [1966] 1981. *Warrant for Genocide.* Chico, CA: Scholars Press.

Langmuir, Gavin. 1990. *Toward a Definition of Antisemitism.* Los Angeles: University of California Press.

Massing, Paul W. 1949. *Rehearsal for Destruction.* New York: Harper & Brothers.

Poliakov, Leon. 1975–85. *The History of Antisemitism.* Vols. 1–4. Philadelphia: University of Pennsylvania Press.

Samuel, Maurice. 1940. *The Great Hatred.* New York: Knopf.

Sartre, Jean-Paul. [1948] 1976. *Anti-Semite and Jew.* New York: Schocken.

Smith, David Norman. 1996. "The Social Construction of Enemies: Jews and the Representation of Evil." *Sociological Theory* 14(3):203–40.

Wilson, Stephen. 1982. *Ideology and Experience.* Rutherford, NJ: Farleigh Dickinson University Press.

APARTHEID

Apartheid (literally "apartness" in Afrikaans and Dutch) refers to a system of racial segregation enforced in South Africa by the white National Party from its election in 1948 until the first election open to all races in 1994. A high degree of de facto racial separation existed before 1948, including controls on black movement originally introduced by the British in the Cape Colony during the 19th century, the Land Acts of 1913 and 1936 limiting black land rights, and the "civilized labor" policies introduced in 1924–26 to protect poor whites, leading some to use the term *apartheid* in relation to earlier periods. More recently, the term also describes policies or systems of racial segregation elsewhere in the world, but it remains associated primarily with South Africa, where its application amounted to an ambitious attempt to remold the country's social, economic, and political geography to enable "separate development" of four designated race groups—white, colored (mixed-race), Indian, and black African or "Bantu"—in a manner that ensured continuing white domination.

The Nature of Separation

Separation affected all spheres of life, including marriage and sexual intercourse (illegal between whites and other races), health and welfare, education, job opportunities, recreation, transport, and much more. Inter-racial social mixing was difficult and, when it did occur as in some of the English-speaking churches, was often self-conscious, given the essentially separate lives that people led. Geographically, apartheid was applied at three spatial scales, all of them distinguishing primarily between white and non-white. Micro-scale or "petty apartheid" measures segregated facilities and amenities such as transport, beaches, post offices, cinemas, and even park benches. Meso-scale segregation involved racial zoning in urban areas, using the Group Areas Acts of 1950 and 1966 to segregate whites, coloreds, and Indians. Macro-scale segregation allocated 10 *Bantustans* ("homelands") to the officially recognized black ethnic groups and attempted to minimize the black population elsewhere to that which was indispensable to the white economy. Rural black spots—small areas of black settlement surrounded by white farms—were excised, with their inhabitants resettled in the homelands, while many blacks were expelled from urban areas if they did not qualify to remain there. Altogether, 3.5 million people were forcibly relocated under apartheid policies between 1960 and 1983.

The homelands gradually became self-governing, and four of them became officially independent but recognized only by South Africa. As descendants of earlier colonial policies creating reserves for those depending on subsistence agriculture, all the homelands were peripheral to the major centers of the South African space economy and, with the partial exception of Bophuthatswana (a significant platinum producer), all remained economically dependent on South Africa for both financial subventions and employment.

Macro-scale territorial segregation of coloreds and Indians was impracticable given their high levels of urbanization, although interprovincial movement of Indians was restricted until 1975, and Indians were prohibited from living in the Orange Free State and northern Natal until 1985. The policy of parallelism established colored and Indian political institutions whose representatives were initially nominated and subsequently elected but essentially advisory to an all-white national government elected only by whites. In 1984, a new constitution created separate Indian and colored houses of parliament with sovereignty over their own affairs, including education, health, and welfare. These houses depended on budgetary allocations from the national government, and their territorial authority, based on the Group Areas Act of 1950, was highly fragmented. Only a small minority of eligible Indians and coloreds voted in elections for these bodies in 1984 and 1989.

Urban segregation involved the forcible movement of some 125,000 families, mainly colored and Indian, under the group areas legislation, together with an unrecorded but probably larger number of blacks moved under pre-apartheid legislation to designated townships. Whites received disproportionately large areas of each city or town, including the most desirable parts, with blacks typically located close to the industrial areas where they worked. Attempts also at ethnolinguistic segregation of black groups met with limited success. Some blacks—5.5 million by 1986 when racially discriminatory influx controls were repealed—acquired rights to permanent urban residence, giving them better placement in terms of employment. For the majority, the operation of influx control strongly discouraged in-movement to the cities, with large numbers arrested under the pass laws. Special restrictions applied to black movement to the western Cape Province, home to most colored people and designated a colored labor preference area between 1962 and 1985. Elsewhere, blacks from homelands or white rural areas could seek employment in the mines or the towns only as migrant laborers, leaving their families behind in their designated homelands. However, many managed to stay in urban areas illegally, lodging with township families, while natural increase led to continuing growth of the black urban population. From 1968 onward, municipalities were expected to meet black housing needs across homeland boundaries wherever possible. This led to large black formal and informal settlements in homeland areas close to major cities, such as Mdantsane (Ciskei, near East London), and in the Winterveld of Bophuthatswana, where nearly half the homeland population lived within 50 kilometers of Pretoria. Frontier commuters who crossed daily into white South Africa to work numbered 773,000 by 1982.

Pressures Leading to Transition

President P. W. Botha attempted to reform apartheid in the 1980s, to make it more acceptable to blacks as well as coloreds and Indians who had benefited materially from the "own affairs" budgets of their new houses of parliament. The main incentives were rapid increases in black education spending (but no end of segregated schools), repeal of influx control and major indirect state support for black housing, and the creation of regional services councils mandated to spend new sources of taxation where the need was greatest.

Such material improvements were unlikely to satisfy black aspirations, both economic and political. Black resistance, hitherto largely repressed by the banning of the African National Congress (ANC), Pan Africanist Congress (PAC), and South African Communist Party (SACP) in 1960 and harsh security laws within the country, increased massively from 1984 to 1986. It not only tested the state security apparatus but attracted world attention, leading to the escalation of sanctions and other pressures against the apartheid regime. The refusal in 1986 by American and European banks to roll over short-term loans led to a net outflow of capital in the late 1980s and accelerated already serious economic problems. A new president, F. W. de Klerk, stunned the country in February 1990 by announcing the unbanning of the ANC, PAC, and SACP and the release of Nelson Mandela and other political prisoners with a view to negotiations on a new political dispensation. These negotiations took 4 years, with many setbacks and much violence, some of it probably sponsored by the dying apartheid regime, but South Africa's first open elections in April

1994 ended the apartheid era and ushered in a Government of National Unity comprising the ANC, which won 62 percent of the poll, the National Party, and the Zulu-dominated Inkatha Freedom Party.

The legacy of apartheid will pervade South Africa for many decades. It remains one of the most unequal countries in the world, with class gradually replacing race but intra-racial inequalities increasing since 1994. Desegregation is certainly occurring in residential areas and schools, but almost entirely "up" the apartheid racial hierarchy, leaving most blacks as poor (or poorer) and as segregated as before. Politically, however, the achievement of relatively peaceful political transition has been consolidated through three democratic general elections, in 1994, 1999, and 2004.

Anthony Lemon

See also Discrimination; Ethnicity; Ethnocentrism; Hypersegregation; Nation Building; Pluralism; Race; Racism; Segregation; Stratification, Race; White Supremacy

Further Readings

Beinart, William. 2001. *Twentieth-Century South Africa.* New York: Oxford University Press.
Lemon, Anthony. 1987. *Apartheid in Transition.* Aldershot, England: Gower.
———. 1991. *Homes Apart: South Africa's Segregated Cities.* Bloomington, IN: Indiana University Press.
Posel, Deborah. 1991. *The Making of Apartheid 1948–1961.* Oxford, England: Clarendon.
Smith, David M. 1982. *Living under Apartheid.* Boston: Allen & Unwin.

ARMS CONTROL

Arms control is a means of addressing a major and enduring global social problem: arms proliferation. This entails the production and spread of weapons, ranging from small arms and light weapons, through missiles and military aircraft, up to weapons of mass destruction. Arms control involves a variety of efforts to restrict or ban the development, stockpiling, proliferation, and use of these weapons. While much of the literature on arms control focuses on formal negotiations and treaties, this should neither refute the importance of claims making by peace and disarmament organizations nor obscure the importance of informal controls and, at the extreme, the use of force to prevent proliferation.

States arm themselves because of what is called the "security dilemma." States exist in an anarchical international system where there is no central authority capable of providing them with security. Hence they must try to protect themselves against external foes as well as the threat of civil violence (by guerrillas, warlords, etc.). Security measures can take many forms, but typically they involve maintaining armed forces and forging alliances. Other states may see arms and alliances as a threat, and they in turn normally seek their own arms and alliances to protect themselves. The upshot is to augment general mistrust and insecurity and to foster arms races.

Arms are easily available, as about 100 countries manufacture small arms. Virtually every industrialized country manufactures an array of weapons to supply its own military; most of these countries also sell arms internationally, with the United States in particular, followed by European nations, Russia, and China, as the major world suppliers of armaments. The global arms trade—legal and illegal—is, by some estimates, approaching a trillion dollars annually, and arms industries are clearly of major economic and often strategic importance to supplying countries.

Here we see a further manifestation of the security dilemma. While selling arms potentially serves the national interest of seller states—beyond profit, there is the hope of strengthening allies—this is not the case when opposing states buy arms or contribute to regional or national instability. Hence arms-supplying nations often try to curb the sales of specific weapons to particular countries by a mixture of collaboration and the exertion of pressure. Such informal arms controls work reasonably well with advanced computers and sensitive electronic components but have minimal impact on small arms and light weapons. Selective sales, which can be considered a primitive form of arms control, sometimes backfire. Following the Soviet invasion of Afghanistan in 1979, the United States supplied the latter with anti-aircraft missiles and other sophisticated weapons that subsequently became part of the arsenal of groups that the United States came to regard as enemies.

At the other extreme is the use of force to impose arms controls. Perhaps the outstanding example is the 1981 Israeli bombing of the Osirak nuclear reactor in Iraq. Saddam Hussein started a clandestine nuclear program in the 1970s and likely would have acquired nuclear weapons if the reactor had not been destroyed. The U.S.-led invasion of Iraq in 2003 was supposedly motivated by the fear that Saddam had developed weapons of mass destruction after having expelled UN weapons inspectors in 1998. The inspections, however, proved to have been effective. The possibility that Iran might be developing nuclear weapons has generated pressure from the United Nations as well as implied threats of military action by the United States and Israel.

Beyond selective sales and force, arms control has been effectuated mostly through multilateral treaties. Arms control agreements are meant to check the security dilemma by providing transparency, (relative) equality, stability, and trust among participating states. While the ultimate aim is to prevent war, arms control can arrest the development or spread of particular weapons, limit the damage done in conflicts, obviate arms races, and reduce military spending. Although there are many problems in getting nations to ratify treaties and to adhere to them, arms control has proven to be effective in at least some instances.

Looking at past successes, the Geneva Protocol prohibiting the use of poisonous gases was signed on June 17, 1925. Although it took many years for the protocol to be ratified by most nations, the prohibition has generally held, and it has been updated by Biological (in 1972) and Chemical (in 1993) Conventions. All of these examples involve weapons of mass destruction. Notably, most arms control treaties since the end of World War II deal with such weapons rather than conventional ones. This is significant and relates to the sociology of social problems.

Sociologists studying social problems commonly observe that responses to issues are often independent of their "objective seriousness." Whereas 10 cases of mad cow disease in England became a global celebrity issue, close to 3 million annual deaths from tuberculosis attract almost no media attention. With arms control, most of the negotiations and the vast majority of media coverage focus on weapons of mass destruction, particularly nuclear arms. The latter draw on deeply embedded anxieties (the mushroom cloud, invisible radiation poisoning), as well as the risk of almost unimaginable numbers of deaths should such weapons ever be used. Yet small arms and light weapons—think of the Soviet/Russian AK-47 assault rifle—are responsible for the vast majority of combat deaths in recent wars and are central to civil violence.

Still, it has proved almost impossible to get any agreements to regulate such arms. Thus the United Nations Conference to review the implementation of the Programme of Action on the Illicit Trade in Small Arms and Light Weapons ended on July 7, 2006, without agreement on an outcome document. The original UN Programme of Action, adopted in 2001, is still in operation, but it has inadequate controls. Indeed, the United States has vetoed UN attempts to limit international trade in small arms, citing the right of citizens to bear arms for self-defense.

A significant exception is the 1997 Ottawa Convention that bans anti-personnel land mines. The Mine Ban Treaty became binding under international law in just 2 years, doing so more quickly than any treaty of its kind. This success was due in good part to the extensive publicity the issue received, with claims-making by celebrities that included Princess Diana, as well as by a host of nongovernmental organizations from around the world. Most arms control agreements, in contrast, gain limited publicity and are engineered mostly in closed meetings among government bureaucrats. The United States, China, and Russia are among 40 countries that have not signed the Ottawa Convention. Another nonsignatory, Pakistan, has generated so much opposition to its plan to land mine its border with Afghanistan that it appears to have backed away from the idea.

The bulk of arms control agreements deal with nuclear weapons and related delivery systems. Since the United States and the Soviet Union conducted scores of atmospheric nuclear tests, public pressures led to the 1963 Partial Test Ban Treaty, limiting testing to underground sites. Subsequent treaties aimed to prevent nuclear proliferation and have had mixed success in the context of several dilemmas. A key dilemma is how to prevent arms proliferation while allowing countries to develop nuclear power for peaceful purposes. Although this was the goal of the 1968 Nuclear Non-Proliferation Treaty (NPT), it created the further dilemma of enshrining a monopoly by the original nuclear weapons club—the United States, the Soviet Union, Britain, China, and France. While most countries have joined the NPT, others, such as Israel, India, and Pakistan, have developed their own nuclear weapons. There is now concern about a "second nuclear age," as North Korea and Iran pursue nuclear weapons, the United States and Russia maintain about 2,000 launch-ready strategic nuclear missiles, and unsecured nuclear materials in Russia feed fears of a terrorist bomb. Were Iran to develop the bomb, it is likely that neighboring countries would also go nuclear.

Because states are sovereign entities, the security dilemma plays out again in the difficulties in verifying and enforcing arms agreements. States can carry on unauthorized nuclear or other arms activities, and they can always abrogate treaties. In its efforts to develop a Star Wars defense against missiles, the United States is jeopardizing the Anti-Ballistic Missile Treaty and the Outer Space Treaty. China's apparently successful test of an anti-satellite missile in January 2007 points to the vulnerability of arms control agreements as the security dilemma drives efforts to develop newer and more sophisticated weapons. Arms control will never be completed but will remain a challenging endeavor requiring constant input and monitoring. Thus, as a result of an arms buildup by China and a possible North Korean atomic bomb, Japan is contemplating changing the pacifist constitution it adopted after World War II.

Sheldon Ungar

See also Claims Making; Demilitarization; Nuclear Proliferation; Peacekeeping

Further Readings

Forsberg, Randall. 2005. *Arms Control Reporter.* Cambridge, MA: MIT Press.
Lumpe, Lora. 2000. *Running Guns: The Global Black Market in Small Arms.* London: Zed.
Wittner, Lawrence. 2003. *Toward Nuclear Abolition: A History of the Nuclear Disarmament Movement 1971 to the Present.* Stanford, CA: Stanford University Press.

ARSON

Arson is the willful or malicious burning of property, and arson fires also entail the risk of intentional or inadvertent personal injury, including risk to firefighters. In the United States, at least 20 percent (and as much as 50 percent) of fire-related property damage is due to arson. This proportion has been declining due, at least in part, to increased vigilance and investigation.

Considerable scientific knowledge now supports forensic fire investigation, including determination that the cause was arson. Nevertheless, conviction rates for arson are extremely low (2 percent to 3 percent), and about 80 percent of arson cases remain unsolved. Although profit is probably the most common motive for arson, little is known about its perpetrators because of their low likelihood of apprehension. Most of the academic literature has focused on juveniles and mentally disordered firesetters whose actions had little to do with monetary gain. Vandalism is the most common motive among juveniles, whereas among adults apprehended for arson, the leading motives are revenge, anger, and excitement, with fraud accounting for less than 10 percent. The overwhelming majority of apprehended firesetters are male, and at least half are juveniles.

Psychodynamic perspectives dominated the early professional literature on mentally disordered firesetters and declared that pyromania (the recurrent inability to resist impulses to set fires) was a specific disorder responsible for the majority of fires not set for monetary gain. Pyromania was believed to have a sexual root, and clinicians' writings frequently noted the triad of firesetting, cruelty to animals, and enuresis. More recently, empirical approaches to mentally disordered firesetters show that pyromania, as defined in the *Diagnostic and Statistical Manual of Mental Disorders,* is extremely rare. Moreover, although mentally disordered adult firesetters frequently set fires as children, little evidence exists that enuresis or cruelty to animals is especially related to adult firesetting.

Compared with other mentally disordered offenders, firesetters are younger, less intelligent, more socially isolated, less assertive, and less physically attractive. Although mentally disordered firesetters have a slightly lower risk of violent recidivism than other mentally disordered offenders, the available research suggests that approximately one third committed subsequent violent offenses over an 8-year period, while another third committed only nonviolent offenses. Although treatments designed to improve assertion and social competence show promise, no convincing evidence yet exists that any therapies reduce arsonists' criminal, specifically firesetting, recidivism.

Marnie E. Rice and Grant T. Harris

See also Juvenile Delinquency; Property Crime; Vandalism

Further Readings

Faigman, David L., David H. Kaye, Michael J. Saks, and Joseph Sanders. 2005. "Fires, Arsons, and Explosions." Pp. 657–728 in *Modern Scientific Evidence: The Law and Science of Expert Testimony,* vol. 4, 2nd ed. St. Paul, MN: West Publishing.

Geller, J. L. (1992). "Arson in Review: From Profit to Pathology." *Clinical Forensic Psychiatry* 15:623–45.

Quinsey, Vernon L., Grant T. Harris, Marnie E. Rice, and Catherine A. Cormier. 2006. "Fire Setters." Pp. 115–29 in *Violent Offenders: Appraising and Managing Risk.* 2nd ed. Washington, DC: American Psychological Association.

Rice, Marnie E. and Grant T. Harris. 1996. "Predicting the Recidivism of Mentally Disordered Firesetters." *Journal of Interpersonal Violence* 11:351–63.

ASSAULT

Assault is a type of violent crime against a person, its degree classification based on the use of a weapon, the seriousness of the injury sustained, and/or the intent to cause serious injury. Whereas battery is the application of physical force, assault is the attempt or threat to commit battery. The Federal Bureau of Investigation (FBI) distinguishes between aggravated assault and nonaggravated assault, the latter of which may include simple assault and intimidation. Aggravated assault refers to the unlawful attack by one person upon another for the purpose of inflicting severe or aggravated bodily injury. Typically accompanying this type of assault is the use of a weapon or means likely to produce death or great bodily harm. Attempted murder is an example of aggravated assault. Non-aggravated simple assault refers to assault that does not involve the use of a dangerous weapon and in which the victim does not suffer apparent serious injury. Intimidation is a form of assault wherein a person threatens the victim without actually using or displaying a weapon.

The FBI's Uniform Crime Reporting (UCR) program tabulates aggravated assaults reported to law enforcement and provides a basis for examination of trends across time as well as across geographic areas, such as cities, states, or metropolitan areas. However, because the UCR program is voluntary and provides data on only aggravated assault, it may not reveal the true extent of assault in the United States. To gauge the incidence of assault, both reported and not reported to law enforcement, one can use the National Crime Victimization Survey (NCVS). The NCVS is the primary source of data on assault victimization for households in the United States.

During the late 1980s and early 1990s, the assault rate increased, and then declined sharply beginning in 1994 for both simple and aggravated assault. Historically, simple assault occurs at higher rates than aggravated assault. However, of the four types of violent crime classified by the FBI (murder, forcible rape, robbery, and aggravated assault), aggravated assault accounts for the greatest percentage. According to UCR data, aggravated assault accounted for 60.7 percent of all violent crime in 2006. Victimization rates of assault by sex, race, and age show that in 2005, males had a higher rate than females (21.5 vs. 14.3); blacks had a slightly higher rate than whites (20.6 vs. 17.2); and young adults ages 20 to 24 had the highest rate of all age-groups (40.3), while older adults (50 to 64 and those 65 and older) had significantly lower rates (9.3 and 1.9, respectively).

Danielle C. Kuhl

See also National Crime Victimization Survey; Uniform Crime Report; Victimization; Violent Crime

Further Readings

Catalano, Shannan M. 2006. *Criminal Victimization, 2005.* Washington, DC: U.S. Department of Justice, Bureau of Justice Statistics.

U.S. Department of Justice. 1992. "Uniform Crime Reporting Handbook." NIBRS ed. Washington, DC: U.S. Department of Justice, Federal Bureau of Investigation.

———. 2004. "Uniform Crime Reporting Handbook." Washington, DC: U.S. Department of Justice, Federal Bureau of Investigation.

———. 2007. "Crime in the United States 2006." Washington, DC: U.S. Department of Justice, Federal Bureau of Investigation.

ASSIMILATION

Assimilation is making a comeback as a major concept in the study of immigrant groups' processes of adjustment to a receiving society. This development is most evident in the United States, but it is to some extent occurring in western Europe as well, where multiculturalism is declining sharply in favor. This comeback reverses the trend at the end of the 20th century, which saw assimilation frequently criticized as an outmoded, ethnocentric notion.

Reconceptualizing Assimilation

Assimilation's return is associated with significant changes in the way it is conceptualized, reflecting an updating to take into account the criticisms of the recent past. Earlier versions of the concept originated with the studies of early 20th-century immigrants in American cities conducted by sociologists of the Chicago school, who saw immigrants and their children, usually called the "second generation," changing in tandem with upward social mobility and migration away from immigrant residential enclaves into better and more ethnically mixed neighborhoods. This view crystallized in the book *The Social Systems of American Ethnic Groups* of 1945, by W. Lloyd Warner and Leo Srole, which, however, added the jarring note that assimilability depended crucially on skin color and that, therefore, the assimilation of southern Italians, for instance, would require six generations. The assimilation of African Americans, according to Warner and Srole, was not foreseeable without revolutionary changes in U.S. society.

The concept originating with the Chicago school received its canonical post–World War II formulation at the hands of sociologist Milton Gordon in *Assimilation in American Life* of 1964, a book still widely cited. Gordon conceived of assimilation as a multidimensional process, in which two dimensions, cultural and structural assimilation, are the most determinative. Cultural assimilation is a largely one-way process, by which immigrants and their children divest themselves of their original cultures and take on the cultural features of the mainstream society, which are those of middle-class white Protestants, in Gordon's view. Structural assimilation refers to the integration of immigrant-group members with their majority-group counterparts in friendship circles, neighborhoods, and other forms of noneconomic relationship. Gordon hypothesized that in the United States, (a) cultural assimilation is inevitable in all domains other than religion; and (b) once structural assimilation occurs, then the overall assimilation process is destined to complete itself in short order. With this last hypothesis, Gordon had in mind the collapse of prejudice and discrimination against the group, a surge of intermarriage involving group members, and the disappearance of salient differences between the immigrant group and the host majority.

In this brief account, one can readily see some of the problematic aspects of the older concept that critics attacked. First, assimilation seems to require a complete transformation by the *immigrant-origin group* (a term used here to refer to the immigrants and their descendants), which must drop all of its original characteristics to become carbon copies of the host society's majority group, white Anglo-Saxon Protestants. Second, assimilability depends upon skin color, and thus the older concept reserves full assimilation for European-origin groups, which could be seen as racially "white" (although there were initially doubts about the whiteness of some of the southern and eastern European groups). Hence, the verdict of many critics was that assimilation was hopelessly racist and ethnocentric.

A new version of the assimilation concept, developed by Richard Alba and Victor Nee, adapts it to the multiracial America of the 21st century, while remaining faithful to the historical experiences of integration into the mainstream that gave rise to it in the first place. Alba and Nee define assimilation, a form of ethnic change, as the decline of an ethnic distinction and its corollary cultural and social differences. *Decline,* in this context, means that a distinction attenuates in salience, and more specifically, that the occurrences for which it is relevant diminish in number and contract to fewer and fewer domains of social life. As ethnic boundaries become blurred or weakened, individuals' ethnic origins become less and less relevant in relation to the members of another ethnic group (typically, but not necessarily, the ethnic majority group), and individuals from both sides of the boundary mutually perceive themselves with less and less frequency in terms of ethnic categories and increasingly only under specific circumstances. Assimilation, moreover, is not a dichotomous outcome and does not require the disappearance of ethnicity; consequently, the individuals and groups undergoing assimilation may still bear a number of ethnic markers. It can occur on a large scale to members of a group even as the group itself remains as a highly visible point of reference on the social landscape, embodied in an ethnic culture, neighborhoods, and institutional infrastructures.

One important aspect of this definition is that it leaves room for assimilation to occur as a two-sided process, whereby the immigrant minority influences the mainstream and is not only influenced by it. The degree to which the assimilation process is in fact two-sided is an empirical question to be answered in specific cases and not a matter to be settled a priori. But there can be no question in the U.S. context that the mainstream culture has taken on layers of influence from the many immigrant groups who have come to U.S. shores, as seen, for instance, in the impact of 19th-century German immigrants on American Christmas customs and leisure-time activities.

The ramifications of the influence of the immigrant minority on the mainstream are developed conceptually by Alba and Nee through the idea of "boundary blurring." A social boundary is an institutionalized social distinction by which individuals perceive their social world and divide others into categories that have the character of "us" or "them." However, not all boundaries are sharply delineated; when boundaries become blurred, the clarity of the social distinction involved has become clouded, and other individuals' locations with respect to the boundary may appear indeterminate or ambiguous. Boundary blurring can occur when the mainstream culture and identity are relatively porous and allow for the incorporation of cultural elements brought by immigrant groups; that is, two-sided cultural change. Under such circumstances, the apparent difference between the mainstream culture and that of the immigrant group is reduced partly because of changes to the former. Assimilation may then be eased insofar as the individuals undergoing it do not sense a rupture between participation in mainstream institutions and familiar social and cultural practices and identities. Assimilation of this type involves intermediate, or hyphenated, stages that allow individuals to feel themselves simultaneously to be members of an ethnic minority and of the mainstream.

A Theory of Assimilation

A reconceptualization of assimilation is not enough: Understanding the potential role of assimilation for contemporary immigrant groups and their descendants also requires a theory of assimilation—an account of the causal mechanisms that produce it. Positing such a theory implies that assimilation is not an inevitable result of the intergroup contacts resulting from migration—an assumption that was unfortunately shared by many of the early 20th-century scholars of the phenomenon—but requires a specification of the circumstances under which it emerges as an outcome. According to Alba and Nee, the pace and success of assimilation depend principally on three factors or mechanisms. First is the crucial effect of informal and formal institutions—customs, norms, conventions, and rules—that establish the underlying framework of competition and cooperation in a society. Second are the workaday decisions of individual immigrants and their descendants—which often lead to assimilation not as a stated goal but as an unintended consequence of social behavior oriented to successful accommodation. And third is the effect of network ties embedded in the immigrant community and family, which shape the particular ways in which their members adapt to American life.

The institutional portion of this account calls attention to the fundamental changes in the societal "rules of the game" that have occurred since the 1960s. Prior to World War II, the formal rules and their enforcement bolstered the racism that excluded nonwhite minorities from effective participation in civil society. For example, Asian immigrants were ineligible for citizenship until 1952 and faced many discriminatory local and regional laws that restricted their property rights and civil liberties. But these blockages have yielded as a result of the legal changes of the civil rights era, which have extended fundamental constitutional rights to racial minorities. These changes have not been merely formal; they have been accompanied by new institutional arrangements, the monitoring and enforcement mechanisms of which increased the cost of discrimination.

Institutional changes have gone hand in hand with changes in mainstream values. One of these is the remarkable decline in the power of racist ideologies since the end of World War II. An examination of more than half a century of survey data demonstrates unequivocally that the beliefs in racial separation, endorsed by a majority of white Americans at mid-century, have steadily eroded. Such institutional and ideological shifts have not ended racial prejudice and racist practice, but they have changed their character. Racism is now outlawed and, as a consequence, has become more covert and subterranean, and it can no longer be advocated in public without sanction.

At the individual level, assimilation is frequently something that happens while people are making other plans. That is, individuals striving for success in

U.S. society often do not see themselves as assimilating. Yet the unintended consequences of practical strategies taken in pursuit of highly valued goals—a good education, a good job, a nice place to live, interesting friends and acquaintances—often result in specific forms of assimilation. It is not uncommon, for instance, for first- and second-generation Asian parents to raise their children speaking only English in the belief that their chances for success in school will be improved by their more complete mastery of the host language. Likewise, the search for a desirable place to live—with good schools and opportunities for children to grow up away from the seductions of deviant models of behavior—often leads immigrant families to ethnically mixed suburbs (if and when socioeconomic success permits this), because residential amenities tend to be concentrated there. One consequence, whether intended or not, is greater interaction with families of other backgrounds; such increased contact tends to encourage acculturation, especially for children.

The network mechanisms of assimilation emerge from the dependence of immigrants and their children on the social capital that develops within immigrant communities and extended family networks. In this respect, it is rare for immigrant families to confront the challenges of settlement in a new society alone, and they frequently go along with the strategies of adaptation worked out collectively within the ethnic group. Frequently enough, these collectivist strategies advance assimilation in specific ways. For instance, Irish Americans, in their effort to shed the stereotype of "shanty Irish," socially distanced themselves from African Americans as a group strategy to gain acceptance from Anglo-Americans, ostracizing those who intermarried with blacks. More recently, South Asians who settled in an agricultural town in northern California evolved norms encouraging selective acculturation, while discouraging social contact with local white youths who taunted the Punjabi youths. The Punjabi immigrants' strategy, according to the anthropologist Margaret Gibson, emphasized academic achievement in the public schools as a means to success, which they defined not locally, but in terms of the opportunity structures of the mainstream.

Alternative Conceptions

The Alba and Nee theorization of assimilation is not the only new approach. Other sociologists have also attempted to reintroduce this concept in ways that overcome the deficiencies in the older versions and adapt it to the contemporary realities of immigration. Thus, Rogers Brubaker has described assimilation as a process of becoming similar to some population, indicating his preference for a population-based approach.

The alternative conception that is most challenging to the Alba and Nee version is "segmented assimilation" as formulated by Alejandro Portes and Min Zhou. Portes and Zhou argue that a critical question concerns the segment of U.S. society into which individuals assimilate, and they envision that multiple trajectories are required for the answer. One trajectory leads to entry into the middle-class mainstream; this is conventional assimilation, compatible with the Alba and Nee conceptualization. But another leads to incorporation into the racialized population at the bottom of U.S. society. This trajectory is followed by many in the second and third generations from the new immigrant groups, who are handicapped by their very humble initial locations in U.S. society and barred from entry into the mainstream by their race. On this route of assimilation, they are guided by the cultural models of poor, native-born African Americans and Latinos/as. Perceiving that they are likely to remain in their parents' status at the bottom of the occupational hierarchy and evaluating this prospect negatively because, unlike their parents, they have absorbed the standards of the American mainstream, they succumb to the temptation to drop out of school and join the inner-city underclass.

Portes and Zhou also envision a pluralist alternative to either "upward" or "downward" assimilation. That is, Portes and Zhou claim that some individuals and groups are able to draw social and economic advantages by keeping some aspects of their lives within the confines of an ethnic matrix (e.g., ethnic economic niches, ethnic communities). Under optimal circumstances, exemplified by the Cubans of Miami, immigrant-origin groups may even be able to attain, within their ethnic communities and networks, socioeconomic opportunities equivalent to those afforded by the mainstream. In such cases, the pluralist route of incorporation would provide a truly viable alternative to assimilation.

The contrast between the Alba and Nee conceptualization and that of Portes and Zhou frames the state of debate and discussion about the trajectories of contemporary immigrant groups and their second generations in the United States. The evidence is far from definitive at present, but what there is seems to indicate that the predominant pattern among the children of immigrants remains that of assimilation toward, if not into, the mainstream as described by Alba and Nee. Although the evidence remains provisional for the time being, it leaves no doubt that the assimilation pattern is certain to be important for contemporary immigrant-origin groups, and any reflection on the American future must take it into account.

Richard Alba and Victor Nee

See also Acculturation; American Dream; Americanization; Pluralism; Segmented Assimilation

Further Readings

Alba, Richard and Victor Nee. 2003. *Remaking the American Mainstream: Assimilation and Contemporary Immigration.* Cambridge, MA: Harvard University Press.

Brubaker, Rogers. 2001. "The Return of Assimilation? Changing Perspectives on Immigration and Its Sequels in France, Germany, and the United States." *Ethnic and Racial Studies* 24:531–48.

Gibson, Margaret. 1988. *Accommodation without Assimilation: Sikh Immigrants in an American High School.* Ithaca, NY: Cornell University Press.

Gordon, Milton. 1964. *Assimilation in American Life.* New York: Oxford University Press.

Kasinitz, Philip, John Mollenkopf, Mary Waters, and Jennifer Holdaway. Forthcoming. *Second-Generation Advantage: The Children of Immigrants Inherit New York City.* Cambridge, MA: Harvard University Press.

Portes, Alejandro and Min Zhou. 1993. "The New Second Generation: Segmented Assimilation and Its Variants." *The Annals* 530:74–96.

Warner, W. Lloyd and Leo Srole. 1945. *The Social Systems of American Ethnic Groups.* New Haven, CT: Yale University Press.

ASYLUM

Asylum refers to a form of sanctuary in which an asylum seeker is granted protection to remain in a host nation after fleeing persecution in his or her homeland. More commonly the term used is *political asylum*, whereby the applicant must complete two major phases within a much more complex set of proceedings carried out by immigration authorities. First, upon arriving at a port of entry (e.g., an international airport), the applicant must clearly identify him- or herself as an asylum seeker, a claim that initiates an interview to determine whether the individual can establish a credible fear of persecution (based on race, ethnicity, religion, political opinions, gender, or sexual orientation). That interview is conducted by a relatively low-ranking officer in the immigration system but one with the authority to admit the applicant for further proceedings in an immigration court or else issue an order for expedited removal (i.e., deportation). In the second stage, the asylum seeker appears before a series of panels or hearings to verify further his or her need for sanctuary. Should the case prove convincing, the judges award asylum along with a range of legal protections. In some instances, entire groups of refugees gain entry and asylum under the auspices of the U.S. Department of State, for example, during periods of humanitarian crisis (e.g., war, genocide, or natural disasters).

Asylum seeking is a social problem due to its social, ethical, and political implications. In the United States and in Western Europe, officials commonly view asylum seekers not as desperate people fleeing persecution but rather as economic migrants abusing the asylum system to gain entry. Influences on the perception of asylum seekers falls along lines of social constructionism shaped by forces such as economics, politics, and public opinion, much like the suspicion about nonwhite immigrants. Indeed, since the attacks of September 11, 2001, asylum seekers face an even greater challenge in attaining asylum because of the power of labeling stemming from anxiety over threats of terrorism.

Greatly informing the social construction process is the societal reaction perspective, more specifically the concept of moral panic: an exaggerated and turbulent response to a putative social problem. Moral panic theory allows sociologists to refine interpretations of negative societal reaction aimed at people easy to identify and dislike because of differences in race, ethnicity, religion, and so forth. Cross-national studies have unveiled the subtleties of moral panic, noting that even though the prevailing notion of such unrest resides in its noisy features (e.g., public outrage), constructions also occur under the public radar. Despite similarities among Western nations in their harsh treatment of those fleeing persecution, differences persist in social constructionism. Recent research extracts the nuances in this moral panic by identifying distinctions between American and British constructions. Among the most striking features is the fact that the invention and dramatization of so-called bogus asylum seekers as a popular stereotype is much more of a British phenomenon than an American one.

Cultural divergence affects a discursive formula of moral panic: Some panics are transparent and others opaque. Societal reaction to asylum seeking in the United Kingdom manifests as a transparent moral panic because "anyone can see what's happening." Whereas spikes of panic occur in the United States over foreigners (most recently those perceived as being Arab and Muslim) and undocumented workers (generally Latino/a) before and after September 11, the putative problem of asylum seeking does not resonate in the public mind. However, U.S. government officials quietly embarked on a detention campaign similar to those in Britain. Although such detention practices were in place prior to 9/11, the War on Terrorism provided U.S. authorities with an urgent rationale for greater reliance on that form of control; specifically, U.S. government officials insist that policies calling for the detention of asylum seekers serve national security interests.

Particularly when of long duration, detention is among the gravest measures the state can take against an individual. Its seriousness is even greater when the person is held not on criminal or immigration charges but rather on fleeing persecution. The detention of asylum seekers, especially when stemming from moral panic, receives wide criticism as costly, unnecessary, and, under many circumstances, a violation of international laws intended to protect those in need of sanctuary. By its very nature, detention compounds a criminalization process by lumping asylum seekers together with prisoners charged or convicted of criminal offenses. Many asylum seekers are held in county jails because the immigration system lacks proper detention capacity. Again, the labeling process figures prominently under such conditions, adversely influencing their cases for asylum. These asylum seekers are not only confined in a correctional facility but must wear a prison uniform and be shackled with handcuffs during visits and transfers to court. Human rights advocates complain that the criminal justice model now dominating that asylum procedure unfairly undermines a system designed to protect people seeking sanctuary.

Finally, issues pertaining to asylum ought to be contextualized in a more global setting that attends to worldwide migration alongside political, economic, and military events that produce refugees in search of sanctuary. At the heart of those developments is the politics of movement, also known as the global hierarchy of mobility, in which freedom of movement is a trait of the dominant, forcing the strictest possible constraints upon the dominated. In the wake of globalization, borders still sustain their symbolic and material impact against the circulation of some classifications of people, most notably asylum seekers (and underprivileged non-Western workers). Therefore, borders are not disappearing; rather, they are fragmenting and becoming more flexible. Borders no longer operate as unitary and fixed entities; instead, they are becoming bendable instruments for the reproduction of a hierarchical division between so-called deserving and undeserving populations, wanted and unwanted others.

Michael Welch

See also Refugees; Resettlement

Further Readings

Cohen, Stanley. 2002. *Folk Devils and Moral Panics: The Creation of the Mods and Rockers.* 3rd ed. London: Routledge.

De Giorgi, Alessandro. 2006. *Re-thinking the Political Economy of Punishment: Perspectives on Post-Fordism and Penal Politics.* Aldershot, England: Ashgate.

Schuster, Liza. 2003. *The Use and Abuse of Political Asylum in Britain and Germany.* London: Frank Cass.

Welch, Michael. 2002. *Detained: Immigration Laws and the Expanding I.N.S. Jail Complex.* Philadelphia: Temple University Press.

Welch, Michael and Liza Schuster. 2005. "Detention of Asylum Seekers in the US, UK, France, Germany, and Italy: A Critical View of the Globalizing Culture of Control." *Criminal Justice: The International Journal of Policy and Practice* 5(4):331–55.

ATTENTION DEFICIT HYPERACTIVITY DISORDER

Attention deficit hyperactivity disorder (ADHD) is a behavior problem that is characterized by hyperactivity, inattention, restlessness, and impulsivity and, until recently, was diagnosed primarily in children. It was first defined as Hyperkinetic Disorder of Childhood in 1957 and was commonly known as hyperactivity or hyperactive syndrome until it was renamed ADHD in 1987. The renaming also represented a shift in focus from hyperactive behavior to the inattention as a major characteristic of the disorder.

In the United States the Centers for Disease Control and Prevention (CDC) estimates 7 percent of school-age (6–10) children have ADHD, with a ratio of 3 to 1 boys to girls. White children tend to have higher rates of ADHD diagnosis than minority children. In recent years the definition of ADHD has broadened. Now, in addition to school-age children, ADHD is diagnosed in preschool children, adolescents, and adults, which contributes to the rising prevalence.

The most common medical treatment for ADHD is with psychoactive medications, especially ethylphenidate (Ritalin) and other stimulant medications (Cylert, Adderall, and Concerta). Treatment rates have increased enormously in recent years; in 2004 the Department of Health and Human Services estimated 5 million children ages 5 to 17 were treated for ADHD in 2000–02, up from 2.6 million in 1994. The diagnosis and treatment of ADHD is much higher in the United States than in other countries, but evidence suggests that since the 1990s it has been rising in other countries as well, for example, in the United Kingdom.

The causes of ADHD are not well understood, although various theories have been offered, including dietary, genetic, psychological, and social ones. In the past 2 decades, medical researchers have reported genetic susceptibilities to ADHD and found differences in brain imaging results from individuals with ADHD and individuals without ADHD. Although biomedical theories of ADHD predominate, the causes of ADHD are still largely unknown. Some contend that even if there are biological differences between children with ADHD and other children, what is observed may be a reflection of differences in temperament rather than a specific disorder.

ADHD and its treatment have been controversial at least since the 1970s. Critics have expressed concern with the drugging of schoolchildren, contending that ADHD is merely a label for childhood deviant behavior. Others grant that some children may have a neurological disorder, but maintain that there has been an overdiagnosis of ADHD. From time to time some educators and parents have raised concerns about

adverse effects from long-term use of stimulant medications. Child psychiatrists see ADHD as the most common childhood psychiatric disorder and consider psychoactive medication treatment as well established and safe. Parent and consumer groups, such as CHADD (Children and Adults with Attention Deficit Hyperactivity Disorder), tend to support the medical perspective of ADHD.

Since the 1990s there has been a significant rise in the diagnosis and treatment of adult ADHD. Whereas childhood ADHD is usually school or parent identified, adult ADHD seems to be largely self-identified. Some researchers have noted that many apparently successful adults seek an ADHD diagnosis and medication treatment as a result of learning about the disorder from professionals, the media, or others, and then seeing their own life problems reflected in the description of ADHD (e.g., disorganized life, inability to sustain attention, moving from job to job). Adult ADHD remains controversial, however. Many psychiatrists have embraced adult ADHD as a major social problem, with claims of tens of billions of dollars in lost productivity and household income due to the disorder, whereas critics have suggested it is "the medicalization of underperformance."

Sociologists view ADHD as a classic case of the medicalization of deviant behavior, defining a previously nonmedical problem as a medical one and the treatment of ADHD as a form of medical social control. Whereas some have pointed out that when a problem becomes medicalized it is less stigmatized, because its origin is seen as physiological or biomedical rather than as linked to volitional behavior, others point to the social consequences of medicalizing children's behavior problems. Some have suggested that medicalizing deviant behavior as ADHD individualizes complex social problems and allows for powerful forms of medical social control (medications) to be used. Secondary gain, accruing social benefits from a medical diagnosis, is also an issue with ADHD. There are reports of adolescents seeking an ADHD diagnosis to gain learning disability status in order to obtain certain benefits, such as untimed tests or alternative assignments. From a sociological view, the definition of ADHD is a prime example of diagnostic expansion, the widening definition of an accepted diagnosis. For many individuals, ADHD is now deemed a lifelong disorder, with an expanding age range for diagnosis (from preschool to adult) and a reduced threshold for psychoactive medication treatment. Although it is possible that the behaviors characteristic of ADHD are increasing because of some kind of social cause, it is more likely that an increasing number of individuals are being identified, labeled, and treated as having ADHD.

Peter Conrad

See also Deviance; Labeling Theory; Learning Disorders; Mental Health; Psychoactive Drugs, Misuse of; Social Control; Stigma

Further Readings

Barkley, Russell A. 1998. "Attention-Deficit Hyperactivity Disorder." *Scientific American,* September, pp. 66–71.

Centers for Disease Control and Prevention. 2002. "Prevalence of Attention Deficit Disorder and Learning Disability." Retrieved February 4, 2008 (http://cdc.gov/nchs/pressroom/02news/attendefic.htm).

Conrad, Peter and Deborah Potter. 2000. "From Hyperactive Children to ADHD Adults: Observations on the Expansion of Medical Categories." *Social Problems* 47:559–82.

Diller, Lawrence A. 1998. *Running on Ritalin.* New York: Bantam.

Automation

Automation is the substitution of self-operating machinery or electronics for manual or animal effort to support or control a broad spectrum of processes. Examples range from automatic teller machines, to robotic farm tractors, to securities transactions, and beyond. Henry Ford's use of the conveyor belt to produce Model T Fords in the early 1900s was a precursor to today's assembly lines that feature robotic assembly stations and automated inventory control, testing, and defect detection, all of which can be quickly reconfigured to accommodate variations of car models. Information technology is a form of automation used to process data, transmit information, or handle transactions, such as to order merchandise, buy or sell securities, or make hotel reservations.

Automation and the technology change that it represents have transformed economic arrangements and human lives in numerous ways. It has profoundly impacted production processes by increasing speed, accuracy, and sheer output volume, while eliminating some kinds of tedious, repetitive work. Automation that extends the reach of information transmission, processing, and control generates economies of scale that lead to firms being larger and allows production in more disparate regions, thereby increasing the intensity of global competition.

Automation has far-reaching consequences for employment opportunities. It generally substitutes for unskilled labor while complementing skilled labor. As such, automation results in the elimination or outsourcing of some jobs and the creation of new ones. As skill requirements change, members of the labor force must be retrained, and across the board, educational demands are raised.

Automation generally has positive impacts on productivity, economic growth, and the quality of life. It also has far-reaching impacts on the consumer side, lowering the prices of existing products and services, while increasing their quality, and creating entirely new products and services such as digital entertainment (CDs, DVDs, MP3s, etc.). Automation also increases the productivity of consumption within the home, contributing to the quality of leisure time. Examples are dishwashers, microwave ovens, and automatic lawn sprinklers.

Automation commonly involves the substitution of prespecified, codified rules for human judgment. This might be fine during normal times, but anomalies can cause breakdowns, and under stressful conditions in particular, human judgment retains its importance. Automation duplicates human actions with machines and electronic technology, but when automated, tasks themselves can change. For example, many secretarial jobs morph into administrative functions in an automated office environment. Electronic technology can blur national boundaries and, in the words of Thomas Freedman, create a flat world. For example, a phone call from New York City to Akron, Ohio, can be routed through India without either party to the conversation knowing it. Automation can accelerate the speed with which events occur. While it is desirable to get tasks done quickly, production processes must be synchronized; thus timing must be coordinated, and speed can have negative consequences. Faster cars, for example, are not necessarily safer cars, especially if they are cruising down the highway at great speed. All told, automation presents new challenges to public policy and governmental regulators.

In recent years, automation has affected many industries in general and some in particular. One of the most important and complex industries, that involving the securities markets, has moved in the past quarter century from the horse-and-buggy era to the jet age. Equity markets are a good example.

In the early 1970s, equity trading was, for the most part, a manual, human-intermediated process. Orders were transmitted to brokers who physically met each other (face-to-face or by phone) to trade shares of a stock. Then, gradually, automation entered the picture. The first role for the computer was to deliver trading instructions and information about the prices (quotes) at which people were willing to buy and to sell, along with the prices and sizes of realized trades. In the United States, in 1971, the National Association of Securities Dealers introduced NASDAQ, its automated quotation system.

Then came automation of the act of trading itself. In 1977, the Toronto Stock Exchange introduced an electronic trading system. Over the following 20 years, European exchanges, from Stockholm to Madrid, including London, Paris, Switzerland, and Germany, replaced antiquated floor-based systems with electronic systems. In the United States, Instinet in 1969 and Archipelago in 1997 were among the first to introduce electronic trading. NASDAQ rolled out its own automated trading system in 2002, and in January 2007, the New York Stock Exchange (NYSE) substantially completed instituting its Hybrid Market, which combines an electronic system with its traditional trading floor. The replacement of manual broker/dealer intermediation functions with electronic systems owned by the exchanges paved the way for exchanges to convert their organizational structures from not-for-profit memberships to privatized, for-profit entities.

Automation in the equity markets facilitated the rapid calculation of price indices such as the Dow Jones Industrial Average and the S&P 500. Virtually continuous information about these continuously changing indices supported the trading of new financial products, such as index futures and options, and exchange-traded funds. Real-time index values are also valuable pricing guides for individual shares. Automated trading provides a faster, more error-free transmission of trade data into clearance and settlement, thereby increasing the efficiency of post-trade operations. The electronic capture of intra-day records of all quotes and transactions facilitated the overview and regulation of trading and enhanced academic equity market research.

Nevertheless, when it comes to equity trading, automation continues to be a challenge. Delivering orders to the market and reporting back quotes and transaction prices are the easy parts to trading; the difficult part is handling orders at the most critical part of the process, when buys meet sells and turn into trades. Trading involves more than simply transferring something (share ownership) from one participant to another at a pre-established price (as is the case when a passenger books an airline seat); it also entails finding the prices at which trades are made, a complex process referred to as "price discovery."

Automating the point of trade for small, retail orders (perhaps 1,000 shares or less) for big capitalization stocks is not difficult. A large trade (perhaps 500,000 shares), on the other hand, can be very difficult to handle. Time, skill, and risk taking are all required. The difficulty of handling large orders for all stocks, and all orders for mid and small cap stocks, explains in part why automation has proceeded slowly in the equity markets and why, as of this writing, the New York Stock Exchange still retains its trading floor.

In general, an electronic environment differs greatly from a human-to-human environment (either telephone connected or face-to-face), and replacing people with machines and computers is not necessarily a simple matter of having computers take over tasks that were previously performed by humans.

In markets around the world, human agents staunchly resist the introduction of electronic technology that, by automating activities, eliminates otherwise profitable jobs. Slowly, however, resistance may be overcome as the role of human agents is transformed.

Electronic information transmission is lightning fast; human-to-human information transmission is considerably slower but can include a broader spectrum of thoughts and emotions (a tone of voice or facial expression can itself convey important information).

Automation that enables people from disparate parts of the globe to access a market virtually instantly with virtually equal facility has flattened the world of trading and commerce.

In equity trading, automation has driven down commission costs, and volumes have exploded. Orders get delivered and trades executed within fractions of a second. However, the sequence in which orders arrive remains important, and subsecond time frames are of no substantive importance per se. Concurrently, large block orders are commonly being shot into the market in protracted sequences of smaller tranches. This practice of "slicing and dicing" and the speed with which events can happen in the automated environment have pressured traders to use new computer tools to time and otherwise handle their order submission. The automated, rules-based procedures, referred to as "algorithmic trading," are both a product of automation and a symptom of the complexities that electronic, high-speed trading can introduce.

Automation offers much promise and, driven by technology developments, impacts economic activities around the world. Automation is indeed a powerful tool, but it can also be a harsh taskmaster. Throughout history, and even today as seen in the equity markets, automation's introduction has rarely escaped controversy. Its transformative power disrupts the status quo and can create new sources of friction even with significant reductions in time, effort, and mistakes.

Robert A. Schwartz and Richard D. Holowczak

See also Cyberspace; Social Change

Further Readings

Carlsson, B., ed. 1995. *Technological Systems and Economic Performance: The Case of Factory Automation.* New York: Springer.

Friedman, Thomas L. 2005. *The World Is Flat: A Brief History of the Twenty-first Century.* New York: Farrar, Straus & Giroux.

Loader, David and Graeme Biggs. 2002. *Managing Technology in the Operations Function.* St. Louis, MO: Butterworth-Heinemann.

Schwartz, Robert A. and Reto Francioni. 2004. *Equity Markets in Action: The Fundamentals of Liquidity, Market Structure & Trading.* Hoboken, NJ: Wiley.

B

BABY BOOMERS

Baby boomers are Americans born between 1946 and 1964. Birth rates fell in the United States during the Great Depression of the 1930s (when uncertain economic prospects discouraged many people from having children) and World War II (when millions of men were away from home serving in the armed forces). When the war ended in 1945, marriages increased and the birth rate rose. In 1946, births jumped to 3,411,000 (up more than half a million from the previous year); they continued rising until 1957, when they hit 4.3 million, and remained above 4 million per year through 1964. Nearly 76 million babies were born between 1946 and 1964.

The baby boom, then, consists of a set of unusually large birth cohorts (those born in a given year). Most people pass through social institutions at roughly the same ages, so that most children attend school from ages 6 to 17, most adults work from sometime in their 20s through their 60s, and so on. Larger cohorts strain institutions: When the baby boomers were of school age, new schools were needed; similarly, when they enter retirement, the baby boomers will place greater demands on Social Security, Medicare, and other services used by the old.

People who belong to the same set of cohorts are sometimes called generations, and they share some historical experiences. The baby boomers grew up in the long period of prosperity that followed World War II, a period marked by the cold war. Television became nearly universal during their childhood, just as personal computers spread during their adulthood.

Commentators contrast these experiences with those of the preceding cohorts, born between, for example, 1925 and 1940, who experienced the hardships of economic depression and wartime. Many commentaries on baby boomers suggest that their common histories led to shared outlooks on life.

Such claims ignore important differences among the baby boomers. Although the oldest baby boomers were in high school when President John F. Kennedy was assassinated in 1963, the youngest were not yet born. The oldest males were subject to the draft during the war in Vietnam, but the draft ended before the youngest baby boomers came of age. Thus, baby boomers did not all have the same experiences at the same points in their lives. In addition, every age cohort contains people of different ethnicities, income levels, political affiliations, and so on. If the baby boomers share some things, they remain a diverse population.

Although commentators also generalize about other generations, such as "Generation X" (those born following the baby boom, roughly 1965–80), similar qualifications are in order. People born at about the same time experience major historical events at roughly the same point in their lives; still, every birth cohort contains people from diverse social circumstances. Yet the sheer size of particular cohorts affects social institutions: Large cohorts will, at different times, require many schoolrooms and nursing home beds, whereas smaller cohorts may require institutions built for larger client populations to shrink.

Joel Best

See also Pensions and Social Security

Further Readings

Gillon, Steve. 2004. *Boomer Nation: The Largest and Richest Generation Ever and How It Changed America.* New York: Free Press.

BACKLASH

Backlash is a term used to describe action taken by individuals and groups to counter an existing social or political development. Although the term may be used to describe efforts seeking progressive effects, such as the move to reform health care in the United States, it is more often used to denote a countermovement aimed at narrowing a group's access to rights and benefits. The point of a typical backlash is to prevent a targeted group from obtaining, or continuing to obtain, certain rights or benefits bestowed through policy or law. The action can take various forms, including voter initiatives, court challenges, demonstrations, and violence.

Among those targeted by recent backlashes in the United States were welfare mothers for existing on welfare, gays and lesbians for seeking the right to marry, women and people of color for having affirmative action policies, and women for legally obtaining abortions. The backlash against welfare mothers led to a federal law, the *Personal Responsibility and Work Opportunity Reconciliation Act,* which reversed long-standing policy by limiting the time a family could receive welfare and mandating that adult recipients work. The move against gay and lesbian rights resulted in the legalization of same-sex marriages in Massachusetts, the refusal of several other states to acknowledge those marriages, and an unsuccessful, proposed constitutional amendment to ban such marriages throughout the nation. Successful efforts to dismantle affirmative action included voter referendums in California, Washington, and Michigan and several rulings by the U.S. Supreme Court, including *Adarand Constructors, Inc. v. Pena* and *Texas v. Hopwood.* Less successful, but considerably more violent, with abortion clinics bombed, several physicians murdered, and scores of women physically and verbally harassed, was the backlash against legalized abortion.

An early example of a backlash in U.S. history involved the federal rights granted to former slaves and their descendants in the aftermath of the Civil War.

Among these were the right to vote, for men, through the Civil Rights Act of 1870, and access to public accommodations for all, through the Civil Rights Act of 1875. The backlash against these and other rights included the rise of the Ku Klux Klan, the institution of Jim Crow laws and social practices by state and local governments, and the support of such laws by the U.S. Supreme Court beginning with its 1896 ruling in the case *Plessy v. Ferguson.* The Supreme Court also invalidated key sections of the 1870 act in *James v. Bowman* in 1903 and the 1875 act in the Civil Rights Cases in 1883. It was not until decades later that the court overturned the separate but equal doctrine established by *Plessy v. Ferguson* through *Brown v. Board of Education* in 1954. Congress eventually restored most of the rights that had been rescinded by the Supreme Court in *James v. Bowman* and the Civil Rights Cases through provisions located in the Civil Rights Act of 1957 and the Civil Rights Act of 1964, respectively.

Dula J. Espinosa

See also Abortion; Affirmative Action; Jim Crow; Same-Sex Marriage; Welfare

Further Readings

Faludi, Susan. 2006. *Backlash: The Undeclared War against American Women.* 15th anniv. ed. New York: Crown.

BAIL AND JUDICIAL TREATMENT

Bail is providing security, usually in the form of money, to guarantee a defendant's return to court for subsequent court dates. When an offender is arrested, that individual must appear before a lower court judge (e.g., a municipal court judge) for an initial appearance or for the first court appearance after arrest. During this court appearance, the judge determines whether or not the defendant is required to make bail to be released pending the defendant's next court date. If a defendant can pay the bail amount, the defendant is released into the community and ordered to return for future court dates. If the defendant cannot pay the bail amount or bail is denied, the defendant is placed in jail for the duration of the case. There is no constitutional right to bail; in fact, the Eighth Amendment to the U.S. Constitution only prohibits the use of excessive bail.

A judge's bail decision rests on four primary factors. Perhaps most important is the seriousness of the offense. The more serious the offense is with which the defendant is charged, the higher the bail amount will be. In most cases, bail is denied for defendants who are charged with first degree murder. Second, flight risk is an important consideration in bail decisions. If the defendant is not a resident of the area in which the offense was committed or if the defendant has been arrested in the past and has not shown up for court dates, the judge may set a high bail amount or deny bail altogether, regardless of the seriousness of the offense. Third, a defendant's prior criminal record plays a role in bail decisions. Defendants with more extensive prior records will typically have higher bail amounts. Finally, public safety is a concern if the defendant appears to be a risk to others if released. If the defendant has made specific threats or has demonstrated risky behavior in the past, bail could be denied.

Defendants have several ways to secure their release while awaiting trial. The first method is a cash bond, in which the defendant pays the entire bail amount up front. If the defendant appears for all court appearances, the money is returned to the defendant. If court appearances are missed, the defendant forfeits the money. Cash bonds are uncommon, as most defendants cannot afford to pay the full bail amount. A second method is a property bond, in which assets are used as collateral. Those who own homes may cash out equity to pay the bail amount. As with a cash bond, a property bond is uncommon, as most defendants do not own any, or enough, assets to use as collateral. A third method uses a bail bondsman, who pays the bail amount to the court in exchange for a fee that the defendant must pay to the bondsman, usually 10 percent of the bail amount. This fee is nonrefundable. The bondsman basically promises the court that the defendant will make future court appearances. A final method does not involve a specific bail amount. A defendant can be released on his or her own recognizance, in which no bail amount is set, but the defendant is released with a promise to return to court for future court dates. Defendants who are released in this manner are usually charged with minor offenses, have strong ties to the community, or both.

Judges have considerable discretion in bail decisions, with the ability to set any bail amount as long as it is not excessive. Critics charge that this discretion allows the decision of one person to have an impact on numerous aspects of a case. For instance, a judge has limited information at the initial appearance and must make a prediction about the defendant's future actions. A judge may underpredict and release a defendant who should not be released. On the other hand, a judge may overpredict and incarcerate a defendant who should be released. This has implications not only for the defendant but also for the judge, the criminal justice system, and the public.

Other criticisms of bail decisions include the issues of preventive detention, jail overcrowding, and social class. Regarding preventive detention, a judge may deny bail to a defendant who he fears would be a risk to public safety if released and place the defendant in jail for the duration of the case. Some critics feel that preventive detention is a form of punishment without trial, in that a judge makes a decision to incarcerate a person for something that might occur, not for something that already has occurred. Sometimes judges face constraints in bail decisions based on the conditions of the local jail. If the jail is overcrowded, the judge may have to lower bail amounts or release defendants on their own recognizance to avoid further overcrowding. Finally, critics complain that, because it is based on a monetary system, those who can afford their bail amounts are able to enjoy release pending their case dispositions, whereas those who cannot afford bail are forced to stay in jail. Those in jail may not be able to assist with their defense and must endure the conditions of the jail even though they have yet to be convicted of a crime. Consequently, critics feel that the criminal justice system, through the use of a bail system, draws distinctions between the rich and poor and makes it more difficult for the poor to defend themselves.

Marian R. Williams

See also Class; Judicial Discretion; Justice; Plea Bargaining

Further Readings

Dhami, M. 2005. "From Discretion to Disagreement: Explaining Disparities in Judges' Pretrial Decisions." *Behavioral Sciences and the Law* 23:367–86.

Walker, Samuel. 1993. *Taming the System.* New York: Oxford University Press.

BANKRUPTCY, BUSINESS

Business bankruptcy occurs when a commercial organization does not have sufficient readily available funds (capital) to pay its current debts. Further, the business is either unable or unwilling to sell its assets, or to use debt (by borrowing capital) or equity (by selling ownership shares), to pay such obligations. As a result, the owner(s) declare(s) the business to be bankrupt. This declaration in most developed countries invokes laws and procedures designed to protect the interests of both the owner(s) and the creditor(s) in an orderly fashion. In the United States, the declaration and resolution of a business bankruptcy is most often governed by the provisions of Chapter 11 of Title 11 of the U.S. Commercial Code. Hence, although a business may also file under the provisions of Chapter 7 or Chapter 13, reference is usually made to a business being "in Chapter 11."

Business bankruptcies are a fact of the life cycle of some businesses and of the economic cycle in general. During the decade from 1995 through 2004, despite such high-profile filings as WorldCom (US$104 billion) and Enron (US$63 billion), the relative rate of business bankruptcies in industrialized countries worldwide decreased by almost 10 percent. The typical rate of business bankruptcy filings worldwide is less than 1 percent of all organized businesses, although it is often difficult to discover data separately reporting business and personal bankruptcy filings. In the United States, bankruptcy filings of all types—both business and personal—from 2000 through 2005 ranged between 1.3 million and 1.7 million each year.

Direct and Indirect Effects

U.S. bankruptcy filings directly affect tens of millions of new persons annually and many more tens of millions of persons indirectly. Those directly affected are generally the laborers, managers, long-term lenders of secured capital, and owners, including shareholders. These individuals and organizations, as direct participants in the business, have a vested interest in the vitality of the business. Thus a business failure usually impacts them more immediately and more severely. However, a business bankruptcy may also harshly affect indirect participants in the business, such as suppliers of raw materials, customers down the supply chain, and especially the residents of the cities, regions, and national economies of the bankrupt business.

The direct effects of bankruptcies are usually reported first, as they are the easiest to measure. Among these are the impacts on the financial investment in and the human capital of the business. The effects on the financial investment tend to be the loss of capital invested, including reductions in revenues and profits and, if it is a publicly traded company, the drop in share pricing. The effects on the human capital are, bluntly, the job losses associated with the bankruptcy and subsequent restructuring or sale of the business.

As an example of indirect effects, an automotive industry analysis stated in June 2006 that 24 percent of parts suppliers to the world's automobile companies themselves faced fiscal danger as a result of the near bankruptcy of their clients, in addition to the US$60 billion in parts supplier company bankruptcies since 2001 in North America alone.

As a specific example of some of the human fallout of a business bankruptcy, consider that all 21,000 Enron employees were eventually fired—5,000 of them the day after the bankruptcy filing. All had their company-paid health insurance coverage terminated upon dismissal, and none of those under the age of 50 was able to sell any of the Enron stock held in his or her pension plan until that stock had lost over 98 percent of its value. While this is dire in itself, the larger picture includes all those persons and their families who had invested their savings directly in shares of Enron or in pension and similar funds that invested heavily in the company. It also includes all those creditors and their employees and their families who had extended credit to Enron. Two years after the bankruptcy filing, the company still owed more than US$31 billion and ultimately never paid most of that debt.

Related Social Problems

While it seems clear that the most obvious effects of a bankruptcy are economic, it also seems reasonable to project that many social ills—physical and mental abuse, development of chemical dependencies, heightened racial or ethnic tensions, criminal activity, and self-destructive behavior—may find key sources in the direct and consequential effects of business bankruptcies. However, little research is readily available that investigates the "social cost" of bankruptcies. Despite the many studies conducted on social issues arising from unemployment and depression, few, if any, link these issues directly to bankruptcy. It is tempting to extend these results to stress, long-term depression, and other ailments that may arise from unemployment, financial uncertainty, or social unease experienced by a person affected by a business bankruptcy.

A recent Harvard University study concluded that illness and medical bills caused half of the nearly 1.5 million personal bankruptcies in the United States in 2001 and affected a total of nearly 2 million people. However, this is the inverse of a research finding that reveals clearly identified cause-and-effect data showing that business bankruptcies create social problems.

A paper published by the European Bank for Reconstruction and Development puts forth the concept that bankruptcy is one of the clearest indicators that an economy is open and market oriented. The rationale is that bankruptcy is the result of the community limiting credit to ventures that do not succeed in producing marketable goods at a sustainable return on investment. It is worthy of note that this rationale is somewhat circular, in that the bankruptcy of a going business concern has multiple and usually profound effects on both the economy in which the business is organized and the lives of those involved in its activity. Further, focused study might help estimate the total cost of a business bankruptcy—not just the financial loss—that the entire community endures.

Jeffrey Whitney

See also Bankruptcy, Personal; Debt Service; Economic Restructuring; Globalization; Outsourcing; Social Capital

Further Readings

Averch, Craig H. 2000. "Bankruptcy Laws: What Is Fair?" *Law in Transition* 26(Spring):26–33. Retrieved December 16, 2006 (http://www.ebrd.com/country/sector/law/insolve/about/fairlaw.pdf).

"Medical Bills Leading Cause of Bankruptcy, Harvard Study Finds." 2005. *Consumer Affairs Online*, February 3. Retrieved December 16, 2006 (http://www.consumer affairs.com/news04/2005/bankruptcy_study.html).

Payne, Dinah and Michael Hogg. 1994. "Three Perspectives of Chapter 11 Bankruptcy: Legal, Managerial, and Moral." *Journal of Business Ethics* 13(January):21–30. Retrieved December 16, 2006 (http://www.springerlink.com/content/jj6782t6066k7056/).

"Q&A: The Enron Case." 2006. *BBC News Online*, May 7. Retrieved December 16, 2006 (http://news.bbc.co.uk/2/hi/business/3398913.stm).

BANKRUPTCY, PERSONAL

Personal bankruptcy occurs when a court of law approves and grants the person's (debtor's) petition or application to legally declare an inability to pay and satisfy monetary obligations (debts) to those owed monies (creditors) for the purpose of eliminating or reducing those debts. In contrast to ongoing income-providing social safety nets, such as welfare or unemployment insurance, to prevent individuals from entering into poverty, bankruptcy has historically been viewed as a means to provide debtors in financial hardship who cannot pay their debts a chance for a fresh start. For example, a person has debts that include credit cards, car loans, a mortgage, and medical bills; loses his or her job; depletes his or her savings; and can no longer meet these debts. The debtor applies to, and seeks the protection of, the bankruptcy court to wipe clean, or at least reduce, those debts. On the opposite side of bankruptcy are creditors and other providers that will not be paid for goods or services already provided, with the result that paying consumers bear the costs of those who cannot, through higher loan and credit card interest rates and prices. Bankruptcy petitions, or filings, have tripled on an annual basis over a 10-year period, culminating in 1.6 million filings in the year 2004.

Social scientists and public policy makers are interested in personal bankruptcy for several reasons: whether or not the factors that contribute to and cause bankruptcies can be identified and somehow lessened; bankruptcy's relationship to other social concerns such as job volatility, income, and family life; the bankruptcy process and its ensuing result as to its fairness, role, and inter-relationship with other social safety nets; and its costs to business in terms of lost revenue, all of which affect social and economic stability.

The factors that contribute to bankruptcy are varied and inter-related. Excessive debt is increasingly a primary factor but is usually not sufficient on its own to trigger a bankruptcy. When coupled with major adverse events like job loss, disability, loss of health care, or other income disruption and additional shocks such as increased medical expenses from illness or injury, the potential for bankruptcy increases significantly. Divorce can also contribute to bankruptcy potential in two-income households that split and become separate economic entities trying to maintain a similar living standard. These factors create a financial vulnerability that increases as individuals save less, reducing their own personal safety net. The vulnerability is compounded as means-based social safety net programs, such as unemployment insurance, health care, and welfare, are restricted due to public policy. Resulting middle-class stability is threatened, and choice of bankruptcy as the final safety net increases in incidence. Research shows that 80 percent of bankruptcy filings result from adverse events like job loss, illness, injury, or divorce and those who filed for bankruptcy were predominantly middle class, with earnings above the bottom 20 percent and below the top 20 percent. This is in contrast to the stereotypical bankrupt debtor who is often viewed as a so-called deadbeat, unwilling to meet his or her debts.

The factors that create personal financial risk and vulnerability are consistent in modern societies, but how a society deals with these risks varies. If the risks are to be socialized and borne collectively, stronger safety nets—before the last resort of bankruptcy—are implied, coupled with laws that restrict bankruptcy. Such is the case in the United Kingdom, with its generally regarded wider safety nets and similar consumer debt levels relative to the United States yet with lower levels of bankruptcy. If the financial vulnerability is to be borne individually, which is consistent with the U.S. open market–based society, bankruptcy remains the final safety net that must distribute debt relief and a fresh start opportunity.

In the United States, the Bankruptcy Abuse Prevention and Consumer Protection Act of 2005 was passed into federal law and is the most significant change in personal bankruptcy since 1978. As personal stigma regarding bankruptcy has lessened and consumer debt has grown, the act was passed to prevent so-called abuse and fraud bankruptcies by debtors who borrow heavily without regard to meeting scheduled obligations while retaining the historical intent of providing those in true financial hardship a second-chance start. The act's most significant provision both limits debtors' ability and makes it more difficult for debtors to completely wipe clean all debts (referred to as a Chapter 7 filing), than previously allowed. It also requires those debtors who can afford to make some payments to do so while having the remaining debts erased (referred to as a Chapter 13 filing). Under a

Chapter 13, the court stops creditors from seizing income and assets of the debtor and assists in devising a repayment plan for up to 5 years. The result is that creditors receive some of the debts owed and more than if the debtor had been allowed to file under Chapter 7. The determining factor of whether a debtor can file under Chapter 7 or is required to file under Chapter 13 is the individual's income level relative to the median income in the state in which he or she resides and excess income after allowable expenses. If the debtor's income exceeds the median income of the debtor's resident state and the debtor has excess income above allowable expenses of $100, that person must file under Chapter 13. The result is that the choice of filing is means-based testing that is consistent with other means-based programs like welfare and unemployment insurance. The means test, however, will not prevent debtors from overextending their credit and may not do much to decrease the need to seek bankruptcy relief as the skills and knowledge required to avoid bankruptcy are not addressed.

Alky A. Danikas

See also Bankruptcy, Business; Living Wage; Means-Tested Programs; Underemployment; Unemployment; Wealth, U.S. Consumer; Wealth Disparities

Further Readings

Dickerson, A. Mechele. 2001. "Bankruptcy and Social Welfare Theory: Does the End Justify the Means?" Paper presented at the Workshop on Bankruptcy, Association of American Law Schools, St. Louis, MO.

Fisher, Jonathan D. 2001. *The Effect of Transfer Programs on Personal Bankruptcy.* Washington, DC: Bureau of Labor Statistics.

Kowalewski, Kim. 2000. *Personal Bankruptcy: A Literature Review.* Washington, DC: Congressional Budget Office.

Sullivan, Teresa A., Elizabeth Warren, and Jay Lawrence Westbrook. 2000. *The Fragile Middle Class: Americans in Debt.* New Haven, CT: Yale University Press.

BASIC SKILLS TESTING

Basic skills tests measure the knowledge and skills examinees have in core areas that will impact future performance. These core areas typically include reading, mathematics, language arts, and sometimes other prerequisite skills.

A fine line exists between exit requirements from one level and entrance requirements to the next level. Basic skills testing straddles that line and can cross over in either direction. Minimum competency tests, especially those required in high schools as part of No Child Left Behind, include basic skills assessment as an exit requirement. College entrance tests, taken at the same time and with similar items and content, serve as predictors of future success based on performance in basic skills areas.

The most common use of the term *basic skills* relates to the 3 R's—reading, writing, and arithmetic—also known as literacy and numeracy. Speaking and computing are sometimes added to the generic list, with the term occasionally expanded for specific jobs. For example, a computer operator would need basic knowledge of computer systems, and a welder would need to know about welding equipment. The military provides basic skills training and tests these skills for future success in the armed forces, particularly in officer candidate schools. Thus, basic skills can be viewed as survival skills ensuring that test takers have the skills for future survival.

Basic skills may be tested at almost any time from elementary school through entrance to upper-division undergraduate training to entrance into a job market. One of the most common tests of basic skills is the Iowa Test of Basic Skills for K–8 students. Three of its fundamental purposes are to describe each student's developmental level, to identify a student's areas of relative strength and weakness, and to monitor year-to-year growth. Skills tested include reading, writing, listening, math, social studies, science, and reference materials.

States also use basic skills tests under a variety of names as an exit requirement from high school. Minnesota calls it a basic skills test, Georgia a high school graduation test, and New Jersey a high school proficiency test. These minimum competency tests use a cutoff score for sorting examinees into dichotomous categories—pass/fail.

College entrance tests also test basic skills, with the most common developed by Educational Testing Service and the American College Testing Service. While these tests are for initial admission at the freshman level, additional tests measure competency in basic skills for exit from sophomore standing and entrance to upper-division standing as well as entrance/exit from some professional programs such as teacher education. Some states develop their own tests, such as the CLAST exam in Florida; others use national tests.

Basic skills testing has become particularly popular as an entrance requirement in teacher education. The most widely used test is PRAXIS I, published by Educational Testing Service, which focuses on reading, writing, and mathematics. National Evaluation Systems also has a teacher basic skills test. Some states, such as Florida, developed their own test for professional licenses, using it not only as an entrance requirement into a professional program but also as an exit requirement from lower-division coursework or a community college program.

Basic skills for professionals and employment are sometimes expanded to include critical thinking skills such as problem solving and decision making. Leadership skills may be included as basic in business, military, or other contexts. Some basic skills tests even incorporate affective traits such as a positive attitude.

When used properly, basic skills tests can be highly effective in diagnosing student needs and ensuring that examinees have the prerequisite skills for future success. Many agencies examine passing rates for these tests as a measure of program or school effectiveness, even though this is controversial. For example, children can become lost if their weak areas are not diagnosed and remediated. Children can also be harmed by teachers who have deficits themselves in the basic skills. Further, when poorly developed or used improperly, basic skills tests can have negative social consequences for low-income, minority, and special needs students, as is most evident when these tests are used as minimum competency tests.

Judy R. Wilkerson

See also Academic Standards; Education, Academic Performance; Educational Equity; Minimum Competency Test

Further Readings

Educational Testing Service. 2007. "The Praxis Series: Teacher Licensure and Certification." Retrieved November 30, 2007 (http://www.ets.org/portal/site/ets/menuitem.fab2360b1645a1de9b3a0779f1751509/?vgnextoid=48c05ee3d74f4010VgnVCM10000022f95190RCRD).

University of Iowa, College of Education. 2007. *Iowa Testing Programs: Iowa Tests of Basic Skills*. Retrieved November 30, 2007 (http://www.education.uiowa.edu/itp/itbs/index.htm).

BEREAVEMENT, EFFECT BY RACE

The increased risk of death among individuals who have lost their spouse is known as the "bereavement" or "widowhood effect." The bereavement effect originates from the difference between the health benefits of marriage and the negative consequences of widowhood. Research shows a strong and long-lasting bereavement effect among white men and women in the United States but no evidence for a bereavement effect among black men and women. The size of the widowhood effect for spouses in black–white interracial marriages may depend on the race of the wife. No research presently exists on the widowhood effect among Asian and Hispanic individuals in the United States.

Among whites married to whites, the death of one spouse increases the risk of death for the surviving spouse by over 50 percent during the first month of widowhood. For at least the first 3 years of widowhood, widowed individuals continue to face a risk of death that is more than 10 percent higher than that of comparable married individuals. The bereavement effect is the same for men and women, at least in old age. Research attributes the bereavement effect among whites to a variety of mechanisms, including emotional distress, difficulties with adjusting to new daily routines, the loss of spousal support, and the loss of health supervision. Traditionally, men lose their primary caregiver, whereas women suffer from reduced economic resources. Widows and widowers report less healthy lifestyles than married individuals and reduced access to high-quality medical care.

As mentioned, research has found no bereavement effect among blacks married to blacks. Because blacks derive similar health benefits from marriage as whites, the absence of a bereavement effect among blacks is likely due to racial differences in the experience of widowhood. Research suggests three possible explanations for this absence. First, blacks are twice as likely as whites to live with relatives in old age (40 percent vs. 20 percent). Coresident relatives may provide care for bereaved individuals, thus effectively substituting for the health services previously rendered by the spouse. Second, the gendered division of labor in marriages among blacks is, on average, less rigid. This may instill greater self-sufficiency, reduce spousal task dependence, and consequently better prepare blacks for widowhood. Third, greater religiosity and religious participation among blacks may provide bereaved individuals with spiritual comfort and social resources for dealing with loss that are less available to whites.

One study suggests that the bereavement effect for men in black–white intermarriage may depend entirely on the race of the wife: Elderly black men who lose a white wife suffer a bereavement effect, whereas white men married to a black wife do not suffer a widowhood effect. This may be explained by differences in kin involvement of racially intermarried spouses, but strong evidence for this or other explanations is presently unavailable.

Felix Elwert

See also Life Course; Life Expectancy; Stressors

Further Readings

Elwert, Felix and Nicholas A. Christakis. 2006. "Widowhood and Race." *American Sociological Review* 71:16–41.

BILINGUAL EDUCATION

Bilingual education, the use of two languages to educate children in a school, is very complex in its nature, aims, approaches, and outcomes. So much as its philosophy and practices vary across schools, regions, states, and nations, the controversial issues and arguments surrounding bilingual education have bewildered not only the general public but also bilingual researchers and practitioners, especially in the United States.

For example, the No Child Left Behind Act of 2001 encourages schools to abandon bilingual instruction, even though researchers have continuously demonstrated the value of bilingual programs for educating language-minority children. English-only advocates do not necessarily deny the effectiveness of bilingual education, but they view bilingual education or bilingualism as a threat to upholding national identity and a trigger to dividing people along ethnolinguistic lines; some of them even question whether anything was wrong with the old "sink or swim" approach that worked for earlier immigrants.

What the anti-bilingual backlash suggests is that many perceive bilingual education as a political issue rather than an educational one. However, unlike the general public's perception, the academic field of bilingual education heavily rests on rigorous empirical research as well as in-depth studies and theories on language acquisition and academic development of bilingual children.

The Field of Bilingual Education

Bilingual education is a multidisciplinary field with various areas of research focusing largely on three areas: (1) a linguistics-based psychological and sociological foundation, (2) a micro-classroom pedagogy and macro-education, and (3) sociolinguistic perspectives.

The area of linguistics-based psychological and sociological foundations examines historical backgrounds and develops and integrates various theories. Researchers in this area emphasize the child's bilingual and cognitive development and the effect that home and neighborhood play in this development; they investigate ways of interfacing bilingual education with minority language maintenance as well as language decay and language revival. The area involving micro-classroom pedagogy and macro-education deals with the effectiveness of bilingual programs of different types. Researchers examine essential features of bilingual classrooms that foster bilingualism and academic learning, investigate various teaching methodologies, and analyze different views of the overall value and purpose of bilingualism in conjunction with the nature of multiculturalism in society, schools, and classrooms. The sociolinguistic perspective concentrates on language planning and policy, raises critical issues reflecting diverse viewpoints about language minorities and bilingual education, investigates factors that generate disparity in preference between the assimilation of language minorities and language diversity, and examines language policies.

In dealing with the previously mentioned areas at the individual and societal levels, the field of bilingual education evolved into various types of bilingual programs. For example, a *transitional bilingual program* facilitates the transition from the language minority's home language to the majority's language. It is important to note that publicly funded U.S. bilingual education is, broadly speaking, transitional in that it aims essentially to move children into English-only instruction within 2 or 3 years. However, some schools offer a *self-contained bilingual program* in which a bilingual teacher provides instruction in two languages in all subject areas. Another interesting form of bilingual education is a *two-way bilingual program* (also named *dual language program*) in which the classes are evenly divided between students who speak English and those who speak another language. Such programs use two languages more or less equally in the curriculum so that both language-majority and language-minority children become bilingual and biliterate. Some ESL (English as a second language) programs are a form of bilingual education in that all the students speak the same language other than English and the teacher speaks the students' home language yet little or no instruction is given in a language other than English.

Bilingual Education in the Political Arena

The field of bilingual education is academically well established, but its conception and operation closely inter-relate with immigration, societal changes, and political movements such as civil rights and equality of educational opportunity. Interestingly, U.S. society generally accepted language diversity, which was encouraged through religious institutions and newspapers, until World War I. In addition, bilingual education was practiced in some states (e.g., German–English schools in Ohio, Pennsylvania, Minnesota, the Dakotas, and Wisconsin). However, when the United States entered World War I, a wave of patriotism led to a fear of foreigners, and aliens' lack of English language skills became a source of social, political, and economic concern. Consequently, public and governmental pressure mounted to require all aliens to speak English and to become naturalized Americans, and for schools to conduct all classes in English.

Societal changes in the mid-20th century led to a more favorable public attitude toward bilingual education. For instance, the Civil Rights Act of 1964 was a significant marker that symbolized the beginning of a less-negative attitude toward ethnic groups and their linguistic heritage. What may be a most noteworthy landmark in U.S. bilingual education in this period was a lawsuit brought on behalf of Chinese students against the San Francisco School District. This case, known as *Lau v. Nichols,* involved whether or not non-English-speaking students received equal educational opportunities when instructed in a language they could not understand. In 1974, the Supreme Court ruled in favor of the students, thereby expanding the language rights of limited-English-proficient students nationwide.

Society keeps changing, and language-related affairs and education assume different forms accordingly. Since the late 20th century, bilingual education has faced political adversity in varying degrees. Senator S. I. Hayakawa of California teamed up with other activists to found the advocacy group U.S. English in the early 1980s. This lobby headed the Official English offensive in Congress, state legislatures, and ballot campaigns. In 1996, the House of Representatives approved a bill designating English as the federal government's sole language of official business, but the Senate did not act, ending the proposed legislation. In 1998, California voters approved Proposition 227, mandating the dismantling of most bilingual education in the state. Voters in Arizona in 2000 and Massachusetts in 2002 also approved similar measures; in Colorado in 2002 voters rejected this initiative. More recently, the trend toward "holding schools accountable" through high-stakes testing, primarily in English as mandated by the No Child Left Behind Act, discourages schools from providing bilingual programs.

Sociopolitical and Educational Outlook

Although high-stakes testing has become a threat to bilingual education, it recasts a fundamental issue: the benefits of a bilingual program. Recently, advocates of bilingual education promoted two-way/dual bilingual programs by stressing their benefit. Unlike the transitional bilingual programs or self-contained bilingual programs initially developed and implemented for children with limited English language proficiency, the dual language program is designed for both language-minority and language-majority students. Each class would be equally composed of students who speak English and those who speak another language, as bilingual teachers aim to keep the two languages separate in their classroom. This dual language program is an interesting sociopolitical challenge in that bilingual education benefits students of the dominant language group as well as language-minority students.

However, interested observers note that the dual language program is limited in serving the school population "at large" because the non-English language in such a program may not be the language that the entire school population wants. For example, a school with many Spanish-speaking immigrants' children may consider offering a Spanish–English dual language program, but parents who are not Spanish-speaking descendants may not want to choose Spanish as the second language for their children: They may want Italian, French, or Polish, for example, which may not be financially or logistically practical.

Bilingual education, then, involves multifaceted issues. Its continuity or discontinuity and the choice of program types are sociopolitical issues as well as educational ones. No doubt consistent efforts will attempt to educate the general public about the societal benefits of developing native-language skills of language-minority children. Yet, U.S. education policy, driven by high-stakes testing and accountability demands, will continue the trend toward all-English programs. Thus the challenges that schools, communities, states, and bilingual professionals face vis-à-vis bilingual education are enormous. The challenges include establishing criteria about programs and services to ensure language-minority children's equal access to education, overcoming the mistaken perception that bilingual education threatens the existing social order, and expanding bilingual education to the dominant language group—the English-speaking children—to enhance their foreign language and intercultural communication skills.

Keumsil Kim Yoon

See also Education, Academic Performance; Education, Policy and Politics; Educational Equity; English as a Second Language; English-Only Movement; Immigration, United States

Further Readings

Baker, Colin. 2006. *Foundations of Bilingual Education and Bilingualism.* 4th ed. Clevedon, England: Multilingual Matters.

Crawford, James. 2000. *At War with Diversity: US language policy in an Age of Anxiety.* Clevedon, England: Multilingual Matters.

Government Accountability Office. 2006. "No Child Left Behind Act: Assistance from Education Could Help States Better Measure Progress of Students with Limited English Proficiency." GAO-06-815, July 26. Washington, DC. Retrieved November 30, 2007 (http://www.gao.gov/highlights/d06815high.pdf).

Krashen, Stephen and Grace McField. 2005. "What Works? Reviewing the Latest Evidence on Bilingual Education." *Language Learner* 1(2):7–10, 34.

Lessow-Hurley, Judith. 2004. *The Foundations of Dual Language Instruction.* White Plains, NY: Longman.

BINGE DRINKING

Most alcohol treatment clinicians use the term *binge drinking* to mean a drinking spree that lasts several days—an episode known colloquially as a "bender." Such drinking is often a diagnostic sign of alcoholism or severe alcohol dependence.

In recent years, medical and public health researchers have defined binge drinking more broadly as the consumption of five or more alcoholic drinks on a single occasion. Some researchers specify a threshold of four or more drinks for women, who typically experience alcohol-related problems at lower consumption levels.

Researchers classify a person as a *binge drinker* if that individual has five or more (or four or more) drinks at least once during a particular time period, typically pegged at 2 weeks or a month. Critics call this research definition too expansive, especially in light of its pejorative connotations. One problem is that the definition fails to differentiate between a true bender and lower levels of heavy alcohol use, which can lead to public misunderstanding when news headlines proclaim binge drinking rates.

In addition, the definition does not account for the drinker's body weight, the pace of alcohol consumption, or whether food is eaten at the same time. As a result, a man of 240 pounds who had one drink per hour would still be labeled a binge drinker even though his blood alcohol concentration (BAC) would remain below high-risk levels commonly associated with mental and physical impairment.

Accordingly, in 2004, the National Institute on Alcohol Abuse and Alcoholism (NIAAA), a U.S. federal agency that sponsors alcohol research, redefined a binge as a pattern of drinking alcohol that brings BAC to .08 percent (i.e., .08 gram of alcohol per 100 grams of blood) or above. This level was chosen because all 50 U.S. states have laws that define a BAC of .08 percent or higher as impaired driving. For the typical adult, a binge would result from consuming five or more drinks (male), or four or more drinks (female), in about 2 hours. NIAAA also distinguished binge drinking from both *risky drinking,* which involves reaching a peak BAC between .05 percent and .08 percent, and a *bender,* which involves 2 or more days of sustained heavy drinking.

Although the NIAAA definition is more precise, researchers have not yet embraced it, in part because of its complexity but primarily to ensure that their research can be compared with prior studies. Growing numbers of researchers no longer use the term *binge drinking* when describing alcohol use that merely exceeds the five-drink (or four-drink) threshold, but no alternative term has taken its place. The *Journal of Studies on Alcohol,* a leading periodical in the field, requires authors to use the term *heavy, episodic drinking,* but this is too cumbersome for everyday use. In this entry the phrase *heavy drinking* is used.

The Behavioral Risk Factor Surveillance System (BRFSS), a health survey organized and supported by the U.S. Centers for Disease Control and Prevention (CDC), defines heavy (binge) drinking as having five or more drinks on at least one occasion in the preceding month. The BRFSS for 2001 found that an estimated 14 percent of U.S. adults 18 years and older (22 percent of men, 7 percent of women) engaged in heavy drinking.

The heavy drinking rate for persons ages 18 to 20 years, who are younger than the U.S. legal drinking age, was 26 percent. Among persons of legal age, those ages 21 to 25 years had the greatest heavy drinking rate at 32 percent. The rate declined with increasing age: For those ages 26 to 34 years, the rate was 21 percent; for those 35 to 54 years, 14 percent; and for those 55 years and older, 4 percent. Heavy drinking rates by racial/ethnic group were as follows: Hispanic, 17 percent; white, 15 percent; and black, 10 percent.

The Monitoring the Future Study (MTF), an annual survey of U.S. middle school and high school students, defines heavy (binge) drinking as having five or more drinks in a row in the past 2 weeks. In 2005, the MTF reported that 28 percent of high school seniors (Grade 12) had engaged in heavy drinking, compared with 21 percent of students in Grade 10, and 10 percent of students in Grade 8. Historically, heavy drinking reached its peak in 1979, with a rate of 41 percent among high school seniors.

Heavy drinking is of particular concern at U.S. colleges and universities. The Harvard School of Public Health's College Alcohol Study (CAS) defines heavy (binge) drinking using the 5/4-plus standard. In 2001, an estimated 44 percent of students attending 4-year institutions reported drinking at that level at least once during the 2 weeks preceding the survey. About one half of these students (23 percent) drank heavily three or more times during that period.

Heavy drinking is associated with increased mortality and morbidity. For example, an estimated 1,700 U.S. college students die each year from alcohol-related causes, including alcohol poisoning, interpersonal violence, and unintentional injury. Roughly 80 percent of these deaths are due to alcohol-related traffic crashes. Heavy drinking is also associated with poor academic performance, unprotected sex, vandalism, and other problems.

Several environmental factors are known to affect heavy drinking rates. Higher alcohol prices—brought about by increasing state excise taxes or eliminating "happy hours" and other low-price promotions—result in lower consumption and fewer alcohol-related problems. Likewise, communities with fewer alcohol retailers per capita also experience fewer alcohol-related problems. Responsible beverage service programs—involving identification checks to prevent underage customers from obtaining alcohol and procedures to avoid overservice—can also lead to lower alcohol use.

Based on data from the CAS, heavy drinking by underage U.S. college students is lower in communities where age 21 is the legal minimum age to buy alcohol. Heavy drinking by underage students is also lower in those communities where four or more of the following six laws are in place: keg registration, a .08 percent BAC per se law (that defines the legal limit by which alcohol-impaired driving is defined), and restrictions on happy hours, open containers, beer sold in pitchers, and billboards and other advertising.

William DeJong

See also Addiction; Alcoholism; Drunk Driving; Fetal Alcohol Syndrome; Gateway Drugs; Temperance Movement; Twelve-Step Programs

Further Readings

DeJong, William. 2001. "Finding Common Ground for Effective Campus-Based Prevention." *Psychology of Addictive Behaviors* 15:292–96.

Johnston, Lloyd D., Patrick M. O'Malley, Jerald G. Bachman, and John E. Schulenberg. 2006. *Monitoring the Future National Survey Results on Drug Use, 1975–2005, vol. 1, Secondary School Students.* NIH Publication No. 06-5883. Bethesda, MD: National Institute on Drug Abuse.

National Institute on Alcohol Abuse and Alcoholism, Task Force of the National Advisory Council on Alcohol Abuse and Alcoholism. 2002. "A Call to Action: Changing the Culture of Drinking at U.S. Colleges." Washington, DC: National Institutes of Health.

Bioethics

Bioethics refers to an interdisciplinary approach used to address quandaries and moral dilemmas that arise from applied biology and medical science. It involves applying societal mores, philosophical principles, religious values, and human judgment to making decisions about human life and death, health and medical treatment, environmental issues, and the relationship of humans to other organisms on our planet. Principles of bioethics arose from secular and religious ethical principles. As medical science and biological technology developed and enabled humans to change their natural environment in dramatic ways, consideration of bioethics principles became more critical to guide applications of the technologies and human behavior.

History of Bioethics

Religious traditions served as the earliest sources to guide individuals and communities in decisions vis-à-vis medical practice, treatment of animals, and the environment. For instance, Judeo-Christian sources such as the Bible address bioethics issues, including injunctions to heal the sick and prohibitions regarding wanton destruction of property. The humane treatment of animals is also emphasized, as are mechanisms to provide reparations for personal harm. Healers and medical practitioners find guidelines in other ancient codes of law and thought as well, including those of Islam, Hinduism, Buddhism, Confucianism, and Taoism.

The Hippocratic tradition, developed in ancient Greece approximately 2,500 years ago, includes guidelines for doctors in their relationships with their patients. The sections of the oath most influential for modern medicine include the prohibition against giving patients deadly drugs, directives against euthanasia and abortion, and most important, the core principle of the oath, the pledge to improve the health of the patient.

Modern codes of medical ethics include Percival's Code, developed by Thomas Percival of Great Britain in 1803, which also emphasized the physician's duty to the patient. With the founding of the American Medical Association in the mid-19th century, that group developed a code of ethics that focused on doctors benefiting their patients, in addition to the physician's role in benefiting society. After World War II, at the Nuremberg trials, the world learned of the unspeakable violations of human rights carried out by Nazi doctors in the name of science. Nazi medical practitioners performed grievous experiments on Jews, Gypsies, and homosexuals—innocent victims and unwilling subjects—imprisoned in concentration and death camps. The Nuremberg Code of 1946 was developed in response to the testimonies at the Nazi doctors' trials. That code stipulated, for the first time, the principle of voluntary and informed consent. The medical community, represented by the World Medical Association, also reacted to Nazi violations of human rights by developing a code in response to Nazi atrocities. Their document, the Declaration of Geneva of 1948, states that the health of the patient is of paramount importance and should be the doctor's first consideration.

Biotechnology and Bioethics

The advent of biotechnology and its myriad new applications in the 1970s and 1980s created a need for reconsideration of bioethics issues. In 1998, the Biotechnology Industry Organization developed a statement of principles to address some of the issues by reaffirming the basic principles of bioethics and declaring that biotechnology should be used in only beneficial ways. It emphasizes the importance of respect for animals, protection of the environment, and observance of the principle of informed consent for patients and the research subjects. The statement recommends that the power of biotechnology be applied to endeavors that lead to improvements in food production and the cleaning up of toxic wastes. The organization also emphasized its opposition to the use of the new technology to develop weapons. These noble concepts of the biotechnology industry clearly arose from general principles of bioethics and from previous codes guiding applied science and medicine.

The Roots of Bioethics

Bioethics rests on a foundation of ethics thousands of years in the making. Codes of law and other guidelines for human behavior have traditionally involved two major approaches: principle-based ethics and casuistry.

Principle-based approaches to ethics are top-down ("here are the rules, follow them"), whereas casuistry is a bottom-up type of ethical approach, which involves the application of case studies ("here are the

situations, figure out the rules for yourself"). Exclusive use of either approach limits flexibility and adaptability to new situations. Thus, many ethicists find combination approaches more acceptable. One such approach, reflective equilibrium, developed by John Rawls in 1971, combines theories, principles, rules, and judgments about specific cases. Many legal and ethical systems are based, at least in part, on casuistry. For instance, legal precedents play important roles in determining the decisions of U.S. courts. But legal and ethical systems also combine case-based reasoning with a clear set of rules. Bioethics likewise developed from both approaches—from a set of principles, and from analysis of cases.

Major Principles of Secular Bioethics

In 1979 Tom Beauchamp and James Childress proposed four principles of modern secular bioethics: respect for autonomy, nonmaleficence, beneficence, and justice. The principles, developed specifically to address issues in medical and environmental science, serve as cornerstones for the development of bioethical codes of behavior.

The *principle of respect for autonomy* includes the patient's or research subject's right to freely choose or reject treatment, and the liberty to act accordingly. Every patient's autonomy is of paramount importance. The right of informed consent represents one aspect of this principle. Accordingly, patients should be educated and allowed to participate in decisions regarding their fate; patients should retain authority to determine what their course of treatment is. However, even patient autonomy has limits; for instance, many would agree that patients must be prevented from harming themselves. Euthanasia on demand is not legal in the United States.

The *principle of nonmaleficence* means that the physician or scientist should do no harm. Patients should not be injured in the course of treatment. This could also be expanded to include the environment and be understood as a directive to protect our natural world.

The *principle of beneficence* directs medical practitioners and researchers to do good, promote patient welfare, devise ways to improve quality of life, and repair the world.

The fourth principle, the *principle of justice,* focuses on fairness in allocating resources. For instance, social benefits such as health care services, including pharmaceutical drugs, diagnostic tests, donated organs, and medical expertise, should be distributed in a just manner. Likewise, social burdens such as taxes should be assessed fairly.

Major Issues in Bioethics

Most bioethics issues fall into five major themes: beginning of life, end of life, rights of patients, animal rights, and environmental protection and preservation.

The beginning of life category includes traditional areas of controversy (such as contraception and termination of pregnancy) and issues that more recently arose as a result of biotechnological advances. The latter category includes cloning, embryonic stem cell research, fetal experimentation, fetal surgery, multifetal pregnancy reduction, artificial reproductive technologies, eugenics, genetic screening, and gene therapy.

End-of-life issues include the injunction to preserve human life, assisted suicide and euthanasia, futility of end-of-life care, and allocation of medical resources.

The rights of patients involve issues such as voluntary participation and informed consent for medical treatment, truth-telling (i.e., sharing all information with patients), doctor–patient confidentiality, autonomy of patients, research on human subjects, the rights of the insured and the uninsured, and the fair allocation of limited resources.

Animal rights issues include questions regarding the use of animals as research subjects, the respectful and humane treatment of laboratory animals, domesticated farm animals and pets, and proper treatment of animals in the wild.

Environmental protection and preservation focus on minimizing the destruction of natural resources and habitats, preserving species, recovering and cleaning up fouled habitats, and reintroducing endangered species. Biotechnological advances have also led to novel bioethical conundrums, such as whether to alter species by genetic engineering and how to safely utilize genetically modified plants and animals so as not to harm humans or the environment or wreak havoc with the natural process of evolution.

The Future of Bioethics

As new technologies evolve, humankind will continue to grapple with new ethical dilemmas that arise. Increased human life expectancies will further stretch limited medical resources. As neonatal medicine improves, fetuses will be viable outside the womb at earlier stages, making abortion issues even more challenging. Genetic screening and gene therapy will permit parents to choose or reject offspring with particular traits, permitting humankind to change the course of evolution. Thus, in bioethics, the breakthroughs of today become the daunting dilemmas of tomorrow.

Miryam Z. Wahrman

See also Abortion; Contraception; Environmental Degradation; Eugenics; Euthanasia; Fertility; Genetically Altered Foods; Genetic Engineering; Genetic Theories; Genocide; Health Care, Access; Life Expectancy; Suicide

Further Readings

Annas, George J. and Michael A. Grodin. 1992. *The Nazi Doctors and the Nuremberg Code: Human Rights in Human Experimentation.* New York: Oxford University Press.

Beauchamp, Tom and James F. Childress. 2008. *Principles of Biomedical Ethics.* 6th ed. New York: Oxford University Press.

Beauchamp, Tom L., LeRoy Walters, Jeffrey P. Kahn and Anna C. Mastroianni. 2007. *Contemporary Issues in Bioethics.* 7th ed. Belmont, CA: Wadsworth.

Levine, Carol, ed. 2006. *Taking Sides: Clashing Views on Controversial Bioethical Issues.* 11th ed. Dubuque, IA: McGraw-Hill/Dushkin.

Mappes, Thomas A. and David DeGrazia. 2006. *Biomedical Ethics.* 6th ed. New York: McGraw-Hill.

Ridley, Aaron. 1998. *Beginning Bioethics.* Boston: Bedford/St. Martin's.

Veach, Robert M. 2003. *The Basics of Bioethics.* 2nd ed. Upper Saddle River, NJ: Prentice Hall.

Wahrman, Miryam Z. 2004. *Brave New Judaism: When Science and Scripture Collide.* Hanover, NH: Brandeis University Press.

BIRACIAL

The term *biracial* refers to a person with parents of two different races. The 1967 *Loving v. Virginia* Supreme Court decision that invalidated laws forbidding inter-racial marriage, the civil rights movement of the 1950s and 1960s, and the opening up of Asian and Latin American immigration in 1965 all contributed to an increase in inter-racial unions and biracial off-spring. In the U.S. Census 2000, when people were given the opportunity to identify with more than one race for the first time, 2.4 percent of all Americans did so. The Census 2000 finding that 4 percent of Americans under 18 are biracial (compared with 2.4 percent of all Americans) is an indication of the relative youth of biracial Americans.

Increasingly, the word *multiracial* is replacing the term *biracial*. However, 93 percent of people who checked off more than one race on the 2000 census checked off only two races. It is also important to remember that the U.S. Census considers Hispanic/Latino an ethnic, rather than a racial, category. So, Latino/a Americans listed as "more than one race" checked off "Hispanic or Latino" *and* two or more racial groups. Most biracial Americans have a white parent because two thirds of Americans are non-Hispanic whites and, therefore, most inter-racial unions consist of a white person and a person of color. However, as a group, white people are least likely to marry outside of their racial group and have biracial offspring.

Most biracial Americans live in states with relatively high levels of diversity and metropolitan centers. According to the 2000 census, 40 percent of biracial persons reside in the West, 27 percent in the South, 18 percent in the Northeast, and 15 percent in the Midwest. Hawaii has the most multiracial persons, with 21 percent. In descending order, the other states with above-average biracial populations are Alaska, California, Oklahoma, Arizona, Colorado, Nevada, New Mexico, Oregon, Washington, New Jersey, New York, Rhode Island, and Texas. Each of these states has a biracial population greater than the 2.4 percent national average.

The literature on biracial Americans was primarily negative before the post–civil rights era "biracial baby boom," focusing on problems biracial Americans might have fitting into a monoracial society. However, recent social science research and popular writing on the topic of biracial Americans provide a much more positive view. Most of today's published work on biracial Americans stresses their ability to bridge racial divides and see both sides of racial issues. The popularity of biracial stars like Mariah Carey and the "Cablinasian" Tiger Woods has also done much to promote the benefits of a mixed-race background. As their numbers and presence grow, more and more biracial Americans are questioning the traditional racial hierarchy in the United States and embracing all sides of their racial heritage.

Kathleen Korgen

See also Race; Racial Formation Theory

Further Readings

Jones, Nicholas A. and Amy Symens Smith. 2001. *The Two or More Races Population: 2000*. Census 2000 Brief No. C2KBR/01-6. Retrieved July 17, 2006 (http://www.census.gov/prod/2001pubs/c2kbr01-6.pdf).

Lee, Sharon M. and Barry Edmonston. 2005. "New Marriages, New Families: U.S. Racial and Hispanic Intermarriage." *Population Bulletin* 60(2). Retrieved July 17, 2006 (http://www.cs.princeton.edu/~chazelle/politics/bib/newmarriages05.pdf).

BIRTH RATE

Birth rates are measures used by social scientists and journalists to provide some indication of the role that new births contribute to a country's total population growth each year, as well as potential future increases when the new cohort reaches childbearing age. The most common form is the crude birth rate (CBR), which is crude in the sense that it compares the number of births to the number of men, women, and children in a given society even though only women of certain ages can reasonably be expected to give birth. The CBR is usually expressed as the number of births in a given period for every 1,000 live persons counted in the midpoint of that period and must not be confused with the total fertility rate (TFR), which includes only women of childbearing ages in the denominator.

In 2006, CBRs ranged from a high of 50.7 births per 1,000 in Niger to a low of 7.3 births per 1,000 in Hong Kong. Birth rates reflect two factors: the proportion of the population composed of fertile women (ages 15 to 44) and the prevalence of childbearing among them. (The TFR is based only on the latter of these). When women of childbearing age constitute a large proportion of the population and exhibit a high prevalence of childbearing, the outcome is predictable: significant population growth due to high levels of childbearing. Small proportions and low prevalence of childbirth among such women will naturally lead to population stagnation or decline due to low levels of childbearing. However, in some instances low prevalence of childbearing among fertile women is offset by their over-representation in the population; sometimes high birth rates are driven not by the high prevalence of childbearing among fertile women but simply by the high number of fertile women in a given society.

In 2005, birth rates were slightly higher in Ireland and Chile (14.4 per 1,000 and 15.2 per 1,000, respectively) than in the United States (14.1 per 1,000) even though childbirth was more common among American women of childbearing age than among women in the other two countries. This paradoxical finding is attributable to the fact that larger proportions of Irish and Chilean women are of childbearing age (45 percent and 46 percent, respectively) compared with women in the United States (41 percent).

Through the 20th century, birth rates fell precipitously throughout the industrialized world, and less developed countries have begun to follow suit. Sudden drops in birth rate have a cumulative effect: The fewer babies born now, the fewer potential mothers there will be later. This has led to stagnant and even declining populations in some countries. This situation is aggravated by the simultaneous decrease in death rates, which has left relatively small birth cohorts charged with providing for larger birth cohorts who are surviving to retirement age, and well beyond, in unprecedented numbers. Immigrants have kept population growth robust in many such countries. However, by 2050 Mexico and other developing countries will experience similar population shortfalls; only time will tell if they can count on immigrants to span the difference between the number of native-born workers and the number needed to support burgeoning senior populations.

Amon Emeka

See also Baby Boomers; Fertility; Life Expectancy; Total Fertility Rate

Further Readings and References

Central Intelligence Agency. 2007. *The World Factbook.* Dulles, VA: Potomac Books.

Preston, Samuel H., Patrick Heuveline, and Michel Guillot. 2000. *Demography: Measuring and Modeling Population Processes.* Malden, MA: Blackwell.

BISEXUALITY

Situated within the heterosexual versus homosexual binary, bisexuality is a sexual orientation or preference consisting of more than incidental amounts of sexual feeling, sexual behavior, or romantic desire for persons of both one's own and the other sex. The term encompasses those who self-define as bisexual, whether or not currently active with both sexes. It also refers to others who experience dual attractions or behavior but identify as heterosexual, gay, or lesbian, or simply reject the use of a sexual label altogether.

Although estimates vary widely and remain unresolved, representative national survey data indicate perhaps 6 percent of men and about 4 percent of women in the United States have had bisexual experiences from adolescence onward. Far fewer report recent sexual activity (in the past year) with both sexes. Likewise, a considerably smaller percentage self-defines as bisexual. Nonetheless, more people across the life course report bisexual behavior than exclusive same sex behavior, but fewer men and women self-define as bisexual than as gay or lesbian.

People who think of themselves as bisexual or who are actively bisexual often are not equally attracted to or equally sexual with both sexes. Evidence suggests there are more heterosexual-leaning bisexuals than homosexual-leaning bisexuals. Among self-defined bisexuals, more report heterosexual attractions and behaviors earlier in life than homosexual attractions and behaviors. The label *bisexual* often is adopted years later, after a period of identity drift and confusion, which results from a lack of acceptance of bisexuality in the larger world.

Bisexual lives are diverse. Serial bisexuality involves switching from a partner of one sex to another one at a time. Simultaneous bisexuality consists of ongoing sexual relationships with partners of different sexes. Whereas some bisexually oriented people practice monogamous relationships, others prefer multiple partners in a group relationship structure, and yet others live with a core primary partner with casual partners outside. Regardless of the structure, heterosexual marriage is common, involved partners of bisexuals often are not bisexual, and outside sex may or may not be openly agreed upon.

People in both the heterosexual and gay and lesbian communities view bisexuality in problematic terms, though for different reasons. On the one hand, during the 1980s, the AIDS crisis emerged and bisexual identified men were viewed as a threat for transmitting the disease to the straight world. In response to the AIDS crisis, many openly identified bisexuals turned to practicing safer sex—using condoms or latex, screening partners, avoiding exchange of bodily fluids, and so forth. Today, AIDS research focuses on men who have sex with men, recognizing that bisexual behavior may occur among gay or heterosexual identified men as well, creating a more complex picture of risk.

On the other hand, despite the proliferation of more inclusive GLBT (gay/lesbian/bisexual/transgender) groups on college campuses and elsewhere, bisexuality still holds a marginalized status in the gay and lesbian world. Perceptions persist that bisexuality is nothing more than a transitional fence-sitting sexuality. Bisexuals are likewise stereotyped as prone to jumping ship and as less capable of forming committed relationships. Additionally, bisexuals who live with or who are married to partners of the other sex are said to hide behind heterosexual privilege and to be politically incorrect. For example, while the issue of same-sex marriage is currently being contested, the question in the case of heterosexual coupled bisexuals is whether or not they are equally involved politically in this debate.

Douglas W. Pryor

See also Gender Identity and Socialization; Homosexuality; Sexuality; Sexual Orientation

Further Readings

Fox, Ronald C. 2004. *Current Research on Bisexuality.* Binghamton, NY: Harrington Park.
Weinberg, Martin S., Colin J. Williams, and Douglas W. Pryor. 1994. *Dual Attraction: Understanding Bisexuality.* New York: Oxford University Press.

BLACK CODES

The term *Black Codes* refers to a collection of laws passed to restrict the civil rights of freed slaves and other persons of African descent. These are most commonly associated with an assortment of local and state laws passed in the Southern states between 1865 and 1866 following the abolition of slavery at the end of the U.S. Civil War. The purpose of these laws was

threefold. First, the laws curtailed the social, occupational, and spatial mobility of African Americans. Geographically varying by state and local jurisdiction, these laws generally denied freed slaves the right to vote, marry whites, bear arms, or assemble after sunset. Other laws proscribed areas where African Americans could purchase or rent property or prohibited them from testifying against whites in court.

Second, the Black Codes operated to reproduce slavery in a disguised form. African Americans who quit their jobs, for example, could be arrested, imprisoned, and leased out as convict labor. Likewise, African Americans could be arrested and fined for other infractions, such as curfew violations or making insulting gestures. Through unfair imprisonment and debt bondage, Southern politicians tried to replicate slavery as closely as possible.

Third, the intent of the laws was to reinforce white supremacy and symbolically reflect the inferior status of blacks in the United States. In Mississippi, for example, railroads forbade "any freedman, negro, or mulatto to ride in any first-class passenger cars, set apart, or used by and for white persons." In short, the Black Codes ensured that African Americans "knew their place" in U.S. society.

President Andrew Johnson, being a white supremacist and supporter of states' rights, encouraged the South in its drafting of the Black Codes. Indeed, every governor whom Johnson appointed to head the new state governments in the South opposed black suffrage and worked to curb the civil rights and civil liberties of African Americans. However, the Republican-dominated Congress, angered by the imposition of the Black Codes, subsequently established a military governance of the Southern states. In effect, this repealed the 1865–66 Black Codes and led to the radical Reconstruction of the South (1867–77).

The postbellum Black Codes were not unique. Indeed, these codes had as antecedents a long history of laws discriminating against African Americans that dated to the founding of the United States. Most obvious, for example, is the congressional decision in 1790 to limit citizenship to whites only. Other legislation limited occupational attainment of African Americans, as seen in the 1810 law barring persons of African descent from carrying the U.S. mail.

Many laws, however, were more local, with the intent of controlling where African Americans could live. In 1717, for example, free blacks were prohibited from residing in any town or colony in Connecticut, and an early North Carolina law required free blacks to register and to carry papers testifying to their legal status. Free blacks were also required to wear patches that read FREE. Any free black who failed to register, or was found without his or her proper paperwork, could be arrested and sold into slavery.

Laws prohibiting inter-racial marriage exhibit an even longer history. In 1662 the Virginia Assembly passed an act that black women's children were to serve according to the condition of the mother. This ensured that children of white fathers and black slave mothers would be assigned slave status. In 1691 Virginia amended this act, specifying that any free English woman who bore a mulatto child would pay a fine of 15 pounds or be sold as a servant for 5 years; the child would be a servant until age 30. These laws were replicated in other colonies. In 1664, for example, Maryland passed a law prohibiting white women from marrying black slaves. Any woman found in violation of this act was to serve the master of the woman's black slave husband during the lifetime of the husband. In addition, any children resulting from the marriage would themselves become slaves.

The Black Codes are not synonymous with the Jim Crow laws. Although similar in intent and practice, Jim Crowism began in 1890 as a response to the ending of radical Reconstruction. These latter laws, which built on and expanded the discriminatory practices of the Black Codes, were accompanied by informal measures of control, including lynchings, beatings, and other forms of harassment. They would continue, legally, until the civil rights movement of the 1950s and 1960s.

James Tyner

See also Jim Crow; Lynching; Miscegenation; Racism

Further Readings

Franklin, John Hope and Alfred A. Moss Jr. 1994. *From Slavery to Freedom: A History of African Americans.* 7th ed. New York: McGraw-Hill.

Woodward, C. Vann. 2001. *The Strange Career of Jim Crow.* Commemorative ed. New York: Oxford University Press.

BLACK NATIONALISM

Often misunderstood and misplaced historically, Black Nationalism (most often directly or indirectly interwoven with Pan-Africanist thought and practice)

has its U.S. origins in the 19th century with Paul Cuffe's (1759–1817) "Back to Africa" voyage of 1815, whereby he sailed to Sierra Leone and founded a colony with 38 free African Americans. This form of self-determination received further emphasis over the following 100 years with the works and lives of several key Black Nationalists: David Walker (1795–1830), Martin R. Delany (1812–85), Henry Highland Garnet (1815–82), Edward Wilmot Blyden (1832–1912), and Bishop Henry McNeil Turner (1834–1915). However, unlike those who wanted to resettle in Africa, Walker felt a strong desire for his people to stay and fight in North America. He contended that African Americans contributed to its growth and development and deserved to be rewarded for that labor and human misery.

Moreover, Frederick Douglass (1818–95) and, later, W. E. B. Du Bois (1868–1963) could not be deemed separatist Black Nationalists, as they spent much of their lives fighting for the democratic rights of African Americans to have a stake primarily in U.S. society. However, they each provided impetus to the Back to Africa discussion and debate. Indeed, Du Bois would eventually become a prominent player in the Pan-Africanist movement.

Black Nationalism and its key ideas in the Back to Africa and Black separatism themes often coexisted with appeals for integrationist strategies for African American progress. In other words, some Black Nationalists argued for a homeland back in Africa, whereas others argued for integration into the U.S. mainstream. Black Nationalists thus do not fit into a tidy theoretical box.

Arguably, Marcus Garvey (1887–1940), a gifted Jamaican orator, encapsulates the breadth of modern Black Nationalism. Garvey led the largest movement involving the black masses (both urban and rural) on a global scale in the 1920s. In 1914, he established the Universal Negro Improvement Association and the African Communities League to unite peoples of African descent. His attempts to provide Africans in the Diaspora with a passage back to Africa and an African continent free from European colonial rule, promote black pride and knowledge of black history, and argue for economic independence and empowerment emboldened subsequent generations of Black Nationalists.

The legacy of Black Nationalism and its meandering path includes Elijah Muhammad (1897–1975), a Garveyite who would model much of the Nation of Islam on the methods used to build the Universal

Negro Improvement Association, and Malcolm X (1925–65), whose father was a staunch Garveyite, who articulated the need for black economic, cultural, and political empowerment in black communities throughout the world. Finally, the mid-20th century brought forth the independence movement in Africa, led by Kwame Nkrumah (1909–72), and the Black Power and Black Panther movements, led by Kwame Ture (aka Stokely Carmichael, 1941–98), Bobby Seale (1936–), Huey P. Newton (1942–89), Angela Davis (1944–), and many other activists. Crucially, then, Black Nationalism today represents an evolution of thought and practice in the notion of African American self-determination.

Mark Christian

See also Black Power Movement; Race; Racism

Further Readings

Abraham, Kinfe. 1991. *Politics of Black Nationalism: From Harlem to Soweto.* Trenton, NJ: Africa World Press.

Christian, Mark, ed. 2002. *Black Identity in the 20th Century: Expressions of US and UK African Diaspora.* London: Hansib.

Essien-Udom, E. U. 1962. *Black Nationalism: A Search for Identity in America.* Chicago: University of Chicago Press.

Van Deburg, William L., ed. 1997. *Modern Black Nationalism: From Marcus Garvey to Louis Farrakhan.* New York: New York University Press.

BLACK POWER MOVEMENT

Black Power signified both a departure from, and a continuation of, the ongoing civil rights movement. Prominent during the late 1960s and 1970s, Black Power promoted an activist-oriented strategy to challenge racial oppression and exploitation. Various individuals and groups identified as part of the Black Power movement include the Black Panther Party, the Republic of New Africa, US, and the League of Revolutionary Black Workers.

The term *Black Power* originated in June 1966. During that year James Meredith, the first African American permitted to attend the University of Mississippi, conducted a one-man march against fear across the state of Mississippi. Two days into the march he was shot by a sniper and unable to complete the march. In his stead, Stokely Carmichael (1941–98), then chair of the Student Nonviolent Coordinating Committee (SNCC), encouraged supporters to continue the march. As state troopers attacked the marchers, SNCC organizer Willie Ricks (now known as Mukasa Dada) advocated that African Americans adopt a strategy of Black Power. In response, Carmichael rallied the marchers with chants of "Black Power."

Within a year Black Power had emerged as an activist-based strategy to challenge white supremacy and to promote self-determination. A critical event in the maturation of Black Power as a strategy occurred in 1967 with the publication of Stokely Carmichael (later known as Kwame Ture) and Charles Hamilton's book *Black Power: The Politics of Liberation in America.* This book not only defined a phrase, it presented the movement with a political framework and encapsulated the idea that social justice was not forthcoming through traditional political processes but rather through more radical practices.

That said, Black Power did not encompass a single ideology, and its proponents did not advocate a single political strategy. Rather, the political orientations included the ideas of Marcus Garvey (1887–1940), Malcolm X (1925–65), Frantz Fanon (1925–61), Mao Zedong (1893–1976), and Karl Marx (1818–83). Drawing on Malcolm X, for example, many advocates of Black Power eschewed integration. Both politically and economically, integration was theorized as a means of retaining and reaffirming racial inequalities and injustices. Likewise, for Carmichael and Hamilton, integration was "a subterfuge for the maintenance of white supremacy."

Common to the many variants of Black Power was a commitment to racial equality and racial pride, as well as self-defense and self-determination. Black Power was thus about putting ideas into practice. This translated into various self-defense and community-empowering projects. The form in which Black Power was put into practice reflected the local conditions confronted by activists. The Black Panther Party, for example, initiated a series of locally based and locally derived programs. These neighborhood programs—later termed *survival programs*—were designed to satisfy the immediate needs and concerns of community residents. Specific programs included petitioning for community control of the police, teaching Black history classes, promoting tenant and welfare rights, establishing health clinics, and investigating reports of police brutality.

An ideology of self-determination did not translate into isolation. Instead, many Black Power proponents, including Huey Newton, cofounder of the Black Panther Party, called for inclusion while advocating autonomy and black liberation. The argument was based on the belief that black equality could not come about while other groups were simultaneously oppressed and exploited. As a result, Black Power advocates established crucial linkages with other organizations, including those supporting women, gays, and lesbians. Furthermore, Black Power proponents, as well as specific Black Power organizations, served as templates for other organizations demanding equality and liberation from oppression and exploitation. The Black Panther Party, as an example, catalyzed other organizations, not only in the United States (e.g., the Brown Berets, the Young Lords, and the American Indian Movement) but in other countries around the world. These later organizations included the Black Beret Cadre (Bermuda), the White Panther Party (United Kingdom), the Black Panther Party of Israel, the Black Panther Party of Australia, and the Dalit Panthers (India).

Black Power should not be seen as the militant counterpart of the broader civil rights movement. To be sure, Black Power, unlike the civil rights movement, focused more attention on racial pride, empowerment, self-determination, and self-defense. Certain proponents of Black Power, moreover, contradicted the goals set forth by mainstream civil rights leaders. Those supporting Black Power, for example, favored a variant of separatism as opposed to integration. There was also a tendency among Black Power proponents to view the United States not as a land of opportunity but rather as a land of racism, prejudice, exploitation, and oppression. Indeed, many participants of the Black Power movement viewed African Americans as living under a form of domestic colonialism.

Despite these differences, however, it is best to conceive Black Power as a locally derived alternative to the civil rights movement. Although its roots stretch to the south, the Black Power movement increasingly was defined by, and focused on, the northern and western portions of the United States. The Black Power movement, consequently, initiated a shift in focus from the rural agrarian South to the more urban industrialized North. This geographic transformation highlighted the spatial variations in racist practices. Whereas African Americans in the South largely confronted de jure racist practices and policies (e.g., Jim Crow laws), those in the North and West more often experienced de facto racism. Consequently, different strategies for racial equality and social justice were required.

Black Power also entailed an important cultural component. Whereas the promotion of racial pride was vocalized through popular slogans such as "Black Is Beautiful," the movement also experienced a flourishing of the arts. Poetry and paintings, songs and novels: All promoted the ideas of black liberation and freedom. The influence of Black Power is especially seen in the changed music styles of the late 1960s. Building on the rhythm and blues of James Brown, Sam Cooke, and Ike Turner, Black Power contributed to the emergence of a distinctly "black" sound: soul music. Influential groups and musicians included the Last Poets, the Isley Brothers, Rusty Bryant, the Temptations, Edwin Starr, Marvin Gaye, Stevie Wonder, and the aforementioned James Brown. Indeed, Brown's 1968 song "Say It Loud (I'm Black and I'm Proud)" served as an official anthem of Black Power.

James Tyner

See also Chicano Movement; Civil Rights; Jim Crow; Segregation, De Facto; Segregation, De Jure

Further Readings

Joseph, Peniel E. 2006. *Waiting 'til the Midnight Hour: A Narrative History of Black Power in America.* New York: Henry Holt.

Ogbar, Jeffrey O. G. 2005. *Black Power: Radical Politics and African American Identity.* Baltimore: Johns Hopkins University Press.

Ture, Kwame and Charles V. Hamilton [1967]. 1992. *Black Power: The Politics of Liberation in America.* New York: Vintage.

Tyner, James A. 2006. *The Geography of Malcolm X: Black Radicalism and the Remaking of American Space.* New York: Routledge.

BLAMING THE VICTIM

Victim blaming is the act of attributing fault, in whole or in part, to a person or group damaged by a social or physical context or situation. It can include those hurt in an accident; victims of crime, mental illness, poverty, or nonfunctional education; and those with "undesirable" physical or cognitive characteristics. Victim blaming can be an inherent side effect of societal and professional remediation, treatment, or both. The act of blaming the victim rests on the belief that individuals are at least partially responsible for safeguarding themselves against foreseeable threats and dangers; therefore, from this perspective, individuals who fail to protect themselves are at least partly responsible for their status.

This premise operates as the basis for many social attitudes, practices, and policies regarding culpability in several spheres. For instance, home buyers are expected to inspect prospective properties for structural damages and weaknesses before finalizing purchases. If a home buyer fails to do so, such an individual must bear some responsibility for any problems with the house predating its purchase. Another example, in the case of natural disaster, is victims who failed to avoid a foreseeable catastrophe. This is also exemplified in cases of critique targeting refugees who are displaced by war and civil unrest yet had refused to abandon their homes in earlier periods of convenience or peace. More generally, it is the act of attributing culpability to individuals who suffer in a variety of contexts. Further, this process may be exacerbated by ameliorative or rehabilitative interventions. This act of attributing fault to victims because of perceived negligence or lack of vigilance against preventable damages is derogatorily referred to as "blaming the victim," especially when organizations are attempting to "help."

William Ryan coined the phrase "blaming the victim" in a 1971 book with that title in a criticism of *The Negro Family: The Case for National Action* by Daniel Moynihan. The so-called Moynihan Report attributed the social conditions and problems of black Americans to poor family structure and the overdependence of blacks on formal social systems, the latter of which Moynihan traced back to slavery. Ryan explained that in the context of the Moynihan Report, which was written by a liberal ideologue, blaming the victim is an ideological process that excuses or even justifies injustices and inequities by focusing on the imperfection of the victim. Blaming the victim then ultimately serves the group interests of those who practice it by displacing culpability for social problems from themselves and allowing the practitioner to enjoy the privileges resulting from sustaining the status quo.

Victim blaming has also received considerable attention from the social psychology field. In the 1972

work *Causal Schemata and the Attribution Process*, H. H. Kelley supposed that individuals can make one of two causal attributions for a person's behavior or circumstance. Individuals can identify personal characteristics as causes for negative outcomes, or they can attribute their conditions to environmental or situational factors. People tend to make external attributions when referring to their own failures or misfortunes yet make internal attributions when referring to their accomplishments or good fortunes. The tendency is the opposite when referring to the successes or failures of others. Victim blaming is therefore a fundamental attribution error, meaning individuals overemphasize personal characteristics and de-emphasize environmental factors in making judgments of others.

Theoreticians later proposed that the tendency to make this error is greater for individuals who strongly believe in a "just world." In a classic just-world experiment, a woman was supposedly subjected to electric shocks while working on a memory problem while participants observed her performance. Observers rated the woman's character more negatively than did observers who had not witnessed the experiment. Such individuals are thus inclined to believe good things happen to good people and bad things happen to bad people; therefore, when others find themselves in a bad predicament, more than likely it is through some fault of their own. Another explanation for attribution errors like victim blaming is that observers only have the victim as a point of reference and not the external forces that affect that victim. Therefore, they focus on the factors that they are aware of, such as character flaws, and not factors they are not privy to, for example, external systems and behaviors.

Researchers in the 1970s and 1980s studied the extent to which specific groups of people were believed to be responsible for social problems endemic to their group. Researchers found that most participants believed personal characteristics of impoverished individuals were greater factors in poverty than were societal attributes. Researchers later conducted a factor analysis of proposed internal and external attributes, deriving individualistic and structuralist scales that respectively blamed poverty on individual or societal characteristics. Similar findings were reported in 1989, suggesting that people were still more likely to choose individualistic attributes in explaining poverty. In a 1985 study of causal attributions regarding racial inequalities, researchers found results that were akin to the studies on perceived causes of poverty. Participants cited differences in levels of personal effort and values required for advancement in society as the root cause of economic and social disadvantages for minorities. In 1992, social scientists conducted a victim-blaming study regarding AIDS victims. Participants were more likely to attribute blame for the disease to individuals than to external factors. Victim blaming in cases of domestic violence and rape has also been extensively studied, with many researchers reporting that individuals with a "just-world" orientation believe victims provoke or somehow deserve an assault.

Victim blaming is contextual and moderated by several factors. Some theoreticians suggest that persons from individualistic cultures—that is, cultures that focus on individuals rather than groups—are more likely to blame the victim. Researchers have also found that moderating victim blaming is the level of tolerance for victim characteristics, social support, age, degree of one's identification with the victim, and severity of harm to the victim. One may identify acts of victim blaming as society blaming, which is also an attribution error, in that individuals overemphasize external factors as the cause of their circumstances. Moreover, one may identify efforts to prevent social problems on behalf of individuals as victim focused rather than change focused on the part of society.

William S. Davidson II and Eyitayo Onifade

See also Domestic Violence; Poverty

Further Readings

Kelley, H. H. 1972. *Causal Schemata and the Attribution Process.* New York: General Learning Press.

Ryan, William. 1976. *Blaming the Victim.* New York: Vintage Books.

BODY IMAGE

Body image refers to a person's self-perception of his or her body type and body size. This image is sometimes in keeping with the reality of a person's body size but often quite disparate from that actuality. When a disconnect exists between perceived and actual body size, harmful eating and dieting behaviors can ensue. Understanding body image provides insight into the underlying cause of severe eating disorders and unhealthy obsession with weight control. These problems are often very severe, especially for girls and women.

Standards of attractiveness have changed in U.S. culture. In the 1940s and 1950s, predominantly full-bodied women and tall, dark-haired men were seen as the most attractive. In the 1960s, a shift to much thinner body types became the norm in the fashion and entertainment industries. Since this shift, popular culture images consistently show thin, or often extremely thin, women as the standard of beauty. For men, muscle strength remains the predominant physical feature of attractiveness. The prevalence of attractive models and characters influences consumers to compare themselves to these images, and this increased focus on ultra-thin women affects the body image of young girls and women.

Gender differences in body image are the focus of much social science research, which consistently shows that compared with men and boys, women and girls are more susceptible to poor body images and the problems associated with a poor self-image. Women are far more likely to be diagnosed with anorexia nervosa and bulimia nervosa. These are harmful, often life-threatening, diseases leading women to cause serious damage to their digestive and central nervous systems by extreme dieting and eating behaviors. Although men and boys are also diagnosed with eating disorders, the statistics show women and girls are at much greater risk.

Some of the risk-taking behaviors associated with eating disorders are self-induced vomiting, excessive use of laxatives and appetite suppressants, and self-starvation. Some unhealthy eating and dieting practices are also associated with weight gain. Overeating (or bingeing) and steroid use cause the individual to bulk up. Overeating leads to obesity, a major cause of disease in North America. Steroid use is associated with myriad health problems and is far too common among athletic males who desire to bulk up their muscle mass. Social science research must consider the different techniques used to control weight, including the consumption of food, the use of drugs, and exercise habits.

Media representations of beautiful people continue to show men and women differently. For women and girls specifically, we see a demand for thin women with big breasts and little tolerance for overweight women. For men, on the other hand, popular culture images of overweight men meet with much less resistance. Studies show that women in the entertainment industry must achieve and maintain thin waistlines, large breasts, toned skin and muscles, perfectly coiffed hair, and well-defined facial features. This ideal is largely consistent across all media of popular culture. Women who do not meet these criteria are hidden from public display. Men, however, may be overweight and short, yet featured prominently on television and in film. Although product advertisements still rely heavily on male models who are tall, thin, and muscular, more roles in television and film exist for men who do not fit into those images than for women not fitting the attractiveness standards. This leads to an overabundance of popular images of thin women.

The media images of thin women, combined with the increased attention to health concerns regarding weight, result in an increase in women engaging in extreme measures to become or stay thin. Women may also overexercise in an effort to obtain the ideal body size. A woman suffering from anorexia nervosa can achieve an overly thin body size by excessively exercising and undereating. While self-starvation has historically been the major symptom of anorexia, counselors and doctors now also pay attention to extreme exercising habits.

Health professionals and organizations, such as the Centers for Disease Control and Prevention, highlight the problem of overweight Americans because of their concern about obesity and related diseases. For children, especially, problems associated with obesity are increasing in number. Critics call the United States a "culture of excess," with large meals and food portions, easy access to fast foods and sweets, and little time for physical activity. In an effort to combat obesity, specifically among children, experts advocate physical fitness and exercise. Gym memberships, exercise programs, and diet plans are big business. For women with poor body image, extreme efforts to be thin hide behind the guise of healthy lifestyle. For others, of course, this health-conscious approach to life is a welcome change and a needed benefit for health improvement. Society should give more attention to the contradictory messages regarding weight and appearance, particularly the unrealistic images of thin women as portrayed in popular culture. Combined with a societal "push" to be active and

physically fit, these unrealistic images contribute to a nation of women engaging in unhealthy eating and dieting behaviors. Whether overweight and overeating, or super thin, starving, and overexercising, women and girls struggle with their body image.

In other parts of the world, similar beauty standards exist. While some variation occurs between cultures of how women and men display beauty, thin bodies prevail in both Western and non-Western cultures as the female ideal. Skin tone, facial features, hair texture, and overall figure also determine beauty according to cultural standards. Given the global diversity of men and women, standardizing these individual features becomes problematic. The Western model woman is typically tall and thin, with straight hair and smooth skin tone. Facial features are proportionate with a small thin nose, with full lips and white straight teeth. Eye color is usually a light blue or green. For men, specific facial features receive less attention. Tall men with dark hair, white teeth, and muscular yet thin bodies remain as the standard of attractiveness. In essence, the Westernized image of attractive is now a global one.

One standard of attractiveness—based on a white ideal of beauty—results in problems for women and men of different racial/ethnic identities. Early research concluded that African American women value a larger female body type than do white Americans. The explanation purported that the black culture prefers full-figured, overweight, black women; therefore, black women were less susceptible to eating disorders. Several problems exist with this conclusion. First, even if we accept the assumption that there is a fundamental difference in the African American culture regarding attractiveness, black women may still be at risk for unhealthy eating and dieting. Obesity is statistically higher among the black American population, putting black men, women, and children at much greater health risk. Additionally, the "cultural differences" conclusion precludes continued discussion of racial/ethnic differences in body image.

Social science research must continue to address the racial/ethnic differences in body image and efforts to modify or maintain appearance. More research, for example, needs to be done on Asian Americans, Latinos/as, and other groups to uncover the influence of the popular image of attractiveness on body image. Finally, the earlier conclusions about black America dismiss the increased pressure on African American women, and *all* women, to obtain the thin, white ideal body size and type. Hair straightening, teeth whitening, skin toners, and plastic surgeries all exist in a society that overvalues appearance and undervalues achievement.

Body image is a complex issue. The personal trouble of an unhealthy or unrealistic self-image can lead to serious mental and physical health concerns. The larger concern, however, is the social problem of competing pressures and ideals that result in a culture of poor self-worth and body image dysfunction. Social science must focus research on an improved understanding of the gender and racial differences in body image and efforts to achieve the cultural standard of beauty. With this improved understanding should come improved efforts to address the problems of negative body image and unhealthy eating and dieting behavior.

Kim A. Logio

See also Eating Disorders; Mass Media; Media; Obesity; Social Constructionist Theory

Further Readings

McCabe, Marita P. and Lina A. Ricciardelli. 2003. "Sociocultural Influences on Body Image and Body Changes among Adolescent Boys and Girls." *The Journal of Social Psychology* 143:5–26.

Poran, Maya A. 2006. "The Politics of Protection: Body Image, Social Pressures, and the Misrepresentation of Young Black Women." *Sex Roles* 55:739–55.

Thompson, Becky W. 1996. *A Hunger So Wide and So Deep: A Multiracial View of Women's Eating Problems.* Minneapolis, MN: University of Minnesota Press.

Wolf, Naomi. 2002. *The Beauty Myth: How Images of Beauty Are Used against Women.* New York: William Morrow.

BOOMERANG GENERATION

The Boomerang Generation refers to a trend in North America of young adult children, generally between the ages of 18 and 30, returning home to reside with their middle-aged parents in greater numbers than young adults in previous generations. Tied closely to social psychological life course theory, the concept offers a visual metaphor of young adults who "boomerang"—returning to and leaving the family home on several occasions before forming their own households. This pattern violates age-norm expectations that children separate physically from their parents and make their own lives sometime between age 18 and age 24.

If the transition to adulthood is defined by a series of milestones that include completing education or training, achieving economic independence, and forming long-term partnerships or establishing one's own family, the young adult who lives at home can be seen as not fully adult. Delays in home leaving, and returns home after one has left, signify new expectations about adulthood and what it means for the different generations in the household. Research on the family life course examines several questions about this phenomenon: To what extent are young adults today more likely to live at home with their parents? To what extent does this family arrangement represent something new? Who is helping whom with what; that is, what is the familial exchange (parents to child, child to parent, mutual aid)? Finally, what is the impact of such a family arrangement on coresident adults of different generations?

The most recent U.S. Census Bureau figures show that of the youngest young adults, 18 to 24 years old, more than 50 percent of young men and 43 percent of young women lived at home in 2000. Among "older" young adults, 25 to 34 years old, 12 percent of men and only 5 percent of women lived with a parent. This continues a trend first noted in the 1980s when the age of home leaving increased. It is harder to ascertain how many young adults leave home and then return home more than once, but their chances of doing so doubled between the 1920s and the 1980s. One group of researchers estimate that 40 percent return home at least once. The younger the young adult, the greater the likelihood that he or she will return on several occasions, suggesting a more nuanced pattern of establishing independence than in the past.

Why are young adults today more likely to live with their parents? The timing and frequency of standard reasons for leaving home have changed. Generally, adult children still leave home to take a job, to get married, to go to college or university away from home, or to join the military. The typical permanent path to home leaving—getting married—is occurring later, around age 25 or 26, which means more young adults than ever before have never married. Other reasons that may contribute to young adults returning home include economic ones: poorly paid employment, high cost of housing, and the trade-off between the child's loss of privacy and the ability to save money while living with parents. Leaving home expressly because the adult child wants to be independent, which can include cohabitation with a lover or roommates or living alone, is more likely to lead back to living with parents at a later date. There are also marked cultural differences within some immigrant groups, where children are expected to live at home well into adulthood, and across native-born racial/ethnic groups.

The presence of adult children has implications for middle-aged parents or older parents whose children return to live with them. Except for the frail elderly, parents are more likely to provide the home, help, and support to their adult children than the reverse. The likelihood of being welcome at home depends on the parental situation as well as the reasons why the child lives at home. Those parents in intact, first marriages are more likely to welcome adult children back than are divorced or remarried parents. Parents who have small families are more likely to offer an adult child support than those who have large families. The unhappiest parents are those whose children have left and returned on several occasions, returning because of failure in the job market or in pursuit of education. Otherwise, parents of younger adults do not report marital problems or unhappiness specifically related to having their children back in the nest.

Thus, the idea of middle-aged parents, sandwiched between their elderly parents and demanding young adult boomerang kids who refuse to grow up or who are unable to do so, may overstate a gradual trend in families and households. Leaving home sooner or later and leaving home for good are largely related to changes in marriage patterns and to specific historical events that shaped the young adulthood of particular generations, such as world wars or access to higher education. Although some young adults will take a longer time to leave the nest completely, returning and leaving on occasion, and others will stay longer than in earlier generations, most young adults continue to endorse the norm of living independently as soon as possible.

Elizabeth Hartung

See also Cohabitation; Family; Family, Extended; Life Course; Sandwich Generation

Further Readings

Fields, Jason. 2004. *America's Families and Living Arrangements.* Current Population Reports, P20-553. Washington, DC: U.S. Government Printing Office.
Goldscheider, Frances, Calvin Goldscheider, Patricia St. Clair, and James Hodges. 1999. "Changes in Returning Home in the United States, 1925–1988." *Social Forces* 78:695–721.
Messineo, Melinda and Roger Wojtkiewicz. 2004. "Coresidence of Adult Children with Parents from 1960 to 1990: Is the Propensity to Live at Home Really Increasing?" *Journal of Family History* 29:71–83.

BOOT CAMPS

Correctional "boot camps" have existed as part of the U.S. penal system for the past quarter century. In most states, young, first-time offenders participate in lieu of a prison term or probation; likewise, in certain jurisdictions, an adolescent can be sentenced to serve time (ranging from 90 to 180 days) in a boot camp instead of being given a prison sentence of up to 10 years. How the offender serves his or her time (either in jail or at a penal boot camp) differs among facilities and individual states. Prisoners not finishing a program must serve the original prison sentence.

Although still considered punishment, being sentenced to a boot camp became accepted as an alternative sentencing choice because many pundits felt it offered a better outcome (for adults and adolescents) than did traditional sentencing. It was hoped that by inserting nonviolent, low-risk offenders into a highly disciplined environment for a short time, these perpetrators (as envisioned) would learn new skills that would help prevent them from returning to a life of crime. Depending on the specific program, a boot camp's composition involved inmates learning discipline, experiencing regimentation and drill, physical conditioning, hygiene and sanitation, work, education, treatment, and therapy.

The average individual thinks of the military model when hearing the term *boot camp*, though other approaches exist as well. To recognize the wide range of methods, the definition expanded to include "work-intensive correctional programs" that did not technically qualify as boot camps but had related features: for instance, a 16-hour workday filled with laborious work, arduous physical training, studying, and counseling. Experiential programs (camps providing young offenders with a mixture of physical activity, athletic contests with fellow detainees, and challenging outdoor experiences) were the norm, not the exception. However, when the public thought about boot camps, the concept centered on military discipline to generate respect for authority while emphasizing good support services once an inmate was released—with an overriding purpose of reducing recidivism.

Boot camps were referred to as "shock incarceration" (someone becomes so frightened that he or she voluntarily obeys the law). Usually, drill instructors forced inmates dressed in army fatigues to perform push-ups, chin-ups, and pull-ups for breaking any of the many rules. The program's primary goal was to give young offenders a "taste" of prison for a short period and then release them back into the community under supervision.

Even at the beginning, boot camps' success was guarded. Evaluation research produced mixed results, suggesting that the boot camp approach did not achieve its objective as originally hoped. Evaluations in Louisiana and Georgia indicated that boot camp graduates did no better in terms of re-arrests than inmates freed from prison or on probation and were, in fact, more likely to have parole revoked for technical violations. More serious, however, were deaths that were caused by drill instructor negligence, for example, thinking an adolescent was "malingering" when he or she was dying from dehydration.

Cary Stacy Smith, Li-Ching Hung,
and Cindy Tidwell

See also Juvenile Delinquency; Juvenile Justice System

Further Readings

Benda, Brent B. and Nathaniel J. Pallone, eds. 2005. *Rehabilitation Issues, Problems, and Prospects in Boot Camp.* New York: Haworth.

Cromwell, Paul, Leanne Fiftal Alarid, and Rolando V. del Carmen. 2005. *Community-Based Corrections.* 6th ed. Florence, KY: Wadsworth.

Langan, Patrick A. and David J. Levin. 2002. *Recidivism of Prisoners Released in 1994.* Washington, DC: U.S. Department of Justice, Bureau of Justice Statistics.

MacKenzie, Doris L. and Eugene E. Herbert, eds. 1996. *Correctional Boot Camps: A Tough Intermediate Sanction.* New York: Diane Publishing.

BOOTSTRAP THEORY

Bootstrap theory refers to social practices and laws dedicated to helping people help themselves; these practices range from the Puerto Rican industrialization project titled "Operation Bootstrap" in the mid-20th century to U.S. ideology and social policy in the post–welfare reform state.

Bootstrap theory was first intimated in an official policy called Operation Bootstrap (Operación Manos a la Obra), an ambitious project to industrialize Puerto Rico in 1948. The architect of Operation Bootstrap was Teodoro Moscoso (1910–92), a supporter of the then recently established Popular Democratic Party, who argued that a densely populated island like Puerto Rico could not subsist on an agrarian system alone. Therefore, U.S. companies were enticed to build factories that provided labor at costs below those within the United States, access to U.S. markets without import duties, and profits that could enter the mainland free from federal taxation.

To entice participation, tax exemptions and differential rental rates were offered for industrial facilities. As a result, Puerto Rico's economy shifted labor from agriculture (food, tobacco, leather, and apparel products) to manufacturing and tourism (pharmaceuticals, chemicals, machinery, and electronics). Although initially touted as an economic miracle, Operation Bootstrap, by the 1960s, was increasingly hampered by a growing unemployment problem and global free-market competition.

In more recent years, bootstrap theory reached a high level of mainstream acceptance as welfare came to represent an unpopular token commitment to a poor, disproportionately minority population that was thought to unfairly usurp government resources and tax dollars. After President William J. Clinton signed the Personal Responsibility and Work Opportunity Reconciliation Act on August 22, 1996, welfare was abolished and replaced with a bootstrap theory–motivated structure called "workfare." First, workfare forced people who had been on welfare to enter the labor market, and second, it shunned the "paternalism" of welfare by allowing citizens to remove themselves from a possible cycle of dependency.

Under these circumstances, "bootstrap capitalism" became a main rationale for ending federal or state support for the impoverished. Bootstrap capitalism was manifested in three distinct modalities: wage supplements, asset building, and community capitalism. First, bootstrap theory was realized in wage supplements from tax credits for both low-wage workers and their employers. Second, asset building from promoting institutional development accounts to microenterprises was a key facet of bootstrap theory. Third, bootstrap theory relied upon the idea of community capitalism whereby federal aid gave earmarked funds to create community financial institutions, as well as *block grants*—federal funds given to individual states for applications of their choice. Bootstrap theory is an overall commitment to individualism, meritocracy, a strong work ethic, free-market competition, and private ownership.

Matthew W. Hughey

See also Welfare; Welfare Capitalism

Further Readings

Cordasco, Francesco and Eugene Bucchioni. 1973. *The Puerto Rican Experience: A Sociological Sourcebook.* Totowa, NJ: Littlefield, Adams.

Fernandez, Ronald. 1996. *The Disenchanted Island: Puerto Rico and the United States in the Twentieth Century.* New York: Praeger.

Maldonado, Alex W. 1997. *Teodoro Moscoso and Puerto Rico's Operation Bootstrap.* Gainesville, FL: University Press of Florida.

Meléndez, Edwin and Edgardo Meléndez. 1993. *Colonial Dilemma: Critical Perspectives on Contemporary Puerto Rico.* Cambridge, MA: South End Press.

Rivera-Batiz, Francisco L. and Carlos E. Santiago. 1997. *Island Paradox: Puerto Rico in the 1990s.* New York: Russell Sage Foundation.

Servon, Lisa J. 1999. *Bootstrap Capital: Microenterprises and the American Poor.* Washington, DC: Brookings Institution Press.

Stoesz, David. 2000. *A Poverty of Imagination: Bootstrap Capitalism, Sequel to Welfare Reform.* Madison, WI: University of Wisconsin Press.

BRACERO PROGRAM

The U.S.–Mexico Bracero Program was a temporary worker program that began in 1942 and lasted until 1964. Designed to be a wartime labor relief measure, agricultural producers successfully pressured the United States into extending the program for 22 years. During that time, 4.5 million individual work contracts were signed by approximately 2 million Mexican farmworkers. During World War II, the U.S. railroad industry also employed *Braceros* (a term referring to arms or *brazos* in Spanish and translating as "worker"). Although the vast majority of workers went to three states (California, Arizona, and Texas), 30 U.S. states participated in the program, and every state in Mexico sent workers northward. Workers were severely disempowered in their attempts to secure the rights guaranteed to them in the agreements made between both governments.

The Bracero Program began on August 4, 1942, in Stockton, California, as a result of the U.S. government responding to requests by southwest growers to recruit foreign labor. Nine months later the railroad industry secured the importation of Mexican laborers to meet wartime shortages. The agreement between the federal governments of Mexico and the United States laid out four general guidelines for the Mexican contract workers: (1) no U.S. military service; (2) protection against discriminatory acts; (3) guaranteed transportation, living expenses, and repatriation along the lines established under Article 29 of the Mexican labor laws; and (4) their employment would not displace domestic workers or reduce their wages.

The first guideline quelled Mexican popular discontent and apprehension based on earlier abuses (during World War I) of Mexican labor that occurred during the first Bracero Program. The second guideline, which explicitly banned discrimination against Mexican nationals, served as the key bargaining chip that the Mexican government utilized to promote the decent treatment of Braceros by U.S. growers. From 1942 to 1947, no Braceros were sent to Texas because of documentation of such mistreatment. Only after a series of anti-discrimination assurances by the Texas government were growers there allowed to import Braceros. The Mexican government also blacklisted Colorado, Illinois, Indiana, Michigan, Montana, Minnesota, Wisconsin, and Wyoming until the 1950s because of discriminatory practices documented in those states.

The third guideline guaranteed workers safe passage to and from the United States as well as decent living conditions while working in the United States. Braceros thus did not pay transportation costs from the recruitment centers in Mexico to the U.S. processing centers and eventual job sites. They did shoulder the traveling costs from their hometowns to the Mexican recruitment centers, and these costs varied depending on where the recruitment centers were located and how long men waited before receiving a contract. The U.S. government preferred recruitment centers near the border to reduce their costs, whereas the Mexican government wanted centers in the major sending states of Central Mexico where the majority of Braceros originated.

The final guideline reduced competition between domestic and contracted labor. To ensure that Braceros received the same wage as U.S. citizens, determination of the prevailing wage in each locale prior to the harvest season established the wage that Braceros received. Labor organizer Ernesto Galarza noted that although the Department of Labor set the prevailing wage, it was growers who collectively determined the prevailing wage they were willing to pay.

With regard to all four guidelines, workers experienced a much different Bracero Program than the one designed on paper. Scholars have documented the inadequate housing; dehumanizing treatment; substandard wages; exorbitant prices for inedible food; illegal deductions for food, insurance, and health care; inadequate and unsafe transportation; and lack of legal rights and protections.

After potential Braceros secured the necessary paperwork from their local officials, their first stop was in Mexico at a recruitment center designed to assemble a qualified labor force of experienced, male workers, who were assigned numbers and processed by those numbers. Next, in the U.S. processing centers, the men stripped for inspection for hernias, sexually transmitted diseases, and communicable diseases such as tuberculosis. If they passed, a delousing spraying with DDT followed before they dressed. The weeding out of "undesirables" even included inspections of workers' calloused hands to ensure they were adept at agricultural tasks. Representatives of growers' associations then chose which men they would employ as workers and what work they would do.

The transportation, housing, and boarding of Braceros were an extension of the batch-handling. Living conditions for Braceros were similar to the military, as Braceros typically lived in barracks complete with a mess hall that served institutionally prepared meals. Less-desirable living arrangements included tents, chicken coops, barns, Japanese internment camps, high school gymnasiums, and stockyards. If Braceros lodged a complaint about negative treatment, they had to fear reprisal in the form of deportation. No shifts to other jobs were possible because contracts explicitly tied them to a specific employer, and Braceros were powerless to negotiate with their employers.

Given limited options for active protest, Braceros' main form of resistance was the exit option. Low wages, bad food, excessive deductions from paychecks, poor housing, domineering supervisors, or on-the-job injuries prompted many Braceros to leave their contracts. An estimated 20 percent to 33 percent exited the Bracero Program. A significant (but uncounted) number who stayed refused to return to the United States for other crop seasons.

Since 2000, former Braceros have organized to recoup losses suffered during the program. A march on Mexico City first brought the savings program issue to the Mexican public (10 percent of their wages were deducted automatically and placed in Mexican national banks to encourage men to return). A more recent pilgrimage to the border, like the former march to the original soccer stadium where Braceros were processed during World War II, followed the earlier path north to the border recruitment centers. *Alianza Braceroproa,* National Assembly of Ex-Braceros, and the Binational Union of Former Braceros are the main social movement organizations placing pressure on the Mexican government for monetary redress.

Ronald L. Mize

See also Chicano Movement; Discrimination; Labor, Migrant; Social Movements

Further Readings

Calavita, Kitty. 1992. *Inside the State: The Bracero Program, Immigration and the I.N.S.* New York: Routledge.

Galarza, Ernesto. 1956. *Strangers in Our Fields.* Washington, DC: United States Section, Joint United States–Mexico Trade Union Committee.

———. 1964. *Merchants of Labor: The Mexican Bracero History.* Santa Barbara, CA: McNally & Loftin.

Gamboa, Erasmo. 1990. *Mexican Labor and World War II: Braceros in the Pacific Northwest, 1942–1947.* Austin, TX: University of Texas Press.

Mize, Ronald L. 2004. "The Persistence of Workplace Identities: Living the Effects of the Bracero Total Institution." Pp. 155–75 in *Immigrant Life in the US: Multidisciplinary Perspectives,* edited by D. R. Gabaccia and C. W. Leach. New York: Routledge.

BROWN V. BOARD OF EDUCATION

Brown v. Board of Education, 347 U.S. 483 (1954), was a landmark Supreme Court case that overturned the "separate but equal" doctrine of *Plessy v. Ferguson,* 169 U.S. 537 (1896), ruling that blacks and whites be allowed to attend the same public schools. The decision was a major blow to the system of southern de jure segregation, which required by law that blacks and whites be separated in all areas of public facilities, such as waiting rooms, restaurants, hotels, buses and trains, drinking fountains, and even cemeteries.

Racial segregation in public schools was especially problematic because it was clear that schools for white children and schools for black children were not equal and could not be made equal if they were to retain racial separation. The average amount spent by southern cities for each black pupil was usually less than half that spent on each white pupil. In many parts of the South, black children were forced to travel long distances to attend schools lacking basic facilities and qualified teachers. Some rural schools provided instruction for only 3 months out of the year; others provided no high school for black children. Even in urban areas of the South, schools were overcrowded and lacked the amenities of whites-only schools.

The case of *Brown v. Board of Education* rested on a class action suit filed in 1951 against the Board of Education of the City of Topeka, Kansas, by the local NAACP (National Association for the Advancement of Colored People) on behalf of 13 plaintiffs. Among those plaintiffs, Oliver Brown—for whom the case is named—served on behalf of his daughter, Linda Brown. Miss Brown lived in a racially mixed neighborhood but had to travel more than an hour to attend school because her neighborhood school was segregated white. Because Kansas was a border state, and Topeka was not racially segregated in all areas of public facilities (e.g., waiting rooms), the NAACP strategically chose the city as its next battleground in the effort to desegregate public life. It was just one of five cases decided within the *Brown* decision, which included cases from South Carolina (*Briggs v. Elliott*), Delaware (*Gebhart v. Belton*), Virginia (*Davis v. County School Board of Prince Edward County*), and Washington, D.C. (*Bolling v. Sharpe*). Out of the five cases, *Brown v. Board of Education* was the only case predicated on black parents' constitutional right to send their children to local neighborhood schools.

This was a major shift in the argument for dismantling a system of racial inequality and segregation: that racial segregation is inherently unequal regardless of the quality of public facilities.

One of the compelling arguments used in the *Brown* decision against segregated schools was that segregation causes psychological harm to individuals forced into segregation by the dominant group. This argument was based on the social scientific work of psychologists Kenneth B. Clark and Mamie Phipps Clark. Clark and Clark conducted experiments in which they showed black children in segregated schools and nonsegregated schools pictures of brown and white dolls. A majority of black children tested in a southern segregated school said that they preferred white dolls over brown dolls, leading the researchers to conclude that segregation caused self-loathing and acceptance of racist stereotypes in these black children.

Clark and Clark also argued that the lack of cross-status contact inherent in segregation causes hostility and suspicion between races. The historical assumption behind racial segregation was that segregated groups are intellectually and socially inferior and thus should be separated from the dominant group. The Clarks and other social scientists questioned this assumption by making the point that segregation produces inequality by creating different and unequal environments resulting in observable differences between races. This was effectively argued in an appendix (signed by 32 prominent psychologists) to the appellants' briefs in the *Brown, Briggs,* and *Davis* cases. A number of other social scientific works were cited in these briefs, including Gunnar Myrdal's famous work on U.S. racial inequality, *An American Dilemma,* of 1944.

Brown v. Board of Education was decided in a unanimous 9–0 vote on May 17, 1954, in favor of the plaintiff. Chief Justice Earl Warren delivered the opinion of the court. He argued that public education was an increasingly important right of U.S. citizens and that individuals who are denied equal access to education are denied full citizenship in violation of the 14th Amendment of the U.S. Constitution, which guarantees equal protection under the law. Although the separate facilities for black and white children in Kansas were not measurably different, Warren argued that forced legal segregation makes black children feel inferior, retarding their "educational and mental development," and concluded that separate but equal facilities in education are inherently unequal.

The *Brown* ruling was a victory for civil rights, but it was not until 1955 that the Supreme Court ordered states to comply with the ruling "with all deliberate speed" (in an ambiguous, open-ended ruling often referred to as *Brown II*). Not until the 1970s did many southern schools become desegregated, by which time many white students had fled to private schools. Subsequent critiques of the *Brown* ruling question the effectiveness of public school desegregation, which some argue did nothing to solve the problem of racial inequality, institutional racism, and segregation in other, nonpublic areas of life.

In 2006, the Supreme Court reassessed Brown's legal interpretation in two cases, dealing with Seattle, Washington, and Louisville, Kentucky. Both cities had color-conscious policies that specifically sought to create a more balanced and racially integrated school system. Although students in each city had school choice, they could be denied admission based on race if their attendance would disrupt the racial balance in the school. On June 27, 2007, the Supreme Court ruled by a 5–4 vote along ideological grounds that school admission programs in Seattle and Louisville violated the Constitution's guarantee of equal protection to individuals. Because this decision stipulates race cannot be used to decide where students go to school, educators believe it may lead many districts to drop efforts at racially balancing schools.

Meghan Ashlin Rich

See also Jim Crow; *Plessy v. Ferguson;* Racism; School Segregation; Segregation, De Facto; Segregation, De Jure

Further Readings

Barnes, Robert. 2007. "Divided Court Limits Use of Race by School Districts." *Washington Post,* June 29, p. A01.

Clark, Kenneth B., Isidor Chein, and Stuart W. Cook. 2004. "The Effects of Segregation and the Consequences of Desegregation: A (September 1952) Social Science Statement in the *Brown v. Board of Education of Topeka* Supreme Court Case." *American Psychologist* 59(6):495–501.

Myrdal, Gunnar. 1944. *An American Dilemma: The Negro Problem and Modern Democracy.* New York: Harper & Brothers.

Patterson, James T. 2001. Brown v. Board of Education: *A Civil Rights Milestone and Its Troubled Legacy.* New York: Oxford University Press.

BUDGET DEFICITS, U.S.

Demographic conditions profoundly affect the U.S. federal budget. Roughly one half of spending outside of interest on the debt and defense goes to people age 65 and over. In 2006, combined Social Security, Medicare, and Medicaid spending averaged over $30,000 per capita for the older population. The first baby boomer will apply for Social Security in 2008 and for Medicare in 2011, and shortly after, spending pressures will soar.

Just as spending pressures will accumulate rapidly, tax revenue growth will decline because of a slowing in the growth of the working population. The slowdown will be the result of baby boomer retirements and a scarcity of younger entrants into the labor force. Simply put, the boomers did not have enough children to support them comfortably in their old age.

The combination of accelerating spending and decelerating revenue growth will place enormous upward pressures on budget deficits unless spending programs for the elderly are reformed, tax burdens are raised far above historically normal levels, or other government programs are cut to almost nothing. If deficits are allowed to drift upward continually, international financial markets will eventually become concerned about the future of the U.S. economy. At best, international and U.S. domestic investors will then demand higher interest rates and higher returns on U.S. equities before they are willing to buy U.S. bonds and stocks. At worst, investor concerns could cause a financial panic and do grave harm to the U.S. economy.

It is important to differentiate two very different types of economic cost imposed by deficits. Mild deficits erode a nation's wealth and therefore its standard of living in the long run. That is because deficits are financed by selling debt to either Americans or foreigners. If Americans did not use their savings to buy this debt, they probably would invest in housing or in business equipment and buildings in the United States and that would add to American wealth and productivity in the long run. Added productivity results in higher wages and therefore higher U.S. living standards.

To the extent that foreigners buy the debt, the United States will have to pay them interest in the future. The U.S.-generated income used for this purpose will not be available to Americans, and again, U.S. living standards will suffer. The erosion of U.S. living standards caused by mild deficits occurs slowly and is barely noticeable in the short run. But over the long run, it slowly accumulates and eventually becomes quite significant.

However, the negative effect on living standards is not the main concern raised by growing deficits. As deficits grow, the nation's debt will eventually start to grow faster than its income. Then interest on the debt will also grow faster than income. If a nation starts to borrow to cover a growing interest bill as well as a portion of its noninterest spending, it can quickly get into very serious trouble. An ordinary household would too under similar circumstances. The interest bill begins to explode, and at some point, a household declares bankruptcy. A nation has another recourse. It can print money. But then inflation explodes and can easily reach 10,000 percent per year, or even more than 1,000,000 percent, as it did in the case of the Weimar Republic in the 1920s.

At what point should investors become worried about a debt explosion leading to hyperinflation? The ratio of the government's debt to the nation's gross domestic product (GDP) is an important indicator. If a government borrows enough every year to cause its debt to grow faster than the nation's total income, there is some reason to worry. Of course, this need not be an intense worry if the nation starts with a very low ratio of debt to GDP, and the United States' ratio is quite low relative to that of most other developed nations. Nevertheless, if the United States does nothing to reform its programs for the elderly or to raise taxes dramatically, the ratio will begin to rise at a very rapid rate after about 2015.

At what point do deficits raise the national debt faster than income? Economists focus on something called the *primary surplus* or *deficit*, which is noninterest spending minus revenues. Why is interest spending ignored in this calculation? In the long run, the interest rate on the public debt gravitates toward the growth rate of the economy. Let us assume that both the interest rate and the economic growth rate equal 5 percent. If the government borrows just enough to cover the interest bill on the debt, the debt will grow 5 percent. With the economy also growing at 5 percent, the ratio of debt to GDP will be constant. If the government borrows less than the interest bill, that is to say, runs a primary surplus, the ratio of debt to GDP is likely to fall in the longer run. Thus, it is considered prudent to always strive for a primary surplus.

That does not mean that government should never allow the debt-to-GDP ratio to rise over limited time periods. It would be very wasteful to raise and lower tax rates with every wiggle in expenditures. If a country is confronted by a temporary surge of spending because of a war or a major investment project, it makes sense to borrow temporarily even if the ratio of debt to GDP rises for a time. The same is true when a recession temporarily reduces revenue. Raising taxes could worsen the recession, although that theory is more controversial than it once was.

The budget duress caused by the aging of the population is not temporary. The problem will persist and worsen rapidly if there is no significant change in policy. It would be better to implement the necessary policy changes gradually and deliberatively rather than hastily when frightened by a panic in financial markets.

Rudolph G. Penner

See also Bankruptcy, Business; Bankruptcy, Personal; Debt Service; Population, Graying of

Further Readings

Kotlikoff, Laurence J. and Scott Burns. 2005. *The Coming Generational Storm.* Cambridge, MA: MIT Press.

Penner, Rudolph G. and C. Eugene Steuerle. 2003. *The Budget Crisis at the Door.* Washington, DC: Urban Institute.

Rivlin, Alice M. and Isabel Sawhill, eds. 2005. *Restoring Fiscal Sanity 2005.* Washington, DC: Brookings Institution Press.

BULLYING

Bullying refers to aggressive behavior intended to harm the physical well-being of the victim or to create a feeling of fear and intimidation. Bullying includes physical assaults, physical intimidation, psychological intimidation, name-calling, teasing, social isolation, and exclusion. Two characteristics distinguish bullying from other forms of aggressive behavior. The first is the repetitive and prolonged nature of the bullying act; hence, not all name-calling is a form of bullying. Many students experience verbal insults by their peers, but the name-calling does not rise to the level of bullying until the student experiences it regularly over a period of time. The second characteristic that distinguishes bullying from other forms of aggressive behavior is the status inequality between bully and victim. In comparison, the victim is physically, psychologically, and socially more vulnerable, which allows the bully to engage in the behavior with little concern for reprisals or other consequences. For example, physical assaults might be classified as acts of bullying if the victims were selected because they lacked the resources to defend themselves due to their physical stature, psychological profile, or social skills.

Until the 1970s, the problem of bullying received little attention from educators, researchers, or the general public. Bullying behavior was viewed as almost a rite of passage that most young people experience at some point during their childhood, adolescence, or both. Such a perception led to the belief that bullying behavior had no long-term consequences for either the victim or the bully. Today, the research suggests that neither perception is true. Both bullies and their victims are socially and psychologically different from their peers, and there are lasting implications for both. Not only has the traditional view of bullying as a rite of passage undermined our understanding of the causes and consequences of bullying; it may also have supported a "culture of bullying" within our education system.

A Culture of Bullying

Research suggests that the environment within schools is inadvertently supportive of bullying, thus creating a "culture of bullying." For a school's environment to be so described, it must possess two critical components that undermine the school's ability to act as a protector against bullying and instead allow development of a milieu that not only tolerates bullying behavior but also allows bullies to enhance their social standing through aggression without fear of consequences. First, it must possess an administration and faculty that are unaware of the extent of bullying behavior and therefore fail to effectively protect vulnerable students from being victimized or to punish those students who engage in bullying behavior. The research is consistent in suggesting that the schools' response to bullying is often ineffective in curbing the problem. In addition, schools rarely hold bullies responsible for their behavior when their behavior is brought to the attention of the faculty. This lack of effective response may be due to other social problems to which the schools must respond,

such as teen pregnancy, alcohol and drug use, and other forms of violence. However, by focusing on these more "serious" problems within the schools, administrators may be ignoring an important precursor to these behaviors.

The second component that creates a culture of bullying within the educational system is the reaction of the student witnesses. Although some student eyewitnesses will intervene on behalf of the victim, the majority of students either become passive bystanders or else active participants in the bullying. Students who act as passive bystanders usually fear the consequences for themselves in an environment where the adults cannot be relied on to punish the bullies. Therefore, victims of bullying usually cannot depend on their fellow students to act as capable guardians against bullying behavior. Students who become active participants in the bullying act do so because the victim may be viewed by their peers and the faculty as an acceptable target because of an outcast status within the school social system. The culture of bullying evolves because both the school and the student body fail to send the message that bullying behavior is unacceptable behavior. Instead, they may be sending the message that aggression against a social outcast is tolerated, if not condoned, as a means of resolving problems and improving one's social standing.

The Bullies

The psychological profile of bullies suggests that they suffer from low self-esteem and a poor self-image. In addition, bullies can be described as angry or depressed and tend to act impulsively. In comparison to their peers, bullies possess a value system that supports the use of aggression to resolve problems and achieve goals. Finally, school is a negative situation for the bullies, who tend to perform at or below average in school and are unhappy in school. Further, teachers and peers view them as a disruptive influence. Due to their psychological profile, value system, and attitude toward school, bullies rely on aggression to solve school-based problems and to establish their position in the school hierarchy. While the research clearly demonstrates that bullying behavior is most common among middle school students and steadily declines with age, bullies may nonetheless graduate into more serious anti-social behaviors, including drug and alcohol use/abuse, delinquency, spousal abuse, and adult criminal behavior.

The Victims

Bullies do not select their targets at random; rather, they select targets specifically for their vulnerability. Victims are typically shy, socially awkward, low in self-esteem, and lacking in self-confidence. Furthermore, these characteristics reduce the victims' social resources and limit the number of friends they have. This makes them a desirable target for the bullies because the victims are unlikely to successfully defend themselves or have the social resources to force the bullies to cease their behavior. They are also less likely to report the behavior to an authority figure. In contrast, bullying victims who are successful in terminating the victimization typically rely on friends to intervene on their behalf with the bully or report the behavior to an authority figure. For victims, the act of bullying can have lasting consequences, including persistent fear, reduced self-esteem, and higher levels of anxiety. In addition, the research suggests that those students targeted by bullies in school are more likely to experience adult criminal victimization than those students who were not bullied in school.

Ann Marie Popp

See also Juvenile Delinquency; School Violence

Further Readings

Bosworth, K., D. L. Espelage, and T. R. Simon. 1999. "Factors Associated with Bullying Behavior in Middle School Students." *Journal of Early Adolescence* 19:341–62.

Elsea, M., E. Menesini, Y. Morita, M. O'Moore, J. A. Mora-Merchan, B. Pereira, and P. K. Smith. 2004. "Friendship and Loneliness among Bullies and Victims: Data from Seven Countries." *Aggressive Behavior* 30:71–83.

Olweus, D. 1999. "Sweden." Pp. 7–27 in *The Nature of School Bullying: A Cross-national Perspective*, edited by P. K. Smith, Y. Morita, J. Junger-Tas, D. Olweus, R. Catalano, and P. Slee. New York: Routledge.

Unnever, J. D. and D. G. Cornell. 2003. "The Culture of Bullying in Middle School." *Journal of School Violence* 2:5–27.

BUREAUCRACY

A bureaucracy is a form of organization with designated rules, hierarchy or chain of authority, and positions. Max Weber identified bureaucracy as a particular ideal-type, or an abstracted model, with the following characteristics: a division of labor in which tasks are specified and allocated to positions, a hierarchy of offices, a set of rules that govern performance, a separation between personal and official property and rights, the assignment of roles based on individuals' technical qualifications, and membership as a career. These specifications allow members to perform tasks without awaiting approval from a central authority, build organizational memory through routines, coordinate individual expertise, and ascend a career ladder. Rather than drawing upon authority based on tradition (such as a monarchy) or charismatic leadership, a bureaucracy relies on rules and formal positions to exert control over its members.

Bureaucracy's Spread

Weber argued that the bureaucracy exhibited greater technical efficiency, stability, and "fairness" than other organizational forms. He and others attributed bureaucracy's spread to its superior effectiveness at coordinating large numbers of members, inputs, and outputs. Some have attributed the proliferation of contemporary bureaucracies not to efficiency but to normative pressures. When confronted by the demands of governments, regulators, suppliers, vendors, and other actors in the organizational environment, organizations tend to adopt accepted organizational forms, namely, bureaucracy. Whereas most researchers categorize the majority of modern, complex, and large organizations as bureaucracies, cross-cultural studies document the existence of other organizational forms.

Drawbacks of Bureaucracy

Although a few argue that the effects of bureaucratic structures are contingent, much research has critiqued bureaucracy as inevitably exerting undesired consequences. Most notably, Weber lamented increasing bureaucratization as subjecting individuals to an "iron cage" of control. Others warn that bureaucracies consolidate and legitimize corporate or elite control at the expense of individuals and minorities. Using their access to resources and power, leaders can redirect organizing efforts toward elite interests. Oligarchy, or "rule by a few" may thus overtake collective interests. Organizational maintenance activities such as fundraising further divert efforts away from substantive goals.

Unchecked bureaucratic rationality can also generate suboptimal outcomes. Under a chain of authority, members' efforts may benefit only their immediate supervisor and unit, rather than serve larger organizational interests. Lower-ranking members may have little recourse for expressing dissenting views or protesting superiors' orders. To do their work, members may have to break the rules. If members mindlessly apply rules, then rules can become an end rather a means of reaching an end. This means–ends inversion can worsen goal displacement. Setting rules and procedures may only temporarily alleviate conflict between management and employees about appropriate activities. In addition, bureaucratic procedures can foster depersonalization. Bureaucracies ignore, or try to minimize, informal relations, or relationships among members that are not based on formal positions. They also fail to provide a group identity and meaning, aspects that some members seek. Although a division of labor and rules offer members some protection against intrusive requests by superiors and clients, they can also restrict members from applying their talents and interests. Those who labor in repetitive, assembly line work may experience their limited activity as particularly stultifying. Specification and standardization can generate "trained incapacity" or difficulties dealing with change intended to improve organizational performance.

Some critics blame bureaucratic dysfunction for imposing high societal costs. Hierarchy and a division of labor allow members to disavow responsibility and knowledge of problematic activities. Members may also use bureaucratic practices to normalize rather than correct deviance. For instance, repeatedly overlooked problems contributed to the NASA space shuttle disasters and chemical and nuclear plant accidents, corporate misconduct allowed for unsafe products and white-collar crime, and abuse of power sustained genocide and other atrocities. Furthermore, bureaucratization can homogenize the production and distribution of goods and services worldwide, thus eliminating local diversity. Finally, bureaucratic structures can reproduce and exacerbate larger societal inequality, including gender, ethnic, and class divisions.

Attempts to Redress the Ills of Bureaucracy

Collectivist Organizations

To counter bureaucracy's negative effects, some practitioners have designed organizations to respond to the interests of their members and the communities served. Known as co-operative, collective, democratic, or collectivist organizations, these organizations endorse practices that are explicitly antithetical to bureaucratic practices. Instead of a strict division of labor, members rotate tasks. Rather than establishing a hierarchy with top-down decision making, members practice consensual or democratic decision making. Flexible and modifiable rather than set rules govern performance. Blended personal and group property and rights afford members collective ownership of the organization. Members can learn skills "on the job" rather than having to qualify for positions. A reliance on a "value-rational" form of authority binds members through a collective commitment to the organization's mission.

Collectivist organizations face both external pressures and internal pressures to adopt standard organizational forms. Ironically, practices intended to support participation and group solidarity, such as decision making by consensus or reliance upon expressive friendship ties, exert their own unintended consequences and reproduce larger societal inequalities. Many collectivist organizations have dissolved or replaced collectivist practices with bureaucratic practices, although a few exceptions—the Mondragón co-operatives, the two-party International Typographical Union, the Burning Man organization, and Open Source projects—suggest that collectivist organizations can persist.

Contemporary Organizations

Contemporary organizations are increasingly adopting modified collectivist practices, such as worker participation, flattened hierarchy, and organizational missions. During the 1980s and 1990s, small decentralized organizations were heralded as superior to large bureaucracies in innovating and responding to change. To improve production, "lean production" practices capitalized on workers' otherwise untapped experiences and innovation by giving workers more control over their work. Corporations also attempted to instill meaning in employees' work through corporate culture and mission statements. However, some critics deem these changes symbolic and as masking exploitation under the guise of worker empowerment. Researchers recommend larger structural changes, such as establishing stronger unions and worker councils to represent employee interests. Others propose that professional and team forms of organizations can increase member input and autonomy and that such organizations can work in tandem with conventional bureaucracies to improve both organization and production.

Katherine K. Chen

See also Corporate Crime; Inequality; Oligarchy; Total Institution; White-Collar Crime

Further Readings

Adler, Paul S. and Bryan Borys. 1996. "Two Types of Bureaucracy: Enabling and Coercive." *Administrative Science Quarterly* 41(1):61–89.

Rothschild, Joyce and J. Allen Whitt. 1986. *The Cooperative Workplace:. Potentials and Dilemmas of Organizational Democracy and Participation.* New York: Cambridge University Press.

Scott, W. Richard. [1981] 2003. *Organizations: Rational, Natural, and Open Systems.* 5th ed. Englewood Cliffs, NJ: Prentice Hall.

Weber, Max. [1946] 1958. "Bureaucracy." Pp. 196–204, 214–16 in *Max Weber: Essays in Sociology,* edited and translated by H. H. Gerth and C. Wright Mills. New York: Oxford University Press.

BURGLARY

The crime of burglary, also called "breaking and entering," is rooted in common law, originally designed to protect both the property within the home and the safety of its occupants. Modern-day burglary has expanded from a common law definition of entering the dwelling house of another during the night with the intent to commit a crime to now include illegal entry of any structure with criminal intent. The intent is most typically to commit a larceny, but it can be for assault, rape, vandalism, or any other criminal transgression. Most state criminal codes delineate degrees of seriousness based upon factors such as time of day, whether the structure serves as a dwelling, and whether the burglar is armed.

Burglary is a rather widespread crime with more than 2 million offenses recorded by the police annually and more than 3 million reported in victimization surveys. The gap between these measures is rather large because burglaries are rarely solved. If not for supporting insurance claims, the rate of reporting to the police would undoubtedly be even lower. The average take in a burglary is around $1,200, and the total annual loss is more than $4 billion.

Burglars vary widely in their skills, planning, and success. Criminologists generally identify several subsets of offenders. One sizable group is those with drug addictions looking for quick sources of funds to support their habit. Juvenile offenders constitute another significant group. Neither of these sets of offenders plan very well, and consequently, their risk is high and profits tend to be low. On the other hand, a segment of the burglar population plans quite carefully, gathering information about items present in a home or business and the occupying patterns of the residents or proprietors.

The single most important criterion to burglars is that persons are not present in the premises to be burglarized. Whether there is careful planning or only cursory observation of indicators, the goal is to break into unoccupied sites. Once entry is gained, a second dictum of the burglar is to work fast to minimize the risk of being caught. The most prized targets of the burglar are items that are portable, of high value, and readily convertible to cash. Jewelry, silver, and guns are prime examples. The overwhelming motivation for burglary is to profit from the theft to fulfill needs, or perceived needs, for money.

Many criminologists portray burglars primarily in terms of rational choice theory, whereas others view them as often impacted by emotion and other factors that undermine rational decision making. Offenders motivated by less-rational factors such as a desire for revenge, being under the influence of alcohol or drugs at the time of the offense, or desperation are at greatest risk of discovery. Those who are more rationally motivated are more likely to take environmental cues regarding the susceptibility of sites and their own risks into account.

Stephen E. Brown

See also Crime; Property Crime; Rational Choice Theory; Theft

Further Readings

Tunnell, Kenneth D. 2000. *Living Off Crime.* Chicago: Burnham.

Wright, Richard T. and Scott Decker. 1994. *Burglars on the Job: Street Life and Residential Break-ins.* Boston: Northeastern University Press.

BURNOUT

Job burnout is one of the top 10 health problems in today's workplace in the United States and is a persistent problem in other developed nations. Although definitions of *burnout* vary, generally it is a chronic and persistent feeling of emotional exhaustion related to stressful job conditions. The personal and organizational costs associated with burnout can be quite high. The factors related to the onset of burnout and to associated job and personal changes are discussed in this entry, as are ways to ameliorate burnout.

The Nature of Job Burnout

Use of the term *burnout* helps researchers describe a state of emotional exhaustion caused by overwork. Burnout can be seen as a negative outcome of excessive levels of perceived stress on the job. During the 1970s, researchers examined burnout in the context of early findings about its connection to decreased performance, particularly as identified in the helping professions (e.g., counseling). Recent research reports burnout in a broad array of jobs. Since the early 1990s, U.S. workers have reported a dramatic increase in their experiences of job stress, and the general public has embraced the term for those experiencing a high degree of stress or feeling frazzled, at their wit's end, and so on. The common thread is the feeling of emotional exhaustion.

Burnout as a Construct

Christina Maslach has been one of the major proponents of a three-pronged theory of burnout, in which the three prongs are emotional exhaustion, depersonalization, and diminished personal accomplishment. Emotional exhaustion still remains the most fundamental component of burnout. Individuals experiencing depersonalization start to see and treat people as objects, and individuals experiencing a diminished sense of personal accomplishment are unable to take pride in what they do. Current research suggests that burnout should once again be viewed as a single concept highlighted by emotional exhaustion. Recently, some attempts to study job burnout focused on exhaustion. Some theories expand the concept of exhaustion to include physical, emotional, and cognitive aspects. Other recent studies focused on both exhaustion and disengagement from personal relationships as job burnout symptoms, dropping only the diminished sense of personal accomplishment from the three-pronged approach.

Precursors of Job Burnout

Research has identified a variety of factors that contribute to the development and severity of job burnout. These problems fall into two major areas: work factors and personality factors.

Work Factors Related to Burnout

The most common work responsibility factor is work overload: having too much to do over an extended period of time. It depletes an individual's physical, cognitive, and emotional resources and leads to exhaustion. A second major contributor to burnout is the loss of personal control in the job environment. The final set of problems relates to the roles established and maintained by individuals at work: role ambiguity, role conflict, and role overload. Role difficulties often link closely to both work overload and control problems. These role-related difficulties lead to increased stress levels. Clearly, these are areas where organizations have the ability to change and thereby reduce the potential for burnout. However, such changes are in potential conflict with organizational trends like downsizing and cost-saving adjustments.

Interpersonal relationships in the workplace are another major source of stress and, therefore, burnout. Most of these problems fall into the categories of lack of social support and conflict. Interactions with supervisors, peers, subordinates, and clients are all potential sources of stress and may range from lack of support to interpersonal conflict. Whereas in its lesser forms interpersonal peer issues are often mild and produce lower levels of stress, their more conflict-laden forms are a major source of stress to people.

Personality Factors Related to Burnout

In addition to the job environment, individuals have certain traits, conditions, and histories that may further heighten the effects of certain job factors leading to burnout. These traits are often referred to as "personality" factors and can range from work–family issues to transportation problems. Substantial evidence exists about the association of certain personality traits with increased incidence of job burnout. The most consistently found traits include Neuroticism, which predicts greater degrees of burnout, and Hardiness, which buffers the effects of burnout. Clearly, some people have predispositions to burnout, but job factors remain the most potent predictors of burnout.

The potential list of general conditions that affect workers' tendency to experience burnout is long. Several factors seem particularly potent in today's workplace. Work–nonwork balance is one of those factors. Individuals who are unable to balance their nonwork and work commitments are more likely to experience job burnout. Nonwork factors, such as financial difficulties, commuting time, multiple jobs, personal relationships, worries about war and terrorism, and even more "positive" stressors such as getting married or having children, are just a few of the issues that can elevate stress levels and contribute to burnout. The most likely outcome of these factors is a higher incidence of stress and burnout over time. However, job factors remain the major predictor of stress and burnout.

Consequences of Burnout in the Workplace

Job burnout creates problems with workers' performance and attitudes about their jobs. These problems on the job fall into three broad categories: emotional, biological, and behavioral.

Consistent with the emotional exhaustion associated with burnout, other psychological changes occur. The most consistent job attitudes where declines occur include job satisfaction, job involvement, job commitment, organizational commitment, and increased job frustration. These negative attitudes often connect strongly to negative health outcomes (e.g., hypertension), behavioral changes (e.g., wanting to leave the organization), and, at the most extreme end, aggression and violence.

As with all negative stress-related circumstances, physical problems occur. These problems result in increased health care costs for the individual and possibly increased health care rates. Clearly, the organization can incur increased costs from these consequences of burnout.

Finally, stress and burnout may create additional behavioral changes in workers which directly affect organizational productivity. Burnout has been linked to

increased accident rates, which result in decreased productivity and, in some cases, increased health care costs. Burnout decreases job performance, with individuals accomplishing less. In some cases, burnout can lead individuals to engage in negative activities that can cause decreased unit performance (e.g., being rude to customers). Because burnout is a health problem, companies may have difficulties firing a "sick" individual.

Coping With Burnout

While burnout is a negative outcome of stress, the question still remains: Why are some individuals more likely to experience burnout than others do when they experience the same sources of stress? Current research suggests that coping strategies and resources may reduce an individual's risk of experiencing burnout. Different ideas abound regarding identification and categorization of these different coping strategies and resources. These varying categories and definitions of coping strategies find conflicting support for models, suggesting coping decreases the perception of stress and, thus, burnout. Coping plays a sizable role in explaining why some individuals experience burnout whereas others do not. However, it remains unclear just how coping works.

Future Directions

The previous focus on individual stress reduction techniques, such as coping, health promotion, and counseling, may place too much responsibility for stress reduction on the individual versus the organization. Needed are more programs directed at primary organizational causes of stress and burnout. Such programs could be directed at identifying factors affecting stress and burnout, such as selecting, training, and developing supervisors and managers; providing interpersonal communication training to all levels of employees; and reducing work and role overloads.

Future research could examine such factors as how resilient a person will be to stressors (the hardy personality) and matching people and environments (organizational fit). The key might be to design programs that are flexible and that recognize the important individual differences that influence job burnout.

Alternatively, along with psychology's recent refocus on positive psychology, a new way to view this situation has emerged: focusing on individuals who are *engaged* in their jobs. Current debate centers on the construct definition of engagement between engagement as simply the opposite of burnout and engagement as an entirely separate and distinct construct. This view provides a way to apply the knowledge gained from the burnout literature without risking negative consequences that may be seen as stemming from employers admitting to possibly having a stressful work environment.

Ronald G. Downey, Dianne E. Whitney,
and Andrew J. Wefald

See also Job Satisfaction; Role Conflict; Role Strain; Stressors

Further Readings

Barling, Julian, E. Kevin Kelloway, and Michael R. Frone. 2005. *Handbook of Work Stress.* Thousand Oaks, CA: Sage.

Quick, James C., Jonathon D. Quick, Debra L. Nelson, and Joseph J. Hurrell Jr. 1997. *Preventive Stress Management in Organizations.* Washington, DC: American Psychological Association.

Shirom, Arie. 2003. "Job-Related Burnout." Pp. 245–65 in *Handbook of Occupational Health Psychology,* edited by J. C. Quick and L. Tetrick. Washington, DC: American Psychological Association.

———. 2005. "Reflections on the Study of Burnout." *Work & Stress* 19:263–70.

Capital Flight

The phenomenon of capital flight refers to the movement of money—as capital—across national boundaries. This can be money leaving one country to be invested in financial assets in another country, or it can be foreign direct investment, whereby a company invests directly into a foreign country's domestic structures, equipment, and organizations (nonfinancial assets). What makes capital movement "flight" is either the magnitude of the movement or the reason for the movement; that is, that the capital is "fleeing" something. However, no consensus exists on either what this magnitude or these reasons must be for capital movements to constitute flight. Thus, in general, *any* cross-national movement of capital may be considered capital flight.

When capital moves between countries, opposite economic impacts occur in the two affected countries. There are primarily positive effects for the country that is receiving the invested capital. For them, money is pouring into their economy, pumping it up and expanding economic activity. If the capital is invested only in financial assets, however, the money may just get lost in a speculative bubble of some sort, with no real net benefit for the economy. For the country from which capital is leaving, on the other hand, there are mainly negative effects. Falling investment will tend to retard economic growth, reducing the demand for labor and increasing unemployment. The money flowing to another country is that much money that cannot be used to expand the economy.

A striking example of capital flight is the East Asian financial crisis of 1997. This world region was greatly expanding for a generation leading up to this debacle, with capital pouring in from the rest of the world. At some point, however, investors became wary and started to pull out, trying to jump from what they perceived as a sinking ship. For the five countries of South Korea, Indonesia, Malaysia, Thailand, and the Philippines, the net private capital flow for 1996 was +$93 billion, and in 1997 it dropped to –$12 billion, which represented a 1-year turnaround of $105 billion in capital flowing out of these countries—in other words, capital flight. The economic consequences for these countries were severe. Indonesia's economy, for example, grew 4.9 percent in 1997 and contracted 13.7 percent in 1998, while Malaysia's growth rate fell from +7.8 percent in 1997 to –6.8 percent in 1998. Reversals of growth of these magnitudes can only be devastating for an economy. In addition, for these five countries, real wages dropped, unemployment increased significantly, and poverty rates rose dramatically; in Indonesia the poverty rate nearly tripled from 1997 to 1998.

The threat of capital mobility can be used as a tool of capitalists both to keep labor in line and to keep environmental costs in check. If workers demand higher wages and benefits, or better working conditions, the owners of capital can respond by threatening to move to a more congenial location, preferably one with lower wages and more docile workers. Given the extremely unequal distributions of income and wealth in the world, this threat is more than credible. For example, a U.S. worker making $20 per hour is effectively competing against a Chinese worker who makes perhaps 50 cents per hour. If that U.S. worker fights for a wage increase, the Chinese worker may become irresistible to the U.S. manufacturer—50 cents an hour can offset all sorts of financial obstacles to relocating abroad.

Further skewing this asymmetric relationship is the fact that workers do not have the same sort of mobility that capital has. It is legally very difficult and not very desirable to a worker to emigrate to another country simply to find a better job: Animate workers do not have the same mobility as inanimate capital. There is no "labor flight" comparable to "capital flight." The difficulties encountered by Mexican workers in their movement to the United States underscore this asymmetry.

Within a country, the consequences of capital flight can be quite localized. For example, during the past 20 years U.S. auto companies shut down many assembly plants in Michigan to shift production to low-cost locations abroad. A well-known example of this is the city of Flint. Once a vibrant city where General Motors (GM) employed over 80,000 workers, Flint now has a poverty rate of over 25 percent, an unemployment rate of 12 percent, and only a few thousand workers still at GM. The devastation wreaked by capital flight has been overwhelming in Flint.

The ability of capitalists to move capital freely between countries is enhanced by free trade agreements. For example, the 1994 North American Free Trade Agreement (NAFTA) lifted trade restrictions not only on goods and services but also on capital flows between Mexico, the United States, and Canada. The removal of nearly all cross-border restrictions on both financial investment and foreign direct investment opened the door for capital to go wherever capitalists desired in order to reduce costs and increase profits. Restrictions on the movement of labor, in contrast, were not lifted: Most Mexican workers still have to enter the United States illegally to take advantage of the higher U.S. wages.

One result of NAFTA's elimination of restrictions on the movement of financial capital was the Mexican financial debacle of 1994. Investors poured money into Mexico in the early 1990s, but with the enactment of NAFTA, it was very easy for these investments to flee Mexico as the speculative bubble burst. Reductions in Mexico's output and employment followed this capital flight.

The dictates of the free market point toward unrestricted capital mobility. Along with arguing for free trade in goods and services, proponents of the free market generally argue for complete capital mobility. This, in turn, increases the probability of capital flight, especially of the sort associated with financial speculation. Capital flight thus becomes a logical result of international free trade.

Paul A. Swanson

See also Globalization; Multinational Corporations; Urban Decline

Further Readings

Baker, Dean, Gerald Epstein, and Robert Pollin, eds. 1998. *Globalization and Progressive Economic Policy.* Cambridge, England: Cambridge University Press.

Krugman, Paul. 2000. *The Return of Depression Economics.* New York: Norton.

Offner, Amy, Alejandro Reuss, and Chris Sturr, eds. 2004. *Real World Globalization.* 8th ed. Cambridge, MA: Dollars & Sense.

CAPITAL PUNISHMENT

Unlike most industrialized nations that severely restrict or have banned the practice completely, the United States continues to use capital punishment. Despite international pressures, internal protests, and some compelling arguments against this practice, the United States remains the only industrialized democracy still executing prisoners.

Historical Use of Capital Punishment

The death penalty was used widely in the ancient world. In the 18th century BCE, Babylon prescribed the death penalty for 25 crimes. Even the celebrated ancient democracy in Athens relied heavily on capital punishment in its legal code developed in the 7th century BCE. Roman law is well known for its executions, using various methods, including crucifixion. In England, during the reign of King Henry VIII in the 16th century, approximately 72,000 people were executed.

In Britain during the 1700s, there were more than 20 crimes punishable by death, including many trivial property offenses. Because of this severity, juries often refused to convict many of these offenders. Britain ultimately abolished capital punishment in 1971. France joined in abolishing its execution method by guillotine in 1981. Indeed, currently the

European Union prohibits its member states from maintaining death penalty legislation.

This European aversion to capital punishment may well have something to do with the millions of Jews executed by the Nazi state in Hitler's gas chambers. In addition, 200,000 to 300,000 of the disabled were murdered as were nearly 25,000 homosexual men, 226,000 "Gypsies," up to 200,000 Freemasons, 5 million Russians, 3 million Ukrainians, 1.5 million Belarusians, and 1.8 million non-Jewish Poles. With these staggering figures in mind, one can understand why the new free German state (Federal Republic of Germany) abolished capital punishment in 1949, shortly after the end of the war. As soon as East Germany (the German Democratic Republic) joined the West in 1990, the death penalty was abolished there was well. The remnants of Nazi concentration camps scattered around Germany remind all residents of the horrors of state executions.

Contemporary International Use of the Death Penalty

Amnesty International reported in 2006 that 86 nations had abolished the death penalty for all crimes, while an additional 37 had abolished the death penalty in actual practice. Seventy-three nations still retain the death penalty, but the number actually executing prisoners is much smaller. The list of abolition states (together with their year of abolition) is long and impressive. It includes Iceland (1928), Austria (1968), Sweden and Finland (1972), Poland (1976), Portugal and Denmark (1978), Norway, Luxemburg, and Nicaragua (1979), the Netherlands (1982), Australia (1985), New Zealand (1989), Ireland (1990), Switzerland (1992), Greece (1993), Italy (1994), Spain (1995), and Belgium (1996). Forty countries have abolished capital punishment since 1990, including nations as diverse as Cyprus, Armenia, Serbia, Samoa, Senegal, Canada, Mexico, and Greece.

At the other extreme, the People's Republic of China (PRC) executed at least 3,400 people in 2004, most by shooting. Indeed, one PRC government representative claimed that nearly 10,000 were executed per year in China. Other leaders include Iran (at least 159 executions), Vietnam (at least 64), and the United States (59 executions). The death penalty is typical of dictatorships such as China, North Korea, and Saudi Arabia.

Contemporary U.S. Death Penalty Debates

Arguments for and against the death penalty revolve around two issues: the constitutionality of such punishment and how effective a deterrent it is.

Constitutionality

U.S. Supreme Court decisions have weighed in on this issue. The 1972 *Furman v. Georgia* decision ruled that existing death penalty laws were unconstitutional as representing cruel and unusual punishment. Yet, in 1976, the *Gregg v. Georgia* decision determined that there was a constitutional formula allowing states to resume executions. In 1986, *Ford v. Wainwright* banned executions of the insane. Most recently, in 2005, *Roper v. Simmons* banned the execution of those who have committed their crimes before the age of 18.

Deterrence

Although the issue is still hotly debated, there is no scientific evidence that the death penalty is a deterrent to murder or that it results in lower homicide rates. Attempts to correlate capital punishment statutes or actual executions to murder rates have been unsuccessful. The United States is the only industrialized democracy using capital punishment and has far higher rates of homicide than any of these nations. Among U.S. states, most that abolished capital punishment have low murder rates, although Alaska and Michigan have relatively high levels of murder. Texas executes far more than any other state and still has a high rate of homicide. In the New York state legislature, the death penalty was debated annually from 1977 through 1995. Arguments primarily revolved around whether the death penalty was a deterrent to murder. Every year there were enough votes to approve the death penalty but not enough to override a gubernatorial veto. A new pro–death penalty governor took office in 1995 and he signed the bill into law.

Death Rows

In the United States it is not unusual for prisoners under sentence of death to remain on death row for more than 20 years. A convict may even come within days, hours, or a few minutes of being executed only to have the execution stayed by court decision. Opponents argue that preparing to die, then being temporarily spared, only to die later, represents extreme cruelty. Although U.S. legal authorities may not intend this, the long isolation under sentence of death nonetheless provides for a special torture not found anywhere else in the modern world.

Innocence and Reversal of Sentence

In 2003, Illinois Governor George Ryan commuted the death sentences of all state prisoners on death row. He did this because others awaiting execution had been released after their innocence was determined from DNA analysis. Investigations revealed that some innocent people have been executed in the United States in recent years, due in part to the illegal acts of police and prosecutors in withholding evidence or asking prosecution witnesses to give false statements. The innocent have also been sentenced to death on the basis of the incompetence and dishonesty of some forensic scientists working in state crime laboratories. U.S. legal authorities have yet to realize the political consequences of such error. Once a death sentence is carried out, there is, of course, no way of rectifying the error.

Economic Costs of Capital Punishment

It is generally agreed that the cost of administering the death penalty as punishment for murder is greater than the cost of life in prison without parole. These costs are a consequence of protracted trials, appeals, and increased security expenses for those under sentence of death. An increased guard-to-prisoner ratio is often found on death rows to prevent the embarrassment to government officials of suicides by convicts. In those cases when death-sentenced prisoners attempt suicide, the prison staff makes heroic attempts to save their lives so they can survive to be properly executed as specified by law.

Public Versus Private Executions

During much of the 19th century, most U.S. executions were conducted in public. Hangings often occurred in the county seat in the middle of the day to attract the maximum number of onlookers. The logic was that these ceremonies provided warnings to all would-be felons and thus were significant deterrents. However, during the late 19th and early 20th centuries, executions in the United States began to be conducted behind prison walls and typically in the middle of the night to attract as little attention as possible. Further, American courts have ruled that there is no legal right for a prisoner to insist on a public or televised execution. Some argue that if U.S. policymakers took the deterrent effect of executions seriously, executions would be conducted with a maximum amount of publicity rather than in secret.

Racism and the Death Penalty

There is widespread evidence that the death penalty is much more likely to be imposed on those convicted of murder when the victim is white than when the victim is black. This pattern indicates that white life is valued more highly than the lives of black citizens. One counterpoint that is sometimes mentioned is that the courts, prosecutors, and juries should be encouraged to use the death penalty more in cases with black victims rather than abandon executions involving white victims.

Religion and the Death Penalty

Many Christian denominations publicly oppose capital punishment, including the Roman Catholic Church, whose leadership has become especially active since it joined the American anti-abortion wars beginning in the 1970s. The Roman Catholic emphasis on being "pro-life" gives this body little choice but to oppose the death penalty. Many Protestant denominations also oppose capital punishment, including Baptists, Episcopalians, Lutherans, Methodists, Presbyterians, and the United Church of Christ. Yet Evangelical, Fundamentalist, and Pentecostal churches support the death penalty, citing the Old Testament as support.

Methods of Modern Execution

During the 19th century most U.S. executions were by hanging. Shooting was also an option used in several states. As technology advanced, electrocution became an option, and in 1888, New York became the first state to use this technique. Lethal gas was introduced in Nevada in 1924. By the late 20th century lethal injection had become the dominant method of execution. Every new method of execution has been justified as a more humane method of killing. Lethal injection is sometimes seen as more humane than other execution techniques because it uses the antiseptic techniques of medicine, including a hospital gurney, drugs, and an intravenous line. Still, it is the object of current litigation as the source of suffering and cruel and unusual punishment.

History of U.S. Capital Punishment

From the beginning of the American colonial experience, the New World has been no stranger to capital punishment and reflected variation from colony to colony. A prime example of enthusiastic execution is found in the killing of those suspected of witchcraft in the Massachusetts Bay Colony during the 1600s. On the other hand, in colonial Maine the death penalty was never very popular.

The United States is unique it that it allows its member states choice in use of this most extreme punishment. At this writing, 9 of the 50 states (Michigan, Wisconsin, Maine, Minnesota, North Dakota, Alaska, Hawaii, West Virginia, and Iowa) have abolished laws allowing capital punishment, 5 have had their death penalty laws declared unconstitutional (Vermont, Rhode Island, New York, Kansas, and Massachusetts), and 2 have a moratorium on executions (Illinois and New Jersey).

Michigan and Wisconsin were the first states to abolish capital punishment, in 1847 and 1853 respectively. In 1876, Maine abolished its death penalty, reinstated it in 1883, and finally abolished capital punishment in 1887. In all three states there existed great concern about racial and ethnic discrimination in the application of the death penalty.

Progressive Era Abolition, Lynching, and Reinstatement

The Progressive Era is generally defined as the first 2 decades of the 20th century and was a time when many legislative reforms were initiated. Two states abolished their death penalty laws and have made no changes since that time. Minnesota abolished its death penalty in 1911; North Dakota followed suit in 1915 and, with one of the lowest crime rates in the nation, it has had little motivation to resume executions. In some other states that abolished the death penalty during this era (Colorado, Arizona, Missouri, and

Tennessee), post-abolition lynching typically went unpunished until reinstatement of capital punishment as the better of two "bad" alternatives. Political radicals and economic depressions were responsible for reinstatement in Washington, Oregon, Kansas, and South Dakota.

When Alaska and Hawaii joined the union in 1957, both exercised their option to abandon capital punishment. Legislators in both states worried that, if a death penalty were established in law, local ethnic minorities would bear the brunt of such executions, as this had been the pattern prior to statehood.

Iowa abolished the death penalty in 1872, reinstated it in 1878, and then abolished it again in 1965. Iowa has both a low crime rate and a homogeneous population. Like Iowa, West Virginia abolished its death penalty law in 1965 and, with its similarly low crime rates and largely white population, reinstatement is seldom an issue.

Ambivalent States

Several urban states with large, heterogeneous populations have high homicide rates and many death row prisoners, yet drag their feet when it comes to actual executions. This profile applies to California, Pennsylvania, and Ohio. All three states have hundreds of prisoners awaiting execution, but each state has executed only a few since the Supreme Court found a constitutional formula for capital punishment statutes.

The South

In many Deep South states of the former Confederacy, there has recently emerged some respectability for those opposing capital punishment. In many of these states, calls have recently been made for a moratorium on executions until research can determine if the state's death penalty laws are being fairly administered. This is significant because the death penalty has been more frequently used in this region than in other parts of the nation. In these regions the Roman Catholic Church and others have become increasingly vocal critics of executions.

Texas

In the "Lone Star State," there is a sizable death row population, but that state has also executed more than a third of all prisoners in the United States since 1977. While other states have been slowing the execution process, Texas moves forward, ever increasing the percentage of American prisoners put to death there. Over the past 30 years, a Hispanic member of the state legislature has regularly introduced death penalty abolition bills that have been routinely ignored. An African American member of the legislature who sponsored such abolition fared worse, getting condemned by the press, the state Bar Association, and the Internal Revenue Service.

Predicted Future of U.S. Capital Punishment

Many social observers predict that the death penalty will be abolished in a few years. There are several grounds for this prediction rather than simple wishful thinking.

1. All other Western nations have abolished this practice, putting pressure on the United States to rise to the same standard.

2. Numerous states in all sections of the nation have passed or are seriously considering moratorium bills.

3. In some states many prisoners are being released from death rows because of serious legal questions about the quality of their trials.

John F. Galliher

See also Innocence Project; Murder; Prison; Subculture of Violence Hypothesis

Further Readings

Amnesty International. 2006. "Facts and Figures on the Death Penalty." Retrieved December 14, 2007 (http://www.amnesty.org/en/report/info/ACT50/006/2006).

Bedau, Hugo Adam, ed. 1964. *The Death Penalty in America: An Anthology.* Garden City, NY: Doubleday.

———. 1997. *The Death Penalty in America: Current Controversies.* New York: Oxford University Press.

Death Penalty Information Center. (http://www.death penaltyinfo.org).

Galliher, John F., Larry W. Koch, David Patrick Keys, and Teresa J. Guess. 2005. *America without the Death Penalty: States Leading the Way.* Boston: Northeastern University Press.

Innocence Project. (http://www.innocenceproject.org).

CARJACKING

Carjacking is the theft of a motor vehicle from another person by force, violence, or intimidation. Although often viewed as a hybrid offense—maintaining elements akin to both robbery and auto theft—carjacking is counted as a robbery in the Federal Bureau of Investigation Uniform Crime Reports because force is used to accomplish the theft. Defining carjacking in this way is problematic because it hinders systematic understanding of the prevalence, distribution, and nature of the offense. Although some states (e.g., Maryland and New Jersey) collect statewide carjacking data each year, most data about carjacking come from victimization surveys and offender interviews.

Recent estimates from the National Crime Victimization Survey (NCVS) indicate that carjacking is a rare offense. On average, 38,000 carjackings occurred annually between 1993 and 2002, a rate of 1.7 carjackings per 10,000 persons. This compared with 24 robbery victimizations per 10,000 persons and 84 motor vehicle thefts per 10,000 households in 2005. As with other forms of violent crime, carjacking has declined in recent years. For example, the NCVS reported an annual average of 49,000 carjackings between 1992 and 1996, a rate of 2.5 per 10,000 persons. From 1998 to 2002 the rate dropped to 1.3 per 10,000 persons.

As in other types of robbery, weapon use is inherent in carjacking. About 75 percent of carjacking victims interviewed by the NCVS between 1993 and 2002 reported that their assailant was armed. The most common weapon was a firearm (45 percent of cases). Despite the high likelihood of weapons, only 24 percent of all victims reported an injury and only 9 percent reported serious bodily injuries. Those most vulnerable to carjacking tend to be male, young, African American, never married or divorced/separated, and living in urban areas. The carjackers themselves are much like their victims: male, young, and African American. The NCVS reports more than half of carjackings involve two or more assailants, and interviews with offenders indicate that carjacking is a crime of opportunism and spontaneity rather than carefully planned, probably due to the mobility of their targets.

The term *carjacking* was virtually unknown until the early 1990s when several atypical, albeit, well-publicized and horrific carjacking cases brought national attention to the subject. In the wake of these events, media reports described carjacking as a national epidemic brought on by a new type of auto thief whose misdeeds resembled a symbolic attack on the fabric of people's lives. Such depictions helped to legitimize carjacking as an important social problem and acted as an impetus for passage of the Anti-Car Theft Act of 1992, which made carjacking a federal offense punishable by sentences ranging from 15 years to life. In 1994, an amendment included the death penalty in carjackings resulting in homicide. Several states also enacted legislation. For example, Louisiana passed the "shoot-the-carjacker" law, giving citizens the right to use lethal force during a carjacking. Florida passed a law to protect its tourism industry after media reports suggested carjackers were purposely targeting tourists in rental cars.

Michael Cherbonneau

See also National Crime Victimization Survey; Property
    Crime; Theft; Violent Crime

Further Readings

Bureau of Justice Statistics. 2004. "Carjacking, 1993–2002."
    Washington, DC: U.S. Department of Justice. Retrieved
    May 18, 2007 (http://www.ojp.usdoj.gov/bjs/pub/
    pdf/c02.pdf).
Cherbonneau, Michael and Heith Copes. 2003. "Media
    Construction of Carjacking: A Content Analysis of
    Newspaper Articles from 1993–2002." *Journal of Crime
    and Justice* 26:1–21.
Jacobs, Bruce A., Volkan Topalli, and Richard Wright. 2003.
    "Carjacking, Streetlife and Offender Motivation." *British
    Journal of Criminology,* 43:673–88.

CHARTER SCHOOLS

Charter schools are publicly funded schools that operate under a legally binding agreement or "charter" between an independent stakeholder (charter operator) and an authorizing agency (charter sponsor). Stakeholders may be, among others, a group of parents, a team of educators, a community organization, a university, or a private nonprofit or for-profit corporation. On the other hand, the charter authorizing agency is usually a public entity such as a state department of education or local school district. The charter, usually lasting 3 to 5 years, exempts a school from various rules and regulations that normally apply to district-operated public schools. In this way, a charter school receives increased control over school governance and management in areas such as budget, internal organization, staffing, scheduling, curriculum, and instruction. In exchange for this increased autonomy, however, the school must comply with the stipulations outlined in the charter document, including goals related to student academic achievement.

Minnesota lays claim to opening the first charter school in 1992. Since then, the number of charter schools has steadily increased. According to the Center for Educational Reform, as of September 2006, about 4,000 charter schools were serving more than 1 million students in 40 states and the District of Columbia. Nonetheless, charter school legislation varies widely from state to state, affecting the number, characteristics, and level of autonomy of charter schools in each state.

A charter school may be established for numerous reasons. Nonetheless, realizing an alternative vision of schooling, serving a specific population, and gaining greater autonomy have been among the most common reasons cited for starting a new charter school or converting a preexisting public or private school into a charter school. Seeking to support the growth and development of the charter school movement, the U.S. Department of Education created the Public Charter Schools Program in 1995 to help schools deal with costs associated with planning, start-up, and early operation—stages at which charter schools seem to face their most difficult challenges.

In practice, charter schools implement a hybrid design that combines elements traditionally associated with either public or private schools. As public schools, charter schools are nonsectarian and tuition free. These schools have no mandatory assignments of students; instead, parents or guardians voluntarily choose them to enroll their children. Also, charter schools tend to be much smaller and have greater control over internal educational philosophies and practices than district-operated public schools. Because charter school legislation frequently allows flexibility in hiring and other personnel decisions, charter school teachers are also less likely than their counterparts in district-run schools to meet state certification requirements and to have membership in a labor union. Furthermore, some charter schools may tailor their programs to emphasize a particular learning approach (e.g., back-to-basics, culturally relevant curriculum) or to serve a specific population (e.g., special education students). In addition, charter schools often contract out services with educational management organizations (EMOs). An EMO may be nonprofit or for-profit, and contracted services may range from the management of one to all of a school's operations.

For supporters, charter schools, by expanding the options currently available in public education, foster healthy competition and thereby encourage innovation, efficiency, and greater response to "consumer" preferences. In this form, accountability is not only to a public body granting the charter but also to parents and students who, by choosing enrollment, ultimately decide a school's survival. Opponents, however, contend that charter schools represent a stepping-stone toward full privatization and see the introduction of market dynamics in the education system as a threat to democratic values endorsing universality and equal access to educational opportunity. Furthermore, as the market dictates the range and quality of educational services, some critics fear that charter schools may add layers of stratification and exacerbate class and racial isolation.

As charter schools continue to strive for a permanent space in the U.S. educational landscape, their impact on student academic achievement is still uncertain. As of today, studies have produced mixed results. Whereas some show that charter schools outperform district-run public schools, others indicate just the opposite or no significant differences. A reason for these discrepancies is that charter schools are relatively new in most states, so not enough data are available to properly evaluate their effectiveness and draw definite conclusions. Similarly, the influence of charter schools on their surrounding districts remains vague. Although advocates expected that districts would enhance their systems and practices in response to competition from charter schools, little evidence supports this claim. Systemic effects, if any, may emerge in the future, but at this point it is still too early to identify any. Several opinion surveys, nonetheless, show that, overall, teachers, students, and parents are satisfied with their charter schools.

Victor Argothy

See also Education, Academic Performance; Education, School Privatization; School Vouchers

Further Readings

Center for Education Reform. 2006. "Charter Schools." Washington, DC: Center for Education Reform. Retrieved December 14, 2007 (http://www.edreform.com/index.cfm?fuseAction=stateStats&pSectionID=15&cSectionID=44).

Finn, Chester E., Jr., Bruno V. Manno, and Gregg Vanourek. 2000. *Charter Schools in Action: Renewing Public Education.* Princeton, NJ: Princeton University Press.

Miron, Gary and Christopher Nelson. 2002. *What's Public about Charter Schools? Lessons Learned about Choice and Accountability.* Thousand Oaks, CA: Corwin.

Nathan, Joe. 1996. *Charter Schools: Creating Hope and Opportunity for American Education.* San Francisco: Jossey-Bass.

Wells, Amy S., ed. 2002. *Where Charter School Policy Fails: The Problems of Accountability and Equity.* New York: Teachers College Press.

CHICANO MOVEMENT

Understanding the Chicano movement requires an understanding of the past. Often heard among Mexican Americans is the saying, "We did not cross the border; the border crossed us." This refers to the 1848 Treaty of Guadalupe Hidalgo that ended the war between the United States and Mexico and ceded much of the Southwest to the U.S. government for a payment of $15 million. The treaty guaranteed the rights of Mexican settlers in the area, granting them U.S. citizenship after 1 year and recognizing their property rights. However, the Senate would not ratify the treaty without revisions. It eliminated articles that recognized prior land grants and reworded articles specifying a timeline for citizenship. The result was the eviction of Mexicans from their lands, their disenfranchisement from the political process, and the institutionalization of more than a century of discrimination.

During the late 19th and early 20th centuries, mutual aid societies and other associations in Mexican American communities advocated for the rights of community members and provided social solidarity. In 1911, the First Mexicanist Congress attempted to unify the groups under a national organization. The assembly resolved to promote educational equality and civil rights for Mexican Americans, themes that would reemerge in the Chicano civil rights movement of the mid-1960s.

Between the 1930s and the 1950s, numerous local, regional, and national organizations were socially and politically active in promoting the rights of Mexican Americans. A few key organizations included the Community Service Organizations (CSO), the G. I. Forum, and the League of Latin American Citizens (LULAC). In California, community service organizations were successful in sponsoring Mexican American candidates in bids for local and state offices. The G. I. Forum, limited to Mexican American war veterans, was involved in politics and anti-segregation class action suits. Founded in 1929, LULAC fought against discrimination in education, law, and employment. LULAC was involved in several landmark civil rights cases including *Mendez v. Westminster* of 1947, which legally ended the segregation of Mexican American children in California schools. LULAC was also involved in *Hernandez v. Texas* of 1954, which affirmed the 14th Amendment rights of Mexican Americans to due process and equal protection under the law.

El Movimiento:
The Chicano Civil Rights Movement

The 1960s Chicano movement criticized these earlier organizations as largely urban, middle class, and assimilationist, who neglected laborers, students, and recent migrants. Like other ethnic social movements of the time, the Chicano movement embraced the culture and identity of Mexico. Leaders of the movement initiated many legal and political maneuvers, union strikes, marches, and student protests.

César Estrada Chávez (1927–93) joined the CSO in California as a community organizer in 1952. He rose to the position of regional director by 1958. Chávez resigned from the CSO in 1962 when they voted not to support the Agricultural Workers Association led by a former CSO founding member, Dolores Huerta. Together, Chávez and Huerta formed the National Farm Workers Association, which later became the United Farm Workers of America. Chávez became famous in the late 1960s with a series of work stoppages, marches, boycotts, and hunger strikes centered on the working conditions and low pay for grape pickers and other farmworkers. Chávez and the United Farm Workers launched a 5-year strike against grape growers (1965–70), successfully convincing 17 million people to boycott nonunion California grapes. In the 1980s he led protests against the use of dangerous pesticides in grape farming. Chávez became a symbol of

the movement and was supported by other unions, clergy, student activists, and politicians such as Senator Robert F. Kennedy. He died in 1993, and in the years since, he has been honored by the naming of many streets, schools, and community centers, as well as with murals and a commemorative stamp.

After Pentecostal minister Reies López Tijerina (1926–) failed in his attempt to create a utopian religious cooperative in Arizona, he moved to New Mexico and established the *Alianza Federal de Mercedes* (Federal Land Grant Alliance) in 1963, with the goal of regaining legal ownership of land lost since the Treaty of Guadalupe Hidalgo. After failing to petition the courts to hear its case, Tijerina and *Alianza* members claimed a part of the Carson National Forest previously held by members in a land grant. They detained two forest rangers and declared the land an autonomous state but surrendered 5 days later. While out on bond, Tijerina and 150 *Alianza* members stormed the county courthouse to free imprisoned members of their group. In the raid they shot two officials and took two hostages. The largest manhunt in New Mexican history ended a week later when Tijerina surrendered. Achieving his goal of drawing attention to the land-grant cause, he represented himself at trial and won an acquittal in the courthouse raid but was later sentenced to 2 years for charges related to the occupation of the Carson National Forest. While confined, he became a symbol of the Chicano movement. Released in 1971, Reies Tijerina continued to press for recognition of Chicano land rights; he has resided in Mexico since 1994.

Rodolfo "Corky" Gonzales (1929–2005) was a leader of the urban youth movement. First known as a professional boxer in the late 1940s and early 1950s, he became active in the Democratic Party as a district captain and coordinator of a *Viva Kennedy* club in 1960. By 1966, he left the Democrats and founded *La Crusada Para la Justicia* (the Crusade for Justice), an organization that supported Chicano civil rights, education, and cultural awareness. He authored *Yo Soy Joaquín* (I Am Joaquín), one of the most defining writings to come out of the Chicano movement. The poem voiced the conflicted nature of Chicano identity and inspired the nationalist tone of the movement. Gonzales also organized the First National Chicano Youth Liberation Conference in 1969 in which *El Plan Espiritual de Aztlán* (Spiritual Plan of Aztlán) was adopted. The goals of this manifesto were to promote Chicano nationalism and a separatist Chicano political party. In 1970, Gonzales helped to organize the Colorado *La Raza Unida* Party, and in 1972 he attempted to create a national *Raza Unida* Party. However, Gonzales left the party in 1974 after it had become factionalized into those wanting it to promote Chicano political candidates and those who wanted radical social reform. Gonzales continued to work on behalf of Chicano rights issues until his death in 2005.

Legacy

The civil rights movements of the 1960s established legal and political rights of minority ethnic groups in the United States. The Chicano movement also had the effect of broadening the class structure of existing Mexican American social and political organizations to recognize migrants, laborers, and urban youth. It also brought about a reversal of the assimilationist goals of previous decades and an acute awareness of Chicano identity and nationalism. Several of the institutions of that period are still active today, including numerous Chicano and Mexican American Studies programs at major universities that began as a result of those earlier student protests. Vestiges of the movement were also evident in the marches and rallies of the National Day of Action for Immigrant Rights on April 10, 2006.

Stephen J. Sills

See also Assimilation; *Brown v. Board of Education;* Civil Rights; Labor Movement; Racism; Social Movements

Further Readings

Chávez, Ernesto. 2002. *"¡Mi Raza Primero!" (My People First!): Nationalism, Identity, and Insurgency in the Chicano Movement in Los Angeles, 1966–1978*. Berkeley, CA: University of California Press.

Gonzales, Manuel G. 2000. *Mexicanos: A History of Mexicans in the United States*. Bloomington, IN: Indiana University Press.

Rosales, Francisco Arturo. 1997. *Chicano! History of the Mexican American Civil Rights Movement*. Houston, TX: Arte Público.

CHILD ABDUCTION

Child abduction occurs when, in violation of lawful authority, a child is transported or detained, even if for a short period of time. Whereas news media often focus on dramatic stranger kidnappings, the problem of child abductions is more complex, often involving noncustodial family members. Despite this, much of the impetus for studying child abductions has been in response to public outcry in the wake of noteworthy abduction cases. In the past 2 decades, missing children emerged as a public concern, leading to the increased study of child abductions and the variety of missing children.

Although abducting a child is typically a criminal offense, the family court, a branch of the civil court system, determines custodial rights. Except for the most clear-cut cases, this distinction makes development of policies to combat abductions rather complex. In recent years, authorities quickly instituted action programs designed to combat child abductions, such as AMBER Alert and Code Adam, both named after kidnapped and murdered children.

Child abductions fall into three varieties. Familial abductions occur when, in violation of a custody order or other legitimate custody right, a child's family member absconds with or fails to return a child in a timely fashion. A nonfamily abduction occurs when, without parental consent, a nonfamily perpetrator takes a child by force or coercion and detains that child for at least 1 hour. Stereotypical kidnapping, a subcategory of nonfamilial abduction, occurs when a stranger or slight acquaintance holds a child overnight with the intention to hold the child for ransom or to physically harm the child.

Much of what is known about the child abduction problem comes from studies known as the National Incidence Studies of Missing, Abducted, Runaway, and Thrownaway Children, or NISMART. An estimated 68,000 to 150,000 cases of child abduction occur each year in the United States, although the three types of abductions occur with varying frequency. Familial cases are by far the most common, occurring an estimated 56,000 to 117,000 times annually. Nonfamilial abductions also occur with high frequency, between 12,000 and 33,000 cases yearly. Although they are most frequently covered in the news media, stereotypical kidnappings are extremely rare, occurring 90 to 115 times each year.

Research indicates that children themselves often thwart attempted abductions, and this reinforces the importance of teaching "stranger danger." In a series of partnerships between mass media and law enforcement, AMBER Alert plans now exist in all 50 states. When a child is abducted, law enforcement may broadcast the description of the victim and perpetrator on television and radio, via highway signs, and via cellular phones. In addition, many large retail chain stores have instituted Code Adam plans, restricting people from exiting from the premises until a lost child is found.

Glenn W. Muschert and Melissa Young-Spillers

See also Abuse, Child; Family, Dysfunctional; Missing Children

Further Readings

National Center for Missing and Exploited Children. (http://www.missingkids.com/).

Sedlak, Andrea J., David Finkelhor, Heather Hammer, and Dana J. Schultz. 2002. *National Estimates of Missing Children: An Overview.* NISMART Bulletin No. NCJ 196465. Washington, DC: Office of Juvenile Justice and Delinquency Prevention, U.S. Department of Justice. Retrieved December 14, 2007 (http://www.ncjrs.gov/pdffiles1/ojjdp/196465.pdf).

CHILD ABUSE

See ABUSE, CHILD

CHILD CARE SAFETY

Child care safety refers to children's safety from injury or death from accidents or acts of violence, or from emotional or sexual abuse, while in child care settings. Child care is defined as paid care provided by nonrelatives.

Nearly 8 million children of employed mothers in the United States are in some form of child care provided by nonrelatives. Despite this large enrollment in child care, little has been known until recently about children's level of safety in care, as no national government or private agency collects data on injuries or fatalities in child care. Whereas extensive research exists on issues such as airline safety and risks posed in the nuclear or chemical industries, much less is known about safety issues in human services.

The United States lacks a developed child care system, instead relying on a patchwork of arrangements differing in their level of formality and government oversight. Child care arrangements involve nannies or babysitters in children's own homes, 7 percent; family

day care providers in the caregivers' homes, 27 percent; and children enrolled in child care centers, 66 percent. Care in the child's home involves the least regulation, with parents hiring caregivers on their own and with no caregiver licensing or required training. Family day care homes may be regulated but may also be exempt because of small size or may operate underground. Child care centers are more formal organizations, the great majority licensed and inspected by the states and with professionally trained directors.

These markedly different organizational types of child care lead to different patterns of risk. This in turn suggests that researchers studying safety in human services can benefit from considering organizational factors that affect the routine circumstances in which care is offered.

Risks by Type of Care and Age of Child

Fatalities are the most serious caregiving failures in child care and the most likely to be reported. The first national study of child care safety of 1,362 fatalities from 1985 to 2003 showed that overall child care was quite safe compared with other environments in which children spend time. It also revealed, however, striking differences in the safety of different types of child care and among children of different ages.

Infants are by far the most vulnerable children in care. Their fatality rate from both accidents and violence is nearly 7 times higher than that of children ages 1 to 4. Equally striking are differences in infant fatality rates across types of care. The infant fatality rate for children in the care of nannies or family day care providers is more than 7 times higher than in centers.

The most dramatic differences across types of care occur in rates of infant deaths from violence. Remarkably, no reports of deaths of infants from violence in centers occurred between 1993 and 2003. Deaths from accidents are more evenly distributed across types of care, although centers also have a safety advantage in this area among the youngest children.

Overall, child care centers offer greater safety than care offered in private homes and, in particular, offer a high level of protection against fatalities from violence, with the protection extending even to infants. The safety of infants is striking: Within children's own families, as well as in types of child care offered in private homes, these are the children at greatest risk of fatalities from abuse or violence.

Risk and the Organization of Child Care

The safety of child care centers does not arise from overall higher-quality care than that offered in family day care or by nannies or babysitters in the child's home. Researchers find that, on average, center care for infants is of lower quality than that offered in the more intimate modes of care provided in private homes. Centers have organizational features, however, that offer multiple forms of safety protection to children even when the centers themselves do not offer particularly responsive or sensitive care.

Most important, staff members in centers do not work alone. They have others watching them and helping them cope with fussy infants or whining toddlers. This helps them maintain their emotional control. It also helps identify an unstable or volatile worker. Center teachers also have more training than most caregivers in private homes, and they are supervised by professionally trained directors. Finally, centers control access by outsiders more effectively to keep out people who might pose risks.

These protections help reduce risks of accidental deaths, such as suffocation and drowning, but they are especially important in preventing violent deaths. Not a single shaken baby fatality occurred in a child care center, whereas 203 happened in private home arrangements. Child care centers are almost completely protective against this impulsive and often lethal form of violence against infants. In types of care offered in private homes, however, it is the single most important mode of death from violence. The stress of an infant crying, in particular, can drive caregivers to impulsive violence. With little professional training, without supervisors or coworkers, and with low earnings for long hours of work, even experienced caregivers can lose control. They can cause serious injuries or death to infants from just 20 seconds of violent shaking. Other members of providers' households can also shake or otherwise abuse infants when confronted with their crying.

Child care centers do not protect against all forms of violence against children or against inattentiveness that can lead to accidents. Children in center care are at greatest risk when they are taken out of the center and lose the organizational protections the institutions provide. Fatalities can occur when children are taken to pools and adults do not notice a struggling child in the water; they can also occur when young children are forgotten in center vans. Children can also suffer injuries in centers when angry or poorly trained teachers grab or push them, but these forms of assault almost never rise to the level of fatal violence.

Improving Child Care Safety

Child care safety could be improved by the provision of more resources and closer regulation of care. In particular, the safety advantages of centers could be recognized and more funding provided for the expansion of center care to the most vulnerable children, infants. In addition, caregivers working in private homes could receive more training and support to increase their empathy toward crying or difficult children. Resources could be expanded for licensing and regulation so that "bad apples" in child care who commit repeated acts of abuse could be more easily identified and excluded from the field. Finally, safety data could be collected so that parents could choose care arrangements wisely, and preventive measures could be developed on the basis of comprehensive information.

More broadly, research on child care safety shows that safety in human services depends crucially on organizational features of care. These may be distinct from the features that determine quality levels. Even the lowest-quality child care centers, for example, provide very high levels of safety protection for infants and almost complete protection against fatalities from violence for all children enrolled in them. By collecting and analyzing data on safety violations in human services, a better understanding can be gained of ways to reduce risk as to well as to increase quality.

Julia Wrigley and Joanna Dreby

See also Abuse, Child; Child Neglect

Further Readings

Wrigley, Julia and Joanna Dreby. 2005. "Fatalities and the Organization of U.S. Child Care 1985–2003." *American Sociological Review* 70:729–57.

Child Neglect

Child neglect is the most frequent form of child maltreatment and results in more fatalities than all other types of child maltreatment in the United States. Child abuse often involves acts of commission, but child neglect often involves chronic acts of omission in care by a parent or caregiver which cause (the harm standard) or create an imminent risk (the endangerment standard) of serious physical or mental harm to a child under 18 years of age. Neglect may be physical, medical, educational, or emotional. It may involve a failure to provide for a child's basic needs of nutrition, clothing, hygiene, safety, or affection. It may involve abandonment, expulsion, inadequate supervision, permitted substance abuse, chronic school truancy, or failure to enroll a child in school. Many neglected children experience various forms of abuse as well. School personnel, law enforcement officers, and medical personnel are the most frequent reporters of child neglect.

Epidemiology

The youngest (most dependent) children are the most frequent victims of neglect, with boys being significantly more emotionally neglected than girls. Mothers (birth parents) are the most frequent perpetrators, given that women tend to be primary caregivers. Studies using the most varied and nationally representative sources of information report no significant race differences in the overall incidence of child maltreatment. Children from single-parent families, those from the lowest income strata (less than $15,000 in the 1990s), and children in the largest families (four or more children) are most likely to be neglected.

Correlates of Child Neglect

A systemic perspective (including the society, community, family, and individual) best encompasses the variety of factors correlated with child neglect. Poor parenting knowledge and skills, such as not engaging in discussions of emotional issues and showing a high degree of negative emotions; parental psychological disorders, especially depression and substance abuse; and a family history of maltreatment are often observed in neglectful parents. When the mother's partner is not the child's father, when there is domestic violence, and when the parents lack support or are socially isolated, the possibility of child neglect increases. Many of these factors are highly correlated with social class and neighborhood characteristics and are more often observed in individualistic than in collectivistic cultures and in societies, such as the United

States, which have lower levels of systemic supports (e.g., national health care) for families.

Effects of Child Neglect

Effects of child neglect depend on the severity, duration, and type of neglect; the age, temperament, and other characteristics of the child; the number of risk factors; and the strengths of the child, family, and larger context.

Child neglect correlates with many physical and psychological problems. Research findings include delayed body and head circumference growth, increased rates of infection and failure to thrive, somatization (expressing emotional problems through bodily ones), and a higher frequency of heart and liver disease in adults who were maltreated as children.

Delayed intellectual, motor, and linguistic development often characterizes neglected children. Neuropsychological tests show deficits in attention, executive functions (e.g., planning), memory and learning, visual–spatial abilities, and sensorimotor functions. Research findings also include poor school performance and lower IQ and academic achievement in adults who were maltreated as children.

Neglected children exhibit both externalizing and internalizing problems. Externalizing problems involve acts that adversely affect others (e.g., aggression). Internalizing problems involve those that adversely affect primarily the child (e.g., depression and anxiety). Neglected children often have difficulty with behavioral and emotional regulation (e.g., the ability to inhibit impulsive behavior) and are more prone to substance abuse as adults.

Neglected children are at a higher risk of social–relational problems. They often demonstrate lower levels of emotional understanding, withdrawal from social interactions, excessive attention seeking, or attachment problems. Childhood neglect is a risk factor for violence against a dating partner and for difficulty in forming intimate relationships in adulthood. The psychological assaults on the child's sense of safety, trust, and self-worth can have long-term consequences for interpersonal relations with peers and adults.

Child neglect is a risk factor for psychopathology. Diagnoses include post-traumatic stress disorder, hyperactivity and inattention, and oppositional-defiance, conduct, and separation anxiety disorders. Various anti-social behaviors also occur in adolescence and adulthood. Adult victims of child neglect use medical, correctional, social, and mental health services more frequently than do non-neglected individuals. People with childhood histories of trauma and maltreatment make up almost the entire criminal justice population in the United States.

Results of recent neuroimaging studies suggest that the brains of children may be negatively impacted by maltreatment. Negative environmental circumstances, such as neglect, may cause anxiety and distress, which impact the neurotransmitter, neuroendocrine, and immune systems. These systems impact the brain's development, adversely affecting the child's psychological and educational development.

Intervention

Most studies on intervention address abuse rather than neglect. However, findings of multisystemic contributions to the etiology of child neglect suggest that intervention has to be multisystemic as well. Earlier intervention enhances the likelihood of success.

Given that children are emotionally attached, even to neglectful parents, intervention work should first help the parents become more caring and responsive caregivers. Intervention starts with an assessment of a family's strengths as well as the factors that contribute to child neglect. Strengths need to be supported and used to address any deficits. Basic needs, such as jobs and housing, and parental problems, such as substance abuse, domestic violence, and psychopathology, need to be addressed. Multidisciplinary teams are often necessary, and intervention work is difficult.

Support is fundamental in effective parenting. Fathers and father figures need support to be involved in child care and to learn appropriate parenting. The availability of supportive others (e.g., relatives, neighbors, teachers) needs to be explored and supported. Provision of child care or parent aides can reduce the stresses on parents; parent support groups can be helpful as well. Provision of opportunities for family fun can also be healing.

Once parents feel supported, they may be more able to address their children's needs. Parenting classes, video feedback, and direct intervention in the family may be helpful. A therapist can observe family interactions and interpret the child's actions for parents in ways that clarify the child's developmental needs for support and limits and age-appropriate ways that parents can address these needs. The parents' own past experience of neglect can be an obstacle that needs to be therapeutically addressed as well.

Therapeutic work with the child varies with the child's age. Identification of children's strengths is important. Play and art therapy allow for nonverbal means through which younger children can express themselves and work through their anxieties or depression. Storytelling techniques can help older children. Adolescents and adults, with more developed verbal skills and rational thought, can work through their experiences in a more traditional verbal therapeutic setting. Children can be taught to express their needs clearly and appropriately and can be offered sources of support in addition to their parents. Big Brother and Big Sister programs can offer attachment opportunities. Peer relations can be fostered through the teaching of social skills and through support groups. Positive experiences with other adults and children and opportunities for pleasure and mastery can provide reparative experiences for neglected children.

Various states have developed time limits for parental change in the cases of child maltreatment. If neglect is severe or if changes are not sufficient or rapid enough to ensure the child's safety, the child may be placed in foster care or placed for adoption. At these times, psychological issues related to separation, reunification, and termination need to be addressed.

Prevention

Prevention programs should reduce risk factors and promote protective factors in the society, community, family, parent, and child. Community-based service programs that help at-risk families in their homes and neighborhoods, even for only 3 months, have shown positive effects in reducing risk (e.g., parental depression) and in promoting protective factors (e.g., parenting competence). These programs offer information, emergency services, parenting support, and education, and they also address existing mental health and substance abuse problems.

Realignment of national budget priorities toward more support for families is vital. Social changes, such as fair living wages and increased availability of quality low-income housing, address poverty issues that affect many neglectful parents. A national health (including mental health) care system and universal quality child care will ease pressures that make it more difficult to be a caring parent. Child Protective Services investigate only a fraction of children reported to them, suggesting that they need additional resources. Increased services to families, such as home visits, early childhood and parenting education, and heightened awareness and resources for work with domestic violence and substance abuse, are essential, as is educating the public about child neglect.

Behnaz Pakizegi

See also Abuse, Child; Family, Dysfunctional; Poverty; Role Conflict; Role Strain; Runaways; Stressors

Further Readings

Dubowitz, Howard, ed. 1999. *Neglected Children: Research, Practice and Policy.* Thousand Oaks, CA: Sage.

Gaudin, James M., Jr. 1993. *Child Neglect: A Guide for Intervention.* Washington, DC: U.S. Department of Health and Human Services.

Pelton, Leroy H. 1985. *The Social Context of Child Abuse and Neglect.* New York: Human Sciences Press.

Sedlak, Andrea J. and Diane D. Broadhurst. 1996. *Executive Summary of the Third National Incidence Study of Child Abuse and Neglect.* Washington, DC: U.S. Department of Health and Human Services.

Winton, Mark A. and Barbara A. Mara. 2001. *Child Abuse and Neglect.* Boston: Allyn & Bacon.

Zielinski, David S. and Catherine P. Bradshaw. 2006. "Ecological Influences on the Sequelae of Child Maltreatment: A Review of the Literature." *Child Maltreatment* 11(1):49–62.

CHILD SEXUAL ABUSE

See ABUSE, CHILD SEXUAL

CHRONIC DISEASES

Chronic diseases are illnesses that characteristically have a slow, progressive onset and a long duration. Chronic diseases impact every aspect of the individual's and family's life and usually result from repeated or prolonged exposure to an environment or substance that does not support the normal structure and functioning of the body.

Chronic diseases are those illnesses that are part of a person's life, with little or no chance for full recovery. In acute disease, treatments focus on returning the individual to full health. With chronic disease, the medical focus is to limit the progression of the disease or to delay any secondary complication that might arise because of the disease.

The body's normal structure and function work like a well-coordinated machine, with each part vital to the whole. The structure and function of the human body of a person with a chronic disease, on both the cellular and systemic levels, is permanently altered. It is due to this permanent, and often progressive, cellular change that the person with the chronic disease has an altered ability to function in activities of daily living. Centers for Disease Control and Prevention (CDC) statistics reveal that 1 out of 10 Americans (25 million people) have severe limitations in their daily activities because they have a chronic disease.

According to the CDC's 2004 data on death in the United States, the current four leading causes of death are heart disease, cancer, stroke, and chronic lower respiratory disease, all chronic diseases. Of the 10 leading causes of death in the United States, only three are not due to chronic illness. More than 1.7 million American deaths, or 7 out of 10, each year are due to a chronic disease. More than 75 percent of the $1.4 trillion spent on U.S. medical care costs is to treat chronic diseases.

Although some chronic diseases transmit during gestation or at birth and others have a genetic link predisposing a person to be more likely to develop that disease, most of the existing chronic diseases are preventable or manageable through lifestyle choices and changes.

Mortality and Morbidity

Mortality refers to the rate of deaths in a given population, and morbidity is the rate of illnesses occurring. These statistics are important when evaluating chronic diseases because we are able to identify trends and shifts in norms. For example, before the discovery of antibiotics, the leading cause of death in the United States was infection, not heart disease. As the population continues to age, the causes of death will change. In the United States, the highest mortality and morbidity rates are due to chronic diseases.

Heart disease, cancer, stroke, upper respiratory disease, diabetes, Alzheimer's disease, kidney disease, liver disease, hypertension, and Parkinson's disease are among the top 15 causes of death. Deaths attributed to accidents, suicide, and pneumonia/influenza may also reflect the impact of chronic diseases such as epilepsy, depression, and AIDS.

According to the 2002 *Chartbook on Trends in the Health of Americans,* life expectancy for Americans increased during the past century from 51 to 79.4 years for females and from 48 to 73.9 for males. Despite this increase, however, the United States still lags behind other developed countries in life expectancy. This gap may be due, in part, to the fact that more Americans live longer with chronic diseases but not as long as healthy people.

Contributing Factors

Contributing factors for chronic disease are those situations, environments, or lifestyle choices that increase the likelihood of developing a chronic disease. Aging is one of the leading contributing factors; other factors are environmental exposure to toxins, secular trends, genetics, stress, diet, race, socioeconomic status, access to health care, and level of education.

This entry divides risk factors into four groups: genetic/familial, social, environmental, and behavioral. For each group, the common factors, associated disease(s), and prevention or containment methods are discussed. Some overlapping occurs between groups, as many factors related to the development of chronic diseases are codependent. Historically not considered contagious, some chronic diseases—particularly newly emerging long-term diseases—have causative agents transmitted through the mixing of body fluids or sexually, such as herpes, HIV, and hepatitis.

Genetics and Heredity

Aging is the process that begins at birth and continues until death. As a person ages the cells mature, reach their peak performance, and then begin to decline or degenerate. As medical science discovers more ways to prolong the healthy life of our cells, the aging process appears to slow down, hence the recently coined phrase "60 is the new 40," allowing baby boomers (those born between 1946 and 1964) to maintain the illusion of youth as they age. The primary way in which we have extended our life expectancy is the reduction of the number of deaths related to infection and accidents and the development of medical interventions to treat chronic diseases.

Some theories propose that aging is genetically programmed into the cell. Symptoms of aging cells are wrinkles, gray hair, and even menopause, demonstrating that aging can be considered a degenerative chronic disease. The process of aging incorporates the issue of prolonged exposure to toxic elements in the environment, increases the risk of organic failure, and raises the likelihood of degenerative diseases such as Alzheimer's.

As a normal part of the aging process, a person becomes more susceptible to illness, is at increased risk of coronary disease and stroke, and has a depletion in bone mass. The aging cell is more vulnerable to opening the door to other acute and chronic diseases, which in turn can accelerate the aging process. In reviewing chronic diseases, it is important to keep in mind that, as our population lives longer (by 2030 one in five Americans will be over age 65), the prevalence of chronic diseases will grow.

Hereditary, Congenital Diseases, and Intrauterine Injury

Birth defects and intrauterine injury may produce chronic diseases such as hemophilia, muscular dystrophy, sickle-cell anemia, congenital heart disease, Tay-Sachs disease, cerebral palsy, and Down syndrome, to name a few. Chromosomal abnormalities genetically determine some diseases and can be tested for during pregnancy. A congenital disease is one that is present at birth but is not necessarily caused by a chromosomal abnormality. Environmental factors during pregnancy can result in birth defects and subsequent chronic diseases, as in fetal alcohol syndrome (FAS), where the child's exposure to the mother's alcoholic intake alters the normal cellular growth and development of the fetus. FAS often results in lifelong, chronic ailments. Any toxic environment or harmful drug or chemical taken by a pregnant woman can result in fetal injury. The best-known case of this was the 1960s use of the drug thalidomide (a tranquilizer), which resulted in very serious congenital malformations.

Essential Hypertension, Stroke, and Coronary Disease

Research revealed an inherited trait predisposing a person to building up fats in major arteries, thus increasing the individual's susceptibility toward stroke and heart disease. Families with a history of cardiac or vessel disease may be more likely to develop heart and vessel disease with aging. Race is also linked to heart disease, with statistics indicating that African Americans are at higher risk for developing heart disease and stroke than people of other races.

Social Factors

Secular trends, or behaviors shared by a group of people over a specific period, demonstrate the ability to change disease patterns over time. Secular trends can increase or decrease the risk of developing or exacerbating a chronic disease. Often, positive secular trends will follow a change in policy or legislation, such as the smoke-free workplace laws, which encourage a decrease in the amount of smoking by employees.

A secular trend increasing the likelihood of developing chronic diseases is Americans' choice of eating at fast food restaurants. As more women enter the workforce, more families eat fast foods. One out of every four Americans reports eating fast food once a day. Research indicates that lower income and lower education levels correlate to higher intake of fast foods. The consumption of deep-fried, high-calorie meals over time increases an individual's likelihood of obesity, diabetes, and cardiovascular disease.

Income and Education

As mentioned earlier, income and education often dictate behavioral choices, as well as environmental hazards. Individuals of a lower income and lower educational level do not have the same choices in access, ability to pay, choice of safe shelter, and understanding of health hazards. According to the National Bureau of Economic Research, poorer, less-educated Americans have shorter life spans than their rich, well-educated counterparts. Income and education, although listed as a social factor, also impacts behavior, genetic/familial, and environmental factors.

Stress

The body adapts to stress, and that adaptation corrupts multiple normal body functions. The brain, sensing stress, releases hormones to deal with the event and then allows for a recovery period. If stress is a chronic condition, however, the absence of recovery means the body's major organs continue to react as if in jeopardy. This heightened level of readiness can ultimately result in high blood pressure, heart disease, diabetes, obesity, and even cancer.

Environmental Factors

The environment is a leading risk factor for developing chronic inflammatory disease. Environmental risk factors include any exposure that presents a danger to health, such as airborne toxins, toxins in foods and paint, radio towers and other electromagnetic energy sources, exposure to sun and other weather-related situations, and access/availability to harmful and beneficial health aids. Prolonged exposure to environmental pollutants increases the likelihood for specific cancers.

Airborne Toxins

Particles in the air that can cause chronic diseases can be a result of ongoing large-scale pollution, like car and factory emissions, can arise from an acute event like the demolition of a building, or may be due to exposure to secondhand smoke. The inhalation of toxins released into the air causes the lung tissues to change, resulting in upper respiratory compromise. Diseases commonly associated with air pollution are lung cancer, asthma, allergies, emphysema, sarcoidosis, and other breathing disorders. Multiple sclerosis has been linked to exposure to heavy metals, which are also found in car exhaust.

Disaster-Related Pollutants

The long-term effects of natural and non-natural disasters that release pollutants into environments can include increased prevalence of chronic diseases. Exposure to gases and other nuclear and non-nuclear toxins during wartime resulted in lifelong medical support to treat both emotional and physical ailments in veterans and affected populations. The stress of experiencing a natural disaster (like a tsunami or Hurricane Katrina) increases the likelihood of developing stress-related diseases or chronic diseases occurring as the result of an acute infection.

Access to Medical Care

The slow onset and long duration of chronic diseases make crucial the access to health promotion education and medical management. Some diseases, like rheumatic heart disease, can result from poor medical treatment of a primary throat infection. Access to medical care, preventive health education, and ongoing monitoring and treatment of chronic disease are the primary methods of handling chronic diseases.

Exposure to UVA and UVB

The reduction in the ozone layer has resulted in an increased exposure to the sun's ultraviolet rays, leading to increased skin cancer rates. The secular trend of using tanning beds further increases a person's susceptibility to developing melanomas and other types of skin cancer. Although some risks for skin cancer link to familial traits (including skin color and family history of skin cancer), the CDC states that skin cancer is the most preventable cancer. Methods to prevent skin cancer are reduction in exposure to UVA and UVB rays and use of sunscreen.

Behavioral Factors

Chronic diseases often relate to our behaviors and personal life choices, which in turn are often influenced by environment, social issues, genetics, and family. However, the ultimate responsibility for what to put into the body rests with the individual.

Alcohol, Tobacco, and Other Drugs

Long-term use of alcohol, tobacco, and other drugs increases the likelihood of developing cirrhosis of the liver and associated liver diseases like hepatitis, as well as specific types of pneumonias and brain deterioration. Tobacco is the leading causative agent for lung cancer, emphysema, and asthma, and secondhand smoke is itself a carcinogen (i.e., cancer-producing agent). Prolonged use of drugs, illegal and recreational, increases the risk for brain degeneration, hepatitis, and mental illness. Infection with HIV, transmitted through the use of infected needles or unsafe sex, can result in multiple chronic diseases.

Food and Exercise

Data from the 1999–2000 National Health and Nutrition Examination Survey and the 2005 CDC reports reveal that almost two thirds of U.S. adults are overweight, and 30.5 percent, more than 60 million people, are obese. Nine million children in the United States are overweight. Chronic diseases related to increased weight and decreased physical exercise are hypertension, high cholesterol, diabetes, heart disease, stroke, gallbladder disease, osteoarthritis, respiratory problems, and some cancers (endometrial, breast, and colon). In fact, experts attribute most chronic diseases today to physical inactivity and improper diet.

Sexually Transmitted Diseases

HIV and herpes are two incurable sexually transmitted diseases that can be precursors to other chronic diseases, such as cancer and specific types of pneumonia. Although HIV and herpes are not chronic diseases, their chronic, ongoing nature and the secondary chronic diseases resulting from them make them appropriate for the list. Sexual abstinence and the use of condoms for those who engage in sexual acts can prevent the transmission of these diseases.

The Challenge

Chronic disease is the leading cause of death in the United States. Its treatment affects us on a national and individual level, impacting our economics, emotions, and daily life. Health care costs continue to rise, the population continues to age, and the responsibility for taking care of family members with chronic diseases falls more frequently on the nearest relative. The more risk factors a person has, the greater the likelihood will be that he or she will develop one or more chronic diseases.

Chronic diseases are the most preventable diseases, according to the CDC, as development of a chronic disease requires repeated exposure over time. Removing the toxins negatively affecting the body, replacing unhealthy behaviors with healthy ones, exercising more, and reducing or stopping the use of alcohol, tobacco, and other drugs can prevent, or at least control, some of the effects of these chronic diseases. Improving health education and increasing access to medical care and information can also reduce or eliminate some of the prevalent chronic diseases.

Many chronic diseases seen in adulthood begin in childhood. Learning proper diet, encouraging physical exercise, removing secondhand smoke and other environmental toxins, and educating youth to make wiser, healthier decisions related to their personal habits and their environment will help combat the development of chronic disease.

Brenda Marshall

See also Environment, Pollution; Environmental Hazards; Health Care, Access; Life Expectancy; Secondhand Smoke; Sexually Transmitted Diseases

Further Readings

Brownson, Ross C., Patrick L. Remington, and James R. Davis, eds. 1998. *Chronic Disease Epidemiology and Control.* 2nd ed. Washington, DC: American Public Health Association.

Crowley, Leonard V. 2004. *An Introduction to Human Disease.* 6th ed. Boston: Jones & Bartlett.

Hamann, Barbara. 2006. *Disease Identification, Prevention, and Control.* 3rd ed. New York: McGraw-Hill.

Hayman, Laura L., Margaret M. Mahon, and J. Rick Turner, eds. 2002. *Chronic Illness in Children: An Evidence-Based Approach.* New York: Springer.

Morewitz, Stephen J. 2006. *Chronic Diseases and Health Care: New Trends in Diabetes, Arthritis, Osteoporosis, Fibromyalgia, Lower Back Pain, Cardiovascular Disease and Cancer.* New York: Springer.

Oxford Health Alliance. 2005. "Economic Consequences of Chronic Diseases and the Economic Rationale for Public and Private Intervention." Draft for circulation at the Oxford Health Alliance 2005 Conference, October 21.

Roberts, Christian K. and R. James Barnard. 2005. "The Effects of Exercise and Diet on Chronic Disease." *Journal of Applied Physiology* 98:3–30.

CITIZEN MILITIAS

Since September 11, 2001, public and political concerns have focused primarily on international terrorism and Al-Qaeda. It is surprising that domestic terrorism has been ignored, considering that it was an important social problem after the Oklahoma City bombing. Timothy McVeigh was a right-wing extremist, and when he murdered 168 people on April 19, 1995, the government focused their terrorism efforts on domestic extremism generally and the militia movement specifically. Although there was clear evidence of the establishment of the militia movement in the early 1990s, one can conclude that the bombing of the Alfred P. Murrah Federal Building in Oklahoma City, and the erroneous inference that McVeigh was a member of the militia movement, led to a public panic regarding this newly discovered group of domestic extremists.

The militia movement emerged in the 1990s, fueled by several significant policy issues and two tragic events. Key policy issues included federal legislation that limited gun rights. The two legislative initiatives of particular concern were waiting period legislation (the "Brady Bill") and the semiautomatic assault weapons ban. Other salient political issues included the election of Bill Clinton as U.S. president, passage of the North American Free Trade Agreement, enforcement of legislation to protect endangered species and the environment, and other statutes that limited individual property rights. Two events that were critical to the emergence and growth of the militia movement were the law enforcement–citizen standoffs at Ruby Ridge, involving Randy Weaver and his family in northern Idaho, and of David Koresh and the Branch Davidians in Waco, Texas. These two events, both of which involved federal law enforcement agents attempting to enforce gun laws, numerous people killed, and evidence of attempted government "cover-ups" to hide mistakes, solidified anti-government concerns and provided the early leaders of the militia movement with convincing evidence in support of their concerns and rhetoric.

Structural and Ideological Characteristics

The militia movement was influenced by key extremist leaders and borrowed well-known extremist traditions. The most influential traditions were adapted from the Ku Klux Klan, Posse Comitatus, the Order, the Aryan Brotherhood, and the Covenant, the Sword, and the Arm of the Lord. Generalizations are difficult, as research indicates that the militia movement is quite diverse, but it is sage to say that there are two types of militia organizations. First, most militia groups are above-ground, paramilitary organizations. The Michigan Militia, for example, has a hierarchical command structure, conducts frequent training exercises, and has public meetings. Such groups criticize the media for demonizing them and claim they are simply community help organizations that focus on community service and preparedness. They discuss how they are preparing to assist the community in times of natural disasters and other crises. Their ideology is moderate—they are less likely to embrace conspiracy theories, are more likely to decry racism and nativism, and claim that they are willing to work within the political system and with extant political leaders to achieve change. Second, a smaller percentage of militia groups operate underground. These groups tend to embrace conspiracy theories and racism and usually intensely distrust government. Many of these groups organize in small underground cells. They have limited contact with other militia organizations and are fearful of being infiltrated by federal law enforcement officers. A very small percentage of these militia groups and their supporters attempt to engage in preemptive strikes against their "enemies" in the government and wider society. Most of these plots have been foiled and the perpetrators arrested by law enforcement before any harm has occurred.

Variations in the ideological commitments of these different types of organization exist, but there are some common themes. Both are interested in celebrating local community rights and protecting the sovereignty of the United States. They are fearful of a growing federal bureaucracy, intrusive government activities, and job-stealing multinational corporations. Some militia members argue that international troops have already invaded American territories as part of a global conspiracy to create a "new world order." They seek to protect "fundamental" rights of individual liberty, property, and gun ownership and are willing to use whatever force is necessary to protect these interests. Militia groups are critical of the news media, blaming them for demonizing them and destroying the minds of the American public. Other prominent issues that flow from these core ideas include federal land regulations, jury nullification, educational and political reform, immigration, anti-abortion, and anti-homosexuality.

Size of the Movement

Members are recruited in several ways. First, many are recruited informally: Contacts are made at hunting and gun clubs, at job sites, and through social networks. Second, some groups publicize their agenda at public meetings and through newsletters, Web sites, and letters to the editor; they also organize public demonstrations. Many groups attend gun shows and gun events to share ideas and recruit members. Third, high-profile celebrity figures of the movement tour the country or appear on talk and radio shows to discuss the beliefs of the movement, encourage involvement, and guide interested parties toward relevant literature. Fourth, some groups have shortwave radio programs to share the militia message and recruit new members.

Because data are not collected about the militia movement (or any other extremist group) in any systematic way and there are legal limits on what law enforcement is able to collect and retain about such groups when lacking a criminal predicate, there is a very limited understanding of the number of groups and membership in these organizations. The only available information about the size of the movement is provided from watch-group organizations, such as the Southern Poverty Law Center (SPLC) and the Anti-Defamation League. Both watch-groups acknowledged that a new movement had emerged and grown rapidly in the early 1990s, but mass media and politicians simply ignored the movement. The SPLC, through its Intelligence Project, claimed that the movement appeared in the early 1990s, grew dramatically after the Oklahoma City bombing, and then declined in the late 1990s. The SPLC claimed that militia groups existed in 20 states in 1994, 42 states by late 1995, and all 50 states by 1996. In 2005, the SPLC estimated that there were 152 "patriot groups" in approximately 30 states.

Steven M. Chermak and Joshua D. Freilich

See also Countermovements; Gun Control; Terrorism, Domestic Spying

Further Readings

Chermak, Steven M. 2002. *Searching for a Demon: The Media Construction of the Militia Movement.* Boston: Northeastern University Press.

Freilich, Joshua D. 2003. *American Militias: State-Level Variations in Militia Activities.* New York: LFB.

Freilich, Joshua D., Nelson A. Pichardo Almanzar, and Craig J. Rivera. 1999. "How Social Movement Organizations Explicitly and Implicitly Promote Deviant Behavior: The Case of the Militia Movement." *Justice Quarterly* 16:655–83.

Pitcavage, Mark. 2001. "Camouflage and Conspiracy: The Militia Movement from Ruby Ridge to Y2K." *American Behavioral Scientist* 44:957–81.

CITIZENSHIP

Citizenship is both a legal status and a social identity. Legally, citizenship refers to an individual's political status, rights, and obligations in a nation, for example, the right to political representation or participation in the judicial process in that nation. Socially, citizenship refers to an individual's membership in a political organization or community. Whereas legal citizenship is closely linked to nationalism, the social conception of citizenship focuses on individual or group political ideology. In both, however, notions of morals, good standing, and social responsibility elements of so-called active citizenship are central to what it means to be a citizen.

Legal citizenship comprises several types. For example, in the United States, citizenship occurs through birth, naturalization, or, rarely, through an act of Congress and presidential assent. Any person born in a U.S. territory or from U.S. citizen parent(s) automatically becomes an U.S. citizen. In other countries, such as Japan, citizenship is based on *jus sanguinis* (bloodline) rather than birth. Subsequently, only those with biological Japanese parents or ancestors may automatically receive Japanese citizenship. In contrast to citizenship through birth or bloodline, in most countries, the naturalization process is lengthy and citizenship awarded only upon fulfillment of a set of cultural and financial requirements. These requirements measure the applicant's degree of social, moral, and financial responsibility and, thus, worthiness of citizenship status.

Only legal permanent residents who have resided in the United States continuously for a minimum of 5 years, with no single absence of more than 1 year, can initiate the naturalization process. Exceptions are for non-U.S. citizens who have served in the U.S. military since September 11, 2001. These individuals can apply for expedited naturalization, which shortens by 3 years the time period non-U.S. citizen military personnel normally must wait before they can apply for citizenship. Also, expedited naturalization allows applicants to apply without being physically present in the United States during the application process. Nonmilitary applicants must be physically present in the United States for at least 30 months out of the preceding years. All applicants must be persons of "good moral character" for the preceding 5 years (1 year for military applicants and 3 years for applicants married to U.S. citizens). The government defines "good moral character" as lack of a criminal record. Noncitizens are ineligible for naturalization for criminal offenses ranging from murder conviction to involvement with terrorist organizations and for noncriminal activities including alcoholism or testing HIV-positive.

Nationalism is a central element of naturalized citizenship. Applicants must demonstrate proficiency in the English language and a fundamental knowledge and understanding of U.S. history and the principles and form of U.S. government. They must also show "attachment to" (i.e., a willingness to honor and obey) the principles of the U.S. Constitution. Taking the Oath of Allegiance legalizes this attachment. During this oath, applicants officially renounce any foreign allegiances and commit themselves to serve in the U.S. military (e.g., during a draft) and perform civic services (e.g., jury duty) when needed. Whereas some nations—such as Germany, the United Kingdom, and the United States—allow dual citizenship, most require applicants to surrender one in favor of the other. Whether citizenship is achieved through birth or naturalization, in both instances U.S. citizens have both legal rights (e.g., of political representation) and legal obligations (e.g., jury duty). To date, however, only U.S. citizens by birth may run for presidential office, a stipulation that reflects a deterministic (biological) view of nationalism and citizenship.

Supranational citizenship extends the idea of national citizenship to an international level, as in, for example, the European Union (EU). The Maastricht Treaty of 1992 grants EU citizenship to citizens of all EU member countries and entitles them to supranational legal benefits, such as freedom of movement within the EU, the right of residence within any EU member nation, and the right to vote in EU elections. However, supranational citizenship is not a substitute for national citizenship; rather, both coexist. Last, *honorary citizenship* is, on rare occasions, bestowed upon non-U.S. citizens of extraordinary merit through an act of Congress and presidential assent. To this date, only six individuals have been awarded honorary U.S. citizenship, among them Winston Churchill in 1963 and Agnes Gonxha Bojaxhiu (Mother Teresa) in 1996.

The legal definition of citizenship focuses on legal and political rights, representation, and obligations. Social citizenship also involves rights and obligations, but within a social context; it can be used to indicate membership in a particular political community, for example, the lesbian and gay community. Within this social context, citizenship refers to identity politics, political ideology, and the perceived responsibilities that are associated with these politics, such as engaging in political activism or a particular lifestyle. Another form of social citizenship is corporate citizenship. Corporate citizenship does not refer to a corporation's legal status but to its perceived contributions to (particularly the betterment of) a society. Corporate citizenship, like its legal counterpart, is synonymous with social responsibility, and it incorporates notions of "good" and "active" citizenship.

While legal citizenship is more deterministic in nature than is social citizenship, as witnessed in the birth-citizenship requirement to run for presidential office, ultimately both are socially constructed. Legal citizenship requirements and definitions of socially and morally responsible behaviors are culturally and historically specific. Therefore, the main purpose behind legal citizenship is the construction of national identity by forming ingroups and outgroups. Similarly, citizenship of political communities differentiates a specific community's ideological thought or lifestyle from others in a society.

Ultimately, citizenship is as much a legal as it is a social concept and is often used in both contexts. What links the two conceptions together is the centrality of ideas such as social responsibility, political rights, and identity politics.

Marc JW de Jong

See also American Dream; Assimilation; Civil Rights; Identity Politics

Further Readings

Aleinikoff, Thomas A., David A. Martin, and Hiroshi Motomura. 2003. *Immigration and Citizenship: Process and Policy.* St. Paul, MN: West Publishing.
———. 2005. *Immigration and Nationality Laws of the United States: Selected Statutes, Regulations and Forms as Amended to May 16, 2005.* St. Paul, MN: West Publishing.
Ong, Aihwa. 1999. *Flexible Citizenship: The Cultural Logics of Transnationality.* Durham, NC: Duke University Press.

CIVIL RIGHTS

Governments grant civil rights to those considered citizens through birth or naturalization. When rights are not distributed evenly, conflicts arise. The first stage is often a struggle for citizenship and against laws that create and delimit access to citizenship and related rights and privileges. The 1790 Naturalization Law that established whiteness as a requirement for citizenship is a good example.

Throughout U.S. history, women and minorities have been excluded from full participation in civil rights. They protested their exclusion, using the founders' articulations of equality and democracy as American ideals to draw support. Passage of the Civil Rights Act in 1964 was the culmination of a long history of protest. This set into law both the requirement for protection against discrimination and the creation of agencies to oversee the expansion of civil rights.

The federal government, generally responsible for protecting citizen rights, created the U.S. Commission on Civil Rights as an oversight agency. This commission is charged with monitoring other agencies, such as the Department of Education and the Equal Employment Opportunity Commission, to ensure that they enforce the provisions of the Civil Rights Act of 1964 to protect civil rights and combat discrimination. However, their ability to do so remains dependent on political will and the resources given to study and document discrimination and the violation of civil rights.

An Enduring Problem

The acquisition of civil rights for all groups remains inextricably linked to issues of inequality, discrimination, and social justice still plaguing the United States. The denial of civil rights led to mass protest in the country, particularly in the second half of the 20th century. Much of that protest centered on problems of voting and political representation. Protest groups saw political representation and voting as keys to accessing educational opportunity and employment and as a means for confronting discrimination in housing and real estate practices, police brutality, and bias in the judicial system.

Despite substantial progress in the expansion of civil rights to previously disenfranchised groups and dismantling de jure forms of segregation, patterns of social inequality remain. According to recent census data, minorities continue to lag significantly behind the majority group in educational attainment, wealth, occupational prestige, income, and quality of life as indicated by health and longevity. These patterns of inequality remain after controlling for similar educational and occupational standing. Despite increasing political integration, gaps remain. This is especially the case for African Americans, Latinos/as, and Native Americans. These groups are disproportionately impoverished, incarcerated, and underrepresented among political and economic leaders. Despite being citizens, the "first" Americans—members of the American Indian nations—suffer the worst poverty and the greatest marginalization.

Also, jobs in the United States are gendered. Gender segregation in occupations lead to women being relegated to jobs that do not ensure their future economic vitality and are characterized by lower wages. This pattern persists in each racial group. Women also suffer from media treatment that sexualizes and diminishes them. Substantive change in the striking gender imbalance that characterizes economic, political, and cultural institutions has been slow. It is not surprising, then, that sharp gender differences continue in income, wealth, and poverty, as well as in political representation. However, scholars vary significantly, as do the public and policymakers, in how they interpret these figures.

To some, it seems that the struggle for civil rights is no longer as pressing a social problem. However, the new millennium witnessed an expansion of both the definition of civil rights and those calling for their enactment. In the recent media spotlight on officials issuing marriage licenses to same-sex couples and in the massive demonstrations protesting immigration policies that restrict immigration, it is clear that civil rights remain a pressing social problem for those marginalized and excluded from rights and protections extended to others. Given the counterprotests to both these campaigns, it is also clear that civil rights concerns continue to produce conflict over what is meant by citizenship rights and who shall have access to them.

Ideology Versus Reality

Cemented into the founding documents of U.S. society, the Declaration of Independence and the Constitution, was an ideology of liberty and equality. Yet, as many scholars and activists note, social practices that work to reproduce structural inequality contradict this ideology. Because of this, much of the struggle to expand civil rights rests on the notion that U.S. society has not lived up to its creed of equal treatment before the law. Areas of concern include the right to citizenship, the right to vote, the right to own property, and rights to protection from employment and educational discrimination as well as harassment and violence based on group membership. Major

leadership emerged from the African American community, who felt keenly their government's abandonment following the abolition of slavery and the promise of reconstruction.

Despite amendments to the Constitution that (a) abolished slavery (13th Amendment), (b) granted citizenship to those born or naturalized in the United States and provided for "equal protection under the law" (14th Amendment), and (c) granted the right to vote to all *male* citizens (15th Amendment), the southern states were allowed to enact a series of Black Codes that consigned African Americans to a continued diet of repression and exploitation. Chicanos and Asians fared little better, as they too received no protection from segregated schools and relegation to the most exploited forms of labor, while experiencing violent repression and social exclusion.

In a period that had the potential for radical change in modes of political and economic distribution, the government instead opted for containment. It moved swiftly to relocate and relegate native peoples to reservations and to exclude wave after wave of Asian immigrants from settlement. It was not until massive social protest in the 20th century that civil rights became actualized for many.

The Civil Rights Movement

The 1954 Supreme Court decision in *Brown v. Board of Education of Topeka, Kansas* that rendered segregation in public schools unlawful was a dramatic reversal of the 1896 "separate but equal" doctrine announced in *Plessy v. Ferguson,* which legalized segregation. In the decades following *Plessy,* W. E. B. Du Bois's prediction that the major U.S. social problem of the 20th century would be the "color line" was borne out: Social life was characterized by division of the races into segregated and *unequal* schools, neighborhoods, churches, clubs, recreational facilities, and jobs. Whites alone enjoyed privileged access to political representation and the means for simple wealth accumulation through home ownership. The *Brown* decision represented a challenge to this privilege system. As activists responded, despite the widespread effects of race-based oppression, it was African Americans who were the mainstay of the multiracial civil rights movement.

Dramatic confrontations with Jim Crow legislation reveal the courage of activists such as Rosa Parks. Her refusal to cede her bus seat to a white man led to the Montgomery bus boycott, which delivered a significant victory in the battle for desegregation at the start of the civil rights movement. A young Martin Luther King, Jr. rose to leadership of the movement, built upon a coalition of activist groups that included the Southern Christian Leadership Conference, the Student Nonviolent Coordinating Committee, the Congress for Racial Equality, and established groups such as the National Association for the Advancement of Colored People and the Urban League. However, it was the everyday citizens who risked their lives whose heroism should be realized for its contribution to social change. They braved bombings, beatings, police dogs, fire hoses, and jails, laying their lives on the line for justice.

They established a base of support in black churches and drew media attention as they successfully framed the civil rights movement as a moral crusade and recruited a wide base of supporters that included many students. Dr. King drew upon the practice of nonviolent confrontation that Mahatma Gandhi initiated in India's struggle against British colonialism. Involvement in the civil rights movement politicized a nation with tactics of nonviolent, direct disobedience including marches, sit-ins, and arrests that followed consciousness-raising through "rap sessions" and generated international support for the cause.

Civil Rights Legislation

The civil rights movement of the mid-20th century culminated in passage of a broad civil rights act that assured the right to vote and outlawed discrimination in public areas, education, employment, and all federally funded programs. Eventually, protection against discrimination extended to social group membership by race, color, national origin, religion, sex, and age, later expanding to include disability. Related legislation removed the long-standing white preference in immigration quotas, required equal pay for equal work, and established oversight agencies.

Identity Politics and Mass Protest

A host of disenfranchised groups adapted tactics and ideological frames of the civil rights movement as they struggled for equitable treatment and social justice. New social movements emerged based on social group membership, or "identity politics." African Americans organized for Black Power and national liberation, Native peoples organized as the American Indian Movement to create a coalition of indigenous nations that protested the federal government's refusal to honor their treaties, and a Chicano movement also emerged. Women, politicized by their experience in the civil rights movement, organized as feminists to force attention on gender and sex in society. A gay rights movement, accompanied this examination of gender and sex in society. These efforts by activists to extend the agenda initiated by the civil rights movement paralleled the expansion of the scholarly discourse and research on civil rights.

Theorizing Civil Rights

Sharp divisions mark the discourse on civil rights. Scholars debate over how to define the correlation between stratification and differential access to civil rights protections. They interpret outcomes of civil rights legislation differently, leading to contemporary arguments over whose access to civil rights shall be guaranteed and what rights the state shall be bound to protect. Moreover, scholars debate whether a successful conclusion to the campaign for civil rights, their extension and enforcement, can bring about social justice and equality.

Assimilationist scholars dominated the discourse on racial/ethnic inequality and its resolution throughout much of the 20th century. Their prediction of a harmonious outcome to conflicts that accompanied social marginalization based on group membership rested on assumptions that once ethnic minorities adopted the cultural patterns of the dominant group, they would find acceptance throughout society. They saw the denial of full participation in society as the result of irrational prejudices that produced discriminatory treatment and social marginalization, as well as periodic violent confrontations.

For such scholars, passage of the Civil Rights Act resolved inequality based on racial prejudice. Inequality could be legislated away by outlawing discrimination. Any vestiges of inequality were the outcome of individual capabilities, motivation, and training. Where patterns of social inequality persisted, they could be interpreted as arising from cultural differences—not exclusionary practices.

Liberal feminist scholars' positions on the effectiveness of civil rights legislation to resolve women's inequality parallel those of assimilationist scholars. Their central premise is that women should advance in what they view as a meritocratic society without being hampered by discrimination. Civil rights legislation led to the removal of legal barriers to women's education and employment opportunities, thereby resolving their main problems. Further, they argue that resistant problems of occupational segregation and the gender wage gap may result from choices women make due to their socialization as mothers and wives that suppress their human capital.

Critical race scholars, on the other hand, argue that race shapes social institutions and culture, leading to the social construction of race categories imbued with notions of capacity and behavior that emanate from an ideology of white male supremacy. These "racializing" notions are culturally embedded, so legislation is insufficient to counter their effects on social interactions and cultural representations. Given white hegemony, whites would need the will to counter their own privilege for anything to change, and no evidence suggests that this exists. Discrimination continues, though somewhat abated, in covert forms. Segregation in schools and neighborhoods, persistent poverty, police brutality, and mass incarcerations of young men of color are outcomes of a racial hegemony that reproduces white privilege and racial oppression. These problems, they argue, reflect a flawed social structure and mandate social change, but the society instead has exhibited backlash tendencies against the gains of civil rights legislation in the decades that have ensued. Contemporary discourse promoting a color-blind approach to race will only retard struggles for justice. Neither civil rights legislation nor color-blind policies negate the effects of globalization and deindustrialization on the inner cities that remain disproportionately peopled by African Americans and Latinos/as.

Radical feminists, socialist feminists, and multiracial feminists argue, similarly, that legislation can ease, but not resolve, structural inequalities. Though discrimination has been outlawed, women face occupational sex segregation, the "second shift," and sexual violence nurtured by patriarchal culture. Though, like racial minorities, they have benefited from removal of barriers to education and employment, they still do not net the same rewards as white men for their efforts. For example, men who enter feminized occupations such as nursing and education enjoy a swift ride to the top via "glass escalators" while women are shunted into dead-end careers such as clerical work, under a "glass ceiling."

Despite documentation of civil rights complaints and evidence of practices that maintain race and gender stratification, public discourse suggests that civil rights legislation has resolved related problems except those residing within the cultures of marginalized groups. Given recent allegations that African Americans were disenfranchised in the first two presidential elections of the new millennium amid disputes over race and redistricting, even the central civil rights movement promise of voting rights remains in question.

Sharon Elise

See also Affirmative Action; Black Codes; *Brown v. Board of Education*; Citizenship; Disability and Disabled; Discrimination; Educational Equity; Identity Politics; Inequality; Jim Crow; Justice; *Plessy v. Ferguson*; Same-Sex Marriage; Segregation; Women's Rights Movement

Further Readings

Andersen, Margaret. 2008. *Thinking about Women: Sociological Perspectives on Sex and Gender*. 8th ed. New York: Macmillan.

Bonilla-Silva, Eduardo. 2006. *Racism without Racists: Color-Blind Racism and the Persistence of Racial Inequality in the United States*. 2nd ed. Lanham, MD: Rowman & Littlefield.

Brown, Michael K. et al. 2003. *Whitewashing Race: The Myth of a Color-Blind Society*. Berkeley, CA: University of California Press.

Du Bois, W. E. B. 1903. *Souls of Black Folk*. Chicago: A. C. McClurg.

Gordon, Milton. 1964. *Assimilation in American Life*. New York: Oxford University Press.

Hacker, Andrew. 1992. *Two Nations: Black and White, Separate, Hostile, Unequal*. New York: Macmillan.

Haney López, Ian K. 2006. *White by Law: The Legal Construction of Race*. 10th anniv. ed. New York: New York University Press.

Morris, Aldon D. 1986. *The Origins of the Civil Rights Movement: Black Communities Organizing for Change*. New York: Free Press.

Oliver, Melvin L. and Thomas M. Shapiro. 2006. *Black Wealth/White Wealth: A New Perspective on Racial Inequality*. 2nd ed. New York: Routledge.

Omi, Michael. 2008. *Racial Formation in the New Millennium.* New York: Routledge.

Steinberg, Stephen. 2001. *Turning Back: The Retreat from Racial Justice in American Thought and Policy.* 3rd ed. Boston: Beacon Press.

CLAIMS MAKING

Claims making entails the activities by which groups of people (such as advocacy or social movement organizations, community groups, legislators, or journalists) attempt to persuade an audience (such as Congress, other government officials, or the general public) to perceive that a condition is a social problem in need of attention. The concept of claims making originates from the social constructionist theory, which rejects the perception of social problems as objective realities. Rather, conditions, which may or may not exist, or are currently considered the normal state of affairs, are defined or redefined as social problems via social interactions between interested groups and audiences. Consequently, of analytical interest is how or why a condition is or is not constructed as a "social problem" via claims making, and what features of the claims-making activities are likely to facilitate public support of the claims makers' cause.

Using this perspective, social scientists examine various social problems, such as child abuse and abduction, domestic violence, prostitution, and cigarette smoking. Researchers analyzing claims and claims-making activities might explore such questions as follows.

About Claims Makers

Who is making the claims, and what stake do they have in the successful construction of their issue as a social problem? How do their different statuses (such as gender, class, race/ethnicity, political affiliation, professional affiliation, and religion) influence their decision to make claims, the rhetorical features of their claims, and the likelihood that their claims will be heard and either accepted or rejected? How are their claims different or similar to other claims makers approaching the same issue? Do they adjust their claims in response to others' reactions to their claims? What modes of communication (such as television, newspapers, Web sites) are they using to convey their claims, and how do the modes influence the claims?

About Claims

What are the rhetorical features of the claims being made, and what about them are or are not compelling? What types of evidence (e.g., statistics, expert testimony, victims' stories) are being given regarding the nature, magnitude, and reach of the social problem? What solutions are being proposed as a way of addressing the social problem? What values or interests are being reflected in the claims? Are the claims constructing "victims" and "victimizers," and, if so, who are they? What motifs or themes (such as good/evil, right/wrong, justice/injustice, or morality/immorality) are being conveyed in the claims? Do the claims contain broader or localized social, historical, or cultural themes (such as civil rights, value of or protection of freedom), and will these resonate with the target audience(s)? What emotions or ideologies are being appealed to in the claims (such as anger, sympathy, patriotism and freedom, or social/moral responsibility)?

Amanda Swygart-Hobaugh

See also Moral Entrepreneurs; Social Constructionist Theory

Further Readings

Loseke, Donileen. 2003. *Thinking about Social Problems: An Introduction to Constructionist Perspectives.* 2nd ed. New York: Aldine de Gruyter.

Loseke, Donileen and Joel Best, eds. 2003. *Social Problems: Constructionist Readings.* New York: Aldine de Gruyter.

Nichols, Lawrence. 2003. "Rethinking Constructionist Agency: Claimsmakers as Conditions, Audiences, Types and Symbols." *Studies in Symbolic Interaction* 26:125–45.

Spector, Malcolm and John I. Kitsuse. 2001. *Constructing Social Problems.* New ed. New Brunswick, NJ: Transaction.

CLASS

In its broadest sense, class refers to group inequalities based on economic attributes. The specific economic attributes used to define class vary by theoretical perspective, with some focusing on ownership or control of wealth-producing property, and others emphasizing material and cultural holdings, such as income, wealth, occupational prestige, and lifestyle. Class is thus a primary concept for analyzing social inequality and, as such, provides insight for almost all social problems.

Class denotes both a social group and a social force. As a social group, class is researchers' categorization of people by the various economic attributes. Class as a social force refers to its micro- and macro-level patterned influences. Class shapes myriad inequalities experienced individually, such as those in health, health care, residence, vocabulary, speech, crime, criminal justice, education, employment, marriage, family life, and many more. It may also develop, in some, a sense of class identification that may create macro-level social change, as exemplified by business owners' shaping of national tax laws and global trade pacts or workers' achievement of the right to unionize and the 8-hour workday.

Two Main Perspectives on Class

The relationship between class and social problems is explained differently in numerous theories on class. Most of these theories can be arranged into two main camps, notwithstanding differences within and broad areas of agreement between them: one broadly defined as Marxian, the other as distributional.

Marxian Perspective

Based on the ideas of Karl Marx, the Marxian perspective emphasizes class-based exploitation, struggle, and social change. From this perspective, classes are distinct groups defined by relations of production, that is, the roles the groups have in the way a society produces its goods and services. Industrial societies form two major classes based on the relations of production: the capitalist class, which owns and controls the means of production (i.e., production facilities and raw materials) and which employs and manages others for purposes of profit making, and the working class, or proletariat, which owns only the capacity to produce for the capitalist class. Other classes are recognized (e.g., landlords, small-business owners, intellectuals), but it is the capitalist and working classes that are central to the way societies operate and change.

Most important is the unequal and antagonistic relationship between the two main classes: Capitalists need workers to produce goods and services, and workers need capitalists for wages, but capitalists exploit the working class, which means they appropriate more value from the workers than they give them in the form of wages and benefits. Owing to this economic power of exploitation, the capitalist class attains greater social, cultural, and political power. It has a greater ability to ensure that its interests are represented in the public policy, legal order, and dominant values of society, such as the primacy of economic development policies, laws upholding private property, and the social norm of profit maximization. However, Marx saw class relations as the resolution as well as the source of social inequality. Because of its subordinate position, the working class would form strong class solidarity, or class consciousness, and initially struggle against the capitalist class for workplace reform. Ultimately, this class struggle would expand to create an entirely new social order based on public ownership and control of production, thereby abolishing exploitative and antagonistic relations between classes and thus the classes themselves, so defined.

Distributional Perspective

The distributional perspective is an amalgamation of diverse approaches, most of which derive in some measure from Max Weber's notions of class and status. For Weber a social class is a group that shares similar life chances, that is, chances of achieving a socially valued living standard. Life chances are determined by one's income and ownership of various types of material property, including the means of production, but also by the possession of what Weber referred to as status, that is, social prestige and related cultural attributes, such as educational attainment, type of occupation, and lifestyle. In this view the Marxian relations-of-production approach is too broad to address inequalities rooted in the distribution of these multiple cultural attributes. Thus, in the distributional view classes are nuanced social groupings based on distributions of numerous economic and cultural attributes that shape life chances, and identified generally as lower class, middle class, and upper class. Each designation may be further modified (e.g., lower middle class) or alternatively titled to recognize tradition or prestige (e.g., "old money").

The class borders are less distinct and more permeable than as seen in the Marxian view; upward social mobility is both possible and socially expected. Poor life chances, however, are a major obstacle to upward mobility, and they may result from social closure, that is, conscious attempts by groups to control and exclude others from resources, and from weak internalization of achievement norms. In addition, social-psychological problems of class and mobility are examined, such as perceptions of low self-worth or uncertainty of social standing. For example, one may attain the income of a higher class but still be excluded by its members because the important attributes of lifestyle, taste and speech, do not automatically follow.

Class-Based Social Problems

Exploitation

In the Marxian perspective, exploitation of the working class produces surplus value, which is the value workers create during production that goes uncompensated. It is the source of profits for the capitalist class but also the source of economic inequality. This inequality is evidenced in 2004 Census Bureau data showing that after production costs, manufacturers received a value-added total of $1.584 trillion, but the total wages for production workers was $332 billion. This means the average U.S. production worker made about $35,500 per year in wages but created about $170,000 in surplus value for the business owner, thus enabling the capitalist to sell commodities for a profit. The capitalist class keeps the lion's share of its profits for its income, and this share has grown over the past quarter-century, as seen in the ratio between the average pay of chief executive officers and the average pay of workers: from 35:1 in 1978 to 185:1 in 2003. Thus, an average chief executive officer in 2003 could earn in about one and one-half days what the average worker made in the entire year. Working-class families use most or all of their incomes for personal consumption (e.g., food, utilities, clothes). However, the capitalist class may use much of its vastly higher income for further profit-making, such as reinvestment in its operations and investment in other businesses. Ownership of significant (over $5,000) direct stock is dominated by the capitalist class, whereas the wealth of the working class is mainly in the form of houses, cars, or pensions.

The capitalist class is positioned to generate more wealth; the working class is more likely to own more personal debt.

Unionized workers have higher compensation compared with non-unionized workers, but since the 1970s the capitalist class has taken strong and successful anti-union measures, a form of class struggle that has included illegally firing or disciplining more than 20,000 pro-union workers each year since the 1990s. A problem the capitalist class faces from exploiting the working class and from the consequent disparity in income and wealth is a weakened ability to sell the very goods on which its profits depend.

Unequal Life Chances

Since the 1970s, as income and wealth inequality have increased, as union membership has declined sharply, and as employers have reduced health care benefits for their workers, life chances have diminished for most Americans, be it absolute or relative to the upper or capitalist class. From the distributional standpoint, the inability to attain socially valued goods in socially accepted ways poses a threat to the social order, as evidenced by such social problems as crime, decline in community ties, and withdrawal from electoral processes. Higher education, health, and residence are some important yet unequally distributed life chances.

Regarding higher education, the likelihood of applying, being admitted, and graduating, and the type of college considered are influenced by class. The lower the average income of parents, the less likely the children are to apply, and average Scholastic Aptitude Test scores have varied directly by family income brackets since the 1990s. In 2004, 71 percent of students from families in the top income quartile received a bachelor's degree, but the rate was only 10 percent for those from families in the bottom income quartile. Moreover, an early 21st-century trend is that more students from high-income families are admitted into prestigious private colleges, while the number of students from low-income families admitted is declining.

Lower-class families report they are in poor health more often than do upper-class families, and in fact are more likely than upper-class families to suffer morbidity, such as lung cancer and hypertension, and to experience infant mortality, and their members die an average of 7 years earlier. Employer-provided health insurance coverage varies directly by wages: In 2003 more than 3 times as many top-fifth wage earners had job-based health insurance as did those in the bottom fifth.

Homeownership varies directly by income. In 2001, just half of those in the lowest income group owned homes, while in the highest income group the figure was 88 percent. Moreover, the geographical distance between homeowners by income has been growing since 1970 in U.S. metropolitan areas. Upper-class families have the ability to move farther away from central cities and form homeowner associations which help maintain their isolation from the lower classes by such means as "gated communities" that limit residence to those with similarly high levels of income, education, and occupational prestige. Because of such distancing, municipal services (such as education and recreation) for the lower classes in urban centers may be reduced.

Class Reproduction

The Marxian and distributional perspectives see class reproduction as a problem, that is, that most stay within their class position and the class structure tends to remain stable over time. The Marxian view sees class borderlines as mainly impermeable; the possibility of a worker becoming a capitalist is very weak. Through inheritance of wealth-producing property and financial wealth, the offspring of capitalists have the advantage to remain in the capitalist class, while children of working-class families are less likely to accumulate enough capital to become big business owners and employ others. According to this view, education does not resolve this problem because school curricula vary by social class and prepare students for work roles consistent with their class origins.

Given its emphasis on cultural as well as economic attributes, the distributional perspective finds more possibilities for movement between and within classes. For example, movement from the lower class to the capitalist class is unlikely, but attaining income and prestige higher than one's parents is common. Yet, while research has long found intergenerational upward mobility, especially from manual work to white-collar work, most children remain in the same occupational and status group as their parents or move down.

Some researchers attribute this to the ways parents socialize their children for work and future, which is shaped by features of parents' work. Middle-class occupations typically require self-direction (independent judgment and autonomy), whereas working-class occupations are usually closely supervised and require much rule following. Middle-class parents tend to internalize values of self-direction and, in turn, impart these values to their children. Working-class parents, on the other hand, internalize and socialize obedience. Consequently, middle-class parents tend to socialize their young to be curious and attain self-control, which thus leaves them well prepared for middle-class work; working-class parents tend to socialize their young to obey rules and maintain neatness and cleanliness, and thus they are ill prepared for middle-class work. Another explanation for class reproduction concerns the role of cultural capital, which refers to cultural possessions, such as credentials, artifacts, and dispositions. The cultural capital of upper-class families, which includes professional degrees, taste for "high" art, and a reserved disposition, is more highly valued by educators, employers, and other gatekeepers than is the cultural capital of lower- and working-class families. Because children embody the cultural capital of their parents, upper-class schoolchildren tend to receive higher rewards in school, thus gaining better chances for admission into prestigious colleges, which ultimately ensures their upper-class position in adulthood.

Challenges to Democracy

From the distributional and Marxian standpoints, unequal class power threatens democracy. In the distributional view, those with high income and social status wield disproportionate political power, especially at the federal level: Most U.S. presidents were wealthy; about two thirds of cabinet appointments by Presidents John F. Kennedy to George W. Bush were of people from top corporations and law firms; three fourths of Congress in 2001 was composed of business executives, bankers, realtors, and lawyers; and 81 percent of individuals who have donated to congressional candidates since the 1990s had incomes over $100,000, and almost half in this group had incomes over $250,000.

Some hold a pluralist view, finding that those with high socioeconomic status form more powerful lobby groups and raise more money through political action committees than do those from the lower classes and are thereby more successful in achieving legislation favorable to their interests, such as reduced capital gains taxes. Others find that a tripartite elite composed of a small group of wealthy corporate owners, the executive branch of the federal government, and the top military officials form a power elite in the United States. Members of the power elite share similar perspectives and dominate national-level decision making, such as foreign policy, for their unified interests.

The Marxian perspective holds that it is the capitalist class that dominates national political power and is a nation's ruling class. Some with this view find that a segment of the capitalist class purposefully dominates the three branches of the U.S. government financially and ideologically. This is evidenced by their strong financial support of candidates and officeholders and by their creation and domination of large foundations (e.g., the Ford Foundation), policy-formation groups (e.g., the Council on Foreign Relations), and national news media. Others find that the interests of the capitalist class for profit accumulation are so deeply embedded in the culture that little direct influence by the capitalist class is necessary for public policy and legislation to express its interests, as is evidenced in the conventional wisdom that business expansion is the national imperative and must be facilitated by business deregulation.

Vincent Serravallo

See also Class Consciousness; Cultural Capital; Deindustrialization; Economic Restructuring; False Consciousness; Inequality; Intergenerational Mobility; Life Chances; Social Mobility; Socioeconomic Status; Stratification, Social; Underclass Debate

Further Readings

Domhoff, G. William. 2005. *Who Rules America? Power and Politics.* 5th ed. Boston: McGraw-Hill.

Gilbert, Dennis. 2008. *The American Class Structure in an Age of Growing Inequality.* 7th ed. Thousand Oaks, CA: Pine Forge Press.

Grusky, David B., ed. 2008. *Social Stratification: Class, Race and Gender in Sociological Perspective.* 3rd ed. Boulder, CO: Westview.

New York Times Correspondents. 2005. *Class Matters.* New York: Times Books.

Perrucci, Robert and Earl Wysong. 2007. *The New Class Society: Goodbye American Dream?* 3rd ed. Lanham, MD: Rowman & Littlefield.

Sennett, Richard and Jonathan Cobb. 1993. *The Hidden Injuries of Class.* New York: Norton.

Tucker, Robert C., ed. 1978. *The Marx-Engels Reader.* New York: Norton.

Wright, Erik Olin, ed. 2005. *Approaches to Class Analysis.* New York: Cambridge University Press.

Class Consciousness

Class consciousness is an awareness of one's position in the class structure that can be shared by members of the same class. It enables individuals to come together in opposition to the interests of other classes and, therefore, can be important for people challenging inequality and exploitation. Although members of any class can have class consciousness, it is particularly important for those in the working class because they are at the bottom of the class hierarchy and have the most to gain from being unified.

The concept of class consciousness originates in the work of Karl Marx, who emphasized that it is important for the working class (proletariat) to see itself as a group with shared interests in order for workers to come together and overthrow the dominant capitalist class (bourgeoisie) and to take control of the means of production in a revolution. Although Marx never actually used the term *class consciousness,* he distinguished between "class in itself," where workers merely have a common relation to the means of production, and "class for itself," where they organize to pursue common class interests.

In *The Communist Manifesto,* Marx and Friedrich Engels encouraged workers to unite by informing them of their exploitation by 19th-century capitalists who forced them to endure bad working conditions, long working hours, and wages so low that many families had to send their children to work to supplement the family income. Marx and Engels wrote that proletarians faced alienation—estrangement from both their work and the world in general. *The Communist Manifesto* states that because the dominant classes control major social institutions like education and religion, they can shape cultural norms and values so that members of the proletariat will blame themselves for their misfortunes. An individual who blames him- or herself will fail to recognize that others have the same problems and will fail to see a collective solution for them. Thus, Marx and Engels thought that an awareness of the increasingly exploitative nature of capitalism would make class consciousness inevitable and that it would help workers around the world to overthrow the bourgeoisie.

Marxists express concern about the lack of class consciousness among workers, particularly in the most developed nations, where Marx predicted that communist revolution would occur first. Engels introduced the concept of false consciousness to explain how workers can develop a mistaken or distorted sense of identity and their place in the social hierarchy. Because people with false consciousness identify with the bourgeoisie rather than with other workers in the same class, they do not develop a true class consciousness that would disrupt the social order. For example, waiters employed in a five-star hotel may associate and identify with their wealthy customers and fail to recognize that their interests are more aligned with the interests of the hotel's kitchen workers, security and maintenance staff, housekeepers, or other people who make a similarly low wage. This would make waiters less likely to see themselves as working class, to recognize that their wealthy customers and the owners of the hotel mistreat them, to participate in efforts to organize for better pay or working conditions in the hotel, and to support social policies that challenge inequality in society. In contrast, waiters with a class consciousness, who recognize other hotel workers as fellow members of the working class and have interests opposed to those of wealthy customers and owners, would be more likely to work together to demand change.

Michael Mann's work further developed the idea of working-class consciousness by specifying varying levels of class consciousness. He identified four different elements of working-class consciousness: *class identity,* one's self-definition as part of a working class; *class opposition,* the perception that the capitalist class is an enemy; *class totality,* the acceptance of identity and opposition as the defining characteristics of one's social world; and *having a vision of an alternative society without class.* These elements help us to contrast class consciousness in different settings. For instance, Mann compared the working class in Western economies and said that workers in Britain were likely to see themselves as members of the working class, but they were not likely to envision a classless society or work toward worker revolution. In contrast, Italian and French workers were more likely to participate in unions that directly oppose capitalism in favor of socialist or communist platforms. Mann's arguments can help explain why class organizing has been more prominent in some countries than in others, and why socialist or communist parties have been supported only in some societies.

Despite these conceptual advances, class consciousness is considered difficult to study: It is hard to measure using common survey methods, and it is always changing because classes themselves are always in flux as people interact with one another. Class consciousness may change as people learn about their positions in society, about the status of others, and about social stratification in general. What it means to be working class can vary across time and space, making it hard for workers to have a common awareness of class. Recently, some sociologists argued that class consciousness is an overly rigid concept. Instead, they proposed class formation; that is, the dynamic process of interclass relations and how class is practiced, represented, and constructed in daily life. To study class formation, scholars might examine how class is part of the organization of workplaces, family traditions, and neighborhoods, paying attention to how class images and identities affect other perceptions of society and how evolving class formation can increase or decrease the potential for resistance and social change.

Elizabeth Borland

See also Alienation; Class; Countermovements; False Consciousness; Identity Politics; Inequality; Oligopoly; Social Change; Social Conflict; Socialism; Social Movements; Social Revolutions; Stratification, Social

Further Readings

Fantasia, Rick. 1995. "From Class Consciousness to Culture, Action, and Social Organization." *Annual Review of Sociology* 21:269–87.

Mann, Michael. 1973. *Consciousness and Action among the Western Working Class.* London: Macmillan.

Marx, Karl and Friedrich Engels. [1848] 1998. *The Communist Manifesto.* New York: Signet Classic.

CLUB DRUGS

MDMA (methylenedioxymethamphetamine), more commonly called ecstasy, is the most popular in a category commonly called "club drugs." Others are Rohypnol (flunitrazepam), GHB, and ketamine. First synthesized in Germany by the Merck Company in 1912, ecstasy is both a mild stimulant and a hallucinogen. The medical community initially embraced this drug for appetite suppression and psychotherapy.

However, research could not document any reliable benefits, and ecstasy fell out of favor by the late 1970s, only to reappear as a recreational drug about a decade later.

In the United States and Europe in the 1980s, a rave scene emerged featuring all-night dancing to various forms of electronic or "sampled" music (e.g., house, techno, and trance) at unconventional locations (warehouses and abandoned buildings). The scene embraced a community ethos of peace, love, and unity, not unlike the hippie subculture of the 1960s. As an empathogenic, ecstasy promoted the PLUR (peace, love, unity, respect) ethos. "Ravers" were typically between the ages of 13 and 21 (the so-called Generation X children of the baby boomers), and they sought to break down social barriers through the universal language of music at all-night dance parties. Ecstasy, with its stimulant and affective properties, fit perfectly.

Ecstasy's Impact on Public Health

Rates of ecstasy use are relatively low compared with those of marijuana, alcohol, and cocaine. In 2004, about 4.6 percent of the U.S. population over 12 years of age had tried ecstasy at least once, but less than 1 percent in the past month. However, ecstasy use is more prevalent than heroin, particularly among those ages 18 to 25. Although no studies have established an addictive potential, evidence exists of such psychosomatic complications as mood disorders, depression, anxiety, short-term memory problems, and physical problems such as nausea, increased heart rate, and overdose.

Social Control and Crime

Extensive adolescent presence at raves and reports of extensive drug use ignited fear in parents and officials that Generation X would fall victim to drug addiction or suffer other consequences. The anti-rave movement started at the community level. Cities passed ordinances designed to regulate rave activity, including juvenile curfews, fire codes, safety ordinances, and liquor licenses for large public gatherings. Also, rave promoters had to provide onsite medical services and security to prevent drug use.

Several federal measures early in this century took action against the rave scene and club drug use. The Ecstasy Anti-Proliferation Act of 2000 increased penalties for the sale and use of club drugs. In 2003, the Illicit Drug Anti-Proliferation Act, or the Rave Act, focusing on the promoters of raves and other dance events, made it a felony to provide a space for the purpose of illegal drug use.

To date, relatively few arrests and convictions for ecstasy use and sales have occurred, compared with those for drugs such as marijuana, crack, cocaine, and heroin. One reason is that, unlike other drug users, ecstasy users and sellers generally do not engage in much criminal activity other than illegal drug use, although theft, assault, and vandalism have reportedly occurred at raves or dance music events. Also, the drug is sold privately in informal networks that are difficult for police to penetrate, unlike the street-level sales of drugs like crack and heroin.

Tammy L. Anderson

See also Addiction; Drug Abuse; Drug Subculture; Therapeutic Communities

Further Readings

Baylen, Chelsea A. and Harold Rosenberg. 2006. "A Review of the Acute Subjective Effects of MDMA/Ecstasy." *Addiction* 101(7):933–47.

Bellis, Mark A., Karen Hughes, Andrew Bennett, and Roderick Thomson. 2003. "The Role of an International Nightlife Resort in the Proliferation of Recreational Drugs." *Addiction* 98(12):1713–21.

Collin, Matthew. 1997. *Altered State: The Story of Ecstasy Culture and Acid House.* London: Serpents Tail.

COCAINE AND CRACK

Cocaine hydrochloride (a white powder) and crack (a solidified version of cocaine hydrochloride) come from the coca leaf, grown mostly in the mountains of South America. Cocaine and crack are Schedule II stimulants that produce intense but short-term euphoria and increased energy levels. The chief active ingredient in coca leaves is the alkaloid cocaine, which was isolated in pure form in 1844.

Cocaine and crack produce dependency, addiction, and many other physical and psychological problems. They increase the heart rate and can lead to death by cardiac arrest. Both cocaine and crack also spur anxiety, paranoia, restlessness, and irritability. Because of the obsessive use patterns they produce, cocaine and crack increase the risk of sexually transmitted diseases, HIV, and physical assault and victimization among their users.

History

In the late 19th and early 20th centuries, the United States experienced its first cocaine epidemic. Soldiers took it to improve their endurance for battle. Cocaine was packaged in tonics and patent medicines to treat sinus illnesses or for eye, nose, and throat surgery. It was also administered to slaves to secure longer workdays and used as a cure for morphine addiction. Rampant addiction followed, with the drug outlawed in 1914 by the Harrison Narcotics Act.

Cocaine reemerged as a popular recreational drug during the 1970s among the upper class, celebrities, and fans of disco. Significant problems, such as the loss of jobs, savings accounts, and family trust, as well as increased health risks, such as overdose and cardiac arrest, soon followed.

Crack cocaine appeared in the early 1980s in the inner city among the lower class. It was packaged in small pieces called rocks (for as little as $5 each), which could be smoked in a small pipe. Users found themselves bingeing for hours or days, smoking up hundreds of dollars of the product and resorting to crime to fund their habits.

Crime and Social Control

The explosion in these two forms of cocaine, and the related social problems that followed, stunned U.S. public and government officials. Sophisticated criminal networks emerged in the inner city to control crack sales. Their use of violence to protect their profits produced significant spikes in rates of homicide and assault. Users resorted to all kinds of theft and sex work to fund their habits.

The federal government responded with numerous laws. The Comprehensive Crime Control Act of 1984 and the Anti-Drug Abuse Act of 1986 increased funds to reduce the sales and supply of the drug and broadened mandatory minimum penalties for cocaine sales and possession. The Omnibus Drug Abuse Act of 1988 expanded mandatory minimum penalties for drug users and sellers and established a 100-to-1 sentencing disparity between crack and powder cocaine. These laws filled U.S. prisons with small-time crack

cocaine users and did little to curb the cocaine crime problem. In December 2007, the Supreme Court ruled that federal judges could impose shorter sentences for crack cocaine cases, making them more in line with those for powder cocaine. This decision reducing the disparity in prison time for the two crimes had a strong racial dimension, since the majority of crack offenders are black.

Prevalence of Cocaine and Crack Use

Use of cocaine powder persists in the United States, although less so since its reemergence in the 1970s. Although scholars note a drop in crack use as well, they caution against its future escalation because its use also persists in inner-city pockets.

In 2005, approximately 33.7 million Americans reported using cocaine or crack at least once in their lives. This is about one third the amount who ever used marijuana (97.5 million) and 3 times the 11.5 million who ever used club drugs (ecstasy, ketamine, GHB, or Rohypnol). However, cocaine and crack continue to be the most often mentioned illicit drugs in emergency room visits, indicating the problematic nature of their use.

Tammy L. Anderson

See also Addiction; Anti-Drug Abuse Act of 1986; Club Drugs; Drug Abuse; Marijuana

Further Readings

Bureau of Justice Statistics. 2006. "Drug Use and Dependence, State and Federal Prisoners, 2004." Retrieved December 14, 2007 (http://www.ojp.usdoj.gov/bjs/abstract/dudsfp04.htm).

National Institute on Drug Abuse. 2005. "NIDA InfoFacts: Crack and Cocaine." Retrieved December 14, 2007 (http://www.drugabuse.gov/Infofacts/cocaine.html).

CODEPENDENCY

The term *codependency* has two related uses. The first originated in the addiction treatment and family therapy discourses. Until the 1980s, the term described a person involved in a relationship with an alcoholic or drug addict. The codependent engaged in considerable effort, mostly unsuccessful, to manage the problems associated with the partner's addiction. The spouse of an alcoholic might find him- or herself making excuses and telling lies to employers and family members, hiding liquor, struggling with issues of blame, and often trying in vain to figure out how to "fix" the addicted spouse. Domestic violence, as well as verbal and emotional abuse, might also characterize such relationships.

Over time, many nonaddicted spouses and partners came to believe that they had no sense of self apart from the addiction. Whereas the addict depended on substances, the spouse depended on the presence of the addiction for his or her self-worth. Treatment professionals began to label such clients "codependents." Because of the original connection with substance abuse, particularly alcohol, the therapy of choice for codependency was the twelve-step program called Al-Anon, which offers support to relatives and close friends of alcoholics.

In addition to the connotation of "co-alcoholic" or "co-addict," another use of the term *codependency* evolved during the 1980s. The newer use of the term connotes the same relationship difficulties and lack of a sense of self but without the necessity of substance abuse.

During the late 1980s, family therapists claimed to see increasing numbers of clients who felt that their identities were based largely in relationships with problematic spouses. The problems did not necessarily stem from substance abuse or addiction. A person who was drawn to emotionally distant partners, or partners who were consistently unfaithful, might continually attempt to change or fix the undesirable behavior in the other person. Similar to the spouse of the alcoholic or addict, the "codependent" partner began to base his or her sense of self-worth in trying to fix problems in the relationship, while losing touch with his or her own goals and plans. Codependents claimed not to know who they were and reported feeling out of touch with their emotions. Family therapists attributed this behavior to "dysfunctional" families.

According to the systems approach of the therapeutic discourse, all families have secrets and embarrassments, and all create rules to hide them from outsiders. Children internalize these rules, at the expense of trust and self-confidence. The dysfunctional family system results in relationships that lack true intimacy because the child purportedly has no self in which to base that intimacy. Children tried to please parents who could not be pleased. As a result, they did not develop a sense of self-worth apart from trying to please others. Within the therapeutic discourse, this constitutes a form of abuse, regardless of the presence of physical or emotional violence. Children grow up to reenact the various unresolved conflicts and abuses of childhood. They become what family therapists refer to as "adult children," codependent on the dysfunction and abuse much as the co-alcoholic had depended on alcoholism.

Because alcohol and substances did not necessarily play a part in the problems that adult children felt, those seeking therapy felt unwelcome in Al-Anon, with its focus on living with active alcoholism. In 1986, two enterprising codependents noticed this lack and started Codependents Anonymous, or simply CoDA. The group describes itself as a place for people with an inability to maintain functional relationships. CoDA adopted and adapted the twelve steps and traditions of Alcoholics Anonymous (AA), as well as its voluntaristic, democratic organizational structure. However, the two groups have strong ideological differences stemming from the therapeutic origins of codependency and AA's exclusive focus on alcohol. In any case, therapists began sending clients with codependency to CoDA meetings to supplement therapeutic sessions or to replace sessions when insurance would no longer cover them.

The recovery program for codependency differs from that of other addictions in that it does not require abstinence from the presumed cause: relationships. However, the more accurate term is not *recovery* but *management*, for the discourse claims there is no complete recovery. Codependent tendencies never disappear completely, but they can be recognized and addressed before they cause problems again. Doing so depends on finding ways to "get in touch with" one's true self, known in the discourse as the "inner child."

Codependency is a self-diagnosed condition. It does not appear among the disorders listed in the *Diagnostic and Statistical Manual of Mental Disorders*. Regardless of whether codependency constitutes an actual disease, the complaints do respond to real social concerns prevalent during the time. Most people who claim to be codependent are baby boomers, having come of age in a period during which many Americans valued "getting in touch with" the self and understanding one's "true" emotions. In addition, the increase in varieties of therapy and the popularity of self-help literature lionized and democratized self-actualization. Moreover, most codependents have experienced at least one divorce and several other uncouplings, which could lead one to question one's ability to maintain "functional" relationships. Many are single parents, and some struggle with custody arrangements. The resulting disillusionment can understandably produce a suspicion of marriage and other mainstream social institutions. However, these very institutions can offer a context for the strong sense of self that codependents claim to lack.

In short, codependency is a disease of its time. It reveals much about late 20th- and early 21st-century social circumstances.

Leslie Irvine

See also Abuse, Child; Abuse, Intimate Partner; Addiction; Alcoholism; Divorce; Drug Abuse; Family, Dysfunctional; Twelve-Step Programs

Further Readings

Beattie, Melody. 2001. *Codependent No More: How to Stop Controlling Others and Start Caring for Yourself.* 15th anniv. ed. New York: Harper/Hazelden.

Co-dependents Anonymous. 1995. *Co-dependents Anonymous.* Phoenix, AZ: CoDA Service Office.

Irvine, Leslie. 2008. *Codependent Forevermore: The Invention of Self in a Twelve-Step Group.* Chicago: University of Chicago Press.

Rice, John Steadman. 1998. *A Disease of One's Own: Psychotherapy, Addiction, and the Emergence of Co-dependency.* New Brunswick, NJ: Transaction.

COHABITATION

Cohabitation is a tentative, nonlegal coresidential union that does not require or imply a lifetime commitment to stay together. Perhaps as a result, cohabiting unions break up at a much higher rate than do marriages. Cohabitors have no responsibility for financial support of their partner, and most do not pool financial resources. Cohabitors are more likely than married couples both to value separate leisure activities and to keep their social lives independent and are much less likely than husbands and wives to be monogamous. Cohabitors may choose this arrangement because it carries no formal constraints or responsibilities.

A substantial proportion of cohabiting couples have definite plans to marry, and these couples tend to behave like already-married couples. Others have no plans to marry, and these tentative and uncommitted relationships are quite fragile. The tentative, impermanent, and socially unsupported nature of this latter type of cohabitation impedes the ability of this type of partnership to deliver many of the benefits of marriage, as do the relatively separate lives typically pursued by cohabiting partners. The uncertainty about the stability and longevity of the relationship makes both investment in the relationship and specialization with this partner much riskier than in marriage, for the partners themselves and for their extended families, friends, and communities. The lack of sharing typical of cohabitors disadvantages the women and their children in these families relative to the men, because women typically earn less than men; this is especially true for mothers. Cohabitation seems to distance people from some important social institutions, especially organized religion. Young men and women who define themselves as "religious" are less likely to cohabit, and those who cohabit subsequently become less religious.

Parenting and Sex

Cohabitation has become an increasingly important—but poorly delineated—context for childrearing. One quarter of current stepfamilies involve cohabiting couples, and a significant proportion of "single-parent" families are actually two-parent cohabiting families. The parenting role of a cohabiting partner toward the child(ren) of the other person is extremely vaguely defined and lacks both social and legal support.

Cohabiting men and women report slightly more sexual activity than married people. But cohabiting men and women are less likely than those who are married to be monogamous, although virtually all say that they expect their relationship to be sexually exclusive.

Commitment and Housework

Studies show that cohabiting people with no plans to marry are significantly less committed to their partner and to the partnership itself than are husbands and wives. Cohabiting men score lower on commitment than any other group.

One study found that married women spend 14 hours more on housework than married men do, while women who are cohabiting spend about 10 hours more on housework than cohabiting men. On this dimension, then, cohabitation is a better "deal" for women than marriage. Some economists argue that husbands compensate their wives for their time in work for the family by sharing their income with them. But cohabiting women generally do not share their partner's earnings, so they may be doing extra housework without extra pay.

Wealth and Emotional Well-Being

Married couples link their fates—including their finances. Among families with children, cohabiting couples have the lowest average level of wealth, comparable to families headed by a single mother. Intact two-parent families and stepfamilies have the highest level of wealth, followed at a distance by families headed by a single father. Unlike single-parent families, cohabiting couples have two potential earners, so their very low levels of wealth are a cause for concern, especially for the children living in these families. Financial uncertainty, especially low male earnings, reduces the chances that cohabiting couples will marry.

Cohabitors report more depression and less satisfaction with life than do married people. The key seems to lie in being in a relationship that one thinks will last. Marriage is, by design and agreement, for the long run, and married people tend to see their relationships as much more stable than do cohabitors. Relationship instability is often distressing, leading to anxiety and symptoms of depression. Thus, cohabitors with no plans to marry tend to show lower psychological well-being than similar married people. Worrying that one's relationship will break up is especially distressing for cohabiting women with children, who show quite high levels of depression as a result.

Who Cohabits?

Most cohabitors say that ensuring compatibility before marriage is an important reason why they wanted to live together. But people who cohabit and then marry are much more likely to divorce than people who married without living together. People who cohabit tend to have other characteristics that both lead them to cohabit in the first place and make them poor marriage material, accounting for the

higher divorce rates for those who cohabited. But some scholars argue that the experience of cohabitation itself makes subsequent marriages less stable.

Couples who live together with no definite plans to marry are making a different bargain than couples who marry or than engaged cohabitors. The bargain is definitely *not* marriage and is "marriage-like" only in that couples share an active sex life and a house or apartment. Cohabiting men tend to be quite uncommitted to the relationship; cohabiting women with children tend to be quite uncertain about its future. Cohabiting couples have lower earnings and less wealth than married couples, perhaps disadvantaging the children in them. Cohabiting couples with plans to marry, on the other hand, are indistinguishable on most dimensions from married couples.

Linda J. Waite

See also Divorce; Domestic Partnerships; Role Strain

Further Readings

Booth, Alan and Ann C. Crouter. 2002. *Just Living Together: Implications of Cohabitation for Children, Families, and Social Policy.* Mahwah, NJ: Erlbaum.
Smock, Pamela J. 2000. "Cohabitation in the United States: An Appraisal of Research Themes, Findings, and Implications." *Annual Review of Sociology* 26:1–20.
Waite, Linda J. and Maggie Gallagher. 2000. *The Case for Marriage: Why Married People Are Happier, Healthier, and Better Off Financially.* New York: Doubleday.

COLLATERAL DAMAGE

The obligation to distinguish between civilians and civilian objects on the one hand and military objectives on the other is a central tenet of international humanitarian law (the law that applies during an armed conflict). Collateral damage is inflicted when a party to the conflict intends to attack a military objective but kills or injures civilians or destroys civilian objects in addition to, or instead of, destroying the military objective.

Significant collateral damage is a particular risk with respect to aerial bombardment campaigns. There are several ways in which a conflict bombing of legitimate targets may kill and injure civilians. The civilians may be working inside the target, such as workers in a munitions factory, or they may live next to, or simply be passing by, a military target. An example of civilians killed and injured as a result of living near targets is the deaths of, and injuries to, civilians in the 2003 Iraq conflict, when houses in the vicinity of military objectives collapsed as a result of the shock of explosions.

Another risk is that missiles may simply go off course. In the 2003 Iraq conflict, Amnesty International reported that a U.S. missile hit a bus in Western Iraq, killing five civilians and injuring others. A U.S. spokesman reportedly stated that the real target was a nearby bridge. A further threat to civilians from aerial bombardment is the risk of damage caused by defensive measures such as anti-aircraft missiles, which may fall back onto civilian areas.

Collateral damage does not necessarily occur immediately following an attack on a military objective. During the 1990–91 Gulf conflict, many more deaths occurred as a result of the long-term effect of the targeting of power grids, as sewage plants and water purification facilities broke down, than were caused contemporaneously during the bombardment.

An important question in relation to the threat of collateral casualties resulting from aerial bombardment is whether this threat has become practically negligible as a result of the advent of precision-guided missiles. Unfortunately, although precision-guided missiles have the capacity to greatly reduce collateral damage, risks to civilians remain. Weather may affect the accuracy of such missiles, and countermeasures such as smoke or jamming devices may interfere with their targeting system.

International Armed Conflicts

Although treaties and customary international law regarding armed conflicts (i.e., law that results from the general practice of nation-states coupled with the belief that they are legally obliged to so act) prohibit the intentional targeting of civilians, they accept that civilians may be incidentally affected. Part of the reality of war is that innocent people are killed and injured and their property is damaged. International humanitarian law would never be respected if it established unrealistic rules.

The modern expression of the legal restriction on collateral damage in international armed conflicts is set out in Article 51(5) of the 1977 Protocol I

Additional to the 1949 Geneva Conventions. It is prohibited to launch any attack with expectations that it will cause incidental loss of civilian life, injury to civilians or damage to civilian objects, or a combination thereof, which would be excessive in relation to the concrete and direct military advantage anticipated. This means that the death and destruction of innocent civilians and their property which is incidental to an attack on a legitimate military target (i.e., collateral damage) is prohibited only if it is excessive in relation to the military advantage anticipated from the attack. In a recent study on customary international humanitarian law, the International Committee of the Red Cross (ICRC) opined that this rule represents customary international law and so is binding on all nation-states.

Therefore, any commander who authorizes an attack in an international armed conflict which causes excessive collateral damage may be criminally responsible under international law for the commission of a war crime. Indeed, the statute of the International Criminal Court (created in 1998) prohibits, under Article 8(2)(b)(iv), intentionally launching an attack in the knowledge that such attack will cause incidental loss of life or injury to civilians or damage to civilian objects which would be clearly excessive in relation to the concrete and direct overall military advantage anticipated. This only criminalizes very clear incidents of excessive collateral damage when the accused person realizes that the attack would cause such excessive civilian casualties.

Noninternational Armed Conflicts (Civil Wars)

International humanitarian law is generally less extensive and less specific when it comes to noninternational armed conflicts. Historically, nation-states have been jealous of their sovereignty and unwilling to countenance any interference in domestic affairs. Humanitarian law in noninternational armed conflicts is governed by Article 3 common to the four 1949 Geneva Conventions (universally accepted by nation-states). However, owing to the generality of this article, it appears that the only possible bearing on collateral damage is the duty to treat noncombatants humanely, which arguably would be breached by intentionally attacking a target which would cause excessive civilian casualties.

The other treaty which may apply during noninternational armed conflicts (for those nation-states accepting it) is the 1977 Protocol II Additional to the Geneva Conventions. However, although this prohibits intentionally attacking civilians and attacking objects indispensable to the survival of the civilian population, it does not expressly prohibit excessive collateral damage. The statute of the International Criminal Court also fails to refer to excessive collateral damage in noninternational armed conflicts. Therefore, the issue arises as to whether or not customary international law prohibits excessive collateral damage in noninternational armed conflicts. The ICRC study proclaimed that the rule prohibiting excessive collateral damage applies in both international and noninternational armed conflicts, but the extent to which nation-states accept this finding remains unclear.

Christine Byron

See also Arms Control; War; War Crimes

Further Readings

Fenrick, William. 1982. "The Rule of Proportionality and Protocol I in Conventional Warfare." *Military Law Review* 98:91–127.

Lippman, Matthew. 2002. "Aerial Attacks on Civilians and the Humanitarian Law of War: Technology and Terror from World War I to Afghanistan." *California Western International Law Journal* 33:1–67.

Reynolds, Jefferson D. 2005. "Collateral Damage on the 21st Century Battlefield: Enemy Exploitation of the Law of Armed Conflict, and the Struggle for a Moral High Ground." *Air Force Law Review* 56:1–108.

COLLECTIVE CONSCIOUSNESS

Collective consciousness, also known as *conscience collective,* refers to a shared, intersubjective understanding of common norms and values among a group of people. The concept was developed by eminent French sociologist Émile Durkheim (1858–1917). In his magnum opus, *The Division of Labor in Society,* Durkheim employs the term *collective consciousness* to describe a determinate social system in which the totality of beliefs and sentiments are common to the average members of a society. According to Durkheim, collective consciousness possesses a distinctive reality because it is a nonmaterial social construction, which is external to, and coercive of, individuals in a particular social order. Therefore, Durkheim distinguishes collective consciousness from the individual consciousness. Collective consciousness of a given society operates as an external force over the group members and autonomously exists outside of the individual's biological and psychic sphere. Nonetheless, the collective consciousness can only be operationalized through consciousness of the individuals in the community because it is a *social construct.* Thus, although collective consciousness is something totally different from the consciousness of separate individuals, it can be realized only through individual consciousness.

Collective consciousness is a significant concept for the Durkheimian theory of solidarity because it constitutes the basis of social systems of representation and action. Durkheim believes that an act is considered as unlawful when it offends the collective consciousness. He claims that a certain behavior is not condemned because it is criminal; instead, it is criminal because people condemn it. Thus, it is collective consciousness that regulates all social worlds and defines accordingly what is acceptable and what is deviant within the community. Here, Durkheim's discussion over *social facts* is a key text to be considered. According to Durkheim, manners of acting, thinking, and feeling that are external to the individual and exercise control over him or her constitute *social* facts, which are observable in two forms: "normal" and "pathological." Normal social facts are simply the social facts that can be found in almost all cases in a social life, whereas pathological forms can be found in a very few cases for brief transient periods. Durkheim regards a certain rate of crime as a normal fact; however, he considers high crime rates in a certain society as a pathological fact that needs sociological explanation. In this sense, Durkheim sees collective consciousness as a cure for a society that suffers from the mass similarity of consciousness, which may give rise to legal rules imposed on everybody by (re)producing uniform beliefs and practices.

Conscience collective is also a key term to grasp Durkheim's typologies in *The Division of Labor in Society,* where he argues that the degree of collective consciousness varies in regard to characteristics of the solidarity in a certain collectivity. For Durkheim, *mechanical solidarity,* in which similarity of individuals who share a uniform way of life is predominant, is distinguished by its high degree of collective consciousness; on the other hand, *organic solidarity,* which is based on extensive social differentiations and development of autonomous individuals, reflects the reverse characteristics. As Durkheim foresees, as modern societies renounce the mechanical solidarity of their past and transform into societies based on organic solidarity, the collective consciousness declines in strength. As collective consciousness gets weakened in a particular community, the society suffers from a total social disorder, what Durkheim calls *anomie,* wherein the shared meanings of norms and values become nullified. This particular context enables an individual to act as a free rider agent. Durkheim associates, for example, the weakened collective consciousness with an increased rate of anomic suicide. Thus, when individual consciousness does not reflect the collective consciousness, the individual loses a clear sense of which action is proper and what an improper behavior is. Then, the threat of *anomie* in a society emerges from a lack of mechanical solidarity and strong collective consciousness.

Durkheim regards every society as a moral society; thus, his concept of collective consciousness is much related to his theoretical analyses of the sociology of religion as well. For Durkheim, the *conscience collective* manifests itself through totems in a primitive society. Religion plays a remarkable role in the creation and consolidation of the similar consciousness among group members. First, religion provides the necessary link between individual consciousness and the collective consciousness. Second, radical changes in the collective consciousness generally occur during historical moments of transformation in beliefs in the community.

Nevertheless, as Durkheim developed his theory of religion, he began to overwhelmingly emphasize systems of symbols and social representations over collective consciousness. In his subsequent writings during the late 1890s, Durkheim modified the concept of collective consciousness and replaced the concept with a more specific notion: *collective representations.* Durkheim never rejected the term *conscience collective* completely, but his reformulated concept of collective consciousness was remarkably different from the original concept developed in his specific theory of solidarity in *The Division of Labor in Society.* The modification made the individual consciousness relatively less significant and overemphasized the systems of belief. Thus, it may be concluded that Durkheim abandoned the specific theory of collective consciousness but retained the concept of *conscience collective* as a part of his larger theory of social solidarity.

Mustafa E. Gurbuz

See also Anomie; Religion, Civil; Suicide

Further Readings

Alexander, Jeffrey C., ed. 1988. *Durkheimian Sociology: Cultural Studies.* Cambridge, England: Cambridge University Press.

Durkheim, Émile. [1893] 1984. *The Division of Labor in Society.* New York: Free Press.

Jones, Robert A. 2000. "Émile Durkheim." Pp. 205–50 in *The Blackwell Companion to Major Social Theorists,* edited by G. Ritzer. Malden, MA: Blackwell.

Marske, Charles E. 1987. "Durkheim's 'Cult of the Individual' and the Moral Reconstitution of Society." *Sociological Theory* 5(1):1–14.

Némédi, Dénes. 1995. "Collective Consciousness, Morphology, and Collective Representations: Durkheim's Sociology of Knowledge 1894–1900." *Sociological Perspectives* 38(1):41–56.

COLONIALISM

Both the global magnitude of colonialism's expansion and its abrupt, fragmented demise place colonialism at a pivotal phase in human history. Colonialism normally refers to the conquest and direct control of other land and other people by Western capitalist entities intent on expanding processes of production and consumption. In this context, colonialism is situated within a history of imperialism best understood as the globalization of the capitalist mode of production. While colonialism as a formal political process managed through state entities began to unravel following World War II, the global expansion of capitalism continues as a process that informs and often structures national, corporate, and human entanglements on a global scale.

Historically, *colonialism* is a term largely restricted to that period of European expansion lasting roughly from 1830 to 1930. By the early 20th century, Britain,

France, Germany, Italy, Belgium, the Netherlands, Denmark, Spain, and Portugal together claimed control of nearly 84 percent of the earth's surface. The British alone ruled over one fourth of the world's land and one third of its population.

European expansion did not begin, of course, in 1830. It was arguably the Iberian navigators of the 15th century, reaching the Americas in 1492 and India in 1498, who inaugurated the age of colonialism. Furthermore, other empires outside of Europe clearly rose (and fell) prior to the colonial period. By the 1830s, however, a new period of empire building had erupted, sparked by a volatile combination of technologies (of travel, production, and health) and ideologies (including liberalism, enlightenment, scientific racism, and capitalism) that entangled human relationships within the distinct and asymmetrical identifying categories of colonizer and colonized.

Colonial expansion was related to technological advancements driven by the rise of industrialization. Processes of commodity production that required ever larger quantities of raw material and unskilled labor, along with advances in travel technologies, pushed European powers into untapped spaces of labor and material around the world. In the process, colonized lands were reconfigured as spaces of manufacture or plantations for cash crops, and newly landless colonial populations were introduced to the wage economy.

Travel technologies helped make this possible. From the large-hulled sailing ships that took the Portuguese into Southeast Asia during the 1500s to the steam engines that followed 300 years later, people and products began to move through space at a pace the world had never before seen. At the same time, medical discoveries, such as quinine, allowed for relatively sickness-free travel into tropical climates that had before caused great illness for Europeans. In addition, the arms revolution at the end of the 19th century allowed for relatively small forces to take and hold large blocks of land and indigenous populations.

Ideologically, the impetus for colonialism might rest with what has been called capitalism's tendency to expand beyond the confines of a single political system. Yet this push outward was buttressed not only by a belief in the logic of capitalism but also by a belief in the racial and cultural superiority of the colonizers. Colonialism as a "civilizing" project was fueled by Enlightenment beliefs in reason and progress, ideas thought capable of leading humanity out of the darkness of tradition and superstition and into the light of objective truth.

A concurrent scientific obsession with "race" further differentiated between populations already divided by an economic system of exploitation and helped legitimize feelings of superiority for the colonizers over the colonized. In short, an expansion in travel, combined with an ideology of racial difference, resulted in a cultural confusion of space for time, locating indigenous populations temporally behind Europeans in an evolutionary scheme that went beyond biology to include culture and intellect.

The confluence of these ideologies worked to create, at least in the mind of the colonizers, legitimacy for their actions. Colonialism as the "white man's burden" was, for a time, perceived as a legitimate and benevolent enterprise of Europeans civilizing others.

A central component of the colonial project was the production of knowledge about other populations by European powers. To dominate and educate a population, one must construct that population as needing domination and education. Thus, colonialism brought with it a description of indigenous beliefs and behaviors that codified populations in terms of race, culture, tradition, religion, and economy. Knowledge of the world's populations, created within a colonial context, highlighted differences to the benefit of the colonizers and, perhaps more important, continues to inform global relations as well as more intimate understandings of self and other. Area studies and anthropology departments, for example, owe their existence, at least in part, to the colonial process of knowledge production.

The demise of colonialism was in many ways of the colonizers' own doing. A focus on liberalism and nationalism, in particular, had devastating effects on colonial projects in that indigenous populations were being introduced to Enlightenment concepts such as self-attainment and national identity. These ideas gave ideological weight to nationalist youth movements in colonized spaces. These movements often served to organize resistance that eventually turned into postcolonial nationalist projects.

William H. Leggett

See also Global Economy; Globalization; Imperialism; Race; Racial Formation Theory; Racism

Further Readings

Dirks, Nicholas, ed. 1992. *Colonialism and Culture.* Ann Arbor, MI: University of Michigan Press.

Williams, Patrick and Laura Chrisman, eds. 1994. *Colonial Discourse and Post-colonial Theory: A Reader.* New York: Columbia University Press.

Wolf, Eric. 1997. *Europe and the People without History.* Berkeley, CA: University of California Press.

COMMUNITARIANISM

Communitarianism, as a coherent body of thought, is a movement that seeks to resolve social problems by strengthening individual commitment to the broader society. The movement began to coalesce in the early 1990s among predominantly U.S. social scientists. Its chief proponent is sociologist Amitai Etzioni (president of the American Sociological Association, 1994–95), who, along with political scientist William A. Galston, among others, formed the Communitarian Network in 1990. One of the major components of that network is the Institute for Communitarian Policy Studies at George Washington University, which began publishing *The Responsive Community* in 1990. Publication ceased in 2004 after 54 issues.

Communitarianism, in broad terms, is a partial rejection of the liberal ideology that has been a cornerstone of Western political and social thought for approximately 200 years. Liberalism maintains that the rights of individuals supersede the rights of the group and that governments are formed to secure individual liberties. Communitarians claim that the responsibilities individuals have to each other and to the larger society have taken a backseat to individual rights, and this has led to a downward spiral of selfishness, greed, and conflict. In U.S. society, and throughout much of the modern world, rights have trumped responsibilities. Individuals have gained a strong sense of entitlement but with a rather weak sense of obligation to the broader group—whether it be family, community, or society.

However, the communitarian rejection of liberalism is not wholesale. The Responsive Communitarian Platform, adopted in 1991, states that the communitarian perspective "recognizes both individual human dignity and the social dimension of human existence."

Communitarians emphasize the need to understand that individual lives are inextricably tied to the good of communities, out of which individual identity has been constituted.

Etzioni's 1993 book, *The Spirit of Community,* details the communitarian perspective on U.S. social problems and offers a prescription for strengthening moral values. Etzioni argues that law and order, families, schools, and the individual's sense of social responsibility can be restored without the country becoming a police state and that the power of special interests can be curtailed without limiting constitutional rights to lobby and petition those who govern.

The Responsive Communitarian Platform states some of the major principles of the movement:

- Community (families, neighborhoods, nations) cannot survive unless members dedicate some of their attention and resources to shared projects.
- Communitarians favor strong democracy. They seek to make government more representative, more participatory, and more responsive.
- Communitarians urge that all educational institutions provide moral education, that they should teach values that Americans share.
- The right to be free of government intervention does not mean to be free from moral claims. Civil society requires that we be each other's keepers.
- The parenting deficit must be reduced. Parents should spend more time with their children; child care and socialization are not responsibilities that other institutions should take on large scale.
- Education for values and character formation is more "basic" than academic skills.
- Reciprocity is at the heart of social justice.

Gerald Kloby

See also Collective Consciousness; Community; Identity Politics; Social Networks

Further Readings

Etzioni, Amitai. 1993. *The Spirit of Community.* New York: Simon & Schuster.

Zakaria, Fareed. 1996. "The ABCs of Communitarianism." *Slate.com,* July 26. Retrieved November 28, 2007 (http://www.slate.com/id/2380).

COMMUNITY

Theorists do not agree on the precise definition of *community*. Referents for the term range from ethnic neighborhoods to self-help groups to Internet chat rooms. What is broadly agreed upon is that community is a locus of social interaction where people share common interests, have a sense of belonging, experience solidarity, and can expect mutual assistance. Communities are the source of social attachments, create interdependencies, mediate between the individual and the larger society, and sustain the well-being of members. When locality based, such as in a town or neighborhood, they also provide a place for people to participate in societal institutions and, as such, are linked with democracy. Because community is recognized as socially imperative, community absence or weakening becomes a social problem.

In the 19th and early 20th centuries, social theorists, looking at different types of places (a typological approach), observed the shift of population from rural areas to larger, denser, more diverse urban-industrial places. They noted a transition also occurring in the way people related to one another. In smaller, traditional villages, people were bound together by their similarities and sentiments; in cities their ties were based on contracts and they lived a more anonymous existence. The concept of community became identified with that smaller, more intimate locality and the types of relationships within it. In the 1920s the theoretical framework of human ecology, using the city of Chicago as a laboratory, further reinforced the notion of community as a geographic entity.

As a result, community became a social concern as the proportion of the population living in urban areas increased. Social scientists depicted urban dwellers as bereft of involving social ties, emotionally armored against a world of strangers. They were detached individuals, lacking the necessary social supports for psychological well-being. The city thus had a disorganizing effect.

By the mid-20th century, however, research documented the existence of ethnic villages within cities, but more important, in a new conceptualization, community was described as "liberated" from place. Community was reframed as a network of individuals connected to each other possibly in a particular locale or possibly widely dispersed geographically. Researchers sought to uncover the locus of attachments, whether in the neighborhood, workplace, or religious institution. Network theorists gave assurances that people enjoyed necessary social supports but in a more far-flung manner.

Communitarianism

With advances in technology, increased geographic mobility, and the expansion of later-stage capitalism, a concern has emerged among community theorists that societies are becoming dangerously privatized, individualized, and atomized. With a fragmented diversity in postmodern society, no longer is there a consensus on fundamental rules of order. Individuals construct their own social worlds and escape into hedonistic pleasures and narcissism. As civic engagement and social capital decline, the emphasis on individual rights strengthens while the sense of obligation and community responsibility weakens. As the tradition of community disappears, society becomes corroded by self-interest. Atomized individuals become at risk for totalitarian leadership and vulnerable to exploitation by hegemonic market forces." Theorists, defining themselves as "communitarians," call for a reversal of these trends, stressing individual responsibility for the greater common good and the re-assertion of shared values and norms.

Critics call communitarianism morally authoritarian, failing to grapple with questions of social diversity and inequity in the establishment of a normative order. Opponents charge that dominant institutions and power holders are not sufficiently challenged, and in consensus building, some groups could potentially be excluded and differences suppressed, leading to recent attempts to confront differences within and between communities as a starting point for political discourse. Pluralism is at the core, and democratic participation and power differentials are part of the debate. A more radical communitarianism encourages participation in multiple communities—to create dense social networks of solidarity—and attempts to incorporate a theory of social justice.

Most research, however, does not find people isolated and atomized. They still have family and friends and broader organizational contacts. Alarmist calls about declining civic engagement are countered by the assertion that the associations of today are not copies of the Rotary and Lions clubs of the 1950s. People today are more likely to have "loose connections," temporary involvements in a range of social networks, each of which may have a different instrumental end and varying degrees of social solidarity. All institutional realms have become more porous as people, resources, and information flow across their boundaries. Individuals may join self-help groups, which they can abandon at will or reattach with in some other location. Internet connections allow individuals to establish new social contacts, often organized around particular interests or similarities, or to reinforce existing social ties as in e-mails among family members. Still the Internet community can be deleted with a click, subject to individual will. So there are new forms of connecting, reflective of and adaptive to present-day realities. By holding these new types of attachments to the standards of an earlier, geographic place-bound community, they seem weak and decidedly more individualized. The newer conceptualizations leave open to debate whether or not they should be called communities. Research questions remain on whether the essential conditions of democracy and citizenship are served by them.

Security or Freedom

Tension will always exist between the individual and the collective on how much individual freedom must be surrendered for the security and support of the latter. Amid the individualism described by the communitarians, other social theorists describe a contemporary trend where individuals choose to live in enclaves, whether by race, ethnicity, lifestyle, or social class, raising questions about whether these are true communities. The physical boundaries around these enclaves may be arranged on a continuum of permeability, from gated communities (fortresses) with guardhouses and elaborate security systems, to those with streets or other geographic features serving as symbolic borders. Each enclave distinguishes members from outsiders. Individuals are willing to forgo some individual freedoms for the security of knowing their properties are hedged against depreciation and that their neighbors are likely to be similar to themselves. People are fearful of those they perceive as different, especially in a post-9/11 world of terrorism, and seek the security of the homogeneous. In the face of globalization some may retreat into parochial localism.

Locality-Based Actions

With the bias in community research defining it as locality based, it can be studied as the site where social problems occur. Groups tend to be most concerned about their own spaces. At the neighborhood level they may organize to address social problems and their consequences, such as crime or environmental pollution. Community power differentials come into play as to who is claiming that a problem exists. Social class differences may also be prominent in certain kinds of issues, such as those pitting environmental concerns against economic opportunities. The community becomes a geographic arena where a threat elicits a unified response or coalitions form.

Given the multidimensionality of *community,* community development is an umbrella term. Community development may reference early historical designs to plan new communities; more often it has meant an action course to identify problems within a geographic community, assessing the needs of members, locating resources, and coordinating agencies to deliver the necessary goods and services. Earlier community development programs were more paternalistic where governments identified needs and problems and helped local people find solutions. A shift occurred toward an empowerment model where local people—taught necessary organizing skills and encouraged by activists and practitioners—identify their own needs and challenge centers of economic and political power to remedy the situations. Coalitions emerge and social movements begin. As centers of decision making become more distant from localities, especially in transnational corporate boardrooms, community development strategies may require widely dispersed social networks and cybermobilization. The Internet may be an effective means to organize geographically distant parties.

The notion of community development, given the concern about the absence or breakdown of community, may also refer to efforts to strengthen social capital. The communitarian platform urges and applauds strategies to encourage local interaction, civic involvements, and solidarity.

Questions for Research

In the postmodern world, the meaning of community is likely to remain fluid. People's lives are less determined by place, but at the same time, there is more concern about environmentally sustainable local areas. Individuals have more freedom to choose their social attachments. Researchers and community theorists are consequently challenged by at least three questions:

1. Are people connected? What is the nature and degree of their social attachments?

2. Do the multiple communal forms fulfill the prerequisites of a democratic society in terms of citizen participation and social justice?

3. Are contemporary communities able to respond to the major challenges of a globalizing world, particularly the increased diversity and global interdependencies, the retreat of the state from the public sector, the ascendancy of market forces, and the widening gap between the rich and the poor?

Some theorists see ominous trends, whereas others see evolutionary change. Ongoing research will assess whether contemporary social attachments are indeed communities, and whether their presence or absence or the nature of the bonds constitute a social problem.

Mary Lou Mayo

See also Collective Consciousness; Communitarianism; Identity Politics; Postmodernism; Social Networks

Further Readings

Bauman, Zygmunt. 2001. *Community: Seeking Safety in an Insecure World.* Cambridge, England: Polity Press.

Bruhn, John G. 2005. *The Sociology of Community Connections.* New York: Kluwer Academic/Plenum.

Castells, Manuel. 2003. *The Power of Identity.* 2nd ed. New York: Blackwell.

Etzioni, Amitai. 1993. *The Spirit of Community: Rights, Responsibilities, and the Communitarian Agenda.* New York: Crown.

Little, Adrian. 2002. *The Politics of Community.* Edinburgh, Scotland: Edinburgh University Press.

Wuthnow, Robert. 2002. *Loose Connections: Joining Together in America's Fragmented Communities.* New ed. Cambridge, MA: Harvard University Press.

COMMUNITY CORRECTIONS

Community corrections refers to the supervised handling of juvenile and adult criminal offenders, convicted or facing possible conviction, outside of traditional penal institutions. It includes a wide range of programs intermediate between incarceration and outright release, such as probation, parole, pretrial release, and house arrest. It includes diversion from criminal justice to rehabilitative programs, day reporting, and residential centers. Community corrections measures include restitution, community service, fines, and boot camps. Whereas probation and parole are the predominant forms of community-based corrections, they often are considered separately, having long been parts of mainstream criminal justice practice. The resources available for community corrections and the forms they take vary considerably from jurisdiction to jurisdiction.

Community-based correctional programs stand in contrast to jails or prisons—institutions with large numbers of inmates incarcerated for extended periods in enclosed, formally administered settings, apart from society. The goals of punishment, deterrence, and incapacitation through exclusion and isolation prevail in jails and prisons. Physical abuse and other inhumane conditions, including overcrowding and convict-dominated peer cultures, are undesirable aspects of these "total institutions." Incarceration also leads to resentment over perceived unfairness and discrimination in the criminal justice process, the loss of hope and positive aspirations, and inmates further committing themselves to criminal lives as they accept their deviant social identities (social labels) and redefine themselves as essentially criminal. Inmates' isolation from their families and inability to engage in productive work can also foster intergenerational criminogenic patterns. Consequently, the community-based correctional movement sought to alleviate these consequences of traditional correctional practices.

The modern movement toward community-based corrections began in the 1950s and gained impetus in the late 1960s, sparked by a holistic reassessment of the purposes and processes of criminal justice. It was initiated with hopes of achieving restitution, rehabilitation, reintegration, and restorative justice. Low-risk offenders would reap the benefits of remaining in the community. Higher-risk offenders would be subject to more supervision than if simply released into open society. Community-based practices provided levels of punishment intermediary between simple release and confinement, practices allowing for more proportionate responses to both the crimes involved and offenders' individual circumstances. Offenders would receive means by which to reassess their actions and to positively direct their lives. Community corrections programs would offer structured paths by which offenders could reintegrate into the larger society. The threat of alternative punitive criminal justice regimens would encourage offenders to take advantage of rehabilitative regimens.

Financial considerations also prompted interest in community-based programs. By the 1970s, prison expansion and the economics of housing and supervising inmates put severe strains on state budgets, and community correctional programs are much less costly than those involving total confinement. With their diversity of midrange sanctions, community-based programs offered a relatively low-cost panacea to crime problems.

Community-based correctional programs take numerous formats. Pretrial release prevents unneeded jailing of offenders posing no flight risk (e.g., because they have established roots in the community) or threat to society. Offenders may be released on bail or on their own recognizance prior to trial, often under supervision and with restrictions on travel. Pretrial release without bond (release on recognizance), with a penalty incurred only if a court appearance is missed, benefits those who might be jailed simply because they could not afford to put up bond.

Diversion programs may be offered to offenders both before and following criminal justice processing. Either way, the aim is to provide individualized assistance in resolving the problems that generate unlawful behaviors. Offenders may be directed to conflict resolution programs, including mediation services, which focus on the issues that led to criminal charges. Some locales maintain community courts, in which neighborhood residents partner with criminal justice agencies to offer nonadversarial adjudication of low-level offenses and controversies. Diversionary approaches with predominantly rehabilitative aims combine release with participation in a problem-specific diversion program such as substance abuse treatment, mental health counseling, and job training and assistance. In some jurisdictions, substance abusers are initially referred to drug courts. These specialized courts have been successful particularly in providing supervision and treatment for drug offenders, while freeing up criminal justice resources for more serious crimes. Offenders are monitored and face immediate sanctions for continued drug use. Other offenders may be directed to educational programs, as much of the

traditional inmate population is not literate and not apt to have completed high school. Some rehabilitation programs work with all affected family members.

House arrest, another in-community criminal sanction, requires offenders be in their residence during specified times each day. Offenders might be allowed to leave home for work, counseling, education, and other rehabilitation activities. Enforcement of house arrest may be manually through phone calls or electronically through sensors locked to the offenders' ankles or wrists. The latter tracking devices alert authorities when offenders venture from a prescribed territory. These practices allow offenders to engage in legitimate occupations, raise children, and avoid entanglement with criminogenic influences, as would be the case if they were incarcerated.

Offenders assigned to day reporting programs live at home but report regularly—often daily. This regimen allows for rehabilitative treatment and continued employment while under supervised punitive sanctions. Day reporting programs may be based in standalone centers or in residential correctional facilities, such as halfway houses or work-release facilities.

Offenders in residential centers have limited freedom to positively engage in the larger society. Centers range from small, secure, community-based facilities providing a full range of correctional programs, including drug and alcohol abuse treatment and mental health counseling, to loosely structured programs that simply provide low-custody shelter. Programs dealing with participants having multiple personal and social deficiencies have met limited success. The most successful targets of support programs are offenders who want to redirect their lives but need assistance to do so. Some agencies offer "mutual agreement programs," contracts stipulating goals offenders are to achieve and the freedoms they will gain for doing so. Recurrent problems of residential centers include rebellion against rules participants regard as petty, offender codes (similar to inmate codes in prisons) that set offenders against staff, and facilities and neighborhoods offering few opportunities for successful personal upgrading. Virtually all community-oriented correctional formats face common problems of underfunding and understaffing. In nearly all forms of community-based corrections, participants face the risk that relatively minor violations of program and release conditions will lead to reincarceration. The more closely they are supervised, the more likely minor offenses will be discovered.

Day reporting and residential centers may function as halfway houses, intermediary between total incarceration and living at large in the community. Some provide halfway-out measures to increase the mobility of probationers and inmates who are being released early from prison yet still require intensive supervision. Or they can be used as halfway-in programs for offenders found in violation of probation or parole conditions.

Boot camps usually are designed for younger offenders perceived to lack self-restraint and respect for authority, thus requiring external structuring. Camps are typically set in natural settings. Their living conditions, organizational structures, and emphases on discipline and physical fitness are modeled after military training. Advocates of boot camps hope to give participants a sense of accomplishment and to get them off drugs. Critics argue the boot camps are often overly harsh and abusive, leave participants with few additional skills, and bear limited success. Such programs may need to be coupled with extensive postrelease supervision to effectively change offenders' lifestyles.

Fines, restitution, and community service provide retribution and can act as rehabilitation and deterrent. Restitution may require that offenders make reparations for the losses they have caused their victims, or it may require offenders do community service in amends for harms caused society. Setting appropriate financial penalties can be problematic, both in determining amounts proportionate to the offense and in setting amounts appropriate to the economic status of the offender. Some jurisdictions solve such dilemmas by imposing day fines, proportionate to the amount of the offender's earnings. Collecting such debts is problematic: Offenders often are in poor financial state to begin with or come to feel their obligations unfair. Financial penalties can be used to underwrite the criminal justice process.

One of the initial impetuses for community-oriented corrections was the notion of restorative justice, the view that criminal proceedings should focus on the predicaments of all parties involved in a criminal incident, should repair the harm done the actual people involved in a criminal incident, and should focus on the future rather than the past. Restorative justice sees crime as an act that violates individual victims, their families, and the community, rather than the state. It places primacy on offender accountability and responsibility and on reparations rather than punitiveness.

Critics contend that restorative justice processes jeopardize such defendant rights as the presumption of innocence and the right to assistance of legal counsel.

Since the 1980s, in response to shifts in popular sentiment, there has been a trend toward using community-based correctional formats for more traditional correctional ends. Programs that initially sought to rehabilitate and reintegrate offenders have become more concerned with community safety. Some even take on a punitive cast. One of the predicaments of community-based corrections is that it has not necessarily led to a reduction in the number of offenders going to jail or prison. Because of their lower cost and ability to handle more people without increasing prison capacity, community treatment efforts are now sometimes used to bring more people within the scope of criminal justice treatment. Pressure "to do something" has led to community-based programs being used to expand sanctioning to less serious offenders.

Charles M. ViVona

See also Deterrence Programs; Juvenile Institutionalization, Effects of; Parole; Prison; Prisons, Pregnancy and Parenting; Probation; Restorative Justice; Total Institution; Victim–Offender Mediation Model

Further Readings

Cromwell, Paul F., Leanne Fiftal Alarid, and Rolando V. del Carmen. 2005. *Community-Based Corrections.* 6th ed. Belmont, CA: Wadsworth/Thomson Learning.

Latessa, Edward J. and Harry E. Allen. 2003. *Corrections in the Community.* 3rd ed. Cincinnati, OH: Anderson/LexusNexus.

McCarthy, Belinda Rodgers, Bernard J. McCarthy Jr., and Matthew Leone. 2001. *Community-Based Corrections.* 4th ed. Belmont, CA: Wadsworth/Thomson Learning.

Petersilia, Joan, ed. 1998. *Community Corrections: Probation, Parole, and Intermediate Sanctions.* New York: Oxford University Press.

COMMUNITY CRIME CONTROL

Community crime control refers to the use of criminal justice mediums in solving social problems or preventing crime. Examples of this proactive approach to crime control include neighborhood watch, community watch, and beautification projects. A primary assumption is that crime is a social problem, rather than an individual problem, disrupting the community structure.

The goal of community crime control is to empower the community by decreasing the fear of victimization and to foster positive participation in the community through the reduction of crime. These goals connect to theories of social control and social disorganization. Travis Hirschi's social control theory suggests that desistance from offending requires attachment to others, commitment to conformity with pro-social facets, involvement with conventional norms, and the belief that a commonality exists within the community. A corollary is Clifford R. Shaw and Henry D. McKay's social disorganization theory, which proposes that community disorder fosters crime.

The propensity to crime is not an innate individual characteristic; rather, crime is a function of the individual's environment and level of social interaction. If marked by vague ties to community members and a disconnect from the mainstream culture, interaction with community members is often superficial, thus hindering the achievement of social capital. *Social capital* refers to pro-social interaction that fosters conformity to the conventional norms of a community. This lack of interaction may lead to a decrease in trust and cooperation with community organizations and law enforcement and, thus, a decrease in social capital.

This trust that is imperative to the success of community crime control, also known as *collective efficacy,* includes how community members share expectations of social control. The goal of collective efficacy is to increase trust and the level of social control in the community, as community disorder usually indicates a lack of informal social control. With disintegration of the family and isolation from the community and the mainstream comes a greater reliance on formal social control, or the presence of a guardian. The guardian need not be a physical entity, such as a police officer, but could also include surveillance and tracking mechanisms, as well as neighborhood watch.

Decriminalization is an aspect of community crime control. Instead of criminalizing disorder such as homelessness, drug abuse, and mental illness, it seeks to increase positive integration into the community. Otherwise, neighborhood disorder has a threefold impact: the undermining of social control, the increased fear of victimization, and the destabilization

of the housing market. As a result, trust and commitment to the community decreases. Also hindering collective efficacy is overcrowding, demoralization, and hopelessness. The resulting neighborhood instability—linked with socioeconomic status—can foster criminal activity.

One approach in community crime control is *broken windows policing.* Broken windows policing, also known as disorder policing, seeks to rid the community of crimes that diminish the quality of life, which in turn should reduce other crimes. Although this is a popular focus of policing, no data yet show its use actually improves the quality of life or stops the downward community spiral. Another approach, *community policing,* used at least partially by approximately 80 percent of law enforcement agencies, includes participation within the community, citizen empowerment, and partnership with community agencies. Because community crime control is most effective when citizens' opinions and views are considered, community policing focuses on involving the public in defining what disorder is, solving community problems by promoting communication, and increasing decentralization and police responsiveness to the needs of the community. The elements of community policing include protecting citizens' rights, maintaining order, relying on the cooperation of citizens for information and assistance, and responding to community issues.

Because the organization of the community affects voluntary efforts and interaction with law enforcement, the use of these policies differs depending on the neighborhood, with poor, minority neighborhoods tending to be the least involved. Frustration with the frequent changes of policy, the conflicts among community organizations, and distrust of the police are factors that undermine community cooperation.

Another facet of community crime control is community prosecution, such as when the community acts as agents in stopping quality-of-life offenses such as drug involvement. Such community participation, however, is limited to members acting as witnesses. This reactive approach, unlike a proactive one, ignores the root causes of problems such as prostitution, gambling, drug abusing, and loitering.

Community dispute resolution councils and community corrections are also aspects of community crime control. Community dispute resolution councils are neighborhood committees that include residents, attorneys, and service providers in solving community problems. Parole and probation are examples of community corrections. Both refer to methods of sanctions in which the offender serves time within the community while still being responsible to the court. This method helps facilitate offender reentry into the community. Due to get-tough-on-crime policies, intermediate sanctions now include intensive supervision, home incarceration, and electronic monitoring.

The jury is still out on the value of community crime control. The research shows mixed results, with some authorities citing the decrease of fear and others citing an increase of isolation. Critics contend that, instead of helping, community crime control weakens communities and diminishes social capital. Those benefiting from collective efficacy are those who need it least: white, middle-class communities. The challenge is not just to protect the rights of community members but also to find better ways to foster community involvement.

LaNina Nicole Floyd

See also Community; Community Corrections; Community Service; Conflict Resolution; Parole; Policing, Community; Policing, Strategic; Probation; Social Capital; Social Control; Social Disorganization

Further Readings

Akers, Ronald L. 2000. *Criminological Theories: Introduction, Evaluation and Application.* Los Angeles: Roxbury.

Gottfredson, Michael R. and Travis Hirschi. 1990. *A General Theory of Crime.* Stanford, CA: Stanford University Press.

Sampson, Robert J., Jeffery D. Morenoff, and Thomas Gannon-Rowley. 2002. "Assessing 'Neighborhood Effects': Social Processes and New Directions in Research." *Annual Review of Sociology* 28:443–78.

COMMUNITY SERVICE

Community service is compulsory, free, or donated labor performed by an offender as punishment for a crime. This requirement is a community service order. An offender under a community service order must perform labor for a certain length of time (as determined by the crime) at charitable not-for-profit agencies or governmental offices. Community service involves many different types of work, both skilled and unskilled. Most work is physical in nature, such as graffiti and debris removal or outdoor maintenance. Offenders must complete the work within a certain amount of time, such as 3 months. Community service closely aligns with restitution; the offender engages in acts designed, in part, to make reparation for harm caused by the criminal offense, but these acts are directed to the larger community rather than to the victim.

The first documented community service program in the United States began in Alameda County, California, in the late 1960s, when traffic offenders who could not afford fines faced the possibility of incarceration. To avoid the financial costs of incarceration and individual costs in the lives of the offenders (who were often women with families), judges assigned physical work in the community without compensation. The idea took hold, and the use of community service expanded nationwide through the 1970s. Today, community service is a correctional option in every state and at the federal level. Because of the lack of a national survey, exact numbers of offenders with community service orders remain unknown. In Texas alone, more than 195,000 adults participated in community service in 2000.

Community service serves as a criminal sanction for adults and juveniles, males and females, felons and misdemeanants, offenders on probation, offenders in prison or jail, and offenders on parole. Most states use four models for community service. First, community service can be a sole penalty for very minor or first-time offenders, for instance, traffic violators. Second, and most commonly, community service is a special condition of probation or parole, something required of the probationer or parolee in addition to other sentence stipulations. Third, community service may replace incarceration as an intermediate sanction, usually for misdemeanants. Fourth, community service works in conjunction with incarceration, for example, when inmates form work crews removing litter from roads and other public service works.

When enforced properly, community service can serve as meaningful punishment for misbehavior while improving the quality of life in communities. To the benefit of offenders and their families, community service is less intrusive than most other sanctions, and the structured work routines may prove beneficial in the lives of offenders. Even if a community service program does not aim to treat their needs, when offenders remain in their communities performing unpaid labor as a criminal sanction, they are able to maintain their familial, social, and work-related responsibilities and ties. When available to replace short jail terms, especially for repeat but minor property offenders whom the system finds hard to deal with, community service sentencing may also bring relief to overcrowded jails.

Gail A. Caputo

See also Community Corrections; Parole; Probation; Restorative Justice

Further Readings

Caputo, Gail A. 2004. *Intermediate Sanctions in Corrections.* Denton, TX: University of North Texas Press.

COMPARABLE WORTH

Until the late 1970s, an acceptable workplace practice was to pay men more than women, even if they did the same or essentially the same work. The 1963 federal Equal Pay Act mandated equal pay for equal work. Although this law helped those women who did the same or essentially similar work, it had limited impact, because rarely do men and women do the same work. Indeed, the National Research Council of the National Academy of Sciences concluded that not only do women do different work than men, but the work they do is paid less, and the more an occupation is dominated by women, the less it pays. Occupational segregation is pervasive and is a major factor accounting for the gender-based wage gap.

Comparable worth, also known as pay equity, focuses on correcting the gender-based wage gap that is a by-product of occupational segregation. It requires that dissimilar jobs of equivalent work for the employer be paid the same wages. Comparable worth also encompasses a technique for determining the complexity of dissimilar jobs and the value of these jobs to the major mission of a work organization. Comparable worth addresses wage discrimination, that is, the systematic undervaluation of women's work simply on the basis that primarily women do it. Because some men also work in historically female jobs, such as nursing, they too suffer from gender-based

wage discrimination because they choose to work in female-dominated jobs.

Systematic undervaluation or wage discrimination means that the wages paid to those who perform female-dominated work (FDW) are lower than they would be if the typical incumbent of that job were a white male. Thus, wage discrimination involves adjusting the wages paid to those performing female-dominated jobs by removing the negative effect of "femaleness" on the wage rate independent of the complexity of tasks and responsibilities of that job. If implemented, comparable worth would require employers to base their wages solely on the skills, effort, responsibilities, and working conditions of the job.

How, then, is it possible to measure the content of the job and determine its complexity relative to other jobs? The use of job evaluation to determine wages goes back more than 100 years, but those systems in use today have their roots in systems first developed in the 1940s and 1950s. Approximately two thirds of all employers in the United States use some form of job evaluation to establish their wage structure—that is, ranking jobs from lower to higher in job complexity and paying people who work in these jobs less or more money.

Although job evaluation systems rest on the argument that they are scientific and objective in their assessment of job content, they actually embed assumptions about work that contain significant gender bias. Specifically, these systems, developed more than a half-century ago, evolved at a time when approximately 25 percent of all adult women worked, with their wages treated as secondary incomes or "pin money." To develop these systems, evaluators would take existing wage rates, examine the job content of high-wage jobs, and treat the characteristics of those jobs as complex. As a result, either they did not recognize the job content found in historically low-paid women's work as complex, or they did not even define the job content. In these traditional job evaluation systems, there was no explanation or justification provided for either the description of certain job characteristics or the definition of certain characteristics as more complex. Conceptually, the breadwinner–homemaker ideologies of the mid-20th century became institutionalized into the wage structure through conventional job evaluation systems.

Technically, job evaluation orders jobs as more or less complex and, therefore, as more or less valuable to the employer for the purpose of paying jobs according to some systematic procedure. It follows three steps: describing jobs with respect to the characteristics to be evaluated; evaluating jobs as more or less complex relative to the established hierarchy of complexity; and assigning wages based on how many job evaluation points a job receives and what other firms pay for such jobs. The more job evaluation points there are, the higher the wage will be.

Job evaluation is the institutional mechanism that perpetuates wage discrimination, especially in medium-sized and large workplaces. The gender bias of these systems is pervasive. Those pay equity advocates who attempt to measure wage discrimination seek to cleanse traditional job evaluation systems of gender bias. To achieve this objective requires recognition of the social construction of systems of job evaluation and the need for social reconstruction to achieve gender neutrality.

One aspect of gender bias in job evaluation is ignoring or taking for granted the prerequisites, tasks, and work content of jobs historically performed by women. For example, working with mentally ill or dying patients and their families or reporting to multiple supervisors is not treated either as stressful job content or as involving any effort. By contrast, working with noisy machinery is treated as stressful, and solving budgetary problems is treated as involving significant effort. The work of a secretary or office coordinator in running an office remains invisible, especially if she performs her job competently.

Another aspect of gender bias is the assumption that the content of historically female work is innate to all females and does not require skills, effort, or responsibilities. For example, the emotional labor of nurses, nursing assistants, day care workers, and even flight attendants is treated as stereotypically female; thus, it is not necessary to remunerate those who perform these types of jobs. By contrast, those who perform the occupation of math professor—a historically male job—do not receive lower pay because men are supposedly innately good at math.

Gender bias also manifests itself in descriptions of work performed in female-dominated jobs that assume its lesser complexity compared with the content of male-dominated jobs. For example, both women's and men's jobs require perceptual skills and effort. Male-dominated jobs are more likely to require spatial perceptual skills, and female-dominated jobs are more likely to require visual skills. In traditional job evaluation systems, spatial skills are treated as more complex than visual skills without any explanation or justification.

Comparable worth advocates do not question the established hierarchy of complexity as it relates to male work. Rather, they seek to adjust the way women's work is described and evaluated, so that FDW is paid fairly in relation to the actual complexity and value of the work performed. Technical comparable worth advocates first attempted to modify traditional job evaluation systems; now they have begun to design new gender-neutral job evaluation systems to measure job content.

These gender-neutral systems, one of which was developed by Ronnie J. Steinberg, measure both male-dominated work and FDW more accurately, making the invisible components of FDW visible and thus rewarded for the actual work performed in two important ways. First, gender-neutral job evaluation builds new dimensions of job complexity or job factors to capture and positively value the skills, effort, responsibilities, and undesirable working conditions of FDW. An example is the construction of a new evaluation factor for emotional effort, which measures the intensity of effort required to deal directly with clients or their families or coworkers in assisting, instructing, caring for, or comforting them. Within emotional effort, hierarchies of complexity are built and applied consistently to both FDW and male-dominated work. Thus, the work of police officers, as well as of client-oriented direct service workers, is recognized and compensated for this important dimension of their work.

Second, gender-neutral job evaluation includes and revalues unacknowledged or undervalued job content by broadening definitions of job dimensions or factors that already exist in traditional job evaluation. For example, the measurement of human relations skills would not only measure supervision of subordinates but also include and value highly the skill and effort required to deal effectively with, to care for, or to influence others.

However, gender-neutral systems of job evaluation are almost never used in pay equity initiatives undertaken in the United States, and whereas most states have taken some action to assess wage discrimination in public sector employment, only Minnesota has made wage discrimination illegal for all public sector employers. Thus, gender-neutral job evaluation is a technical solution in search of a radically different political climate as well as a political base with sufficient power to implement it.

Why have comparable pay initiatives not used gender-neutral job evaluation and instead used gender-biased traditional job evaluation to measure and correct for gender bias? First, when trendsetter states such as Minnesota and Washington conducted their job evaluation studies, no design for gender-neutral job evaluation yet existed. The studies did find some unexplained wage differences—enough to result in modest wage increases. Politically, women earned more wages and all but a few believed that the problem of wage discrimination had been solved. These first studies set the limits for future studies.

By the time that the second phase of initiatives emerged—partly as a result of these early successes—advocates were developing new job evaluation systems. But, given the previous studies, there was no commitment to do more than states had already done. So the studies were conducted, the results fell far short of removing gender bias from compensation practices, and gender-neutral job evaluation remained on the shelf.

In addition, states conducting studies developed advisory committees or task forces as well as several political strategies to give the appearance of advocate involvement while undercutting advocate power to affect study design or outcomes. In other words, advocates were contained, making it possible to limit the impact of the study on wage adjustments. For example, study directors would pretend that political decisions were technical decisions, thereby blocking advisory committee members from deliberating on key aspects of the study design, or the study directors would withhold information from the task force. Also, comparable worth advocates were in the minority of the advisory committee and, as a result, were unable to garner sufficient votes when a disagreement arose. Yet, their presence on the committee contributed to the legitimacy of the study. Directors often divided proponents from each other, especially representatives from labor organizations and women's groups. Finally, in some states, advocates were completely excluded from a task force, on the argument that they were not directly involved in the wage-setting process.

Truly cleansing compensation systems of their gender bias could put an extra $2,000 to $7,000 per year in the paychecks of those performing FDW. Even flawed studies with gender-biased evaluation systems have resulted in approximately $527 million dispersed

in 20 states, according to the Institute for Women's Policy Research. For many employed in FDW, these adjustments represent the difference between poverty and economic autonomy. Along with raising the minimum wage and the success of the movement for a living wage, comparable worth is a very effective strategy for moving working women out of poverty.

Comparable worth is a matter of economic equity. It affects the political and social power of women. Above all, it is a matter of simple justice.

Ronnie J. Steinberg

See also Gender Bias; Gender Gap; Segregation, Gender; Segregation, Occupational; Wage Gap

Further Readings

England, Paula. 1992. *Comparable Worth: Theories and Evidence.* Piscataway, NJ: Aldine de Gruyter.
Evans, Sara M. and Barbara N. Nelson. 1991. *Wage Justice: Comparable Worth and the Paradox of Technocratic Reform.* Chicago: University of Chicago Press.
Steinberg, Ronnie J. 1990. "Social Construction of Skill: Gender, Power, and Comparable Worth." *Worth and Occupations* 17(4):449–82.
Treiman, Donald and Heidi Hartmann. 1981. *Women, Work, and Wages: Equal Pay for Jobs of Equal Value.* Washington, DC: National Academy Press.

COMPUTER CRIME

The global growth in information technology—alongside unparalleled advances in productivity, commerce, communication, entertainment, and the dissemination of information—has precipitated new forms of antisocial, unethical, and illegal behavior. As more and more users become familiar with computing, the scope and prevalence of the problem grow. Computers and the Internet allowed for the modification of traditional crimes (stalking, fraud, trafficking of child pornography, identity theft) and the development of novel crimes (online piracy, hacking, the creation and distribution of viruses and worms).

The Royal Canadian Mounted Police define *computer crime* as "any illegal act fostered or facilitated by a computer, whether the computer is an object of a crime, an instrument used to commit a crime, or a repository of evidence related to a crime." A computer is an object of a crime in instances of Web site deface-ment, denial of service, network security breaches, and theft or alteration of data. A computer is an instrument used to commit a crime in activities of credit card fraud, auction fraud, phishing, identity theft, counterfeiting and forgery, digital piracy, illegal use of online services, and cyberstalking. A computer is a repository of evidence used to commit a crime when data stored on a system aids or abets traditional criminal activity, as with tax evasion or drug trafficking.

Fiscal and Social Consequences of Computer Crime

As one of the fastest-growing criminal movements in the country, computer crimes cost society and private industry billions of dollars, an amount steadily increasing. Compared with the cost of traditional "street" crimes, the cost of computer and white-collar offenses is astronomically high. Experts estimate that the average bank robber nets $2,500, the average bank fraud nets $25,000, the average computer crime nets $500,000, and the average theft of technology loss is $1.9 million. Moreover, financial losses do not fully capture the extent of harm done to victims and society through such incidents.

Detection and Response

Computer crime is extremely difficult to detect, in part because of the power of computers to process, and the Internet to disseminate, electronic information rapidly and the fact that many people have access to the Internet at universities, businesses, libraries, and homes. When data communications take place at high speeds without personal contact, users are left with very little time to consider the implications of their actions online. Moreover, many computer crimes are relatively effortless and can be accomplished via a few keystrokes or by a simple "drag and drop" mouse maneuver that takes mere seconds. Additionally, temporal and spatial limitations are largely irrelevant in cyberspace, and both personal and property crimes can occur at any time and place because the Internet provides global interconnectivity.

Because they can use chat room pseudonyms, temporary e-mail accounts, multiple Internet venues, and even instant messaging programs, electronic offenders have an advantage in shielding their true identity. Relative anonymity perhaps frees potential and actual perpetrators from traditionally constraining pressures of society, conscience, morality, and ethics to behave in a normative manner. Also, words and actions that an individual might be ashamed or embarrassed to say or perform in a face-to-face setting are no longer off-limits or even tempered when they occur from behind a keyboard in a physically distant location from a personal or corporate victim. Many individuals may actually be emboldened when using electronic means to accomplish wrongdoing, because it perceivably requires less courage and fortitude to commit certain acts in cyberspace as compared with their counterparts in real space.

Furthermore, supervision is lacking in cyberspace. Many of the actions taken and electronic words exchanged are private and outside the purview and regulatory reach of others online or off-line. Both informal (e.g., parents, teachers) and formal (law enforcement) arms of social control have little ability to monitor, prevent, detect, and address instances of computer crime because it occurs largely from locations geographically removed from the privacy of one's personal home or office computer.

There are a host of traditional problems associated with responding to computer crime. First, the law often does not address the intangible nature of the activity and location. Second, it is difficult to foster communication and collaboration between policing agencies on a national or international level because of funding issues, politics, and divergent opinions on criminalization and punishment. Third, prosecutors are also often reluctant to go after all computer criminals because they are limited by few or no resources, societal or political ambivalence, victim uncooperativeness, and the difficulties in case preparation for crimes that occur in cyberspace. Fourth, individuals and business victims are often hesitant to report the crime to authorities. Fifth, law enforcement entities often lack training and practice in recognizing, securing, documenting, and formally presenting computer crime evidence in a court of law.

Sameer Hinduja

See also Cyberspace; Piracy, Intellectual Property; Property Crime; White-Collar Crime

Further Readings

Casey, Eoghan. 2000. *Digital Evidence and Computer Crime: Forensic Science, Computers and the Internet.* San Diego, CA: Academic Press.

D'Ovidio, Robert and James Doyle. 2003. "A Study on Cyberstalking: Understanding Investigative Hurdles." *FBI Law Enforcement Bulletin* 72(3):10–17.

Grabosky, Peter. 2001. "Computer Crime: A Criminological Overview." *Forum on Crime and Society* 1(1):35–53.

Hinduja, Sameer. 2004. "Perceptions of Local and State Law Enforcement Concerning the Role of Computer Crime Investigative Teams." *Policing: An International Journal of Police Strategies & Management* 27(3):341–57.

———. 2006. *Music Piracy and Crime Theory.* New York: LFB.

Rider, B. A. K. 2001. "Cyber-Organized Crime: The Impact of Information Technology on Organized Crime." *Journal of Financial Crime* 8(4):332–46.

Rosoff, Stephen M., Henry N. Pontell, and Robert Tillman. 2006. *Profit without Honor: White-Collar Crime and the Looting of America.* 4th ed. Upper Saddle River, NJ: Prentice Hall.

Taylor, Max and Ethel Quayle. 2003. *Child Pornography: An Internet Crime.* New York: Brunner-Routledge.

CONFLICT PERSPECTIVE

The theoretical foundation of the conflict perspective is the philosophy of Karl Marx and its expression in various schools of intellectual thought that include conflict theory, critical theory, historical Marxism, Marxist feminism, socialist feminism, and radical feminism. At the center of Marx's analysis is an economic perspective of social life that conceptualizes people's ownership of and control over the products and processes of their labor as the origin of social organization (society). In capitalist societies, the unequal distribution of property ownership and control and autonomy over one's work underlies a social organization characterized by inequality, social conflict, subordination, and domination. Individuals similarly located and influenced by particular economic positions constitute a social class and act in their interests. The upper-income classes ensure their privilege over the lower-income classes by influencing and controlling significant components of society— namely, the political, ideological, and cultural spheres. Theorists of the conflict perspective critique these capitalist class relations of production and examine their influence on idea systems (i.e., ideologies), history, politics, gender, race, culture, and the nature of work.

Conflict Perspective and Women

Marxist feminism, socialist feminism, and radical feminism are theoretical strands that employ a conflict perspective in the study of the relations between men and women (gender). Marx and Friedrich Engels's essay titled *The Origin of the Family, Private Property, and the State* serves as a theoretical basis for their work. Influenced by Marxism and feminism, these theoretical strands examine the interplay between capitalism and gender relations. Marxist and socialist feminists believe that *patriarchy,* defined as a system of power in which males have privilege and dominance over women, emerges as a result of the men's ownership of and control over the economic resources of society. Radical feminists believe that patriarchy and a division of labor based on sex preceded, and is the origin of, capitalism. Therefore, Marxist and socialist feminists argue that the transition from capitalism to communism will ameliorate gender inequality, and radical feminists believe a challenge to patriarchy is the solution to women's subjugation.

According to Marxist and socialist feminists, the identification of women with domestic life (e.g., reproduction, childrearing, cleaning, socialization) is a product of capitalist class relations. Marxist and socialist feminists conceptualize the emergence of the association of women with the domestic sphere in the transition from hunting and gathering societies to capitalist ones. During this transition, women's role as the producers of goods and economic providers for the family and community diminished.

In hunting and gathering societies women collected for their social group the greatest portion of the daily sustenance by gathering berries, nuts, fruit, and so on. In agrarian societies women often farmed side by side with men. However, the development of agrarian societies coincided with men's interactions away from home and the creation of a public life in which men controlled politics and the production and sale of goods and services. Consequently, the economic (productive) power of farming women was diminished, and women came to be increasingly associated with domestic life and work.

Capitalism exacerbated the split between private (domestic) and public life by shifting the production process completely away from farming, thereby relegating women completely to the domestic sphere. This split is referred as *the separation of spheres.* As women's role and control over production diminished, so did their social power.

Because poor white women and many black and immigrant women always worked in the public domain, the theory of the separation of spheres has been criticized. Nonetheless, women's public work mirrors, and is an extension of, this association of women with domestic work, for example, women employed as domestic workers, nurses, nannies, secretaries, and so on. Furthermore, Marxist and socialist feminists argue that because capitalism positions women into the private sector of domestic work, women reproduce capitalism by providing food, shelter, and the socialization necessary to maintain an able-bodied and willing workforce.

Conflict Perspective: Race and Ethnicity

Theorists who hold a conflict perspective attribute racial and ethnic prejudice to the operation and benefit of capitalism. According to historical Marxists, racism (and racial consciousness) emerged at the precise historical time in which capitalism developed—in the 15th century. They argue that before the capitalist period, social group differences were not based on race but rather on culture (language, values, and customs), religion, and citizenship/property ownership. Racism emerged as an ideology (i.e., a system of values members of a society believe) to justify the exploitation of African slaves. In other words, the cultural belief in the racial inferiority of black people (racism) enabled capitalists and slave traders in pursuit of economic profit to enslave and subjugate people of African descent. In the Marxian analysis, racism is a fabrication, mythology, and ploy to maintain capitalist power relations. Thus the ideology of racism results from the underlying conflict between capitalists and laborers.

According to the conflict perspective, racism and ethnic prejudice emerge as a result of economic conflict between lower-income groups competing for the same jobs. For example, during the early period of U.S. industrialization (the mid-19th century), Irish and African American conflict over socially desirable factory work resulted in conflict expressed in racial and ethnic terms. The Irish secured their positions in the working class by pointing to their "whiteness," denouncing the abolitionist movement, and sometimes initiating violence against blacks. This racism supported capitalism by diverting potential conflict away from the Irish workers and capitalists and toward the Irish and African Americans. The intraclass conflict between the Irish and African Americans thwarted their development into a unified and class-conscious social group, thereby quelling a working-class rebellion. This competitive situation is called a *split labor market.*

This type of economic competition occurred during the period of U.S. industrialization and mass immigration. From the conflict perspective, ethnic and racial prejudice resulted as Chinese and Japanese immigrants competed with the native-born Americans over mining and laundry work, respectively, and as southern and eastern European immigrants competed with the native-born over factory work in the Northeast. In sum, according to the conflict perspective, racism and ethnic prejudice originated in economic capitalist relations.

Vaso Thomas

See also Class Consciousness; Feminist Theory; Postmodernism; Racism; Sexism; Social Constructionist Theory; Split Labor Market

Further Readings

Collins, Randall and Scott Coltrane. 2000. *Sociology of Marriage and the Family: Gender, Love, and Property.* 5th ed. Chicago: Nelson-Hall.

hooks, bell. 2000. *Feminist Theory: From Margin to Center.* 2nd ed. Boston: South End Press.

Ignatiev, Noel. 1995. *How the Irish Became White.* Cambridge, MA: Harvard University Press.

Roediger, David R. 2003. *Colored White: Transcending the Racial Past.* Berkeley, CA: University of California Press.

CONFLICT RESOLUTION

Conflict resolution refers to a process for ending disputes. A broad spectrum of mechanisms for dealing with conflicts exists across all levels, from interpersonal disputes to international armed engagements. These processes enlist a variety of problem-solving methods to resolve incompatibilities in needs, interests, and goals. Variations in both the methods used and outcomes achieved characterize the differences between conflict resolution and other processes, such as conflict settlement, conflict management, or conflict regulation.

Conflict resolution is an approach to ending conflicts rooted in a normative framework that sees conflict as a normal part of human interactions and thus argues for a particular understanding of resolution. Conflict resolution, when done well, should be productive and maximize the potential for positive change at both a personal and a structural level. Thus, what distinguishes conflict resolution from other dispute resolution processes is its emphasis on participatory processes, party control of solutions, and self-enforcing, integrative solutions. Typical aspects of the conflict resolution process include getting both sides to listen to each other, providing opportunities for parties to meet each side's needs, and finding the means to address both sides' interests to reach a mutually satisfactory outcome.

Designing a conflict resolution process requires a broad definition of "parties" to the conflict. This would include people impacted by the conflict, or those who could be impacted by potential solutions. More narrow definitions of parties, limited to decision makers or power brokers, are insufficient because they often ignore parties who can block decisions or who, if excluded, may choose to wage their own round of the conflict.

Getting to resolution also requires the use of participatory processes in which parties have both voice and vote. Third parties may help facilitate a process, but parties should maintain control over both the development and selection of viable solutions. Conflicts may be settled or regulated when powerful third parties dictate or enforce solutions, but this seldom results in eliminating the causal factors.

Conflict resolution further requires the addressing of the deep-rooted causes of the conflict. Processes that address symptoms rather than underlying causes may temporally manage a conflict, but they do not result in full resolution. Although there can be significant trade-offs in the agreement, these must not sacrifice the key issues and needs.

The final criterion for achieving the resolution of a conflict is the building of integrative solutions. To achieve a successful resolution, both parties must have at least some, if not all, of their underlying needs and interests satisfied. If one side leaves the process feeling it has lost, the actual achievement of resolution did not occur.

Celia Cook-Huffman

See also Social Conflict

Further Readings

Deutsch, Morton, Peter T. Coleman, and Eric C. Marcus, eds. 2006. *The Handbook of Conflict Resolution: Theory and Practice.* San Francisco: Jossey-Bass.

Miall, Hugh, Oliver Ramsbotham, and Tom Woodhouse. 2005. *Contemporary Conflict Resolution.* 2nd ed. Cambridge, England: Polity Press.

CONGLOMERATES

A conglomerate is a company engaged in often seemingly unrelated types of business activity. Two major characteristics define a conglomerate firm. First, a conglomerate firm controls a span of activities in various industries that require different managerial skills. Second, a conglomerate achieves diversification primarily by external mergers and acquisitions rather than by internal development.

There are three types of conglomerate or diversifying mergers: (1) product extension mergers that broaden the product lines of firms, (2) geographic market extensions that result in nonoverlapping geographic areas, and (3) pure conglomerate mergers that involve combining unrelated enterprises. Common motives for conglomerate mergers include financial synergies, taxes, and managerial incentives.

Conglomerate mergers were popular in the 1960s because of low interest rates and favorable economic conditions. Small- or medium-size firms facing diminished prospects for growth and profits decided to diversify into more promising industries. Acquiring firms borrowed low-cost funds to buy businesses outside their traditional areas of interest. The overall return on investment of the conglomerate appeared to grow as long as the target company had profits greater than the interest on the loans. In practice, much of this growth was illusory and profits fell as interest rates rose. During this merger wave, about half of the firms considered as conglomerates were based in the defense and aerospace industries.

In 1968, Congress moved against conglomerate firms by passing hostile anti-trust policies and punitive tax laws. These factors plus declining stock prices brought an end to the conglomerate fad. Because of the lack of success of many conglomerate mergers, managers shifted their focus from diversification to a firm's core competency.

Various arguments exist for and against the diversification achieved by conglomerates. Proponents argue that the conglomerate organizational form allows for allocation of capital in a more efficient way. Other potential advantages include stabilizing earnings, cost and revenue economies of scope, lower tax burdens, sharing of managerial "best practices," and better monitoring and control of capital expenditures. Arguments against diversification include cross-subsidization across business lines, overinvestment in certain projects caused by excess free cash flow and unused borrowing capacity, and conflicts of interest among various activity areas.

An important issue is whether conglomerates create or destroy value. Although some mixed evidence exists, research suggests that diversification does not increase the firm's value in most cases. That is, diversified firms are worth less than the sum of their individual parts. For example, empirical studies of financial conglomerates suggest the presence of a financial discount caused by diversification. Thus, the impact of functional scope is predominantly value destroying. However, the benefits of geographic diversification appear to outweigh its costs and lead to value enhancement.

Today, examples of large conglomerates include Time Warner, AT&T, General Electric, News Corporation, and Walt Disney Company in the United States; Sony and Mitsubishi in Japan; and Siemens AG in Germany. For instance, Time Warner is a leading media and entertainment company, whose businesses include interactive services, cable systems, filmed entertainment, television networks, and publishing.

H. Kent Baker

See also Economic Restructuring; Global Economy; Globalization; Multinational Corporations

Further Readings

Weston, J. Fred, Mark L. Mitchell, and J. Harold Mulherin. 2004. *Takeovers, Restructuring, and Corporate Governance.* 4th ed. Upper Saddle River, NJ: Pearson Prentice Hall.

CONSERVATIVE APPROACHES

The U.S. welfare state and its relation to domestic labor markets changed dramatically at the close of the 20th century. A new group of conservatives shifted the terms of welfare debate away from the logic of need and the logic of entitlement, promoted by Democratic politicians and the social movements of the 1950s and 1960s, to install a new social policy agenda that highlighted the obligations of citizenship. In 1996, after 20 years of political campaigning and policy advocacy, neoconservatives, supported by new conservative think tanks, succeeded in replacing the federal Aid to Families with Dependent Children Program (AFDC), first enacted in 1935, with the Temporary Assistance for Needy Families Program (TANF).

By crafting a synthetic reform program that would both buttress conservative social norms and limit access to public assistance that mitigated the pressures of labor market competition, the neoconservatives succeeded in mobilizing a powerful coalition of social conservatives and free-market proponents discontented with the welfare state expansions that had been enacted as part of the War on Poverty. In contrast to the Nixon administration, which had failed to pass a major welfare reform initiative because its Family Assistance Plan divided these two political factions, by uniting them behind a single reform agenda, neoconservatives were able to pass the Family Support Act in 1988 and then the Personal Responsibility Work Opportunity Reconciliation Act (PRWORA) in 1996.

Neoconservative authors dubbed the first publication laying out their collective reform program the New Consensus, suggesting that by 1987 the nation was ready to reach a new agreement on social policy to replace the previous consensus institutionalized in the New Deal programs of the 1930s. The neoconservatives' new consensus articulated an alternative vision of citizenship from that underlying the New Deal and the subsequent finding by the Supreme Court that the Social Security Act of 1935 had entitled poor, single mothers to public assistance. In contrast to the previous logic of citizenship, which considered entitlement to assistance necessary to protect individual freedom, the neoconservatives called on the state to use public programs to reinforce work and domestic norms that they reformulated as obligations of citizenship.

According to the "New Consensus," social programs should discipline poor family members receiving public assistance to prepare them for incorporation within the polity. Poor single mothers should be required to assist government agencies to identify the biological fathers of their children, and fathers who do not pay child support should be subject to enforcement measures. To be eligible for assistance, poor parents should be required to attend school or to participate in work or work-preparation activities. Anticipating liberal objections to extending government regulation into areas of life that are protected from state intervention if citizens are not poor, neoconservatives noted that once poor parents mastered the skills now considered prerequisite for citizenship, they, like other citizens, would be free to pursue their desires through the market. Neoconservatives also suggested that as the new paternalist poverty programs succeeded in preparing the poor for market entry and citizenship, the number of parents claiming public assistance would decline and the state would transfer fewer resources from taxpayers to poor families.

However, regulating family life and work activities in ways that satisfied both free-market proponents and social conservatives proved problematic. Unlike the Nixon administration's Family Assistance Program, which promised to eliminate the financial incentive for family dissolution by extending benefits to poor families with working fathers, the "New Consensus" proposed eliminating the incentive to remain a single parent by requiring that poor single parents work to receive benefits. But this new policy direction conflicted with social conservatives' aspirations of returning to a family model in which the mother stayed at home to care for the family. The conflict between the demands of capitalist labor markets for low-wage service workers and the caregiving needs of the traditional family posed a problem for the writers of the "New Consensus" that they were unable to resolve, except by prioritizing the needs of the market over those of the family. Unlike earlier Christian defenders of the family who had lobbied for a family wage at the beginning of the 20th century, neoconservative welfare reformers asserted that two wage earners working at the minimum wage were needed to keep working-class families above the poverty line. Because this solution and reliance on paid child care was unsatisfactory to some conservatives, the authors of the

"New Consensus" remained silent on how the new "citizen-mothers" were to balance the demands of the market and domestic work, leaving the problem to be addressed by politicians, government bureaucrats, welfare case managers, and poor parents.

In contrast to matters of family care, the neoconservatives were explicit about how to foster economic self-reliance. The policy challenge, according to neoconservative policy scholar Lawrence Mead, was to build a new institutional network that would replicate, for parents receiving public assistance, the same balance of support and expectation that other Americans face in supporting their families by participating in the labor market. This required conditioning the receipt of assistance on the completion of work or work-preparation activities much like an employment relationship. It also authorized a reorganization of the state and state–citizen interactions to conform to the norms and practices used to govern market interactions. In passing the Family Support Act of 1988, national policymakers created the Job Opportunities and Basic Skills (JOBS) program to engage parents enrolled in AFDC in work or job search activities. As part of the JOBS program, lawmakers suggested that states introduce new employability plans (similar to employment contracts), which specified the conditions parents had to meet to receive public assistance. However, unlike an employment contract that can be voided if an employee fails to meet the stipulated conditions, states could only sanction parents who did not participate; states could not deny financially eligible parents from enrolling in the program until Congress eliminated the entitlement to assistance in 1996. Freed by the PRWORA to develop state-specific TANF programs that no longer included an entitlement to assistance, some states, such as Wisconsin, reorganized their poverty programs to resemble more closely employment practices commonly used in low-wage labor markets, such as making benefit amounts insensitive to family size, issuing benefit payments only after several weeks of participation, and sanctioning parents for each hour of assigned activity they failed to complete at a rate equal to the federal minimum wage rate.

By revoking the entitlement to assistance, Congress authorized state and local agencies to exercise new forms of discretion. Eliminating policies and practices designed to guarantee equal treatment under the previous welfare program and creating new rules to regulate poor mothers' domestic lives, lawmakers reorganized poverty policy to be more like private charitable giving. Under the new TANF policies, states can require poverty agency staff to make distinctions among parents, based on their perceptions of the applicants' ability to work and parents' domestic situations. In some states case managers use these evaluations to determine who can enroll in the program and what types of services and requirements will be incorporated within individualized participation agreements. The 1996 federal poverty legislation also limited the time parents could be eligible for federally subsidized assistance to a total of 5 years and allowed states to impose even shorter time limits.

In addition to recommending that lawmakers restructure government policies and practices to resemble norms and practices exercised by market actors and private charities, neoconservatives also recommended granting new regulatory authority to nongovernmental institutions to supplement the supervisory capacities of the governmental sector. Governments already contracted with for-profit firms and community-based organizations for other types of services, so federal guidelines were in place to regulate contracts with these types of organizations. However, federal and state lawmakers had to pass new legislation to allow state and local governments to contract with faith-based organizations to provide guidance to parents enrolled in the new poverty programs. In addition, some state governments went further in reorganizing the network of local agencies administering the state's new TANF program, shifting from the standard fee-for-service contract arrangement to new market-like fixed-sum contracts or performance-based contracting.

Pursuing changes that remade agencies administering the new poverty programs more like market actors and private charities changed the boundaries between the state, civil society, the market, and the home. Eliminating the entitlement to assistance freed the state from the previous obligation to provide poor parents with cash assistance. This opened the way for new forms of discretion and for a new understanding of receiving assistance as a contractual act in which poor citizens voluntarily agree to new forms of state regulation in exchange for access to cash assistance and other services. However, because U.S. society currently holds public and private institutions accountable for different kinds of performance, the shift to market contracts with an array of governmental and nongovernmental organizations, in the context of new forms of discretion, also raises questions

concerning the level of public representation in policy making, the degree of transparency in program implementation, and appropriate fiscal and employment practices.

Victoria Mayer

See also Aid to Families with Dependent Children; Culture of Dependency; Culture of Poverty; Poverty; Temporary Assistance for Needy Families; Welfare; Welfare Capitalism

Further Readings

Mead, Lawrence. 2001. *Beyond Entitlement: The Social Obligations of Citizenship.* New York: Free Press.
Novak, Michael et al. 1987. *The New Consensus on Family and Welfare.* Washington, DC: American Enterprise Institute.
Starr, Paul. 1988. "The Meaning of Privatization." *Yale Law and Policy Review* 6:6–41.
Weaver, R. Kent. 2000. *Ending Welfare as We Know It.* Washington, DC: Brookings Institution Press.

CONSPICUOUS CONSUMPTION

The term *conspicuous consumption* was coined by Norwegian American sociologist and economist Thorstein Veblen (1857–1929) in his 1899 book titled *The Theory of the Leisure Class: An Economic Study of Institutions.* Conspicuous consumption refers to an individual's public or ostentatious use of costly goods or services to indicate his or her wealth and high social status. In capitalist societies, this practice includes purchasing and publicly displaying expensive goods (commodities or status symbols) that are luxuries rather than necessities. Conspicuous consumption goes beyond simply fulfilling an individual's survival needs (food, shelter, clothing) and is characterized by what Veblen described critically as wastefulness. Veblen conceived of conspicuous consumption as a practice in which men engaged to demonstrate their wealth. However, he also described women as conspicuous consumers whose actions indexed the wealth of their husbands or fathers (in Veblen's time, women did not have a recognized separate social status).

Conspicuous consumption can be a social problem because it has the effect of reaffirming social status boundaries and distinctions based on access to wealth. In some cases, such as the conspicuous consumption of elites in developing countries, this practice can lead to social unrest and even political violence.

Conspicuous consumption is a peculiar feature of industrial and postindustrial capitalism that reflects social inequalities within societies characterized by this system of production. In precapitalist societies, an individual's status within his or her social group could be indexed in a variety of ways: for example, through the exertion of physical force or the size and quality of landholdings. According to economists and sociologists, feudal societies had clear distinctions and direct relations of domination between high-status and low-status individuals, precluding the need for elaborate or symbolic demonstrations of wealth, status, and power on the part of the elite. With the advent of industrial capitalism, however, traditional bases of social power and authority (such as land ownership and titles of nobility) became unstable, and status within a society or social group became increasingly tied to the accumulation of money.

The urbanization that accompanied industrialization in Europe and elsewhere increased population density, placing in close contact individuals and families who were previously unknown to each other and who did not have a basis for judging the social status of their new neighbors. Conspicuous consumption allowed people in urban areas to project a certain degree of wealth or status to those around them. Veblen identified this practice with the *nouveau riche* (newly rich), a class of capitalists who tended to lack traditional status markers, such as noble bloodlines, and who compensated for this fact by buying and ostentatiously displaying consumer goods, such as clothing. In the context of the sudden instability of social status and the crumbling of traditional social distinctions (such as those in the feudal system), conspicuous consumption also became a way for the upper-class elites to reaffirm their place at the top of the social hierarchy.

In the 20th and 21st centuries, conspicuous consumption has become identified not only with the wealthiest members of society but with the middle class as well. In the United States, where no feudal system, nobility, or aristocracy has existed, consumption is the primary manner in which to indicate social status to others. The expansion in consumer purchasing power and the increased availability of a wide range of goods in the United States in the past century enables more individuals to practice conspicuous consumption.

Popular culture encourages conspicuous consumption through magazines, television programs, and films that glorify the lifestyle of the wealthy and celebrities, a lifestyle often emulated by the masses. Scholars have examined critically the increasing links between consumption and identity, stating that in capitalist societies, what one has is often seen as what one is. Some intellectuals view this link between consumption of commodities and identity negatively, lamenting the "commodification" of social relationships and the seemingly never-ending pursuit of the biggest, newest, most expensive goods. This common view sees as futile the attempt to achieve personal happiness or satisfaction or to obtain social mobility by purchasing high-status products. Other scholars do not object to people expressing their sense of self through consumption, seeing instead an element of creativity and fulfillment in the practice of buying and using products. In the current period, with identity and consumption linked, conspicuous consumption not only serves to signal social status but also indicates an affinity with a social group or subculture (a specialized culture within a larger society). For example, consumers may see their driving a Harley-Davidson motorcycle or using a Macintosh computer as situating them within a social group of like-minded people who consume the same goods.

A related concept introduced in Veblen's work is that of conspicuous leisure. Individuals engaging in conspicuous leisure demonstrate to those around them that they are privileged or wealthy enough to avoid working for extended periods of time. A good contemporary example of this practice is tourism, in which people show that they can afford to travel and to be away from work (or that they are wealthy enough to not have to work). When a newly married couple is asked where they will spend their honeymoon or an individual brings in vacation photos to share with his or her coworkers, the logic of conspicuous leisure may be in play.

Erynn Masi de Casanova

See also Class; Social Bond Theory; Social Mobility; Stratification, Social

Further Readings

Bourdieu, Pierre. [1984] 2002. *Distinction: A Social Critique of the Judgment of Taste.* Cambridge, MA: Harvard University Press.

Clarke, David, ed. 2003. *The Consumption Reader.* New York: Routledge.

Veblen, Thorstein. [1899] 1934. *The Theory of the Leisure Class: An Economic Study of Institutions.* New York: Random House.

CONTINGENT WORK

In the United States controversy over contingent work—called precarious work or atypical work in other industrialized countries—has focused on definitions and numbers. Coined in the mid-1980s by economist Audrey Freeman, the term *contingent work* connotes instability in employment. As originally used, contingency suggests an employment relationship that depends on an employer's ongoing need for an employee's services. Applied broadly, however, contingent work has been equated with a range of nonstandard work arrangements, among them temporary, contract, leased, and part-time employment. All are notably different from the standard, regular full-time, year-round job with benefits as part of compensation and the expectation of an ongoing relationship with a single employer.

Much contingent work is far from new. Rather, the workforce has long encompassed work arrangements that are in some way nonstandard. Among these arrangements are on-call work, day labor, seasonal employment, and migrant work, all of which involve intermittent episodes of paid employment and much mobility from one employer to the next. The more recent identification of contingent work as a social problem stems from the perception that many of these forms of employment are expanding, affecting new groups of workers and new sectors of the economy and, therefore, creating greater inequality and new social divisions.

Estimates as Evidence of a Problem

Estimates of the size and scope of the contingent workforce reflect a controversy over the definition of contingent employment. In 1995, the U.S. Census Bureau began collecting data on specific work arrangements, including expected duration of employment and related conditions of work such as earnings, benefits, and union membership. Data were collected several more times in alternating years. Yet analyses of the data have yielded widely divergent counts. Applying a series of narrow definitions, which excluded independent contractors and workers whose arrangements had lasted more than 1 year, researchers at the Bureau of Labor Statistics first estimated that contingent workers comprised 2.2 to 4.9 percent of the total workforce. Using the same data, however, another team of researchers applied a different definition—including most nonstandard work arrangements, regardless of duration—and determined, in contrast, that 29.4 percent of the workforce was in some way contingent.

The debate over numbers and definitions represents different views about the significance of contingent work and, in turn, whether these work arrangements are indeed a social problem. Analysts who apply a narrow definition—and imply little problem—suggest that nonstandard work arrangements provide expanded opportunities for certain segments of the workforce. They focus on workers' social characteristics and identify women, younger workers, and older workers near retirement as those most likely to choose contingent status. Analysts who equate contingent work with a broad range of nonstandard arrangements, in contrast, see evidence of worker subordination and limited opportunity. Comparing the characteristics of standard and nonstandard employment, they identify lower compensation, fewer employment benefits, and lower levels of union membership among contingent workers. Noting that these workers are disproportionately women and racial minorities, they further see contingent status as perpetuating economic inequality and social marginality.

Researchers concerned with inequities in employment, therefore, more often characterize nonstandard, contingent work as "substandard" and equate contingent status with a proliferation of poor-quality jobs. Many further relate contingent work to restructuring across industries, occupations, and sectors of the economy. With employment increasingly unstable and workers insecure, they note, more jobs are temporary—many mediated and controlled by staffing agencies—and a great many entail greater uncertainty, few formal rights, little legal protection, and greater individual responsibility for finding ongoing employment. With these concerns at the forefront, analysts and advocates who see contingent work as a social problem equate it broadly with a shifting of risk from employers to employees and from institutions to individuals. Workers assume greater risk, they argue, because the standard job, which once provided security for a large segment of the workforce, has become increasingly unstable or unavailable to more and more workers.

Framing the Problem

Determining what counts—and who should be counted—depends, in large measure, on framing the problem that contingency creates. Most analysts, advocates, and policymakers point to deepening divisions between social groups. Some have focused on the proliferation of triangular employment relations, in which workers are hired through staffing agencies or contracting companies, as a source of increased control and subordination for some workers. Many identify the flexibility associated with some forms of contingent work as an advantage principally to employers who seek to adjust the size of a workforce as needed. Contingent status, these assertions conclude, leaves large numbers of workers vulnerable and insecure.

Although they continue to disagree about definitions and numbers—and hence about whether contingent work is indeed a problem—most researchers do agree about two key points. One is that that employment in general is undergoing major change, so that the standard job has increasingly eroded as an employment norm. The other is that the size of the contingent workforce, however defined, did not change significantly over the course of an economic cycle, from the boom of the late 1990s through the recession that followed. The contingent workforce thus appears to comprise a stable segment of overall employment. Those analysts and advocates seeking to frame a social problem, therefore, see several main trends associated with contingent work arrangements.

Cost Cutting and Inequality

Analysts agree that contingent work often comes with lower wages, so that employers can cut costs by replacing standard jobs with nonstandard work, sometimes by laying off "regular" employees and replacing them with contingent workers. The result, overall, leads to lower living standards and rising inequality between rich and poor. Good jobs—that is, those that provide living wages and employer-sponsored benefits—are thus harder to find. More people are working for less or are working several jobs.

Contingent work may, therefore, trap workers in low-wage jobs that provide few opportunities for advancement over time.

Legal Loopholes: Gaps in Labor and Employment Law

Many analysts also point to legal loopholes associated with contingent work, arguing that legal rights and guarantees fail to protect many contingent workers. The reasons for these exclusions depend on the specific work arrangement. Most statutes explicitly exclude some workers, especially those classified as independent contractors. Other legal rights become hard to access when workers are employed through a staffing agency, which typically claims legal status as the worker's employer. When staffing agencies divide legal liability with their client firms, workers may find that neither the agency nor its client assumes responsibility under the law.

Disparate Impact on Women and Minorities

Related to a concern over legal rights is evidence of a disparate impact on women and racial minorities. Many contingent workers are employed in temporary or part-time arrangements, which in many cases earn them proportionately less than their counterparts with comparable standard jobs. In some settings, therefore, nonstandard, contingent work may be a pretext for sex or race discrimination, which would otherwise be illegal. Workers who seek flexibility to meet personal or family needs, this reasoning suggests, should not be forced to trade part-time or part-year schedules for equal income and opportunity.

Threat to Competitiveness

A more general concern associated with contingent work is an overall threat to the national economy. Short-term employment, some analysts argue, leads to limited loyalty and lower productivity. Temporary work also rationalizes lower employer investment in the workforce, with limited on-the-job training. The eventual result may, therefore, be an overall lack of skilled labor or the shifting of training costs to the public sector. In a global economy, these analysts suggest, the erosion of workforce skills may mean a falling standard of living in certain countries or regions, as employers can increasingly seek skilled labor in many parts of the world.

Debra Osnowitz

See also Downsizing; Inequality; Labor Market; Outsourcing; Segregation, Occupational; Split Labor Market; Underemployment; Working Poor

Further Readings

Barker, Kathleen and Kathleen Christensen, eds. 1998. *Contingent Work: Employment Relations in Transition.* Ithaca, NY: ILR/Cornell University Press.

General Accounting Office. 2000. *Contingent Workers: Incomes and Benefits Lag behind Those of the Rest of the Workforce.* GAO/HEHS-00-76. Washington, DC: U.S. General Accounting Office.

Hipple, Steven F. 2001. "Contingent Work in the Late 1990s." *Monthly Labor Review* 124(3):3–27.

Kalleberg, Arne L. 2000. "Nonstandard Employment Relations: Part-Time, Temporary and Contract Work." *Annual Review of Sociology* 26:341–65.

Kalleberg, Arne L., Barbara F. Reskin, and Ken Hudson. 2000. "Bad Jobs in America: Standard and Nonstandard Employment Relations and Job Quality in the United States." *American Sociological Review* 65(2):256–78.

Polivka, Anne E. 1996. "Contingent and Alternative Work Arrangements Defined." *Monthly Labor Review* 119(10):3–9.

CONTRACEPTION

Contraception refers to the numerous methods and devices used to prevent conception and pregnancy. For millennia, women and men have relied on such folk and medical methods as condoms, herbs, vaginal suppositories, douching, and magic rituals and potions—along with abortion and infanticide—as means to control the birth of children. Today contraceptives include medically prescribed hormones for women; condoms, diaphragms, and other barriers; behavioral practices, including withdrawal and the rhythm method; and irreversible male and female sterilization. Although there are a number of contraceptive options with varying levels of reliability and effectiveness, use is circumscribed by access and availability, as well as by legal and cultural restraints.

Because contraception separates intercourse from procreation, it raises moral and legal issues. The Catholic Church and some other religious institutions have long morally condemned contraception as a mortal sin. However, legal prohibitions in the United States against contraception and the advertisement and sale of contraceptives did not arise until 1873 with the passage of the Comstock Law. This law made it illegal to distribute "obscene" material through the mail, thus effectively banning contraceptives for Americans.

In 1914, Margaret Sanger, who would go on to found Planned Parenthood, was charged with violating the Comstock Law when she urged women to limit their pregnancies in her socialist journal, *The Woman Rebel,* coining the term *birth control* to emphasize women's agency in procreative decision making. Sanger, along with other birth control advocates, promoted contraception in publications, distributed contraceptives in birth control clinics, lobbied for their legalization, and urged the medical establishment to develop more effective methods. The birth control movement described contraception as a "right" of women to decide if, when, and how many children to bear (a right that would be echoed in the abortion rights movement) without intervention from the state or religious institutions.

Eugenicists were also advocates of contraception in the first half of the 20th century. Contraception, including permanent sterilization, was heralded as a solution to social problems such as poverty, insanity, and criminality because it would ensure that indigent, mentally ill, and otherwise "undesirable" populations would not reproduce. Thus one aspect of the history of contraception in the United States and worldwide has been its link with eugenic programs. Furthermore, just as the term *birth control* emphasized an individual's contraceptive choice, *population control* emphasized contraception as a policy issue for entire populations.

Although the Comstock Law had been overturned in most states by the early to mid-20th century, it was not until the 1965 Supreme Court case of *Griswold v. Connecticut* that the use of contraceptives was legalized throughout the United States. The court decided that couples had the right to privacy and that contraception was a decision that should be left to the individual couple, not the state. The *Griswold* decision was followed 8 years later by *Roe v. Wade,* which legalized abortion in the United States.

Along with the overturning of the Comstock Law, another major development in contraception of the 1960s was the invention and widespread use of the oral hormonal contraceptive known as "the pill." Indeed, demand for the pill precipitated the *Griswold v. Connecticut* decision. The pill further cemented the separation between intercourse and procreation because it is highly effective (between 90 and 99 percent), and its timing is separated from the sexual act.

In the 1990s and 2000s, long-term contraceptive solutions were developed and marketed as scientific breakthroughs. Instead of ingesting pills on a daily basis, hormones could be implanted under the skin of a woman's arm, injected right into her bloodstream, or worn as a patch on her body. Although these methods are highly effective, lasting for anywhere from 1 week to 3 years, and are less subject to user error than is the pill, critics have raised concerns about their side effects. Others emphasize that long-term contraceptives have the potential to be used as coercive or eugenic measures against marginalized populations, such as poor women of color. Furthermore, critics argue that scientists should prioritize developing male contraceptives, lessening the burden on women to be responsible for contraception.

Thus it is largely women today who have a wide range of contraceptive options. According to a 2004 report released by the U.S. Centers for Disease Control and Prevention (CDC), 98 percent of women between the ages of 15 and 44 who have ever had sexual intercourse with a male partner have used at least one contraceptive method or device, and 62 percent are currently practicing contraception. Use of contraceptives, however, varies by socioeconomic status, ethnicity, age, religion, education, and many other factors.

Differences in contraceptive use bear out globally, as well. The UN 2005 World Contraception Report indicates that 60.5 percent of married women of reproductive age worldwide are currently practicing some form of contraception. Contraceptive use is highest in northern Europe (78.9 percent) and lowest in western Africa (13.4 percent).

Contraception continues to be an important issue throughout the world. As indicated by UN data, global disparities exist in use of, access to, affordability of, and availability of contraception. Birth control and family planning may be linked to global development by controlling population growth and by providing women in the developing world with more sexual agency, yet contraception sometimes conflicts with traditional norms about sexuality and childbearing.

In the United States, controversy has arisen around the U.S. Food and Drug Administration approval of the over-the-counter sale of emergency contraception—a pill that is taken after unprotected sexual intercourse—because some religious figures view it as a method of abortion. Those with even more conservative views continue to see all contraception as immoral and aim to restrict it in the United States once again.

Lauren Jade Martin

See also Abortion; Birth Rate; Eugenics; Population Growth

Further Readings

Feyisetan, Bamikale and John B. Casterline. 2000. "Fertility Preferences and Contraceptive Change in Developing Countries." *International Family Planning Perspectives* 26(3):100–109.

Gordon, Linda. 1990. *Woman's Body, Woman's Right: Birth Control in America.* New York: Penguin.

McCann, Carole R. 1994. *Birth Control Politics in the United States, 1916–1945.* Ithaca, NY: Cornell University Press.

CORPORATE CRIME

Corporate crimes include secretly dumping hazardous waste, illegally agreeing to fix prices, and knowingly selling unacceptably dangerous products. These offenses, like other corporate crimes, are deviant outcomes of actions by people working in usually nondeviant corporations.

Identifying true rates of corporate crime is problematic because victims and their victimization are difficult to establish. Toxic dumping, for instance, does not leave maimed or dead bodies at dump sites, and victims of price fixing seldom know they were illegally overcharged. Knowingly selling hazardous pharmaceuticals is particularly difficult to determine because often the harms are insidious—they kill only a tiny fraction of consumers, and harms do not appear until decades after exposure.

Motives for such crimes are equally difficult to predict or identify. Thus, some ordinary employees of one ordinary corporation, Goodrich, on multiple occasions knowingly produced and sold faulty aircraft brakes, although nothing in their biographies would have led observers to predict that they would do so. Likewise, some Enron and Equity Funding Corporation employees violated laws and personal morality by misleading investors into thinking that their failing corporations were profitable.

The structures, cultures, and incentives of their large organizations encouraged these people to commit such anti-social acts. People in these organizations know they are replaceable, and so they are surprisingly malleable. Most of them are average (and sometimes well-intentioned) people committing their crimes in the course of meeting their everyday occupational responsibilities. No data suggest that, as they started their careers, these people were less law-abiding than their peers. And, like other criminals, most devote only a small part of their total time and effort to criminality.

Corporate-generated beliefs, motives, and incentives can help explain their criminal behaviors (just as life experience can help explain street crimes), but these explanations do not absolve participants of their moral or legal violations. They merely explain why participants participated. Research over the past 50 years offers some convincing explanations for the corporation-generated environments that allow or encourage employee participation in corporate crime. It also offers some insights into the social responses that label and penalize some corporate actions as criminal, while ignoring others.

Corporate-Generated Employee Beliefs, Motives, and Incentives

Beliefs, motives, and incentives that employees acquire over many years working in criminogenic occupations greatly increase the chances that they will become criminal participants. Philips Petroleum's chief executive officer, for example, learned the skills and beliefs needed to make illegal $100,000 Watergate-era political contributions as he ascended the corporate ladder over decades in the company.

Beliefs

Employees learn corporate criminal (and noncriminal) beliefs from people like themselves with whom they work and socialize, a pattern known as "differential association." Through differential association, employees create and acquire excuses and justifications for their behaviors. They can attempt to *excuse* their crimes by emphasizing—even exaggerating—their personal powerlessness in large organizations. Like all employees of large corporations, they know they are replaceable cogs filling assigned positions until they retire or are terminated, so they can emphasize their replaceability to justify participating in schemes they consider unsavory. Excuses permit them to participate while believing that their participation is not their fault.

They also learn *justifications* from coworkers. These crime-facilitative rationalizations may be wholly or partly accurate. Thus, price fixers frequently justify their actions as stabilizing unstable markets and protecting employee jobs, which may be true. Nonetheless, their acts are illegal and harm the economy. Justifications facilitate participation because they help participants believe that extenuating circumstances make their actions permissible.

These beliefs do not cause criminal participation—they only provide suitable conditions that make participation more likely. They allow employees to respond reflexively to supervisor authority, standard operating procedures, corporate culture, and patterns that their predecessors established. A learned or innate tendency to obey authority encourages them to participate without serious reflection. Furthermore, the homogeneity, cohesiveness, and differential association of their work worlds can produce "groupthink," a striving for unanimity so strong that it can override recognition that behaviors are criminal. Finally, each of the involved employees, none of whom individually plays a major part or has full knowledge of the crime, might correctly (but immorally or illegally) believe that the crime would occur regardless of his or her personal decisions. And each might conclude that personal interests would be served best by participating, because of perceived rewards for participating or penalties for refusing. This applies even when (as in the cases of Enron and the Dalkon Shield) the crime they didn't expose caused the bankruptcy of their employers and the loss of their own jobs.

Motives and Incentives

More immediate forces also encourage criminal participation, such as pressure to provide a product on time despite unforeseen problems that undermine its safety. Hoping that problems will not be detected or can be corrected before they are detected, employees faced with deadlines conclude that corporate crime is their best available option. Production pressures to meet demand and keep costs low for the disastrous Dalkon Shield, a poorly designed and manufactured intrauterine contraceptive device for which testing was woefully inadequate, thus led to killing at least 33 women, injuring 235,000 others, and bankrupting the device's producer.

"Bounded rationality" limits employees' ability to collect all needed information, foresee consequences of their actions, or act rationally in light of what they believe. Few employees can make individual criminal decisions that would substantially increase their employers' stock prices, and few own so much stock that they would benefit greatly even if their crimes did increase stock prices. Furthermore, employees' rational self-interests seldom favor stockholder interests. Employees at all but the highest ranks have little incentive to risk fines, their jobs, or even prison sentences, by committing crimes altruistically for the benefit of the company's stockholders. Though profit-seeking to maximize shareholder income undoubtedly encourages some corporate crimes, its importance in today's large corporations is easily overstated.

Thus, the job incentives of involved Dalkon Shield and Dow Corning breast implant employees encouraged them to please immediate supervisors by making small cost-reducing choices for products contributing relatively minor profits. Lawful incentives encouraged these employees to produce outcomes harmful to stockholders and customers alike. Ultimately, lawsuits caused unforeseen bankruptcy of their employers, making stockholders' investments in the companies worthless.

In corporate crime cases, incentives are usually indirect. Employees believe their participation may ingratiate them to their supervisors, and their refusal might result in them being passed over for promotion. Rarely is a promotion or raise explicitly conditional on participation in a specific crime. In sum, corporate crimes may be directly, indirectly, or unknowingly encouraged by situations, supervisors, and coworkers.

Separation of corporate ownership from corporate control provides additional incentives for crime. In theory, corporate employees act only as agents for corporate owners (i.e., stockholders), maximizing, whenever possible, the profits that go to those owners. In practice, however, an "agency problem" exists, because employees cannot be counted on to act as agents of their stockholders. Employees' interests generally conflict with stockholder interests; stockholders do not make management decisions, and increased employee incomes can readily reduce stockholders' profits. Employees' personal interests may be best served by participating in crimes, even if the end result of exposure might be the demise of the firm, because the perceived likelihood of rewards for participating exceeds penalties for not participating. Employees thus may run corporations in their own self-interests and against the interests of distant and uninvolved stockholders.

Enron employees thus knowingly "cooked the books" with encouragement from their bosses, receiving large bonuses while deceiving stockholders into thinking that the company was so successful that it had become the seventh largest U.S. company. These employees were concealing disastrous failures that ultimately cost Enron's stockholders $60 billion in savings and most of its 21,000 employees their jobs. Similarly, hundreds of corporations recently were investigated for back-dating stock options, a procedure that illegally and secretly showers on corporate elites millions of dollars each at stockholder expense.

Corporate crime motives frequently are defensive attempts to solve intractable problems. Companies in declining industries face extraordinary pressures to solve problems beyond their immediate control, so they are more likely than others to fix prices. Participants in such cases feel they lack noncriminal options, and they often believe that their illegal acts are temporary. Similarly, executives at companies dependent on federal government rulings (e.g., airlines, pharmaceutical companies, and petroleum producers) acquiesced to illegal political contribution solicitations in the Watergate scandal. They feared unspecified future harm to their firms by President Nixon's administration if they did not make requested large cash payments. Executives at firms with less to fear because they were in industries less dependent on the federal government (e.g., retailers) were less likely to acquiesce.

When reasonable decisions produce unexpected failures, managers often gamble by making corporate criminal decisions because they already are deeply committed to a course of action. Escalating commitment encourages participants who have so much ego or time invested in the product that they don't feel free to quit. In fact, almost all known cases of corporate bodily harm crimes are best described as the product of escalating commitment. The many pharmaceutical company decision makers at Merck and elsewhere who concealed adverse drug reactions did not expect those drug reactions when they began marketing their products.

Participants, in many cases, are novices unfamiliar with actual industry norms, so they can exaggerate the degree to which crimes occur elsewhere in their industries. They are highly trained in business or science, leading to a "trained incapacity" to consider everyday rules of behavior. Employees with recent graduate business degrees are generally assumed to be ambitious people who favor the short-term, quantitative, and data-manipulating skills they learned, while ignoring long-term, nonquantifiable, and ethical issues they should also consider.

Such participation illustrates the "banality of evil," where crimes are committed comfortably by a cross-section of normal, malleable, and ambitious individuals who were not recruited for their criminal tendencies or skills. Most of these people would not commit corporate crimes if they were employed in roles that lacked incentives, opportunities, or cultural support for these crimes. Furthermore, their sense of personal responsibility is reduced by "authorization" from their bosses, as they unthinkingly conform to what they think their bosses want.

Whistleblowers

Whistleblowers are encouraging exceptions to these tendencies. Corporate whistleblowers are employees or former employees who risk being demonized and ostracized, or in a few cases fired, for informing outsiders about their employers' wrongdoing. They manage to avoid the groupthink, fear, loyalty, escalating commitment, and other banal tendencies to which ordinary employees submit, thereby retaining their independence of action. Dr. Jeffrey Wigand, for example, was a tobacco company vice president for research who braved the anger of seemingly invincible tobacco companies by disclosing that his employer knowingly manipulated and enhanced the addictive power of nicotine.

Emergent Corporate Crimes

Many firm, industry, and societal traits appear to encourage corporate crime. Crimes are more common in unusually hierarchical firms that enhance employees' fears or need to operate on tight schedules. Crime is further encouraged by having weak controls and lucrative and contradictory incentives. Industries with low profit potentials, only a handful of companies, or undifferentiated products (e.g., business envelopes, where brand loyalty is minimal) are particularly susceptible to price fixing. Also, poor societies with histories of corruption and natural resources needed by large multinational corporations are prone to corporate bribery of local officials.

No person founded a tobacco company intent on selling a dangerous product. Tobacco producers were well-established corporations for 2 centuries before tobacco's health hazards were recognized by even the harshest critics of smoking. Each employee hired filled a narrowly defined organizational role and could rightly assert that his or her contribution was minor. Even if a person left the company for moral reasons, his or her activity would continue as another person readily filled the vacancy. As a collection of positions, not of persons, the corporation thus has a dynamic all its own.

Social Responses to Corporate Crimes

The current American penchant for incarcerating offenders increasingly applies to corporate employees. In 2002, an otherwise divided Congress overwhelmingly approved the Sarbanes-Oxley Act in response to Enron and similar corporate financial frauds. The act mandates that corporate financial reporting safeguards be strengthened, with most attention directed to its felony provisions making corporate elites legally responsible for the accuracy of their firms' financial statements. And it tries to provide significantly longer jail sentences and stiffer fines for violators. Attention to it has been great—a Google search in early 2007 produced 12.2 million hits—and its future impact on corporate financial criminality may be significant. Such stiffer penalties in response to scandals is not new; similar penalty and prevention changes occurred earlier in response to Dalkon Shield contraceptive device deaths and to preventable coal mine accidents.

Nonetheless, the law remains a limited tool for gaining corporate legal compliance. For punishment to effectively deter, prospective criminals must consider possible discovery and punishment *before* deciding whether to commit crimes. But much corporate crime results from a "slippery slope" where egos, time investments, or fears encourage participants to gradually escalate the illegality of their actions.

These criminals know that their crimes are likely to go undiscovered and unpunished because, for example, pollution takes time to kill, and price fixing is usually hidden. Limiting enforcement is the imbalance of resources favoring the aggregate of corporations over the government. (But this imbalance can be overstated—the Food and Drug Administration, Securities and Exchange Commission, and other sanctioning bodies have significant resources, dedicated personnel, and strong interests in showing their effectiveness.) Punishment is limited despite survey results showing public outrage toward corporate crime in general, because members of the public who happen to serve on juries are relatively sympathetic toward accused well-spoken middle-class and wealthy executives with no known previous violations and exemplary family, community, and occupational biographies. Jurors view defendants' transgressions as caused by their jobs because they received no direct or immediate personal financial gain for their criminality.

M. David Ermann

See also Deviance; Environmental Crime; Groupthink; White-Collar Crime

Further Readings

Braithwaite, John. 1984. *Corporate Crime in the Pharmaceutical Industry.* London: Routledge & Kegan Paul.

Clinard, Marshall B. and Peter Yeager. 2005. *Corporate Crime.* Somerset, NJ: Transaction.

Ermann, M. David and Richard J. Lundman, eds. 2002. *Corporate and Governmental Deviance.* New York: Oxford University Press.

Fisse, Brent and John Braithwaite. 1983. *The Impact of Publicity on Corporate Offenders.* Albany, NY: State University of New York Press.

Geis, Gilbert. 2007. *White-Collar and Corporate Crime.* Upper Saddle River, NJ: Pearson Prentice Hall.

Geis, Gilbert, Robert F. Meier, and Laurence M. Salinger. 1995. *White Collar Crime.* New York: Free Press.

Simon, David R. 2005. *Elite Deviance.* Boston: Allyn & Bacon.

Simpson, Sally S. 2002. *Corporate Crime, Law, and Social Control.* Cambridge, England: Cambridge University Press.

Yeager, Peter C. 2002. *The Limits of Law: The Public Regulation of Private Pollution.* Repr. ed. Cambridge, England: Cambridge University Press.

CORPORATE STATE

The concept of the corporate state closely relates to pluralist philosophy. As opposed to monist philosophy, pluralist philosophy claims the existence of more than one ultimate principle that may serve as the basis of decision and action at the same time. Monist philosophy, in contrast, recognizes that all decisions and actions proceed from one consistent principle; otherwise, action would be impossible.

The core of state corporatism is to integrate different social classes and groups—often with contradictory interests—into the policy-making process. As a theory of social partnership closely connected historically to Catholic social theory, it also served as a basis for utopian socialists such as Saint-Simon to argue that the working classes should be included in decision- and policy-making processes. Catholic social theory seeks to reconcile social classes and conserve the existing social order by mitigating the radicalism of social conflicts. Utopian socialists, however, want to overcome social classes by establishing, in the long run, a socialist society.

During two periods in modern history, the concept of the corporate state became popular. In the 1890s, under pressure from growing working-class and socialist movements, the Catholic Church tried to popularize the concept against the opposing concept of class conflict or war. In the 1970s the concept (neo-corporatism) again became popular, particularly among academics responding to the growing influence of international socialist and communist movements. Each time the goal was to incorporate the usually excluded working classes, subordinate cultural groups, and extra-parliamentary movements into the decision- and policy-making processes.

The concept of the corporate state found voice among fascists. Mussolini, for example, claimed to have a corporate theory of the state. Similar but less explicit claims may be found in German fascist theories of the state. Marxists, however, find this to be merely demagoguery to conceal the real aims of fascism. They maintain that, if neoliberalism is the most radical polity under representative democracy to enforce the interests of the monopolist bourgeoisie, then fascism is the most radical and open polity with military force and violence to the same end. In other words, fascism is the most radical conservative and monist theory of politics, despite its efforts to conceal its ideology.

Marxism explores a monist theory of politics also. However, it differs from fascism radically in that it wants, like utopian socialists, to change the existing social order rather than to conserve it. It seeks to take political power in the name of the working classes and subordinated groups to establish a socialist society without any subordinated social classes or groups. In this view, socialism is the essential solution to all structurally caused social problems, offering the kingdom of freedom as opposed to the kingdom of subordination and suppression.

Doğan Göçmen

See also Class; Collective Consciousness; Communitarianism; Socialism; Social Revolutions

Further Readings

Crouch, Colin and Wolfgang Streeck, eds. 2006. *The Diversity of Democracy: Corporatism, Social Order and Political Conflict.* Northampton, MA: Edward Elgar.

Williamson, Peter J. 1989. *Corporatism in Perspective: An Introductory Guide to Corporatist Theory.* Thousand Oaks, CA: Sage.

CORRUPTION

Corruption is the abuse of public power for private benefit. Corruption occurs if a government official has the power to grant or withhold something of value and—contrary to laws and normal procedures—trades this thing of value for a gift or reward. Among corrupt acts, bribery gets the most attention, but corruption can also include nepotism, official theft, fraud, certain patron–client relationships, and extortion.

Examples of corruption would include cases in which a high-level government official accepts cash bribes from firms to reduce competition from imports, middle-level bureaucrats favor suppliers who promise them jobs after they leave government service, a judge rules in favor of an organization because it employs his child, a customs official speeds up the administrative processing of an import shipment in return for receiving part of the shipment, or a junior health inspector accepts free meals to ignore a restaurant's sanitary violations. Some researchers extend the definition of corruption to include violations of private trust such as insider trading. Although it is sometimes difficult to draw a clear line between where public corruption ends and private violations begin, the usual understanding is that corruption is limited to violations of public trust.

The World Bank further divides corruption into "state capture" and "administrative corruption." State capture occurs when firms or persons pay officials to revise laws in the favor of the bribe payer, whereas administrative corruption refers to the payment of bribes to distort the execution of existing laws. Another common distinction is that "grand corruption" involves major programs at the highest levels of government, whereas "petty corruption" is associated with less important programs and officials.

Costs of Corruption

At the individual level, corrupt acts are inequitable. They allow some to avoid laws, regulations, and practices that others must follow. Thus, corruption undermines people's confidence that success results from individual effort rather than from bribery or political connections. In addition, a growing body of research shows that corruption tends to have an adverse impact on a country's economy.

Besides its adverse impact on democratic processes, widespread corruption tends to reduce economic growth and worsen the distribution of income (the poor must pay bribes but rarely receive them). It tends to increase government spending and reduce tax receipts. Because great opportunities for bribery exist in new construction, excessive unproductive investment in infrastructure often occurs at the sacrifice of necessary maintenance of existing infrastructure. Resources are diverted into the negotiating, paying, and, if necessary, attempting to enforce bribes. Finally, corruption tends to reduce the confidence of people in their own government as well as the willingness of foreigners to invest in, lend to, or trade with firms in the corrupt country.

Even crude analysis points to a significant negative relationship between corruption and the level of economic development. Figure 1 shows the relationship between Transparency International's Corruption Perceptions Index and income per capita adjusted for differences in the cost of living (purchasing power parity [PPP]) for 150 countries.

There are no very corrupt rich countries and there are no very honest poor ones. In fact, the correlation between perceived corruption and income per capita is –.8. Of course, correlation is not causation, and it

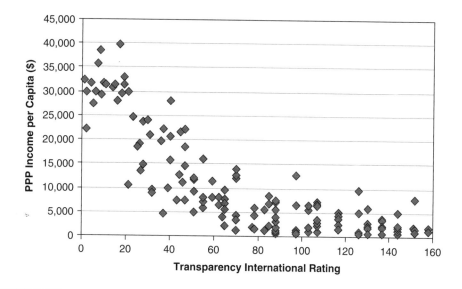

Figure 1   Relation of Perceived Corruption to Purchasing Power Parity (PPP) Income per Capita

is possible that the causation runs the other way (low incomes provide a fertile environment for corruption).

Corruption is rarely static; in the absence of an effective anti-corruption drive, it tends to worsen over time (the "ratchet effect"). Corrupt officials continuously attempt to increase the inclusiveness and complexity of laws, create monopolies, and otherwise restrict legal, economic, or social activities in order to extract even larger bribes or favors in the future. Perhaps the most damaging aspect of corruption is that it increases the level of uncertainty and forces individuals and organizations to expend extensive effort in attempts to reduce this uncertainty. For example, investors must worry not only about changing market conditions but also whether various unknown officials will seek to block their investment to extract additional bribes.

Measuring Corruption

Estimating the amount of corruption in a society is difficult because this offense often lacks a victim. For example, private citizens may find themselves excluded from business opportunities because of the length of time, expense, or complex procedures required to pursue the opportunity legally. If, to speed up the bureaucratic process, citizens either offer bribes or agree to a public official's demands, then the citizens often see the officials as doing favors—not imposing burdens. Even if bribe-paying citizens feel

victimized, they may hesitate to report corruption for fear of retaliation or legal sanction. Under most legal systems, both the public officials and the private persons who engage in corrupt transactions are legally vulnerable if the corrupt acts are uncovered.

Because victims rarely report the crime of corruption, almost all studies of corruption rest on either publicized corruption investigations or surveys. Publicized investigation reports tend to grossly underestimate actual levels of corruption because only a fraction of corruption cases are investigated. Further complicating the analysis is the fact that in many countries, decisions to institute corruption investigations are political in nature.

For these reasons, most of the widely accepted studies deal with the perception of corruption as measured in surveys. Probably the best known is Transparency International's Corruption Perceptions Index (TI/CPI), an annual listing of the perception of international business people and country analysts of the degree of corruption in more than 160 countries. The TI/CPI is a survey-of-surveys and excludes some of the most corrupt countries where few surveys are available (e.g., North Korea). The TI/CPI score ranges from 10.0, most honest, to 0.0. In 2006, Finland, Iceland, and New Zealand were perceived as the least corrupt countries with a TI/CPI score of 9.6, while Haiti had the dubious honor of placing 163rd (last) with a score of 1.8. Other subjective estimates of corruption are the International Country Risk Guide and Control of Corruption measures.

Although important methodological differences exist among these three measures, their results tend to correlate closely.

Determinants of Corruption

Although no consensus exists on why some nations suffer more from corruption than others, researchers can identify certain national attributes that correlate with greater amounts of corruption: low levels of income per capita, low literacy, hostile or disease-ridden physical environments discouraged from effective oversight of colonial administrators by their home governments, noncommon law (Napoleonic code) legal systems, socialist/statist economies, Catholic or Muslim religious beliefs, weak press, lack of economic competition (either internal [monopolies] or external [trade restrictions]), misvalued currency, and lack of political competition.

When corruption is viewed as an economic decision, the willingness of officials to accept or solicit bribes becomes a function of both the size of the bribe and the consequences of being caught. The size of the bribe relates to the scale of the benefit sought by the bribe payer, whether the official must share the bribe with colleagues, and whether other officials might provide competition by offering to provide the same illegal benefit for a smaller bribe. The consequences of being caught accepting a bribe are a function of the likelihood of being discovered, investigated, prosecuted, and convicted as well as the seriousness of the punishment if convicted. In many developing countries, although statutes may call for extremely severe punishment for bribery, the chances of being caught and convicted are effectively zero.

Fighting Corruption

Not only is the eradication of corruption impossible; many attempts to reduce it to tolerable levels have also failed. Anti-corruption policies primarily composed of exhortations to virtue and a spurt of well-publicized investigations tend to have little long-term effect. Often, various political factions will usurp the anti-corruption campaign to settle scores with their opponents.

Successful anti-corruption campaigns, such as Hong Kong's, take into account the particular country's cultural, social, political, historical, and economic situation. Successful campaigns include institutional changes to reduce the economic incentives for corruption combined with improved governance, transparency, and an aggressive effort to communicate the purpose and progress of the campaign to the public. Successful anti-corruption campaigns must have widespread support for them to move forward in the face of tenacious covert opposition. Finally, lasting results require a serious effort to change the culture of corruption. A free press that uncompromisingly seeks to expose corruption at every level and improved political competition are critical to changing this culture.

However, even well-designed anti-corruption campaigns tend to stall. A common cause of failure is a weakening of political will brought about by a corruption "J" curve effect. A J curve effect occurs when the announcement of a new anti-corruption campaign initially causes corruption to worsen. Corrupt officials, who believe that they will lose opportunities for future bribes, will seek to maximize their current corruption earnings. Such corrupt officials may also attempt to "capture" a new anti-corruption campaign by inserting themselves or their clients into the investigation process and turning it into another means of extracting bribes from the guilty (or innocent).

International Anti-Corruption Efforts

The international community, through its technical advice and financial aid, can either encourage or discourage corruption in developing countries. Foreign aid or loans that are granted without appropriate conditions give corrupt officials other funding streams to divert into their own pockets. Over the past decade, the World Bank and other international and nongovernmental organizations have increased their efforts to ensure that their aid is not stolen and that recipient countries improve their anti-corruption efforts.

Since 1977, U.S. companies that pay bribes abroad have faced legal sanctions in U.S. courts. Although other developed countries are gradually imposing similar restrictions, it is not clear whether such efforts will have a significant impact. Not only does the nature of the restrictions differ dramatically with respect to activities forbidden; as well, analysts suspect that such restrictions simply shift bribe-paying activities from the parent company to subcontractors in the developing country. International efforts can assist but not substitute for a country's effective anti-corruption campaign.

Frank R. Gunter

See also Capital Flight; Corporate Crime; Economic Development; Global Economy; Multinational Corporations

Further Readings

Elliott, Kimberly Ann, ed. 1997. *Corruption and the Global Economy.* Washington, DC: Institute for International Economics.

Rose-Ackerman, Susan. 1999. *Corruption and Government: Causes, Consequences and Reform.* New York: Cambridge University Press.

Speville, Bertrand de. 1997. *Hong Kong: Policy Initiatives against Corruption.* Paris: Development Center of OECD.

Svensson, Jakob. 2005. "Eight Questions about Corruption." *Journal of Economic Perspectives* 19:19–42.

COUNTERMOVEMENTS

As social movements gain strength, they almost inevitably spark opposition, which can become organized as countermovements. These oppositional groups typically become active when a social movement's success challenges the status quo, threatening the interests of a cohesive group with its strong potential for attracting political allies. The emergence of an opposition group and the complicated dance of actions and reactions with the original movement that results can change the trajectory of a social movement's path and even derail it.

Countermovements emerge in many different kinds of social movements, such as abortion rights and civil rights. Operation Rescue and other anti-abortion groups formed in the years after *Roe v. Wade* to battle with pro-choice groups, sometimes violently, to stop women from obtaining legal abortions. The civil rights movement gained not only legislative and judicial successes in the 1960s but also a cadre of opponents, who staged their own protests and lobbying efforts to stop desegregation efforts made possible by *Brown v. Board of Education* and the Civil Rights Act of 1964. By advocating for change and threatening established interests, social movements also stir up a reaction among those established interests, who aim to fight back as vigorously as possible.

What factors lead to the development of opposition groups, and when are they most effective at blocking the social change advocated by a social movement? What tactics do opposition groups usually take, and what impact do those activities have on the course and outcome of a social movement?

When Do Countermovements Form?

Looking at the history of social movements that sparked intense opposition reveals three factors that tend to lead to the formation of a countermovement. Opposition groups are most likely to develop and become active when a social movement gains some measure of success, though not a total victory, that threatens the interests of a population who are unable to block the social movement through normal institutional channels and when political elites are available and willing to support the countermovement.

A social movement must meet some measure of success in attaining its goals to be taken seriously enough to spawn an opposition movement. Advocates of the availability of safe and legal abortions did not attract much reaction until the U.S. Supreme Court ruling in *Roe v. Wade,* which overturned state laws banning the procedure. Fierce opposition formed in the wake of the court ruling, as the movement's goals became attainable. But total victory would squelch opposition by making resistance seem hopeless. The success of the civil rights movement in light of the landmark ruling in *Brown v. Board of Education,* which outlawed segregated public schools, led to the creation of several countermovements, such as the citizens councils in the South. The councils vanished after mobilization of federal marshals to enforce school desegregation efforts.

Countermovements are also more likely to develop if those threatened by a social movement's goal cannot block the threat through existing institutions. For example, agricultural growers, frustrated by the inability of law enforcement officials to stop labor strikes and protests staged by farmworkers seeking to unionize in California in the 1930s, formed an opposition group known as Associated Farmers (AF). Farmworkers staged more than 200 labor strikes between 1933 and 1939, but these were so peaceful that the local sheriff had no grounds to break them up. Frustrated growers, whose economic interests were at risk, formed the AF and organized vigilante groups to terrorize and intimidate the farmworkers.

The brutal AF illustrates a third factor often found in the formation of countermovements: support of political elites. The opposition group was made up of members of the Los Angeles Chamber of Commerce, wealthy growers, groups such as the American Legion, and industrial organizations. In fact, the local power elite formed the core of the AF, which originated as a subcommittee of the Chamber of Commerce. It was able to draw on the support of transportation and power companies, whose economic fortunes were linked with the growers.

Boston city officials were active in the anti-busing movement that mobilized in the 1970s to block the use of busing to achieve school desegregation. City officials held key positions in the organizations that opposed busing, and many countermovement activities were held in city buildings. But although city officials provided the necessary resources, they were able to dissociate themselves from the sometimes violent actions taken by more militant members. Those protestors hurled rocks at buses carrying black students and taunted the students as they went in and out of school, but city officials did no more than offer tacit support.

Elite support, however, can be a double-edged sword, as pro–nuclear power groups formed by nuclear power industries learned in the 1970s. The pro-nuclear movement was spawned largely by companies involved in the production of nuclear equipment and trade associations in the face of the anti-nuclear protest movement. Demonstrations at Seabrook, New Hampshire, Rocky Flats, Colorado, and Three Mile Island, Pennsylvania, drew hundreds of protestors. Opposition groups launched a major campaign to counter those voices but were often publicly scorned as shills for the nuclear industry. The active engagement of companies, such as Westinghouse, affected their legitimacy in the eyes of the public.

Actions and Reactions

The interaction between movements and countermovements is a dynamic, fluid process of thrusts and parries, as each side attempts to disarm and delegitimize the other. Countermovements can try to raise the costs of mobilization for social movements by blocking their access to resources, damaging their public image by casting movement goals in a negative light, and directly intimidating and threatening movement activists.

Pro-nuclear organizations responded to the anti-nuclear movement by organizing "truth squads" to promote their position that nuclear power was safe and discredit their opponents as wrongheaded. The

pro-nuclear movement also tried to block activists' access to federal funding to intervene in regulatory proceedings, and several campus chapters organized efforts to block the use of student fees to fund the activities of campus anti-nuclear groups. The pro-nuclear organizations also tried to intimidate protestors by hiring security firms to photograph license plates at rallies, disseminating derogatory information about activists, and pursuing trespassing charges against activists protesting at nuclear power plants. More recently, conservative groups such as the Capital Research Center have tried to discredit anti-corporate globalization groups by writing derogatory articles about them and embarrassing foundations that fund movement groups into cutting off their financial support.

Anti-abortion groups worked hard to reframe the abortion debate to discredit their opponents. A movement that thought it was advocating for safe and legal medical procedures for women seeking to terminate a pregnancy was eventually recharacterized as "baby killers" as the terms of the debate shifted from the rights of women to the rights of the unborn. Demonstrators ringed abortion clinics with signs showing gruesome pictures of aborted fetuses, and some abortion opponents turned to violence by bombing abortion clinics.

Countermovements also use conventional political methods to block social movements. The AF not only physically attacked striking farmers but also worked to convince state and local governments to pass anti-picketing ordinances, withhold relief payments from striking farmworkers, and prosecute labor leaders for their organizing activities. Anti-abortion groups have turned to the courts to seek favorable judicial rulings to uphold limits on the availability of abortion through such avenues as requiring minors to obtain parental consent or mandating counseling before a procedure can be performed. Opponents of the civil rights movement created private academies for white children in the South in the 1970s to circumvent federal demands that public schools be desegregated.

Opposition movements such as the anti-abortion movement can change the path of a social movement by changing the terms of the debate and can even ultimately defuse an activist group. A countermovement formed by scientists and professional associations to battle against animal rights activists in the 1980s was eventually able to prevail, blocking activists from shutting down animal experiments. A group of animal protectionists was able to stop two animal research projects in the 1970s and 1980s, but opposition groups formed to defend the use of animals in research.

Professional associations began discussing ways to counter the animal rights movement and to counsel research institutions to defend their practices. They were able to reframe the issue as one of helping the sick, particularly children, giving support to other universities and research centers.

Yvonne Chilik Wollenberg

See also Anti-Globalization Movement; Black Power Movement; Chicano Movement; Fathers' Rights Movement; Social Movements; Transnational Social Movement; Women's Rights Movement

Further Readings

Andrews, Kenneth. 2002. "Movement-Countermovement Dynamics and the Emergence of New Institutions: The Case of 'White Flight' Schools in Mississippi." *Social Forces* 80:911–36.

Jasper, James and Jane Poulsen. 1993. "Fighting Back: Vulnerabilities, Blunders, and Countermobilization by the Targets in Three Animal Rights Campaigns." *Sociological Forum* 8:639–57.

Meyer, David S. and Suzanne Staggenborg. 1996. "Movements, Countermovements, and the Structure of Political Opportunity." *American Journal of Sociology* 101:1628–60.

Pichardo, Nelson. 1995. "The Power Elite and Elite-Driven Countermovements: The Associated Farmers of California during the 1930s." *Sociological Forum* 10:21–49.

Zald, Mayer N. and Bert Useem. 2006. "Movement and Countermovement Interaction: Mobilization, Tactics, and State Involvement." Pp. 247–72 in *Social Movements in an Organizational Society,* edited by M. Zald and J. McCarthy. New Brunswick, NJ: Transaction.

CRIME

Recent figures from the Bureau of Justice Statistics (BJS) National Crime Victimization Survey (NCVS) report that violent and property crime are declining. For example, from 2003 to 2004, the index for violent crime indicates a drop of 2.2 percent. Perhaps more telling is that between 1995 and 2004 the same index reports an overall decline in violent crime of 32 percent. The trend for property crime is equally noteworthy. Figures from the NCVS report a 2.1 percent decrease from 2003 to 2004. Moreover, the rate of property crime from 1995 to 2004 fell by 23.4 percent. Clearly, these data suggest that the problem of crime is increasingly under control and that the mechanisms to contain it are working effectively. However, interpreting the data reveals another story.

For instance, if the focus is on the incarceration rate, the BJS reports that the number of persons in federal and state prisons rose by 1.9 percent in 2004. While this rate of increase is lower than the average rate of growth during the past decade (3.2 percent) and slightly lower than the growth rate during 2003 (2 percent), the total convict population is currently in excess of 2.4 million (approximately 1.5 million in federal and state facilities, another 800,000 in local jails, and another 100,000 in juvenile settings).

Complicating these incarceration trends are the increasing number of overcrowded facilities and concerns related to both the types of offenses committed most frequently and those identified as responsible for them. As of the end of 2004, 24 state prisons were operating at or above their highest capacity. Additionally, 40 percent of federal facilities were operating above their capacity. According to the BJS, half of those persons serving time in state prisons were incarcerated for violent crimes, 20 percent for property crimes, and 21 percent for drug offenses. Moreover, as of December 31, 2004, 104,848 women were confined in state and federal prisons. This is an astonishing 65 percent increase when compared with the 68,468 women in prison in 1995. The BJS also indicates that women represented 7 percent of all persons incarcerated in 2004. This is a 6.1 percent increase from the figure reported in 1995.

When tracking race, the incarceration trends are also quite revealing. The BJS reports that as of December 31, 2004, approximately 8.4 percent of all black males living in the United States who were between the ages of 25 and 29 were incarcerated. Hispanics made up 2.5 percent for this same age group, and whites constituted 1.2 percent for this age cohort. When combining the figures for male and female convicts, 41 percent were black, 19 percent were Hispanic, and 34 percent were white. The remaining percentage was composed of people who were either of another race or of some grouping of two or more races.

What these incarceration data suggest is that the story behind recent declining rates of crime is related to the swelling number of people criminally confined. Overwhelmingly, these individuals are poor, young, and of color. Moreover, state and federal trends in arrest, prosecution, and conviction show that persons subjected to these criminal justice practices are typically males who also are disproportionately poor, young, and of color. How should the problem of crime be understood, given society's emphasis on incarceration?

The Problem of Definition

Different approaches to crime result in different interpretations for when (and by whom) a violation has occurred. This creates a problem with defining criminal behavior. Broadly speaking, three approaches or paradigms are discernible. The first of these is the legalistic view. The legalistic paradigm argues that if an action violates the criminal law, then that action is a crime. For example, if a federal, state, or local code exists prohibiting the smoking of cigarettes in places of business, then engaging in this behavior violates the criminal law. Thus, if a law exists banning murder, rape, torture, or school violence, then behavior that is consistent with these actions represents a transgression against the law. Criminal sanction can follow. This legalistic paradigm on crime dominates the field.

Critics identify three shortcomings with this approach. First, given that the legalistic view is the most prevalent, this means that politicians, the media, and other agents of socialization focus the general public's attention on certain types of criminality often to the near exclusion of other types of criminality. For example, most people believe that victimization brought about by person-on-person violence is the most rampant and damaging to the long-term well-being of society. Although this sort of criminality is certainly worth noting, the societal harm that follows in the wake of corporate, white-collar, and environmental wrongdoing is far more devastating. This is because the number of persons affected is considerably greater than the number affected by street crime. Thus, the legalistic view acts much like a "blinder," because those with power and influence draw our attention to some crimes and criminals (e.g., street crime, inner-city gang members) while distracting us from the illicit activities of governments, industry, and corporate America.

Second, by focusing only on those behaviors officially defined by law as criminal, actions that are harmful but not defined by law this way can continue to exist and, quite possibly, flourish. This would include actions that amount to social harm or social injury, not the least of which would include violations of human and moral rights. If the definition of crime

encompassed this standard (as opposed to the strictly legalistic view), then the presence of poverty, racism, sexism, and other expressions of discrimination; the absence of safe, fair, and clean working conditions; and the lack of access to food, clothing, shelter, housing, and medical care all would be criminal.

Third, the legalistic definition of crime includes some behaviors that are not fundamentally harmful or behaviors in which there is little consensus on the extent of injury, if any, that occurs. Whereas most people would agree that rape, murder, robbery, arson, and burglary are crimes, there is far less agreement on such things as prostitution, drug use, pornography, and gambling. In most sectors of society, however, these actions are recognized as criminal. Despite this, some criminologists suggest that these latter behaviors are victimless, especially as there is no clear indication of an offender or a victim. Instead, what typically exists are willing consensual participants. Critics thus contend that the legalistic paradigm does nothing more than legislate morality in these instances.

Two alternative approaches have emerged in response to the limits of the legalistic paradigm. One of these is the social construction perspective. In this view, crime does not exist independent of what people think or how people act. Instead, crime is a product of human construction. Consequently, the "reality" of crime (e.g., definitions of lawbreaking, types of criminal offenders) is regarded as an artifact of culture and history and, thus, subject to change. Further, the social construction paradigm maintains that because these definitions vary, no act, in and of itself, is categorically or universally lawful or unlawful. Changing societal views on abortion, homosexuality, prostitution, alcohol consumption, and slavery amply demonstrate this point. These views may be linked to shifting political, economic, and social influences. In each instance what changes is not the behavior itself but how people collectively define and act toward the behavior at different periods, given the pressure from various societal influences. What changes, then, is the construction of what these actions mean supported by people's thoughts and feelings as linked to several societal forces that then reinforce these constructions as if they were objective, stable realities. Eventually, changes in language, custom, habit, socialization, and education institutionalize favored ways of perceiving these constructed realties.

The other approach that has developed in response to the shortcomings of the legalistic view is the critical paradigm. This perspective endorses the social reality of crime but adds to it the notion that definitions of law, of criminal wrongdoing, and of criminals function to support status quo interests. These interests advance the aims of powerful segments in society. Examples of these segments include government, business, the military, industry, the medical establishment, and the media. According to the critical paradigm, certain types of offenses are less likely to be identified as crime (e.g., unfair labor practices, medical malpractice), and certain types of offenders are less likely to be arrested, prosecuted, and punished for harmful actions (e.g., corporate executives, government officials), because those with economic and political influence shape such definitions in favor of their own material and symbolic needs. There are various strains of thought within the critical paradigm (e.g., feminist criminology, left realism, anarchism, critical race theory, postmodernism); however, each emphasizes the way that those who represent the status quo structure definitions of crime so that they do not lose their accumulated power, despite committing acts that are unlawful. Supporters of the critical paradigm suggest that one example of how the crimes of the powerful are concealed, distorted, or minimized is through the reporting of the media. Television, radio, print, and various other electronic outlets—owned and operated by elite business interests—disseminate the message that certain types of crimes and criminals warrant the public's attention. The media's selective attention to these behaviors, then, dramatically shapes public sentiment such that the public is led to believe that the "real" crime problem is that which has been defined for them. As proponents of the critical paradigm explain, the selective attention on such offenses as murder, robbery, arson, and rape diverts the focus away from those social harms (criminal acts) that are the most devastating to the health and welfare of society (e.g., toxic waste dumping, global warming, corporate fraud, governmental abuses).

The Problem of Theory

The problem of crime is not limited to the choice of definition. Closely linked to this issue is the type of theory employed to explain, predict, prevent, and control offender behavior. Contemporary theories of crime fall into one of three approaches. These include neoclassical criminology, the positivist school, and the critical/postmodern orientation. Each of these three approaches focuses on certain aspects of understanding crime to the exclusion of other considerations.

Neoclassical criminology maintains that crime is a rational choice best understood through the routine activities of victims upon whom offenders prey. These activities include the availability of suitable targets (e.g., homes, businesses), the absence of capable guardians (e.g., police, pedestrians), and the presence of motivated offenders (e.g., unemployed, semiskilled, and undereducated workers). The interaction of these three conditions produces "hot spots" for criminality. Neoclassical criminology suggests that informal mechanisms of deterrence (e.g., neighborhood watch groups, community policing efforts) and shaming practices (e.g., public apology, compensation, and the victim's forgiveness) are essential to preventing and controlling crime.

Positivist criminology draws on insights from biology, sociology, psychology, religion, politics, and economics. The positive approach argues that crime is an objective, concrete reality that can be defined as such. Emphasis is placed on understanding the causes of criminality that are said to determine one's behavior. Supporters maintain that the application of the scientific method (hypothesis generation, theory testing, and empirical observation) results in the researcher's ability to explain these causes and to prevent and predict their likely reoccurrence. Adherents of positive criminology draw attention to such things as genetic predisposition, social disorganization, personality deficiencies, development failures, poor self-control, differential opportunity, and group affiliation to account for criminal wrongdoing. Positivist criminology dominates the contemporary study of crime.

The critical/postmodernism approach emphasizes the presence of differential power found among various segments of society. Power assumes many forms. Examples include economic wealth, social standing, patriarchy, heterosexist norms, race privileging, and dominant systems of communication (e.g., law, medicine, science). Critical criminological theories demonstrate how different segments in society (especially white, well, and straight men of privilege) use their power to shape a reality supportive of their group's interest, invalidating, dismissing, or otherwise controlling the needs of other, less powerful societal collectives. Consistent with this orientation, postmodernists show how the exercise of power is mediated by dominant forms of speech; this is language that structures and regulates how people think, act, feel, and exist.

This disciplining of identities supports those in positions of power.

The Problem of Research Focus

Concerns for both an agreed-upon definition of crime and the dilemma associated with the utilization of a criminological theory that best expresses this definition leads to a third fundamental issue. This is the problem of research focus. The concern for research focus addresses what criminologists should study. Several responses have been put forth, but three appear most promising: These are (1) an emphasis on conceptual models of integration, (2) strategies for restoration and offender reentry, and (3) a return to the philosophical foundations of crime.

Integration considers whether there are strategic ways to unify various (and competing) criminological theories so as to increase overall explanatory and predictive capabilities. One noteworthy recommendation along these lines argues that the multidisciplinary nature of crime requires the development of models that synthesize discipline-specific theories based on shared assumptions. Efforts at restorative justice and offender reentry attempt to make peace with crime by pursuing interventions that reconnect offenders, victims, and the communities to which both belong. One solution consistent with this logic encourages ex-offenders to engage in personal, intimate storytelling as a way of owning harm to self and others, and as a way of reconstituting their identities. The return to the philosophical foundations of crime entails a reconsideration of the rationale that informs definitions of crime and theories pertaining to it. One proposal supportive of this strategy suggests revisiting the ontological, epistemological, ethical, and aesthetic dimensions of the crime construct, especially as understood in ultramodern society.

Bruce A. Arrigo

See also Class; Crime, Fear of; Crime Rates; Crime Waves; Drug Abuse, Crime; National Crime Victimization Survey; Policing, Strategic; Postmodernism; Power; Race; Restorative Justice; Subculture of Violence Hypothesis; Victimization; Victim–Offender Mediation Model

Further Readings

Arrigo, Bruce A., ed. 1999. *Social Justice/Criminal Justice: The Maturation of Critical Theory in Law, Crime, and Deviance*. Belmont, CA: Wadsworth.

Arrigo, Bruce A., Dragan Milovanovic, and Robert C. Schehr. 2005. *The French Connection in Criminology: Rediscovering Crime, Law, and Social Change*. Albany, NY: SUNY Press.

Arrigo, Bruce A. and Christopher R. Williams, eds. 2006. *Philosophy, Crime, and Criminology*. Urbana, IL: University of Illinois Press.

DeKeseredy, Walter and Barbara Perry, eds. 2007. *Advances in Critical Criminology: Theory and Application*. Lexington, MA: Lexington Books.

Guarino-Ghezzi, Susan and A. Javier Trevino, eds. 2006. *Understanding Crime: A Multidisciplinary Approach*. Cincinnati, OH: LexisNexus Anderson.

Lynch, Michael J. and Raymond J. Michalowski. 2006. *Primer in Radical Criminology: Critical Perspectives on Crime, Power, and Identity*. 4th ed. Monsey, NY: Willow Tree.

Milovanovic, Dragan. 2003. *Critical Criminology at the Edge: Postmodern Perspectives, Integration, and Applications*. Monsey, NY: Criminal Justice Press.

Quinney, Richard. 2001. *The Social Reality of Crime*. 2nd ed. Somerset, NJ: Transaction.

Reiman, Jeffrey. 2005. *The Rich Get Richer and the Poor Get Prison: Ideology, Class, and Criminal Justice*. Boston: Allyn & Bacon.

CRIME, DRUG ABUSE

See DRUG ABUSE, CRIME

CRIME, FEAR OF

Fear of crime is widespread among people in many Western societies, affecting far more people than the personal experience of crime itself, and as such, it constitutes a significant social problem. Although researchers note that it is a somewhat problematic measure, the question most frequently used to assess fear of crime is "Is there anywhere near where you live where you would be afraid to walk alone at night?" Over the past 3 decades, roughly 40 to 50 percent of individuals surveyed in the United States responded affirmatively to this question (or slight variations of it). An international survey conducted in 17 industrialized nations in 2000 found that overall, 17.5 percent of respondents expressed moderate to high fear of crime, ranging from a high of 41 percent in Switzerland to a low of 5 percent in Finland and Sweden.

The single most common reaction to fear of crime is spatial avoidance—that is, avoiding places perceived to be dangerous. In some situations, fear can serve as a beneficial, even life-saving, emotion. However, in other circumstances, fear is an emotion that unnecessarily constrains behavior, restricts personal opportunity and freedom, and, ultimately, threatens the foundation of communities. In addition to generating avoidance behaviors, fear of crime can also lead to significant attitudinal changes—including support for more stringent criminal justice policies and negative attitudes toward members of minority groups, who are frequently portrayed by the media as the main perpetrators of crime.

One of the first large-scale studies of the fear of crime, conducted under the auspices of the President's Commission on Law Enforcement and the Administration of Justice in the late 1960s, found that fear of crime was based less on actual personal victimization and more on inaccurate beliefs about the extent of crime. This study suggested that individuals assess the threat of victimization from information communicated to them through a variety of interpersonal relationships and the media, and from interpretations of symbols of crime to which they are exposed in their local environments. Recent studies of the fear of crime show that, somewhat paradoxically perhaps, individuals who experience the lowest actual rates of criminal victimization (women and the elderly) tend to report the greatest fear of crime, whereas those with higher rates of victimization (especially young minority males) express significantly less fear.

The majority of the general public obtains the bulk of their information about crime from the mass media—including movies, crime drama shows, and news reports. One of the first sophisticated theoretical explanations of the effects of media consumption on individuals was posited by George Gerbner and Larry Gross, whose cultivation hypothesis asserts that television viewing cultivates a "mean world view" characterized by a heightened fear of crime and inflated estimations of personal risks. Although more recent studies have refined this hypothesis and pointed out that media effects are somewhat more nuanced and vary according to the sociodemographic characteristics of media consumers, this mean world view is generated by the media's exaggeration of the frequency and seriousness of crime and major emphasis on violent crime, particularly murder. For instance, although the U.S. murder rate decreased by 20 percent between 1990 and 1998, during the same period the major television network newscasts increased the number of their stories about murder by 600 percent. In addition to a disproportional focus on murder, at various points in time, the media have generated moral panics (and hence fear among the general public) surrounding alleged threats to elderly people's safety, child abductions, and sex offenders, among others. These media depictions also frequently portray the perpetrators of crime as members of marginalized groups such as racial minorities and homeless people, when in reality these individuals most frequently demonized in the media are more likely to be victims than perpetrators of crime. Perhaps even more problematically, the media's disproportional focus on young black males as the perpetrators of crime can serve to justify more stringent criminal justice policies and expenditures and the elimination of social support systems, such as welfare and job creation programs.

In addition to the role of the media in generating fear of crime, it is important to note that politicians and legislators exploit fear of crime as a political tool. One of the first elections in the United States to utilize crime and fear of crime for advantage was the 1968 campaign of Richard Nixon. Similarly, influencing the 1988 election of George H. W. Bush in the United States were advertisements implying that presidential candidate Michael Dukakis was soft on crime. The political uses of generating fear of crime have been particularly manifest in the post–September 11, 2001, period, during which the governments of several Western countries, especially the United States and Britain, have emphasized their vulnerability to terrorism, thereby often generating fear among the general public and to justify the passage of several laws that eroded civil liberties. Similar to the depictions of crime being associated with members of minority groups, the portrayal of terrorists as primarily Muslim and Arab has led to increased incidents of racism against members of these groups.

Clayton Mosher and Scott Akins

See also Community Crime Control; Crime; Crime Rates; Crime Waves

Further Readings

Baer, Justin and William Chambliss. 1997. "Generating Fear: The Politics of Crime and Crime Reporting." *Crime, Law and Social Change* 27:87–107.

Biderman, A. D., L. A. Johnson, J. McIntyre, and A. W. Weir. 1967. *Report on a Pilot Study in the District of Columbia on Victimization and Attitudes toward Law Enforcement.*

President's Commission on Law Enforcement and the Administration of Justice. Washington, DC: Government Printing Office.

Gerbner, George and Larry Gross. 1976. "Living with Television: The Violence Profile." *Journal of Communication* 26:173–99.

Glassner, Barry. 2004. "Narrative Techniques for Fear Mongering." *Social Research* 71:819–26.

International Crime Victimization Survey. 2000. Retrieved August 6, 2006 (http://www.unicri.it/wwd/analysis/icvs/statistics.php).

Shirlow, Peter and Rachel Pain. 2003. "The Geographies and Politics of Fear." *Capital and Class* 80:15–26.

Warr, Mark. 2000. "Fear of Crime in the United States: Avenues for Research and Policy." *Criminal Justice 2000.* Washington, DC: National Institute of Justice.

CRIME RATES

Crime rates are standardized measures of crime levels. In mathematical terms, a crime rate can be expressed as $(M/N) \times K$ where M is an estimate of the amount of crime occurring in a particular setting during a specified period of time, N is an estimate of the population at risk, and K is a constant determined by the analyst. So, if for hypothetical Community A, we determine that for the last calendar year, there were 9,300 crimes committed against property, and if the population of Community A is 458,000, the property crime rate per 100,000 for this community for the year in question is calculated as $(9,300/458,000) \times 100,000 = 2,030.6$. Using this general approach, crime rates can be calculated for any size social unit from the neighborhood to the nation-state and for any temporal period.

Unlike raw counts of crimes, rates take the size of the at-risk population into account. Whereas a comparison of the raw or absolute numbers of crimes across communities or within any particular community over time might suggest significant variations, a comparison of crime rates allows the analyst to determine whether the differences are real or merely a function of differences in population size.

Crime rates are useful for a number of reasons. As standardized measures of crime levels, they can serve as useful indicators of the quality of community life. Policy planners utilize crime rate measures to assess the need for social interventions and the relative success of crime control policies. Academic investigators rely on crime rate data as they attempt to investigate the relative value of empirical predictions associated with competing criminological theories.

In a fundamental way, the value of crime rate measures is reliant upon the appropriateness of the estimates of the numerators and denominators used in rate construction. Estimates of the former tend to be derived from one of three sources: the data collected by police, the reports of members of the general public who are asked about their victim experiences in surveys, and the reports of offenders. It has been well established in the research literature that each of these sources of crime data has characteristic flaws. As a result, it is prudent to think of these numerator estimates as somewhat biased samples of all crimes occurring.

The denominators of crime rates also present some formidable problems. Although so-called crude crime rates (like the hypothetical example given in the first paragraph of this entry) offer several advantages over the use of raw numbers, they fail to take account of information regarding the internal structure of the at-risk population. For instance, because most crime is committed by people in early adulthood (ages 18–26), it might make more sense to standardize the rates with reference to the size of this segment of the population rather than with reference to the overall population. Thus, two communities of similar size might differ with respect to their crude crime rates because one is truly more lawless than the other, or because one of the communities might have much more of its population clustered in younger age groups. A comparison of age-specific crime rates would permit an assessment of the value of these two accounts.

Vincent F. Sacco

See also Crime; Crime Waves

Further Readings

Mosher, Clayton J., Terance D. Miethe, and Dretha M. Phillips. 2002. *The Mismeasure of Crime.* Thousand Oaks, CA: Sage.

CRIME WAVES

The term *crime wave* has two distinct (but related) meanings in criminological and popular discourse. The most familiar meaning associates the term with relatively rapid and abrupt upward (and subsequent downward) shifts in rates of crime. A second usage suggests that the term refers not to actual crime rate increases—in any narrow sense—but to changes in levels of public fear, anxiety, and publicity surrounding the problem of crime. Whereas the former usage emphasizes an understanding of crime waves as "objective" phenomena, the latter emphasizes their "subjective" character.

As a measure of actual crime rate change, this concept has no specific, agreed-upon meaning. However, most commonly, it references crime rate variations occurring over the shorter term rather than the longer term. In this respect we can speak of crime waves in reference to relatively distinct, historically specific episodes, such as the increases in gangsterism in the Midwest during the 1930s, the nationwide post–World War II urban crime rate increase, or the rapidly escalating rates of extortionate crime that plagued Italian neighborhoods in large American cities during the first decades of the 20th century. We can assess crime waves objectively as mathematical entities through several key dimensions, including length (How long does it take crime waves to rise and fall?), shape (Do crime waves rise and fall with equal rapidity?), linearity (Do the factors that affect crime rate development have consistent effects?), and synchronicity (Is the crime wave just a local or is it a more general phenomenon?).

Efforts to explain sudden and rapid shifts in crime levels focus on processes of social change. Researchers have shown three major types of relevant variables. One group of explanations relates to various social dislocations, such as war, rapid economic change, or institutional breakdown. A second explanation focuses on the diffusion of cultural patterns. So-called copycat crimes are perhaps the clearest example of such a dynamic. A third type stresses the ways in which the various kinds of social and technological innovations facilitate the commission of crimes posing a serious challenge to the existing social control apparatus. An alternative way of thinking about crime waves is as social constructions. In other words, crimes waves can be said to exist when there are widespread public perceptions that they exist—irrespective of what more objective measures of crime level variation might indicate. In this sense, crime waves imply increased public anxiety, higher levels of media attention, and eventually more coercive forms of social control reactions. Although this meaning of crime wave might be less intuitive, it is actually the formulation

with which the term has been most often associated in recent years.

A naive interpretation of the relationship between these two kinds of crime rates might suggest highly correlated empirical realities. However, this does not appear to be the case. The social dynamics that drive changes in crime rate levels appear, in many cases, to be only tangentially related to the dynamics that drive shifts in fear and perception.

Vincent F. Sacco

See also Crime; Crime Rates

Further Readings

Sacco, Vincent F. 2005. *When Crime Waves*. Thousand Oaks, CA: Sage.

CULTS

Cults, more appropriately called "new religious movements" in sociology, have emerged since the 1950s in the United States (and elsewhere) and have gathered much media attention. Many of these faiths provide religious alternatives to mainstream Protestantism, Roman Catholicism, and Judaism and are popular with young adults. New religions, such as the Unification Church ("the Moonies"), Scientology, Hare Krishna, and the People's Temple, garner negative press and public antipathy for three primary reasons.

First, many people—especially family members of these young adults—are concerned about the nature of their conversion. Have they freely decided to convert, or has the cult pressured them to join? Worse, has the cult brainwashed these new members, robbing them of free will? With little information forthcoming, from the faith or the convert, family members often perceive that brainwashing has occurred. It seems impossible that their beloved has freely chosen such an odd faith, so the group must have done something nefarious. If or when family members are able to question these new recruits, they cannot articulate their new faith's theology clearly, and the family members' worries grow.

But conversion theories would predict such a problem. Although there is some debate, much sociological research on conversion states that adults convert not for theological reasons but because they have developed social bonds with members. Individuals who convert often meet the new faith at an emotionally perilous moment, such as a romantic breakup, the first year away at college, and so on. The new religion tends to envelope the person with hospitality (pejoratively, this was known as "love bombing") and praise for seeking the correct path to spiritual enlightenment. Conversely, as these affective bonds grow with the new faith, ties to family and friends not involved in the new religion weaken. Families often feel isolated from their loved ones once they convert and wonder how much of the isolation is ordered by the new religious movement to hide them away from those who might talk them out of the faith. When families reunite, questioning about the conversion is often the topic of conversation, and new converts feel interrogated by those who claim to love them. They respond by further reducing contact, which only increases their families' suspicions.

The second reason that cults are perceived as worrisome is the range of behaviors members pursue after they have been converted. Caught up in the fervor of saving the world, practitioners of new religious movements often engage in constant recruitment. Even worse, at least one new religion (the Children of God, now known as The Family) encourages female members to use their sexuality to convert wealthy men, a practice known as "flirty fishing." Fundraising is viewed suspiciously by outsiders, especially practices such as selling flowers in airports. After some members of The Family left the group and went to the press, nearly all complained about exhausting schedules, wherein they would rise before dawn and not return home until late. Questions were raised by family members and in the press about where all the money had gone; was it financing extravagant lifestyles of the charismatic leaders?

Other behaviors that are perceived by outsiders as odd are dietary practices, such as vegetarianism (Hare Krishna); the use of chemicals/drugs (the Love Israel family's ritual use of toluene); the practice of spiritual counseling using E-meters to become "clear" (e.g., Scientology); unfamiliar clothing norms and trance possession (e.g., Bhagwan Shree Rasjneesh); the belief in extraterrestrial life (e.g., Heaven's Gate), and so on.

Even more serious allegations have been raised about some new religious movements. Children who grew up in the Children of God told of horrific physical and sexual abuse in the boarding schools used by the group. While never proven, allegations of child sexual abuse were among the reasons the government used to justify its 1993 raid against the Branch Davidians in Waco, Texas. Female ex-members of many movements have given accounts of being asked to sexually service leaders, in part to demonstrate their religious commitment. Undoubtedly physical and sexual abuse occurred in the People's Temple, led by Jim Jones, especially during its time in Guyana. Perhaps the best-known examples of new religious movements using violence are Aum Shinrikyo's 1995 attack on the Japanese subway system and the 1978 People's Temple assassination of a U.S. congressman, Leo Ryan, followed by the murder-suicide of the nearly 1,000 members.

The third reason that cults are perceived as worrisome concerns if and how members are able to leave: Are they free to simply walk away? Or must families hire experts, called deprogrammers, to help members leave? In part, the debate over leaving these new religious movements mirrors the conversion debate. Those who feel that cult members freely choose to belong tend to believe that they are free to leave. Those who feel that the group has nefariously done something to the convert to facilitate joining the cult, naturally assume that the person will need intervention to leave. Initially, deprogrammings were often forcibly accomplished, by kidnapping the member and taking him or her to an undisclosed location prepared for the intervention. The deprogrammer, assistants, and the family engaged in emotional dialogue with the believer, until the member chose to leave (adherents to the brainwashing hypothesis tend to use the phrase "snapped out of the cult" to express what happened during the deprogramming). After some members of various cults, who had been kidnapped but managed to escape, sued the deprogrammers and their families for kidnapping, a "gentler" form of deprogramming, called "rational evaluation," emerged.

One of the many misconceptions about the emergence of these so-called cults is that this was a unique time in U.S. history and that they burst forth, primarily in the post–Vietnam War era, as young adults struggled in the changed sociopolitical landscape. This claim, notwithstanding its popularity, is false. A careful examination of religious history has shown that new religious movements have long been a part of U.S. history, as any student of the First and Second Great Awakenings knows. While many movements arose, only to die off, others evolved into established religions, such as the Church of Latter-day Saints (the Mormons).

Kathleen S. Lowney

See also Anomie; Social Exclusion

Further Readings

Dawson, Lorne, ed. 1998. *Cults in Context: Readings in the Study of New Religious Movements.* Toronto, ON: Canadian Scholars Press.

Lofland, John and Rodney Stark. 1965. "Becoming a World Saver: A Theory of Conversion to a Deviant Perspective." *American Sociological Review* 30(6):862–75.

Wilson, Bryan, ed. 1999. *New Religious Movements.* New York: Routledge.

CULTURAL CAPITAL

The concept of cultural capital, which examines the interactions of culture with the economic class system, originated with French sociologists Pierre Bourdieu and Jean-Claude Passeron. Although conceived within the context of French culture, much of Bourdieu's writing has been translated into English, resulting in the extensive use of his concept in sociological and educational research in the United States and elsewhere.

In "Cultural Reproduction and Social Reproduction" Bourdieu sought to understand why children from different social classes in the 1960s exhibited unequal scholastic achievement. He examined how children from the upper class profit in school settings from the activation and distribution of cultural knowledge their parents directly transmitted to them.

In a subsequent writing, "The Forms of Capital," in 1983, Bourdieu discussed three interrelated and inextricably linked types of capital—economic capital, social capital, and cultural capital. Cultural capital similarly encompasses three forms: the embodied state, the objectified state, and the institutionalized state.

Embodied Capital

In its most fundamental form, cultural capital is "linked to the body," partly unconscious and acquired early on in life. Individuals must often exert effort to incorporate it. In his description of embodied cultural capital, Bourdieu borrowed a related concept, "habitus." Habitus can be understood as culturally learned performances that take the form of taken-for-granted bodily practices, ways of thinking, dispositions, or taste preferences. Embodied capital includes such things as manners, habits, physical skills, and styles that are so habitually enacted as to be virtually invisible. Embodied capital enacts values and tendencies socialized from one's cultural history that literally become part of the individual. Knowledge itself, Bourdieu suggested, is actively constructed as habitus, influenced by individual cultural history, and available to be mobilized by experiences in everyday life.

Objectified Capital

Things or possessions owned or acquired by people are objectified capital, but the objectified form of cultural capital cannot be understood without acknowledging its relationship to embodied capital and habitus. This form of capital is not of the body but rather lies outside of the body. The concept is similar to the Marxist or economist concept of capital: things that can be used, exchanged, or invested and may provide an advantage in societal interactions. Individual persons are not the only possessors of objectified capital. Social institutions and social systems acquire objectified capital that affects their value and social status, for example, the built environment of schools and the social networks and connections of students, faculty, and alumni. Objectified capital operates to maximize benefits in a wide variety of social situations.

Institutionalized Capital

Institutionalized cultural capital manifests as academic qualifications that recognize and legitimate the embodied and objectified forms of cultural capital possessed by a person. Institutionally sanctioned capital implies what Bourdieu called "cultural competence." Therefore, persons possessing academic qualifications can be compared and exchanged, and monetary value can be placed on their qualifications. Bourdieu asserted that the value of institutionalized cultural capital is determined only in relation to the labor market, where the exchange value of cultural capital is made explicit.

Cultural Capital and Societal Consequences

In all its forms cultural capital is an accumulation of resources that cannot be acquired as instantaneously as economic capital. Resources acquired over time can, theoretically, be mobilized and invested to gain an advantage in various fields. *Fields*, or *social contexts*, in Bourdieu's use of the term, are complex and fluid institutions, customs, and social rules. Depending on the field in which one is operating, the value of the person's cultural capital changes. The social issues where the concept of cultural capital is helpful include social class, education, inequality, power, and exclusion.

Cultural capital becomes mobilized and reproduced through primary and secondary socialization processes. For this reason childrearing practices and parental involvement in schools have been extensively investigated. Various forms of cultural capital, when activated through interaction with social institutions, may be valued unequally. For example, schools may not reward the embodied capital of working-class parents who practice rigid distinctions between work and play. Social institutions reward, ignore, or punish different types of cultural capital, thereby creating and perpetuating inequality.

Uses and Misuses of Cultural Capital

Bourdieu's concept of cultural capital is fluid and multidimensional, with various forms nested in such a way that they are inseparable within the individual; however, the concept also evolved over time in his writings. Moreover, as a "grand theory" in the sociological tradition of Karl Marx and Talcott Parsons, cultural capital has been critiqued for the overabundance of definitions and lack of empirical referents. Application and misuse of the concept of cultural capital has led to confusion and a lack of clarity as to what the term actually means.

The use of the concept of cultural capital, as intended by Bourdieu, is paramount to the explanation and description of one vein of influential factors relating to social problems and issues in the social sciences and in educational research, in particular. Cultural capital harnesses the intrapersonal as well as the extrapersonal knowledge and experiences that help shape a person's interaction with others and with

social institutions, such as the school. However, if defined too narrowly, as in the case of deeming valuable only the cultural capital of the upper class, maximal potential of the concept cannot be reached. Given the social diversity of U.S. society, what constitutes cultural capital should be examined in context and both inside and outside the boundaries of social class.

One major weakness with respect to the use of cultural capital in the exploration of social problems is that so many people misunderstand the concept and use it within a deficit paradigm to point out the failures of working-class parents to properly educate their children. Therefore, it is important for researchers and practitioners to identify both the positive and negative aspects of cultural capital from all types of social groups. This practice can give these aspects value, broaden the understanding of an individual's interactions with social institutions, and give strength to the concept of cultural capital.

The versatility of the concept of cultural capital provides fertile ground for future research across disciplines and is especially useful in the fields of education and sociology. The notion of cultural capital is also connected to discussions of social, intellectual, and human capital. Future research that examines these connections will further develop the concept of cultural capital and its potential value for understanding current social issues.

Gina Pazzaglia and Eric Margolis

See also Class; Cultural Values; Social Capital

Further Readings

Bourdieu, Pierre. 1977. "Cultural Reproduction and Social Reproduction." Pp. 487–511 in *Power and Ideology in Education,* edited by J. Karabel and A. H. Halsey. New York: Oxford University Press.

———. 1984. *Distinction: A Social Critique of the Judgment of Taste.* Trans. Richard Nice. Cambridge, MA: Harvard University Press.

———. 1987. "The Forms of Capital." Pp. 241–58 in *Handbook for Theory and Research for the Sociology of Education,* edited by J. G. Richardson. New York: Greenwood.

Bourdieu, Pierre and Jean-Claude Passeron. [1970] 1990. *Reproduction in Education, Society, and Culture.* Trans. Richard Nice. Newbury Park, CA: Sage.

CULTURAL CRIMINOLOGY

Cultural criminology combines theories of culture, subculture, and crime. This field of crime study draws on a mixture of classical and contemporary theoretical and methodological perspectives. In doing so, cultural criminology provides a holistic approach to the study of crime, not only to gain insight into the social construction of crime but also to analyze the intersections of subculture, popular culture, politics, and institutions where meanings about crime and criminals are shaped and produced.

One area of cultural criminology thus focuses on the construction of criminal subcultures, categories of criminal conduct, and crime control strategies through media portrayals and how each influences the others. Analysts view the media as playing an important role in shaping, but not creating, shared understandings of crime and criminals. An ongoing process of image and information dissemination creates meaning about crime and criminals, continually reinventing and reinforcing stories about illicit subcultures, crime, and criminals, thereby establishing identity within these situated media portrayals.

It is not that crime has become fashionable as a result of the media attention given to certain subcultures and crimes. Rather, the media play a role in shaping what crimes and deviant behaviors become popularized and associated with particular populations. Of interest is the extent to which the popular culture adopts those representations. It is popular culture—shaped but not created by the media—that influences the construction of criminal identities and vice versa. This interplay constructs meaning about crime and deviance. Cultural criminologists thus analyze this interplay to understand how the situated meanings of subcultural groups evolve and also how this process informs debate about deviant and criminal categories and control strategies.

The influential power of the media and popular culture is not limited to their ability to shape and influence styles of crime. Cultural criminologists also view the media as politically oriented, promoting elite perspectives through stereotypes about marginalized groups. Cultural criminologists point to the selection of certain subcultural styles to be criminalized, even though the behavioral characteristics of these groups often do not differ significantly from other subcultural movements and actions. Enterprises acting as moral entrepreneurs mediate social control and thus favor the control of certain groups over others.

The media subsequently produce shared understandings about the intersections of criminals and institutions of control. Crime control strategies are the product of a media-saturated culture influenced by selected portrayals of deviance, crime, and criminals. As a result, cultural criminologists focus on how the media and popular culture shape a culture of crime and how this, in turn, influences the culture of policing and policing strategies.

T. Patrick Stablein

See also Crime; Deviance; Mass Media; Racial Profiling; Rational Choice Theory; Scapegoating; Self-Fulfilling Prophecy; Social Constructionist Theory; Subculture of Violence Hypothesis

Further Readings

Ferrell, Jeff. 1999. "Cultural Criminology." *Annual Review of Sociology* 25:395–418.
Ferrell, Jeff and Clinton R. Sanders, eds. 1995. *Cultural Criminology.* Boston: Northeastern University Press.
Presdee, Mike. 2000. *Cultural Criminology and the Carnival of Crime.* New York: Routledge.

CULTURAL DIFFUSION

In its simplest form, cultural diffusion is the borrowing of cultural elements from one culture by another. Aspects of material culture include clothing styles, musical structures, medicine, and agricultural practices, whereas normative traits such as ideas, behavioral patterns, religion, language, and values are another component of culture. Borrowing occurs either between two different cultures (intercultural) or within the same cultural grouping (intracultural). For example, in the case of intercultural borrowing, a nondemocratic developing country can borrow the political processes and structures of democracy and feminism to change tyrannical rule. Intercultural diffusion is a result of patterns of involuntary and voluntary migration. On the other hand, an example of intracultural borrowing would be baby boomers adopting iPod technology from the MySpace Generation. Ideas and material culture can also spread independently of population movement or direct contact between the inventor and receptor cultures.

Process of Cultural Diffusion

Borrowing from one culture to another is common although the donor culture is not necessarily the original inventor. For example, of the many new academic books and articles published every year, an analysis of these "new" texts and themes will reveal few ideas that can be labeled "original." The history of thought and creativity must thus be taken into consideration while exploring the parameters of cultural diffusion. Does the borrowing culture fuse or merge with the contributing culture wherein both cultures lose their single identity? Why, in fact, do cultures have a need to borrow from other cultures? Is it out of necessity? An underlying assumption is that borrowing makes a culture better, stronger, more evolved as in adapting to constantly changing physical environments, more modern, and hence, more civilized. This assumption leads to the observation that some cultural elements do not diffuse.

Several social issues are important when considering the process of diffusion. Is the borrowed cultural element a basic need, such as technology that harvests food crops for human consumption? Does it enhance the quality of life, as in the case of people who use in vitro fertilization as a family planning option? Just because the scientific community argues the importance and immediate use of stem cell research, does it mean that a culture's normative structure needs rules on sanctions for this technology? What has happened to individuals' civil liberties around the world in a post–9/11 world surveillance culture? Also, when religious institutions televise their services, are these efficient means to reach and shepherd larger congregations? Perhaps an even more fraught argument to technological intervention in social institutions would be the tenuous use of teaching social science classes online or offering them through televised satellite centers. What happens to the affective, effusive, volatile, provocative, soul searching, compassion, and empathy building in both of these cases? The impulse for efficiency is positive, but an arguable consequence is the loss of accountability and a diminished sense of human connectedness. Guiding the adaptation of the imported cultural element are evaluative considerations, the mechanics of

implementation, and the terms of transfer decided upon by the receptor culture.

If the cultural element under consideration is not compatible with the values of the dominant culture, key decision makers, or gatekeepers, its importation is unlikely. This power elite can also force change on groups not in agreement with the imported practice. Obliging elderly people not computer literate to order their medication online and have it delivered to their homes is a good example of borrowed cultural elements forced on receptor cultures. Although this process may eliminate the need to pick up medicine in person, the reality that the elderly are more familiar with typewriters than with computers suggests that there are some overlooked details in implementation. Subcultures thus can retain their identity, while losing their autonomy, with a borrowed element used as a social control mechanism.

Cultural diffusion occurs quickly, given the speed and reach of telecommunications. For example, other countries as well as U.S. cities addressed post–9/11 security strategies through cultural borrowing facilitated by the immediacy of ubiquitous mass-mediated communication. Instant communications also enable inventor cultures to advertise and market their ideas to receptor cultures who feel compelled to borrow so they can keep apace with swiftly changing world trends in a competitive post–9/11 global economy.

The Politics of Cultural Appropriation

Cultural diffusion is not devoid of political ramifications. For example, when a dominant group steals from a minority through diffusion and still controls and oppresses the subordinate group, this is exploitation. Consider the case of white rappers in America borrowing from the black hip-hop culture. With its cultural elements stolen, co-opted, appropriated, and uncredited, the contribution of the subordinate (inventor) culture becomes diminished and diluted to the point of lacking social significance. However, it could also suddenly have social meaning because the dominant group now engages it.

The appropriating culture can take the borrowed element and apply new, different, and insignificant meanings compared with its intended meaning, or the meaning can be stripped altogether. Examples of cultural appropriation through diffusion are naming athletic team mascots, musical subcultures borrowing or stealing from one another, and baggy clothing in urban culture becoming mainstream in suburban America. Once again, this also raises the issue of how original the culture of invention is and who owns certain cultural elements. Some practices are transcontinental, and no one should own or claim them as exclusive and profit from them, although these things do, indeed, happen.

Cultural diffusion is not always political. When cultures borrow from one another, they can develop and refine the element that they are adopting. They can also fall on new discoveries as they customize elements for use within their own culture. Creative development becomes a part of invention and is a result of serendipity rather than of calculated intent and design. For example, labanotation is a system of notation for dance movement, but architects can borrow elements of this system to design spatial models for creative urban architectural design. Whether it is U.S. football borrowing from British rugby by allowing players to touch the ball, Impressionist musical composers borrowing from medieval modal scale structures, Elvis Presley or Eminen borrowing from black musical subcultures, or cotton developed and refined from one culture to another, the idea and politics of borrowing from cultures is not new and will continue.

H. Mark Ellis

See also Cultural Lag; Cultural Relativism; Cultural Values; Culture Shock; Culture Wars; Social Change

Further Readings

Power, Dominic and Allen J. Scott, eds. 2004. *The Cultural Industries and the Production of Culture.* London: Routledge.

Rogers, Everett. 2003. *Diffusion of Innovations.* 5th ed. New York: Free Press.

Cultural Imperialism

Cultural imperialism refers to the practice by which one society forwards or imposes its cultural beliefs, values, normative practices, and symbols on another society. Generally, cultural imperialism involves a power relationship, because only those groups enjoying economic, military, or spatial dominance have the ability to inflict their systems upon another.

The roots of cultural imperialism are commonly traced to the ancient regimes of Greece and Rome. The Greeks, for example, built amphitheaters, gyms, and temples in the lands they conquered, attempting to centralize these distinctly Greek cultural rituals in the lives of those they controlled. Likewise, the Romans worked to "Romanize" every land they annexed. As they invaded new regions, the Romans bombarded the conquered with the glittering standards, towering temples, and marble statues that embodied Roman ideals. Coins bearing pictures of Caesar kept the chain of command fresh in the minds of the conquered, while official rituals and festivals replaced the religious practices of non-Romans.

After 1500, when the exploration of the Americas, Africa, and Asia thrived, Western European nations worked aggressively to expand their economic bases. Cultural imperialism often served as the tool by which these nations secured resource-rich lands. Language was key in this regard. England, for example, imposed the Book of Common Prayer on all peoples it conquered. They did so in an attempt to obliterate native languages such as Cornish, Manx, and Gaelic and establish English as the official tongue of new "acquisitions." The English believed that as the languages of the conquered slipped into obscurity, so too would many elements of the non-English cultures that sustained them. The Spanish took a similar position, going so far as to rename the populations of the regions they colonized. In the Philippines, for example, a Spanish governor replaced the surnames of native peoples with Spanish names taken from a Madrid directory. He viewed the strategy as a means of forcefully imposing Spain's cultural standards on those whom he now administered. In the 20th century, the Japanese implemented a similar strategy in Korea. After years of occupying Korea, the Japanese mandated a policy which replaced traditional Korean names with those of Japan, and mandated Shinto worship in place of Korean religious practices. The Japanese viewed these strategies as a way of absorbing Korea, giving Japan an additional workforce and strength as it pursued the imperialist policies that contributed to World War II.

Of course, cultural imperialism is not always forced. Often, the culture of a dominant power is voluntarily embraced by those exposed to it. Corporations such as Coca-Cola or McDonald's are often accused of homogenizing diverse cultures and inflicting an ethos of consumerism across the globe. Others, such as Estee Lauder and Christian Dior, are accused of imposing Western values of beauty. Yet, these products are often welcomed by populations as symbols of progress and modernization. For many, these products represent complements to the host culture rather than replacements of it.

Karen Cerulo

See also Cultural Diffusion; Cultural Values; Hegemony; Multinational Corporations; Social Change; Values

Further Readings

Ritzer, George. 2007. *The McDonaldization of Society.* 5th ed. Thousand Oaks, CA: Pine Forge.
Said, Edward. 1994. *Culture and Imperialism.* New York: Vintage.

Cultural Lag

Cultural lag occurs when the proliferation of technological and material advancement outpaces the normative dimensions of a civilization's blueprint for social existence. When technology advances more quickly than the social expectations and considerations surrounding new innovations, cultural lag is present.

Although technological development and knowledge for knowledge's sake are indicators of heightened human evolution, without shared rules and understandings to govern such creations, these developments can nullify any potential social improvement. Without social consensus of new folkways, mores, and laws to understand, contextualize, and utilize new technology, knowledge without immediate application or without foresight of consequences prior to its development and introduction into a society can be deleterious to a culture's well-being. For example, computerizing tollbooth collections can result in more efficient highway vehicular movement and aid in the reduction of environmental pollution, but changing the behaviors of drivers to convert and conform to this change cannot be done with technology. In fact,

driving accidents and billing mishaps may initially increase at the onset of implementing this technological innovation.

Technological change and advancement encompass all areas of social life, including warfare, engineering, transportation, communication, and medicine. Social beliefs and the need for immediate change often dictate the rate of introducing these changes into a society. When considering the merit of these changes, one must take into account the consequences of displacement of the old with the new. Does the innovation offer more utilitarian value, and are moral and ethical conditions improved? Are innovators producing change without regard to consequences? For example, is the rate of semiskilled labor displacement considered when computerizing tollbooth collections or retooling workers to keep pace with technological change? What happens to the profit margin when calculating a cost–benefit analysis, and what happens to unemployment rates in society? At what rate can new technology be introduced into a society without having adverse effects? Also, if human embryonic stem cells provide better material for fighting degenerative diseases than do adult stem cells, does the potential of curing and understanding chronic disease outweigh the extinguishing of the embryo during the stem cell harvest? Who gets to define and put a value on life? Who gets to prioritize various stages of the life course? Is society better and more efficient as a result of these changes and possessing this type of technical know-how?

Proponents of technological development view technology as advancement and key to improving social conditions, for example by reducing poverty and economic dependence. They see technology as making social processes more efficient, where individuals would have access to better living conditions and more leisure time, thus providing expanded opportunities for all under the banner of democratic idealism. Individual citizens would also benefit by having more freedom and not having to rely on traditional social arrangements and interactions within socially established institutions.

For example, the introduction of in vitro fertilization (IVF) as an alternative in the procreative process and in family planning led to contested legal issues and trials. IVF forced society to reconsider the definitions of family, fetal ownership, motherhood, and parenthood. Another new definitional reconsideration was using the body for economic gain (prostituting oneself), as some thought that renting out a womb and being a gestation mother (also called "surrogate mother") for the money or the joy of allowing a childless person or couple to experience parenthood were honorific uses of the body. Yet traditional sex workers who used their bodies (sex/reproductive organs) for financial gain in the name of sex for recreation remained stigmatized as morally debased. At the same time, many people consider gays and lesbians who use this reproductive technology as contributing to the decay of the traditional family, morally scrutinizing them differently than they would a single and financially successful female who might choose single parenthood. However, to be a gestation/birth/surrogate mother, an egg donor, a sperm donor, and so on was not considered sexualized or corrupt. Instead, the initial issues raised by this technology were embedded in the threat to the traditional family structure, fetal ownership, and adoption law.

Just because a society possesses this knowledge and skill, does it make life better? Single people do not have to wait for marriage, do not need a partner to rear a child, and infertile couples can have more alternatives to traditional adoption. While these technologies give adults more personal choice in family planning, what are the long-term effects on children who enter family structures under these technologies? Is the fact that we possess this knowledge a precursor to other forms of genetic engineering and manipulation where we will see other eugenics movements? Will such medical innovations fall into nefarious hands? The fact that we can know the sex of a fetus in utero also should not lead to selective abortion because some believe that it is harder to rear girls or that girls are of a lower social status than boys. Is this dangerous knowledge, or is it information for individuals to make informed personal choices? Should a couple have the option of whether or not to bring a special-needs child into this world, or should they simply play the hand that they are dealt?

Advancements in medical technologies continue to raise unaddressed social expectations and sanctions. What social issues must be taken into account when considering the priority of organ, facial, and limb transplantation or vaccine testing on human subjects? As social adaptations to new technologies occur, adjustments also occur in the context of public debate where regulatory agencies oversee public safety while not interfering with economic profitability. For technological advancement to benefit society, it must evolve alongside a social system that sees its full potential.

When we consider the benefit of offering online degrees promoting extra hours in the day by minimizing transportation to traditional classrooms, we must also consider the impact that distance learning has on academic integrity, intellectual ownership, and the potential decline of conflict resolution skills in face-to-face encounters when experiencing highly effusive, affective, and emotive subject material and real-life situations. Creating more hours in the day creates more opportunity for self-definition around the acquisition of things. When we do not achieve these new and heightened standards of success, we have more ammunition to contribute to a poor self-image.

Making printed books available on audio should not increase illiteracy or aliteracy. Televised religious services should not promote social disconnection and isolation, nor should the availability of fast food be blamed for weakening familial relationships. The military strategy during time of war to eradicate oppressive political regimes while minimizing collateral damage is not an exact science. Civilian casualties are bound to happen. Is technological advancement in warfare a just endeavor to bring about political change? Are condoms now a form of birth control and death control (with respect to AIDS)? How do we currently understand and utilize this technology? Is the warehousing of knowledge without immediate application and full public understanding and awareness of this knowledge contributive to anomie (the social condition in which behavioral expectations are not present or are unclear or confusing, and people do not know how to behave or what to expect from one another)? Technological advancement, its rate of infusion into a society, and how willingly, quickly, and thoughtfully a society addresses the social consequences and implications of these innovations will dictate the level of cultural lag that a society experiences.

H. Mark Ellis

See also Anomie; Cultural Diffusion; Cultural Values; Genetic Engineering; Social Change; Social Control; Social Disorganization

Further Readings

Friedman, Thomas L. 2005. *The World Is Flat: A Brief History of the Twenty-first Century.* New York: Farrar, Straus and Giroux.

Gilbert, Scott F., Anna L. Tyler, and Emily J. Zakin, eds. 2005. *Bioethics and the New Embryology: Springboards for Debate*. Sunderland, MA: Sinauer.

Jukes, Ian. 2001. *Windows on the Future: Educating in the Age of Technology*. Thousand Oaks, CA: Corwin.

Roberts, Dorothy. 1998. *Killing the Black Body: Race, Reproduction and the Meaning of Liberty*. New York: Vintage.

Taverner, William I., ed. 2006. "Should Health Insurers Be Required to Pay for Infertility Treatments?" In *Taking Sides: Clashing Views on Controversial Issues in Human Sexuality*. 9th ed. New York: McGraw-Hill/Dushkin.

CULTURAL RELATIVISM

Cultural relativism is a methodological concept rooted in social theory. The term indicates that a society's beliefs, values, normative practices, and products must be evaluated and understood according to the cultural context from which they emerge. No society should be evaluated with reference to some set of universal criteria, and no foreign culture should be judged by the standards of a home or dominant culture. Based on these ideas, cultural relativists would never deem a particular thought or behavior to be "right" or "wrong." Rather, they would argue that rightness or wrongness is *relative to* a specified group or society.

Roots of the Concept

Cultural relativism can be traced to the writings of philosopher Immanuel Kant and, later, works by Johann Gottfried Herder and Wilhelm von Humboldt. These scholars defined the mind as a critical mediator of sensate experience. They argued that when the mind apprehends stimuli from the environment, it molds perceptions with reference to (a) the specifics of one's spatial surroundings, (b) the cultural practices and artifacts that define those surroundings, and (c) the temporal or biographical lineage that places one in those surroundings. From this perspective, reality cannot be defined as a universal or objective phenomenon. Culture and biography add a subjective dimension to reality.

In the mid-1900s, anthropologist Franz Boas took the aforementioned ideas and used them to establish a formal research methodology. Under his methodology he urged a rejection of universal evaluative criteria.

He advised researchers to adopt an objective, value-free stance, to free themselves from the conscious and unconscious bonds to their own enculturation. Boas also demanded that no culture be considered superior or inferior. Rather, all cultures must be viewed as equal. For Boas, the purpose of research was not moral evaluation but the discovery and understanding of cultural differences.

Boas's ideas stood in direct contrast to popular comparative methods of the day—methods more concerned with the evolutionary foundations of cultural similarities. But cultural relativism was steeped in political issues as well. Its tenets directly addressed what many believed was a Western European tendency toward "ethnocentrism." Ethnocentrism, as defined by sociologist William Graham Sumner, refers to the perception of one's group as the center of civilization and, thus, a gauge by which all other groups should be judged. In the 1900s, a period in which international contact was becoming increasingly routine, distinguishing between observation and evaluation proved a critical task.

Examples From the Field

One can invoke many concrete examples to illustrate the usefulness of cultural relativism in field research. Consider a common gesture—sticking out one's tongue. Americans commonly interpret this gesture as a sign of defiance, mockery, or provocation. Yet, if American researchers applied this meaning while engaged in global studies, they would likely miss important information about their object of inquiry. Anthropologists tell us, for example, that in Tibet, sticking out one's tongue is a sign of polite deference. In India, it conveys monumental rage. In New Caledonia, sticking out one's tongue signifies a wish of wisdom and vigor. And in the Caroline Islands, it is a method of banishing devils and demons. To garner the variant meanings of this single behavior, researchers must immerse themselves in the culture they are studying. They must draw meaning from the target culture's inhabitants as opposed to making assumptions drawn from their own cultural dictionaries.

Cultural relativists claim that language is at the center of their studies, in that a society's structure emerges from the structure of its language. British explorer Mary Kingsley forcefully illustrated this idea in her writings on Samoan culture. As an unmarried woman, Kingsley discovered that spinsterhood was a foreign concept to Samoans. A woman alone was viewed as a taboo presence. Once discovering this belief, Kingsley proved able to circumvent the problem. When she needed to travel, she would tell the Samoans that she was looking for her husband and point in the direction she wished to travel. By presenting herself as a married woman wishing to reunite with her spouse, she conformed to the social structure established by the Samoan language. With Samoans now happy to facilitate her reunion, Kingsley regained her ability to move throughout the country.

Demographer David Helin notes that failing to consider the relative nature of culture can prove costly. Many American businesses have learned this lesson the hard way. For example, ethnocentrism blinded General Motors to the reasons behind the poor international sales of its Chevrolet Nova. Within Spanish-speaking nations, the automobile's name *Nova* translated to the phrase "No Go." A similar disaster befell American chicken mogul Frank Purdue. While his slogan "It Takes a Tough Man to Make a Tender Chicken" enjoyed success in the United States, when translated to Spanish, Purdue's slogan became "A Sexually Excited Man Will Make a Chicken Affectionate." With these examples, we learn the importance of avoiding simple translation of one's ideas to cultures with different meaning systems.

The Moral Debate

The objectivity to which cultural relativists aspire is admirable for some. Yet, many feel that the method introduces problems of its own. For example, Robert Edgerton asks, If practices such as cannibalism, infanticide, genital mutilation, genocide, and suicide bombings are normative to a particular cultural context, does that make them right? The cultural relativist position, taken to its extreme, would frame events such as the Holocaust, the 9/11 attacks, torture at Abu Ghraib, and ethnic cleansing in Darfur as normative to the cultures from which they emerge and, thus, morally justifiable. Edgerton supports the notion of objective evaluation. But he also argues that once such data are gathered, researchers must carefully review their findings. If a culture's values, beliefs, and behaviors are different yet beneficial and adaptive, then they must be respected. But according to Edgerton's point of view, if values, beliefs, and behaviors endanger people's health, happiness, or survival,

ranking cultures in terms of their moral health becomes necessary.

Karen Cerulo

See also Cultural Values; Ethnocentrism; Relative Deprivation

Further Readings

Benedict, Ruth. 1934. *Patterns of Culture*. Boston: Houghton Mifflin.

Boas, Franz. [1940] 1982. *Race, Language and Culture*. Chicago: University of Chicago Press.

Edgarton, Robert. 1992. *Sick Societies: Challenging the Myth of Primitive Harmony*. New York: Free Press.

Helin, David W. 1992. "When Slogans Go Wrong." *American Demographics* 14(2):14.

CULTURAL VALUES

The notion of "cultural values" brings together two powerful social science concepts to produce a concept that is seductive yet slippery and contentious. It is seductive in that it purports to explain or interpret human behavior, especially differences in behavior between groups, through an emphasis on how human lives are also differently valued moral lives. It accomplishes this through deploying the concept of value as that which makes people conceive of what is right, beautiful, and good and, hence, what is desirable. Thus, groups with behavioral differences are viewed as different because of differing values or cultural values. The concept of value becomes further sharpened by distinguishing the desirable from the desired; the former is based on a strong notion of moral justification, whereas the latter restrictively refers to nothing more than a preference. Such an emphasis on value as valuable for the understanding of social action assures a critical space for cultural approaches to human behavior as distinct from conventional sociological, political, and economic approaches, which emphasize social institutions, social relations, power, and market or nonmarket commodity transactions.

Nevertheless, the carefully crafted notion of value, when qualified as cultural value, quickly becomes slippery and contentious when used uncritically. Whereas intense debate over the precise scope, meaning, and valence of the concept "culture," especially within the discipline of anthropology and the sociology of culture, makes its users mindful of overstating its explanatory value, the same cannot be said for the concept "cultural value." While debate over cultural values usefully seeks to distinguish between moral evaluation and factual cognition, or between the desirable and the desired, seldom does one encounter questions as to whether and how values relate to structures of power. For example, can one indeed separate a cultural value from, say, a political value? Those knowledgeable in social and anthropological thought have pointed out that to value is to introduce hierarchy. Hence, values are very much political, concerned with the organization of power and inequality by definition. In what sense, then, can a value be cultural? In other words, the problem with the concept "cultural values" is not that people do not operate with values that influence their actions, but rather that it is difficult to demonstrate what exactly is a cultural value, and hence it is intellectually misleading to assume that this is self-evident. That such fundamental distinctions are not clear in the use of the term is not due to an oversight in the development of the concept but is more a result of overstating the case for cultural values by treating the concept "cultural" uncritically. Consequently, it fatally leaves open fundamental questions about its own explanatory or interpretive validity.

Even a cursory appreciation of the debates around culture (taking this to be somewhat more problematic than the use of the term *value* by itself) ought to, at least minimally, caution us against using the term *cultural values* easily. This entry first delineates the development of the concept "culture," then highlights examples of how cultural values frame popular discourses on social problems, and finally poses the problem of human rights as an example of how cultural values may not be the best way to look at social problems. Throughout this entry, the term *cultural values* is viewed as problematic.

Culture has surely earned its place among the most difficult terms in history. Etymologically related to the sense of *cultivate* as in *agri-culture*, this early sense of culture denoted an activity, a production (one needs to work on cultivation), and simultaneously a product or set of products—the cultivated or cultured artifacts. However, this dual sense was gradually repressed over the following 2 centuries as 18th- and 19th-century European theorists of the cultural "Other"

emphasized only the sense of culture as product. Culture came to be viewed as a kind of property that humans possessed (or not) and in varying degrees. It is crucial to note that these latter theorizations were intimately associated with the experience of Europeans with colonialism in the Americas, Asia, and Africa, and the emergence of new forms of class divisions and patriarchy within European societies.

This classic notion of culture, most clearly represented by the 19th-century English literary critic Mathew Arnold, held that culture referred to the best achievements and thoughts of humans, in short the set of perfect values or perfection itself that emerged from a people. This, of course, left the issue of who decides what is perfection or what is the best of values relatively unexamined, leading to a notion of "high culture" and its obverse, "low culture," that proved useful for the civilizing mission of colonialism as well as for the ruling elites in any society. Culture, in the Arnoldian sense, was then viewed as "property of the few," as some people were deemed to have more of it than others, and a large number of wretched were thought not to have any of it at all. Notions of "savage" and "barbarian" as the opposite of "civilized" were strengthened in this view of culture. More generally, culture came to mean the finer products of any group, specifically referring to the products in the realm of ruling-class understandings of art, music, literature, dance, poetry, sculpture, and so on.

It was in this classic context that some anthropologists explicitly developed another notion of culture as distinct from the elitist notions of culture. At least three breaks (or waves) can be identified over the next century or so. The first break in the mid-19th century was symbolized by the Tylorian view of *culture* as an all-inclusive term for all human beliefs and behavior that are learned rather than inherited biologically. Culture in this sense was an entire way of life—beliefs, practices, ideals, norms, and values that spanned the economic, political, kinship, religious, and aesthetics. One still possessed culture, and hence culture was still viewed as property, except that culture was now considered as a property of all. All have culture, albeit of different kinds. Such a notion of culture as an entire way of life contained an evolutionary sense, as now there were "primitive" cultures and advanced ones—qualitative evaluation rather than a quantitative measure. This sense of culture was further developed in a nonevolutionary direction by the Boasian anthropological enterprise, which seriously built up "scientific" ways to study different cultures. Notably, the Boasian sense of cultures, in the plural, assumed cultural difference along the same racial lines it was designed to refute, leading to a problem of the culturalization of race, wherein culture comes to play the same classificatory function as the now scientifically dubious notion of race played. Thus, what distinguishes one race or ethnicity or nationality from another is its purported culture, and also, what distinguishes one culture from another is its different race, ethnicity, or nationality. This problematic with the Boasian notion of culture continues despite the fact that it strenuously distinguished biological ideas of race from culture.

A second break from the classical view of culture distinguished the *cultural* from other aspects of life. Culture acquired its own experiential and analytical sharpness, and this move was akin to the earlier Durkheimian carving out of a special space for "the social." This break was best exemplified by Clifford Geertz, who used culture to refer to those human activities specifically engaged with meaning construction via symbols. According to Geertz, humans are suspended in a web of meaning that we have spun ourselves, and this web is culture. The Geertzian turn made it possible for culture (in the singular) to be viewed widely not as a property that one has or not, but as an aspect of living, an ordinary condition of being for all humans. We thus have two different notions—cultures and culture. The former refers to groups that are culturally different, whereas the latter refers to an aspect of how all humans live.

Although the Geertzian understanding of culture succeeds brilliantly in demarcating a distinct realm of culture as concerned with meaning, it failed to answer some questions. Whose web was it? Who makes the web? Do all people who are suspended in it contribute equally to its production? Most important, Geertz's view was critiqued for not taking into account the—fact that culture was not only a product—the web—or a production—the weaving of the web but actually a struggle or a contest over production. In other words, the Geertzian emphasis on culture as shared unfortunately masked the fact of power, as culture is not simply shared by all within its boundaries but is actually a dynamic site of contestation over meanings including the question of cultural group boundaries. Consequently, over the past 2 decades, we have seen a third break from the classical view of culture that has now made the notion of different cultures itself problematic.

In this third break, a culture is no longer assumed to be a group that shares a cultural way of life. Instead, culture (the activity) and culture (the group) are viewed as constituted by power (struggles over meaning making), thus making margins and borders between cultures blurred or contested, highlighting interstitial spaces, making the hybrid into the normal condition of being, and turning the focus of anthropologists to the process of Othering rather than simply the study of the already existing Other. It is now a "normal" anthropology (in the Kuhnian sense) that speaks of the production of the Self and the Other and hence views culture itself as a production of, among other things, difference. Difference is thus historicized and shown as both constitutive of and constituted by group formation and identities in such a discourse of culture. An example of such a use of the term *culture* is that of the Mexican anthropologist Nestor Garcia Canclini, who views culture as the social production of meaning through symbolic (semiotic) representation of material structures to understand, reform, and transform the social system. Culture is thus a dynamic concept that reminds us that claims of tradition are always constructed through sites of power and struggle over meanings.

Returning to the concept of "cultural values," we see that this concept is used popularly as an explanatory device for a wide range of social problems, such as poverty, modernization, ethnic and religious conflict, gender and racial inequality, and, most recently, democratization. Despite being roundly critiqued for their scholarly content, many theses based on cultural values abound in the popular imagination. Examples of such theses include the Huntington thesis, or the clash of civilizations thesis, which invokes cultural values in the guise of civilizational units to explain all kinds of conflict on a world scale; the culture of poverty thesis, which holds the value-based actions and decision-making behavior of the poor as explanations for their poverty; the modernization thesis, which identifies "backward," or the more euphemistically termed *traditional*, values of people in developing countries as the shackles that prevent them from enjoying the fruits of modernization and modernity; and the endless discussions on gender and racial differences that, while taking care not to seemingly biologize gender or naturalize race, actually come very close to doing so by speaking in particular ways of the essentially different values embraced by men and women, or by members of so-called different and hence separate races. The most dubious and pernicious misuse of the concept is in the debates over family values, where no awareness seemingly exists about the constructed nature of any such claims. It all seems to naturally flow from an unspecified human nature that is insidiously raced, classed, and gendered.

None of these uses of the term *cultural values* take account of the intellectual backdrop of the term *culture* discussed earlier in this entry. The term *cultural* in the notion "cultural value" operates in two senses—as an aspect of life (connected with production of meanings) and as a reference to the basis of group difference. In this discourse of cultural values, each group is assumed to share a cultural way of being or values, and groups are differentiated from each other purportedly on the basis of these given values. Both of these are problematic assumptions. In other words, cultural values, by definition, are never universal. They are always particular because they are associated with groups of people who supposedly operate as a group because they share cultural values.

Such a formulation of the self-evident existence of cultural groups (based on different cultural values) has led to intense debates over the claim to cultural rights, especially in the context of more universalizing human rights. This debate is crucial in an era of globalization where borders seem to be crossed with impunity by flows of finance, goods, services, and images, even as they are newly (re)erected as barriers to the flow of people viewed as cultural Others and the diversity of interpretations of what it means to be democratic. In such a context, social problems such as child labor or female genital mutilation get to be viewed too easily as differences of cultural values of cultural groups. The dual pitfalls of ethnocentrism or plain bigotry, and its obverse of cultural relativism, both share the assumption that these problems are indeed manifestations of cultural values as opposed to sociopolitical and economic problems. While the former position condemns such practices based on a racist and bigoted prejudging of all cultures different from one's own, the latter position majestically refuses to condemn even those practices that oppressed members within any cultural group struggle against. The result is that particular groups are assumed to be the cultural Others of a panoptic Self that only observes and is never observed. Both ethnocentrism and cultural relativism share dubious assumptions about culture and social problems. Both of them are incapable of implicating the Self in the degradation of the Other. While one is triumphalist in proclaiming its own superiority, the other is many times a weak call for viewing all practices with equanimity and ultimately runs into both ethical and logical problems.

Alternative approaches call for understanding such social problems as the effects of historically constructed and contingent struggles over meanings and material control of economic, political, and legal conditions of existence of culturally hybrid groups. The problem then becomes one of viewing cultural values as serious and discursive claims rather than actually existing facts of social life. Consequently, the task becomes one of evaluating claims to cultural rights in the context of how group norms are shaped in complex ways by power differentials within and between groups, and how dispositions to act are cultivated among individuals experiencing power and values in ways that are difficult to separate in the din of everyday life.

Balmurli Natrajan

See also Cultural Relativism; Culture of Poverty; Culture Wars; Ethnocentrism; Postmodernism; Power; Values

Further Readings

Abu-Lughod, Lila. 1991. "Writing against Culture." Pp. 137–62 in *Recapturing Anthropology: Working in the Present*, edited by R. G. Fox. Santa Fe, NM: School of American Research Press.

Boggs, James. 2004. "The Culture Concept as Theory, in Context." *Current Anthropology* 45(2):187–209.

Cowan, Jane K., Marie-Benedicte Dembour, and Richard A. Wilson, eds. 2001. *Culture and Rights: Anthropological Perspectives*. Cambridge, England: Cambridge University Press.

Geertz, Clifford. 1973. "Thick Description: Toward an Interpretive Theory of Culture." Pp. 3–30 in *The Interpretation of Cultures: Selected Essays*. New York: Basic Books.

Markus, Gyorgy. 1993. "Culture: The Making and the Make-up of a Concept (An Essay in Historical Semantics)." *Dialectical Anthropology* 18:3–29.

Roseberry, William. 1994. "Balinese Cockfights and the Seduction of Anthropology." Pp. 17–29 in *Anthropologies and Histories*. New Brunswick, NJ: Rutgers University Press.

Sewell, William. 1999. "The Concept(s) of Culture." Pp. 35–61 in *Beyond the Cultural Turn: New Directions in the Study of Society and Culture,* edited by V. E. Bonnell and Lynn Hunt. Berkeley, CA: University of California Press.

Sökefeld, Martin. 1999. "Debating Self, Identity, and Culture in Anthropology." *Current Anthropology* 40:417–47.

Visweswaran, Kamala. 1998. "Race and the Culture of Anthropology." *American Anthropologist* 100:70–83.

Wilson, R. 1997. "Human Rights, Culture and Context: An Introduction." Pp. 1–27 in *Human Rights, Culture and Context: Anthropological Perspectives,* edited by R. Wilson. London: Pluto.

CULTURE OF DEPENDENCY

A culture of dependency is defined as a type of culture that relies upon, and comes to expect, state benefits and other support to maintain it. Overall the usage is best related to the neoconservative supply-side view of welfare in the 1990s. The argument of a culture of dependency assumes the position that entitlements lead to poverty by reducing the work ethic and regenerating dependency on state benefits. Following the lead of Margaret Thatcher and Ronald Reagan in the 1980s, political attacks on a culture of dependency in Europe's social democratic states began with Tony Blair in Great Britain and Gerhard Schröder in Germany in the 1990s.

In the United States, policies reducing welfare payouts by the Ronald Reagan administration and, later, Bill Clinton's welfare reform bill of 1996, titled Temporary Aid for Needy Families (TANF), were predicated on the concept of changing a culture of dependency. Along with TANF, the Personal Responsibility and Work Opportunity Reconciliation Act was passed to reduce welfare dependency and encourage work. The policies required individuals to become "job ready" and work to be eligible for welfare benefits. Between 1996 and 2002 there were 4.7 million fewer welfare-dependent Americans as defined by having 50 percent or more of a family's income coming from TANF, food stamps, or Supplemental Social Insurance. The U.S. welfare reform laws also limit cash awards to 5 years.

The attack on welfare and a culture of dependency occurred as Western countries moved toward neoliberalism, fiscal conservatism, and free-market strategies. Along with attempts at reducing the size of government in Western nations came an emphasis on decentralization and deregulation. The 1994 conservative U.S. Congress played a key role in the philosophy of welfare reform and the attack on the idea of a culture of dependency. The policies of workfare were a result of this critique of dependency culture.

Welfare Reform and the Third Way

The culture of dependency argument holds that chronic low income among entitlement recipients results from welfare benefits and not personal inadequacies. The generosity of the welfare state reduces self-reliance and responsibility. The main ideas of this perspective originated with the concept of a culture of poverty argument in the 1960s, along with debates on the existence of an underclass in the 1980s. Both held that poverty in third world countries and poor communities in developed countries rested on a set of behaviors learned inside those poor communities. The culture of dependency argument draws on historical attacks on welfare, with a central focus on the undeserving poor and abuse of entitlements. According to advocates of the culture of dependency argument, welfare reduces the will of individuals to work. Other aspects of the argument are that welfare causes a decline in family values linked to child illegitimacy and a rise in the number of single-parent families. The assumption is that, when faced with opportunity, individuals with entitlements will not work if it requires too much effort to secure a small rise in income.

Social theorists identify a culture of dependency with other social problems, including family breakdown, addiction, and educational failure. Those critical of socialist welfare states and entitlements make the argument that the welfare state leads to passive actors and inhibits enterprise among dependents. The welfare reforms of the 1990s thus evolved with ideas of creating a new contract making recipients accountable, while using market solutions to end poverty. Supporters of the doctrine of the Third Way argue for a smaller role for the state, while emphasizing accountability and personal responsibility. They argue for a stakeholder approach to entitlements where the state does not guarantee long-term support. In Australia and New Zealand, social reforms also led to critical responses to the welfare state and the culture of dependency.

Critics of the Culture of Dependency Argument

Critics of this stance argue that welfare has not created dependency as much as it has produced an isolated population with few options. They point to welfare as a form of social control for capitalism and the idea of dependency as a myth used to dismantle the system under neoliberalism. Liberals and leftists argue that many single parents are trapped not by dependency on benefits but by the absence of affordable child care and a lack of decent jobs.

The idea of a culture of dependency has also been applied in international development perspectives on social problems faced by developing nations. Perspectives on poverty reduction strategies use the idea to describe the culture of dependency of poor people, including indigenous populations faced with colonialism, uneven development, and exploitation due to global capitalism. Development theorists point to dependency on limited benefits as a by-product of land concentration, debt, and other social problems. World system and dependency perspectives criticize neoliberalism as a main cause of a culture of dependency in developing nations. Unlike the Third Way, they draw on dependency theory emphasizing the role of power and conflict in creating a culture of dependency. These approaches concentrate on development initiatives which include capacity building and institutional accountability.

Chris Baker

See also Poverty; Welfare; Welfare States

Further Readings

Dean, Hartley and Peter Taylor-Gooby. 1992. *Dependency Culture: The Explosion of a Myth.* London: Harvester Wheatsheaf, Hemel Hempstead.

Giddens, Anthony. 2000. *The Third Way and Its Critics.* Oxford, England: Polity Press.

Midgley, James. 1997. *Social Welfare in Global Context.* Thousand Oaks, CA: Sage.

Robertson, James. 1998. *Beyond Dependency Culture.* Westport, CT: Greenwood.

CULTURE OF POVERTY

The culture of poverty, originally termed the *subculture of poverty*, is a concept that first appeared in 1959 in the work of North American anthropologist Oscar Lewis. As the name implies, this theory focuses attention on the cultural aspects of poverty. The theory holds that adaptation to the economic and structural conditions of poverty promotes the development of deviant social and psychological traits which, in turn, act as barriers to overcoming poverty. Once a culture of poverty emerges, it is reproduced through the transmission of traits to future generations. This perspective leads to the conclusion that economic solutions are limited in their ability to end poverty. Lewis suggested that social work and psychological interventions accompany economic responses to poverty. Culture of poverty theory has had a powerful influence on U.S. poverty policies and programs. A great deal of criticism surfaced as this theory gained prominence as an explanation for poverty in the United States.

Conditions That Promote a Culture of Poverty

Culture of poverty theory is a class-based theory. That is, the structure of the economy is posited as the initial condition that gives rise to a culture of poverty. It is most likely to emerge during transitional periods such as the shift from an agrarian to an industrial society or when rapid economic and technological shifts occur within a given society. Although racial discrimination can be a factor, it is not a necessary condition for a culture of poverty to emerge. (Lewis claimed that cultures of poverty formed among ethnically homogeneous populations in Latin America and among poor rural whites and poor African Americans in the United States.) Low-wage, unskilled workers who experience high rates of unemployment or underemployment in capitalist societies that stress social mobility are thought to be at greatest risk for developing a culture of poverty.

Culture of Poverty Traits

By the time he had fully formulated his theory, Lewis had compiled a list of 70 characteristics thought to be common to groups who live in cultures of poverty. He characterized members of these cultures as people who do not form their own local organizations and are isolated from participation in mainstream social institutions. For instance, the theory posits that people who live in cultures of poverty have high rates of unemployment, do not use banks or hospitals, and rely on dubious businesses like pawn shops. Such social isolation initially results from structural conditions of poverty (e.g., unemployment). However, when opportunities do arise, cultural values that develop in response to isolation work against future integration into mainstream society.

Family illustrates another way that the values of the poor are said to deviate from mainstream society. The theory holds that cultures of poverty are characterized by community and family disorganization. Male unemployment is thought to discourage formal marriage and encourage female-headed households. In addition to recognizing economic disincentives to marry, women may view poor men as too punitive and immature for marriage. The theory also contends that no prolonged period of childhood occurs, and consequently, children experience early initiation into adult activities such as sexual relations. High rates of adult illiteracy and low levels of education contribute to the inferior academic performance of children raised in a culture of poverty. Impulsivity, a present-time orientation, and an inability to set goals further impede educational attainment.

Not all impoverished groups form a culture of poverty. A connection to local organizations or national movements hinders such development by providing the poor with a greater purpose. For example, Lewis claimed that a culture of poverty is less likely to form in socialist countries like Cuba, where neighborhood committees helped to integrate the poor into the national agenda.

Criticism of Culture of Poverty Theory

Criticism surfaced as a culture of poverty framework gained dominance among U.S. academics and policymakers. Critics focused their attention on methodological concerns and on poverty policies and programs influenced, in their development, by culture of poverty theory.

Critics suggest that the popularity of culture as an explanation for poverty is inappropriate, because Lewis based his theory on findings from a small number of interviews with Latin American families. Moreover, critics suggest that scholars who employ this theory filter their observations through a white, middle-class understanding of "appropriate" cultural values, a form of classism and ethnocentrism. In fact, findings from subsequent research studies that employed in-depth fieldwork called into question the claims put forth by Lewis and his contemporary

adherents. Family and community disorganization is an example of one theme targeted by critics. Critics claim empirical evidence shows that poor groups who have been depicted as disorganized actually live in highly organized neighborhoods and rely on extended kin and friendship networks. Moreover, research finds that poor women value marriage as much as their middle-class counterparts do. Although critics agree that in recent years, inner-city family and neighborhood networks have eroded, they trace this pattern to structural causes such as the loss of living-wage jobs and cuts to the social safety net.

Critics are concerned that the focus on behavior gave rise to ineffective poverty policies and programs. For instance, recent growth in job programs that center on developing a work ethic and teaching the poor how to dress and behave in a work environment exemplifies the type of behavioral approaches that critics view as ineffective. These approaches contrast sharply with the decline in structural solutions like the creation of living-wage jobs and the expansion of the social safety net (e.g., unemployment benefits, subsidized health care).

The extent to which behavioral solutions are reflected in poverty policies and programs shifts over time. The influence of culture of poverty theory on U.S. poverty policy is rooted in 1960s War on Poverty programs. Culture of poverty theory shaped Senator Daniel Patrick Moynihan's 1965 report, *The Negro Family: The Case for National Action* (more commonly known as the Moynihan Report), and Michael Harrington's 1962 book, *The Other America: Poverty in the U.S.* Both of these scholars influenced President Lyndon B. Johnson's War on Poverty campaign and the consequent passage of the 1964 Economic Opportunity Act, which established federal funding for, and oversight of, anti-poverty programs.

Critics contend that the Moynihan Report racialized culture of poverty theory. After the publication of the report, poverty became equated with race, and an image of the black matriarch as the cause of black poverty became firmly rooted in the popular imagination. Despite the uncritical acceptance of characterizations of the poor, critics point out that the 1960s anti-poverty programs still addressed the structural causes of poverty. For instance, both Head Start and the Job Corps were War on Poverty programs. Irrespective of his portrayal of black family "pathology," Senator Moynihan argued for the extension of welfare benefits to black single mothers. Addressing the economic causes of poverty was viewed as necessary to achieve the desired behavioral changes.

Behavioral solutions to poverty gained prominence in the conservative climate of the 1980s. The anti-poverty programs of the 1960s came under attack as conservative politicians advanced the view that these programs encouraged economic dependence. Critics argue that it is no accident that the focus on behavior as the cause, not the consequence, of poverty coincides with the call to end the era of "big government" by cutting spending on poverty programs. Welfare reform, enacted with the 1996 passage of Personal Responsibility and Work Opportunity Reconciliation Act, illustrates this trend. Research shows that congressional debates on welfare reform excluded discussions of economic trends. Racialized images of poor single mothers who eschew work and marriage dominated both political and public discussions. Critics charge that the focus on behavior resulted in the passage of a law that failed to make sufficient provisions for the impact of low-wage jobs on women who now face restricted access to welfare benefits.

Scholars and policymakers continue to debate the relationship between poverty and culture. Social scientists face the difficult task of studying culture without losing sight of the complex relationship between culture and structure. In addition, they face the task of attending to the impact of poverty without reinforcing harmful socially constructed views of the poor.

Patricia K. Jennings

See also Cultural Capital; Life Chances; Personal Responsibility and Work Opportunity Reconciliation Act; Poverty; Relative Deprivation; Social Capital; Working Poor

Further Readings

Battle, Juan J. and Michael D. Bennett. 1997. "African-American Families and Public Policy." Pp. 150–67 in *African Americans and the Public Agenda,* edited by C. Herring. Thousand Oaks, CA: Sage.

Goode, Judith. 2002. "How Urban Ethnography Counters Myths about the Poor." Pp. 279–95 in *Urban Life: Readings in the Anthropology of the City,* edited by G. Gmelch and W. P. Zenner. Prospect Heights, IL: Waveland.

Kaplan, Elaine Bell. 1997. *Not Our Kind of Girl: Unraveling the Myths of Black Teenage Motherhood.* Berkeley, CA: University of California Press.

Lewis, Oscar. 1959. *Five Families: Mexican Case Studies in the Culture of Poverty.* New York: Basic Books.

———. [1966] 2002. "The Culture of Poverty." Pp. 269–78 in *Urban Life: Readings in the Anthropology of the City,* edited by G. Gmelch and W. P. Zenner. Prospect Heights, IL: Waveland.

CULTURE SHOCK

The term *culture shock* was first introduced in the 1950s by anthropologist Kalvero Oberg, who defined it as an illness or disease. Later studies focused on cognitive, behavioral, phenomenological, and psychosociological explanations. In general, culture shock is a consequence of immersion in a culture that is distinctly different from one's own background or previous experiences. Typically, these encounters involve new patterns of cultural behaviors, symbols, and expressions that hold little or no meaning without an understanding of the new social setting. The most common usage of the term today is in discussing the effects of students' studying abroad or immigration. Although in the short term culture shock may have adverse effects, in the long run it can enhance one's appreciation of other cultures, foster self-development, and help a person gain greater understanding of diversity.

Several important factors intensify the effects of culture shock. Greater ignorance of foreign contexts and stronger integration in one's own native culture contribute to the difficulty of acculturating in a new cultural context. Other variables include intrapersonal traits, interpersonal group ties, the ability to form new social groups, the degree of difference between cultures, and the host cultural group's perceptions of the new member.

First, intrapersonal factors include skills (e.g., communication skills), previous experiences (e.g., in cross-cultural settings), personal traits (e.g., independence and tolerance), and access to resources. Physiological characteristics, such as health, strength, appearance, and age, as well as working and socialization skills, are important. Second, embracing a new culture includes keeping ties with one's past social groups, as well as forming new bonds. Those who can maintain support groups fare better in unfamiliar contexts. Third, variance in culture groups affects the transition from one culture to another. Acculturation is more challenging when cultures hold greater disparities in social, behavioral, traditional, religious, educational, and family norms. Finally, even when an individual's physical characteristics, psychological traits, and ability to socialize are favorable, culture shock can still occur through sociopolitical manifestations. The attitudes of the citizens in a foreign culture may exhibit social prejudices, acceptance of stereotypes, or intimidation. Furthermore, social presumptions may couple with legal constructions of social, economic, and political policies that enhance hardships for those interacting in new settings.

Culture shock develops through four generally accepted phases: the "honeymoon" (or "incubation") phase, problematic encounters, recovery and adjustment, and finally, reentry shock. In the honeymoon stage, the new environment initially captivates the individual. For example, fast-paced lifestyle, food variety, or tall skyscrapers of a large city may initially awe a newcomer coming from a small town. In the second stage, the area becomes increasingly uncomfortable. Within a few days to a few months, the difference in culture becomes acute and often difficult. Misinterpretation of social norms and behavior leads to frustration or confusion. Reactions could include feelings of anger, sadness, discomfort, impatience, or incompetence. In this phase, the newcomers feel disconnected from the new setting. However, by the third phase, individuals experience their new context with better understanding. They become more familiar with where to go and how to adapt to daily life, for example, knowing where to buy stamps and send a letter. Finally, for those returning to their home locale, they commonly experience "reshock." In this phase, they must readjust to their previous lifestyle. Things may have changed in their absence, and they must resocialize into their previous cultural setting.

To combat the more distressful aspects of culture shock, the individual must be open-minded to new cultural experiences, must develop flexibility and adaptability skills, and must be capable of building tolerance. Furthermore, he or she must hold positive but realistic expectations. Communication development, whether it be through understanding social norms or decreasing language barriers, is critical to acculturation in a new environment.

Although travelers and study-abroad students often experience culture shock, the extent of cross-cultural interactions goes beyond such narrow conceptualizations. Culture shock also affects many others, such as military personnel, immigrants, minorities entering college, parolees from prison, and married couples who divorce. Additional factors include an individual's social and class mobility, occupational change, or migration between urban and rural environments.

In particular, immigrants can experience culture shock in a variety of ways. First and foremost is the manifestation of cultural differences in traditions, holiday observations, rituals, and other practices that involve distinct religious differences or educational beliefs. Second, accepted behaviors in both public and private settings may be fundamental to one's native culture but socially unacceptable in the new environment. An additional hardship may include distance from friends and family and other social support networks. Third, what is particularly difficult for some immigrants is the language barrier. Despite finding comfort and adaptability in the physical environment, they may not be able to communicate successfully. Macro structures of new cultural ideologies, reproduced through micro interactions, can affect the personal psyche of the individual. Further exacerbating the situation may be an underlying racist or stereotypic assumption, which further reinforces insecurity. In addition, a new immigrant may have feelings of anxiety in unfamiliar contexts as a result of a lack of knowledge of cultural behavior cues.

The study of culture shock becomes increasingly important as the globalization process continues. Greater exposure to other cultures requires a better understanding of cultural differences. Furthermore, understanding culture shock can help lessen social problems that are not cross-national. For underprivileged groups, such as minorities, those in poverty, and English language learners, growing accustomed to new environments can be extremely difficult. In addition to problems in day-to-day lifestyles, these groups also may experience culture shock along a continuum ranging from treatment as "the other" to racism, sexism, rejection, or violence.

Educational programs that address cultural differences can minimize culture shock to make the transition phase less overwhelming. Gaining greater understanding of other cultures not only facilitates the acculturation process but also helps build bridges between diverse groups.

Heather Zaykowski

See also Acculturation; Assimilation; Cultural Values; Immigration

Further Readings

Adler, Peter S. 1975. "The Transitional Experience: An Alternative View of Culture Shock." *Journal of Humanistic Psychology* 15(4):13–23.

Anderson, Linda E. 1994. "A New Look at an Old Construct: Cross-Cultural Adaptation." *International Journal of Intercultural Relations* 18(4):293–328.

Hofstede, Geert. 2004. *Cultures and Organizations: Software of the Mind.* 2nd ed. New York: McGraw-Hill.

Searle, W. and C. Ward. 1990. "The Prediction of Psychological and Socio-cultural Adjustment during Cross-Cultural Transitions." *International Journal of International Relations* 13:449–64.

CULTURE WARS

The phrase *culture wars* refers to the conflicts between individuals or groups who see themselves as either preserving or, in some measure, changing fundamental cultural understandings and practices. These conflicts play out in the political arena and in the battle for public opinion. The earliest use of the term *culture war*, or *cultural struggle*, was in the context of Otto von Bismarck's unification of modern Germany in the late 19th century. At that time, *Kulturkampf* was deployed approvingly by liberal, largely Protestant forces to describe a variety of legal efforts aimed at separating church and state and limiting Roman Catholic clerical power. The phrase is now most often associated with U.S. cultural controversies, gaining popular currency in the United States in the 1990s. It is, however, occasionally applied to such controversies in other developed countries. In the United States and elsewhere, the culture wars are a main locus of social and political tension.

The issues implicated in the U.S. culture wars are many, including abortion, artistic and personal expression, crime and punishment, education, ethnicity, family relations, gun ownership, immigration, language, media bias or objectivity, medical ethics, national identity, popular culture, race, religion, and sexuality. Both sides in the culture wars tend to identify the mid- to late 20th century as the time of important changes in popular attitudes, legislative constraints, and political consensus on each of these issues. The preservationists generally see this as change for the worse. In this sense, they seek to retrieve and preserve what they claim to be an earlier U.S. cultural consensus, which they often see as rooted in unchanging moral, theological, and political truths. Meanwhile, advocates of change tend to argue for continuous evolutionary progress toward new understandings that they claim are more consonant with contemporary mores.

Contemporary Usage

The currency of the phrase *culture wars* in the United States is largely traceable to sociologist James Davison Hunter and media personality and political candidate Patrick J. Buchanan. Hunter argued, in 1991, that significant fault lines in U.S. society no longer correspond with old cleavages such as class, or religious or partisan affiliation, but with new divisions over cultural questions that transcend the old cleavages. He contended that the United States is polarizing into two hostile camps, defined by their orthodoxy or progressivism on these questions. To members of these camps, the old divisions are less salient than the new. Moral and political allegiances and alliances are therefore subject to reconfiguration, and new social solidarities and political movements emerge. Groups united by these new identities and common purposes define themselves according to their answers to cultural questions and their tactical responses to cultural controversies.

At the Republican National Convention in 1992, Buchanan gave a widely noted speech in which he claimed the culture wars are, at root, religious in character and that only by stopping or reversing a host of cultural shifts that had occurred since the mid-20th century could the United States follow God's will. For many on the left, such rhetoric amounted to hate speech; for many on the right, it was a symbolic call to arms for a nation in crisis. Indeed, the terms *left* and *right*, or *liberal* and *conservative*, are increasingly used in the United States to define opposing factions in the culture wars, in contrast to their earlier application to different philosophical and policy orientations on economic or foreign affairs questions.

Cultural Divisions

The new fault lines manifest themselves in various ways. In religious terms, preservationists understand themselves to be orthodox or traditional rather than modernist. If Christian, they tend to be evangelical rather than mainstream. Advocates of cultural change are more likely to identify themselves as non-orthodox or secularist. The culture wars also have distinct political implications in the United States. Preservationists are more likely to support the Republican Party, whereas advocates of cultural change gravitate toward the Democratic Party. Preservationists are more likely to defend and ally with popular or common opinion, whereas advocates of change find more common ground with elite opinion. Institutionally, preservationists tend to be suspicious of the judicial branch of government, which they see as pushing the culture too far too fast in the direction of unconstitutional and indeed immoral change. By contrast, advocates of cultural change are more likely to be sympathetic to judicial alterations of the cultural landscape. Indeed, particular judicial decisions are rallying points for those engaged in the culture wars. For many preservationists, cases identified as fundamentally altering a cultural status quo, such as the abortion decision *Roe v. Wade,* are abominations; for many advocates of cultural change, they mark out sacred ground not to be ceded.

The Culture Wars Internationally

In Australia and Canada, some issues associated with the U.S. culture wars, and occasionally the phrase itself, enjoy currency. In Canada, a variety of scholarly and populist organizations have emerged since the 1980s to combat what they see as cultural drift and decadence, including the perceived liberal activism of the Supreme Court of Canada. In European nations too, cultural issues have gained increasing traction, particularly in relation to Muslim immigration into Europe. With this immigration has come the threat, from the point of view of preservationists, to European national identities that is posed by the injection of Islam into largely secularized polities. France, Germany, the Netherlands, Spain, and Denmark, among other countries, have all seen explosive cultural controversies in recent years, sometimes spurred by actual violence or the threat of violence by Islamist forces fundamentally hostile to the dominant culture. These forces themselves cannot be considered to be engaging in the culture wars, however, because of their willingness to move from the arena of ideological and political struggle to the arena of actual warfare.

Assessment

Whether one is preserving or changing culture depends on how one defines it. Complex questions of political and social theory as well as historical interpretation are bound to arise. The nature of the struggle, as well as the relative strengths of the parties, are therefore controversial. In the United States, those who understand themselves to be preserving the culture often claim they are on the defensive against the hegemony of elite forces hostile to older but worthy understandings and practices, which forces they claim dominate many or most media and educational institutions. By contrast, those who understand themselves as changing U.S. culture often claim they are persecuted minorities who are simply reflecting newer but more legitimate interpretations of understandings and practices, or bringing out what has always been latent in the society.

The culture wars arguably have the potential to be more divisive than previous social conflicts in U.S. history. Partisans in the culture wars tend to concentrate on particular issues and the reorientation of public opinion and policy on those issues, rather than seeking broad-based accommodations and compromises. The relative lack of attention to compromise stems from the fact that these issues are linked to the very origins and sense of identity of the partisans. To them, they are issues of the highest possible salience because they speak to the question of ultimate moral standards and authority.

On the other hand, some political scientists argue that members of the U.S. political classes, including party activists, may be polarized, but average Americans are not. These experts contend that most Americans do not embrace the extremes of either cultural conservatism or liberalism, and their opinions continue to be relatively stable on a variety of issues, including abortion and homosexuality. Furthermore, at the mass as opposed to the elite level, these opinions tend to converge in the center. Thus consensus rather than conflict may best describe contemporary U.S. attitudes on cultural questions.

What can be said for certain is that forces of preservation and change have routinely vied with each other for the ability to define authoritatively the mores of virtually all societies throughout history. It is highly likely that the contemporary culture wars will, for many years to come, result in seesaw battles waged in and for legislative chambers, courtrooms, and public opinion.

Bradley C. S. Watson

See also Abortion; Affirmative Action; English-Only Movement; Euthanasia; Feminism; Gun Control; Homosexuality; Immigration, United States; Multiculturalism; Politics and Christianity; Pornography; Religion and Politics; Same-Sex Marriage; School Prayer; Values

Further Readings

Fiorina, Morris P. 2005. *Culture War? The Myth of a Polarized America.* New York: Pearson Longman.

Fonte, John. 2005. "Is the Purpose of Civic Education to Transmit or Transform the American Regime?" Pp. 73–111 in *Civic Education and Culture,* edited by B. C. S. Watson. Wilmington, DE: ISI.

Graff, Gerald. 1992. *Beyond the Culture Wars: How Teaching the Conflicts Can Revitalize American Education.* New York: Norton.

Hunter, James Davison. 1991. *Culture Wars: The Struggle to Define America.* New York: Basic Books.

Watson, Bradley C. S., ed. 2002. *Courts and the Culture Wars.* Lanham, MD: Lexington.

Wolfe, Alan. 1998. *One Nation, after All: What Middle Class Americans Really Think about God, Country, Family, Racism, Welfare, Immigration, Homosexuality, Work, the Right, the Left, and Each Other.* New York: Viking.

CURRENT ACCOUNT DEFICIT

The current account deficit is broader than the generally well-known trade deficit because it includes the deficit (or surplus) on investments and both personal (think foreigners sending money home) and government (think foreign aid or military assistance) transfer payments. A *current account* is the difference between exports and imports plus the difference between interest and dividends received from foreigners or paid to foreigners plus the difference in transfer payments paid or received. It is a current account deficit when the total amount of money leaving a country across these three categories exceeds the amount coming in; most commonly this occurs when imports exceed exports. The current account deficit and the federal budget deficit are often erroneously linked in discussions of the "twin deficits."

As Figure 1 shows, the United States has experienced a current account deficit for all but one quarter (the first quarter of 1991) over the past 25 years. Virtually all forecasters expect this deficit to continue for years to come.

The one positive number came about when several countries (most notably Germany, Japan, and Saudi Arabia) offered to contribute billions to the United States to pay for the cost of the Persian Gulf War on the condition that the contributions be used solely for the defense budget and not in any way to reduce the overall federal budget deficit. Then Defense Secretary Dick Cheney discovered that the Feed and Foraging Act of 1864 was still the law governing such contributions and that it allowed donations of money or goods and services to be used only for defense (or war) purposes. So much money came in that it gave the United States a one-quarter surplus on the current account. It also meant the United States made a profit on that war.

The basic economic principle to keep in mind is that the balance of payments for every country in the

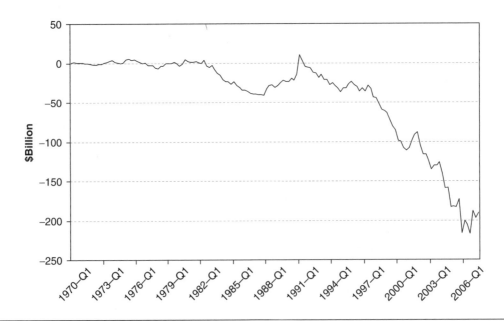

Figure 1   The Current Account Deficit

Source: Data from Bureau of Economic Analysis.

world is identical, namely, zero. This is an iron law of international accounting and has nothing to do with any theory.

This simply means that every country that has a current account deficit has a capital account surplus (an inflow of foreign money) of exactly the same amount. Any country with a current account surplus (such as China, Germany, or Japan) has a capital account deficit (an outflow of money to other countries) that exactly offsets the current account surplus.

The data do not provide any way to separate which side is driving the situation. Some commentators argue that because the return on investment that foreigners expect to earn by investing in the United States is so attractive, they continue to pour money into the United States at a rapid rate. So much of this has gone into direct investment that the Bureau of Labor Statistics now estimates as many as one out of every six employed people in the United States works for a foreign company such as BMW, British Petroleum, Four Seasons, Nissan, Shell, or Toyota.

If these people are correct, then the U.S. current account deficit will remain huge. Of course, trends that become unsustainable must stop and turn around, so sooner or later this will change.

Figure 2 shows the current account deficit as a share of gross domestic product (GDP), the total value of all the goods and services produced for final demand within the borders of the United States. The current account deficit appears to have stabilized in 2006 at approximately 6.6 percent of GDP.

Other analysts believe that it is the appetite of U.S. consumers for foreign goods that drives the current account deficit. Figures 3 and 4 show the huge and growing discrepancy between imports and exports of goods. The largest part of this trade deficit is due to motor vehicles (think of all the Jaguar, Lexus, and high-end BMW and Mercedes-Benz vehicles in the United States), and the largest deficit with a single country, which is unrelated to motor vehicle sales, is the one with China, which was $201.5 billion in 2005.

Figures 5 and 6 show that in the realm of services (education, entertainment, health care, travel, and so on), the United States has a large surplus. This surplus was $66.0 billion in 2005.

Much research has shown that approximately 70 percent of U.S. imports of goods are from affiliates of the same company. These imports are part of complicated corporate supply chain strategies and are not likely to change much due to normal ups and downs in the value of the dollar.

The best example of this is U.S. vehicle producers. The United States and Canada have had a free trade agreement since 1988, and this has led to a complete interchange of vehicles and parts between the two countries. After the North American Free Trade Agreement (NAFTA), which began on January 1, 1995, went into full effect, the same became true of vehicle and parts production in Mexico.

The United States and Canada are the world's two largest trading partners. Total trade between the two countries was a little over $500 billion in 2005 as

Figure 2   The Current Account Deficit: Percentage of GDP

Source: Data from Bureau of Economic Analysis.

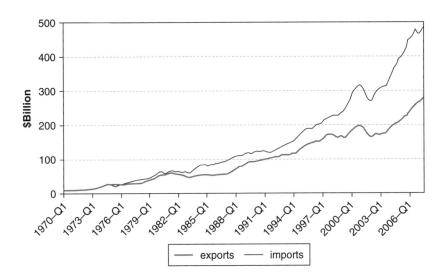

Figure 3   Exports and Imports: Goods

Source: Data from Bureau of Economic Analysis.

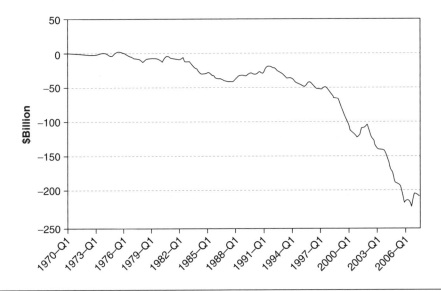

Figure 4   The Trade Deficit: Goods

Source: Data from Bureau of Economic Analysis.

compared with $290 billion with Mexico, $285 billion with China, and a little over $193 billion with Japan.

The group that thinks it is imports of goods driving the current account deficit always argues for a decline in the dollar to reverse or at least ameliorate the situation. However, this remedy is unlikely to work because the magnitude of decline for the dollar needed is too large and because so many corporate supply chain relationships would have to change dramatically.

Of course, if it is the attractiveness of the United States as a place to invest that is driving the current account deficit, then a decline in the dollar would only exacerbate the situation. This is frustrating to some people.

The Bureau of Economic Analysis of the U.S. Department of Commerce publishes updated information on the current account every 3 months. It also publishes monthly estimates of the trade deficit.

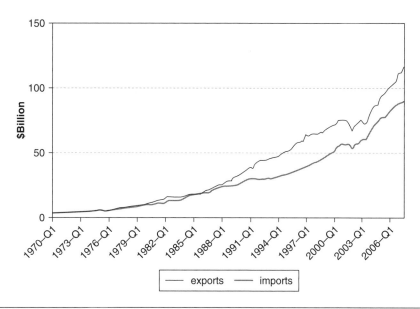

Figure 5   Exports and Imports: Services

Source: Data from Bureau of Economic Analysis.

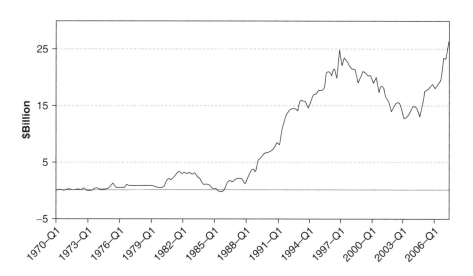

Figure 6   The Trade Surplus: Services

Source: Data from Bureau of Economic Analysis.

It seems likely the United States will have a current account deficit for many years to come. It will probably shrink as a share of GDP, but it is unlikely to disappear for a long time, if ever.

James F. Smith

See also Capital Flight; Global Economy

Further Readings

Bureau of Economic Analysis. (http://www.bea.gov).

Houthakker, Hendrick S. and Stephen P. Magee. 1969. "Income and Price Elasticities in World Trade." *Review of Economics and Statistics* 51:111–25.

Mann, Catherine L. 1999. *Is the U.S. Trade Deficit Sustainable?* Washington, DC: Institute for International Economics.

CYBERSPACE

Cyberspace is an invisible realm occupied by electronically mediated communication. Coined by science fiction writer William Gibson as a tool to describe a global computer network, the term *cyberspace* closely identifies with the age of the information revolution. Derived from the Greek verb *Kubernao* (to steer), the term commonly refers to the perceived freedom afforded users by the Internet and can involve any form of communication that involves computers or networking, ranging from text to multimedia and machine-generated data exchanges.

Computer-mediated communication can be thoughtful, edifying, and unifying, bringing far-flung families together and bridging continental divides. But cyberspace does not always carry positive connotations. Web sites supporting racial, gender, and religious stereotypes engender hatred and encourage social instability. E-mail has replaced traditional mail in many sectors, and legitimate e-mail is overwhelmed by unwanted "spam," which clogs in-boxes and has the potential of carrying destructive viruses. In addition to spreading computer viruses, malicious coders have used computer networks to generate denial-of-service attacks that can cripple Web sites and businesses.

Governments have used cyberspace to violate the civil rights of citizens and also have been victimized themselves. Some countries have censored what digital content is available to their citizens, and others have been accused of spying on citizens in the name of national security. Cyber sleuths suspect both China and Russia of backing a series of attacks on U.S. government and corporate sites in espionage cases known as "Moonlight Maze" and "Titan Rain." The potential for social, political, and economic conflict resulting from cyber espionage is daunting.

Cyberspace can involve both the positive and the negative. U.S. workers protest that cyberspace allows jobs, which once provided domestic employment, to be outsourced to Asia, where the process dramatically improves the lives of workers, their families, and the economies of those nations. Whereas this instance of communication in cyberspace has caused dislocation in one sector, it has brought prosperity to another, highlighting the ambiguous nature of the tool.

Robert Harris

See also Computer Crime; Digital Divide

Further Readings

Gibson, William. 2004. *Neuromancer.* 20th anniv. ed. New York: Ace.

Heylighen, Francis. 1993. "Cyberspace." In *Principia Cybernetica Web*, edited by F. Heylighen, C. Joslyn, and V. Turchin. Brussels: Principia Cybernetica. Retrieved February 4, 2008 (http://pespmc1.vub.ac.be/CYBSPACE.html).

Sterling, Bruce. 2002. *The Hacker Crackdown: Law and Disorder on the Electronic Frontier.* New York: Bantam.

Suler, John. *The Psychology of Cyberspace.* Retrieved February 4, 2008 (http://www.rider.edu/~suler/psycyber/psycyber.html).

Debt Service

In this entry, *debt service* is defined as the repayment of principal and interest on loans to sovereign entities such as cities and nation-states. This restriction of the definition facilitates a focus on social issues precipitated or aggravated by the repayment of such obligations.

Most commonly, governments fund their activities by borrowing the funds needed, usually via sale of obligations, such as treasury bills with terms under 1 year for financing current year operations, or treasury bonds with longer terms. Purchasing governmental obligations allows the buyer to "lock in" a return on the investment made for a long period of time or, if needs change, to resell what should be a widely held, well-regulated investment.

Governments borrowing funds must then repay them according to the terms and conditions of the obligation. Repayment usually requires transferring amounts greater than those borrowed—in other words, repaying both the amount borrowed (principal) and the interest thereon, or "servicing the debt." When servicing debt starts negatively to impact the provision of social services, the social dimension of debt service begins.

Debt Service in Developing Countries

Debt service in developing countries that causes extended, seemingly intractable social issues is usually the result of one of three scenarios: (1) Funds were lent to countries with a poor governmental structure, meaning with leadership not beholden to the population for its decisions; (2) debt was transferred that arose during colonialism, meaning historical costs incurred by the colonizing country were transferred to the newly independent colony at its independence; or (3) loaned funds were not properly managed, usually meaning that the lenders (in the wealthier countries), instead of ceasing to lend, actually lent more funds as economic or political situations deteriorated.

According to data presented in a 2005 news article by the British Broadcasting Corporation (BBC), total debts amassed by the world's poorest countries increased more than 20 times in the 3 decades from the early 1970s to the beginning of this decade, rising from—in U.S. dollars—$25 billion in 1970 to over $520 billion in 2002. Specifically to Africa, its share of the total in 1970 was less than $11 billion, not even half the total owed by poor nations. But, by 2002, total African debt stood at $295 billion, over half the total owed by all poor countries. Perhaps the bleakest fact is that, although the world's poorest countries have repaid $550 billion in principal and interest over the past 3 decades, on $540 billion of loans, these same countries are currently spending $13 on their debt repayments for every $1 they receive in grants.

Obviously, a country whose government cannot use its revenues, including (and especially) any grants received as humanitarian aid, for any current activity other than debt service, will have social issues. Because all three scenarios (described earlier in this section) seem to be caused by the actions of foreigners, social unrest is also often stoked.

Debt Service as a Political Issue

Debt service as the root cause of social problems has its origin in the creation of the system of exchange rates brought into effect with agreements reached at the conference at Bretton Woods, New Hampshire, in 1944. The representatives of the sovereign states in attendance created the International Monetary Fund (IMF) as an independent organization monitoring monetary flows among sovereign states, agreeing to certain principles for measurement of those flows—and either to assist or to threaten to sanction any state's monetary policy as it affected world prosperity. Because the member states are generally represented at the IMF by their most senior treasury or finance official—usually an unelected cabinet member or other appointee—virtually every intervention has both monetary and political dimensions.

Thus populations in countries in which debt service markedly diminishes the amounts spent on social costs (health care, housing, public transport, education, etc.) tend to blame their government or the governments of the lending countries—usually members of the Organisation for Economic Co-operation and Development—or the IMF itself. Strikes and riots, resulting from increased intolerance of such situations and impatience in awaiting their resolution, tend to exacerbate the overall problem by reducing the creditworthiness of the nation-state. In turn, this increases interest rates assessed on outstanding debt, further reducing the government's ability to service its debt.

Issues in Debt Relief

One way to remove issues created by debt service is for lenders to forgive outstanding debt. In theory, funds exported for debt service may then be used immediately to address social issues in-country. But there are at least two problems in relieving debt. First, the real lender—meaning the financial entity—usually requires settlement. This means the government of the lender must use public-sector funds to pay what is generally considered a private-sector debt. This is not very popular among taxpayers, as it seems their government is using their money to rescue big banks from imprudent lending, lending often made to unpopular or dictatorial regimes. Second, debt relief seems to rescue countries that have mismanaged funds or, worse, have misappropriated

funds or, worst, continue to commit significant human rights abuses. For example, between 1998 and 2000, Uganda received $374 million in debt relief—while troops were widely reported to be killing white minority farmers.

This situation has caused the World Bank and the IMF to require the government requesting debt relief to create a comprehensive poverty reduction strategy paper (PRSP) that the two organizations must approve before recommending debt relief. The PRSP contains requirements, among many others, for a democratically elected government. This can generate additional resistance at both the leadership and popular levels of such governments: Requiring an approvable PRSP is usually seen as further foreign interference in sovereign affairs.

Still, progress is occurring. The Paris Club is a voluntary gathering of creditor countries that coordinates handling of the debt owed them by developing countries. Since 1983 alone, it has canceled or rescheduled debts worth $509 billion. In January 2007, the Paris Club announced agreements to cancel 100 percent of Sierra Leone's $240 million in debt. Unfortunately, the Paris Club still has over $500 billion of developing nation debt to go.

Jeffrey Whitney

See also Colonialism; Human Rights; Social Revolutions

Further Readings

Katsouris, Christina. 2000. "New Conditions Slow Debt Relief." *Africa Recovery* 14(1):6. Retrieved March 4, 2007 (http://www.un.org/ecosocdev/geninfo/afrec/subjindx/141debt.htm).

Madslien, Jorn. 2005. "Debt Relief Hopes Bring Out the Critics." *BBC News,* June 29. Retrieved March 4, 2007 (http://news.bbc.co.uk/1/hi/business/4619189.stm).

Paris Club. "Description of the Paris Club." Retrieved March 4, 2007 (http://www.clubdeparis.org/sections/qui-sommes-nous).

"Pillars of Peace. Documents Pertaining to American Interest in Establishing a Lasting World Peace: January 1941–February 1946." 1946. United Nations Monetary and Financial Conference at Bretton Woods: Summary of Agreements. July 22, 1944. Pamphlet No. 4, pp. 30–31. Carlisle Barracks, PA: Army Information School. Retrieved March 4, 2007 (http://www.ibiblio.org/pha/policy/1944/440722a.html).

DECRIMINALIZATION

Decriminalization broadly refers to the removal or reduction of criminal penalties from particular substances or activities. Although the two terms are sometimes used interchangeably, *decriminalization* and *legalization* are not the same thing. Legalization implies complete removal of governmental control, whereas acts or substances that are decriminalized are still subject to state control even if the acts are no longer considered criminal. Commentators often vary on their interpretation of the term, based on the extent to which the state is involved in regulation. Terms such as *partial decriminalization* and *full decriminalization* specify the extent of state enforcement.

Decriminalization often takes place in response to social change. A society may change its political or moral views regarding an act, thereby no longer viewing the act as harmful, deviant, or worthy of intervention by the criminal justice system. Acts that are subject to decriminalization are typically victimless or public order crimes. A victimless crime refers to an act that is regarded as illegal and potentially harmful to society despite the lack of a victim. Prostitution, homosexuality, abortion, pornography, and illicit drug use are examples of acts that are, or were considered, victimless crimes and have been, or are, subject to decriminalization.

Although the concept of decriminalization can be applied to a wide variety of acts and substances, most of the discussion regarding the topic involves the debate over the decriminalization of illicit drugs. Those in favor of drug decriminalization often refer to the lack of success enjoyed by the current prohibition policy in the United States. Current policies, they argue, tend to overcrowd prisons, cost a great deal of money to enforce, and cause an increase in drug-related violence. Others argue that decriminalizing drugs would allow the state to place some regulations on the quality and purity of substances, as is the case with alcohol and tobacco, thus reducing the dangers that drug users face in consuming unregulated substances. Opponents of decriminalization suggest that such measures would drastically increase drug use or that decriminalization may not actually decrease drug-related violence.

Also relevant to the discussion of drug decriminalization is the issue of civil liberties. Those in favor of decriminalization note that prohibition not only results in restricting one's right to use psychoactive substances but also encourages unconstitutional practices by law enforcement, given the discrete nature of drug distribution and use. The varying levels of government control, coupled with the uncertainties over whether drug use is an individual right or a societal problem, make for varying perspectives on decriminalization at both ends of the political spectrum.

Jamie Longazel

See also Drug Abuse, Crime; Prohibition; Victimless Crimes

Further Readings

Goode, Erich. 2007. *Drugs in American Society.* 7th ed. New York: McGraw-Hill.

Husak, Douglas N. and Peter de Marneffe. 2005. *The Legalization of Drugs.* New York: Cambridge University Press.

Inciardi, James A. and Karen McElrath. 2004. *The American Drug Scene.* 4th ed. Los Angeles: Roxbury.

DEFORESTATION

Deforestation is the clearing and destruction of forests. The Food and Agriculture Organization of the United Nations (FAO) estimates that deforestation accounts for the loss of 13 million hectares of forests annually. At this rate, nearly all of the world's tropical rain forests will be depleted by the year 2050. Forests are important for a number of reasons, including the production of wood products, soil and water conservation, conservation of biodiversity, and social services such as recreation, tourism, and education. Forests, and the natural resources held within them, are essential for the survival of the human race.

Forests contain a number of advantages for the planet Earth. More than 20 percent of the world's oxygen, essential for survival of the human race, originates in the Amazonian rain forests. Forests are also a significant source of food for the human species, including fruits, vegetables, nuts, grains, and even fish. The number of species of fish in the Amazon, for example, is higher than the number found in the entire Atlantic Ocean. In terms of medicine, the benefits of forests are immense. Rain forests provide 25 percent of drugs currently used by Western pharmaceutical companies. Over 70 percent of the plants identified as active in fighting cancer originated in the rain forests, including periwinkle, which has significantly reduced childhood leukemia. Yet scientists have assessed only 1 percent of the trees in the rain forests for potential medicinal purposes, meaning that deforestation may lead to the permanent loss of lifesaving drugs.

Much of the deforestation is due to an increase in population, slash-and-burn techniques to clear land for agriculture and cattle grazing, and logging for paper, wood, and fuel products. More than 11 million acres of forest are cleared annually for commercial and property purposes. In Brazil alone, 70 percent of the tropical rain forests cleared have fallen to medium and large-scale ranches. Large corporations from the United States and other industrialized nations have also cleared land in rain forests for land production. In the United States, 90 percent of the virgin forests have been converted into firewood, shingles, furniture, railroad ties, and paper. Other causes of deforestation are acid rain, pollution, cash crops that require large tracts of land and deplete soil nutrients quickly, and industrialization.

Deforestation threatens the planet Earth in many ways. Tropical forests cover only 2 percent of the world's surface but account for 90 percent of the world's biodiversity. The current rate of deforestation has led to the loss of 50 to 100 animal and plant species daily. Of additional concern is the immediate impact of deforestation on our natural resources, including soil erosion, water treatment, fisheries protection, and pollination. The world's poorest people rely on these natural resources for their survival, and deforestation affects their quality of life and survival. The long-term consequences of deforestation include the decrease in biodiversity and significant increases in climate changes, both of which threaten the human race.

Deforestation has a significant impact on soil erosion. Forests act as a sponge, soaking up rainfall and providing a humid environment for plants and animals. As forests are cleared, water runoff and drought increase. The effects of Hurricane Mitch on Nicaragua and Honduras in 1998 provide a good example of the dangers. The extent of deforestation in Central America led to landslides, flooding, and the destruction of entire villages in areas in which land had been cleared. In many cases this destruction was at the expense of the poorest individuals in the countries with the least number of resources for survival.

Climate change also is a consequence of deforestation. Trees are a natural "sink" for carbon dioxide, a greenhouse gas that contributes to the rise in temperatures on the planet Earth. As forests are depleted, greater concentrations of carbon dioxide are present in the atmosphere and the threat of drought increases. The loss of freshwater can have a serious impact on human consumption, industry, and national security. As countries compete for less freshwater, the risk of global conflicts increases. Deforestation alone accounts for 25 to 30 percent of the world's global warming.

The habitats and livelihood of people in this world are being lost to deforestation. Indigenous populations in many parts of the world rely on tropical rain forests for cultural, medicinal, and spiritual purposes. Five hundred years ago there were 10 million indigenous people living in Amazonian rain forests. Today, because of deforestation, fewer than 200,000 individuals live there. Often it is the poorest countries that suffer the worst consequences of deforestation.

A correlation exists between a reduction in deforestation and a reduction in poverty. The preservation of forests provides individuals with more capital in terms of natural resources, more opportunities to earn their livelihood through better agroforestry techniques, improved wildlife management, and an increase in levels of fire management. As individuals acquire more wealth, they are less likely to depend on forests for survival.

Conversely, better forest management reduces poverty by increasing income, improving people's health, and giving them tools to increase protection of their natural resources. In assessing the positive impact of forests on people in poverty, three areas are important: land tenure rights, effective governance of these rights, and the community's capacity to manage their natural resources.

The rate of deforestation is declining, although the process is still continuing. The FAO reports that from 2000 to 2005 the net loss of forests was 7.3 million hectares per year, down from 8.9 million hectares annually from 1990 to 2000. Contributing to this decrease are greater conservation efforts, reforestation efforts, and the natural growth of forests. Industries such as recreation and ecotourism also contribute to an increase in efforts to preserve forests and biodiversity. The longevity of the human species is dependent on such efforts to halt the rate of deforestation.

Wendy Sellers Campbell

See also Environmental Movement; Erosion; Global
    Warming; Population Growth; Sustainable Development

Further Readings

Fearnside, R. 2006. "Deforestation in Brazilian Amazonia; History, Rates, and Consequences." *Conservation Biology* 19:680.

Kerr, Suzi, Alexander Pfaff, Romina Cavatassi, Benjamin Davis, Leslie Lipper, Arturo Sanchez, and Jason Timmins. 2004. *Effects of Poverty on Deforestation: Distinguishing Behavior from Location*. ESA Working Paper No. 04-19. Retrieved December 20, 2006 (ftp://ftp.fao.org/docrep/fao/007/ae401e/ae401e00.pdf).

Matthews, Christopher. 2006. *Deforestation Causes Global Warming*. New York: FAO Newsroom. Retrieved December 21, 2006 (http://www.fao.org/newsroom/en/news/2006/1000385/index.html).

DEINDUSTRIALIZATION

Deindustrialization is a term that describes the decline in manufacturing (or goods producing) employment occurring in the United States and other industrialized countries since the 1970s. Indeed, between the late 1970s and 2000s, the share of workers employed in goods-producing industries declined from approximately one third to one fifth of the workforce. Some scholars also define deindustrialization in terms of increased trade deficits, associated with increased foreign investment and production. Deindustrialization—closely associated with globalization and postindustrialization—has generated increases in earnings inequality, higher unemployment, and higher poverty rates in the United States. Furthermore, deindustrialization has undermined the strength of unions and has financially devastated some local cities and communities.

Whereas some economists argue that deindustrialization is a normal component of economic development, many scholars attribute deindustrialization to globalization. These scholars argue that economies are deindustrializing because firms face increasing competition in the world market. In the late 20th century, U.S. firms lost their competitive advantage in the global economy, and they responded by reducing costs. Innovations in information technology, production, and transportation permitted firms to move capital and jobs overseas where they could hire cheap labor and enjoy tax breaks, as well as relaxed labor and environmental laws.

The second associated process, postindustrialization, is the shift toward service employment. The deindustrialized, postindustrial economy is unique with its polarization of the new service industries into high-wage, knowledge-intensive service industries—such as finance, insurance, and real estate—and low-wage service industries, including personal services. During the latter part of the 20th century, the share of employment in service-producing industries increased dramatically. The largest share of these service jobs is characterized by lower pay than manufacturing jobs, and they are more likely to be part-time with few benefits.

As a result of deindustrialization and the simultaneous shift toward a postindustrial economy, wage and income inequality increased. The manufacturing sector had offered a more egalitarian wage structure than the service sectors. To illustrate, in 2005, the average hourly compensation for goods-producing employment was $29, ranging from $27 per hour in nondurable manufacturing (which includes textiles and food production) to $31 in durable manufacturing (which includes machinery, computer, and furniture production) and $37 in mining. Average wages in service industries were $24 per hour, ranging from $15 in retail to $33 in the finance, insurance, and real estate industries, to $36 in information industries (which includes publishing, printing, and motion picture production).

According to numerous scholars, deindustrialization has disproportionately harmed lower-skilled workers in inner cities. The substantial job loss in inner cities, particularly in blue-collar occupations found primarily in manufacturing industries, has not been offset by the growth in jobs in service industries, because many of these jobs require extensive education. Thus they do not provide sufficient opportunities for displaced workers. This, along with the suburbanization of manufacturing jobs and residential segregation, has led to an education mismatch between the supply of labor and the available jobs, particularly among young, inner-city youth.

The vast majority of jobs that moved overseas required little education and offered low wages. The loss of these jobs has reduced the demand for low-income and less-educated workers in the United States. This has resulted in stagnating wages for these workers. Indeed, among men who completed only high school, the entry-level wage declined between 1973 and 2005, dropping from $13 per hour in 1973 to $11 per hour in 2005. In contrast, the average entry wage for male college graduates rose between 1973 and 2005, increasing from $18 per hour in 1973 to $20 per hour in 2005. These patterns are similar for women. In addition to stagnating wages, deindustrialization has increased long-term unemployment among low-income workers. As a result, long-term dependence on governmental assistance has increased. However, the government attempted to reduce this dependence through the 1996 Personal Responsibility and Work Opportunity Reconciliation Act, which created the Temporary Assistance for Needy Families program.

In addition to its deleterious effects on workers, particularly low-income workers, deindustrialization has negatively affected unions because the manufacturing sector is one of the most heavily unionized sectors. The loss of jobs in this sector has undermined union strength, particularly because firms have relocated, in part, in an effort to escape the wage demands of unions. As unionized firms have closed and the volume of unemployed workers has increased, the negotiating power of existing unions has declined.

The negative impact of deindustrialization on unions is a key reason that deindustrialization has harmed lower-income workers. Historically, wages were relatively high among unionized workers and industries, particularly when comparing the incomes of unionized and nonunionized workers at the bottom of the income distribution. However, unionization rates declined most dramatically among low-income workers, due in part to the loss of low-wage manufacturing jobs. This in turn served to reduce the wage premium of unionization among low-wage workers.

Finally, deindustrialization can have devastating effects on cities and communities, particularly when entire towns or sections of towns are dependent on a manufacturing firm or industry for economic vitality. A number of ethnographic studies illustrate the impact of deindustrialization on families and communities, showing that when cities lose manufacturing employment, their economies suffer because lost jobs result in reduced consumerism, a depleted tax base, and an increased need for public support. Lost jobs inhibit the ability of displaced workers to contribute to the local economy. Thus many other businesses that rely on manufacturing workers as consumers, such as restaurants and retail shops, feel the ripple effects of deindustrialization through reduced profits. In addition, deindustrialization depletes the city's tax base because cities lose revenues from business taxes and individual income taxes. This further undermines the vitality of the city. In sum, while deindustrialization

allows U.S. firms to remain competitive in the global economy, it also has broad detrimental effects on individuals, organizations, businesses, and in some instances, entire communities.

Stephanie Moller

See also Current Account Deficit; Global Economy; Globalization; Income Disparity; Inequality; Postindustrialism; Temporary Assistance for Needy Families; Urban Underclass; Wage Gap; Welfare; Working Poor

Further Readings

Alderson, Arthur S. 1999. "Explaining Deindustrialization: Globalization, Failure, or Success?" *American Sociological Review* 64:701–21.

Bluestone, Barry and Bennett Harrison. 1982. *The Deindustrialization of America: Plant Closings, Community Abandonment, and the Dismantling of Basic Industry.* New York: Basic Books.

Kasarda, John D. 1989. "Urban Industrial Transition and the Underclass." *Annals of the American Academy of Political and Social Science* 501:26–47.

Mishel, Lawrence, Jared Bernstein, and Heather Boushey. 2006. *The State of Working America: 2006/2007.* Washington, DC: Economic Policy Institute and Cornell University Press. Retrieved December 8, 2007 (http://www.stateofworkingamerica.org).

Nash, June C. 1989. *From Tank Town to High Tech: The Clash of Community and Industrial Cycles.* New York: State University Press.

Wilson, William Julius. 1987. *The Truly Disadvantaged: The Inner City, the Underclass and Public Policy.* Chicago: University of Chicago Press.

Deinstitutionalization

Deinstitutionalization—the movement of mentally disabled people from mental institutions into a community- or family-based environment—is a concept that transformed in a generation from a solution to a problem. Introduced in the early 1960s as a way to reduce societal reliance on state institutions, the policy itself became a problem by the early 1980s. Increases in homelessness, poor community services for the mentally ill, the placement of the chronically mentally ill in nursing homes, the increase in the mentally ill in jails and prisons, and a general increase of incivility in large cities were all seen as consequences of deinstitutionalization. For many, the reform caused more problems than it solved.

The United States, by the mid-20th century, had become a country reliant on "total institutions" to control and treat deviance and dependency. State mental hospitals counted more than a half million patients and had long waiting lists in most states. Institutions for children dominated care for dependent and neglected minors. Prisons were the answer to criminality. Although the poorhouses of the 19th century had disappeared, their replacement—public housing projects and federal welfare programs—segregated the poor in minority communities. Started during the second quarter of the 19th century, these public institutions lost their legitimacy as a reasonable way to care for the needy and troubled. They were expensive, overcrowded, and generally seen as failures. They neither rehabilitated nor protected. That consensus led to new ideas about care and containment. Moral entrepreneurs from both the left and the right stepped in with proposals to close institutions. Scholarship emphasis on institutions shifted from seeing them as agencies of reform to seeing them as producing the very problems earlier reformers thought they would fix. If institutions were causing the problems they were supposed to ameliorate, then closing those institutions, or at least reducing the reliance on them, would improve the situation greatly. *Deinstitutionalization* was the name given to those efforts.

By the 1980s deinstitutionalization had become a bad word. Officials emptied the mental hospitals and closed down children's institutions. The median length of stay in state mental hospitals dropped by almost 44 percent during the 1970s. Between 1974 and 1984 the number of beds in state mental hospitals dropped by more than 58 percent. But community mental health services intended to replace mental hospitals and foster care in place of children's institutions failed to improve conditions for mentally ill or dependent children. Journalistic reports revealed that many of the mentally ill were living on the streets, and children in foster care were trapped in a permanent limbo. Homelessness increased 300 percent in the 1980s, and fear of the mentally ill intensified as involuntary commitment receded. Prison populations skyrocketed, and the mentally ill filled the jails. Nursing homes became repositories for the chronically mentally ill in many states. By the 1990s few spoke of deinstitutionalization

as a remedy, and most spoke of it as a problem. Little could be done to reverse the trends, though. Case law made reinstitutionalization a legal impossibility. The Supreme Court limited the use of institutions, and state courts were reticent to reverse this trend away from exclusion and confinement. By the 21st century, society had transitioned into a world of care and containment that included the deviant in society (with prisons as the notable exception).

Nevertheless, deinstitutionalization left society with a new set of serious and persistent problems. Whereas some scholars could look back and see progress, many citizens could only see communities that did not have the tools to care for and contain the chronically mentally ill. For them, deinstitutionalization failed to protect society from the troubled and troubling. With involuntary commitment greatly restricted and most state mental health systems committed to community care, even the most difficult mentally ill persons were assigned community care or no care at all. After a quarter century of experience, few would call it a success. Yet, the society seemed incapable of moving beyond the rhetoric of inclusion and the reality of weak social control capacity.

From the variety of explanations for this turn of events, some argue that deinstitutionalization was flawed in its conceptualization. Built on symbolic interactionist theory of the self and its production, the very idea misspecified the source of the deviance and the process that brought it into being. Many important works on deinstitutionalization assumed that mental illness was less a disease and more a learned social role. Given that fundamental theoretical mistake, they argued, the policies that followed could not help but be flawed. Acting mentally ill did not disappear when the socializing institutions that taught the role disappeared. Others felt that the theory was correct but that the implementation was woefully inadequate. Most mental health care is provided by state systems. Although the 1970s saw a rapid decline in patient censuses at state hospitals, the saved dollars were slow in being transferred to community services. The community services that developed were poorly integrated, as most states relied on private organizations to deliver community care. The idea of deinstitutionalization was solid; the implementation was deplorable. States failed to put the resources into the new community services, and the results were unsurprisingly devastating.

Deinstitutionalization is part of a major transformation of social control strategies that occurred in the last quarter of the 20th century. Desegregation of schools and deconcentration of public housing combined with deinstitutionalization of mental hospitals to absorb deviant and dependent populations back into civil society. The exclusion that was the hallmark of institutionalization was replaced by the push for inclusion. Stimulated by the civil rights movement and a desire to correct the abuses of the institutional system of care, the push to mainstream those on the fringes of society has won the day. Today the deviant are hidden away downtown as opposed to out of town in institutions. But the mentally ill and other deviant groups did not disappear. Nothing in the move to inclusion reduced the number of people who experience mental illness or the ravages of poverty and racism. Today, they are hidden among us waiting for a new generation of social problem researchers to tear away the camouflage and expose the reality of a deinstitutionalized system of care.

Dan A. Lewis

See also Mental Health; Total Institution

Further Readings

Lewis, Dan A., Stephanie Riger, Helen Rosenberg, Hendrik Wagenaar, Arthur J. Lurigio, and Susan Reed. 1991. *Worlds of the Mentally Ill: How Deinstitutionalization Works in the City.* Edwardsville, IL: Southern Illinois University Press.
Winerip, Michael. 1994. *9 Highland Road.* New York: Pantheon.

Dementia

Originating from the Latin word *demens,* meaning "without a mind," the term *dementia* historically designated social and intellectual deterioration associated with old age. However, beginning in the late 19th century, the medical characterization of *dementia* increased in specificity with the rise of biological sciences and the advent of new technologies to study the brain. As a diagnostic category, the term now encompasses about 70 different conditions associated with abnormal cognitive decline. Seminal in this evolution was the 1906 description by German neuropathologist Alois Alzheimer of a presenile form of dementia in a younger woman in her early 50s. In 1910, famous psychiatrist Emil Kraepelin reviewed Alzheimer's findings and claimed them to be suggestive of a new condition he called "Alzheimer's disease" to distinguish it from senile dementia, a disease experts then believed to occur only at a later stage in life. Later research revealed that Alzheimer's disease and senile dementia shared similar clinical and histological features, and by the 1970s, the medical community reached a consensus to use the term *Alzheimer's disease* to designate both conditions, irrespective of age of onset.

The 1980s marked the development of standardized diagnostic criteria under the impetus of the Alzheimer Disease and Related Disorders Association and the National Institute of Neurological and Communicative Diseases. This development allowed more precise clinical identifications of distinct forms of dementia, including Alzheimer's disease, vascular dementia, and Pick's disease, among others. It also permitted more accurate estimates of the number of dementia cases within the general population.

Current findings put the prevalence of dementia in Western countries at between 2 and 9 percent of people over the age of 65, with rates for those age 85 years and over as high as 50 percent. Alzheimer's disease is by far the most common form of dementia and accounts for approximately three quarters of all cases. In the United States alone, the Alzheimer Society reports that Alzheimer's disease currently affects an estimated 4.5 million Americans, and projections for 2050 put this number at between 11.3 and 16 million. Worldwide, dementia affects an estimated 28 million individuals, a figure projected to increase to 80 million by 2040. These estimates make dementia one of the most common causes of morbidity in elderly people.

The Geneticization of Alzheimer's Disease

A significant recent development in dementia research has been the discovery of several genes associated with familial and sporadic types of Alzheimer's disease. Familial Alzheimer's disease implicates the action of a number of mutated genes that follow an autosomal dominant pattern of inheritance whereby each child has a 50 percent chance of inheriting the disease if one of the parents is a carrier. Individuals with familial Alzheimer's disease account for about 10 percent of all cases and typically develop the disease before the age of 60. By contrast, sporadic Alzheimer's disease involves a combination of genetic factors not necessarily mutational that likely interact with a host of poorly understood environmental factors. Sporadic Alzheimer's disease accounts for the majority of cases of the disease, and onset typically occurs after the age of 60. So far, only a variant of the apolipoprotein E gene, called apoE4, has been determined to increase susceptibility for sporadic Alzheimer's disease.

A number of caveats have prevented the widespread use of genetic testing for Alzheimer's disease in clinical settings. First, testing to identify asymptomatic individuals who will develop the disease later in life is only useful for a small subset of familial cases. Predictive testing in sporadic cases remains problematic because apoE4 is an unreliable marker for Alzheimer's disease. Also found in individuals who do not develop the disease later in life, this variant likely needs to interact with other factors to cause the disease. A key concern with genetic discoveries is their potential for redefining Alzheimer's disease as an inherited condition that clinicians can accurately detect early in life. This mischaracterization of the predictive power of genetic testing raises concerns about the misguided use of test results by employers and health care insurers for eliminating high-risk cases from their rosters.

Dementia as Loss of Self

The neuropathological consequences of dementia have been well documented in the medical literature as a gradual decline in intellectual function that affects memory, thinking, and behavior. Through the artifacts of computer tomography scans, autopsied brain matter, and psychometric scores, biomedicine has legitimized dementia as a disease that unfolds independently from social circumstances, gradually erasing the identity of those afflicted by its pathology. In the popular imagination, dementia exists as rhetoric of irrevocable decline that robs afflicted individuals of self and dignity. Yet, this inevitability is increasingly being challenged by research that seeks to understand the influences of culture, social location, organizational practices, and health policies on how dementia is interpreted, and responded to, by both diagnosed persons and their social partners. Adhering to the tenets of social constructionism, this perspective critically interrogates the different discourses that construct dementia in relation to social, historical, and political

contexts. The suggestion is that a nihilistic understanding of dementia sets expectations and responses that undermine the moral status of those afflicted and creates the conditions under which expressions of the self are subsumed to pathology. This alternate conceptualization acknowledges the impact of pathology but also recognizes people with dementia as having the ability to maintain a sense of valued self when supported by person-centered care practices.

The Treatment of Dementia

One of the most significant developments in dementia care has been the introduction of pharmacological interventions to slow mild to moderate cognitive decline in Alzheimer's disease. The majority of these drugs are designed to interfere with the process by which the Alzheimer pathology breaks down acetylcholine, a neurotransmitter essential for optimal brain functioning. The introduction of drug treatment coincided with an interest in studying dementia in its earliest manifestations, when cognitive loss deviates from normal functioning but at levels insufficient to meet criteria for a diagnosis of dementia. This phenomenon, described almost half a century ago as "benign senescent forgetfulness," has in the past decade received a surge of interest, with nearly 20 new diagnostic categories characterizing more or less the same type of impairment.

The attraction in detecting dementia at an early stage lies in the possibility of introducing pharmacological intervention to retard decline into full-blown disease. With an increasingly aging population, early detection represents a potentially lucrative market for pharmaceutical companies that have invested in the development of dementia treatments. However, a key challenge has been to develop neuropsychological tests that are sufficiently accurate to distinguish the types of impairment that convert to dementia from those associated with normal aging. Inaccurate diagnosis could lead to the unwarranted use of potentially harmful drugs and cause psychological distress to those mistakenly identified as being at risk for dementia and their families. The stigma of being labeled as "dementing" early in life also has repercussions in terms of employment and access to adequate health insurance coverage. Rising public awareness of these new diagnostic categories could also potentially cause healthy older individuals to needlessly worry about their memory function.

The Future of Dementia

The definition of *dementia* remains contested as biomedicine continues in its quest to categorize cognitive decline into increasingly specific disorders. Social scientists have drawn attention to the social and moral dimensions associated with the diagnosis, genetic testing, and treatment of dementia disorders, with particular emphasis on Alzheimer's disease. Epidemiological findings about the prevalence of dementia disorders in an increasingly older population raise concerns about the allocation of health care resources worldwide.

André P. Smith

See also Chronic Diseases; Discrimination; Discrimination, Institutional; Health Care, Access; Health Care, Costs; Health Care, Insurance

Further Readings

Ballenger, Jesse F. 2006. *Self, Senility, and Alzheimer's Disease in Modern America: A History.* Baltimore: Johns Hopkins University Press.

Gubrium, Jaber F. 1986. *Old Timers and Alzheimer's: The Descriptive Organization of Senility.* Greenwich, CT: JAI.

Kitwood, Tom. 1997. *Dementia Reconsidered: The Person Comes First.* Buckingham, England: Open University Press.

Leibing, Annette and Lawrence Cohen, eds. 2006. *Thinking about Dementia: Culture, Loss, and the Anthropology of Senility.* New Brunswick, NJ: Rutgers University Press.

Sabat, Steven R. 2001. *The Experience of Alzheimer's Disease: Life through a Tangled Veil.* New York: Blackwell.

Traphagan, John W. 2000. *Taming Oblivion: Aging Bodies and the Fear of Senility in Japan.* Albany, NY: State University of New York Press.

DEMILITARIZATION

Demilitarization refers to the dismantling or deconstruction of militarism. Militarism is the influence of the military as an institution and of the preparations to use military force on the overall social organization of society. Demilitarization can be seen as taking place along several dimensions, which may or may not be aligned with each other. The implication is that a society might be in the process of becoming demilitarized in some areas but not in others.

One key element of militarism is the direct participation of the armed forces in the governing structures of society. In this case, demilitarization signifies the reduction of this practice by the introduction of new legislation, stronger democratic electoral procedures, and the strengthening of other norms encouraging civilian participation, or by the actions of citizens who become less inclined to vote or otherwise support military leaders. Since the end of the cold war, Latin America and some parts of Africa have seen a dramatic reduction of this form of militarism.

Militarism also finds expression as an aggressive foreign policy that relies on the actual and threatened use of armed force. In this respect, demilitarization is proceeding, at least in parts of the world where international organizations such as the United Nations and International Criminal Court, new treaties between nations, and commercial transactions, tourism, and professional and educational exchange are gradually replacing geopolitical competition. At the same time, it should be noted that some powerful nations continue to rely on the projection of military force. Furthermore, many parts of the globe remain violent. The demilitarization of some countries and some features of international relations is not incompatible with continued economic, political, and cultural inequality.

Demilitarization also includes the replacement of values and norms that glorify military conduct and the reduced impact of preparations to use military force on key institutions. During World War II, defense spending accounted for 40 percent of the gross national product of the United States; now it is about 5 percent (although the absolute size of military spending remains very significant). The process of demilitarization is also likely to limit conscription and the search for external and internal enemies. Fully demilitarized societies are also more likely to embrace formal and informal forms of conflict resolution, nonviolence, and a more elaborate peace culture. These developments may be the result of institutional changes or more deliberate efforts to create political will through concerted peace movements and other forms of activism.

Paul Joseph

See also Militarism; Military-Industrial Complex

Further Readings

Fellman, Gordon. 1998. *Rambo and the Dalai Lama: The Compulsion to Win and Its Threat to Human Survival.* Albany, NY: SUNY Press.

Marullo, Sam. 1993. *Ending the Cold War at Home: From Militarism to a More Peaceful World Order.* New York: Lexington Books.

Meyer, David. 1990. *A Winter of Discontent: The Nuclear Freeze and American Politics.* New York: Praeger.

Shaw, Martin. 1991. *Post-military Society: Military Demilitarization and War at the End of the Twentieth Century.* Philadelphia: Temple University Press.

Democracy

Democracy is an ancient Greek word meaning the rule (*kratos*) of the people (*demos*). It refers primarily to a form of government in which political decisions are made by a majority of the citizens (direct democracy) or their elected representatives (representative democracy). Democracy also signifies a country, society, or culture that possesses or tends toward a democratic form of government. Thus one might say that the future states of America knew democracy before officially gaining independence from the British Empire.

Varieties of democracy and of democratic theory abound, but a remarkable consensus exists as to the value of democracy: To call a country democratic today is virtually synonymous with saying its government is legitimate. Since World War II, almost all countries, however authoritarian, have called themselves democratic and have held elections—even if fraudulent—to maintain this reputation.

Direct democracy requires a small and close-knit society and is generally associated with historical polities, such as ancient Athens or the Italian city-states of the Renaissance, though it also survives today in town meetings and plebiscites, such as referenda, initiatives, and recalls. Most democracies now use representation, which is organized according to one or a mixture of two models. In presidential systems such as the one used in the United States, government is divided into branches—legislative, executive, and sometimes judicial—separately elected or appointed, with distinct but overlapping responsibilities and powers. This produces a system of "checks and balances" in which different representations of the popular will struggle to prevail or achieve compromise in public policy. Parliamentary systems such as Great Britain's instead give the bulk of effective powers to a single branch—the "lower" or popular branch of the legislature—with executive and judicial authority subordinated to its membership and laws, respectively. This tends to facilitate the formation of centralized, energetic administrations that founder only when public opinion demonstrably turns against them or when intraparliamentary alliances and loyalties fail.

From the first accounts of democracy in ancient Greece, the concept has been associated with the claim to equal freedom on the part of each member of the *demos,* or qualified citizenry. The meaning and social impact of democracy thus changes with the definition of citizenship. Factors such as race, gender, age, education, and economic condition have historically been applied to limit political participation and its concomitants, now referred to as civil liberties. Today the prevailing tendency is to enfranchise all adults, with some exceptions; for instance, in the United States resident aliens and felons may not vote, there are minimum ages for political office, and only natural-born citizens may run for president.

The concepts of equal freedom and majority rule are not perfectly congruent, as citizens who tend to be in the minority need not be treated fairly by democratic majorities. Examples include those whose race, ethnicity, religion, or way of life gives them interests truly or seemingly contrary to those of their fellows, a problem long noted. Aristotle and the American founders both warned, for example, that unrestrained majorities might seek to use government to divest the wealthy of their property and redistribute it to the people, undermining the economic system upon which politics relies. Political philosophers have insisted on the distinction between the good of the majority and the good of all; when the former supplants the latter, it is often called the "tyranny of the majority."

Solutions to majority tyranny are numerous but entail two broad strategies. Classical political philosophy sought to curb the excesses of the democratic faction by recommending a mixed regime—one in which government is divided among offices representing members of the various social classes. The modern approach eschews any institutional recognition of class, relying instead on various procedural mechanisms to guard against majority tyranny. These include (a) requiring a supermajority or qualified majority vote on certain important measures, (b) the aforementioned checks and balances among branches or levels of government, (c) the concept of enumerated powers outside of which government may not act, (d) proportional representation of various groups within society, and (e) the provision of individual rights, which the government may be barred from infringing. Governments that employ such strategies to protect minority interests are often referred to as liberal democracies.

Most democracies today are liberal democracies, and it could be argued that the spirit that animates them is as much liberal (focused on individual rights) as democratic (focused on majority rule). When U.S. leaders speak of promoting democracy in the Middle East, for example, they are thinking of government with constitutional protections for women and ethnic and religious minorities, not of regimes such as that of Iran, an Islamic Republic in which key offices are elected, but Shi'a Islam is the official religion, and councils of clerics apply Islamic law to legislative, executive, and judicial decisions. Liberal democracy, by contrast, is generally thought to be incompatible with an establishment of religion or legal restrictions on the religious beliefs of individuals.

One consequence of the focus on liberal democracy has been the gradual enhancement of the power of courts in deciding political issues. The United States pioneered this trend when its Supreme Court claimed the power of judicial review: the ability to negate laws or governmental acts that, in the Court's judgment, conflict with the Constitution. Originally, this power was defended by noting that laws passed by popular representatives are subordinate to the Constitution, embraced as a "higher law" by a supermajority of eligible citizens at the time of its ratification (the same applying to subsequent amendments). Today, the Court argues more broadly that modern democracy implies the "rule of law," including vital but indeterminate constitutional rights, and that as the final interpreter of these rights, the Supreme Court serves an indispensable function within democracy. In the United States and elsewhere, this trend has empowered courts vis-à-vis elected officials.

L. Joseph Hebert

See also Citizenship; Civil Rights; Inequality; Political Fragmentation; Religion and Politics; Voter Apathy

Further Readings

Aristotle. 1984. *Politics.* Translated and edited by Carnes Lord. Chicago: University of Chicago Press.

Tocqueville, Alexis de. 2000. *Democracy in America.* Translated and edited by Harvey C. Mansfield and Delba Winthrop. Chicago: University of Chicago Press.

Zakaria, Fareed. 2004. *The Future of Freedom: Illiberal Democracy, at Home and Abroad.* New York: Norton.

DEMOGRAPHIC TRANSITION THEORY

Prior to the 20th century, many social scientists believed that at some point the carrying capacity of the earth would be outstripped by the needs of the rapidly growing human population. However, during the 20th century, data became available that led social scientists to abandon the idea that the human population would continue to grow in an unsustainable manner. This change came about with the realization that, from the late 18th through the 19th century, numerous European countries experienced dramatic demographic transitions that were eventually mimicked by countries in other parts of the world. These demographic transitions might ultimately stabilize the world population.

Demographic transition theory posits that populations ultimately stabilize by way of a three-phase process (see Table 1). Characterizing the first of these phases are high rates of mortality offset by high rates of fertility to create a balanced mortality–fertility regime with slow population growth. Characterizing the second phase is rapid population growth brought about by continued high levels of fertility and declining levels of mortality. Historically, dramatic population growth has most often resulted from lower death rates, not higher birth rates. Characterizing the third and final stage of demographic transition are low levels of fertility and low levels of mortality.

While general agreement exists that preceding declines in fertility are declines in mortality, no consensus exists as to the cause of fertility decline. Some argue that high levels of fertility reflected strategies of familial and self-preservation in the face of high mortality levels at all stages in the life course. Others focus on structural changes in societies, namely industrialization and urbanization, as the main causes of fertility decline. In agricultural

Table 1	The Three Phases of Demographic Transition Theory		
Phase	*Mortality*	*Fertility*	*Population Growth*
I	High	High	Slow/Stable
II	Low	High	Rapid/Unstable
III	Low	Low	Slow/Stable

societies children were, among other things, economic assets—crucial to family and household economics. Young children could provide substantial manual labor, infant and child care, and elder care. To the extent that this is true of preindustrial societies, it is not surprising to find high fertility levels among them. In the urban-industrial context, however, children become economic liabilities because economically productive activities are generally removed from the household where children can easily contribute. Modern child labor laws and compulsory schooling have further undermined the ability of children to contribute to household economics. Still others attribute fertility decline to cultural changes in societies, namely, modernization and secularization, which are not necessarily tied to the structural changes described earlier.

Irrespective of the causes, much of the world is moving into the third stage of the demographic transition. In the space of two generations, Mexico and other less-developed countries cut their fertility rates in half—from more than five children per woman to less than three. All of this has led population experts to less frequently ask, "What must be done about the population explosion?" and more often to ask, "How do societies work when people stop replacing themselves?"

Amon Emeka

See also Birth Rate; Mortality Rate; Population Growth

Further Readings

Chesnais, Jean-Claude. 1992. *The Demographic Transition: Stages, Patterns, and Economic Implications.* New York: Oxford University Press.

Morgan, S. Philip. 2003. "Low Fertility in the Twenty-first Century." *Demography* 40:589–603.

DEPENDENCY RATIO

The dependency ratio is the number of elderly people and children as a fraction of the number of working-age adults. For example, a dependency ratio of 30 percent would indicate that there are 30 children and elderly people for every 100 working-age adults. The definitions of the age groups may vary. For example, some calculations treat people between the ages of 20 and 64 as working-age adults, whereas others define this group as people ages 15 to 64. The ratio is intended to capture the size of the population that is too old or young to work, relative to the population that is capable of producing economic output; that is, it reflects the number of children and elderly who must be "supported" by each working-age adult. The aged (or old-age) dependency ratio is similar but includes only the number of elderly people as a fraction of the number of working-age adults.

An increase in the dependency ratio typically places additional stress on the public sector, as the working-age population must bear an increased tax burden to support programs for children and the elderly. The aged dependency ratio has particular significance for policy debates in the United States and other industrialized countries, where aging populations are putting a strain on public retirement programs and other programs targeted toward the elderly.

Trends and Forecasts

The aged dependency ratio in the United States (using the 20–64 working age definition) rose from 13.8 percent in 1950 to 20.3 percent in 2005. According to the latest projections of the Social Security Board of Trustees, this dependency ratio will rise rapidly between 2010 and 2030, reaching 34.9 percent in 2030. After that, it should increase more slowly, to 38.0 percent in 2050 and to 42.1 percent in 2080. However, significant uncertainty surrounding such forecasts exists. The Social Security trustees estimate that the dependency ratio in 2080 could be as high as 58.1 percent (the "high-cost" scenario) or as low as 31.6 percent (the "low-cost" scenario). A similar trend is occurring around the world, particularly in industrialized countries. According to official UN estimates, the aged dependency ratio (using working age as 15–64) for developed countries could rise from 22.6 percent in 2005 to 44.4 percent in 2050.

Changes in a country's dependency ratio can result from a number of demographic factors, including fertility, mortality, and immigration. Affecting the projected rapid increase in the U.S. dependency ratio prior to 2030 is the aging of the baby boom generation. Driving the more gradual, long-term upward trend is increasing life expectancy due to medical advances, combined with a low fertility rate. The period life expectancy for a 20-year-old in the mid-20th century was 71.2 years; by 2003 this increased to 78.4 years. Whereas the total fertility rate varied greatly over the past century, it has remained at around 2.0 children per woman recently (below the rate of 2.1 required to maintain zero population growth in the absence of immigration and changes in life expectancy).

Relevance for Fiscal Policy

The upward trend in the dependency ratio has significant implications for public sector programs, particularly Social Security and Medicare. In a pay-as-you-go (PAYGO) retirement program, the following mathematical relationship holds at every point in time:

$$twN_y = bN_o$$

Here, t is the payroll tax rate, N_y is the number of workers covered by the program, w is average covered earnings per worker, b is the average benefit per retiree, and N_o is the number of retirees. The equation implies that all payroll taxes collected in the current period are paid out as benefits to current retirees; this is the defining characteristic of a PAYGO system. This equation can be rearranged as follows:

$$t = (b/w)(N_o/N_y)$$

Here, the side to the left of the equal sign is the payroll tax rate, and the side to the right of the equal sign is the product of the replacement rate (fraction of the average worker's earnings that the retirement benefit replaces, or b/w) and the aged dependency ratio (retirees per worker, or N_o/N_y). This equation shows that the payroll tax required to support the system is directly proportional to the dependency ratio.

Currently, the payroll tax rate for Social Security's Old-Age and Survivors Insurance (OASI) program is 10.6 percent, while the replacement rate is approximately 42 percent for a worker with average earnings.

Taken together with the dependency ratio of 20.3 percent, one can see that the left-hand side of the equation is larger than the right-hand side, indicating that OASI is running a surplus. As the dependency ratio rises to 42.1 percent (its expected value in 2080), the right-hand side grows larger than the left. This indicates that OASI will run deficits (drawing down the trust fund) unless either the payroll tax is raised or benefits are cut. The Social Security trustees estimate that the OASI program will begin to run deficits in 2018 and that the trust fund will be exhausted in 2042. The Medicare Hospital Insurance program, which operates in a similar manner, also is greatly affected by increases in the dependency ratio. Medicare trustees predict that the hospital insurance program will begin to run deficits in 2010 and that the trust fund will be exhausted in 2018. The sizes of the long-run imbalances are significant, with Social Security's unfunded obligations amounting to $13.4 trillion and the Medicare Hospital Insurance program's amounting to $28.1 trillion.

Sita Nataraj Slavov

See also Baby Boomers; Birth Rate; Fertility; Life Expectancy; Medicare; Mortality Rate; Pensions and Social Security

Further Readings

UN Department of Economic and Social Affairs. Population Division. 2005. "World Population Prospects: The 2004 Revision." Vol. 3, Analytical Report. New York: United Nations.

U.S. Department of Health and Human Services. Centers for Medicare and Medicaid Services. 2006. "The 2006 Annual Report of the Boards of Trustees of the Federal Hospital Insurance and Federal Supplementary Medical Insurance Trust Funds." Washington, DC: U.S. Government Printing Office.

U.S. Social Security Administration. Office of the Chief Actuary. 2006. "The 2006 Annual Report of the Board of Trustees of the Federal Old-Age and Survivors Insurance and Disability Insurance Trust Funds." Washington, DC: U.S. Government Printing Office.

DEPORTATION

The U.S. Department of Homeland Security deports more than 1 million nonresident aliens annually, including about 150,000 to 200,000 "formal removals." A formal removal occurs when an alien is decreed deportable in an administrative proceeding within the U.S. Citizenship and Immigration Services. Deportability may be due to undocumented entry, visa overstay, or criminal conviction. More than two thirds (69.5 percent) of formal removals in 2005 were Mexican nationals, with nationals of Honduras (7.0 percent) and Guatemala (6.0 percent) a distant second and third. More than one third of formal removals (36.2 percent) resulted from attempts to enter without proper documents (see Table 1). A similar offense, "present without authorization," resulted in an additional 34.6 percent of removals. Only about one fifth (19.2 percent) of formal removals were due to criminal violations. Thus undocumented migrants account for the majority of formal removals. Nonetheless, nearly 90 percent of deportations are termed *voluntary departures*. This occurs when foreign nationals are permitted to depart the United States without formal proceedings. By far the greatest number of these deportations occurs when the U.S. Border Patrol returns undocumented Mexican nationals directly to Mexico.

History of Deportation

The history of deportations interrelates with conditions that cause xenophobia: periods of financial insecurity, war, and mass immigration. The first legal grounds for deportation came through passage of the Alien and Sedition Acts of 1798. In preparation for a possible war with France, the United States passed An Act Concerning Aliens, granting authority to the president to order the deportation of any alien deemed "dangerous to the peace and safety of the United States." The president was also granted the power to remove aliens who had been imprisoned. Another related law passed in the same year was An Act Respecting Alien Enemies. This act gave the president the power to detain or deport aliens if their country of citizenship was at war with the United States. Whereas three of the acts passed in this series were repealed or allowed to expire, the Alien Enemies Act is still enforced in a modified form today.

Early Immigration Laws

Faced with the growing diversity of immigrants from non-European countries, the United States instituted a

Table 1   Aliens Formally Removed by Administrative Reason for Removal: 2005

Administrative Reason for Removal	N	%
Attempted entry without proper documents or through fraud or misrepresentation	75,532	36.2
Present without authorization	72,229	34.6
Criminal violations	40,018	19.2
Previously removed, ineligible for reentry	18,203	8.7
Failed to maintain status	1,042	0.5
Public charge	824	0.4
Smuggling or aiding illegal entry	540	0.3
Other	120	0.1
National security and related grounds	10	0.0
Unknown	3	0.0
Total	208,521	100.0

Source: "Table 40: Aliens Formally Removed by Administrative Reason for Removal: Fiscal Years 1996 to 2005." Department of Homeland Security, Office of Immigration Statistics. Retrieved January 13, 2007 (http://www.dhs.gov/xlibrary/assets/statistics/yearbook/2005/table40.xls).

series of laws, including the Chinese Exclusion Act of 1882 and the Immigration Acts of 1891, 1903, 1907, and 1917. These laws restricted immigration and barred Chinese and many Asian migrants. These laws expanded the reasons for the apprehension and deportation of undocumented immigrants, enemies of the state, and criminal aliens. There were relatively few formal removals in the early period of the laws (between 2,000 and 5,000 annually), and voluntary departures were not tracked. Following the Immigration Act of 1903, in which the Bureau of Immigration was moved to the Department of Commerce and Labor, the number of formal removals doubled to nearly 10,000 deportations. By 1910 there were 27,000 removals, climbing to a peak of 37,000 in 1914. Deportations dropped dramatically during World War I to fewer than 10,000 annually by the end of the war. Yet, during this period, demands in the

United States required the importation of undocumented laborers from Mexico as many U.S. workers had gone to Europe to fight in the war. By 1924, labor demands had decreased and deportations nearly reached pre-war levels.

The Great Depression and Operation Wetback

The Great Depression saw a surge in deportations as labor surpluses led to extreme competition for jobs. Although official immigration statistics show about 351,000 deportations of all nationalities between 1929 and 1939, estimates place the number of Mexican laborers deported or repatriated at between 1 and 2 million persons. Deportations again declined following the Depression, as the United States entered into World War II. Farm labor shortages during the war led to implementation of the Bracero Program, the legal importing of as many as 400,000 temporary Mexican guest workers annually. Even more undocumented workers entered the country during the same time period seeking employment. Yet, growing xenophobia

in the early 1950s and the post–Korean War recession caused President Eisenhower to launch a campaign of mass deportations of Mexican workers. Under General Joseph Swing, the Immigration and Naturalization Service instituted a series of raids recording more than a million deportations in 1954 of persons of Mexican origin, even including some legal residents and U.S.-born children of immigrants (see Figure 1).

Recent Immigration Legislation

The Hart-Celler Immigration Bill of 1965 (aka the Immigration Act of 1965) radically restructured the U.S. immigration system to one that favored family reunification and immigrants with needed skills. The law also removed preferences for European countries, permitting a greater influx of immigrants from Asia, Latin America, the Middle East, and elsewhere. As the flow of legal immigrants increased after 1965, so too did the number of deportations for illegal entry (officially "entry without inspection"), visa overstay, and other reasons. The number of deportations quadrupled from 82,209 in 1964 to 320,817 in 1970.

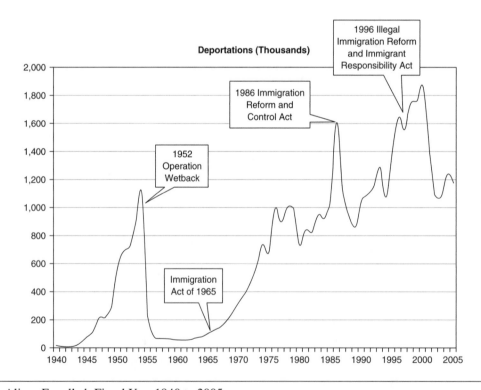

Figure 1   Aliens Expelled: Fiscal Year 1940 to 2005

Source: "Table 38: Aliens Expelled: Fiscal Years 1892 to 2005." Department of Homeland Security, Office of Immigration Statistics. Retrieved January 13, 2007 (http://www.dhs.gov/xlibrary/assets/statistics/yearbook/2005/table38.xls).

In the 1980s negative public opinions of undocumented migrants and the fear of the rapid growth of the foreign-born population compelled Congress to consider changes to immigration laws. The Immigration Reform and Control Act of 1986 sought to control the flow of immigration by penalizing companies that hired undocumented workers while regularizing the status of those already in the United States without permission. It also contained a provision for increasing the Border Patrol to curb further entry without inspection. In that year nearly 1.7 million deportations occurred, partly as a result of the addition of more than 1,000 new Border Patrol agents. The reforms proposed by the Immigration Reform and Control Act of 1986 had the unintended consequences of increasing migration flows through family reunification. Likewise, employers were able to avoid penalties and fines as they did not "knowingly" hire undocumented workers. In 1996 the Illegal Immigration Reform and Immigrant Responsibility Act was passed, adding 5,000 new Border Patrol agents by 2001, appropriating more funding for border control, and introducing a process of expedited removal in which officers of the then Immigration and Naturalization Service (now Department of Homeland Security) could remove undocumented aliens without judicial oversight.

Stephen J. Sills

See also Asylum; Bracero Program; Chicano Movement; Human Trafficking; Immigration; Immigration, United States; Labor, Migrant; Nativism; Repatriation; Sanctuary Movement; Terrorism; Undocumented Immigrants; War; Xenophobia

Further Readings

Balderrama, Francisco and Raymond Rodriguez. 1995. *Decade of Betrayal: Mexican Repatriation in the 1930s.* Albuquerque, NM: University of New Mexico Press.

Dillin, John. 2006. "How Eisenhower Solved Illegal Border Crossings from Mexico." *The Christian Science Monitor,* July 6. Retrieved January 13, 2007 (http://www.csmonitor.com/2006/0706/p09s01-coop.html).

Dougherty, Mary, Denise Wilson, and Amy Wu. 2006. *Immigration Enforcement Actions: 2005 Annual Report.* Department of Homeland Security Office of Immigration Statistics. Retrieved January 13, 2007 (http://www.dhs.gov/xlibrary/assets/statistics/yearbook/2005/Enforcement_AR_05.pdf).

Garcia, Juan R. 1980. *Operation Wetback: The Mass Deportation of Mexican Undocumented Workers in 1954.* Westport, CT: Greenwood.

Tichenor, Daniel J. 2002. *Dividing Lines: The Politics of Immigration Control in America.* Princeton, NJ: Princeton University Press.

DEPRESSION

See MENTAL DEPRESSION

DEREGULATION

Deregulation is the easing or elimination of governmental restrictions on economic activity. In the past century, in advanced capitalist economies such as that of the United States, governments instituted many rules restricting business behavior. As these rules always seemed onerous to businesses, businesses have always been in opposition to them. This opposition became effective in the past 30 years, leading to deregulation policies to remove the fetters on market activity and let markets determine economic outcomes. From this point of view, regulation stifles the economy, creating inefficiencies and lowered output.

The Interstate Commerce Commission (ICC), created in 1887, was the first federal regulatory agency in the United States. At that time the railroad industry was fixing rates, controlling markets, and favoring large customers, that is, acting in noncompetitive ways. The federal government tried to reintroduce competition into this industry by setting rules and regulations concerning fares and routes. However, these rules had little effect, essentially creating a protected, noncompetitive market for the railroads under the aegis of government regulation.

Since then, many different federal regulatory agencies have emerged to regulate most economic activity. For example, the oil, steel, agriculture, banking, air travel, pharmaceutical, construction, and chemical industries have all been subject to regulatory scrutiny, with varying results. Some agencies, like the ICC, have been failures; others, like the Environmental Protection Agency (EPA), have been quite successful in achieving their stated goals.

Regulation is a response to the functioning of the market. Certain undesirable outcomes may be the result of free-market activity. These kinds of outcomes can be considered as market failures, which the market itself is inherently incapable of correcting. A classic example of this is air pollution. In the refining of oil into gasoline, toxic chemicals are discharged into the air. Because the oil companies do not own the air and need not pay anyone for its use—it is commonly held by society—little incentive exists for them to limit their discharges. Whatever they spew into the air costs them nothing and therefore is not taken into account by them or consequently by the market. There may very well be costs associated with this air pollution, in the form of increased payments for health care, but they are not reflected in any market calculations. If left to the market, this problem is insoluble. Thus it becomes necessary for the government—an agent outside of the market—to step in to solve the problem.

Not wanting to eliminate markets (e.g., by replacing them with government planning), the U.S. government tries to alter these negative outcomes by limiting what businesses can do. Market failure is one main reason why a government may regulate. In addition to pollution (regulated by EPA), other examples of market failure are unwanted income distribution (not regulated in any way); lack of product information, such as the efficacy and safety of drugs (regulated by the Food and Drug Administration); and monopoly power (regulated by various antitrust laws promoting competition). A second reason for regulation would be to prevent discrimination—the Equal Employment Opportunity Commission, established in 1961, oversees this. A third reason is to promote the health and safety of workers on the job—the Occupational Safety and Health Administration sets myriad rules that employers must follow regarding worker safety. With the establishment of these more recent agencies, the federal government now regulates virtually all business in the United States in one way or another.

Not surprisingly, a backlash against this extensive regulation soon followed. Businesses chafed at having to follow all of these rules imposed by agents outside the market. The only impact that they could see was the increased costs associated with compliance with these rules. Widespread regulation seemed to be an unfair governmental intrusion into private business. The move toward deregulation was born.

While the primary objection to regulation on the part of business is the increased cost and resultant lower profits, an economic–philosophical argument also exists against this sort of government interference. Economists who believe in the free market argue that market outcomes are the most efficient and desirable of all outcomes; government involvement can only make things worse. They have faith that by following the rules of the market, letting supply and demand freely determine prices and output, the economy will be the best that it can be. This became the intellectual underpinning of the deregulation movement beginning in the late 1970s.

The first major deregulation legislation was the Airline Deregulation Act of 1978 that removed many rules governing air travel, presumably opening up this industry to more competitive forces. Within the 1980s satellite transmissions, trucking, natural gas, crude oil prices and refined petroleum products, radio, and the financial industry were all deregulated. Generally speaking though, rules concerning safety (both worker and product) and discrimination remained.

In addition to changing laws, deregulation can also occur through government neglect. If the government does not enforce the regulatory laws—by not monitoring industry for safety violations, for example—this is, effectively, deregulation. The George W. Bush administration, which strongly supported deregulation, used this as a primary tactic in its fight against what it saw as governmental interference in the free market.

The results of deregulation have been mixed. Commercial airfares have gone down, but bankruptcies and labor problems plague the airline industry. The main goal of deregulation—lower prices—occurred in some cases, while the opposite occurred in others. A striking failure of deregulation was the savings and loan debacle of the 1980s. After 1982, when Congress took oversight controls off of savings and loan institutions, those institutions responded with an orgy of speculative investments resulting in massive bankruptcies, with taxpayers ultimately paying $160 billion for this experiment in market freedom.

Paul A. Swanson

See also Conservative Approaches; Megamergers; Multinational Corporations; Oligopoly

Further Readings

Belzer, Michael. 2000. *Sweatshops on Wheels: Winners and Losers in Trucking Deregulation.* New York: Oxford University Press.

Friedman, Milton and Rose Friedman. 1980. *Free to Choose.* Orlando, FL: Harcourt.

Hardin, Garrett. 1968. "The Tragedy of the Commons." *Science* 162:1243–48.

Kahn, Alfred. 2004. *Lessons from Deregulation: Telecommunications and Airlines after the Crunch.* Washington, DC: Brookings Institution Press.

Kuttner, Robert. 1999. *Everything for Sale.* Chicago: University of Chicago Press.

DESERTIFICATION

Of all the global environmental problems, desertification is, perhaps, the most threatening for poor rural people. The most accepted definition of *desertification* states that it is land degradation in arid, semiarid, and dry subhumid areas (hereafter called "drylands") resulting from various factors, including climatic variations and human activities. Drylands cover almost 40 percent of the total land surface of the world and are inhabited by approximately 1 billion humans dispersed over more than 100 countries. These people include many of the world's most vulnerable, marginalized, and politically weak citizens. In spite of the progress in the understanding of the ecological dimension of this phenomenon, few communities' well-being has improved by the myriad action plans and activities carried out by local, regional, or national organizations, particularly in Africa. A growing body of evidence suggests that a closer look at the social system and the role of its components is critical to understanding this frequent outcome.

Drylands are characterized by water scarcity stemming from the conjunction of low water offer (i.e., precipitation) and high water demand (i.e., water lost to the atmosphere as water vapor from soil via evaporation and from plants through transpiration). Drylands' precipitation is highly variable through the year and occurs in infrequent, discrete, and largely unpredictable events. In turn, the high evaporative demand of the atmosphere, resulting from high air temperatures, low humidity, and abundant solar radiation, determines that water availability is the dominant controlling factor for biological processes such as plant growth and herbivore productivity. Thus drylands, though not barren, are ecosystems of low and highly variable productivity capable of limited human settlement and vulnerable to anthropogenic disturbance.

The proximate causes of desertification are complex and vary from region to region. The European Mediterranean region has a long history of human misuse. War, urbanization, farming, and tourism have, over the years, altered vegetation to such an extent that, at present, virtually no natural vegetation exists there and soil erosion is ubiquitous. In contrast, Australian drylands have experienced extensive degradation only recently. The introduction of domestic livestock by Europeans in the late 1880s, together with the fences used to concentrate these animals and the suppression of fire, drastically reduced the abundance of perennial grasses, leaving more soil exposed to erosion by water or wind, and triggered shrub encroachment. In the Sahelian region of Africa, where the concept of desertification was first coined at the beginning of the 20th century, the replacement of the original vegetation by crops, the increase of grazing pressure over the remaining lands, and the collection of wood for fuel resulted in a reduction of the biological or economic productivity of the land. In particular, inappropriate use of heavy machinery, deficient irrigation schemes, and grazing management practices led to soil erosion, salinization, and overgrazing.

Any attempt to assess the impact of desertification on human societies should first acknowledge the difference between the ways water-limited ecosystems shape the functioning of social systems and the effects of desertification itself. Desertification imposes an additional constraint on human well-being by further reducing the limited ecosystem goods (e.g., food, timber, water) and services (e.g., soil maintenance, erosion control, carbon sequestration) that drylands provide. Failure to address this difference would lead to an overestimation of the desertification effects. Additionally, the manifestations of desertification vary widely, depending on the capacity of each country to mitigate its impacts. For example, in Africa it resulted in declining productivity and intensifying food insecurity and widespread famines, whereas in the Mediterranean region desertification seriously threatens water supply, while many regions of northern Europe are experiencing an increase in dust deposition due to north African soil erosion. In poor countries with a large proportion of their territory in arid and semiarid regions, desertification may trigger a downward spiral where a significant amount of a nation's human and financial resources are devoted to combating past desertification effects, leaving less available to invest in health, education, industry, and governmental institutions. The ultimate precarious social conditions thus developed generally lead to migrations, exacerbating urban sprawl, and may bring about internal and cross-boundary social, ethnic, and political strife.

Approaches to the desertification problem broadly fall into two competing perspectives: the predominant global environmental management (GEM) discourse and the populist discourse. Whereas the former discourse rests on neoliberal values and Malthusian thinking, the latter has its philosophical roots in the self-reliant advocacy derived from the dependency schools of the 1970s and 1980s. The GEM discourse depicts overpopulation in drylands as the main problem leading to the degradation of the ecosystems on which they depend. As seen in the GEM discourse, the global problem of desertification requires a global solution. Therefore, GEM supporters promote top-down, interventionist and technocentrist solutions implemented through international institutions and conventions, such as the UN Convention to Combat Desertification. On the contrary, the populist discourse—populist in the sense that it positively portrays the acts of local people—emphasizes that the marginalization of smallholders and pastoralists started during the colonial period and was subsequently deepened by global capitalism, transnational corporations, and northern consumers as the principal causes of land overexploitation and degradation. International assistance in the form of debt per nature exchanges or technological transferences is regarded as part of the problem itself. Rather, the populist discourse focuses on local or traditional knowledge and community-based action as major sources to overcome environmental problems. However, despite its diametrically opposed explanations of the desertification problem, neither discourse denies an impending crisis caused by desertification.

Why, almost a century after its first detection, does desertification continue to be among the most important environmental problems faced by humankind? Though no single answer exists, there are some arguments to sketch an answer. Undoubtedly the inherent complexity of the desertification phenomenon hampers almost every phase of the sequence leading to the mitigation or control of an environmental problem (i.e., first detection, general recognition, agreement on regulation). For instance, a long period elapsed between when French foresters first perceived what they called "the desert advance" and the widespread diffusion of the desertification tragedy that took place in the Sahelian region of Africa after a series of drought years at the beginning of the 1970s; today improvements in our understanding of rangelands functioning and climatic variability allow

for faster detection and prevention. These advances show that vegetation dynamics in drylands may remain seemingly unaffected by an increase in land use pressure until there is a sudden shift to a lower-productivity stable state, with stochastic climate events, such as severe droughts, acting as triggers. Additionally, incomplete or inadequate scientific knowledge, together with the urgent need of integrative solutions for the Sahelian drama, may have driven actors to resort to the first workable options, leading to erroneous regulations at that time. However, regulations of this kind are not dependent on scientific knowledge alone but also on political pressure mechanisms. Thus an explanation of the failure to achieve sound regulation needs to consider political issues as well.

The predominance of the GEM discourse, despite the poor performance of top-down solutions to "unsustainable" resource management, can be explained by its convenience for the interests of three main groups involved in the desertification issue: national governments, international aid donors, and scientists. National governments benefit not only from foreign financial aid but also from the use of desertification as the basis for severely repressive social control. International donors and institutions find the problem of desertification a reason unto itself for their involvement, whereas scientists may highlight the global nature and severity of the desertification problem as a means to obtain research funds. On the contrary, the bottom-up approaches promoted by the populist discourse do not fit the terms and conditions of bilateral and multilateral funding and instead stress the principles of participation and decentralization.

It is apparent that the progress achieved in our comprehension of desertification has not been matched by an improvement in the regulations aimed at mitigating its consequences. While the accumulation of knowledge generated during the past decades provides evidence against both discourses' main tenets, they nonetheless remain influential in the political and scientific arenas. Future contributions to the solution of the desertification problem require the synthesis of recent social and ecological advances into a new synthetic framework that overcomes the constraints upon the solutions imposed by the GEM and populist discourses. Social scientists hope that a new desertification paradigm—that is, the dryland development paradigm, which represents a convergence of insights from both discourses—is emerging.

Santiago R. Verón

See also Deforestation; Ecosystem; Environmental Degradation

Further Readings

Adger, W. Neil, Tor A. Benjaminsen, Katrina Brown, and Hanne Svarstad. 2001. "Advancing a Political Ecology of Global Environmental Discourses." *Development and Change* 32:681–715.

Herrmann, Stefanie M. and Charles F. Hutchinson. 2005. "The Changing Contexts of the Desertification Debate." *Journal of Arid Environments* 63:538–55.

Reynolds, James F. and D. Mark Stafford-Smith. 2002. *Global Desertification: Do Humans Create Deserts?* Berlin: Dahlem University Press.

Verón, Santiago R., José M. Paruelo, and Martín Oesterheld. 2006. "Assessing Desertification." *Journal of Arid Environments* 66:751–63.

DETERRENCE PROGRAMS

Deterrence programs rest on the belief that society can reduce crime by taking action that makes it more difficult for a criminal to commit a crime or by developing punishment that is so severe that an individual will not commit the crime so as to avoid the stated punishment. Philosophers during the latter part of the 18th century originated this belief. Jeremy Bentham stated in his "Utilitarianism" that people, after reviewing the benefits and possible detriments of committing a crime, will always seek pleasure and avoid pain. Cesare Beccaria echoed Bentham's words in his "On Crime and Punishment" essay, in which he stated that people want to achieve pleasure and avoid pain. Therefore, to deter crime, the pain administered as punishment for the crime must be in a proportionate amount to offset the pleasure obtained from the crime. Beccaria also taught that the certainty and swiftness of the punishment is even more important than the level of severity of the punishment in deterring crime, thus making the stated purpose of punishment to be the prevention of crime.

General deterrence is the belief that effective public action reduces crime within the general population. If people fear being caught and punished for committing a crime, they will not commit the crime. The fear of apprehension is tied to the certainty of being caught and the swiftness of the trial and punishment, as much as it is to the severity of the punishment. When people believe that they are not going to be caught for committing a crime, they have little incentive to obey the law. Therefore, if a society can increase the certainty of apprehension and punishment, it can logically expect a reduction in the amount of crime.

Specific deterrence is the belief that, for certain crimes, if the chance of being caught and convicted is great enough or the punishment is severe enough, the rate for that specific crime will be reduced. This design includes harsher punishment for specific crimes that the public finds to be especially offensive and for repeat offenders. Whereas many believe that the severity of punishment will decrease crime, studies show that the correlation between the severity of punishment and crime reduction is not proportional in relation to crime rates.

Incapacitation is an action that eliminates the possibly of a crime being committed. A criminal cannot commit the crime if the methods, the opportunity, or the tools needed to commit the crime are eliminated. Such deterrence programs may take a number of different forms: incarceration, capital punishment, or police activity.

Selective incapacitation is a deterrence program based on the premise that a small number of offenders commit a large amount of crime. If society can eliminate the opportunity to commit crime for this selective group of offenders, then the crime rate will decrease. One example of this type of program is the Supervision for Life Program, now existing in many states for sex offenders. Parole authorities supervise convicted sex offenders even after they complete their periods of incarceration. The program rests on the belief that such extended supervision will reduce the opportunity of the sex offender to re-offend.

Incarceration is the primary method of incapacitation used in the United States. Because U.S. culture places great value on freedom of movement, the greatest deprivation that society can inflict as punishment is to imprison someone. Public officials express the belief that, as the number of imprisoned criminals increases, a corresponding drop in the crime rate follows. Today, more than 2.2 million people are in federal, state, and local correctional institutions. Although a causal relationship is still unproven, since the use of imprisonment for felons has increased, the crime rate has, on average, dropped each year since 1990. In addition, the belief that strong punishment reduces crime led to enactment of mandatory sentencing laws in every state. The "three strikes and you're out" law for repeat offenders operates on the assumption that offenders will make a stronger effort to stay within the law and avoid a third conviction if that conviction means an automatic life sentence.

The most commonly recognized deterrence program is capital punishment, the ultimate form of punishment. During the U.S. colonial period, the death penalty was the punishment for more than 245 different types of crime. Over the years the public's attitude toward capital punishment and findings from additional criminal justice research led to reduced application of the death penalty to crimes of murder at the state level and treason at the federal level. Public support for the death penalty appears to be based more on the issue of revenge than a general belief that capital punishment really is a deterrent.

Another form of deterrence program is police activity. Many people believe that the simple presence of additional police will reduce crime because criminals will be less likely to commit a crime if they are aware of a police presence. However, studies show that mere presence is not as effective as directive assignment or a change in police tactics. However, the redeployment of police resources to specific troubled areas reduces crime in those areas if the police officers enforce the laws aggressively. Another approach, *community policing,* encourages police officers to patrol on foot or on bikes to reduce the isolation between officers in cars and the community. Improved communication between officers and community members has reduced crime rates in select neighborhoods because it enlists the help of the community in preventing and solving crimes, which in turn increases the chances of apprehension of the criminal. Also, the increased use of guns and the growing amount of violence in life has made gun control into a major deterrence program. Officials believe that by reducing the number of firearms in the community, the number of murders, particularly of young people, will decrease. Many states have enacted legislation to reduce the number of firearms and to restrict those who can possess firearms.

Raymond R. Rainville

See also Community Corrections; Community Crime Control; Crime

Further Readings

Champion, Dean J. 2004. *Corrections in the United States.* 4th ed. Upper Saddle River, NJ: Prentice Hall.

———. 2007. *Probation, Parole, and Community Corrections.* 6th ed. Upper Saddle River, NJ: Prentice Hall.

Dunham, Roger G. and Paul F. Cromwell, eds. 2001. *Crime & Justice in America: Present Realities and Future Prospects.* 2nd ed. Upper Saddle River, NJ: Prentice Hall.

Fairchild, Ericka and Harry R. Dammer. 2005. *Comparative Criminal Justice Systems.* 2nd ed. Belmont, CA: Wadsworth.

Kane, Robert J. 2006. "On the Limits of Social Control: Structural Deterrence and the Policing of Suppressible Crimes." *Justice Quarterly* 23(2):186–213.

DEVIANCE

Generally speaking, deviance is behavior that a group or society considers inappropriate. Approaches to deviance are primarily biological, psychological, or sociological. Typically, biological and psychological approaches view deviance as a result of a defect or character flaw within the individual. Sociological explanations accept that individuals have free choice but emphasize that often societal forces shape one's choices, including the choice to engage in deviant behavior.

Every group or society attempts to regulate its members' behavior and actions through norms of acceptable and unacceptable behavior. Such general norms, often classified as folkways or mores, with the latter deemed more important and carrying strict penalties for violators, find enforcement through both positive and negative sanctions. Positive sanctions are rewards for acceptable behavior, while negative sanctions are punishments for undesirable behavior.

Because of the highly relative nature of societal norms from society to society and through time, deviance is a highly relative concept. For example, U.S. society today does not view premarital intercourse by a female as a violation of significant norms and thus cares little for any punishment. More traditional cultures, such as in the Middle East, consider this as highly deviant behavior punishable by death, even if government criminal laws may prohibit such punishment. Various studies show that the public considers a wide range of behaviors as deviant, depending on the respondents' culture and socioeconomic status.

White-Collar and Corporate Crime

Deviance exists at all socioeconomic levels. Typically, property crimes correlate more often with the lower class, and white-collar and corporate crime is more characteristic of the middle and upper classes. White-collar crime refers to the violation of law by individuals of high social position as part of their day-to-day professional activities. Typical types of white-collar crime include insider trading and financial fraud and also can include an attorney who deliberately over-bills clients or doctors ordering unnecessary tests for fees. The most popular examples in the media focus on the illegal activities of corporate executives who defraud their own companies, the public, and often the government. Enron's top executives provided an extreme example in which fraudulent activities led to the ultimate collapse of one of the largest U.S. corporations.

Corporate crime differs from white-collar crime in that the corporation as an institution engages in deliberate violations of law. Victims of such crime include consumers, government, and employees. Common examples of corporate crime include environmental pollution through inappropriate disposal of waste, the sale of products known to be unsafe, and various forms of financial fraud. In extreme cases corporations have even violated international laws governing national sovereignty to protect their financial interests when threatened. For example, International Telephone & Telegraph in the 1970s collaborated with the Central Intelligence Agency to overthrow the democratically elected government of Salvador Allende in Chile. It then installed Augusto Pinochet, one of Latin America's most brutal dictators.

Both white-collar and corporate crime is committed primarily for financial gain. What distinguishes these types of deviance from others is that the perpetrators often do not see themselves as committing crimes. Rather, they see themselves as industry innovators persecuted for their business success. Ex-Enron chief executive officer Jeffrey Skilling, convicted of fraud and insider trading, consistently characterized his activities as innovative rather than illegal.

Drugs and Deviance

Another major area concerning deviance relates to drug abuse and efforts by law enforcement to curb distribution. Drug abuse is not limited to illegal substances such as heroin and cocaine. It also includes abuse of over-the-counter and prescription drugs, most commonly pain medications. Reasons for drug abuse are varied, ranging from escapism to recreational

use. Drug abuse occurs throughout all socioeconomic levels, but social class is a factor in the type of drug used. For example, professional and middle- to upper-class abusers typically use cocaine, whereas lower-class abusers more commonly use crack, a cocaine derivative.

A major issue related to drug abuse is how society determines which drugs are legal. This question is often not answered based on the actual effects of the drug but rather the perceived harm. For example, tobacco and alcohol are legally available in the United States, but marijuana is not. Compared with other illegal substances, marijuana use is not addictive, and its negative health impacts are more comparable to legalized tobacco than to other illegal drugs. Moreover, marijuana has been found to have various positive effects especially for medicinal use, such as treating loss of appetite associated with cancer therapies, and as an effective painkiller without the severe side effects of prescription drugs. Although tobacco and alcohol kill many times more people than all illegal drugs combined, they are nonetheless legally sold. The reason often given for this contradiction is that society's reaction to a drug is based on perception and moral beliefs rather than scientific evidence.

Functions of Deviance

Not all deviance is necessarily negative. For example, one can be a deviant but for a noble cause, such as those who engaged in civil disobedience to promote racial equality in the 1960s. Émile Durkheim was one of the first social scientists to recognize that deviance could also have functional benefits for society at large. First, identifying deviance sets the moral boundaries between right and wrong. Second, by defining deviance we also define acceptable norms and values. Third, the concept creates a sense of group cohesion in terms of "us versus them." Finally, deviant behavior often functions as a mechanism for change by challenging existing ways of thinking. For example, art is often shocking in that it challenges our way of thinking about various issues.

Major Perspectives

Historically, people viewed deviance as a result of demonic possession, biological defects, and psychological problems. Seventeenth-century Salem, Massachusetts, residents saw lesbians and assertive women as deviants, attributing their behavior to witchcraft or demonic position, and so burned them to death. In late 19th-century Italy, Cesare Lombroso, a physician, hypothesized that deviance had biological origins. As such, he believed that deviants could be identified by common physical characteristics, such as low foreheads. Lombroso reached these conclusions by examining the body types of prison populations without realizing that such traits were common in the general population. By the mid-20th century, William Sheldon believed criminality could be predicted by body structure. In contrast, psychologists identify internal psychological problems as the cause of deviance, but in the second half of the 20th century, sociological explanations of deviant behavior became more widely accepted.

Positivist Perspectives

The positivist perspective, generally associated with the natural sciences and law enforcement, defines deviance as intrinsically real and makes three assumptions about it. The first is absolutism, the belief that something intrinsically real regarding the deviants' behavior sets them apart from conventional society. Second is objectivism, the reality that deviance can be objectively studied and quantified, such as with statistical police reports. Third is determinism, the belief that variables outside of the deviant's control will cause the deviant act. Examples of positivist theories would include Robert Merton's strain theory, Edwin Sutherland's social learning theory, and control theory, exemplified by Hirschi's social bond and self-control theory.

Strain Theory

This positivist theory exemplifies the sociological perspective called structural-functionalism. Merton had argued that every society encourages its citizens to pursue certain legitimate goals, such as wealth, with corresponding legitimate means, such as obtaining an education and a career. However, some people may experience a disconnect between the legitimate means and goals and thus experience strain, prompting five modes of adaptation (responses). First is conformity, when the goals and means are accepted (e.g., a college graduate pursuing wealth through a career). Second is innovation, where a person "innovates" new illegitimate means toward the goal (e.g., becoming a drug dealer or prostitute). Third is ritualism, by which

a person accepts the means but cares little about the goal (e.g., doing enough to keep a job without extra effort or interest in obtaining promotions and bonuses). Fourth is retreatism, where the individual rejects all legitimate means and goals, (e.g., by becoming a hermit or severe drug user). Fifth is rebellion, when a person rejects both means and goals and replaces them with his or her own alternative set (e.g., the hippies of the 1960s who rejected American materialism in favor of a natural way of life).

Social Learning Theory

Differential association is an interactionist sociological perspective which treats deviance as a socially learned behavior through interaction with deviants. Edwin Sutherland argued that individuals associating more with people who have deviant ideas than with conformists are more likely to become deviant themselves. This is more likely to occur within small primary groups. Associating with deviants is only a first step, however. A person must also identify with the deviants and act accordingly before becoming one of them.

Control Theory

Control theory argues that conformity results from social controls placed on the individual by society. Travis Hirschi argued that everyone has an innate tendency to deviate from social norms. However, if our bond to society is strong, we will choose to conform. Accordingly, people bond to society in four ways, namely (1) attachment to conventional people; (2) commitment to conformity by investing in conventional activities such as an education; (3) involvement in conventional activities, which reduces the time available for other activities; and (4) a belief in the validity of the existing social rules.

Constructionist Perspectives

This more recent perspective, which emerged in the 1960s, sees deviant behavior as a social construct, determined by how society reacts to certain behaviors, which in and of themselves are not intrinsically bad or good, such as getting a tattoo. Constructionists also make three assumptions regarding the nature of deviance. First is relativism, the belief that deviance is not intrinsically real but rather a socially imposed label upon that behavior. Second is subjectivism, the idea that there is nothing objective regarding deviant behavior, thereby requiring its study from the subjective perspective of the deviants themselves. Third is voluntarism, a view of deviant behavior as a result of free will without external causes. Examples of constructionist theories include labeling, relativist, phenomenological, and power theory.

Labeling Theory

Labeling theory fits within the sociological perspective of symbolic interactionism. This theory argues that what is important is neither the cause nor the deviant act in itself but the meaning that people attach to it, who applies the label, and the resultant consequences on the labeled and labelers. According to this theory, those with power define and impose the label of deviant or conformist on others who may or may not actually deserve it. The labeled, in turn, may eventually come to accept the deviant label in a self-fulfilling prophecy. A person who commits an initial deviant act (primary deviation) will face societal sanctions even though the person may not see himself or herself as a deviant at the time. If the person repeats the behavior (secondary deviation), society will impose harsher penalties and eventually stigmatize the violator as a deviant. The violator may eventually come to accept the label and continue the expected deviant behavior.

Conflict, Marxist, and Power Theory

Conflict theorists argue that deviance results from differences in either social class or culture. Marxists believe that capitalism, as an economic system and in its coercive control over the working class, induces deviant behavior caused by alienation from production, society, and oneself. Conflict theorists maintain that the wealthy and powerful elite of a society define as deviant any behavior that poses a threat to their wealth or privileged social position. For example, laws protecting private property benefit the rich and their extensive wealth more than they do the working class, who may not have any property. Power theorists argue that the extent of one's power determines the type of deviant action. For example, the powerful—encountering weaker social controls—have a greater deviant opportunity because of their skills and position in society. Combined with higher expectations of success, this may cause feelings of relative deprivation and a stronger deviant motivation. Thus the powerful

are more likely to engage in more profitable white-collar and corporate crime. The powerless, who face greater social controls and who have fewer skills and lower positions, are more likely to engage in less profitable blue-collar crime like robbery.

Deviance is difficult to define because of the relative nature of societal norms governing behavior. In general, a high social consensus exists regarding some forms of deviance, such as murder and rape. In these cases, the focus tends to be placed on prevention, deterrence, and containment of the deviant. In other instances, a lower degree of social consensus exists as to what *is* deviant. These cases generally involve behaviors regulated by informal codes of everyday behavior, such as cell phone use in public places.

John Asimakopoulos

See also Alienation; Anomie; Corporate Crime; Crime; Differential Association; Drug Abuse; Illegitimate Opportunity Structures; Labeling Theory; Pornography; Social Bond Theory; Social Constructionist Theory; Social Control; Stigma; Strain Theory; Terrorism; Victimless Crimes; White-Collar Crime

Further Readings

Akers, Ronald L. and Gary F. Jensen, eds. 2003. *Social Learning Theory and the Explanation of Crime: A Guide for the New Century.* New Brunswick, NJ: Transaction.

Becker, Howard S. 1953. "Becoming a Marijuana User." *American Journal of Sociology* 59:235–42.

———. 1997. *Outsiders.* New York: Free Press.

Braithwaite, John. 1989. *Crime, Shame and Reintegration.* New York: Cambridge University Press.

Chambliss, William. 1973. "The Saints and the Roughnecks." *Society* 11:24–31.

Curra, John. 1999. *The Relativity of Deviance.* Thousand Oaks, CA: Sage.

Gaylord, Mark S. 1987. *Edwin Sutherland and the Origins of Differential Association Theory.* New Brunswick, NJ: Transaction.

Goffman, Erving. [1963] 1986. *Stigma: Notes on the Management of Spoiled Identity.* New York: Simon & Schuster.

Hirschi, Travis. 2001. *Causes of Delinquency.* New Brunswick, NJ: Transaction.

Lilly, Robert J., Francis T. Cullen, and Richard A. Ball. 2006. *Criminological Theory.* 4th ed. Thousand Oaks, CA: Sage.

Martin, Clarence Augustus. 2006. *Understanding Terrorism: Challenges, Perspectives, and Issues.* 2nd ed. Thousand Oaks, CA: Sage.

McLean, Bethany and Peter Elkind. 2003. *Smartest Guys in the Room: The Amazing Rise and Scandalous Fall of Enron.* New York: Portfolio.

Merton, Robert K. 1968. *Social Theory and Social Structure.* New York: Free Press.

DIFFERENTIAL ASSOCIATION

Edwin Sutherland's theory of differential association, the first learning theory of crime, continues to stimulate research today. In 1947, Sutherland stated the theory as a set of nine propositions, which introduced three concepts—normative conflict, differential association, and differential group organization—that explain crime at the levels of the society, individual, and group.

Societal Level: Normative Conflict

For Sutherland, primitive, undifferentiated societies are characterized by harmony, solidarity, and consensus over basic values and beliefs. Such societies have little conflict over appropriate behaviors. They also have little crime. With the industrial revolution, societies developed with advanced divisions of labor, market economies, and inevitably conflict. These societies are characterized by specialization rather than similarity, coercion rather than harmony, conflict rather than consensus. They have high rates of crime. Sutherland hypothesized that high crime rates are due to normative conflict, in which groups conflict over the appropriateness of the law. Some groups define the law as rules to be followed under all circumstances; others define the law as rules to be violated under certain circumstances. When normative conflict is absent in a society, crime rates are low; when it is pervasive, crime rates are high. Thus crime is ultimately rooted in normative conflict.

Individual Level: Differential Association

The differential association process provides a social psychological explanation of how normative conflict translates into individual criminal acts. Criminal behavior is learned through communication in an intimate group, and the content of learning includes two important elements. First are the requisite skills and techniques for committing crime, which can range from complicated, specialized skills of insider trading to the simple, readily available skills of purse snatching. Such techniques are a necessary but insufficient condition of crime.

Second are definitions favorable and unfavorable to crime. These are motives, verbalizations, or rationalizations that make crime justified or unjustified. For example, definitions favorable to income tax fraud include "Everyone cheats on their taxes" and "The government has no right to tax its citizens." Definitions favorable to drunk driving include "I can drive fine after a few beers" and "I only have a couple of miles to drive home." Definitions favorable to violence include "If your manhood is threatened, you have to retaliate" and "Sometimes in the heat of the moment, you can't help yourself." These definitions favorable to crime help organize and justify a criminal line of action in a particular situation. They are offset by definitions unfavorable to crime, such as "Income tax fraud deprives citizens of important programs that benefit society," "Turn the other cheek," "Friends don't let friends drink and drive," and "Any violation of the law is wrong." Some definitions pertain to specific offenses only (e.g., drunk driving), others refer to a class of offenses (e.g., fraud), and still others refer to virtually all law violation. Definitions are not merely ex post facto rationalizations of crime but rather operate to justify committing or refraining from crime.

Sutherland identified four modalities on which definitions vary in importance (weight): (1) frequency (the number of times a definition is presented), (2) duration (the length of time of exposure to a definition), (3) priority (the earlier a definition is presented in one's life), and (4) intensity (the more intense one's relationship with or the more prestigious is the person presenting the definition). Therefore, the individual-level hypothesis of differential association states that individuals will engage in criminal behavior if the following three conditions are met: (1) They have learned the requisite skills and techniques for committing crime. (2) They have learned an excess of weighted definitions favorable to crime over unfavorable to crime. (3) They have the objective opportunity to commit the crime. If all three conditions are present and crime does not occur, or a crime occurs in the absence of all three conditions, the theory would be wrong and in need of revision. Thus, in principle, the theory can be falsified.

Group Level: Differential Social Organization

Differential social organization—the extent to which a group or society is organized against crime versus organized in favor of crime—explains how normative conflict translates into group rates of crime. Here, Sutherland reconceptualizes Clifford R. Shaw and Henry D. McKay's concepts of social disorganization (weak organization against crime) and cultural transmission (strong organization favoring crime). Shaw and McKay observe that disorganization arises in inner cities when rapid urban growth undermines informal social controls by increasing mobility, poverty, family disruption, immigration, and physical deterioration. Residents tend to be transient, fail to develop a sense of community, and consequently, are unable to build strong and linked families, schools, and neighborhood associations. Such social disorganization, in which a community is unable to control local youth, is equivalent to "weak organization against crime."

But disorganization is only half of the equation. The other half is "organization in favor of crime," which consists of structures that foster criminal behavior—such as cultural transmission, in which older street gangs in disorganized areas transmit a delinquent tradition to younger groups, resulting in high rates of delinquency across generations of youth. Differential social organization refers to both forms of organization and can be applied to any group to determine its crime rate. Thus, compared with suburban neighborhoods, inner-city neighborhoods are weakly organized against street crimes and strongly organized in favor of such crimes. Compared with the United States, Japan is strongly organized against violence and weakly organized in favor of violence. Moreover, differential social organization is not static, and its dynamics can be explained by theories of collective action.

Differential social organization explains group crime rates by determining the availability of definitions favorable and unfavorable to crime within a group. Groups strongly organized in favor of crime and weakly organized against crime will present an abundance of definitions favorable to crime and few definitions unfavorable to crime (and vice versa). Members of such groups have a high probability of learning an excess of definitions of crime (and vice versa), which can determine their criminality. Thus

the group- and individual-level explanations are inextricably linked.

Ross L. Matsueda

See also Crime; Crime Rates; Cultural Criminology; Illegitimate Opportunity Structures; Juvenile Delinquency; Social Disorganization; Subcultures; Theory; Violent Crime

Further Readings

Akers, Ronald L. 1998. *Social Learning and Social Structure.* Boston: Northeastern University Press.

Matsueda, Ross L. 1988. "The Current State of Differential Association Theory." *Crime & Delinquency* 34:277–306.

———. 2006. "Differential Social Organization, Collective Action, and Crime." *Crime, Law and Social Change* 46:3–33.

Sutherland, Edwin H. 1947. *Principles of Criminology.* Philadelphia: Lippincott.

DIGITAL DIVIDE

Digital divide is a metaphor for the cleft between people with access to technology and those without. Although the term originated in the mid-1990s to describe differences in technological infrastructure of U.S. schools, it has grown to describe various forms of alienation predicated on class, race, and national identity. Some analysts see a problem rooted in access, or the lack thereof, to computers and Internet services, whereas others suggest a more persistent gulf between developed and developing nations. Still others deny the existence of a divide at all, arguing that market forces have created an abundance of services and products that serve to render the issue moot. Finally, some authors maintain a "change over time" approach, pointing out that although the term may have had some cogency when it was coined, various government and social initiatives are working to narrow the divide.

A 2005 study by the Pew Internet & American Life Project found that two thirds of U.S. adults go online, and white, educated, affluent people without a child living at home are more likely to have regular access to the Internet from home. Older citizens, African

Americans, and the less educated are not as likely to go online, although only one in five reported never having been online at all. The report suggested that the current digital divide resides with access speed; connection speed is a more important factor in Internet use than experience. The report also suggested three degrees of Internet access: cold, tepid, and hot. The first group has no access and does not go online, the second has a tenuous or modest connection to the Internet, and the third is considered highly wired.

Some critics contend that figures such as those reported by the Pew Center are important but miss the deeper issues of understanding and social inclusion. Despite well-meaning attempts to improve people's lives through the introduction of information and communication technology, meaningful access entails much more than just the provision of computers and Internet connections. Rather, a complex interaction among variables, including physical, digital, human, and social resources and relationships, must be considered as critical components to the problem of, and the solution to, the disparity between technological haves and have-nots.

An international study released in 2005 by the UN Conference on Trade and Development combines many of these arguments. The report finds that wealthy, predominantly Caucasian (and some Asian), relatively educated countries do better than poorer countries, especially those in Africa. While the technological rift today may be due to the presence or absence of, and access to, dependable, high-bandwidth connections, information and communication technology is slowly becoming more available and accessible to all. Case studies of China, Chile, Botswana, Singapore, India, and the United States have explored how various social, institutional, and governmental strategies interacted to create diverse solutions and equally varied results to technological disparities. Although market-based solutions have been important tools in bridging the digital divide, the report suggests that private enterprise solutions may have reached the point of diminishing returns, and new solutions need to be explored to continue the advances already under way.

Optimists offer a market-based panacea to take on the assumption of the growing alienation between the well-connected and those who are not, typically citing the prevalence of free or almost free hardware to Internet connections as proof that the divide is a myth and attempts to reconcile it are wasted. Most studies,

however, suggest this argument reflects more wishful thinking than rigorous analysis. When one third of Americans lack access to the educational and journalistic information provided by information and communication technology and when developed and developing countries support radically different technology infrastructures, alienation within and between nations is likely.

Robert Harris

See also Cyberspace; Social Change

Further Readings

National Telecommunications and Information Administration. 1999. "Falling through the Net: Defining the Digital Divide." Retrieved December 8, 2007 (http://www.ntia.doc.gov/ntiahome/fttn99/).

Pew Internet & American Life Project. "Reports: Digital Divisions." Retrieved December 8, 2007 (http://www.pewinternet.org/PPF/r/165/report_display.asp).

United Nations Conference on Trade and Development. "The Digital Divide Report: ICT Diffusion Index 2005." Retrieved December 8, 2007 (http://www.unctad.org/en/docs/iteipc20065_en.pdf).

Warschauer, Mark. 2003. *Technology and Social Inclusion: Rethinking the Digital Divide.* Cambridge, MA: MIT Press.

DILLINGHAM FLAW

The Dillingham Flaw is a relatively new concept to describe a centuries-old phenomenon of faulty logic when nativists misinterpret and react to the presence of immigrants in their midst. It ignores diversity and assumes homogeneity, thereby setting a framework for negativity about newcomers.

The term draws its name from a special commission created in 1907 by President Theodore Roosevelt to look into the "immigration problem." Chaired by Senator William P. Dillingham of Vermont, the commission, over a 4-year period, listened to testimony from civic leaders, educators, social scientists, and social workers and made onsite visits to Ellis Island and New York's Lower East Side. In 1911, the commission issued a 41-volume report of its findings. Unfortunately, the report was flawed in its application and interpretation of the data that the commission had so tirelessly collected. Social scientists agree that the commission erred in its use of simplistic categories for diverse immigrant groups. Their second error was in an unfair comparison of "old" and "new" immigrants despite the changed structural conditions and longer time interval that previous immigrants had to assimilate and achieve some measure of economic security.

Quite simply then, the term *Dillingham Flaw* refers to inaccurate comparisons based on simplistic categorizations and anachronistic observations. This erroneous thinking can occur in assessments of the past, present, or future.

The Past

Applying modern classifications or sensibilities to a time when they did not exist, or, if they did, had a different form or meaning is one version of the Dillingham Flaw. In this instance, we utilize our modern perceptions to explain a past that its contemporaries viewed quite differently. For example, today's term *British* refers collectively to the people of Great Britain (the English, Welsh, Scots, and Scots-Irish). However, in the 18th century, *British* had the much narrower meaning of only the English, and for good reason. The English, Scots, and Scots-Irish may have been English-speaking, but significant cultural and religious differences existed among them and they did not view each other as "similar." For us to presume that the colonial British, even just the colonial English, were a single cohesive entity and thus the 13 English colonies were homogeneous would be to fall victim to the Dillingham Flaw.

Similarly, we fall into this trap if we speak about either African slaves or Native Americans as single, monolithic entities. Such ethnocentric generalizations fail to acknowledge that these groups actually consisted of diverse peoples with distinctive languages, cultures, and behavior patterns. Similarly, European immigrants were not alike, despite their collective groupings by mainstream society. Instead, all of these groups—African American, Native American, and immigrant—were diverse peoples with many distinctions that set them apart from one another.

The Present

Similar misconceptions can, and often do, occur in one's own time. Here, the faulty logic about the past

just described is used to evaluate the present. Working from a false premise about past rapid assimilation and cultural homogeneity, individuals employ what they believe is an objective comparison with the present scene, which they find troubling in its heterogeneity and supposedly nonassimilating groups. Like the 1907 presidential commission (mentioned earlier in this entry), they are susceptible to mistaken impressions about a "threat" posed by recent immigrants whose presence and behavior they view as different from earlier immigrants.

The most common examples are expressed views that today's steadily increasing ranks of Africans, Asians, Hispanics, and Muslims in the United States present an unprecedented challenge to an integrative society. Reacting to the increasing presence—even in many nonurban settings—of nonwhite newcomers speaking a foreign tongue, including many from a non-Judeo-Christian background, nativists view with alarm these demographic changes. Such fears are echoes of those raised about earlier groups, such as the racist responses to the physical appearance of southern Europeans or the anti-Semitic reactions to eastern European Jews. In reality, studies consistently reveal rapid English language acquisition among all immigrants groups and higher naturalization rates among non-Westerners.

The Future

Using oversimplified categorizations and imposing present-day sensibilities—the essence of the Dillingham Flaw—also can occur when individuals engage in demographic projections. For example, the U.S. Census Bureau projects that Hispanics will compose about one fourth of the total U.S. population in 2050. Given past patterns and current trends, however, we cannot be certain that today's group categories, such as Hispanic, will still be valid by then.

Currently, most white Americans bear witness to mixed European ancestry, but two generations ago, Americans of southern, central, and eastern European backgrounds were far more likely to be of a single national lineage and religion. Their single-group identities evolved into multiple-group identities, as large-scale intermarriages generated such a blending of peoples that "whites" and "European Americans" became synonymous. Further, their mixed heritage is now more likely to be passively acknowledged, except for occasional symbolic celebrations. It is no longer an element of everyday ethnicity, subcultural participation, or minority status.

Each succeeding year shows greater numbers of exogamous marriages among ethnic, racial, and religious groups. Therefore, it is not unreasonable, for example, to suggest—given the annual increase in Hispanics marrying non-Hispanics—that in two generations many of the descendants of today's Hispanic Americans will claim a mixed heritage, partly Hispanic and partly non-Hispanic. Projections that the mid-21st century will find the United States with a one-fourth Hispanic population suggests a demographic categorization by today's realities that may well not fit the reality then.

A similar argument could be made for other groups, as racial intermarriages continue to create a growing multiracial population. Using today's categories for Americans living in 2050 can easily be another unwitting application of the Dillingham Flaw. Projecting our perceptions and the existing social distance between groups onto a distant future carries a presumption that they will remain the same. Our present-day categories may be inadequate or irrelevant to our descendants.

Vincent N. Parrillo

See also Acculturation; Americanization; Assimilation; Nativism; Xenophobia

Further Readings

Parrillo, Vincent N. 1994. "Diversity in America: A Sociohistorical Analysis." *Sociological Forum* 9:523–35.
———. 2008. *Diversity in America.* 3rd ed. Thousand Oaks, CA: Pine Forge.

DISABILITY AND DISABLED

Approximately 54 million people, one in five Americans, have a disability, according to the U.S. Census Bureau. The size of this population group would rank people with disabilities among the largest minority groups in the United States. Disability knows no limitation by race, ethnicity, religion, or gender. It is an experience that touches upon every corner of society. Indeed, as average life spans trend upward, disability prevalence is also increasing as a natural phenomenon of aging. However, people with disabilities remain in the shadows of the general public, largely ignored as people with an undesirable characteristic and condemned to inequality of opportunity. This entry offers insight into the disability identity and its future direction.

Medical Model of Disability

Conventionally, disability refers to an individual's physical or mental limitations. For example, the World Health Organization defines disability as any restriction or lack of ability (resulting from an impairment) to perform an activity in the manner or within the range considered normal for a human being. With the deficiency construed as inherent, biological, and abnormal, the focal point was to repair or mitigate the functional limitation to the extent medically possible. Disability became primarily a challenge for the medical profession, to "cure" people of their physical and mental shortcomings.

Whereas many types of disability cause physical hardship and affect the quality of personal health, most disabilities are relatively benign and manageable with the proper supports. Although the provision of health care is a humane effort that is a foundation of civilization, the well-being of people consists of more than the functionality of their body parts. The narrow and heavy emphasis on the medical aspects of disability created a social understanding and attitude about people's well-being as diminished if they have a disability.

In cases where medical intervention into disabling conditions was limited by research, technology, capacity, or resources, frequently charitable or governmental institutions would attempt to bridge the gap by providing funds. For charitable organizations, a particularly effective means for collecting contributions was appealing to the public's sense of empathy and pity by portraying people with disabilities as victims of natural tragedy. Petitions for support from governmental institutions typically described people with disabilities as unfortunate wards of the state requiring care by society. Collectively, those approaches created a social mind-set that a physical or mental limitation condemns one to a lower standard and quality of life, and their recourse is dependence on society's largesse if they are not medically restored. Educational institutions and employers thus doubt their ability to successfully educate and employ people perceived as below the mainstream of society.

In response, people with disabilities often develop low self-esteem and low expectations for how they may assert themselves in life. Compounding this situation is the fact that members of their families or communities are likely not to share the same condition, removing them from any opportunity for a shared cultural identity with respect to a distinguishing characteristic. Unless people lay claim to a different model of experiencing their disability, they are more likely to become isolated, impoverished, undereducated, and out of place with society.

Social Model of Disability

In 1962, the University of California at Berkeley admitted Ed Roberts and arranged for him to live in the campus medical facility out of concern for his polio-related condition. He had almost no functional movement and was dependent on a respirator. A year before, Ed had been rejected by the California state vocational rehabilitation department as too severely disabled and considered "unemployable."

Ed organized other students with disabilities in a group called "The Rolling Quads." Together, they started a self-determination movement which would radicalize perceptions of people with disabilities and how they perceived themselves. Stating that he was tired of well-meaning noncripples with their stereotypes of what he could or could not do in deciding his life choices, Ed explained his desire for "cripple power," where the disabled would direct their own programs and be able to train other disabled persons to direct new programs. He insisted that achieving independence was not a functional limitation or medical issue but rather a sociological, political, and civil rights one.

In 1972, Ed and others established a community-based self-help program called the Berkeley Center for Independent Living (CIL). The fundamental philosophy of the Berkeley CIL—dignity, consumer direction, peer support, and civil rights advocacy—sparked an independent living movement that has since resulted in nearly 500 CILs throughout the country. The term *center for independent living* is now commonly understood to mean a consumer-controlled, community-based, cross-disability, nonresidential private nonprofit agency that is designed and operated within a local community by individuals with disabilities and provides an array of independent living services.

The independent living movement pushed for the "demedicalization" of disability by shifting from a controlling medical model to an approach of individual empowerment and responsibility for identifying and fulfilling one's own needs. There was growing awareness that environmental and attitudinal issues produced the greatest challenges and barriers to the independence and full participation of people with disabilities, more so than their physical and mental conditions. Solution efforts focused not on people with disabilities but on altering and remedying societal and environmental barriers.

People with disabilities began to view themselves as capable, self-directed, and with opportunity, as opposed to being afflicted, less than normal, victims of external barriers, objects of charity, and passive beneficiaries of governmental support. Evolving society began to view disability as a natural and common human experience, not a tragedy.

As an ironical footnote, in 1975 California Governor Jerry Brown appointed Ed Roberts as the state director of the Vocational Rehabilitation Agency, which originally had refused to serve him as being too severely disabled ever to work.

Civil Rights Movement

In the United States, the disability rights movement emerged in the 1970s as a substantial tool in eradicating the societal and attitudinal barriers afflicting people with disabilities. Modeling the African American and women's civil rights movements, groups of people with disabilities became fierce advocates in gaining the right to be free from discrimination and to pursue equal opportunity. A series of national disability rights laws were enacted:

- Architectural Barriers Act: prohibits architectural barriers in all federally owned or leased buildings.
- Rehabilitation Act: particularly Title V, Sections 501, 503, and 504, prohibits discrimination in federal programs and services and all other programs or services receiving federal funding. Also provides for independent living centers and the Client Assistance Program, an advocacy program for consumers of rehabilitation and independent living services.
- Developmental Disabilities Bill of Rights Act: among other things, establishes protection and advocacy.
- Education of All Handicapped Children Act (Pub. L. No. 94-142): requires free, appropriate public

education in the least restrictive environment possible for children with disabilities. This law is now called the Individuals with Disabilities Education Act.

- Mental Illness Bill of Rights Act: requires protection and advocacy services for people with mental illness.
- The Civil Rights of Institutionalized Persons Act: authorizes the U.S. Attorney General to investigate conditions of confinement at state and local government institutions, such as prisons, jails, pretrial detention centers, juvenile correctional facilities, publicly operated nursing homes, and institutions for people with psychiatric or developmental disabilities.
- Air Carrier Access Act: prohibits discrimination on the basis of disability in air travel and provides for equal access to air transportation services.
- Telecommunications Act: requires manufacturers of telecommunications equipment and providers of telecommunications services to ensure that such equipment and services are accessible to, and usable by, persons with disabilities, if readily achievable.
- Voting Accessibility for the Elderly and Handicapped Act: generally requires polling places across the United States to be physically accessible to people with disabilities for federal elections.
- Fair Housing Amendments Act: prohibits discrimination in housing against people with disabilities and families with children. Also provides for architectural accessibility of certain new housing units, renovation of existing units, and accessibility modifications at the renter's expense.
- Americans with Disabilities Act: provides comprehensive civil rights protection for people with disabilities; closely modeled after the Civil Rights Act and Section 504 of Title V of the Rehabilitation Act and its regulations.

Political Force

People with disabilities have made great strides in recent years, which saw the emergence of nationally recognized disability rights laws that propelled awareness of the desire for people with disabilities for full inclusion in the mainstream of society. Disability advocacy groups, such as the American Association of People with Disabilities, used its several thousand membership base to become a force in promoting political and legislative responsiveness to the issues of people with disabilities.

The disability rights movement is now global, as recently highlighted in March 2007, when the United Nations adopted the Convention on the Protection of the Rights of People with Disabilities. The convention reflects the evolving concept of disability and fully represents the human right of people with disabilities to determine and direct their destinies.

Jeff Rosen

See also Medicalization; Prejudice; Self-Fulfilling Prophecy; Social Constructionist Theory

Further Readings

American Association of People with Disabilities. (http://www.aapd-dc.org/index.php).
Disability Social History Project. (http://www.disability history.org/).
Institute on Disability. (http://bss.sfsu.edu/disability/).
National Council on Disability. (http://www.ncd.gov/).
Smithsonian Museum of American History, the Disability Rights Movement. (http://americanhistory.si.edu/disabilityrights/welcome.html).
UN Enable. (http://www.un.org/esa/socdev/enable/).

DISASTERS

A disaster is an event generating exceptional social and structural disruption characterized by four main elements. First, humans play a significant role in effects of disaster impact. Whether technological (e.g., a nuclear reactor leak) or natural (e.g., a hurricane), humans modify their environment in a manner that may facilitate or hinder the impact of a disaster. Second, disasters have a "before," "during," and "after," as opposed to existing as a singular event or moment in time. Although many commonly think of a disaster as lasting for a specified time, there is a lead time before impact, the impact, and the aftermath. Third, disasters are exceptional in their altering of previous routines of action, interaction, and ritual. By focusing on disasters as exceptions, researchers can assess social change before, during, and after disaster. Finally, disasters are socially and structurally disruptive; they significantly disrupt routine patterns of action as well as the social structures and built environment. In fact, some previous patterns of action and physical structures either change significantly or may no longer return or exist. For this reason, some scholars, such as

Robert Merton and Gary Kreps, have argued that disasters may be social catalysts for change that offer researchers a unique opportunity to understand social action and social structures under extreme pressure over a relatively short duration.

Distinctions of Disaster

A disaster is different from a hazard in that a hazard such as a flood, hurricane, tornado, fire, earthquake, volcanic eruption, or tsunami may occur but have little impact on the social or structural environment. In contrast, a disaster necessitates exceptional social and structural disruption. Thus, if a tornado strikes a pristine forest without social disruption, it is a hazard, but if the same tornado were to later strike a community and generate exceptional social and structural disruption, it is a disaster.

Disaster is uniquely located in the context of social and structural disruption. For example, a complex emergency such as a large traffic accident or a plane crash may result in exceptions to routines, but not to the extent that it constitutes a significant disruption to communities and social structures. Thus authorities and emergency professionals can respond to complex emergencies without adversely impacting most members of a community and social institutions.

On the other hand, a disaster is not sufficiently as large as a catastrophe. In contrast to a disaster, a catastrophe impacts most or all of the community. Local officials are unable to undertake their usual work roles; help from nearby communities cannot be provided due to the scale of impact; most, if not all, of the community's routines are disrupted; the community undergoes a period of prolonged inoperability, and the role of the political institution emerges as increasingly significant in dealing with the catastrophe. Thus disaster may be understood not merely as an exceptional social and structural disruption but as fitting along a continuum ranging in severity from emergencies, to complex emergencies, to disaster, to catastrophe.

History of Disaster

Disaster evolved from two Latin words (*dis* and *astro*), which together roughly mean "formed on a star." In the 16th century, *disaster* made reference to unfavorable negative effects, usually of a personal nature, resulting from a star or planet. However, following the 1775 Lisbon earthquake, the outlook that disaster was an uncontrollable force that humans were powerless against began to change, as the disaster evoked a coordinated state response and a comprehensive plan for reconstruction. Thus some professionals and elites of Western Europe began to view disasters as something humans and societies could attempt to prevent or mitigate through a secular and protoscientific framework.

Despite the acknowledgment of a secular and protoscientific approach, the first known social scientific research on disasters did not occur until 1909 when Eduard Stierlin studied the psychological consequences to survivors of a mining disaster and the 1908 Messina earthquake. Although some disaster research continued through the first half of the 20th century, not until after World War II did a more systematic study of disaster take place. This research began with military-sponsored strategic bombing studies of civilian communities and their responses and continued with the establishment of the first social science disaster institution, the Disaster Research Center, in 1963.

As a research interest within the social sciences, the study of disaster has, until recently, always been at the periphery. This was largely due to the conceptualization of disaster as exceptional and divergent from normative behavior, and thus an area not of considerable interest to most social scientists. However, even in research traditions such as social problems where normative deviance is of considerable interest, disaster had trouble gaining widespread acceptance. For example, Robert Merton and Robert Nisbet's highly influential *Contemporary Social Problems* of 1961 originally featured a well-written and substantive chapter dedicated to the social problem of disasters. In preparation for the second edition, a survey of its readers found the chapter to be the most difficult to teach to students and the least familiar to those in the subfield of social problems. Consequently, disaster was dropped from subsequent editions and, until recently, rarely studied as a social problem. Recent occasions such as the September 11, 2001, attacks on New York and Washington, the Indian Ocean tsunami, and Hurricane Katrina have again provided the opportunity to a larger audience for disaster research within the social sciences. The renewed interest in disaster is indicative of both the changing interests of social scientists and the changing nature of disaster. Because current research emphasizes exceptional social and structural disruption, the potential for additional study of occasions such as terrorist attacks, biological accidents, economic destabilization, or pandemic disease offers an expansion of disaster as well as greater opportunity for social science collaboration.

John Barnshaw

See also Pandemics; Stressors; Terrorism

Further Readings

Dynes, Russell. 2000. "The Dialogue between Voltaire and Rousseau on the Lisbon Earthquake: The Emergence of a Social Science View." *International Journal of Mass Emergencies and Disaster* 18:97–115.

Kreps, Gary. 1992. *The Contributions of Sociology to Disaster Research.* Williamsburg, VA: College of William and Mary.

Perry, Ronald. 2006. "What Is a Disaster?" Pp. 1–15 in *Handbook of Disaster Research,* edited by H. Rodriguez, E. Quarantelli, and R. Dynes. New York: Springer.

Perry, Ronald and Enrico Quarantelli. 2005. *What Is a Disaster? New Answers to Old Questions.* New York: Xlibris.

Qurantelli, Enrico. 1998. *What Is a Disaster? Perspectives on the Question.* New York: Routledge.

DISCRIMINATION

Discrimination is one of the most studied social phenomena within the social sciences because of its serious social, political, economic, psychological, and physical consequences and implications. It is the action of distinguishing and categorizing individuals in a society based on perceived cultural, social, or physical characteristics and subsequently preventing certain categories or groups of people equitable access to social, economic, and political resources.

As with all social constructions, the role of perception is central to the understanding of discrimination, as discriminatory practices differ according to the circumstances in which they occur. For example, in the 19th- and early 20th-century United States, Italian and Irish Americans and immigrants were actively discriminated against. Justification for these discriminatory practices rested in commonly accepted stereotypical perceptions that Irish and Italians were lazy, drunk, dirty members of a budding criminal class and unable and perhaps unwilling to assimilate into U.S. culture.

Yet, in the 21st-century United States, discrimination against these two groups based on such stereotypical perceptions of their ethnicity is almost nonexistent. While the status of Irish and Italian Americans has improved, perhaps because of their assimilation into mainstream U.S. society, others have taken their place. For example, in the post–9/11 climate, most Americans justify the racial profiling of Arab Americans as serving homeland security purposes. Many Americans agree with the existence of "no-fly" lists that actively discriminate against those suspected as terrorists, and they regard the fact that the vast majority are of Arab descent and not affiliated in any way with terrorist organizations as a necessary inconvenience, even if such a list is clearly discriminatory. In fact, after the attacks of 9/11, reported incidences of discrimination and hate crimes against Muslims in the United States increased to such a degree that the Civil Rights Division of the U.S. Department of Justice placed a priority on the prosecution of bias crimes and acts of discrimination against perceived Muslims, including Sikhs and persons of Arab and South Asian descent. And although the status of Irish Americans has significantly improved, prejudicial attitudes toward people of Irish descent in the United Kingdom are still widespread, suggesting once more that discrimination should be understood in specific historical, cultural, economic, and political contexts.

In the United States and other racially and ethnically diverse societies, race and ethnicity are often at the root of discrimination. A partial explanation is the visibility of racial phenotype, but in the United States, another factor is the fact that the nation's social structures and institutions are still experiencing the lingering effects of such racially discriminatory practices as slavery and segregation. Thus, in historically racialized societies like the United States or South Africa, discrimination is an inherent part of their social existence. Discrimination, however, is not only rooted in racial prejudice but in a wide range of social prejudices such as homophobia, sexism, ageism, disability discrimination, and religious intolerance.

The key to understanding the social function of discrimination is marginalization. Although anyone can become a victim of discriminatory practices, ultimately the essence of discrimination lies in power and privilege. Socially marginalized groups in society tend to be the most likely targets of discriminatory practices. This characteristic, with its roots in the perpetuation of power and privilege, makes discrimination of particular relevance to the study of social problems. For instance, historical examination of anti-discrimination laws can provide an analytical framework to examine why and how certain groups in society are disadvantaged and what groups set out to benefit from this marginalization.

The Problem of Power and Privilege

Whereas discrimination is often grounded in political ideology (e.g., religious or sexual discrimination) or opportunity (e.g., scarcity of jobs), in all instances its underlying principle is power, especially the perpetuation of power. Examinations of the roles of power and privilege are essential to the understanding of the social function of discrimination. Only those with social or economic power, the socially dominant groups, have the ability to actively discriminate in ways that prevent individuals or groups of people access to social, economic, or political resources.

Discrimination occurs on two levels: institutional and individual. On the institutional level, discriminatory practices are embedded in the social structures of a society, whereas on the individual level, discrimination takes place during direct interactions among individuals or groups. Unlike individual discrimination, which tends to be overt, intentional, and direct, institutional discrimination is often covert and unintentional, and this invisibility makes it much harder to detect. Standardized testing in schools, for example, may exclude certain historically marginalized groups from succeeding in academic settings. Although the government may not have intentionally established testing standards that are culturally or class biased, in practice these standards tend to have a disproportionate negative effect on ethnic minority students. Furthermore, institutional discrimination often has a generational or cyclical impact on certain ethnic minority groups and therefore its consequences are as severe, if not more so, than for those suffering individual discrimination.

Social scientists often employ the power/privilege framework to provide theoretical explanations of the role of discrimination in society. Three sociological perspectives—structural-functionalism, conflict theory, and symbolic interaction—examine this social phenomenon. Conflict sociology, grounded in Marxist thought, suggests that society is in a constant class struggle for scarce resources. Those controlling economic, political, and cultural resources safeguard their economic and social privilege through discriminatory practices that establish and perpetuate inequality. Elites thus reproduce their own advantages and privileges by limiting the distribution of resources and supporting the dominant value system.

Social classes conflict with each other as they vie for power and economic, social, and political resources. Elites shape societal beliefs to make their unequal privilege appear legitimate and fair, thereby constructing a false consciousness to perpetuate their hegemony. This unquestioned acceptance serves to perpetuate racial or gender privileges in a society. Similarly, the false consciousness inhibits many in the lower classes from questioning the fairness of the economic system and their social status in society. Conflict theorists would argue that inequality is an inevitable consequence of class conflict, due to the economic exploitation built into the social system.

Unlike conflict theorists, sociologists who adhere to the structural-functionalist theoretical approach do not see inequality or discrimination as an unnatural state of society. Functionalists view society as an organism in which all of its elements (social institutions) serve to maintain its stability and thus work toward survival of the society. Although discrimination may be deplorable and has certain dysfunctions, these theorists suggest that it does serve an important social function. For instance, supporters of assimilation theories may believe that marginalization occurs because of certain groups' failure to conform to the normative (cultural) standards and values in a society, a failure that contributes to a lack of social cohesion and, in its most extreme form, to anomie—a state of normlessness. Discrimination, in this case, forces these marginalized groups to conform to the socially accepted standards, morals, and values and thus fosters social (cultural) cohesion. Functionalists may also argue that in a capitalist society, discrimination maintains economic stability by creating and maintaining a cheap manual labor force. Unlike conflict theorists, who argue that, because inequality is built into the social system, only a complete restructuring of society can rid it of social and economic inequality, functionalists are more optimistic. They would point to ethnic groups, such as the Irish, Italians, Japanese, or Korean Americans, who overcame their historical social marginalization through hard work and cultural assimilation. They generally maintain, for example, that if society determines that racial discrimination is no longer socially functional, then the norms regarding its existence will be reevaluated.

Functionalist and conflict theories are structural concepts used to explain the purpose of discrimination by examining its roots in social institutions and structures. However, a micro-level analysis can also serve as a theoretical perspective. Symbolic interaction theorists, for example, focus on the role interpersonal communication plays in the construction of stereotypes and social prejudices. They see society as constantly created and re-created through interactions and subsequent negotiation of meaning. They may, for instance, argue that sexual identities are not biologically constructed but rather learned behaviors or "performances." Thus, from a related perspective, labeling theory, discrimination does not occur because of attributes inherent to marginalized groups but because of dominant groups' reactions to these perceived attributes. Power inequality, therefore, rests in a dominant group's ability to label certain perceived behaviors as deviant and to enforce and perpetuate such labeling through social control and legal enforcement (e.g., implementation of anti-sodomy statutes or anti-miscegenation laws). Symbolic interactionists would thus maintain that discrimination, in this instance, is a socially constructed practice rooted in interaction and perception rather than biological determinism.

Types of Discrimination

In U.S. history, many racial and ethnic groups have been victims of racial discrimination, particularly those "visibly" or racially identifiable. As discussed earlier, discriminatory practices can either express themselves individually (e.g., through hate crimes or the lynching of African Americans during the 19th and 20th centuries) or in an institutionalized way (e.g., by subsequently failing to prosecute those responsible for these lynchings). Other examples of institutionalized discrimination include the enactment of laws barring Native Americans from owning land (1898 Curtis Act), the disenfranchisement of African Americans from voting (until the enactment of the 1965 Voting Rights Act), the barring of Chinese from entering the country (1882 Chinese Exclusion Act), or the classification of Japanese Americans as enemy aliens allowing for their subsequent internment during World War II (under Executive Order 9066). Of course, the United

States does not stand alone in its history of legal and social discriminatory practices against ethnically marginalized groups. Other examples include Germany's treatment of Jewish Europeans, culminating in the Holocaust; South Africa's system of apartheid; the treatment of Muslim citizens during the war in the former Republic of Yugoslavia; the Turkish genocide of Armenians between 1915 and 1917; and the current genocide in the Darfur region in Sudan.

Furthermore, in most countries discrimination based on sexual orientation is still socially acceptable and in some cases legalized. Whereas the Netherlands, Canada, Belgium, and Spain recognize same-sex marriage, same-sex intercourse carries the death penalty in Saudi Arabia, Iran, Mauritania, Yemen, Sudan, and Somalia. Also, in the United States, until 2003 when the Supreme Court ruled that *Bowers v. Hardwick* of 1986 unfairly criminalized "same-sex sodomy," 13 states had prohibited lesbians and gay men from engaging in sexual activities. Same-sex couples, however, still are unable to marry legally in most places, and private schools may deny admission to lesbian or gay students if their same-sex lifestyle conflicts with the school's religious convictions. While many nations have some form of institutionalized discrimination, many countries have recognized and negated discrimination by adopting legislation banning discrimination in employment, housing, and education, as well as legislation on hate crimes.

In the United States, several federal laws prohibit discrimination in employment. For example, Title VII of the Civil Rights Act of 1964 prohibits employment discrimination based on race, color, religion, sex, or national origin in companies consisting of 15 or more employees. Also, the Equal Pay Act of 1963 protects men and women who perform equal work in the same work establishment from sex-based wage discrimination. The Age Discrimination in Employment Act of 1967 protects individuals who are 40 years of age or older from workplace discrimination, and Titles I and V of the Americans with Disabilities Act of 1990 prohibit discrimination in employment against qualified disabled individuals in the private sector and in state and local governments. The Equal Employment Opportunity Commission (EEOC) oversees and coordinates federal equal employment opportunity regulations, practices, and policies and enforces these laws.

Despite some fluctuations, the number of sex-based discrimination charges between 1992 and 2005 remained relatively stable. In 1992, the EEOC received

21,796 sex-based discrimination complaints as compared with more than 25,000 in 1994, 2001, and 2002, and 23,094 in 2005. Last, whereas federal laws still fail to protect lesbian, gay, bisexual, and transgender employees from workplace discrimination, many states offer anti-discrimination protections that are often more expansive than those offered under federal law. Seventeen states and the District of Columbia, for example, have laws protecting gay and lesbian employees from discrimination in privately owned companies.

In the United States and many European countries, significant strides have been made to protect historically marginalized groups against discriminatory practices. However, despite these advances, much work remains, as reflected by the still prevalent gender gap in wage earnings, the increase of hate crimes against Muslims in the aftermath of 9/11, continuing debates surrounding the legality of same-sex marriage in the United States, and the religiously, racially, and ethnically charged armed and political conflicts that continue around the world. Discrimination, especially struggles over power and privilege, remains a relevant field of study in the (global) social sciences.

Marc JW de Jong

See also Affirmative Action; American Dream; Apartheid; Ethnic Cleansing; False Consciousness; Gender Bias; Gender Gap; Genocide; Hate Crimes; Hate Groups; Hate Speech; Homophobia; Inequality; Jim Crow; Minority Group; Multiculturalism; Native Americans, Cultural Degradation; Nativism; White Supremacy

Further Readings

Doob, Christopher Bates. 1996. *Racism: An American Cauldron.* 2nd ed. New York: HarperCollins.

Gregory, Raymond F. 2001. *Age Discrimination in the American Workplace: Old at a Young Age.* New Brunswick, NJ: Rutgers University Press.

———. 2003. *Women and Workplace Discrimination: Overcoming Barriers to Gender Equality.* New Brunswick, NJ: Rutgers University Press.

Lindgren, Ralph J., Nadine Taub, Beth Anne Wolfson, and Carla M. Palumbo. 1993. *The Law of Sex Discrimination.* St. Paul, MN: West Publishing.

Plaus, Scott, ed. 2003. *Understanding Prejudice and Discrimination.* New York: McGraw-Hill.

Poliakov, Leon. 1985. *The History of Anti-Semitism: From the Time of Christ to the Court Jews.* New York: Vanguard.

Silvers, Anita, David Wasserman, and Mary B. Mahowald. 1998. *Disability, Difference, and Discrimination: Perspectives on Justice in Bioethics and Public Policy.* Lanham, MD: Rowman & Littlefield.

DISCRIMINATION, INSTITUTIONAL

The term *institutional discrimination* broadly refers to the systematic and unequal treatment of people within the ongoing operations of society's institutions. Entrenched in customs, laws, and practices, these discriminatory patterns can exist in virtually any private or public entity, including schools, corporations, hospitals, financial institutions, and the government. Institutional discrimination is often "invisible" and difficult to document as it is deeply rooted in the norms and values of society. As such, institutional discrimination often appears logical to the members of society. Because it stems from widely held, but incorrect, assumptions about groups of people, institutional discrimination is unlike other forms of discrimination, in that prejudice may not be intentional on the part of the individual and may not be fueled by bigotry.

For example, many women today find themselves discriminated against in the workforce. A number of large, high-profile class action suits were consequently filed against large corporations claiming that women receive less pay for the same jobs that men hold and pointing to the widespread absence of women in managerial positions. Sometimes referred to as the "glass ceiling," this situation is gradually improving, with more females becoming chief executive officers of Fortune 500 companies. Another manifestation of institutional discrimination against women in the corporate world lies in pay disparities. However, a May 2007 Supreme Court ruling in *Ledbetter v. Goodyear* made it harder for workers to sue their employers for discrimination in pay. In this case, the only woman among 16 men at the same management level was paid less over a 20-year period than any of her colleagues, including those with less seniority. The Court ruled that employees must make their complaint within 180 days of when their pay is set. Ms. Ledbetter thus learned too late in her career that she was making 40 percent less than the lowest-paid man.

Of course, institutional discrimination is not limited to gender. Court and historical documents offer numerous cases of institutional discrimination against other minority groups. Institutional racism in Black Codes and Jim Crow laws denied African Americans access to the same institutional resources that others have enjoyed. Bias against ethnic minorities has often been built into society, from the blatant job discrimination in "No Irish need apply" signs of past years to ongoing real estate discrimination steering minority clients away from mostly white housing areas. Homosexuals have experienced denial of equal rights in marital, religious, legal, and employment institutions. Senior citizens have often encountered systematic discrimination in the workplace because of the perception by employers and many in society that they are "obsolete."

Because institutional discrimination hinges on the norms and values of society, the more these norms are evidential in society, the more they are reinforced and the harder it becomes to recognize the manifestation of institutional discrimination. In fact, it often becomes so widespread that even those engaged in such practices may be completely unaware of their existence.

Faye Allard

See also Ageism; Discrimination; Glass Ceiling; Racism; Sexism

Further Readings

Feagin, Joe R. and Douglas Lee Eckberg. 1980. "Discrimination, Motivation, Action, Effects and Context." *Annual Review of Sociology* 6:1–20.

DISENGAGEMENT THEORY

Disengagement theory defines the aging process as a period of mutual separation between the old and the young. The theory predicts that the social order requires a transformation among those advancing into old age, from a state of active involvement in society to one of steady withdrawal. It suggests that the elderly desire both psychological and social separation from the young, and this comes at a time in their lives when societies tend to devalue the importance of their contributions. As a result, those advancing into old age tend to seek isolation at the same time in which society is discouraging their continued participation. The most compelling evidence in support of

disengagement theory may be its apparent usefulness for explaining why elders seem to prefer early retirement, leisure, and isolation. According to the theory, these choices represent successful and adaptive responses for older people who normally find their lifestyles and philosophies inconsistent with those maintained by popular culture or mainstream society.

This theory envisions the disengagement of those advancing into old age as natural because it occurs in all societies, regardless of the high status that the elderly possess in some cultures. It is also inevitable since growing old leads to unavoidable death, the ultimate separation from society. Perhaps most significantly, disengagement is a necessary function of the aging process because it facilitates the replacement of old ideas with newer and more advanced knowledge. By withdrawing from society, disengagement theory suggests that the elderly assist in the modernization of science and technology and also in the creation of new job opportunities for the young.

Intense criticism, beginning as early as the theory's inception in the 1960s, led to the near universal abandonment of disengagement theory by the field of gerontology. Functionalist theorists argued that disengagement theory overlooks the presence of dysfunctions inherent in its assumptions. For example, disengagement theory neglects the negative outcomes for the elderly that are associated with isolation. Critics also contend that societies do not advance any more effectively by casting the elderly aside. To the contrary, gerontologists believe that societies bring harm to themselves by discouraging participation among older members of society. Such exclusionary practices are a common result, however, of negative stereotypes based on age (or ageism). Many believe that this results in the false notion that disengagement is a typical and socially acceptable course of action for those who are growing old. In fact, empirical research reveals great diversity in the routes that people follow into old age and that little or no basis exists for the notion that disengagement leads one to age successfully.

Christopher Donoghue

See also Activity Theory; Ageism; Life Course

Further Readings

Adams, Kathryn B. 2004. "Changing Investment in Activities and Interests in Elders' Lives: Theory and Measurement."

International Journal of Aging and Human Development 58:87–108.

Cumming, Elaine and William E. Henry. 1961. *Growing Old: The Process of Disengagement.* New York: Basic Books.

DIVORCE

Divorce is the legal dissolution of a marriage, as initiated by one or both partners. The social acceptability of divorce has varied widely across historical periods, religious faiths, and cultures. Whereas the United States has allowed divorce, under certain conditions, since the establishment of the nation, Chile legalized divorce in 2004, and a handful of other countries still prohibit the practice. Because sociological theory traditionally views the family as a basic building block of society, social scientists are interested in many aspects of divorce. Some scholars view the right to divorce as an indicator of women's rights, whereas others attempt to explain the social and cultural causes and consequences of rising divorce rates in the United States and elsewhere. Still other researchers examine families' internal dynamics preceding or following divorce. Accompanying the rise in divorce rates since the mid-20th century have been other changes in family forms, including the rise of single-parent households, an increase in age at first marriage, lower fertility rates and fewer children in families, the rise of cohabitation, and the formation of gay and lesbian families.

Accurately estimating the incidence of divorce is difficult because of the varying lengths of marriages, the related challenge of tracking individual marriages over time, and confusion over how to define a couple who divorces and then remarries. Recent U.S. statistics from the National Center for Health Statistics show that there were 7.5 new marriages per 1,000 people and 3.6 divorces per 1,000 people in 2005, giving rise to the conventional wisdom that "half of all marriages end in divorce." These rates have remained relatively constant since the 1960s.

Divorce reform was a major concern of the U.S. women's movement of the mid-20th century, commonly referred to as the "second wave" of feminism. Prior to major reforms undertaken by individual states since the 1970s, U.S. laws followed the British legal tradition of finding one partner at fault for the breakup of a marriage. The advent of no-fault divorce laws

made divorce a simpler process by allowing reasons such as "irreconcilable differences" as grounds for divorce.

Advocates of women's rights pursued expanding the availability of divorce, based on an understanding of marriage as an institution based on gender inequality, in which the woman is the weaker partner and at risk of exploitation, domination, or violence by her husband. Many feminists view marriage as an inherently unequal social institution in which the man has more power than the female because of greater social status, higher income, or greater physical strength. Women have traditionally been responsible for care of the home and children, increasingly in addition to paid work outside the home. Because of these disadvantages, women are more likely than in past generations to seek a divorce or separation. Thus the legal right to break marital bonds emerged as key to women's autonomy and independence.

Consequently, divorce has become more socially acceptable in the United States since the women's movement in the 1960s. Before that time, a social stigma was attached to divorced families, especially to divorced women and their children, rather than to the men. Divorced families constituted "broken homes," a phrase still in use today. Illustrating the normalization of divorce are not only higher divorce rates but also the often positive or sympathetic portrayal in popular culture of divorced men and women.

Regardless of the causes of divorce, its social and economic consequences are a source of concern for both conservative and liberal politicians, policymakers, and intellectuals. Whereas some studies show strong negative effects on children, other studies argue that differences between children of divorced parents and children of continually married parents are overestimated. Most experts agree that children of divorce tend to have more negative outcomes in terms of educational achievement, delinquency and crime, psychological well-being, teenage pregnancy, and behavior when compared with children of "intact families." In addition, children who experienced parental divorce have higher divorce rates than those whose parents remained married. Experts debate about whether there are gender differences in these long-term effects. Moderating the risks for children from divorced families can be attentive and supportive parenting and low levels of conflict between divorced parents. Despite these protective factors, the period immediately following divorce is stressful for children and can lead to anxiety and depression that typically fade within 2 years. The long-term outcomes of children from divorced families are partially caused by the decrease in standard of living and socioeconomic status after divorce. Households composed of never-married or divorced women and their children are much more likely than two-parent households to live in poverty, a trend sociologists refer to as the "feminization of poverty."

The debate over whether the negative outcomes of children of divorce stem from family structure (i.e., living in a home with one rather than two parents) or poverty is far from settled. Some scholars argue that poverty leads to divorce as well as increasing the likelihood of negative outcomes for children. Others claim that it is the absence of a father in the home that leads to both poverty and children's problems. Still other scholars of family life state that it is increasingly difficult for men, especially working-class and minority men, to fulfill the socially expected role of breadwinner. Lack of economic opportunities may thus cause men to leave marriages to which they feel they are not contributing financially. In terms of the effects of divorce, both popular and academic discussions tend to emphasize either culture or economics.

Aside from the question of the economic effects of divorce, the termination of a legal marriage generally involves some process of negotiation over the married couple's finances. Interactions between husbands and wives can become conflictual about dividing up the couple's assets and determining whether spousal support (referred to as alimony in the past) or child support will be required. Due to assumptions about gender roles and the actual gendered division of labor among married couples, the husband has typically been the partner required to pay alimony and child support to compensate for the family's expected drop in income after divorce. With many women employed and possibly the higher-earning partner, the granting of spousal support (alimony) does not always occur and is not always in the direction of husband to wife, although this is still a common occurrence. Child support enforcement varies from state to state. Failure of divorced fathers to pay child support is one of the reasons for high poverty rates in families composed of divorced women and their children.

Custody of children is often another point of conflict during the process of divorce. As with alimony and child support, assumptions about gender roles have been inherent in judges' decisions over which partner legally becomes the primary parent after a divorce. Because most cultures recognize the woman as the primary parent who takes on most of the parenting responsibilities (caring for children's emotional and physical needs), the courts typically favor mothers as custodial parents. The famous Oscar-winning film *Kramer vs. Kramer* of 1979 dramatized this tendency: In the film, the mother was awarded full custody although the father had shown himself to be an exemplary and caring father. Although mothers are more likely to obtain custody, U.S. courts also favor fathers' involvement in children's lives and will generally allow fathers the right to visit and interact with their child or children on a regular basis. Despite the rights of fathers to visit their children, only about one quarter of fathers have regular contact with their children after divorce.

One result of the increase in divorce rates is the increase in the rates of formation of stepfamilies. A stepfamily is made up of a married couple with one or both partners having children from a previous marriage or relationship. Although stepfamilies can form after the death of one partner's spouse, most stepfamilies are the result of a previous divorce. Also, the mother with custody of her children generally remarries, meaning that most step-parents living with stepchildren are men (stepfathers). Step-parents not residing with children tend to be stepmothers. Stepfamilies are more likely to end in divorce than are first marriages, which means that the children in these families may experience multiple divorces in their lives, an experience that some scholars argue can affect their educational and social outcomes. In most states, step-parents who do not legally adopt their stepchildren do not have special rights, privileges, or responsibilities toward the children. Adoption of stepchildren is only possible if the nonresident parent has died or given up his or her parental rights. Despite this fact, stepchildren are often eligible for Social Security or military benefits through their step-parents.

Erynn Masi de Casanova

See also Family; Family, Blended; Family, Nuclear; Fathers' Rights Movement; Feminization of Poverty; Single Mothers

Further Readings

Hackstaff, Karla B. 1999. *Marriage in a Culture of Divorce.* Philadelphia: Temple University Press.

Mason, Mary Ann and Steven Sugarman, eds. 2003. *All Our Families: New Policies for a New Century.* New York: Oxford University Press.

Popenoe, David, Jean Bethke Elshtain, and David Blankenhorn, eds. 1996. *Promises to Keep: Decline and Renewal of Marriage in America.* Lanham, MD: Rowman & Littlefield.

Yalom, Margaret and Laura L. Cartensen. 2002. *Inside the American Couple: New Thinking/New Challenges.* Berkeley, CA: University of California Press.

DOMESTIC PARTNERSHIPS

Domestic partnership ordinances are a form of licensed cohabitation in the United States, typically available to both same-sex and opposite-sex couples. Currently, couples may register their unions in approximately 60 cities, 9 counties, and 6 states. Hawaii in 1997, California in 1999, Vermont in 2000, Maine and New Jersey in 2004, and Connecticut in 2005 were the first to confer some form of official recognition on same-sex couples, as well as on unmarried opposite-sex couples, who may also be licensed domestic partners. At the national level, proposed domestic partnership legislation in 2001, the Domestic Partnership Benefits and Obligations Act, was referred to the House Subcommittee on the Civil Service and Agency Organization but never reached the floor; so far no one has introduced a similar bill.

The first domestic partnership ordinance—implemented in Berkeley, California, in 1984—provided official acknowledgment of the unions of same-sex couples, at a time when legal marriage did not exist elsewhere. Since 2004, Massachusetts has permitted same-sex couples to legally marry and, to date, remains the only state to do so, although no other state yet legally recognizes these Massachusetts marriages. Berkeley extended the option of becoming licensed partners to opposite-sex couples as well, as legislators asserted that heterosexual cohabiting couples also need legal acknowledgment of their unions, particularly when couples dissolve their unions and disagree over property division and "spousal" maintenance (commonly referred to as "palimony"). Most locales actually do permit both same-sex and opposite-sex couples to register. Currently, domestic partnership legislation in five cities and three counties (in addition to the states of Hawaii, Vermont, and Connecticut) specifies that only same-sex couples are eligible.

In most locales, becoming licensed partners requires the completion of an affidavit; couples attest that they are financially interdependent adults who share a single residence, are not biologically related, are not related through legal marriage or adoption (and are not legally married to anyone else), share an intimate relationship, and agree to be mutually responsible for each other's well-being. Some locales have additional requirements. For example, currently in the states of California and New Jersey, the partners in same-sex unions must be at least 18 years of age to register their unions. At least one partner in opposite-sex unions, however, must be at least 62 years of age (as a function of the eligibility requirements under the Social Security Act). Other locales are less restrictive. For example, some do not require that the partners be residents of the locale, as long as they meet the other requirements to become licensed. Regardless of additional requirements, to register the union in most locales, couples must submit the completed affidavit, along with a small registration fee, to the appropriate government records office (e.g., the city clerk's office), though in some locales, couples may have their affidavits notarized to register their partnerships.

Despite the legal acknowledgment of licensed partnerships, most locales grant few tangible benefits to the partners. Indeed, although all states with domestic partner registries offer some benefits, only a handful of cities do so. Benefits typically include the option of including a partner under one's health insurance plan, visitation rights in hospitals and correctional facilities, and bereavement leave. Additionally, some state and local governments provide health insurance benefits to their employees and their partners even without enactment of a domestic partnership ordinance.

The proportion of licensed couples that are same-sex or opposite-sex is unknown, as most locales do not request this information on the affidavit. Thus, estimates rest on determining the sex of each partner on the basis of first names, but even then such methodology is not conclusive. Furthermore, because of confidentiality issues, about half of all locales refuse to release information about how many couples register their partnerships. From the available data of domestic partnership records from the locales that release such information, approximately 8 percent of all registered couples are in heterosexual unions.

Individuals can legally leave licensed domestic partnerships more easily than they can leave marital situations. The only requirement to terminate the license is that one of the partners inform the government records office where the partnership was registered. Termination of the license does not require the consent (or knowledge) of both partners, and the legislation does not include guidelines with regard to property division or palimony. In most locales, a new licensed partnership may be registered 6 months after the termination of the previous one. Furthermore, couples must terminate their license with the government records office even if the couple has subsequently married, though it appears that many couples fail to do so.

Legal challenges concerning domestic partnership ordinances focus on the debate surrounding the legal recognition of same-sex unions, with little attention paid to opposite-sex unions. Court decisions have come down on both sides of this issue. In *Baker v. State of Vermont* in 1999, the state supreme court ruled in favor, leading to the implementation of civil unions in that state. In *Goodridge v. Massachusetts* in 2003, the state court extended eligibility for legal marriage to same-sex couples. However, in *Knight v. Schwarzenegger* in 2005, the California Supreme Court ruled in favor of licensed domestic partnerships. In this case, the petitioners argued that the state's Domestic Partners Act, in effect, amended Proposition 22, the defense of marriage initiative approved by a majority of California voters that defined legal marriage as existing only between one man and one woman. The petitioners argued that allowing same-sex couples to register as licensed partners redefines marriage without voter approval. The California Supreme Court disagreed, ruling that marriages and licensed partnerships were two legally distinct institutions. Other cases include *Snetsinger v. Montana* in 2004 and *Tyma v. Montgomery County Council* in 2001. Both cases were unsuccessful attempts to deny benefits such as insurance coverage to the domestic partners of homosexual employees.

Marion C. Willetts

See also Cohabitation; Family; Homosexuality; Norms; Same-Sex Marriage

Further Readings

Bowman, Craig A. and Blake M. Cornish. 1992. "A More Perfect Union: A Legal and Social Analysis of Domestic Partnership Ordinances." *Columbia Law Review* 92:1164–1211.

Human Rights Campaign. "HRC: Domestic Partners." Washington, DC: Human Rights Campaign. Retrieved August 23, 2006 (http://www.hrc.org/Template.cfm?Section=Domestic_partners1&Template=/TaggedPage/TaggedPageDisplay.cfm&TPLID=23&ContentID=10326).

Willetts, Marion C. 2003. "An Exploratory Investigation of Heterosexual Licensed Domestic Partners." *Journal of Marriage and the Family* 65:939–52.

Williams, Hannah Koopman and Rachel E. Bowen. 2000. "Marriage, Same-Sex Unions, and Domestic Partnerships." *Georgetown Journal of Gender and Law* 1:337–59.

Domestic Violence

Domestic violence—usually defined as intentional physical, sexual, or emotional harm by an intimate partner or family member—likely has always been part of human history. The construction and reconstruction of this social problem in the United States occurred in several ways, beginning as the problem of wife abuse.

Claims makers concerned with wife abuse emerged during the 1970s out of several other moral entrepreneurial campaigns, particularly those of the second wave feminist consciousness-raising groups, the anti-rape social movement, and the child protection movement. The first two focused their attention on challenging the secondary status of women in society. Consciousness-raising groups gave women time and space away from their busy lives to share stories of harassment, victimization, and often, abuse. These groups let many women see that what they had experienced was not unusual but rather was typical of many women's experiences. These groups gave women a discourse with which to analyze their individual and collective pain: how patriarchal institutions such as the family, the criminal justice system, and religion controlled women's lives and how women and girls were vulnerable to male power from birth until death, among other issues. The anti-rape movement's claims deepened the political analysis, showing how law enforcement often revictimized women when they reported sexual assaults and how police and prosecutors often did not follow through with investigations of incest and what came to be called "date rape." Some other women shared the humiliation and frustration of rape by their husbands; even if they called on law enforcement for protection and justice, they were often turned away for lack of an offense that could be prosecuted. Thus many women did not report intimate wife abuse or rape; they feared not being believed and they were loath to suffer the humiliation of police investigative techniques.

Emboldened by the sheer numbers of stories of terror at the hands of men told in consciousness-raising groups, feminist activists initiated social change by creating sexual assault centers and training law enforcement officers to understand trauma and victimology; in time, they began to advocate for shelters where victims of wife abuse could go to be safe and to gain a time away to rethink their lives and their futures. With much hard work, the shelter movement grew across the United States. With its successes came awareness that the term *wife abuse* did not adequately capture the essence of what women were enduring. Not all victims were married to their abuser; as sexual mores changed, more women were living with a male partner without benefit of marriage, and thus the term *wife abuse* was a misnomer. The shelter movement—now a freestanding social movement—began to refer to the problem as "family violence." Family was understood, in a holistic way, as anyone with whom a person creates an intimate bond; this normally meant a sexual relationship between two consenting heterosexual adults. But family violence was different in another way; there was a growing recognition that children were also victims, even if they were only witnesses to the adults in their lives hitting each other. Learning lessons from the child protection movement, family violence activists emphasized that such children were more likely to grow up to be violent with an intimate partner (if a boy) or to allow a partner to hurt them (if a girl). Thus the intergenerational cycle of violence theory was born, and it resonated with many in the general public.

Activists strove to find ways to keep their claims about this kind of violent act fresh and in the public's consciousness. So by the 1990s, they reconstructed the social problem yet again, this time calling it "domestic violence." This new term incorporated the earlier elements of the claim: Males were the perpetrators, while females and children remained as victims, but the new term allowed for expansion of the possible kinds of victimization and, therefore, created more possible victims and more accused perpetrators. *Domestic violence* became the umbrella term for other acts of interpersonal violence: Emotional abuse, fiscal abuse, even spiritual abuse were new ways that males could hurt their female partners. The success of these claims allowed for construction of new types of domestic violence: Sibling abuse, elder abuse, even roommate abuse also became instances of domestic violence. Nevertheless, for most people, domestic violence meant aggressive behavior between those who were—or had been—in romantic relationships.

When asked to identify the causes of domestic violence, experts focused on two. First, there was a societal explanation: U.S. society was thoroughly patriarchal. Major institutions such as the criminal justice system, the labor market, and education were infused with "male is superior" values and minimized women's contributions, complaints, and suffering. Those institutions, undergirded by chauvinistic mass media, further socialized each sex into what patriarchy felt was its natural status. Not surprisingly, public policy also endorsed male superiority; this could be best illustrated by the few domestic violence shelters that existed and the difficulty they had in finding stable funding. Such limited societal resources to help victims of domestic violence often meant that women had to return to their abusers. Feminist experts—especially when they appeared in the media—explained repeatedly how this high rate of victim return did not mean that "women were asking for it" or that "they were masochists who enjoyed being hurt." Individual causation, experts opined, was the second reason that domestic violence occurred: A man decided to hurt the woman he loved. Even though he had been socialized into patriarchy, every male faced a choice: He could channel his anger, jealousy, frustration, or other emotions into behaviors that fostered healthy communication and a healthy relationship, or he could choose to do harm to his intimate partner, whom he viewed as his inferior. Even if the man felt powerless in his other statuses in the public sphere, it was not acceptable, these experts claimed, to turn those feelings of powerlessness on innocent victims within his family. These experts also rejected male explanations for losing control, such as alcohol or drug usage, arguing that they were simply rationalizations to cover the men's deliberate decision to hurt their partner.

By the mid-1990s, domestic violence claims makers had made significant gains in shaping public policy. Shelters were present in many more communities; passage of state and federal laws offered more protection for victims in areas as wide-ranging as mandatory insurance coverage, temporary protective orders, child custody, and so on. The public, thanks to several well-known cases covered by the media, such as the Nicole Brown–O. J. Simpson case, became much more sensitized to the harm that domestic violence could cause.

Such high-profile cases also added two new elements to the social problem of domestic violence. The first new element was stalking; perpetrators did not allow their victims to leave the relationship voluntarily. Instead, they followed their former partners, tracing their every movement in person, via the mail, or via the Internet, and threatened to commit, or committed, violence against their exes. Stalking behaviors were simply one more example of the male's need to control his female partner, even after the relationship had ended. That led directly to the second new element, that without intervention, domestic violence would continue to escalate, culminating in the murder of one partner or ex-partner, most often the woman.

More recently some sociologists have critiqued the feminist construction of domestic violence as men exhibiting power over women, by studying interpersonal violence within same-sex relationships and violence perpetrated by females against their male partners. Their analyses show that although patriarchal values are woven through many relationships, not all violence between partners can be attributed to patriarchy.

Kathleen S. Lowney

See also Abuse, Child; Abuse, Elderly; Abuse, Intimate Partner; Abuse, Sibling; Family, Dysfunctional; Violence

Further Readings

Cho, Hunkag and Dina J. Wilke. 2005. "How Has the Violence Against Women Act Affected the Response of the Criminal Justice System to Domestic Violence?" *Journal of Sociology and Social Welfare* 32:125–39.

Gondolf, Edward W. 1998. *Battered Women as Survivors: An Alternative to Treating Learned Helplessness.* Lanham, MD: Lexington Books.

Hoffman, Kristi L., K. Jill Kiecolt, and John N. Edwards. 2005. "Physical Violence between Siblings: A Theoretical and Empirical Analysis." *Journal of Family Issues* 26:1103–30.

Renzetti, Claire. 1992. *Violent Betrayal: Partner Abuse in Lesbian Relationships.* Newbury Park, CA: Sage.

DOWNSIZING

Downsizing refers to the reduction of employees in a business enterprise for economic or business reasons. In contrast to being fired, to be downsized is usually not strictly related to personal performance but rather to economic cycles or a company's need to restructure itself. Eliminating a downsized employee's job and not refilling it occurs because the company wishes to reduce its size or operations, not because the employee failed to perform. Downsizing is a permanent or large-scale workforce reduction and is distinguished from a layoff, which typically is a more individualized or temporary job loss. A "mass layoff" implies laying off a large number of workers and is similar to downsizing. A plant closing or relocation, in contrast to downsizing with the elimination of some positions and the retention of others, occurs when the entire workforce, at least at a particular location, is eliminated.

Industrial "restructuring," that is, job churning rather than net job reductions, or change in composition rather than change in size, is what occurs in many circumstances broadly termed *downsizing*. In fact, while the manufacturing industry has experienced significant downsizing, nonmanufacturing industries, even in the midst of large-scale downsizing, have experienced significant "upsizing" in terms of actual net company size. Nevertheless, both downsizing and restructuring entail individual job termination. Downsizing is one cause of worker *displacement*, a comprehensive term that refers to all forms of involuntary job loss that result from economic and business conditions largely beyond the control of the individual worker, including downsizing and restructuring, layoffs, and closing or relocating plants.

Rightsizing is downsizing accompanied by the firm belief that a given enterprise should operate with fewer people. Some contention exists that downsizing has become too closely associated with the process of organizational decline and that downsizing can be a purposive strategy, undertaken and designed to improve organizational efficiency, productivity, and competitiveness. Downsizing thus defined falls into the category of management tools for achieving desired change, like rightsizing or "reengineering."

Further Definitional Issues

The narrowest definitions of worker displacement include the points that (a) the workers have been displaced as the result of a structural cause, including but not limited to international trade, technology, and government regulations, rather than due to cyclical downtown or economically motivated firm-specific idiosyncrasies and (b) the workers are firmly attached to the sector in which they were employed and have a limited ability to return to a comparable job in a reasonable time span. Empirical research, however, rarely uses these narrow criteria.

The distinction between voluntary quits and involuntary displacement is not always clear-cut. Firms may wish to reduce costs without downsizing workers and may reduce or fail to increase wages. This may prompt some workers, presumably those with less job loss risk-aversion, to quit, whereas other workers, presumably those workers with more job loss risk-aversion, may choose to work for lower wages.

Data Sources

The Mass Layoff Statistics program of the U.S. Department of Labor's Bureau of Labor Statistics collects reports on mass layoff actions that result in worker–job separations. Monthly mass layoff numbers come from establishments that have at least 50 initial claims for unemployment insurance filed against them during a 5-week period.

Since 1984, the Employment and Training Administration of the U.S. Department of Labor has sponsored the Displaced Worker Surveys (DWSs) that collect information on workers who were displaced from their jobs. The DWSs are conducted biennially as supplements to the Current Population Survey, a monthly survey of households that is the primary source of information on the nation's labor force. The DWS defines displacement as an involuntary job separation based on operating decisions of the employer, such as a plant closing, an employer going out of business, or a downsizing or layoff from which the worker was not recalled. DWS data have the benefit of a large sample of displaced workers. But DWS data suffer from several limitations; most important, the data are cross-sectional, making it difficult to study causal relationships.

The most widely used longitudinal data in empirical studies of downsized workers come from the Panel Study of Income Dynamics and the National Longitudinal Surveys. The primary advantage of longitudinal data is that they allow the construction of comparison groups; the primary disadvantage is the small sample sizes relative to the DWS. Other data sources on downsized workers include regional data, data from administrative sources on workers and their firms, and case studies of plant closings. These data are rich in detail and narrative but tend not to generate a representative portrait of the broader experience of downsizing.

Effects on Workers

Roughly 2 million workers a year were displaced in the early 1990s from jobs that they held for at least 3 years. According to the Bureau of Labor Statistics, during the January 2001 through December 2003 period, another 5.3 million workers were displaced from jobs they held for at least 3 years. With the tenure restrictions relaxed, the number is significantly larger. Other data show an increase over the past 3 decades in downsizings, plant closings, and layoffs that is independent of the business cycle.

Downsizing correlates with serious career losses for workers. The most reliable estimates indicate that the average displaced worker experiences a substantial period of nonemployment, a period that lasts longer during recessions than expansions. The length of nonemployment has a high degree of variance; some workers experience rapid reemployment at comparable (or improved) pay, whereas others experience prolonged periods of unemployment or reemployment at reduced wages. Researchers also found an increased probability of part-time employment following displacement. Substantial earnings losses are also incurred, and these generally are more persistent than nonemployment effects. The degree to which displaced workers suffer earnings losses is cyclical. Moreover, labor market conditions in a downsized worker's industry and local area conditions are important factors in the extent to which downsized workers suffer earnings losses. Some studies also found that downsized workers experience declines in other properties of jobs that signal quality, such as occupational status, job authority and autonomy, and employer-offered benefits.

The risk of being downsized varies along a number of dimensions that in turn condition the extent to which the event damages a worker's career. First, men are more likely to be downsized than women, although debate persists over the question of whether men or women experience greater losses following displacement. Second, studies find that less educated workers are more likely to lose a job due to downsizing than are more educated workers, spend more time unemployed, and suffer the greatest wage losses. Third, the risk of job loss and transition difficulties corresponds to occupation: Semiskilled, blue-collar workers disproportionately endure long-term unemployment and the largest earnings reductions. However, as the incidence of downsizing events for more educated and white-collar workers increases, the transition difficulties for such workers increase as well.

Some theories of why workers are downsized and unable to replace lost jobs with comparable reemployment include (a) technological innovation and the structural transformation of manufacturing; (b) foreign competition, including international trade and the pressure that low-wage labor abroad puts on U.S. labor markets; (c) a shift in consumer spending from goods to services; (d) a weakening of labor unions; and (e) a change in the social contract between labor and capital such that workers are seen as costs that need to be minimized in an effort to increase profits.

Policy Response

The unemployment insurance system, although not directly targeted at downsized workers, is the most consequential policy effort. One policy targeted at displaced workers is the Worker Adjustment Retraining Notification (WARN) Act, which requires employers to provide 60 days notice of a plant closing or mass layoff. The Trade Adjustment Assistance Act, originally enacted by Congress in 1962, provides income replacement support above levels provided by unemployment insurance, targeting workers downsized from jobs as a result of the relaxation of trade restrictions. The 1994 North American Free Trade Agreement Transitional Adjustment Assistance Program also is a response to concerns about job loss following trade liberalization; it provides income replacement and reemployment services. The Job Training and Partnership Act, amended in 1988 as the Economic Dislocation and Worker Adjustment Assistance Act, provides job search assistance and retraining. Research on existing training programs shows no clear evidence that such programs provide many benefits to downsized workers. Also, programs have generally failed to address the most critical component of worker's costs: earnings losses after reemployment.

Jennie E. Brand

See also Deindustrialization; Economic Restructuring; Globalization; Outsourcing; Social Mobility; Underemployment; Unemployment

Further Readings

Addison, John T., ed. 1991. *Job Displacement: Consequences and Implications for Policy.* Detroit, MI: Wayne State University Press.

Bernhardt, Annette, Martina Morris, Mark S. Handcock, and Marc A. Scott. 2001. *Divergent Paths: Economic Mobility in the New American Labor Market.* New York: Russell Sage.

Bluestone, Barry and Bennett Harrison. 1982. *The Deindustrialization of America: Plant Closings, Community Abandonment, and the Dismantling of Basic Industry.* New York: Basic Books.

Fallick, Bruce. 1996. "A Review of the Recent Empirical Literature on Displaced Workers." *Industrial and Labor Relations Review* 50:5–16.

Farber, Henry S. 2005. *What Do We Know about Job Loss in the United States? Evidence from the Displaced Worker Survey, 1984–2004.* Working Paper No. 498. Princeton, NJ: Princeton University, Industrial Relations Section.

Newman, Katherine S. 1999. *Falling from Grace: The Experience of Downward Mobility in the American Middle Class.* Berkeley, CA: University of California Press.

DRUG ABUSE

What is a drug? For social science purposes, a drug must be defined in context. In the medical context, a drug is a chemical substance used to heal the body and mind, one that is physician approved in medical therapy. In this sense, Lipitor, a cholesterol-fighting agent, Zoloft, an anti-depressant, and Celebrex, an anti-arthritis agent, are drugs. Within a legal context, a drug is an illicit or controlled substance, one whose possession and sale are subject to legal penalties; this makes marijuana, LSD, and heroin drugs. In a psychopharmacological sense, a drug is a chemical substance that is psychoactive, that significantly influences the workings of the brain and hence the mind; it has an impact on mood, emotion, and cognitive processes. By this definition, alcohol, methamphetamine, and cocaine are drugs. Even tobacco induces a psychic state, while not an intoxication or "high" per se, that causes pleasurable sensations in the user that entices him or her to continue consumption.

To the analyst of social problems, the third of these definitions is most relevant. The psychoactive property of drugs induces a substantial number of people to use them for recreational purposes, that is, to achieve a particular state of intoxication, which often produces harmful medical and psychological effects and dangerous behavior that generate concern in the public, negative attention from the media, and calls by legislators for controlling such use. In addition, the medical administration of drugs generates social problems when their overuse or misuse causes harm, leading to still other calls for corrective remedies.

Social problems can be measured objectively and subjectively. Objectively measured, concrete indicators such as death, disease, monetary cost, and an incapacity to work or attend an educational institution define a social problem. Subjectively measured, defining a social problem is its social construction, that is, how the members of a society—including the general population, the media, lawmakers and law enforcement, social movement activists, and the medical and psychiatric professions—define and react to a given condition or supposed condition. Also referred to as the "social construction" of a social problem, this subjective definition often finds expression through emotions such as fear and dread, which may or may not be related to a condition's objective harm.

Measuring the Drug Problem Objectively

The Drug Abuse Warning Network (DAWN) collects data from emergency departments on untoward nonlethal drug effects that cause users to seek medical care. This program also collects data from medical examiners on drug-related lethal overdoses. DAWN's data only cover sudden, direct, or acute untoward drug episodes, or "overdoses," such as unconciousness, convulsions, and psychotic episodes. DAWN does not tally chronic or long-term harmful effects, such as cirrhosis of the liver, AIDS, and hepatitis. In addition, DAWN's program, especially its data collection effort on lethal overdoses, does not cover the entire population, and so its statistics are incomplete. Still, untoward effects remain one of several objective measures of drug use as a social problem.

In 2005, DAWN tallied 816,696 nonlethal drug abuse–related emergency department episodes in U.S. metropolitan areas. A total of 31 percent involved illicit drugs only; 27 percent involved pharmaceutical drugs only; 14 percent involved alcohol plus one or more illicit drugs; 10 percent involved alcohol with pharmaceuticals; 8 percent involved illicit drugs with pharmaceuticals; 4 percent involved a three-way combination of alcohol, pharmaceuticals, and illicit drugs; and 7 percent were in a separate category: alcohol-only patients under the age of 21.

DAWN also collects drug-related mortality data from medical examiners in 35 metropolitan areas; as of this writing, 2003 statistics are the latest available. Of the roughly 7,000 deaths by overdose on which DAWN collected information, 70 percent involved one or more opiate or narcotic drugs, including heroin; 43 percent involved cocaine; 30 percent involved alcohol; 17 percent involved benzodiazepines, a category of tranquilizers; and 17 percent involved anti-depressants. (These percentages do not add up to 100 percent because these deaths involved more than one drug.) Clearly, with respect to death by overdose, these drugs or drug types represent a social problem.

More than 100 epidemiologists and biostatisticians from the World Health Organization surveyed the available data and isolated roughly 20 leading risk factors for premature death in countries around the world. The risk factors were somewhat different for developing countries as compared with developed countries. In such developing countries as Nigeria, Indonesia, and Bolivia, factors such as malnutrition and poor sanitation were the leading causes of premature death. But in the developed or industrialized countries such as France, the United States, and Japan, tobacco consumption accounted for 12.2 percent of the years of life lost to all the risk factors, and excessive alcohol consumption accounted for 9.2 percent. Tobacco and alcohol were the number one and number three factors in this respect. In contrast, illicit drugs only accounted for 1.8 percent of years of life lost. In other words, in the industrialized world, the legal drugs, taken together, contribute more than 5 times as much to premature death as do the illegal drugs.

Because DAWN's data are incomplete, the Robert Wood Johnson Foundation estimates the total number of direct deaths (mainly overdoses) in the United States per year as a result of taking illicit drugs at 15,000 to 20,000. The foundation estimates the number of deaths caused by illegal drug-taking from all sources (AIDS, hepatitis, tuberculosis, homicide, injury, suicide) at 25,000 to 30,000. The number of direct deaths from alcohol consumption are estimated at 20,000 per year, and the foundation's tally of alcohol's total contribution from all sources is 100,000. The federal Centers for Disease Control and Prevention estimate the number of deaths caused by long-term cigarette smoking at just under 440,000. (Smoking causes virtually no sudden or acute deaths.) Of the 2.4 million deaths that occur in the United

States each year, approximately one in four is caused by alcohol, tobacco, and illicit drug use. The Robert Wood Johnson Foundation calls substance abuse the nation's number one health problem.

The National Institute on Alcohol Abuse and Alcoholism has calculated the risk or chance of being killed in a single-vehicle crash, given a specific level of blood alcohol concentration (BAC). At the 0.08 to 0.09 BAC level, DWI (driving while intoxicated) or DUI (driving under the influence [of alcohol]) in all states, for 16- to 20-year-old males, that chance increases 52 times; for females at the same age, the chance increases 15 times. At the 0.15 BAC level or higher, for males 16 to 20 years old, this risk increases by over 15,000 times; for females, this figure is 738 times. For the older age categories, the risk is less elevated. After 1982, the number of alcohol-related fatalities in the United States declined by some 10,000 per year, but between 1999 and the early 2000s, it increased slightly each year. In contrast, teenage alcohol-related fatalities consistently declined after 1982, for under-16-year-olds, from 1,269 to 573 in 2002, and for persons 16 to 20, from 5,244 to 2,329. Nonetheless, drinking and driving remains a major social problem.

Death, effects that trigger emergency department admissions, and automobile accidents are but three of many objective measures of drugs as a social problem. Estimates place the U.S. economic cost of substance abuse at a half trillion dollars in the value of lowered on-the-job productivity due to illness and injury, health care expenditures, motor vehicle crashes, fire, and violence; 40 percent of that total is from alcohol abuse, a third from smoking, and a quarter (27 percent) from illicit drug use.

High school students who use illicit drugs and engage in binge drinking are more likely to experience impaired personal relationships and difficulties in their mental and physical health. The relationship between drug use and criminal behavior, while causally complex, is nonetheless an epidemiological fact: People who commit crime are *hugely* more likely to use drugs than the population at large, and it is possible that drug use may be causally implicated in the commission of criminal behavior.

Clearly, the contribution of substance abuse to death, disease, monetary cost, educational and occupational impairment, accidents, and violence is considerable. Drug use is a social problem of major proportions.

The Social Construction of the Drug Problem

A measure of independence exists between the subjective and the objective as it does for all other conditions that cause harm and damage to the society. For instance, given the nearly 600,000 deaths caused by the use of alcohol and tobacco compared with the 20,000 or 30,000 deaths caused by illicit drug use, why does the latter generate so much more concern than the former? Considering solely the objective harm caused by a given condition—using death as one measure of harm—why should the *less* serious problem generate *more* public concern and dread?

The answer to this question does not stem solely from irrational factors. Some of them seem entirely reasonable. For one thing, on a dose-for-dose basis, several of the illicit drugs (most notably, heroin, and to a lesser extent, PCP, cocaine, and methamphetamine) are more damaging and dangerous than alcohol and cigarettes. A single episode of heroin use is vastly more likely to kill the user than a single episode of alcohol consumption and, even more emphatically, a single episode of cigarette consumption. Second, heroin and cocaine tend to kill earlier in the user's life for each death than is true of alcohol and, especially, cigarettes. Hence, with respect to number of years of life lost, to equal one crack cocaine death, it would take 10 cigarette deaths and perhaps three to five alcohol deaths. It seems entirely reasonable that the former would generate more public concern than the latter. Third, most cigarette deaths result from chronic conditions, such as lung cancer, whereas most cocaine and heroin deaths result from sudden, acute conditions, and sudden, dramatic deaths attract more attention than long-term, chronic deaths. Last, illicit drugs are implicated in maladies other than, and in addition to, direct drug-induced medical death: maladies such as drive-by and bystander shootings, robbery, burglary, holding a neighborhood hostage to drug dealers, addicted babies, and the spread of HIV/AIDS. Of course, some of these harms can be traceable to the illicit status of illegal drugs. Nonetheless, illegal drugs, especially cocaine, heroin, and methamphetamine, are implicated in other objective social problems more than the legal drugs are. And many of these conditions are what people worry most about.

One indicator of the subjective or constructionist perspective defining a social problem is the public's designation of drug abuse as the number one problem facing the country today. Between January 1986 and September 1989, the Gallup poll and the *New York Times*/CBS polls reported that the proportion of Americans naming drug abuse as the country's most important problem catapulted from 2 to 64 percent. Clearly in the late 1980s, the crack cocaine epidemic had caught the public's attention. In just 2 months, however, this figure had slipped to 38 percent; by July 1990, it had decreased to 18 percent and in August 1990, to only 10 percent. Throughout the 1990s and into the first 2 years of the new century, up until September 2001, the percentage of the U.S. population indicating drug abuse as the most important problem facing the country today remained in the 5 to 10 percent range. After the attack on the World Trade Center towers and the Pentagon on September 11, 2001, the public's priorities shifted. A Gallup poll taken in November 2001 revealed that more than a third of the respondents (37 percent) named terrorism as the nation's top problem, and from then until today, somewhere between 1 and 3 percent of Americans, depending on the specific date of the survey, list drug abuse as the country's top social problem.

What the roller-coaster ride of drug abuse as a major social problem indicates is that conditions compete with one another for public attention and concern. In other words, a "carrying capacity," or saturation point, of public attention means only so many issues can rank near the top and, obviously, only one can be number one. The war in Iraq and the War on Terrorism crowded out drug use as a major social problem, causing its decline on the list of the public's major concerns.

Another way drug abuse is socially constructed as a social problem is through the criminal justice system. In 1970 the number of prisoners in state and federal penitentiaries totaled 200,000. As of 2006 the nation's prisons housed 1.5 million inmates; its jails held nearly 800,000 detainees. This enormous increase did not come about as a result of an increase in the crime rate; in fact, the country's crime rate declined sharply. In 1994, the violent crime victimization rate was 51.2 per 1,000; in 2005 it was 21.2. In 1977, the country's property crime victimization rate was 544.1; in 2005, it was 154.0. Likewise, the country's drug use has not increased since the 1970s; in fact, it has decreased. In 1979, 14.1 percent of respondents said they had used at least one illicit drug in the past month; in 2005, the

figure was 8.1 percent. The figure for cocaine in 1979 was 2.6 percent, but in 2005 was 1.0 percent. What has happened is that arrests and incarcerations for drug possession have skyrocketed. In 1970, the country's drug arrests totaled 322,000; in 2004 they were more than 1.7 million. In 1970, 16 percent of all inmates housed in federal penitentiaries were sentenced for drug offenses; today, the figure is 55 percent. In the state prison system (whose population makes up 90 percent of all prisoners), there are more inmates incarcerated for a drug offense than a violent offense. The federal justice system spends $20 billion a year fighting the drug war; states spend roughly the same amount. Clearly, the country is waging a drug war, and that war is a measure of drug use as a social problem, an indicator of public concern about drug use.

The subjective recognition of substance abuse as a social problem does not mean that its designation is arbitrary or fanciful. Saying that drug use is a constructed problem is not to say that it is "just" a construction; not all social constructions are equal. Still, we must be alert to disjunctions between claims and evidence, and drug use represents one condition for which such discrepancies are especially striking. In general, such discrepancies are normal because claims issue from interested parties, interest groups, political activists, and ideological and moral entrepreneurs, as well as a variety of other sources, whereas objective measures of material harm issue from social, medical, and natural scientists. By any criteria, drug abuse is a major social problem, but the claims made about the degree of harm it causes do not always match up with material reality. Indeed, this is one of the more intriguing features of drug use as a social problem.

Erich Goode

See also Alcoholism; Binge Drinking; Club Drugs; Cocaine and Crack; Drug Abuse, Crime; Drug Abuse, Prescription Narcotics; Drug Abuse, Sports; Drunk Driving; Heroin; Marijuana; Smoking

Further Readings

Becker, Howard S. 1963. *Outsiders: Studies in the Sociology of Deviance.* New York: Free Press.

Best, Joel. 2000. "The Apparently Innocuous 'Just,' the Law of Levity, and the Social Problems of Social Construction." *Perspectives on Social Problems* 12:3–14.

Goldstein, Paul J., Henry H. Brownstein, Patrick J. Ryan, and Patricia A. Bellucci. 1989. "Crack and Homicide in New York City, 1988: A Conceptually Based Event Analysis." *Contemporary Drug Problems* 16(Winter):651–87.

Himmelstein, Jerome J. 1983. *The Strange Career of Marihuana: Politics and Ideology of Drug Control in America.* Westport, CT: Greenwood.

Hingson, Ralph and Michael Winter. 2003. "Epidemiology and Consequences of Drinking and Driving." *Alcohol Research and Health* 27(1):63–78.

Horgan, Constance, Kathleen Carley Skwara, and Gail Strickler. 2001. *Substance Abuse: The Nation's Number One Health Problem.* Princeton, NJ: Robert Wood Johnson Foundation.

Krug, Etienne G., Linda L. Dahlberg, James A. Mercy, Anthony B. Zwi, and Rafael Lozano, eds. 2002. *World Report on Violence and Health.* Geneva, Switzerland: World Health Organization.

DRUG ABUSE, CRIME

Drugs and crime are undeniably linked. Not only are manufacturing, distributing, and purchasing drugs illegal, but the misuse of drugs often increases the need and likelihood of committing additional criminal acts. Overwhelming evidence indicates a connection between drug misuse, criminal activity, and arrest. However, the nature of the relationship is complex, and no one explanation or pathway accounts for everyone's experiences with drug misuse and crime.

The criminalization of drug use has long been the official policy of the U.S. government. The prevailing viewpoint of the addiction that drives drug use and the associated criminal activity is largely through a criminal, rather than medical, paradigm; the people addicted to drugs who commit crimes are not sick or ill but offenders in need of punishment, not treatment.

Characterizing the U.S. War on Drugs are increased penalties for crimes associated with so-called hard drugs and narcotics. With the crack epidemic of the 1980s largely subsided, today law enforcement pursues not only drugs such as heroin, cocaine, and marijuana but also methamphetamine and designer drugs such as Ecstasy. The focus of criminal justice policy is on crimes committed in association with drug use, whether driven by the pharmacological effect of the drug, an economic need to obtain more of the drug, or violence committed while participating in the illegal drug market. Perhaps the most significant characteristic of the War on Drugs is its well-documented differential impact on society's poor and nonwhite.

History of Drug Use as Crime

The criminalization of U.S. drug use parallels the sociopolitical events in the country's history. Drug use as a federal crime began with the Harrison Narcotics Tax Act of 1914 that taxed the manufacture, importation, and distribution of opiates and coca. Motivated by the government's desire to control opium users after seizing the Philippines at the end of the Spanish-American War, Congress expanded the act in 1924 to include the importation of heroin. At that time the United States was experiencing an influx of immigrants who brought their culture, including their patterns of drug use, with them. Asian immigrants introduced opium to the United States, and Mexican immigrants brought marijuana. With the societal belief that blacks favored cocaine, the false image of a crazed black man, high on cocaine and raping white women, helped fuel the public's moral panic.

The government's leading spokesperson for the criminalization of drug use was Harry J. Anslinger, who served as the first head of the Federal Bureau of Narcotics, later the Drug Enforcement Agency (DEA), from 1930 to 1962, and fervently promoted the criminal model of addiction. Through a series of improper research studies, false testimony given to Congress, and successful use as a legal defense, marijuana became known for inducing insanity and homicidal tendencies in users. The 1937 Marijuana Tax Act made it illegal to distribute marijuana without a stamp or license from the federal government. Because the government would not issue stamps, this essentially made marijuana illegal, punishable by a significant fine and prison term. The Boggs Act of 1951, passed during the cold war and while the country was fighting the Korean War and motivated by fear that the enemy was using drugs to sabotage the country's youth, increased penalties for drug crimes fourfold. The Daniel Act of 1956 followed the first televised Senate hearings on the topic of organized crime in the United States and increased penalties eightfold. In Virginia, for example, conviction of rape mandated a 10-year sentence, whereas drug possession mandated a 20-year sentence.

Despite the increasingly severe punishment of drug crimes, use of illegal drugs skyrocketed in the 1960s as the country faced cultural upheaval and challenges to the status quo. President Lyndon Johnson's Commission on Law Enforcement and the Administration of Justice, referred to as the President's Crime Commission, and comprising criminal justice experts, members of law enforcement, and authors from across the country, culled scientific research regarding crime and the criminal justice system response. According to the commission's 1967 report, crime resulted from poverty and social disorganization, thus requiring increased integration and services to provide support to offenders and those at risk of offending. During the 1960s and early 1970s these policy recommendations began to take hold within the criminal justice system. The seemingly enlightened tone of the report and the political era may have influenced passage of the Comprehensive Drug Abuse Prevention and Control Act, more commonly known as the Controlled Substances Act of 1970, the first piece of legislation to reduce penalties associated with drugs. It also classified drugs, except tobacco and alcohol, according to their medical use and potential for misuse.

Shortly after passage of the Controlled Substances Act, 1964 presidential candidate Barry Goldwater inserted the fear of street crime into national politics. Although Goldwater lost to Lyndon Johnson, Richard Nixon returned to the message in 1968 and laid the foundation for a get-tough era in the White House that culminated with Ronald Reagan in the 1980s. Reagan declared a national war on drugs in 1982 and called for its renewal in 1986. The Reagan and first Bush administrations increased funding for law enforcement budgets, pouring resources into international drug interdiction and domestic programs that ranged from increased drug testing in the workplace to assigning more law enforcement officers to pursue drug crimes. President Reagan initiated the expansion of criminalization to private or casual drug use, arguing that society should not have to bear the burden of anyone's addiction. However, with prisons funded by tax dollars, the public did not escape responsibility for drug addicts. Between 1985 and 1995 the number of state prisoners convicted of a drug crime increased 478 percent and accounted for 35 percent of the total increase in the overall prison population during that time. At the federal level, drug offenses increased 446 percent and accounted for 74 percent of the increase during the same period.

The federal government maintained pace with the changing drug scene. A powerful tool in that effort is the Controlled Substances Analogue Enforcement Act of 1986 that enables drug enforcement officials to bypass traditional administrative requirements and immediately classify a substance as illegal. The Chemical Diversion and Trafficking Act of 1988 empowers the DEA to regulate the distribution of the chemicals and equipment often used to manufacture illegal drugs. Similarly, the Comprehensive Methamphetamine Control Act of 1996, in addition to increasing the penalties associated with manufacturing and distributing the drug, regulates the chemicals and equipment most commonly used in its production. More recently, GHB, often referred to as the "date rape drug," and the weight-loss drug ephedrine, were classified as controlled substances.

The control of drugs and crime expanded beyond any one political orientation. The 1994 Violent Crime Control Act, sponsored and signed into law by President Bill Clinton, a Democrat, increased penalties for drug crimes and provided states with funding if their inmates convicted of violent crimes served at least 85 percent of their sentence. Despite society's concern with violent crime, contemporary drug laws are such that people convicted of nonviolent drug offenses can serve sentences longer than those who commit violent street crimes.

Ample evidence shows that the increased penalties for drug crimes have had disproportionately negative effects based on race and class. Differential punishment of drug users, based on the type of drug, as incorporated into the 1986 Anti-Drug Abuse Act, established harsh mandatory sentences for possessing less than $100 worth of crack, a relatively cheap drug viewed as favored by poor urban dwellers. Until 2007, federal law set the sentence for possession of 1 gram of crack at the equivalent of that for 100 grams of cocaine, an expensive drug favored by wealthier, white drug users. Research shows that differential treatment continues in the courtroom, where, among those convicted of drug felonies in state court, whites are less likely than nonwhites to be sent to prison and generally more likely to receive shorter sentences when they are punished. Nearly half of all state prison inmates serving time for drug offenses are black; whites and Hispanics each make up about one quarter of state prison inmates. Nonwhite drug users would appear to be over-represented in the criminal justice system as, according to self-report studies, nearly three quarters of drug users are white; blacks represent approximately 15 percent and Hispanics about 10 percent of U.S. drug users.

Drug-Related Crime

Violation of drug laws is not the only intersection between drug misuse and crime. Whether drug users are viewed as criminal or as suffering from addiction, crime perpetrated by them is not as uniform as once thought. Not until the 1970s and 1980s did research become sophisticated enough to reveal the range of differences among drug users. As the types of drugs people use vary, so do the types of crimes committed. Most research on drug-related crime has concentrated on heroin, as it was found that hallucinogens and marijuana do not consistently increase criminal activity; the research is mixed regarding tranquilizers and stimulants.

Another focus of research regarding drug misuse and crime has been on violent offenses. The most widely accepted model outlines a three-pronged relationship between drug use and violent crime. The psychopharmacological or biochemical effects of drug use can lead to violence, as can the economic need or compulsion created by addiction; violence can also result from the illegal activities related to drug markets. According to the National Institute of Justice, in 2002 approximately 25 percent of convicted property and drug offenders reported that they committed their crimes to get money for drugs, while 5 percent of both violent and public order offenders reported an economic motivation. Authorities generally agree that most drug-related violent crime is the result of the prohibition against drugs, rather than the drugs themselves. Support for this comes from the violence and criminal enterprise surrounding alcohol that flourished during the years of Prohibition and quickly dissipated after its repeal.

From 1986 until 2004, under the Arrestee Drug Abuse Monitoring program, the Justice Department collected information about the illegal drug use of arrestees. In nearly 40 cities across the country, urine testing for illegal drug use during the 72 hours preceding arrest revealed that approximately two thirds had at least one illegal drug in their bodies at the time of arrest; females had slightly higher rates of use. In 2000, for example, men were generally more likely than women to test positive for marijuana, whereas women were more likely to test positive for cocaine. During the same year, methamphetamine use was more common in the West and used more frequently by women than men.

Alcohol and Crime

Although not a target in the War on Drugs, alcohol use strongly relates to criminal activity and is the only drug regularly shown to increase aggression. Instead of violations of drug laws or offenses associated with its distribution, alcohol-driven crime is most frequently interpersonal and violent. Approximately 40 percent of violent crimes and fatal car accidents involve alcohol. Two thirds of violent crime victims attacked by an intimate reported alcohol was a factor in the offense. Among domestic violence victims, approximately 75 percent of offenders used alcohol. Violence results not only because of intoxication but also through learned expectations about how drinking and violence are paired.

Unlike prohibitive drug laws, those regulating alcohol deal primarily with the legal age of consumption. After Prohibition, most states adopted a minimum legal drinking age of 21. When 29 states lowered the age between 1970 and 1975, researchers found car crashes significantly increased among teens in those states. In response to mounting public pressure, most but not all states returned the age to 21. The federal government enacted the Uniform Drinking Age Act in 1984, stipulating receipt of federal transportation funds as dependent on a minimum state legal drinking age of 21. Despite such laws, underage drinkers consistently report it is relatively easy to obtain alcohol.

Drug Treatment

Mandatory or involuntary treatment ordered by the criminal justice system is a much debated issue. Research shows coerced treatment is generally effective but that issues of motivation are important for determining individual success. An often-cited RAND Corporation study found that treatment is 10 times more cost-effective than efforts at interdiction in reducing the societal costs of cocaine addiction, including crime and loss of productivity. Recently, several states adopted alternatives to incarceration, including mandatory treatment, for nonviolent offenders who misuse drugs.

Because of the heterogeneity among drug-using offenders and the range of challenges in employment, education, and health care that drug users face, a variety of interventions exist. Drug treatment for offenders may take place in residential or inpatient programs, in community-based outpatient programs, or in programs administered in prison. These intervention programs vary greatly in terms of the types of services provided and the quality of those services. Programs differ in the extent of staff training, the levels of rewards and punishment incorporated, whether psychological and medical care is provided, and whether medication, such as methadone, is administered. No single, specific approach consistently results in success for all drug users; rather, programs offering a variety of integrated services, those of longer duration, and those administered in the community, not prison, are generally more effective. Overall, treatment for incarcerated addicts appears to have decreased in recent years.

Since 1989, drug courts have addressed the multiplicity of issues faced by drug-using offenders by combining supervision, drug testing, and treatment governed by a system of rewards and punishment. Patterned after a social work caseload model, the courts are effectively coordinating multiple services and decreasing rates of relapse and recidivism. However, little support from the public presently exists for drug legalization and treatment or for clean needle exchanges. An alternative to the prohibition policies of the United States is the harm reduction approach favored in Western Europe, Australia, and Canada.

Gennifer Furst

See also Addiction; Anti-Drug Abuse Act of 1986; Club Drugs; Cocaine and Crack; Crime; Drug Subculture; Gangs; Heroin; Juvenile Delinquency; Marijuana; Uniform Crime Report

Further Readings

Boyum, David and Mark Kleiman. 2003. "Breaking the Drug-Crime Link." *The Public Interest* 152:19–38.

Bureau of Justice Statistics. 2005. "Drugs and Crime Fact Sheet." Washington, DC: Bureau of Justice Statistics. Retrieved December 9, 2007 (http://www.ojp.usdoj.gov/bjs/dcf/duc.htm).

McBride, Duane C., Curtis J. VanderWaal, and Yvonne M. Terry-McElrath. 2003. *The Drugs-Crime Wars: Past, Present, and Future Directions in Theory, Policy, and Program Interventions*. Washington, DC: National Institute of Justice. Retrieved January 7, 2007 (http://www.ncjrs.gov/pdffiles1/nij/194616d.pdf).

National Center on Addiction and Substance Abuse at Columbia University. 2006. "'You've Got Drugs!'

Prescription Drug Pushers on the Internet: 2006 Update." New York: CASA. Retrieved January 7, 2007 (http://www.casacolumbia.org/absolutenm/templates/Press Releases.aspx?articleid=492&zoneid=65).

Roth, Jeffrey. 1994. *Psychoactive Substances and Violence*. Washington, DC: National Institute of Justice. Retrieved January 7, 2007 (http://www.ojp.usdoj.gov/nij/pubs-sum/145534.htm).

Rydell, C. Peter and Susan Everingham. 1994. *Controlling Cocaine*. Santa Monica, CA: RAND. Retrieved January 7, 2007 (http://www.rand.org/pubs/monograph_reports/MR331/).

Sabol, William J. 2007. *Prisoners in 2006*. Washington, DC: Bureau of Justice Statistics. Retrieved December 9, 2007 (http://www.ojp.usdoj.gov/bjs/abstract/p06.htm).

DRUG ABUSE, PRESCRIPTION NARCOTICS

Prescription narcotics include a number of opiates, including morphine, codeine, hydrocodone (Vicodin), and oxycodone (OxyContin). OxyContin and Vicodin—Schedule II and III painkillers, respectively—represent the most widely abused prescription narcotics in the United States. Both have significant abuse potential. Recreational users take them orally in pill form, crushed and snorted, or dissolved in water and injected. Effects of Vicodin include feelings of well-being by reducing tension, anxiety, and aggression ("high"). Effects of OxyContin are stronger than those of Vicodin and similar to the effects of heroin.

Hydrocodone and oxycodone were first manufactured and marketed in the United States in the 1920s, as an answer to the number of Americans who were addicted to opium-derivative cough medicines such as heroin and morphine. The addictive potential of hydrocodone and oxycodone has been a major concern since the early 1960s. However, the introduction of the Vicodin and OxyContin preparations in the mid-1990s radically boosted illicit use and abuse due to a major marketing push by numerous pharmaceutical companies. The problem of Vicodin and OxyContin abuse became widely recognized by the media in 2003 when conservative radio host Rush Limbaugh admitted abusing these drugs.

Hydrocodone products are the most frequently prescribed pharmaceutical opiates in the United States.

Despite their medical utility, they are also the most popular pharmaceuticals associated with trafficking, abuse, and addiction. In every geographical area in the country, the U.S. government lists Vicodin among the most commonly diverted. OxyContin has been popular among the narcotic-abusing population since its introduction in 1995. Medical misuse of both Vicodin and OxyContin is most common among the elderly, whereas illicit use is most common among youth. However, recent concern has grown among federal, state, and local officials about the increase in illicit availability and abuse of both Vicodin and OxyContin, particularly in the eastern United States.

Millions of dosage units of Vicodin and other hydrocodone products get diverted by theft, doctor shopping, fraudulent prescriptions, and Internet fraud. Chronic long-term use of Vicodin can cause severe liver damage, and hydrocodone-related deaths are widespread and increasing. Emergency room admissions for hydrocodone-related problems have increased by 170 percent since 1994. Consequently, the U.S. government has recently moved to enact regulations reclassifying Vicodin and other hydrocodone products as Schedule II controlled substances.

OxyContin abuse has also led to increased instances of pharmacy robberies, thefts, shoplifting incidents, and health care fraud incidents. Most OxyContin-related deaths result from ingestion of high quantities of the drug in combination with depressants such as alcohol. In the eastern United States, OxyContin is the drug of greatest concern to law enforcement, although reliable data on actual abuse incidence are difficult to establish. More recently, a number of states have enacted or proposed more stringent regulatory guidelines and increased penalties for its illegal sale.

Philip R. Kavanaugh

See also Deviance; Drug Abuse

Further Readings

Ball, Judy and Dana Lehder Roberts. 2004. *The DAWN Report: Oxycodone, Hydrocodone, and Polydrug Use, 2002.* Washington, DC: Substance Abuse and Mental Health Services Administration, Office of Applied Studies.

National Drug Intelligence Center. 2004. "Intelligence Bulletin: OxyContin Diversion, Availability and Abuse." Johnstown, PA: National Drug Intelligence Center. Retrieved December 9, 2007 (http://www.usdoj .gov/ndic/pubs10/10550/10550p.pdf).

Drug Abuse, Sports

Drug use and abuse, including alcohol abuse, are considerable public health problems. One societal domain where this problem has received particular attention is in the realm of sports. This attention is due, in part, to numerous alcohol- and drug-related incidents involving well-known sports figures, and the problem encompasses both performance-enhancing and recreational drug use. Scholars have conducted numerous studies on the prevalence rates and reasons for drug abuse among athletes at various competitive levels, although many important questions remain unanswered.

Performance-Enhancing Drugs

Performance-enhancing drugs are substances that give an athlete some type of competitive advantage and are deemed illegal by a sport's governing body or state or federal law. Examples of commonly used performance-enhancing drugs include steroids, human growth hormone, amphetamines, and painkillers. These drugs are generally used to increase strength and speed, provide extra energy for practice and competitions, allow an athlete to train harder and recover more quickly from training, and enable an athlete to compete when hurt or injured.

The use of drugs for enhancing athletic performance is not a new phenomenon, as historians have uncovered evidence of stimulant use among ancient Greek athletes for competitive advantages. Steroid use to increase strength was documented among Olympic, professional, and intercollegiate athletes in the 1960s and 1970s, and the first Olympic drug-related suspensions occurred during the 1968 Summer Olympics. The first most notable performance-enhancing drug suspension involved Canadian sprinter Ben Johnson being stripped of his 100-meter gold medal at the 1988 Summer Olympics, although throughout the 1990s and into the 21st century a number of Olympic and professional athletes continued to be suspended for performance-enhancing drug abuse. In 2007, Marion Jones—the first woman to win five medals at one Olympics (in Sydney, Australia, in 2000)—admitted to using steroids and was stripped of her medals. No comprehensive studies, however, have been conducted among professional or other elite athletes to gauge the overall prevalence rate of performance-enhancing drug use among this population, although the 2007 Mitchell Report revealed that some professional baseball athletes had used illegal performance-enhancing substances. Recent studies among college and high school athletes have found that 1 to 4 percent of athletes in these groups reported steroid use or amphetamine use for performance-enhancing purposes.

The most obvious reasons for performance-enhancing drug use among athletes are self-evident: to become a better athlete and have enhanced sport-related outcomes. Athletes also report that they use such substances to recover from and prevent injuries, to improve their appearance, and in some cases in response to pressures from coaches. Stimulants may be used for energy purposes or as a weight loss aid, the latter reason being particularly relevant for sports where appearance can be judged (e.g., gymnastics) or where weight requirements exist (e.g., wrestling). Athletes may abuse painkillers in an effort to conform to a cultural norm that suggests being injured is explicitly or implicitly met with disapproval and playing through pain or injury is rewarded.

Abuse of performance-enhancing drugs can have multiple negative impacts on an athlete's health. Some substances, such as painkillers and amphetamines, can result in physiological and psychological dependence. Steroid use has been linked with a number of physical and psychological problems, including cardiovascular disease, genital shrinkage (among men), development of masculine physical characteristics (among women), and increased mania and rage. It should be noted, however, that most of the research on the long-term effects of steroid use comes from case reports and not well-designed, comprehensive studies.

Aside from the potential negative health impacts, performance-enhancing drug use compromises fundamental assumptions associated with athletic contests. One of the most important assumptions of competitive sport is that all participants are adhering to a standard set of rules and laws. Individuals who intentionally violate these rules in an effort to gain a competitive advantage compromise the integrity and fabric of the activity in which they participate. If those who participate in and are fans of a sport cannot be certain that the competitions are "clean," the resulting decline in credibility could have a considerable negative impact on the sport's popularity and acceptability within the larger culture.

Recreational Drugs

Unlike substances such as steroids, there are generally no physiological performance-related advantages to using recreational substances like alcohol, marijuana, or cocaine. Nonetheless, recreational drug use, especially alcohol use, has long been linked with athletics. In Europe a formal relationship between the alcohol industry and athletics goes back several hundred years, and today alcohol companies are among the most important commercial sponsors of organized sports. Additionally, there have been several high-profile athlete deaths involving recreational drug use, including cocaine overdoses and auto accidents when driving while intoxicated.

A number of research studies have found those who participate in athletics consume more alcohol and engage in more high-risk drinking than those who do not. Several national research studies on college students in the United States have found that intercollegiate athletes are considerably more likely than other students to engage in heavy drinking. Not surprisingly, these studies have also found that college athletes are more likely than non-athletes to experience negative health, social, and legal consequences as a result of their drinking. Studies among youth, high school, professional, and recreational athletes are not as comprehensive, but most indicate that those who participate in athletics consume more alcohol than those who do not. Others studies have shown that sports fans drink more heavily than do non-fans. In contrast, research seems to indicate that participating in sports serves as somewhat of a protective factor against other recreational drug use, as studies have shown that youth and college-aged individuals participating in sport are less likely than others to use substances such as marijuana and cocaine.

There are several theoretical explanations as to why athletes tend to drink more than non-athletes. These include athletes being under more pressure than non-athletes (e.g., balancing academics and athletics), athletes having high levels of personality traits associated with alcohol use (e.g., impulsivity), the larger cultural link between alcohol and sport, athletes having more social opportunities than other individuals, and a perceived norm regarding the social behaviors expected of athletes. Few research studies have explored these possibilities, however, so the exact reasons athletes tend to drink more than non-athletes remain unknown.

The reasons that athletes seem to use drugs (other than alcohol) less often than non-athletes do are also largely unknown. Many professional and collegiate sporting organizations engage in random drug testing that could serve as a deterrent, although comprehensive research studies on the effects of drug testing programs in sports are lacking. Some research indicates that one of the common reasons college athletes report not using recreational drugs is concern for their health, so it is possible that the negative health effects of substances like cocaine and marijuana are salient for those participating in athletics. Finally, it is possible that the overall culture of athletics, while somewhat permissive regarding alcohol use, implicitly and explicitly discourages the use of other recreational drugs.

Preventing Substance Use Among Athletes

Over the past 10 years research studies have shown that brief, individualized interventions are effective in the general population at reducing alcohol and other drug use, especially those that utilize the motivational interviewing framework or alcohol and drug skills training. Motivational interviewing is a nondirective approach, often incorporating personalized feedback regarding one's behaviors, which is designed to enhance one's desire to change his or her behaviors. Alcohol and drug skills training programs are designed to help the individual develop specific strategies for reducing his or her substance use. Research studies have shown that many athletes are exposed to education-based substance abuse prevention programs, but these education-only programs generally have been shown to be ineffective at reducing substance use. However, a handful of recent studies have provided promising support for using motivational interviewing or skills training programs to reduce substance use, specifically among athletes. Adaptations of these types of programs that address considerations unique to athletes, such as the impact of substance use on an athlete's sport performance, may prove to be particularly effective.

Matthew P. Martens

See also Binge Drinking; Drug Abuse; Drug Subculture

Further Readings

Damm, John and Patricia Murray. 2002. "Alcohol and Other Drug Use among College Student-Athletes." Pp. 185–220 in *Counseling College Student-Athletes: Issues and Interventions*, 2nd ed., edited by E. F. Etzel, A. P. Ferrante, and J. W. Pinkney. Morgantown, WV: Fitness Information Technology.

Elliot, Diane L., Esther L. Moe, Linn Goldberg, Carol A. DeFrancesco, Melissa B. Durham, and Hollie Hix-Small. 2006. "Definition and Outcome of Curriculum to Prevent Disordered Eating and Body-Shaping Drug Use." *Journal of School Health* 76:67–73.

Mottram, David R., ed. 2006. *Drugs in Sport*. 4th ed. New York: Routledge.

National Collegiate Athletic Association. 2001. "NCAA Study of Substance Use Habits of College Student-Athletes." Retrieved December 9, 2007 (http://www .ncaa.org/library/research/substance_use_habits/ 2001/substance_use_habits.pdf).

Nelson, Toben F. and Henry Wechsler. 2001. "Alcohol and College Athletes." *Medicine and Science in Sports and Exercise* 33:43–47.

Peretti-Watel, Patrick, Valérie Guagliardo, Pierre Verger, Jacques Pruvost, Patrick Mignon, and Yolande Obadia. 2003. "Sporting Activity and Drug Use: Alcohol, Cigarette and Cannabis Use among Elite Student Athletes." *Addiction* 98:1249–56.

Stainback, Robert D. 1997. *Alcohol and Sport*. Champaign, IL: Human Kinetics.

DRUG SUBCULTURE

Culture refers to the commonly held beliefs, shared language, history, and systems of meanings that link large groups of people together. The concept of a subculture refers to a definable, recognizable group within a larger culture that can be distinguished by its own beliefs, customs, and values. Members of a subculture recognize that they are within the larger culture and often define or describe the values or customs of their subculture in opposition to the larger social world. Insider knowledge of the subcultural argot provides members with a kind of cultural capital that helps them to recognize one another, reinforces group solidarity, and confers degrees of status as a member of the group.

Do drug users, or users of some drugs, constitute a unique drug subculture? There is evidence to suggest both yes and no.

Drug use is often a social activity in which groups of users are known to one another but not publicly identified. At each stage of the process, from finding dealers, to purchasing drugs and equipment, to finding a safe space to use, to the consumption itself, drug use is characterized by elaborate and mostly secret symbols and slang. Furthermore, both police and researchers have observed unique etiquette, some say rituals, surrounding the distribution of drugs and the sharing of equipment ("works") among groups of users. Finally, groups of drug users accord each other status for drug-related achievements—such as eluding the police, serving time, or surviving harrowing drug use experiences—that would not be bragged about by nonusers. All of these features imply that unique subcultures exist around the use of particular drugs.

Despite the superficial similarities, there are many reasons to reject the subculture label as applied to drug use. First, drug use is illegal and aggressively prosecuted. Shared signals and slang exist to avoid detection and arrest, regardless of any presumed histories or shared meanings. Slang, in particular, allows dealers to arrange sales over phone lines or in public spaces without actually providing evidence of a crime when the conversations are recorded. The behaviors are hidden out of necessity. Hiding them does not clearly indicate a desire to separate oneself or to form a unique group.

The hypothesis that drug use is ritualistic, particularly that injecting drug users share syringes as a statement of community, with status conveyed through the order of use, was explored closely in the wake of HIV/AIDS. If users preferred to share equipment, researchers worried, then it would be much more difficult to reduce the spread of HIV among them. Research has indicated, however, that the opposite is true. Users are aware of the medical risks that come with reusing syringes. That is why those who invest the most money or take the greatest risk in procuring the drugs will often insist on shooting up first. A cost–benefit analysis explains more than the "etiquette" argument. As most U.S. states have decriminalized syringe possession or allowed the introduction of syringe exchange programs, users have taken advantage of the opportunities to use clean needles whenever possible.

Do drug users actively reject the value systems of their social worlds? Probably not, because most users are employed and lead stable lives. Others, occasionally referred to as junkies or "chaotic" users, appear to have fallen out of the mainstream social world due to their chaotic dependencies rather than having chosen to leave it. Drug use is often an aspect of the lives of many people who otherwise have little in common.

Patterns of drug use have social and cultural aspects to them. Although it is not uncommon for drug users to have experience with multiple drugs, medical and ethnographic research has found that most users have a "drug of choice." Club drug users prefer particular types of drugs in particular social settings. Crack cocaine use follows very different patterns, as does youth pot smoking and other drug use settings from high school bleachers to shooting galleries. These social worlds do not routinely come into contact. Drug dealing, of course, is a separate social sphere altogether from drug use. Much of the drug subculture research has had a hard time separating drug use from other social, economic, or cultural contexts. The "hang loose" ethic that researchers of the 1960s associated with pot smoking among college students turned out to be very difficult to distinguish from the "youth culture" of the time or the self-described youth "counterculture." Sociologists of the period also attempted to distinguish the cultural worlds of the self-described "heads" (pot and LSD) versus "freaks" (speed), which demonstrated differences between them but did not show complex cultures defined around the drugs.

Critics point out that it is often unclear who is in a subculture and who is not, that by defining deviant behavior as a choice people are obscuring the social, political, and economic factors that constrain those choices, and that, by extension, one of the main accomplishments of the subculture explanation is that it absolves mainstream society of responsibility. That is, this is not a society with drug users, thieves, gangs, and tax cheaters; this is a society of good people who have subcultures of drug users, tax cheats, and so forth, living among them. Thus, the subculture label stigmatizes groups rather than explaining them.

Anti-drug campaigns and literature still use the concept of a drug subculture. This literature represents drug use as the "lifestyle choice" of a subculture whose members seek to recruit other users. The drug subculture is here defined to include research organizations and drug policy reform groups that criticize the zero-tolerance policies that the United States has adopted since the mid-1980s, presumably as part of a secret campaign for complete drug legalization. There are little data to support this approach.

Howard Lune and Pedro Mateu-Gelabert

See also Club Drugs; Cocaine and Crack; Cultural Capital; Drug Abuse; Gateway Drugs; Subcultures

Further Readings

Bourgois, Philippe. 1989. "Crack in Spanish Harlem: Culture and Economy in the Inner City." *Anthropology Today* 5(4):6–11.

Covington, Jeanette. 1995. "Racial Classification in Criminology: The Reproduction of Racialized Crime." *Sociological Forum* 10(4):547–68.

Currie, Eliot. 1993. *Reckoning: Drugs, Cities and the American Future.* Berkeley, CA: University of California Press.

Ferrell, Jeff. 1999. "Cultural Criminology." *Annual Review of Sociology* 25:395–418.

Gelder, Ken and Sarah Thornton, eds. 1997. *The Subcultures Reader.* London: Routledge.

Johnson, Bruce D., Flutura Bardhi, Stephen J. Sifaneck, and Eloise Dunlap. 2006. "Marijuana Argot as Subculture Threads: Social Constructions by Users in New York City." *British Journal of Criminology* 46(1):46–77.

DRUNK DRIVING

Traffic crashes are the cause of more fatal and debilitating traumatic injuries than any other modern activity in the United States, and today few are blind to the fact that alcohol-impaired drivers pose a significant risk to themselves and others. The deaths and injuries that drunk driving causes are frequently inflicted upon innocent victims; as there is no justification for drunk driving, these are particularly pointless and tragic occurrences. But broad recognition of the problems drunk drivers cause has not led to an easy crafting of effective strategies to combat them; indeed, the path remains contentious. Even fundamental issues, such as defining the term *drunk driving*, spark sometimes-heated battles among researchers, activists, industry, and the government. Nonetheless, great strides have occurred in preventing deaths from drunk driving. Of concern, though, is the apparent recent stall in the decline in drunk driving and the identification of tools for further prevention success.

Drunk driving is the act of driving after being impaired by alcohol, placing the driver at a higher risk of crashing than normal, given the same driving conditions. This is a more general term than a legal definition, which requires impairment to be identifiable by an enforcement officer, or a per se definition of driving under the influence (DUI) based on a specific blood alcohol concentration (BAC). States vary in their definitions of DUI and driving while impaired (DWI). Further, the U.S. National Highway Traffic Safety Administration (NHTSA) uses the term *alcohol related* to mean a crash that occurs where at least one driver, pedestrian, or pedalcyclist has a BAC greater than or equal to .01 (g/dL). To avoid confusion, statistics in this entry include the terms and definitions of the statistic's source.

The NHTSA compiles alcohol-related traffic fatalities within a database, the Fatality Analysis Reporting System (FARS), formerly known as the Fatal Accident Reporting System. FARS is a valuable resource for understanding the prevalence of drunk driving within the United States. Each state reports to this system its fatal road crashes, along with important details about the drivers, other vehicle occupants, the vehicles, and the crash itself. Included within the driver data set are the results of any alcohol level testing. The NHTSA uses an imputing scheme to replace missing data from states' reports.

According to the NHTSA analysis, in 2005, 16,885 fatalities stemmed from alcohol-related crashes. Most of these crashes (85.3 percent) involved drivers whose BAC was .08 (g/dL) or greater. In fact, more than half of the crashes (57.6 percent) involved a driver with a BAC of .15 (g/dL) or greater. Relative to their risk of being in any fatal crash, males and those between ages 20 and 39 are at a disproportionate risk of being in an alcohol-related fatal crash. Motorcyclists are also disproportionately involved in alcohol-related crashes.

Physiology

Alcohol is usually absorbed quickly through the stomach and intestines and thus enters the bloodstream within 20 minutes of consumption. Food in the stomach acts to slow this absorption. The concentration of alcohol within the blood is usually measured in the proportion of grams of alcohol per deciliter of blood (g/dL). This fraction is often referred to as blood alcohol concentration (BAC). A number of formulas can estimate the resulting BAC from the consumption of varying amounts of alcohol. The actual attained BAC that results from consumption is a function of the drinker's physiology (including weight and sex), the quantity of alcohol consumed, and the time over which the consumption occurred. Time plays two roles: latency of absorption and time that it takes for removal of the alcohol by the liver.

In 2000, the U.S. Congress mandated that states adopt a legal limit of BAC 0.08 g/dL. Since then, all states have adopted this standard, many lowering it from their previous limit of BAC 0.10 g/dL. Also, mandatory "zero tolerance" laws now make it illegal for drivers under age 21 to have virtually any BAC at all.

The amount of impairment alcohol causes is directly related to the BAC, though people differ with respect to the concentration needed to observe particular impairments. The effects of low BAC levels (below .04 g/dL) are difficult to observe without baseline performance assessments. Generally, these impairments involve attentive and cognitive functions. Such impairments, while mild, may account for some of the increased risk of crashes such BAC levels appear to produce, as driving is a behavior that requires the ability to divide one's attention among a number of important tasks.

At moderate BACs (.05 to .08 g/dL), cognitive impairments become more pronounced, affecting not only attention but judgment. Some drinkers experience gross motor impairment at this level too. Above a BAC of .08 g/dL, gross motor coordination problems are usually observable. Perceptual impairments may also be present as attentiveness impairments become severe. Judgment becomes impaired as cognitive effort becomes too great to consider multiple alternative choices within the decision process.

An innovative research protocol, known as the Grand Rapids Study, estimated the increased risk associated with various BAC levels. Breath alcohol tests were conducted on drivers who matched accident-involved drivers on environmental exposure to road conditions. Thus the researchers were able to control for a variety of external factors related to the crashes and estimate the role of alcohol. Their data showed that as measured BACs rose above .04 g/dL, a clear increase in accident involvement risk emerged and rose exponentially. Looking at accident causation, by BAC .10 g/dL the relative probability of causing an accident was estimated at more than 5 times greater than having a BAC 0.0 g/dL. By BAC .16 g/dL, the probability increases by a multiple of 35. The stark results of this seminal study have been credited for spurring the adoption of laws regarding BAC levels in the United States.

Recognition of the Problem

Concerns about drunk driving date back to the introduction of the automobile. Early 20th-century temperance movement literature mentions drunk driving as a justification for avoiding alcohol. One 1917 temperance publication lauded the American Automobile

Association's contest board policy of prohibiting the use of alcohol among "drivers, mechanicians [sic] and officials of races." It laments, however, that alcohol was still sold to spectators, indicating that the American Automobile Association's policy reflected a driving-related safety concern and not a general affinity for the temperance cause. At the end of Prohibition, temperance movements again raised the issue of drunk driving concurrently with other social ills associated with alcohol. The Kansas United Dry Forces produced poster stamps with messages like "Death rides the highway" and "Alcohol belongs in the radiator" in 1939. An early anti–drunk driving poster commissioned by the WPA Federal Arts Project in 1937 depicted a skull, whiskey bottle, and gas pump with the caption reading "DON'T MIX 'EM."

Although early research pointed out the inherent hazards of drunk driving and government-funded anti–drunk driving programs had been around for decades, there was little advocacy for a collective approach to the problem. That changed with the founding of Mothers Against Drunk Driving (MADD) in 1980. Candy Lightner, whose daughter Cari was killed by a drunk driver, launched the organization after encountering mostly indifference from state officials about the issue. That indifference launched a quickly growing sense of outrage spurred by MADD, as it rapidly became a national organization. Lightner's effective use of television news events is credited for bringing the staggering statistics of the true impact of drunk driving into the social consciousness and changing the perception of the nature of drunk driving.

The Drunk Driver

Drunk driving cuts across all racial, ethnic, age, and socioeconomic categories. It is a crime that a substantial proportion of the U.S. population commits at least occasionally. However, certain risk patterns remain fairly consistent. According to the Substance Abuse and Mental Health Services Administration (SAMHSA), female drivers 21 and over are less likely than their male counterparts to report having driven under the influence within the past year (11.4 percent vs. 22.0 percent respectively; SAMHSA). The prevalence generally declines with age, though reporting of ages within most studies tends to group ages into broad categories, making it difficult to be certain that the decline is linear. Both the National Survey on Drug Use and Health (NSDUH) and the FARS data show declines with age, though the NSDUH data on self-reported DUI (SAMHSA) appear to show a steeper slope than the FARS crash data (NHTSA). Native American drivers and non-Hispanic white drivers report the highest rates of driving under the influence (SAMHSA).

Though most incidents of drunk driving do not end in either a crash or an arrest, when they do, it is often a wake-up call for the driver to modify his or her behavior. However, a substantial proportion of DUI arrests are for drivers who have already been arrested at least once before. This recurrence of arrests indicates that drunk driving behavior has a persistence that some drivers find difficult to break. In fact, over half of one sample of interviewed DUI offenders admitted to driving under the influence again during the penalty phase of their DUI convictions.

James E. Lange

See also Alcoholism; Prohibition; Temperance Movement

Further Readings

Kelly, Erin, Shane Darke, and Joanne Ross. 2004. "A Review of Drug Use and Driving: Epidemiology, Impairment, Risk Factors and Risk Perception." *Drug and Alcohol Review* 23:319–44.

Moskowitz, Herbert. 1973. "Laboratory Studies of the Effects of Alcohol on Some Variables Related to Driving." *Journal of Safety Research* 5:185–99.

Ross, H. Laurence. 1982. *Deterring the Drinking Driver: Legal Policy and Social Control.* Lexington, MA: Lexington Books.

Williams, Allan F. 2006. "Alcohol-Impaired Driving and Its Consequences in the United States: The Past 25 Years." *Journal of Safety Research* 37:123–38.

DUAL-INCOME FAMILIES

Dramatic changes in the workforce participation of women and men and, to a lesser extent, in the division of labor in the home have occurred in recent decades. The traditional family of the male breadwinner and female homemaker, the norm among middle-class married couples in the 1950s and 1960s, evolved into families where both the husband and wife often work for pay—the dual-earner family or dual-income family. Dual-earner families include two-career couples and couples who do not see their jobs as careers. Careers differ from jobs in requiring a deeper commitment of time, energy, and education; the payoffs are higher salaries. Thus, despite the difficulties dual-earner families experience because of career demands, the added income can buy many services.

Working wives and mothers are not new. Since the 1850s working-class, minority, and immigrant women have found employment as factory laborers or domestic servants, or have taken in boarders or laundry or performed other home-based jobs. What is new are the numbers of middle-class women and mothers of preschool children who are employed outside the home. Among adults today, dual earners comprise over 60 percent of all families compared with 30 percent with one earner. In 1963, the reverse was true, with 60 percent of families having one earner.

Currently, over 70 percent of married mothers of preschoolers work for pay at least part-time, and one third of these mothers are full-time employees. Their paychecks lift some families out of poverty and permit others to enjoy a middle-class standard of living. Typically, the family income for dual-earner households is twice that of single earners at similar skill levels.

The experiences of dual-earner couples are both positive and problematic. When their jobs are challenging and provide status and autonomy, mothers and fathers feel involved and they experience positive self-esteem at work and at home. These women work not because they are unhappy at home but because they gain personal satisfaction from the job.

However, dual-income parents tend to work long hours and are forced to sacrifice time with their families to satisfy the demands of the workplace. U.S. dual-earner couples work an average of 81 hours per week, and 12 percent of couples work 100 or more hours per week. Forty-one percent of the couples report going to work early or working late, nearly 60 percent take work home, and 54 percent report that they feel pressured to keep up.

Employed parents complain that there are not enough hours in the day—they feel "harried" and "hurried." Such working parents remain connected via their cell phone, Blackberry, or laptop; many often go to work early, stay late, and carry work home. The long hours and spillover of work into the home drains parents emotionally and leaves them feeling stressed and resentful of their work intruding into family life.

Gender Differences

Although both men and women struggle to balance work and family and men currently do more housework than previous male cohorts, women still do almost twice as much housework as men. Among couples with children, especially young children, the women spend more time on child care. Typically the woman makes the greater adjustment, reducing her work hours or even leaving the workforce. As children grow older, many women increase their work hours, but usually their work hours will never again match those of their spouses.

Tradition also continues when couples are faced with making choices between his and her career. In one sample of professional couples, the career of the husband was most often given priority over the wife's career. Husbands are more likely than wives to travel for work and relocate their families for a new job; mothers are more concerned about disrupting family life than are fathers. Moreover, relocation moves can lead to underemployment for the wife, and having young children at home also decreases the probability that the mother will travel for work.

However, there is an upside to being in a dual-earner couple. Studies show that, in addition to enjoying enhanced self-esteem and a buffer from home stress, women who are employed full-time experience less anxiety and depression and report better physical health than full-time homemakers.

How do husbands respond to their wives' employment? Some men are relieved to share economic responsibilities and to have added income. Others feel emasculated and may lower their share of housework. Not surprisingly, divorce rates are higher for dual-earner than for single-earner couples. This higher divorce rate may reflect the difficulties in negotiating the division of labor, as well as reflecting the wife's ability to support herself and, therefore, to leave an unhappy marriage. Sharing household work is especially important for the emotional health and marital satisfaction of working wives, benefits that also accrue to husbands.

Who Cares for the Children?

Child care arrangements are another major consideration in the dual-earner family. Studies indicate that almost half of all children are cared for by the husband or wife when the couple works split shifts; a grandparent may take over if both are working at the same time.

Another 20 percent of children are cared for in a private residence, called family day care. Only 30 percent of children are in a formal day care center at the mother's place of work, operated by a nonprofit community organization, or run by a commercial chain.

Regardless of the type or quality of the child care center, all suffer from extremely high staff turnover, primarily due to low pay. By contrast, in most Western European countries, preschool is universal and publicly funded, and the teachers earn the same pay and prestige as kindergarten teachers. Year-round child care workers in the United States are paid about half of what public school teachers earn. U.S. parents fend for themselves, a situation that strongly favors wealthier families who can afford quality child care.

When the shortcomings of the U.S. day care system are explored, the media and some political leaders tend to blame working parents, especially working mothers. Critics tend to focus on the behavioral problems of some children rather than the research, which indicates that the great majority of youngsters (83 percent) show no significant behavioral problems. Children's language skills and other cognitive abilities also improved when the children were in day care for 20 hours or more per week. Child advocates contend that investing more money in universal, early childhood education would benefit children from low-income families and could narrow the education and income gaps that grow wider as the children age.

Managing Work–Family Conflict

Another solution to help dual earners balance competing demands, which today may also include the needs of aging parents, lies in supportive workplace policies. Many mothers prefer a schedule that reflects the local school day. The relatively few U.S. corporations that have instituted "family friendly" policies such as flexible time schedules, part-time work with benefits, compressed workweeks, and job sharing, have benefited from lower absenteeism, lower turnover, higher employee morale, and increases in psychological and physical health.

Studies show that the most egalitarian relationships in dual-earner families occur when both husbands and wives find work that requires a "moderate amount of time," allowing them to balance work and family demands. Working long hours is not necessarily desirable, and at least one study found that 64 percent of mothers are actually interested in working part-time.

However, many employers and employees believe that only full-time workers are seriously committed to the company and their careers and are therefore resistant to such changes. Most experts agree that there is a dramatic need to change the culture of the workplace, which now requires employees to work unconditionally and place work demands above family concerns. What many sociologists have shown is that work–family conflicts are structural problems, stemming from existing institutional arrangements, not from individual shortcomings. If middle-class families with considerable resources experience problems in balancing their work and home lives, parents with more limited resources struggle even more.

Dual-earner families need a more equitable balance between the demands of work and family life. The major challenge for U.S. newlyweds today is to find that mutually compatible balance between breadwinning and home and child care tasks.

Peter J. Stein

See also Family; Family Leave Act; Labor Force Participation Rate

Further Readings

Glass, Jennifer. 2000. "Envisioning the Integration of Family and Work: Toward a Kinder, Gentler Workplace." *Contemporary Sociology* 29:129–43.

Jacobs, Jerry and Kathleen Gerson. 2004. *The Time Divide: Work, Family, and Gender Inequality.* Cambridge, MA: Harvard University Press.

Moen, Phyllis, ed. 2003. *It's about Time: Couples and Careers.* Ithaca, NY: Cornell University Press.

Schneider, Barbara and Linda J. Waite, eds. 2005. *Being Together, Working Apart: Dual-Career Families and the Work-Life Balance.* New York: Cambridge University Press.

Eating Disorders

Eating disorders include anorexia nervosa (self-starvation) and bulimia nervosa (binge-purge syndrome). Although anorexia nervosa and bulimia nervosa represent different types of disordered eating, both entail a distorted body image and fear of fatness.

Specifically, anorexia nervosa involves self-starvation alone or in combination with excessive exercising, occasional binge eating, vomiting, or laxative abuse. An individual with anorexia nervosa refuses to maintain minimum weight for age and height and is at least 15 percent below expected weight. Bulimia nervosa is a pattern of bingeing and self-induced purging. This eating disorder consists of binge eating, followed by vomiting, laxative abuse, enemas, or ipecac use. One's weight is usually normal or close to normal.

The reported occurrence of eating disorders increased markedly over the past 30 years. Eating disorders do not exist equally across populations; they have very specific patterns of distribution and are most prevalent in certain cultural contexts and sociodemographic categories.

Sociodemographic and Cultural Context

In general, eating disorders most commonly occur among young, white, affluent females in modern, industrialized countries. Concerning the gender distribution of eating disorders, 90 percent of individuals with eating disorders are female. Cultural norms of the body are critical to understanding why females are more vulnerable to eating disorders than are males. Specifically, the pervasive thinness norm for women is a major contributor to gender differentiation. The ideal body norm for males, in contrast, is to be muscular and not skinny or weak. Rather than desiring weight loss and thinness, males want to gain weight and size from muscle.

Females perceive themselves as overweight even when they are not. For example, over half of college females believe they are overweight when a much lower percentage actually is. In addition, nearly three out of four college females of normal weight report their wanting to be thinner. This striving for thinness develops early. For example, girls as young as 6 years old choose as ideal image silhouettes of girls who are thinner than they are and already falsely think of themselves as overweight.

The ideal body type of thinness is also crucial to understanding the international distribution of eating disorders. Within developing countries, many people do not get enough to eat; only the affluent can afford to be fat or corpulent. So, fatness becomes a symbol of wealth and an ideal body shape. Therefore, eating disorders, with their fear of fatness, are unlikely. Further, the eating disorder of bulimia nervosa is less likely, due to the expense of buying large quantities of food for bingeing. Also, it seems improbable in a developing country that one would have anorexia nervosa, or deliberate self-starvation, when forced starvation is evident.

In contrast, in modern, industrialized nations, fatness no longer symbolizes affluence because people generally obtain enough to eat. In fact, it is possible to eat too much. Thus, being slim becomes a symbol of discretionary eating, and appearance ideals shift from plumpness to thinness. Affluent groups in particular have the resources to eat as much, as or little, as they want.

In the United States, whites compose most of the affluent classes, which helps to explain why eating disorders are more prevalent among whites. Also, larger-size body norms for women may be more prevalent among certain ethnicities, such as African Americans and Hispanics. Eating disorders are more common among individuals of color as they become more upwardly mobile, and among recent immigrants to the United States who experience acculturation.

Another major sociodemographic pattern in the occurrence of eating disorders concerns age. The teens and early 20s are the most reported ages of onset and prevalence. This time is one in which individuals form their identity and are quite vulnerable to peer group influences and appearance expectations. Problems with self-esteem also occur more often during this age period. Thus, manipulating one's weight and being extra compliant with thin body norms are more likely occurrences in young age groups.

The Social Construction of Eating Disorders

The great majority of writings on eating disorders focuses on the medical and psychological dimensions of the conditions. This attention facilitates the belief that eating disorders require medical intervention and control, thus viewing anorexia nervosa and bulimia nervosa as illnesses or diseases that need to be treated by the medical profession. Such a construction of eating disorders promotes the medicalization of these conditions. Medical professionals become the experts in treating the conditions, and individuals who have eating disorders become patients. Examining cultural and societal context becomes secondary to medical testing and treatment, and eating disorders become another societal condition that the medical profession can claim as its own. Notably, both eating disorders are included in the *Diagnostic and Statistical Manual of Mental Disorders* with specific diagnostic features.

In the medicalization of eating disorders, attention is paid to the immediate, medical treatment of the problem and to medical and psychiatric etiology. Many hospitals now have special floors or wings for patients who have eating disorders and often remove these patients from family and friends while they receive psychiatric counseling and medical treatment.

Once released and away from this controlled environment, patients often relapse and find themselves back in the hospital. Other popular medical treatments are drug therapies to deal with the diagnosis of depression that often accompanies eating disorders, as well as with the reported obsessive and compulsive nature of the diseases.

Cultural Messages

In contrast to being viewed as grounded in biological processes, eating disorders can be seen as a mirror of culture. Several aspects of the sociocultural context perpetuate attempts to conform to the slim standard and facilitate the occurrence of eating disorders. The factors contributing to eating disorders are heavily engrained in the normative structure of society. Prominent among societal influences are the multimillion-dollar diet industry, the mass media, and role models.

Many women believe it is a role obligation to be visually attractive. On a given day in the United States, more than half of all women report that they are dieting; however, the main reason for dieting is cosmetic concerns, not health or fitness. Dieting has become a cultural preoccupation among females of all ages. Even among 10- and 11-year-old girls, nearly four out of five diet. Not surprisingly, a proliferation of weight-reducing centers and spas, as well as diet drugs, guides, aids, and plans, have emerged. As a weight loss measure, cigarette smoking has increased among teenage girls. Eating disorders represent extreme concern about body shape and weight and are thus extensions of slim body ideals. In fact, a history of dieting is common among anorexics and bulimics.

Concerning the mass media, magazine models are uniformly slim, and dieting and weight-control books and magazines are ubiquitous. Even women's magazines not devoted to dieting offer a pervasive amount of food ads and articles on dieting and body shape. Such inclusion encourages weight control preoccupation, through the dual emphasis on eating and staying thin. Compared with men's magazines, women's magazines include a much larger number of food articles and ads, as well as ads and articles on dieting and body shape. Further, in television programs, most females are thinner than the average woman, and in contrast to males, few female characters are overweight.

Regarding the influence of role models, standards for women generally became less curvaceous in the latter part of the 20th century. Contestants in the

Miss America pageant as well as *Playboy* centerfolds have less of an hourglass shape, which reflects an overall decrease in their bust and hip measurements. In addition, many winners of Miss America are thinner than the average contestant. Further, two thirds of *Playboy* centerfolds weigh 15 percent or more below expected weight for height, one of the criteria for anorexia nervosa.

Rather than focus on eating disorders as a medical problem, a critical examination would direct attention to the social conditions and cultural context that promote the genesis and maintenance of anorexia nervosa and bulimia nervosa. Eating disorders are most prevalent in societies that both visually objectify females and endorse pervasive, powerful industries and media that support a cult of thinness.

Diane E. Taub and Penelope A. McLorg

See also Body Image; Cultural Values; Gender Identity and Socialization; Mass Media; Medical-Industrial Complex

Further Readings

American Psychiatric Association. 2000. *Diagnostic and Statistical Manual of Mental Disorders IV–TR.* Washington, DC: American Psychiatric Association.

Gordon, Richard A. 2000. *Eating Disorders: Anatomy of a Social Epidemic.* 2nd ed. Oxford, England: Blackwell.

Morris, Anne M. and Debra K. Katzman. 2003. "The Impact of the Media on Eating Disorders in Children and Adolescents." *Paediatrics & Child Health* 8:287–89.

Sypeck, Mia Foley, James J. Gray, and Anthony H. Ahrens. 2004. "No Longer Just a Pretty Face: Fashion Magazines' Depictions of Ideal Female Beauty from 1959 to 1999." *International Journal of Eating Disorders* 36:342–47.

Taub, Diane E. and Penelope A. McLorg. 2007. "Influences of Gender Socialization and Athletic Involvement on the Occurrence of Eating Disorders." Pp. 81–90 in *Sociological Footprints: Introductory Readings in Sociology,* 10th ed., edited by L. Cargan and J. H. Ballantine. Belmont, CA: Thomson Wadsworth.

ECONOMIC DEVELOPMENT

Encompassing the nexus between political, economic, cultural, and social trends, the study of economic development has been one of the most contentious in sociology. The intellectual course of this field resembles Karl Mannheim's institutionalization of ideas.

Academics and public intellectuals from both industrial and less-developed societies have quarreled for more than half a century over topics related to nation building. The tumultuous intellectual debates that ensued resulted in one of the first instances of international public sociology.

Early Developments

The field of economic development exploded in earnest after World War II. A particular historical conjunction gave rise to the preoccupation with promoting some measure of prosperity among developing nations. The first obvious political event was the process of decolonization, which resulted in the birth and rebirth of new nations, such as Korea regaining independence in 1945 after 40 years of Japanese rule and the emergence of African nation-states in the 1950s and 1960s. The plight of newly independent developing societies and the disparities of the world economy became the focus of much public and academic debate. One result of the resonance of this intellectual trend was the remarkable growth of institutions dedicated to the study of the challenges associated with economic development. Two such emerging organizations, the UN Economic Commission for Latin America and the Social Science Research Council (SSRC) Exploratory Committee on World Areas Research, and its successor, the Committee on Comparative Politics, would later, irrespective of each other, compete in their economic development theorizing.

In addition, several contextual international developments also facilitated the explosion of development thinking. After the outbreak of the cold war and the Chinese revolution, economic development policies were inserted into the overall peripheral containment strategy. Since then, the juxtaposition of political economic interests and humanitarian intentions has resonated in the minds of pundits and academics.

Meanwhile, the foundations of development studies were grounded in Western philosophy. Liberals argued that the wealth of nations depended, in large part, on their ability to capitalize on free trade policies. Mercantilists became ardent supporters of state-sponsored development. Malthusians correlated living standards with population size. Years earlier, Max Weber, in his *Protestant Ethics and the Spirit of Capitalism,* had laid out the foundations for a cultural approach to national development, while Marxists argued that developing nations are often enmeshed in financial and diplomatic networks that sustain their own dependency.

Competing Paradigms

Several competing paradigms offered their own pre-scripts of the causes as well as the policies to overcome the adverse effects of underdevelopment. The first was the modernization perspective. Modernization theory grew out of behaviorist standpoints and the structural-functionalist persuasion that dominated U.S. social sciences for much of the 1940s and early 1950s. Modernization scholars were devout anti-communists, and as such, they conformed to the view that liberalism was absolutely necessary to deflate any stipulations other than a Western approach to development. Modernity, they argued, was essentially the engine to transform backward traditions into Western-style progress. Modernization scholars envisioned this transformation incrementally and linearly. They espoused the conviction that Western development models, particularly the American model, were replicable anywhere in the world. For this reason, modernization scholars fervently supported development aid policies and embedded liberalist programs like the Alliance for Progress.

Some proponents encouraged the emergence of an entrepreneurial elite capable of transforming traditional values into concrete economic growth and development. For them, entrepreneurs were the innovators who restructure the production process. Others went to considerable efforts to foster basic tenets of achievement and modernity to jettison "backwardness."

Needless to say, the ethnocentrism embedded in this line of thinking quickly came under attack for sanitizing the complex and overwhelming reality that developing nations confronted. As a result, a structural version of modernization later gained some currency in the social sciences. Scholars affiliated with the SSRC Committee on Comparative Politics promoted a framework that explored structural obstacles and other conditions affecting economic development without seriously questioning the effects of the world economy. In a widely cited and controversial study, Seymour M. Lipset found a positive correlation between levels of industrialization and democracy. Another provocative study examined how the effectiveness of states facilitates economic development. Another group of scholars scrutinized the modernizing capacity and latent functionality of development.

Modernization was quickly criticized for misunderstanding the distortions of the Western experiment in other parts of the world. Take, for example, Lipset's argument. Supposedly, industrialization promotes the expansion of the middle class, so pivotal for the functioning of democratic politics. Yet, others quickly pointed out that pressure to lower production costs and the desire of transnational capital to remain competitive depressed middle-class wages, resulting in a more sophisticated brand of authoritarianism. In one of the most pointed critiques of modernization, Guillermo O'Donnell, an Argentine sociologist, illustrates how the new authoritarianism unfolds when—to satisfy demands from multinationals—the military, civilian technocrats, and the entrepreneurial elite forge coalitions and transnational pacts with foreign capital that adversely impact the national interest.

Another equally mesmerizing perspective was dependency. As its name implies, the dependency perspective represented the antithesis of liberal modernization. Early on, many *dependentistas* rejected the assumptions of modernization and shared the premise that the predicaments of development must be examined within the broader context of regional and global relations that often inflict developing nations. These relations, essentially sustained by hierarchical structures of power, trap less-developed countries in the periphery of the world economy. Conversely, revolutionary change, not incremental evolution, serves as the most viable way out of underdevelopment conditions.

The dependency movement was a radical outgrowth of the basic "terms of trade" argument proposed by Raul Prebisch and his Economic Commission for Latin America associates. The condition of underdevelopment was largely determined, they argued, by the unequal exchange between exporters of raw materials and manufactured goods. The strategy of development they advocated was industrialization through import substitution. Politically, this policy resulted in the rise of mercantilist states, command economies, and populist social mobilizations. However, scholars within the dependency tradition went further to anticipate such conditions as associated-dependent development, development of underdevelopment, marginality, and internal colonialism.

The dependency movement soon fell under criticism from the right for its lax methodology and its historicism and from the radical left for not going far enough in exploring the inner workings of the international division of labor. An outgrowth of this perspective, therefore, pushed for further understandings of the historical legacy of global capitalism.

Immanuel Wallerstein's world system, even though it did not quarrel with some of the basic premises of dependency, underlines how the economic development *problematique* lies within the organization, nature, and scope of the global economy, not with the nation-states. Conversely, this position argues that while the location of nations in relation to the world system may change over time from the periphery to the semiperiphery—or in a few cases, as with the United States, to the core—the capitalist raison d'être and its patterns of exploitation remain. A foregone conclusion, then, was that the only way to promote more equitable forms of development was by changing the capitalist structure, not the bilateral relations among individual units as the dependency movement earlier proposed. This ominous conclusion eventually cast doubts on the capacity of national development theories to promote viable solutions to the question of underdevelopment.

Recent Directions

More recently, the sociology of national development literature no longer attempts to understand micro and macro structures alone or to chart radical policies. With the advent of globalization, the Asian export–led development model, and the modernization under way in China, the possibility of relative national development growth is again in the minds of scholars and policymakers. Globalization has also gravitated to the study of more technical middle-range development issues, such as the volatility of fiscal reforms, production networks, and the magnitude of trade liberalization. Especially welcomed are the recent examinations of neoliberal policy formations. Finally, another popular line of research discerns the impact of transnational population movements and communities.

This new twist in national development theory also contradicts some of the most impious premises advocated by liberal and neo-Marxist scholars. One noteworthy example is the recent work of Peruvian social scientist Hernando de Soto, who dismisses the myths of prevailing lack of entrepreneurial values among marginal classes in developing societies by demonstrating how transaction costs adversely impact economic development. De Soto concludes instead that development bottlenecks lie within the thick bureaucratic layers devised by rent-seeking states to protect their interests and those of their benefactors.

Enrique S. Pumar

See also Global Economy; Globalization; World-Systems Analysis

Further Readings

Cardoso, Fernando H. and Enzo Faletto. 1979. *Dependency and Development in Latin America.* Berkeley, CA: University of California Press.

Collier, David. 1979. *The New Authoritarianism in Latin America.* Princeton, NJ: Princeton University Press.

De Soto, Hernando. 2000. *The Mystery of Capital.* New York: Basic Books.

Huntington, Samuel. 2006. *Political Order in Changing Societies.* New Haven, CT: Yale University Press.

Portes, Alejandro and A. Douglas Kincaid. 1989. "Sociology and Development in the 1990s: Critical Challenges and Empirical Trends." *Sociological Forum* 4:479–503.

Tarrow, Sidney. 2005. *The New Transnational Activism.* New York: Cambridge University Press.

Wallerstein, Immanuel. 1979. *The Capitalist World Economy.* Cambridge, England: Cambridge University Press.

Weaver, James and Kenneth Jameson. 1981. *Economic Development.* Lanham, MD: University Press of America.

Wood, Charles H. and Bryan R. Roberts. 2005. *Rethinking Development in Latin America.* University Park, PA: Pennsylvania State University Press.

Economic Restructuring

Economic restructuring refers to any major reconfiguring of the primary way in which goods, services, capital, and jobs get produced, distributed, or consumed. Over the past 70 years, the U.S. economy changed from one dominated by manufacturing and farming to one dominated by industries that provide services rather than producing goods. As early as 1955 the percentage of employees in the service sector passed the 50 percent mark, and that trend has continued ever since. In 2004, service industries accounted for 70 percent of the gross domestic product (GDP) and for 75 percent of all employed persons. The Bureau of Labor Statistics projects that by 2014, that employment figure will increase to 78.5 percent.

What are the service industries? As tracked by the U.S. Census Bureau, they are retail and wholesale trade; transportation and warehousing; information, finance, and insurance; real estate and rental and leasing; professional, scientific, and technical services; administration and support, waste management and remediation services; health care and social assistance; arts, entertainment, and recreation; and other services.

The Current U.S. Occupational Structure

Not all service occupations are alike. The diversity in compensation and skills ranges widely and includes occupations such as nurses, child care workers, software engineers, postsecondary teachers, cashiers, and truck drivers. Certain service occupations require highly skilled, highly educated workers, but a majority of the occupations (measured as the number of people in those occupations) do not require a postsecondary degree, although many do require some technical training beyond a high school degree. The top 10 occupations listed in Table 1 employ nearly 20 percent of the total workforce.

As of May 2005, 130 million people were in the workforce. More than 70 percent were in occupations with an average hourly wage under $18.39 or $38,500 a year; 50 percent were in occupations with an

average hourly wage below $15.77 or $32,500 annually; and 24 percent of all workers earned wages at or below the poverty level.

The trend by which low-skill jobs dominate the U.S. labor market will continue, with projections that two thirds of U.S. job growth will come from occupations requiring only on-the-job training. Those with the most projected growth are some of the lowest-paying occupations (see Table 2).

Historical Causes of Economic Restructuring

Why has manufacturing become less of an important economic engine for the United States? In the 1980s many countries, including the United States, changed the international financial rules, making it easier for corporations to move capital and goods from one nation to another. The legal opening of markets also increased competition for U.S.-based companies, as "open" markets are not necessarily equal. U.S. corporations—with the salaries and benefits of their employees and the legal limits on labor, safety, and environmental practices—were at a competitive disadvantage with companies in the developing world. As a result, many U.S. producers utilized

Table 1   Top 10 Largest Occupations in the United States

BLS Occupation	Number Employed (in Millions)	Median Hourly Wage
Retail sales	4.3	9.50
Cashiers	3.5	8.08
General office clerks	3.0	11.40
Registered nurses	2.4	27.54
Laborers and freight, stock, and material movers, hand	2.4	10.20
Food preparation and service workers (including fast food)	11.0	7.90
Waiters and waitresses	2.3	7.14
Janitors and cleaners	2.1	9.58
Customer service representatives	2.1	13.62
Bookkeeping, accounting, and auditing clerks	1.9	14.69
Total	35 million	

Source: Data from Bureau of Labor Statistics Report "Occupational Employment and Wages, May 2005."

Table 2   Top 10 Occupations Projected to Grow

BLS Occupation	Number of Projected New Jobs by 2014	Training Required	Current Median Hourly Wage
Retail salespersons	750,000	On the job	9.20
Registered nurses	700,000	Associates degree	26.28
Postsecondary teachers	510,000	Ph.D.	
Customer service representatives	450,000	On the job	13.22
Janitors and cleaners	425,000	On the job	9.32
Waiters and waitresses	400,000	On the job	6.83
Food preparation service workers	390,000	On the job	7.11
Home health aides	380,000	On the job	9.04
Nursing aides, orderlies, attendants	370,000	Vocational degree	10.31
General and operations managers	300,000	Bachelor's degree and work experience	45.90

Source: Data from Bureau of Labor Statistics *Occupational Outlook Handbook 2006–2007.*

cost-cutting practices called offshoring and outsourcing. *Outsourcing* means buying services from another company—often in another country. *Offshoring* is when companies opt to move their production facilities to foreign countries—often to what are called economic processing zones. Compared with their U.S. counterparts, workers in economic processing zones receive significantly less pay, have fewer health and safety protections, and have fewer rights to act collectively.

At the same time that manufacturing jobs declined, service industries expanded their workforce and also created new areas of work that included jobs for computer programmers, web designers, and Internet technology specialists. Thus manufacturing experienced a twofold shrinkage in terms of its contribution to GDP and percentage of workers it employs.

Service industries are also less susceptible to offshoring and outsourcing pressures. The services they provide, the customers they serve, and the goods they move usually exist at the local level. However, although less susceptible to pressures to outsource or offshore, services are not immune to the competitive pressures to cut labor costs by outsourcing. For example, U.S. tax servicing companies, like H&R Block, hire accountants in India to process U.S. income tax returns; customer service call centers can and do relocate anywhere in the world a company can find English speakers. As technology increases the ability to relocate services to secure cheaper sources of labor, corporations will probably outsource whatever they can.

Effects on Income Inequality

Since the 1970s income inequality in the United States has steadily increased and is now at an all-time high. The Census Bureau reported that 50.5 percent of all income in 2006 went to the top 20 percent of U.S. households; the bottom fifth had a share of just 3.4 percent of all income. Debate continues as to whether or not economic restructuring caused this inequality to grow. Most likely, economic restructuring, combined with the dominant, neoliberal economic assumptions in the 1980s, brought a rise in income inequality. Neoliberalism is the belief that creating open or free markets—which is the absence of, or limit to, regulations on commodity and capital markets—would raise everyone's living standard.

Like the United States, many Western European countries—including France, Germany, and Sweden—have economies where over 70 percent of the GDP comes from service industries. Unlike the United States, however, they do not have the attendant rise in inequality. Some scholars suggest that each government faced a trade-off among economic equality, full employment, and budgetary restraint. U.S. leaders, as opposed to their Western European counterparts, opted for full employment and some comparative budgetary constraints at the expense of economic equality.

Effects on Workers

Opening national borders to trade in goods from other countries made goods cheaper, and hence many economists argue Americans are better off overall, despite growing inequality. But there have been major trade-offs, particularly for low-skilled U.S. workers, their families, and in particular, women-headed households. Historically, manufacturing jobs offered workers some protection through their unions that were able to negotiate job security, living wages, and benefit packages including health care and pensions. All these conditions are less likely in today's job market. Many of today's workers face more job insecurity as employers move to a flexible workforce backed by a philosophy of retaining employees only when they are really needed. By using temporary employees through outside agencies, fewer employers offer benefits. In 2006, for example, only 59.7 percent of workers had health insurance coverage through their employers.

These forces affect subgroups in the U.S. population in different ways depending on race, gender, and education level. The most recent census data show that men who did not graduate from high school earned 22 percent less in 2006 than in 1979, while those with a high school degree or with some college saw their wages remain stagnant. Families with a two-parent household have coped by sending an additional worker out into the workforce. In 2006, 63 percent of women with children under the age of 6 were working, compared with 39 percent in 1975. Female-headed households have fared the worst as women across all levels of education earn, on average, less than men. In 2005, 22.4 percent of working families headed by women were earning wages below the poverty line. This compares with 11.7 percent for households headed by single men and 8.3 percent for married-couple families.

A high correlation exists between race and class and inequality. Blacks and Latinos/as, historically shut out of the good paying jobs, have had a harder time in the shift to a service economy. They are over-represented in the poorest paid and least secure occupations. Even when controlling for education, Latinos/as and blacks make approximately 82 percent of whites' weekly median earnings.

Lorna Mason

See also Deindustrialization; Deregulation; Feminization of Poverty; Global Economy; Inequality; Labor Market; Outsourcing; Postindustrialism; Segregation, Occupational; Service Economy; Split Labor Market; Trickle-Down Economics

Further Readings

DeNavas-Walt, Carmen, Bernadette D. Proctor, and Jessica Smith. 2007. *Income, Poverty, and Health Insurance Coverage in the United States: 2006.* U.S. Census Bureau, Current Population Reports, P60-233. Washington, DC: U.S. Government Printing Office. Retrieved December 24, 2007 (http://www.census.gov/prod/2007pubs/p60-233.pdf).

Tonelson, Alan. 2002. *The Race to the Bottom: Why a Worldwide Worker Surplus and Uncontrolled Free Trade Are Shrinking American Living Standards.* Boulder, CO: Westview.

U.S. Department of Labor, Bureau of Labor Statistics. 2007. *Charting the U.S. Labor Market in 2006.* Retrieved December 24, 2007 (http://www.bls.gov/cps/labor2006/chartbook.pdf).

———. 2007. *Occupational Outlook Handbook 2008–2009.* Washington, DC: U.S. Government Printing Office. Retrieved December 24, 2007 (http://www.bls.gov/oco/home.htm).

———. 2007. "A Profile of the Working Poor, 2005." Report 1001. Retrieved December 24, 2007 (http://www.bls.gov/cps/cpswp2005.pdf).

———. 2007. "Women in the Labor Force: A Databook." Report 1002. Washington, DC: U.S. Government Printing Office. Retrieved December 24, 2007 (http://www.bls.gov/cps/wlf-databook2007.htm).

Wilson, William J. 1996. *When Work Disappears: The World of the New Urban Poor.* New York: Knopf.

ECOSYSTEM

The science of ecology is the study of organisms, their relationship with the physical environment, and the interactions among organisms. Ecosystem is a concept in ecology. An ecosystem consists of both nonliving and living components. The abiotic parts include the atmospheric gases, all forms of water, and sediment. The 28 chemical elements required by living organisms are contained in these three interconnected physical spheres. The biotic segments of an ecosystem are the living organisms in five biological kingdoms: Monera (bacteria and blue-green cyanobacteria), Protista (algae and protozoa), Fungi (mushrooms, molds), Plantae (green plants), and Animalia (animals).

The living organisms in an ecosystem may be divided into two functional groups: producers, which are the photosynthetic plants and algae, and consumers, which are the heterotrophs. Heterotrophs are macro consumers and micro consumers. Macro consumers are herbivores and carnivores. Micro consumers are bacteria and fungi; together they are the decomposers of the ecosystem. The role of the decomposers is to break down dead organic matter into molecules and inorganic compounds. This mineralization results in chemical components that are reused by living organisms. Thus the required chemical nutrients are continually recycled through ecosystems.

Energy flow and nutrient cycling are the dynamic processes that maintain an ecosystem. Solar energy is the source of energy for ecosystems on Earth, and this energy enters the ecosystem through the process of photosynthesis of algae and plants. Pigments in the cells of algae and plants capture solar energy and change it to chemical energy during photosynthesis:

$$6CO_2 + 6H_2O \xrightarrow[\text{pigment}]{\text{sunlight}} C_6H_{12}O_6 + 6O_2$$

$$\text{carbon} + \text{water} \xrightarrow[\text{pigment}]{\text{sunlight}} \text{sugar (glucose)} + \text{oxygen gas}$$

Carbon dioxide gas from the atmosphere is taken in by the plant and algal cells and, in a complex set of biochemical reactions, combines with water to form carbohydrates and to release oxygen gas back to the atmosphere. This primary productivity provides the energy base of the food web in ecosystems. The greater the rate of primary productivity there is, the more energy there will be available to herbivores and carnivores. Light energy must be continually provided to ecosystems for them to survive, because the energy flow is one-way: It enters the ecosystem and is released via cellular respiration at each trophic level and is not recycled.

Aerobic cellular respiration is a metabolic process that occurs in the cells of all living organisms:

$$C_6H_{12}O_6 + 6O_2 \longrightarrow \text{energy released} + 6CO_2 + 6H_2O$$

$$\text{Glucose} + \text{oxygen gas} \longrightarrow \text{energy released} + \text{carbon dioxide} + \text{water}$$

In this process, oxygen is used to break down carbohydrates in the cells to produce energy that the organisms use for normal maintenance, reproduction, and growth. Carbon dioxide gas is released as a by-product of cellular respiration. All organisms undergo cellular respiration. It occurs in heterotrophs all the time and occurs in plants and algae mainly in the dark. The greatest amount of energy in an ecosystem resides in the first trophic level, consisting of plants and algae. The more productive the bottom level is, the more productive the entire ecosystem will be.

Ecosystems are ranked by ecologists in order of their primary productivity, which is the rate at which carbon, from carbon dioxide gas, is incorporated into the chemical structure of the cells of algae and plants. Examples of natural ecosystems are the temperate deciduous forest, coniferous forest, tropical rain forest, grassland prairie, arctic tundra, desert, wetland, lake, stream, estuary, and ocean. An ecosystem can be as small as a quart-size aquarium and as large as an ocean, as long as there exists a food web of interacting autotrophs, heterotrophs, and decomposers, and a light energy source. In natural ecosystems, populations of organisms interact in a complex food web in which energy flows through, nutrients recycle, and decomposers break down organic compounds. Thousands of species may live and interact in one ecosystem. The interactions among populations and the interactions between organisms and the physical environment are incredibly complex, and no system has ever been completely studied.

Ecosystems vary in complexity. For example, a tropical rain forest is very complex and has high biodiversity (many species of organisms). Ecologists have determined that tropical rain forests have more species of organisms than any other ecosystem. On the other end of the scale, the Arctic tundra has relatively low biodiversity. In between are deciduous forests and lakes.

Ecosystems also vary in the number of trophic, or feeding, levels. The least complex system might have only two trophic levels: producers and herbivores that feed on them. Decomposers are always present, but they are not considered a separate level, because they are part of all trophic levels as these bacteria and fungi break down the dead organic matter. Available energy limits the number of trophic levels in an ecosystem. When primary productivity is high in the producer level and energy is transferred efficiently between trophic levels, the total number of trophic levels may reach seven or even eight in an ecosystem such as the ocean. However, three to five trophic levels are most common. The first level is always the producers (algae and plants), the second level consists of all the herbivores lumped together, and the third and higher levels are carnivores (see Figure 1).

Energy flow in ecosystems follows the two laws of thermodynamics. The first law states that energy can neither be created nor destroyed, only changed in form. The second law entails that when energy is transferred from one form to another, some is lost as heat, so the transfer is not 100 percent efficient. Ecosystems obey the laws of physics, and as energy is transferred from one lower level to the next higher level, energy is lost as heat of cellular respiration from the living organisms. Therefore, the upper level always has less available energy than the lower level. This is why light energy must continually enter at the producer level via photosynthesis of algae and plants. Energy is a one-way flow; it does not cycle and must always be replenished. As a rule of thumb, approximately 90 percent of the energy is lost through heat of cellular respiration at each trophic level. Thus only 10 percent of the energy in a lower level is available to the next higher trophic

level. Energy quickly diminishes through the web and, as a result, limits the number of trophic levels in ecosystems.

All systems are connected either directly or indirectly. An example of close connection is a forest that contains a lake and streams to and from the lake. In this example, three ecosystems are directly interconnected. Some organisms and nutrients travel throughout the three systems and between them and the atmosphere above. Ecosystems have no natural boundaries. The biosphere of Earth is a continuum of ecosystems that are determined by the climate and soil type. For example, in eastern North America, the arctic tundra gradually becomes the boreal coniferous forest of Canada and New England to the south, which further south becomes the eastern deciduous forest of the Mid-Atlantic states. All natural ecosystems have been affected by humans, and the impact continues as human activities result in more pressure to modify them. With such influence on Earth, the human species needs to maintain and protect these ecosystems.

Social Obligations Solutions

Human activities threaten the Earth's natural ecosystems. Scientific evidence shows conclusively that increasing concentrations of gases such as carbon dioxide cause climate change that will increase the average temperature of the atmosphere and oceans. The varying consequences include undesirable weather patterns, desertification in some areas and increased precipitation in others, sea level rise with flooding of developed coastal areas and inhabited islands, destruction of wetlands, decreased agricultural production, and species extinction. Deforestation, particularly in the Amazon rain forest, will affect global climate. Deforestation everywhere on the planet affects soil erosion, stream destruction, flooding, and decreased groundwater recharge. Large-scale mining eliminates ecosystems outright and pollutes the remaining ones. Overfishing has decimated most of the ocean's fisheries, which may never recover. In many areas, urban sprawl and habitat destruction are the greatest threats to natural ecosystems, including filling or flooding valuable wetlands.

Humans are the ecosystem destroyers, and we must learn to become the caretakers instead. Most protectors of the environment today are people who played, camped, fished, or hunted in the outdoors and

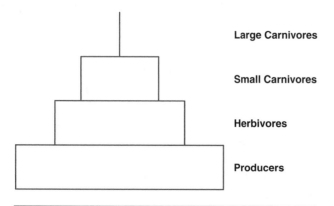

Figure 1   Energy Pyramid Showing Four Trophic Levels and the Decrease in Available Energy From Lower to Higher Levels

thereby developed a love of the environment when they were young. However, there are too few, and they are getting older. Thus the key to the future protection and restoration of natural ecosystems is to have today's children spend much time outdoors playing, camping, hiking, fishing, and hunting. Such environmental education of young people will help develop and maintain a critical mass of voters and lawmakers to ensure environmental protections and the maintenance of our natural ecosystems.

Michael J. Sebetich

See also Acid Rain; Deforestation; Desertification; Environment, Hazardous Waste; Environment, Pollution; Environment, Runoff and Eutrophication; Environment, Sewage Disposal; Environmental Degradation; Environmental Hazards; Extinction; Global Warming; Nonrenewable Resources; Water Organization; Water Quality; Water Resources

Further Readings

Louv, Richard. 2006. *Last Child in the Woods: Saving Our Children from Nature-Deficit Disorder.* Chapel Hill, NC: Algonquin.

Molles, Manuel C., Jr. 2005. *Ecology: Concepts and Applications.* New York: McGraw-Hill.

Ricklefs, Robert E. 2007. *The Economy of Nature: Data Analysis Update.* New York: W. H. Freeman.

Edge Cities

Coined by Joel Garreau in 1991, the term *edge cities* describes the suburbanization of office work, retail trade, and industrial production that followed residential relocation out of urban areas after World War II. More than 200 edge cities exist in the United States and several in Canada, typically located on highway corridors outside central cities. Some commercial clusters were intensifications of land use in formerly rural settlements; others were planned developments on agricultural land. Highway intersections centered some, but most were strip formations along arterial corridors without sharp boundaries or restriction to a single municipality.

Developers used edge cities to capture the increase in value that public highways brought to land on the urban fringe, while satellites and fiber optic networks kept these new entities linked to the national and global economy. Highways made these complexes accessible to suburban workers and consumers, but their automobile dependence added to regional sprawl and highway congestion. Shifting the locale of much office work, they depleted the job and tax base of core cities.

In their early phase, core cities allowed suburban residents to avoid commuting to central cities and permitted developers to erect signature buildings in campus-like environments without the limitation of existing street grids. But as each project stimulated subsequent development on the metropolitan frontier, the costs became apparent. Their low density made them more costly to service than older city locations, they displaced agriculture from prime soils near urban markets, and their dependence on cars led to clogged highways and air pollution. As commercial islands beyond efficient mass transit, they required aprons of grade-level parking that disconnected them from the street and pedestrian fabric of community life. This isolation, initially a cost advantage for speculators, entailed inefficiencies for suppliers and customers and even for employees seeking a restaurant lunch. As a locus of capital investment, they drained economic activity from city locations where schools, housing, and mass transit were already in place. The brownfield locations in older cities, created by concurrent deindustrialization, offered more rational locations for many edge city projects.

Edge cities were not safe from their own obsolescence. Office complexes continued to be built further out on arterial highways, even as firms outsourced staff functions to domestic and foreign suppliers. As business shifted from a national to an international focus, the most competitive business locations proved to be those that provided face-to-face interaction between management and financial and marketing support firms as well as a rich cultural environment. This dynamic stimulated a commercial and residential revival of globally oriented central cities.

In response, some edge cities altered their design. Orange County's John Wayne Airport area, with more than 25 million square feet of office space and a large retail mall, added a performing arts center and plans light rail mass transit to compete with Spectrum, a nearby high-tech industrial park. Upping the ante, Spectrum added office buildings, a cinema complex, and an Amtrak station. Addison, Texas, an office park on the highway north of Dallas, added rapid transit, a conventional street grid, stacked parking, apartments, and retail stores to make it a 24-hour city. Under competitive pressure, edge cities are trying to resemble traditional urban areas in their mix of uses and texture of street life.

Charles R. Simpson

See also Urban Decline; Urban Infrastructure; Urbanization; Urban Sprawl

Further Readings

Abrahamson, Mark. 2004. *Global Cities.* Cambridge, England: Oxford University Press.

Barnett, Jonathan. 2002. "Turning Edge Cities into Real Cities." *Planning* 68(11):11–16.

Garreau, Joel. 1991. *Edge City: Life on the New Frontier.* New York: Doubleday.

EDUCATION, ACADEMIC PERFORMANCE

The past 2 decades witnessed a marked increase in public attention to academic performance. Historically, concern about quality of the U.S. educational system has fluctuated, but rarely has there been a period of such intense interest in measuring and comparing performance of students, teachers, and schools. Whereas in earlier eras the measurement of performance focused on summary indicators, such as graduation from high school, recent efforts utilize more refined measures. Examining the current state of academic performance—defined broadly as how well students in schools achieve the goals established by and for them—requires examination of changes in performance measurement and the changes in the consequences of performance.

Measurement Changes

Two broad reforms in U.S. education over the past decade drive the current focus on academic performance: the development and implementation of standards-based education and the implementation of the No Child Left Behind Act of 2002 (NCLB). Both reforms sharpened policy focus on measuring educational performance.

Standards

Stemming from anxiety about the conditions of U.S. schools following the publication of *A Nation at Risk* in 1983, the standards-based movement emerged. The report warned that the educational foundations of the nation were being "eroded by a rising tide of mediocrity" and that a primary factor contributing to this condition was the lack of rigorous standards in U.S. schools.

Developing and implementing a set of educational standards was held to be the key to addressing the mediocrity identified in *A Nation at Risk.* The core idea of educational standards is that there are sets of basic knowledge and skills that students of a particular grade level should master, such mastery to be evaluated using a series of tests. Reform rests on the notion that educational improvement will occur when rigorous academic (content) standards are set, student performance against these standards is assessed, and then students and teachers are held accountable for meeting these standards. The 1990s thus witnessed a substantial investment of energy by educational policymakers in the development and implementation of content and performance standards. Nearly all states have implemented academic standards and all but two states now have academic standards in the core subjects of mathematics, language arts, science, and social studies.

No Child Left Behind

Following the initiatives of standards-based reforms, particularly the framework of establishment of performance standards, NCLB brought about a number of significant changes in the U.S. education system, particularly in substantially expanding the role of the federal government.

The first of NCLB's four key program elements is stronger accountability for results. The act established a system of requirements for states to fulfill, including the creation of standards for what children in Grades 3 through 8 should know in the subjects of mathematics and reading, as well as a set of assessments to measure how many children have met the state standards. This translated to a substantial expansion of the testing required in school, with students (excluding some exceptions) tested each year in Grades 3 through 8 and at least once during Grades 10 through 12.

The passage of NCLB also served to increase interest in the performance of educational institutions.

Schools must submit annual state-, district-, and school-level "report cards" of how many children achieved acceptable scores on the assessment. Under federal law, local districts must make available achievement data for each school through these report cards. As discussed in the next section, the data carry consequences, with rewards and penalties based on performance. Under NCLB, schools are also required to make adequate yearly progress (AYP) toward improvement in student performance. Although the formulae used to calculate and assess AYP are too complex and opaque to explore here, the central idea of the requirement is that districts must make annual gains in reducing the percentage of students who do not achieve at a proficient level.

The NCLB law is designed so that the primary consumers of data from the report cards are teachers, administrators, and parents; however, data on educational performance have found a much broader audience, with aggregated measures of test scores, graduation rates, and similar data now available in newspaper articles, and even as part of real estate ads.

Consequences of Performance

The increase in policy focus on performance has been accompanied by changes in the use of academic performance measures, with policies basing rewards and sanctions on test performance at the level of individual student, classroom, school, and district. At the student level, the past decade witnessed the widespread adoption of policies whereby grade retention is tied to performance on standardized assessment. Students in the majority of states are now subject to educational statutes that tie promotion to performance on a standardized assessment—and those who are unable to attain a minimum score on such an assessment are required to repeat the school grade. Similarly, a number of states and districts are working to create systems to tie teachers' pay and other career goods to measures of school or classroom performance. These efforts, however, face significant difficulty in their creation and implementation, as teacher rewards historically rest exclusively on tenure and level of education.

Moreover, under NCLB individual districts are now held accountable for the performance of the schools, as measured by standardized assessments in a method analogous to school-level accountability. The law specifies that 95 percent of the students in the district must be tested, as well as 95 percent of

subgroups. With the performance system as constructed, there are specific sanctions for schools and districts that do not meet AYP goals. Schools that do not make AYP goals by this measure are subject to an increasing set of sanctions, such as replacement of school staff, implementation of a new curriculum, and complete "restructuring" of the school, a step involving dissolution of the school.

Unintended Consequences

Although the intent of the policy changes is to increase the measurement and consequences of academic performance to influence instructional practice and effort, these efforts to tie rewards and sanctions also have yielded a number of unintended consequences. Newspaper accounts report a number of episodes of students, teachers, and even administrators cheating on high-stakes exams. Similarly, other reports have revealed students being classified as special needs (a category with special testing provisions under NCLB) to avoid their inclusion in the school's performance measures.

Another unintended consequence of the high-stakes testing regime is that teachers and schools may focus resources disproportionately on those students at the margin of passing the test. For example, one study of students in a Texas public school told of teachers focusing the bulk of their effort on students identified as "bubble kids," those who were just below passing but could conceivably pass with additional help. All of these triage and cheating actions are understandable in light of the heightened stakes of performance, as tangible rewards and penalties are tied to test results.

Persistence of Performance Differences

Proponents argue that both standards-based reforms and NCLB can serve as the basis for improving both excellence and equity in education. The NCLB Web site explicitly makes this point: The law is "designed to help close the achievement gap between disadvantaged and minority students and their peers." Yet, despite the attention to the measures of student performance and revisions in the measurement and consequences of performance, significant gaps in performance persist—and they persist in the face of a federal program designed to address the historical gaps in educational performance. One innovative aspect of NCLB is that it requires performance results to be disaggregated by gender, race/ethnicity, English language proficiency, migrant status, disability status, and socioeconomic status. However, gaps in assessed performance persist. Moreover, there is evidence that poor and nonwhite students are increasingly classified as special education or having educational needs that exclude them from the pool of students tested, a strategy designed to meet performance targets without addressing students' educational needs.

Future of Academic Performance

While academic performance will almost certainly remain a topic of importance in the future, it is not clear whether or how the current system of performance measurement, rewards, and sanctions will persist. NCLB is up for reauthorization in 2008 and, at present, its prospects for renewal are uncertain. A growing chorus of critics of testing programs have repeatedly made the argument that these programs limit student learning to only those topics tested and that what is tested is a narrow slice of what students should know, ignoring skills such as problem solving and critical thinking. Whether and to what extent these criticisms bring about changes in the measurement and consequences of educational performance remains an open question.

Christopher Weiss

See also Academic Standards; Charter Schools; Education, Inner-City Schools; Education, Policy and Politics; Education, School Privatization; Education, Special Needs Children; Educational Equity; Magnet Schools; No Child Left Behind Act; School Dropouts; School Funding; School Segregation; School Vouchers

Further Readings

Booher-Jennings, Jennifer. 2005. "Below the Bubble: 'Educational Triage' and the Texas Accountability System." *American Educational Research Journal* 42(2):231–68.

Carnoy, Martin and Susanna Loeb. 2002. "Does External Accountability Affect Student Outcomes? A Cross-State Analysis." *Educational Evaluation and Policy Analysis* 24(4):305–31.

Jacob, Brian A. and Steven D. Levitt. 2003. "Rotten Apples: An Investigation of the Prevalence and Predictors of Teacher Cheating." *Quarterly Journal of Economics* 118(3):843–77.

Ravitch, Diane. 1995. *National Standards in American Education: A Citizen's Guide.* Washington, DC: Brookings Institution Press.

EDUCATION, INNER-CITY SCHOOLS

Because the vast majority of U.S. students reside in urban areas, their education and indeed the preservation of the values of democracy are intrinsic to the success or failure of U.S. inner-city schools. Such schools are historically overpopulated and underfunded, leading to problems relating to the quality of education and learning activities offered in comparison with suburban schools. Of concern are large classes affecting discipline, motivation, teaching effectiveness, and morale, as well as having sufficient school supplies and attractive learning facilities. Maintaining a safe environment and recruiting and retaining good teachers are other primary concerns.

Like their suburban counterparts, inner-city schools address the usual pressures of preparing students for productive lives upon graduation. In many instances, contemporary inner-city student bodies are multiracial, multiethnic, and socially and ethnically diverse. Complicating "normal" teaching and administrative challenges—for example, the practical enactment of classroom authority—is the need to nurture positive academic and racial/ethnic identity and the ongoing negotiations between teachers and students. These teacher–student relations are socially constructed and linked to social problems in the wider society.

Public schools located in densely populated urban areas contend with challenges that are indistinguishable from the broader social environments in which the schools and their students exist. Crime and gang activity, particularly activities related to the selling and using of illegal drugs, coupled with low societal expectations of inner-city students, make up an almost insurmountable barrier to school—and student—success. Recent empirical and ethnographic studies of drug-related social problems, linked to the rising incidence of violent crime, point to potentially dire consequences for poor students of color in inner-city neighborhoods situated in urban centers. However temporary they may be, the complex social and economic benefits of participation in the local drug and gang cultures in inner cities can be an irresistible lure to young people with few family or financial resources. Although a thriving drug and gang culture creates myriad problems, including poverty, drug addiction, homelessness, and the like, such a culture also can offer a sense of belonging and even a sense of social structure to the community.

Findings from recent research on low-income African American and Latino/a students identify key factors that influence racial/ethnic identity formation in inner-city schools. Such findings link racial/ethnic identity formation with student achievement and, ultimately, school success and describe student responses as falling into one of three general categories: (1) cultural mainstreamers, (2) cultural straddlers, and (3) noncompliant believers.

Cultural mainstreamers express themselves culturally in race-neutral terms and, as might be expected, tend to achieve at higher levels in comparison with the other two groups. The cultural mainstreamers appear to acknowledge an essential racist environment while simultaneously accepting the structural limitations of assimilation. The implication is that cultural assimilation—accommodation to the norms, values, and cultural behaviors of middle-class white society—place such students at odds with their racial/ethnic peers.

Those in the second group, the *cultural straddlers,* inhabit two worlds. They honor the school's cultural code while at the same time constructing an alternative meaning for their everyday academic experience as students. Furthermore, the enrolled children of immigrants often have limited English proficiency, and the language barrier often constrains their parents' interaction with the school and reinforcement of these children's learning.

The *noncompliant believers*, predictably the group least likely to experience school success, paradoxically strongly believe in education, especially its potential for upward mobility. As might be expected, students who resist the premium placed by schools on academic work tend to do poorly academically. However, contemporary qualitative studies have uncovered a more nuanced appreciation for the processes whereby cultural complexities are implicated in a racial/ethnic dynamic that implicitly rejects the academic values of white society. In particular, noncompliant students tend to acutely struggle with the norms of the school— its dress code, the policing of student behavior, or an irrelevant school curriculum.

Issues of student and cultural diversity complicate the consolidation of professional authority in the classroom. This leads, potentially, to the academic underachievement of straddlers and noncompliant students, or worse, ultimately pushing many young black and Latino males into criminal activity and probable eventual incarceration. The broad social challenge is to achieve educational and social equity in an increasingly multiracial and multicultural society. Given the educational and political challenges of narrowing the achievement gap, the central goal of the No Child Left Behind Act, both a conceptually more sophisticated understanding of teachers' authority and the application of this legitimate authority in relation to student identity are crucial.

Luis Mirón

See also Education, Academic Performance; Educational Equity; Ethnicity; No Child Left Behind Act; Race; School Dropouts; School Funding; School Segregation; School Violence; School Vouchers; Social Constructionist Theory

Further Readings

Anyon, Jean. 2005. *Radical Possibilities: Public Policy, Urban Education, and a New Social Movement.* New York: Routledge.

Carter, Prudence L. 2005. *Keepin' It Real: School Success beyond Black and White.* Oxford, England: Oxford University Press.

Lauria, Mickey and Luis F. Mirón. 2005. *Urban Schools: The New Social Spaces of Resistance.* New York: Peter Lang.

Lipman, Pauline. 2003. *High Stakes Education: Inequality, Globalization, and Urban School Reform.* New York: Routledge.

Mirón, Luis F. 1996. *The Social Construction of Urban Schooling: Situating the Crisis.* Cresskill, NJ: Hampton.

Noguera, Pedro A. 2003. *City Schools and the American Dream: Reclaiming the Promise of Public Education.* New York: Teachers College Press.

Sentencing Project. 2003. "The Economics of Drug Selling: A Review of the Research." Washington, DC: Sentencing Project.

EDUCATION, POLICY AND POLITICS

The professional standing of educators in U.S. society is particularly conflicted, and this situation weakens their voice in shaping educational policy at the national, state, and even local levels. As a result, decisions made often reflect political considerations rather that professional, academic insights.

Public school teachers, who are the most visible and largest segment of the profession, offer a prime example of how the defining characteristics of professional status are insufficiently established and, as a consequence, how the status of educator as a professional is absent or compromised. Historians and social commentators since de Tocqueville have noted a number of reasons why teaching has not fully attained the standing of fields such as medicine, law, nursing, pharmacy, and others. These include the sheer number of persons in public school instruction, the local genesis and control of the schools, the popular conceit that no specialized knowledge is necessary for the teaching role, and the convention of allowing untrained persons to teach under "emergency" conditions. Also blurred are the lines between certified teachers practicing in their specialization and those who are either uncertified or teaching out of their field. Many thus casually use the term *teacher* to refer to anyone who offers instruction of any kind, as opposed to protected titles such as physician, attorney, and nurse. Teachers have strength in numbers, but they suffer from an unclear societal identity, which gives them a tenuous grip on professional status.

To a large extent, these conditions spill over onto professors of education, particularly onto those in teacher education. The education professoriate is numerous, like teachers, which lends some influence. Their *knowledge base*—to employ the field's own term—undergoes much internal debate, however, and receives outside challenges over its very existence. Even the question of the need for the field of teacher education is continually at issue. One need not be a scholar in the field to verify the phenomena that challenge the field. For example, no universal, mandatory accreditation for teacher preparation exists. Competing accrediting bodies take radically different approaches to their mission. Furthermore, numerous states accept alternative pathways to certification. Such alternatives may require, for example, no more than acquisition of a bachelor's degree and passing a standardized test of general knowledge. Part-time instructors without terminal degrees or scholarly credentials often conduct teacher education in transported "storefront" programs. A new movement matriculates elementary teachers at community colleges, reverting to a pre–World War II standard of preparation. These challenges to teacher education are unique: No other major field faces such threats of de-professionalization and de-skilling.

Phenomena such as these have a profound influence on education policy and politics and contribute to a destructive cycle affecting the profession. Assigned low status and struggling with an uncertain identity, educators are often bypassed by elected officials in the formation of policy that affects their practice. Such action prevents educators from overcoming challenges of identity and autonomy, allowing further incursions to take place. Perceived as low status and quasi-professional, educators seem to need only minimal preparation, so the cycle replicates itself at the levels of teacher education and policy development.

Some recent events in reading provide an important example. On the federal level, the National Institutes of Health, specifically under the National Institute of Child Health and Human Development, assembled a research strand in reading. By determining that literacy was a "health concern," this study of research in reading thus distanced itself from the teachers and professors of reading and literacy. The researchers, named the National Reading Panel, drawing on paradigms identified with educational psychology but distant from the practice of teaching reading, presented a lengthy, prescriptive report on reading instruction. Complementing the report was a summary and an executive summary, each of which deviated from the content of the report and neither of which the panel vetted. The report quickly affected policy and funding in reading across the United States. Even as the scholarly community of reading specialists called the report (and especially the summaries) into question, the U.S. Department of Education moved quickly to encourage applications for discretionary funding based on the recommendations of the summaries, thereby narrowly restricting educational policy and practice at the state and district levels. The net result was a redirection of federal money to prescriptive, textbook-oriented programs published by corporations active in the world of Washington lobbyists. Sloganeering, with such phrases as "Reading Wars" and "Phonics vs. Whole Language," reduced the discussion of improving literacy to a publicity battle rather than a public discussion of the substance and subtlety of what was at issue.

What was wrong with this process? It co-opted scholarly processes in the selection process of the panel as well as its means of deliberating. Later, the process compromised the report's validity when popularized, and slanted versions of the report were put forward to influence policy formation. Politics and public relations were disguised as scholarship for the purpose of "feeding the voter base" of phonics advocates and steering government funding to campaign donors. The experience, expertise, and perspectives of teachers were excluded except for the marginalized voice of dissent, in this case, from one panel member who had been a teacher of reading. The voices and views of reading scholars express grave concerns in the literature, but these remain primarily within the academic research community and have little influence on policy implementation.

In another example, on a statewide level, legislators ordered the California Commission for Teacher Certification to create a set of objectives in reading for preservice teachers as well as a standardized test that would serve as a gatekeeper for entry to the profession. The commission, to its credit, salvaged the process by introducing a list of expectations and an assessment, the Reading Instruction Competency Assessment, which surpasses conventional standardized tests in determining competence in professional practice. Professors of education in reading methods courses, however, were confronted overnight with a prescribed curriculum for much of their preservice coursework in reading. This is another example of a process that provides a stunning message to universities about the degree of control of the curriculum that the legislature is able to assume when so motivated. Rarely does much resistance or response emerge from faculties of education or higher education at large in such cases, yet the vulnerability of faculties of education to imposition from the political world should attract the attention of all faculty.

Characterizing education policy and politics in the United States is the marginalization of professional educators from the process of consultation and decision making. Even though teachers' unions are among the top donors to the Democratic Party, the voices of teachers and teacher educators and their organizations are notably absent from both the writing of policy and the debates that lead to legislation. Today, in a period marked by the heightened infusion of public relations techniques into politics, policy such as No Child Left Behind (NCLB) is distinguished not only by its neglect of professional education expertise but also by its undermining of the public education establishment.

Education policy has departed so far from informed, collaborative decision making among educators and politicians that it has become the vehicle for creating wedge issues in political life and a means for manipulating the public treasury for the benefit of publishing houses and other campaign donors with no professional responsibility to students and society.

The statistically questionable thresholds of annual yearly progress have made NCLB a fool's game for public education in which there are countless ways to be deemed a "failed school" and the paths to success are few and improbable. This high-stakes scenario extended the federal tradition of unfunded mandates by setting high standards without providing the additional funding known to be necessary for meaningful reforms to take place. NCLB also has not addressed what are recognized as the chronic and "savage inequalities" of the U.S. school funding system that distributes per student support in a highly inequitable fashion that is particularly disadvantageous to urban, minority schoolchildren.

Without an acknowledged and significant place in policy formation for professional educators and an honest, in-depth presentation and discussion of issues before legislators and the public, education policy and politics will continue to be subject to exploitation for purposes other than the welfare of children and youth. As the inadequacies of the current political era continue to draw criticism and public discussion nationally and internationally, educators may have an opportunity to take their rightful place as informed and experienced professionals in the arena of policy formation and political process. Progress of this type cannot occur, however, unless teachers and professors of education and their organizations are persistent and assertive in their pursuit of professional respect and autonomy.

Paul Shaker

See also Education, Academic Performance; Education, Inner-City Schools; Education, School Privatization; Education, Silencing; Educational Equity; No Child Left Behind Act; School Dropouts; School Funding; School Vouchers

Further Readings

Apple, Michael. 2006. *Educating the 'Right' Way: Markets, Standards, God, and Inequality*. 2nd ed. New York: Routledge.

Cochran-Smith, Marilyn and Kenneth M. Zeichner, eds. 2005. *Studying Teacher Education: The Report of the AERA Panel on Research and Teacher Education*. Mahwah, NJ: Erlbaum.

Garan, Elaine M. 2004. *In Defense of Our Children: When Politics, Profit and Education Collide*. Portsmouth, NH: Heinemann.

Nichols, Sharon L. and David C. Berliner. 2007. *Collateral Damage: How High-Stakes Testing Corrupts America's Schools.* Cambridge, MA: Harvard University Press.

Spring, Joel. 2004. *Conflict of Interests: The Politics of American Education.* 5th ed. New York: McGraw-Hill.

EDUCATION, SCHOOL PRIVATIZATION

A controversial and often politically tinged idea, school privatization in the United States describes a range of proposals to transfer K–12 education from the public to the private sector. These proposals stem mostly from conservative critiques of public education that in turn sparked reforms such as school vouchers, charter schools, and school choice. Such measures attempt to bring public schools into the sway of market forces—supply and demand—in a bid to reward good educational practices and penalize bad ones.

Implicitly, such measures usually reflect the belief that the public sector is less efficient and less effective than private institutions, whether the latter are non-profit or for profit. They may also draw on the libertarian notion that education and social programs are not a proper concern of government, which should be limited to only the most basic necessities of public order and defense. Privatization plans also appeal to advocates of religious education as a means to fund and legitimize their cause, and such plans offer an opportunity to circumvent certain teachings in public schools that they oppose on religious grounds, like human evolution and sex education.

Chartered and Privately Managed Schools

Charter schools represent the most widespread effort at privatization in the United States. As of 2007, an estimated 4,000 elementary and secondary charter schools were in operation. Charters first appeared in the 1990s as a solution to various problems perceived in the public schools. Some are effectively private, whereas others are more directly supervised by a local school district. A related practice is privately managed public schools, where a so-called education management organization (EMO), often a for-profit company like Edison Schools, Inc., runs one or more schools in a district. In either case, these schools may depart from certain rules and practices of ordinary public schools to carry out innovations as their organizers see fit. For example, charters usually have different rules for admission, different staffing and management policies, and not infrequently, they are run entirely by EMOs. Often they adopt a mix of several "alternative" practices, either in pedagogy or management, although some adopt few or no such measures at all. In theory, though, all are held accountable for student progress and risk losing their charter if students fail to meet state-mandated levels of achievement.

In fact, the sheer breadth of different organizations, structures, curricula, and pedagogies of these schools poses a major hurdle for evaluating their effectiveness. Although they all have special legal status with respect to public schools, they are far from having a single, coherent policy or educational strategy to assess. To treat them all as one method of schooling is to ignore the vast differences among them.

Research Evaluations

Social scientists have not, for the most part, painted a flattering portrait of either the motives or the outcomes of privatization efforts. Public schools, however imperfect, have long been perceived as a leveling mechanism to reduce inequality in society; some social philosophers argue that education is a basic right and a requirement of democracy, no matter how inefficient public schooling may be. In the ideal case, public schools allow people of limited means to develop skills and talents which, in turn, allow them to compete effectively for placement in higher education and desirable jobs. Public schools' success at attaining this ideal, though, has been roundly criticized; according to many observers, they have not leveled the playing field enough. Hence one rationale for privatization: If public schools have not lived up to their promise, so the theory goes, more rigorous and dynamic private schools could fill the gap. However, this is not the conclusion of most scholars when considering the question from the standpoint of equal opportunity for socially and economically disadvantaged groups. To the contrary, privatization appears to them a retreat from the goal of universal education. Drawing on theories of class and inequality, they argue that privatization only widens the opportunity gap. Moreover, some scholars dispute the free-market logic on which most privatization plans are based. They cite imperfect information about which school is "best" and wealthier parents' ability to intervene more effectively to have their students placed in the preferred schools, thereby reproducing inequality along class lines. Meanwhile, on the supply side, scholars question whether a truly competitive industry could ever emerge to set off a "race to the top" in terms of quality, as opposed to a "race to the bottom" aimed at consolidating profits and market share.

Depending on the locale, privatized schools can "drain" the public schools of better prepared students, who, for example, may seek out a charter school for higher academic quality. This appeared to happen in Arizona, where white, non-Hispanic students disproportionately chose charter schools over regular public schools, and these same students were more likely to have higher test scores. But privatized schools might also have higher concentrations of students who are struggling, as in cases where a charter school has replaced a local public school that was considered below par. In either scenario, the population of the privatized school is unlike that of surrounding schools, the result of a selection bias that can affect both privatized and public schools. Studies also show that the rise of charter schools may have a negative effect on student–teacher ratios at nearby conventional schools. Thus the problem becomes one of finding an adequate comparison to measure any private school advantages over conventional schools.

One solution is to compare student achievement within categories of ethnicity, sex, language background, and past academic performance—for example, comparing high-achieving black students at a charter school with high-achieving blacks at a conventional public school. Other approaches include comparing learning growth rates to national averages and following individual students through school to measure their particular gains. In the case of vouchers, random assignment—the optimal solution—has led to more compelling data in cities like New York. In short, any meaningful comparison must take both policy differences and potential selection bias into account. Unfortunately, some published evaluations have failed to do so, leading at times to prematurely negative or positive assessments of the benefits they might offer.

Overall, research in this area has been contradictory despite the level of funding and attention directed toward charter schools, vouchers, and similar efforts. Most careful studies on these issues find that privatization has, at best, a small advantage, usually as measured in performance on standardized tests. Still, a few well-researched econometric studies attribute higher student gains to privatization measures, although not always across all groups of students. Most often, comparisons turn up essentially no difference between privatized ventures and conventional public schools, and in a few cases, the private efforts appear worse. Strikingly similar results appear in studies of voucher programs (e.g., Wisconsin), charter schools (Arizona), and privately managed schools (multiple sites managed by Edison Schools, Inc.). Further dampening the prospects of privatization reforms is evidence that private efforts, and specifically charter schools, can actually harm public schools by taking away resources and increasing ethnic segregation. In short, the upside for privatization appears to be small, and it may be outweighed by the potential downside.

Scott Heil

See also Charter Schools; Income Disparity; Inequality; School Funding; School Segregation; School Vouchers

Further Readings

Carnoy, Martin. 1998. "National Voucher Plans in Chile and Sweden: Did Privatization Reforms Make for Better Education?" *Comparative Education Review* 42:309–37.

Dee, Thomas S. and Helen Fu. 2004. "Do Charter Schools Skim Students or Drain Resources?" *Economics of Education Review* 23:259–71.

Hoxby, Caroline M. 2003. *The Economics of School Choice.* Chicago: University of Chicago Press.

Miron, Gary and Brooks Applegate. 2000. *An Evaluation of Edison Schools Opened in 1995 and 1996.* Kalamazoo, MI: Western Michigan University, The Evaluation Center.

Sanders, Nicholas M. 2002. "Would Privatization of K–12 Schooling Lead to Competition and Thereby Improve Education? An Industrial Organization Analysis." *Educational Policy* 16:264–87.

Travers, Paul D. 1996. "Academic Privatization and Choice in Public Education, K–12." *Education* 116:471–75.

Woods, Philip A., Carl Bagley, and Ron Glatter. 1998. *School Choice and Competition: Markets in the Public Interest?* New York: Routledge.

EDUCATION, SILENCING

Silencing in education (as verb) refers to the state of being forgotten; to put to rest; to be quiet, as with selected voices of students, public school teachers, and professors. *Silence* (as noun) suggests concealment or secrecy; the absence of sound or noise; omission of mention or expressed concern.

In its theoretical variations, silence has been categorized as either cultural or ontological. Within the cultural—for example, socioeconomic, feminist, and postcolonial theory—silence is used to expose hegemonic workings, linguistic dispossession, and sites of repression. In contrast, Western ontological theory imbues silence with a transcendental signifying capacity, disassociated from language's contingency, or, following post-structuralism, grants it a constitutive role at the heart of language. Silence, like meaningfulness, has both an absence and a presence. It requires one to rethink, to welcome in, to host difference, for it is neither literal silence, as in the absence of speaking, nor epistemological silence, as when faced with the unspeakable, but ontological silence, the silence of Being or Life itself. This entry addresses the theoretical variations and the implications of silence in education.

In cultural terms, silence is a form of resistance. For example, some researchers describe a continuum of women's perspectives on knowledge, where silence is a position of unconsciousness. Silence as such reflects a position in which women experience themselves as mindless and voiceless and subject to the whims of external power. Silence is thus contingent upon the individual's relationship to a community of speakers, institutional structures, and the individual's relationship to power and language. Silences also express power struggles because certain voices or accounts count while others are discounted. For instance, preservice teachers express their practice in what they name and what remains unnamed. Since enactment of the *No Child Left Behind* legislation, there have been widespread efforts to silence those whose views challenge current political polities and initiatives, to restrict forms of research by funding and supporting only those aligned with current policy, and to curtail what public school teachers can say and do in the classroom.

Michel Foucault's description of silence captures some of the implicit power dynamics of discourse. Power lies not only with the things one declines to say or is forbidden to name, but also with the authorized type of discourse or form of discretion required by those who can and cannot speak of such things. He emphasizes there is not one but many silences, and they are an integral part of the strategies that underlie and permeate discourses.

Foucault considers silence essential to speech. Silence is meaning without language and can be a substance with meaning, just as language can be without meaning. Silence is not mere background to speech; it is a state of being shaped and colored by meanings. When institutionally sanctioned, discourse becomes powerful because it positions the subject in relation to what and how something is said and in relation to a community that favors and makes available particular practices. When the powerless use silence to avoid conflict, it is not a deficit of language but a counter-language of critique.

Janet Miller explains that the silence of both her students and herself belies the claim that educators have overcome historical, social, cultural, economic, racial, gender, and class constraints that deny them the power to decide about curriculum and what counts as knowledge. Professors, preservice teachers, and those in public schools continue to be constricted by hierarchical structures of schooling and the legacy of a behaviorist-oriented curriculum field that requires the separation of classroom experiences from everyday lives. Such unnatural silence may envelop educators and researchers in a comforting sense of supposed completeness or a muffling of questions.

Curriculum, critical, queer, and feminist theorists are moving not only into areas that may break that unnatural silence but also into the silencing aspects of communication features in studies across the social sciences, especially in clinical, psychotherapeutic, and experimental psychology. In organization studies, scholars frequently note that organizations with a deeply embedded patriarchal discourse are generally intolerant of dissent, so employees are often reluctant to speak about problems. The silence sustained within such discourse, argues Adrienne Rich, severs women from their history and constitutes one of the ways in which women's work and thinking are made to seem sporadic, errant, and orphaned of any tradition of their own. This belief is true not only of women but also of various groups, including racial and ethnic minorities. The result is not just to render them voiceless but to blame them for not having a voice, thereby weakening their relationship to a community and their relationship to power and language. This silence in organizations can make people unable to articulate certain types of experience, such as the aesthetic, or the emotional, when silence seems governed by norms or rules that dissuade people from speaking out. This structure has led to a focus on organizational conspiracies, cultures, and climates of silence. Silence is a feature of all organizations, including schools and universities, which may be theorized as an effect of both power and management.

Alexandra Fidyk

See also Conflict Perspective; Culture Wars; Education, Policy and Politics; Feminist Theory; Hegemony; Hidden Curriculum; No Child Left Behind Act; Queer Theory; Standpoint Theory

Further Readings

Belenky, Mary F., Blythe M. Clinchy, Nancy R. Goldberger, and Jill M. Tarule. 1996. *Women's Ways of Knowing: The Development of Self, Voice, and Mind.* 10th ed. New York: Basic Books.

Bollnow, Otto. 1982. "On Silence—Findings of Philosophico-Pedagogical Anthropology." *Universitas* 24(1):41–47.

Dauenhauer, Bernard P. 1980. *Silence: The Phenomenon and Its Ontological Significance.* Bloomington, IN: Indiana University Press.

Foucault, Michel. 1980. *The History of Sexuality.* Vol. 1. Translated by R. Hurley. New York: Vintage.

Jaworski, Adam. 1993. *The Power of Silence: Social and Pragmatic Perspectives.* Newbury Park, CA: Sage.

Miller, Janet L. 2005. *Sounds of Silence Breaking: Women, Autobiography, Curriculum.* New York: Peter Lang.

Polanyi, Michael. 1969. *Knowing and Being.* Chicago: University of Chicago Press.

———. [1974] 1998. *Personal Knowledge: Towards a Post-critical Philosophy.* New ed. New York: Routledge.

Rich, Adrienne. [1979] 1995. *On Lies, Secrets and Silence: Selected Prose 1966–1978.* New York: Norton.

EDUCATION, SPECIAL NEEDS CHILDREN

Throughout history, there has been an enormous disparity in attitudes toward and treatment of individuals with disabilities in the workplace and the community. The advent of universal public education during the 19th century added another area in which this disparity would play out.

Similar to many other universal rights, publicly supported education was denied to many individuals with disabilities in the United States up through the first half of the 20th century. In the 1950s, organizations of parents and professionals coalesced to press for the right of children with disabilities to receive a public education, and political leaders gradually began to acknowledge that right through legislation and court decisions. Educators responded by establishing special education programs and the bureaucracy by which students in need of special education could be identified and provided with services. The first significant federal legislation was Public Law No. 94-142, The Education of All Children. Passed in 1975, this law established three bedrock principles of special education. These principles have since expanded through several critical court decisions and the reenactments of the law. The current version is the Individuals with Disabilities Education Improvement Act, commonly known as IDEA 2004.

The first principle is that all children, regardless of ability, are entitled to a free, appropriate public education. Districts must provide programming with a suitable curriculum and instruction for each individual child with special needs. A continuum of services now exists, ranging from assistance within the regular education classroom to placement in a hospital or institution.

The second principle is a criterion for placement known as the least restrictive environment. This means that, of the range of settings where appropriate services can be provided for an individual child, the first choice must be the setting that is as close as possible to the setting the child would be educated in if the child had no disability.

The third principle is that children's right to be educated with their peers must not be infringed upon without their consent, or more typically, that of their parents. Federal law clearly defines the procedural safeguards in the provisions for obtaining informed parental consent before any decision is made regarding evaluation, classification, or placement.

Embedded in these principles is the intent to provide services that are nondiscriminatory in nature and designed to enable individuals to lead productive and independent lives as adults. However, progress in the education of students with special needs has not resolved many of the issues that confront individuals with disabilities. In addition, the classification and placement procedures of children have produced uncertainty and conflict among parents and educators. At best, the process can be categorized as a work in progress.

Changes in terminology reflect efforts to avoid unfairly categorizing children receiving special education services. Replacing the term *handicapped* is the term *disabled*, making a finer distinction between the two terms. A disability refers to a condition where an individual is unable to perform certain life skills because of a loss of function in one of the bodily systems. Handicap is situation specific; children with an attention deficit disorder may have a handicap where they are required to sit and listen for long periods of time, whereas on the playground no handicap is evident. In addition, leaders in the field of special education maintain that the language used in speaking about children in special education is important. Naming children by their diagnosis, as in "a learning disabled child" or "the autistic," suggests that the disability is the major aspect of the child's life. Advocates instead promote the use of nomenclature that emphasizes the person rather than the disability, as in "individuals with disabilities" or "a child with autism."

A more intense debate focuses on the practice of labeling children by their diagnosis in the process of identifying those in need of special education services. Supporters of this practice maintain that the use of a diagnosis to categorize a child helps to suggest means of remediation and programming. Opponents criticize the stigmatizing nature of the process of labeling; labels gradually slip into public use and often acquire a pejorative connotation. In addition, within disability categories, wide variations exist in ability, motivation, and attitude that are masked by a label. Labels also influence expectations. These can limit consideration of all the strengths and weaknesses of a child in formulating individualized goals and services.

Another issue related to labeling is the disproportionately higher classification of students from minority groups. African Americans constitute 16.6 percent of the school-age population but a larger proportion (20.5 percent) of the students classified for special education, a fact that engenders widespread concern and criticism. African American students are 2.99 times more likely to be classified as having mental retardation and 2.21 times more likely to be classified as having an emotional disturbance than all other racial groups combined. Some experts link this disproportion in classification to income; 25 percent of students with disabilities live in poverty compared with 20 percent of the general population. Social welfare programs, preschool programs such as Head Start, and increased preparation in helping teachers teach children from diverse cultural and linguistic backgrounds attempt to reverse the trend.

Debate over the setting for delivery of special education services reflects concerns over both the discriminatory nature of isolating children from their peers and the effectiveness of instruction in a special education setting. *Inclusion* is the term to denote the trend to keep a classified child in the general education classroom with the delivery of appropriate services. The debate largely focuses on the second aspect of this issue: the effectiveness of instruction in inclusive settings. Advocates of inclusion point to the stimulation of interaction of peers who model learning and behavior and the benefits for children without disabilities to learn to interact with a wider range of abilities. Opponents argue that the goals and pace of the curriculum in the general education classroom are too far removed from what children with moderate to severe disabilities need to learn and that their presence in the classroom is disruptive to the learning of their nondisabled peers. Research has not provided definitive answers because it is not entirely acceptable to place children in control groups, and challenges remain to providing remedial services within the general education classroom. However, as a result of this push, the number of classified students spending 79 percent or more of their day in the regular class increased from 33 percent to 46 percent between 1990 and 2000.

Concern over the effectiveness of special education has been an issue since initial efficacy studies in the 1950s. Part of this concern is related to budget issues. On average, it costs approximately $6,000 in additional funds to educate a child with a disability. It is evident too, that despite extensive interventions, most students in special education continue to lag behind their nondisabled peers on measures of achievement. For example, on the National Assessment of Educational Progress administered in 2002, 36 percent of classified eighth graders scored at the proficiency level, compared with 79 percent of their nondisabled peers.

This concern with efficacy manifests itself in two ways. The first is an increase in the degree of accountability in special education. Children with disabilities are required to work toward the same curriculum standards as their nondisabled peers. As a corollary, progress toward those standards must be measured and documented. P.L No. 107-110, the No Child Left Behind Act (2001), mandates assessment of children with disabilities and establishes requirements for corrective action if targets are not reached. Opponents of No Child Left Behind have criticized the assumption that, with effective instruction, nearly all students with disabilities can meet grade-level curriculum standards.

Special educators and laypeople are also troubled by signs that transition to a productive adulthood for individuals with disabilities is often an unrealized dream. Nationally, only 48 percent of classified students leave high school with a diploma. They also endure rates of unemployment at significantly higher rates than the general population, ranging from 55 to 79 percent of those students with moderate to severe disabilities. Studies tend to show that classified students are often unprepared for the world of work. As a result, new legislation requires an increased emphasis on transition planning from age 14 on up. Components of the planning include consideration of a student's abilities and preferences, the provision of school experiences that would help students achieve occupational goals, and collaboration between school, family, and public agencies to identify postsecondary resources for education, employment, and recreational activities.

Peter Griswold

See also Education, Academic Performance; Education, Policy and Politics; Educational Equity; No Child Left Behind Act

Further Readings

Heward, William. 2006. *Exceptional Children: An Introduction to Special Education.* Upper Saddle River, NJ: Prentice Hall.

Individuals with Disabilities Education Improvement Act, P.L. No. 108-446 (IDEA 2004). Retrieved December 24, 2007 (http://www.copyright.gov/legislation/pl108-446.pdf).

Ysseldyke, James, Bob Algozzine, and Martha Thurlow. 2000. *Critical Issues in Special Education.* Boston: Houghton Mifflin.

EDUCATIONAL EQUITY

Educational equity refers to equal access, opportunities, and expectations in education for all persons, irrespective of their backgrounds or status. As a democratic nation, the United States offers a system of "universal" and free public education as a primary mechanism for providing equal educational access and opportunities to all persons, for preparing its people for civic participation in society, and for the socialization of immigrants.

The basic premise of public schooling in the United States is that students at all grade levels are entitled to equal learning opportunities irrespective of advantages, disadvantages, or liabilities linked to skin color, ethnicity, disability, or socioeconomic status. An open system of public education serves as a key compensatory strategy to minimize individual differences and to equalize potential achievements and life outcomes for all. To achieve this end, attendance in public schools became compulsory in most states by the start of the 20th century.

Rooted in the principle of human equality in a democracy, educational equity identifies with the basic liberties and constitutional rights of all citizens, allowing them to participate on an equal footing in a competitive, capitalist economy, with the freedom to move, as desired, in a stratified social system in pursuit of their goals in life. Colloquially referred to as the American Dream, this principle finds expression in the Declaration of Independence as every person's entitlement to "life, liberty, and the pursuit of happiness."

Specifically, the words *equality* and *equity* have different meanings. Equity speaks to public actions and policies in the cause of fairness and social justice. It requires a sufficient distribution of social resources to rectify initially unequal conditions for different groups of people.

Equal access to educational opportunity has been a central issue of legal, educational, and social debates since the landmark *Brown v. Board of Education* U.S. Supreme Court decision in 1954. Affirmative action policies like busing, a strategy for balancing racial distributions in public schools, are examples of public actions aimed at improvement of educational equity through desegregation.

Fiscal equity and educational adequacy lawsuits represent other examples of legislative action in the pursuit of educational equity. These cases challenge inequitable allocation of dollars by U.S. states for public schools located in rich versus poor localities or in inner-city versus suburban areas. Because school financing is largely dependent on local property taxes, plaintiffs successfully argued that children in school districts with low assessable property values receive a lower-quality education than that available to children in wealthier districts. Observers document that larger classes, fewer certified or qualified teachers, run-down physical plants, low teacher pay, and limited or out-of-date teaching materials are found more often in schools located in poorer areas.

The 1980s standards movement in the United States focused educators, policymakers, and the courts on equality of educational outcomes and on "achievement gaps" among different socioeconomic, ethnic, gender, and disability groups, as measured on standardized achievement and ability tests. The bipartisan No Child Left Behind (NCLB) Act of 2001 followed 2 decades of standards-based reforms in U.S. education. NCLB was passed on the premise that higher standards alone had not resulted in higher levels of achievement, and achievement gaps still persisted in various ethnic and socioeconomic subgroups. Comprehensive visions of educational equity in the United States now advocate broadening resource allocations to achieve student outcomes beyond raising test scores. Recent proposals aim to equalize access of families to an array of health, educational, and supplemental services, both in and out of school, to improve students' cognitive and noncognitive outcomes more comprehensively.

Globally, the notion of educational equity found voice in the Millennium Development Goals (MDG) of the United Nations, signed by all member nations in 2002. The MDG calls for universal primary education and equal educational access for girls and boys in developing nations worldwide.

As a social problem, the analysis of educational equity can be approached from multiple perspectives. Issues for investigation may be situated in ethical, legal, political, sociological, economic, or institutional policy frameworks. The appraisal standards for educational equity vary in different contexts, such as in public schools, higher education, and professional or private institutions, both in the United States and overseas.

Madhabi Chatterji and Edmund W. Gordon

See also Academic Standards; *Brown v. Board of Education*; No Child Left Behind Act; School Funding; School Vouchers

Further Readings

Center on Education Policy. 2006. "From the Capital to the Classroom: Year 4 of the No Child Left Behind Act." Washington, DC: Center on Education Policy.

Fuller, Bruce, Kathryn Gesicki, Erin Kang, and Joseph Wright. 2006. *Is the No Child Left Behind Act Working? The Reliability of How States Track Achievement.* Berkeley, CA: University of California Press.

Gordon, Edmund W. 1999. *Education and Justice: A View from the Back of the Bus.* New York: Teachers College Press.

Gordon, Edmund W., Beatrice L. Bridglall, and Aundra Saa Meroe, eds. 2005. *Supplementary Education: The Hidden Curriculum of High Academic Achievement.* Lanham, MD: Rowman & Littlefield.

ELDERLY SOCIOECONOMIC STATUS

Most observers agree that the elderly suffered a loss in status during the periods of modernization and industrialization in the 18th and 19th centuries. According to modernization theory, older members of society failed to maintain their economic standing in the nations that were developing economically during this time, as new skills and technology replaced more primitive forms of production. These nations mainly include those on the European continent and the United States, which were transforming their economies during that time from agriculture to industrial manufacturing. These changes led to an emphasis on factory labor, which required long hours, fixed working schedules, manual dexterity, and often great physical endurance. Elders were not well equipped to compete for these jobs or to remain in good health under that stress. Modernization theorists believe that these trends led to widespread poverty among the elderly during this time, thereby giving rise to age-based prejudice as younger people sought to replace older people in the labor market.

Another suggestion is that in the United States, elders lost their traditionally venerated status prior to industrialization, when the young sought to reverse social standing based on age in the interests of equality and free enterprise. Historians have identified several trends indicating that old age was becoming a less-desirable condition (such as the enactment of mandatory retirement ages for judges and the rising popularity of clothing styles that accentuated youth); many of these trends predate the U.S. industrial era. Critics of this perspective charge, however, that because it is not known exactly when these trends began, modernization as the cause cannot be dismissed.

The financial situation only worsened for elders in the decades following industrialization. In the absence of centralized public pension systems, most of the older people worked as long as their health allowed. When they became out of work and poor, they relied on family and local welfare services. In the midst of the Great Depression, Congress passed the Social Security Act of 1934, which offered some hope for the future well-being of the aged in the form of public pensions granted to workers who retired at the age of 65. Although some European nations had already initiated such programs, U.S. leaders had been reluctant to enact social welfare programs because of their perceived potential to undermine the capitalist incentive to work for a living. In a political compromise, President Franklin Delano Roosevelt supported a plan that rewarded only those elderly retirees who had contributed to the system through compulsory salary deductions for a period of at least 10 years.

Eligibility for U.S. public pension benefits expanded in the 1940s and 1950s to cover not only the old but also the disabled and the children and living spouses of deceased workers. Private pensions also grew immensely during this time. Public health insurance became available to the elderly and the disabled in the 1960s with the passing of Medicare and Medicaid; Supplemental Security Income offered welfare checks to elders and people with disabilities who did not have an adequate work history for regular Social Security benefits but were poor. Cost of living increases to Social Security pensions improved in the 1970s, and the regulations concerning mandatory retirement for the collection of benefits were relaxed by the end of the 20th century. By this time, the Medicaid program had also begun paying for about half of the costs incurred by the rising nursing home population.

These increases in government spending on senior benefits and services drastically reduced the proportion of elders living in poverty. Historical data from the U.S. Census Bureau indicate that the percentage of people over 65 below the poverty line was approximately 35 percent in the 1960s. By 2000, that proportion dropped to about 10 percent. Still, many elders continue to suffer from financial constraints that persist because of the rising costs of housing, health services, and pharmaceuticals. Women tend to experience these problems more than men do, because their higher life expectancy makes them more likely to become widowed and to live on their own in old age.

Population Aging

During the 20th century, it became clear that lower death rates and lower birth rates would soon mean that most nations of the world would experience exponential growth in the age of their populations. Many demographers and economists believe that aging populations will be prone to economic crises as they experience a shortage in the availability of working-age people and an abundance of older people who are dependent upon their labor. In response, many nations have begun to formulate plans to restructure their old age pension, insurance, and health benefit plans or to seek greater efficiency in these programs through privatization.

Critical aging theorists believe that the recent interest in privatizing or restructuring these senior health benefits actually represents a political movement to curb further increases in spending on programs that benefit the elderly. By implying that economic crisis is an inevitable result of population aging, the proponents of these spending cuts are believed to be seeking a political foothold to foster more conservative spending reforms. Although they face fierce opposition from their politically active elder constituents and advocacy groups for the aged, their efforts have so far led to the introduction of incremental reforms, such as the increase in the retirement age for full Social Security benefits. The prospect for more severe cuts in social welfare programs for the aged may depend upon both the nature of the public's image of the elderly and the ongoing extent of age-based prejudice.

Christopher Donoghue

See also Discrimination; Life Course; Minority Group; Population, Graying of; Prejudice; Stereotyping; Stratification, Age

Further Readings

Cowgill, Donald O. 1974. "The Aging of Populations and Societies." *Political Consequences of Aging. Annals of the American Academy of Political Social Science* 415(1):1–18.

Estes, Carol L. and Associates. 2001. *Social Policy and Aging: A Critical Perspective.* Thousand Oaks, CA: Sage.

Federal Interagency Forum on Aging-Related Statistics. 2004. "Older Americans 2004: Key Indicators of Well-Being." Washington, DC: U.S. Government Printing Office.

Fischer, David H. 1978. *Growing Old in America.* Oxford, England: Oxford University Press.

Hummert, Mary Lee, Teri A. Garstka, Ellen Bouchard Ryan, and Jaye L. Bonnesan. 2004. "The Role of Age Stereotypes in Interpersonal Communication." Pp. 91–114 in *Handbook of Communication and Aging Research,* edited by J. F. Nussbaum and J. Coupland. Mahwah, NJ: Erlbaum.

EMINENT DOMAIN

Eminent domain refers to the government taking private property without the owner's permission for specified, legitimate purposes and just compensation. This entry explores various conceptualizations of eminent domain and its background and then discusses controversies surrounding its key components.

Related concepts to eminent domain exist in other countries with common law systems. In the United Kingdom, New Zealand, and the Republic of Ireland, a similar procedure is called compulsory purchase, and in Australia it is called resumption. In Canada and Louisiana, a concept similar to eminent domain is expropriation.

In the United States, eminent domain receives legal support from the Fifth Amendment to the U.S. Constitution, which reads, in part, "nor shall private property be taken for public use, without just compensation." Eminent domain is often considered an inherent governmental power, even without legislation saying so. Governments, however, must use due process to appropriate the property, often taking private property through a condemnation proceeding. Government can take property only for public uses, and it must compensate the property owner. The courts usually defer to the legislative branch in deciding what a public use is.

In the United States, it is without controversy that governments possess an inherent power to exercise eminent domain but that due process must be followed beforehand. Experts conceptualize four kinds of property takings: complete, partial, temporary, and easements. A complete taking is a total and permanent taking of property, whereas a partial taking is a permanent taking of a portion of the owner's property, such as land on one edge of the property. A temporary taking means the owner is compensated for temporary loss of the property, but the property eventually returns to the owner. An easement gives another entity access to the property, but the owner can continue to use the property if it does not interfere with the other entity's use. An example of an easement is that a utility company can install power lines over a property; the property owner can continue to use the property under the power lines as long as he or she does not interfere with the utility's service.

Contemporary controversies surrounding eminent domain revolve around what are legitimate public uses and what is fair compensation. The notion of a legitimate public use has changed dramatically over time, from a notion of universal availability, to a definite, direct public benefit, and more recently, to a potential, indirect public benefit. State governments have exercised eminent domain since the nation's founding, but one of the first U.S. Supreme Court cases, *Kohl et al. v. United States*, 91 U.S. 367, was concerned with what is a legitimate public use. Decided in 1876, the Supreme Court concluded that the federal government could appropriate private property in Cincinnati, Ohio, to develop a building that would house a federal post office, courthouse, pension office, customhouse, and other federal government facilities. In this instance, the Court was concerned with the potential access of all Americans to these public properties.

Eventually, the focus of legitimate public use was less on universal access and more on the interest of the public. It became no longer necessary that everyone have access to the property but rather that everyone would benefit from the property. This change was sometimes characterized as arising from government's police power, that government can legitimately secure the safety, health, and welfare of its citizens by maintaining public order. In *Berman v. Parker,* 348 U.S. 26, the U.S. Supreme Court considered whether the District of Columbia Redevelopment Land Agency could use its powers of eminent domain to take blighted property in Washington, D.C. The specific area subject to eminent domain proceedings was characterized as one in which "64.3 percent of the dwellings were beyond repair, 18.4 percent needed major repairs, only 17.3 percent were satisfactory," and the Supreme Court noted that most had outdoor toilets, over 60 percent did not have baths, and over 80 percent did not have laundry facilities or central heating. In ruling that eminent domain proceedings were appropriate, the Supreme Court noted in this 1954 case, "Miserable and disreputable housing conditions may do more than spread disease and crime and immorality. . . . They may indeed make living an almost insufferable burden."

Attempts to construe public use to an indefinite, indirect public one have recently dominated the legal and policy arenas. Notably, in the 2005 case *Susette Kelo, et al. v. City of New London, Connecticut, et al.,* 545 U.S. 469, the U.S. Supreme Court decided a city could appropriate private property for a public purpose, even if that private property is turned over to private developers whose ultimate aims may or may not result in fulfilling a public purpose.

Rather than condemning the property to build a public facility as in the *Kohl* case, or condemning a building because of public health concerns as in the *Berman* case, the New London city government wanted to appropriate the private property and then sell it to real estate companies, who would then develop the property. Two public purposes were to result from this transaction: economic development and increases in tax revenue. The U.S. Supreme Court previously did hold that economic development is a public purpose for which condemnation proceedings are legitimate. An important difference in the *Kelo* case is that government was conveying the private property to a private developer, whose objectives only indirectly put the property to a public use. The public purpose that would be served would be economic development and an increase in tax revenue. Logically, the *Kelo* case stands for the proposition that government can legitimately force a family to convey their home to a private entity that promises but cannot guarantee economic development and consequent tax revenue.

Another reason the *Kelo* case is controversial is that the city government of New London used condemnation proceedings against homes that were not dilapidated but were in a working-class neighborhood that, by all accounts, was not blighted. Some members of the New London neighborhood had assented to purchase of their property by the City of New London, but other neighborhood residents had not. The city government condemned the holdouts' properties, despite the lack of evidence that the neighborhood or homes were falling apart.

Not surprisingly, hostile responses to the *Kelo* case were swift and strong. The Property Rights Protection Act, passed by the U.S. House of Representatives in 2005, has since languished in the Senate. If it ever becomes law, it would prevent local governments from receiving economic development funds to use for eminent domain proceedings for private development. Across the United States, several state legislatures passed legislation to prevent governments from using the strategy of designating a home or neighborhood as "blighted" to condemn private property when the primary purpose is economic development.

The other important debate arises from just compensation. Typically a government must pay fair market value to the owner of the private property; eminent domain proceedings force market prices onto the property owner. Given that the owner of the private property is not willing to sell the property, often he or she will value the property higher than what he or she can receive on the market. Thus the property owner will believe an eminent domain proceeding does not provide full compensation. Taxpayers, the group that funds the local government's purchase, will overpay for the property if they pay more than the market value. As a result, typically neither the private property owner nor the taxpayers receive fair treatment through eminent domain proceedings.

Eminent domain fundamentally raises questions about boundaries separating public and private actors. A key ingredient of a capitalist-oriented economy is private property. In the United States, the original intent of eminent domain was for situations when property would have the greater purpose of serving an entire community, and the U.S. Supreme Court was reluctant to permit government officials to take private property unless the use would benefit everyone. In contrast, today local governments can take private property from a private owner and convey the property to another private owner because the government anticipates the end result will be greater tax revenue, arguably a greater good. Ironically, in these situations the advantage gained by the new owner seems to have fallen out of the equation.

Brian Gran

See also Equal Protection; Gentrification; Urban Renewal

Further Readings

Bell, Abraham and Gideon Parchomovsky. 2006. "The Uselessness of Public Use." *Columbia Law Review* 106(6):1412–49.

Cohen, Charles E. 2006. "Eminent Domain after *Kelo v. City of New London*: An Argument for Banning Economic Development Takings." *Harvard Journal of Law & Public Policy* 29(2):491–568.

Epstein, Richard. 2005. *Takings: Private Property and the Power of Eminent Domain.* Cambridge, MA: Harvard University Press.

Talley, Brent E. 2006. "Restraining Eminent Domain through Just Compensation: *Kelo v. City of New London,* 125 S. Ct. 2655 (2005)." *Harvard Journal of Law & Public Policy* 29(2):759–68.

ENGLISH AS A SECOND LANGUAGE

English as a second language (ESL) is a multifaceted term associated with several aspects in the area of English language teaching and learning. Broadly speaking, it refers to the use or study of English by speakers of other languages who are permanently or temporarily residing in English-dominant countries, such as Australia, Canada, England, New Zealand, and the United States. In a narrow sense, it refers to the field of study in applied linguistics that brings together aspects from theoretical linguistics, language acquisition, and teacher education; it is a discipline with its own theories, methodologies, and approaches for teaching and learning.

ESL is one of the possible ways to refer to the learning and teaching of English to native speakers of other languages. Due to the range of meanings subsumed under ESL, many other terms and acronyms have been coined over time, including *English as a second or other language (ESOL), teaching of English to speakers of other languages (TESOL), teaching of English as a second language (TESL),* and *English language teaching (ELT).* In the past few years, however, the tendency has been toward an acknowledgment of the increasing presence of multilingual speakers for whom English becomes their third, fourth, or fifth language. As a result, *English as an additional language (EAL)* has been replacing *ESL* as an umbrella term in the latest professional literature.

ESL learners can be found at all levels. From prekindergarten to graduate studies, programs aim at meeting the needs of their particular population of language learners. ESL programs typically fall into three main categories: ESL in elementary and secondary schools, ESL in higher and professional education, and adult ESL. Regardless of the type of model, successful ESL programs always take into account the elements that influence the process of English language teaching and learning. Crucial factors to consider are that learners have different needs, learning abilities, levels of education, and literacy, and they vary depending on age, socioeconomic background, and sociolinguistic variables.

Elementary and Secondary Schools

In K–12 public schools, educators identify students whose native or home language is not English as English language learners (ELLs) or limited English proficient (LEP) students. These students include both foreign-born and U.S.-born students reared speaking a language other than English. ELLs can receive either traditional ESL instruction, which has English as the subject matter, or content-based ESL instruction, which focuses on teaching English through grade-level content. Neither of these program models should be confused with bilingual education programs, which involve the use of the students' first language to provide academic instruction.

Traditional ESL programs treat the learning of English as an isolated topic, that is, devoid of content area subject. In high school, ELLs have separate ESL class periods. In elementary school, however, ESL programs generally include *pull-out* classes. Students leave their regular classroom daily to receive 40 to 50 minutes of English language instruction in self-contained classrooms with limited or no first language support, while their classmates continue with their regular schedule. Although pull-out programs are the most implemented type of ESL instruction, research shows that they are the least effective. This approach provides students with English language instruction, but students miss some of their regular class time to receive such instruction. To avoid this loss of instructional time, some school districts have implemented inclusionary or *push-in* programs. These programs bring the ESL teacher into the regular classroom to provide English language instruction as the classroom teacher covers the grade-level content. Evaluation of this new approach is limited, but initial observations indicate it may be even less effective than pull-out programs. Coordinating the activities of two teachers with two distinct foci teaching together in the same classroom seems to be a highly complex enterprise.

In content-based ESL programs, ELLs receive content area instruction based on the students' level of English language proficiency. English language development (ELD) programs are geared to ELLs with low levels of English language proficiency. ELD programs use content as a means to acquire English, focusing on developing language skills. ELLs with intermediate levels of English language proficiency have a wider range of options. These include programs such as structured English immersion (SEI), specially designed academic instruction in English (SDAIE), the cognitive academic language learning approach (CALLA), and sheltered instruction observation protocol (SIOP). These programs allow the development of language skills as students learn content area knowledge in a more understandable way. In high school, ELLs are in classes taught by teachers with dual certifications—subject area and ESL. In primary school, content-based instruction is self-contained and leads to mainstreaming, that is, a gradual shift of students to all-English classes, as they become fully proficient in English.

Higher and Professional Education

Most higher education institutions have ESL programs for their international, resident, and U.S.-born ELLs. These programs concentrate on general language skills needed for general academic work across disciplines as well as learning and study skills. Courses range from academic reading and writing to oral presentation skills. The majority of the undergraduate students are U.S.-born and long-term U.S.-resident ELLs who, despite graduating from U.S. high schools, are still in the process of learning English. These students are known as *generation 1.5* students because their cultural world and everyday experiences place them in the world of both the first and second generation of immigrants. Depending on the institution, these undergraduates take ESL classes as a prerequisite to the general English requirement or as an optional course in lieu of general English courses.

Graduate students, on the other hand, are mostly international students who need to develop further their written or oral communication skills in English to meet the language demands of their academic discipline. These students have an array of ESL classes specifically designed for the language requirements of their disciplinary community. These courses, which range from oral communication skills for teaching assistants to dissertation writing, are housed in English for academic purposes (EAP) programs—one of the divisions of English for specific purposes (ESP). The primary focus of ESP programs is ESL courses tailored to the specific learning and language use needs of students, most of whom are educated adult learners. In addition to EAP, ESP programs include English for occupational purposes (EOP) programs, which concentrate on the teaching and learning of either English for workers in nonprofessional contexts (vocational English) or English for professionals, such as English for business and economics, English for science and technology, English for medical purposes, and English for legal purposes.

Adult Education

Adult immigrants and refugees interested in learning ESL find themselves taking courses in adult education programs. Located in community centers, schools, and churches, these programs respond quickly to the changing needs of fluctuating immigrant populations and diverse adult learners. Most of these students are working adults who need to acquire basic skills in English. Others are preparing for citizenship or trying to complete a general education diploma. Classes are typically multilevel, meet in the evening or on weekends, and have open enrollment to allow students to register and drop the class at any point in the term. Although ESL is crucial in facilitating the adjustment to the new environment and integration to U.S. society, great challenges still remain to be overcome in terms of program design, teacher preparation, instructional strategies, and learner assessment.

Gladys V. Scott

See also Bilingual Education

Further Readings

Chamot, Anna U. and J. Michael O'Malley. 1994. *The CALLA Handbook: Implementing the Cognitive Academic Language Learning Approach.* White Plains, NY: Addison-Wesley Longman.

Echevarria, Jana, Mary Ellen Vogt, and Deborah J. Short. 2007. *Making Content Comprehensible for English Learners: The SIOP Model.* 3rd ed. Boston: Allyn & Bacon.

Haley, Marjorie H. and Theresa Austin. 2004. *Content-Based Second Language Teaching and Learning: An Interactive Approach.* Boston: Allyn & Bacon.

Harklau, Linda, Kay M. Losey, and Meryl Siegal, eds. 1999. *Generation 1.5 Meets College Composition: Issues in the Teaching of Writing to U.S.-Educated Learners of ESL.* Mahwah, NJ: Erlbaum.

Hawkins, Margaret R. 2005. "ESL in Elementary Education." Pp. 25–44 in *Handbook of Research in Second Language Teaching and Learning,* edited by E. Hinkel. Mahwah, NJ: Erlbaum.

Hinkel, Eli. 2005. *Handbook of Research in Second Language Teaching and Learning.* Mahwah, NJ: Erlbaum.

Thomas, Wayne P. and Virgina P. Collier. 2002. *A National Study of School Effectiveness for Language Minority Students' Long-Term Academic Achievement.* Center for Research on Education, Diversity & Excellence, University of California, Berkeley. Retrieved October 29, 2006 (http://repositories.cdlib.org/crede/finalrpts/1_1_final).

ENGLISH-ONLY MOVEMENT

The goal of the English-only movement is to make English the official language of the United States and to restrict the use of non-English languages in schools and for government services, such as interpreters and voting materials. The movement is based on the belief that encroachment on English by minority languages has reached such a level that English is in danger of losing its primacy as the nation's dominant language. A widespread campaign to make English the official language and to restrict the use of minority languages began in 1983, with the founding of US English by John Tanton and the late U.S. Senator S. I. Hayakawa (R-CA).

Two years prior, Senator Hayakawa had proposed an English Language Amendment to the Constitution of the United States. Hayakawa gave three primary reasons for why English needed to be an official rather than a de facto national language: (1) English is a common language that can unify people, and separate languages can fracture and fragment a society. (2) All immigrants who come to live in the United States should learn English. (3) Immigrants can fully participate in democracy only if they learn English.

Although Hayakawa's amendment proposal failed, the assertions he made about the unifying power of a common language resonated with many Americans who saw the provision of bilingual schooling for immigrant children and bilingual voting ballots for naturalized citizens as contradictory to the requirements for citizenship: ability to read, write, and speak English. Hayakawa's message also resonated with English speakers who were concerned with the burgeoning language and ethnic diversity in the United States. Dr. John Tanton, a Michigan ophthalmologist, founder and head of the Federation for American Immigration Reform (FAIR), teamed up with Senator Hayakawa to form US English, mainly as a way to expand his efforts to restrict immigration, particularly among Latinos/as, whom he believed were not only unwilling to learn English but also reproducing with such speed and numbers that they threatened the ability of white people to maintain their dominance.

In his work with FAIR, Tanton financed negative propaganda about immigrants, especially Mexican immigrants, whom he described as having low educability and little interest in civic affairs. He also advocated policies of eugenic sterilization for immigrant groups. Tanton and his connection to FAIR became a liability for US English, and he was forced to step down after the executive director of US English, Linda Chavez, when learning of his anti-Hispanic and anti-Catholic views, resigned in protest. At that time, US English claimed to have approximately 400,000 dues-paying members, but its membership climbed to 1.8 million by 2007. The organization added the US English Foundation to disseminate information on English teaching methods, develop English instructional materials, and promote opportunities for people living in the United States to learn English. Today, US English lists Senator Hayakawa as the sole founder of US English, omitting any mention of Tanton or connections to FAIR. Parenthetically, Tanton later founded a competing English-only organization, initially called English Language Advocates, and now known as ProEnglish. US English is careful not to use language that could be construed as racist toward any particular minority group. However, the organization continues to use quotes from conservative and neoconservative supporters that capture the group's belief that English is a unifying language and that U.S. nationhood depends on having a common language.

Arguments for English as the Official Language

Motivating the campaign to make English the official language of the United States are two types of fear: (1) Some suggest that English is under siege and in jeopardy of losing its place of dominance, and (2) others suggest that bilingualism, biliteracy, bilingual communities, and any educational approach promoting the acquisition and use of languages other than English promote ethnic hostility and divisiveness. To overcome these fears, proponents of English-only argue that English must become the official, common language of the nation so that Americans of diverse backgrounds can communicate with one another and, in this manner, assimilate into U.S. society (an appeal to those who fear that the English language will be replaced by Spanish). A second argument is that, because new immigrants, as opposed to early 20th-century immigrants, refuse to learn English, there must be a concerted effort to eliminate government-sponsored bilingual education, which encourages immigrants not to learn English (an appeal to white Europeans whose immigrant ancestors supposedly assimilated quickly). Third, all immigrants should be taught English only through intense immersion in the language, where they are forced to use it for communication (an appeal to conservatives who fear the spread of bilingualism and bilingual communities). Fourth, ethnic politicians promote bilingualism and biliteracy for selfish ends: to provide jobs for constituents and to keep immigrants dependent by encouraging them to keep their native language and not learn (an appeal to those who fear the growing populations of Latinos/as across the United States). Finally, proponents insist that language diversity always leads to group conflicts and competition over goods and services, to ethnic hostility, and to political separatism (an appeal to both sets of fears).

US English presents these arguments with no reference to evidence or research, which is understandable since studies consistently disprove their claims. It is clear, for example, that the overwhelming majority of immigrants, both new and old, shift to English-only within three generations, and many lose their native language abilities by the second generation. Research shows that the idea that "new" immigrants, especially Latinos/as, refuse to learn English is simply not the case. What is true, however, is that many of those who are supportive of English-only proposals are also anti-immigration, and particularly, anti-Mexican.

Accordingly, the main objectives of US English and the English-only movement are to adopt a constitutional law establishing English as the official language of the United States; repeal laws mandating multilingual ballots and voting materials; restrict federal funding of bilingual education, and wherever possible, encourage English-only immersion education; and strengthen the enforcement of English language oral and written requirements for naturalization.

Support for the English-Only Movement

Across the nation, 60 to 90 percent of Americans answer "Yes" to the simple question, "Should English be the official language?" Latinos/as are the only group of Americans to consistently answer "No." However, when Americans are asked whether the government should restrict the use of languages other than English or terminate bilingual services for people who need them, support declines significantly for all demographic categories—age, ethnicity, sex, income, education level, and political affiliation. This is an important pattern because it shows that while non-Latino/a Americans tend to favor some kind of official language policy, when it comes to enforcing English-only policies through restrictions on minority language use, few seem willing to support an enforcement measure. Accordingly, the English-only movement has yet to garner enough votes in Congress to support a constitutional law, mainly because most Americans do not support enforcement efforts, which are in conflict with First Amendment rights concerning freedom of speech.

As of 2007, 30 states had passed a law declaring English the official language. However, voters in only three states had passed anti–bilingual education laws to restrict the use of non-English languages for academic instruction and to enforce a strict English-only mandate for public schools.

Because the English-only movement is tied to the national concern over immigration, especially what to do about the burgeoning numbers of undocumented workers and families from Mexico and Central America, and because US English portrays these same groups of immigrants as reticent English learners who choose not to assimilate, it is likely that more states will make English official. It remains to be seen, however, whether Americans nationwide will favor restrictions on non-English language use. The United

States is not, and has never been, a country with one language. While English is undeniably the dominant language of the United States, it is not in any danger of being overtaken by other languages. Moreover, many Americans are critical of past restrictions on the use of Native American languages and other non-English languages in school and in the workplace and may be reluctant to place limitations now on the use of languages other than English for legal, political, and educational purposes.

Christian Faltis

See also Acculturation; Americanization; Assimilation; Bilingual Education; English as a Second Language

Further Readings

Crawford, James. 1996. "Anatomy of the English-Only Movement." Paper presented at the University of Illinois at Urbana-Champaign, March 21. Retrieved May 1, 2006 (http://ourworld.compuserve.com/homepages/ JWCRAWFORD/anatomy.htm).

———. 2004. *Educating English Learners: Language Diversity in the Classroom.* 5th ed. Los Angeles: Bilingual Educational Services.

Faltis, Christian and Cathy Coulter. 2004. "Bilinguaphobia in the New Millennium." Pp. 211–34 in *Marketing Fear in America's Public Schools,* edited by L. Poyner and P. M. Wolfe. Mahwah, NJ: Erlbaum.

Lakshmi, Rama. 2006. "House Panel Examines the Future of English." *Washington Post,* July 27. Retrieved July 27, 2006 (www.washingtonpost.com/wp-dyn/content/ article/2006/07/26/AR2006072601375.html).

May, Stephen. 2001. *Language and Minority Rights: Ethnicity, Nationalism and the Politics of Language.* New York: Longman.

Tanton, John. 1986. Unpublished memorandum for WITAN IV attendees, October 10, 1986. Excerpted in James Crawford's "Anatomy of the English-Only Movement," 1996.

US English, Inc. 2007. "Making English the Official Language." Retrieved December 24, 2007 (http://www .us-english.org/inc/).

ENTRAPMENT

Entrapment in law occurs when an enforcement officer or other government agent suggests, encourages, or aids in the production of a crime that otherwise would not have been committed. The defense is recognized in federal law and also in most states. Alaska statute §11.81.450, for instance, allows an affirmative defense if, to obtain evidence of the commission of an offense, a public law enforcement official, or a person working in cooperation with the official, induces the defendant to commit the offense by persuasion or inducement that would be effective to persuade an average person, other than one who is ready and willing, to commit the offense.

The U.S. Supreme Court in 1932 upheld the entrapment defense in *Sorrells v. the United States,* 287 U.S. 485. A federal agent had approached the defendant in his rural North Carolina home and claimed that he was a furniture dealer from Charlotte and had served in the same army unit as David Sorrells. The agent persistently sought to have the defendant sell him liquor, a violation of the National Prohibition statute. Sorrells maintained at first that he did not drink whiskey, but after several visits and persistent requests, he provided the agent with half a gallon of whiskey and was arrested and sentenced to 18 months in prison. The Supreme Court decision stressed that the aim of the government should not be to create crime in order to punish it but rather to prevent crime, and it called for a retrial in which the jury could evaluate Sorrells's claim to having been entrapped.

To overcome an entrapment defense, the state must convince the judge or jury that the individual had a predisposition to commit the criminal act and that the inducement offered was not sufficient in itself to produce that result. This criterion is known as the "subjective test" of entrapment. Some commentators regard this standard as unfair because it places persons with a previous criminal record at a disadvantage because their earlier illegal behavior can be used to demonstrate a predisposition to offend. There also is some philosophical uneasiness about the courts' acknowledgment of the entrapment defense as criminal law rests on free will doctrines that maintain that, except for gross inadequacies such as mental deficiency, all persons, whatever the circumstance, are to be held responsible if they choose to violate the law. If entrapment is a legitimate excuse, it can be argued that growing up in poverty in a crime-ridden neighborhood also ought to be seen as an excusatory circumstance on the ground that it propelled a person into criminal behavior that would not have occurred had that person lived an affluent existence in a crime-free suburb.

The "objective test," advocated by several judges in the *Sorrells* case, focuses on the decency and persuasive power of the tactics used by law enforcement personnel to determine whether an entrapment defense will prevail. Its aim is not to excuse defendants but to monitor police behavior so that it adheres to acceptable standards of morality.

Procedures such as radar equipment to detect speeding motorists and two-way mirrors in supermarkets to discover shoplifters are not regarded as entrapment. Police, at times, will use decoys in sites with high crime rates or where a pattern of specific offenses has emerged. The decoys may assume roles such as derelicts, shoppers, or drunks. For example, in a case in which patients complained that a dentist had sexually molested them while they were under an anesthetic, an undercover policewoman posed as a patient, was anesthetized, and was kept under surveillance by a hidden camera, which captured evidence of the dentist's criminal act.

Tactics that arguably represent illegal entrapment typically are employed against persons engaged in activities defined as "crimes without victims," particularly narcotics violations where there are no complaining witnesses and the police have to resort to proactive enforcement efforts. Similarly, female detectives, posing as prostitutes, engage in dragnets to apprehend johns who patronize prostitutes. Those accused can prevail with an entrapment defense only if they can convince a judge or jury that the law enforcement officer acted so aggressively and seductively that, but for this, the arrested person would not have solicited her services.

For social scientists, entrapment raises complex issues of causation and responsibility. If the temptation seems virtually irresistible, such as a wallet deliberately left by police detectives in a telephone booth in a ghetto neighborhood, should the youth who keeps the contents of the wallet be allowed to claim entrapment?

Entrapment figured in two prominent cases in recent decades. The Abscam sting operation targeted primarily lawmakers believed to be susceptible to bribery. Federal Bureau of Investigation (FBI) agents posed as representatives of a make-believe wealthy Arab sheikh, offering considerable sums to members of Congress for the sheikh's alleged desire to obtain asylum in the United States, to invest in U.S. enterprises, and to launder money. The ruse resulted in the conviction of a U.S. senator, six members of the House of Representatives, and three other officeholders. Only Florida Congressman Richard Kelly succeeded with an entrapment defense, and this was only

temporarily, because an appellate court reversed the original decision and Kelly went to prison.

John DeLorean was accused in 1982 of putting up $1.8 million to buy 100 kilos of cocaine that, if resold, would have netted him $24 million, enough to bail out his failing automobile manufacturing company. DeLorean was caught in an FBI sting operation that had a former drug smuggler-turned-informant offer him the opportunity to finance the drug import transaction. The judge dismissed the case on the ground of entrapment, with DeLorean not needing to call a single witness on his behalf.

Gilbert Geis

See also Affirmative Action; Corruption; Power Elite; Victimless Crimes; White-Collar Crime

Further Readings

Caplan, Gerald. 1983. *ABSCAM Ethics: Moral Issues and Deception in Law Enforcement.* Cambridge, MA: Bollinger.

Fallon, Ivan and James Srodes. 1985. *Dream Maker: The Rise and Fall of John Z. DeLorean.* New York: Putnam.

Holmes, Bill. 1998. *Entrapment: The BATF in Action.* El Dorado, AR: Desert Publications.

Marcus, Paul. 2002. *Entrapment Defense.* 3rd ed. Newark, NJ: LexisNexis.

ENVIRONMENT, ECO-WARRIORS

In recent years a set of related movements, sometimes referred to as "radical environmentalism," has appeared on the global stage. Despite precursors in history, what is new about these movements is the confrontational nature of the tactics they often employ, including blockades, tree spiking, forest occupations, and property destruction. Sometimes referred to as "eco-warriors," or more pejoratively by authorities as "ecoterrorists," the individuals in these movements directly confront the social problem of environmental degradation, yet also at times generate new social problems through their choice of tactics and strategies.

Some observers suggest the radical environmental movement found its initial inspiration in Edward Abbey's writings, which popularized the term *monkeywrenching*. Despite the linguistic logic to this, more philosophical discourses such as "deep ecology" have had an equally profound impact on modern eco-warriors. Indeed, the radical environmental movement appears to be a product of equal parts wide-ranging ecological thought and explicit calls to action. Combining theory and practice, eco-warriors call attention to serious issues such as pollution, species extinction, nuclear waste, and deforestation through the use of dramatic actions aimed at simultaneously educating the public and preventing further environmental harm.

Rik Scarce characterizes an eco-warrior as someone who generally believes in "direct action" instead of incremental or legislative change, strongly embraces the values of biological diversity, disdains bureaucratic hierarchy in favor of self-organization, works tirelessly to save the environment despite long odds and great personal risk, and maintains an ecological consciousness that often includes a spiritual component. Eco-warriors also generally adhere to a philosophy of nonviolence toward all living entities; nonetheless, highly confrontational tactics are part of the movement's identity. Eco-warriors have, for instance, vandalized animal testing laboratories, chained themselves together to block logging roads, damaged bulldozers and other machinery, picketed outside the homes of animal researchers, and disrupted power lines to mining operations. Still, experts generally agree that these environmentalists have not caused serious physical harm to any humans during their campaigns, except perhaps to themselves on rare occasions.

Dave Foreman, one of the founders of the radical environmental entity Earth First!, asserts that monkeywrenching—the direct resistance to the destruction of the earth and its life forms—is nonviolent, in that it never aims to harm any living being, with care taken to minimize any possible physical threat to people. He further argues that monkeywrenching itself is diverse, as anyone can do it and a wide range of movements on both the left and the right actively use it. Movement activists themselves also accept direct action strategies such as monkeywrenching as part of a "diversity of tactics" to employ, depending upon the situation, and that sometimes radical actions can help more mainstream activists accomplish their stated aims and goals. However, this remains a controversial point in environmental circles and in movement literature.

In addition to Earth First!, eco-warriors also include groups such as Greenpeace, the Sea Shepherds,

People for the Ethical Treatment of Animals, the Redwood Alliance, Stop Huntingdon Animal Cruelty, and Friends of the Earth. While at times employing strategies like boycotts and blockades, these entities also utilize less-controversial tactics, such as media campaigns, legislative lobbying, and mobilizing around environmental issues ranging from animal exploitation to ocean health to nuclear power. Whereas some view these groups as radical extremists, others see them as an institutionalization of environmental concerns and a more viable alternative to movement radicalism.

In the 1990s, more directly confrontational animal rights and environmental movement groups appeared, sometimes under the rubrics of the Animal Liberation Front and the Earth Liberation Front. These entities claimed credit for numerous acts of strategic property destruction, including the sabotage of development projects that threatened endangered species, the destruction of laboratories experimenting with genetically modified organisms, and arsons at dealerships that sold sport-utility vehicles. These activists appear to take more literally the notion that protecting the environment is a matter of war and that nature needs dedicated defenders if it is to survive. These sentiments, sometimes accepted as doctrinal in the radical environmental movement, justify the construction of eco-warriors as a specific class of activists and partly explain the increasing frequency of acts of ecological sabotage (also known as "ecotage").

These more confrontational tactics have brought an increased interest on the part of law enforcement. Numerous legislative acts and federal interdiction efforts focus on eradicating "ecoterrorists," resulting in the dramatic increase in criminal penalties for acts of ecotage against commercial enterprises. Also, anti-terrorist laws passed after 9/11 have, at times, been used against radical environmentalists. This led some activists to speak of a "Green Scare," drawing an analogy to the anti-Communist Red Scare of the 1950s in the United States. Despite the many arrests made, authorities acknowledge the difficulty of curtailing these activities entirely, as there are no formal group structures involved and it is difficult to intervene in actions of autonomous individuals. This view is consistent with the characterization of an eco-warrior as someone who disdains organizational hierarchy in favor of self-defined actions, yet it can also leave practitioners open to allegations of terrorism in its apparent randomness. Nonetheless, eco-warriors generally hold to their stated principle of avoiding physical harm to human life, which for some has made the invocation of the terrorist label problematic.

Eco-warriors are thus a diverse and complicated part of the modern environmental movement. Whereas many admire their motivations and goals, others criticize their tactics as dangerous and divisive. As befits such contradictions, it is difficult to measure the effectiveness of eco-warriors in promoting the values of ecology and sustainability. And as with many social problems, this one evidences a great deal of ambiguity and consternation, bringing to mind the aphorism that one person's terrorist is another person's freedom fighter.

Randall Amster

See also Deforestation; Environment, Pollution; Environmental Crime; Environmental Degradation; Environmental Justice; Environmental Movement; Global Warming; PATRIOT Act; Social Change; Social Movements; Terrorism; Terrorism, Domestic Spying; Toxic Waste

Further Readings

Abbey, Edward. 1975. *The Monkey Wrench Gang.* New York: Avon Books.

Amster, Randall. 2006. "Perspectives on Ecoterrorism: Catalysts, Conflations, and Casualties." *Contemporary Justice Review* 9(3):287–301.

Devall, Bill and George Sessions. 1985. *Deep Ecology: Living as if Nature Mattered.* Salt Lake City, UT: Peregrine Smith.

Foreman, Dave and Bill Haywood, eds. 1993. *Ecodefense: A Field Guide to Monkeywrenching.* Chico, CA: Abbzug.

Scarce, Rik. 1990. *Eco-warriors: Understanding the Radical Environmental Movement.* Chicago: Noble.

Shevory, Thomas C. 1996. "Monkeywrenching: Practice in Search of a Theory." Pp. 183–204 in *Environmental Crime and Criminality: Theoretical and Practical Issues,* edited by S. M. Edwards, T. D. Edwards, and C. B. Fields. New York: Garland.

ENVIRONMENT, HAZARDOUS WASTE

Hazardous wastes are among the by-products of industrial production in societies in which there is intensive use of chemicals (e.g., acids, bases, chlorinated hydrocarbons) and materials (heavy metals [e.g., mercury] or paint pigments) that are toxic and can cause poisoning and death. Official definitions of hazardous waste promulgated by state and federal environmental protection agencies usually require that the material have at least one of four characteristics: ignitability, corrosivity, reactivity, or toxicity.

Hazardous wastes can become severe social problems for entire societies and smaller populations within them. Unregulated industrial dumping of such wastes can poison large land areas and residential neighborhoods, or foul drinking water or swimming beaches, with potential or real damage to human and other populations. Even when placed in special dump sites, some wastes can dissolve into groundwater and soils, a process known as leaching. Once transported by streams or tides, dissolved wastes can endanger populations far from the original dump site.

Industry is not the only major source of hazardous waste. Household waste often contains corrosive, toxic, ignitable, or reactive ingredients like paints, cleaners, oils, batteries, and pesticides, all of which contain potentially hazardous ingredients. These require special care in disposal, and consumers must be continually educated about safety in the use of these products, as well as the proper procedures to follow in disposing of them. Improper disposal of household hazardous wastes often results from pouring them in drains, on the ground, or into storm sewers or mingling them with other trash. Such improper disposal of these wastes can pollute the environment and pose a health threat, which is why communities in the United States and other industrial nations now offer a variety of options for their safe disposal.

Most hazardous wastes have histories of earlier public, and even scientific, ignorance about their potential dangers. For most of the industrial age, people paid little attention to the consequences of indiscriminate dumping of the by-products of mining and manufacturing. As late as the 1960s, containers of pesticides, household insulation materials containing asbestos, old car batteries, and used paint cans—all containing extremely hazardous materials—were handled and disposed of quite casually. Quantities of poisonous materials were transported in unsafe containers and disposed of in public dump sites or even in vacant lots. Industrial corporations frequently dumped hazardous wastes into rivers and streams, resulting in long-term damage to plants and animal species and eventually to humans. In the developing world these unsafe practices often continue and present a growing danger to the world's oceans and animal species.

Public awareness about hazardous materials and wastes in the United States was almost nonexistent until publication of Rachel Carson's book *Silent Spring* in 1962. Drawing extensively on new scientific studies of the dangers of pesticides and other toxic chemicals to human and other animal species, Carson exposed the dangers of the insecticide DDT to the earth's food chains. The tragic case of widespread mercury poisoning in the Japanese fishing village of Minamata in the 1950s and 1960s brought world attention to problems of hazardous waste disposal and indiscriminate dumping of hazardous wastes by private companies. Not until the 1978 crisis of environmental poisoning and the high incidence of children with birth defects in the community of Love Canal in New York State, near Buffalo, did the federal government pass effective legislation to identify and begin cleaning up areas of land polluted and empoisoned by hazardous wastes. In response to the Love Canal disaster, Congress in 1980 passed the Comprehensive Environmental Response, Compensation, and Liability Act, known most commonly as the Superfund Act.

The federal Superfund pays for toxic waste cleanups at sites where no other responsible parties can pay for a cleanup. Its funds come from a special tax on the petroleum, chemical, and other industries that routinely use or produce toxic materials and wastes. The Superfund Act also provides broad federal authority to clean up ongoing releases or potential releases of hazardous substances that may endanger public health or the environment. The majority (65–70 percent) of uncontrolled U.S. waste sites are waste storage and treatment facilities (including landfills) or former industrial properties. Typically these properties have been abandoned, and most have more than one major chemical contaminant. Another category of hazardous waste sites is found in federal government facilities in such as military bases, armament testing grounds, and nuclear energy complexes.

The substances most commonly released into the environment from uncontrolled hazardous waste sites are heavy metals and organic solvents: lead (59 percent of sites), trichloroethylene (53 percent), chromium (47 percent), benzene (46 percent), and arsenic (45 percent). The U.S. Environmental Protection Agency (EPA) has identified more than 15,000 sites that qualify for Superfund remediation. About 1,400 of these sites are currently proposed for

listing or are listed already on the National Priorities List. Assessment and remediation of these sites is proceeding under the direction of EPA, with support of the national Superfund Trust. As of this writing, Congress has failed to renew some of the fees collected from the oil and related industries, and the Bush administration is the first in the history of the program to oppose making polluting industries fund the Superfund toxic waste cleanup program.

The burdens of living with hazardous wastes are not shared equally in the United States or in most other industrial nations. Contaminated Superfund sites in the United States are most commonly found adjacent to poor communities, often populated by ethnic and racial minorities with relatively large numbers of children. Research commissioned by EPA estimates that approximately 11 million Americans live within 1 mile of a high-priority contaminated Superfund site, and between 3 and 4 million of these persons are children under 18 years of age. This puts them at risk of exposure to chemical toxicants released from these sites into the air, groundwater, surface water, and surrounding communities. Because they are growing rapidly and their bodies are building new tissue more rapidly than are adults, children are uniquely susceptible to health injury resulting from exposures to chemical toxicants in the environment.

EPA has identified more than 1,000 hazardous waste sites on military bases and proving grounds and in 1997 ordered Camp Edwards in Massachusetts to cease firing live ammunition because munitions chemicals were leaching into the drinking water for all of Cape Cod, where more than 500,000 people spend the summer. In response, the Pentagon has repeatedly, but so far unsuccessfully, requested legislation that would exempt more than 20 million acres of military land from key facets of the Clean Air Act and the two federal laws governing hazardous-waste disposal and cleanup. State environmental officials widely oppose this legislation, fearing that it will interfere with the ability of states to enforce environmental laws that protect drinking water and otherwise protect public health.

Nuclear waste is particularly hazardous and presents some of the most difficult problems of disposal. Exposure to radioactivity can cause cancer and birth defects and also has potential uses by terrorists. Nuclear waste results from the use of radioactive metals in nuclear power plants and military nuclear weapons facilities. Throughout the world are nuclear power plants nearing the end of their operating lives, particularly in the United States, where most of these plants are approaching the end of the operational time period allowed in their licenses. The close of the cold war in the 1990s left a legacy of radioactive waste from decommissioned nuclear missiles, but hospitals and nuclear research facilities also generate a great deal of nuclear waste.

Nuclear waste is classified as either "low-level" or "high-level" radioactive waste. Low-level nuclear waste includes material used to handle the highly radioactive parts of nuclear reactors (i.e., cooling water pipes and radiation suits) and waste from medical procedures involving radioactive treatments or X-rays. The level of radioactivity in low-level waste is relatively small, and the materials are relatively easy to dispose of. Storing the waste for a period of 10 to 50 years will allow most of the radioactive isotopes in low-level waste to decay, at which point the waste can be disposed of as normal refuse. High-level radioactive waste comes from the core of the nuclear reactor or nuclear weapon. This waste includes uranium, plutonium, and other highly radioactive elements made during fission. Most of the radioactive isotopes in high-level waste emit large amounts of radiation and have extremely long half-lives (some longer than 100,000 years), creating extensive periods before the waste will settle to safe levels of radioactivity. In consequence, waste disposal facilities for high-level nuclear wastes must be extremely secure and well protected. Few cities or regions welcome the location of hazardous waste treatment facilities, particularly nuclear waste facilities, in their vicinity. This makes the problem of transport and disposal of these materials a particularly difficult political problem.

William Kornblum

See also Environment, Pollution; Environment, Sewage Disposal; Environmental Racism; Water Quality

Further Readings

Carson, Rachel. [1962] 2002. *Silent Spring.* Anniversary ed. New York: Mariner Books.

Landrigan, Philip J., William A. Suk, and Robert W. Amler. 1999. "Chemical Wastes, Children's Health, and the Superfund Basic Research Program." *Environmental Health Perspectives* 107(6):423–71.

McGowan, Keith. 2001. *Hazardous Waste.* San Diego, CA: Lucent Books.

U.S. Environmental Protection Agency, Hazardous Waste Web Site. (http://www.epa.gov/osw/hazwaste.htm).

ENVIRONMENT, POLLUTION

The environment is an important part of life that must be safeguarded and preserved in the best way possible, because without it there would be no life. People have always used the environment to advance their own goals, but this can lead to environmental pollution, which in turn affects the world's population. In other words, human beings must be consciously concerned with the environment—whether air, water, or soil—because it affects them as much as they affect it. To assess the health of the environment and the effects of environmental pollution, we must look at the environment's different facets individually and how they interact. Discussing environmental pollution is only one part of the whole. The other component is assessing the extent of its negative effects on people.

Pollution Trends

Today, pollution is occurring on a vast and unprecedented scale worldwide, impacting virtually everyone and everything. We can best understand the dramatic changes or increase in pollution in the 20th and 21st centuries in terms of four long-term trends.

First, the world's population increased more than threefold in the 20th century, along with a twentyfold increase in the gross world product. These increases caused a demand on the use of fossil fuels, thereby increasing the release of both sulfur dioxide and nitrogen oxide into the atmosphere. These emissions are the principal components of smog and give rise to acid rain.

The second long-term pollution trend recognized in the 20th century is the shift from gross environmental results to micro toxicity. Before World War II, the major public health issues centered on smoke and sewer-related issues. One incident, the killer fog over Donora, Pennsylvania, in 1948, sickened thousands and killed 20 people. An even more ominous micro-level threat has existed since the advent of nuclear technology. The ushering in of the nuclear age, chemical, biological, and nuclear warfare, and the peacetime applications of these technologies—such as agribusiness fertilization and power generation—has led to the development and widespread use of chemical, biological, and radioactive material, thus creating waste storage issues for generations to come.

The third environmental pollution trend is its global spread. Once thought to be a problem of the rich or more developed nations, pollution is now a serious problem for less-developed countries as well. For example, with the explosion of industrialization in both China and India, these countries are experiencing environmental pollution problems on a national scale that threaten the quality of life for both rural and urban residents. Moreover, data from the UN Global Environmental Monitoring System indicate that, by and large, cities in eastern Europe are more polluted with sulfur dioxide and other particles than most cities in Western developed countries. In essence, developing world citizens rank high in their exposure to pollutants, particularly toxic chemicals. Many of these impacted people reside in Mexico, India, and China.

The fourth trend in global environmental pollution is how localized environmental contamination becomes a larger, more global environmental assault, such as the Exxon Valdez oil spill in 1989, the burning of oil wells during the Gulf Wars, and the Chernobyl nuclear disaster in 1986. Such incidents, despite their having occurred in confined geographical regions, have had wider global environmental impacts.

Attention to global environmental issues approached critical mass with the Rio de Janeiro Earth Summit in 1992. The major crises of focus were the depletion of the stratospheric ozone layer, climate change, rapid shrinkage of tropical rain forests, the loss of biodiversity, the spread of deserts, and the decline of global fisheries. During the early 1990s scientists adopted the wider concept of global change to signify the level of impact humans have on global environmental conditions and their potential to alter permanently the functioning of the ecosystem on earth. To combat the aforementioned issues, the 116 heads of state attending the 1992 summit adopted a revised set of principles and action statements called "Agenda 21" and a host of environmental treaties on climate change and biodiversity as well as a statement on forest principles. To strengthen Agenda 21, the UN General Assembly created the Commission on Sustainable Development. Although its progress is questionable, the Commission on Sustainable Development works to improve environmental quality worldwide, as do

other organizations, international nongovernmental organizations, government think tanks, scientific and professional societies, and the European Union (as a collective).

Air Pollution

Air pollution is almost impossible to contain because of its ability to spread rapidly over a large area. There are many different pollutants in the air, and their effects range from environmental damage to health issues. The effect of pollution on the ozone layer is one example of environmental damage. The ozone layer is a part of the atmosphere that helps absorb radiation from the sun and a portion of ultraviolet light that is responsible for causing, among other things, various types of skin cancer and cataracts. Because substances such as carbon dioxide, chlorofluorocarbons, and sulfur dioxide (the chief cause of air pollution) are being released into the air, the ozone layer is being reduced and could possibly be destroyed. These pollutants are by-products of industrialization, such as the combustion of fossil fuels and exhaust from automobiles and factories.

The U.S. Environmental Protection Agency (EPA) has taken steps to prevent and reduce several sources of air pollution, such as supporting the passage of legislation to ban the use of lead in gasoline in the United States. Furthermore, the Clean Air Amendment of 1990 mandated a 50 percent reduction in pollutants such as sulfur dioxide by the year 2000 in an attempt to reduce future occurrences of acid rain. Despite action taken, a common problem that the EPA encounters is that many strategies used to reduce one type of pollution can lead to the introduction of a different pollutant into the environment.

The danger of air pollution is not only how rapidly it spreads but also how it affects other parts of the planet, such as the ozone layer. The atmosphere is such a critical part of the environment that experts now view it as a resource in the same way as land, forests, and water.

Water Pollution

Like air pollution, water pollution spreads quickly over a large area. Surface water and groundwater both serve as sources of drinking water, and both are uniquely affected by pollution. As a general rule of thumb, surface waters are more polluted than groundwaters due to disinfection by-products and the heavy industrialization of river and lake basins. However, the contamination of groundwater generally involves higher concentrations of chemicals because of the low amount of underground dispersion, mixing, and dilution.

Because surface water is readily available to companies, lakes and rivers tend to be more polluted; however, because water constantly moves, the foreign materials are dispersed over a larger area, making the concentration of pollution smaller. Groundwater moves more slowly than surface water, so contamination tends to be more concentrated and recorded in higher levels than in surface water. Groundwater is not moved by wind and it does not normally encounter air, making the underground water reservoirs (aquifers) stagnant. Therefore, when toxic chemicals or foreign materials enter that water supply, they are not diluted or dispersed over larger areas as they are in surface water. Although all groundwater sources eventually run into rivers and lakes, the water used for drinking is most often acquired while it is still underground and the pollution is at its most concentrated, causing the most harm to the people who drink water from such underground sources.

Because of its availability and the low cost of extraction, groundwater is a popular choice of industries to extract and turn into drinkable water. However, the downside to this is that although groundwater may have a higher availability rate, it is not a quickly renewing source such as surface water. This causes companies to tread with caution when extracting groundwater because if too much is taken, the entire source could be depleted indefinitely. Precipitation and runoffs make surface water a renewable source of drinking water. However, before it is usable as potable water, surface water usually requires extensive treatment (purification) to remove all pollutants. Although pollution is increasing the cost of extracting surface water and purifying it, surface water's ability to renew itself through precipitation makes it a preferred source of drinking water.

The main source of water pollution is poor disposal of industrial waste, which often leads to the contamination of both groundwater and surface water sources. Industrial waste accounts for more than 18 billion gallons of wastewater daily and 800 million pounds of pollutants yearly. The inadequate construction of disposal sites, such as landfills and injection wells, also contributes to water pollution. Injection wells are pipes lined with concrete that are dug deep into the ground, past the layer of earth where groundwater reservoirs reside that many industries use to dump waste. Contamination occurs when these pipes are constructed or operated incorrectly, thus leaking waste into the groundwater system. Without better care, the available drinking water resources also become contaminated from pathogens that enter the water from sources such as untreated sewage, storm drains, and boats that dump sewage into the water.

Ground Pollution

Ground pollution is closely tied with water pollution because of its close proximity to sources of water. Many sources of water contamination come from pollution originally introduced into the ground. The chief source of ground pollution comes from the inadequate operation and construction of waste disposal facilities, such as landfills and injection wells. This inadequate disposal of wastes leads to ground pollution, which leads to the contamination of rivers, lakes, and groundwater reservoirs. Improper discharge of pollutants in the air (which can become acid rain) can also lead to contamination of water supplies. Incineration, a waste disposal method meant as an alternative to land-based disposal facilities, further contributes to air pollution, as it creates airborne particle contaminants and leaves heavy metal residues for waste disposal, which can result in the contamination of the surrounding environment. However, poor waste management is only a part of the overall pollution affecting the environment.

Some of the pollution contaminating the soil and damaging vegetation is caused by humanmade pesticides and herbicides. Although used primarily for agricultural purposes, these pesticides and herbicides are dangerous if people are exposed to a high enough concentration of the product. During the Vietnam War, the United States developed a strong herbicide, code named Agent Orange, to destroy the jungle canopies and vegetation the Vietcong used as cover. Agent Orange was successful in its destruction of the vegetation, but the region had difficulty recovering from its effects. So toxic was the chemical that few new plants grew for several years after the spraying, and restoring the forests will apparently take several decades. The use of Agent Orange not only had long-term effects on the environment but also affected the people exposed to it; these people subsequently developed higher rates of liver problems, cancer, and immune system disorders than those not exposed.

The lessons to be learned are the realities of an interrelationship among different forms of environmental pollution and of the interdependence of humans and their environment. The combustion of fossil fuels and factory emissions contribute to air pollution. Herbicides damage vegetation in ways from which it could take years to recover. Water pollution is influenced by ground pollution, which in turn is created by poor waste disposal. People cause all this pollution that harms not only the environment but also themselves. Few, if any, can escape the far-reaching effects of pollution. People in all countries are dependent on the Earth's ecosystem and its resources. Although all people are harmed by damage to these resources and ecological systems, the harm is much greater for individuals who are poor, those who live in developing countries, women and children, and racial/ethnic minorities.

Society needs to develop a proactive attitude in dealing with environmental pollution, instead of merely reacting to an environmental crisis. This will be difficult when the wealthiest countries (the United States, Canada, Western European countries, Japan, and Australia), who contain only about 22 percent of the world's population, disproportionately consume the largest portion of the world's resources (nearly 88 percent of the natural resources each year, including 73 percent of the world's energy resources). The best way to treat pollution is to eliminate its source. If people act first and eliminate the sources of pollution, rather than reacting to crises and scrambling to contain the already widespread pollution, the environment will have a better chance of survival.

DeMond S. Miller and Joel Yelin

See also Acid Rain; Deforestation; Desertification; Ecosystem; Environment, Hazardous Waste; Environment, Runoff and Eutrophication; Environment, Sewage Disposal; Environmental Crime; Environmental Degradation; Environmental Hazards; Environmental Racism; Water Organization; Water Quality; Water Resources

Further Readings

Gardner, Gerald and Paul Stern. 1996. *Environmental Problems and Human Behavior.* Boston: Allyn & Bacon.

Hodges, Laurent. 1977. *Environmental Pollution.* New York: Holt, Rinehart & Winston.

McBoyle, G. R. 1973. "Meteorological Aspects of Air Pollution." Pp. 36–48 in *Ecological and Biological Effects of Air Pollution,* edited by G. M. Woodwell. New York: MSS Information Corporation.

Moeller, Dade W. 2004. *Environmental Health.* 3rd ed. Boston: Harvard University Press.

Socha, Tom. 2006. "Air Pollution: Causes and Effects." Retrieved September 19, 2007 (http://healthandenergy.com/air_pollution_causes.htm).

Soroos, Marvin. 1999. "Global Institutions and the Environment: An Evolutionary Perspective." Pp. 27–51 in *The Global Environment: Institutions, Law and Policy,* edited by N. Vig and R. Axelrod. Washington, DC: Congressional Quarterly Press.

Speth, James. 1998. *Environmental Pollution: A Long-Term Perspective.* Washington, DC: World Resource Institute of the National Geographic Society.

Stewart, John C. 1990. *Drinking Water Hazards: How to Know If There Are Toxic Chemicals in Your Water and What to Do If There Are.* Hiram, OH: Envirographics.

U.S. Environmental Protection Agency. 2006. "Ozone Science: The Facts behind the Phaseout." Retrieved September 19, 2007 (http://www.epa.gov/ozone/science/sc_fact.html).

Vancil, L. 1994. *Agent Orange.* Retrieved December 26, 2007 (http://www.vvvc.org/agntor.htm).

Environment, Runoff and Eutrophication

Eutrophication, or cultural eutrophication, is the enhancement of the natural process by which streams, lakes, reservoirs, and estuaries become enriched with nutrients (phosphorous and nitrogen), enabling the ecosystem to support higher rates of production as measured by biomass or energy per unit area over time. This natural process of enrichment can take thousands of years and result in the succession of a glacial lake into a bog and, eventually, a prairie. However, this process can be greatly accelerated by human activities; while natural eutrophication occurs on geologic timescales, a reservoir undergoing cultural eutrophication can evolve into a bog in less than a hundred years.

This accelerated enrichment can have many detrimental ecological, aesthetic, and human health effects. Excess phosphorous and nitrogen can disrupt the natural balance of the aquatic ecosystem by spurring population explosions of nuisance algae and aquatic plants. As these algal populations sink and die, they create an oxygen demand in the underlying water where bacteria deplete oxygen supplies to decompose the dead algae. The oxygen-depleted bottom waters become poor fish habitat. In freshwater ecosystems, sudden, short-term episodes of low oxygen levels can cause fish kills, and extended periods of low bottom-water oxygen concentrations can cause a shift in fish populations from desirable sport fish to low-oxygen-tolerant species such as carp. In marine ecosystems, this phenomenon is seen in the Gulf of Mexico's "dead zone," where nitrogen from the Mississippi and Atchafalaya Rivers stimulates high rates of algal growth in the upper water layers, which cause oxygen depletion in the underlying waters.

Nutrient enrichment has also been cited as the cause of coral reef destruction, degrading both the ecological and recreational value of these marine resources. In freshwater ecosystems, nuisance algal blooms can diminish the aesthetic and recreational value of the water body by forming surface scums and producing earthy and musty tastes and odors, which can persist in finished drinking water. In addition to ecological and aesthetic degradation, some algal blooms can pose risks to human health. These harmful algal blooms (HABs) can produce potent toxins, and scientists have implicated them in wildlife, livestock, and pet deaths after the animals had drunk contaminated water. Long-term low dose exposures of a hepatotoxin, microcystins-LR produced by HABs of *Microcystis,* is suspected to contribute to high rates of liver cancer in certain parts of China. A short-term acute poisoning of the neurotoxin anatoxin-a, produced by an HAB of *Anabaena,* was the likely cause of death for a Wisconsin teenager in July 2002. In marine ecosystems, HABs have resulted in human exposures to the neurotoxins brevetoxin and saxitoxin, which are produced by the algae *Karenia brevis* and *Alexandrium fundyense,* a known cause of paralytic fish poisoning.

The causes of nutrient enrichment can be categorized into two main sources: point source pollution (i.e., from a pipe) and non-point source (i.e., diffuse) pollution. As all streams, lakes, reservoirs, and estuaries receive water from their respective watersheds (area of land that drains into a water body), any upstream or up-watershed sources of pollution can become pollution sources to the receiving water body. In the United States, the point source release of plant (and algae) nutrients, phosphorus and nitrogen, into the environment is controlled by the National Pollutant Discharge Elimination System (NPDES), a provision of the Clean Water Act.

Although the NPDES program has achieved much improvement in nutrient pollution control, recent assessments of the nation's water quality have shown continued water quality degradation caused by these nutrients (e.g., a 1999 U.S. Geological Survey study showed that the nation's median stream phosphorous concentration was still greater than the 0.100 mg L^{-1} threshold for reduced phytoplankton growth), demonstrating a need to manage both point and non-point sources of nutrient pollution. Non-point source pollutants are transported to the receiving waters via subsurface water, surface water (i.e., streams and rivers), or runoff (direct overland flow).

U.S. Environmental Protection Agency (EPA) studies have shown that in a natural forested area, 40 percent of rainwater returns to the atmosphere through evapotranspiration, 50 percent filters into subsurface flow, and 10 percent runs off the land surface into a receiving water body. However, with the removal of vegetation and its replacement with impervious surfaces (land cover that does not allow for the water to soak into the ground, e.g., rooftops, parking lots, and streets), the amount of water transported via runoff increases: Suburban land cover results in 30 percent rainwater runoff and urban land cover results in 50 percent rainwater runoff.

In 2000, EPA stated that the most common sources of pollution affecting U.S. streams and rivers were agricultural runoff, animal feeding operation runoff, hydrologic modification (e.g., channelization, dredging, and dam construction), habitat modification (e.g., removal of stream bank vegetation), urban runoff from lawns and impervious surfaces, erosion from urban development, and urban storm sewer overflows. These sources of non-point pollution can transport more than just nutrients to receiving waters: Pesticides from agricultural and suburban uses, bacteria and pathogens (e.g., *E. coli* and *Cryptosporidium*) from animal feeding operations, and oil and trash from parking lots can be transported as well.

Social Dynamics of Addressing Eutrophication and Runoff

EPA's 2000 National Water Quality Inventory showed that, of the U.S. water bodies assessed, 47 percent of rivers, 53 percent of lakes, and 52 percent of estuaries were polluted or threatened. In 1996 and 2000, nutrients and siltation (sedimentation) were among the top five causes of impairment for streams, rivers, lakes, ponds, reservoirs, and estuaries. Both nutrient enrichment and siltation can lead to eutrophication, but in many cases, the nutrient enrichment and siltation caused by human manipulation of the environment can be prevented or minimized through the use of best management practices (BMPs). However, even though safe drinking and recreational waters are social necessities, a lack of understanding of causes and effects of pollution often inhibits stakeholder investment in BMPs.

Case studies by the Iowa Department of Natural Resources on Squaw Creek Watershed in 2002 and Cedar Lake Watershed in 2001 showed that perceptions of good water quality varied widely between water quality specialists and local landowners based on different ideas of how the water body should function. Whereas participants from Squaw Creek Watershed said that stream water quality was adequate (or not harmful) to wildlife but not okay for human consumption, water quality specialists measured good water quality on the basis of a broad set of physical, chemical, and biological characteristics. This discrepancy in determining the health of the watershed ecosystem impacted the importance stakeholders placed on water quality improvement efforts.

In the Cedar Lake study, water quality specialists identified agricultural operations as the main cause of excess nitrates in the lake water. (Studies implicate nitrates as a cause of the Gulf of Mexico's dead zone.) However, the discrepancy between farmers' and water quality managers' perceptions of water quality led to only 50 percent of the farmer participants believing that agricultural activities were the cause of elevated nitrate levels. The farmers cited the many conservation practices they already employed as proof that their activities were not the cause of the high nitrate levels. As such, project managers focused efforts on educating stakeholders on the complexity and differences of different pollutant transport.

To be fair, this discrepancy in attitudes between water quality managers and stakeholders toward water resources is not unique to farming communities. Similar attitudes toward pollution exist in suburban and urban communities. From development practices that remove or redirect headwater streams and build retention ponds to homeowners who improperly fertilize their lawns or fail to maintain septic systems, many people do not recognize the link between an individual's actions and the broader context of cumulative ecological effects. In an EPA 1997 study, urbanization was shown to have a direct impact on stream ecology. Therefore, recent efforts have focused on

reducing runoff from suburban and urban areas, resulting in the implementation of urban BMPs such as EPA's Low Impact Development program. This program, like agricultural BMPs, requires landowner buy-in, where the homeowner or homeowner's association is responsible for maintaining the BMP.

Denise Lani Pascual

See also Ecosystem; Environment, Pollution; Environmental Degradation; Erosion; Urbanization; Urban Sprawl; Water Quality

Further Readings

Committee on the Causes and Management of Eutrophication, Ocean Studies Board, Water Science and Technology Board, and National Research Council. 2000. *Clean Coastal Waters: Understanding and Reducing the Effects of Nutrient Pollution.* Washington, DC: National Academies Press.

Sharpley, A. N., T. Daniel, T. Sims, J. Lemunyon, R. Stevens, and R. Parry. 2003. *Agricultural Phosphorous and Eutrophication.* 2nd ed. ARS-149. Washington, DC: U.S. Department of Agriculture, Agricultural Research Service.

U.S. Environmental Protection Agency. 2000. "National Water Quality Inventory." EPA-841-R-02-001. Washington, DC: U.S. Environmental Protection Agency, Office of Water.

Wetzel, Robert G. 2001. *Limnology: Lake and River Ecosystems.* 3rd ed. San Diego, CA: Academic Press.

Environment, Sewage Disposal

The history of civilization, especially urban civilization, is the history of water—of the fundamental need to supply clean, fresh, disease-free drinking water while simultaneously disposing of vast quantities of disease-ridden, foul human and animal waste. From at least the time of the Phoenicians up to the present day, the growth of the world's major metropolitan centers—Rome, Paris, London, New York, Beijing— has been defined by how well they solved that dilemma of water supply and waste disposal.

The challenge of water supply and disposal is directly related to population density. In prehistoric time, and in many impoverished areas even today, "night fertilization" of open field and cropland is not uncommon and may not pose an unwarranted risk of disease to the population or a heavy burden to the environment. Under rural farm conditions, both the supply of potable water and the safe disposal of waste are only minor difficulties. More often than not, nature itself, without the need of human intervention, provides the mechanisms by which water is filtered and cleansed of contaminants. Simple precautions such as keeping the outhouse far from the water well are adequate to ensure human health wherever population density is low.

Increasing population density demands increasingly complex treatment solutions. There are at least three major environmental issues that have to be addressed when disposing of human and animal waste: (1) reducing organic and inorganic solids, (2) reducing the demand for oxygen in wastewater that is a consequence of its dissolved and suspended load of organic matter, and (3) minimizing the concentration of nutrients and chemicals that always characterize waste materials.

As population density increases above rural, farm levels, some sort of engineered solution to the waste disposal problem must be found. Cesspools and septic systems have long provided such solutions in many suburban areas of the world. A cesspool is little more than an underground tank with many holes in it. Household waste enters one (settling) chamber of the tank from which overflow is allowed to escape into the soil surrounding the tank. Natural or introduced microbes and enzymes within the cesspool tank decompose the organic matter in the waste stream while the tank itself provides storage for any indigestible materials. Soil organisms and vegetation around and above the tank provide further filtering of the wastewater and take up some, if not all, of the chemical burden. Cesspools have the drawback of becoming clogged over time and require periodic cleaning and flushing to work efficiently. Septic systems are a slight improvement over cesspools—the overflow wastewater stream from a septic tank exits through a gridded system of perforated pipe that is laid out in soil at shallow depth. The slow flow of water through the septic-field grid enhances the decomposition of organic matter and the absorption of nutrients and chemicals by soil organisms and vegetation. Septic systems require less maintenance but demand large areas of lawn or open field not often available in urban centers.

Both cesspools and septic systems cannot remove 100 percent of the burden of organic matter, nutrients, and chemicals from typical household waste. The increasing use of detergents, soaps, and other chemicals in modern households has placed an additional and growing burden on the ability of house-specific waste disposal systems. At some point on the population growth curve of urban systems, cesspools and septic systems are no longer a viable alternative and some other approach has to be taken to sewage treatment. One of the most spectacular examples of this transition in modern times is provided by Nassau and Suffolk Counties on Long Island, New York. What was once rural farmland was rapidly suburbanized following World War II. Initially the waste disposal of homes was served by cesspools and septic systems—one or the other depending primarily on lot size. Over time, however, these house-specific systems dispensed an ever-increasing load of nutrients into the groundwater system of the island—a drinking water supply on which the suburban community was totally dependent. The concentration of one particular nutrient, dissolved inorganic nitrate, was the trigger that led to a complete reengineering of the two counties' waste disposal systems—a construction project of immense size that is still under way. High levels of nitrate had led to "blue-baby syndrome," a condition under which newborns have difficulty breathing. The solution was to place the homes in every community in the two counties on sewerage systems connected to central processing plants. Nearly every street and highway had to be excavated, every household lawn dug up, and sewer lines installed. In addition, a place had to be found for the huge and not-always-welcome treatment plants.

Sewage treatment plants have been built in major cities since the 19th century. Basically sewerage systems consist of a network of collection pipes from an urban environment directed by gravity to the central facility typically located at the lowest elevation available—either on the coastline or next to a river. Initially the treatment facilities consisted of little more than settling tanks in which "floatables" and sediment were accumulated and later disposed of as sludge. This "primary" treatment did little for overall concentration of organic matter, nutrients, and chemicals in the water. The outflow of these plants was dumped directly into the ocean, stream, or river to be dealt with by natural decomposition. In some urban and suburban environments, sewer lines were merged with storm drains from streets in what is known as "combined sewer overflow" systems.

During a rainstorm the huge quantities of runoff, rapidly developed in urban environments, mixed with sewage and were discharged directly to streams and rivers without any treatment. U.S. cities are still dealing with the legacy of these combined sewer overflow systems today.

Few natural aquatic ecosystems are capable of dealing with the heavy demands for decomposition placed on them by the influx of large amounts of primary-treated sewage. As decomposition proceeds within the natural system, the demand for oxygen to fuel the microbial decomposition process exceeds the capacity for the absorption of oxygen through the water's surface or the generation of oxygen via photosynthesis by plants. An "oxygen sag" develops downstream from the wastewater treatment plant outflow. Depending on several factors—the load from the treatment plant, the discharge of the stream or river, and tidal flushing of bays and estuaries—the depletion of oxygen in water can reach critical levels, typically set at below 4 mg/L of dissolved oxygen. At those low levels, fish, and the insect life on which they depend, die. Other pollution-tolerant organisms replace those fish and "higher-order" insects. Eventually all oxygen-dependent life can be extinguished and the aquatic system can descend into anoxia, capable of supporting only anaerobic organisms. Those anaerobic organisms, more often than not, produce foul-smelling hydrogen sulfides among other noxious chemicals.

In the United States and Europe this sad state of affairs for most urban streams and rivers was reached sometime during the 1960s and 1970s and led directly to the passage of water-quality legislation such as the Clean Water Act in the United States. Existing sewage treatment plants were upgraded, and new plants were built nationwide. This upgrading consisted chiefly of the addition of "secondary" treatment at each facility. Secondary treatment is designed to reduce the dissolved and suspended organic matter in the waste stream. This is accomplished in a variety of ways. The simplest way is to aerate the wastewater in huge tanks, either by mixing or by direct aeration with bubblers. Some treatment plants employ anaerobic digestion, that is, enclosed tanks from which oxygen is excluded. Inside these tanks bacteria reduce organic matter to methane, which can fuel the treatment process itself. In addition, anaerobic digesters, as they are called, emit far less odor than open-tank oxygen-decomposition facilities. They are more expensive to maintain, however, and can require periodic injections of microbes if, for example, antibiotics enter the tanks from the sewer lines.

Secondary treatment is effective at reducing the level of organic matter in wastewater plant discharge, but it has little effect on the nutrient and chemical load of the plant discharge. In fact, secondary treatment may even increase the levels of nutrients such as nitrates and concentrate and elevate existing loads of phosphate in the plant discharge. This discharge of nutrients can promote the rapid growth of algae and macrophytes in streams and rivers. If those plants grow excessively and if conditions (such as a drought) in the aquatic environment lead to the wholesale death of those plants, the stage may be set for a calamitous decline in dissolved oxygen concentrations. Such oxygen-depletion events have caused repeated occurrences of huge die-offs of fish in modern times.

Thus, today, we are faced with the problem of going beyond secondary treatment of sewage to tertiary treatment—the removal of nutrients—an expensive process that will involve rebuilding nearly all of the thousands of treatment facilities throughout the world.

Richard R. Pardi

See also Environment, Pollution; Environment, Runoff and Eutrophication; Water Organization; Water Quality

Further Readings

Arundel, John. 1999. *Sewage and Industrial Effluent Treatment.* 2nd ed. Boston: Blackwell.

Dunne, Thomas and Luna B. Leopold. 1978. *Water in Environmental Planning.* San Francisco: W. H. Freeman.

Phelps, Earle B. 1944. *Stream Sanitation.* London: Wiley.

United Nations World Water Assessment Programme. 2006. "Water: A Shared Responsibility: The United Nations World Water Development." Report 2. New York: Berghahn Books.

ENVIRONMENTAL CRIME

Environmental crime is among the most controversial categories of illicit activity within the parameters of defining social problems. Some scholars simply classify it as a form of white-collar crime, because the motivating factor behind committing such offenses is frequently financial gain. Federal enforcement entities consider the term more broadly, deeming actions such as killing endangered wildlife or illegally releasing toxic substances into public drinking water or agricultural production as posing serious risk to the public because of the long-term harm such actions may pose to society. Last, human rights advocates proffer that workers exposed to hazardous materials without proper health and safety equipment or training, and the deliberate placement of chemical plants and hazardous waste treatment, storage, and disposal facilities in economically disadvantaged areas, are forms of *political* crime because those at the lowest stratum of the socioeconomic scale lack a voice in protecting themselves and their families when compared with constituents from wealthier communities. Collectively, this problem is referred to as the challenge of attaining environmental justice.

Financial Motivation

What induces large manufacturing corporations, small home contracting companies, and individuals to commit acts such as illegally dumping hazardous waste, improperly removing asbestos and lead-based paint, and poaching rare and exotic flora and fauna? In each case, the response is but one word: money.

The proper treatment, storage, and disposal of hazardous wastes are expensive, and many businesses are willing to chance getting caught because the risks outweigh the costs. For example, in a 2001 U.S. district court judgment against ExxonMobil, the company acknowledged that from 1991 to 1993, it had improperly stored and disposed of benzene—a known cancer-causing agent found in petroleum products—at its product storage and distribution facility in Staten Island, New York. Although ExxonMobil paid a hefty US$11.2 million in penalties (one of the largest settlements in U.S. history), it was the equivalent of just 3 months' salary enjoyed by ExxonMobil chairman and chief executive officer Lee R. Raymond.

For smaller companies such as home contractors, meeting strict environmental regulations may prove cost prohibitive when compared with their larger competitors. Consider the disposal of asbestos-containing materials (ACMs) found in household pipe insulation, boilers, and furnaces. To properly manage ACMs requires laboratory testing, removal by a state-licensed technician, and a postremediation inspection

by a certified professional. A self-employed home remodeling contractor may be willing to risk his own health (or worse yet, the long-term health of the household's unsuspecting occupants for whom the work was completed) to bring the job in at a lower estimate than that of his larger competitor.

Profit is also the primary motivation for wildlife poachers and for those who illegally traffic in wildlife parts. For example, the gallbladder of a common black bear can net anywhere from $2,000 to $10,000 on the underground market because some cultures believe it has medicinal value. An individual bowl of bear paw soup can cost as much as $1,000 in Asia. Worldwide, the profit associated with threatened and endangered species is even greater, as seen, for example, in the $2,300-per-pound premium for African rhino horn (purportedly an aphrodisiac in some cultures) or the sale of more than 5,000 elephant tusks in 1999, which netted traffickers about $5 million. At present, the World Wildlife Fund estimates that the global trade in illegal wildlife parts exceeds $20 billion annually.

Enforcement

To reduce the profit motivation for large corporations and smaller businesses and individuals engaging in the improper disposal of hazardous wastes, Congress enacted a variety of environmental laws from the 1970s through the early 1990s. These statutes protect air, soil, and water from the risks of contamination posed by industrial chemical residues and heavy metals common in the manufacturing process.

Among the most important of the initial laws passed during this era were the Clean Air Act of 1970 (CAA) and the Clean Water Act of 1972 (CWA). The CAA radically improved upon previous air quality laws passed in the 1950s and 1960s by mandating acceptable levels of airborne contaminants that could be released by manufacturers, energy producers, and industrial facilities into the environment. It also established a timetable by which facilities must meet these thresholds and imposed civil and criminal penalties for those entities unable or unwilling to do so.

Similarly, the CWA created a permit requirement system for releasing toxins into the environment, especially in areas where surface waters may be located or rainfall runoff could feed into riverways, lakes, ponds, or drinking water reservoirs. By mandating that businesses obtain effluent discharge permits via the

Environmental Protection Agency (EPA) or its authorized state representative, the government was better able to control potential pollutant risks to humans and wildlife. The CWA also provided federal funding to build and upgrade sewage treatment plants throughout the United States, further reducing contamination posed by bacteriological and chemical hazards.

Following the successes of the CAA and CWA, Congress enacted the Safe Drinking Water Act in 1974 and the Solid Waste Disposal Act—commonly referred to as the Resource Conservation and Recovery Act—in 1976. The Safe Drinking Water Act was designed to protect the nation's drinking water supply from the risk of contamination posed by faulty public water supply piping (which often contained high levels of lead or copper). The Resource Conservation and Recovery Act also strove to reduce contamination to drinking water wells and groundwater from public landfills (e.g., from leaking batteries, cleaning products, solvents, thinners, pesticides). Last, the Safe Drinking Water Act established specific maximum allowable concentrations for heavy metals and chemicals in drinking water, while the Resource Conservation and Recovery Act specifically banned substances that were deemed toxic, reactive, ignitable, or corrosive from public landfills and required that these substances instead be taken to EPA-licensed treatment, storage, and disposal facilities for proper handling.

Armed with these laws and the addition of the Comprehensive Environmental Response, Compensation and Liability Act of 1980 and the Oil Pollution Act of 1990, both of which prohibit unauthorized releases of hazardous substances and petroleum products into the environment, EPA and the U.S. Coast Guard have exercised extensive environmental enforcement authority, making arrests, shutting down facilities, and imposing civil and criminal penalties for violations of environmental regulations. High-profile cases such as the 1998 $8 million settlement against W. R. Grace for polluting drinking water wells in Woburn, Massachusetts, and ExxonMobil's payment of $900 million in punitive damages for their involvement in the 1989 tanker disaster in Valdez, Alaska, demonstrate that the environmental enforcement community takes its mission seriously.

Although less media attention is paid to the quiet victories of wildlife inspectors, special agents, park rangers, and other environmental enforcement specialists from the U.S. Fish and Wildlife Service, National Park Service, Bureau of Land Management, and Department of Agriculture, their work is equally demanding and the breadth of laws available in their regulatory arsenal just as powerful. Often combined with extensive undercover operations, federal statutes such as the Lacey Act and the Endangered Species Act frequently yield large criminal penalties for those trafficking in wildlife parts both within the United States and abroad. Similarly, park rangers monitor large tracts of public land via truck, horse, and foot patrol and through aircraft and electronic surveillance to enforce the Federal Land and Management Policy Act and the Archaeological Resources Protection Act. These guardians of U.S. natural, cultural, and historic resources ensure that hazardous substances are not unlawfully disposed of in critical wildlife habitat, marijuana is not being cultivated on federal property, and artifacts are not removed from battlefields and Native American burial grounds.

Environmental Justice

The financial motivations for corporations and individuals who pollute, poach, or traffic in animal parts are clear. Moreover, the corresponding enforcement strategy on the part of the U.S. government to protect human health and the environment is also readily apparent. What is far more elusive is the concept of environmental justice, that is, ensuring that those persons in the lowest socioeconomic stratum of society are afforded the same health, safety, and environmental protections under the law as are society's wealthiest members. Much of this concern dates back to the mid-1960s, when workers in a variety of industrial settings such as shipyards, chemical manufacturing plants, and the textile industry began to experience illnesses based on years of exposure to asbestos, solvents, and heavy metals. Lawsuits gave way to legislation such as the 1970 Occupational Safety and Health Act, which guarantees all workers a right to a workplace reasonably free from industrial hazards. Yet, more than 30 years later, employees in many of these high-risk settings still face challenges such as receiving basic respiratory protection gear and chemically resistant gloves and goggles, obtaining training on how to properly use these items, and participating in medical monitoring programs to track their long-term health.

Legislation such as the Emergency Planning and Community Right-to-Know Act of 1980 and the Federal Facilities Compliance Act of 1992 granted leaders in the most economically disenfranchised areas empirical evidence to support what they had long suspected: Many chemical manufacturing plants, hazardous waste storage areas, and energy production facilities are located in or adjacent to those locations with the highest rates of minorities and lowest socioeconomic status. Community activists responded by amending their rallying cry pertaining to the siting of such industrial facilities from "Not in my backyard" to "Not in *anyone's* backyard."

The term *environmental crime* is complex, and it evokes images ranging from the midnight dumping of 55-gallon drums in a local stream behind an elementary school to the wholesale slaughter of threatened and endangered species for sale on the black market. Whatever one's perspective is on this issue, only through the examination of the nexus between financial motivations, regulatory enforcement, and equal protection for all of society's members can this important social problem be explored with the richness it so rightly deserves.

Hank J. Brightman

See also Environment, Hazardous Waste; Environment, Pollution; Environment, Sewage Disposal; Environmental Justice; Environmental Movement; Environmental Racism; NIMBYism; Occupational Safety and Health

Further Readings

Carson, Rachel. 1962. *Silent Spring.* New York: Fawcett.

Clifford, Mary. 1998. *Environmental Crime: Enforcement, Policy, and Social Responsibility.* Frederick, MD: Aspen.

Gore, Albert. 2000. *Earth in the Balance: Ecology and the Human Spirit.* Boston: Houghton Mifflin.

Swendsen, David. 1987. *Badge in the Wilderness: My 30 Years Combatting Wildlife Violators.* Mechanicsburg, PA: Stackpole.

ENVIRONMENTAL DEGRADATION

Theoretically, as many proposals exist for tackling the origin of the phenomena of environmental degradation as do different views on how to define it. First, this plethora of theoretical approaches always begins with an interest in identifying certain variables suitable for strategic policies of intercession, that is,

environmental amelioration. Thus, the very question of how to define environmental degradation is contentious because it innately promotes particular policies and de-legitimizes others.

Second, besides having raw politics determine environmental degradation policy first and then popularize a theory to justify such policy afterward, the definition of environmental degradation also wrestles with difficulties in the organization of Western institutionalized divisions in academia. Particular methodological cultures compete against one another to reduce environmental degradation to their discipline instead of working together on defining environmental degradation. The topic of environmental degradation thus became divided across separate disciplines of biology, physical sciences, and social sciences (social sciences itself divided across sociology, political science, economics, and anthropological divisions of methodology). Thus the topic of environmental degradation tends to mirror reductionisms inherent in this disciplinary division, with each providing a reductionist construct on most occasions.

In short, what has passed historically for analysis of much environmental degradation has been a series of cultural filters and viewpoints that influenced approaches to its treatment. The environmental degradation construct historically determined what should be done—if anything—to ameliorate environmental degradation. What is being reacted to, in many cases, is this environmental degradation construct.

However, taking the question of the definition of environmental degradation into account as a historical issue of change in the construct, a pattern emerges of moving from arguments about philosophical primacy of a single factor of population—with monotonic, monocausal, ahistorical, and quantitative/mathematical requirements of timeless "unalterable" issues— toward explanations of environmental degradation more multivariate (multiple variables without any of them being reducible to another), historical, strategic, and highly interdisciplinary. Arguably, as multiple variables enter the definition, the robustness of the model improves toward relational and interscientific definitions of environmental degradation. With multiple variables involved in modeling environmental degradation, the areas or variables to deal with expand. Instead of only one recognizable venue of intercession, a far more problematized, political, relational, and interscientific model of environmental degradation with multiple areas for intercession comes to the fore—demoting previous reductionist attempts to link environmental degradation to philosophical conjecture about only one factor of population and its preeminence instead of its relation with other factors.

Early Reductionist Constructs

Though many other literate cultures throughout world history left records observing environmental degradation and theoretical state approaches to alleviate it, with European imperialism and scientific culture having such a wide effect on the world in the past 500 years, it is impossible to ignore the importance of the freshly minted and highly acclaimed culture around—and even substitutionary religious status for—quantification. Quantification was popularized within Europe as a more reliable method of thought for establishing "stable, timeless, true" knowledge in the wake of mutual Protestant and Catholic disenchantment of the Wars of Religion conducted in Europe over the period of the French Wars of Religion (1550s–1598) into the generalized European Thirty Years' War (1618–1648). Nevertheless, the selected factors that came to be measured in the model were still subjective.

The Venetian lapsed-Camaldolese monk and mathematical philosopher Giammaria Ortes (1713–1790) was the first to take quantification of population and apply it to political philosophical issues and "social science." Ortes provided the first mathematical theory of what he considered the penultimate variable for environmental degradation: population. Why was it so? Because to Ortes, population was imminently quantifiable and could be fitted to methods he wanted to utilize. To be sure, Giovanno Botero (c. 1544–1617), in *On the Greatness of Cities* of 1588, foreshadowed the dynamic Ortes describes, though he was writing before European popularized mathatized arguments were framed as static, inescapable, counterbalanced, zero sum game equations imported with great status into political argument. By the 1750s, Ortes published the first instance of a mathematized argument implying exponential population growth versus arithmetic food resources leading to both starvation/poverty on one side and wealth consolidation on the other. He argued that geometric population growth "had to," by logic of his mathematical models, outstrip the assumed slower arithmetic progress of food production. In the last year of his life, 1790, Ortes published *Reflections on the*

Population of Nations in Relation to National Economy, setting an unalterable construct of an upper limit for the world's human population at 3 billion—after moving through a series of mathematical arguments and tables. Ortes is the first to employ the term *carrying capacity* as well. Thus, Ortes is the father of "overpopulation" theory.

Due to high political Venetian–English political alliances and other points unmentioned for lack of space, it is certain that Rev. Thomas Robert Malthus (1766–1834), himself a cleric with a greater interest in mathematics, plagiarized ideas of mathematic ex-monk Ortes. In Rev. Malthus's famous work, *An Essay on the Principle of Population* of 1798, he makes identical religio-moral mathemetized arguments as "proof" about population outstripping food as inevitably decreasing food per capita. Without any intrusion of other variables, Malthus, like Ortes, claims this inevitably leads to famine, environmental degradation, and social and moral degradation. Malthus even calculated his own Ortesian "carrying capacity," which was to be broached sometime in the mid-19th century. Like Ortes, Malthus proposed that late marriage and abstinence should be state policies as a check on "geometric" population growth. The larger context is that while all other major continental states in Europe, like Colbertian France, Linnaean Sweden, and Frederick the Great's Prussia, were cameralist (meaning, among other points, supporting population growth politically as the means to make a state wealthy), the maritime empires of Venice and England—without comparable political economic situations linking their larger transoceanic empires' elite wealth to the well-being of their territorial inhabitants—took to anti-cameralist arguments against their continental cameralist enemies. Hired in 1805 as the first chair of political economy in Britain soon after his essay was published, Rev. Malthus worked until his death at the Haileybury school, created by the British East India Company (BEIC) to indoctrinate its corporate management staff in the business of running a global anti-cameralist empire, with such management ideologies continuing into the British Raj. In short, Rev. Malthus's construct of environmental degradation as a populationist idea of "natural timeless famines" and as a nonpolitical check on population encouraging wealth conservation was applied as the main anti-cameralist policy justification for the global BEIC/British Empire's food, poverty, population growth, and famine response (or lack thereof) from Ireland, to India, to China, to Africa.

Though most social scientists no longer seriously consider single-variable causal model solutions of social problems, construct environmental degradation as populationism continues to have considerable political policy influence regardless of the fact that rarely any "calculations" came true over the past 200 years showing population as a direct variable of environmental degradation. The common application and thread in this population policy-based construct of environmental degradation is as a useful anti-cameralist policy for maintaining a global corporate state empire from the 1700s to the present. However, even the United Nations, long maintaining such anti-cameralist constructs concerning environmental degradation/population, by 2002 moved toward more multivariate models to make sense of the reality of negative population growth evident across many countries since the 1990s. Charitably, population as a proxy for environmental degradation has been, at most, an indirect relationship even if government workers acted upon construct populationism.

The earliest, more sociological, models of environmental degradation are elaborations of direct inexorable populationist arguments, however sociologically adapted—namely, the work of Ehrlich, O'Connor, the Club of Rome group, Schnaiberg/Gould, or Catton.

Intercession Variables

More multivariate models of environmental degradation and intercession have been aired since the 1970s. These include a plethora of other proposed direct variables of environmental degradation which are equal pressure points for environmental intercessions. This entry proposes a relational and interscientific definition of environmental degradation to encapsulate these many variables. Regardless of the theoretical-methodological approach to the construct of environmental degradation, any statement of environmental degradation must include issues of the organization of human consumption and pollution. The devil has always been in the multivariate details, however. This is despite a long history of attempts to popularize environmental degradation strictly, with populationism being politically paramount instead of being just one factor among many. The tendency of many sociological theories of the environment has been to ignore multivariate aspects and ignore case-specific issues, that is, to aim toward a grand theory. Grand theories

or plans typically fall apart in the analysis of particular cases or applications to real-world issues. A multivariate appreciation of environmental degradation is more appropriate, particularly in summing all the different variables analyzed in environmental degradation as well as toward applications of environmental amelioration.

Summarizing much of the literature that talks at cross-purposes, it will be noted that the empirically multivariate issue of human consumption shows we are (1) populations that consume (2) choices of physical and biological materials through which we have (3) chosen to create particular pollution wastes, in (4) social networks via mostly (5) institutionalized and habitual frameworks (6) contentiously legitimated or delegitimated among ourselves, employing (7) choices of available knowledge and choices of technological interfaces, influenced by the (8) history of (9) politics and (10) weather/geographic pattern changes. In the political variable concerning environmental degradation, it is particularly clear how formal institutions and formal policy change to respond to, or to shore off response to, the aforementioned variables. As a result, in the past decades scholars have moved toward more (11) infrastructural views on environmental degradation, as well as, in turn, more infrastructural views of human consumption. This requires changing many basic epistemological views, particularly how we define and analyze commodities, commodity choice, socioeconomic change, the origins of technological change, and environmental degradation as politically contentious developmental issues instead of as neutral economic presuppositions and methods employed in these areas.

None of these numbered intercessions that influence environmental degradation can be reducible to another. All are, to various degrees, independent sites of intercession and are relational. They are politically negotiated, problematic, and historically iterative in their effects instead of timelessly stable or given. All have been aired—either together or separately, either as direct or indirect variables involved in environmental degradation. A simpler statement is that human population is always mediated through these organizational factors of consumption, making such organizational issues of consumption direct variables of environmental degradation and intercession, whereas population scale/reduction is, at best, an indirect variable. It is quite possible, in other words, to reduce or expand population and to have little or zero change in the institutionalized patterns of environmental degradation, because human consumption is mediated by many sociopolitical, cultural, and technological issues. Humans are networked and mediated creatures in their consumption across multiple ecologies; however, many attempts have been made to take 18th-century populationist models or 20th-century population ecology models and "plug in" human numbers.

Mark D. Whitaker

See also Environment, Hazardous Waste; Environment, Pollution; Environment, Runoff and Eutrophication; Environment, Sewage Disposal; Environmental Hazards; Environmental Movement; Environmental Racism

Further Readings

Bijker, Wiebe. 1997. *Of Bicycles, Bakelites, and Bulbs: Toward a Theory of Sociotechnical Change.* Cambridge, MA: MIT Press.

Davis, Mike. 2001. *Late Victorian Holocausts: El Niño Famines and the Making of the Third World.* New York: Verso.

Dunlap, Riley E., Frederick H. Buttel, Peter Dickens, and August Gijswijt, eds. 2002. *Sociological Theory and the Environment.* Lanham, MD: Rowman & Littlefield.

Lappe, Frances Moore, Joseph Collins, Peter Rosset, and California Institute for Food and Development Policy. 1998. *World Hunger: Twelve Myths.* 2nd ed. New York: Grove.

McDonough, William and Michael Braungart. 2002. *Cradle to Cradle: Remaking the Way We Make Things.* New York: North Point.

Mol, Arthur P. J. and Gert Spaargaren. 2005. "From Additions and Withdrawals to Environmental Flows: Reframing Debates in the Environmental Social Sciences." *Organization & Environment* 18(1):91–107.

Pye-Smith, Charlie. 2002. *The Subsidy Scandal: How Your Government Wastes Your Money to Wreck Your Environment.* Sterling, VA: Earthscan.

Sen, Amartya. 1983. *Poverty and Famines: An Essay on Entitlement and Deprivation.* New York: Oxford University Press.

Spaargaren, Gert, Arthur P. J. Mol, and Frederick H. Buttel, eds. 2006. *Governing Environmental Flows: Global Challenges to Social Theory.* Cambridge, MA: MIT Press.

Watts, Sheldon. 1999. *Epidemics and History: Disease, Power, and Imperialism.* New Haven, CT: Yale University Press.

Weisman, Alan. 1999. *Gaviotas: A Village to Reinvent the World.* White River Junction, VT: Chelsea Green.

Whitaker, Mark. 2005. *Toward a Bioregional State: A Series of Letters on Political Theory and Formal Institutional Design in the Era of Sustainability.* Lincoln, NE: iUniverse.

ENVIRONMENTAL HAZARDS

An environmental hazard is a threat posed by the natural or built environment to humans and the things that are valued in human society. An environmental hazard becomes a disaster when the threat is realized and causes significant human loss. Death, injury, and psychological harm are judged to be more serious than economic or property loss, and threats to nonhuman environments and their flora and fauna are considered to be the least severe and are frequently left out of measures of environmental hazard unless they lead to a secondary threat to humans or their property.

Environmental hazards are categorized as either natural or technological, though multiple hazards may be linked to one another. Natural hazards include geologic events, like earthquakes, landslides, and volcanic eruptions; hydrologic events, like floods and drought; meteorological events, such as tornadoes and hurricanes; and biologic events, like wildfires, infestations, and diseases. Technological hazards arise from within human systems and are usually accidental in nature. They include industrial failures that release toxic materials into the environment, structural collapse of buildings and bridges, and transportation disasters like plane crashes and train derailments.

A third category of environmental hazard has been increasingly employed to describe events with the potential for catastrophic impact on the global environment. Sometimes referred to as "context hazards," these include not only unpredictable occurrences like meteor impacts or the mutation of a virus into a deadly pathogen but also chronic, ordinary events. For example, deforestation and the release of industrial contaminants are increasingly implicated in the complex environmental threats posed by global warming.

The connection between human action and natural disaster was first explored at the University of Chicago during the 1950s by geographer Gilbert F. White, who argued that disasters cannot be understood in isolation from human society. Social scientists using a human ecology framework began to investigate disaster prevention and the mitigation of its consequences. Geographers took up a "hazards-based" approach to disaster, analyzing perceptions of hazards and subsequent behavioral responses. Psychologists compared perceptions of risk for hazards that are involuntary (like breathing air pollution) and voluntary (like smoking cigarettes), while anthropologists noted that perceptions of hazard are substantially influenced by cultural tradition. At the same time, sociologists were preoccupied with collective behavior and the dynamics of social organizations that might influence disaster preparedness and response. Earth scientists continued to focus on the physical causes of disasters. Geologists, meteorologists, and hydrologists were developing better systems of disaster prediction, while civil engineers worked on designing more effective technological defenses.

By the 1970s social scientists challenged the "behavioral paradigm" associated with the hazards-based approach and criticized its emphasis on individual action and its minimization of the power of social and economic forces. The new theoretical paradigm (also known as the critical or political economy view) asserted that environmental hazards are not caused by natural or technological processes but by structural inequalities within and between nations that systematically increase the risk to some social groups while sheltering others from threat.

The term *risk* refers to the probability that a particular hazard will be realized, combined with the severity of its consequences. For example, the coastal landing of a hurricane presents the same hazard to rich and poor; however, the risk of suffering serious harm as a result of the hurricane is significantly greater for the poor than for the rich because they are more vulnerable to the consequences. Vulnerability is the key variable used to measure susceptibility to the harms associated with environmental hazards and to calculate risk. Less-reliable technological systems (those with frequent system failure) and less-resilient social systems (those with reduced capacity for recovery following disaster) are considered to be most vulnerable. Studies that chart the distribution of risk across demographic groups demonstrate that it is the very old and the very young within the lowest socioeconomic and culturally marginalized groups who are the most vulnerable to disasters' harmful effects. The least vulnerable are those with the greatest access to financial, technological, and informational resources.

Although most disaster researchers and policymakers share many of the same practical goals, there remains a substantial divergence in philosophy and strategy. Echoing the globalization debate between modernization and dependency theorists, the behavioral view of disaster attributes the vulnerability of less-developed nations to their failure to modernize, whereas conflict theorists point to unequal global trade relations. Arguing that wealthy industrialized nations use economic and political pressure to force economically dependent nations to exploit their own natural resources, these theorists claim that it is not underdevelopment that creates vulnerability to environmental hazard, but poverty. Behavioralists assume that vulnerability can be reduced through technological innovation, whereas conflict theorists call for social changes, including redistribution of wealth and power and greater reliance on local knowledge in preference to imported expertise. Finally, there is sharp disagreement about the extent to which environmental hazards and their realized disasters occur as a result of unusual occurrences or whether they reflect chronic circumstances. Having as a post-disaster goal a return to "normalcy" is problematic if normal conditions are implicated in creating the environmental hazard in the first place.

The United Nations has developed the International Strategy for Disaster Reduction, a plan of action for the 21st century that acknowledges the complex social contexts that color perceptions and influence calculations of vulnerability and risk. The plan takes a pragmatic view, advocating the use of both behavioral and structural strategies to reduce the losses associated with environmental hazards.

Judith Pintar

See also Disasters; Environmental Justice; Modernization Theory

Further Readings

Beck, Ulrich. 1992. *Risk Society: Towards a New Modernity.* London: Sage.

Blaikie, Piers, Terry Cannon, Ian Davis, and Ben Wisner. 2003. *At Risk: Natural Hazards, People's Vulnerability, and Disasters.* 2nd ed. London: Taylor & Francis.

Burton, Ian, Robert W. Kates, and Gilbert F. White. 1993. *The Environment as Hazard.* 2nd ed. New York: Guilford.

Inter-agency Secretariat of the International Strategy for Disaster Reduction (UN/ISDR). 2004. "Living with Risk: A Global Review of Disaster Reduction Initiatives." Geneva: United Nations. Retrieved December 26, 2007 (http://www.unisdr.org/eng/about_isdr/bd-lwr-2004-eng.htm).

Smith, Keith. 2004. *Environmental Hazards: Assessing Risk and Reducing Disaster.* 4th ed. London: Routledge.

ENVIRONMENTAL JUSTICE

Environmental justice seeks to assess the fairness of the distribution of environmental risks and benefits. Of primary concern are the negative effects of nearby activities that generate pollution or risk in some form and that have health or nuisance impacts on people who live or work in the neighborhood. Most research and public policy dealing with environmental justice seeks to determine whether low-income or minority populations are disproportionately and negatively impacted by polluting activities.

Primarily since the 1970s, a number of research projects in the United States have investigated whether or not a systematic inverse relationship exists between pollution exposure and income or racial minority populations. Many of these studies examined the population characteristics of areas in the vicinity of solid waste transfer stations and disposal sites.

Criticisms of many of these investigations concern their (a) dealing with population areas larger than the likely spatial extent of the negative spillovers, (b) employing inadequately defined control areas to assess if disadvantaged people were disproportionately impacted, (c) depending too heavily on case studies with limited external validity, and (d) not addressing whether nearby sources of pollution or risk did indeed have negative health or nuisance effects on neighboring populations.

Other studies employing sound research designs have demonstrated that in some geographic areas, low-income and minority groups in the population *do* live closer to some kinds of environmental hazards than other groups. For example, a national study in the mid-20th century used a comprehensive listing of waste storage and disposal facilities and census tract data for a 20-year period, comparing tracts with and without hazardous sites. In general, the findings were that surrounding these sites were primarily working-class neighborhoods with mostly white populations extensively employed in manufacturing. However, this was more the case in northern urban areas than in the southeastern portion of the United States, where neighboring tracts had larger black populations.

The most reliable studies account for market forces and land use controls, using census tracts in the same urban area but without waste sites as the basis for comparison. Although even these largely fail to establish the public health effects of this proximity, they do point out what needs to be considered to have a reliable empirical basis for assessing the distributional implications of local decisions and thus for public policy.

Public policy applications of findings from sound environmental justice research focus not only on remediation and mitigation of existing conditions but also on current and future decisions that can impact environmental quality. This is the primary purpose of Executive Order 12898: Federal Actions to Address Environmental Justice in Minority and Low-Income Populations, signed by President Clinton in 1994.

This order directs each federal agency to adopt, as part of its mission, responsibility for evaluating and mitigating "disproportionately high adverse human health or environmental effects of its programs, policies, and activities on minority and low-income populations in the United States." This order also requires both informing these populations about these likely health and nuisance impacts and involving them in assessing these impacts and in developing ways to minimize or mitigate them.

The National Environment Policy Act requires environmental impact assessments on anything that the federal agencies sponsor, fund, permit, or undertake, which includes many programs and projects implemented at the local level. Legal action can occur in the case of unequal treatment under Title VI of the Civil Rights Act of 1964, which requires nondiscrimination in relation to sex, age, disability, race, color, and national origin.

Although Executive Order 12898 establishes the principles concerning factors to consider in assessing environmental justice, it stops short of specifying the strategy that agencies must use or prescribing the methodology for evaluating the performance of alternative plans or project designs. Instead, agencies can initiate a range of approaches on an experimental basis. Even so, the principles of the order suggest a sequence of at least four analytical tasks.

First is identifying and mapping the spatial extent of negative environmental impacts, such as air and water pollution, noise and vibration, displacement of homes or businesses, degraded aesthetic values, disrupted natural and man-made resources, traffic congestion, and disrupted community cohesion or economic vitality. The second task is identifying the demographic profile of those living and working in the impacted area. Next is defining a baseline or control population, usually for a larger area such as a jurisdiction. The final analytical task is calculating and comparing the percentage of low-income and minority people in the impact area and the larger area, to determine if those impacted by the action are disproportionately disadvantaged.

As noted earlier, the order requires both these analytical tasks and public outreach and involvement in identifying, reviewing, and understanding the negative environmental effects. It also requires engaging stakeholders in designing ways to reduce these effects, to mitigate those effects that remain, and perhaps to compensate for effects that are otherwise difficult to mitigate.

This executive order was a unique initiative by a central government to address and act on environmental justice. Furthermore, it provided a definition of environmental justice that grew out of studies that examined who was especially adversely impacted by the location of hazardous facilities. Finally, this definition led to an analytical and outreach procedure to assess the environmental justice implications of alternative designs for programs and projects involving the federal government.

Donald H. Miller

See also Environmental Movement; Environmental Racism

Further Readings

Cole, L. and S. Foster. 2001. *From the Ground Up: Environmental Racism and the Rise of the Environmental Justice Movement.* New York: New York University Press.

Federal Register. 1994. "Executive Order 12898, Federal Actions to Address Environmental Justice in Minority Populations and Low-Income Populations." *Federal Register,* 59:32. Retrieved December 26, 2007 (http://www.labtrain.noaa.gov/ppguide/ffpp_53.htm).

Miller, Donald. 2005. "Methods for Evaluating Environmental Justice—Approaches to Implementing U.S. Executive Order 12898." Pp. 25–44 in *Beyond Benefit Cost Analysis—Accounting for Non-market Values in Planning Evaluation,* edited by D. Miller and D. Patassini. Burlington, VT: Ashgate.

Oakes, John M., Douglas L. Anderton, and Andy B. Anderson. 1996. "A Longitudinal Analysis of Environmental Equity in Communities with Hazardous Waste Facilities." *Social Science Research* 25:125–48.

Rhodes, Edwardo Lao. 2005. *Environmental Justice in America—A New Paradigm.* Bloomington, IN: Indiana University Press.

ENVIRONMENTAL MOVEMENT

The environmental movement is a social movement dedicated to the management, protection, and restoration of the natural environment. Also referred to as the conservation movement, or more recently, the green movement, it is one of the more successful social movements of the 20th century, for it secured widespread public support and influenced governments to establish agencies and pass legislation consistent with the goals of the movement.

Although the movement is rooted in many ideas from the conservationist movement of the early 20th century, what can be called the modern environmental movement did not begin until the late 1960s and early 1970s. During this time the movement benefited from the increased political mobilization and cultural climate that accompanied the civil rights and anti-war movements. Also helping to launch the environmental movement was new scientific evidence increasingly indicating that human activity was harming the natural environment. Environmentalists pointed to river fires, gas station lines, and factory soot as examples of avoidable human behavior that was damaging to the environment.

Numerous highly publicized disasters occurred during the 1970s and 1980s that further increased public awareness. Two of these events—the near meltdown at Three Mile Island, Pennsylvania, in 1979 and the explosion at Chernobyl, Ukraine, in 1986—involved mishaps with nuclear energy. Both events received considerable media and public attention, resulting in a decline in public support for nuclear energy. In 1989, an oil tanker, the *Exxon Valdez,* hit a reef off the coast of Alaska, resulting in leakage of an estimated 11 million gallons of oil into the sea, one of the largest oil spills in U.S. history. The images of sea animals covered in oil further outraged the public and produced increasing support for the environmental movement into the 1990s.

Government agencies were established and legislation was passed near the beginning of the environmental movement, and these agencies and laws remain in effect today. In 1969 came the National Environmental Policy Act and establishment of the Environmental Protection Agency as a federal agency devoted to protecting and preserving the environment. In 1973, the Endangered Species Act sought to save species who were threatened by environmental destruction.

Various organizations promoting environmentalism have also had a profound impact. Two of the first organizations, the Sierra Club and the National Audubon Society, have been promoting environmental issues for more than a century. Sporadic grassroots protests, referred to as Not In My Backyard (NIMBY) movements, reflect local concerns of the environmental movement by discouraging the establishment of waste sites and trash incinerators in local communities. Earth Day—first held on April 22, 1970—continues to serve as a day encouraging Americans to be particularly cognizant of environmental issues.

Recently, the environmental movement began focusing on such macro-level concerns as global warming, ozone depletion, and rain forest loss. In 2005, an agreement among more than 160 countries, known as the Kyoto Protocol, went into effect. Countries ratifying this protocol agreed to reduce emissions of carbon dioxide and other greenhouse gases considered harmful to the environment. The United States has not ratified this protocol despite being the world's most significant producer of greenhouse gases.

Demographically, the environmental movement is primarily a middle-class movement. Many attribute the affluent nature of this movement to the greater amount of time devoted to recreation by the middle class and the tendency for the middle class to focus on aesthetics. A recent trend in the movement, however, has been an emphasis on environmental justice, which emphasizes racial and class disparities in the level of harm caused by pollution and waste. Those participating in the movement tend to be younger in age than participants in most other social movements. Despite the rural nature of the early conservationist movement, those participating in the environmental movement are more likely to reside in urban areas.

Although the environmental movement receives a great deal of public support, some groups resist the movement. Businesses with economic incentives to engage in what many consider to be environmentally harmful practices oppose the movement, typically stating that claims made by environmentalists are exaggerated or mythical. Recently, however, businesses have begun to alter their practices and images to act and appear more environmentally friendly. As a result, the culprit has become the general public, and emphasis has shifted to individual responsibility for environmental concerns.

Jamie Longazel

See also Environment, Eco-Warriors; Environmental Degradation; Environmental Justice; Environmental Racism; Global Warming; NIMBYism; Social Movements

Further Readings

Dryzek, John S. 2005. *The Politics of the Earth: Environmental Discourses.* New York: Oxford University Press.

Dunlap, Riley E. and Angela G. Mertig. 1992. *American Environmentalism: The U.S. Environmental Movement, 1970–1990.* New York: Taylor & Francis.

Hannigan, John A. 2006. *Environmental Sociology: A Social Constructionist Perspective.* 2nd ed. New York: Routledge.

ENVIRONMENTAL RACISM

Environmental racism refers to the disproportionate distribution of environmental hazards and toxic facilities resulting from governmental or corporate policies and regulations that deliberately target poor and minority communities. The seminal 1987 study, *Toxic Waste and Race in the United States,* conducted by the United Church of Christ's Commission for Racial Justice, found that race was the most significant variable in deciding where hazardous waste facilities were to be located. Subsequent research has largely confirmed that race, even more than economic class, is the strongest predictor of placement for waste-producing facilities. In effect, environmental racism can be seen as mirroring existing patterns of social inequality; the most polluted communities tend to be the ones populated by minority residents of low socioeconomic status.

The disparate geographic distribution of environmental hazards means that toxic facilities emanating high levels of pollution are apt to be situated near neighborhoods with low property values and high minority populations. Individuals in these communities are more likely to be exposed to inordinately high levels of contamination and work in jobs that subject them to increased environmental risk. Furthermore, children are particularly vulnerable to health risks from higher levels of pollution; illnesses such as asthma, lead poisoning, leukemia, and encephalitis are being detected with increasing frequency among young children living in highly polluted regions. Whereas many of the most polluted areas can be found in and around urban neighborhoods—"cancer alley," for example, is the vicinity along the Mississippi River near Baton Rouge, Louisiana— nuclear waste and other toxic materials and garbage are often disposed of on Native American reservations, which are particularly vulnerable because they are not subject to state jurisdiction. Environmental regulations on Native American lands are more lax, making them prime targets for nuclear waste disposal, landfills, and other toxic facilities.

Environmental justice advocates argue that toxic facilities tend to be placed in nonwhite communities because these are more likely to be impoverished areas where residents are disenfranchised, possess little political power, and offer the least amount of resistance. Furthermore, research suggests that minority communities receive less protection from the enforcement of environmental laws. According to a 1992 report in the *National Law Journal,* penalties for hazardous waste were 500 percent higher in white communities, and penalties for pollution law violations were almost 50 percent higher in white communities than in areas with large minority populations. Environmental justice advocates argue that this disparity, which has been found to occur regardless of whether communities are middle class or poor, is a result of governmental regulations that are enforced in a discriminatory manner.

Still, critics suggest that there is nothing discriminatory about the placement of hazardous waste facilities, arguing instead that market forces ultimately determine where toxic sites are located. As a result, incinerators, landfills, and other waste facilities tend to be found in areas where land is cheaper. These areas, in turn, are also where inexpensive housing is available for lower-income households. Hence, critics argue that toxic facilities are not disparately situated in poor and minority communities, but rather that poor people and people of color tend to move to those areas because they offer the most affordable housing. However, environmental justice activists are critical of the market forces approach, arguing that people in poor and minority neighborhoods do not make a freely rational choice to live in those areas where the risks from environmental hazards are most severe.

Advocates further argue that the effects of "NIMBYism" (based on an acronym for "not in my backyard") have exacerbated the disparate effects of environmental hazards on racial minorities. While middle- and upper-class communities have exhibited the political power to stop the intrusion of hazardous waste facilities, these successes have led to the increased development of toxic sites in poor and minority neighborhoods. According to the 2001 Supreme Court decision in *Alexander v. Sandoval,* 532 U.S. 275, individuals are unable to sue to enforce federal regulations that prohibit disparate racial impacts. In other words, it is not sufficient to simply show harm or discriminatory impact as evidence of environmental racism. Instead, courts also require evidence of discriminatory intent, meaning individuals must prove that they were disproportionately affected by environmental harms resulting from acts of purposeful discrimination. Because most poor and minority communities lack the financial resources and political power needed to maintain a legal challenge against polluters, many environmental justice advocates argue that existing laws and regulations simply serve to maintain the status quo.

In hopes of effecting change, increasing support can be found within the environmental justice movement for grassroots activism that empowers traditionally passive and marginalized neighborhoods. Historically, environmental activists have fought to block the placement of hazardous sites without any communication or consultation from those residents who live in the communities that will be most affected by the presence of harmful toxins. However, grassroots environmental justice organizations are increasingly working with the people living in vicinities affected by environmental degradation. The goal is to encourage the active participation of residents in historically disenfranchised areas in the struggle against placing toxic facilities in their neighborhoods. As the fight against environmental racism continues to evolve at the grassroots level, the hope is that poor and minority residents living in marginalized communities will continue to have more prominent voices in the fight for environmental justice.

Ray Maratea

See also Discrimination; Discrimination, Institutional; Environment, Hazardous Waste; Environment, Pollution; Environmental Degradation; Environmental Hazards; Environmental Justice; Environmental Movement; NIMBYism; Race

Further Readings

Cole, Luke W. and Sheila R. Foster. 2001. *From the Ground Up: Environmental Racism and the Rise of the Environmental Justice Movement.* New York: New York University Press.

Lester, James P., David W. Allen, and Kelly M. Hill. 2001. *Environmental Injustice in the United States: Myths and Realities.* Boulder, CO: Westview.

Visgilio, Gerald R. and Diana M. Whitelaw, eds. 2003. *Our Backyard: A Quest for Environmental Justice.* Lanham, MD: Rowman & Littlefield.

Westra, Laura and Bill E. Lawson, eds. 2001. *Faces of Environmental Racism: Confronting Issues of Global Justice.* Lanham, MD: Rowman & Littlefield.

EPIDEMICS, MANAGEMENT OF

The standard biomedical definition of *epidemic* is the sudden spread of a disease among a number of people in excess of normal expectancy. Unlike most social problems, infectious disease epidemics are grave social problems not only because of the possible deadly nature of the disease but also because of the element of surprise and the social context of contamination. For most communities affected by an infectious disease epidemic, the outbreak is unexpected. The mode of contamination tends be a simple daily life activity involving social relations and practices that are innocuous under normal circumstances but that must be halted once the link with the disease becomes evident (e.g., preparing, buying, and selling food; collecting, storing, and drinking water; sharing garments or eating utensils; or engaging

in close social and physical contact). The disruption of normal social and economic activities in the affected communities is one of the major consequences of epidemics that transform what begins as one person's illness episode into a large-scale social problem or crisis.

Thus the management of epidemics as a crisis is a problem of governance. Generally, governance refers to the management of the affairs of the collective to ensure safety, fairness, and equality of opportunity for all its individual members. Seen from the perspective of crisis management, unforeseen epidemics are real-time tests of the effectiveness of a country's governance in a time of crisis, and foreseen epidemics testify to the country's level of preparedness. Either way, the political leaders' style of governance becomes a definitive factor in the country's efforts to prevent or contain the epidemic. Consequently, the political and health authorities in the country or region affected by an epidemic are major stakeholders as they are naturally expected to find a solution and implement the measures necessary to deal with the crisis.

The world's experiences with bubonic plague, cholera, typhoid, yellow fever, and countless other infectious disease epidemics of the ancient past have been amplified by encounters with recent epidemics such as HIV/AIDS, SARS (severe acute respiratory syndrome), and the threat of human transmission of the H5N1 virus, commonly known as "avian influenza" or "bird flu." It is a sign of the times that, compared with past generations, although the world might still be caught unaware by an epidemic in the 21st century, economically advanced countries today are in a better position to manage epidemics. Still, the ability to manage epidemics varies widely across countries depending on the nature of the disease, economic resources, technical expertise, and the overall level of preparedness, among other things.

The accumulated knowledge and experiences with past epidemics highlight three important areas of attention in their management: the scientific and biomedical efforts to develop an effective cure and vaccine against the infectious disease; the types of people affected by the disease; and the leadership actions and decision making that affect the level of success in managing the crisis. The biomedical and scientific efforts to find cures and vaccines are beyond the scope of this entry. The objects of attention here are the other two areas: people and the decision-making process.

Concerning the types of people involved, four types of stakeholders are crucial in the management of epidemics: the group or community directly affected by the outbreak, including infected persons, their families, and immediate social networks both formal and informal; the larger population at risk of infection; the medical and other health care personnel; and the political authorities, including policymakers, health authorities, and all levels of policy implementation personnel. The active cooperation of these important stakeholders is necessary to deal successfully with the epidemic. Medical sociology and social policy studies show that the cooperation of these groups tends to fluctuate due to the influence of many factors, but more significantly with the level of trust citizens have in their national leaders.

Regarding actions and decision-making processes, the management of epidemics requires two kinds of knowledge: (1) knowledge on the nature of the virus or bacteria involved and its clinical features, and (2) knowledge on the population affected. Historical records show that lack of both types of knowledge was among the reasons for the failure of communities and nations waging war against a succession of many epidemics such as bubonic plague in the 14th century; typhus, scurvy, and dysentery in the 16th and 17th centuries; and pulmonary tuberculosis for most of the 19th century.

Today we have HIV/AIDS, SARS, and avian influenza ("bird flu"), among other major infectious diseases. Managing these epidemics means preventing and controlling the infectious disease outbreaks, and this is a race against time. The ability of viruses to evolve and move across species represents an ever-increasing danger in a time of considerable population movements through global travel, immigration, and forced exodus propelled by large-scale natural and human-caused disasters. As a result, scientists around the world are scrutinizing the microcosm of viruses and bacteria with an increasing sense of urgency and intensity. Yet, while scientific advances are crucial, they are insufficient. The battle against infectious disease epidemics must be fought simultaneously outside the laboratory on a wider, social front involving the attitudes and actions of ordinary individuals and groups. People's image of a disease influences their attitudes toward illness and may even become part of the community's folklore. Research by medical sociologists and other social scientists indicates that the successful management of epidemics involves knowledge of factors such as cultural values, beliefs, and practices; socioeconomic and demographic features of the population; the public image of the infectious disease; and the political will to intervene. Cultural norms on disease causation, diagnosis, and treatment (including social stigma, privacy issues, and ability to obtain prompt and affordable medical care) are very important. These norms and beliefs influence people's behavior and the level of success in preventing and containing an infectious disease epidemic.

A final point deserves specific mention. Given the dual nature of epidemics as both biomedical and social problems and given the two types of knowledge (biomedical and social) required for their prevention and management, it is clear that effective governance of epidemics can be attained only by close and dynamic collaboration between biomedical and social science experts on the one hand and leaders and the public on the other hand.

Stella R. Quah

See also Bioethics; Health Care, Access; HIV/AIDS, Reaching High-Risk Populations; Pandemics

Further Readings

Quah, Stella R., ed. 2007. *Crisis Preparedness: Asia and the Global Governance of Epidemics.* Stanford, CA: Shorenstein Asia-Pacific Research Centre and the Brookings Institution.

Quah, Stella R. 2007. "Public Image and Governance of Epidemics: Comparing HIV/AIDS and SARS." *Health Policy* 80:253–72.

Rosenberg, Charles E. 1992. *Explaining Epidemics and Other Studies in the History of Medicine.* Cambridge, England: Cambridge University Press.

Wills, Christopher. 1996. *Plagues:. Their Origin, History and Future.* London: HarperCollins.

World Health Organization. 2006. *SARS: How a Global Epidemic Was Stopped.* Geneva: World Health Organization.

EQUAL PROTECTION

The concept of *equal protection* originates in the 14th Amendment of the U.S. Constitution. In part, it reads: "No State shall make or enforce any law which shall abridge the privileges or immunities of citizens of the

United States, nor shall any State deprive any person of life, liberty, or property, without due process of law; *nor deny to any person within its jurisdiction the equal protection of the laws*" (emphasis added).

The seemingly simple clause has generated significant public debates over its interpretation and usage. Among these is whether the framers were concerned primarily with *equality* of the laws or *protection* of the laws. Various alternative framings and interpretations have generated a vocabulary of common expressions such as *separate but equal* and its converse of separate as *inherently unequal, color-blind*, or *race conscious*, as well as the terms *equal opportunity, affirmative action*, or *preferential treatment* and its corollary *reverse discrimination*. These competing conceptualizations frame larger social, political, and legal debates spawned by the equal protection clause.

Historical Perspective

The 14th Amendment was ratified in 1868, just 3 years after the 13th Amendment, which abolished slavery and involuntary servitude, and 2 years before the 15th Amendment, which prohibited denying citizens the right to vote "on account of race, color, or previous condition of servitude." This trio of post–Civil War amendments served many purposes, but a central focus was protecting newly freed slaves, particularly in those States that had constituted the Confederacy.

So on its face, the 14th Amendment's equal protection clause seemed intended to provide recently freed slaves the same protection under the laws as white citizens. Surprisingly, the earliest litigation involving the 14th Amendment had little to do with race. Today, litigation under the equal protection clause involves questions about gender, age, disability, and sexual orientation, among other classifications. Nonetheless, examining the application of the equal protection clause to race is illustrative.

In 1877, when federal troops withdrew from the South, abruptly ending a period of Reconstruction, many Southern and Border States enacted regulations known as Jim Crow laws (which prohibited blacks from using the same public facilities as whites) and Black Codes (which impinged on blacks' civil rights and civil liberties). In 1896, one such Jim Crow law was the focus of a notorious U.S. Supreme Court case known as *Plessy v. Ferguson*. This case gave rise both to the doctrine known as "separate but equal" and to a contradictory minority view that the Constitution was "color-blind."

Using the equal protection clause of the 14th Amendment, Homer Plessy challenged a Louisiana law that mandated that railway coaches be segregated by race. State law required black customers to ride in separate, third-class passenger cars. Plessy, an "octoroon" (meaning he was one-eighth black), was arrested when he boarded the train with a first-class ticket usually reserved for white patrons. The Court upheld the law, finding that the equal protection clause did not extend to "equality in social arrangements" but rather protected only "equality of civil rights."

In this reading of the equal protection clause, the notion of *protection* of the laws trumped the idea of *equality* of the laws. Justice Brown, writing for the majority, identified "the underlying fallacy" of Plessy's argument as based on an assumption that "separation of the two races stamps the colored race with a badge of inferiority." The only dissenting justice, John Harlan, wrote, "Our Constitution is *colorblind,* and neither knows nor tolerates classes among citizens" (emphasis added). Two decidedly conflicting views thus emerged. The majority permitted separate treatment by race if that treatment was equal; Harlan objected to the very notion of *separate,* where people were sorted by race.

Ostensibly, *Plessy* permitted separate treatment only when groups were treated *equally.* In reality, the *Plessy* decision legitimized racial discrimination in virtually all aspects of social life and resulted in inferior treatment of blacks. Separate accommodations extended well beyond transportation and included all types of public facilities and institutions (e.g., water fountains, swimming pools, schools, hotels, and lunch counters). These laws flourished into the 1960s.

Interpretation Change

The "separate but equal" interpretation of the "equal protection" clause was finally successfully challenged in 1954 in the landmark case of *Brown v. Board of Education of Topeka.* In this case, involving segregated public schools, the U.S. Supreme Court held that separate schools were "inherently unequal" and explicitly violated the equal protection clause of the 14th Amendment. Note the significant shift to interpreting the equal protection clause as discriminatory merely by virtue of treating minority groups separately. The Court acknowledged that racial classifications could not be considered independently from the social context that perpetuated inferior treatment.

During the 1960s, civil rights advocates expressed concern about institutional or structural discrimination.

Advocates argued that race-neutral or color-blind policy—which might appear fair and impartial on its face—actually perpetuated institutional discrimination (on the basis of race, gender, or age) as a practical matter by replicating the status quo. These advocates argued that race-conscious policies were necessary to correct historic inequities. They sought to provide equal opportunities for historically marginalized populations through affirmative action programs and policies. Under these initiatives, special preferences could be given to under-represented groups. The point of affirmative action was to correct, compensate, or redress past discrimination for social injustices by giving preferential treatment to individuals based on membership in a group to ensure their equal opportunity to participate in social and political institutions (education, employment, etc.). The object was to increase the representation of the minority groups in areas where they had been traditionally excluded or under-represented. Unequal treatment was seen as a way to promote equal protection as it related to distribution of opportunities.

By the 1970s, concern that some groups were receiving preferential treatment led opponents to reframe the issue and introduce the idea of reverse discrimination. In general, "reverse discrimination" was conceptualized as the practice of discriminating against members of a majority or dominant group by favoring members of a minority group. Affirmative action or preferential treatment programs and policies were challenged as violating the equal protection interests of members of the majority.

For example, in *Regents of the University of California v. Bakke,* another landmark Supreme Court case, Allen Bakke—a white male applicant to the University of California at Davis School of Medicine who was twice denied admission—argued that the school's affirmative action program, which set aside 16 seats for minority candidates, violated his equal protection guarantees because the policy discriminated based on *his* race. Notably, he argued it was race alone that barred him from competing for one of those 16 reserved seats. The court agreed, holding that a quota system that reserved a specific number of seats based on race was an unconstitutional violation of the 14th Amendment.

Recent Developments

More recently, the Supreme Court returned to the issue of affirmative action policies and university admissions. In 2003 the court held in *Grutter v. Bollinger* that the University of Michigan Law School's affirmative action policy was constitutional and did not violate the equal protection clause. Barbara Grutter, a white woman who was denied admission, argued that the university's race-conscious admissions policy violated her 14th Amendment equal protection rights. The university argued that diversity—broadly defined to include more factors than race, such as socioeconomic status, gender, age, and religion—was necessary to obtain a diverse student body. In order not to run afoul of *Bakke,* the University of Michigan argued that it did not have a quota system but rather that each person was individually evaluated based on a number of factors including, but not limited to, race and that each had an equal opportunity to compete for every seat.

Although race serves as the primary example in this entry, the equal protection clause has been broadly applied—with greater and lesser success—to many other kinds of groupings, such as gender, age, sexual orientation, and disability. The Supreme Court has established a three-tiered theory of equal protection depending on what group is being considered and the importance of the interest threatened. *Strict scrutiny,* the highest standard, is reserved for cases involving race, and the unequal treatment must meet a *compelling state interest.* The lowest standard of review is known as *rational scrutiny.* Under this minimal standard, there must be some sort of reasonable relationship between the unequal treatment and a legitimate government purpose. The middle tier has been used exclusively for cases involving gender, where the unequal treatment must be *substantially related* to an important state objective. Thus, as simple as the idea of equal protection sounds, it applies differently based on group membership and the interests at stake.

Karen M. Staller

See also Affirmative Action; Black Codes; Civil Rights; Jim Crow; Race-Blind Policies; Segregation, De Facto; Segregation, De Jure

Further Readings

Baer, Judith A. 1983. *Equality under the Constitution: Reclaiming the Fourteenth Amendment.* Ithaca, NY: Cornell University Press.

James, Joseph B. 1984. *The Ratification of the Fourteenth Amendment.* Macon, GA: Mercer University Press.

tenBroek, Jacobus. 1951. *Antislavery Origins of the Fourteenth Amendment.* Berkeley, CA: University of California Press.

EROSION

Erosion can refer to either the effects of human and natural processes or the human–natural interactive processes, the latter serving here as the focus in discussing soil erosion and biodiversity loss, particularly as a result of surface water runoffs in both urban and rural environments. When humans disrupt soil creation processes, habitat fragmentation, habitat destruction, and general ecological unraveling begin in the soil gradient's plant and animal life specific to it. Worldwide, the majority of biologists blame anthropogenic (resulting from human influence) soil erosion and biodiversity loss for the current sixth major mass extinction event in the history of planet Earth. This is the first anthropogenic mass extinction event, and it is far more rapid than any of the "Big Five" in past geologic times.

Natural Erosion and Soil Creation

In different soil gradients, a specific slow, organic and inorganic physical process of natural soil creation occurs that involves beneficial erosion. This process jockeys increasingly with a faster, human soil erosion and sheet runoff that kill plant and animal life within a soil gradient—carrying the slowly formed soil away. Thus anthropogenic soil erosion and associated biodiversity loss start in the alteration of this balance in the creation or destruction of soil and in how humans affect water dynamics.

Understanding soil creation chemically and physically is necessary if one wishes to understand and arrest the process of soil destruction. Soil creation results from a mixture of decayed organic and inorganic matter relationships, which create an all-important macro-molecular chelate arrangement of humic acids. Humic acids are a major component required for making humic substances, created via microbial degradation of once-living matter. A large number of humic molecules are hydrophobic, meaning they innately allow, in the presence of water, clumping into "water-avoiding" supramolecular nodes.

Only the acidic component of humic substances, mainly carboxylic acid, gives soil a capacity for *chelation,* a capacity to "store" inorganic minerals as ions without them having a strong chemical bond with anything else. Chelated inorganic ions are more readily bioavailable for plants or are sequestered away

from them if they are poisons. Thus one of the most important properties of humic acid is this chelation ability to solubilize many ions into hydrophobic cations (water-avoiding, chemically positive ions). For bioavailability chelation, ions like magnesium, calcium, and iron are made available for plant absorption. For *sequestering* chelation, humic acid holds apart as ions many elements that otherwise would form toxic molecular salts to poison the soil without positive biological effect (like cadmium and lead). For instance, sodium and chlorine ions naturally want to combine to form a salt. Instead, in good fertile soil they are attached as separate ions to humic acids and clay—rendered harmless by chelation. Thus many good soils contain large quantities of safely chelated "salt," held apart in ionic form from precipitating out in this way. Plant growth thrives in such "theoretically saline" soils, in many cases. In short, humic acid chelation capacities have an important dual role for living systems: They make biological uptake of nutrients possible, and they sequester poisons. Chemistry of varied humic acids has a profound influence on chelation capacities as well.

On the contrary, human soil erosion processes chemically have in common destruction of the humic acid creation process. This causes (1) loss of chelation capacity and (2) loss of water permeability and loss of soil infiltration capacities as a consequence. For agriculture, the latter can lead to (3) forced excessive watering, and in turn, a raised pH. Water as slightly alkaline (chemically positive) as well as dilutive would demote the slightly acidic (chemically negative) environment that encourages humic acid creation and would thus demote chelation action further. Such watering as a consequence can lead to (4) artificially raised water tables that can bring in external salts to precipitate from below, creating a hardpan and encouraging erosion of the drier soil above it. These four interactive soil destruction factors cause increased salt precipitation in chelated soil. This encourages a chemical and physical change toward poorer soil and less water-absorbent soil in both urban and rural areas. This primes the conditions that cause soil erosion, whether by sheet water runoff or wind.

Erosion: Just Add Water or Wind

Poor land or soil uses such as those involving deforestation, overgrazing, styles of chemical and physical agriculture (tilling), unmanaged construction activity, and urban impermeable surfaces demote humic acid formation. This leads to erosion because less humic acid means less hygroscopic soil, resulting in an innately dry soil—regardless of climate. Human-created poor soils facilitate ongoing natural water erosion and wind erosion above rates of natural soil formation. In heavily eroding water conditions, it is not water alone that erodes, but also suspended loads of abrasive particles of poor loose soil, pebbles, and boulders, which expand the power of erosion as they traverse and scrape soil surfaces. Waterborne soil erosion in these conditions is additionally a function of water speed and suspended particle dynamics.

Wind erosion occurs in areas with little or no vegetation, often in areas without sufficient rainfall. However, the common factor of a less humic-acidic hygroscopic soil facilitates wind erosion regardless of climate. One example is provided by the long-term shifting dunes in beaches or deserts, which advance to bury any plant life even when underground sources of water may be sufficient. Huge areas of western China are experiencing expanding desertification and wind-based erosion, whipped into incredible dust storms caused by mostly anthropogenic climate change. Both water and wind erosion cause further biodiversity loss from receiving water sedimentation and ecosystem damage (including fish kills).

Anthropogenic soil erosion and biodiversity loss expand from *edge effects,* the ecological juxtaposition between contrasting environments. Edge effects are boundaries between natural habitats and disturbances by poor land use choices. When an edge is created to a natural ecosystem and the area outside is a disturbed system, even the natural ecosystem fragment is affected for great distances inward from the edge. This edge effect area is called the "external habitat" and has a different microclimate than the residual "interior habitat." This partially compromised external habitat starts a feedback loop process, leading to further soil erosion and microclimate change unraveling and exposing more interior habitat to further habitat destruction. For example, Amazonian areas altered by edge effects exceed the area actually cleared, and fires are more prevalent in the external habitat area as humidity drops and temperature and wind levels rise. Increased natural fire frequency from the 1990s in the Amazon, Indonesia, and the Philippines is an edge effect.

In such contexts, an ecosystem unravels toward a simpler, *emergy* state (i.e., embedded or sequestered biomass energy). Intrusive exotic species are part of this, further causing biodiversity loss to levels of lower complexity. Exotics are hardly to blame. The blame is human soil-erosive processes that create edge effects and biodiversity loss that exotics opportunistically utilize.

Shifting Blame and Shifting Cultivation

The blame for much of the world's soil and biodiversity erosion usually focuses on the poor—the slash-and-burn cultivators, mostly of the developing world. However, the developed world engages in transnational corporate logging, mining, export-driven grazing of cattle, and plantation agriculture linked to a war economy demoting political expression of local ecological self-interest. These factors in combination are to blame for soil and biodiversity loss, as well as for keeping such degradation in place. In short, current faulty and unsustainable developed world models and associated warfare are the larger origin of soil erosion, defoliation, and biodiversity destruction. Another example of misplaced priorities of exclusive blame (though a matter of proper concern) on peasant slash-and-burn for erosion is its false magnification by politicized developed world research institutions. Despite the largest blame for soil erosion and biodiversity loss coming from developed world developmental models, the Food and Agriculture Organization of the United Nations (FAO) assessed shifting cultivation of the last independent natives to be the main cause of deforestation—ignoring more invasive and destructive unsustainable developed world logging. The apparent discrimination and policy focus against independent shifting cultivators (whom the FAO recommend be forced to work on export economy rubber plantations) caused a confrontation between the FAO and environmental groups who saw the FAO supporting unsustainable commercial logging and plantation interests against local rights of indigenous people to be independent economically.

The lesson here is that the infrastructural and cultural adherence of more than 3 to 4 billion people (at least ambivalently) supportive of developed world political economic models and commodity choices is far more dangerous to soil erosion and biological diversity than the estimated mere 250 million people subsisting on slash-and-burn. Instead of nomadic slash-and-burn sustenance-minded shifting cultivation villages, it is the expansion of permanent agricultural monocropping techniques—particularly in export frameworks of high herbicide/pesticide commodities, mining pollution, transnational corporate logging, and tree plantations—that has led to more soil erosion and biodiversity loss. Massive export-oriented sheep and cattle herding, for instance, led to soil erosion and biodiversity loss in Australia, New Zealand, the United States, and the Amazon. In less than 150 years in Australia, export-oriented monocrop agriculture in New South Wales led to clearing 90 percent of native vegetation. The same chosen agricultural strategy and chosen commodities removed 99 percent of tallgrass prairie in North America in the same period, leading to extreme habitat fragmentation and massive *suspended loads* (sediment) flowing down the Mississippi River. In the past 50 years, erosion has been affecting even oceans, with more than 60 massive dead zones of deoxygenated ocean water appearing off the littorals of the developed world. In short, organizing developmental paradigms of more locally attenuated human–environmental commodity relationships to maintain local natural soil gradient formation processes and to maintain soil infiltration are two generalized goals common to addressing soil erosion and biodiversity loss. There are already many land use techniques developed in urban and rural areas to allow for quick sedimentation and decreased water speed. Wider goals are to demote contexts that allow suspended loads or soil destruction in the first place—by altering agricultural and construction practices to mitigate loosened soil or heavy watering. There are frameworks of urban water handling and agricultural water and soil handling already developed to allow for more water infiltration, less (sometimes zero) soil tilling, and elimination of chemical pesticides and herbicides.

Integrating ecological relationships into urban infrastructural relations and making rural extraction sustainable by encouraging soil-creating human activities instead of soil destruction are both crucial. This seems to be the only route to demote the massive soil erosion and biodiversity loss that follow soil gradients. Comparatively, soil and biodiversity survive with human societies, or all will fall together.

Mark D. Whitaker

See also Environment, Runoff and Eutrophication; Environment, Sewage Disposal; Environmental Degradation; Environmental Movement; Water Organization; Water Quality

Further Readings

Ascher, William. 1999. *Why Governments Waste Natural Resources: Policy Failures in Developing Countries.* Baltimore: Johns Hopkins University Press.

Diamond, Jared. 2005. *Collapse: How Societies Choose to Fail or Succeed.* New York: Viking.

Hillel, Daniel. 1991. *Out of the Earth: Civilization and the Life of the Soil.* New York: Free Press.

Ponting, Clive. 1992. *A Green History of the World: The Environment and the Collapse of Great Civilizations.* New York: St. Martin's.

Potter, Christopher S. and Joel I. Cohen. 1993. *Perspectives on Biodiversity: Case Studies of Genetic Resource Conservation and Development.* Washington, DC: AAAS Press.

Pye-Smith, Charlie. 2002. *The Subsidy Scandal: How Your Government Wastes Your Money to Wreck Your Environment.* Sterling, VA: Earthscan.

Quammen, David. 1997. *The Song of the Dodo: Island Biogeography in an Age of Extinction.* New York: Scribner.

Steensberg, Axel. 1993. *Fire-Clearance Husbandry: Traditional Techniques throughout the World.* The Royal Danish Academy of Sciences and Letters' Commission for Research on the History of Agricultural Implements and Field Structures. Herning, Denmark: Poul Kristensen.

ETHNIC CLEANSING

Ethnic cleansing refers to the act of purging a region or area of a particular group based on its ethnic or racial identity, through violence and intentional oppression against the targeted group. Activities associated with ethnic cleansing include forced migrations, population transfers, appropriation of property, establishment of resettlement camps, threats of violence, and acts of violence (rape, torture, murder) on an individual and mass scale. Smaller-scale but equally insidious acts include prohibitions against citizenship and work; restricted civil rights; and restrictions on the right to bear arms, own property, use public resources, and communicate with the outside world. The intent of these deliberate acts is to alienate and exclude the target group.

The purpose of ethnic cleansing, a type of extreme action on behalf of nationalism or national self-determination, is ostensibly to purify a region or place. A majority or dominant group empties a region to occupy it. The offered justification for such a goal is often presented in either historical terms—in which the group taking the action considers itself bereft of past glory—or in racial terms—in which the dominant group claims that the victim has no right to exist within a territory. This drive to homogenize a place is not new, but the widespread and increasingly problematic use of the term is rather recent.

Vocabulary referring to the victims of ethnic cleansing includes such innocuous-sounding terms as *émigrés, deportees, refugees, war refugees, migrants, immigrants,* and *displaced persons.* Norman Naimark and others have traced the meaning of the term *ethnic cleansing* in European languages, including *chishchenie* (Russian) and *cicenja* (Serbo-Croatian), as referring to political purges. The term compares with the German word *Säuberung,* which conjures up the concepts of eugenics and race as well as political persecution. The term emerged during the Balkan Wars of the late 20th century, when it appeared in use by journalists in 1992 to describe Serbian activities against Croats and, later, Bosnian Muslims, with the clear intent to convey that a population was being expelled by means of force and terror. It became a pervasive term in the press, from the *New York Times,* to the *Financial Times* and the *Economist,* to the London *Times* and the *Guardian,* to the BBC, CNN, and wire services like the Associated Press and Agence France. By the summer of 1992, *Newsweek* and *U.S. News and World Report* used the term. This proliferation produced a debate about whether journalists had sanitized the term *ethnic cleansing,* rendering it an illegitimate synonym for genocide. A perhaps simplistic response would be that genocide may be a tactic of ethnic cleansing, but not all ethnic cleansing is genocide. The term has since been formalized by its use in war crimes cases. For example, items 138 to 140 of the World Summit Outcome, adopted by the United Nations on September 15, 2005, fell under the heading "Responsibility to protect populations from genocide, war crimes, ethnic cleansing and crimes against humanity," thus demonstrating that the term has acquired legal status.

Since its introduction into the vocabulary of politics and the media, the term *ethnic cleansing* has been applied to cases ranging from the former Yugoslavia to Rwanda. These may be the simplest applications, whereas others—such as the population transfers during the partition of India and Pakistan in 1947, the exile of Germans from the Volga region in 1941 and the later deportation of the Chechen-Ingush and the Crimean Tatars in 1944, the expulsion of Ukrainians from Poland after 1945, the genocide of Armenians in 1915, and the ongoing crisis in Palestine—are more complex and contested instances of ethnic cleansing. Some point to events such as the Spanish Inquisition as evidence that "cleansing" against Jews, Muslims, and "the Other" has long been a legacy of Western civilization. Other postwar applications include attacks on Kurds in Iraq, crimes of the Khmer Rouge in Cambodia, and the Sudan crisis of Darfur. This has led to a debate about whether it is appropriate to apply the term retroactively.

The question of morality also comes into play when equating ethnic cleansing with genocide or the Holocaust. Assigning the role of victim to a population is a weighty task and one fraught with pitfalls. For example, only after the reunification of Germany did a real discussion emerge which allowed for the investigation of ethnic Germans as suffering ethnic persecution after the war. Likewise, populations of other ethnic groups, including Poles, Lithuanians, and Ukrainians, registered complaints regarding postwar population transfers intended to homogenize territories as a prophylactic against future petitions from a large ethnic minority and as a means for the Soviet Union to force East Europeans into a condition of dependency.

The justification of acts of ethnic cleansing can be interpreted as a perversion of the Wilsonian concept of national self-determination, taking various forms. In former colonial territories, it involves the invention or rediscovery of indigenous culture and power structures, which are then interpreted, or reinterpreted, along ethnic lines. In the immediate aftermath of World War II in Europe, acts identified as ethnic cleansing were a direct result of Nazi or fascist interpretations of historical destiny as inextricably linked to ethnic identity and Aryan superiority, as well as oppressive expansionist and genocidal activities in occupied territories. Thus, at both the macro and micro levels, invoking both legal justifications and illegal persecution, ethnic cleansing was practiced in Europe and elsewhere, both before and after 1945.

Elizabeth Morrow Clark

See also Genocide; Holocaust; Human Rights; Mass Murder; Refugees; Resettlement

Further Readings

de Zayas, Alfred-Maurice. 2006. *A Terrible Revenge: The Ethnic Cleansing of the East European Germans.* 2nd ed. New York: Palgrave Macmillan.

Gourevitch, Philip. 1998. *We Wish to Inform You That Tomorrow We Will Be Killed with Our Families: Stories from Rwanda.* New York: Picador.

Naimark, Norman M. 2001. *Fires of Hatred: Ethnic Cleansing in Twentieth-Century Europe.* Cambridge, MA: Harvard University Press.

Power, Samantha. 2002. *"A Problem from Hell": America and the Age of Genocide.* New York: Basic Books.

ETHNIC GROUP

An ethnic group is a large group of people that defines itself, or is delineated by outsiders, as separate or set apart socially and sometimes geographically. The separation of this group of people is due to differences in national or geographic origin, religion, or other cultural factors, and race. National origin refers to the country or geographic region, for example, in Europe or Asia, where a person's family came from originally or at least at one point in the past. Cultural factors that create ethnic group boundaries include language, dress, family structure, and values, as well as religion. Ethnic groups are also set apart by race. Although race is a socially manufactured concept, it has been, and continues to be, an important factor in creating and maintaining ethnic group boundaries in many societies.

Although everyone may not know the term *ethnic group,* the concept is very important to many people for everyday interaction. When someone asks, "What are you?" or "What kind of name is that?" the question indicates a desire to know one's ethnic group affiliation.

Interestingly, the term *ethnic group* is often mistakenly equated only with recent immigrants. People who are newcomers to society and who might speak a different language, have different cultural or religious practices, or have different racial features are seen as "ethnics," meaning that the newcomers are members of an ethnic group, whereas native residents are not. In fact we are all members of an ethnic group even though one person's group affiliation might not be as apparent as another's. For example, a white Protestant who has no idea when his or her ancestors first came to America, nor from where in the world they originated, might consider him- or herself as having no ethnicity compared with recently arrived Mexican Americans who seemingly have a clear ethnic group membership. But everyone has an ethnic group affiliation. To those Mexican Americans, for example, "ethnic group" could refer to white, Protestant Americans.

However, not everyone's ethnic group holds the same degree of importance. Ethnic group membership plays a significant role in the everyday lives of recently arrived immigrants. Furthermore, ethnic group affiliation is meaningful to other groups that have been severely oppressed for many years, such as African Americans. Often Native Americans remain bounded by clear and significant social and geographic boundaries.

As in the United States, many societies claim to be egalitarian, arguing that their members do not discriminate on the basis of ethnicity. However, to varying degrees, it is important for many people who hold stereotypical views to be able to place individuals in the proper ethnic group. Just as awareness of gender is important for many people in trying to relate to others, ethnic group affiliation is important for those holding stereotypical beliefs of the people with whom they are seriously interacting.

The passage of time often makes a difference. Whereas the German American ethnic group was sharply set apart in many U.S. communities from the mid-1800s to the early 1900s, today the German American ethnic group is largely symbolic.

John P. Myers

See also Ethnicity; Ethnocentrism

Further Readings

Gordon, Milton. 1964. *Assimilation in American Life.* New York: Oxford University Press.

Spickard, Paul R. 1997. *Japanese Americans: The Formation and Transformations of an Ethnic Group.* New York: Twayne.

Warner, W. Lloyd and Leo Srole. 1945. *The Social Systems of American Ethnic Groups.* New Haven, CT: Yale University Press.

ETHNICITY

Ethnicity is a descriptive concept. One's ethnicity is something like a residential address. When you reveal that you live at 1402 River Street, Philadelphia, Mississippi, in the United States, the listener knows more about you, can locate you in the geographic world, and perhaps from this address can detect some clues about your social placement as well. However, what we might call one's "social address" is equally important to many people. Ethnicity makes up an important part of one's social address along with class, gender, and other factors, such as the community in which one lives.

When people ask, "What are you?" or "What kind of name is that?" they want to know your ethnicity. "Ethnicity" refers to the phenomena that create boundaries that separate a large group of people from other groups. The ethnic group itself, as well as outsiders, can create and maintain this separation. Some groups, such as Amish Americans, ardently maintain their ethnicity. Other groups, such as African Americans, encounter ethnic boundaries maintained by the larger groups in power through formal and informal practices and norms.

The phenomena generating ethnicity are national or geographic origin, religion or other cultural factors, and race. National origin refers to the country or geographic region, for example, in Asia, Europe, or Latin America, where a person's family came from originally or at least at one point in the past. Cultural factors that create ethnicity include language, dress, family structure, values, and religion. Race may also be a defining part of ethnicity. Although race is a socially manufactured concept, it has been and remains an important factor in creating and maintaining ethnicity in many societies.

Ethnicity is not like an illness that comes and goes. We all have an ethnic background that is always part of us. Some often think that only recent immigrants possess an ethnicity, but this is wrong. Newcomers who might speak a different language, have different cultural or religious practices, or have different racial features are certainly visible "ethnics," openly revealing themselves to be members of an ethnic group not that of native residents. However, we all possess ethnicity even if it might not be as apparent. For example, a white Protestant American with no idea when his or her ancestors first arrived, nor from where in the world they originated, might consider him- or herself as having no ethnicity compared with recently arrived immigrants. Yet that white, Protestant American group possesses cultural attributes that are recognizable by others.

Not everyone's ethnicity is a conscious daily reality, however. One's ethnicity plays a significant role in the everyday lives of recently arrived immigrants compared with the occasional ethnic self-awareness of fully assimilated individuals. Furthermore, ethnicity is usually most meaningful to members of groups that were severely oppressed for many years. Thus, being African American is very meaningful in the United States. Often Native Americans still experience clear and significant social and geographic boundaries.

John P. Myers

See also Cultural Values; Ethnic Group; Ethnocentrism; Subcultures

Further Readings

Goldstein, Eric L. 2006. *The Price of Whiteness: Jews, Race, and American Identity.* Princeton, NJ: Princeton University Press.
Jacobson, Matthew Frye. 2006. *Roots Too: White Ethnic Revival in Post-Civil Rights America.* Cambridge, MA: Harvard University Press.

ETHNOCENTRISM

The meaning of *ethnocentrism* is revealed by the smaller words that make up the larger one: *ethnicity* and *center*. Ethnocentrism means placing your ethnicity at the center. In this case *center* means "most important." Ethnocentrism is the practice of judging other cultures and ethnic groups against your own culture and ethnic group while seeing your own group and culture as the ideal.

For example, many Americans hold the viewpoint that the English language is the best language, the most natural language, and certainly the only language to be spoken in the United States. Those imbued with ethnocentrism would conclude that other languages are inferior. The same holds true with many cultural practices. Those possessed by ethnocentrism would conclude that their religion, their holidays, their economic system, and their family structure are clearly the best ones.

Ethnocentrism results in prejudice and discrimination based on culture and ethnicity. Racism and ethnocentrism are parallel concepts and processes, both having to do with attitudes and behaviors. Both imply a sense of superiority of one race or ethnic group to others. Both become justifications to oppress groups.

Sociologist Andrew Greeley sees ethnocentric people concluding, "Why can't they be like us?"

Invidious comparisons are inevitable when viewing members and practices of other ethnic groups through the lens of ethnocentrism, which sees all other cultures and groups as lacking and inferior. This often leads to frustration and hostility for those who are ethnocentric. Prejudice, discrimination, proselytizing, verbal hostility, and violence are ways ethnocentrism may be made manifest. In the United States, hate crimes are one of the outcomes of ethnocentrism. Indeed, ethnicity and race account for the great majority of hate crimes.

Being ethnocentric may facilitate regrettable decisions. For example, on a large-scale level, country "A," which is led by ethnocentric rulers, makes war on country "Z." The leaders in country A believe that the Zs are suffering under a bad government, subject to an oppressive religion, and the citizens are impoverished because the economic system in country Z is outdated and needs to be modernized. The leaders of country A expect the population of Zs to be supportive of the invasion and "liberation" of their country. They expect Zs to embrace a new and "better" form of government and support the new Z leadership installed by the As. However, the As find out that even though most Zs were not totally happy with their lives, overall the Zs were fairly satisfied and so they resist the invasion by the As. As a micro-level example, ethnocentric U.S. college student Bill takes a semester abroad in Mexico. Bill attempts to convince the members of his host family that they should shower at least once a day, work longer hours, forgo their siesta, allow the young women to date without chaperones, and increase the amount of meat in their meals. In addition, Bill was only trying to help the members of the host family when he told them about the "one true religion."

John P. Myers

See also Cultural Values; Prejudice; Racism

Further Readings

Chan, Sucheng, ed. 2006. *The Vietnamese American 1.5 Generation: Stories of War, Revolution, Flight and New Beginnings.* Philadelphia: Temple University Press.

Hagopian, Elaine C., ed. 2004. *Civil Rights in Peril: The Targeting of Arabs and Muslims.* London: Pluto.

ETHNOMETHODOLOGY

Ethnomethodology is a sociological paradigm (perspective) that views the social world as a phenomenon that individuals must constantly construct and reconstruct in thought, process, and action. It is a micro-analytic perspective that focuses on breaking taken-for-granted rules.

History and Definition

In the United States in the 1960s, Harold Garfinkel first coined the term and developed the school of ethnomethodology. The term means the study (*ology*) of people (*ethno*). Its foundation lies in Europe, generally based on the work of phenomenologists Edmund Husserl and Alfred Schutz. Schutz's writings redevelop Max Weber's *verstehen* (sympathetic introspections or understanding behavior from the perspective of those engaged in it). Phenomenology is the counterpart to scientific positivism, which views the social world as objective reality. Positivism perceives society as external to, and dominant over, the individual. In ethnomethodology, nature and culture influence human experiences in an intersubjective manner, given that interaction with others creates social worlds. Early ethnomethodological studies involved college students "bargaining" in a grocery store by insisting on paying more for jelly beans than the sale price indicated and pretending to be boarders in their own homes.

Focus and Application

Although ethnomethodology links symbolic interaction and dramaturgy, it differs in methodology and focus. It requires that the researcher shed preconceived notions of how social order is maintained and instead focus on the fluidity, the constantly changing nature of social structure. Social order occurs through member interaction and cooperation; it is not something detached from, and imposed on, members.

People tend to share the manner in which they experience the social world. Our culturally shared understanding of how social life is conducted facilitates interaction. Interaction rests not on anonymous relationships but on the subjectivity of membership categories (e.g., mother, employer, female, white, etc.) that identify those engaged in the interaction.

In human interaction, nothing in the interactive process is completely objective or subjective. Explanations individuals provide result from their cultural and personal experiences and expectations (biographies).

Ethnomethodology thus focuses on the documentary evidence (accounts) that members provide by questioning the taken-for-granted to reveal the norms that help maintain social order. Ethnomethodologists analyze mutually related factors regarding the interrelations of actors in a given situation in everyday life. These factors refer to the indexical and reflexive character of the interaction process. *Indexicality* is a term used to explain the interpretive nature of human interaction. The context in which, or vantage point from which, to view an individual or social situation impacts the "construction" of the "reality." The term *reflexivity* refers to the intuitive nature and common-sense component of interaction. Based on the appropriateness of manner and circumstance, individuals are accountable for engaging in socially acceptable behavior.

Communication in general, and the use of language in particular, play important roles in ethnomethodology, as these reveal the organization of people's ideas. Words have meaning in the context of their use; that is, individuals use words that fit their circumstances and the language patterns of those with whom they interact. Labels attached to behavior are given symbolic meaning through the subjective understanding of situations in everyday life.

Two rules help to process and categorize information: consistency and economy. Once a person or situation receives a category or label, individuals will perceive, construct, and reconstruct past and future situations so that the definition of the situation seems "objective" and "real." Using ethnomethodology, the researcher must provide a logical analysis (a reasonable account) of the individual by interpreting the information provided in the given interaction in conjunction with physical appearance, official records and reports, and standard categorizations or typifications (i.e., homeless, manic depressive, homosexual, felon, etc.).

Ethnomethodologists see past records and labels solely as products of social structure, or indicators of organizational norms, not as the reality of the social problem. To understand social order, the researcher should also identify the members of the society who have the daily responsibility for maintaining that specific component of social structure. For example, if the problem is homelessness, the researcher would seek out social workers to uncover the social norms and manner prompting the typification "homeless."

Some may question how a generally classified micro-method perspective can provide an understanding of macro-sociological issues. It is important to note that the context in which the phenomenon occurs determines the categorization (micro or macro). What is a micro phenomenon in one situation is macro in another. To determine whether or not an ethnographic study is appropriate, the researcher must clearly delineate the goals of the research; the major goal of the research should drive the methodology. Once the research goal is identified, researchers can use an ethnomethodological approach to analyze poverty, social welfare, homelessness, pregnancy, alcoholism, crime, or any social problem or form of deviant behavior.

Susanna Tardi

See also Social Constructionist Theory; Standpoint Theory

Further Readings

Francis, David and Stephen Hester. 2004. *An Invitation to Ethnomethodology: Language, Society, and Interaction.* Thousand Oaks, CA: Sage.

Garfinkel, Harold and Anne Rawls. 2007. *Studies in Ethnomethodology.* Expanded and updated ed. New York: Paradigm.

Liska, Allen. 1987. *Perspectives on Deviance.* 2nd ed. Englewood Cliffs, NJ: Prentice Hall.

Pfohl, Steven. 1994. *Images of Deviance and Social Control: A Sociological History.* 2nd ed. New York: McGraw-Hill.

EUGENICS

Eugenics is a broad term for policies aimed at the genetic improvement of the human race. Whereas most people are familiar with the eugenic practices of the Nazi Party, fewer realize the widespread international use of such practices, both before and after World War II. Derived from the Greek word meaning "well born," eugenics falls into two types: positive and negative. Positive eugenics is encouraging people with "good genes" to reproduce, whereas negative eugenics refers to discouraging reproduction by people with "bad genes." Often these policies are couched in terms of the "fit" and the "unfit."

Unlike social Darwinism, which argues that social systems will, if left alone, provide checks against poor breeding, eugenics implies an active role for the state. Eugenic programs include forced sterilization for those deemed unfit, as well as the criminalization of abortion for the fit. The definition of fitness is, of course, socially constructed and reflects the biases and agendas of those in power, as well as the state of scientific knowledge at the time of implementation. Although overt eugenics programs, such as murder and compulsive sterilization, fell out of favor (at least publicly) after World War II, the ideology of eugenics is still very much alive.

Programs of selected breeding have existed since the time of the ancient Greeks. Plato wrote in *The Republic* that the "best men" should reproduce with the "best women" as often as possible and that the "inferior" should reproduce as little as possible. The Spartans also practiced passive eugenics, leaving newborn infants in the elements to determine their physical hardiness. During the 1860s, Sir Francis Galton, a cousin of Charles Darwin, systematized the ideas behind this history and titled them *eugenics*. Galton argued that behavioral and personality traits, such as criminality and intelligence, were linked to genes. As social welfare programs grew, he argued, society was effectively preventing the human species from ridding itself of the genes responsible for society's ills.

The American Eugenics Movement

American eugenicists appropriated Galton's ideas in the 1880s when radical social change brought by increased immigration and economic changes created unease in the minds of Americans. Eugenics quickly became a popular ideology, attracting many highly respectable supporters. For example, Alexander Graham Bell studied the rates of deafness at Martha's Vineyard and determined (correctly) that deafness in this community was genetic in nature. Incorrectly extending his findings to all deaf people, he argued for prohibitions on marriage and childbearing for anyone with deafness in their family.

In 1896, Connecticut passed the first law prohibiting marriage on eugenic grounds. Charles B. Davenport, a prominent U.S. biologist, received funds from the Carnegie and Rockefeller Institutes. Using that money in 1910 to found the Eugenics Record Office, he began to promote eugenics nationwide. In 1914 his partner, Harry Laughlin, published a model eugenics law. This model law called for legalized sterilization for the "socially inadequate" (those supported in part or entirely at public expense), and it was the blueprint for the German eugenics program in 1933.

Eugenics became more explicitly tied to racism and xenophobia when eugenicists served as expert witnesses for the passage of the Immigration Act of 1921. Because of their congressional testimony regarding "unfit races," immigration from southern, central, and eastern Europe decreased from an annual average of 780,000 to 155,000 annually. But eugenicists did not focus solely on outside threats. Although there were no federal eugenics statutes, many states engaged in forcible sterilization of the unfit. Evidence of unfitness included such things as disability and criminality, as well as sexual deviance and poverty. African Americans and Native Americans were sterilized in large numbers and were often the subject of laws preventing their marriages.

In the 1927 Supreme Court case *Buck v. Bell,* the court upheld the rights of states to sterilize "imbeciles" (i.e., the mentally deficient). Ruling on a 1924 Virginia law, Justice Oliver Wendell Holmes determined that it was in the best interest of the society to actively improve the gene pool and commented, "Three generations of imbeciles is enough." Although little hard evidence existed as to Carrie Buck's actual mental state, only one justice dissented, thereby laying the legal groundwork for new and more expansive state laws. Those considered unfit could legally be sterilized without consent and often were segregated into asylums where they were victims, sometimes fatally, of neglect and abuse.

The American eugenics movement did not exist solely within the courts, however. It was also an integral part of U.S. culture. The movement had displays at many local and state fairs and encouraged people to take part in its "Fitter Family" contests, where families competed in categories of attractiveness, vitality, and intelligence to be deemed the most "fit" and appropriate to reproduce. Films like *The Black Stork* entertained viewers and educated them about the dangers of ill-advised breeding. Mobile exhibits demonstrated the cost of poor genetics through displays with flashing lights next to statements like "Every fifteen seconds 100$ [sic] of your money goes to the care of persons with bad heredity such as the insane, feeble-minded, criminals, and other defectives."

Eugenics Through the Back Door

After world awareness of the atrocities of the Nazi regime, overt eugenics fell from favor. However, the ideology did not go away completely. The Eugenics Record Office closed in 1944, and all of its records went to the Institute for the Promotion of Human Genetics at the University of Minnesota. Eugenics was, in effect, made over but not eliminated. Today many scholars speak of eugenics "coming in from the back door." Replacing the language of "fitness," associated with overt eugenics programs, is a more humanitarian language, with a focus on alleviating the suffering of individuals or society.

For example, although compulsory sterilization for poor women was no longer lauded as the salvation for the human race, it was still practiced in many U.S. cities well into the 1970s. Doctors pressured poor African American women, particularly those on welfare, to have the operation. Others still were sterilized without their consent when they went in for unrelated medical treatments. This practice, justified as a social cost-saving measure, was so common, it was given a name: the "Mississippi appendectomy."

But sterilization and immigration restrictions are not the only way to affect the gene pool. With more advanced scientific testing, doctors can diagnose certain conditions in utero and perform selective abortions. The work of the Human Genome Project suggests that at some point in the future, couples may create a "designer baby" with preselected traits, an idea sometimes referred to as "reprogenics." In the 1990s, the Repository for Germinal Choice, more commonly referred to as the "Genius Sperm Bank," opened its doors, promising carefully screened and morally upright women the chance to bear the child of a Nobel Laureate.

Eugenicist beliefs about race, while not as overt as those in the first part of the 20th century, are still active. Richard J. Herrnstein and Charles Murray, in *The Bell Curve* of 1994, explored intelligence in America by examining IQ scores and concluded that minorities, particularly African Americans, were inherently less intelligent and therefore less successful than whites. Given their findings, the authors argued that the U.S. welfare system promoted the overbreeding of an unfit class of people. They argued for the elimination of welfare benefits because they subsidize "births among poor women, who are also disproportionately at the low end of the intelligence distribution." Two years later the federal programs they referenced were substantially cut.

Resistance

While eugenic modes of thinking still exist, so does resistance to them. The disability rights movement decries selective abortion on the grounds that many individuals with these "selected" conditions live full and productive lives. Racial equity and pride movements focus on the reproductive options of women of color, particularly the coerced usage of long-term birth control such as Norplant and Depo-Provera. Some bioethicists caution against blanket acceptance of genetic testing and manipulation without an appropriate examination of the social forces that cause particular genes to be considered "unfit." Social scientists argue that the majority of a person's life chances are determined by social forces irrespective of genetic makeup, citing the fact that health and welfare outcomes are most strongly influenced not by racial factors or prenatal defects but instead by the zip code area in which the person lives.

Jes Peters

See also Abortion; Bioethics; Civil Rights; Contraception; Disability and Disabled; Genetic Engineering; Holocaust; Immigration; Intermarriage; Mental Health; Nature–Nurture Debate; One-Drop Rule; Racism; Welfare

Further Readings

Black, Edwin. 2004. *War against the Weak: Eugenics and America's Campaign to Create a Master Race.* New York: Four Walls Eight Windows.

Duster, Troy. 2003. *Backdoor to Eugenics.* New York: Routledge.

Image Archive on the American Eugenics Movements. Retrieved December 26, 2007 (http://www.eugenicsarchive.org/eugenics/).

Katz Rothman, Barbara. 1998. *The Book of Life: A Personal and Ethical Guide to Race, Normality, and the Implications of the Human Genome Project.* Boston: Beacon Press.

Kevles, Daniel J. 1985. *In the Name of Eugenics: Genetics and the Uses of Human Heredity.* New York: Knopf.

Kincheloe, Joe L., Aaron Gresson, and Shirley R. Steinberg, eds. 1997. *Measured Lies:* The Bell Curve *Examined.* New York: St. Martin's.

Nelson, Jennifer. 2003. *Women of Color and the Reproductive Rights Movement.* New York: New York University Press.

Pernick, Martin S. 1996. *The Black Stork: Eugenics and the Death of "Defective" Babies in American Medicine and Motion Pictures since 1915.* New York: Oxford University Press.

EUTHANASIA

The Greek roots of the term *euthanasia* denote "good death." Though it is common to think of death as unequivocally bad—it is, after all, our most severe punishment—one can easily distinguish between dying processes that are mercifully tolerable and others that are agonizing beyond endurance. During the events of 9/11, scores of people trapped in the World Trade Center leaped out of windows to escape the heat and smoke, some holding hands with others as they fell. Presumably, knowing their lives had come to an end, they chose deaths better than the ones they would suffer if they remained inside. Though it was tragic that so many luckless people met death in this way, few, if any, publicly argued that it was impermissibly wrong.

Euthanasia requires a second person's involvement. In these so-called mercy killings, one person acts for the benefit of another. Many people think that, except for self-defense and a few other cases, it is a grave wrong to cause the foreseeable death of another human being. But one can imagine oneself struggling through the heat and smoke to reach a window at the World Trade Center. A coworker who uses a wheelchair is also there, but unable to get past the debris and into the air outside. She asks for your assistance. Now if it is permissible to do some one thing oneself, why would it not, by implication, be equally permissible to lend assistance to one who reasonably desires to do that same thing but is unable to do so?

Euthanasia, as an ethical problem, focuses on whether and, if so, when killing another person can be excused or justified on the grounds that it benefits the person killed. Except in some European countries, euthanasia is a crime. Those who end the lives of the intractably suffering, even when they follow urgent requests, will be charged with homicide. Should the law be changed to permit some beneficent killings?

Three issues muddy the waters. First, "euthanasia" was the euphemism the Nazis used to sanitize their early extermination of those they deemed defective. The program quickly evolved to kill millions: Jews, Romani, homosexuals, Communists, and more. Treated as vermin, the people involuntarily and secretly gassed in the concentration camps were not killed beneficently. "Involuntary euthanasia"—killing another *against* his or her will—seems a contradiction in terms. While some fear that loosening the law of homicide will send us down the slippery slope to holocaust, such prognostications require careful examination.

The second issue concerns what some still call "passive euthanasia": the discontinuation of life-prolonging measures, often the removal of a ventilator (a mechanical breathing device). When a patient or an authorized proxy withdraws consent to treatment, then doctors, no longer at liberty to continue, may lawfully withdraw life support, causing death. Some maintain these patients die from their underlying diseases rather than from the doctor's action. But if death is a foreseeable consequence, then the clinical removal of a ventilator kills a patient just as surely as the removal of a regulator kills a deeply submerged scuba diver. The law of homicide already includes this exception for doctors, and much of the literature on death and dying treats the patient's legal and ethical power to refuse treatment. Although withdrawing life support can sometimes avert suffering, this strategy is often unavailable and the deaths so obtained may not be as tolerable as those medically induced. Nonetheless, it is nearly everywhere unlawful to administer medications for that purpose. Should this be changed?

The third issue, physician-assisted dying, refers to doctors who provide the means to end life: commonly a prescription and special instructions. Such assistance is legal in Oregon. Note that the doctor does not take the final, life-ending step. Should we amend the law on homicide to permit beneficent killing?

Intractable Suffering

Suffering commonly affects patients with progressive illness—metastatic cancer, multiple sclerosis, Huntington's disease, and so on—where the diagnosis is firm and the prognosis dire. Patients often understand what lies in store. Much of the euthanasia literature fixates on pain, and the sufferings brought on by severe illness come in many flavors: dizziness, diarrhea, disfigurement, itching, insomnia, incontinence, exhaustion, strains upon relationships, shortness of breath, anxiety, cognitive impairment and dementia, debt, depression, disabilities of all kinds, dependency, loss of control, nausea, offensive odors, and the losses of dignity that can accompany these.

Sometimes—but not always—symptoms can be managed while preserving positive elements that give value and richness to a waning life, for example, talking with loved ones, listening to music, or enjoying a sunset. But residual abilities too can succumb, even as a patient retains sensitivities that can make life intolerable. One strategy is "terminal sedation." Doctors render a patient unconscious while withholding nutrition and hydration: Death ensues in a matter of days. However, not every patient prefers such "care" to a timely passing. There is a difference between having a life and being (biologically) alive: The former—the life one has—may be of supreme value to a patient. As with those trapped on 9/11, that life can come to an end before death occurs.

When a human life deteriorates to the point where one reasonably desires to end it, the argument for the permissibility of euthanasia turns on autonomy, that is, the ethical and legal power, within civic constraints, to chart the course of one's own life, especially in areas where the stakes that others have in one's action are not as great as one's own. The root political idea is that, unless sound and proportional countervailing reasons exist, adults should be free to make their own choices. The presumption is in favor of liberty, that is, the liberty of informed, suffering, competent individuals to choose the manner and time of their death. In the face of intractable suffering and an expressed and settled preference for death, advocates argue strongly (a) that voluntary euthanasia should be permitted and (b) that it is cruel to prohibit charitable assistance to those who are relevantly similar to the luckless coworker in her wheelchair. Those acting out of compassion in these cases are surely not the criminals we have in mind when we build prisons. Accordingly, public policy should regulate, but not prohibit, voluntary euthanasia.

Forced Abandonment

The second type of case occurs in the context of medical catastrophe. During a disaster the flow of patients into a hospital can temporarily exceed its carrying capacity. Doctors then focus on the patients who will likely live if treated but die if untreated, setting aside those without life-threatening injuries and those who will likely die despite treatment. They do not abandon this last group—"expectant" patients commonly identified with black tags—but give only ongoing comfort care (pain medications) and medical reassessment, especially if they unexpectedly survive the period of scarcity.

During forced military retreats and sometimes massive civilian disasters like Hurricane Katrina, health care settings can collapse catastrophically and care professionals and their patients can be compelled to evacuate. Should it prove impossible to relocate black-tagged patients, physicians have only three choices:

1. They can, at great personal risk, stay behind with these doomed individuals even though there is little or nothing that can be medically done for them. By abandoning other treatable patients, health care professionals may be violating obligations toward them.

2. They can abandon the black-tagged patients, leaving them to die unmedicated and unattended (or, during forced military retreats, in the hands of the enemy), thereby violating legal and ethical obligations toward those patients.

3. They can beneficently kill expectant patients who cannot be evacuated. Patients able to decide could opt for abandonment, but those incapable of giving and withholding consent would receive nonvoluntary euthanasia.

This situation highlights two weighty medical norms: the prohibition against killing patients and the prohibition against abandoning them. Where it is impossible to evacuate patients and too dangerous to remain with them, one of the two norms must give way. Given this tragic moral uncertainty, it seems both compassionate and reasonable for the law to refrain from condemning those who try heroically to render honorable assistance under these rare but appalling circumstances, even though they deliberately end the lives of some.

Objections

It is useful to distinguish between "yellow-light" objections (urging caution) and "red-light" objections (admonishing one to stop): Euthanasia can be said to pose a risk of adverse consequences or it can be said to be impermissible on its face.

There are many yellow-light objections. This is a slippery slope down which we can slide to holocaust. Compassionate homicide might erode the professional commitments of physicians as well as our trust in doctors. Patients could be depressed or pressured at the time of decision, or misdiagnosed, or haste in ending patients' lives could prevent possible recoveries, or relatives and health care providers might conspire to end the lives of the ill, or protective measures might be unequal to the task of preventing carelessness and misconduct. The definitive assessment of these objections requires that we examine the effectiveness of specific protections. Here the Oregon record, as it becomes available, and the experience of the Dutch, Belgians, and Swiss become useful. Unlike the Nazis, we can require publicity in the implementation of protocols. Should adverse consequences occur following legalization, they must be measured against the adverse consequences of prohibition.

Many red-light objections emerge within particular religious traditions. These we can set aside because, in a pluralist society, the arguments that settle important public issues should be ones that can persuade any reasonable person, not just those who embrace some sectarian view. The sectarian arguments often maintain that human life is sacred and not to be discarded lightly. But if the closely related idea of human dignity can somehow be given a secular interpretation—one that is broadly persuasive and sufficiently weighty—and if the favored understanding of that idea somehow precludes euthanasia, then it may be reasonable to keep the law of homicide as it is. Again, such arguments require close examination.

The problem of euthanasia arises in extreme circumstances. In the first case, the life of a suffering person approaches a ruinous and horrific end. In the second, a collapsing health care system is unable to minister to the most grievously afflicted. It is distressing to ponder what it is like when such important matters go so dreadfully awry and to discern our responsibilities when they do. But such tragedies do befall us, challenging our capacities to craft decent and just social practices and to act rightly out of charity, compassion, and respect.

Kenneth Kipnis

See also Bioethics; Disability and Disabled; Disasters; Eugenics; Holocaust; Hospices; Murder; Suicide

Further Readings

Battin, Margaret P. 2000. *The Least Worst Death: Essays in Bioethics on the End of Life.* New York: Oxford University Press.

Brock, Dan W. 1992. "Voluntary Active Euthanasia." *Hastings Center Report* 2(March/April):10–22.

Dworkin, Ronald. 1993. *Life's Dominion: An Argument about Abortion, Euthanasia, and Individual Freedom.* New York: Knopf.

Foot, Philippa. 1977. "Euthanasia." *Philosophy and Public Affairs* 6(Winter):85–112.

Kipnis, Kenneth. 2003. "Overwhelming Casualties: Medical Ethics in a Time of Terror." Pp. 95–107 in *In the Wake of Terror: Medicine and Morality in a Time of Crisis,* edited by J. Moreno. Cambridge, MA: MIT Press.

Rachels, James. 1986. *The End of Life: Euthanasia and Morality.* New York: Oxford University Press.

Sulmasy, Daniel P. 1994. "Death and Human Dignity." *Linacre Quarterly* 61:27–36.

Swann, Steven W. 1987. "Euthanasia on the Battlefield." *Military Medicine* 152:545–49.

EVALUATION RESEARCH

Evaluation research originally emerged in the education and human services arenas as a means for improving social programs, but it now focuses more on determining the overall effectiveness of programs. Both approaches are valuable in that they yield evidenced-based research to secure funding or develop and implement effective programs.

One type of evaluation research, *formative evaluation,* deals with influencing the beginning stages of program development. The evaluation researcher collects and interprets data about how a program operates in its early stages and then translates this information into concrete suggestions for improvement to be shared with program staff. For example, if a local school board requests a formative analysis of a new Holocaust Education program, the researcher would carefully review the program's goals, objectives, curriculum, and instructional materials as well as collect data from students, teachers, and administration about how the program functions. After analyzing and interpreting the data, the evaluator could offer program improvement suggestions in such areas as curriculum, instructional materials, and overall program management.

The second type of evaluation research, *process evaluation,* determines whether a given program was implemented as designed. Understanding the sources of variation in program delivery allows evaluators to understand better how a program works. Process evaluations are especially important when trying to understand multisite programs such as the Gang Resistance Education and Training program. The focus is not to determine if a program works, but rather to determine how it works and what variations in its delivery could potentially contribute to its overall effect.

Summative evaluation, the third type of evaluation, focuses on determining the program's outcomes. In other words, did the program work? Did it meet its professed goals and objectives? This type of evaluation research resonates strongly with funding agencies. For example, in the 1990s, the National Cancer Institute funded several health promotion programs reaching out to Hispanic women to raise awareness, increase knowledge, and improve access to cancer screening opportunities. For funding eligibility, each proposed program had to include a summative evaluation component. The proposal design comparing the intervention group with another group had special appeal to the funding agency.

Program evaluations, regardless of type, typically encompass a sequence of stages. The initial two stages involve understanding the essence of the program. More specifically, stage 1 involves the formulation of the program's goals and objectives, while stage 2 involves developing an understanding of the program's delivery, setting, and participants. Stage 3 focuses on designing the evaluation. The design can include both qualitative and quantitative research methodologies. Choice of methodologies depends on several factors, including purpose of the evaluation and type of information needed. The fourth stage involves collecting, analyzing, and interpreting the data. The fifth and final stage of the evaluation involves utilizing the evaluation results to improve the program or to verify that it works.

Evaluation Research Designs

Evaluation researchers typically use a variety of research designs when evaluating a program. Design choices depend on several aspects of the evaluation, including the intended audience, available resources, and ethical concerns. Three main types of evaluation research designs exist: experimental designs, quasi-experimental designs, and qualitative research designs.

Experimental designs use summative evaluations to assess whether the program worked. Because this design involves the random assignment of participants to an experimental or a control group, researchers can be reasonably certain that any outcome differences between the two groups result from program participation as opposed to preexisting group differences. For example, if an elementary school principal applies for funding for a social-skills training program for fifth-grade students, she must include an evaluation design in her proposal. Recognizing that experimental design is a stringent, respected means for evaluating program effects, she proposes that her school's fifth-grade students will be randomly assigned to either an experimental group or a control group. She hypothesizes that those students assigned to the experimental group will demonstrate more positive social skills than those in the control group.

Quasi-experimental designs are more commonly utilized than the more stringent experimental design. Examples of quasi-experimental designs include nonequivalent control groups and time series. Like experimental designs, the nonequivalent control group design involves both an experimental and a control group. However, because random assignment is not possible, the researcher must find an existing "control" group that is similar to the experimental group in terms of background and demographic variables. Despite the matching process, the two groups may still differ in terms of important characteristics. Because of the nonequivalent nature of the groups, pretests will determine baseline differences on the outcome variable. Controlling for these differences allows the researcher to isolate program effects. Another type of quasi-experimental design, time-series, involves measurements made over a designated period of time, such as the study of traffic accident rates before and after lowering the speed limit. Time-series designs work in those situations in which a control group is not possible.

Qualitative research methodologies are another means for obtaining evaluation research data. These methodologies are especially useful because they can provide in-depth information about program processes, which in turn can inform program modifications. Focus groups, in-depth interviews, and content analyses of program materials are all useful tools for the program evaluator. For example, in a process program evaluation of a school-based parent-involvement program, Spanish-speaking parents are less likely to attend sessions than English-speaking parents, despite the fact that sessions are available in Spanish. An evaluator decides to find out why this is the case by setting up focus groups with Spanish-speaking parents. Results indicate that although Spanish-speaking parents want to be involved in their children's schooling, they view their lack of English proficiency as a barrier to effective involvement. Program staff can use this information to modify recruitment strategies, ensuring communication to Spanish-speaking parents that their involvement encompasses more than schoolwork assistance.

From Research to Practice

It might appear that evaluation research would have a significant impact on whether a program continues. However, this is not always the case, particularly when a program is immensely popular and taps into the public's perception of what should work. The Drug Abuse Resistance Education (D.A.R.E.) program provides a good example of a program that receives continued funding despite a plethora of evaluation research indicating that it has no long-term effects for preventing and reducing adolescent drug use. The D.A.R.E. case illustrates that program evaluation research can only be effective when program stakeholders, those with a vested interest in the program's success, actually utilize the results either to modify the existing program or to design a more effective one.

Vera Lopez

See also Focus Groups; Latent Functions; Manifest Functions

Further Readings

Adler, Emily S. and Roger Clark, eds. 2007. *How It's Done: An Invitation to Social Research.* 3rd ed. Belmont, CA: Thomson/Wadsworth.

Birkeland, Sarah, Erin Murphy-Graham, and Carol Weiss. 2005. "Good Reasons for Ignoring Good Evaluation: The Case of the Drug Abuse Resistance Education (D.A.R.E.) Program." *Evaluation & Program Planning* 28:247–56.

Fitzpatrick, Jody, James R. Sanders, and Blaine J. Worthen. 2004. *Program Evaluation: Alternative Approaches and Practical Guidelines.* 3rd ed. Boston: Allyn & Bacon.

Patton, Michael Q. 2002. *Qualitative Evaluation and Research Methods.* 3rd ed. Thousand Oaks, CA: Sage.

Rossi, Peter H., Mark W. Lipsey, and Howard E. Freeman. 2003. *Evaluation: A Systematic Approach.* 7th ed. Thousand Oaks, CA: Sage.

EXTINCTION

Extinction—the permanent disappearance of a species from the earth—can be thought of as the ultimate social problem. When our neighbors disappear from the planet forever, our potential social interactions are forever diminished. Extinction is not a new phenomenon. What is new, however, is the current *rate* of extinction, which is dramatically higher than any in the geologic record, and the fact that for the first time ever, a single species—our own—is the *cause* of this high rate of extinction. This is why extinction represents a serious social and environmental problem.

Extinction in Context

Just as every person will die someday, so too will every species eventually go extinct. In fact, almost all species that have ever existed on earth have already gone extinct. Paleontologist David Raup has estimated that 99.9 percent of all species in Earth's history have gone extinct (or, conversely, that today's living world represents only 0.1 percent of the variety of species that have existed at one time or another). Studies of marine fossils—the most continuous and reliable record of life on earth—indicate that the average "life expectancy" for a species is approximately 1 to 10 million years.

Simple microscopic life (formed of prokaryotic cells—those without cell nuclei, like today's bacteria) began appearing some 3.8 billion years ago. More complex unicellular life—formed of eukaryotic cells, those with cell nuclei and organelles—began to appear approximately 2 billion years ago. More recognizable, larger multicellular forms of life—fishes, plants, and the like—began proliferating about 542 million years ago (at the start of the Paleozoic era). Throughout the history of the Earth, species have arisen and faded like the blossoming and wilting of generations of flowers. Even though extinction is inevitable, species have different fates. Some morph into new, better-adapted species, becoming the ancestors of vital living lines. Others find themselves in evolutionary dead ends, the last of their kind. The interaction of living species with the ever-changing environments on Earth, through the process of natural selection, creates ever-better-adapted organisms, usually resulting in greater diversity of life.

While extinction is almost as old as life, it has not always occurred at a uniform rate. Geologists and paleontologists have been able to decipher a "background extinction rate" throughout the geologic past—an average rate of species loss, which turns out to be approximately 2 to 3 extinctions per year globally. In general, though, new species have been generating much more rapidly than old ones have been going extinct. Creation, then, has generally been outpacing loss. (Accordingly, biological diversity on this planet is higher than ever before.) But there have been five "moments" in the geologic past when huge numbers of species became extinct at roughly the same time ("same time" in this case referring to a period of a few million years). Scientists refer to these as "mass extinctions." From most ancient to most recent, these mass extinctions occurred in the geologic ages known as Ordovician (440 mya [million years ago]), Devonian (365 mya), Permian (245 mya), Triassic (210 mya), and—best known—the end of the Cretaceous (65 mya). Two of these have drawn special attention from biologists.

The episode at the end of the Cretaceous (usually referred to as the "K-T" mass extinction, because it straddled the boundary between the Cretaceous—which geologists symbolize with a "K"—and the Tertiary periods) is familiar to the general public because this was the end of dinosaurs (many earlier forms of which had already gone extinct). The abruptness of this massive change in life forms had long been recognized, because of fossil evidence, but had long puzzled scientists. Evidence suggests that this mass extinction was precipitated when a meteorite approximately 6 miles (10 kilometers) wide struck the planet, in what is now the Gulf of Mexico, causing enormous climatic and habitat shifts. The meteorite's impact created thick dust clouds, which initiated a dramatic reduction in levels of photosynthesis. Other consequences of the meteorite impact included immense tidal waves, large-scale fires, and atmospheric changes leading to "acid rain."

The Permian extinction crisis represented the closest brush that life on earth ever had with total annihilation. The history of extinction is usually examined through study of marine animal fossils. Marine environments have been present throughout Earth's history, and many marine animals fossilize well. When looking so far in the past, biologists tend to focus on organisms at the level of the family—two steps more general than species in the hierarchy of biological taxonomy—because they can have greater confidence in their conclusions about this more general grouping. During the other four mass extinction crises, roughly 12 percent of marine animal families went extinct, but during the Permian, well over half the families disappeared. Extrapolations suggest that this represents somewhere between 77 percent and 96 percent of *species* lost. It took almost 100 million years for species diversity to regain previous levels. But of course these were new species. One of the starkest realities of extinction is that it is truly forever—once a species and its complex genetic coding is lost, it will never be seen again.

Extinction Today

What is of concern today is that humans have initiated the sixth great extinction crisis in the history of the planet. While this point is occasionally argued in popular media, there is remarkable scientific consensus that this rate of extinction is much higher than anything seen in the fossil record. Humans' impact has been much greater than that of a meteorite smashing into the earth. It is difficult to be exact, of course, when predicting the future. And predicting extinction is especially challenging because the vast majority of species have yet to be described. Approximately 1.7 million species have been described and named by scientists, but no one thinks that is even close to the true measure of biological diversity. Well-reasoned estimates range from approximately 5 to over 100 million species on earth today. Why such confusion? Because Western science emerged from Europe and North America, the temperate zones have been studied much more carefully than other parts of the world. Certain habitats have only recently begun to be explored—the canopies of tropical rain forests, for example, and deep-sea thermal vents. As it turns out, these new biological frontiers are, in many cases, immensely more diverse than anything in Europe or North America. Also, certain groups of organisms—vertebrate animals, especially—are relatively well-known, whereas many other groups are just now being discovered.

In some cases, we are losing species before we even know they exist. One poignant example: In 1978 two botanists visited a ridge in Ecuador and found almost 90 species of plants that were known from nowhere else. Within 8 years the ridge had been cleared for agriculture, and most of those species were gone forever. If not for that one visit, we would be ignorant of this loss.

In spite of these predictive challenges, many scientists have attempted to predict the short- and long-term future of extinction. Harvard biologist E. O. Wilson provided one of the most painstakingly calculated examples, estimating our current rate of extinction to be 2,700 times higher than the average "background rate" in the geologic record. Other estimates have asserted a current extinction rate "only" hundreds of times higher than the background rate. Actually, all these estimates are remarkably similar: All declare that the current extinction trend is at least an order of magnitude higher than ever before, and all estimates are based on conservative assumptions on numbers of species and optimistic assumptions on crucial changes in human behavior patterns. Thus the reality could be worse.

Not only is the future hard to predict in relation to extinction, but the recent past can elude certainty as well. For one thing, it is difficult to know exactly when a species *has* gone extinct. For another, as stated above, we cannot know true rates of past extinctions when we are only aware of the existence of a fraction of the world's species. Nevertheless, biologists do their best to maintain records of species loss. The International Union for the Conservation of Nature Red List—an authoritative database of loss and endangerment—documents a minimum of 844 extinctions since 1500. Alarmingly, the rate of loss increased dramatically in the most recent century.

Why do species go extinct? While some species have been directly and intentionally exploited, the most common cause of extinction is destruction or fragmentation of habitat. Certain characteristics of species predispose them to be more vulnerable to extinction. Species with more general food and habitat preferences are able to adapt to environmental changes—including those induced by humans—more readily than specialists. Species with limited geographic ranges, such as islands, are at special risk. In fact, 75 percent of the animal species that have gone extinct in the past 4 centuries were island dwellers. Species that specialize in a particular habitat become vulnerable when people desire that habitat. Many species from the prairies of the North American Midwest, for example, almost all of which have been

plowed under for large-scale agriculture, have either gone extinct or hang on in remaining shreds of prairie—in pioneer cemeteries and along remote roadsides. Passenger pigeons were once the most abundant bird in North America; individual flocks, numbering millions of individuals, were known to darken the sky at midday. Their extinction would have been unthinkable to early settlers. Yet the pigeons relied on extensive tracts of eastern deciduous forest; once these forests were cleared away for settlement and agriculture, they did not last long. Some species are victims of direct hunting and persecution; those that taste good or scare us are especially vulnerable. Some species, especially large predators such as bears and mountain lions, have problems because they require large areas to roam. Some species are vulnerable for several of these reasons. Wolves, for example, require large home ranges of relatively wild country, and they have been persecuted for centuries because people consider them fearsome beasts. Whatever the initial causes of endangerment, when a population becomes very small, it becomes especially susceptible to extinction. Chance occurrences can exert critical influence on a species' survival. Random sorting of gametes can unbalance a species' sex ratio, lowering its probability of ongoing successful reproduction. Small populations are more likely to inbreed (mating between closely related individuals), which can accentuate harmful genetic traits (as was seen in some European royal families). And unpredictable events, such as forest fires or hurricanes, can be catastrophic for a species with only a few individuals.

Extinction as a Social Problem

As terrible as wars, injustice, and poverty are, no form of human violence and indiscretion will have such long-lasting and irreversible consequences as the extinction of species from our planet. As Wilson has pointed out, this is the only human-caused problem that will take literally millions of years to compensate, and then only incompletely. The forms of life we lose will never come back, a folly for which Wilson believes our descendants will be least likely to forgive us. His calculations, described earlier in this entry, on extinction rates work out to a prediction of losing 10 to 25 percent of the species in the world in the next 50 to 100 years. This relatively conservative prediction is based on an assumption of stabilizing human population and reducing excessive consumption in developed nations. Without achieving those laudable goals, the losses will be much greater, perhaps even worse than losing a quarter of the species in the world in the next two human generations.

Why does this matter? Foremost is the simple tragedy of so much loss. Forms of life that evolved over the course of millions of years, through the interactive forge of natural selection, have an intrinsic right to exist for their own sakes. More pragmatically, the loss of biodiversity creates both direct and indirect problems for humanity. Biodiversity has several types of instrumental (utilitarian) value for people. It directly provides *goods,* such as food, medicines, fuel, and fiber. It also provides ecosystem *services*—for example, climate regulation, pollination of crops, and fixation and cycling of crucial chemical elements. Without these services, life on earth as we know it would cease to exist. Moreover, wild species hold *information* of untold usefulness to humans—potential templates for genetic engineering and future medicines, for example. For this reason, environmental philosopher J. Baird Callicott has likened the mindless destruction of biodiversity to book burning. Finally, the world's biodiversity holds *psychospiritual* value for people: in the sheer aesthetic beauty of the world, as the source, in some cases, for religious awe, and as a sanctuary for mental and spiritual well-being. For all these reasons, a world of human-hastened extinction of species is a tragically diminished world. But because humans are the cause of this problem, we are also the source of solutions.

Thomas L. Fleischner

See also Deforestation; Desertification; Environment, Pollution; Environmental Degradation; Global Warming; Nonrenewable Resources; Population Growth; Water Quality

Further Readings

Callicott, J. Baird. 2006. "Conservation Values and Ethics." Pp. 111–35 in *Principles of Conservation Biology,* 3rd ed., edited by M. J. Groom, G. K. Meffe, and C. R. Carroll. Sunderland, MA: Sinauer.

Hunter, Malcolm L. Jr. and James P. Gibbs. 2007. "Extinction Processes." Pp. 130–49 in *Fundamentals of Conservation Biology,* 3rd ed. Malden, MA: Blackwell.

———. 2007. "Mass Extinctions and Global Change." Pp. 114–29 in *Fundamentals of Conservation Biology,* 3rd ed. Malden, MA: Blackwell.

Jablonski, D. 1991. "Extinctions: A Paleontological Perspective." *Science* 253:754–57.

Pimm, Stuart L. 1998. "Extinction." Pp. 20–38 in *Conservation Science and Action,* edited by W. L. Sutherland. Oxford, England: Blackwell.

Raup, David M. 1991. *Extinction: Bad Genes or Bad Luck?* New York: Norton.

Wilson, E. O. 1992. *The Diversity of Life.* Cambridge, MA: Harvard University Press.

EXTRAMARITAL SEX

Extramarital sex refers to any sexual activity, but usually intercourse, that takes place outside of a legally sanctioned marriage. Even though general use of the term is with respect to heterosexual partnerships, it can also apply to homosexual relations when one of the individuals is in a heterosexual marriage. Furthermore, extramarital sex is a broad concept that encompasses sex that takes place in a cohabiting relationship; teenage sex; any other form of premarital sex; and adulterous sexual relations between two people, at least one of whom is married.

The 20th century witnessed increases in all the forms of extramarital sex, which eventually helped normalize sexual activity outside of marriage. A vocal group of commentators and scholars decried these increases as a sign that the American family was in decline. The 1960s, in particular, witnessed a marked increase in the rates of cohabitation, nonmarital births, and divorce. College students in the 1960s and 1970s were prime movers with respect to cohabitation and premarital/teen sex. By the 1990s most of the trends had stabilized, indicating that despite concerns, marriage remained a lasting American institution into the 21st century.

According to demographers, overall trends in extramarital sex since World War II are primarily the result of the long-term process of women's growing employment outside the home and their better access to birth control. Social scientists also draw on shifts in social and cultural values—such as the decline in the power of religious norms to affect individual behavior and changing opinions on the permanency of marriage—to explain the increase in extramarital sex.

One of the most common forms of extramarital sex is cohabitation, the sexual union between an unmarried man and woman. Cohabiting partners share the same living quarters for a sustained period of time, though their arrangement does not normally invoke any legal rights and obligations; as such, it is less stable than marriage. In the late 1960s only 8 percent of first marriages began as cohabiting relationships, but by the 1990s that number had jumped to 56 percent. Cohabitation became commonplace during the 1970s and 1980s, as younger people began to postpone marriage but not sexual relations or life with a partner.

As with other forms of extramarital sex, cohabitation increased due to a variety of social, cultural, economic, and technological changes. These include the change in values about sexual relations outside of marriage (again, partly attributable to the weakening of religious influence on individuals' decision making); the increased employment opportunities for women, which gave them greater bargaining power in relationships; and the development and availability of various forms of birth control that freed couples from having to get married following an unexpected and unwanted pregnancy.

Development of effective contraception, along with the legalization of abortion in particular, made it more likely for women to engage in extramarital sex at various points in their life course, beginning in their teen years. While there has been much hand-wringing over teenage sexual activity, mainly because of concerns over poverty and high school dropout rates, the current rates of teenage pregnancy in the United States are down from previous highs. Still, the United States has the highest incidence of teen pregnancy in the developed world; in 2004 approximately 41 out of 1,000 girls ages 15 to 19 experienced pregnancy, almost always as a result of extramarital sex. Although there have been efforts, especially with teens, to sign virginity pledges promising not to have sex outside of marriage, teenage sex continues to persist. Efforts now focus on helping to prevent teenage pregnancy through the effective use of contraception—a sign of tacit acceptance that extramarital sex for teens is here to stay.

The sex lives of older adults also changed in the second half of the 20th century. Increases in extramarital sex among older men and women can be attributed to two related trends: the delay of age at first marriage and the increase in the divorce rate. As young people wait until their late 20s and into their 30s to get married for the first time, there is a subsequent rise in the incidence of extramarital sex, which in this case is defined as premarital sex.

Even though the likelihood of divorce is lower for those who marry later, divorce rates remain quite high in the United States. In many cases, divorce occurs because one or both partners engage in extramarital sex. Increases in adultery can be partially understood as a result of the same changing social and cultural values that promote the other forms of extramarital sex. A shift in views of marriage allows people to view marriage as a changeable state rather than a permanent one. This means that as soon as one person feels unhappy or attracted to another person, he or she feels able to leave the marriage or to stray sexually without concerns about social censure. Additionally, such feelings are often legitimated for people when they are protected from pregnancy and disease through contraception and prevention and when the woman can independently support herself financially. In effect, partly as a result of economic and technological changes, some see marriage less as a permanent partnership and more as the temporary union of two individuals.

Despite the seeming retreat from marriage through cohabiting relationships and sex outside of matrimony in its various forms, the institution continues to persist. One scholar has written that there is still strong sentimental strength in marriage, especially when children are involved, even though marriage may no longer be seen as an economic necessity for women or as a cultural imperative. But so long as marriage continues to be important, extramarital sexual relations will persist, for teens, single young adults, and divorcés and widowers.

Hilary Levey

See also Cohabitation; Contraception; Divorce; Premarital
Sex; Teenage Pregnancy and Parenting

Further Readings

Casper, Lynne M. and Suzanne M. Bianchi. 2002. *Continuity and Change in the American Family.* Thousand Oaks, CA: Sage.
Cherlin, Andrew J. 1992. *Marriage, Divorce, Remarriage.* Cambridge, MA: Harvard University Press.
Waite, Linda, ed. 2000. *The Ties That Bind.* New York: Aldine de Gruyter.

FAITH-BASED SOCIAL INITIATIVES

Faith-based social initiatives are forms of social and community support that religious institutions such as mosques, churches, and synagogues provide to help solve social problems. For some, religious institutions are a main source of support and guidance. This support can include building and funding elementary schools, providing health care, sponsoring local neighborhood watch programs, operating soup kitchens, providing clothing for the needy, and building low-income housing and neighborhood renewal.

For quite some time, religious and community leaders and politicians alike have argued for more governmental support for their programs because of the impact they have on their communities. Indeed, when most people think of faith-based social initiatives, they think of the fairly recent federal programs that allow churches and other religious institutions to seek funding to support their charities and community works. These programs encourage faith-based institutions to apply for and receive federal funds from the U.S. Departments of Agriculture, Education, Housing and Urban Development, Justice, and Labor and the U.S. Agency for International Development, in addition to any funding from state and local sources.

These programs evolved after January 29, 2001, when President George W. Bush issued Executive Order 13199, establishing the White House Office of Faith-Based and Community Initiatives. This office, under the executive branch of the federal government, oversees the government's efforts in encouraging both religious and community-based institutions to supply social services as well as provide financial and even, in some cases, technical support for social service programs. Another function of this office is to ensure that policy developed is in accordance with administrative goals that encourage charity and community action and identify and replicate successful community service programs.

Origins of Federal Aid

Discussions about federal funding of faith institutions began with welfare reform proposals in the 1990s that sought to have individuals take more control over their well-being and also to reduce welfare fraud. In 1996, President Clinton signed legislation that reduced government funding for welfare by limiting the length of time that people can receive welfare support. Section 104 of this welfare reform law, the Charitable Choice provision, removed barriers preventing religious institutions from applying for federal welfare funds. Simultaneously, this provision also stressed the separation of church and state by allowing these religious institutions to promote their religious beliefs without government intervention yet stipulating government funds could not be used for religious activities such as religious instruction or missionary work.

Because of attention paid to the more dramatic aspects of the welfare reform overhaul, for the most part, Charitable Choice fell between the legal cracks until the 2000 presidential campaign, when both candidates, Al Gore and George W. Bush, endorsed such funding of religious institutions for social service programs. Immediately after taking office, Bush established the aforementioned Office of Faith-Based and Community Initiatives to implement the Charitable Choice provision.

Controversy and Opposition

These initiatives quickly became highly controversial. Civil libertarians, secularists, and opponents on both ends of the political spectrum argued that federal funding of faith organizations violated the First Amendment's "separation between church and state." They feared that federal taxpayer funds could be used to support proselytizing, discrimination in hiring, and the building of houses of worship. Such concerns extended not only to the separation of church and state issue but also to the fear of some that public funding would go to support religious institutions with whom other taxpayers disagree, whether it be a clash of religious values and beliefs or atheists unwilling to support any religion. Indeed, little, if any, federal monitoring has occurred to ensure compliance with the safeguards against proselytizing.

Debates surrounding employment discrimination increased in 2001 when the Salvation Army requested an exemption in hiring gays and lesbians, maintaining that homosexuality went against their religious beliefs and morals and that receiving federal funds should not force religious institutions to change their beliefs. A New York Federal Court subsequently ruled that the organization could use religious criteria in its hiring. Critics of the decision argue that, theoretically speaking, the Salvation Army is willing to accept tax dollars from all Americans, including gays and lesbians, but is unwilling to hire all Americans, including homosexuals.

Concerns about public funding for religious buildings proved legitimate to critics when, in 2003, the Bush administration, through the Department of Housing and the National Parks Service, allowed the allocation of federal funds for the construction or rehabilitation of such edifices, as long as community service programs would be enacted.

Although some religious institutions may have beliefs that discriminate against other groups and others are controversial—for example, Hare Krishnas, Wiccans, the Nation of Islam, Scientologists, or even religious cults—all are eligible for federal funding. Because no definition exists as to what constitutes a religious institution and what types deserve funding, the current position of the White House Office of Faith-Based and Community Initiatives is that, as long as these religious institutions develop programs to create positive social change, they are eligible for funding.

Although federal funding of faith-based initiatives is part of federal law, the controversy still continues. Few would deny the influential role that faith-based institutions play within their communities to ease social problems; they reach people in ways that other service organizations, government agencies, and even community-based organizations cannot. However, the church–state separation issue remains, and challenges to the constitutionality of such public funding continue as of this writing. Only time will tell if a change in national leadership or future Supreme Court rulings will alter or reaffirm this approach to improving society.

Angelique Harris

See also Politics and Christianity; Religion and Conflict; Religion and Politics

Further Readings

Black, Amy E., Douglas L. Koopman, and David K. Ryden. 2004. *Of Little Faith: The Politics of George W. Bush's Faith-Based Initiatives.* Washington, DC: Georgetown University Press.

Formicola, Jo Renee, Mary C. Segers, and Paul Weber. 2003. *Faith-Based Initiatives and the Bush Administration: The Good, the Bad, and the Ugly.* Lanham, MD: Rowman & Littlefield.

Kuo, David. 2006. *Tempting Faith: An Inside Story of Political Seduction.* New York: Free Press.

FALSE CONSCIOUSNESS

False consciousness is a complex cognitive-epistemological and socioeconomic political concept. First explored by the philosophers of the Scottish Enlightenment, notably Adam Smith and Adam Ferguson, its most common association is with the work of Karl Marx and Friedrich Engels.

Although *false consciousness* is one of the most central Marxian terms, Marx and Engels use it only once each in their published works to refer to distorted knowledge or inadequate expression of reality. Marx used the term in his 1854 essay, "*Der Ritter vom edelmütigen Bewußsein*" (The Knight of Noble-Minded Consciousness). However, he uses it not in a conceptual way to categorize a certain phenomenon but to refute a slanderous article by August Willich, claiming the latter attempted to detect "a false consciousness behind a correct fact." The connotation of Engels's usage of the term is something more substantial. In a letter to Franz Mehring dated July 14, 1893, he discusses the genesis of ideology (superstructure) and how it affects structure. He admits that he and Marx emphasized how structure determines superstructure but neglected to work out how superstructure affects structure. In this context he asserts that ideology is a process accomplished by the so-called thinker. Consciously, it is true, but with a false consciousness. The real forces impelling him remain unknown to him; otherwise it simply would not be an ideological process. Hence he imagines false or seemingly motivating forces.

Thanks to the first generation of Marxist philosophers, particularly Georg Lukács, the concept of false consciousness assumed its current preeminence. In his classical essay "Class Consciousness," Lukács suggests that Marx's concept of false consciousness arises as a reply to bourgeois philosophy and sociology of history, which reduce progress to the role of individualities or supernatural forces like God. Now, Marx resolves this dilemma of bourgeois theory of history, Lukács suggests, by developing his concept of historical materialism and by presenting human relations in capitalist society as reification. Then, by referring to Engels's letter to Mehring, Lukács introduces the concept of false consciousness. He poses the question whether historical materialism takes into account the role of consciousness in history. In this connection he speaks of a double dialectical determination of false consciousness. On the one hand, considered in the light of human relations as a whole, subjective consciousness appears justified because it is something that can be understood. That is, it gives an adequate expression of human relations, but as an objective category, it is a false consciousness as it fails to express the nature of the development of society adequately. On the other hand, this consciousness in the same context fails to achieve subjectively determined goals because they appear to be unknown, unwanted objective aims determined by some mystical, supernatural alien forces.

The work of Marx and Engels explores how human relations can be brought into an agreement with human consciousness. The mature work of Marx on this question is *Das Kapital,* most particularly the first chapter on commodities. In his analysis of commodity, Marx differentiates between value in use and value in exchange. The use value of commodities is obtained by transforming natural objects into useful objects, say, by transforming wood into tables through useful or productive labor to satisfy various human needs. The exchange value is the relative value of commodities, or the socially necessary labor time to produce them, and is realized in the consumption of commodities. The exchange value is realized in the exchange process; that is, by relating commodities to one another and exchanging them for one another. Now, in his analysis of the relationship of use value and exchange value, Marx sees a mutual negative relationship. He thinks that this negative relationship results from reversal of the exchange process, going from the aim of production (satisfaction of needs) into the obtaining of exchange values. The aim of production, then, is no longer satisfaction of human needs but rather production and realization of exchange values. This gives rise to the fact that products as commodities dominate humans rather than humans their products. This is, in turn, the reason why everybody strives to realize exchange values and becomes commodity fetishists. As a result, human relations take the form of social relations between products.

The commodification of products, however, also requires the commodification of human labor. The commodification of human labor, in turn, requires the separation of laborers from their means of production and monopolization in the hands of the few (original accumulation) so that the laborers have nothing to sell but their labor forces, that is, the physiological and intellectual functions of their bodies. This is also the source of the rise of social classes in capitalist society with their class consciousnesses or ideologies. In capitalist society, then, there are two contradictory sets of ideologies: on the one hand, the institutionalized ideology of the ruling class claiming to represent the whole of society and, on the other hand, the subaltern ideology of subordinated classes. In short, ideology as a form of consciousness arises from social class relations.

Marx's concept of ideology is often equated with false consciousness. But as Theodor W. Adorno showed in the early 1930s and as Hans Heinz Holz and István Mésáros reinforced in the 1970s, equating ideology with false consciousness is undertaken in the tradition of Weberian sociology—in particular in the sociology of knowledge of Karl Mannheim. Ideology in Marxian thought has many meanings, and false consciousness is just one of them. To introduce a historical perspective into the debate on false consciousness, Lukács suggests considering Marx's concept of ideology in the light of class position vis-à-vis the means of production. Only in this manner, Lukács thinks, can one obtain objectivity to overcome consciousness as ideology and false consciousness. He thinks that, because of its position vis-à-vis the means of production, the only class that is objectively interested in overcoming consciousness ideology and false consciousness is the working class, an idea Marx and Engels formulated as early as 1848 in *The Communist Manifesto*.

Doğan Göçmen

See also Conflict Perspective; Socialism; Social Movements; Social Revolutions

Further Readings

Mésáros, István. 1986. *Marx's Theory of Alienation*. London: Merlin.
———. 2005. *The Power of Ideology*. New York: Zed.

FAMILY

One of the most contentious issues facing us today is the impact of changing norms and values on the bedrock of society: the family. The structure of the family has changed significantly over the past 50 years, so much so that it is often difficult for both individuals and social institutions to keep up and adapt. Replacing the traditional breadwinner–homemaker model that at one time epitomized the family are a multitude of family forms—single-parent households, stepfamilies, cohabitating couples, extended and multigenerational families, same-sex partnerships, and grandparents raising grandchildren. In response to these changes, some bemoan the demise and decline of the nuclear family and push for the promotion of marriage as salvation, whereas others see an opportunity for wider acceptance of diversity in family households and advocate for public policy to accommodate families in all shapes and sizes. So, how did we get to this crossroads, in feeling that we have lost touch with the form and function of this cornerstone institution?

What Is the "Family"?

The term *family* carries with it plentiful social and cultural meanings, and it also has profound and personal significance for most people. Most discussions about the family, however, define it in practical terms as two or more people living together who are related by blood, marriage, or adoption. The most common assumption about households (defined as one or more people who occupy a house, apartment, or other residential unit, except dormitories) is they should consist of two-parent families. However, various social and economic transformations in society have also led to a transformation of the family in recent decades, which has resulted in a decline in the traditional family share of households.

In 1960, 85 percent of households were family households; by 2000, just 69 percent were family households. Most of this decline reflects the decrease in the share of married-couple households with children. Explanations for this shrinking proportion include declines and delays in fertility within marriage, postponement of first marriage, an increase in cohabiting and single households, and a consistent divorce rate. Two-parent family households with children dropped from 44 percent to 24 percent of all households between 1960 and 2000.

The changes in household composition began gradually in the 1960s, which coincided with radical social changes in U.S. society, including the civil rights movement and the women's liberation movement, and particularly with the baby boom generation heading into adulthood. The biggest decline in the share of family households was during the 1970s when the baby boomers entered their 20s. By the 1980s, change was still occurring but at a less rapid pace; by the 1990s, household composition reached a still-continuing equilibrium. So with these structural changes and the eventual quieting that occurred, why are we still concerned about the state of the family and where does this alarm stem from?

Nostalgia for Families Past

In many public policy discussions surrounding marriage and the family, the common underlying theme is a desire for simpler times. This time warp in mind-set harks back to the 1950s, when a prosperous post-war economy existed and families fared well overall in comparison with an earlier generation that faced the hardships and challenges of the Great Depression. In this era between the 1950s and the late 1960s, changes

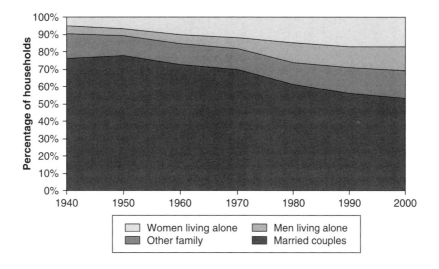

Figure 1   Trends in U.S. Households, 1940 to 2000

Source: U.S. Census Bureau. "Households by Type, 1940 to Present." Retrieved December 26, 2007 (http://www.census.gov/population/socdemo/hh-fam/hh1.pdf).

occurred in family structure from times past, where marriage rates increased and the baby boom occurred. The revision of the breadwinner–homemaker model came about; no longer were women told they did not need to work outside the home in order for the family to make ends meet. What we need to remember about this time, however, is what it represents: a blip in our nation's history. A precursor to the women's liberation movement from this time was "the problem that has no name," which was Betty Friedan's call to a generation of women about complacency and adherence to

conformity. Still, what is often recalled from the 1950s is a romanticized version of the family, not how things really were.

Much discussion continues about the save-the-marriage movement promoted by the Bush administration, in offering financial incentives for marital counseling, the push for covenant marriages and stricter divorce laws in several states, and the continued impetus for the decline in welfare benefits for single-parent households but no change in assistance to working-poor families, as well as the endorsement of the "defense of marriage" laws defining marriage as being between a man and a woman. However, the real problem does not necessarily lie with the structural appearance of the family but with how well families are faring underneath the surface impressions. What are we doing, as a society, to support the infrastructure of the family?

Table 1   Trends in Single-Parent and Two-Parent Families With Children Under Age 18, 1950 to 2000

Year	Single Mother	Single Father	Two Parents
	Percentage Distribution of Families		
1950	6	1	93
1960	8	1	91
1970	10	1	89
1980	18	2	80
1990	20	4	76
2000	22	5	73

Source: U.S. Census Bureau. "Families, by Presence of Own Children under 18: 1950 to Present." Retrieved December 26, 2007 (http://www.census.gov/population/www/socdemo/hh-fam.html).

Note: Includes only families who maintain their own households.

Reality of Present-Day Families

The institution of the family continues to persist and evolve, as families continue to be an important anchor for both individual and collective well-being in our society. Modern norms refuse to dissipate in discussions about the desirability of marriage, the optimal timing of children, and the involvement of fathers in childrearing and of mothers in breadwinning. Families of today are taking on changing and varied forms of adaptation; what we are seeing is how the institution of marriage and family has become more flexible and fluid in reaction to the reality of the choices and opportunities that are available to individuals. Research continues to show an overall transformation in attitudes toward family behaviors; people have become more accepting of divorce, cohabitation, and sex outside of marriage; more tolerant of blurred gender roles; and more open-minded about a variety of living arrangements, family configurations, and lifestyles.

The biggest challenge that families face in society today is economic well-being, as economic fortunes and the health of family relationships remain ever intertwined. Other issues of great importance include how families will balance paid work and childrearing and whether the workplace will become more accommodating to family needs, what income inequality will do to the potential fortunes and life chances of the next generation, and also how relationships between the generations will be altered by the increase in life expectancy, with the impact resting on the sandwich generation to meet the needs of their aging parents as well as their children. Over the generations, the family has changed in response to economic conditions, social change, and such changing demographics as the graying of the population. Therefore, it is not unreasonable to expect families to continue to be adaptive and resilient in the future as well.

Pamela McMullin-Messier

See also Adoption; Child Care Safety; Divorce; Domestic Partnerships; Dual-Income Families; Family, Blended; Family, Dysfunctional; Family, Extended; Family, Nuclear; Family Leave Act; Family Reunification; Same-Sex Marriage; Single Mothers; Transnational Families

Further Readings

Casper, Lynne M. and Suzanne M. Bianchi. 2002. *Continuity and Change in the American Family.* Thousand Oaks, CA: Sage.

Coontz, Stephanie. 2000. *The Way We Never Were: American Families and the Nostalgia Trap.* 2nd ed. New York: Basic Books.

Demo, David H., Katherine R. Allen, and Mark A. Fine, eds. 2000. *Handbook of Family Diversity.* New York: Oxford University Press.

Jasper, James A. and Jeff Goodwin, eds. 2006. "Special Issue on Families." *Contexts* 5(4).

Milardo, Robert M., ed. "Decade in Review: Understanding Families in the New Millennium." 2000. Special Issue of *Journal of Marriage and the Family* 62(4).

Roseneil, Sasha and Shelley Budgeon. 2004. "Cultures of Intimacy and Care beyond 'the Family': Personal Life and Social Change in the Early 21st Century." *Current Sociology* 52:135–59.

Family, Blended

Blended families are the result of two adults establishing a union, with at least one having had a child or children previously. Because the concept of family itself is evolving to include gay partnerships, "commuter" relationships with separate households, and cohabiting couples, the definition of the blended family is also fluid. Blended families reflect all the nuances of the modern nuclear family, while bearing the additional impact of members' prior family relationships.

Sociologists characterize family by long-term commitment, strong group identity, and an economic structure that provides for any children within the union. Kinship, common ancestry, or marriage are traditionally, though not always, present. The exceptions to these guideposts are apparent in the blended family. In most, a previous commitment has already ended; identifying with the new family unit is a lengthy process and not guaranteed; possibly, there is economic involvement, with all its implications, from outside the new family, in terms of child support. The strength of blood and legal bonds is especially ambiguous in the blended family.

Considering the overall 50 percent divorce rate in the United States and the fact that 50 percent of marriages are remarriages, blended family dynamics are an influential social phenomenon. One in three Americans is now part of a stepfamily, and demographers predict that the aging baby boomers (those born between 1946 and 1964) will have to rely more on stepchildren than biological children for elder care. Thus, resolving complicated blended family relationships is culturally significant.

Three types of blended families and several variations thereof exist and are reflected in popular culture: (1) the biological mother–stepfather arrangement (most common, as divorced mothers usually gain custody of their children); (2) the biological father–stepmother; and (3) the couple who each brings biological children to the new union, as in the popular TV series from the 1960s and 1970s, *The Brady Bunch.* In the book-based movie *Yours, Mine and Ours,* a widowed couple also each had their own children and went on to have mutual biological children. A recent remake of that film depicted the wife's adopted children of various races and ethnicities, calling to mind the real-life celebrity union of Brad Pitt and Angelina Jolie, whose biological child followed and preceded single and joint multiracial adoptions, respectively. An even more intricate—and controversial—family configuration was the nonmarital, noncohabiting relationship of Woody Allen and Mia Farrow and her multiple adopted children, some of whom were also his legally adopted children, and the ensuing marriage of Mr. Allen and one of his own children's adopted siblings, the legal daughter of his former romantic partner. Social reaction, both positive and negative, to such multilayered connections is indicative of the blended family experience.

Without diminishing their delicate, interpersonal dynamics, the notoriety of the blended families described in the previous paragraph helped dispel stepfamily myths. Historically wrought with negative connotations underscored by fairy tales like Cinderella, the archetype of the stepmother, in particular, has given way to more benevolent images. However, the possible pitfalls of step-parenting are an aspect of the blended family that cannot be overlooked. Preexisting parent–child allegiances and the influence of family members outside the home or held in memory weaken loyalties to, and the authority of, step-parents. Moving to a different community may be part of the new arrangement, and transitional strains may result. Indeed, the term *blended family* itself may be a misnomer, as families do not so much blend as they expand, potentially encompassing residential and nonresidential stepsiblings and half siblings, additional sets of grandparents, and other extended stepfamily members, and, in the case of "serial" couplings and breakups, ex-stepfamily members. *Binuclear family* is another term used to describe two families joining to form a new one.

New family members are often of unfamiliar backgrounds, and the lack of homogeny in second and third marriages increases their rate of failure to 60 percent, while shortening the expected duration from 8 years for a first union, to 7. A couple's compatibility strongly depends on familiarity with one another's culture, but because people are older at the time of successive marriages or cohabitation (mid- to late 30s vs. early to mid-20s for first unions), the pool of available partners has diminished, and they may marry outside their generation, social class, ethnicity, or religion. Adding children to the mix, especially adolescents, without sufficient time for couple adjustment, increases stress.

Ironically, most blended families involve cohabitation, rather than marriage, yet the remarriage model, and related research, is the only reference available to institutions like school and church. One case study illustrates confusion over family ties: A single mother's live-in boyfriend coached her daughter's sports team. The community questioned his relationship with the child, as the parents were not legally married, and ruled that he could not coach because he was not part of any team member's family. Yet, this man had served as stepfather to the child all her life.

Theorists acknowledge that lack of biology between some blended family members can be problematic. The family—that basic unit of civilization—is an intimate, stressful, and potentially dangerous experience. Some social scientists who subscribe to the biosocial perspective, which posits that genetics and evolution govern roles and relationships, assert that society should not encourage the formation of stepfamilies, as danger increases when no biological ties rule behavior. Indeed, 30 percent of adult–child sexual assault cases involve a stepfather, and higher incidence of child abuse statistically links to a mother's cohabiting boyfriend. The issue of incest becomes a concern also, especially whenever revelations of sexual activity, even marriage, between stepsiblings becomes known.

Nonetheless, blended families help those divorced or widowed reorganize their lives and maintain familial structure. Women living in poverty may raise their socioeconomic status through subsequent family formation. People are more mature when they remarry, and such relationships are more egalitarian. Children benefit from the commitment, communication, cohesion, and effort required of successful blended families.

Sarah E. Murray

See also Abuse, Child Sexual; Divorce; Family

Further Readings

Booth, Alan and John N. Edwards. 1992. "Starting Over: Why Remarriages Are More Unstable." *Journal of Family Issues* 13(2):179–94.

Ganong, Lawrence H. and Marilyn Coleman. 2004. *Stepfamily Relationships: Developments, Dynamics and Interventions.* New York: Kluwer Academic/Plenum.

Giles-Sims, Jean. 1997. "Current Knowledge about Child Abuse in Stepfamilies." Pp. 215–30 in *Stepfamilies: History, Research, and Policy,* edited by I. Levin and M. B. Sussman. New York: Haworth.

Herbert, W. 1999. "When Strangers Become Family." *U.S. News and World Report,* November 29, pp. 58–67.

FAMILY, DYSFUNCTIONAL

Dysfunctional family refers to a family pattern generally associated with lower levels of health, well-being, happiness, and positive outcomes, compared with other families. Conceptualizing a dysfunctional family should be not as a dichotomy but as a continuum, viewing it in terms of degrees of dysfunction. Some families may be more or less dysfunctional than other families, with the extent and severity of dysfunction varying.

Many disciplines—such as sociology, psychology, social work, medicine, and criminology—study dysfunctional families. Because several disciplines study dysfunctional families, many different definitions, viewpoints, and solutions to dysfunctional families exist.

Many different types of dysfunctional families exist, as do various forms of family violence commonly classified as dysfunctional. For example, all forms of chronic or severe child abuse—sexual, emotional, and physical—are considered dysfunctional, as is child neglect, perhaps the most common form of child abuse. Spousal violence is also dysfunctional because of the physical and emotional harm inflicted on the victim and the negative and threatening environment in which the children live.

Chronic and abusive use of drugs or alcohol within the family is dysfunctional because of the action affiliated with such activity. Such chronic and abusive use correlates with higher levels of emotional and physical violence as well as diminished parent–child interaction. The net results for offspring are lower levels of academic success, self-esteem, and other indicators of overall well-being. Moreover, a higher likelihood of drug or alcohol abuse among children and adult children of drug- or alcohol-addicted parents is another negative outcome.

Dysfunctional families often result from chronic poverty, particularly in areas that offer few economic opportunities, inadequate educational programming, and an overall lack of hope for the future. Such families experience low levels of academic achievement, few plans for the future, high levels of criminal activity, drug and alcohol addiction, unemployment, and homelessness. With fewer means to achieve success, families in chronic poverty are more likely to be considered dysfunctional.

Some research findings suggest that families experiencing emotional or physical disabilities have higher rates of stress, marital breakup, and second generations of emotional disorders (among families with emotional/psychological disorders, such as depression). However, many families in similar situations do not become dysfunctional. No particular event or social circumstance appears to cause or create a dysfunctional family, despite such assumptions. More likely, the way a family or family member views the event or social circumstance is the determining factor as to whether or not the family remains more functional. Thus, one family may experience a family member becoming disabled and yet remain highly functional, whereas another family may experience the same event and become dysfunctional because of inadequate support, self-definition of the event as a crisis, and lack of previous positive experiences.

Where on a dysfunctional family continuum families fall relates to the number of dysfunctional characteristics present within the family. That is, families with several elements associated with being dysfunctional would fall in the "more dysfunctional" category. For example, a family in chronic poverty, headed by a drug- or alcohol-addicted parent where child and spousal abuse are also present, is more dysfunctional than a family where one event of non-life-threatening couple violence occurred. The more dysfunctional the family, the more challenging it is for the offspring to have successful outcomes in life.

Dysfunctional families are a social problem for two main reasons. First, the immediate members of a dysfunctional family may experience harm or hardship because of the nature of the family. Second, the pattern of dysfunctional families may be transmitted to the second generation, in what is known as "intergenerational transmission." However, intergenerational transmission is not an absolute; whereas some family members will repeat the dysfunctional family pattern, many will not.

Perhaps most important in determining whether or not intergenerational transmission occurs are individual characteristics of children. Substantial research documents the resilience of some people to harsh or unhealthy environments. These individuals generally have several protective factors that aid in minimizing the long-term impact of dysfunctional families. These protective factors include high intelligence, external social supports, an internal sense of locus of control, the ability to recognize opportunities for change, and an awareness of the ability to have better outcomes. Recognition of the dysfunctional nature of family actions is essential but does not necessarily prevent intergenerational transmission of family dysfunction.

Recent research indicates that disidentification with dysfunctional family members may aid in preventing repetition of the dysfunctional behaviors. Disidentification comes about by the offspring recognizing the problem behavior and taking steps and making a commitment to break the cycle. Sometimes disidentification involves limiting contact with the dysfunctional family members. The presence of role models who may or may not be family members also seems to be important in preventing intergenerational transmission of dysfunctional family patterns. Less frequently, removal of children from the dysfunctional family is necessary to prevent permanent physical or mental harm to the children, resulting in their placement with alternative family members or foster care families.

Donna Dea Holland

See also Abuse, Child; Domestic Violence; Foster Care; Poverty

Further Readings

Luthar, Suniya W., ed. 2003. *Resilience and Vulnerability: Adaptation in the Context of Childhood Adversities.* New York: Cambridge University Press.

Martinez, Cindy. 2006. "Abusive Family Experiences and Object Relations Disturbances." *Clinical Case Studies* 5(3):209–19.

Pollock, Joycelyn M., Janet L. Mullings, and Ben M. Crouch. 2006. "Violent Women: Findings from the Texas Women Inmates Study." *Journal of Interpersonal Violence* 21(4):485–502.

Reiss, David. 1991. *The Family's Construction of Reality.* Cambridge, MA: Harvard University Press.

Rutter, Michael. 1995. "Psychosocial Adversity: Risk, Resilience, and Recovery." *Southern African Journal of Child and Adolescent Psychiatry* 7(2):75–88.

Werner, E. E. 1994. "Overcoming the Odds." *Developmental and Behavioral Pediatrics* 15(2):131–36.

FAMILY, EXTENDED

The extended family consists of two or more generations of the same family residing in the same household. Members of the extended family can consist of, but are not limited to, husband and wife, their children, maternal and paternal grandparents, aunts, uncles, and cousins. The extended family is also referred to as the "consanguine family" because most of its members include those of the same bloodline.

Sociologists once believed that the extended family was the norm in preindustrial societies, an economic unit that produced and distributed goods. In addition, extended families relied on one another for economic survival, support, and services, such as care for the sick and the elderly, services that society did not yet provide.

With industrialization, family members leave home to seek work that pays wages, leading to the end of the family as an economic unit and the breakdown of the extended family. This gives rise to the nuclear family, consisting of husband and wife and their children residing in a home of their own. The nuclear family is also known as the "conjugal family" because it centers on marriage.

The assumption that the extended family thrived prior to industrialization may be a myth. Records of households in Europe and America during the 17th century show that the nuclear family was actually the most common family form of the time. The idea of the extended family as dominant may have derived from the most common living arrangements of the time, in which the nuclear family may have had servants, slaves, boarders, lodgers, or apprentices living within the same household and contributing economically to the household.

The industrial revolution may have actually promoted the extended family, as members of nuclear families left home to seek work in urban areas and sought out relatives to live with, out of economic need. In addition, some working-class families in urban areas shared living spaces in order to share living expenses.

Today variations of the traditional extended family can be seen among different racial, ethnic, and social groups throughout U.S. society. Many extended families live within the same geographical location and rely on each other to provide financial and social support, child care, and protection. In poor urban and rural areas, extended families develop in response to economic needs and to provide support for one another. Among the elite, extended families provide a sense of community and maintain the family's wealth.

As many extended families no longer live within the same household, the U.S. Census Bureau and the Internal Revenue Service do not recognize these families as extended but rather as separate family households. As a result, there are no public programs or policies in place to support the extended family.

Although not always the dominant form of family within society, the extended family has always existed in response to economic factors. With the increase in single-parent households, the high divorce rate, stagnating wages, and the high costs of housing and child care, extended family households have been on the rise.

Cheray T. W. Teeple

See also Divorce; Family, Nuclear; Role Conflict; Single Mothers

Further Readings

Coontz, Stephanie. 2000. *The Way We Never Were: American Families and the Nostalgia Trap.* 2nd ed. New York: Basic Books.

Hansen, Karen V. 2005. *Not-So-Nuclear Families: Class, Gender, and Networks of Care.* New Brunswick, NJ: Rutgers University Press.

Hughes, Michael and Carolyn J. Kroehler. 2005. *Sociology: The Core.* 7th ed. New York: McGraw-Hill.

Ojeda, Auriana. 2003. *The Family.* Farmington Hills, MI: Greenhaven.

Ruggles, Steven. 1987. *Prolonged Connections: The Rise of the Extended Family in Nineteenth Century England and America.* Madison, WI: University of Wisconsin Press.

FAMILY, NUCLEAR

The nuclear family consists of a married couple and their children, either natural or adopted, who reside within the same household. Because the nuclear family is based on marriage, it is also called the "conjugal family." Nuclear families form around marriage, a legal relationship that includes economic cooperation, sexual activity, and childbearing and childrearing, which people expect to last. Although many different types of family exist in North America, the nuclear family has long been considered the norm.

The origin of the nuclear family is connected to the economic and social changes of the industrial revolution. The nuclear family's smaller size, in relation to the larger extended family, was considered better suited for moving closer to the occupational opportunities the industrial revolution created.

The traditional view of the nuclear family consisting of a husband and wife and their dependent children living within the same household is based on the ideal of the husband/father breadwinner and the wife/mother as the family caretaker. However, the male breadwinner/female caretaker nuclear family was only possible when men could earn enough to support their families. Throughout history, many nuclear families have had to rely on wages earned by women in order to remain economically stable.

With specific gender roles, the nuclear family becomes a distinctive group, whose function in society is to socialize the children and to provide emotional support, love, and affection for the family members. As the family members turn to each other for emotional gratification, the home is seen as a safe haven and private retreat from the larger community.

The prevailing view of the nuclear family coming about with the industrial revolution may be a myth. The examination of birth, death, and marriage records from 17th-century English and American households shows that the dominant family form was nuclear. Sociologists now believe that the concept of childhood, a period of time to train and prepare children to become adults, emerged during the 17th century. The increased importance given to the welfare of children necessitated the formation of close bonds among family members and the stability of the family unit.

The nuclear family is also seen as an isolated, independent unit that is self-reliant within society. This view assumes that the nuclear family's association with relatives is distant and that the extended family does not play an important role in the nuclear family. However, many nuclear families do remain within the same geographic location as their relatives. Extended family members often provide services, such as child care and financial assistance. For families that are scattered across the United States, modern transportation and communication help families maintain their bonds.

Today, many feel that the stability of the nuclear family is being threatened by divorce, cohabitation, single parenthood, and gay and lesbian couples. It is feared that the breakdown of the nuclear family will lead to the breakdown of society. Despite these "threats" to the nuclear family, most people still want to be a part of this family structure. The nuclear family will likely remain a foundation of U.S. society for some time to come.

Cheray T. W. Teeple

See also Family, Blended; Family, Extended

Further Readings

Adams, Bert A. 1995. *The Family: A Sociological Interpretation.* 5th ed. Fort Worth, TX: Harcourt Brace.

Coontz, Stephanie. 2000. *The Way We Never Were: American Families and the Nostalgia Trap.* 2nd ed. New York: Basic Books.

Hutter, Mark. 1998. *The Changing Family.* 3rd ed. Needham Heights, MA: Allyn & Bacon.

FAMILY LEAVE ACT

The Family and Medical Leave Act (FMLA) of 1993 was the first piece of legislation signed into law by President Bill Clinton. Prior to its enactment, the legislation went through numerous iterations, with nearly a decade of congressional debate, and was vetoed twice by President George H. W. Bush. The FMLA allows a qualified worker up to 12 weeks of unpaid leave during a 12-month period to attend to various health-related conditions: the birth or adoption of a child, serious personal health conditions, or the care of a sick child, spouse, or seriously ill parent. The bill guarantees relative job security and requires employers to maintain the same level of employee health benefits paid prior to the leave. Companies with fewer than 50 employees are exempt from providing the benefit; employees working for companies that fall under the mandate of the FMLA must be employed for 1 year, must give 30 days notification in advance of the leave, and may be required to reimburse the company for all benefits if they do not return to work.

The final contours of the FMLA reflect the compromises worked out among various stakeholders involved during its evolution during the 1980s and early 1990s, including the business community, labor groups, feminist organizations, advocates for the elderly, and partisan politicians. Its ultimate passage was proclaimed to affirm the needs of an increasingly feminized workplace; yet an analysis of its provisions, in comparative perspective, reveals the extent to which the policy reflects patterns of social stratification and power distribution in the United States. Although the FMLA recognizes the intersection of work and family obscured for nearly a century by the ideology of separate spheres, the patterns of usage reveal the extent to which care work within families is still defined as women's responsibility—the gender neutrality of the law notwithstanding.

Unlike medical leave policies in other industrialized nations, the U.S. policy has a family focus rather than a specification toward pregnancy and early child care. The first iterations of the legislation (e.g., the Parental and Medical Leave Act) were formulated in response to the increasing labor force participation of women of childbearing age. The rapid aging of the baby boom demographic and the political strength of elder care advocates are linked to the inclusion of caring for elderly parents in the revised law by 1990. Indeed, this reformulation acknowledged women on the so-called corporate granny track: primarily white, middle-class professionals who bear responsibility for the care of aging parents. The narrow definition of family, however, excludes both extended family members and fictive kin potentially in need of care and excludes gay and lesbian partners.

The other characteristics of the FMLA that differentiate it from leave policies in other countries are that the benefit is tied to size of company and, most significant, it is unpaid. Studies show that fewer women than men in the labor force are eligible, although men are less likely to take family leave. Workers who report the most need, including single mothers, seasonal and temporary workers, and other low-income laborers, are less likely than middle-class professional workers to meet eligibility requirements. African American workers report the most need, yet they are the least likely among all racial groups to qualify. In fact, research shows that although a majority of workers who need leave take it, only single-digit percentages of workers actually do so through the FMLA. Research also suggests that the costs of the policy have not appreciably affected the costs of doing business; ostensibly this is related to both low eligibility rates and low usage.

Research also suggests that the FMLA, when compared with the provisions of welfare reform under the Personal Work and Responsibility Reconciliation Act, reinforces patterns of stratification by class, gender, and race. Within the dual labor market, the FMLA covers employees with top-tier jobs, who are more likely to have the financial resources and familial support to take leave without income replacement. On the other hand, welfare reform legislation requires low-income mothers to work full-time for limited pay in low-mobility and generally peripheral jobs. One group of privileged mothers is given the security to suspend work for child and family care, whereas another group is compelled to work or face dire financial straits. Thus, existing patterns of stratification that privilege primarily white, middle-class families over lower-class and largely minority families are reproduced within the two-tiered welfare system.

Critics suggest the FMLA is a prime example both of "policy minimalization" and of a typical U.S. response to social problems. Similar policies in European countries that provide paid leave and extended allocations of time may reflect the higher likelihood of their workers to be unionized and the normativity of state and employer redistribution of economic resources to workers. Widespread support for family-friendly policies exists in the United States, but the FMLA is so exclusive that the primary constituents in need of its benefits are the least likely to receive them—low-income, contingent, racial minority, and women workers. As such, it primarily represents the interests of the organized business community and economically privileged families and is a less than effective policy in relation to the problem that it was initially formulated to address.

Laura L. O'Toole

See also Dual-Income Families; Mommy Track; Sandwich Generation; Welfare

Further Readings

Gerstel, Naomi and Katherine McGonagle. 1999. "Job Leaves and the Limits of the Family and Medical Leave Act: The Effects of Gender, Race, and Family." *Work and Occupations* 26(4):510–34.

Hudson, Robert B. and Judith G. Gonyea. 2000. "Time Not Yet Money: The Politics and Promise of the Family Medical Leave Act." *Journal of Aging and Social Policy* 11(2–3):189–200.

U.S. Office of Personnel Management. 2006. *Family and Medical Leave.* Retrieved December 26, 2007 (http://www.opm.gov/oca/leave/HTML/fmlafac2.asp).

Wexler, Sherry. 1997. "Work/Family Policy Stratification: The Examples of Family Support and Family Leave." *Qualitative Sociology* 20(2):311–22.

Wisensale, Steven K. 2003. "Two Steps Forward, One Step Back: The Family and Medical Leave Act as Retrenchment Policy." *Journal of Policy Research* 20(1):135–51.

FAMILY REUNIFICATION

U.S. immigration laws are based on the 1952 Immigration and Nationality Act and subsequent amendments. These laws grant priority for permanent residence status to immediate relatives of U.S. citizens or legal permanent residents for family reunification. Priority is also given to applicants with critical job skills, refugees and asylum seekers, and applicants from countries with low levels of immigration to the United States (diversity immigrants). The Immigration Act of 1990 specifies an annual limit of between 416,000 and 675,000 for family-sponsored preferences, employment preferences, and diversity immigrants. The annual limit for family-sponsored preferences is from 226,000 to 480,000 immigrants, accounting for more than half of all immigration priorities. There are also per country and dependent area limits of 7 percent and 2 percent respectively, for the total number of family-sponsored and employment preferences.

Family reunification consists of two categories: immediate relatives of U.S. citizens and family-sponsored preferences. Immediate relatives of U.S. citizens include spouses of U.S. citizens, unmarried minor children of U.S. citizens, and parents of U.S. citizens. Immediate relatives of U.S. citizens account for 40 percent or more of the annual legal permanent residence status. This category has no numerical limit. Family-sponsored preferences consist of four numerically limited categories: (1) unmarried, adult sons and daughters of U.S. citizens and their children; (2) spouses, minor children, and unmarried, adult sons and daughters of legal U.S. permanent residents; (3) married sons and daughters of U.S. citizens and their spouses and children; and (4) brothers and sisters, including their spouses and children, of adult U.S. citizens.

A Petition for Alien Relative (Form I-130), submitted by a U.S. citizen or legal permanent resident, must be approved by the U.S. Citizenship and Immigration Services (USCIS) to receive legal permanent residence as an immediate relative of a U.S. citizen or as a family preference immigrant. Filing the petition establishes a priority date for the immigrant. The U.S. State Department monitors the availability of visas within the categories and country limits, and issues a permanent immigrant visa (green card) to the immigrant if there is no administrative backlog. Before issuing the visa, the State Department completes criminal history background checks and ensures that the immigrant is not a security threat and is admissible to the United States.

Current immigration laws and practices regarding family reunification may warrant further review, as families typically experience lengthy periods of separation while waiting for reunification. In 2000, the Immigration and Naturalization Service (INS), now known as USCIS, had 1,190,768 pending I-130 applications, as compared with 747,369 applications in 1994. This administrative backlog, caused by insufficient human resources and the increasing numbers of various application types filed, contributes to a minimum processing time of 24 months for permanent resident visas. Further, as the demand for visas exceeds the number of visas available for family-sponsorship preferences, a second backlog results from the discrepancy between the demand for visas and the actual availability of visas. Except for the immediate relative category, with no country or category limits, all other categories of family-sponsorship immigration have processing delays.

In 2000, partially addressing the consequences of backlog, Congress approved the Legal Immigration Family Equity Act (LIFE Act), granting temporary nonimmigrant status (V status) to spouses and minor children of lawful permanent residents waiting for longer than 3 years for an immigrant visa. Persons granted V status would receive employment authorization and would be allowed to remain in the United States until they received permanent residence status. However, these visas had limited availability. Solutions to lessening the number of administrative backlogs also include giving immigration agencies more resources to handle their workload. Backlogs caused by the quota system could be alleviated by raising the limit on the first and second preference categories so that the number of visas available better meets demand. Proposed measures of reform also include broadening the definition of *immediate relative* so that more visas could be available to the remaining categories of family-sponsored immigrants, and not counting immediate relatives in the family-sponsored preferences limit.

Immigration law requires that the sponsor must file a Form I-864, *Affidavit of Support,* and prove an income level minimally at 125 percent of the federal poverty level before filing for a relative. If the sponsor's income does not meet the requirement, other financial assets can be considered. The income of certain other household members can also be considered if they sign a Form I-864A, *Affidavit of Support Contract Between Sponsor and Household Member.* Although this financial requirement is intended to ensure that immigrants will be provided for by family members and will not depend on public assistance, it may be an additional constraint to family reunification.

The Illegal Immigration Reform and Immigrant Responsibility Act of 1996 instituted a 5-year bar to admission for aliens unlawfully present in the United States for more than 180 days but less than 1 year and a 10-year bar for aliens unlawfully present in the United States for 1 year or more. The act stipulates a waiver for immigrants who are spouses or children of U.S. citizens and legal permanent residents if they can satisfactorily establish to federal authorities that refusal of admission would result in extreme hardship to the citizen or lawfully resident spouse or parent of the immigrant. Although given sole discretion to waive the clause, the attorney general may not adjust the status of more than 4,000 aliens annually. Reports of recent increases in the number of denials of these waivers may constitute a further barrier to family reunification.

Danielle Taana Smith

See also Citizenship; Immigration; Immigration, United States

Further Readings

Catholic Immigration Network. "Barriers to Family Reunification." Washington, DC: Catholic Immigration Network. Retrieved December 11, 2007 (www.cliniclegal.org/Advocacy/barriers.html).

McKay, Ramah. 2003. *Family Reunification.* Washington, DC: Migration Information Source, Migration Policy Institute. Retrieved December 11, 2007 (http://www.migrationinformation.org/feature/display.cfm?ID=122).

National Immigration Forum. 2005. "Immigration Backlogs Are Separating American Families." Washington, DC: National Immigration Forum. Retrieved December 26, 2007 (http://immigrationforum.org/documents/TheDebate/ImmigrationReform/FamilyBacklogBackgrounder.pdf).

U.S. Department of Homeland Security. 2005. "Fact Sheet: Characteristics of Family-Sponsored Legal Permanent Resident Residents: 2004." Washington, DC: Office of Immigration Statistics.

———. 2006. "Annual Flow Report: U.S. Legal Permanent Residents: 2005." Washington, DC: Office of Immigration Statistics.

U.S. General Accounting Office. 2001. "Immigration Benefits: Several Factors Impede Timeliness of Application Processing." Washington, DC: U.S. Government Printing Office.

FAMINE

Famines are complex processes, usually arising from a combination of several causes over an extended period. Their effects on different households and social groups vary greatly according to levels of anticipation and preparedness, capacity to cope with sustained adversity, and ability to return to previous livelihood patterns once the crisis period has passed. The difficulty of pinpointing critical causes and effects, other than on a case-by-case basis, makes it hard to define what famine is or when it starts and stops. As a result, there are no agreed-on mechanisms to trigger appropriate interventions to prevent or mitigate famines, and the question of responsibility for relief is normative and politicized.

Definition Problems

The simplest way to define famine is as a significant increase in mortality from starvation or starvation-related disease over an extensive geographical area. This is hard to measure, however, because famines often occur in regions where mortality rates are variable and poorly recorded. Disputes arise over deaths resulting from behaviors in response to hunger—for example, from eating venomous wild foods. Diseases such as cholera are common when people migrate en masse toward dwindling water sources—and epidemics can last for years after food crises have passed—but it is a matter for debate which disease deaths should count as famine mortality. It is tricky to distinguish between deaths from starvation and from gastric diseases.

More important, if famine is defined by mass mortality, famine relief will always be too late. Interventions early enough to prevent starvation can be described as famine prevention, but without a specific phenomenon to which to respond, both governments and international agencies often fail to achieve them. It would also be useful to differentiate between successful but last-ditch humanitarian efforts and long-term programs designed to make people food secure. However, an instrumental definition of famine vulnerability would require ongoing assessment of several aspects of people's livelihoods, which would be difficult in practice.

Because famines do not start suddenly and are difficult to define objectively, it usually falls to national governments to declare their existence. The World Food Program, like all United Nations agencies, can only intervene in sovereign states by invitation. Yet governments have an in-built incentive not to acknowledge that they have allowed famines to occur under their watch, at least until they have to, when it is again usually too late for some. National and regional vulnerability assessment committees are attempting to redress this problem, as are donor-funded schemes, such as the Famine Early Warning System Network (FEWSNET). Both, however, depend primarily on measurement of rainfall and crop yields rather than on social indicators. Vulnerable people themselves are more likely to label famines by their sociopolitical causes, such as land theft, or by strategies used to survive them.

Causes of Famines

In this context, it is no longer helpful to distinguish between natural and man-made famines. Even when drought is a proximate trigger, a famine will occur only if both markets and political systems fail to respond to food shortages. The likelihood of drought or other disasters has itself been increased by human forces, including both local and global climate change. Since the groundbreaking work of Amartya K. Sen in the early 1980s, most analysts have focused on the ability of individuals and households to command food rather than on aggregate food availability. This usefully switches the focus away from technological solutions to a technical problem and onto socioeconomic and political understandings of famine causation. For example, development of commercial farming for export can increase the vulnerability of nearby smallholders left on the poorest land.

Overpopulation in poor areas can leave too little food to go round, but the effect of HIV/AIDS has shown that reduced populations are sometimes more vulnerable, when it is the most productive members of households who are stricken. Temporary or permanent migration by young men to urban areas in search of paid employment can also contribute to chronic food shortages, though it may improve individual households' entitlement to food. Thus famines can be engendered by ordinary, unspectacular economic or social processes. From the 1970s until the early 21st century, almost all famines were associated with conflict or political repression. More recent crises, however, reflect the declining capacity of governments to respond to disease, worsening terms of trade, and infrastructural gaps.

Effects of Famines

Famines affect different social groups in varying ways, depending on the range and reliability of their entitlements to food. Particular professional classes whose work is dispensable in times of hardship, such as barbers, may suffer more than poorer laborers who are better able to adjust the nature or location of their work. People's own coping strategies are critical to their chances of survival but can involve taking risks. Migration and crime are both common responses that involve increased mortality rates, as suggested by the fact that more men than women die in most famines. Vital indigenous knowledge of which wild foods are safe to consume is likely to be limited in areas where famine is unprecedented, and this knowledge is diminishing, even in chronically vulnerable areas, because of the impact of HIV/AIDS.

Mortality patterns are further confused because deaths from starvation-related disease are far more common than from starvation itself. While the likelihood of dying from disease is greatly increased by hunger, the chance of becoming infected in the first place is less strongly correlated with food intake. As a result, starving people perceive their chances of survival to be arbitrary and beyond their control. They are therefore liable to protect their long-term livelihoods in preference to maximizing their consumption in response to prolonged hunger. For example, it is rare for key productive assets such as land or cattle to be sold until famine crises are acute. Savings, jewelry, and unessential tools are usually disposed of first, though this is made more difficult by declining prices for household assets, particularly relative to the cost of food.

Recently, humanitarian agencies have attempted to match their relief efforts to people's coping strategies, for example, by providing food for work programs close to homes. However, these are hard to target and organize and attract far more women than men, who prefer to work for cash. Care also needs to be taken not to encourage extreme behaviors. Coping strategies can be divisive or violent—for example, household breakups and murder rise sharply during famines. They are also finite. Households surviving one famine by selling assets may not be able to cope with a second, even many years later. Relief therefore needs to start before people have made decisions that will permanently affect their livelihoods. This suggests a need for better cooperation between humanitarian and development agencies. Long-term sustainable development would reduce the risk of famines. Again, however, it is important to consider poor people's priorities. Poverty reduction strategies may be rejected if they are perceived to increase risk, even if they are designed to improve household food production or profits. Examples include genetically modified seeds and projects encouraging diversification into high-value nonfood crops.

Responses to Famines

For relief to be timely and effective, it is essential to establish who bears primary responsibility for it. Ideally it should be the government, provided it has sufficient capacity and will. However, we cannot assume that all nation-states will take the (often difficult and expensive) measures necessary to prevent starvation in every case, especially if the threat of famine is in a remote or politically unimportant area. Indeed, where a local population is from a minority ethnic group or tends to support political parties opposed to the government, leaders may even see benefits in allowing famine to develop. Many authors now argue that the politics of relief has a greater bearing on the likelihood and extent of famine mortality than any other factor.

Famine prevention therefore becomes a question of how to provide incentives for states to uphold their populations' right to sufficient food, as established in the UN Declaration of Human Rights (Article 26.1). One way could be to establish such rights legally. Supreme Court cases in India and South Africa have held specific governments accountable for failures to prevent starvation. However, only 22 nations guarantee this right in their constitutions, and scarcely any have specific legislation to ensure that it is enforced. The International Criminal Court could investigate cases where governments have been directly culpable for famines, but the court is unlikely to see them as straightforward or as taking priority.

An alternative would be to rely on democracy and free media to punish governments that fail to prevent famines. Although the fear of losing power would be a powerful incentive, this may not help where famines only affect minority groups. Though shocking, recent famines will not be the only issue in most elections and may not be the main one in voters' minds. Moreover, underfunded local media organizations—and notoriously fickle and uninformed international ones—rarely provide early enough warnings of imminent famines to prompt preventive action. Taking responsibility for famine response away from governments, however, would be problematic. International agencies or nongovernmental organizations may exacerbate political problems associated with food insecurity, as recently happened, for example, when President Mugabe disputed FEWSNET's warnings of severe shortages in Zimbabwe.

David Hall-Matthews

See also Desertification; Food Insecurity and Hunger; HIV/AIDS, Reaching High-Risk Populations; Human Rights

Further Readings

Devereux, Stephen. 2007. *The New Famines: Why Famines Persist in an Era of Globalization.* London: Routledge.

De Waal, Alexander. 1989. *Famine That Kills.* Oxford, England: Clarendon.

Edkins, Jenny. 2000. *Whose Hunger? Concepts of Famine, Practices of Aid.* Minneapolis, MN: University of Minnesota Press.

Howe, Paul and Stephen Devereux. 2004. "Famine Intensity and Magnitude Scales: A Proposal for an Instrumental Definition of Famine." *Disasters* 28(4):353–72.

Keen, David. 1994. *The Benefits of Famine: A Political Economy of Famine and Relief in Southwestern Sudan, 1983–1989.* Oxford, England: Blackwell.

Sen, Amartya K. 1981. *Poverty and Famines: Essays in Entitlement and Deprivation.* Oxford, England: Clarendon.

FATHERS' RIGHTS MOVEMENT

The fathers' rights movement is an international movement, though concentrated in Western countries, that seeks to protect the legal rights of biological fathers. This primarily involves advocating for custodial rights for divorced fathers on the part of local, state, and national organizations, such as the American Coalition for Fathers and Children.

During the 1990s there was an increase in the number of single-father families; by 2002 they accounted for one in five single-parent families in the United States. However, the movement predates the recent increase in the number of father-led families. Born in the 1970s in the United Kingdom and in the United States, it was mainly a reaction to the rise in divorce rates, coupled with the increased economic independence of women through employment in the labor market and the women's rights movement. In the United States, many states moved to no-fault divorces in the 1960s, which also led to a rise in the number of divorces and hence the number of single fathers.

Historically, fathers were responsible for both the physical and financial fitness of their children, but this changed in the 20th century due to a social and cultural shift that saw mothers as better caregivers. As a result, in recent decades, physical custody of children has almost always been awarded to women. Those in the fathers' rights movement consider the legal system now unfairly biased in the direction of mothers, and they advocate for joint physical custody of children, arguing that it is in the best interest of the child to have a healthy relationship with both biological parents.

Frustration exists among many organizers and those active in the movement that the trend toward joint legal custody has been slow to take hold, even though certain types of fathers are more likely to receive either sole custody or shared physical custody of their children. This group includes high-income families, families in which the parents owned a home together, and families with older children who are boys.

As father-only families remain a small proportion of all families, the fathers' rights movement has also begun to move in a new direction, that is, emphasizing that the father is important in all families and that married fathers also need support and representation in their attempts to balance work and a meaningful home life. This involves promoting awareness about the importance of family time and pushing for paternity leave policies. In general, the increase in mothers who

work outside of the home and a cultural shift that resulted in the decline in patriarchal attitudes about and within families combined to allow the fathers' rights movement to gain a foothold to advocate for all kinds of fathers in the legal arena and beyond.

Hilary Levey

See also Divorce; Single Mothers

Further Readings

American Coalition for Fathers and Children. (www.acfc.org).
Garasky, Steven and Daniel R. Meyer. 1996. "Reconsidering the Increase in Father-Only Families." *Demography* 33:385–93.

FELONY

A felony, in contrast to a misdemeanor, is a more serious and harmful offense to society. Rooted in common-law tradition, felonies in most states are offenses punishable by imprisonment for one or more years or death. Misdemeanor offenders receive sentences for less than a year and serve their time in local jails. However, the same offense can be either a felony or a misdemeanor, depending on the degree of harm, potential danger to society posed by the offender, number of times an offender commits the same offense, or amount of property stolen.

Felony convictions first appeared in England in the 12th century and, following common-law practice, led to forfeiture of assets or death. The United States remains the only major common-law nation making a distinction between a felony and a misdemeanor. Other English-speaking countries distinguish between a petty crime (not requiring an indictment or jury) and an indictable offense (requiring a jury).

Most U.S. jurisdictions impose felony penalties based on the gravity of the offense, as stipulated in federal criminal law statutes or state penal codes, vehicle codes, and health and safety codes. The list of felonies is extensive, ranging from theft to drug possession to computer crimes to murder. The underlying rationale of classification schemes is that felonies are intentional, purposeful acts with multiple elements of harm, danger, and severity. Yet little research examines the role of felony classifications in punishment philosophy and practice.

Unlike other crimes, felonies receive differential treatment, both substantively and procedurally. Offenses like burglary require intent to commit a felony as a critical element in their definitions. Crime classifications can change if accompanied with a felony. The most controversial and widely debated example is the felony-murder rule whereby a death, even if accidentally occurring during the commission of a felony, is treated as murder. Many argue this rule disregards intent and contradicts *mens rea* (literally "guilty mind"), which is at the heart of criminal law. Multiple convictions for nonfelony offenses can also become felony offenses under state "three strikes" laws popularized in the 1990s.

Guided by court rulings and interpretations, law enforcement agents can use deadly force in arresting felons and may even arrest felons without a warrant if there is probable cause. Due process considerations are critical in felony cases and guide policy and practice, often requiring a preliminary hearing and sometimes a grand jury indictment.

The implications and consequences of definitional, substantive, procedural, and conviction decisions are numerous, including loss of voting rights, disqualification from holding public office, and prohibition against serving on juries or in the military, practicing law and some other professions, and owning firearms. Civil rights activists challenge this disenfranchisement of convicted felons, citing its anti-democratic character. The stigma and resulting deprivations and life-altering consequences associated with a felony conviction are difficult to overcome, prompting debate in research and policy circles about recidivism (relapse into criminal behavior) and societal reintegration. The charging and transferring of violent juvenile offenders to adult felony courts is another current controversial issue.

Sanjay Marwah

See also Juvenile Justice System; Misdemeanor; Recidivism; Three Strikes Laws

Further Readings

Manza, Jeff and Christopher Uggen. 2006. *Locked Out: Felon Disenfranchisement and American Democracy.* Oxford, England: Oxford University Press.
Simon, Jonathan. 2007. *Governing through Crime: How the War on Crime Transformed American Democracy and Created a Culture of Fear.* New York: Oxford University Press.

FEMALE GENITAL CUTTING

Female genital cutting (FGC; also known as "female circumcision" or "female genital mutilation") has sparked enormous debate because the issue lies at the crux of many other critical issues: globalization, sovereignty, women's and children's rights, democracy, and modernity. The precise origins of the practice, which dates back to antiquity, are unclear. FGC is deeply embedded in the culture of a number of eastern and central African nations and can be found in other parts of the world as well. The practice continues primarily because it is a tradition. At the turn of the millennium, FGC was practiced widely in 25 countries. The World Health Organization (WHO) has estimated that more than 130 million women and girls have undergone some form of genital cutting worldwide. Since the 1970s, eradication efforts have been particularly intense.

FGC is typically delineated into categories that vary by type of procedure. "Sunna" is most comparable to male circumcision. It involves the removal of the prepuce, or hood, of the clitoris. "Genital excision" or "clitoridectomy" is the removal of the entire clitoris and the labia minora, leaving the labia majora intact. "Infibulation," the most extreme form of FGC, is the excision of the clitoris, labia minora and labia majora, followed by the sewing together of the raw edges of the vulva so that only a small hole remains through which urine and menstrual fluid may pass. Mothers have typically taken responsibility for having their daughters circumcised. A traditional midwife often performs the circumcisions, but in some places, health professionals are circumcisers.

FGC creates a number of short- and long-term health consequences. Severe bleeding is the most common immediate complication. Many other complications, such as urine retention or keloids, can lead to discomfort and disfigurement but are typically not life-threatening. Nearly all forms of FGC interfere with women's sexual response. However, they do not necessarily eliminate the possibility of sexual pleasure or climax. Infibulated women are especially vulnerable to more serious health consequences. Much of the literature on FGC exaggerates such harmful or negative health consequences because it often assumes that all circumcised women are infibulated. In fact, estimates suggest that this extreme form of FGC occurs among only 15 to 20 percent of circumcised women. Further,

the incidence of infibulation has decreased in recent years. In some parts of the world, increased medicalization has reduced the incidence of negative health complications.

Three different cultural frameworks for FGC exist. Frequently, the practice is promoted to ensure the virginity of women upon marriage. The idea is that a clitoridectomy will help women keep their sexual desires in check; in some societies, infibulation is an added precaution because it makes intercourse uncomfortable and difficult. In communities where virginity is of paramount importance, girls are often circumcised in a private ceremony. The second cultural framework treats FGC as a rite of passage into adulthood. In this case, entire cohorts of girls are circumcised at the same time at a certain age. A cohort of boys is also often circumcised at the same time. When FGC is a rite of passage, a period of seclusion often follows, in which elders educate girls about community requirements. Under either of these cultural frameworks, FGC is usually a requisite for finding a marriage partner. A much less common cultural framework for FGC is the fad. Young women in a number of countries (including the United States and Chad) are undergoing the procedure to be fashionably different. This type of FGC is the least prevalent and tends not to have a lasting impact on the communities in which it occurs.

Mobilization Against Female Genital Cutting

Western feminists and women's international organizations were critically important in the 1970s in raising international interest in FGC. African opponents of the practice had been present for some time but had been unsuccessful in getting the attention of international organizations. The Western women who initially took up the issue argued that FGC was a tool of patriarchy and a symbol of women's subordination. Although some African women were part of this early mobilization, many African women objected to this framing of FGC. For example, at the international women's conference in Copenhagen in 1980, African women boycotted a session featuring Western feminist Fran Hosken, calling her perspective ethnocentric and insensitive to African women. As a consequence, international organizations eschewed the feminist rhetoric in their eradication efforts. Instead, they couched their interventions in a purportedly more neutral medical discourse.

Eventually, in the late 1980s and early 1990s, activists returned to the women's rights discourse. A relationship between gender equality and human rights had been developing, and gender equality was becoming an appropriate basis for international action. Feminist arguments that the state was responsible for protecting women and children from abuses suffered in the private sphere had been rejected or downplayed earlier, but now these arguments became the overriding ideology of international organizations. By the mid-1990s, a women's rights frame was dominating the anti-FGC discourse.

In a dramatic policy reversal, a joint statement of WHO, UNICEF, UNFPA (UN Population Fund), and UNDP (UN Development Programme) in 1995 even labeled the medical basis for anti-FGC policies a "mistake." The reasoning of the joint statement suggested that much of the medical discourse—at least as it was applied locally—was exaggerated and consequently counterproductive. The second problem with the medical reasoning was more surprising. Essentially, medicalization had been *too* effective. By making FGC safer, the international community had undermined the urgency that originally motivated the eradication of the practice. The organizations attempted to recapture some of that urgency in their repackaged message: FGC had negative health consequences, but—more important—it was a violation of women's rights.

The popular media in the West were particularly amenable to this message and to dramatizing FGC. In 1994 Cable News Network (CNN) broadcast live the circumcision of a 12-year-old girl in Cairo. The footage prompted promises of action from the Egyptian government. It also launched a global media frenzy. In the United States, FGC was suddenly featured on many popular television talk shows, such the *Oprah Winfrey Show,* and in popular magazines, such as *Cosmopolitan.* These popular media stories were grossly ethnocentric, often involving stories of U.S. women "saving" the women of Africa from FGC.

In 1996 the United States made FGC illegal. In addition to forbidding FGC in the United States, the law also made loans and aid to other countries contingent on the development of eradication policies. Soon all of the countries where FGC occurred (except those which had no government) had policies opposing the practice. These policies were often very controversial and frequently had to be implemented without formal parliamentary approval. For example, in Egypt, where mid-1990s estimates suggested that 97 percent of women had been circumcised, the Egyptian parliament was unwilling to pass a law criminalizing FGC. Ultimately, the anti-FGC policy in Egypt took the form of a "Health Ministry Decree." Although some women were able to use the laws as leverage to forgo circumcision, a lack of popular support undercut their effectiveness in many countries.

In fact, the media hype, combined with the coercive measures of countries like the United States, created a backlash against intervention in some parts of the world. Leading African proponents of eradication began to call for more local solutions. A number of scholars began to argue that FGC was not an issue that should concern individuals outside the societies where it occurs. These scholars have been at the forefront of exploring FGC within a cultural context and of calling for more culturally sensitive anti-FGC interventions.

Changing Behavior

One widespread impact of international intervention has been to increase the medicalization of FGC. In other words, chances have increased that parents will go to a health professional to have their daughters circumcised, and even traditional midwives now frequently use antiseptics and other medical aids.

In terms of raw rates of circumcision, the overall effect of eradication efforts has been uneven. For example, a recent study conducted in Egypt indicated that the percentage of circumcised Coptic Christian girls had decreased, but the percentage of circumcised Muslim girls had remained relatively stable. The same study also found that education only led to a decrease in daughters' circumcisions among Christians. This suggests that for some groups FGC has become an important cultural marker to distinguish "us" from "them." In other countries, such as Uganda, eradication efforts appear to be very effective. The most recent demographic health surveys coming from countries where FGC is practiced tend to show no change or slight decreases in the prevalence of the practice (from 2 to 6 percent) at the aggregate national level. Overall, interventions that are narrowly tailored and culturally sensitive to empower women appear to be the most effective at eradicating FGC.

Elizabeth Heger Boyle

See also Feminism; Women's Rights Movement

Further Readings

Boyle, Elizabeth Heger. 2005. *Female Genital Cutting: Cultural Conflict in the Global Community.* Baltimore: Johns Hopkins University Press.

Gruenbaum, Ellen. 2001. *The Female Circumcision Controversy.* Philadelphia: University of Pennsylvania Press.

Shell-Duncan, Bettina and Ylva Hernlund. 2000. *Female "Circumcision" in Africa.* Boulder, CO: Lynne Reinner.

U.S. Agency for International Development. 2006. "FGC Data from DHS Surveys, 1990–2004." Retrieved December 12, 2006 (http://www.measuredhs.com/topics/gender/FGC-CD/start.cfm#Disaggregation).

Yount, Kathryn M. 2004. "Symbolic Gender Politics, Religious Group Identity, and the Decline in Female Genital Cutting in Minya, Egypt." *Social Forces* 82:1063–90.

FEMINISM

Feminism is both a theoretical perspective and a social movement. As a theoretical perspective, feminism provides an explanation of social behavior and social phenomena, particularly those having to do with gender. As a social movement, feminism seeks to bring about social change, specifically gender equity.

Feminism as a social theory is not a single, unified perspective. Rather, there are multiple feminisms (e.g., liberal feminism, socialist feminism, standpoint feminism). However, there are several principles common to all feminist perspectives. One principle is that gender is socially created rather than innately determined. This is not to deny the fact that humans are biological beings and that our biological makeup influences who we are as women and men. However, from a feminist perspective, there is a complex interaction between biology and culture, and biological traits may be modified by environmental or social conditions. Feminism defines gender as a set of social expectations that is reproduced and transmitted through a process of social learning.

A second feminist principle is that gender is a central organizing factor in the social world. Gender is embedded in all social interactions and processes of everyday life as well as all social institutions. At the institutional level, gender is shaped by a society's economic and political structure. In every society, a specific set of gender norms is dominant, even though these norms may vary from society to society—further evidence that gender is socially constructed. According to the feminist perspective, no gender is inherently better or superior to any other. However, the culture of a society may imbue one gender with a higher value than another gender. In the United States and most Western societies, for example, masculinity (i.e., behaviors and traits associated with being male) is valued more highly than femininity (i.e., behaviors and traits associated with being female). Men, therefore, are accorded greater access to resources and rewards in these societies, simply because they are (masculine) men. Thus differential valuing produces gender inequality.

A common misconception about feminism is that it focuses only on women or "women's issues." It is the case that feminism's primary goal, as a theoretical perspective, has been to study and explain the position of women in society, largely because women and the behaviors and traits associated with them have historically been devalued or ignored. Nevertheless, feminism recognizes that men have gender, too, and that although virtually all men benefit in some way from gender privilege, some groups of men are disadvantaged by other social factors. A third principle of feminism, therefore, is that gender inequality does not have the same consequences for all women and men. The feminist perspective examines how gender inequality intersects with other types of inequality—racism, social class inequality, heterosexism, ageism, and inequalities based on physical and intellectual abilities—to affect different groups of women and men differently. For instance, a man who behaves effeminately is viewed as deviant and is punished for this deviation in various ways, which include social ostracism; discrimination in employment, housing, and other areas; and sometimes even violence. Similarly, poor men of color have less access to societal resources and rewards than white middle-class women do, because the negative effects of racism and social class inequality in their lives outweigh the advantages of gender privilege.

Because feminism understands gender to be socially constructed, this perspective holds that any aspects of current constructions of gender or gender norms that are harmful or destructive can be changed. And because gender norms are institutionalized, this change must occur not only at the individual level but also at the institutional level. Feminists are advocates for social change that brings about gender equity, and they have mobilized to bring about such change through collective action. In this way, feminism is more than a theoretical perspective; it is also a social movement.

Although feminist theory and resistance to gender inequality have been found in early Christian writings, as well as in writings from the Middle Ages, the Renaissance, and the Reformation, historians date the emergence of feminism as a social movement toward the end of the 18th century. It was during the late 1700s that some women began publicly demanding equal rights with men, especially in the area of education. During the first half of the 19th century, women working in anti-slavery organizations in the United States, Great Britain, and Europe became angry when their male peers prohibited them from speaking in public and segregated them at meetings and conventions. Armed with the organizational and administrative skills they had acquired through anti-slavery activism and using abolitionism as an ideological framework for understanding their own inequality relative to men, these women began to hold conferences and stage protests demanding equal rights for women. The most famous women's rights conference was held at Seneca Falls, New York, on July 19 and 20, 1848. There about 300 women and some sympathetic men adopted the Declaration of Sentiments, modeled on the Declaration of Independence, along with 12 resolutions that supported equality between the sexes and opposed laws and customs that discriminated against women. But as this "first wave" of the feminist movement developed, its focus narrowed on winning women the right to vote. This effort took nearly three quarters of a century to achieve its goal. Ratification of the 19th Amendment occurred on August 26, 1920.

Following ratification of the 19th Amendment, feminism as a social movement became dormant. Although small groups of feminists, such as the National Women's Party, continued to lobby for women's rights, including the passage of the Equal Rights Amendment, it was not until the 1960s that a second mass mobilization occurred. A number of factors contributed to the resurgence of feminism as a social movement at this time, including the appointment by President John F. Kennedy of a Presidential Commission on the Status of Women that documented widespread and severe labor force discrimination

based on sex, as well as the publication in 1963 of the bestseller *The Feminine Mystique,* by Betty Friedan. Feminism also appealed to women involved in the civil rights movement and the anti–Vietnam War movement, who were motivated by their personal experiences of gender discrimination in these social movements as well as in the larger society.

This second wave of feminism was not homogeneous. It included, for example, lesbians as well as heterosexual women, and pro-feminist men were involved. However, one serious criticism of contemporary feminism—a criticism that was also leveled against the first wave of feminism—was racism. Critics maintain that feminism as a social movement was composed of mostly white, economically privileged, well-educated women, who disregarded or deliberately excluded the concerns of women of color as well as poor and working-class women of all races and ethnicities. At the same time, by focusing largely on winning formal legal rights for women—and often succeeding—second wave feminism also overlooked the concerns of younger generations of women, who came after them.

Although it has been argued that most young women today reject feminism, research documents the development of a third wave of feminist activism that is rebellious against conventional gender norms and that also embraces inclusiveness. Studies of third wave feminism emphasize its celebration of sexuality, women's agency and autonomy, and multiculturalism. Third wave feminists have adopted a multiracial emphasis and address problems resulting from racism, social class inequality, homophobia, and other inequalities in addition to gender inequality. In fact, the inclusiveness of third wave feminism is likely to be key to the continued viability of feminism as a social movement in the 21st century.

Claire M. Renzetti

See also Gender Bias; Gender Gap; Sexism; Women's Rights Movement

Further Readings

Lorber, Judith. 2005. *Gender Inequality: Feminist Theories and Politics.* Los Angeles: Roxbury.

Renzetti, Claire M. and Daniel J. Curran. 2007. *Women, Men and Society: The Sociology of Gender.* 6th ed. Boston: Allyn & Bacon.

Feminist Theory

Feminist theories are varied and diverse. All analyze women's experiences of gender subordination, the roots of women's oppression, the perpetuation of gender inequality, and remedies for gender inequality.

Liberal feminism argues that women's unequal access to legal, social, political, and economic institutions causes women's oppression. Liberal feminists advocate women's equal legal rights and participation in the public spheres of education, politics, and employment.

Radical feminism claims women's oppression originates in men's power over women (patriarchal power). They argue that men control women's bodies through violence, objectification, and men's status in social institutions, such as medicine and religion. Radical feminists see sexism as the oldest and most pervasive form of oppression; they argue that the eradication of patriarchy and compulsory heterosexuality are key to ending gender oppression. This would be accomplished by increasing women's control over their bodies, including transforming sexuality, childbirth, and motherhood, and by eliminating patriarchal social relations.

Marxist and socialist feminists root gender inequality in capitalism. They argue that capitalists and individual men exploit women's unpaid reproductive labor—both within the family and in the workplace. Women are exploited as a low-wage and expendable reserve army of labor. Marxist feminists claim capitalism produces patriarchy that will end with capitalism's demise. Socialist feminists argue that patriarchy and capitalism are separate systems of oppression but that they do intersect. They call for economic and social change, specifically of relations within the family, as well as changing access to education, health care, economic opportunities, and political power.

Psychoanalytic feminism applies Freudian theories to gender inequality. It seeks to correct the male bias in psychoanalytic theory, producing theories that explore women's experiences with their emotions, bodies, and sexuality. Theorists argue that early childhood experiences shape women's psyches and create differences between men and women, especially because of the different roles of men and women within the family. They argue that the phallus, a symbol of male power, dominates Western culture. Solutions call for an androgynous society, possibly created through dual parenting.

Women of color criticize feminist theories for ignoring coexisting forms of oppression. This perspective includes black, Chicana, multicultural, and third world feminisms. They integrate analyses of gender oppression with systems of inequality based on race, class, gender, and sexuality. They show how privilege and disadvantage are built into a matrix of domination and intersect to produce unique forms of oppression. They advocate for remedies that focus on the survival of entire peoples rather than solely on women. Postcolonial feminism elaborates on intersectionality by emphasizing Western colonization. Here, sexism results from modernization and economic restructuring; it includes women's exploitation as workers and sexual beings. Postcolonial feminists focus on the roles of women as mothers within communities who can use their position to advocate for education of girls, adequate health care, and environmental protection.

Postmodern feminists avoid overarching causes or solutions of gender inequality and focus on plurality and difference. They challenge inevitable and fixed characteristics of gender, including heteronormativity (assumption that heterosexuality is "natural"), and the undifferentiated category of "woman." They argue that performativity—the repetition of gendered identity and display—perpetuates gender inequality. They advocate *queering,* a blending of gendered characteristics, and questioning "normal" forms of gender and sexuality as remedies for gender inequality.

Katherine Castiello Jones and Michelle J. Budig

See also Feminism; Standpoint Theory; Theory

Further Readings

Lorber, Judith. 2005. *Gender Inequality: Feminist Theories and Politics.* 3rd ed. Los Angeles: Roxbury.

Tong, Rosemarie. 1998. *Feminist Thought.* Boulder, CO: Westview.

Feminization of Poverty

The term *feminization of poverty* was first coined by Diana Pierce in 1976 in an attempt to describe the changing demography of the poor in the United States since 1960. Whereas the poverty rate for all families in the United States had declined quite rapidly (from 18.1 percent in 1960 to 9.4 percent in 1976), the number of female-headed households in poverty had dramatically increased (from 1.9 million households to 2.6 million households), and one third of all female-headed households were in poverty. The question became why a disproportionate number of the poor or near-poor (those between 100 percent and 125 percent of the poverty line) were women and their children, and how the demography of the poor had changed so swiftly.

One key explanation for the feminization of poverty in the early 1970s was a change in family structure, particularly in the number of female-headed households created by divorce. The divorce rate steadily climbed from the 1960s until 1979, and in divorces where children were involved, women were more likely to receive custody. Although many of the women were in the labor force, women earned on average about 62 percent of what men earned in the 1970s. This gender gap in income, coupled with the loss of male income, accounts for much of the rapid increase in the number of female-headed households falling into poverty. Although the divorce rate has declined since 1981, data from the 2000 census suggest that there were about 3.2 million female-headed households living in poverty; the poverty rate for female-headed households continued to be disproportionately high, around 25 percent.

At the same time that divorce created more female-headed households, births to unmarried women became more pervasive in the United States. In 1960 about 6 percent of all births were to unmarried couples, but by 1996, over a third of births were to unmarried couples, with the largest increase among black families. While black women are more likely to be unmarried mothers than are white women, the trend of more births to unmarried women is similar across racial and ethnic lines. Black female-headed households are more likely to be in poverty than are white female-headed households. This disparity is related to historical differences in access to good jobs and residential segregation, both resulting in part from racism and discrimination.

The feminization of poverty is not solely the experience of single women and their children. The elderly compose a nontrivial proportion of the poor or near-poor, with elderly women disproportionately represented. Although the poverty rate among the elderly has been declining as a result of federal programs such as Social Security and Medicare, elderly women do not accrue the same benefits as do elderly men, especially if those women are divorced and did not remarry. On average, women born before 1930 have limited work histories, thus having contributed little to Social Security and having less access to pension benefits. Widowed women could expect access to their husbands' benefits; divorced women could not. Longer life expectancy among women, as well as an increased desire to live independently, place elderly women at a greater risk of living at or near the poverty line.

The U.S. government implemented many policies with the goal of reducing poverty, some of which were targeted toward women and children. Early means-tested welfare policies, such as Aid to Families with Dependent Children (AFDC), provided cash transfers to low-income mothers caring for their children that could be used for housing, food, or other expenses. Temporary Assistance to Needy Families replaced AFDC in 1997, but the goal of the program is generally the same: to provide temporary aid to families caring for children as the caretakers search for employment, acquire additional skills, and more generally, work to move out of poverty. Medicaid is a means-tested program that provides access to medical care for the poor. Comprehensive child support enforcement legislation has been implemented by the federal government as well as in many states. This legislation works to ensure that children who deserve financial support from a nonresidential parent have access to that support, with the goal of reducing the need for support from the federal (and state) government. As noted earlier, Social Security benefits and Medicare are governmental programs that have helped elderly women move out of poverty.

As women and children continue to be disproportionately represented among the poor, social scientists have suggested other policies and policy reforms that target the proximate causes of poverty. Policies that encourage a strong and growing economy that includes well-paying jobs with benefits will help reduce poverty overall, not just among women and children. Low-cost, high-quality child care would allow women to work while providing safe caregiving environments for children. Policies encouraging the building of affordable housing, offering affordable health care, and providing access to education and skills training will also work to stem the tide of families moving into poverty.

Shannon N. Davis

See also Aid to Families with Dependent Children; Divorce; Gender Gap; Poverty; Temporary Assistance for Needy Families; Wage Gap; Widowhood; Working Poor

Further Readings

Casper, Lynne M., Sara S. McLanahan, and Irwin Garfinkel. 1994. "The Gender-Poverty Gap: What We Can Learn from Other Countries." *American Sociological Review* 59:594–605.

Christopher, Karen, Paula England, Sara McLanahan, Katherine Ross, and Tim Smeeding. 2001. "Gender Inequality in Poverty in Affluent Nations: The Role of Single Motherhood and the State." Pp. 199–220 in *Child Well-being, Child Poverty and Child Policy in Modern Nations*, edited by K. Vleminckx and T. Smeeding. London: Policy Press.

McLanahan, Sara S. and Erin L. Kelly. 1999. "The Feminization of Poverty: Past and Future." Pp. 127–45 in *Handbook of the Sociology of Gender*, edited by J. Chafetz. New York: Plenum.

Tomaskovic-Devey, Donald, ed. 1988. *Poverty and Social Welfare in the United States*. Boulder, CO: Westview.

FERTILITY

Fertility is the process of producing live births. Because of their roles in shaping population dynamics and change, fertility, migration, and mortality are central concepts in the field of demography. Demographic transition theory attempts to trace populations as they move from high or low birth and high or low death rates; however, researchers now recognize that the process is more complicated than the theory suggests.

While counting births can be straightforward, exposure to the risk of becoming pregnant is not universal, complicating the denominator in measures of fertility. Although both men (or at least sperm) and women are necessary to create a live birth, measurement is simplified by relating fertility to one sex, usually women. The crude birth rate, a basic measure, counts the number of live births per 1,000 women of childbearing age (usually 15–49 years old) in the population of interest. The age-standardized fertility rate and total fertility rate (TFR) are two measures that directly account for age variation in fertility. The proximate determinants framework attempts to quantify a woman's exposure to the risk of becoming pregnant as it varies by four factors: marital/union status (exposure to sexual intercourse), postpartum infecundability (the inability to become pregnant directly after giving birth, as breast-feeding further slows the

return of menstruation), contraception use, and abortion (spontaneous and induced).

Fertility levels can be characterized in a number of ways. Populations with high birth rates are often referred to as those with natural fertility, suggesting that there is no conscious effort to control family size. Theoretically, women could begin childbearing in their mid-teens, having a child each year until their late 40s, resulting in 35 births. Yet, even in natural fertility populations like the Hutterites (United States/Canada) and the !Kung (Kalahari Desert), TFR was far below this biological maximum, at 10 to 12 and 4.5 births, respectively. Replacement fertility occurs when TFR is 2.1 (a woman has two children over her lifetime, thus replacing the children's parents; the one tenth accounts for child mortality under age 15). Today a number of countries, including many in Europe and East Asia, have total fertility rates below replacement: On average women have fewer than two children over their lifetime.

Fertility research often focuses on (a) ways populations control family size, (b) access to and unmet need for modern contraception, and (c) understanding changing fertility levels. An interest in fertility control through natural and modern contraception and the processes behind fertility decision making drives a number of quantitative and qualitative studies in diverse populations. For example, the World Fertility Surveys (60+ countries, 1974–86) and the Demographic and Health Surveys (mid-1980s–present, 70+ countries, many with multiple surveys) provide data to explore some of these issues. Understanding the influence of gender dynamics and social contexts on fertility and the impact of emerging reproductive technologies are central to future understandings of fertility and infertility.

Enid Schatz

See also Abortion; Birth Rate; Contraception; Demographic Transition Theory; Population Growth; Total Fertility Rate

Further Readings

International Family Planning Perspectives [Journal]. (http://www.guttmacher.org/journals/aboutper.html).

Poston, Dudley L. and Michael Micklin, eds. 2005. *Handbook of Population*. New York: Springer.

Studies in Family Planning [Journal]. (http://www.blackwell publishing.com/journal.asp?ref=0039-3665&site=1).

FETAL ALCOHOL SYNDROME

Fetal alcohol syndrome (FAS) is a cluster of birth defects related to prenatal alcohol exposure. There are four diagnostic criteria for FAS: prenatal and/or postnatal growth deficiency, central nervous system abnormalities (most typically mental retardation), a set of characteristic craniofacial features, and confirmed maternal alcohol use during pregnancy. Estimates of the prevalence of FAS vary widely, in part because there is no gold standard for recognizing a child affected by FAS. In the United States, the Centers for Disease Control and Prevention estimate that FAS affects 0.2 to 1.5 births per 1,000. FAS tends to be concentrated among minority and disadvantaged populations. For example, in the United States the reported prevalence of FAS is highest among African Americans and American Indians. Reports of FAS are particularly prevalent in South Africa, in Russia, and among Native Peoples of Canada. However, numerous studies have documented both overdiagnosis and underdiagnosis of FAS in certain population groups. Moreover, FAS is subject to ascertainment bias, meaning that physicians may be more inclined to see it in some groups than in others.

Not all women who drink heavily during pregnancy have babies with FAS; the syndrome is correlated with poverty, race/ethnicity, advanced maternal age, and high number of children. Researchers have hypothesized that factors such as nutritional status, exposure to environmental toxins, smoking, and stress may exacerbate the adverse effects of alcohol. Despite widespread public belief that any alcohol exposure during pregnancy is dangerous, there is considerable uncertainty about the exact etiology of FAS. Binge drinking (the consumption of five or more drinks in a single episode) is highly correlated with FAS.

In 1973, physicians at the University of Washington discovered FAS, based on similar defects observed among eight children of alcoholic mothers. Over the past several decades the diagnosis has expanded to include categories such as "fetal alcohol effect," "alcohol-related birth defects," and "alcohol-related neurodevelopmental disorder." There are no clear diagnostic criteria for these labels.

Governments around the world have responded in disparate ways to the policy issues raised by FAS. In the United States the surgeon general first issued a warning advising pregnant women not to drink in 1981 (updated in 2004), and congressionally mandated warning labels have appeared on all alcoholic beverages since 1989. Rates of FAS have not decreased since implementation of these measures. European countries tend to have more permissive attitudes about prenatal alcohol use, whereas drinking during pregnancy is today a highly stigmatized behavior in the United States. South Dakota and Wisconsin permit civil detention of women who drink during pregnancy; several states have brought criminal charges against women whose babies have allegedly been born with FAS or a related diagnosis. None of these prosecutions has been successful.

Elizabeth Mitchell Armstrong

See also Alcoholism; Binge Drinking; Social Control

Further Readings

Armstrong, Elizabeth M. 2003. *Conceiving Risk, Bearing Responsibility: Fetal Alcohol Syndrome and the Diagnosis of Moral Disorder.* Baltimore: Johns Hopkins University Press.

Bertrand, Jacquelyn, R. Louise Floyd, and Mary Kate Weber. 2005. "Guidelines for Identifying and Referring Persons with Fetal Alcohol Syndrome." *Morbidity and Mortality Weekly Report* 54(RR-11):1–14.

FETAL NARCOTIC SYNDROME

Fetal narcotic syndrome refers to the effects on the fetus and newborn of exposure to illicit substances—particularly cocaine, crack cocaine, and heroin—during pregnancy. Narcotic use during pregnancy poses risks to both the woman and the fetus, including miscarriage, poor fetal growth, placental problems, premature delivery, low birth weight, and stillbirth. In addition, infants born after exposure to drugs may develop symptoms of withdrawal, including excessive crying, irritability, trembling, and breathing or gastrointestinal problems. These symptoms, known as "neonatal abstinence syndrome," are short-lived. National surveys find that about 4 percent of pregnant women in the United States report using illicit drugs. In contrast, about 18 percent of pregnant women report smoking cigarettes. Women ages 15 to 25 are substantially more likely than women ages 26 to 44 to use illicit drugs during pregnancy.

The mass media, health care workers, and legislators became particularly concerned about the consequences of prenatal drug use during the crack cocaine epidemic in the 1980s. Initial reports suggested that infants born after prenatal exposure to crack cocaine, labeled "crack babies" by the media, suffered permanent brain damage and lifelong behavioral problems, raising fears of a generation of unteachable children in the inner cities. However, more thorough epidemiological research later established that children exposed to cocaine and other drugs in utero do not suffer lasting cognitive deficits. Moreover, many pregnant women who use illicit substances also use alcohol and tobacco and may experience extremely poor nutrition, sexual abuse, domestic violence, and homelessness. These factors make it difficult to discern the effect of narcotics alone on fetal development and birth outcomes.

The policy response to prenatal drug use has been mainly punitive. In the past 2 decades, more than 200 women in 34 states have been prosecuted in criminal courts for substance use during pregnancy. Many others have been jailed, faced charges of child endangerment or neglect in civil proceedings, or had their children removed from their care because they tested positive for drugs at the time of the birth. Some women have been prosecuted for murder after their babies were stillborn. The majority of women targeted by these policies are poor and nonwhite. Many child advocacy, public health, and medical organizations—including the March of Dimes, the American Public Health Association, the American Academy of Pediatrics, and the American College of Obstetricians and Gynecologists—oppose this criminal justice approach, arguing that it scares women away from prenatal care and other needed services.

Elizabeth Mitchell Armstrong

See also Addiction; Cocaine and Crack; Drug Abuse; Heroin; Social Control

Further Readings

Frank, Deborah A., Marilyn Augustyn, Wanda Grant Knight, Tripler Pell, and Barry Zuckerman. 2001. "Growth, Development and Behavior in Early Childhood following Prenatal Cocaine Exposure: A Systematic Review." *JAMA* 285(12):1626–28.

Gomez, Laura E. 1997. *Misconceiving Mothers: Legislators, Prosecutors, and the Politics of Prenatal Drug Exposure.* Philadelphia: Temple University Press.

Substance Abuse and Mental Health Administration (SAMHSA). 2005. "Substance Use during Pregnancy: 2002 and 2003 Update." The NSDUH Report, June 2. Research Triangle Park, NC: Office of Applied Studies, SAMHSA, and RTI International.

FLEXTIME

Flextime refers to an arrangement permitting full-time employees to negotiate hours of employment, allowing for an arrangement of the start and end times of the workday and workweek in such a way that they vary from the standard work schedule. Flextime arrangements benefit both the employee and the employer, as such programs resolve conflicts between work and family responsibilities with the intention of promoting productivity. Women are the main benefactors of flextime, as these programs offset family demands traditionally assigned to women.

As originally conceived, flextime policies aim at reducing the pressures on women to leave the labor market to bear and rear children. Through such policies, women would not be subject to derailed career paths, loss of wages, and lack of employment consideration as a result of family demands. Flextime policies thus create greater equity between men and women in the workplace.

Working women are not the only ones who benefit from flextime policies. Employers benefit from such programs in numerous ways. By controlling their own work schedules, employees can reduce the stress and distraction that comes from competing home and work responsibilities, thereby lowering tardiness and absentee rates. Accommodating schedules also result in lower turnover rates. Moreover, offering the option of flextime allows employers to be competitive in their hiring practices, making their company more attractive to potential employees and putting themselves in a better position to hire and retain valuable employees.

Flextime arrangements may be of a formal or informal nature, although formal flextime arrangements are more common in large organizations, with policies outlining flextime options and arrangements. Usually, employers make flextime available only to employees holding certain types of positions least affected by such an arrangement. Within smaller organizations, flextime arrangements are often worked out informally among a work group.

Studies of the impact of flextime arrangements on negative spillover, job satisfaction, and salary rates and parity between men and women are inconclusive. To the extent that women remain the primary responsible parties for home responsibilities and the ones more likely to take advantage of flextime, the policy seems to perpetuate much of the inequity it was designed to alleviate. Until flextime is seen as a viable option for men and women and the stigma associated with its use eliminated, the goal of reducing inequity in the workplace remains unattained.

Barbara Feldman

See also Income Disparity; Mommy Track; Second Shift

Further Readings

Giele, Janet Bollinger and Leslie F. Stebbins. 2003. *Women and Equality in the Workplace.* Santa Barbara, CA: ABC-CLIO.
Weeden, Kim A. 2005. "Is There a Flexiglass Ceiling? Flexible Work Arrangements and Wages in the United States." *Social Science Research* 34:454–82.

FOCUS GROUPS

A focus group includes either strangers or acquaintances and typically 8 to 12 participants.

Focus group interviewing is a valuable method for studying how particular categories of people think about social issues and social problems. The goal in such research is often to examine how claims making in the public arena influences the consciousness of particular categories of people.

As a research technique, the focus group has advantages and disadvantages relative to alternative approaches to the study of public opinion. In contrast to random sample surveys, focus groups (like other qualitative methods) enable the researcher to observe not just *what* people think and say but also *how* they think and say it. Thus, transcripts of focus group discussions can be analyzed for the constituent elements of everyday social problems talk, including media imagery, popular wisdom, and everyday personal experience. The technique thus permits analysis of how claims making in the public arena interacts with other factors in shaping how people think and feel relative to particular problems. However, focus groups do not constitute a random sample and therefore cannot be reliably generalized to total populations.

The focus group also has advantages and disadvantages relative to its qualitative cousins, the intensive interview and the ethnography. Ethnographies provide more naturalistic observations but are more time-consuming to conduct and provide fewer instances of relevant social problems talk. Intensive interviews enable greater attention to the views and experiences of particular individuals but serve as weaker indicators of how people talk in their everyday social groups. Located at a conceptual midpoint between the intensive interview and the ethnography, the focus group enables researchers to exercise control over the topic of conversation, while preserving certain elements of the naturally occurring social environment, including the gallery of peers.

In studies that do not compare subgroups, focus groups involve individuals with a particular trait or characteristic, for example, elementary school teachers, parents of young children, or baseball coaches. In studies that compare subgroups, the focus groups are generally homogeneous with respect to the variable under examination (e.g., race, marital status) and heterogeneous in relation to other variables. In general, groups should be added within each subcategory until the point of theoretical saturation (i.e., the point at which adding groups yields little additional information). To preserve the "insider" character of the discussion group, the moderator is typically attached to the group in relation to the critical research variable. The interview format tends to include relatively few open-ended questions (e.g., 4–6 questions for an hour-long discussion) rather than many short-answer questions. The interview format design also encourages free-flowing conversation among the discussion participants rather than between the moderator and the individuals in the group. Discussion prompts from the public discourse (i.e., campaign advertisements, political cartoons or posters) can help sharpen and focus the discussion. Discussions are typically recorded or videotaped and transcribed for subsequent analysis.

Theodore Sasson

See also Claims Making; Collective Consciousness; Ethnomethodology; Mass Media; Media; Public Opinion

Further Readings

Gamson, William. 1992. *Talking Politics*. New York: Cambridge University Press.

Morgan, David. 1996. "Focus Groups." *Annual Review of Sociology* 22:129–52.

FOOD INSECURITY AND HUNGER

Food security is access by all people in a population at all times to a reliable supply of food from socially acceptable sources sufficient for an active and healthy life. In contrast, *food insecurity* is the involuntary shortage of food due to economic constraints. When this food shortage progresses to the point that physical symptoms are felt, *hunger* occurs. Since the 1990s, these terms have largely come to replace a focus on *malnutrition*, a physiological condition that can arise from both shortages of food and disease processes. Worldwide, population levels of food insecurity tend to be associated with gross domestic product; within the United States, ethnic minorities and families with children have higher levels of food insecurity.

Hunger and food insecurity were rediscovered in the United States during the 1960s as physicians supported by the Field Foundation visited poor populations and reported widespread nutritional problems previously assumed to exist only in developing countries. These problems became the targets of Lyndon B. Johnson's War on Poverty. Federal resources were directed to programs to assist low-income families with job training, nutrition, and health care needs. These programs highlighted social inequality, particularly that linked to racial discrimination. Due to the activities of such programs as the Food Stamp Program, Head Start, and the Women, Infants, and Children feeding program, the prevalence of frank malnutrition was reduced, but it was replaced with food insufficiency that is chronic or cyclic in many poor households.

In the 1980s in developing countries, the discussion of food insufficiency was redefined. Experts noted that "famine" and "malnutrition" were not the same as food insufficiency, but rather, a complex range of factors kept households from having access to sufficient food. The change in focus to factors regulating access has been instrumental in producing national and international efforts to increase access.

In 1996, the Food and Agriculture Organization of the United Nations convened the World Food Summit. This summit affirmed poverty as the major source of food insecurity and its eradication as a critical step in reducing food insecurity. Participants set a goal of reducing food insecurity by one half by 2015 and acknowledged three core concepts—food availability, food access, and food utilization—each a necessary but not sufficient condition for the next. Cross-cutting these concepts is a set of risks (e.g., conflict, climatic fluctuations, job loss, and epidemic disease) that can disrupt any of the three cores. A second summit in 2002, called to assess the reasons for poor progress toward the 2015 goal, cited a lack of will by the signing countries. However, critics cited the need for "food sovereignty," the rights of poor countries to grow food for their own countries' consumption, rather than for export through multinational corporations. These proceedings highlight the web of factors that regulate availability, access, and utilization of foods: land ownership and control, access to credit for agricultural inputs, and national policies regarding food exports.

At the same time as efforts focused on economic development as a means of ensuring food access, private efforts in the United States focused on food banking, soup kitchens, and other means of providing emergency food to the poor. The number of such programs has increased dramatically since demand spiked with the recession of the 1980s. Food banks were established to receive surplus food supplies, gleaned produce, and food donated through local and national food drives. The food banks supply a wide network of public and private food pantries and soup kitchens, staffed by volunteer organizations that distribute food directly to those in need. Analysts point out that such programs have allowed contributors to believe they are helping to solve the problem of hunger, while not directly addressing the complex circumstances (e.g., low-wage employment, mental illness and drug addiction, social stratification, declining government support for social programs) that lead to household food insufficiency.

Measurement of Food Insecurity

Food insecurity has several core experiential domains common across cultures. They include uncertainty and worry, inadequate quality, insufficient quantity, and social unacceptability. The cross-cultural comparability of these domains makes it possible to construct questionnaires to measure food insecurity that make sense cross-culturally. Reflecting these domains, the U.S. Household Food Security Survey Module (HFSSM) contains 18 questions that measure levels of food insecurity in the United States. Since 1995, the annual Current Population Survey and other government-sponsored surveys have included it.

The HFSSM module is based on ethnographic research that indicates that food insecurity is a process managed by households. "Belt-tightening" measures such as changing to low-cost foods and reducing food variety occur before more extreme measures occur, such as decreasing meal size or skipping meals. The steps in this management process serve as the basis for the behaviors and experiences assessed by items in the HFSSM module. These include worrying that food will run out, cutting the size of meals, and feeding children before feeding adults. Research shows that these behaviors and experiences occur in a predictable order as households manage their declining food availability.

Changes in the interpretation and labeling of the HFSSM results were introduced in 2006. They included eliminating the terms *food insecurity* and *hunger*. Instead, households are labeled as being *food secure*, having *low food security*, and having *very low food security*. The intent of these changes is to reduce the confusion of food security as an economic concept with hunger, a physiological phenomenon.

Consequences of Food Insecurity

The experience of chronic food insecurity and hunger appears to have long-term consequences for physical health. Data from a variety of studies suggest that children and women in food-insecure households are more likely to be obese than those in food-secure households. Because most data on food insecurity and obesity are collected at the same time, it is difficult to establish causation. However, several suggested potential mechanisms may explain this association of food insecurity and obesity. Eating patterns of food-insecure families appear to be more binge-like, with food deprivation leading to greater overeating when food supplies are adequate. Analyses of food costs suggest that energy-dense foods of refined grains, fats, and added sugars cost less than less-dense foods such as fruits and vegetables. Thus, consumption of energy-dense food in poor households as a cost-saving measure may lead to overconsumption of calories and obesity.

Other effects of food insecurity on physical health are more difficult to measure. Elderly persons in the United States report making choices between purchasing food and medications. Seasonal variation in food insecurity, particularly for the elderly, has also been linked to costs of heating and, to a lesser extent, cooling, suggesting that households must pay for heating and cooling utilities rather than food.

Mental and social health has also been linked to food insecurity. Children from food-insecure households have problems in school, including greater anxiety and irritability, more absences, difficulty in learning, and lower grades and test scores. They are also more likely to be hospitalized.

Sara A. Quandt

See also Famine; Human Rights; Inequality; Living Wage; Poverty

Further Readings

Coates, Jennifer, Edward A. Frongillo, Beatrice Lorge Rogers, Patrick Webb, Parke E. Wilde, and Robert Houser. 2006. "Commonalities in the Experience of Household Food Insecurity across Cultures: What Measures Are Missing?" *Journal of Nutrition* 136:1438S–48S.

Drewnowski, Adam and Nicole Darmon. 2005. "Food Choices and Diet Costs: An Economic Analysis." *Journal of Nutrition* 135:900–904.

Food and Agriculture Organization of the United Nations. 2006. "The State of Food Insecurity in the World 2006." Rome, Italy: Food and Agriculture Organization of the United Nations. Retrieved December 12, 2007 (ftp://ftp.fao.org/docrep/fao/009/a0750e/a0750e00.pdf).

Nord, Mark, Margaret Andrews, and Steven Carlson. 2006. *Household Food Insecurity in the United States, 2005.* Economic Research Report No. 29. U.S. Department of Agriculture, Economic Research Service. Retrieved December 29, 2006 (http://www.ers.usda.gov/Publications/ERR29/ERR29.pdf).

Panel to Review the U.S. Department of Agriculture's Measurement of Food Insecurity and Hunger. 2006. *Food Insecurity and Hunger in the United States: An Assessment of the Measure,* edited by G. S. Wunderlich and J. L. Norwood. Washington, DC: National Academies Press.

Poppendieck, Jane. 1998. *Sweet Charity? Emergency Food and the End of Entitlement.* New York: Penguin.

Sen, Amartya K. 1981. *Poverty and Families: An Essay on Entitlement and Deprivation.* Oxford, England: Clarendon.

FOSTER CARE

The protection and nurturance of children is a universal goal shared by all human cultures. Children thrive best when they live in safe, stable, and nurturing families. However, many children in the United States lack this type of home environment. For these children whose families are not safe havens, a caring society needs to find alternative foster care placements.

Foster care refers to the system that provides protection for minor children who are unable to live with their biological parents. Currently there are over 500,000 children in foster care in the United States. The goal of the foster care system is to provide abused and neglected children with an environment of safety, permanency, and nurturance.

The Purpose of Foster Care

In many states the foster care system makes provisions for both voluntary and involuntary foster care. Voluntary foster care involves circumstances stemming from parental problems that render parents unable to care for their children (e.g., illness, substance abuse, AIDS, incarceration, or death) or from situations when a child's behavioral or physical problems require specialized treatment and parents are unwilling to care for their children.

Involuntary foster care requires the removal of children from their parents to ensure the children's safety. The children are usually victims of abuse or neglect whom the court removes from their homes and places in the state's custody. Young children tend to be placed in homes with foster families, while teens tend to be placed into residential facilities or group homes.

Children in Foster Care

Removal from their homes and placement into a foster care setting is both difficult and stressful for children. Although they come into foster care because of their exposure to serious abuse and maltreatment, family problems, and any number of risk factors, many children struggle with feelings of guilt and blame for being removed from their homes.

Many children also experience a sense of confusion, anxiety, stress, and loss. In addition, they may feel unwanted and helpless about their placement in a foster care setting; they may have difficulty attaching themselves to the many different foster parents they encounter as they move from one placement to another; and they may be insecure about their future. Prolonged and multiple foster care placements can contribute to negative outcomes for some of these children. For example, children—especially adolescents—who have been in foster care for an extended time have difficulty developing self-sufficiency and independence in adulthood.

Children need consistency, connectedness, and a sense of belonging to have a successful, healthy development. Providing a safe, stable, nurturing environment can bolster resilience and the short- and long-term adjustment of children.

Permanency Planning

The foster care system provides only a temporary living arrangement for vulnerable children to ensure their safety and well-being. Children remain in foster care placements until the problems that caused their removal are solved. Decisions made about the future for foster care children are called "permanency planning."

A successful resolution enables children to return home. However, if no successful resolution to the problem occurs, the court may terminate parental rights and free the children for adoption, or else provide long-term care with foster parents or relatives. Fortunately, more than half of children in the foster care system get reunited with their birth parents or primary caregivers. In addition, more than 2 million children live with grandparents or other relatives because they were not able to return to live with their parents.

Approximately half of the children in foster care spend at least 2 years in the system and one in five children remains in the system for 5 years or more. Some children in foster care move between families as many as seven times during their stay.

The Foster Care System

The number of children in the foster care system continues to increase. While the foster care system is essential in helping abused, abandoned, and neglected children, many children remain in foster care for long periods of time when family reunification or adoption is planned. Court delays can often extend the time between when children enter the foster care system and when they are placed into permanent homes.

Significant differences exist in the quality of care and outcomes for children depending on their race and ethnicity. The percentage of children of color in the foster care system is larger than the percentage of children of color among the general U.S. population. However, the occurrence of child abuse and neglect is at about the same rate in all racial/ethnic groups.

The foster care system tends not to be a cohesive system; it is a combination of many different intertwining agencies whose responsibilities include the provision of services, financial support, and other services to children and families. Many foster care agencies find themselves unable to provide adequate, accessible, and appropriate services for these children and families. In addition, many of these agencies have high caseloads and high staff turnover.

Over the past 40 years, an evolution occurred in the development of the U.S. policy that influences the protection, placement, and care of children in foster care. However, serious gaps still exist in areas such as the provision of adequate, accessible, and appropriate community-based services for families; the development and implementation of individualized service plans for birth parents; the provision of supportive training programs for foster parents; and the high caseloads of caseworkers. As society continues to struggle with problems such as poverty, violent crimes, substance abuse, HIV/AIDS, homelessness, and racism, the need for foster care services also continues to grow. Although the foster care system is not the most desirable parental option for a child, the system is an alternative that usually provides a safe, stable, and nurturing home for children who otherwise would be exposed to detrimental and traumatic circumstances.

Myra Robinson

See also Adoption; Adoption, Gay and Lesbian; Adoption, Transracial; Family

Further Readings

Courtney, Mark E., Richard P. Barth, Jill D. Berrick, Barbara Needell, and Linda Park. 1996. "Race and Child Welfare Services: Past Research and Future Directions." *Child Welfare* 75(2):99–137.

Kortenkamp, Katherine and Jennifer Ehrie. 2002. *Well-Being of Children Involved with the Child Welfare System: A National Overview.* Washington, DC: Urban Institute.

Roberts, Dorothy. 2001. *Shattered Bonds: The Color of Child Welfare.* New York: Basic Civitas Books.

U.S. Department of Health and Human Services, Administration for Children and Families. 2003. "Child Welfare Outcomes 2000." Washington, DC: U.S. Department of Health and Human Services.

FOSTER CHILDREN, AGING OUT

Foster care is one remedy for the social problem of child abuse, neglect, and dependency. Designed as a short-term solution to ensure the safety of children, critics have assailed foster care as creating additional social problems for children and families, including for young adults who transition out of foster care, referred to as "aging out." Children who age out of foster care reach the maximum age of service by the foster care system, 18 years of age in most states, or 21 for persons with developmental disabilities, or somewhere between 18 and 21 after completing high school.

Aging out becomes a social problem in the failure of the foster care system to secure permanent adoptive families for these children earlier, leaving them to become adults who have no permanent legal families. Children not successfully reunified with families of origin or alternative family members—such as an aunt, uncle, or grandparent—leave foster care, transition directly into adulthood, and lack placement with permanent families.

About 20,000 individuals age out of foster care each year. Their living conditions and outcomes, compared with those of individuals who have never experienced foster care placement, are typically worse. Because the foster care system seldom adequately prepares aging-out youth for independence, they often experience other social problems in adulthood and suffer lower levels of overall well-being compared with the general population.

The foster care system fails in several ways to prepare youth for independence. First, many people who age out of foster care complain that the initial reasons they were placed in foster care—child abuse, neglect, and dependency—were never adequately processed by the foster care system. Many complain that they were left to manage all of the psychological impact of experiencing child abuse and neglect by themselves. While the long-term effects of child abuse and neglect vary, the effects do tend to be negative. Those individuals who were provided counseling services for the effects of child abuse, neglect, and dependency frequently claim that the therapeutic approaches used by counselors were ineffective and that they struggled and still struggle with the long-term effects of child abuse, neglect, and dependency.

The foster care experience itself seems to be related to negative life outcomes for aged-out adults. It may be that reentry and drift impair independent living skills acquisition by interrupting both formal education and other important learning experiences, such as independent living skills training that would have more adequately prepared aging-out youth for independence. As a result, child welfare professionals have developed independent living skills training to better prepare older foster children for more successful transitions to adulthood. Although there are many foster care agencies providing excellent independent living skills training, many adults who have aged out of foster care indicate the training was inadequate because it relied on generic workbooks, was not community specific, did not require long-term learning by foster children, and was not ongoing long-term training.

Aged-out adults may contribute to other social problems in adulthood. Individuals who aged out of foster care are likely to move from foster care to public assistance. Indeed, aged-out adults are more likely to need public assistance over the life course compared with the general population. Thus, it appears that society pays high costs because many aged-out adults are not able to make it independently. This may be due to some other negative outcomes aged-out adults experience, such as lower levels of education, high unemployment, poverty, low-wage jobs, homelessness, and a disproportionate involvement in criminal activity. That is, they are more likely to be victims or perpetrators of violence and to serve jail time. Aged-out adults are also more likely, when compared with the general population, to experience young parenthood, divorce, and relationship instability.

Overall well-being is lower among people who have aged out of foster care than among the general population. For example, aged-out adults are more likely to experience depression and other mental health problems, lower self-esteem, lower aspirations for the future, lower levels of social support, less knowledge and understanding of family histories, and lower overall life satisfaction than the general population.

Aging out of foster care is therefore a social problem for many reasons. The inadequacy of the foster care system, the long-term impact of child abuse, neglect, and dependency, the overarching negative life outcomes experienced by aged-out adults, and their contributions to other social problems over the life course provide some evidence of the problematic nature of aging out of foster care. Aging out of foster care often generates difficulties that challenge aged-out adults throughout their lives.

It is important to note, however, that even though many individuals who have aged out of foster care experience fewer pro-social adult outcomes in general, many others can and do become successful adults. Furthermore, it is not clear that aged-out youths actually have worse adult outcomes than individuals who were reunified with family.

Donna Dea Holland

See also Abuse, Child; Foster Care; Poverty

Further Readings

Blome, W. W. 1997. "What Happens to Foster Kids: Educational Experiences of a Random Sample of Foster Care Youth and a Matched Group of Non-Foster Care Youth." *Child and Adolescent Social Work Journal* 14(1):41–53.

Buehler, Cheryl, John G. Orme, James Post, and David A. Patterson. 2000. "The Long-Term Correlates of Family Foster Care." *Child and Youth Services Review* 22(8):595–625.

Holland, Donna Dea. 2005. "A Life Course Perspective on Foster Care: An Examination of the Impact on Variations in Levels of Involvement in the Foster Care System on Adult Criminality and Other Indicators of Adult Well-Being." Ph.D. dissertation, Bowling Green State University, Bowling Green, OH.

FUNDAMENTALISM

Fundamentalism is the strict maintenance of ancient or fundamental doctrines of any religion. The term *fundamentalism,* though, was originally an Anglo-Saxon Protestant term applied to those who maintained that the Bible must be accepted and interpreted literally.

In popular usage, the term *fundamentalism* connotes both religious conservatism and traditionalism, and by extension, various strands of thought in politics, economics, government, and also scientific and academic perspectives that advocate strict adherence and maintenance of traditional perspectives in reaction against secularism and modernism. Although the term came into popular usage in the early 20th century, the concept and ideology trace back to early Christian and European history.

Origins and Purpose

As a movement, fundamentalism began in the United States as a Protestant movement to repel liberalism and developments perceived as threats to the purity, integrity, and authority of God's word as found in the Bible. In 1878, the Niagara Bible conference drew up 14 fundamentals of the faith, later reduced to five central doctrines: the inspiration and inerrancy of the Bible, the virgin birth, the physical resurrection of Jesus, the death of Christ as atonement, and the physical return of Christ to preside on Judgment Day. The resulting controversy ranged across all denominations, but it was most intense among Baptists and Presbyterians.

In the so-called monkey trial of 1925, a Tennessee teacher, J. T. Scopes, was found guilty of teaching evolution in public schools; other attempts to banish modernism and evolution from schools and society were unsuccessful. Unfavorable press reports quickly turned public opinion against fundamentalists, rendering their victory a short-lived one. Many dissociated themselves from the movement, not wanting to be labeled anti-intellectuals and fanatics. Gradually, the movement lost its cohesiveness and degenerated into splinter (independent) groups. From the late 1940s through the 1960s, fundamentalists redefined themselves in a movement known as neo-evangelicalism and sought broader participation within the U.S. political system. Billy Graham epitomized this new trend in evangelicalism.

Since the 1970s fundamentalists have reaffirmed their beliefs and initiated political actions to shape the nation accordingly. They used the ballot box, the airwaves, the mega-churches, and the power of the purse to restore what they saw as the unquestionable role of religion in society. Their position is that most

social institutions of today's secular society and most contemporary social issues—such as abortion, same-sex marriage, family and divorce, the spread of pornography, the ban on school prayer, homosexual lifestyle, feminism, gender equality, priesthood for women, and ordination of gay and lesbian ministers—are incompatible with religion. Consistently, they seek to include the teaching of creationism or "intelligent design" theory in public schools alongside evolution and to defeat politicians they view as liberals contributing to moral decadence in the nation. In their effort to reconstruct society, fundamentalists developed strategies that transcended borders. For example, Jerry Falwell, a fundamentalist Baptist minister, founded the Moral Majority in 1979, which enabled fundamentalist organizations to become a formidable force in U.S. politics. Together with other New Christian Right groups and political conservatives, fundamentalists supported the candidacy of Ronald Reagan and helped elect him president in 1980. Ever since then, they have influenced the U.S. political process.

Fundamentalism has its parallels in Islam, Judaism, Hinduism, and Buddhism in attracting followers reacting against secularization and modernism. Fundamentalism in Islam has a strong political component as Muslims view Islam as a comprehensive way of life, making their religion an integral part of politics, state, law, and society. The most influential fundamentalist movement was the Muslim Brotherhood, founded in 1928 by Hasan al-Banna as a reaction against the collapse of the Ottoman Empire and emergence of European imperialism. Sayyid Qutb was its most prominent thinker. A similar ideology underlines today's fundamentalist movement Al-Qaeda, headed by Osama bin Laden. Originally established in 1988 in Afghanistan as a resistance movement against Russian occupation, it had the support of Saudi Arabia, Pakistan, and the United States. In recent years Al-Qaeda has expanded globally and seeks to rid Muslim nations of all foreign elements and to reestablish the primacy of Islam.

Global Fundamentalism Today

Although fundamentalism has been a recurrent phenomenon in religious history, its recent characteristics are strident militancy, confrontation, and all too often, violence. Increasingly radicalized, fundamentalist extremists thus pose a serious threat, especially to developing nations and those experimenting with democracy.

The past 2 decades have witnessed continuous but steady growth in religious fundamentalism and revivalist movements. The growing Arab and Islamic presence in Europe, especially in Germany and France, once a bedrock of Christianity, has prompted concern among European Union nations. While seeking understanding of the emergence of fundamentalism, militancy, and extremism among many European Muslim groups, some Western nations also are asking if the time has come to take a defensive position.

Fundamentalism in the 21st century is a complex phenomenon characterized by several factors that combine socioeconomic and religiopolitical dimensions. Many traditionalist and conservative believers, including some of the better educated, deeply believe that they are in danger of losing their identity and culture because of the erosive forces of secularism and modernism. Thus, sparking today's resurgence in fundamentalism is a reaction against the social upheaval caused by globalization and technology. Fundamentalists view their world and belief system as falling deeper into moral and social decadence and believe that a return to the true religion in its orthodoxy would solve all social problems.

Because fundamentalism offers a simple solution to the complexities of many contemporary moral and social issues, it appeals to certain individuals and has the potential of mobilizing groups for action. As a movement attracting devout adherents, fundamentalism must be recognized as a major social force. Many fundamentalist groups view contemporary problems from a perspective quite different from other observers in their society.

Gabriel Maduka Okafor

See also Religion and Conflict; Religion and Politics; Religious Extremism

Further Readings

Armstrong, Karen. 2000. *The Battle for God: A History of Fundamentalism.* New York: Ballantine.

Marsden, George M. 1991. *Understanding Fundamentalism and Evangelicalism.* Grand Rapids, MI: Eerdmans.

Marty, Martin E. and R. Scott Appleby, eds. 1994. *The Fundamentalism Project.* Chicago: University of Chicago Press.

Watt, W. Montgomery. 1989. *Islamic Fundamentalism and Modernity.* London: Routledge.

G

GAMBLING

This is a vice which is productive of every possible evil, equally injurious to the morals and health of its votaries. It is the child of avarice, the brother of inequity, and father of mischief. It has been the ruin of many worthy families; the loss of many a man's honor; and the cause of suicide. . . . The successful gamester pushes his good fortune till it is overtaken by a reverse; the losing gamester, in hopes of retrieving past misfortunes, goes on from bad to worse; till grown desperate, he pushes at everything; and loses his all. In a word, few gain by this abominable practice (the profit, if any, being diffused) while thousands are injured.

—George Washington in a
letter to his nephew, January 15, 1783

The father of his country would be dismayed 225 years later to look upon his child. Legal lotteries in 41 states, horse racing in 43—these would have been familiar even to Washington. But the past quarter-century has seen an explosion in the availability of other forms of gambling, with full casinos legal in 10 states and on Indian lands in 16 others, card rooms in 5 states, and gambling machines (video poker, etc.) by the thousands in convenience stores and other locations in 6 states. And these are only the legal forms of gambling. Sports betting, at least 90 percent of it handled by illegal bookmakers, may run as high as $380 billion annually (the low-end estimate is closer to $80 billion). Most recently, the Internet has made all these forms of gambling available to anyone anywhere.

In assessing the impact of gambling, it is useful to distinguish between places—the neighborhoods, cities, or states where legalized gambling has taken hold—and people. After all, proponents of legalization have never argued that gambling benefits individuals, though subsequent advertising usually appeals precisely to that idea. Instead, they promote gambling as an economic enhancement to the general community. Lotteries and machines ("electronic gaming devices") would provide money for education and other worthwhile government projects; casinos would be the core of a tourist-like industry, reducing local unemployment, bringing money to other local businesses, and generally improving the local economy. Opponents argue that casinos would also have negative effects on the area, attracting crime and perhaps other illegal commerce, like prostitution and drugs.

The results of various forms of legalization are mixed. Revenues from lotteries, even when dedicated to education, often merely allow states to cut back on other sources of revenue, thus shifting the tax burden to lottery players, who come disproportionately from the ranks of the poor, the black, and the uneducated. Lotteries function in effect as a regressive tax. Casinos, however, do reduce unemployment (though this may not hold for tribal casinos), and casino jobs are generally good jobs, better than what these employees could get otherwise. Casinos raise the value of commercial property, especially property close to the casinos, but not residential property. Particularly for economically depressed areas, introduction of casinos can spark community renewal, but the net effect on business is not always like that of general tourism, with local restaurants and shops flourishing. Often the revitalization affects a narrow slice of the region, as the history of Atlantic City shows. Twenty years after the glitzy casinos opened, the number of bars and restaurants had fallen by 80 percent, and many of the businesses that survive more than a few steps from the casinos are pawn shops and other downscale establishments—the gold coast and the slum, with little in between.

As for the attendant problems of crime, and so on, evidence, especially evidence of direct causation, is lacking. Some gambling centers—for example, Atlantic City and Las Vegas—have high rates of property crime because, as in nongambling tourist areas, the hotel rooms, cars, and sometimes tourists themselves make attractive targets. The crimes committed by losing gamblers desperate for money are likely to be nonviolent—embezzlement mostly and check fraud—and do not have great impact on the localities. Nor is there evidence that gambling adds to other forms of social blight.

If gambling has not brought problems to the areas where it has been legalized and in some ways has brought benefits, the same cannot be said of its effects on gamblers themselves. Most people who gamble lose money—an outcome assured by the odds; over the long run, the house wins, and the gamblers, collectively, lose. Moreover, the games played most frequently, state lotteries, take out the largest house percentage. Still, most people who gamble say they do so for the enjoyment rather than to win money (71 percent vs. 21 percent) and see their losses as a cost similar to that of other forms of entertainment.

For some people, however, gambling becomes a problem. In a typical cycle, even if the gambler starts off winning, he or she eventually loses and then gambles more in hopes of getting even; further losses lead to attempts to recoup, with the gambler tapping into other sources of money—savings, money that should have gone for household expenses (mortgage, rent, food), then credit card debt, loans, and even crime, in a logical if insidious downward spiral. Attendant problems can include loss of job, bankruptcy, divorce, arrest, substance abuse, and suicide, all of which affect not just the gambler but also his or her family and others.

Estimating the incidence of this kind of gambling is difficult. Researchers must rely on self-reports of embarrassing, shameful, or even criminal behavior, and they must be somewhat arbitrary in defining the condition and selecting a time frame. Most analyses distinguish "problem" gambling from "pathological" gambling according to the number of criteria among the 10 listed in the authoritative *Diagnostic and Statistical Manual of Mental Disorders* (e.g., preoccupation, chasing, lying). Researchers also estimate both "lifetime" incidence (whether the person has *ever* been a problem or pathological gambler) and "past year" incidence. The population estimates for lifetime incidence range from 0.8 to 1.5 percent for pathological gambling; for problem gambling, estimates cluster around 3.5 percent. Past-year estimates are of course lower: 0.6 to 1.2 percent for pathological gambling and 1.9 to 3.7 percent for problem gambling. The difference between lifetime and past-year rates—anywhere from 50 percent to 300 percent—suggests that many or most problem gamblers overcome the problem, whether by self-reform programs or by just aging out. These incidence rates translate to anywhere from 3 to 8 million Americans with a gambling problem, numbers which are dwarfed by other addictions like alcohol and drugs but which still constitute a social problem.

Undoubtedly, some causes of problem and pathological gambling lie within the individuals, their psychology, and perhaps their brain chemistry. But gambling is affected by external, social factors, notably the availability of gambling, the structure of the game itself, and the social situation of the gambler.

As gambling has become more available, the number of problem gamblers has increased. Areas within 50 miles of casinos have double the prevalence of problem and pathological gamblers. Games where payouts come faster are more likely to "hook" gamblers. In the old days, a horse-race gambler had to wait a half hour between bets. Now, at a track, an off-track parlor, or even from home, one can bet legally on races at several different tracks, and at many tracks, one can play slot machines as well. Casino games (blackjack, craps, roulette) offer one payout per minute. At slot machines, video poker, and other electronic gaming devices, a player can make 10 to 12 plays per minute. More important, with these machines available in ordinary stores, gamblers do not have to make a special trip, as they would to a casino. One Las Vegas psychologist has called the machines the crack cocaine of gambling.

The Internet makes all forms of gambling even more available than video poker machines in 7-Eleven convenience stores. Several factors about Internet gambling suggest that it will increase problem gambling. Because of its newness, however, evidence of its impact is thin. The Internet offers gamblers every form of gambling except state lotteries. Internet gamblers can play at a variety of sites simultaneously at any hour and from any location—home, school, or work. The anonymity and privacy of the Internet allow the gambler to keep the problem secret. By contrast, brick-and-mortar casinos train staff to identify problem gamblers among customers and employees, and even illegal bookmakers may try to help the problem gambler, interventions that are impossible from Internet sites. Finally, the Internet is more accessible to young people, who are more at risk of becoming problem gamblers.

The crucial link for Internet gambling may well be the credit card companies. The most important factor allowing losing gamblers to become problem and pathological gamblers is access to credit. If credit card companies and Internet money transfer companies like PayPal limit or ban payments to gambling sites, players will find it much harder to chase after lost money. Such a ban was at the heart of the 2006 Unlawful Internet Gambling Enforcement Act (UIGEA), which targeted the link between offshore gambling sites and U.S. financial institutions. As of this writing, the impact of the UIGEA on gambling, both pathological and conventional, and on land-based casinos remains unknown.

Jay Livingston

See also Bankruptcy, Personal; Deviance; Values

Further Readings

American Gaming Association. 2006. "State of the States, the AGA Survey of Casino Entertainment." Retrieved December 26, 2007 (http://www.americangaming.org/assets/files/2006_Survey_for_Web.pdf).

National Gambling Impact Study Commission. 1999. "Final Report." Retrieved December 26, 2007 (http://govinfo.library.unt.edu/ngisc/reports/fullrpt.html).

National Research Council. 1999. *Pathological Gambling: A Critical Review.* Washington, DC: National Academies Press.

Pew Research Center. 2006. "Gambling: As the Take Rises, So Does Public Concern." Retrieved December 26, 2007 (http://pewresearch.org/assets/social/pdf/Gambling.pdf).

Shaffer, Howard J., Matthew N. Hall, and Joni Vander Bilt. 1997. *Estimating the Prevalence of Disordered Gambling Behavior in the U.S. and Canada: A Meta-analysis.* Boston: President and Fellows of Harvard College.

Washington, George. 1938. *The Writings of George Washington from the Original Manuscript Sources, 1745–1799*, vol. 26, p. 40, edited by J. C. Fitzpatrick. Washington, DC: U.S. Government Printing Office.

GANGS

Gangs composed of young persons, as distinct from organized criminal syndicates, arose in America by the mid-19th century and were a concern for city leaders from the time they first appeared. The first serious piece of research on the subject did not come until Frederic Thrasher's book *The Gang* was published in 1927. Since then, research on the subject has become quite prevalent.

Though not easily summarized, there appears to be consensus on two points. First, gangs are far more likely to be found in "disorganized communities." These would be places that have few, if any, homegrown institutions and groups to guide and constrain their residents, especially their young people, so they will behave in more "conventional" ways. A corollary of the disorganization hypothesis is that the people living in "disorganized communities" are likely to be members of a minority population, be overwhelmingly poor (or certainly not well-off), and have unclear or questionable values. Second, the only way to control gangs is to cut off the supply of members or break up the groups. Efforts to suppress gang activity often combine a variety of carrots (e.g., programs that attract youngsters to conventional groups and styles of behavior) and sticks (e.g., police harassment and incarceration). Sometimes the whole neighborhood or community at risk is the target of these initiatives. On other occasions, it is the gang or its members that are targeted.

Although local people sometimes help implement plans to discourage gang activities, it usually is outside agencies and experts that assume most of the responsibility for fashioning intervention strategies and carrying them out. That is because much of the money to support these programs comes from one or another federal, state, or local government agency, and the noncriminal residents inside the targeted "gang areas" are often thought to be almost as problematic as the gangs and their members. Be that as it may, most gang intervention programs have not been effective. In some cases, the use of repressive tactics actually emboldens gang members or makes gangs more attractive to young persons. In other instances, gang activity flares back up once programs intended to discourage gang activity or help children stay out of gangs are curtailed or, in the case of legal efforts to incarcerate gang members for a period of years, members are released from jail.

In the 1990s there was a renewed sense of urgency to do something about youth gangs. That is because many new minority populations arrived in urban areas, and their children formed gangs that both mimicked and diverged from gangs formed by earlier ethnic groups. Although not as much is heard today, as compared with the end of the 20th century, about gangs like the "Crips" and "Bloods," those organizations are still out there, and new gangs and confederations of local gangs have emerged in the 21st century. Armed with even bigger weapons and seemingly less concerned than ever about the havoc they create in the neighborhoods where they are located, contemporary gangs are considered every bit as dangerous as, and perhaps even more indiscriminately violent than, their late 20th-century counterparts.

Historically, some gangs have had a "gang tradition" in a particular neighborhood where several generations of gang members are tied to members of their own families and closest neighbors (e.g., in some Hispanic and Chinese gangs). Others have been more independent and not as well tied in to the ongoing routines of their community or its conventional adult-run groups (e.g., gangs composed of African American youth and more recent Asian immigrants). Some, like many white working-class gangs rooted in older ethnic enclaves, have a tradition of defending their neighborhood against "outsiders." Others, like the drug-dealing gangs affiliated with the Crips or Bloods, are viewed more as predators than defenders of their community. There are ample variations around each of these patterns, to be sure, with gangs sometimes being more protective of the people living around them and on other occasions holding people as virtual hostages in their own neighborhood.

Other changes in gangs occurred in the late 20th century. Girls are now creating their own gangs instead of serving as the female auxiliary to boy gangs. Gangs have also appeared in suburbs and even small towns located some distance from any large city. Some gangs are now more deeply involved than ever in serious illegal activities; use deadly force to solidify their control over an area more readily than they did earlier in the 20th century; and are more mobile, too. In short, the number and variety of gangs has grown, and there appears to be little that can be done to curtail them much less remove them from most of the communities where they take root. One well-known expert at the end of the 20th century had grown so despondent over the prospect of finding any intervention strategy that would work that he recommended abandoning the pretense of trying to curtail gang activity in major urban centers and focusing instead on smaller cities where gangs were just beginning to emerge.

To the degree that gang experts are right (and there is plenty of evidence to suggest that their assessment of the spread of gangs is not wildly exaggerated), something important is going on in American culture. To begin, it would seem that the social disorganization hypothesis is either wrong or now can be extended to cover virtually every kind of American community. On its face, the latter explanation seems implausible. True, American intellectuals at the tail end of the 20th century and the beginning of the 21st were prone to see American culture as worn out, if not altogether corrupted, and its civic routines as being suspect. At the same time, however, most Americans were not moving to small, out-of-the-way places or out of the country, and those who did were not making those moves to escape youth gangs.

There is an alternative explanation for what has been going on in American civic life and with American youth. Basically, civic routines and values may not be as worn down as social critics imagine, and young men and women, boys and girls may not be as problematic as many observers think. By extension, youth gangs would not be so alien a creation as people have been led to believe.

The foundation of this alternative way of looking at youth gangs is laid in the work of American scholars who have studied the rise of different kinds of unscripted and disruptive forms of civil unrest (e.g., mobs, protest marches, boycotts, and gangs) in European history. It turns out that virtually all these seemingly unscheduled and upsetting displays of public discord and the groups that use them are not as irrational, unorganized, and threatening as many persons have theorized and feared. Indeed, these activities have many features in common with those undertaken by more conventional groups, meet similar needs for their members, and do not discourage members from becoming "normal" adults. The boundary line between conventional and unconventional groups, individuals, and behavior is a lot fuzzier and easier to cross than had been imagined.

That is why so many youngsters "mature out" of gangs as they age. Most young people who live in communities with gangs do not belong to such groups, even though they may be on very good terms with youngsters who are. And most young people who join gangs do not become career criminals; rather, they grow up and out of gangs and move into more conventional adult roles like "employee" or "parent."

Gangs fit in this cultural landscape in a very important and telling way. Over the past 200 years, they have managed to change or keep up with the ways other unconventional groups have changed and managed to "fit in" with the larger, more conventional culture. They do this by combining elements of so-called primitive forms of corporate action (e.g., feuds and brawls) with "reactionary" kinds of civic disturbances (e.g., hostility toward "outsiders," particularly powerful outsiders, who might threaten customary ways of doing things) and, more recently, more "modern" types of corporate action (e.g., labor and union unrest) that are designed to garner new resources and rights for those groups initiating the actions. Gangs cannot be compared to labor unions or political parties. However, many contemporary youth gangs mimic modern corporations by forming far-reaching confederations and making lots of money, even as they defend their market or "turf" with a great deal of seemingly "primitive" brawls and feuds. It is the act of combining different kinds of unconventional and even violent behavior in the same groups that distinguishes Americans' use of disruptive community acts from those thought to be used by Europeans, which and has rendered them more conservative and less upsetting of the status quo than their European counterparts.

Contemporary youth gangs carry on the European tradition of forming age-segregated youth cliques. They do this by providing their members with opportunities to make their presence felt and their arrival as full-fledged "adults" known to a much larger and potentially indifferent public. Gang members, like teenagers generally, have presented themselves increasingly in adult-like ways, like assuming the right to take a life, despite being unprepared to accept the responsibilities that come with the assumption of such prerogatives. Thus, in their stylized dress, ritualistic declarations of brotherhood, indecipherable graffiti, harshly violent ways, and crude capitalization of home-grown entrepreneurs, contemporary youth gangs are, in a broadly cultural sense, a cruel parody of 18th- and 19-century male fraternities.

The point is not to dismiss the dangerous activities and harm that a gang does or to embrace gang members' views of the world; it is rather to appreciate the ways in which gangs and gang members fit into a long and surprisingly conservative tradition in the uses of group violence and displays of public bravado. It also is to recognize this singularly important way in which young people from very different backgrounds and in all kinds of communities have come to assume the rights and prerogatives of adults without being prepared by adults to accept the obligations and consequences that come with such privileges.

From what is known about the conduct of gangs and gang members in different settings, several conclusions can be drawn about the relation between gangs and the communities in which they are rooted. First, communities with relatively stable working-class or lower-middle-class populations have fewer gangs, and the gangs they have act in more restrained ways. Second, communities with a lower *or* higher economic profile and less stability in their population (i.e., people move in and out with great frequency) have more gangs, or the gangs they have act out in less-restrained ways.

What stands out most clearly about the relation between gangs and the communities where they are found is that the wealth and status of the persons living there are not the most critical factors in determining how gangs will act. What matters most is the ability and willingness of adults working through informal groups, voluntary organizations, and local businesses to engage their young people in more constructive ways. This is the most effective gang intervention strategy. It will not "save" every youngster, but it will make the transition between childhood and adulthood smoother and kinder than it has been for many young people.

The frightening thing about this assessment is that social scientists had very strong hints that this was the case as early as Frederic Thrasher's pioneering study of youth and adult gangs in 1920s Chicago. Millions of dollars have been spent since then in efforts to create more and better ways to suppress gang activity and lead gang members down a more conventional path to adulthood. The irony is that even as more and more expensive remedies (which ultimately do not work) are suggested and tried, the answer—having adults engage youth in more constructive ways—continues to be ignored.

Daniel Joseph Monti

See also Violence

Further Readings

Cummings, Scott. 1998. *Left Behind in Rosedale*. Boulder, CO: Westview.

Cummings, Scott and Daniel Monti. 1993. *Gangs: The Origins and Impact of Contemporary Youth Gangs in the United States*. Albany, NY: State University of New York Press.

Matza, David. 1964. *Delinquency and Drift*. New York: Wiley.

Monti, Daniel. 1994. *Wannabe: Gangs in Suburbs and Schools*. Oxford, England: Blackwell.

———. 1996. "Gettin' Right with Humpty: Or How Sociologists Propose to Break Up Gangs, Patch Broken Communities, and Make Scary Children into Conventional Adults." *Free Inquiry in Creative Sociology* 24:133–43.

———. 1997. "On the Relation between Gangs and Social Organization." *Free Inquiry in Creative Sociology* 25:3–8.

GANGSTA RAP

Gangsta rap is a subgenre of hip-hop music which emerged in South Central Los Angeles and Compton during the 1980s. N.W.A., Ice-T, DJ Quik, and others rapped about urban poverty, police brutality, unemployment, gang violence, drugs, prostitution, and other social problems in the inner city. Today, gangsta rap has grown into a multibillion-dollar industry and has become a part of popular culture. At the same time, opponents of gangsta rap also grew in numbers and influence. Several critics have argued that gangsta rap celebrates violence and misogyny, initiating a debate over its merits and consequences that still continues.

It is important to understand the broader social conditions from which gangsta rap emerged. During the 1980s, inner-city communities were devastated by deindustrialization and the rise of a service sector economy. Many working-class blacks lost their jobs and could not find employment when manufacturing plants closed. These trends were particularly visible in inner-city Los Angeles, which experienced record highs in unemployment and crime during the 1980s and 1990s.

Gangsta rap reflects many of these themes. Los Angeles– and Compton-based groups like N.W.A. and South Central Cartel and solo artists like MC Eiht rap about street violence in their neighborhoods. Others, such as Ice-T, DJ Quik, and Eazy-E, rapped about pimping and the emergence of an underground economy in "the hood." Many of the same themes continue in today's generation of rappers. For example, Snoop Dogg and The Game carry on the legacies of previous gangsta rappers.

Negative Responses to Gangsta Rap

The growth of gangsta rap also fueled different social responses. Several journalists decried gangsta rap, arguing that it has a negative effect on today's youth. Similarly, in the 1990s former civil rights advocate and (then) president of the National Congress of Black Women, C. Delores Tucker, led a crusade against gangsta rap, arguing that it encouraged violence and misogyny among youth. This resulted in a series of court cases against record labels for distributing controversial rap albums.

Law enforcement also responded negatively to the commercial rise of gangsta rap. Many saw gangsta rap as a threat to mainstream U.S. values. In 1989, N.W.A. released their second album, "Straight Outta Compton," which contained several critiques of the police. In particular, "Fuck the Police" described the inner-city black community's sense of alienation and frustration with local police and other institutions. The Federal Bureau of Investigation (FBI), however, did not see this song and others as valid social commentary. In the same year, the FBI sent critical letters to Ruthless and Priority Records about N.W.A.'s lyrics.

Some academics also criticize gangsta rap. Public health researchers argue that exposure to gangsta rap increases the likelihood one will engage in "risky behaviors" such as premarital sex, drug abuse, and other anti-social behaviors. Black feminists such as bell hooks argue that gangsta rap essentializes blackness by perpetuating the image of violent, over-sexed, and misogynistic black men. Others criticize gangsta rap for encouraging youth to reject mainstream values, some linking black underachievement in schools to the negative values promoted in gangsta rap music. The underlying assumption is that gangsta rap socializes youth away from the mainstream and encourages them to adopt anti-social or oppositional behaviors.

The Social Merits of Gangsta Rap

While the lyrics in gangsta rap are controversial, some argue that they shed light on social problems—poverty, violence, drugs, and gangs—that occur in the inner city. In addition, hip-hop sympathizers argue that critics misunderstand gangsta rap's message. Detractors often take lyrics about violence and misogyny literally and rarely acknowledge the playful and ironic nature of gangsta rap. Although often characterized as such, gangsta rap is not an aberration in urban black culture. Indeed, rap music draws from black nationalist ideology and black oral traditions such as playing "the dozens," signifyin', and other informal communicative practices.

Gangsta rap also provides an alternative space for individuals to express their political, economic, and social frustrations. Despite its portrayal by critics as a uniformly negative musical culture, gangsta rap also discourages individuals from the street life. Some, like Ice Cube, encourage young blacks to think critically about racialized struggles over space and political power in the United States. Others claim that their music informs the general public about issues that communities of color face.

Whichever side one takes, gangsta rap has left an indelible mark on popular culture. Record sales continue to grow each year, gangsta rappers continue to branch out into other kinds of media, and scholars continue debating the consequences and merits of gangsta rap. As it grows in visibility and importance, it becomes important to move beyond simple caricatures of gangsta rap.

Jooyoung Lee

See also Black Nationalism; Deindustrialization; Gangs; Police

Further Readings

Alim, H. Samy. 2006. *Roc the Mic Right: The Language of Hip Hop Culture.* New York: Routledge.

Chang, Jeff. 2005. *Can't Stop Won't Stop: A History of the Hip Hop Generation.* New York: St. Martin's.

Forman, Murray. 2000. "'Represent': Race, Space and Place in Rap Music." *Popular Music* 19(1):65–90.

Henderson, Erol A. 1996. "Black Nationalism and Rap Music." *Journal of Black Studies* 26(3):308–39.

hooks, bell. 1994. *Outlaw Culture: Resisting Representations.* New York: Routledge.

Martinez, Theresa A. 1997. "Popular Culture as Oppositional Culture: Rap as Resistance." *Sociological Perspectives* 40(2):265–86.

McWhorter, John. 2005. *Winning the Race: Beyond the Crisis in Black America.* New York: Penguin.

Quinn, Michael. 1996. "Never Shoulda Been Let out the Penitentiary": Gangsta Rap and the Struggle over Racial Identity." *Cultural Critique* 34:65–89.

Richardson, Jeanita W. and Kim A. Scott. 2002. "Rap Music and Its Violent Progeny: America's Culture of Violence in Context." *The Journal of Negro Education* 71(3):175–92.

GATEWAY DRUGS

The term *gateway drugs* suggests that low-classified drugs are precursors to use of addictive and dangerous "hard" drugs. This theory originated in 1975 as a response to concerns that cannabis use leads to the use of harder drugs, such as heroin and cocaine. Leading gateway theorists statistically substantiated the relationship between marijuana and the use of other illegal drugs as well as the relationship between the use of licit drugs (alcohol and cigarettes) and illicit ones (marijuana and cocaine). The researchers found that licit drug use of either alcohol or cigarettes precedes the use of marijuana, and marijuana use precedes the use of other illegal drugs. The identification of this pattern led to the designation of alcohol, cigarettes, and marijuana as "gateway" drugs.

Determining the order in which respondents used the drugs (the sequencing of drug use) was an important aspect of these studies, as it positioned the use of drugs that appear early in the sequence as causal factors to further drug use. However, many other analysts challenge that causal presumption. An association does not mean cause. To illustrate, most bank robbers drink coffee and smoke cigarettes, but this does not mean that caffeine and nicotine cause robbery.

In two follow-up studies of this cohort in 1984 and 1992, the researchers found that the proportion of men and women (in the sample) who had used illicit drugs increased by 30 to 50 percent respectively, substantiating their general findings that drug use is progressive and that initiation into the use of gateway drugs might lead to a lifetime of drug use. The authors found that the *age* of initiation to gateway drugs was related to further progression of drug use. Men and women who first consumed alcohol or cigarettes at the age of 14 or under remained at that stage in the progression as compared with those who were initiated at age 16 or over, substantiating the progression thesis of the scientists. The *extent* of drug use in the early part of the progression was also correlated to the rate of drug use later in the respondents' lives. Furthermore, the researchers found that males were more likely to use alcohol before cigarettes and marijuana, and women were more likely to use *either* alcohol or cigarettes before marijuana. Alcohol played a greater role for men in the progression. The use of medically prescribed drugs followed the delineated sequence. Over 60 percent of respondents who used medically prescribed drugs used legal and illegal drugs at least 10 times in their lifetime.

In contrast, a 12-year University of Pittsburgh study released in 2006 challenged the findings of gateway theorists by revealing that the sequential progression of the gateway hypothesis was inconsistent in a population of 214 boys, ages 10 to 12. The researchers found that a significant number of the young boys used harder, more dangerous drugs before they smoked marijuana or smoked cigarettes or drank alcohol. Because each stage of drug-use progression in the gateway theory hypothesis is a component of both a temporal and a hierarchical sequence, the University of Pittsburgh study challenged the causal relationships between licit and illicit drugs as well as the hysteria surrounding the smoking of marijuana. As part of their study, the researchers compared a set of boys who had followed the gateway sequence (used tobacco or cigarettes first and then used marijuana) with a set of boys who followed a reverse sequence (used marijuana first and then smoked cigarettes or drank alcohol) and found no relationship between either of these patterns and the development of a substance abuse disorder. In other words, neither of these patterns can predict the probability of continued drug use. Instead the researchers hypothesized and statistically proved that environmental factors, such as drug availability in the neighborhood, and individual factors, such as a predisposition for delinquency, play critical roles in the progression toward substance abuse. The boys were compared on 35 variables measuring psychological, family, peer, school, and neighborhood characteristics. Given the fact that gateway theory has strongly influenced anti-drug policies and informed clinical approaches to drug prevention in the United States, the findings of the University of Pittsburgh study shift away the focus from marijuana as a gateway drug and toward a behavioral and structural approach focusing on early socialization, individual and familial predisposition, and neighborhoods as precursors of a lifetime of drug abuse.

Proponents of the decriminalization of marijuana movement heavily criticize gateway theory. Legalization advocates argue that there is an unwarranted hysteria surrounding marijuana use and that marijuana does not predict the progression to harder drugs. They further argue that mediating the statistical relationships that legitimate gateway theory are factors such as the illegality of marijuana, which sensitizes marijuana users to a world of illegal drugs. In other words, it is the act of criminalizing pot smokers rather than the pharmacological properties of the drug itself or its assumed insidious nature that is the gateway to harder drugs. Nevertheless, institutions such as the National Center on Addiction and Substance Abuse at Columbia University, the Partnership for a Drug-Free America, Drug Watch, the Food and Drug Administration, and the White House Office of National Drug Control Policy have embraced gateway theory as a conceptual foundation for their research and public advocacy.

Vaso Thomas

See also Club Drugs; Drug Abuse; Drug Subculture; Marijuana; Smoking

Further Readings

Kandel, Denise, Kazuo Yamaguchi, and Kevin Chen. 1992. "Stages of Progression in Drug Involvement from Adolescence to Adulthood: Further Evidence for the Gateway Theory." *Journal of Studies on Alcohol* 53:447–57.

National Center on Addiction and Substance Abuse. 1994. *Cigarettes, Alcohol, Marijuana: Gateway to Illicit Drug Use.* New York: National Center on Addiction and Substance Abuse at Columbia University.

Tarter, Ralph, Michael Vanyukov, Levent Kirisci, Maureen Reynolds, and Duncan B. Clark. 2006. "Predictors of Marijuana Use in Adolescents before and after Licit Drug Use: Examination of the Gateway Hypothesis." *The American Journal of Psychiatry* 163(12):2134–40.

GENDER BIAS

Gender bias refers to the socially constructed preference for one sex/gender over the other. The practice of gender bias can be unconscious or conscious. For example, in a grade school classroom, a teacher (female or male) can be gender biased by calling on young boys more than young girls to answer questions or to encourage boys' participation in class discussion. The teacher's gender bias may stem from the belief that male students might have more to contribute to the classroom environment than females. As a social problem, gender bias can appear in various social contexts: the educational system, the work environment and economy, families, the criminal justice system, politics, religion, and medicine. Even how spoken and written language is structured reflects gender bias, such as use of the pronoun *he* as the generic word to represent both men *and* women. Although instances occur where gender bias favors females over males (e.g., mothers awarded child custody instead of fathers in divorce proceedings), research shows that gender bias disproportionately affects women, mainly because of the patriarchal system embedded within the social structure of a given society.

Gender-Based Stereotypes

Notably, gender bias does not occur in isolation. Often driving gender bias in society is the influence of gender-based stereotypes. These are socially constructed overgeneralizations of particular behaviors attributed to a group, and they play a significant role in the formation of gender bias. These "traditional" gender stereotypes reflect expected feminine and masculine attitudes and behaviors attributed to women and men. Female stereotypes generalize women as emotionally supportive, irrational, physically inferior, and economically and socially dependent upon males. Conversely, male stereotypes generalize men as rational, intelligent, physically superior, and independent. These gendered stereotypes become part of a larger cultural belief system within a given society and serve as templates for how women and men should and should not behave in society. Simply, gender bias represents the culturally formed predispositions that individuals, groups, organizations, and societal institutions place upon women and men.

Consequences of Gender Bias

Economically, workplace gender bias contributes to the gender wage gap that exists between women's and men's earnings. For instance, in 2006, women earned 77 cents for every dollar a man earned. Women receive less pay than men, even when both have the same educational and occupational achievement. Another manifestation of gender bias is overlooking individuals for promotion or tenure. At universities, for example, when compared with male faculty members, female faculty members experience fewer opportunities for promotion and tenure. Female faculty members are also less likely than men to hold high-level administrative positions. These differences are especially significant when female faculty work within "male-oriented" fields of study, such as math and science. In addition, women collide with the "glass ceiling," an invisible boundary that prevents them from moving up the occupational ladder. This happens in the workplace because of the patriarchal assumption that women provide child care; in turn, many women are overlooked for promotions and pay raises because employers do not want to "invest" in a worker who is going to leave the workforce temporarily or permanently.

Gender bias also has noneconomic consequences. First, there is a lack of prestige attached to certain social roles in society, depending upon who fills the role. For example, men in female-dominant professions or roles—such as nursing, cosmetology, elementary school teaching, child care, or stay-at-home parenting—are considered less masculine and are therefore viewed as less valuable in society. Second, gender bias affects self-esteem. For instance, educational studies have shown that young girls and young adult women who experience gender bias in the classroom have lower self-esteem. As a result, females construct negative self-perceptions, believing that they are not as intelligent as males.

How Gender Bias Can Be Reduced or Eliminated

Since the 1960s, the U.S. government has implemented anti-discriminatory policies to ensure the equal treatment of women and men. One such policy is the Equal Pay Act of 1963, which states that employers should pay women and men the same salary for doing the same type of job with similar skill sets. Another example of federal policy is Title IX, implemented in 1972, which disallows sex discrimination in educational environments that receive funding from the federal government. Federal affirmative action policy (Executive Order 11246) prohibits sex, race, religion, national origin, and color discrimination in the workplace. Moreover, under affirmative action policy, employers must actively seek out women (and other minorities) to reinforce equity in the work and educational environments.

Despite the implementation of the aforementioned policies, these measures have not been sufficiently enforced to completely eliminate gender bias as a social problem in U.S. society. Although reducing gender bias in specific social contexts is vital, the overarching solution would be to radically transform the existing gender-based stereotypes defined in contemporary society.

Rhonda E. Dugan

See also Gender Gap; Gender Identity and Socialization; Patriarchy; Segregation, Gender; Segregation, Occupational; Sexism; Title IX; Wage Gap

Further Readings

Acker, Joan. 1990. "Hierarchies, Jobs, Bodies: A Theory of Gendered Organizations." *Gender and Society* 4(2):139–58.

Bielby, William T. 2000. "Minimizing Workplace Gender and Racial Bias." *Contemporary Sociology* 29(1):120–29.

Frawley, Timothy. 2005. "Gender Bias in the Classroom: Current Controversies and Implications for Teachers." *Childhood Education* 81(4):221–27.

Heilman, Madeline E. 2001. "Description and Prescription: How Gender Stereotypes Prevent Women's Ascent up the Organizational Ladder." *Journal of Social Issues* 57(4):657–74.

Renzetti, Claire and Daniel J. Curran. 2008. *Women, Men, and Society.* 6th ed. Boston: Allyn & Bacon.

GENDER GAP

When social scientists write of a "gender gap," they mean a systematic difference or disparity between women and men. Frequently discussed gender gaps are those in the labor market and paid employment as well as in family work and relationships. The gender gaps in these areas are not constant but instead vary across time and place; moreover, within a given place or time, the gaps often differ by group membership (e.g., one's race or social class). Because of such variation, explanations of gender gaps tend to focus on social factors rather than biological or other natural causes.

The Labor Market and Families

Men are still more likely to be employed for pay than are women. The gender gap in U.S. labor force participation dropped over the past century, with increasing numbers of women but fewer men reporting they work outside of the home (although the proportion of women entering the labor force peaked in the year 2000). Today, approximately 60 percent of women and 75 percent of men are in the civilian labor force. The numbers and proportions have increased most dramatically for married, white women with children.

The hours women spend on paid work have also steadily risen, but the gender gap in hours worked for pay remains. In the United States, employed men spend an average of 43 hours a week on the job. Employed women work an average of 36 hours per week for pay.

Often receiving even more attention is the gender gap in income and earnings. Over that same time period as the gap in employment declined, the gender gap in income narrowed. Women today, however, still make approximately 77 cents for every dollar that men earn. Moreover, in about three quarters of dual-earner couples, the husband still earns more than his wife; although the numbers are growing, in only about one third of couples in which both spouses work full-time does the wife earn more than the husband. This gender gap varies by race. For example, black wives provide almost $4 out of every $10 of household income, compared with about $3 out of $10 for both white and Latina working wives.

While the gender gap "favors" men in paid work, housework remains women's work more than men's: Wives still cook, clean, shop, and manage domestic routines more than their husbands. Although even single women do more housework than single men, the gap grows when they marry—men start doing even less, and women begin to do even more.

The gender gap in caring for children also remains strong. Over the past few decades, residential fathers (i.e., fathers who live with their children) have begun to spend more time caring for their kids. Nonetheless, just as women in two-parent households continue to do most of the housework, such mothers continue to do most of the parenting. The gap intensifies when single parents are taken into account: Across race, mothers head the vast majority of single-parent families. Even though the number of single fathers is increasing at an even faster rate than is the number of single mothers, there are still five times as many single mothers as single fathers.

A gender gap also exists in caregiving to relatives. Far more than men, women call, write, invite, and take care of kin—whether elderly mothers and fathers, brothers and sisters, aunts or uncles. Matching a gender gap in the amount of time spent giving care is a difference in the kinds of care given. Although women do many and varied caregiving tasks for a significantly larger number of relatives than do men, there is not a single such task that men do more than women for a significantly larger number of people.

Gender Gaps: Explanations

What accounts for these gender gaps? A variety of explanations—emanating from different academic disciplines—address them. The so-called essentialist theories argue that gender gaps in paid work, as well as in family life, are bound up with the biological makeup of women and men and are, by consequence, if not exactly invariant, at least deep and tenacious. Often rooting gender differences in early childhood socialization, psychological theories allow far more room for variation among women and among men than do essentialist biological arguments. Much psychological research, however, explains uniformity among women and among men on grounds of invariance in gender-specific childrearing practices within a given society. Sociologists widely criticize such arguments and theories for ignoring the variation among women and among men.

Attending to such variation, sociological theories of gender gaps tend to emphasize two sets of explanations: structural forces and cultural influences operating in adult life. Most common are the arguments focusing on structural forces: that array of material and objective constraints and opportunities external to individuals. For example, according to this argument, growing educational opportunities available to women help account for the reduction in the gender gap in both employment and wages. Whereas in 1960, male college graduates outnumbered female graduates by five to three, by the year 2005, over half of those attending college were women. Because the gender gap in years of schooling declined, the wage gap between women and men diminished over those same years. Structural explanations also suggest both that the growing similarities between women's and men's paid work explain some of the reallocation of unpaid work and that remaining differences in unpaid work result in the remaining dissimilarities in paid work. Because women and men still spend different amounts of time on their jobs and have different types of jobs, men's jobs more likely pull or push them away from family responsibilities than do women's jobs. The amount and proportion of household income that women earn, the time they spend on the job, and their job prestige are negatively associated with the time they spend on housework.

Some suggest the gender gap in caring for kin also can be traced to employment. For example, compared with employed women, the "traditional woman" who does not work for pay is especially likely to provide care for her relatives. Further, the types of tasks for kin that a housewife does are different from those an employed woman does: Employed women give relatives more money and gifts, whereas housewives do more time-consuming, hands-on chores, like taking care of relatives' children. In this sense, employed women are beginning to look a little like employed men, as the structural model would predict. At the same time, a large portion of this gender gap relates to differences in men's and women's job conditions, especially their wages. When men make the same amount of money as women, for example, men's caregiving to kin begins to resemble women's. This also reaffirms a structural explanation for the gender gap.

Others, however, emphasize that even when women work for pay, the gender gap remains. The "traditional" man—who holds a paying job—continues to do significantly less housework, child care, and kin work than his employed female counterpart. The second set of explanations trace these remaining gender gaps in paid employment and unpaid family labor to the cultural factors that operate in adult life—especially three sets of cultural beliefs: (1) gender ideologies (especially those attitudes concerning what men's and women's roles and power should be in paid and unpaid labor and nurturance), (2) beliefs concerning the importance of employment, and (3) beliefs concerning the importance of family obligations. These types of explanations suggest that women still do significantly more housework, child care, and kin work than men, even if their employment conditions are similar, because women and men have different views about gender, employment, and family obligations.

Any discussion of culture and structure, however, must emphasize that womanhood and manhood are not monolithic. For example, the difference in housework between black men and black women is smaller than the gap between white women and white men. Depending on their race/ethnicity, men and women are held accountable to different standards concerning gender, family, and employment just as they encounter different privileges and opportunities.

Overall, the gender gap in family and paid work has narrowed but still exists. A gender gap also remains in other realms of personal and social life—in physical and mental health (women get depressed more often than men while men develop what are called antisocial personalities and express anger more often than women), in crime (men are still much more likely to commit a variety of crimes, but women are catching up), and in politics (women are more likely than men to vote Democratic). Social forces can explain these, too. A gender gap does not necessarily mean attachment of a lower value to either women or men. Some of these gaps are simply markers of differences. Others are, however, indicators and enactments of inequality associated with different rewards and costs.

Naomi Gerstel

See also Gender Bias; Gender Identity and Socialization; Pink-Collar Occupations; Second Shift; Segregation, Gender; Segregation, Occupational

Further Readings

Bianchi, Suzanne, John Robinson, and Melissa Milkie. 2006. *Changing Rhythms of American Family Life.* New York: Russell Sage Foundation.

Goldin, Claudia. 1990. *Understanding the Gender Gap: An Economic History of American Women.* New York: Oxford University Press.

Padavic, Irene and Barbara Reskin. 2002. *Women and Men at Work.* Thousand Oaks, CA: Pine Forge.

Rosenfield, Sarah, Jean Vertefuille, and Donna D. McAlpine. 2000. "Gender Stratification and Mental Health: An Exploration of Dimensions of the Self." *Social Psychology Quarterly* 63:208–23.

Sarkisian, Natalia and Naomi Gerstel. 2004. "Explaining the Gender Gap in Help to Parents: The Importance of Employment." *Journal of Marriage and the Family* 66:431–45.

GENDER IDENTITY AND SOCIALIZATION

The term *gender identity* generally refers to an individual's feelings of being a man or a woman; it is a self-identification of gender. *Socialization* is the process through which infants develop into mature adults by learning the norms and values of the society. *Gender socialization* represents the idea that gender is socially constructed and that individuals learn gender roles and develop gender identity through human interaction. Through gender socialization, social expectations about what are appropriate masculine and feminine behaviors are communicated to members of society. Socialization processes transmit definitions of proper gender roles to individuals and shape their relationships to others in society as well as understandings of their place in it.

Some scholars argue that gender socialization can act as a mechanism of social control which defines and sanctions behaviors and attitudes about gender. Gender norms guide and restrict people's understanding and actions about what it means to be a male or a female as defined by culture. Researchers have found that extreme pressure to conform to traditional gender norms results in negative consequences for both men and women in U.S. society. For instance, boys who display femininity are often subject to severe social sanctions to reinforce norms of heterosexual masculinity. Some scholars explain that this is due to the coercive system of homophobia, defined as the fear and hatred of homosexuality. For girls, traditional gender expectations are embodied in beauty myths and the normative ideal of a thin body. These rigid and forceful gender role expectations can lead to social problems. Researchers associate high mortality rates among men in U.S. society, and high depression and proliferation of dieting and eating disorders among women, with gender ideologies.

Gender Socialization Literature

The pairing of the terms *gender identity* and *socialization* reflects a particular perspective on gender in the history of gender studies. The idea that gender is not biologically determined but socially created and learned through socialization processes was the central theoretical tenet of gender role theories and developmental literature on gender. According to gender socialization literature, gender refers to behaviors and attitudes associated with being a man or a woman, as distinguished from biological sex. Here, gender is considered a role, or a set of expectations associated with a particular status or position in society.

Young members of society learn gender norms and expectations and grow to identify with the gender category that corresponds to their biological sex. Based on this understanding, gender socialization theories pay analytic attention to the developmental processes by which children form a sense of themselves as individuals with a particular gender. Psychoanalytic theories, social learning theories, and cognitive theories may be included in this school of thought because of their focus on human interaction and the socialization process and their linear perspective on human development. Although akin in that regard, the theories diverge somewhat in their focal interests and explanations on how gender identity formation occurs.

Psychoanalytic Theories

The principal perspective of psychoanalytic theories is that gender identity develops first from genital awareness and then through the psychological imperative to identify with a same-sex parent. In Sigmund Freud's theory, gender identity development is set in motion by recognizing one's particular set of genitals. Subsequent identification with a same-sex parent follows through complex psychosexual processes guided by a fear of the father's intervention prompted by the child's desire for the mother. By way of different psychological fantasies about their relationships to parents, boys eventually gender-identify with their fathers while girls gender-identify with their mothers so as to establish their own gender identity.

Other theories in the psychoanalytic tradition commonly emphasize parent–child relationships as the key process of gender identity formation. These theories focus on explaining why boys and girls develop different gender identities and roles, but they rarely question the link between biological sex and gender identity. In addition, the mechanism of socialization into gender roles is largely unspecified in psychoanalytic theories.

Social Learning Theory

Social learning theory focuses on analyzing the specific mechanism of socialization by which gender identity is developed. Applying principles of learning theory in behavioral science to gender socialization, social learning theory posits that gender-typed behaviors are learned through patterns of reward and punishment in social environments. According to this framework, children learn the gendered behaviors of their parents by mimicking. As children imitate parents' gender-related behaviors, they are either encouraged or discouraged depending on whether they are girls or boys. Girls may be praised for mimicking

mothers' feminine behaviors, whereas boys would be reprimanded for displaying those behaviors.

After learning gender-appropriate behaviors through repeated patterns of reinforcement, children learn the label "girl" or "boy" as associated with the encouraged behaviors, and they internalize the appropriate label as their own gender identity. In essence, social learning theory postulates that children develop their appropriate gender identities through differential treatment given by parents and others in society. Socialization is perceived to be the key to mastering the knowledge about how one should behave appropriately, knowledge that then helps individuals identify with the particular gender that corresponds to the behavioral expectations.

Cognitive Developmental Theory

Whereas social learning theory focuses on adults' influence, cognitive developmental theory emphasizes children's own understanding of, and self-socialization into, gender identity. Cognitive developmental theory is based on Jean Piaget's theory of children's cognitive development. According to this theory, children develop a gender identity, around age 5 or 6, when they begin to understand the notion of gender invariance despite different behavioral displays. For example, a boy who likes to play with robots also may enjoy playing with kitchen sets, but the gender identity of this boy does not change with changing behaviors. When this understanding forms, children begin to know to which gender they belong, and they begin to associate people and behaviors with one sex or the other. Children then start to use gender categories as a lens, or an organizing scheme, to understand reality. As a result, they start to model their own behaviors after those who fall in the same gender category as their own.

Critiques of Gender Socialization

Although gender socialization literature demonstrates its strength in its analytic probing of how individuals are incorporated into the existing social order through gradual adoption of cultural norms, there are several shortcomings. For instance, gender socialization perspectives maintain the linear view on human development that children's ideas of gender are imperfect and must be molded to resemble those of adults before their socialization becomes complete. Furthermore, socialization literature's fundamental failure to see gender as one of several interlocking systems of inequality opens itself to vehement criticisms by later gender theories. Several contemporary theories of gender challenge socialization theories' supposition that gender identity is an attribute to be obtained and become fixed for life at some point. Strong critiques are also made on the socialization literature's assumption of two (and only two) static categories of sex as well as gender, its reliance on universal definitions of manhood and womanhood, its disregard of changing definitions of values and norms, and most important, its failure to see gender as a system of power that is shaped by other structures of inequality.

Contemporary Approaches to Gender Identity

Gender scholars continue to analyze gender identity, albeit from a different perspective than socialization theorists. Gender identity is a social problems theme in today's social science scholarship not only in the sense that it represents individual struggles with cultural norms but also in the sense that gender identity construction is a site of challenge and struggle over existing inequality and power dynamics among diverse social groups. This perspective on gender identity is based on the contemporary view that gender is fundamentally a matter of inequality and domination. Many recent studies conceptualize gender as everyday practices that construct unequal relations of power and therefore emphasize the analysis of power, social structures, and the interplay of gender with class, race, and other systems of inequality.

In analyzing micro dynamics of gender, studies make conceptual distinctions between gender identity (self-attribution of gender), gender assignment (gender attribution at birth, based on genital characteristics), gender attribution (perceived gender by others in everyday interactions), gender role (appropriate behavioral expectations associated with gender categories), and gender practice ("doing gender" in everyday interaction). These conceptual distinctions challenge many taken-for-granted assumptions about gender, including the link between gender assignment and gender identity, the link between sexuality and gender identity, and the interaction between everyday gender practices and larger structures of inequality. On the macro level, analyses of gendered institutions; the mobilization of multiple gender and sexual identities, including ambiguous gender and sex identities; and

the interactions between gender and other social hierarchies have come to replace interests in individuals' acquisition of gender identity through socialization.

Keumjae Park

See also Bisexuality; Identity Politics; Sexual Orientation; Social Constructionist Theory; Transgender and Transsexuality

Further Readings

Andersen, Margaret L. 2008. *Thinking about Women: Sociological Perspectives on Sex and Gender.* 8th ed. Boston: Allyn & Bacon.

Fausto-Sterling, Anne. 2000. *Sexing the Body: Gender Politics and the Construction of Sexuality.* New York: Basic Books.

Kessler, Suzanne J. and Wendy McKenna. 1985. *Gender: An Ethnomethodological Approach.* Chicago: Chicago University Press.

Kimmel, Michael S. 2007. *The Gendered Society.* 3rd ed. New York: Oxford University Press.

Lorber, Judith. 1994. *Paradoxes of Gender.* New Haven, CT: Yale University Press.

Throne, Barrie. 1993. *Gender Play: Girls and Boys in School.* New Brunswick, NJ: Rutgers University Press.

GENETICALLY ALTERED FOODS

Genetically modified organisms (GMOs) are produced by transferring genetic material from one species to another. Genetically altered or modified (GM) foods contain materials derived from such processes. Whereas traditional plant and animal breeding involves the crossing of individuals with desirable traits within a single species, genetic engineering allows more rapid and radical transformations. Examples include the transfer of genes from Arctic halibut into tomatoes to confer frost resistance, and the incorporation of *Bacillus thuringiensis* bacteria into corn or potatoes as a "natural" pesticide. Genetic engineering has also made possible the cheap and rapid synthesis of common food ingredients, such as yeasts, and of products like recombinant bovine growth hormone (rBGH), which vastly increases an animal's milk production.

The criteria for classifying genetically altered foods vary among countries, depending on the strictness of their regulatory systems. Broadly speaking, these foods include genetically modified crops that people consume directly (ranging from strawberries to radicchio to rice); processed foods containing ingredients made from GM crops or products (corn syrup, soy flour, cheese made with GM rennet); and meat or produce from genetically modified or treated animals (GM salmon or rBGH milk). Some people would also include meat or produce from animals fed GM cereals.

The world's first GM crop, the Flavr-Savr tomato, was patented by the U.S. biotech company Calgene and approved by the U.S. Department of Agriculture in 1994. By 2005, 90 million hectares of GM crops, predominantly soy, corn, canola, and cotton, were grown globally; the United States was world leader, with 50 million hectares. The Grocery Manufacturers of America estimate that roughly 75 percent of U.S. processed foods contain GM ingredients; however, less than half the population is aware that GM foods are sold in supermarkets. In the United Kingdom, by contrast, supermarkets label foods containing GMOs, and pubs and restaurants proclaim their dishes "GM-free." In Brazil, farmers smuggled in GM soybean seed from Argentina to overcome an official ban, whereas French cheese makers and South Indian rice farmers demolished buildings in campaigns against GM crops. Biotech corporations insist that GM crops are essential to prevent world hunger, yet when famine loomed in 2002, the government of Zambia, after a public debate, chose to refuse GM corn sent by the United States as food aid. Why are there such radically different responses to GM foods?

GM crops and foods are new life-forms that promise great benefits, including higher yields, longer growing seasons, greater disease resistance, lower pesticide use, or extra vitamins. Any new technology also carries a spectrum of risks, however, and most battles over GM foods concern how risk should be defined and evaluated, and by whom. Proponents of GM foods try to restrict the debate to immediate health and environmental effects. Opponents insist that long-term effects and social and political impacts must also be considered.

No serious health risks related to GM foods have been demonstrated to date, and for developed world consumers, the advantages of GM foods would seem to outweigh the risks. From a farmer's perspective, however, the cost–benefit analysis is more complicated. One contentious issue is intellectual property rights. There are some public research programs working on

GM subsistence crops for unrestricted use by poor farmers—for example, virus-free potatoes in Peru. But the design and testing of GM crops is expensive.

Highly capitalized biotech corporations thus produce most of the new varieties. For highest returns they concentrate on important commercial crops; design new varieties to respond only to their own agrichemical products; patent the gene sequences; and sell seed to farmers as the equivalent of software, bringing damages for any infringement of copyright, like replanting or exchanging seed. The promise of lower overall costs and better output led to rapid adoption by commercial farmers in the United States, but peasant farmers around the world passionately oppose GM seeds as a tool of corporate dominance and control, deliberately designed to deprive them of ownership of their seeds and control of their production methods.

In all organized protests against GM food, including the refusal of U.S. corn as food aid by the Zambians, there is an element of resistance to what is portrayed as American corporate imperialism: Although French and Swiss companies number among the biggest biotech corporations, the industry figurehead is the U.S. company Monsanto.

Another political formulation of risk is prominent in Europe, where issues of trust and governance come to the fore. The U.S. public generally has faith in the virtues of technology and business enterprise and trusts its regulatory bodies, but few Europeans trust government institutions or corporations to assess or manage technologies in the public interest. Citizen groups opposed government licensing of GMOs without public consultation as an example of "democratic deficit." The national debates that ensued broadened the issues from primarily health concerns to encompass environmental risks, citizen rights, the critique of industrial farming, definitions of a healthy society, and concerns for global justice. Consumer boycotts of GM products and of retailers who stocked them drove the message home, and sustained public pressure rapidly brought much stricter regulation of GMOs. Public action in other nations, such as Thailand, Japan, and New Zealand, followed similar patterns, linking consumer, producer, and citizen rights and building transnational coalitions. The global knock-on effects have impacted markets, dented the confidence of GM food producers, and forced biotech corporations to reconfigure their strategies.

Biotech corporations and U.S. trade officials like to argue that foreign opposition to GM foods stems from irrational emotionalism and scientific ignorance. Yet research shows that the more technical information individuals acquire about GM crops and foods, the more likely they are to oppose them. A better understanding of how GMOs are designed, produced, and controlled inevitably extends perception of risks beyond the narrow framework of space, time, and stakeholders that the GM industry and its supporters have sought to impose. The case of GM foods thus illustrates intrinsic tensions between technocracy and scientific literacy within contemporary democracies.

Francesca Bray

See also Genetic Engineering; Multinational Corporations; Transnational Activism; Transnational Social Movement

Further Readings

Bray, Francesca. 2003. "Genetically Modified Foods: Shared Risk and Global Action." Pp. 185–207 in *Revising Risk: Health Inequalities and Shifting Perceptions of Danger and Blame,* edited by B. Herr Harthorn and L. Oaks. London: Praeger.

Conway, Gordon. 2000. "Genetically Modified Crops: Risks and Promise." *Conservation Ecology* 4(1):2. Retrieved December 26, 2007 (http://www.ecologyandsociety.org/vol4/iss1/art2/).

Gutteling, Jan, Lucien Hanssen, Neil van der Veer, and Erwin Sydel. 2006. "Trust in Governance and the Acceptance of Genetically Modified Food in the Netherlands." *Public Understanding of Science* 15:103–12.

Murphy, Joseph, Les Levidow, and Susan Carr. 2006. "Understanding the US-European Union Conflict over Genetically Modified Crops." *Social Studies of Science* 36(1):133–60.

Mwale, Pascal Newbourne. 2006. "Societal Deliberation on Genetically Modified Maize in Southern Africa: The *Debateness* and the *Publicness* of the Zambian National Consultation on Genetically Modified Maize Food Aid in 2002." *Public Understanding of Science* 15:89–102.

GENETIC ENGINEERING

Genetic engineering is the concept of taking genes and segments of DNA from one individual or species (e.g., a spider) and inserting them into another individual or species (e.g., a goat). The biotechnology of genetic engineering has created a broad spectrum of ethical issues, ranging from genetically modified organisms, as in crops, to animal and human cloning, genetic screening for diseases, prenatal and preimplantation diagnosis of human embryos, xenotransplantation, and gene replacement therapy.

Genetic engineering presents an exciting range of possibilities. For example, genetic engineering can give plants and crops desirable traits, such as drought resistance and additional nutrients. Such promises are not without their potential perils; some environmental groups raise concerns that the creation and use of these genetically engineered plants amounts to "genetic pollution" and that they should not be released into the environment until there is a full scientific understanding of their long-term impact on the environment and human health.

The stakes rise even higher when applying genetic engineering to animals or humans or animal–human combinations. For example, by inserting a spider's gene into a goat embryo, a biotech firm created Biosteel, a unique high-performance spider fiber, prized for its toughness, strength, lightness, and biodegradability. Possible applications include the medical, military, and industrial performance fiber markets. However, bioethicists raise concerns about crossing species boundaries and question whether or not we are creating long-term effects on the environment, inflicting harm on these creatures that we create, and whether or not we should place some ethical, social, and legal controls or reviews on such research.

The engineering or combination of animal and human genes (also referred to as "transgenics") represents a booming aspect of biotechnology. For example, genetically engineered pigs provide potential organs for transplantation (known as "xenotransplantation"). Researchers are also exploring the use of cell transplantation therapy for patients with spinal cord injury or Parkinson's disease. However, several drawbacks to xenotransplantation exist, for example, the small but significant risk of the transmission of usually fatal zoonotic diseases, such as bovine spongiform encephalopathy (also known as "mad cow disease"). The U.S. Food and Drug Administration has banned xenotransplantation trials using nonhuman primates until adequate demonstrations that the procedure is safe and sufficient public discussion of the ethical issues take place.

Some groups advocate the use of genetic engineering for the enhancement of the human species, but this raises the specter of eugenics, once used as an excuse for genocide and the creation of the "perfect race." Others call for a ban on species-altering technology enforced by an international tribunal. Part of the rationale for a ban is the concern that such technology could create a slave race, that is, a race of exploited subhumans. In April 1998, activist scientists opposed to genetic engineering applied for a patent for a "humanzee," part human and part chimpanzee, to fuel debate on this issue and to draw attention to potential abuses. The U.S. Patent and Trademark Office denied the patent on the grounds that it violated the 13th Amendment to the U.S. Constitution, which prohibits slavery. These activists appealed the decision, but the appeal has not yet reached a court, and it may never do so, because the appeal may be dismissed on other technical grounds.

A question for the future is how the ethical, legal, and social implications of genetic engineering will challenge traditional notions of personhood.

Linda MacDonald Glenn

See also Eugenics; Genetically Altered Foods; Genetic Theories

Further Readings

Baylis, Françoise and Jason Scott Roberts. 2006. *Primer on Ethics and Crossing Species Boundaries.* Washington, DC: American Institute of Biological Sciences. Retrieved December 26, 2007 (http://www.actionbioscience.org/biotech/baylis_robert.html).

Glenn, Linda MacDonald. 2004. *Ethical Issues in Genetic Engineering and Transgenics.* Washington, DC: American Institute of Biological Sciences. Retrieved December 26, 2007 (http://www.actionbioscience.org/biotech/glenn.html#Primer).

Rasko, John, Gabrielle O'Sullivan, and Rachel A. Ankeny, eds. 2006. *The Ethics of Inheritable Genetic Modification: A Dividing Line?* Cambridge, England: Cambridge University Press.

Rollins, Bernard E. 1995. *The Frankenstein Syndrome: Ethical and Social Issues in the Genetic Engineering of Animals.* Cambridge, England: Cambridge University Press.

GENETIC THEORIES

Genetic theorists assert that we can explain human characteristics, health, and/or behavior, to a significant degree, by the deoxyribonucleic acid (DNA) sequence present in the genes of a person or of a group of people presumed to have meaningful genetic similarity.

Since the beginning of the 20th century, when they rediscovered the earlier published work of Czechoslovakian monk Gregor Mendel, Western scientists have agreed that recessive and dominant factors of heredity govern numerous human traits (such as eye color). Two contributing alleles determine these traits, one from each parent, with dominant factors always physically expressed, as they have the power to mask recessive ones. Scientists call these factors *genes*—although this term was (and some argue still is) quite imprecise—and they conceptualize genes as clustered together on chromosomes. By the 1950s, biologists had demonstrated that the DNA *within* genes influences heredity, and in 1953, scientists James Watson and Francis Crick published their famous double helix model, which is still used today, to conceptualize how discrete strands of DNA interlock with matching base pairs of adenine, thymine, cytosine, and guanine.

Today, common agreement exists that a gene is a stretch of DNA that produces a code specifying the amino acid sequence of one of the many proteins essential to the structure and function of the human body. DNA sequences in genes (the genotype) have some relationship to the physical expression of the human organism (the phenotype). However, disagreement persists about the degree of influence biological heredity has in determining who people are and how they behave. Some geneticists, biologists, and other scientists assert the dominance of a genetic paradigm in explaining human phenomena at both the individual and the societal level. Critics often argue that such assertions are greatly exaggerated and that factors such as family, natural, and social environments and economic and political structures have much more explanatory value. "Nature versus nurture" and "genes versus the environment" are frequently invoked shorthand terms for describing the tension between these points of view.

In the early 21st century, the pendulum between nature and nurture inclines quite steeply toward the former. Genetic explanations figure prominently in dominant understandings about what differentiates humans from one another as well as what determines health and behavior. Nonetheless, what is asserted by some as genetic *knowledge* is contested by others as genetic *theory.* This struggle over definitions and explanatory power is an ongoing social problem with both practical and theoretical implications.

Debates About the Fundamental Assumptions and Politics of Genetics

Behind debates over particular genetic issues lie several fundamental assumptions that are themselves contested. One is the premise that we best generate meaningful knowledge by examining the smallest parts of organisms—the DNA on genes. Proponents of genetic theories assert that the information gathered in this process can reveal the very essence of human life in an objective manner buffered from social or political influence. An opposing point of view is that reducing people to tiny parts ("reductionism") does not allow for a more holistic and useful understanding of humans as complete and relational beings. Reductionism has been central to most traditional forms of scientific endeavor, but many view genetics as its ultimate expression. Critics also extend to genetics a long-standing critique of scientific objectivity, arguing that all knowledge is in fact constructed through such processes as deciding how to define issues, what questions to ask, and how to examine and interpret data.

A second contested point is the relationship between knowledge and concrete interventions to improve human health. Much genetic research receives broad public and political support on the assumption that knowledge about micro processes in the body will benefit all through targeted tests and medical interventions. Critics counter that the ability to test for and diagnose real or predicted problems has always been far greater than the capacity to treat them and that there is a problematic tendency to produce tests and use them as the capacity to do so emerges, without adequate consideration of the ethical, legal, and social consequences of such actions.

A third issue is the exercise of human agency. Do genetic theories lead to a sense of fatalism because genetic endowment cannot be (and should not be) controlled by individuals? Or conversely, do they lead to a sense of hope because they may ultimately lead to greater control over intractable diseases, over the kinds of babies people have, and over what can be predicted about people's behavior and talents?

Also at stake in debates about genetics are questions about the allocation of social resources. Genetic research of all kinds, like many forms of scientific research, successfully attracts enormous financial investment. Are these dollars well spent, or might they yield greater benefit if they were used to address other problems?

Genetics and Genomics

In 2003 scientists completed the multibillion-dollar Human Genome Project, which resulted in a description or "map" of all the genes on all the chromosomes in a prototypical human body. With this massive enterprise came a shift in scientific discourse from a focus on *genetics,* characterized as single gene disorders or characteristics, to a focus on *genomics,* which takes into account both the interaction among genes and the complex interaction between genes and the environment. This shift opened the door for genetic theories to move from explanations featuring direct, linear causality (i.e., gene X causes manifestation Y) to more complex hypotheses. Recognition that the way many genes will express themselves is integrally connected to environmental factors is a particularly notable aspect of the movement from genetics toward genomics.

However, some argue that the shift to genomics greatly expanded the reach of genetic explanations and bolstered assumptions that genomic research can best illuminate and address ever-larger arenas of our social world. For example, genetics traditionally focused on relatively rare disorders, such as Huntington's disease, which are associated with mutations of just one gene. Genomics, in contrast, focuses on the genetic component of nearly all common illnesses, including diabetes, heart disease, schizophrenia, and cancer. The concern is that emphasis on the genetic component of these conditions detracts attention and resources from factors that exert greater influence over health outcomes, such as poverty and environmental toxins.

Genetic Issues in the Early 21st Century

Genetics and genomics are central to a growing number of emerging practices across arenas as diverse as medicine, criminology, special education, employment, and informatics. Two of the most salient of these issues will illustrate how genetic theories apply to concrete social problems.

Predictive Screening and Testing

Predictive screening and testing is perhaps the most tangible form genetics takes in the lives of individuals. These tests identify genetic mutations or information that is presumed to meaningfully predict a person's "risk" for disease. For example, pregnant women now routinely test their fetuses for various mutations and make deliberate decisions about which babies to have and not have. Women identified with the "breast cancer gene" (BRCA1 or 2) may increase the frequency of visits to doctors for screening, or they may have prophylactic mastectomies. Parents whose babies get positive newborn genetic screens may act to prevent, mediate, or even anticipate disease. Proponents argue that these tests illustrate the promise of the genetic revolution. Critics argue that both the accuracy of the tests and the availability of effective treatments or prevention strategies are highly questionable, as increased testing results primarily in greater numbers of people who think of themselves or their children as sick or deviant despite no manifest symptoms of disease. Further, critics contend, mass testing programs function not just as medical procedures but also as mechanisms for categorizing individuals (e.g., as "normal" or as "deviant").

Genetics and Race

Genetic theories also play a prominent role in contemporary debates about race. On the one hand, the Human Genome Project's discovery that little genetic variation exists among people (about .1 percent) received extensive publicity. On the other hand, research on what genetic differences *do* exist among people continues at a rapid rate. Examples include studies to determine genetic components of health disparities; studies to develop "race-based" therapeutics such as BiDil, the first drug to be developed and marketed specifically for blacks; and the Human Genome Diversity Project, which is looking at DNA from groups around the world to understand evolutionary history. Despite care taken to differentiate contemporary genetic theories about race from historical precedents such as Nazi eugenics, such theories do continue to assert that we can meaningfully understand the differences among people through analysis of DNA. Critics contend that social inequality is a much more useful frame for analyzing difference and promoting equality and that genetic theories about race are both scientifically questionable and socially misguided.

Rachel N. Grob

See also Eugenics; Family; Genetic Engineering; Power; Race; Social Constructionist Theory

Further Readings

Duster, Troy. 2003. *Backdoor to Eugenics.* 2nd ed. New York: Routledge.

Hubbard, Ruth and Elijah Wald. 1999. *Exploding the Myth: How Genetic Information Is Produced and Manipulated by Scientists, Physicians, Employers, Insurance Companies, Educators and Law Enforcers.* Boston: Beacon Press.

Kevles, Daniel and Leroy Hood, eds. 1992. *The Code of Codes: Scientific and Social Issues in the Human Genome Project.* Cambridge, MA: Harvard University Press.

Nelkin, Dorothy and Laurence Tancredi. 1994. *Dangerous Diagnostics: The Social Power of Biological Information.* New York: Basic Books.

Rothman, Barbara Katz. 2001. *The Book of Life: A Personal and Ethical Guide to Race, Normality and the Implications of the Human Genome Project.* Boston: Beacon Press.

GENOCIDE

Raphaël Lemkin (1900–59), a Jewish lawyer from Poland who wrote extensively about international law and crimes against humanity, coined the term *genocide* in his most famous work, *Axis Rule in Occupied Europe*, published in 1944 by the Carnegie Endowment for International Peace. In his extensive analysis of German rule during the Holocaust, Lemkin derived the term *genocide* from the Greek root for tribe or nation (*genos*) and the Latin root for killing (*-cide*). Predating his creation of the term was Lemkin's work on earlier forms of genocide, such as the Armenian genocide during World War I and the mass murder of Assyrians in Iraq in the 1930s.

Lemkin not only contributed a conceptual understanding of genocide but also campaigned for its criminalization at the international level. His definition of genocide provided a legal basis for the Nuremburg trials. Furthermore, his work helped inspire the United Nations to establish, on December 9, 1948, the Convention for the Prevention and Punishment of the Crime of Genocide, which became effective on January 12, 1951, with passage of Resolution 260. Article 2 defines genocide as certain "acts committed with the intent to destroy, in whole or in part, a national, ethnical, racial or religious group, as such." The convention delineates these acts of genocide as killing members of a group or causing them serious bodily or mental harm; deliberately inflicting conditions of life on the group that are calculated to bring about its physical destruction in whole or in part; imposing measures intended to prevent births within the group; and forcibly transferring children of the group to another group.

This legal definition thus classified the crime of genocide in three distinct parts: actions, intent, and victimization. The first of these include murder, causing serious harm, creating conditions for the destruction of a particular group, preventing the biological reproduction of a particular group, or removing children from the group, the latter two aimed at destroying the group's continued existence. The second part of the UN definition, intent, is controversial, as legal scholars point out that intent is typically difficult to prove and therefore hard to prosecute. Most often, proof of a perpetrator's intent lies in the terms of a political program aimed at systematic brutality against the group in question. The third element in the definition, racial, ethnic, or religious group victimization, makes genocide distinct from other kinds of murder and brutality.

Initial debates over the UN convention's definition of genocide were intensely political, and the definition itself remains widely criticized, especially for its failure to include political and social groups. The first draft of the convention included political groups, but the USSR contested its inclusion and ultimately prevailed. Moreover, whereas Lemkin's definition of genocide included the intentional destruction of cultures and political groups, the UN definition did not.

The destruction of a group's cultural identity is commonly called *cultural genocide* or *ethnocide*. During the genocide in former Yugoslavia in the early 1990s, the term *ethnic cleansing* entered into popular parlance, but it remains undefined in legal terms. For example, while often used to describe genocide, it may also involve mass deportation without mass murder. Native Americans endured both ethnic cleansing and ethnocide during the 19th and 20th centuries. Ethnic cleansing policies forced native populations onto reservations, while white Americans seized millions of acres of their land. By the late 19th century, the federal government instituted a now-discontinued policy of forced assimilation, with the ultimate goal of eradicating native cultures and societies.

Some scholars classify genocides in terms of their history and the reasons for such action. *Instrumental genocide* refers to mass murder aimed at achieving specific goals, a motivation often associated with premodern genocides. *Ideological genocide,* on the other hand, refers to situations in which mass murder operates as an end in itself. It is often associated with more modern instances of genocide, including those based on religious or ethnic fundamentalism. The most infamous example of genocide involved the mass killing of Jews, so-called Gypsies, Communists, and other groups based on the Nazis' extreme nationalism and claims to racial superiority. As many scholars have noted, although the Nazis were not the first to engage in genocidal activity, the Holocaust was unprecedented in terms of its modern, distinctly nationalist and industrial character.

Other modern examples include the Cambodian genocide perpetrated by the Khmer Rouge, which took place between 1975 and 1979 as part of Pol Pot's pro-Communist purge. Much of the population was forced into labor camps or killed. This genocide, among the most deadly of the 20th century, resulted in the deaths of nearly one fourth of the nation's population (1.7 out of approximately 7 million). The Rwandan genocide, occurring over a mere 100 days (April to July 1994), provides a more recent example of ideological genocide. In Rwanda, extremist members of the country's Hutu majority attempted to wipe out the Tutsi minority and succeeded in killing an estimated three fourths (850,000) of the country's Tutsi population. The Rwandan genocide presents an extreme instance of a remarkably large number of people killed in such a short period of time.

In terms of prosecution, the UN convention—presently accepted by 135 nations—obligates its signatories to take actions to prevent genocide and punish those involved in it. The UN convention states that violators can be tried in courts in the country where the acts in question occurred or by international tribunal. In the 1990s, the UN Security Council created ad hoc tribunals to try international crimes, specifically the genocides in Yugoslavia and Rwanda. In 2002, the International Criminal Court was established to try such cases, thereby making genocide subject to universal legal standards. The convention's historical significance lies in its role as a foundation for an international system of human rights legislation and enforcement. Despite the UN's success in trying war criminals involved in genocidal activity, the international community remains concerned about the continued development of policies and strategies to prevent genocide and adequately provide for its victims.

Heather Gautney

See also Ethnic Cleansing; Holocaust; Human Rights; Scapegoating

Further Readings

Chalk, Frank and Kurt Jonassohn. 1990. *The History and Sociology of Genocide: Analyses and Case Studies.* New Haven, CT: Yale University Press.

Fein, Helen. 1999. *Genocide: A Sociological Perspective.* London: Sage.

Kuper, Leo. 1981. *Genocide: Its Political Use in the Twentieth Century.* New Haven, CT: Yale University Press.

Lemkin, Raphaël. 1944. *Axis Rule in Occupied Europe.* Washington, DC: Carnegie Endowment for International Peace.

Sartre, Jean-Paul. 1968. *On Genocide.* Boston: Beacon Press.

Totten, Samuel, William S. Parsons, and Israel W. Charny, eds. 1995. *Genocide in the Twentieth Century: Critical Essays and Eyewitness Accounts.* New York: Garland.

GENTRIFICATION

Gentrification refers to the process in which members of a highly educated, professional class move into formerly working- or lower-class city districts, populated largely by members of minority groups. The term *gentrification* derives from the European concept of "gentry" and the "gentry class" and suggests, historically, a class whose manners, tastes, and sense of leisure, refinement, and gentility mirrored and emulated the values and habits of the aristocracy.

Contemporary discussions of gentrification take on added importance because of the American ambivalence toward cities as centers of cultural, political, and economic life. If, as Georg Simmel suggests, cities are the greatest representation of societal culture and civilization, they also represent heightened diversity, crowds, noises, anonymity, and a loss of privacy. For these reasons, members of the middle and upper classes have historically sought refuge beyond city boundaries for more space and to engage in activities with members of their own class. However, in the 1950s and 1960s, a series of political, educational, and economic changes occurred that significantly affected the health and prosperity of many U.S. cities. These changes would play a dramatic role in urban gentrification.

First were the government programs in the post–World War II era to address the housing shortage created by returning veterans and the resultant baby boom. These set in motion a suburban building boom that enabled builders to construct housing developments on vacant land outside the cities and hundreds of thousands of families to buy an affordable home of their own. In the years to follow, shopping centers, office parks, and industrial parks would move outward also, all of which would have a negative impact on most cities.

Next came the 1954 *Brown v. Board of Education* decision, initially directed toward the South, but which, under the efforts of Martin Luther King, Jr. and others, applied likewise to northern schools. This increased the outflow of white middle-class residents who sought refuge outside city limits where integration was not mandated. In the 1960s a series of urban riots further accelerated a white exodus and led to the growth of series of satellite suburbs encircling cities and towns. As "white flight" occurred, a simultaneous inflow of blacks came into many U.S. cities, as well as tens of thousands of Puerto Ricans into the New York metropolitan region. This demographic shift had an almost revolutionary impact on the political, economic, and cultural landscape of U.S. cities.

Cities faced several problems. As homes and apartment buildings built in the late 19th and early 20th centuries began to age and deteriorate, cities were losing their tax base: the white middle class. The influx of mostly rural blacks and Puerto Ricans, and the existence of the small, black middle class in most U.S. cities, could not offset the lost tax revenues caused by white flight. Furthermore, President Eisenhower's massive highway construction program made it possible, and easier, for whites to move back and forth between their residence in suburbia and their workplace in the cities from which they had exited.

Urban politicians and businessmen appealed to the federal government for assistance in reshaping their cities and for relieving the traffic jams that resulted from suburbanites (many ex-city dwellers) traveling back and forth between work and home. As a result, in the 1960s and 1970s, cities across the country initiated massive urban renewal programs and built intra-city expressways that destroyed historic and long-existing neighborhoods and communities, homes, churches, community centers, and schools. Some areas not in the path of renewal and expressways were also affected, as cities sought to upgrade building codes, especially those concerned with plumbing and electrical wiring. This became an expensive venture, especially for apartment building landlords or working-class people who had inherited the family home and could not afford the expenses of bringing their properties up to contemporary code standards.

As a consequence, cheap housing—in comparison with escalating suburban home costs—became available in the inner cities. This enticing inducement attracted two groups that spurred on the gentrifying process: ex-urbanites wanting to return to the city and young, highly educated professionals. As they grew older, the ex-urbanites, now empty nesters, sought a more intense interaction with people, activities, and institutions which in the aggregate could only be found in cities. The second group, nicknamed "yuppies," worked in the cities' banks, businesses, colleges and universities, and hospitals. These childless couples and single individuals loved city life and its amenities—theaters, restaurants, parks, museums and galleries, and shops—and did not want the hassles of long commuter drives. Also, unlike the previous generation of white middle-class parents, those with young children in the late 20th century had model schools, which many cities created largely to retain their small and dwindling white middle class. Some of these model schools were excellent and enticed many parents to move into cities and have their children attend one of them.

Consequently, with loans, savings, financial gifts, or money borrowed from family members, these groups began a massive remodeling program to reshape old communities and create new ones. They moved into old, often dilapidated buildings, many just shells, and spent millions to refashion some of the old Victorian homes and brownstone buildings back to what they were 50 to 70 years ago. The results were impressive; eyesores disappeared, street activity and safety returned, and the neighborhood economy thrived.

But the gentrification process came at a human cost. From urban renewal to the building of expressways, the poor were shuttled from place to place, often with their new housing more dilapidated than the old. Poor and minority communities, who had complained for years over the lack of sufficient streetlights and the invisibility of police patrols, now saw an abundance of both in these gentrified neighborhoods and communities. In addition, men not involved with drugs, who would congregate peacefully on corners and stoops,

with gentrification now found themselves harassed by the police, who demanded that they move on. And working-class and lower-middle-class renters and owners who had lived in their neighborhoods for years often faced insurmountable financial stress as their rents and real estate taxes increased. Once the gentrifiers improved their properties, higher rents and property taxes followed. Thus, for many whose income did not match the increased expenses, the only choice was to move away. In some cities, such as Charleston, South Carolina, the gentrifying process grew to such an extent that it became virtually impossible for even middle-class blacks and whites to purchase homes in the peninsular portion of the city. Instead, the middle class moved to the area west of the Ashley River, whereas the working, lower classes moved to the less expensive and not yet gentrified city of North Charleston.

Because gentrification is intricately linked to matters of class, race, and ethnicity, this process has its pluses and minuses. Had urban politicians and the state and federal officials been more attentive to matters related to housing in inner cities, the consequences of gentrification in certain cities might not have been so detrimental to inner-city residents. The question is whether it is necessary to destroy a community in order to save it. Upscale buildings and restored homes unquestionably revitalized the cities, but holistic urban planning might have prevented destruction of the sense of community among low-income people and the networks around which they built their lives.

Rutledge M. Dennis

See also *Brown v. Board of Education*; Community; Inner City; Inner-Ring Suburb; Segregation, Residential; Urban Decline; Urban Renewal; Urban Sprawl; Urban Underclass

Further Readings

Bassand, Michel. 1990. *Urbanization: Appropriation of Space and Culture.* New York: Graduate School and University Center, City University of New York.

Castells, Manuel. 1983. *The City and the Grassroots.* Berkeley, CA: University of California Press.

Coates, Rodney and Rutledge M. Dennis, eds. 2007. *The New Black: Alternative Paradigms and Strategies for the 21st Century.* Oxford, England: Elsevier.

Downs, Anthony. 1976. *Urban Problems and Prospects.* Chicago: Rand McNally.

Harvey, David. 1973. *Social Justice and the City.* Baltimore: Johns Hopkins University Press.

Savage, Mike and Alan Warde. 2003. *Urban Sociology, Capitalism and Modernity.* 2nd ed. New York: Palgrave.

Schnore, Leo, ed. 1975. *Social Science and the City.* New York: Praeger.

Tabb, William and Larry Sawers, eds. 1984. *Marxism and the Metropolis.* 2nd ed. New York: Oxford University Press.

Willie, Charles and Susan Greenblatt, eds. 1981. *Community Politics and Educational Change.* New York: Longman.

GERRYMANDERING

Gerrymandering is the practice of drawing political boundaries—especially the boundaries of legislative districts—in such a way as to obtain political advantage. The term derives from the claim of critics that a legislative district drawn by supporters of Massachusetts Governor Elbridge Gerry in 1812 was shaped like a salamander, or "Gerry-mander."

Consider the hypothetical region shown in Figure 1, with supporters of party A indicated by the light squares and supporters of party B by the dark squares. In proportional voting systems, the fact that 22/36 of the voters support party A would mean that party A would get that proportion—22/36—of the representation. But in a winner-take-all voting system (as in the United States), the region must be divided into a fixed number of single-winner districts. Assume that by virtue of its population, the region is entitled to three legislators, and hence the region must be divided into three legislative districts.

If the district lines are drawn as in Figure 2, then party B will win two out of the three districts (because it has a majority of the votes in each of the two lower districts, while party A has all the votes in the upper district). On the other hand, if the district lines are drawn as in Figure 3, then party A will win two out of the three districts (the top two districts). And if they are drawn as in Figure 4, then party A will carry all three districts. Thus, whoever gets to draw the lines can maximize partisan advantage.

Different district lines yield different political outcomes because, under winner-take-all voting, a

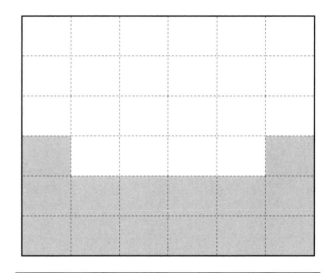

Figure 1   Region With Supporters of Party A (Light Squares) and Party B (Dark Squares)

Note: Each square represents 100,000 voters.

party wins a district whether it has a large majority (with many wasted votes) or a narrow majority. So by arranging for one's own party to win its districts as narrowly as possible and for one's opponents to win their districts with as many wasted votes as possible, one can maximize the number of districts won. (Of course, a party might not want to make its winning edge too narrow, lest a shift in voter sentiment lead to an electoral loss.) With modern computer technology and detailed voter databases, it is possible to manipulate political boundaries with great precision.

Several mathematical procedures exist for neutrally drawing district lines—for example, the shortest split-line algorithm. However, it is sometimes thought desirable to have a district made up of people sharing a community of interest (say, living in the same municipality or county, or on the same side of a mountain), factors that cannot readily be accounted for mathematically. Once discretion is allowed, the opportunity exists for manipulation to suit partisan interest.

In Canada and Britain, independent commissions draw the electoral boundaries. In most U.S. states, the state legislatures—which are partisan bodies—draw the congressional district lines. In a few states, a nonpartisan or bipartisan agency—such as Iowa's Legislative Service Bureau, the Washington State Redistricting Commission, and the Arizona Independent Redistricting Commission—is responsible for

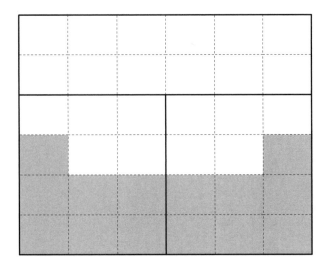

Figure 2   Party B Wins Two out of Three Districts

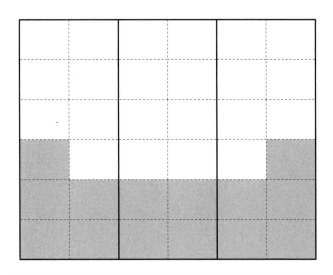

Figure 4   Party A Wins All Three Districts

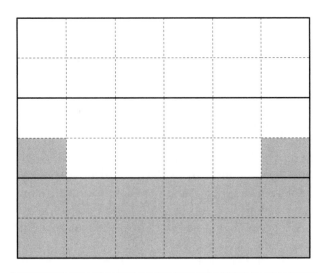

Figure 3   Party A Wins Two out of Three Districts

drawing the lines. Such agencies are often prohibited from considering any demographic data other than population headcount. In some cases these agencies have the last word; in others the state legislature can amend the commission's plan within specified limits.

In the United States, after a new census is conducted every 10 years, the states engage in "redistricting," that is, redrawing their district lines to ensure that each district has roughly equal population. Thus, gerrymandering was once a decennial concern. In 2006, however, the Supreme Court ruled (in *League of United Latin American Citizens v. Perry*)

that there was nothing to prevent a state legislature, when its political control switched from one party to another, from engaging in mid-decade redistricting to change districts drawn earlier in conformity with the census.

The U.S. Supreme Court ruled that boundary drawing must result in "compact districts of contiguous territory" with roughly equal population. In practice, however, districts have been permitted in all sorts of bizarre shapes. Although the Court barred redrawing district lines so as to obtain excessive partisan advantage, it failed to offer a standard for determining whether a partisan gerrymander is excessive, and it has even allowed patently partisan line drawing to stand. Some Supreme Court justices urge that a standard of excessive partisanship be developed; others believe that no such standard can be constructed.

The Supreme Court has prohibited the drawing of district lines where the intent is to disenfranchise racial or ethnic minorities. Some states created legislative districts where a majority of voters are members of a racial or ethnic minority (so-called majority-minority districts) to ensure that some legislators will be minorities. Republicans often support such "racial gerrymandering," with the hope that concentrating minority voters (who tend to vote Democratic) will reduce the number of Democratic legislators statewide.

Gerrymandering need not always be done for partisan advantage; sometimes it is used for the *bipartisan* advantage of incumbents. That is, incumbents of both parties might support a redistricting scheme that makes all incumbents more likely to win reelection. For example, if representatives from party A and party B have been elected from two adjoining districts, each district having voter sentiment divided approximately 50–50 between the two parties, the district lines could be redrawn so that each has a comfortable 70–30 edge, thus assuring reelection.

Stephen R. Shalom

See also Redistricting, Congressional Districts

Further Readings

Cox, Gary W. and Jonathan N. Katz. 2002. *Elbridge Gerry's Salamander: The Electoral Consequences of the Reapportionment Revolution.* New York: Cambridge University Press.

Forgette, Richard and Glenn Platt. 2005. "Redistricting Principles and Incumbency Protection in the U.S. Congress." *Political Geography* 24(8):934–51.

GINI COEFFICIENT

The Gini coefficient is a popular statistical measure of income inequality. It was developed by an Italian statistician, Corrado Gini, in 1912 as a measure of concentration applicable to the distribution of wealth, income, or any other continuous variable. Gini coefficients can range from a minimum of 0 (perfect equality) to a maximum of 1 (perfect inequality). Higher values of the Gini indicate greater income inequality, or income concentration, whereas lower values indicate more equality. In a hypothetical society with perfect equality, the Gini = 0 and all families or persons receive an income equal to the average, whereas in a society with perfect *inequality,* Gini = 1 and a single family or person receives all income.

Gini coefficients have an intuitive interpretation because the measure can be represented graphically on a Lorenz curve (see Figure 1). A Lorenz curve has several components: a 45-degree line representing the line of perfect equality, the cumulative proportion of the population plotted on the horizontal axis, and the cumulative proportion of income plotted on the vertical axis. The Lorenz curve plots the degree of deviation from the 45-degree line of perfect equality. The Gini coefficient is sometimes called a ratio because it reflects the ratio between the 45-degree line of equality and the Lorenz curve relative to the total area. Thus, if the area between the line of perfect equality and the Lorenz curve is A, and B represents the area below the Lorenz curve, then the Gini ratio is equal to A/(A+B).

The Gini coefficient is satisfactory on a number of grounds. It follows the principle of transfers because when income is redistributed from a richer person or family to a poorer one, the Gini index decreases, and when income is redistributed from a poorer to a richer individual or family, it increases. Gini coefficients are also scale-invariant in that when all incomes are increased by some constant, the Gini coefficient yields the same result. In practical terms, this means that Gini coefficients are not affected by inflation.

The Gini coefficient of U.S. family income has been reported by the Census Bureau since 1947. In 1968 the Gini coefficient reached a low of 0.348, whereas in 2005 the Gini coefficient reached 0.440. The increase reflects the general trend of rising income inequality in the United States. A calculation of the Gini coefficient using 2005 data from the U.S. Internal Revenue Service, based on a more comprehensive income definition than the census, yields a Gini coefficient of 0.587.

Despite its strengths, the Gini coefficient is not without criticism. Social scientists have pointed out that the Gini index is more sensitive to the middle of a typical income distribution. In other words, when transfers occur between very rich or very poor individuals, the Gini coefficient will be less sensitive (i.e., will not register much change) than when changes occur among middle-income families or persons. Another problem is that the Gini coefficient does not have an intuitive method for decomposing inequality into an additive within-group and between-group component, but social scientists (mostly economists) have provided potential techniques for decomposing the index.

Thomas W. Volscho

See also Income Disparity; Inequality

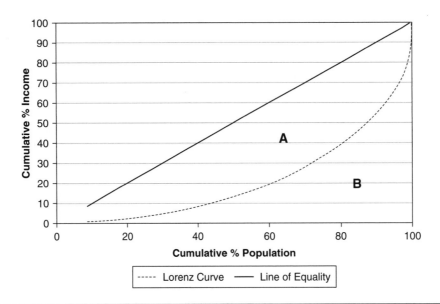

Figure 1   Lorenz Curve of U.S. Adjusted Gross Income, 2005

Further Readings

Allison, Paul D. 1978. "Measures of Inequality." *American Sociological Review* 43:865–80.

Firebaugh, Glenn. 2003. *The New Geography of Global Income Inequality.* Cambridge, MA: Harvard University Press.

GLASS CEILING

The glass ceiling is a metaphorical reference to systemic obstacles created in the workplace that prevent the socioeconomic advancement of minority groups by blocking them from reaching the upper echelons of leadership and management. This concept suggests that individuals who are otherwise qualified for higher-level positions are unfairly limited in their advancement through the organizational ranks. Traditionally, the glass ceiling metaphor pertained exclusively to women, but contemporary definitions now extend it to include minority groups as well. As the term *glass ceiling* implies, the barriers that limit these individuals are not immediately apparent but are tantamount to bumping one's head against a glass ceiling. The opposite term, *glass escalator,* refers to men's more rapid upward movement in organizations, suggesting a gender bias.

Historical Perspective

Coined in 1986 by the *Wall Street Journal,* the glass ceiling characterized organizational constraints that limit the movement of women to assuming leadership and managerial positions. The term quickly worked itself into the public vernacular as women earned promotions to middle management positions in increasing numbers while few advanced further. The glass ceiling metaphor has since been repeatedly stretched and molded to also apply to career mobility for those of minority group status based on race, ethnicity, disability, or sexual orientation. While there have been numerous interpretations of this phenomenon, the fundamental and underlying concept has remained the same: the scarcity of women's movement into top management positions in the workplace.

In its definition of the glass ceiling, the U.S. government views the glass ceiling as any artificial barriers that prevent qualified individuals from advancing upward in their organization into management-level positions because of an attitudinal or organizational bias. With this definition, the glass ceiling now applies to all minorities, and not exclusively to women. The importance of this concept is that it implies that minority group members experience greater resistance to their advancement as they climb their organizational ladders. Although the experience of career impediments is common for all minorities, the patterns differ depending on minority group membership. For example, minority men are not as likely to experience sexual harassment, a barrier to mobility, as their female counterparts do.

The glass ceiling is a reality when certain preconditions exist in the workplace. First, workplace inequalities based on race, ethnicity, gender, or other minority indicators cannot be explained by the employee's job performance. Second, racial and gender disparities in representation are more evident at higher organizational levels than at lower levels. Third, advancement becomes more difficult for minorities as their careers progress.

Research

Some research analyzes the glass ceiling phenomenon by examining quantitative and experiential representations of minorities occupying top management positions. In comparison with conventional barriers to career advancement, such as educational qualifications and job performance reviews, barriers that constitute the glass ceiling are frequently rooted in cultural, societal, and psychological factors. Because of the transcendent and subjective nature of the glass ceiling phenomenon, research analysis has produced mixed and varied results. However, its existence in the corporate world is less questioned than its constituent elements, which continue to be a subject of debate among researchers.

Society as a whole presents a major hurdle to the movement of minorities through the corporate ranks. Discrimination arising from strongly held attitudes, biases, and stereotypes toward women and minorities, as well as varying perspectives of normative behaviors associated with gender and social groups, directly contribute to the glass ceiling.

Researchers have identified three interrelated and panoptic hindrances to the upward mobility of females and members of minority groups on the corporate ladder in their examination and inquiry into the glass ceiling phenomenon. One barrier involves societal and cultural aspects or socialized attitudes or social psychological factors that can impose restrictions. A second barrier deals with organizational limitations or structural factors, and the third barrier addresses the personal, individual, and psychological factors that may interfere with the promotion process.

The supply barrier is the pervasive social force that acts to directly hinder women and members of minority groups from attaining the credentials necessary to move forward in their professional development. This, in turn, leads to a deficiency in the number of skilled and qualified women and minorities. Empirical research shows that each group has differential access to resources, educational and work opportunities, and status. As a result, women and minorities are frequently relegated to the confines of a narrow range of restrictive occupations, a pattern known as "occupational segregation."

The difference barrier arises from the social and cultural preconceptions associated with certain individual differences, such as gender, color, and culture. These barriers can interfere with job performance and employer evaluations. For example, prejudices associated with gender are frequently anchored in the traditionally held views of women's roles in society. Cultural and racial biases are also rooted in the established values and norms of the majority.

Individual and psychological barriers are the result of internalizing the generally held perceptions and stereotypes about women and minorities that employers may hold. Individual and societal barriers are deeply interwoven as lack of self-confidence, motivation, and aspirations. These usually stem from the generally held perceptions and stereotypes about women and minorities which these group members then internalize. One consequence can be development of an inferiority complex.

Organizational barriers occur within the workplace and its structures, a pattern known as "institutional discrimination." Institutional discrimination is systemic and ingrained in policies, laws, and procedures within an organization and is designed to keep individuals or groups of individuals subordinated. This can be intentional or unintentional by design and can include recruitment and hiring practices in the workplace. This barrier also extends to systems which may not be intentionally discriminatory but which generate the effect of depriving women and members of minority groups. These include corporate environments that alienate and isolate those in minority groups.

Future Directions

Networking is an important process that contributes to the entrenchment of the glass ceiling. Employees typically become aware of open positions through word-of-mouth networking, and many organizations routinely hire from word-of-mouth referrals. In predominantly white male organizations, referrals will generally produce more white males for available opportunities. Under current federal guidelines, therefore, organizations must maintain responsibility for general awareness and enforcement of equal opportunity and affirmative action mandates.

Despite growing awareness among leaders in the corporate world of the intrinsic economic value of including women and minorities in senior corporate positions, progress remains slow in penetrating glass ceiling barriers. While each individual company is clearly different and must evaluate its own particular needs, advocates insist that all companies must address each of the glass ceiling barriers, that they must embrace diversity and inclusion from the top down. They also suggest that corporate leaders work to change the climate of the work environment by including a mentoring process to assist in the success and upward mobility of women and minorities.

DeLois "Kijana" Crawford

See also Affirmative Action; Discrimination, Institutional; Feminism; Feminist Theory; Gender Bias; Gender Gap; Hostile Environment; Pink-Collar Occupations; Segregation, Gender; Segregation, Occupational; Sexism

Further Readings

Catalyst. 1990. *Women in Corporate Management: Results of a Catalyst Survey.* New York: Catalyst.

Cotter, David, Joan A. Herman, Seth M. Ovadia, and Reeve Vanneman. 2001. "The Glass Ceiling Effect." *Social Forces* 80(2):655–82.

Federal Glass Ceiling Commission. 1995. "Good for Business: Making Full Use of the Nation's Human Capital." Washington, DC: U.S. Department of Labor.

———. 1996. "Solid Investment: Making Full Use of the Nation's Human Capital." Washington, DC: U.S. Department of Labor.

Phelps, Rosemary E. and Madonna G. Constantine. 2000. "Hitting the Roof: The Impact of the Glass-Ceiling Effect on the Career Development of African Americans." Pp. 161–75 in *Career Counseling for African Americans*, edited by W. Walsh, B. Bingham, R. P. Bingham, M. T. Brown, and C. M. Ward. Mahwah, NJ: Erlbaum.

U.S. Department of Labor. 1991. "A Report on the Glass Ceiling Initiative." Washington, DC: U.S. Department of Labor.

Wellington, Alison J. 1993. "Changes in the Male/Female Wage Gap." *Journal of Human Resources* 38:383–411.

Wieand, Paul. 2002. "Drucker's Challenge: Communication and the Emotional Glass Ceiling." *Ivey Business Journal* 66(5):32–37.

GLOBAL ECONOMY

The global economy refers to the increasing economic interdependence of the countries and regions of the world. The most recent form of the global economy emerged in the 1970s as a result of advancements in information technologies combined with expanding neoliberal, political-economic philosophies and policies. The extent of the global economy is very uneven, with some regions of the world largely bypassed by the process.

A functionalist perspective of the global economy views these trends as virtuous because of the economic efficiencies gained through the global division of labor based on comparative advantage combined with the advancement of democracy worldwide. From this perspective the global economy is a natural evolution of the modernization of societies. This evolution reduces social inequality and enhances the living standards of people across the globe.

A conflict perspective views these trends as vicious, as transnational corporations adopt flexible accumulation strategies to avoid democratic protections, resulting in a "race to the bottom" as countries deregulate to attract foreign direct investment. This process results in the decreased ability of nation-states to coordinate their internal economic and political affairs and in a reduction in substantive democracy. From this perspective, the global economy has led to an increase in stratification within countries of the North, as well as between the North and South.

The global economy is grounded in a long historical process of increasing political and economic integration of the countries and regions of the world. The spice trade of the 1400s led to the first global economy. Technologies such as the sextant, ocean sailing vessel, and cannon/musket allowed the European nations to embrace their "manifest destiny" and send out their fleets in the name of church, king, and country. This process accelerated in the 1700s as a result of the industrial revolution in Europe and the accompanying colonization of much of the non-European world. The international division of labor consisted of a manufacture-based system in the core countries and a mining/agriculture-based system in the colonies. At its peak in the early 1900s, this global economy divided the globe into a system of two unequal components based on asymmetrical power relations of trade, imperialism, and racist ideologies. Capitalist development in the core countries produced underdevelopment in the periphery.

The second global economy was linked to World War I and the Russian Revolution of 1917. As the core countries focused on the war, liberation movements grew in the old colonies. The Soviet Union served as a model and ally for colonial nations to challenge their core counterparts. These events began a reversal of the global concentration of capital, power, and manufacturing in the core. World War II accelerated this process. Italy and Japan lost their colonies and England, France, Belgium, and the Netherlands realized that they could not quell the rising liberation movements. Several former colonies tried collective ownership and centralized planning. It was in this setting that China embraced the path of communism. By the 1960s close to one half of the world's population lived in communist countries. Several other former colonies did not reject markets but abandoned most of the laissez-faire doctrines of the colonial system and adopted a variety of state-managed interventionist measures to support development. A decentralization of power occurred, resulting in the second global economy centered on the bipolar communist and capitalist models of development.

After World War II numerous events set the stage for the current form of the global economy. First, in 1946 political and economic officials from the United States and Great Britain developed a management plan for the postwar global economy. The Bretton Woods Agreement led to the creation of the World Bank, the International Monetary Fund (IMF), and the General Agreement on Tariffs and Trade (GATT) and linked the U.S. dollar to the gold standard as the basis for international currency exchange rates. Second, the United States created the Marshall Plan to rebuild Europe and the McArthur Plan to rebuild Japan. Both of these plans instilled neoliberal economic policies and democratic political systems in these regions. Similar initiatives were taken in Korea in the 1950s, Vietnam in the 1960s, and other countries throughout the world. The creation of the North Atlantic Treaty Organization cemented the military alliance between the United States and the rebuilding countries in Europe to counter the growing power of the USSR. This "global development project" became the major mechanism utilized by the capitalist countries to ensure that communism did not take root in these areas. From the 1950s through the 1980s, the "cold war" was the label given to this contest for world

domination. In the late 1980s the USSR broke apart due to economic bankruptcy and social unrest; the capitalists won.

The Bretton Woods system of global management, based on neoliberal economic policies, laid the groundwork for the blossoming of the current global economy. The World Bank provided loans for infrastructure development projects and the IMF provided loans to stabilize developing countries' currencies in the South. At the same time the GATT worked to decrease trade and tariff barriers and foster increased foreign direct investment. Over time these loans included requirements that developing countries liberalize their political and economic systems. This neoliberal restructuring peaked in the 1980s, as debt crises led to structural adjustment programs that included the deregulation of national protectionist policies and a privatization of national industries, two processes that facilitated increased foreign direct investment by the transnational corporations of the North.

A similar process also occurred in the North, especially in the United States. In the 1960s and 1970s, the rigidities of the Fordist system of socioeconomic development fostered a fiscal crisis of the nation-state and an accumulation crisis of capital. The long run of economic prosperity that began after World War II weakened, as the Fordist system of mass production linked to mass production coordinated via an interventionist state could no longer provide for economic accumulation and societal legitimation. Profits for corporations in the North were constrained by powerful labor unions, environmental regulations, growing competition from Asia (Japan and Korea), and the rise of a third world social movement in the form of OPEC (Organization of Petroleum Exporting Countries). Additionally, the high costs of the cold war (Vietnam and other venues) and the War on Poverty generated a fiscal crisis of the state in the United States, as well as a legitimation crisis, as anti-war, environmental, and civil rights movements protested government policies. In 1973, the "dollar linked to gold standard" was abandoned, and global currencies began to fluctuate wildly. The fluctuations led to currency speculations that became a central aspect of the current global economy.

In response to the more tightly regulated economies and strength of unions in the North that limited corporate profits, many major corporations expanded their global business ventures in an attempt to revive economic accumulation. Capital flight, the decentralization of production, the informalization of labor, and global sourcing became the dominant strategies of transnational corporations. Information technologies allowed for the development and coordination of global-commodity chains. The sphere of influence of the polity no longer matched that of the economy. Through the hypermobility of capital, the economy went global, but the nation-states remained constrained within their jurisdictional boundaries.

In the 1980s the Thatcher and Reagan administrations introduced neoliberal restructuring programs centered on deregulation of government policies and privatization of government-owned enterprises, thereby weakening unions and environmental protections while lessening regulations limiting corporate expansion and concentration. These actions were attempts on the part of the highly regulated nations in the first world to open their economies to re-attract capital investment to the North.

The final pieces of the current global economy are the emerging global governance structures. In 1995, the GATT was reconfigured as the World Trade Organization (WTO), the supranational state-like coordinating mechanism for the global economy. The WTO continues the function of the GATT in lowering tariffs but also acts as a governance body regarding trade disputes. Similarly, the European Union, North American Free Trade Agreement, and Association of South East Asian Nations are examples of the emergence of regional statelike entities that emulate the historical functions of the nation-state in mediating economic accumulation and societal legitimation. Anti-globalization activists resist both the regional organizations and the WTO.

Douglas Harbin Constance

See also Economic Development; Economic Restructuring; Globalization; World-Systems Analysis

Further Readings

Agnew, John. 2001. "The New Global Economy: Time-Space Compression, Geopolitics, and Global Uneven Development." Working Paper No. 3. Los Angeles: Center for Globalization and Policy Research, School of Public Policy and Social Research.

Alam, M. Shahid. 2003. "A Short History: The Global Economy since 1800." *Counterpunch*, July. Retrieved December 26, 2007 (http://aslama.org/Econ/EconGlobalEcon.pdf).

Harvey, David. 1990. *The Condition of Post-modernity*. Oxford, England: Basil Blackwell.

International Monetary Fund. 2001. "World Economic Outlook: December 2001—The Global Economy after September 11." Washington, DC: International Monetary Fund.

McMichael, Philip. 2004. *Development and Social Change: A Global Perspective*. Thousand Oaks, CA: Pine Forge.

Piore, Michael J. and Charles Sabel. 1984. *The Second Industrial Divide: Possibilities for Prosperity*. New York: Basic Books.

GLOBALIZATION

Today's dominant account about economic globalization in media and policy circles, as well as in much economic analysis, emphasizes hypermobility, global communications, the neutralization of place and distance, and the growth of a new professional transnational class. But this emphasis on abstract capabilities of systems and on the demand for highly educated workers leaves out many significant aspects of globalization. Globalization—economic, cultural, political—localizes in multiple concrete settings, and it does so through a broad range of venues and actors. Viewed this way, many more components to globalization exist than those that prevail in the dominant account. It is not only the powerful who are actors in these processes of globalization.

Global and Subnational Scalings

Two distinct sets of dynamics constitute globalization. One set involves the formation of explicitly global institutions and processes, such as the World Trade Organization, global financial markets, and the War Crimes Tribunals. These vary greatly in their aims, from narrow self-interest to enhancing the common good. They operate at the scale usually associated with the term *globalization*. For many, globalization is about these types of conditions and institutions.

But there is a second set of processes that does not necessarily scale at the global level as such, but rather takes place deep inside territories and institutional domains that have largely been constructed in national terms in much, though by no means all, of the world. This largely subnational and translocal form of globalization has received less attention from mainstream scholarship and is far less likely to be conceptualized or recognized as part of globalization; one important exception is the rapidly growing scholarship on world cities and global cities. What makes these processes part of globalization even though localized in national, indeed subnational, settings such as cities is that they involve transboundary networks and domains connecting or articulating multiple local or "national" processes and actors. These include transnational immigrant households and communities; cross-border networks of activists in specific localized struggles with an explicit or implicit global agenda, as is the case with many human rights and environmental organizations; and, generally, cross-border cultural, economic, and political circuits constitutive of the multiple globalizations seen today.

Thus, global processes get constituted at various scales, ranging from supranational and global to subnational and local, and there are many globalizations, from economic to cultural. Many of the globally scaled dynamics, such as the global capital market, actually are partly embedded in subnational scales and move between globally scaled levels (such as electronic financial networks) and locally embedded conditions (such as the actual on-the-ground financial centers). Many localized entities, such as immigrant communities, can be part of transnational circuits and thereby part of globalization; these are a kind of horizontal globalization rather than the vertical forms represented by the International Monetary Fund (IMF), for instance.

In this more complex understanding of globalization, it is then possible to see how the global can also involve subnational places and the many local conditions, processes, and actors this brings with it. Thus the global economic system is partly embedded in specific types of places and partly constituted through highly specialized cross-border networks connecting the 40 or so major business and financial centers (global cities) in the world today (from cities such as New York and London to São Paulo, Shanghai, and Johannesburg). Recapturing the geography of places involved in globalization allows us to recapture people, workers, communities, and more specifically, the many different work cultures, besides the corporate culture, involved in the work of globalization.

It is important to note that globalization is also enabling liberating activities and practices, for example, specific aspects of the human rights and environmental movements as well as particular activities of the anti-globalization network. Globalization also enables the formation of countergeographies of globalization,

some exploitative and others emancipatory. The focus of this entry is on the problematic aspects of globalization, which also means a greater emphasis on the global economy.

Recovering Places and Workers in the Global Economy

Hypermobility and the neutralizing of place have indeed taken place. But they are only half of the story. The other half is the territorial centralization of top-level management, control operations, and the most advanced specialized services in a network of global cities. National and global markets, as well as globally integrated operations, require central places where the most complex tasks required by the global economy get done. Further, information industries require a vast physical infrastructure containing strategic nodes with hyperconcentration of facilities. Finally, even the most advanced information industries have a work process involving many different types of workplaces and workers.

The capabilities for global operation, coordination, and control contained in the new information technologies and in the power of transnational corporations need to be produced. By focusing on the production of these capabilities, a neglected dimension is added to the familiar issue of the power of large corporations and the new technologies. The emphasis shifts to the *practices* that constitute what is called economic globalization and global control: the work of producing and reproducing the organization and management of a global production system and a global marketplace for finance.

A focus on practices draws the categories of place and work process into the analysis of economic globalization. These are two categories easily overlooked in accounts centered on the hypermobility of capital and the power of transnationals. Developing categories such as place and work process does not negate the importance of hypermobility and power. Rather, it brings to the fore the fact that many of the resources necessary for global economic activities are not hypermobile and are, indeed, deeply embedded in place, notably places such as global cities and export processing zones. Global processes are structured by local constraints, including the composition of the workforce, work cultures, and political cultures and processes within nation-states.

Once this production process is brought into the analysis, secretaries are seen as part of it and so are the cleaners of the buildings where the professionals do their work and the buildings where they live. An economic configuration very different from that suggested by the concept of information economy emerges. The material conditions, production sites, and place-boundedness, which are also part of globalization and the information economy, are recovered.

The Other Workers in the Advanced Corporate Economy

One of the localizations of the dynamics of globalization is the process of economic restructuring in global cities which has generated a large growth in the demand for low-wage workers and jobs that offer few advancement possibilities. This has occurred amid an explosion in the wealth and power concentrated in these cities—that is to say, in conditions where there is also a visible expansion of very high income jobs.

In the day-to-day work of the leading sectors in global cities, a large share of the jobs involved are lowly paid and manual, many held by immigrant women. Even the most advanced professionals require clerical, cleaning, and repair workers for their state-of-the-art offices, and they require truckers to bring not only the software but also the toilet paper. Although these types of workers and jobs are never represented as part of the global economy, they are in fact part of the infrastructure of jobs involved in running and implementing the global economic system, including such an advanced form of it as international finance.

High-level corporate services, from accounting to decision-making expertise, are not usually analyzed in terms of their work process. Such services are usually seen as a type of output, that is, high-level technical knowledge. Thus insufficient attention has gone to the actual array of jobs, from high-paying to low-paying, involved in the production of these services. A focus on the work process brings to the fore the labor question. Information outputs must be produced, and the buildings that hold the workers must be built and cleaned. The rapid growth of the financial industry and of highly specialized services generates not only high-level technical and administrative jobs but also low-wage unskilled jobs. In New York and other cities, between 30 and 50 percent of the workers in the leading sectors are low-wage workers.

Further, the similarly state-of-the-art lifestyles of the professionals in these sectors have created a whole new demand for a range of household workers, particularly maids and nannies. The presence of a highly dynamic sector with a polarized income distribution has its own impact on the creation of low-wage jobs through the sphere of consumption (or, more generally, social reproduction). The rapid growth of industries with strong concentrations of high- and low-income jobs has assumed distinct forms in the consumption structure which, in turn, has a feedback effect on the organization of work and the types of jobs being created. The expansion of the high-income workforce, in conjunction with the emergence of new lifestyles, has led to a process of high-income gentrification that rests, in the last analysis, on the availability of a vast supply of low-wage workers. High-price restaurants, luxury housing, luxury hotels, gourmet shops, boutiques, French hand laundries, and special cleaning services are all more labor-intensive than their lower-price equivalents. This has reintroduced—to an extent not seen in a very long time—the whole notion of the "serving classes" in contemporary high-income households. The immigrant woman serving the white middle-class professional woman has replaced the traditional image of the black female servant serving the white master. All these trends give these cities an increasingly sharp tendency toward social polarization.

The Globalizing of Survival Circuits

Crucial to the formation of a global supply of caretakers and other kinds of low-wage workers in demand in global cities is the fact of systemic links between the growth of global survival circuits and negative economic conditions in countries of origin that have been amplified by economic globalization. Among these conditions are a growth in unemployment, the closure of a large number of typically small and medium-sized enterprises oriented to national rather than export markets, and large, often increasing, government debt. (Although these economies are frequently grouped under the label "developing," they are in some cases struggling, stagnant, or even shrinking.)

Globalized survival circuits have grown in number and diversity at a time when major dynamics linked to economic globalization have had significant impacts on developing economies, including the so-called middle-income countries of Latin America. These countries have had to implement a bundle of new policies and accommodate new conditions associated with globalization: structural adjustment programs

(SAPs), the opening up of these economies to foreign firms, the elimination of multiple state subsidies, and, it would seem almost inevitably, financial crises and the prevailing types of programmatic solutions put forth by the IMF. It is now clear that in most of the countries involved, not only in Latin America but also in countries such as South Korea or Thailand, these conditions have created enormous costs for certain sectors of the economy and of the population and have not fundamentally reduced government debt among those that implemented these programs in the 1980s nor those that did so in the 1990s. In addition, a growing number of middle-income countries are also caught in this debt trap. The actual structure of these debts, their servicing, and how they fit into debtor countries' economies suggest that it is not likely that most of these countries will, under current conditions, be able to pay this debt in full. SAPs seem to have made this even more likely by demanding economic reforms that have added to unemployment and the bankruptcy of many smaller, national market–oriented firms.

Ratios of debt service to gross national product (GNP) in many of the so-called HIPC countries (hyper-indebted poor countries) exceed sustainable limits; many are far more extreme than what were considered unmanageable levels in the Latin American debt crisis of the 1980s. Debt-to-GNP ratios are especially high in Africa, where they stood at 123 percent, compared with 42 percent in Latin America and 28 percent in Asia. It is these features of the current situation that suggest that most of these countries will not get out of their indebtedness through such current strategies as SAPs. Indeed it would seem that the latter have in many cases had the effect of raising the debt dependence of countries. Further, together with various other dynamics, SAPs have contributed to an increase in unemployment and in poverty. For over 15 years the major global lenders resisted recognizing the impossibility of debt repayment by most of the 41 HIPCs. But in January 2006, they finally recognized that the 18 poorest of these countries needed to have their debts cancelled, and eventually probably many of the remaining 23 will also have their debts cancelled.

One way of articulating this in substantive terms is to posit that (a) the shrinking employment opportunities in many of these countries, (b) the shrinking opportunities for more traditional forms of profit making in these same countries, as they increasingly open up to foreign firms in a widening range of economic sectors and are pressured to develop export industries, and (c) the fall in revenues for the governments in many of these countries, partly linked to these conditions and to the burden of debt servicing, have all contributed to raising the importance of alternative ways of making a living, making a profit, and securing government revenue. The IMF asks HIPCs to pay 20 to 25 percent of their export earnings toward debt service. In contrast, in 1953 the Allies cancelled 80 percent of Germany's war debt and only insisted on 3 to 5 percent of export earnings debt service. These more general terms have also been evident in recent history when Central Europe emerged from under communism.

All of these conditions have emerged as factors in the lives of a growing number of men and women in Latin America, Asia, and Africa. A key aspect here is that through their work and remittances, migrants enhance the government revenue of deeply indebted countries; in 2006 total remittances sent back home through the banking system (thus this figure does not cover other ways of getting money back home) were US$230 billion, according to the World Bank. The work of migrating is itself a source of profit for those who trade in people—it offers new profit-making possibilities to "entrepreneurs" (though increasingly it is murderous criminal syndicates who control the trade) who have seen other opportunities vanish as a consequence of global firms and markets entering their countries, or a chance to longtime criminals who can now operate their illegal trade globally. In 2006 criminal syndicates are estimated to have earned US$20 billion from trafficking in people.

These survival circuits are often complex, involving multiple locations and sets of actors constituting increasingly global chains of traders and "workers." There is an emergent and distinct gendering at work in the globalizing of these survival circuits. Both in the global city and in these survival circuits, women emerge as crucial actors for new and expanding types of economies. It is through these supposedly rather valueless economic actors that key components of these new economies have been built.

Globalization plays a specific role here in a double sense, contributing to the formation of links between sending and receiving countries and enabling local and regional practices to become global in scale. On the one hand, the particular dynamics that come together in the global city produce a strong demand for these types of workers, while the dynamics that mobilize women into these survival circuits produce an expanding supply of workers who can be pushed, or are sold, into those types of jobs. On the other hand, the technical infrastructure and transnationalism that underlie some of the key globalized industries are also making it possible for other types of actors to deploy their activities at global scales, whether money laundering or people trafficking.

In brief, the major processes covered in this entry involve both the richest and the poorest countries, and the most powerful actors (whether institutions such as the IMF or criminal syndicates) and the most vulnerable (such as immigrant women trafficked from poor countries to rich global cities). This is just one window into the negatives. There is much more, including dynamics that enable the weak and the poor.

Saskia Sassen

See also Global Economy; Multinational Corporations; Transnational Families; World-Systems Analysis

Further Readings

Sassen, Saskia. 2001. *The Global City: New York, London, Tokyo.* 2nd ed. Princeton, NJ: Princeton University Press.
———. 2006. *Territory, Authority, Rights: From Medieval to Global Assemblages.* Princeton, NJ: Princeton University Press.

Global Warming

One reason the earth is teeming with life is the existence of a natural greenhouse effect. The earth is heated by the sun. After the sun's rays strike the earth, many of them bounce back into space, and the planet would be much colder if there were not gases in the atmosphere to trap part of the heat from these reflected rays. Since the start of the industrial revolution, changing economic activities have been increasing the concentrations of heat-absorbing greenhouse gases (GHGs) in the atmosphere. Computer-generated climate models suggest that the buildup of these additional GHGs, particularly carbon dioxide (CO_2) from burning fossil fuels, will warm the earth's surface. The hypothesis that there will be rising global temperatures from increased human emissions of GHGs and that temperature increases will in turn melt global ice

caps, raise sea levels, and increase extreme weather events like hurricanes and floods is what has come to be termed *global warming*.

According to the Intergovernmental Panel on Climate Change (IPCC)—a worldwide network of scientists set up in 1988 by the World Meteorological Organization and the UN Environment Program to report on all aspects of global warming—global average surface temperatures have increased about 1.0° F since the late 19th century. The 10 warmest years of the 20th century all occurred in the last 15 years of that century, with 1998 being the warmest year on record. Globally, sea levels have risen 4 to 8 inches over the past century. These observations appear to be consistent with what climate models predict: increased concentrations of greenhouse gases in the atmosphere will act like a heat-trapping blanket and raise global temperatures, the heat will cause the oceans to warm and expand, hurricanes will increase in intensity, and so on.

As a result of this apparent congruence between theoretical expectations and observations, many scientists, policymakers, and environmentalists believe that action to reduce future emissions of temperature-raising GHGs is imperative. Since 1997, more than 150 nations have ratified the Kyoto Protocol, which aims to reduce emissions of CO_2. The Kyoto Protocol is a first step toward mitigating global warming, but given that it falls far short of the large and costly reductions of GHGs recommended by the IPCC, some warming is seen as inevitable. This will necessitate adaptation strategies to prevent or reduce undesired consequences. Possible adaptations include defenses against rising sea levels and hurricanes, as well as assuring food security. Overall, then, the framing of global warming as a social problem can be deemed a partial success. Its main limitations include the absence of the United States from the Kyoto process, the probable withdrawal of Canada from it, the likelihood that many countries in the European Union will not meet their reduction targets, and the challenge of incorporating China and India into the Kyoto process.

Marketing Social Problems

Conditions like ozone depletion and global warming can exist without much awareness of them. In both cases, it took scientific theorizing and observations to transform the putative condition into a threat seemingly worthy of attention. Scientific warnings that

GHG emissions could warm the planet began in the late 1950s and continued sporadically until 1988. For the most part, these warnings were ignored. To transform such warnings into a viable social problem—one that commands considerable political, policy, and public attention with concrete links to action—requires a host of conducive conditions and phenomena. These include a much larger cast of claims makers than just scientists, collaboration by the media, dramatic real-world events to piggyback on, bridging metaphors to the popular culture, and an institutional context and an issue culture that support the social problem. Under ideal circumstances, these factors generate a cultural whirlwind—a rapidly evolving and progressive sequence of dynamic and often surprising events that create a vortex, hurling through a variety of arenas, creating a strong conversational and practical presence around the social problem. Clearly, issue cultures, bridging metaphors, and cultural whirlwinds cannot be concocted at will. Global warming has some real liabilities as a marketable social problem.

Issue Cultures and Real-World Events

Issue cultures are sets of related social problems that become commanding concerns in society. Perhaps the clearest example is *anything* to do with security in the United States after the 9/11 terror attacks. Another issue culture has developed around the fear of emerging diseases, ranging from Ebola and mad-cow disease to the West Nile virus, SARS (severe acute respiratory syndrome), and avian flu. Scientific findings or real-world events related to these problems are immediately selected for coverage by the media and attention from spokespersons in different public arenas. Social problems that can be linked to an extant issue culture are thus far more likely to attract sustained attention than problems that do not fit or resonate with any current issue culture. Clearly, proponents of a social problem would prefer to hook up with an existing issue culture and thereby garner attention. Such linkages, of course, are not automatic or assured.

Through the 1980s, an issue culture built up around the atmosphere, as a number of social problems from this domain rose in rapid succession. The popular theory that climatic change caused the extinction of the dinosaurs was followed by a furor over the threat of nuclear winter. But the cold war began to wind down after 1985, just in time for the discovery of the ozone

hole. Here the timing was remarkable. With the successful negotiation of the Montreal Protocol in 1987, the ozone problem was largely resolved, just in time for climate change to emerge as a celebrity problem. Before the "greenhouse summer" of 1988, claims making about global warming received little attention. But that summer's severe heat and drought in North America, accompanied by the burning of Yellowstone National Park, put the issue on the map. There were numerous calls for action, and surveys revealed that the public was aware of the threat.

In subsequent years, despite a host of extreme weather events, such as the 1993 Mississippi floods, climate change became a secondary issue in the United States. This is in direct contrast with the European Union, which assumed a leadership role and promoted the Kyoto Protocol. Real-world events were central in Europe, as England had the Great Storm of 1987 and Germany experienced floods and storms that each caused more than a billion U.S. dollars' worth of damage. German scientists drew an extreme picture of an "impending climatic catastrophe"—a *Klima-Katastrophe*—and the term gained incredible momentum in political and media discourse. The emerging EU consensus, an effort in part to create a strong and unified international presence for the bloc, was forged in a very different institutional context than found in the United States. The U.S. political system is much more open to outside lobbying interests (such as oil companies), and a few powerful senators heading key environmental committees can block legislation. In addition, a relatively small number of "climate skeptics" who challenged the global warming consensus attracted considerable attention in the United States but were largely absent in the European Union. The electoral success of Green Parties in Europe also led the major political parties to try to preempt green issues. Finally, the precautionary principle has made considerable headway in Europe and serves to promote action under conditions of uncertainty. The United States, in contrast, has stressed the need for further study and opted for voluntary actions.

Bridging Metaphors and Scientific Uncertainty

While the factors outlined in the previous section congealed to create an early consensus and a degree of closure about global warming in the European Union, there was a backlash against the issue in the

United States following the greenhouse summer of 1988. Whereas public pressure made a significant difference in responding to the ozone hole, the U.S. public has a poor understanding of global warming and, indeed, often confuses it with the ozone hole. The latter had a clear advantage as it is linked to a very familiar "penetration" metaphor found in video games and Star Wars. Stated succinctly, the hole leads to the increased bombardment of the earth by lethal rays. It is apparent to anyone that a "hole" is an aberration, something that a protective shield should not have. The greenhouse effect, in contrast, seems like a benign and essential natural phenomenon. Global warming is an extension of this phenomenon, creating the problem of finding the human "fingerprint" amid highly variable and complex natural processes.

Overall then, there are apparently no ready-made metaphors in the popular culture—as with genetically modified "Frankenfoods"—that provide a simple schematic for understanding the science of climate change. Global warming remains a very complex scientific issue, and it is not surprising that research reveals that the public has little knowledge of either the factors that cause it or the possible means of combating it. This is most visible in the surging sales of sport-utility vehicles (SUVs) just as scientists warned of the need to reduce CO_2 emissions.

While much of the discussion in North America and England is about global warming, scientists prefer the concept of "climate change," since computer models predict that some parts of the globe could get cooler as others get warmer. Indeed, it is theorized that melting ice caps could slow the Atlantic conveyor belt—a massive stream of water in the ocean that moderates climate in North America and Europe—and create global cooling. This was the idea behind the Hollywood movie *The Day After Tomorrow,* though it greatly exaggerated the speed and magnitude of the transformation. Differential predictions about whether the planet might cool or boil in a runaway greenhouse effect—accompanied by huge variations in estimates of phenomena like sea level rise—serve to create confusion, undermine the authority of the science, and provide ammunition for critics challenging the ostensible consensus.

While it is clear that the concentration of GHGs in the atmosphere is increasing and that the earth's temperature has increased about 1.0° F in the past century, both the amount of warming that is likely to occur and the extent to which it can be attributed to human influences remain uncertain. The IPCC, over a number of reports, has asserted with more confidence that the human impact is discernible and significant. But climate models, which ultimately try to link the atmosphere, the oceans, and the earth's surface, are at once extraordinarily complex and yet primitive. For example, there is great uncertainty about how clouds will affect future temperatures. There is also considerable controversy over how much of the temperature increase can be attributed to changing solar radiation.

In recent years these controversies have become increasingly apparent in public arenas. The IPCC has been challenged both internally and externally, in part for its attempts to create a consensus around issues where debate still prevails. It has also been criticized for too readily creating an icon out of the "hockey stick" graph, which appears to show a sudden and dramatic warming in the past 100 years. Claims making by climate skeptics has also escalated, though the approach of many of those who question the IPCC position can be problematic. Specifically, these critics find and hammer away at a specific fault or puzzle—such as the hockey stick model or research on temperatures in the Medieval period—and foster the impression that the reality of global warming rides or falls with this single concern. Once the issue is "resolved," they shift to a new "fault" and repeat the process.

The Current Standing of Global Warming

Despite such controversies, global warming has been revitalized as a celebrity issue in the early 21st century. Again, it has piggybacked on real-world events, encompassing heat waves, forest fires, floods, and hurricanes, particularly Katrina. Whereas there is a raging scientific debate over whether hurricanes have become more frequent or more intense, in the public realm Hurricane Katrina is largely accepted as a sign of the dangers of a warming planet. Amid record-breaking costs from extreme weather impacts, insurance companies have been the first to jump on the global warming bandwagon. With a *Time* magazine cover of April 3, 2006, warning, "Be Worried—Be Very Worried," and the relative success of Al Gore's film, *An Inconvenient Truth,* global warming is now widely seen as the most significant threat facing humankind.

This revived interest does nothing to resolve disputes about how to respond to the threat. Whereas most countries have signed the Kyoto Protocol, the

United States has rejected it. In lieu of federal action, many cities and some states in the United States have formulated their own strategies to cut back on GHG emissions. Defenders of Kyoto argue that it is a first step, although the European experience suggests that it may be quite costly to meet emission reductions. In all of this, almost no attention is being devoted to adaptation strategies. Future Katrinas are likely to become expectable events.

An alternative to mandatory reduction targets comes from the promise of energy efficiency and alternative energy sources. The rapid development of new technologies—along the line of the Manhattan Project perhaps—combined with the rapid application of the best available technologies, appears to be the response of choice at this point. This encompasses everything from using the best available technology for coal-burning plants to the production of fuel-efficient vehicles down to the selection of lightbulbs. Thus Hollywood stars recently have made it trendy to own fuel-efficient hybrid vehicles like the Toyota Prius. Solutions along these lines could help the United States reduce its dependence on foreign oil, which is proving to have a variety of political, military, and economic costs. The extraordinary economic growth found in China and, to a lesser extent, India threatens any possible benefits of Kyoto. Given the conspicuous effects of pollution in both of these countries, it is imperative that they adopt a clean energy path as soon as possible. At the global conference on climate change in Bali, Indonesia, in December 2007, the assembled nations agreed on reducing GHG emissions but set no specific targets to do so.

Proposed solutions to global warming must of course be sold, and claims makers may not have an easy time here. Although there were net savings in costs as a result of energy efficiencies introduced following the large increases in oil prices in the 1970s, this knowledge is largely absent from public discourse. Indeed, there has been an unfortunate tendency to link energy efficiency with a return to the simple life. As fossil fuels lose some of their allure, efforts are being made to revive nuclear energy as the only realistic solution, and this will engender further conflict. Clearly, providing clean, affordable, and secure energy supplies will be an abiding challenge with no simple answers.

Sheldon Ungar

See also Ozone

Further Readings

Flannery, Tim. 2005. *The Weather Makers: The Past and Future Impact of Climate Change.* Melbourne, Australia: CSIRO.

Houghton, John. 2004. *Global Warming: The Complete Briefing.* Cambridge, England: Cambridge University Press.

Moser, Susanne C. and Lisa Dilling, eds. 2007. *Creating a Climate for Change: Communicating Climate Change and Facilitating Social Change.* Cambridge, England: Cambridge University Press.

Ungar, Sheldon. 1998. "Bringing the Issue Back In: Comparing the Marketability of the Ozone Hole and Global Warming." *Social Problems* 45:510–27.

———. 2000. "Knowledge, Ignorance and the Popular Culture: Climate Change versus the Ozone Hole." *Public Understanding of Science* 9:297–312.

GRADE INFLATION

The term *grade inflation* refers to an increase in grade point averages over time without a corresponding rise in achievement. Grade inflation illustrates a concern about declining academic standards in high schools, colleges, and universities over the past 15 years, particularly at elite institutions. For example, fewer than 10 percent of all grades given at Stanford University since 1992 have been below B; similarly, 91 percent of the grades earned at Harvard University are B– or above, and over 90 percent of Harvard graduates received honors in 2001. Applying the term *grade inflation* to these trends suggests that the grades are artificially high with a consequential decrease in the relative value of high grades.

Some researchers identify the source of this grade inflation within the dynamics of student–teacher relationships. For example, most U.S. universities use student evaluations of teacher performance in their tenure considerations; thus, teachers are reluctant to give poor grades for fear of negative feedback. Additionally, some professors fear that giving low grades puts students at a disadvantage when applying for jobs or graduate school. Finally, researchers note that many professors dislike facing students who are upset with their low grades and will grade higher simply to avoid these confrontations. These practices are problematic because artificially high grades can mask a student's true ability. Students may have trouble handling an upper-level course if graded leniently in the lower-level prerequisite. More broadly, students may appear on paper as better educated or better qualified for a job than they actually are, which can cause problems when they are confronted with a task they may be unable to perform.

As with many social problems, however, conflicting evidence abounds. Some researchers assert that the grade inflation problem is not clear-cut, as the development of certain university programs may be causing grades to rise legitimately. For example, the expansion of financial aid programs may motivate students to achieve in order to maintain their aid packages. Faculty development programs that help professors to plan effective syllabi, state explicit expectations, and foster student learning may also contribute to rising grades. Further, a rise in the median age of the U.S. college student may indicate that today's students are more mature and better able to handle college material. Finally, studies of inflation at elite colleges may overestimate the extent to which inflation occurs at a national level. Studies that include community colleges paint a different picture of inflation. For example, during the 1999–2000 school year, only about 14.5 percent of students across all types of colleges received mostly A's, while more than one third received C– or below. Though grades may be on the rise, it is not clear whether this is due to artificial inflation, lack of reliable research, or simply greater teaching and learning over the period in question.

Bridget Rose Nolan

See also Academic Standards; Education, Academic
Performance

Further Readings

Boretz, E. 2004. "Grade Inflation and the Myth of Student Consumerism." *College Teaching* 52:42–46.

Horn, Laura, Katharin Peter, and Kathryn Rooney. 2003. "Profile of Undergraduates in U.S. Postsecondary Education Institutions: 1999–2000." *Education Statistics Quarterly* 4(3).

Marsh, Herbert W. and Lawrence A. Roche. 2000. "Effects of Grading Leniency and Low Workload on Students' Evaluations of Teaching: Popular Myth, Bias, Validity, or Innocent Bystanders?" *Journal of Educational Psychology* 92:202–27.

GREENHOUSE EFFECT

See GLOBAL WARMING

GROUPTHINK

Groupthink refers to the psychological group dynamic that can lead to disastrous decision making. Developed by Irving Janis, the concept of groupthink explains how well-intended political leaders have made notoriously bad foreign policy decisions, such as the Bay of Pigs invasion of Cuba. Others have since invoked groupthink as an explanation for U.S. involvement in the Vietnam War and the post–9/11 invasion of Iraq. Groupthink also offers a more general explanation for disastrous decision making such as launching the doomed space shuttles Challenger and Columbia in the face of contradictory evidence, the Nixon Watergate cover-up, and lack of disaster preparedness despite warnings of impending danger, such as the federal government response before and after Hurricane Katrina struck Mississippi and Louisiana, particularly New Orleans, in 2005.

People who succumb to groupthink typically emphasize the importance of a uniting cause, a uniquely gifted leader, and a strong but vague sense of moral or intellectual superiority. Group members reinforce one another's optimism, believe they cannot fail, and confidently make risky decisions. The symptoms of groupthink include discounting warnings of negative outcomes, self-censoring of doubts, marginalizing critics, ignoring alternatives, disregarding risks, reinterpreting information, and refusing to make contingency plans in case of failure. Individuals adopt particular roles within the group, most notably a "mind guard," a person who detects and punishes others who threaten the group's cohesiveness. Proposed countermeasures to help groups resist succumbing to groupthink are appointing someone to play the role of devil's advocate, staying open to criticism, maintaining an open leadership style, valuing ideological diversity, and actively seeking opinions from sources outside the group.

Criticisms of groupthink fall into three general categories: the use of case studies for theory development, the dangers of hindsight bias, and the validity of the conditions necessary for groupthink. Experimental tests have produced mixed support, yet the idea of groupthink is so well known that some researchers, ironically, suggest that many people believe in the idea far more enthusiastically than empirical tests of the evidence warrant. The criticisms produced refinements of Janis's original idea, particularly in an effort to clarify the conditions associated with the development of groupthink. They include the need for a strong social identity, cognitive dissonance, an abusive organizational structure, and personality characteristics such as hubris and a high level of confidence in the group's ability to make proper decisions. Despite the criticisms, use of the concept of groupthink continues as an explanation for defective group decision making that produces disastrous results.

Tom Heinzen and Susan Nolan

See also Cults; Mass Murder; Power Elite

Further Readings

Choi, Jin Nam and Myung Un Kim. 1999. "The Organizational Application of Groupthink and Its Limitations in Organizations." *Journal of Applied Psychology* 82(2):297–306.

Janis, Irving L. 1972. *Victims of Groupthink.* Boston: Houghton Mifflin.

———. 1982. *Groupthink: Psychological Studies of Policy Decisions and Fiascoes.* Boston: Houghton Mifflin.

Gun Control

Gun control is one of the most commonly proposed methods for reducing violent crime. Defined narrowly, it is the enactment and enforcement of laws regulating firearms. More broadly, it is any organized effort to regulate firearms, which could also encompass civil suits aimed at the firearms industry and voluntary gun turn-ins and buybacks.

Effects of Guns on Violence

The purpose of gun control is to reduce the frequency or seriousness of violence by preventing dangerous persons from obtaining guns. The main rationale for believing that this will reduce violence is the idea that firearms are more lethal than other possible weapons, so denying guns to violent persons will reduce the likelihood that any injuries they inflict will be fatal. Gun use or possession may also facilitate attacks that otherwise would not have occurred by weaker or fewer aggressors against more powerful or numerous victims. On the other hand, an aggressor's possession of a gun can make it unnecessary for the possessor to attack the victim to gain control—a mere threat suffices, reducing the likelihood of an attack. Gun use can also facilitate robbers tackling better defended but more lucrative targets, allowing them to gain a given amount of money with fewer robberies.

Further, guns in the hands of crime victims and prospective victims can deter attempts at crime or reduce the harmful consequences of those attempted. Victims who use guns to defend themselves are less likely to be injured or lose property than are nonresisting victims. Widespread ownership and carrying of guns may also deter some criminals from attempting crimes, by making the crimes seem riskier. These violence-reducing effects complicate efforts to control firearms because they imply that gun possession among largely noncriminal victims has violence-reducing effects, just as possession among criminals has violence-increasing effects. Consequently, the effects of gun controls are likely to differ depending on whether they restrict guns only among criminals and other high-risk groups, or limit gun possession among noncriminals as well. Efforts aimed at exclusively high-risk groups such as convicted criminals are more likely to have purely violence-reducing effects, whereas prohibitionist efforts that would disarm both victims and offenders would have mixed effects on violence.

Varieties of Gun Control

Americans support a wide array of moderate regulatory controls aimed at keeping guns away from criminals, juveniles, and other high-risk groups but oppose prohibitionist controls that would preclude them from legally acquiring or owning guns. As a result, the United States has many gun control laws but virtually none that ban guns or seriously limit access to guns among noncriminal adults. Although three large cities—Washington, D.C., Chicago, and New York City—effectively ban the private possession of handguns, no federal or state laws ban ownership of all guns or even just handguns.

Federal gun laws are less numerous and less restrictive than those prevailing in most states. Under federal law, all persons in the regular business of selling guns must have a federal firearms dealer's license. Anyone purchasing a gun of any kind from a licensed dealer must pass a background check for a criminal conviction and other disqualifying attributes. A convicted felon cannot legally purchase a gun, and a dealer cannot sell a gun to a felon. It is illegal for a convicted felon to possess a gun of any kind, regardless of how it was obtained. It is also unlawful, everywhere in the United States, for a juvenile to possess a handgun and for a dealer to sell a gun to a juvenile. Deliberately, no national policy exists for a national registry of guns, as gun owners fear its potential use to facilitate the mass confiscation of guns. Perhaps the most significant limitation of federal gun law is that gun transfers between private persons (i.e., no licensed dealer is involved) are not subject to any background check.

Each of the 50 states has a different array of gun laws. While some states have controls stricter than the average level prevailing among democracies outside the United States, others have only limited controls. No state bans the private possession of guns, or of handguns. A few states ban the purchase or possession of certain models of semi-automatic firearms (loosely labeled "assault weapons") that fire just one shot at a time but that look like, or were adapted from, military guns that could fire like machine guns. Almost all states forbid possession or purchase of handguns by convicted felons and juveniles, and most also do so with respect to various other higher-risk categories of persons, such as mentally ill persons and illicit drug users.

Some states require a permit to purchase a handgun, and a few of these also require a permit to buy a long gun (rifle or shotgun). Although many states require the reporting of gun sales to state or local authorities, only a few have state-mandated handgun registration systems, and even fewer also register long guns. Some states require a minimum waiting period of anywhere from 1 to 14 days before buyers may take delivery of handguns; a few of these states also mandate waiting periods for long guns.

There are also diverse laws governing the concealed carrying of firearms in public places. In more than two thirds of the states, adult residents without a criminal record may get a permit allowing a concealed gun. In a few states, concealed carrying by civilians is completely forbidden, whereas in the remaining states, permits are technically available at the discretion of authorities but rarely granted in practice, making these states effectively identical to those banning the carrying of guns.

Gun Control Laws and the Supply of Guns to Criminals

Much of U.S. gun law regulates the transfer of guns to keep them away from criminals. Most of these controls apply only to transactions involving licensed gun dealers. This is problematic because many guns are acquired through private channels. Even among members of the general, mostly noncriminal, population, about one third of guns are acquired from private parties. Although nominally regulated in some jurisdictions, these transactions are largely invisible to legal authorities under existing law and, among criminals, are a common means of acquiring guns. One study found that, among felon handgun owners, 44 percent acquired their most recently acquired handgun through a purchase, usually from a source other than a dealer; 32 percent stole the gun; 9 percent rented or borrowed it; and 8 percent each obtained it in trade or as a gift. Only 16 percent of the total obtained their handgun by a purchase from a conventional retail dealer.

Although many criminals get their guns from unlicensed sources, few get them from illicit dealers regularly engaged in the business of selling guns—only 2.9 percent of the felons got their gun from a "black market source" and only 4.7 percent from a "fence" (dealer in stolen goods). The federal agency charged with enforcing the federal gun laws, the Bureau of Alcohol, Tobacco, Firearms and Explosives, devotes a significant share of its resources to suppressing illicit gun trafficking activity, yet its own data indicate an annual capture of fewer than 15 traffickers who dealt in more than 250 guns and that the average number of guns trafficked per trafficking case was just 15 in fiscal year 2000. The "illicit gun dealers" that come to law enforcement attention are numerous, but each one handles so few guns that arresting them is unlikely to have much effect on the availability of guns to criminals. Criminals do occasionally sell guns for profit, but this is mostly a low-volume activity done as a byproduct of other criminal activities, such as burglary, drug dealing, or trafficking in stolen property.

Because Americans own enormous numbers of guns, hundreds of thousands are stolen in a typical year; at any one time, millions of stolen guns circulate among criminals. The volume of gun theft is so large that, even if all voluntary transfers of guns to criminals were eliminated (including either lawful or unlawful transfers and involving either licensed dealers or private citizens) and if police could confiscate all firearms from all criminals each year, a single year's worth of gun theft alone would be sufficient to rearm all gun criminals with enough weapons to commit the current number of gun crimes (about 430,000 in 2000). As a result, large-scale gun trafficking (as distinct from burglars occasionally selling guns they have stolen) is largely superfluous to supplying criminals with guns in most areas.

The Impact of Gun Control Laws on Violence

The enormous variation in strictness of controls across different states and cities makes the United States a natural laboratory for evaluating the impact of gun control laws. Most studies of the impact of gun control laws have found little impact on violence rates. For example, in one comprehensive evaluation, researchers assessed the effects of 19 major types of gun control on rates of homicide, robbery, aggravated assault, rape, suicide, and fatal gun accidents, separately examining gun and nongun violence (e.g., gun homicide vs. nongun homicide), as well as the impact of gun laws on gun ownership levels. They found that none of the 19 common types of gun laws showed consistent evidence of reducing gun ownership. Of course, many gun regulations, such as carry controls or add-on penalties, are not intended to reduce gun ownership. Other gun controls restrict ownership only among high-risk groups, such as criminals or alcoholics.

Gun control laws did not show consistent evidence of reducing violent crime, gun accidents, or suicide. Although some laws appear capable of inducing people to substitute nongun weapons for firearms in violent acts, they do not reduce the total number of violent acts. For example, some laws may reduce the number of gun suicides but not the total number of suicides, because suicide attempters substitute other methods. In particular, two of the most popular gun control measures, waiting periods and gun registration, do not reduce violence rates to any measurable degree. On the other hand, the gun control strategy favored most by gun owner groups—mandatory add-on penalties for committing crimes with a gun—also is ineffective.

The many varieties of gun control laws appear to have no impact on violence for several reasons. First, gun laws intended to reduce gun ownership levels, either in the general population or, more usually, within various high-risk subsets, may fail because they do not achieve their proximate goal of reducing gun availability enough to matter. With more than 260 million guns in private hands, almost anyone who strongly desires a gun can get one.

Second, given that the best research indicates that general gun ownership levels have no net positive effect on crime and violence, even if gun laws did reduce general gun ownership, this reduction would not decrease total violence rates. On the other hand, laws that reduced gun availability among criminals, without disarming noncriminal victims, might reduce violence. Unfortunately no research has effectively distinguished gun availability among criminals from that among noncriminals.

Third, many U.S. gun laws regulate only handguns or regulate handguns more stringently than the more numerous long guns. This permits the substitution of the less-regulated long guns for the more heavily regulated handguns. The harmful effects of some criminals substituting these more lethal firearms could outweigh the beneficial effects of denying handguns to other criminals and produce a net increase in homicide.

Finally, local or state controls over gun acquisition may fail because guns from jurisdictions with weaker controls "leak" into those with stricter controls. Gun control advocates argue that federal measures are therefore necessary. Research on the relatively weak Gun Control Act of 1968, however, generally found it to be ineffective, and an early evaluation of the 1994 federal Brady Act pointed to the same conclusion.

Selected Recent Developments

At the state level, one of the most highly publicized developments in recent years was the widespread passage of "right to carry" or "shall issue" laws, which made it easier for noncriminals to get permits to carry concealed weapons in public. Critics feared that the increase in authorized gun carrying would result in increased acts of violence involving permit holders, but these fears were not realized; only a handful of permit holders committed unlawful acts of violence with their guns in public places. On the other hand, these laws also probably did not reduce crime rates.

The enactment of "state preemption" laws in most of the states, however, was arguably of greater significance, though it received little publicity. These state laws forbid local governments from passing their own gun controls. Their significance is that, while most political struggles over gun control involve just a single control measure in one jurisdiction, these laws forbade the future enactment of almost any kind of gun control, eliminated many existing local controls, and did so for hundreds of local jurisdictions within each state.

In response to defeats in legislatures, the best-known gun control advocacy organization, the Brady Center to Prevent Gun Violence, recently shifted much of its efforts to the courts, helping to bring lawsuits against the gun industry. If widely successful, the lawsuits could either bankrupt gun makers and thereby produce a de facto ban on the further manufacture of firearms, or make guns prohibitively expensive and thereby bring about a de facto ban on gun buying, without benefit of new legislation. The suits rest on novel legal theories that manufacturers or distributors were negligent in (a) producing and selling guns lacking certain safety devices (e.g., "personalized gun" technologies intended to prevent anyone but the authorized user from firing the gun), (b) marketing guns to prohibited buyers such as criminals or juveniles, (c) marketing guns based on supposedly false claims that guns can be useful for self-defense, or (d) manufacturing too many guns, in excess of the demand among noncriminals. Municipal governments also brought suits based on a public nuisance theory that manufacturers should be held liable for the costs to city governments of gun violence—the costs of police and courts, medical care of the wounded, and so forth. Although lawsuits against gun manufacturers are occasionally won on more orthodox legal grounds, such as defects (as conventionally understood) in design or manufacture, U.S. courts have not yet accepted any of these new theories.

Gary Kleck

See also Crime; Crime, Fear of; Crime Rates; Violence; Violent Crime

Further Readings

Bruce-Briggs, Barry. 1976. "The Great American Gun War." *The Public Interest* 45:37–62.

Kleck, Gary. 1997. *Targeting Guns: Firearms and Their Control.* New York: Aldine de Gruyter.

Kleck, Gary and E. Britt Patterson. 1993. "The Impact of Gun Control and Gun Ownership Levels on Violence Rates." *Journal of Quantitative Criminology* 9:249–88.

Newton, George D. and Franklin Zimring. 1969. *Firearms and Violence in American Life: A Staff Report to the National Commission on the Causes and Prevention of Violence.* Washington, DC: U.S. Government Printing Office.

Vizzard, William J. 2000. *Shots in the Dark: The Policy, Politics, and Symbolism of Gun Control.* Lanham, MD: Rowman & Littlefield.

Wright, James D. and Peter H. Rossi. 1986. *Armed and Considered Dangerous: A Survey of Felons and Their Firearms.* New York: Aldine de Gruyter.

H

HARM REDUCTION DRUG POLICY

Harm reduction is a broad term applied to a variety of programs and policies, so there is no clear consensus on its meaning, although its aim is to reduce the adverse consequences of drug use and even of drug control policies. The term originated in the Netherlands in response to the HIV/AIDS epidemic and is the cornerstone of not only Dutch drug policy but drug policy throughout most of the industrialized world (other than the United States).

Harm reduction is a pragmatic policy aimed at minimizing the damage that drug users do to themselves, other persons, the community, and society at large. Harm reduction approaches reject a drug-free society as unachievable, recognizing that drug use has always been present in human societies. Although the official U.S. view tends to place harm reduction in the same camp as legalization, most advocates of harm reduction do not support legalization, expressing concern that it would increase drug use. Yet, they recognize that drug prohibition not only is insufficient to stop drug use but actually creates crime and marginalizes drug users.

Harm reduction interventions thus focus on integrating or reintegrating drug users into the community, taking care not to further isolate, demonize, or ostracize them. Priority is placed on maximizing the number of drug users in contact with drug treatment, outreach, and other public health services. Practitioners evaluate drug policies in terms of their potential effects on minimizing the harms of drugs to the user and to society.

Harm reduction tactics include programs such as methadone maintenance and needle exchange programs. Harm reduction can also include street outreach programs to "hidden" populations of drug users, treatment instead of incarceration, safe injection rooms staffed by medical professionals, and heroin maintenance programs. Most EU nations make treatment widely available and have a policy of street outreach to drug users to prevent further marginalization of drug users and to improve their health and encourage participation in treatment. Most industrial countries do not incarcerate individuals for simple possession of drugs, and the incarceration of drug users and sellers, while increasing, has not contributed to an epidemic of incarceration, as is evident in the United States.

Obligatory treatment, practiced primarily in the U.S. criminal justice system, is rarely considered harm reduction and is a topic of considerable debate in other industrialized countries. Several industrialized countries utilize controlled heroin maintenance, practiced in a manner similar to methadone maintenance, for those who have had multiple failures (drop out) from methadone maintenance. Research in these countries suggests these types of programs are not appropriate as a first response but rather are helpful to a small number of addicts and to their communities, as they help reduce crime.

Lana D. Harrison

See also Drug Abuse; Drug Abuse, Crime; Drug Subculture; Heroin

Further Readings

European Monitoring Center for Drugs and Drug Addiction (EMCDDA). 2005. "EMCDDA Thematic Papers—Illicit Drug Use in the EU: Legislative Approaches." Lisbon, Portugal: EMCDDA.

Harrison, Lana D. 2002. "Harm Reduction." Pp. 819–22 in *Encyclopedia of Crime and Punishment,* edited by D. Levinson. Thousand Oaks, CA: Sage.

Inciardi, James A. and Lana D. Harrison, eds. 2000. *Harm Reduction: National and International Perspectives.* Thousand Oaks, CA: Sage.

Korf, Dirk, Heleen Riper, M. Freeman, R. Lewis, I. Grant, E. Jacob, C. Mougin, and M. Nilson. 1999. *Outreach Work among Drugs Users in Europe: Concepts, Practice and Terminology.* Lisbon, Portugal: EMCDDA.

HATE CRIMES

The term *hate crime* first appeared in the late 1980s in response to a racial incident in the white, working-class Howard Beach section of New York City, in which an African American man was killed while attempting to evade a violent mob of teenagers shouting racial epithets. Originally employed by journalists and politicians, the term was used soon thereafter by the Federal Bureau of Investigation and a number of other law enforcement agencies across the United States to characterize any criminal offense motivated either entirely or in part by the fact or perception that a victim is different in socially significant ways from the perpetrator.

The term *hate crime* can be misleading, because it implies incorrectly that hatred is invariably a distinguishing characteristic of this type of offense. Although it is true that many hate-motivated crimes involve intense animosity toward the victim, many others do not. Conversely, many offenses involving hatred between the offender and the victim are not hate crimes in the sense intended here. For example, an assault that arises out of a dispute between two coworkers who compete for a promotion might involve intense hatred, even though it is not based on any racial or religious differences between them.

Hate Crime Laws

Limited federal legislation exists in the United States, thus leaving it primarily to the states to formulate hate crime legislation. Forty-five states and the District of Columbia presently have some form of hate crime statute; among them, a wide variation in the specifics of the laws exists. For example, in the area of protected groups (i.e., designated groups protected in the statute), most states list crimes targeted toward individuals because of their race, religion, or ethnicity as prohibited. However, a number of states also include sexual orientation, disability, gender, and age. The implication of this lack of uniformity is that members of a particular group may be protected by a hate crime statute in one community but not protected in a neighboring community in an adjacent state.

Another legal distinction among state laws involves the penalty structure of the statutes. In some states, a separate statute exists that prohibits hate crime behavior. In other states the hate crime law is a "penalty enhancement." Thus, for the commission of a crime motivated by bias, the penalty may increase. Penalty enhancements may also apply to crimes committed with a gun or by individuals with long criminal histories, or crimes committed against vulnerable victims such as children.

Types of Hate Crimes

Some degree of variation exists among the offenses known as hate crimes. Some target particular victims, others all members of a group. Some have an expressive function, in order to provide excitement in the lives of the perpetrators; others are designed rationally to satisfy a specific objective. A precipitating event inspires some; others require no external catalyst to provoke their occurrence. Based on the offenders' motivations, hate crimes can be categorized as defensive, retaliatory, thrill-seeking, and mission.

Defensive

In defensive hate crimes, the hatemongers seize on what they consider to be a threatening incident, which serves as a catalyst or precipitant for the expression of their anger. They rationalize that by attacking an outsider they are in fact taking a protective posture, a defensive stance against intruders. Indeed, they often cast the outsiders in the role of those actively menacing them, while they regard themselves as pillars of the community. Such crimes frequently involve attacks on individuals and families who move into, or travel through, a neighborhood where they "do not belong." From the point of view of the perpetrators, it is their community, means of livelihood, or way of life that is threatened by the mere presence of members of some other group. The hatemongers therefore feel justified, even obligated, to go on the "defensive."

Retaliatory

In a number of communities, the police have recorded specific hate crimes perpetrated against victims because of a perceived previous hate crime against their group. The thinking is "You got one of us; we will get one of you." In such cases specific victims are seldom targeted; offenders look to attack any member of the targeted group. Another kind of retaliatory hate crime often follows an international incident such as an act of terrorism. For example, many communities witnessed an increase in anti-Arab, retaliatory hate crimes in the months following the terrorist attacks of September 11, 2001.

Thrill-Seeking

Youthful hatemongers sometimes look merely to have some fun and stir up a little excitement, but at someone else's expense. In a thrill-seeking hate crime, no precipitating incident need occur. The victim does not necessarily "invade" the territory of the assailant by walking through his neighborhood, moving onto his block, or attending his school. On the contrary, it is the assailant (or group of assailants) looking to harass those who are different, who searches out locations where the members of a particular group regularly congregate. In recent years, a common location for thrill-motivated hate crimes has been gay bars, a venue to which hatemongers can travel to locate vulnerable victims. The payoff for the youthful perpetrators is psychological as well as social: In addition to gaining a sense of importance and control, they also receive a stamp of approval from their friends.

Mission

On occasion, hate crimes go beyond what their perpetrators consider thrill-seeking, defensive, or retaliatory, at least in the narrow sense. Rather than direct their attack at those individuals involved in a particular event or episode—moving into the neighborhood, taking a job at the next desk, attending the same party—the perpetrators are ready to wage "war" against any

and all members of a particular group of people. No precipitating episode occurs; none is necessary. The perpetrator is on a moral mission: His assignment is to make the world a better place to live.

The offenders therefore are concerned about much more than simply eliminating a few blacks or Latinos/as from their workplaces, neighborhoods, or schools. Instead, they believe that they have a higher purpose in carrying out their crimes. They have been instructed by God or, in a more secular version, by the Imperial Wizard or the Grand Dragon to rid the world of evil by eliminating all blacks, Latinos/as, Asians, or Jews, and they must act before it is too late. Mission hate crime offenders are likely to be associated with an organized group such as the National Socialist Movement, the Ku Klux Klan, or the National Alliance.

Organized Hate Groups

Only 5 percent of all hate crimes are perpetrated by the members of organized hate groups. According to the Southern Poverty Law Center's Intelligence Project, there are slightly more than 800 active hate groups in the United States. Yet most of these hate groups are small; the average has fewer than 20 members. In total, there are probably no more than 20,000 members of hate organizations in the United States. Given a national population exceeding 300 million people, the 20,000 figure represents a minuscule proportion of Americans.

Numbers do not, however, tell the entire story of organized hate. Thanks to the Internet, a small group of hatemongers can now have disproportionate influence in reaching the young people of America. Hate groups have established more than 500 Web sites. In addition, they create and distribute white power CDs that sanction violence against Jews and people of color. Organized hate groups take advantage of local access cable television and shortwave radio. They often provide the propaganda for youthful hatemongers not only in the United States but around the world.

The findings of recent behavioral science research aimed at understanding the causes and characteristics of hate crimes may, in part, reflect a worsening of intergroup relations during the 1980s and early 1990s, as traditionally disadvantaged groups began to make claims for equal treatment. However, such efforts to explain hate crimes probably also reflect a heightened sensitivity to violence perpetrated against vulnerable members of society—especially women, gays, and people of color. Because of the recent convergence of new social movements involving civil rights, women, gays and lesbians, and victims in general, increased efforts are being made to confront the destructive consequences of hate crimes, especially those committed against the most vulnerable.

The research to date suggests that the best approach to combating hate crimes involves a coordinated and comprehensive approach, incorporating federal and state statutory protection for potential victims and an aggressive reaction from law enforcement. Most important, a truly effective strategy includes a grassroots community effort in which residents support targeted groups both before and after incidents of hate violence have occurred.

Jack Levin and Jack McDevitt

See also Hate Groups; Hate Speech; Homophobia; Prejudice; Racism; Violent Crime

Further Readings

Anti-Defamation League. 2005. "Anti Defamation League State Hate Crime Statutory Provisions." Retrieved December 27, 2007 (http://www.adl.org/learn/ hate_crime_ laws/state_hate_crime_statutory_provisions_ chart.pdf).

Federal Bureau of Investigation. 1999. *Hate Crime Data Collection Guidelines: Uniform Crime Reporting.* Washington, DC: U.S. Department of Justice.

Levin, Jack and Jack McDevitt. 2002. *Hate Crimes Revisited: America's War on Those Who Are Different.* Boulder, CO: Westview.

McDevitt, Jack, Jack Levin, and Susan Bennett. 2002. "Hate Crime Offenders: An Expanded Typology." *Journal of Social Issues* 58(2):303–17.

Potok, Mark. 2006. "The Year in Hate, 2005." *SPLC Intelligence Report,* Spring. Retrieved December 27, 2007 (http://www.splcenter.org/intel/intelreport/article.jsp?aid= 627&printable=1).

HATE GROUPS

According to the Southern Poverty Law Center, more than 800 hate groups are active in the United States. The Intelligence Project estimates that the number of hate groups has grown by about one third since 2000, although most are small, with the majority having fewer than 20 members.

The growing presence of hate groups is hardly confined to the United States. In Germany, for example, the Federal Office for the Protection of the Constitution reported in 1991 the presence of 4,400 neo-Nazis in Germany, most of whom were skinheads. By adding in all other right-wing extremist and Nazi groups in the country, this figure swelled to approximately 40,000. A 2005 German government report indicates that this number of right-wing extremists has remained stable for the past 2 decades.

Apparently, as indicated by voting patterns, hundreds of thousands of individuals in many different countries agree to many, if not all, of the principles of white supremacy, even if they would never join a hate group. However, white supremacist groups represent a fringe element among those who commit hate crimes. Research shows that only a small number of reported hate offenses are committed by members of organized hate groups. Statistically, the membership of all organized hate groups combined constitutes a tiny fraction of the population, most of whom would not consider burning a cross or wearing a swastika. Even so, the influence of white supremacist groups such as Posse Comitatus, the National Socialist Movement, Aryan Nations, and the Ku Klux Klan may be considerably greater than their numbers might suggest. It takes only a small band of dedicated extremists to make trouble for a large number of apathetic middle-of-the-roaders. Today these groups increasingly use the Internet to communicate their philosophy of hate and influence youngsters. The Southern Poverty Law Center estimates that more than 2,000 such Internet sites are currently active.

The newer organized hate groups do not always come so easily to mind for their bizarre uniforms or rituals. Followers of such white supremacist groups as John and Tom Metzger's White Aryan Resistance have shed their sheets and burning crosses in favor of more conventional attire. They often disavow the Klan and the Nazi movement in favor of a brand of "American patriotism" that plays better among the working people of America. In France, one of the original organizing slogans of Jean-Marie Le Pen's right-wing party was an utterly respectable idea: "Two million foreigners, two million Frenchmen out of work."

Moreover, white supremacist organizations now often cloak their hatred in the aura and dogma of Christianity. Followers of the religious arm of the hate movement, the Identity Church, are only "doing the work of God." At Sunday services, they preach that white Anglo-Saxons are the true Israelites depicted in the Old Testament, God's chosen people, while Jews are actually the children of Satan. They maintain that Jesus was not a Jew but an ancestor of the white, northern European peoples. In their view, blacks are "pre-Adamic," a species lower than whites. In fact, they claim that blacks and other nonwhite groups are at the same spiritual level as animals and therefore have no souls.

In recent years white supremacist groups such as the National Alliance and the Creativity Movement have suffered a crisis of leadership. Matthew Hale, who heads the Creativity Movement (formerly known as World Church of the Creator) is serving a lengthy prison sentence for his part in a conspiracy to murder a federal judge. The longtime leader of the National Alliance, William Pierce, died, leaving a vacuum of leadership in the organization yet to be filled effectively. Defections of members in both hate groups contributed to the rising popularity of a neo-Nazi organization known as the National Socialist Movement and a resurgence of membership in racist skinhead groups across the United States.

Jack Levin and Jack McDevitt

See also Hate Crimes; Hate Speech; White Supremacy

Further Readings

Levin, Jack and Jack McDevitt. 1993. *Hate Crimes: The Rising Tide of Bigotry and Bloodshed.* New York: Plenum.

Office for the Protection of the Constitution. 2000. "Annual Report of the Office for Protection of the Constitution 2000." Berlin: Federal Ministry of the Interior. Retrieved December 18, 2007 (http://www.verfassungsschutz.de/download/SHOW/vsbericht_2000_engl.pdf).

Potok, Mark. 2003. "Against the Wall." *SPLC Intelligence Report* (Fall):12.

———. 2006. "The Year in Hate, 2005." *SPLC Intelligence Report* (Spring):1.

HATE SPEECH

Although no widely recognized definition of the term *hate speech* yet exists, its traditional interpretation included any form of expression that any racial, religious, ethnic, or national group found offensive.

This definition broadened in the 1980s to include groups based or age, gender, sexual preference, marital status, and physical ability.

Most commonly, hate speech involves racial and ethnic slurs when referring to the members of a group. Other examples may include jokes that demean or ridicule a particular group or speeches by members of organizations, such as the Ku Klux Klan or the Christian Identity Church, that demonize groups such as blacks, Jews, or Hispanics by depicting them as animals or subhumans.

Most nations have laws that restrict offensive speech, including words targeted at vulnerable groups. Germany and France, for example, prohibit many expressions of hate. The German statutes, introduced after World War II, prohibit many Nazi symbols as well as statements of Holocaust denial. More recently, expansions of legal restrictions on speech include a much broader ban on various forms and targets of hate speech.

By contrast, the United States has a tradition of safeguarding individual rights as codified in a constitutional amendment protecting freedom of expression. U.S. courts have consistently found that hate speech, while extremely offensive, does not violate the First Amendment. In 1992, in a widely cited decision, *R.A.V. v. the City of St. Paul,* the U.S. Supreme Court ruled that a local community ordinance prohibiting cross burning was unconstitutional, because it interfered with expressions of free speech. Moreover, unlike most other countries, the United States has powerful advocacy groups such as the American Civil Liberties Union, whose mandate requires that it assist in preserving the First Amendment. As a result, American popular culture is free to be as hate-filled and offensive as its producers wish. Hate speech continues to be heard in both Europe and America, so one approach is no more effective than the other.

Late in the 1980s hate speech became a concern on U.S. college campuses, resulting in codes of student conduct at many universities. By prohibiting expressions of hate on increasingly diverse college campuses, these codes sought to encourage an environment conducive to learning. Challenges by civil rights organizations and local groups of faculty and students led to the repeal or nonimplementation of most codes. However, they did increase awareness of the potential injury expressions of hate can inflict on an entire community.

The American Civil Liberties Union and many other concerned groups reached consensus about ways to react to hate speech. These organizations believe that hate speech is wrong; but they also believe that prohibiting hate speech is just as wrong. As an alternative, they recommend that people of goodwill confront hate speech not with silence but with speech articulating tolerance and respect for differences. If a racist group holds a rally in a town, the members of that community should sponsor a larger and louder rally in another venue denouncing racism. When dealing with individual expressions of hate or bias, proponents of tolerance cite the necessity of letting bigots know that their hate speech is offensive. On a one-to-one basis, this may be difficult to do, but it may be the most effective way to foster change in individuals who are unaware that their words are hurtful.

Jack Levin and Jack McDevitt

See also Hate Crimes; Hate Groups

Further Readings

Boeckman, Robert J. and Jeffrey Liew. 2002. "Hate Speech: Asian American Students' Justice Judgments and Psychological Responses." *Journal of Social Issues* 58(2):363–81.

Cowan, Gloria, Miriam Resendez, Elizabeth Marshall, and Ryan Quist. 2002. "Hate Speech and Constitutional Protection: Priming Values of Equality and Freedom." *Journal of Social Issues* 58(2):247–63.

Leets, Laura. 2002. "Experiencing Hate Speech: Perceptions and Responses to Anti-Semitism and Antigay Speech." *Journal of Social Issues* 58(2):341–61.

Levin, Jack and Jack McDevitt. 2002. *Hate Crimes Revisited: America's War on Those Who Are Different.* Boulder, CO: Westview.

R.A.V. v. City of St. Paul, Minnesota. 1992. 505 U.S. 377.

Walker, Samuel. 1966. *Hate Speech: The History of an American Controversy.* Lincoln, NE: University of Nebraska Press.

HEALTH CARE, ACCESS

Several indicators measure the level of access to health care. Among these, typically using a 12-month period of focus, are an individual's health care coverage and whether or not an individual saw or spoke to a doctor or visited an emergency room. In addition, determining who uses certain preventative health care, like dental services, prescription drugs, mammograms, cancer screenings, and pap smears, also gauges health care access.

Among adults ages 18 to 64, about 17 percent have no usual source of health care. In a given year, about 16 percent of adults do not see a doctor, visit an emergency room, or have home health care. About 20 percent of Americans ages 18 to 64 visit the emergency room once, and 7 percent visit it 2 or more times. Two thirds of adults see a dentist annually, 70 percent of women over the age of 40 have a mammogram once every 2 years, and 79 percent of women over the age of 18 have a pap smear once every 3 years.

Disparities in Health Care Access

Health care is stratified by certain social characteristics, especially race and social class. Nonwhites are less likely to have a regular source of health care. Hispanics—in particular, Mexicans—have the highest percentage of noncoverage: Almost one third do not have a regular health care provider. Blacks and Native Americans are more likely than whites to have used the emergency room in the past 12 months. Members of all racial minority groups are less likely than whites to have seen a dentist in the past 12 months. Minorities, especially blacks, are less likely to have invasive cardiac procedures, even when their insurance and illness characteristics are the same as those of whites.

Substantial percentages of the poor (23 percent) and near poor (22 percent) have no usual source of medical care. By contrast, 14 percent of the nonpoor have no usual source of medical care. One in five poor adults report they did not see a doctor, visit an emergency room, or receive home health care in the past year. The poor and near poor are more likely to use the emergency room than a doctor's office as their main source of medical care, especially when they qualify for Medicaid. Thirteen percent of the poor and 10 percent of the near poor have visited an emergency room in the past year compared with only 5 percent of the nonpoor. Among those with Medicaid, almost 40 percent have been to an emergency room at least once, and 22 percent have been at least twice in a given year. Poor adults are also less likely to have access to preventative care, like dental services, prescription drugs, mammograms, cancer screenings, and pap smears.

Determinants of Health Care Access

Health insurance coverage and lack thereof largely determine access. In 2007, 44.8 million Americans were uninsured, most of them with little or no access to health care. Forty-seven percent of uninsured adults had no regular source of health care within the past year, and 38 percent had no health care visits in a 12-month period. This percentage is 3 times that of the insured population. Adults without insurance are also less likely to get preventative services, like regular mammograms or pap smears.

Costs also affect access to health care. About 6 percent of the population is unable to obtain necessary medical care because of high costs, and this percentage has been increasing over the past several years. Additionally, 8 percent of Americans delay medical care because of financial difficulties. Among the uninsured, the percentages with health care access difficulties because of costs are even higher. In one study, 47 percent of the uninsured postponed seeking care in a 12-month period because of costs, and 37 percent of them did not fill a prescription because of cost.

Implications

The barriers to health care experienced by the uninsured directly impact their health. Having health insurance reduces mortality rates by 10 to 15 percent. The uninsured have less access to preventative care and therefore are diagnosed later and die earlier from cancer. The uninsured are also less likely to receive lifesaving surgical interventions for cardiac illnesses. Because 20 percent of the uninsured use the emergency room as their usual source of care, they are also more likely to spend time in a hospital for avoidable health conditions.

Many of those who experience barriers in access because of costs delay or go without necessary health care, which can exacerbate existing health conditions. More than 4 in 10 adults report having a chronic condition, like cancer, heart disease, and diabetes. These individuals are more likely to report that they or a member of their household delayed or skipped treatment because of costs: 38 percent compared with only 22 percent of their healthier counterparts. In another study, of the 13 percent with an unmet health need, 7 percent reported it was because of cost.

Christine Caffrey

See also Health Care, Costs; Health Care, Ideological Barriers to Change; Health Care, Insurance

Further Readings

Kaiser Family Foundation. 2006. "The Uninsured and Their Access to Health Care." Washington, DC: Kaiser Family Foundation. Retrieved December 27, 2007 (http://www.kff.org/uninsured/upload/The-Uninsured-and-Their-Access-to-Health-Care-Oct-2004.pdf).

Lasser, Karen E., David U. Himmelstein, and Steffie Woolhandler. 2006. "Access to Care, Health Status, and Health Disparities in the United States and Canada: Results of a Cross-National Population-Based Survey." *American Journal of Public Health* 96(7):1300–1307.

U.S. Department of Health and Human Services. 2007. "Health, United States, 2007." Hyattsville, MD: U.S. Department of Health and Human Services.

HEALTH CARE, COSTS

Officials measure health care costs in two major ways: total expenditures and per person (or per capita) spending. They report total expenditures either in dollars or as a percentage of the gross domestic product (GDP), or else as a growth rate percentage compared with the growth rate percentage of the GDP. Reports on per capita spending are often in dollars, in terms of total medical costs or total out-of-pocket costs, or as a percentage of individual income. A final means of measurement is the share of individual spending paid out-of-pocket. Total expenditures and per capita health costs can also be projected.

Estimating Health Care Costs

Total expenditures are growing at an alarming rate. In 2003, they were $1.7 trillion, with government projections to grow to $2.16 trillion in 2006 and over $4 trillion by 2015. Total health spending as a percentage of the GDP grew from 7.2 percent in 1965 to 16.2 percent in 2005, with projections to be 20 percent by 2015. Health expenditures are growing at a faster rate than is the overall economy. Projections are that health spending between 2006 and 2015 will grow annually by 7.2 percentage points while the GDP will grow annually only by 4.9 percentage points.

Per capita health care costs have also been increasing at a fast rate. In 2005, per person health spending was $7,110, up from $6,280 in 2004. Individual spending may increase to $12,320 by 2015. Out-of-pocket costs rose from $647 in 1999 to $788 in 2004, with projections to increase to $1,287 by 2015. Thirty-five percent of per capita spending is paid out-of-pocket.

Explaining Higher Health Care Costs

One of the major explanations for the increase in health care costs is the rise in the costs of providing services. Hospital care accounts for over 30 percent of national health expenditures. In 2003, hospital costs were $551 billion, and they are projected to increase to $1.01 trillion by 2014. Attempts to decrease or control hospital costs include improvements in the efficiency of administration and a reduction in the care done on an inpatient basis. As a result, other health care providers, such as those engaged in home health care, have seen a rise in their share of health care costs. Between 1990 and 2000, home health care, as a percentage of total health costs, rose from 1.8 percent to 2.5 percent. Nursing home expenses will also rise. Physician and clinical services make up 22 percent of total health expenditures, and these costs may more than double, from $370 billion in 2003 to $783 billion in 2014, because of increased demand for physicians, heightened specialization within the field, and the cost of malpractice insurance.

The emphasis on medical technology in the U.S. health care system also leads to an increase in costs. Expensive tests and highly advanced medical procedures are commonplace and sometimes done when not necessary. Examples of these procedures include invasive cardiology, organ transplantation, and imaging.

Prescription drug costs are another important contributor to rising health care costs. In 2004, they totaled $188.5 billion, but by 2015, expectations are that they will increase to $446.2 billion. The annual growth in prescription drug costs, at around 8 percent, is thus higher than the annual growth in hospital and physician costs. Advances in, and increased demand for, pharmaceutical research and technologies lead to greater medical costs, a trend expected to intensify in the future.

Demographic factors explain some of the rise in health care costs. The aging of the population will greatly impact the financial structure of the health care system. The 65+ population will increase from 13 percent in 2006 to 20 percent in 2030. This growth is caused by increases in life expectancy and the aging of the baby boom population, a cohort of 76 million born between 1946 and 1964. The 85+ population, the population in most need of health care, will more than double in numbers, from 4.2 million in 2000 to 8.9 million in 2030.

Finally, cultural factors play a role in rising medical costs. Lifestyle factors, like heavy tobacco and alcohol use, sedentary work and leisure behaviors, and unhealthy diets are linked to higher health care costs. Smoking and obesity are the two leading lifestyle factors associated with high health care costs. Unequal access to health care also explains growing health care costs. Individuals with insufficient or no health insurance coverage are less likely to seek medical care, especially preventative services. Thus, they are more likely to be treated for illnesses that could have been avoided.

Implications of Higher Health Care Costs

Health care costs are challenging the major payers, that is, the private and public health insurance systems. Private health insurance costs may well double, from $706 billion in 2005 to $1.39 trillion in 2015. Private health coverage companies responded to these increasing costs by implementing several new strategies. Most of these shifted more of the responsibility to their patients and providers. They changed their management of high-cost patients; introduced wellness, disease management, and medical technology information programs; reduced payments to providers; and implemented higher cost sharing.

Public health insurance costs will also rise, from $914.6 billion in 2005 to $1.93 trillion in 2015. Several attempts at curbing these costs slowed but did not stop the spending growth. Reform of Medicare (a federal program for those over the age of 65, certain disabled people under age 65, and those with permanent kidney failure treated with dialysis or a transplant) slowed some of the growth by cutting back payments to providers and shifting enrollees to managed care, both of which restricted benefits. However, the addition of a drug benefit in 2006 increased Medicare costs. Medicaid, a state-funded health program for the poor, greatly burdens the states, and states may respond by further restricting eligibility.

With this current climate of curbing costs, individuals must accept more and more of the financial burdens of the health care system. Two thirds of insured adults reported that their insurance premiums increased in the past 5 years. Copayments and deductibles are also rising for the majority of insured people, and for many individuals, high medical costs can have a huge impact on their lives.

Not only are rising medical costs a major stressor; they can also create significant barriers to health care. In the past year, almost one quarter of Americans had problems paying health care bills. Most of the unpaid bills were for physician services, lab fees, and prescription drugs. In a given year, almost 30 percent of adults report that they or a member of their household skipped medical treatment or either did not complete or cut the dosage of a drug prescription because of high costs. Individuals in disadvantaged social positions experience even greater access problems because of rising costs. Poor people, women, and individuals with chronic illnesses all report delaying or not getting necessary health care because of costs.

Christine Caffrey

See also Health Care, Access; Stressors

Further Readings

Administration on Aging. 2005. "A Profile of Older Americans: 2005." Washington, DC: Administration on Aging. Retrieved December 27, 2007 (http://www.aoa .gov/prof/Statistics/profile/2005/profiles2005.asp).

Centers for Medicare and Medicaid Services. 2007. "National Health Expenditures Projections: 2006–2016." Washington, DC: Centers for Medicare and Medicaid Services. Retrieved December 27, 2007 (http://www.cms.hhs .gov/NationalHealthExpendData/downloads/ proj2006.pdf).

Heffler, Stephen, Sheila Smith, Sean Keehan, Christine Borger, M. Kent Clemens, and Christopher Truffer. 2005. "U.S. Health Spending Projections for 2004–2014." *Health Affairs* Web Exclusive, February 23. Retrieved December 27, 2007 (http://content.healthaffairs.org/ cgi/content/abstract/hlthaff.w5.74).

Kaiser Family Foundation. 2005. "Health Care Costs Survey." Washington, DC: Kaiser Family Foundation. Retrieved December 27, 2007 (http://www.kff.org/ newsmedia/pomr090105pkg.cfm).

HEALTH CARE, IDEOLOGICAL BARRIERS TO CHANGE

Researchers consistently document U.S. disparities in health care access according to race and ethnicity, socioeconomic status, gender, sexual orientation, and disability. Inadequate health care access contributes to poor health outcomes over the life course, leading to higher incidence of disease and chronic conditions and, consequently, to lower life expectancy among some population segments. Although a leader in technological innovation and development and among the highest in per capita health care expenditures, the United States consistently ranks among the worst in national health and health care outcomes compared with other developed countries. In 2006, U.S. Census Bureau estimates placed the number of non-elderly uninsured at approximately 46.1 million, a figure that does not include individuals experiencing discontinuous coverage. Further, costs continue to rise due to increases in chronic health conditions, an influx of expensive new technologies, and expanding definitions of what is medically treatable.

Policymakers, health professionals, consumers, and others recognize the need to reform the U.S. health care system. Strategies to improve health care quality generally take the form of incremental changes to the structure of health care financing or introduction and improvement of health care quality data collection and feedback mechanisms. Still, health care quality improvements from these reforms have been modest. Critics argue that these reform efforts neglect existing sets of beliefs at institutional and interpersonal levels that both impede meaningful health care reform and maintain the current system of inequitable care delivery. The failure of reform efforts points to the need to identify and understand ideological barriers to health care change.

Health Care Reform

Many argue that the only way the United States can achieve substantial improvements in health care quality is through the development of national health insurance (NHI). Successful adoption of NHI would establish the right to health care. Despite high levels of support for some sort of NHI among the public, previous efforts to institute NHI failed. Historically, labor unions and physician opposition, concretized in the lobbying efforts of the American Medical Association, helped undermine early reform efforts. Conservative political opposition, frequently aligned with the Republican Party, also rejects the notion that health care is a right, preferring to treat health care like other goods and services optimally provided through competitive markets. In support of this perspective, the American Medical Association, conservatives, and other opponents have been successful in mobilizing "myths" about the quality of the U.S. health care system as rhetorical devices to persuade policymakers that NHI is simply not a politically feasible option. These myths play upon commonsense beliefs about the U.S. health care system, including generalized beliefs that U.S. health care is "the best in the world," any existing problems are "not that bad," and the best solutions to any problems lie in privatization and the market. The dominance of such ideologies has led to the failure of significant reform attempts, ensuring that the current system of health care rationing, according to ability to pay rather than clinical need, continues.

Health Care Access and Quality

A growing body of evidence suggests that even with the adoption of reforms such as NHI, inequities in the delivery of health care will persist. Some argue that a major problem overlooked by most reform efforts is the chronic undersupply of minority and female physicians. Regardless of good intentions, a health care delivery system reliant upon physicians who are, by and large, white, upper-class, able-bodied, and heterosexual males will inevitably yield poorer health care outcomes for patients who fall outside these categories. Others argue that even if a ready supply of physicians outside these privileged groups existed, inequities sustained by the existing system of medical beliefs remain unaddressed. These barriers stem from the nature of medical training and the ways in which medical knowledge is applied within health care delivery. Medical professionals are trained to complete the process of diagnosis and treatment by taking symptoms presented by a patient and using them as clues to construct a diagnosis for which they can then prescribe treatment. Thus, patients who receive the best care are those who can most skillfully cooperate in the construction of these standardized medical narratives. Patients who are unfamiliar with the appropriate medical terms and phrases, whose cases are complicated, or who attempt to present alternative narratives to the standard medical ones are less likely to receive good care.

Ideological barriers to improvements in the U.S. health care system do not exist solely in the opposition to large-scale policy reform but also in health care delivery. Traditionally, research limited its focus to structural barriers such as health care financing and discrimination in patient–provider interactions. At the level of patient–provider interactions, the focus has been on difficulties arising from factors such as differences in communication styles due to class, race, or gender, or from conscious or subconscious discrimination, which can lead to insufficient information or misinformation, improper or inadequate provision of care and referrals for treatment, and erroneous assumptions about either the patient or the provider. Thus, most reforms have addressed financial barriers or training and reporting policies aimed at the prevention of discriminatory practices. Ideological barriers impeding health care reform and enabling gaps in care are the most pervasive yet the most challenging for reformers to address.

Julia A. Rivera Drew

See also Health Care, Access; Health Care, Costs; Health Care, Insurance

Further Readings

Geyman, John P. 2003. "Myths as Barriers to Health Care Reform in the United States." *International Journal of Health Services* 33(2):315–29.

Institute of Medicine. 2003. *Unequal Treatment: Confronting Racial and Ethnic Disparities in Health Care,* edited by Brian D. Smedley. Washington, DC: National Academies Press.

Mechanic, David. 2006. *The Truth about Health Care: Why Reform Is Not Working in America.* New Brunswick, NJ: Rutgers University Press.

Schuster, Mark A., Elizabeth A. McGlynn, and Robert H. Brook. 1998. "How Good Is the Quality of Health Care in the United States?" *The Milbank Quarterly* 76(4):517–63.

Starr, Paul. 1982. *The Social Transformation of American Medicine.* New York: Basic Books.

HEALTH CARE, INSURANCE

Health care insurance is a contractual arrangement through which individuals spread the financial risk of unexpected and costly medical events. By enabling the voluntary pooling of health-related financial risks, health insurance enhances social welfare. However, incentives inherent in a health insurance contract can result in the inefficient use of health services, leading to reductions in social welfare. Additionally, disparities in information about health status between persons seeking insurance and entities providing coverage can affect the efficient and equitable pricing and provision of health insurance and result in welfare losses. Consequently, the conflict between the welfare gains from risk pooling and the welfare losses from the inefficient use of medical care (known as moral hazard) and asymmetric information (the problem of adverse risk selection) remains an ongoing tension in the design of health plans and in efforts to expand coverage.

Standard Theory of Health Insurance

According to standard theory, risk-averse individuals prefer a monetary loss with certainty to a gamble with the same expected value. To protect against health-related financial losses, such individuals are willing to transfer income (pay a health insurance premium) to a risk-bearing entity (an insurance company) to protect themselves against monetary losses associated with illness. When these income transfers capture the expected value of an individual's medical care expenses over a contractual period, they represent an actuarially fair health insurance premium. Because such monetary transfers are voluntary, the pooling of resources by individuals with similar risk profiles is welfare enhancing.

Standard theory also suggests that risk-averse individuals will pay a "risk premium" above the actuarially fair premium to obtain health insurance. This additional payment enables insurers to make coverage available, because it compensates them for their administrative and marketing costs and allows a margin for profit. This insurance "load" represents the true economic price of insurance as it is the minimal monetary transfer above an actuarially fair premium

necessary to induce insurers to provide coverage. An individual's demand for coverage will depend on its price (in theory, the insurance load, but in practice, the out-of-pocket premium), the individual's risk aversion, and the probability and size of a health-related financial loss.

Setting Health Insurance Premiums

Despite the theoretical construct of an actuarially fair health insurance premium, controversy remains as to how premiums should be established. Some view health insurance as a form of mutual aid and social solidarity among citizens and believe that premiums should be community rated, reflecting the health care experience of an entire insured group. Under this principle, all individuals pay the same premium regardless of their own health care experience. In contrast, others suggest that premiums should more appropriately reflect the actuarial value of individual health care experience (or the experience of a group of very similar individuals) and should be experience rated. These analysts assert that community rating is unfair because it imposes an implicit tax on low risks that is used to subsidize high risks. Such pricing also results in the inefficient provision of coverage as the low risks purchase too little insurance and high risks overinsure.

Moral Hazard and Adverse Selection

Because health insurance reduces out-of-pocket costs, individuals and their providers have an incentive to overuse health care. In doing so, individuals obtain additional health services whose value to them is less than the resource costs incurred in its production. This moral hazard welfare loss represents a major source of inefficiency in the provision of health care.

Efforts to address moral hazard include the use of deductibles and coinsurance. The growth of managed care added a number of innovations to control utilization, including constraints on provider choice, capitated or fixed-dollar payments for the care of each enrollee, utilization review, and case management and quality assurance activities.

Most recently, efforts to instill greater cost consciousness on the part of consumers have led to the development of consumer-driven health plans, typified by health savings accounts combined with high-deductible health plans. Individuals and their employers make tax-free contributions to a health savings account up to a proscribed dollar limit. By assuming responsibility for substantial first-dollar expenditures, the expectation is that consumers will use services prudently. However, some individuals with these plans have delayed or postponed care and have expressed dissatisfaction with such plans. Concern also exists that tax-free health accounts will attract high-income persons in good health, leaving low-income persons with health problems in traditional insurance plans.

Moral hazard remains a concern, and its interpretation and policy implications may be more complex than generally appreciated. A distinction exists between inefficient moral hazard (resulting from the insurance-induced reduction in out-of-pocket price) and efficient moral hazard (resulting from the income transfer the ill receive from members of the insurance pool). Efficient moral hazard is welfare enhancing, as it enables individuals to overcome barriers to affordability.

In certain cases, such as the treatment of chronic illnesses, cost-sharing provisions to address moral hazard may need to be relaxed. The out-of-pocket costs of such provisions may deter compliance with treatment and lead to future health care costs.

Informational asymmetries between potential enrollees and insurers regarding enrollee health status can contribute to adverse risk selection. Because potential enrollees are often better informed than insurers, they may be able to enter health plans and pay premiums that do not reflect their expected health care use. Instead, they may pay the lower premiums faced by good risks. Such behavior can yield inefficiencies over time, as enrollment by poor risks causes health plan costs to rise and low-risk enrollees respond by seeking lower-priced but more restrictive coverage. In the extreme, adverse selection may lead to unsustainable health plans as low-risk enrollees defect and plans become dominated by high-risk enrollees.

To avoid adverse selection, health insurers compete by selecting favorable health risks. Such behavior is inefficient because it diverts resources from efforts to reduce plan costs and enhance quality and may leave certain individuals uninsured. State and federal reforms have sought to counter such insurer behavior by requiring open enrollment and guaranteed renewal of coverage and by limiting exclusions and waiting periods for preexisting health conditions.

Efforts to counter adverse selection have included reinsuring the expenses of high-cost enrollees, establishing high-risk insurance pools, and risk-adjusting payments to health plans.

Health Care Insurance in the United States

Whereas most industrialized countries have established national health insurance systems, the United States stands out as providing a patchwork of private and public sources of coverage that leave a sizable proportion of its citizenry uninsured (15.3 percent, or 44.8 million persons in 2005). Of the insured U.S. population in 2005, coverage from employers represents the largest source (60.2 percent, or 176.3 million persons), followed by Medicare (13.7 percent, or 40.1 million persons), Medicaid (13 percent, or 38.1 million persons), and private health insurance purchased directly from an insurer (9.2 percent, or 26.9 million persons).

The lack of a uniform health insurance system in the United States has resulted in significant gaps in coverage. Persons most likely to lack insurance are young adults (ages 19 to 34), racial and ethnic minorities (especially Hispanics), persons with low educational attainment, persons with low incomes, those in fair or poor health, low-wage earners, workers in small firms, and the self-employed. Compared with insured persons, the uninsured are less likely to have a usual source of health care, more likely to report difficulties obtaining timely care, and less likely to use medical care.

The provision of health insurance in the United States has also raised a number of equity and efficiency issues, especially with regard to employment-based coverage. For example, employer contributions to an employee's health insurance premium are tax deductible, representing a revenue loss of $209 billion in 2004. This "tax subsidy" exacerbates moral hazard by creating incentives for individuals to purchase more generous coverage. Because the value of the tax deduction depends on an individual's marginal tax rate, it represents a regressive subsidy favoring higher- rather than lower-income workers.

Providing coverage through the workplace also yields labor market inefficiencies. Workers may be discouraged from changing jobs or retiring early, and they may alter their labor force activity to qualify for coverage. Means-tested public insurance, such as

Medicaid and the State Children's Health Insurance Program (SCHIP), can also create perverse incentives whereby individuals adjust hours of work and earnings so that family members qualify for coverage. Expanded Medicaid eligibility and SCHIP implementation have also resulted in private insurance "crowd out." In this case, privately insured low-income workers with dependents eligible for public coverage substitute public for private coverage.

Although the United States has failed to address these problems through comprehensive health insurance reform, public policy has not been entirely passive. Medicaid expansions and SCHIP implementation during the 1990s contributed to a reduction in the number of uninsured children. In 2007, however, President Bush vetoed legislation that had bipartisan support to expand the number of children covered by SCHIP. Moreover, recent policy initiatives stressing voluntary enrollment in private coverage through the use of tax credits, small-group and individual insurance market reforms, and premium subsidies for employers have not reduced the number of uninsured. In response, several states have mandated that individuals obtain private coverage. In addition, outreach efforts have sought to provide information to those eligible but not enrolled in public coverage. It remains to be seen whether public policy can effectively expand coverage and address the problems of moral hazard and adverse selection.

Alan C. Monheit

See also Health Care, Access; Health Care, Costs; Health Care, Ideological Barriers to Change

Further Readings

Cutler, David M. and Richard J. Zeckhauser. 2000. "The Anatomy of Health Insurance." Pp. 563–644 in *Handbook of Health Economics,* edited by A. J. Culyer and J. P. Newhouse. Amsterdam: Elsevier.

Newhouse, Joseph P. 2006. "Reconsidering the Moral Hazard–Risk Avoidance Tradeoff." *Journal of Health Economics* 25(5):1005–14.

Nyman, John A. 2004. "Is Moral Hazard Inefficient? The Policy Implications of a New Theory." *Health Affairs* 23(5):317–18.

Selden, Thomas M. and Bradley M. Gray. 2006. "Tax Subsidies for Employment-Related Health Insurance: Estimates for 2006." *Health Affairs* 25(6):1568–79.

HEGEMONY

The term *hegemony* has a long and rich history. Etymologically, *hegemony* derives from the Greek *hegemon,* meaning "leader." The most extensive and influential elaboration of hegemony is that of the Italian theorist and political activist Antonio Gramsci (1891–1937); indeed one can argue that hegemony has become synonymous with Gramsci's theory of hegemony.

Gramsci was one of the leaders of the Italian Communist Party (PCI, founded in 1921). His steadfast refusal to align the PCI with Mussolini and his outspoken criticism of fascism landed him in prison. Gramsci occupied his time in prison reflecting upon, and writing about, a series of political concerns; foremost among these was why the working class in the most industrialized nations had failed to develop a revolutionary consciousness. It is in the course of these writings, which have come to be known as the *Quaderni del Carcere* or *Prison Notebooks,* that Gramsci developed his theory of hegemony.

Gramsci used *hegemony* in his *Prison Notebooks* in two different but related senses. First, he referred to a form of rule characterized by a consensual basis within civil society, the social terrain intermediary between the economy and the state, and contrasted it to a monopoly of the means of violence or control of the state. Second, hegemony referred to the development of class consciousness and, in particular, to the movement of a class from an "in-itself" to a "for-itself" status. Each of the two senses of hegemony relates to a set of key terms. As a form of rule, hegemony relates to *consent, civil society, historical bloc*, and *war of position*. As the development of class consciousness, it relates to *organic intellectual, intellectual/moral bloc, common sense/good sense*, and the party as *collective intellectual.* Gramsci argued that the modern Western bourgeoisie rules not only, or even predominantly, through brute strength (domination) but also through intellectual and moral direction (hegemony). Consequently, a frontal attack on the state—for example, Lenin's military strategy during the Russian revolution—would be inadequate in the nations of the industrialized West because it would leave the bourgeoisie's hegemony intact. In such a situation, a war of position focused on civil society and the formation of an alternative hegemony is the only viable military strategy.

With Gramsci, the concept of hegemony moves beyond a description of a form of rule to a prescription for liberation. And it is precisely Gramsci's emphasis on liberation that accounts for the widespread influence of his theory of hegemony. According to Gramsci, the movement of a class from subordination to hegemony is a long and arduous process whose starting point is the consciousness of the aspiring hegemonic group. Gramsci, like W. E. B. Du Bois and Frantz Fanon, described the consciousness of subaltern or subordinate groups as divided or contradictory. For example, wage workers have one consciousness implicit in their practical activity, and another superficially explicit or verbal, that they have inherited from the past and uncritically absorbed. Gramsci referred to the consciousness inherited from the past and uncritically absorbed as "common sense." Gramsci's treatment of common sense or subordinate cultures was distinctive because it avoided the romanticization/othering dichotomy that characterizes most scholarship on this subject and because it viewed these cultures as dynamic rather than static and as incoherent rather than as patterned wholes possessing a distinctive logic.

Common sense is a confused agglomerate of fragments from religion as well as from the history of philosophy and science. Gramsci argued that common sense is good enough to allow the subalterns to function successfully in their immediate surroundings, but it cannot provide them with any critical insight into their subordinate status and, consequently, poses no threat to the dominant group. However, within all commonsense conceptions of the world or subaltern cultures, there is a kernel of good sense that is the intuition of a future philosophy, and it is in this good sense that one finds the rough beginning of a possible counterhegemony.

For a class to launch a successful counterhegemony—that is, acquire self-consciousness and develop the intellectual and moral order consonant with its practical activity—it must produce its own set of indigenous or organic intellectuals. By *intellectual,* Gramsci means not simply a thinking being—indeed Gramsci argued that all human beings are intellectuals in this sense—but an individual who has the social function of producing or instilling knowledge in others. Any subaltern group that aspires to hegemony must create intellectuals from its ranks who can liberate it from common sense and elaborate its good sense into a coherent worldview.

Organic intellectuals, once formed, need to enter into intellectual-mass dialectics; that is, they must stay in constant interaction with the group they represent, educating, organizing, and developing more organic intellectuals. Intellectuals and education are considered so essential to social transformation that Gramsci envisioned the Communist Party as a collective intellectual. The final step on the road to the creation of a counterhegemony is the creation of a historical bloc; that is, the winning over of other subaltern groups to the newly constructed worldview of the aspiring hegemonic group. Gramsci emphasized that a historical bloc is not a loose association of disparate subaltern groups, each of which maintains its identity, but a fusion of subaltern groups with the aspiring hegemonic group through the appeal of the latter's intellectual and moral worldview.

Gramsci's theory of hegemony has had widespread influence. Within leftist—communist, socialist, and labor—political circles, it persuaded political leaders to acknowledge culture and consciousness as vital for any revolutionary transformation of society. The importance it places on education persuaded many leftist political parties throughout the South, and especially in Argentina and Brazil, to launch massive education campaigns and to make literacy among workers and peasants into a political priority. Within the academy it strongly influenced British cultural studies and, in particular, the Centre for Contemporary Cultural Studies at the University of Birmingham, one of the first and most prolific centers for cultural studies. Although Gramsci wrote within a Marxian paradigm and used class as his basic unit of analysis—because the theory of hegemony places the issue of power firmly at the center of any discussion of culture—his theory has also been utilized in the study of racism, sexism, and postcolonialism.

Wilma Borrelli

See also Class Consciousness; Cultural Imperialism; Social Control

Further Readings

Burgos, Raul. 2002. "The Gramscian Intervention in the Theoretical and Political Production of the Latin American Left." *Latin American Perspectives* 29(1):9–37.

Crehan, Kate. 1977. *The Fractured Community: Landscapes of Power and Gender in Rural Zambia.* Berkeley, CA: University of California Press.

Genovese, Eugene. 1976. *Roll Jordon Roll: The World the Slaves Made.* New York: Vintage.

Gramsci, Antonio. 1971. *Selections from the Prison Notebooks,* edited by Q. Hoare and G. N. Smith. London: Lawrence & Wishart.

Guha, Ranajit and Gayatri Chakrovarty Spivak, eds. 1988. *Selected Subaltern Studies.* New York: Oxford University Press.

Hall, Stuart. 1980. "Cultural Studies: Two Paradigms." *Media, Culture and Society* 2:57–72.

Williams, Raymond. 2000. *Marxism and Literature.* Upper Saddle River, NJ: Prentice Hall.

HEROIN

Heroin is a semisynthetic substance derived from the resin of opium poppies, which are grown widely in South America, the Middle East, and Asia. Heroin can be injected, smoked, or sniffed. Reported effects include vomiting and nausea for first-time users, followed by intense euphoria ("rush") accompanied by flushed skin, dry mouth, and impaired mental functioning.

Heroin was first manufactured in 1898 by the Bayer pharmaceutical company and marketed heavily as a treatment for respiratory ailments. Heroin was originally believed to cure morphine addiction, but doctors soon realized it was more potent and addictive than morphine. Its addictive potential was an important factor in U.S. restriction under the Harrison Narcotics Act in 1914 and in its full criminalization in 1919. Presently, the U.S. Drug Enforcement Agency classifies heroin as a Schedule I narcotic, with high abuse potential and no accepted medical utility.

Most U.S. heroin comes from Mexico and Colombia, with New York, Chicago, and Los Angeles being the primary market areas for domestic heroin distribution. Abuse rates are highest in East Coast metropolitan areas, where higher-purity powder is available. For many years, injection was the dominant method of use, due in part to low purity levels. In the early 1990s higher-quality heroin entered the United States, making snorting and smoking more attractive routes of administration. The result has been an overall increase in heroin consumption rates in the latter years of the 20th century. New use methods also helped combat the social stigma associated with injection and helped broaden heroin's appeal to new and more affluent groups, such as suburban whites.

Despite an increase in overall rates of use, heroin remains one of the least used illegal drugs in the United States. Adolescent use has remained relatively stable over the past 25 years, with use by high school seniors fluctuating between 1 and 2 percent. However, emergency room admissions for heroin have increased 35 percent since 1995, mostly among youth. Drug treatment admissions have also increased steadily since 1992, mostly among middle-aged white males.

Heroin became associated with criminality in the 1970s based on the reasoning that users will turn to burglary, fraud, shoplifting, and prostitution to obtain money to maintain their addictions. Such reports emerged during the Nixon administration and still remain popular in anti-drug campaigns. Heroin use is also associated with violent crime. Research indicates that episodes of prostitutes assaulting and robbing clients are connected to the withdrawal experience. There is also substantial violence associated with heroin trafficking, although this is attributed to the inherent violence associated with drug markets rather than the pharmacological effects of heroin.

Health risks associated with heroin include fatal overdose, addiction, collapsed veins, and withdrawal sickness. An addict typically begins experiencing withdrawal symptoms within 8 hours after discontinuation of use. Withdrawal symptoms are similar to a severe flu, include sweating, anxiety, cold sweats, vomiting, diarrhea, and fever. Another significant problem with heroin use is the high risk of contracting blood-borne diseases, such as hepatitis and HIV/AIDS, from injection and needle sharing. Nationally, roughly 75 percent of new AIDS cases among women and children stem from the injection of illegal drugs such as heroin. Many countries have instituted programs supplying sterile needles to injectors to combat these diseases. The U.S. federal government does not currently support needle exchange programs, although some city and local governments do.

Philip R. Kavanaugh

See also Addiction; Drug Abuse, Crime

Further Readings

National Institute on Drug Abuse, Community Epidemiology Work Group. 2005. "Epidemiologic Trends in Drug Abuse, Advance Report." Bethesda, MD: National Institute on Drug Abuse.

Substance Abuse and Mental Health Services Administration. 2007. "Results from the 2006 National Survey on Drug Use and Health: National Findings." Rockville, MD: Substance Abuse and Mental Health Services Administration.

HIDDEN CURRICULUM

Hidden curriculum is a subset of theories of socialization that investigate how society reproduces culture from generation to generation. Primary socialization encompasses the teaching of children by parents who use direct instruction and modeling to inculcate language, moral beliefs and values, social roles, and so on. At the end of the 19th century, Émile Durkheim noted that schools had become central institutions helping the child to transition from family to society, from primary to secondary socialization, where socialization is increasingly accomplished by contact with adults and peers. Durkheim also advanced the notion that more is learned in schools than is specified in the official curriculum of books, manuals, and mission statements. Researchers from both the conservative structural-functional and radical critical traditions agree that schools accomplish social reproduction, both in formal curricula, where history, literature, and other forms of cultural capital necessary to fully participate in society are taught, and in informal or hidden curricula, which inculcate equally important elements of social reproduction, particularly discipline and stratification along the lines of intelligence, race, gender, and social class.

The Structural-Functional Approach

In a germinal 1959 article, Talcott Parsons described school classes as agencies of "manpower allocation" where academic achievement and ascribed qualities like family class background contribute to the reproduction of social stratification. In U.S. schools, he argued, children had to be inculcated with particular views of "achievement" and "equality of opportunity." Parsonian structural-functionalism contended that schools must teach that inequality is the *legitimate* consequence of differences in educational attainment. Following Parsons, qualitative researchers observed public grade school classrooms in efforts to identify the actual practices that accomplished socialization and sorting. Philip Jackson described values, dispositions, and social behaviors that were rewarded by teachers, and coined the term *hidden curriculum* to describe disciplines that were essential for school progress, for example, waiting quietly, exercising restraint, trying, completing work, keeping busy, cooperating, showing allegiance, being neat, being punctual, and being courteous. Other hidden elements of curriculum are embedded in mechanisms and apparatuses, including the built environment of the school and classroom; textbooks; uniforms; gender roles enacted by students, teachers, and administrators; tracking systems; the hierarchy of knowledge and school subjects; and the competitive/cooperative lessons of sports, contests, and academic performance.

The Neo-Marxist Approach

Beginning in the 1970s, neo-Marxist educational researchers reexamined hidden curricula. Social reproduction, they contended, includes the reproduction of illegitimate inequalities including social class, race, and gender. Two economists, Samuel Bowles and Herbert Gintis, wrote an influential study showing how school norms "corresponded" with capitalist class structures of workers, managers, and owners. Students from different social classes are subject to different curricula, scholarly expectations, types of schoolwork, and treatment by teachers. Schools send silent but powerful messages to students with regard to intellectual ability, personal traits, and occupational choice. Here also, qualitative researchers examined how students in upper-class communities were inculcated with the drive to achieve, whereas those in working-class schools rehearsed disciplines appropriate for low-skill, low-autonomy work.

Resistance Theory

By the 1980s both functionalist and Marxist structuralist accounts were challenged by a group of critical theorists who criticized the concept of hidden curricula for assuming that students were passive recipients and failing to acknowledge their ability to contest socialization or to make meaning of it for themselves. Moreover, school curricula were the location of struggles and conflicts between students, teachers, administrators, and the citizenry. Hidden curriculum was thus an incomplete theory because it ignored human agency and conflict. The notion of "resistance" was proposed to challenge the oppressive nature of schooling.

Resistance theorists developed a theoretical framework in which students and teachers were conceptualized as active agents able to subvert, reject, or change socialization agendas. The hidden curriculum did not constitute a coherent structure but rather a variety of conflicting and contradictory messages. Thus the plural *hidden curricula* was a better descriptor. Resistance theorists attended not only to how students produced meaning and culture but also to how students and teachers challenged even deeply hidden structures, creating their own hidden curricula. Resistance theory thus countered reproduction theory by emphasizing human agency, resistance, and contestation.

Some theorists have also attended to "hiddenness" itself. Noting that the socialization agendas of discipline—following abstract rules, submerging personal identity, being consigned as a member of a group, and so on—have been repeatedly exposed by educational researchers, these theorists ask, "Who are the curricula hidden from?" Interrogating the various types of hiddenness—intentional, undiscovered, hiding in plain sight, known to some but not others—they inquire about the consequences of revealing these pervasive structures of schooling.

There are still fertile fields for social research into the intended and unintended consequences of schooling. Particularly now, when the issues of privatization, vouchers, and charter schools promise to offer choices, it seems important to consider the hidden curricula of schooling in relation to socialization.

Eric Margolis

See also Ability Grouping; Education, Academic Performance; Education, Policy and Politics; Educational Equity; School Dropouts; School Segregation

Further Readings

Anyon, Jean. 1980. "Social Class and the Hidden Curriculum of Work." *Journal of Education* 162:67–92.

Bowles, Samuel and Herbert Gintis. 1976. *Schooling in Capitalist America: Educational Reform and the Contradictions of Economic Life.* New York: Basic Books.

Durkheim, Émile. [1925] 1961. *Moral Education.* New York: Free Press.

Freire, Paulo. 1973. *Pedagogy of the Oppressed.* New York: Seabury.

Giroux, Henry. 1983. "Theories of Reproduction and Resistance in the New Sociology of Education: A Critical Analysis." *Harvard Educational Review* 53:257–93.

Jackson, Philip W. 1968. *Life in Classrooms.* New York: Holt, Rinehart & Winston.

Martin, Jane R. 1976. "What Should We Do with a Hidden Curriculum When We Find One?" *Curriculum Inquiry* 6(2):135–51.

Parsons, Talcott. 1959. "The School Class as a Social System: Some of Its Functions in American Society." *Harvard Educational Review* 29:297–313.

Portelli, John P. 1993. "Dare We Expose the Hidden Curriculum?" Pp. 171–97 in *Reason and Values: New Essays in Philosophy of Education,* edited by J. Portelli and S. Bailin. Calgary, Alberta, Canada: Detselig.

Willis, Paul. [1977] 1981. *Learning to Labor: How Working Class Kids Get Working Class Jobs.* New York: Columbia University Press.

HIERARCHY OF NEEDS

Abraham Maslow's hierarchy of needs is a humanistic theory of motivation based on his observation that humans are a perpetually wanting animal. Maslow proposed five basic needs that become goals that guide human behavior. Lower-level needs are biological and experienced by everyone, whereas upper-level needs are psychological, experienced more rarely, and by fewer people. Typically portrayed as a pyramid (see Figure 1), the five basic needs are inter-related but arranged in order of their relative potency to influence behavior: physiological needs (level 1); safety needs (level 2); love needs (level 3); esteem needs (level 4); and the need to self-actualize (level 5). Thus, physiological needs are more influential than safety needs, and so on, up the hierarchy of needs. The theory posits that human

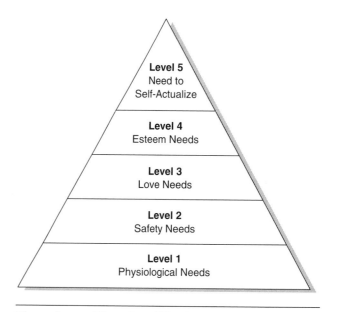

Figure 1   Hierarchy of Needs

behavior is motivated by the desire to achieve and maintain the conditions that make it possible to satisfy these needs.

Maslow proposed subhierarchies within each of the five levels. The physiological needs will be met according to the relative urgency to eat, drink, dispose of bodily waste, sleep, and breathe. If those needs are sufficiently satisfied, safety needs then begin to influence human behaviors, such as maintaining shelter, joining a labor union, and buying health insurance. Love needs are associated with belongingness and motivate individuals to create and maintain intimate relationships, have a family, and join a street gang or religious organization. The esteem needs may be satisfied by both negative and positive social behaviors, such as committing crimes to gain recognition or educating yourself to increase self-confidence. The need to self-actualize refers to maximizing one's potential and experiencing periods of peak achievement. Some psychologists refer to self-actualization as "flow," athletes describe "being in the zone," and artists describe their sensation of time becoming irrelevant while experiencing peak creativity. Maslow's hierarchy of needs unites physiological needs with psychological needs within an easy-to-understand humanistic theory of motivation.

Critics attack Maslow's hierarchy of needs both conceptually and empirically. For example, the stereotypical self-actualizing, starving artist seems to contradict the necessity of first satisfying safety needs or physiological needs. A response to that argument asserts that Maslow's hierarchy explains why there probably are not many self-actualizing, starving artists and that individuals differ in their perception of and need for safety. Researchers have had difficulty creating an empirical test of self-actualization, although creativity researchers have been addressing that issue, partly through brain imaging. Some researchers report different needs within the hierarchy, whereas others have found cross-cultural evidence in support of Maslow's theory. In spite of these criticisms, Maslow's hierarchy of needs has been widely adapted as a guide to individual therapy as well as human relations in the workplace, and as a general explanation of human motivation.

Tom Heinzen and Susan Nolan

See also Gangs; Job Satisfaction

Further Readings

Archives at Brandeis University. *Abraham Maslow & Harry Rand Lecture.* Retrieved December 27, 2007 (http://lts.brandeis.edu/research/archives-speccoll/findingguides/archives/soundrecordings/lectures/Maslow.html).

Maslow, Abraham H. 1943. "A Theory of Human Motivation." *Psychological Review* 50:370–96.

———. 1958. *Understanding Human Motivation.* Cleveland, OH: Howard Allen.

HIV/AIDS, REACHING HIGH-RISK POPULATIONS

Twenty-five years into the global HIV/AIDS epidemic, HIV infection rates remain alarmingly high, with more than 4 million new infections every year. Despite the rapid global spread of HIV, most people in both industrialized and developing countries are at relatively low risk of HIV infection. Comprehensive prevention programs directed at all segments of the general population can help to improve awareness, change social norms, reduce stigma and discrimination, promote less risky behavior, and reduce new infections. However, careful analysis of the sources of new infections in subpopulations is essential in order to focus relevant interventions and maximize their impact. A combination of risk avoidance (abstinence, mutual fidelity) and risk reduction (reduction in the number of sexual partners, treatment of sexually transmitted diseases, correct and consistent condom use, male circumcision, and needle exchange) have proven to be successful all over the globe.

Effective targeted prevention interventions can also lower the number of patients requiring costly drug treatments and boost the sustainability of expensive antiretroviral therapy (ART). At the same time, successful ART makes prevention more acceptable and helps in reducing stigma and discrimination.

To control HIV infections, the focus should be on the populations experiencing the highest rate of infections—often referred to as "high-risk populations," "most at risk populations," or "most vulnerable populations" (MVPs). Interventions tailored to specific populations reach a smaller audience than those aimed at the general population, yet they have the possibility to make a disproportionate impact on the course of the epidemic.

MVPs are a relatively smaller segment of the general population that is at higher than average risk of acquiring or transmitting HIV infections. They include discordant couples, sex workers (SWs) and their clients, injection drug users (IDUs) and other drug users, men who have sex with men (MSM), individuals in the armed forces, prisoners, and children of sex workers. A larger group of MVPs, especially in high-prevalence countries, may include HIV-positive pregnant women, sexually active and out-of-school youth, minority populations, migrant and displaced persons, and large populations of women.

There are compelling reasons to reach MVPs:

- They are often marginalized, criminalized, victimized, and discriminated against by law enforcement agencies as well as the general population. As a result they are difficult to reach and have poor access to relevant public health and other services.
- Segmentation of the various subpopulations allows for more specific, appropriate, and effective interventions.
- There are numerous proven interventions that can control the epidemic in IDUs, SWs, and MSM.

Risk and Vulnerability

An individual's risk of acquiring or transmitting HIV is affected by a variety of factors, such as sexual behavior, drug use, male circumcision, and leaving sexually transmitted diseases (STDs) untreated. High-risk individuals engage in behaviors that expose themselves to the risk of HIV infection, such as unprotected casual sex with multiple partners, sharing needles, and commercial sex.

Risk can be further compounded when the HIV-positive individual is suffering from acute HIV infection. Acute infection refers to the period of time immediately after a person is infected with HIV. Characterizing this phase is prolific viral replication and an acute drop in the CD4 count. Persons with acute HIV infection are extremely infectious, as the potential for an individual to transmit the virus increases eight- to tenfold.

In addition to individual risk behaviors, some vulnerable populations face greater susceptibility to HIV/AIDS. Societal factors, often beyond the control of the individual, may also increase the risk of infection. These include poverty, unemployment, illiteracy, gender inequities and gender-based violence, cultural practices, human rights abuses, and lack of access to information and services.

Women face increased vulnerability to infection due to biological, social, and economic factors. They often lack the power to negotiate safer sex with their partners. Because of economic inequalities, some women enter sex work or perform transactional sex for economic survival. Furthermore, women are more vulnerable to infection than men because of biology: The female genital tract has more exposed surface area than the male genital tract, semen has a greater HIV concentration than vaginal fluids, and a larger amount of semen is exchanged during intercourse than vaginal fluids.

Orphans and children of MVPs are also particularly vulnerable. Whether the parent is a SW or IDU, HIV-positive or HIV-negative, living or deceased, these children need special attention. MVPs with children may not be coherent enough to support a child emotionally or financially. They may not be physically present, may be ill due to HIV, or may have died. Many times, children of HIV-positive parents serve as caretakers.

Understanding the Local Dynamics of the Epidemic

The population of MVPs differs by the type and level of epidemic. Through investigation of the incidence, distribution, and causes of HIV in a society, epidemiologists can predict which populations are most vulnerable to, and at risk of, HIV infection.

In lower-prevalence countries, containing the epidemic in MVPs can have a wide-reaching effect on how the general population experiences HIV and AIDS. Accurate epidemiological and behavioral data can pinpoint which populations are at high risk and, therefore, which targeted interventions should be implemented to address those populations. By targeting MVPs, the progression from low HIV prevalence to higher HIV prevalence in the general population may be prevented.

In higher-prevalence countries, with an increased pool of infected individuals, a more effective strategy would be to identify those infected through targeted counseling and testing and other community-based interventions. In this environment, programs should focus on discordant couples and other at-risk

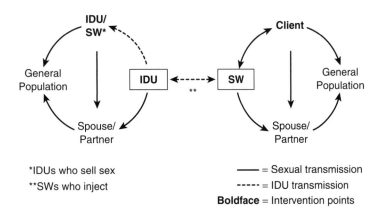

*IDUs who sell sex

**SWs who inject

———— = Sexual transmission

----- = IDU transmission

Boldface = Intervention points

Figure 1   HIV Transmission Through Sex Work and Injection Drug Use

populations such as sexually active youth, young adults, and women and provide both risk avoidance and risk reduction programs.

In many contexts, the relationship between sex work and injection drug use is quite close (Figure 1), and prostitution and injection drug use have been the engines that have fueled the epidemic. Many SWs use injection drugs and many drug users resort to sex work to pay for their injection drug use. These IDU/SWs not only risk transmitting HIV through the sharing of injection drug paraphernalia but also can pass the infection sexually. HIV infections will then reach bridge populations and allow the virus to infect the general population.

Overall, targeted interventions may take various forms, depending on the social, cultural, economic, political, and legal specifics of the high-risk group. The discussion that follows focuses on some most at risk populations and appropriate interventions.

Sex Workers

SWs are a diverse and sizable population. They can be male, female, or transgender and work in a variety of environments, including brothels, bars, or on the streets. In some societies, such as in Amsterdam, Senegal, and Nevada, sex work is legal or decriminalized. These legal SWs have access to health and social services. In some societies, sex work is likely to be a personal choice. In many others it may be due to poverty or a lack of education and employment opportunities, or it may be fueled by trafficking of girls and

women. Sex work is also often used as a survival tactic during severe societal disruption caused by civil wars or natural disasters when no services are available and necessities are scarce.

In many countries, sex work is a driving factor fueling the HIV epidemic. Sustained and meaningful interventions are complicated by a variety of factors, including a lucrative commercial sex industry, low condom use, high levels of STDs, a hard-to-reach, highly mobile population of SWs and clients, and the absence of an atmosphere that encourages access to prevention programs. Awareness and understanding of a particular community's environment is essential in tailoring a relevant, effective message.

The focus should be on harm reduction and increased knowledge among SWs as well as parallel interventions for clients and partners of SWs. Interventions should include the promotion of condom knowledge, access, and use as well as improved health care, including antiretroviral therapy, STD screening, checkups, and treatment. Other critical areas for targeting and scaling up interventions include building the capacity of community organizations; facilitating policy change to reduce discrimination and stigmatization; creating an enabling environment; harmonizing interventions with other HIV/STD, reproductive health, and drug prevention programs; and providing ongoing technical support and effective management and monitoring.

Men Who Have Sex With Men

As with interventions targeting SWs, interventions targeting MSM are essential, as well as challenging. This population is largely neglected in most countries and in urgent need of targeted, relevant HIV interventions. Because MSM often have sex with women, they possess the potential to spread HIV to the general population.

Reaching the MSM population is a difficult task for several reasons. First, this group faces a high level of stigma and discrimination by medical service providers and the general population. In many countries, homosexuality is illegal, and fear of legal repercussions drives the population further underground. Also, MSM do not often self-identify as "homosexual." Cultural perceptions of what constitutes homosexuality can vary widely, and men adopt different definitions based on these perceptions. Lastly, the MSM population is extremely diverse in nature. MSM may include monogamous homosexuals, male bisexuals, transgender individuals, heterosexual SWs, homosexual SWs, and MSM who are IDUs.

Injection Drug Users

IDUs are another key risk population for contracting and transmitting HIV. There are approximately 13 million IDUs worldwide, and the number is rising. Many lack adequate resources or access to sterile needles and syringes, especially in developing countries. They are treated as criminals in many societies and denied access to basic services and support. IDUs face considerable legal obstacles, such as laws prohibiting the possession of drug paraphernalia and drugs, and laws against aiding and abetting. An additional complication is that drug use is often accompanied by sex work.

Though sex is the chief mode of transmission in the spread of HIV, at least 10 percent of new infections globally are those contracted through injection drug use. In some countries, especially those with a low prevalence of HIV such as China and the countries of eastern Europe, IDUs are at the center of the epidemic. Historically a problem of rich countries, HIV transmission through IDUs is now observed throughout the world.

Considering this growing trend of injection drug use, new and scaled-up interventions are imperative to prevent the spread of HIV within and from IDUs. In low-prevalence countries, interventions targeting IDUs can limit transmission to SWs and therefore prevent a generalized epidemic. In countries already battling a high-prevalence epidemic, IDU interventions are critical to prevent an increase in incidence.

Harm reduction interventions should include ART, drug substitution therapy, needle exchange and distribution, condom and bleach distribution, outreach, peer education programs, and social network interventions. Though needle distribution programs are recognized as a cost-effective way to reduce HIV transmission, they remain controversial in many countries, including the United States. Opponents of needle exchange or distribution view the practice as "enabling" and encouraging drug use. As an alternative, bleach distribution programs have been implemented in countries with laws prohibiting or restricting needle distribution.

Individuals in the Armed Services

The armed forces, police, and other uniformed services around the world face a serious risk of HIV and other STDs, with infection rates significantly higher than the general population. Members of uniformed services can serve as a core transmission group for these infections to the general population. The nature of their work often requires that they be posted or travel away from home for extended periods of time, or they must await proper housing before sending for their families. Confronting risk daily inspires other risky behaviors, and a sense of invincibility may carry over into personal behavior. These groups tend to have more frequent contact with SWs, which increases the likelihood of passing on HIV and STDs to other partners, including their wives or girlfriends. The frequent and excessive use of alcohol and other behavior-modifying drugs plays a major role in risky sexual behavior.

Other High-Risk Populations

Other vulnerable populations include prisoners, migrants, refugees and internally displaced persons, truck drivers, transgender individuals, and out-of-school youth. To prevent transmission within these groups and to the general population, early targeted interventions should be implemented.

HIV/AIDS care and treatment are essential; however, prevention interventions are equally crucial. If large-scale and effective HIV prevention interventions are properly supported, the cost and need for treatment decreases.

Lower-level prevalence areas offer public health professionals an opportunity to act swiftly and avoid further expansion of the epidemic. Even in higher-prevalence countries, targeting the most at-risk individuals is important to prevent the further spread of the epidemic in the general population. National HIV prevention efforts need to be prioritized, directed, and scaled up to the populations most vulnerable and at risk of infection.

Many factors improve the ability for targeted interventions to succeed. Laws and policies directly challenging stigma and discrimination against people who have HIV, or are perceived to be at a risk for HIV, are essential. Interventions must also address contextual issues and be sensitive to local cultural and social perceptions surrounding HIV/AIDS. New technologies such as microbicides, male circumcision, and preexposure prophylaxis may become extremely valuable tools in preventing HIV among the most vulnerable populations.

All in all, HIV interventions must focus on the populations most vulnerable to HIV, irrespective of the level of the epidemic. This basic tenet of public health continues to be a cost-effective approach to controlling HIV.

Peter R. Lamptey and Rebecca G. Dirks

See also Drug Abuse; Harm Reduction Drug Policy; Homosexuality; Prostitution

Further Readings

Ball, Andrew L., Sujata Rana, and Karl L. Dehne. 1998. "HIV Prevention among Injecting Drug Users: Responses in Developing and Transitional Countries." *Public Health Reports* 113:170–81.

Barnett, Tony and Justin Parkhurst. 2005. "HIV/AIDS: Sex, Abstinence, and Behavior Change." *Lancet: Infectious Diseases* 5:590–93.

Burris, Scott. 2006. "Stigma and the Law." *Lancet* 367:529–31.

Chatterjee, Patralekha. 2006. "AIDS in India: Police Powers and Public Health." *Lancet* 367:805–6.

Joint United Nations Programme on HIV/AIDS (UNAIDS). 2006. "Report on the Global AIDS Epidemic." Retrieved December 27, 2007 (http://www.unaids.org/en/KnowledgeCentre/HIVData/GlobalReport/Default.asp).

Lamptey, Peter L. and David Wilson. 2005. "Scaling Up AIDS Treatment: What Is the Potential Impact and What Are the Risks?" *PLoS Medicine* 2(2):e39.

Monitoring the AIDS Pandemic (MAP) Network. 2005. "MAP Report 2005: Drug Injection and HIV/AIDS in Asia." Retrieved December 27, 2007 (www.mapnetwork.org/docs/MAP_IDU%20Book%2024Jun05_en.pdf).

———. 2005. "MAP Report 2005: Male to Male Sex and HIV/AIDS in Asia." Retrieved December 27, 2007 (www.mapnetwork.org/docs/MAP_&M%20Book_04July05_en.pdf).

Parker, Richard, Peter Aggleton, Kathy Attawell, Julie Pulerwitz, and Lisanne Brown. 2002. *HIV-Related Stigma and Discrimination: A Conceptual Framework and an Agenda for Action. Horizons Report.* Washington, DC: Population Council.

Rekart, Michael. 2005. "Sex-Work Harm Reduction." *Lancet* 366:2123–34.

Roura, Maria. 2005. "HIV/AIDS Interventions in Low Prevalence Countries: A Case Study of Albania." *International Social Science Journal* 57(186):639–48.

HOLOCAUST

The Holocaust was the systematic, state-organized persecution and murder of nearly 6 million Jews by Nazi Germany, its allies, and collaborators. They destroyed two thirds of Europe's Jews and one third of the world's Jewish population. If Nazi intentions had fully prevailed, all Jewish life and tradition would have been annihilated globally, because Adolf Hitler (1889–1945) and his most dedicated followers took the Jews to be so threatening and unwelcome—racially, economically, and politically—that their total destruction became the plan.

The Holocaust shows where racism can lead. According to Nazi ideology, Jews were the lowest of the low in the Nazis' extensive racial classification, which put Germans at the top but also fueled twin fears: (1) that German superiority could be harmed by race mixing, which would pollute German "blood," and (2) that "inferior" races had to be controlled, if not destroyed, to ensure that German power and culture were triumphant. As a result, Nazi Germany's genocidal policies destroyed millions of other defenseless people who were also regarded as inferior and threatening. These included Roma and Sinti (gypsies) and Polish citizens as well as homosexuals, the handicapped, Jehovah's Witnesses, and other political and religious dissidents. Thus, while the Holocaust refers primarily to the Nazi destruction of the Jews, it also encompasses other groups who, for racial, cultural, or political reasons, became Nazi targets in ways that were related but not identical to the Jews' fate under Hitler.

The Holocaust has more than one name. Its perpetrators took part in what the Nazis eventually called the "Final Solution" (*die Endlösung*) of their so-called Jewish question. In the early 1940s, eastern European Jews turned to Jewish scripture and used a Yiddish word, *Churb'n,* which means "destruction," or the

Hebrew term *Shoah,* which means "catastrophe," to name the disaster confronting their people. Although *Shoah* is used widely in Israel and the official Holocaust remembrance day is called *Yom Hashoah,* the term *Holocaust,* which began to achieve prominence in the 1950s, remains the most common name. Its diverse sources include derivation from the Septuagint, an ancient Greek translation of the Hebrew Bible, which employs *holokauston* for the Hebrew word *olah.* Those biblical words refer to a completely consumed burnt offering.

Racism and Religion

Hitler and his followers were racists because they were anti-Semites looking for an anti-Jewish stigma deeper than any religious, economic, or political prejudice alone could provide. For if Jews were found wanting religiously, it was possible for them to convert. If their business practices or political views were somehow inappropriate, changed behavior could, in principle, correct their shortcomings. But anti-Semites such as Hitler and the Nazis believed that Jews were a menace no matter what they did. Racial theory "explained" why the Jews, no matter what appearances might suggest to the contrary, were a threat that Germans could not afford to tolerate.

Contrary to Nazi ideology, Jews are not a race. Any person, irrespective of "blood" or any other biological feature, can become a Jew by conversion. Nevertheless, the belief that Jews were a race caught on in the 19th and early 20th centuries. Once linked, anti-Semitism and racism energized each other. Racial anti-Semitism, however, could never have arisen had it not been for nonracial forms of anti-Jewish prejudice and hatred that were at its roots. Among those roots, none was more important than Christianity.

Not all Jews are religious, but historically Jewish identity is scarcely imaginable apart from Judaism and its traditions, which unintentionally led to Christianity, a competing religious tradition, some 2,000 years ago. The history of the Holocaust shows that while Christianity was not a sufficient condition for the Holocaust, it was necessary for the actual catastrophe that took place. That statement does not mean that Christianity caused the Holocaust. Nevertheless, apart from Christianity, the Holocaust is barely conceivable because Nazi Germany's targeting of the Jews cannot be explained apart from the anti-Jewish images ("Christ-killers," willful blasphemers, unrepentant sons and daughters of the devil, to name only a few) that have been deeply rooted in Christian teaching and practices until post-Holocaust reforms uprooted them. Existing centuries before Nazism, Christianity's negative images of Jews and Judaism—supported by the institutions and social relationships that promoted those stereotypes—played key parts in bolstering the racial and genocidal anti-Semitism of Hitler and his Third Reich.

The "Final Solution"

In late 1941, the Nazi leader Reinhard Heydrich issued invitations to important German government and SS (*Schutzstaffel*) officials for a meeting to be held on December 9. Heydrich's invitations contained copies of the document he had received from Hermann Göring, his Nazi superior, on July 31, 1941. That document authorized Heydrich to plan the "Final Solution" of the "Jewish question." The Japanese bombing of Pearl Harbor on December 7, 1941, and the entry of the United States into World War II forced the postponement of the December meeting. But on January 20, 1942, Heydrich convened the Wannsee Conference at Am Grossen Wannsee 56/58, a comfortable lakeside villa in an affluent Berlin suburb.

Many of the men attending the meeting held doctorates from German universities. Most knew that mass murder of Jews had become state policy. Heydrich's meeting ensured that all of the leaders in attendance, and the bureaucracies they supervised, were on the same page. The report that emerged from the Wannsee Conference sanctioned the industrialization of death. To those who had to know, its euphemistic language made clear that the Third Reich had sentenced every European Jew to die, either by attrition, extermination through work, or outright murder.

As 1942 unfolded, six major Nazi killing centers were operational in occupied Poland: Chelmno, Belzec, Sobibor, Treblinka, Maidanek, and Auschwitz-Birkenau. At each of those places, gas chambers—some using carbon monoxide, others using a pesticide called Zyklon B—were destroying Jewish lives. During 1942 alone, the most lethal year in Jewish history, approximately 2.7 million Jews perished in the Holocaust.

The Nazis' racist anti-Semitism eventually entailed a destruction process that required and received cooperation from every sector of German society. On the whole, moreover, the Nazi killers and those Germans who aided and abetted them directly—or indirectly as bystanders—were civilized people from a society that was scientifically advanced, technologically competent, culturally sophisticated, efficiently organized, and even religiously devout.

Some Germans and members of populations allied with the Nazis resisted Hitler. Many others, however, played either a silent or an active role in the Holocaust. There were, for example, pastors and priests who led their churches in welcoming Nazification and the segregation of Jews it entailed. In addition, teachers and writers helped to till the soil where Hitler's racist anti-Semitism took root. Their students and readers reaped the wasteful harvest. Lawyers drafted and judges enforced laws that isolated Jews and set them up for the kill. Government and church personnel provided birth and baptismal records that helped to document who was Jewish and who was not. Other workers entered such information into state-of-the-art data processing machines. University administrators curtailed admissions for Jewish students and dismissed Jewish faculty members. Bureaucrats in the finance ministry handled confiscated Jewish wealth and property. Art dealers bought and sold treasures looted from Jewish families. Scientists performed research and tested their racial theories on those branded subhuman or nonhuman by German science. Business executives found that Nazi concentration camps could provide cheap labor. Railroad personnel scheduled and drove the trains that transported Jews to their death. If the destruction process had not been halted by the Third Reich's crushing military defeat, the "Final Solution" would probably have continued until it was finished.

Reverberations and Aftereffects

The Holocaust's impact has been immense. It undermined confidence in religious beliefs (Where was God?), political institutions (What happened to law?), and ethics (In what sense do human rights exist?). Toward the end of the 1990s, an upsurge of concern arose about reparations for Holocaust survivors and former slave laborers and about the restitution of property stolen from Jewish families and communities during the Holocaust years. This modicum of justice is important but also far from perfect.

The Holocaust played a part in the development of the 1948 United Nations Convention on the Prevention and Punishment of the Crime of Genocide,

but the world has not heeded the post-Holocaust imperative, "Never Again," at least not sufficiently to prevent the ethnic cleansing and genocide that have plagued the world after Auschwitz in the Balkans, Rwanda, and Darfur. The Holocaust was also decisive in the establishment of the state of Israel. Repeatedly, however, that aftereffect of the Holocaust has led to volatility and violence as Israelis, Palestinians, and their neighbors in the Middle East try to cope with each other's existence.

Once it was thought that memory of the Holocaust would check anti-Semitism, if not eliminate it. That hope has proved to be naive, especially with regard to the Arab and Muslim worlds, where it is often alleged that Jews, and Israelis in particular, use appeals to the Holocaust to legitimate policies that violate human rights. Holocaust denial—the unfounded view that the Holocaust is a myth, that it never happened, or that claims about its extent are exaggerated—used to be restricted to fringe groups, located primarily in Europe and North America, whose disrespect for sound historical research was disguised as a form of scholarly revisionism. In the early 21st century, however, Holocaust denial has become much more widespread and dangerous because it is so frequently found in radical Islamic ideologies that encourage suicide bombers and seek Israel's destruction. The Holocaust was not over when World War II ended in 1945. Its history and significance are still in the making.

John K. Roth

See also Anti-Semitism; Ethnic Cleansing; Genocide; Human Rights; Religious Prejudice; State Crimes; War Crimes

Further Readings

Berenbaum, Michael. 2006. *The World Must Know: The History of the Holocaust as Told in the United States Holocaust Memorial Museum.* Washington, DC: U.S. Holocaust Memorial Museum.

Bergen, Doris L. 2003. *War & Genocide: A Concise History of the Holocaust.* Lanham, MD: Rowman & Littlefield.

Dwork, Debórah and Robert Jan van Pelt. 2002. *Holocaust: A History.* New York: Norton.

Hilberg, Raul. 2003. *The Destruction of the European Jews.* 3rd ed. New Haven, CT: Yale University Press.

Patterson, David and John K. Roth, eds. 2004. *After-Words: Post-Holocaust Struggles with Forgiveness, Reconciliation, Justice.* Seattle, WA: University of Washington Press.

Roth, John K. 2005. *Ethics during and after the Holocaust: In the Shadow of Birkenau.* New York: Palgrave Macmillan.

Rubenstein, Richard L. and John K. Roth. 2003. *Approaches to Auschwitz: The Holocaust and Its Legacy.* Louisville, KY: Westminster John Knox.

HOMELESSNESS

Small groups of people tending to makeshift structures of an encampment, disheveled men rummaging through garbage cans for food, and young women with small children lining up outside of shelters have become common sights across the world's leading cities. This widespread growth in homelessness has been linked with economic, demographic, and cultural trends that have come to be known as "globalization"—the spread of manufacturing and financial activity across borders, heightened immigration, and the global ascendance of neoliberal ideology which favors free markets over government intervention. However, it is clear that these global trends interact with local conditions, such that the number and characteristics of people who become homeless may vary greatly across locales. Taking the United States as a case, what are the specific structural and demographic manifestations and correlates of its homeless problem? What factors influence whether or not homelessness is perceived as a social problem? Also, what are the different types of public policy responses that have emerged to address this persistent problem?

Structural Precipitants and Demographic Characteristics

As homelessness significantly increased throughout America's urban landscape in the early 1980s, two opposing explanations emerged. The first laid blame on individual characteristics such as human capital deficits (e.g., limited education and job skills), substance abuse, mental illness, and criminality. The second pointed to broad structural changes in labor and housing markets and welfare provisions. However, it is now generally understood that homelessness is the result of the interaction of structural and individual factors. Structural factors help explain why the prospect of homelessness, particularly among some categories of individuals, has increased in recent years; individual

factors help to identify who, among those groups most vulnerable to homelessness, is at greatest risk of becoming homeless.

Structural Precipitants

Economic Changes

As American manufacturing stagnated throughout the 1970s because of increased international competition and a series of oil shocks, firms began to close domestic plants and restructure workforces, displacing workers and driving up unemployment. Newly created jobs were more likely to be nonunion and concentrated in services, low paying, and unstable. A surge in immigration increased competition for low-skill jobs, especially disadvantaging urban residents with low educational attainment. A cheap form of cocaine called "crack" flooded the streets and significant numbers of inner-city residents used or trafficked the drug, rendering some of them vulnerable to addiction, felony conviction, and homelessness. In the early 1980s, early 1990s, and in the early post–9/11 period, cyclical economic recessions produced spikes in unemployment and forced firms to reduce labor costs to remain competitive.

Welfare Retrenchment

At the same time, the welfare state was being scaled back, beginning most notably in the early 1980s. While deinstitutionalization of large-scale state mental hospitals had begun decades earlier, sufficient funding for community-based mental health facilities, intended to replace large mental institutions, never materialized. As a result, many persons who would have been in mental hospitals in previous decades received insufficient mental health treatment and cycled through the streets, shelters, and jails. Also in the early 1980s, the federal government took measures to keep benefit levels low for households in the Aid to Families with Dependent Children (AFDC) program and restricted eligibility for benefits through the Supplemental Security Income program. Later, the Personal Responsibility and Work Opportunity Act of 1996 replaced AFDC with Temporary Assistance for Needy Families, a program with time limits on receipt of welfare benefits and job training. Although many participants in this program have found employment, evidence suggests that many find jobs that fail to lift them out of poverty.

Disappearing Affordable Housing

A decline in affordable housing intersected with economic polarization and stagnation and welfare retraction to increase vulnerability to homelessness. The federal government, already a minor investor in public housing compared with Europe and Asia, retreated from the rental housing market by reducing rental subsidies and all but halting the creation of public housing projects. At the same time, rising income inequality and population growth, trends more intense in major urban areas, pushed rents upward as lower-rent districts were gentrified. As a result, America's urban poor faced a major housing affordability crisis.

Estimated Size and Characteristics of the Homeless Population

Population Size

Researchers at the Urban Institute have estimated the size of America's homeless problem at two points in time, using similar definitions and methodologies. They counted persons using relief services for the extremely poor and homeless and used a moderately broad definition of homelessness that included people who were staying outside or in a car, an abandoned building or place of business, emergency or transitional shelter, a hotel or motel paid by a shelter voucher, or a place where they could not sleep for the next month without being asked to leave. A count in 1996 of the service-using adult homeless, which is estimated to include about 85 percent of the street homeless population, enumerated upward of 842,000 homeless people throughout the country at a single point in time. A comparison with a similar count conducted in 1987 shows that the national point-in-time homeless population did not decline over this 9-year period but remained approximately at the same level, despite a substantial growth in programs and the continuous economic growth of the late 1990s. Also, researchers using a national representative survey sample of U.S. adults estimated that 3.5 million people experience homelessness over a yearlong period.

Population Characteristics

The contemporary homeless population of the United States is diverse in terms of gender, family status, race and ethnicity, age, and disability status. According to the Urban Institute data, approximately 70 percent are male and 30 percent are female. About 75 percent are single individuals, 15 percent adults with children, and 10 percent adults living with one or more persons other than minor children. Many studies have found that adults with children are growing in proportion among the homeless. In terms of race and ethnicity, blacks are over-represented, making up 40 percent of the homeless population but 23 percent of the adult poor population. Whites are the largest group but are under-represented, making up 41 percent of the homeless population but 52 percent of the poor population. Latinos/as are also under-represented at 11 percent of the homeless population but 20 percent of the poor population. Native Americans are over-represented at 8 percent of the homeless population but 2 percent of the poor population. Although this study did not include data for Asians, local surveys consistently report substantial under-representation. Persons in their prime working years make up the majority of the adult homeless population, with approximately 80 percent between the ages of 25 and 54. Homelessness is rare among the elderly, likely because of social security programs, with only 2 percent of the homeless population over 65 years old. Alcohol, drug, and mental health problems are common among homeless persons, with only a third of homeless adults having no such problems and between 25 and 40 percent having struggled with one or more of these problems. The homeless of today, just as in the past, are located primarily in urban areas, particularly in central city neighborhoods.

Public Response to Homelessness

The manifestation of homelessness as a social problem has shown considerable variation across historical contexts. For example, homelessness was thought of as a minor problem, affecting only older alcoholic men in "skid row" neighborhoods in the early post–World War II period. However, by the early to mid-1980s, activists in urban communities were in an uproar about the increasing number of people fending for themselves on the streets and in emergency shelters.

What explains the shifts in prominence of homelessness as a social problem? Certainly increasing numbers and visibility of the homeless are critical. However, other factors are operative as well. First, who becomes homeless often affects the extent and nature of public reaction, as occurred when increasing numbers of women and children became homeless in the late 1980s and 1990s. The fact that many members of this new wave of homelessness were mentally ill, engaged in some form of substance abuse, or both, also affected how the public looked at the homeless.

The level and nature of attention that homelessness receives by the public is also influenced by the extent to which the public encounters homeless people in their daily lives, as well as the nature of the space in which the two groups confront one another. Some scholars have argued that public reaction to homelessness is influenced by the instrumental use and symbolic meaning of the space in which they negotiate their daily lives. When homeless persons eke out their subsistence mainly in "marginal spaces," which have little, if any, economic, political, or symbolic value, they are not very likely to provoke a response by authorities. However, they are more likely to provoke a response when they move into "prime spaces" that are used by the domiciled for residential, recreational, or commercial purposes, or "transitional spaces" that have ambiguous use or are in the process of being transformed into prime space. When homeless persons enter prime and transitional spaces, they are likely to provoke two different responses. Political officials and their agents often try to contain the homeless population or reduce their visibility through differentially monitoring the spaces where they hang out, enforcing anti-panhandling and other ordinances, and disrupting their daily routines. Private citizens and commercial establishments also often engage in exclusionary, NIMBY (not in my backyard) activities that prevent homeless populations, or facilities serving them, from entering and settling in prime and transitional spaces.

It has also been noted that more sympathetic responses to homelessness are not constant, but wax and wane over time. Research has shown that both media attention to homelessness and participation in volunteer efforts to aid homeless persons tend to surge around the holiday season, increasing around Thanksgiving and peaking at Christmas time. It has been noted as well that as mass homelessness has persisted in urban America, public concern about it as a pressing problem has faded due to "compassion fatigue." A slightly different take on this fading concern for homelessness is that it suffers a "liability of persistence." This argument holds that it is not necessarily that the public has tired of being sympathetic to the homeless, but that the duration of the problem has caused people to believe that homelessness is a fixed

aspect of contemporary urban society rather than a solvable problem. However, the emergence of recent local and national campaigns to "end homelessness" suggests that at least some citizens have not succumbed to compassion fatigue or the sense of hopelessness that often accompanies the persistence of a social problem.

Policy Efforts to Address Homelessness

Policy responses to persistent homelessness can generally be divided into at least four often coexisting categories. First, an "emergency" or "accommodation" response involves expanding shelters and food providers to lessen the hardship of homelessness but without doing much to help persons escape the streets. This approach was characteristic of the initial response to homelessness in the early 1980s. Out of this approach emerged a "restorative" response, which provides an extensive array of supportive services to remedy the individual shortcomings of persons who are homeless so they can compete, or at least function, in mainstream housed society. This is basically the approach of the Continuum of Care program, created by the U.S. Department of Housing and Urban Development under the Clinton administration, which encouraged localities to provide mental health and substance abuse treatment, employment counseling, case management, and household and parenting courses to guide persons through emergency and transitional shelters to permanent housing. A third type of response is "preventive" and aims to address the structural causes of homelessness by promoting the creation of affordable and subsidized housing, closing gaps in social service systems, and increasing the stock of living wage employment. This response is championed by advocacy groups and many researchers and is evident in the July 2003 Bring America Home Act (HR 2897). A final policy response consists of efforts to "criminalize" homelessness through ordinances that give police authority to cite both homeless persons for subsistence activities, such as panhandling and sleeping in public, and service providers who provide health care services and distribute meals in public parks. This NIMBY-like response is usually advocated by businesses, residents, and their political representatives in areas with sizable homeless populations.

To date, accommodative, restorative, and criminalizing responses have dominated, forming a two-pronged but contradictory approach in which a limited number of services are available to help persons subsist amid homelessness or exit their situation, and punitive efforts seek to discourage persons from living on the street, especially in prime spaces. However, recent campaigns to end homelessness have gained momentum. These efforts basically combine the preventative approach to "close the front door" into homelessness and the restorative approach to "open the back door" out of homelessness. While these plans to end homelessness incorporate both professional expertise regarding best social service practices and broader consciousness of structural causes, estimates of the cost to prevent future incidences of homelessness and move the currently homeless off the streets are far beyond what is presently devoted to the problem. Thus, the realization of the goal to end homelessness depends on the ability of partnership members to mobilize public concern about the problem and secure sufficient resources to implement all of the components of their ambitious plans.

Matthew D. Marr and David A. Snow

See also Cocaine and Crack; Deindustrialization; Deinstitutionalization; Globalization; Homelessness, Youth; Housing; Marginality; Poverty; Race; Welfare

Further Readings

Bunis, William K., Angela Yancik, and David A. Snow. 1996. "The Cultural Patterning of Sympathy toward the Homeless and Other Victims of Misfortune." *Social Problems* 43:301–17.

Burt, Martha. 1992. *Over the Edge: The Growth of Homelessness in the 1980s.* New York: Russell Sage.

Burt, Martha, Laudon Y. Aron, and Edgar Lee, with Jesse Valente. 2001. *Helping America's Homeless: Emergency Shelter or Affordable Housing?* Washington, DC: Urban Institute Press.

Koegel, Paul, M. Audrey Burnam, and Jim Baumohl. 1996. "The Causes of Homelessness." Pp. 24–33 in *Homelessness in America,* edited by J. Baumohl. Phoenix, AZ: ORYX.

Lee, Barrett A. and Townsend Price-Spratlen. 2004. "The Geography of Homelessness in American Communities: Concentration or Dispersion?" *City and Community* 3:3–27.

Link, Bruce G., Jo Phelan, Michaeline Bresnahan, Ann Stueve, Robert Moore, and Ezra Susser. 1995. "Lifetime and Five-Year Prevalence of Homelessness in the United States: New Evidence on an Old Debate." *American Journal of Orthopsychiatry* 64:247–354.

National Coalition for the Homeless. 2006. *A Dream Denied: Criminalization of Homelessness in U.S. Cities.* Washington, DC: National Coalition for the Homeless.

Shinn, Marybeth and Colleen Gillespie. 1994. "The Roles of Housing and Poverty in the Origins of Homelessness." *American Behavioral Scientist* 37:505–21.

Snow, David A. and Leon Anderson. 1993. *Down on Their Luck: A Study of Homeless Street People.* Berkeley, CA: University of California Press.

Snow, David A. and Michael Mulcahy. 2001. "Space, Politics, and the Survival Strategies of the Homeless." *American Behavioral Scientist* 45:149–69.

Wright, James D., Beth A. Rubin, and Joel A. Devine. 1998. *Beside the Golden Door: Policy, Politics, and the Homeless.* New York: Aldine de Gruyter.

HOMELESSNESS, YOUTH

Homeless youth are generally defined as persons unaccompanied by an adult caregiver for extended periods of time and generally under the age of 21. This term encompasses a variety of unaccompanied youth such as runaways and throwaways. The term *throwaway* refers to youth who are put out on the street as a result of abuse, neglect, or victimization by parents or primary caregivers. Homeless youth can also include system youth (individuals under the age of 18 who are currently in the care or custody of state agencies). Not all homeless youth are actively living on the street. For example, unaccompanied youth may be considered homeless if they currently do not have a permanent residence but are temporarily living with friends, acquaintances, or relatives. Most homeless youth have a combination of these characteristics and routinely find themselves in transitional living situations. Whereas some youth are chronically homeless, many experience episodic homelessness, meaning that their periods of actual homelessness consist of small durations of time spent on the street augmented by semipermanent living situations with family or friends or under the supervision of social service or state agencies.

The varied categories and classifications of homeless youth and the episodic and transient nature of this population make it difficult for researchers to estimate their actual numbers. Also, many homeless youth simply may not want to be found and avoid social service agencies for fear of being placed either back in the situation from which they have run away or in a similar or worse situation. As a result of these factors, estimates of the number of homeless youth vary. Estimates can also be influenced by the counting method. As a result, counts of homeless youth in the United States range from the hundreds of thousands to millions.

When comparing homeless youth with homeless adults, homeless youth tend to cite different reasons for leaving home, such as family problems, abuse, and victimization. Homeless youth populations also experience more instances of sexual and physical victimization and abuse while living on the street. This increased vulnerability on the street may be related to their relative inability to navigate life on the street. As a result, homeless youth construct and utilize informal social networks of peers for two reasons. First, peer group and network ties provide homeless youth with a sense of safety and security. Second, social networks help homeless youth minimize the stigma associated with their marginalized position. Newly homeless youth lack the experience of living on their own and lack knowledge of where to go and what to do while on the street. Many have had real or perceived negative experiences with primary caregivers and social service agencies and so choose to avoid social services. Their choice to form strong bonds with fellow homeless youth is a logical one. Such ties not only enable young homeless individuals to identify with one another but also minimize the impact of negative consequences associated with life on the street.

T. Patrick Stablein

See also Abuse, Child; Abuse, Child Sexual; Family, Dysfunctional; Foster Children, Aging Out; Homelessness; Missing Children; Runaways

Further Readings

Moore, Jan. *Unaccompanied and Homeless Youth: Review of Literature (1995–2005)*. Greensboro, NC: National Center for Homeless Education. Retrieved December 27, 2007 (http://srvlive.serve.org/nche/downloads/uy_lit_review.pdf).

Whitbeck, Les B. and Dan R. Hoyt. 1999. *Nowhere to Grow: Homeless and Runaway Adolescents and Their Families*. New York: Aldine de Gruyter.

HOMOPHOBIA

George Weinberg, in *Society and the Healthy Homosexual* of 1972, coined the term *homophobia* to refer to the psychological fear of homosexuals and homosexuality. That definition, however, is limited in its focus, as it neglects wider structural sources behind the taboo of same-sex sexual relationships and the negative attitudes and intolerance shown toward any gender or sexual nonconformity in society. Additionally, this concept should also include internal manifestations of self-hatred in GLBTIQ (gay, lesbian, bisexual, transgender, intersexed, or questioning) individuals because of the stigma associated with their sexuality or gendered orientation.

Newer terms, such as *heterosexual hegemony*, come across as better expressions to describe an ideological system that denies, denigrates, and stigmatizes any nonheterosexual form of behavior, identity, relationship, or community. At issue is sexual prejudice, the negative attitudes based on sexual orientation, whether the target is homosexual, bisexual, or heterosexual (e.g., "fag" discourse among boys). Unlike homophobia, it conveys no a priori assumptions about the origins, dynamics, and underlying motivations of anti-gay attitudes. Also, using the construct of sexual prejudice does not require value judgments that anti-gay attitudes are inherently irrational or evil.

Homophobia includes bias against family forms that do not conform to heteronormativity. One cited example of such bias was the threat by U.S. Secretary of Education Margaret Spellings to stop federal funding of a PBS kids' show, *Postcards From Buster*, because of a controversial episode. The airing of the 2005 "Sugartime!" episode (also called "Sugarland") was halted because it featured a lesbian couple and their family on a maple sugar tree farm in Vermont. The show is about a cartoon character, Buster, who encounters real-life diverse families, as representative of different regions, religions, and racial/ethnic groups across the United States. The bias in U.S. society against same-sex marriage is also a form of homophobia, particularly with the "defense of marriage" policy arguments that these types of families will lead to the destruction of society.

Other structural examples of homophobia exist in the "don't ask, don't tell" policies used by the military to ban homosexuality; widespread lack of legal protection from anti-gay discrimination and hostility toward individuals and their families in employment, adoption, custody, health care, housing, and other services; the differential treatment of homosexual and bisexual people with HIV or AIDS; and the existence of sodomy laws in more than one third of U.S. states. Extreme forms of homophobia can also be found in hate crimes and anti-gay violence, such as the murders of Matthew Shepard and Billy Ray Gaither because of their sexual orientation.

Complicating any charges or discussion of homophobia is the fact that some people believe homosexual behavior is a sin. Believing that is not necessarily homophobic, but it often gets charged as such when a minority person's reaction might be that of sensitivity toward a perceived prejudice. It is a difficult issue we face as a society, as some people are unwilling to approve of a lifestyle or orientation that they do not believe in or understand, but that does not make them homophobic. However, there is a difference between remaining true to one's moral values and attempting to impose one's values or judgments upon others.

Homosexuality was listed as a mental illness in the American Psychiatric Association's *Diagnostic and Statistical Manual of Mental Disorders* (*DSM*) until 1973. However, many still uphold sexual conversion therapy (aka sexual reorientation) as a cure for what is still perceived to be an identity disorder characterized by distress over one's sexual or gender orientation or from outside pressure from society or family to change. Research shows that homosexual and bisexual men and women are at a higher risk for mental health problems because of the stigma and stress that they face. Suicide rates among gay or questioning teens remain at relatively high levels in comparison with their peers.

Advocates insist that a real need exists to change the way in which society frames sexuality and gender orientations, as there is much misunderstanding over "nature versus nurture" in sexual orientation (e.g., Do gay parents affect their child's well-being?) as well as misconceptions about sexuality (e.g., Is there a link between homosexuality and child sexual abuse?). Some suggestions for eradicating sexual stigma and prejudice include education; getting to know gay, lesbian, bisexual, and transgendered people and their families (e.g., through the organization PFLAG [Parents, Family and Friends of Lesbians and Gays]) by listening to their coming-out stories and experiences; and developing an "allies" support network among heterosexuals for GLBTIQ communities.

Pamela McMullin-Messier

See also Hate Crimes; Homosexuality; Same-Sex Marriage; Sexuality; Sexual Orientation

Further Readings

Adam, Barry D. 1998. "Theorizing Homophobia." *Sexualities* 1(4):387–404.

"Assault on Gay America: The Life and Death of Billy Ray Gaither." 2000. *Frontline* Video Archives. Retrieved December 27, 2007 (http://www.pbs.org/wgbh/pages/frontline/shows/assault/).

Blumenfield, Warren J., ed. 1992. *Homophobia: How We All Pay the Price*. Boston: Beacon Press.

Fone, Byrne. 2000. *Homophobia: A History*. New York: Picador.

Herdt, Gilbert and Terry S. Stein, eds. 2004. "Homophobia and Sexual Prejudice." Special Issue of *Sexuality Research and Social Policy* 1(2).

Herek, Gregory M. "Beyond Homophobia" Blog. Retrieved December 27, 2007 (http://www.beyondhomophobia.com/blog/).

Sears, James T. and William L. Williams, eds. 1997. *Overcoming Heterosexism and Homophobia: Strategies That Work*. New York: Columbia University Press.

HOMOSEXUALITY

Homosexuality is a sexual orientation in which one experiences sexual attraction primarily toward members of one's own sex and is also sexual behavior with partners of the same sex. The prefix *homo-* is from the Greek word for "same." The general term *gay,* and the gender-specific terms *gay man* and *lesbian,* are commonly used to describe people who identify as homosexual. Homosexuality contrasts with heterosexuality, the sexual attraction to members of the other sex, and bisexuality, where there is sexual attraction to members of both sexes.

A variation on these categories derives from the work of Alfred Kinsey and colleagues in the late 1940s. Kinsey allowed people to describe their sexual interests on a 7-point scale from exclusively heterosexual to exclusively homosexual, with bisexual as the midpoint. It is also common to distinguish aspects of homosexual experience: sexual behavior, attraction, romantic interest, and social preference. Intimate same-sex interactions also inevitably create a challenge to gender-role expectations, whether by denying or confirming them, but with a clash between sex and gender role. Given the centrality of gender-role conflict, the acronym LGBT is often used to include lesbians, gay men, bisexuals, and transgendered people under a common banner.

One way in which different perspectives on homosexuality can be framed is in terms of the debate between essentialism and social constructionism. The essentialist position presents homosexuality as a relatively fixed orientation held by a proportion of the population, with continuity of experience across history and culture, and with some basis in biology or very early social development. The social constructionist view proposes that sexualities, like gender and other important social categories, are constructed as part of processes of social power that are heteronormative and that homosexuality as a sexual orientation is a modern construction. There are many variations on these two approaches, adopting more or less of the perspective from each side of the argument and reflecting the diverse ways in which members of the gay and lesbian community experience their own sexual identity, interests, and history.

This diversity of views also informs social conflicts and the operation of social forces, which create ongoing inequities and threaten the liberty, and even life, of many homosexual people. In many cultures, religion plays a central role in these conflicts. For example, many Christians see homosexuality as a direct challenge to aspects of social order based on scripture and tradition, and, indeed, some political movements arising from "queer theory" actively challenge the assumptions underlying that social order. Other members of the gay and lesbian community affirm shared beliefs about the ideal nature of relationships, seeking a point of connection with the dominant social order in order to participate in social institutions such as marriage. Within the Christian tradition itself, homosexuality has also been a source of internal conflict and schism. More broadly, the status and legitimacy of homosexuality has varied across time as well as across cultures. Homosexuality continues to be an important domain of social conflict and social change, with ongoing reverberations through many aspects of individual and social life.

Kenneth I. Mavor

See also Adoption, Gay and Lesbian; Bisexuality; Homophobia; Queer Theory; Same-Sex Marriage

Further Readings

Boswell, John. 1980. *Christianity, Social Tolerance and Homosexuality: Gay People in Western Europe from the Beginning of the Christian Era to the Fourteenth Century.* New ed. Chicago: University of Chicago Press.

Herek, Gregory M. 1998. *Stigma and Sexual Orientation: Understanding Prejudice against Lesbians, Gay Men and Bisexuals.* Thousand Oaks, CA: Sage.

HOSPICES

Hospice emerged in response to improvements in medicine and technology to address the needs of the dying more effectively than hospitals can. Caring for only the terminally ill, hospices can be independent, hospital-affiliated, nursing home based, in an extended care facility, or home health agency based.

The modern hospice movement began in Great Britain. Its origins trace back to the Middle Ages when clergy operated houses or shelters for strangers, soldiers, and pilgrims. In 1842 a group of Catholic women established a hospice in France for poor women who had terminal illnesses. This model inspired Dame Cicely Saunders to establish St. Christopher's Hospice in Sydenham, England, in 1967. In 1963 she had introduced the hospice concept to Yale medical students, leading Florence Wald, dean of the Yale University School of Nursing, to found the first U.S. hospice in New Haven, Connecticut, in 1974.

Hospice Care

Hospice gives the dying some control over their lives, pain, and medications, and it removes the isolation that often characterizes dying in hospitals. To enter hospice programs, the patient and family acknowledge the probability of the patient dying and that a cure is unlikely. Hospice can provide people dying at home with the care, comfort, and dignity that they need in their dying process.

Hospice care begins where traditional medicine ends, allowing the dying a dignified death with less pain and more ability to truly live until they die. Hospice may increase communications between patient, physician, and family to improve pain relief and symptom management. The challenge is to give the dying meaning, dignity, and life during a time of great fear and apprehension in the face of pain, distressing symptoms, dependency, extended suffering, loss of dignity, endless meaningless days, dying alone, and financial disaster.

Dame Saunders saw pain management as the first goal of hospice. If their pain is managed, patients can take care of unfinished business and attend to aspects of their lives and important relationships. Pain increases death anxiety and depression. Those without pain are better able to think and to resolve at least some of their fears.

Fear often keeps us from thinking clearly and discovering alternatives to our situation. Hospice thus pursues aggressive pain and symptom management and creates a comforting environment without rigidity in the caregiver's approach. Unlike hospitals, which typically offer aggressive life-prolonging treatments not always in keeping with the values and preferences of patients and their families, hospice need not try to prolong life or provide painful treatments that may cause additional suffering.

Hospice tries to make patients as comfortable as possible by allowing them to stay at home or, if this is not possible, to stay in a homelike setting where patients can have treasured possessions, family, and friends. Even if hospitals allowed pets and did not have visiting regulations, they would be unable to offer the care and dying with dignity that hospice can provide. The hospice team approach encourages adaptations to different cultural groups, honors traditions, and makes families an integral part of the process. Hospice encourages families to be as involved as they wish to the extent that they are able, and it works around the families' and patients' schedules.

Hospice tries to improve the physical and spiritual quality of life of the patient as a person rather than as a disease, including physical pain, relationships, communications, and dignity. Hospice staff volunteers work as much with the family as with the patient. They may have to teach family members how to change dressings, remove a catheter, administer medicine, use bedpans, use a hospital bed, or assist the dying person in other ways. Because relationships in families are unique, there is no set pattern as to what hospice teaches, who does which task, or how exactly to administer to the needs of the dying. Unlike hospitals, follow-up care for the families continues after the patient's death to aid the families in their grief.

Hospitals and Hospices

Hospital death is typically more impersonal than death under hospice care. Medical schools teach a professional persona that leads to distancing from patients. Medical students learn to use precise medical terms that often leave patients and families confused about diagnoses, treatment, symptoms, and even what the illness might actually be. It is not that physicians cannot care effectively for the dying and their families, but rather that the system is not designed to allow them to have the time and setting to offer the level of compassionate care that hospice can provide. Living until you die is a goal of hospice. Healing and delaying death is the goal of hospitals. Yet people most often die in hospitals.

Staying at home is typically less expensive than being cared for in a hospital. Often programs exist to enhance in-home care, by providing equipment, medicine, meals, and other needs at little or no cost to the dying or their families. Although nurses may be expensive, treatment is still cheaper at home than in hospitals. For most families, economics is not the issue but rather the ability of family members and the staff who assist them to provide quality care, pain management, and a good quality of life and still maintain their own lives, jobs, and quality of life. End-of-life care is demanding and includes limiting the length and numbers of visitors for the terminally ill person, managing neighborhood noise, helping the ill person negotiate stairs, bathing, changing catheters, dealing with emotional outbursts and the person's fear of the caregiver leaving to go shopping or do other required errands, and avoiding family disagreements. Consequently, despite the costs, some family members would prefer not to have the person die at home. Also, hospitals may make families more secure in their belief that they did everything possible for the dying person.

Most families want to care for their dying, but many are not physically, financially, spiritually, or emotionally able to aid the dying. While physicians first seemed to avoid hospice and perhaps saw it as a failure on their part, now most physicians seem to have embraced the approach. Hospice has even had an impact on hospitals, where death is not as impersonal and bureaucratic as it once was. The growth of medical ethics, advanced directives, palliative care, and bereavement services in hospitals is evidence of the impact of hospice, which stretches far beyond the dying.

Gerry Cox

See also Bereavement, Effect by Race; Medicaid; Medicare

Further Readings

Connor, Stephen R. 1998. *Hospice: Pitfalls, and Promise.* Bristol, PA: Taylor & Francis.

Saunders, Cicely M. and Robert Kastenbaum. 1997. *Hospice Care on the International Scene.* New York: Springer.

HOSTILE ENVIRONMENT

Hostile environment is a concept describing a workplace environment that has become intolerable to an employee, due to treatment based on that employee's race, ethnicity, sex, religion, or ability. The idea that some employees suffer discrimination in the form of a "hostile environment" developed in the context of struggles for workplace equality. These struggles led to legislation that protects employees from discrimination. Title VII of the Civil Rights Act of 1964 provides protection from discrimination to ensure equal employment opportunities. The Civil Rights Act provided for the establishment of the Equal Employment Opportunity Commission, which aimed to protect citizens from race and sex discrimination through prevention and response to complaints.

The existence of a hostile environment, then, is considered an aspect of employment discrimination because of its association with exclusionary practices that interfere with the normal functioning of employees complaining of abuse. Hostile environment may also describe a generally abusive workplace culture. The existence of a hostile environment often correlates with occupational segregation and the efforts of more privileged workers to keep women or racial minorities from entering the "neighborhood" of their job.

Scholars of occupational segregation by race and gender pinpoint barriers to workplace integration that include harassment by some employees to exclude others. However, harassment can also be less intentional, as behavior that is offensive to some group members is not necessarily understood as offensive by its perpetrator, such as publicly displaying nude "calendar girls" in a mixed-gender work environment.

Hostile environment most often relates to charges of sexual harassment. Related behaviors may be verbal or nonverbal, physical or nonphysical, but have in common their consequence: making the complaining employee uncomfortable. However, a hostile environment for women need not include sexual harassment. As with racial minorities, a broad spectrum of verbal and nonverbal behavior can constitute harassment in the workplace. The significant aspect of the hostile environment is that it be understood as a set of practices by some employees that block members of protected groups from equal opportunities in the workplace. Thus, the creation of a "hostile environment" links to other modes of segregation and exclusion that contribute to overall patterns of stratification.

One challenge to confronting hostile work environments lies in creating new workplace cultures where employers take responsibility for providing anti-harassment policies, employees familiarize themselves with forms of harassment, and victims of harassment feel comfortable using the established complaint process. When charges are levied, problems in enforcement of the law may occur. This is due both to the problem of interpreting the law and to fluctuations in the burden of proof that reflect the variability of society's commitment to race and gender justice. However, cases of harassment may also be difficult to resolve because of significant variations in judgment of how a "reasonable person" would interpret these social interactions.

Sharon Elise

See also Discrimination; Inequality; Racism; Segregation, Occupational; Sexism; Sexual Harassment

Further Readings

Andersen, Margaret. 2008. *Thinking about Women: Sociological Perspectives on Sex and Gender.* 8th ed. New York: Allyn & Bacon.

Greene, Jeanie Ahearn. 2006. *Blue-Collar Women at Work with Men: Negotiating the Hostile Environment.* Portsmouth, NY: Praeger.

U.S. Equal Opportunity Employment Commission. (http://www.eeoc.gov/).

HOUSING

Housing refers to buildings or other types of shelter construction in which people live. Types of housing have varied across time and geographic location. Housing also varies by structure, layout, building material, shape, and, to some extent, function, depending on location, culture, and socioeconomic status. A house provides semipermanent residence for one or more people, and many consider their house their home—meaning where they return every day, socialize, eat, and sleep. Housing is considered essential for physical and psychological survival in modernized societies. Modern structures generally include single-family homes (detached and sometimes on privately owned parcels of land); semidetached houses (attached to one or more houses, each including one or two housing units); multi-unit dwellings (structures with multiple separate self-contained units, sometimes referred to as tenements, apartments, flats, condominiums, or cooperatives); single-room occupancy units (a room in a multi-unit building that is rented by the week or month and does not include a bathroom or kitchen); and mobile homes (factory-built structures that are purchased and then transported to a specific location, quite often a trailer park that permits mobile homes). Housing units (regardless of type) can be owned by the resident(s) or rented (meaning someone else owns the unit and charges others a monthly fee to live there).

Housing can become the source of social problems for a number of reasons. First there are issues of affordability. If total housing costs exceed the income of those residing in the unit, then the unit is not affordable. In places where the demand for housing exceeds the supply, the cost of housing goes up. This is characteristically the case in large cities with a continual influx of people looking for employment (e.g., New York, London, and Tokyo, among others). In the United States, an accepted guideline for housing affordability is a housing cost that does not exceed 30 percent of a household's gross annual income. However, since the late 1970s, an increasing number of households have had to pay 50 percent or more of their income for housing. Rising costs can thus result in increased foreclosures and evictions, possibly causing homelessness.

People who become homeless are forced to reside in public shelters or other temporary accommodations. Because the number of beds does not meet the need and because length of stay in many public shelters is limited, homeless people are frequently forced to sleep outdoors or find alternative nonconventional lodging, including abandoned buildings, tunnels, tents, and cardboard boxes, all of which are generally unsafe. During the Great Depression of the 1930s, shantytowns known as "Hoovervilles" emerged in major cities across the United States. Families and individuals evicted from their homes would construct

makeshift, temporary housing structures with whatever they could find. Hoovervilles were normally located on vacant land right outside the city limits.

For others, rising housing costs result in "shelter poverty." This is the circumstance in which households are forced to use a substantial proportion of their income to cover housing costs, leaving little to cover other essential nonshelter needs. Rising housing costs can also result in doubling up, where families or unrelated individuals share a housing unit initially built for fewer occupants. This can lead to overcrowding. Extreme overcrowding has health and safety issues associated with it.

Related to affordability is substandard housing. Although the definition of substandard housing will vary across cultures, typically such housing is without what is deemed adequate in terms of shelter or utilities, such as running water, heat, and electricity. Substandard housing can also include structures located on environmentally contaminated land. Habitat for Humanity defines substandard housing as dwellings with structural deterioration of the roof, foundation, porch, exterior walls, windows, or doors, all of which render it unsafe and unfit for occupancy. Housing becomes substandard when property owners neglect upkeep, typically either to save money or to make a bigger profit from rents collected. Over time, as the property deteriorates further, the cost of repair becomes too high to make rehabilitation of the structure economically feasible.

Substandard housing conditions were commonplace in the United States during the 1800s and the first half of the 20th century when immigrants flocked to big cities like New York and Chicago and were forced to live in squalid structures known as tenements, often associated with serious health problems and epidemics of typhoid and other highly contagious diseases. These dwellings were also prone to fires and other safety dangers. Federal and state housing legislation enacted during the mid-20th century brought about stricter building code enforcement, resulting in improved housing conditions, particularly in urban areas. However, experts argue that substandard housing remains commonplace in the United States, despite the fact that the United States also has some of the best housing in the world.

Discrimination in housing markets can indirectly result in affordability and housing quality issues. Property owners, real estate agencies, and lenders may discriminate based on characteristics of those seeking housing, including characteristics of race, gender, nationality, sexual orientation, and disability. In the United States, one of the most pervasive publicly acknowledged forms of housing discrimination is that based on race. African Americans have been vulnerable to housing discrimination in urban areas since the late 1800s. Large influxes of African Americans from the rural South to the big northern cities led to widespread discrimination in housing, forcing migrants into specific geographic areas where they had to pay inflated rents for frequently substandard housing. This process resulted in widespread residential segregation where all-black or all-white neighborhoods became visible on urban and suburban landscapes and remain so today. The term *American apartheid* describes this phenomenon. Among the harmful consequences of segregation is the consignment of racial minorities to inferior dwellings and neighborhoods where the public schools may not be adequately funded and where property values depreciate rapidly. Although housing discrimination was officially made illegal with the Fair Housing Act of 1968 and reinforced with the Fair Housing Amendment Act of 1988, it is still pervasive and particularly focused on racial minorities.

Displacement is another housing-related problem. Displacement in the United States became an issue during the 1950s and 1960s with federally sponsored urban renewal programs. Urban renewal programs authorized slum clearance to make way for freeways and new commercial development, displacing the inhabitants, who were typically poor racial minorities. Displacement can also occur through the process of gentrification. Gentrification occurs when developers or individuals with financial means buy up housing in poor inner-city areas and renovate, eventually increasing the property values of the area and driving up the property taxes and monthly rents. This leads to the displacement of lower-income property owners and tenants who cannot afford the rising prices. This also occurs when properties, including single-room occupancy housing, are converted to condominiums.

Natural disasters cause another form of displacement. Earthquakes, floods, hurricanes, landslides, or fires can result in the destruction of homes, sometimes leaving entire communities without shelter. Mobile home communities or those with deteriorating buildings are particularly vulnerable to the effects of natural disasters. Geographic locations, such as low-lying areas near large bodies of water, are particularly vulnerable. For example, Hurricane Katrina left the entire Ninth Ward of New Orleans without shelter, an area that housed many of the city's poor. Although temporary shelter is generally provided to victims of natural disasters, the pathway back to permanent housing can be a long and difficult one, particularly for people with lower incomes.

Policy solutions to housing problems have been varied. Subsidized housing, in which the government pays a portion of total housing costs, is the most common policy solution. In the United States subsidized housing has taken the form of public housing, which is run by government-funded local housing authorities, and Section 8, where private landlords are given a monthly subsidy to provide reduced rents to qualified tenants. These policies have had mixed results. Location of public housing has resulted in increased residential segregation for racial minorities. In addition, since the early 1980s, public housing has been underfunded, resulting in lack of building maintenance and ultimately substandard housing. During the late 1990s, many cities began to tear down public housing, displacing those public housing residents who were unsuccessful at obtaining Section 8 subsidies or other housing.

Although Section 8 relies on the private market for housing, there is never enough Section 8 housing vis-à-vis the needs. In Chicago, for example, the waiting list for Section 8 housing has contained more than 40,000 people. In addition, not all landlords accept Section 8 vouchers, often therefore confining participants to the poorer urban areas. Nonenforced building code violations are also commonplace with Section 8 housing, rendering some of these units substandard.

Deirdre Oakley

See also Discrimination; Gentrification; Homelessness; Poverty; Segregation, Residential

Further Readings

Bratt, Rachel, Michael Stone, and Chester Hartman, eds. 2006. *A Right to Housing: Foundation for a New Social Agenda.* Philadelphia: Temple University Press.

Friedricks, Jürgen, George Galster, and Sako Musterd, eds. 2005. *Life in Poverty Neighbourhoods: European and American Perspectives.* New York: Routledge.

Massey, Douglas and Nancy Denton. 1993. *American Apartheid: Segregation and the Making of the Underclass.* Cambridge, MA: Harvard University Press.

Miller, Henry. 1991. *On the Fringe: The Dispossessed in America.* Lexington, MA: Lexington Books.

Stone, Michael E. 1993. *Shelter Poverty: New Ideas on Housing Affordability.* Philadelphia: Temple University Press.

U.S. Department of Housing and Urban Development. 1994. "Priority Home! The Federal Plan to Break the Cycle of Homelessness." Washington, DC: U.S. Department of Housing and Urban Development.

van Vliet, Willem, ed. 1998. *The Encyclopedia of Housing.* Thousand Oaks, CA: Sage.

HUMAN RIGHTS

The concept of human rights is not a modern phenomenon. Through codes, decrees, or laws, rulers of empires in ancient India, Mesopotamia, and Persia, for example, established certain rights and privileges for their citizens. Also, some of the oldest written sources on rights and responsibilities are in the documents of many of the world's major religions.

The modern notion of human rights gained strength during the 18th-century Age of Enlightenment, as confidence in human reason increased. European philosophers, most notably John Locke, developed the concept of "natural rights" in the 17th and 18th centuries. Locke believed that people, as creatures of God, possessed certain rights by virtue of their humanity, regardless of race, culture, religion, or ethnicity. Natural rights further played a key role in the 18th- and 19th-century struggles against political absolutism and the divine right of kings, which restricted the principles of freedom and equality. The notion of natural rights, therefore, was important in the eventual development of human rights.

The term *human rights* is a relatively new one, gaining acceptance with the founding of the United Nations in 1945. This term replaced *natural rights*, partially because of the latter's frequent association with religious orthodoxy and growing disenchantment with the term by philosophical and political liberals. Natural rights entailed a select few rights—such as Locke's abstract notions of the rights to "life, liberty, and property"—which found similar expression in the U.S. Declaration of Independence. In comparison, the concept of human rights is much more diverse and specific. Adopted, in part, as a reaction to the atrocities committed by the Nazis during World War II, the UN Universal Declaration of Human Rights of 1948 established what most nations would accept as the list of modern-day human rights.

Consisting of 30 articles, the UN Declaration of Human Rights lists the rights and fundamental freedoms to which all men and women, everywhere in the world, are entitled, "without any discrimination." These specific rights fall into one of six sections: *Security Rights* protect against crimes (such as murder, torture, and rape); *Due Process Rights* protect against abuses of the legal system (imprisonment without trial, secret trials, and excessive punishments); *Liberty Rights* protect freedoms (such as belief, expression, association, assembly, and movement); *Political Rights* protect the liberty to participate in politics by communicating, assembling, protesting, voting, and serving in office; *Equality Rights* guarantee equal citizenship (i.e., equality before the law); and *Social/Welfare Rights* are nondiscriminatory rights for all (such as education for all children and protection against starvation).

Additionally, human rights fall into two main subsections: negative and positive. Negative rights are primary or "first-generation rights" and generally encompass the idea that one is entitled *not* to be abused by another person or state. Such rights are embedded in the U.S. Bill of Rights, the English Bill of Rights, and the Canadian Charter of Rights. A common example is the notion that states should refrain from denying due process of law or equality to their citizens. A positive right (or "second-generation right"), however, is one that states or individuals are obligated to follow. Such positive rights include education, health care, and a minimum standard of living. To compare the two types of rights, consider the example of the right to life: A "negative right" to life would require a state or individual to refrain from killing or critically injuring someone; a "positive right" to life would require the state or individuals to act to save the life of someone who would otherwise die.

However, one must question the practicality and legitimation of some positive rights. For example, when a positive right of citizens to be provided with an adequate diet is not fundable or feasible, is the state committing a human rights violation? Should the state therefore take any surplus from selected individuals to provide for those who are starving? And if so, would that action not itself be a human rights violation against those whose property is taken? One might argue, therefore, that positive human rights have the tendency to be moralistic and for the collective good of societies.

At the national level, enacted laws and their enforcement, supported through judicial decisions, protect citizens' human rights. On a global level, international law, supported through treaties, creates human rights norms and protection. However, even if a country adopts certain human rights laws, that does not ensure it will always follow those laws. And if a government were to break an international human rights law, what would be the consequence? Whose duty is it to intervene and enforce the rights upon that society?

Although human rights developed, in part, as a reaction to mistreatments of citizens by their state, obvious conflicts would arise if another state or international entity were to impose its own beliefs (cultural imperialism) on the perceived "rogue state." One state cannot simply ignore state sovereignty and invade or attack another because of alleged or real human rights violations; this action would, itself, potentially be a human rights violation. Therefore, although international human rights organizations (such as Amnesty International, Human Rights Watch, and Freedom House) document and report perceived human rights violations, no entity has the power to stop those violations. Short of warfare, the most common tactics employed by modern nation-states are economic sanctions, political pressure, and social ostracism.

A major criticism of human rights comes from its presumed moral foundation. Because cultural beliefs and morals vary among societies, the idea of human rights' universalism becomes arguable. Although certain individuals or societies as a whole may embrace certain absolute moral or ethical practices, one must question what would occur if two such individuals or societies, with different beliefs and morals, clashed. The attempt to impose one's beliefs on another has led to immeasurable violence and warfare throughout history. The most recent example is what Samuel Huntington calls a "clash of civilizations" between the West and the rest of the world, particularly Islam. Although Western religions and Islam essentially share the same roots and have a vast majority of shared beliefs and practices, the root of conflicts between these two entities appears to stem more from the cultural differences between, and practices of, traditional Western and Islamic states. Therefore, although a great consensus may exist among societies as to what constitutes a universal human right, trying to impose those beliefs on societies with different views may have negative and such potentially dire consequences as social unrest, anarchy, or warfare.

Jennifer M. Koleser

See also Inequality; Islam and Modernity; Justice; Life Chances; Religion and Conflict; State Crimes; War Crimes

Further Readings

Donnelly, Jack. 2005. *Universal Human Rights.* 3rd ed. Mumbai, India: Manas.

Human Rights Watch. 2007. *Human Rights Watch World Report 2007.* Rev. ed. New York: Seven Stories Press.

Ishay, Michael. 2004. *The History of Human Rights: From Ancient Times to the Globalization Era.* Berkeley, CA: University of California Press.

Lauren, Paul Gordon. 2003. *The Evolution of International Human Rights: Visions Seen.* 2nd ed. Philadelphia: University of Pennsylvania Press.

Steiner, Henry and Philip Alston. 2007. *International Human Rights in Context: Law, Politics, Morals.* 3rd ed. New York: Oxford University Press.

HUMAN TRAFFICKING

Human trafficking is a widespread global human rights problem and refers to the recruiting, transporting, harboring, or receipt of human beings by use of force, coercion, or fraud. Trafficked persons are subjected to labor exploitation, sexual exploitation, or both. Exploitation may include forced labor, debt bondage, slavery, abuse within the commercial sex industry, private parties who demand work and sex, and removal of organs. For children, trafficking may also include trafficking for early marriage, illegal adoption, child prostitution, recruitment as child soldiers, or recruitment for religious cults.

This modern-day slavery is most prevalent in agriculture, mining, and forced prostitution, but it also exists in industries such as construction, domestic servitude, food services, and manufacturing. There are various routes to human trafficking, but the common theme is that the trafficker uses force or coercion to control the trafficked person. Some people are captured and exploited; others are forced to work without pay to erase an illegal "debt." Some voluntarily migrate in search of better economic or political situations but subsequently find themselves in oppressive situations once they get to the destination country. Women and young girls are often tricked into migrating by traffickers who promise a better life through marriage, employment, or educational opportunities. As a means of control, traffickers sometimes keep them locked up away from the public or their families, take away passports or other necessary documents, and use violence or threats of deportation.

The International Labor Organization estimates that more than 12 million people worldwide are in forced labor, debt bondage, forced child labor, or sexual servitude. Depending on the methodology and definition used, other estimates of trafficked persons are as high as 27 million. The U.S. government estimates that the number of people trafficked annually across international borders is approximately 800,000, with millions more trafficked within their own country's borders. Women and children are particularly vulnerable and comprise the majority of trafficked persons. The UN Office on Drugs and Crime reports that human trafficking occurs in at least 127 countries and trafficked persons are exploited in 137 countries.

Supply and Demand

Human trafficking is one of the fastest-growing and most profitable illicit industries, second only to drug trafficking. Global profits from human trafficking are estimated at $44.3 billion per year. Globalization has allowed for greater movement across borders of people, money, goods, and services. The proliferation of human trafficking is due to several interconnected factors on both the supply side and the demand side.

On the supply side, the increase in the world population, rapid social and economic change in countries around the world, and government policies or inaction have all played a role in the conditions that allow human trafficking to prosper. Struggling economies of developing countries and enormous political changes have created economic circumstances that have perpetuated extreme poverty and desperate situations, leaving many people with no choice but to accept work under oppressive conditions. In particular, postcommunist societies have experienced much economic and political instability, and the weakening of law enforcement has allowed organized crime to proliferate and engage in widespread global human trafficking. Other factors such as war, civil unrest, and natural disasters may lead to

population displacement and an increase in orphans and street children who are easy prey for traffickers. Further, lack of opportunities for education and lack of a living wage increase the number of individuals competing for low-skilled jobs.

At the same time, developed countries are experiencing a decrease in birth rates. Countries such as Japan and the nations of western Europe are not able to replenish their labor force, leaving them with unskilled labor shortages. Nonetheless, restrictive immigration policies contribute to the reduction in the flow of labor to countries to fill this gap. As a result, the demand remains high in developed countries for low-skilled labor, and migrants who are desperate for jobs turn to smugglers to get them to these countries. As the risks and costs to smuggle people into developed countries increase, some smugglers become traffickers who sell the migrants or hold them in debt bondage or forced labor to recover the high costs of smuggling.

The situation for women and girls is particularly dire. They are especially vulnerable because the demand remains high for women and girls to work in the commercial sex industry, in sweatshops, and in domestic servitude. The continued subjugation of women economically, socially, and politically in many countries feeds this demand and accounts for some of the increase in human trafficking. For example, some families continue to see girls as a burden and may sell their female children or relatives to brothels or traffickers to support their sons or feed their families. Other families may sell their children believing that this will be the best opportunity for them to escape poverty. Research has shown that most trafficked women are under the age of 25, but traffickers are recruiting younger and younger girls in response to the fear of HIV/AIDS infection among customers. The majority of internationally trafficked women and girls come from Asia. Other source regions include the former Soviet Union and southeastern Europe, Latin America, the Caribbean, and Africa. Trafficked women and girls are often sent to North America, Asia, Western Europe, and the Middle East.

International and Domestic Laws and Policies

The international community has used various mechanisms to address trafficking. In particular, the UN Convention on the Rights of the Child requires countries to take steps to prevent the abduction, sale, or trafficking of children and to protect children from all forms of sexual exploitation. The United States still has not ratified this convention, although it has ratified the convention's Optional Protocol on the Sale of Children, Child Prostitution and Child Pornography and the Optional Protocol on Children in Armed Conflict. To protect women, the Convention on the Elimination of All Forms of Discrimination against Women requires countries to curb all forms of trafficking in women, prevent exploitative prostitution, and ensure healthy and safe working conditions. Although the United States has signed this convention, it is one of the few countries that has not ratified it. The Protocol to Prevent, Suppress and Punish Trafficking in Persons, Especially Women and Children, was adopted by the Convention against Transnational Organized Crime in 2000. The United States ratified the trafficking protocol in December 2005. Various international organizations have programs in place to combat human trafficking worldwide.

In the United States, the Trafficking Victims Protection Act (TVPA) was passed in 2000 and reauthorized in 2003 and 2005. This legislation addresses human trafficking in the United States through prevention, prosecution, and protection. Since the enactment of this policy, however, it has actually helped very few trafficked persons in the United States. One criticism of the TVPA is that it focuses on a law enforcement approach rather than the needs of the trafficked person. Many of the provisions in the TVPA seek to protect the witness primarily so that law enforcement can successfully prosecute the case. Some trafficked persons who cannot provide evidence or refuse to cooperate out of fear are deported rather than helped. Further, this law requires that the trafficked person cooperate with law enforcement immediately and provide detailed accounts of the trafficking. Trafficked persons may be distrustful of law enforcement or traumatized, particularly when first released from trafficking. If law enforcement cannot determine that the person has been trafficked, the person is then deported. Although the TVPA sought to end deportation of trafficked persons, this practice continues to be common.

Despite estimates of up to 17,500 persons trafficked into the United States every year, since 2000 only 675 have been counted as such. This low number accounts only for the number of people who met the definition of a trafficked person within the TVPA and received a T visa, which is a temporary visa granted upon cooperation with law enforcement. Excluded from this count are those who do not report to or assist law enforcement, those who do not require immigration relief, those who are U.S. citizens, those who cannot meet the requirements for a T visa, and those denied a T visa because law enforcement refused to offer support for the application. Although prosecution of traffickers is a worthy goal, the needs of trafficked persons should also be addressed in a way that helps restore their humanity and reintegrates them into society.

A more balanced global approach is needed to address the imbalance of wealth and poverty and labor supply and demand. In particular, social scientists believe that governments in the developed world of destination countries such as the United States need to take a more proactive approach to address the confluence of unstable global economies, lack of labor laws protecting low-skilled workers' rights, lack of availability of living wages, and restrictive immigration policies.

Emily S. Ihara

See also Globalization; Immigration; Labor, Child; Labor, Migrant; Migration, Global; Poverty; Poverty, Children Worldwide; Prostitution; Prostitution, Child; Refugees; Sex Trafficking; Slavery

Further Readings

Bales, Kevin. 2005. *Understanding Global Slavery: A Reader.* Berkeley, CA: University of California Press.

Naim, Moisés. 2005. *Illicit: How Smugglers, Traffickers and Copycats Are Hijacking the Global Economy.* New York: Doubleday.

UN Office on Drugs and Crime. 2006. "Trafficking in Persons: Global Patterns." Vienna, Austria: UN Office on Drugs and Crime. Retrieved September 7, 2007 (http://www.unodc.org/pdf/traffickinginpersons_report_2006ver2.pdf).

U.S. Department of State. 2007. "Trafficking in Persons Report." Washington, DC: United States Department of State. Retrieved December 27, 2007 (http://www.state.gov/documents/organization/82902.pdf).

HYPERSEGREGATION

When a group is so segregated that its members have little chance of contact with outsiders, that group is hypersegregated. In the case of residential location, hypersegregation means that the members of different groups are extremely unlikely to live together. U.S. experts primarily pay attention to the spatial distances between whites and blacks, with increasing attention also paid to the residential patterns of growing Asian and Latino/a populations (some studies have also examined the segregation of Native Americans). Of key concern has been the fact that many whites do not live in neighborhoods with members of other groups, a form of urban segregation documented also in other countries, including Canada, England, France, and Germany.

Identifying Hypersegregation

In an often-cited 1988 study, Douglas Massey and Nancy Denton compiled 20 existing segregation measures and identified five dimensions of residential segregation: evenness, exposure, concentration, centralization, and clustering. *Evenness* refers to the distribution of groups across neighborhoods according to their proportion of the population. Thus, if 10 percent of the population of a given city is Asian, then 10 percent of each neighborhood should be Asian for there to be no segregation. *Exposure* refers to the probability that members of a group will have any form of interaction with other groups. *Concentration* refers to how much space a minority group occupies; if a minority group lives primarily in a few neighborhoods, they are very concentrated. *Centralization* refers to how close to the center of an urban area a group lives. In many U.S. metropolitan areas, living in the suburbs (as opposed to the central city) is associated with a higher standard of living and better access to high-quality schools and amenities. *Clustering* refers to the extent to which a group lives in contiguous or adjoining neighborhoods.

Researchers typically use census data to measure segregation, mainly because such measures require geographically detailed population counts (such as in neighborhoods) that are collected in decennial censuses. More specifically, segregation measures usually take into account the distribution of various groups in particular neighborhoods in a metropolitan area relative to their numbers in the total metropolitan population. Neighborhoods are most often defined in terms of "census tracts," which contain 1,500 to 8,000 people, though sometimes in smaller geographic units, such as blocks or block groups. The statistical indexes developed to measure each of these dimensions typically range from 0 to 1, with 0 indicating complete integration on a particular dimension and 1 indicating complete apartheid or segregation on a particular dimension. Massey and Denton (1989) defined

hypersegregated metropolitan areas as those where indexes exceed .60 on at least four of the five dimensions of segregation.

To date, hypersegregation appears to be a phenomenon that applies almost exclusively to blacks who reside in certain U.S. metropolitan areas. Although blacks are also segregated from whites in other countries, the levels are not as high as they are in many U.S. metropolitan areas. Table 1 provides a list of U.S. metropolitan areas where blacks are hypersegregated from whites, by year. In 2000, Chicago, Cleveland, Detroit, Milwaukee, Newark, and Philadelphia had segregation scores above .60 on all five dimensions of segregation. Also worth noting are the metropolitan areas where African Americans were persistently hypersegregated for several decades: Baltimore, Buffalo, Chicago, Cleveland, Detroit, Gary, Los Angeles, New York, and St. Louis. Two metropolitan areas in 2000 also had Hispanic-white hypersegregation (Los Angeles and New York).

Causes and Effects of Hypersegregation

The hypersegregation of African Americans in so many U.S. metropolitan areas is largely the result of racism and discrimination by whites (though other groups may also engage in similar practices). In addition to their reticence to move into neighborhoods where blacks reside, whites also move out of neighborhoods when they believe too many blacks are moving in. Other practices that have historically served to segregate and thus hypersegregate blacks include discriminatory mortgage lending practices (e.g., some banks will not provide mortgages to black customers with the same income as white customers), neighborhood redlining (mortgages cannot be obtained for certain neighborhoods—usually those deemed "black"), telling potential renters who are black that apartments in white neighborhoods have been taken, and violently attacking and threatening blacks who attempt to move into white neighborhoods. Although racial and ethnic discrimination in the housing market was outlawed with the passage of the Fair Housing Act in 1968, research has documented the persistence, even if at somewhat diminished levels, of discrimination against minorities in the United States.

Larger metropolitan areas, those where blacks make up a large percentage of the population, as well as those in the Midwest, are more likely to be hypersegregated.

Table 1   Metropolitan Areas With Hypersegregation of African Americans, 1980–2000

1980	1990	2000
	Albany, GA	Albany, GA
Atlanta		Atlanta
Baltimore	Baltimore	Baltimore
	Baton Rouge	Baton Rouge
	Beaumont–Port Arthur	Beaumont–Port Arthur
	Benton Harbor	
	Birmingham	Birmingham
Buffalo	Buffalo	Buffalo
Chicago	Chicago	Chicago
	Cincinnati	
Cleveland	Cleveland	Cleveland
Dallas–Fort Worth		
		Dayton–Springfield, OH
Detroit	Detroit	Detroit
	Flint	Flint
Gary	Gary	Gary
Indianapolis	Indianapolis	
Kansas City	Kansas City	
Los Angeles	Los Angeles–Long Beach	Los Angeles–Long Beach*
	Miami	
Milwaukee	Milwaukee	Milwaukee
		Mobile
	Monroe, LA	Monroe, LA
	New Orleans	
New York	New York	New York*
Newark	Newark	Newark
	Oakland	
Philadelphia	Philadelphia	Philadelphia
	Saginaw	Saginaw–Bay City
	Savannah	
St. Louis	St. Louis	St. Louis
	Trenton	
	Washington, DC	Washington, DC

*Also had Hispanic–white hypersegregation in 2000.

To date, the known metropolitan characteristics associated with lower levels of black hypersegregation are the proportion of new housing in a metropolitan area and the proportion of the workforce employed by the military. Why might these two metropolitan characteristics reduce hypersegregation? Some older neighborhoods have a predominantly black population. Others are predominantly white and have a reputation of being unwelcoming or hostile to blacks. Newer neighborhoods do not have this type of preexisting reputation and hence attract a more mixed group of potential residents, which leads to lower levels of segregation. The presence of a large military population also lowers segregation because the military often selects housing for its members, and race plays little role in where people are assigned to live.

In 2000, the combined African American population of the metropolitan areas listed in Table 1 was 13.3 million. This amounts to approximately 38.5 percent of the total black population in all of the United States. Thus hypersegregation clearly affects a very large proportion of the African American population in the United States. Hypersegregation increases the isolation of African Americans from other members of society. It concentrates African Americans in neighborhoods that often have a host of issues associated with poverty, including exposure to crime, poorer access to health care, inadequate access to public transit, poor policing, dilapidated and substandard housing, and poor schools with few resources.

Rima Wilkes and John Iceland

See also Housing; Segregation, Residential

Further Readings

Denton, Nancy. 1994. "Are African-Americans Still Hypersegregated in 1990?" Pp. 49–81 in *Residential Apartheid: The American Legacy,* edited by R. Bullard, C. Lee, and J. E. Grigsby III. Los Angeles: UCLA Center for Afro-American Studies.

Massey, Douglas S. and Nancy A. Denton. 1988. "The Dimensions of Residential Segregation." *Social Forces* 67:281–315.

———. 1989. "Hypersegregation in US Metropolitan Areas: Black and Hispanic Segregation along Five Dimensions." *Demography* 26:373–92.

Wilkes, Rima and John Iceland. 2004. "Hypersegregation in the Twenty-first Century." *Demography* 41:23–36.

I

IDENTITY POLITICS

Identity politics refers to political activism of various social movements including, but not limited to, the civil rights movement, feminist movements, gay and lesbian movements, ethnic separatist movements for political recognition, self-determination, and elimination of discrimination. The term suggests that people who have suffered from actual or perceived social injustice can share a collective consciousness that stimulates them to take further action to advance their particular group's interests. In the social sciences, *identity politics* refers to any social mobilization related to politics, identity, and culture. Depending on the school of thought, the term sometimes means cultural activism, other times political activism, and sometimes both. In any case, however, identity politics focuses on the contrast between the assumed social, political, and occupational privileges of the dominant group as compared with perceived discrimination against the oppressed group.

Historical Synopsis

During the 1960s, unprecedented large-scale political movements—such as second wave feminism, civil rights movements, gay and lesbian liberation activism, and the American Indian movements—launched their attack on the systemic injustices and inequalities that alienated them. These social movements developed a rich literature of questions about the nature, origin, and future of the particular identities traditionally left out of studies. Identity politics as a base for collective behavior was closely connected to the idea that some social groups were historically oppressed because of their particular identities; for example, one's identity as a woman or as a Native American made him or her vulnerable to cultural imperialism (including stereotyping, stigmatizing, erasure, or labeling), violence, exploitation, marginalization, or powerlessness.

Defenders of identity politics called for new analyses of oppression and gave voice to those long silenced as they sought to reconstruct, redescribe, and transform the dominant discourse that stigmatized particular minority group(s). Intersections of race, gender, class, sexual orientation, and ethnicity were the bases of new identities that began to draw the attention of social scientists. Although the description of identity politics goes back to intellectual writings of famous critics such as Mary Wollstonecraft and Frantz Fanon, sociologist Renee R. Anspach first employed the term in 1979. For the past several decades, however, the phenomenon of identity politics attracted numerous scholars. This focus on cultural identities marked a significant shift from the economically and politically based analyses that had long dominated the social sciences. Identity-based movements became the "new social movements" in sociology literature and drew the interest of both U.S. and European scholars. Works of Alain Touraine and Alberto Melucci, for example, hypothesized that the new social movements were "identity oriented" rather than "strategy oriented," and these "expressive" movements were partially a product of the information age and postindustrial era of the Western, developed societies.

Critics of Identity Politics

Identity politics as a base for organized behavior and a set of political philosophical positions draws criticism from various divergent schools of thought, including liberalism, Marxism, and post-structuralism. Criticism of identity politics dates back to the 1970s when scholars began systematically outlining and defending the philosophical underpinnings of identity politics.

Obscurity of the Term

Critics argue that use of the phrase *identity politics* as popular rhetoric belies more possible analytical explanatory power of the term. Because the term is primarily descriptive rather than explanatory, rigorous empirical analyses of identity politics are absent in the field. Using or misusing *identity politics* as a blank term invokes a range of tacit political implications, making identity claims by some early political activists seem lacking in analytical content, misleadingly totalizing, and un-nuanced. As the notion of identity has become indispensable in contemporary political discourse, even as the public rhetoric of identity politics empowered the new social movement activism, it failed to produce coherent theoretical analyses on political inclusiveness and models of the self. In this regard, identity politics increasingly became a derogatory synonym for anti-racism, feminism, and anti-heterosexism.

Critics From the Right

Critics from the political right claim that it is inappropriate for an identity-based group to expect an enumeration of unprecedented rights. Particularly for Enlightenment liberal democratic theory, if a "right" extends to only a portion of society, it is no longer a right but a "privilege." Thus, from the point of view of the political right, identity politics does not contend for "rights" as certain minority groups claim; instead, it functions as rhetoric to strengthen the discourses of some interest groups that demand special privileges.

Critics From the Left

Marxists, both orthodox and revisionist, often interpret the perceived ascendancy of identity politics as representing the end of radical materialist critique. For these critics, identity politics is factionalizing and depoliticizing, drawing attention away from the ravages of late capitalism toward superstructural cultural accommodations that hinder the reality of unchanged economic structures. A parallel criticism of identity politics comes from the radical leftists, who argue that identity politics unnecessarily divides the working class, who are the agents of the revolution against capitalism. As a result, identities are pitted against identities, creating an ideal condition for the ruling class.

"Queer" Dissent

Some lesbian, gay, bisexual, and transgender (LGBT) activists criticize the identity politics approach on the basis of the argument that identity politics has marginalized LGBT people rather than emancipating them. Although LGBT activists employed an "identity politics" approach to gain mainstream culture's full recognition of sexual orientation freedom, their strategy essentially declared themselves as outside of the mainstream. These activists contend that identity politics is a counterproductive strategy, perpetuating discrimination and societal prejudices against LGBT people.

Post-Structuralist Challenge

Post-structuralist criticism of identity politics is perhaps the most philosophically developed and profound challenge to date. Post-structuralists claim that identity politics fallaciously regards actors as metaphysics of substance; that is, cohesive, self-identical subjects that can be identified and reclaimed from oppression. This essentialist position, they suggest, misrepresents both the psychology of identity and its political significance.

The alternative view offered by post-structuralists is that the subject is constantly reconstructed and redefined as a product of discourse. The post-structuralist view of agency reiterates the mutual construction of the opposites, as self versus other and identity versus difference. The danger of identity politics, then, is that it reifies "self" as a category of analysis, which is, rather, a category of practice, fluid, and always subject to interpretation.

Future Directions

Research on identity politics raises significant questions on individual experiences, cultural mobilization, and sociopolitical movements. Scholars of collective action have recently paid more attention to the complex nature of relationships between actors' perceptions, preferences, and strategies and their identities. Analysts of identity politics, as Mary Bernstein suggests, should be careful when they assume that social movement actors' *strategic* deployment of their identities shows the revelation of the identity in essentialist ways. The depiction and reconstruction of essentialist identities might not indicate that the actors are naive to realize that these identities are socially constructed; rather, it can reveal the dynamic of relationship between identities and strategies. In this regard, post-structuralist criticism of identity politics is in need of reassessment. In any case, the debate over identity politics invites scholars of all sorts to investigate how local discourses are produced, perceived, and consequently realized in the actors' lifeworlds, which only in-depth case studies can explore.

Mustafa E. Gurbuz

See also Cultural Imperialism; Ethnocentrism; Feminism; Multiculturalism; Oppositional Culture Theory; Pluralism; Social Movements; Subcultures

Further Readings

Bernstein, Mary. 2005. "Identity Politics." *Annual Review of Sociology* 31:47–74.

Butler, Judith. [1990] 1999. *Gender Trouble: Feminism and the Subversion of Identity.* New York: Routledge.

Calhoun, Craig, ed. 1994. *Social Theory and Politics of Identity.* Cambridge, MA: Blackwell.

Larana, Enrique, Hank Johnston, and Joseph R. Gusfield, eds. 1994. *New Social Movements: From Ideology to Identity.* Philadelphia: Temple University Press.

Monroe, Kristen R., James Hankin, and Renée B. Van Vechten. 2000. "The Psychological Foundations of Identity Politics." *Annual Review of Political Science* 3:419–47.

Ryan, Barbara, ed. 2001. *Identity Politics in the Women's Movement.* New York: New York University Press.

Schlesinger, Arthur M. Jr. 1998. *The Disuniting of America.* New York: Norton.

IDENTITY THEFT

Although identity theft is often heralded as a new crime threat, the phenomenon itself is by no means unique to the information age. Throughout history, criminals have used false identities to commit their crimes. However, as identity theft emerges as a growing crime problem in the 21st century, it has new characteristics which are closely linked with the features of a global and technologically advanced society. The Internet, e-mail, and mobile phone technology have transformed the ways in which we live our everyday lives and, in many ways, have facilitated the criminal enterprise. With all of these changes come new risks and, with them, new challenges. Increasingly, we are required to prove our identities as we interact with others in both real and virtual environments, and the identification process is more important now than it has ever been. Consequently, different aspects of an individual's identity have themselves become attractive commodities in the criminal world. The emergence of identity theft as a recognized social problem shows how the changing value of personal data in modern society has had an impact on the nature of crime.

Definitions of Identity Theft

There is no single accepted definition of identity theft, and it is common to find broad definitions presented in the media and policy documents. Broadly defined, identity theft occurs when a criminal uses another person's personal information (such as name, address, social security number, or credit card details) without permission to commit fraud or other crimes. It is often, therefore, referred to as an "enabling offense"—the identifying information is a tool that the criminal needs to commit the "target offense." The problem with broad definitions, however, is that they ignore the important fact that the target offense can range from simple credit card fraud to the permanent adoption of a false identity and the more complex activities of organized criminal networks. As a result, by treating all offenses where an identity has been misused under one category, we fail to properly understand the motivations and methods of identity thieves. Moreover, there is a danger that we will confuse the quite different impacts on the victims of the enabling versus target offenses.

A better approach is to distinguish between two different types of identity theft. *Identity frauds* are temporary offenses in which personal data are borrowed to commit a fraudulent offense. Here, the identifying information serves merely as a tool for the criminal to use to commit another offense. The motivation for these offenses tends to be financial, either to obtain goods or services or to establish credit or a loan, and the impersonation is temporary. *Identity thefts* are cases in which the victim's entire identity is permanently appropriated (often referred to as "Day of the Jackal" cases). The identity of another individual is "hijacked" by the fraudster with the aim of a permanent appropriation. This may be for financial reasons, for example, to escape an existing record of bankruptcy, or it may be to hide a criminal record or escape a previous life.

Extent of the Problem

Despite repeated claims that identity theft is one of the world's fastest-growing crimes, relatively little is known about the true extent of identity theft and identity fraud when compared with other crimes. The best estimates come from the United States, which recognized identity theft as a statutory offense in 1998 with passage of the Identity Theft and Assumption Deterrence Act and where a number of national surveys on the subject have been conducted. The Federal Trade Commission administers a central repository for identity theft complaints and, in 2005, reported 255,565 incidences of identity theft, totaling losses of $56.6 billion. However, victim surveys (including the National Crime Victimization Survey) estimate the victimization of between 3 and 4 percent of Americans annually.

In Europe, where identity theft is not yet considered to be a widespread problem, data are scarce. The exception is the United Kingdom, which has recently prioritized identity theft as a serious and fast-growing crime problem in need of urgent addressing. Early estimates from the Home Office suggest that 137,000 people are "affected" by identity theft each year, costing £1.7 billion annually, but there is little evidence to support these claims. Other studies suggest the victimization of 1 in 10 people and as many as 1 in 4 experiencing identity theft (either directly or indirectly).

Studies on both sides of the Atlantic suggest that young people are most vulnerable. In the 2004 National Crime Victimization Survey conducted by the U.S. Bureau of Justice Statistics, households where the head was between age 18 and 24 were significantly more likely to be victimized, as were high-income households. Rural households were less likely to be victimized. U.K. studies concur that people under the age of 30 are most vulnerable.

Impact on the Victims

For each episode of identity theft or fraud, there are multiple victims: the individual whose information is borrowed or appropriated (the *primary* victim) and any individual, business, or institution that is subsequently defrauded or duped by the perpetrator (the *secondary* victim or victims).

The primary victim may experience a range of different forms of harm. Although the immediate loss of large sums of money is a commonly held fear, it is actually quite unlikely for the primary victim to be held liable for hefty debts incurred where an identity theft has taken place. More likely is the damage caused to the victim's credit history, which will have a negative impact on his or her future financial autonomy. Also, the primary victim of identity theft faces the challenge of restoring his or her personal identity profile, a process that can be costly in terms of time and effort. Research shows that the loss of control of personal information is potentially damaging to an individual's sense of self and quality of life. For the secondary victims, the loss suffered will, more often than not, be directly financial. Indeed, members of the retail, communications, and finance industries are the ones absorbing the costs of identity theft.

Responses

In the mid-1990s the United States became the first country to formally recognize identity theft as a crime; other countries have been slow to follow suit. Although identity theft swiftly emerged as a key issue on the crime agendas of governments across the Western world, few have followed the U.S. lead on policy. In the current climate of fear of terrorism, the urgent need for reliable processes and methods of identification is apparent. Government agencies and businesses around the world need to work together to examine the practices of document-issuing authorities and those who are involved in the processing of personal data.

It is important for the responses to the problem to be designed and applied in the appropriate context. In the United States, for example, many tailored responses address the vulnerabilities emanating from an over-reliance on the social security number, which is used as a key identifier in a wide range of public and private transactions. In contrast, the United Kingdom does not currently operate a single-identifier system, and therefore the identity theft problem is more strongly associated with extremely high rates of credit or debit card fraud.

On both sides of the Atlantic, significant efforts have been made to provide education and guidance to citizens and consumers in the fight against identity theft and fraud. Increasingly, individuals are encouraged to develop a more responsible attitude toward their personal data. Credit card holders, for example, repeatedly hear that they should keep their card details and personal identification number (PIN) confidential and to shred or burn their statements and receipts. Businesses, too, receive admonitions to think more seriously about the threat of identity theft and the safety of their customers.

Natasha Semmens

See also Cyberspace; National Crime Victimization Survey; Property Crime

Further Readings

Cabinet Office. 2002. "Identity Fraud: A Study." London: HMSO. Retrieved December 27, 2007 (http://www.ips .gov.uk/identity/downloads/id_fraud-report.pdf).

Federal Trade Commission. 2005. "National and State Trends in Fraud and Identity Theft (January–December 2004)." Retrieved December 27, 2007 (http://www.ftc.gov/bcp/ edu/microsites/idtheft/downloads/ clearinghouse_2004.pdf).

Finch, Emily. 2002. "'What a Tangled Web We Weave': Identity Theft and the Internet." Pp. 86–104 in *Dot.con: Crime, Deviance and Identity on the Internet,* edited by Y. Jewkes. Collompton, England: Willan.

Jones, Gareth and Michael Levi. 2000. "The Value of Identity and the Need for Authenticity." In *Turning the Corner.* Foresight Panel. London: Department of Trade and Industry, Office of Science and Technology Crime.

LoPucki, Lynn. 2001. "Human Identification Theory and the Identity Theft Problem." *Texas Law Review* 80:89–136.

Semmens, Natasha. 2004. "Plastic Card Fraud and Identity Theft: Implications of Data Crimes for the Future of Society, Business and Crime Control." *Contemporary Issues in Law* 7:121–39.

ILLEGITIMATE OPPORTUNITY STRUCTURES

During the 1950s two predominant theories of criminal behavior were Edwin H. Sutherland's differential association theory and Robert K. Merton's anomie theory. Sutherland argued that criminal behavior is learned in the same manner as other behaviors; people who are socialized to sanction criminal behavior are likely to become criminals. Merton suggested that criminal behavior results when there is a discrepancy between the goals reinforced by society (e.g., earn a good income) and the institutionalized means for attaining these goals (e.g., complete a good education). Those whose access to legitimate opportunities is blocked in some way, perhaps due to poverty or the unavailability of good schools, may use illegal means to reach culturally valued goals. Richard A. Cloward and Lloyd E. Ohlin agreed that both theories had merit but added that a key channel of access to culturally valued goals was through illegitimate opportunity structures, especially in impoverished inner-city communities where legitimate means may be scarce.

This notion of illegitimate opportunity structures elaborates the notion that differential access to legitimate opportunities explains why some people are more successful than others. Rather than focusing on how access to wealth or social capital leads to financial success, Cloward and Ohlin argued that some people engage in crime and deviance because they have relatively greater access to illegitimate opportunities. These opportunities imply (a) a learning environment in which particular skills and values are acquired, and (b) opportunities to engage in criminal roles. For example, youth may find legitimate opportunities blocked, but those who have learned methods of delinquency and who have opportunities to engage in such practices—perhaps because their peers are delinquent—become delinquents. In the absence of illegitimate opportunity structures, people with blocked opportunities may experience problems of adjustment (e.g., anxiety or depression), withdraw from society, or turn to risky sexual behavior or drug use in an attempt to find other avenues of self-acceptance or peer-evaluated success. Some researchers argued that illegitimate opportunity structures became more prevalent in the 1980s and 1990s as many inner-city areas experienced a concentration of poverty due to the loss of skilled jobs in urban centers. Others pointed out that crime may also result in the attenuation of legitimate opportunities, such as when conventional residents flee high-crime neighborhoods. Hence, residents may be left with few options other than illegitimate opportunities.

In their seminal works, Cloward and Ohlin focused primarily on inner-city gangs and how their members accessed illegitimate opportunity structures as they engaged in particular forms of delinquency. Their studies have been criticized because they describe deviant subcultures with norms that are opposed to the widely accepted norms of the broader culture and focus on gangs as the main facilitator of delinquent behavior. Yet, even members of these presumed subcultures tend to sanction the legitimate norms of society, and most delinquency is not the result of gang behavior. Critics claim that delinquents who maintain that legitimate opportunities are blocked, whereas illegitimate opportunities are not, are engaging in rationalization for their failure to sufficiently inculcate the norms and practices of conventional society.

The notion of illegitimate opportunity structures may be used to account for various types of illegal or deviant activities. For example, transnational criminal organizations may search for porous borders, lax enforcement efforts, or bribery opportunities as they engage in drug trafficking, human trafficking, or money laundering. Hence, they tend to ply their trade in nations that afford ready access to illegitimate opportunities and avoid nations that block such access. Assuming that a cultural drive to financial or political success is part of certain societies, blocked legitimate opportunities may motivate even presumably successful people to draw upon illegitimate opportunity structures. This frequently occurs because people often compare themselves with proximate others, such as those who work in similar occupations, when they judge their relative success. For example, the vice president of a corporation may resort to bribing public officials if his earlier attempts to obtain government contracts were unsuccessful. A lobbyist may provide illegal gratuities to politicians to influence votes, especially if previous efforts at using legitimate means were thwarted. Academic researchers may manipulate data if their earlier research efforts failed. Students who perform poorly on standardized exams may see cheating as a viable alternative if they are eager to be admitted to a particular academic institution. These are examples of using illegitimate opportunity structures when legitimate opportunities are perceived as unavailable.

Although blocked legitimate opportunities and access to illegitimate opportunities may explain some forms of deviant behavior, it remains unclear whether the latter is a necessary or sufficient condition. For instance, access to illegitimate opportunities is often gauged by noting deviant or criminal behavior; this is clearly tautological. However, recent research suggests that providing greater access to legitimate opportunities, such as through vocational training or providing high-quality jobs, results in less criminal behavior. Moreover, moving from an impoverished neighborhood with high rates of joblessness to a better-quality neighborhood has been shown to reduce the probability of delinquency among some youth.

John P. Hoffmann

See also Corporate Crime; Crime; Cultural Values; Differential Association; Inner City; Juvenile Delinquency; Oppositional Culture Theory; Strain Theory; White-Collar Crime

Further Readings

Braithwaite, John. 1989. "Criminological Theory and Organizational Crime." *Justice Quarterly* 6:333–58.

Cloward, Richard A. 1959. "Illegitimate Means, Anomie, and Deviant Behavior." *American Sociological Review* 24:164–76.

Cloward, Richard A. and Lloyd E. Ohlin. 1960. *Delinquency and Opportunity: A Theory of Delinquent Gangs.* New York: Free Press.

McAdam, Doug. 1996. "Conceptual Origins, Current Problems, Future Directions." Pp. 23–40 in *Comparative Perspectives on Social Movements,* edited by D. McAdam, J. D. McCarthy, and M. N. Zald. Cambridge, England: Cambridge University Press.

Merton, Robert K. 1995. "Opportunity Structure: The Emergence, Diffusion, and Differentiation of a Sociological Concept, 1930s–1950s." Pp. 3–78 in *The Legacy of Anomie Theory,* edited by F. Adler and W. S. Laufer. New Brunswick, NJ: Transaction.

Simpson, Sally S. and Nicole Leeper Piquero. 2002. "Low Self-Control, Organizational Theory, and Corporate Crime." *Law & Society Review* 36:509–48.

ILLITERACY, ADULT IN DEVELOPED NATIONS

The last decade of the 20th century witnessed an unprecedented concern for adult literacy in many developed nations. This concern was stimulated by the completion of the first International Adult Literacy Survey (IALS), undertaken in the mid-1990s by the Organisation for Economic Co-operation and Development (OECD) and a number of its member nations, and led to varying government responses. This entry presents the broad outlines of the IALS, its methodology, and general findings, with a focus on responses in three nations—Canada, the United Kingdom, and the United States.

The International Adult Literacy Survey

The IALS methodology was the same as that of the National Adult Literacy Survey of 1993 in the United States. Like that survey, the IALS changed the traditional practice of dividing adults into the dichotomy of "illiterate" and "literate" and instead discussed adult literacy as a continuum from very low literacy to very high literacy. Using the traditional division of adults into illiterate and literate, UNESCO reported illiteracy rates of just 1 to 2 percent for developed nations in the mid-1990s. But using the methodology of the IALS, the percentages of adults in developed nations with very low literacy skills, which earlier would have been called "functional illiteracy," were 10 times as high as the estimates of illiteracy given by UNESCO.

IALS developers defined literacy as using printed and written information to function in society, to achieve one's goals, and to develop one's knowledge and potential. Then, using door-to-door sampling methods, the IALS assessed the literacy skills of adults ages 16 through 65. The IALS developed performance scales composed of tasks for Prose Literacy (e.g., reading text materials such as newspapers, poetry); Document Literacy (e.g., scanning and completing forms or using a train schedule); and Quantitative Literacy (e.g., determining the amount of a tip for a restaurant meal or reviewing a bank statement). Scores on these three scales assign adults to one of five literacy levels (level 1 = very low; level 5 = very high literacy).

For 21 nations assessed in the IALS the percentages of native-born adults in the lowest level of literacy ranged from around 5 percent in Sweden to a high of over 50 percent in Chile, with an average for the 21 nations of about 20 percent on the Prose, Document, and Quantitative Literacy scales. Thus, on average, about one fifth of native-born adults ages 16 to 65 in these developed countries were considered to be "at risk" for social problems because of their low literacy. For foreign-born adults, the percentages were uniformly higher, averaging over 50 percent with Prose, Document, and Quantitative Literacy scores falling in the lowest level of literacy.

Using the Document performance tasks for illustrative purposes, with native- and non-native-born adults combined, 23.7 percent of United States adults ages 16 to 65 fell into the lowest level of literacy, while in Canada this percentage was 18.2, and 23.3

percent in the United Kingdom. Similar percentages, with a little variation, held for the assignment of adults to literacy level 1 on the Prose and Quantitative Literacy scales.

Self-Perceived Literacy and Numeracy Skills

Based on results of the literacy performance tests, about one fifth of adults ages 16 to 65 in the focal nations of Canada, the United Kingdom, and the United States were considered to be at risk for social problems such as unemployment, underemployment, low income, poverty, and poor health due to low literacy. This would come to about 3.3 million adults in Canada, 7.4 million in the United Kingdom, and 32 million in the United States.

However, the IALS did not use only literacy tests to measure adult literacy. Additionally, the IALS developed a scale for the adults' self-assessment of their literacy ability. In this case adults were asked to rate how well they thought their literacy skills matched their needs for these skills at work or in daily life. In making these judgments, adults used the rating categories of poor, moderate, good, excellent, and no response.

Using the adults' self-assessments of their reading abilities for work and daily life, less than 5 percent of adults ages 16 to 65 in either Canada, the United Kingdom, or the United States rated their reading as poor. Using a 5 percent estimate for these three nations, some 8 million adults in the United States, less than 1 million in Canada, and less than 2 million in the United Kingdom considered themselves at risk for poor reading skills. Similar results held for self-assessments of writing and numeracy skills.

In the IALS, then, adults' estimates of their reading ability revealed a considerable discrepancy between the literacy skills as measured by the performance tests and the self-assessments in determining the numbers of adults at risk for poor literacy in these three nations. This discrepancy also occurred in other nations.

Efforts to Increase Access to Adult Literacy Education Programs

For the three developed nations discussed in the previous sections, there were considerable differences in the percentages of adults considered to be at risk and hence in need of literacy or basic skills instruction based on IALS test data and the actual numbers of adults who seek out and enroll in literacy programs. In Canada, for instance, studies reported that only 5 to 10 percent of adults eligible for literacy education had ever enrolled in literacy courses. Some 43 percent of Canadians who sought information about literacy programs did not enroll because of program- or policy-related problems, such as not being called back after calling a literacy telephone hotline, long waiting lists, inconvenient course times, wrong content or teaching structure, and unhelpful program content.

In the United Kingdom, the IALS assigned around 23 percent of adults to literacy level 1 (some 8,000,000 adults) while participants in adult literacy programs around that time included less than 5 percent of that number. To increase access to provision, the United Kingdom set as a target the reduction by 750,000 of the number of adults who had difficulty with literacy and numeracy by 2004. To meet these targets the government set aside up to £1.5 billion over a 3-year period and created a number of special programs for adults.

To determine what might motivate adults with poor basic skills to seek to improve them, the Basic Skills Agency of the United Kingdom conducted a study called Getting Better Basic Skills. The research focused on adults' perceptions of their skills, why they wanted to improve their skills, their access to learning programs, the content of the programs, and what would encourage them to try and improve their skills. Significant findings showed a third of adults thought that their basic skills needed improving, 29 percent said they would definitely take up a basic skills course, and 42 percent said they would probably do so. Factors motivating adults to improve their basic skills included being able to learn on a computer, being able to improve computer skills and basic skills at the same time, getting an education qualification, and being able to attend a course near home.

In the United States, less than 3 million adults enroll annually in the adult education and literacy programs that are funded jointly by the federal government in partnership with the 50 states. Following the National Adult Literacy Survey and the IALS, no special efforts with major funding were undertaken to reach adults with literacy needs in the United States.

In 2003, the OECD conducted a new international survey of adult literacy skills, the Adult Literacy and Life Skills survey. The report of the survey was released in 2005 and indicated that for the most part, there had been little or no improvement in adult literacy skills since the initial IALS in the mid-1990s.

Thomas G. Sticht

See also Illiteracy, Adult in Developing Nations

Further Readings

Blunkett, David. 2001. *Skills for Life: The National Strategy for Improving Adult Literacy and Numeracy Skills.* London: Department for Education and Skills.

Long, Ellen. 2000. *Who Wants to Learn?* Toronto, ON: ABC CANADA Literacy Foundation.

Organization for Economic Co-operation and Development (OECD). 1995. "Literacy, Economy and Society: Results of the First International Adult Literacy Survey." Paris: OECD.

Statistics Canada. 2005. "Learning a Living: First Results of the Adult Literacy and Life Skills Survey." Retrieved December 27, 2007 (http://www.statcan.ca/english/freepub/89-603-XIE/2005001/pdf.htm).

Sticht, Thomas G. 2001. "The International Adult Literacy Survey: How Well Does It Represent the Literacy Abilities of Adults?" *Canadian Journal for the Study of Adult Education* 15:19–36.

Tuijnman, A. 2000. *Benchmarking Adult Literacy in America: An International Comparative Study.* Jessup, MD: U.S. Department of Education, Education Publications Center.

Illiteracy, Adult in Developing Nations

For more than 60 years the United Nations Educational, Scientific and Cultural Organization (UNESCO) has tracked the progress of nations around the globe in achieving higher rates of adult literacy. Though nations may define literacy somewhat differently, most consider literacy as the ability to read and write simple statements in either a national or an indigenous language. Across the latter half of the 20th century, literacy rates of adults ages 15 years and older increased from 56 percent in 1950 to 70 percent in 1980, 75 percent in 1990, and 82 percent in 2004.

UNESCO's compilation of data obtained from member nations during the years 2000 to 2004 indicate that from 1990, illiteracy among adults fell by some 100 million, from around 870 million to 770 million, or about one fifth of the world's adult population. UNESCO data on the worldwide distribution of adult illiterates are presented next, followed by a brief discussion of some of the lessons learned in the years that UNESCO has worked to stimulate adult literacy education, primarily among developing nations.

Adult Illiteracy Worldwide

The overwhelming majority of the world's illiterate adults live in the less-developed regions of the world, including South and West Asia (41 percent of adults are illiterate), sub-Saharan Africa (40 percent), the Arab States (37 percent), Latin America and the Caribbean (10 percent), and East Asia and the Pacific (9 percent). In 1990, which was celebrated around the world as International Literacy Year, UNESCO and its member nations made a major effort to promote the education of women. At that time women comprised about two thirds of the world's illiterate adults. Unfortunately, over a decade later, women still make up about two thirds of the world's illiterate adults. Women are particularly vulnerable to illiteracy in East Asia and the Pacific, where they constitute almost 72 percent of adult illiterates; the Arab States (64 percent); Southern Asia (62 percent); and sub-Saharan Africa, where women constitute about 60 percent of adult illiterates.

Globally, in terms of the extent to which literacy rates for women are at parity with those for men, 88 women are literate for each 100 men, indicating an 88 percent parity rate of women's literacy to men's literacy for the world. These parity rates are lower (.66 to .76) for the regions cited in the previous paragraph.

Some Lessons Learned

Among the important lessons distilled from the international communities' work to raise the world's literacy rate for adults, two are especially important: (1) Adult literacy programs generally produce multiplier effects, meaning that important outcomes beyond the learning of literacy are frequently forthcoming, and (2) adult literacy programs often have intergenerational consequences, meaning that improving adult literacy, especially that of women, increases the likelihood of children's education.

Multiplier Effects in Adult Literacy Education

In 1984 UNESCO awarded a literacy prize to the National Institute for Adult Education of Mexico. In 3 years the institute enrolled nearly 3 million adults, of which some 1 million became literate in that time. In teaching literacy, the institute's instructional materials integrated the teaching of literacy with the teaching of knowledge important in the day-to-day lives of the adults. This way, in addition to acquiring literacy, the participants also acquired knowledge about health, nutrition, education, and other vital concerns.

The National Institute for Adult Education of Mexico program is just one of many recognized by UNESCO for the approach to literacy education that illustrates that governments can expect multiple returns on investments in adult literacy education in at least five areas:

1. Improved productivity at work, at home, and in the community, leading to higher tax bases for communities, decreased violence at home and in the community, and greater participation in citizenship activities by a larger segment of the adult population

2. Improved self-confidence and other psychological and physiological aspects of health of adults, including activities that will help the brain grow throughout adulthood and contribute to reduced medical costs for adults as they age

3. Improved health of children as a result of adults learning in adult education programs, leading to better prenatal and postnatal care, reductions in low birth weight infants, and better home medical care, thereby contributing to lowered medical costs for children and fewer learning problems in school

4. Improved social justice from providing literacy education for marginalized populations to permit them to acquire skills and knowledge needed to take political action that allows them to achieve their civil rights and to overcome social exclusion and join in the mainstream of society

5. Improved productivity in the schools by providing adults with the knowledge they need to better prepare their children to enter school, help them achieve in school, encourage them to stay in school, and increase their opportunities to enroll in higher education

Intergenerational Effects of Adult Literacy Education

The fifth item in the previous list is especially important because it reveals the effects that educating adults can have on the educational opportunities and achievements of children. In 1983 a UNESCO literacy prize was presented to the Department of Adult Education of the Government of Kenya whose program reached more than a million adults, nearly four fifths of whom were women. The prize citation noted the excellent results achieved both directly through the program and indirectly through its impact upon the school enrollment and retention of the children of participants.

Research published by UNESCO illustrates the effects of girls' and women's education on children and their educational development at various stages from before birth to the school years:

Before Pregnancy. Better-educated girls/women show higher economic productivity, better personal health care, and lower fertility rates; hence they produce smaller families. The latter, in turn, is related to the preschool cognitive development of children and their subsequent achievement in school.

During Pregnancy and at Birth. Better-educated women provide better prenatal care, produce more full-term babies, and provide better postnatal care; this results in fewer babies with learning disabilities.

Before Going to School. Better-educated women produce better children's health care; better cognitive, language, and preliteracy development; and better preparation for schoolwork.

During the School Years. Better-educated women produce higher participation rates in schooling, better management of homework, and better advocacy for children's education and negotiation of school–child conflicts. In addition they produce children who achieve higher levels of education and literacy.

Because of these effects of women's education, UNESCO has for decades recommended that nations should pay special attention to the need for resources to provide literacy educational opportunities to the millions of less-literate women who will bring the next generation of children into the world. In 2003, the UN Decade of Literacy was launched with the first year of the decade devoted to issues of gender, with a focus on the literacy needs of girls and women to bring them to parity with the literacy rates of men.

Improving the Monitoring of Adult Literacy

As indicated earlier, adult literacy/illiteracy rates in developing nations are presently determined by a variety of methods. These methods are mostly based on self-reports in census surveys. But studies comparing these self-reports with direct assessments using literacy tests suggest that the traditional methods for determining literacy rates may overstate the extent of literacy. In the 2006 report on UNESCO's Education for All initiative, a report on the monitoring of adult literacy around the world, it is noted,

> In Morocco, 45 percent of respondents in a sample reported being literate, but only 33 percent demonstrated basic competence in literacy. Similar patterns are found in Bangladesh, Ethiopia, Nicaragua and the United Republic of Tanzania. Among Ethiopian women with one year of schooling, although 59 percent were considered literate by household assessments, only 27 percent passed a simple reading test.

Because of the diversity of methods used to indicate literacy rates and the mixed results of studies such as the foregoing, UNESCO is developing new methods of measuring adult literacy to use in monitoring the achievement of adult literacy in developing nations in the coming decades.

Thomas G. Sticht

See also Illiteracy, Adult in Developed Nations

Further Readings

Aksornkool, Namtip. 2001. *Literacy: A Key to Empowering Women Farmers.* Paris: UNESCO.

Sticht, Thomas G. and Barbara A. McDonald. 1990. *Teach the Mother and Reach the Child: Literacy across Generations.* Geneva: UNESCO International Bureau of Education.

United Nations Educational, Scientific and Cultural Organization. 2000. "World Education Report: The Right to Education: Toward Education for All throughout Life." Paris: UNESCO.

———. 2006. "Education for All Global Monitoring Report 2006." Retrieved December 27, 2007 (http://portal.unesco.org/education/en/ev.php-URL_ID=43047&URL_DO=DO_TOPIC&URL_SECTION=201.html).

IMMIGRANTS, UNDOCUMENTED

See UNDOCUMENTED IMMIGRANTS

IMMIGRATION

Immigration is the arrival of citizens from one nation-state who plan on taking or do take up long-term or permanent residence in another country. Thus it is secondary to the preceding migration. Subsequent generations of these immigrants either assimilate and become invisible or maintain features distinguishing them from other members of society as identifiable ethnic, racial, cultural, or religious (minority) groups. Given the historical continuum of global migration, immigration too has a historical continuum, probably observable at any point in history. The concept of immigration, however, is relatively new and corresponds to the emergence of modern nation-states. Nations are founded on various principles, such as blood, culture, fate and destiny, history, or other characteristics supposedly shared by members of a nation. Belonging has either a political or a natural definition, thus making it a matter of choice or of birthright. Therefore, the arrivals of other social or political groups not perceived as holding these commonly shared characteristics make them, in the minds of the natives, either aliens, foreigners, immigrants, or simply "the others."

Immigration, first studied by the Chicago School during the 1920s, raises various issues. These are usually identified with or related to reception, insertion, incorporation (or at times non-incorporation), integration, adaptation, assimilation, and related processes of belonging and identity. Each concept couples with specific beliefs, theories, or policies. While conventional and assimilationist research only examines how immigrants adapt or fail to do so, progressive research also studies the adaptation of host societies. The sociological questions arising are what happens to newcomers and what happens to receiving societies; what is the relationship between indigenous populations, previous immigrants, and newcomers; and what are the social, economic, political, and cultural consequences to all? And the political questions are what is the legal status of new arrivals; which political, civil, and social rights do they have; and how can these rights be acquired?

Integration is an interactive process involving individuals and collectives from both mobile and sedentary populations. The character of the relations, their power relations, their structural positions in society, and their communication processes are crucial. The integration of immigrants into the host society is either a one-way process (the immigrants adapt to the host society) or a two-way process (both parties change). In civic and liberal nations, belonging is a matter of choice: Integration can be negotiated and subsequent belonging acquired, as in the United States or the United Kingdom. In ethnic nations where belonging is related to descent—as, for instance, in Germany, Turkey, Greece, and Japan—this is hardly possible.

Migration and immigration are major forces of global human transformation, alongside globalization and aging. Global migration, defined as the increasing global mobility of people and immigration, significantly increases heterogeneity of ethnic composition and of cultural values and practices. The consequences are manifold: (a) It might or might not increase the size of the population of a host society, depending on net migration, that balance between emigration and immigration; (b) it changes the composition of a host society's population in terms of culture, language, religion, or ethnicity and potentially changes the fabric of a host society; and (c) immigrants increase the labor force, contribute to the economy and tax and social funds, and are consumers and service users. Issues of concern are labor market competition, overcrowding (e.g., in the housing market), drain on public services, and conflicts between indigenous and immigrant cultures. Observers pay specific attention to immigrants who simultaneously hold loyalty to their country of origin and their host country and who are engaged economically, politically, and culturally in both. These are transnational migrants and represent an increasingly relevant group. Another specific challenge relates to those who only temporarily integrate because they intend to return or move on to other destinations, which affects efforts made by both parties.

Three major models and policies of inclusion can be identified: (1) *multiculturalism* (e.g., in Canada and Australia) and its successors *interculturalism* and *transculturalism*, based on diversity, social equality, and participation and emphasizing social integration; (2) *integration* (e.g., in Germany and the Netherlands), emphasizing its structural aspects and based on social equality, participation, and adaptation to a host society; and (3) *assimilation* into a host society (e.g., France), based on (republican) ideas of homogeneity. The difference lies in the level of mutuality in the adaptation process, ranging from one-way assimilation to limited mutuality in integration and high levels of mutuality in multiculturalism.

Antonyms of integration are *social marginalization* and *social or spatial segregation*. All currently practiced models of integration are considered imperfect, at least with respect to implementation: All can lead to alienation, segregation, and (self-)exclusion, which undermine solidarity and social cohesion. While some, such as multiculturalism, pay due respect to mutuality in integration processes, implementation is insufficient because there still is a dominant community. Recent trends show that states prefer skilled immigrants with high levels of human capital and language proficiency, understood as preconditions to successful integration.

Both indigenous populations and immigrants contribute barriers to integration. In most receiving countries, immigrants experience discrimination, often on grounds of racism; hence they are legally, structurally, or socially treated unequally. Consequently, they suffer from such social inequalities as unemployment, poor education, substandard housing, political underrepresentation, overpolicing, and racial violence. Immigrants too might exclude themselves from a host society, and even confront a liberal society with illiberal beliefs, for example, with respect to gender relations. Instead, they might create or integrate into already existing immigrant and ethnic minority communities. These, however, could also be a response to prior rejection by the host society.

Although immigration represents a major challenge to society and community, no coherent theories and policies on integration exist. From the perspective of social scientists, present practices of political organization of humanity are not well equipped to accommodate mobile populations.

Franck Düvell

See also Citizenship; Discrimination; Discrimination, Institutional; Ethnic Group; Ethnicity; Ethnocentrism; Immigration, United States; Multiculturalism; Racism; Segregation

Further Readings

Castles, Stephen and Alistair Davidson. 2000. *Citizenship and Migration: Globalization and the Politics of Belonging.* London: Macmillan.
Schmitter-Heissler, Barbara. 2000. "The Sociology of Immigration." Pp. 77–96 in *Migration Theory: Talking across Disciplines,* edited by C. Brettell and J. F. Hollifield. New York: Routledge.

IMMIGRATION, UNITED STATES

Often described as a nation of immigrants, the United States had a foreign-born population of 12.4 percent in 2005. Before the 19th century, however, people rarely used the term *immigrant.* Instead, the foreign-born came as settlers, pioneers, slaves, or indentured servants.

The Naturalization Act of 1790 first established a centralized process for becoming a citizen, originally open to any free white individual who could demonstrate residence in the country for 2 years. In the mid-19th century, the short-lived Know-Nothing movement emerged as a reaction to a surge in immigration, particularly of Irish Catholics after the potato famine of 1845–1851. No national legislation, however, was enacted in response. Immigration was, for the most part, welcomed as a route to national development until the late 19th century. This changed with the passing of the Chinese Exclusion Act of 1882, which barred Chinese from entering the country and excluded those already in the country from naturalization. From this point forward, who could and could not "become an American" was regulated at the national level. The immigrant became a distinct legal, as well as social, category.

Historically, two major peaks occurred in the foreign-born population as a percentage of the total population. According to U.S. Census Bureau statistics, 9.7 percent of the population was foreign-born in 1850, rising to 14.8 percent in 1890 and 14.7 percent in 1910. Midcentury, the proportion of foreign-born plummeted, representing just 5.4 percent of the total population in 1960 and 4.7 percent in 1970. Since the 1970s, however, the number of foreign-born has risen rapidly. Estimated at more than 35.6 million in 2005, there are now more than twice as many immigrants than at any time before 1980. In addition to the increasing numbers of foreign-born people, there are significant trends in their ethnic and racial composition. In 1910, 87.4 percent of immigrants came from Europe. In 2005, 31 percent of foreign-born arrived from Latin America, 36 percent from Asia, and just 16 percent from Europe.

The gender and age cohorts of immigrants to the United States also varied over the past 100 years. Earlier immigrants were primarily male; in 1910 there were 131.2 males per 100 female immigrants. By 1960, this trend reversed, and in 1970 there were just 84.4 males per 100 female immigrants. The proportion of male immigrants rose again by 1990, with 95.8 males per 100 females, a pattern that continued through 2005. Similarly, the age distribution of the immigrant population shifted over time. In 1910, 5.7 percent of immigrants were under age 15 and 8.9 percent were over age 65. In 1940, less than 1 percent of immigrants were under age 15 and 18 percent were over age 65. By 1990, 7.5 percent of immigrants were under age 15 and 13.6 percent were over age 65.

Scholars analyze the determinants of migration to understand these changing demographic patterns, such as the shift from fewer female migrants in the early 1900s to many more females than males in the 1970s. Researchers also examine the experiences of immigrant groups and their offspring in relation to nonimmigrant populations. They may consider how race and ethnicity shape immigrants' experiences of adaptation and mobility, how an influx of young immigrants impacts the educational system, or how the changing profile of older immigrants affects social security and health care institutions.

Causal Factors in U.S. Immigration

Theoretical approaches to understanding the determinants of immigration include neoclassical economics, world-systems theory, the household strategies models, and social network analysis.

Neoclassical Economics

Neoclassical economic approaches to migration consider the wage differentials between foreign countries and the United States as the root cause of an individual's decision to migrate. Immigrants are often labor migrants; they may be rational actors who weigh the costs and benefits of a move abroad. Immigrants may base their decisions on push and pull factors, the former referring to the causes of economic hardship which make survival in the home country difficult and the latter referring to potential economic opportunity in the United States. As such, fluctuations in immigration can relate to labor markets. For example, expansion of the railroads in the West, starting in the 1860s, provided jobs for Asian and Mexican immigrants before Chinese immigrants and other Asians were barred from entry. More recently, the increasing entrance of women into formal labor markets since the 1970s created job opportunities in child care for many female immigrants.

Immigration patterns also necessarily relate to labor markets in immigrants' countries of origin. In many African countries, for example, civil war and ethnic conflict since the 1980s left professionals with few opportunities for advancement. They often sought work in the United States where they received a greater return for their human capital. In other countries, such as the Philippines and in parts of India, the number of highly educated female nurses exceeded the demands of their national health care systems; many have found work in this expanding U.S. industry since the 1970s.

World-Systems Theories

In the real world, a pure relationship between economic hardship and opportunity is rare. Instead, economic decisions are embedded in social and political structures that may mitigate or intensify hardships and may create or dampen opportunities. A world-systems perspective analyzes the political structures underlying immigration and examines the relations between nations that contribute to creating these structures.

Immigration law and regulation is one key factor that influences migration patterns. For example, the National Origins Act of 1921, which restricted immigration from different countries according to a quota system, and its abolition in 1965 explain the drop in immigration to the United States in the mid-20th century. The abolition of the act also helps explain the greater diversity in the ethnic and racial composition of immigrants since 1965.

Inclusion or exclusion of potential immigrants is also intimately tied to international politics, particularly in the post–World War II era when the United States created refugee and political asylum provisions. For example, Cubans, whose Communist leader Fidel Castro has challenged U.S. intervention in the region since 1959, receive a warm welcome and resettlement support. However, during the 1980s, immigrants from Guatemala and El Salvador, where the United States backed the national governments amid civil war, were routinely denied political asylum. Religious leaders in the United States then illegally provided sanctuary for many Central Americans; their successful challenges to immigration law led to a 1990 provision for political asylum for El Salvadorans and Guatemalans.

U.S. military presence in a country may also spur immigration, particularly by women. The War Brides Act of 1945 allowed GIs to sponsor their foreign-born wives and children, sparking an increase in Korean and Japanese immigration midcentury. Many women from El Salvador first came to the United States in the 1980s as domestic workers for foreign diplomats stationed in their country during the conflict. Today the second largest Salvadoran community is in Washington, D.C.

Household Strategies

In contrast to external imbalances of power, the household migration strategy perspective considers the dynamics within families that shape immigration. Originally, household strategy models were relatively one-dimensional, assuming that families deployed specific members as part of a unified family migration strategy. For example, at the turn of the 20th century, Italian men often left wives and children behind when they immigrated to maintain, and at times increase, the family's holdings via remittances, reducing the risks involved in uprooting the entire family. In contrast, Irish families often sent young unmarried women between 1880 and 1920 to work in domestic service to supplement family income, because inheritance practices limited marriage pools within Ireland.

Today, scholars suggest more complicated household strategy models by tracing the ways power imbalances within families affect decisions to migrate. These scholars argue that a unified family migration strategy may not exist and that migration may not benefit all members of a household equally.

For example, some suggest that because Mexican men generally have more decision-making power than do women in their families, the male breadwinner primarily makes the decision to migrate. Other scholars describe the ways that women from Latin America and the Caribbean actively convince their families to support their moves abroad in order to escape abusive situations at home.

Social Networks

Social networks also shape patterns of immigration. Because the social network is considered as an independent causal factor, social network analysis is a powerful reminder of the ways that informal structures within and between communities and families influence the face of immigration. For example, in recent years, Mexicans living in the United States constituted about 30 percent of the entire foreign-born population, by far the largest immigrant group. Mexican immigration is largely shaped by social networks now institutionalized in migrants' communities of origin.

Consequences of U.S. Immigration

Research on the social consequences of immigration usually pertains to one of three areas: immigrants' experiences of adaptation and assimilation, mobility of immigrant populations, and relationships between immigrant communities and nonimmigrant groups.

Adaptation and Assimilation

At the beginning of the 20th century, the principal stance on immigration was that the United States was a melting pot and that immigrants needed to assimilate to U.S. culture to be successful. Social campaigns during this period often strove to teach immigrant women how to make their families more "American." When immigrants lived in neighborhoods dominated by co-ethnics, enclaves were considered a source of social disorganization that undermined modern development.

By the end of the 20th century, the melting pot paradigm gave way to one of multiculturalism. Rather than a site of social disorganization, ethnic enclaves are now viewed as a source of social support for immigrants. They provide the necessary networks to locate employment and housing. Membership in religious organizations with co-ethnics is one of the primary sites of civic participation among immigrants upon arrival. Ethnic enclaves are also important sources for entrepreneurship, the major means for mobility for some new immigrants. Self-employment rates are particularly high for well-educated Korean and Middle Eastern immigrants, although they may not depend on co-ethnics for business, instead acting as economic intermediaries in other ethnic minority neighborhoods. Yet for other members of immigrant groups, the ethnic enclave can become the principal site of exploitation by co-ethnics. This is particularly true for undocumented workers in Chinatowns across the country, who often must depend on informal, unregulated, and low-wage economic opportunities from co-ethnics.

Recent scholarship examines the increasingly important ways that transnational ties shape immigrant experiences in the United States. From this perspective, immigrants maintain social, political, and economic ties with communities of origin. Transnational studies may involve political ties (hometown associations), economic ties (remittances), technology, cultural identity, or family relationships. The transnational perspective shows that in a globalized world, immigrants' adaptation to life in the United States is intricately linked to the lives of those in their countries of origin.

Mobility

Perhaps the best way to gauge the success of immigrants' adaptations to life in the United States is to study the lives of the second generation, that is, the fate of the children of immigrants. Given the great demographic shifts between the primarily European stock of the earlier waves of immigrants and the influx of immigrants of color since the 1960s, mobility among the children of today's immigrants is particularly indicative of the ways race and ethnicity shape the social structure of the United States.

Among the many factors considered in gauging mobility in the second generation are language acquisition, educational attainment, and socioeconomic status. Despite public concern to the contrary, findings suggest that by the second and third generations, proficiency in English is uniform among children of recent immigrants, much as was the case among the earlier waves of European immigrants. Findings based on other indicators of mobility, however, are mixed. On the one hand, when second-generation immigrants are isolated in ethnic enclaves in inner cities, upward mobility is far less likely. In other cases, immigrant youth may maintain their identity as foreigners to distinguish themselves from minority nonimmigrants.

One of the most important research findings on mobility among second-generation immigrants is that experiences typically differ between and within various groups, a process known as "segmented assimilation." For example, comparative studies of second-generation youth in New York and Los Angeles show that children of different genders and racial/ethnic backgrounds may have vastly different experiences.

Relationships Between Immigrants and Nonimmigrants

A third aspect of the consequences of U.S. immigration is interethnic relationships. Scholars from the Chicago School of sociology at the turn of the century mapped the social ecology of the city as a means of depicting the relationships between immigrant and nonimmigrant groups. Until recently, immigrant settlement patterns have not varied greatly. In urban areas like Chicago, most arrived to ethnic enclaves in the city and only those immigrants who were upwardly mobile, or their children or grandchildren, moved to the suburbs following scenarios of white flight. Moreover, Latino/a and Asian populations were once concentrated in California and in the Southwest. Cubans and other Caribbean immigrants settled in Florida and in the Northeast. In some areas, immigrants worked as migrant farmworkers. For the most part, though, the study of immigrant incorporation was a study of urban communities.

In recent decades, however, immigrants have dispersed rapidly throughout the continental United States, living in rural, urban, and suburban communities. Immigrants, many of them undocumented, have become a major cause of conflict at many of these new destinations. Their presence is associated with various social problems including concentrations of day laborers, bilingual education, health care for the uninsured, and more. Minutemen militia groups have formed at the southern U.S. border with Mexico to try to keep out immigrants. Some municipal governments have passed local ordinances to prevent immigrants from settling in their towns. The

"English only" movement has gained strength. Many fear that these tensions put immigrants' human rights at risk; stories of women and children illegally trafficked into the United States illustrate the ways immigrants may be victimized in the underground economy associated with immigration.

Recently, concerns over terrorism, heightened after the attack on the World Trade Center in 2001, fueled rising tensions over the roles and rights of immigrants in the United States and increased pressures to regulate and monitor immigrants' activities.

Joanna Dreby

See also Americanization; Assimilation; Deportation; English-Only Movement; Ethnicity; Human Trafficking; Immigration; Intergenerational Mobility; Labor, Migrant; Melting Pot; Migration, Global; Refugees; Sanctuary Movement; Segmented Assimilation; Social Disorganization; Transnational Families; Undocumented Immigrants

Further Readings

Foner, Nancy. 2000. *From Ellis Island to JFK: New York's Two Great Waves of Immigration.* New Haven, CT: Yale University Press.

Hondagneu-Sotelo, Pierrette, ed. 2003. *Gender and U.S. Immigration.* Berkeley, CA: University of California Press.

Kasinitz, Philip, John H. Mollenkopf, and Mary C. Waters, eds. 2004. *Becoming New Yorkers: Ethnographies of the New Second Generation.* New York: Russell Sage.

Levitt, Peggy. 2001. *The Transnational Villagers.* Berkeley, CA: University of California Press.

Light, Ivan and Steven Gold. 2000. *Ethnic Economies.* San Diego, CA: Academic Press.

Massey, D., J. Durand, and N. Malone. 2002. *Beyond Smoke and Mirrors: Mexican Immigration in the Era of Economic Integration.* New York: Russell Sage.

Portes, Alejandro and Rubén G. Rumbaut. 1990. *Immigrant America: A Portrait.* Berkeley, CA: University of California Press.

Rumbaut, Rubén G., ed. 2001. *Ethnicities: Children of Immigrants in America.* Berkeley, CA: University of California Press.

Suárez-Orozco, Carola and Marcelo M. Suárez-Orozco. 2001. *The Children of Immigration.* Cambridge, MA: Harvard University Press.

Zúñiga, Víctor and Rubén Hernández-León, eds. 2005. *New Destinations: Mexican Immigration in the United States.* New York: Russell Sage.

IMPERIALISM

Imperialism corresponds closely to the concept of empire and signifies all sorts of expansion policies: economic, political, military, cultural, and so on. In *The Civil War in France,* Karl Marx introduced the concept of imperialism into modern social and political thought. With his classical work *Imperialism: A Study,* John A. Hobson initiated modern theory on imperialism. Because of the close connection between the concept of imperialism and the concept of empire, many scholars assumed a description of human history in terms of imperialism. Hobson's theory of imperialism, on the contrary, is a historical theory of imperialism, describing it as a stage in the development of capitalism. His theory refers to a monopolist stage in the accumulation of capital that he places no later than the 1880s. He differentiates categorically between colonialism and imperialism.

In the colonialist age the driving economic force was the export and import of commodities. In the age of new imperialism, the driving force is exportation of capital, with the pursuit of an imperialist policy in the interest of a small population segment. That is, in the age of imperialism, an increase in the cosmopolitanism of capital occurs, and this should be not mixed up with internationalism. From a national viewpoint, imperialist policy is necessarily irrational. In colonial occupation of foreign countries, the mother country at least attempted to establish a colonial government and extend political and civil liberties to the occupied territories and to raise the state of civilization. Except for a few experiments in India, for example, the tendency of new imperialism goes the other way, seeking more drastic control of annexed territories and destruction of the achieved state of civilization. Politically, new imperialism is an expansion of autocracy. In terms of international relations, imperialism means a permanent rivalry between imperialist countries for the redistribution of natural resources, often a cause of new wars.

V. I. Lenin's contribution to Hobson's theory of imperialism is his illustration of its consistency in the tradition of Marx's critique of political economy. Lenin acknowledged, for example, Hobson's accuracy and deep economic/political analysis of imperialism. What Lenin criticized was what he called Hobson's bourgeois reformism and passivism.

Contemporarily, two closely related debates on imperialism attract interest: one on cultural imperialism and another concerning empire and new imperialism theories. In the first debate the rhetoric is between a critical liberal view of the logic of cultural imperialism and its stigmatization of other cultures, or a Marxist critique of any theory of cultural imperialism. The second debate concerns the nature of imperialism in the stage of globalization, where advocates propose to replace the classical concept of imperialism for a less definable concept of empire. Marxist scholars, in contrast, want to keep the classical concept simply by acknowledging new developments.

Doğan Göçmen

See also Colonialism; Globalization; Socialism

Further Readings

Ahmed, Aijaz. 1994. *In Theory: Classes, Nations, Literature.* London: Verso.

Hardt, Michael and Antonio Negri. 2000. *Empire.* Cambridge, MA: Harvard University Press.

Hobson, John A. 1961. *Imperialism: A Study.* London: Allen & Unwin.

Lenin, V. I. [1916] 1996. *Imperialism, the Highest Stage of Capitalism.* Melbourne, Australia: Pluto Press.

Mészáros, István. 2001. *Socialism or Barbarism.* New York: Monthly Review Press.

Said, Edward W. 1994. *Culture & Imperialism.* New York: Vintage.

INCARCERATION, SOCIETAL IMPLICATIONS

The United States incarcerates a larger share of its population than any other country. Increasingly, the criminal justice system affects not only the lives of convicted offenders individually but also the relative standing of demographic groups and outcomes in the country as a whole. This entry deals with the societal implications of the criminal justice system in the United States, specifically political participation, labor market performance, and black–white wage inequality.

The societal impact of the criminal justice system rests primarily on its size. In 2005, over 7 million individuals were under the supervision of the criminal justice system: 1.4 million in prisons, 0.7 million in local jails, 4.2 million on probation, and 0.8 million on parole. Millions more are identifiable as ex-convicts to authorities and employers. The risk of involvement with the criminal justice system is unequally distributed. Over 90 percent of the incarcerated population is male, most are younger than 45, and nearly half are black. The impact of the criminal justice system on these over-represented groups is naturally greater.

Felon Disenfranchisement

Most states in the United States disenfranchise incarcerated felons as well as nonincarcerated felons on probation or parole. A large minority of states additionally disenfranchises ex-felons after the conclusion of their sentence, and three states disenfranchise all felons for life. Only two states, Vermont and Maine, place no restrictions on the voting rights of convicted offenders, whereas some other states disenfranchise both felons and misdemeanants. Felon disenfranchisement is more common in the United States than in other democratic countries, where it is typically restricted to imprisoned felons for the duration of incarceration. Only Belgium, Chile, Finland, and Germany also disenfranchise (some) felons after release from prison. Although the number of states that disenfranchise ex-felons has sharply decreased since the 1950s, the number of affected individuals has increased because of an increase in the number of offenses classified as felonies and the increased probability of conviction in the sentencing stage of criminal trials. As a result of their over-representation in the criminal justice system, about 12 percent of black men nationwide had lost their right to vote as of 2004.

The impact of felon disenfranchisement on political outcomes hinges on three factors: the size of the disenfranchised population, voter turnout, and political preferences. About 5.3 million current and former felons (2.5 percent of the voting age population) were ineligible to participate in the 2004 presidential election. Approximately 40 percent of these individuals were ex-felons no longer under the supervision of the criminal justice system. Research suggests that voter turnout rates would be an estimated one-third lower among disenfranchised felons than in the general population. The number of votes prevented by felon disenfranchisement, therefore, is large. (Some researchers argue that the apparent decline in voter turnout since the 1970s may be due primarily to felon disenfranchisement: If disenfranchised citizens—mostly felons—are subtracted from the voting age population, which forms the denominator of conventional voter turnout rates, participation rates in the voting-eligible population are essentially constant over time.) One analysis concludes that as a result of the strong preference for the Democratic Party among disenfranchised felons, the 2000 presidential election would have been decided for Democrats in the absence of felon disenfranchisement. No other presidential election, however, is estimated to have hinged on felon disenfranchisement, although a small number of Senate races in the past 30 years may have.

Labor Market Participation and Black–White Wage Inequality

Official labor market statistics in the United States are calculated on the basis of the civilian non-institutionalized population and exclude the incarcerated population. Because economically disadvantaged individuals face much greater risks of incarceration, official statistics may present an incomplete picture of labor market performance.

For example, the employment–population ratio (EPR), which measures labor force utilization, would be lower if inmates were included in the denominator of the rate and counted as nonemployed individuals. The incarceration-adjusted EPR for young black male high school dropouts would have been almost 20 percentage points lower than the official rate in the late 1990s, whereas the incarcerated-adjusted EPR for young white male high school dropouts would have been 6 percentage points lower. The impact is smaller but still sizable for working-age men (4.9 and 0.9 percentage points difference for black and white men, respectively), but not meaningfully different for the national EPR. (Note that this EPR adjustment reverses the logic of the voter turnout adjustment mentioned previously: Whereas the official EPR excludes inmates and the adjustment includes them, conventional voter turnout rates include inmates and the adjusted rates exclude them.)

Mass incarceration also affects conventional measures of black–white wage inequality. Incarceration is selective of individuals with low earnings potential, and it removes relatively more black men than white men from the labor market and hence from official statistics. To account for the economic selectivity of incarceration, researchers have estimated inactivity-adjusted wage distributions, which impute hypothetical wages to nonworking individuals, including inmates of prisons and jails. These statistics are intended to estimate the wage distribution that would prevail if everybody earned wages in the market and nobody was inactive (neglecting general equilibrium effects). One such analysis found that selective labor market inactivity (including incarceration) depressed conventional measures of black–white inequality in log mean earnings by 20 percent among working-age men in 1999 and by almost 60 percent among men ages 22 to 30. The apparent reduction of black–white wage inequality among young men since the mid-1980s, conventionally attributed to economic gains among blacks, may be entirely due to the removal of young black men with low earnings potential from the labor market through incarceration.

Felix Elwert

See also Prison; Prison, Convict Criminology

Further Readings

Manza, Jeff and Christopher Uggen. 2004. *Locked Out: Felon Disenfranchisement and American Democracy.* New York: Oxford University Press.

Pattillo, Mary, David F. Weiman, and Bruce Western, eds. 2004. *Imprisoning America: The Social Effects of Mass Incarceration.* New York: Russell Sage.

Western, Bruce. 2006. *Punishment and Inequality in America.* New York: Russell Sage.

INCEST

Incest refers to sexual relations between closely related persons. The degrees of kinship defined as incestuous vary, but virtually every known society has prohibited father and daughter, mother and son, or brother and sister from having sexual contact or marrying. Only in recent decades, though, has society recognized incest as a social problem. Earlier, the cultural prohibition, known as the "incest taboo," was of primary interest and a topic of considerable theoretical concern. Many leading social theorists, including Sigmund Freud, Émile Durkheim, and Claude

Lévi-Strauss, considered the incest taboo foundational to human social organization.

Consistent with understandings of the taboo, most people long viewed the incidence of incest as extremely rare, and until the 1980s, no prevalence studies of incest occurred. The closest thing to survey data came from general studies of sexual behavior, such as those by Alfred Kinsey, but these studies did not focus on incest and did not separately define or report it. Although incest was prohibited by law in most jurisdictions, the conviction rate of incest offenders was extremely low. As late as the mid-1960s, for example, the annual conviction rate of offenders did not exceed two cases per million persons in any U.S. state. Social scientists recognized that the actual incidence of incest must far exceed the rate of detection by law enforcement. Yet, the available evidence and the cross-cultural studies suggested that the incest taboo was uniquely powerful. Other forms of sexual offenses and sexual pathologies were of professional and occasionally public concern, but not incest.

A series of developments, beginning in the 1960s, led to a changed awareness of sexual offenses within the nuclear and extended family. The emergence of family therapy as a clinical specialty in the 1960s was important in establishing a concern with the child victim of incest. Family therapists initiated a rejection of key elements of Freudian psychoanalysis, particularly with respect to the role of incest fantasies in mental life, and their work led to the first of many treatment programs in which child victims received counseling. The child protection movement, originally organized to draw attention to the physical abuse of children, and the anti-rape movement of the early 1970s drew public and mass media attention to child sexual abuse as a social problem. They also spurred new legislation, such as the Child Abuse Prevention and Treatment Act of 1974, which made it a criminal offense for professionals working with children and public officials not to report suspected instances of child maltreatment. These movements classified incest within the more general category of sexual abuse—sometimes using terms like *intrafamilial child sexual abuse*—and argued that family members and known others, not strangers, committed most abuse. In the ensuing years, research studies, surveys, and increased reporting have confirmed that incest is far more prevalent than previously assumed.

The extent of incest behavior, however, has eluded careful measurement. Studies of such highly stigmatized behavior are notoriously difficult to conduct, and under-reporting is a serious methodological problem. So too is the lack of consensus among researchers about what behaviors and what degrees of kinship define the experience of incest. Some employ narrow definitions of sexual contact—touching or penetration—whereas others use broad definitions that span a wide range of sexual and sexualized activities from penetration to such non-touch behavior as exhibitionism and sexual propositions. There is also wide latitude in what relatives are included, with some researchers adding "father figures" and other unrelated persons. Discrepancies like these have led to great inconsistency in the estimates of the prevalence of incest.

Further, in large-scale studies of sexual offenses and sexual behavior, incest between adults is not separately reported and incest involving a child is counted as a form of sexual abuse. The latter development is also reflected in some state penal codes, where sexual offenses against children by relatives are prosecuted under sexual abuse laws rather than incest statutes. The most comprehensive sources of information on sexual abuse in the United States, for example, come from the Department of Health and Human Services. Mandated studies, including the annual *Child Maltreatment* reports, based on compilations of data from child protective service agencies in individual states, and the periodic National Incidence Studies of Child Abuse and Neglect, based on large nationally representative samples of community professionals, provide the best estimates available on the incidence of sexual abuse. Although these studies offer some breakdown of victimization incidents by the type of perpetrator (e.g., parents, other family members), they do not discuss incest.

With heightened public and professional concern in recent decades, an immense body of research has emerged on the psychological effects of incest, on the dynamics of families in which incest takes place, and on the psychology of offenders. Studies have found that incest can have a wide variety of negative consequences for the victim, in both the immediate and longer term, depending on the frequency, duration, and type of sexual contact; age of the child; relationship to the offender; and other factors. For children, these consequences can include delinquency, anxiety, poor self-esteem, sexual acting out, and other problems. For adult survivors, issues include depression, self-destructive behaviors, and post-traumatic symptoms. Research on families in which incest occurs has centered on complex interaction dynamics and disturbances—intrapsychic, relational, and circumstantial. Men appear responsible for the majority of incest offenses, and much of the research on offenders focuses on various personality types and their conscious and unconscious motivations.

Public controversy and legal battles have erupted periodically since the 1980s over social problem claims of false reports of incest. Parent groups have organized to defend themselves against alleged false reports with respect to children, especially in divorce-custody cases, and by adult daughters or sons claiming trauma-induced amnesia for incestuous victimization as a child. In the latter case, parents criticize psychotherapists for using hypnosis and other "memory enhancement" techniques to induce a condition they call "false memory syndrome." Psychologists in the trauma field remain divided over these claims.

Joseph E. Davis

See also Abuse, Child Sexual; Rape

Further Readings

Davis, Joseph E. 2005. *Accounts of Innocence: Sexual Abuse, Trauma, and the Self.* Chicago: University of Chicago Press.

U.S. Department of Health and Human Services, Administration on Children, Youth and Families. 2007. "Child Maltreatment 2005." Washington, DC: U.S. Government Printing Office.

INCOME DISPARITY

Income disparity refers to differences in income between two or more individuals or aggregates. Aggregates can be defined by relationship (family, household) or by some other attribute (community, nation, gender, ethnicity, age, class). Income disparities are important for several reasons: (a) Income is the primary source of economic well-being in modern societies, so income disparities indicate differences between individuals and groups in the ability to attain a desired standard of living; (b) income disparities are associated with a variety of social problems, including poverty, crime, and social conflict; and (c) large

income disparities, especially between groups defined by ascribed status (e.g., gender, race), are contrary to norms of equity.

Theories of Income Disparity

Explanations of income disparities derive from more general theories of social organization, typically categorized as consensus and conflict theories. Consensus theories posit that social order arises from shared objectives, values, and the evaluation of individual and group behavior. Conflict theories posit that social order is imposed by the exercise of power. Consensus theories include functionalism in sociology and microeconomic price theory in economics. Conflict theories include Marxist and Weberian theories.

Functionalism asserts that, given a complex division of labor, societies must have some mechanisms to allocate individuals to jobs. Jobs can be ranked according to importance and requisite skills, and individuals can be ranked according to their diligence and ability. Inequality is the social mechanism that allocates the most qualified individuals to the most important jobs. Similarly, microeconomic price theory asserts that, in market societies, the price mechanism assures that markets will "clear"; that is, prices will rise or fall until completion of all desired exchanges of goods and services. At this price, supply equals demand, and the wage rate equals the value produced, thus maximizing the total value of production. Income differences represent productivity differences. Each individual, in maximizing his or her income, will obtain the skills which make the best use of his or her abilities.

Conflict theory asserts that disparities in income or, more generally, in life chances, result from conflict among individuals and groups over the distribution of resources. Marx and his theoretical descendants assert that, in all societies, those who own productive assets (land and other forms of capital) exploit those who do not. Those who do not own productive assets cannot acquire necessities, such as food, clothing, or shelter, unless they can access the assets of others. To do this, they must relinquish a share of what they produce to the asset owner (e.g., as rent). Although not explicit in most Marxist accounts, skill (productivity) differences can be incorporated into the theory as "human capital" assets. From this perspective, income disparities reflect disparities in the ownership of productive assets.

Weber and his theoretical descendants do not disagree that property ownership is important, but they assert additional important aspects of power in society: One's relative position in markets for capital and for labor ("class"), the social regard of others ("status"), and collective organization for the rational pursuit of interests ("party"). Any or all of these aspects of power may be used to deny opportunities to others and monopolize opportunities for oneself and those like oneself. Income disparities therefore reflect disparities in the distribution of economic, social, and political power.

Measurement of Income Disparity

The extent of income disparities is measured in a variety of ways, depending on the motivating interest. If interest is in income differences between two persons or social positions, one could simply subtract, but this has the disadvantage of being affected by the value of money (e.g., inflation). A measure of such disparities not affected by the value of money is the ratio of incomes. If, instead, interest is in the distribution of income across a population, numerous statistical indices are available. Quintile income shares are the percentages of income received by each fifth of the population; the standard deviation of income measures average income differences in a population. The Gini coefficient measures departures from perfect equality, where each cumulative percentage of the population receives that cumulative percentage of income. The Gini coefficient is thus a generalization of quintile shares across the entire income distribution.

Extent of Income Disparities

Current and historical data on income inequality in the United States are available on the U.S. Census Bureau Web page. These data show that in 2006, the bottom quintile of households received 3.5 percent of total household income, the third quintile received 14.5 percent, and the top quintile received 50.5 percent of total household income. In 1990, the corresponding income shares were 3.8 percent for the bottom, 15.9 percent for the third, and 46.6 percent for the top quintile; and in 1980 they were 4.2 percent, 16.8 percent, and 44.1 percent, respectively. Between 1980 and 2006, the income share of the bottom quintile of households declined, as did the income share of the third quintile, whereas income share for the top quintile increased. In relative terms, the poor and the middle lost ground, and the top gained ground. Over this period, the Gini coefficient increased from .403 in 1980 to .428 in 1990 and .470 in 2006. Other inequality indices show the same pattern. Since 1980, income disparities among households in the United States have increased.

Consequences of Income Disparities

Consensus theories of income disparities predict that income disparities will not be a cause of social disorder, even if disparities are extreme and widespread. Shared values will produce acceptance of functionally necessary (thus, equitable) disparities in life chances. Conflict theories, on the other hand, interpret disparate life chances as both the outcome of conflict among individuals and groups and the source of future conflict.

Income disparities are associated with disparities in life chances, including physical and psychological health. This is to be expected in market economies, because the goods and services that contribute to life chances must be purchased. However, the consequences of inequality extend beyond the life chances of individuals to affect entire societies. These societal consequences include poverty, social disorder, and crime. Despite debates regarding the measurement of poverty (whether poverty is relative or absolute and what the poverty threshold should be), it is clear that the presence of income disparities is necessary for the existence of poverty.

Research consistently shows an association of between-group inequality (e.g., race, class) and social disruption (riots, strikes). Examples include the labor movement of the 1930s and the civil rights movement of the 1960s. Research also consistently finds a strong association between income inequality and both property and violent crime rates. These research literatures are thus more supportive of conflict theories. Research on the relationship between income inequality and aggregate rates of economic growth has produced mixed results. One strand of this literature finds that inequality reduces economic growth rates; a more recent strand finds the opposite: that inequality increases rates of economic growth. The first is consistent with conflict theories, the second with consensus theories. These literatures differ in their measures, models, and methods, so it is not yet possible to be confident in the findings of either.

Lawrence E. Raffalovich

See also Class; Gender Gap; Gini Coefficient; Life Chances; Poverty; Relative Deprivation; Stratification, Social

Further Readings

Hurst, Charles E. 2006. *Social Inequality: Forms, Causes, and Consequences.* 6th ed. Boston: Allyn & Bacon.

Lenski, Gerhard. 1984. *Power and Privilege: A Theory of Social Stratification.* Chapel Hill, NC: University of North Carolina Press.

U.S. Census Bureau. "Income Data." Retrieved December 27, 2007 (http://www.census.gov/hhes/www/income/income.html).

Wright, Erik Olin. 1985. *Classes.* London: Verso.

INDEX OF DISSIMILARITY

The term *index of dissimilarity* refers to a standard measure of residential segregation, which gauges the extent to which two groups are evenly spread throughout neighborhoods in a given geographic area, usually a city or metropolitan area. It is interpreted as the percentage of either of the two groups that would have to move in order to achieve an even distribution across neighborhoods within the larger geographic unit of interest. An even distribution indicates that all of the neighborhoods would have the same distribution of the two groups as the larger, geographic unit of interest. Values of the index of dissimilarity range from 0 to 100, with values ranging from 0 to 30 indicating low levels of segregation or high levels of evenness, from 30 to 60 indicating moderate levels of segregation, and 60 or more indicating high levels of segregation or very low levels of evenness.

Results from Census 2000 reveal high levels of segregation for blacks and more moderate levels for Hispanics and Asians and Pacific Islanders, relative to non-Hispanic whites. More specifically, 64 percent of blacks, 51 percent of Hispanics, and 43 percent of Asians and Pacific Islanders would have to move to achieve an even distribution with whites, on average, in the metropolitan United States. Trends over time in index of dissimilarity scores reveal that blacks consistently are the most segregated group. In 1980, the dissimilarity scores for blacks, Hispanics, and Asians and Pacific Islanders were 73 percent, 50 percent, and 41 percent, respectively, relative to non-Hispanic whites. Although scores for blacks have declined over time, the level of segregation still remains within the high range, even nearly 40 years after the passage of the Fair Housing Act. Scores for Hispanics and Asians have remained relatively stable, in large part as a result of the trends in immigration of these groups.

Although the index of dissimilarity is a standard measure used to gauge levels of residential segregation, it is not free of limitations. One major limitation is that it can only examine the residential segregation of two groups at a time. Other measures, such as the multigroup information theory index, can measure the evenness of more than two groups. Another is that it is sensitive to the level of geography used as its building blocks. In general, census tract–level data are used as a proxy for the neighborhoods within which evenness is examined. However, an average census tract contains 4,000 residents. Census block groups are smaller areas of geography that are composed, on average, of 1,500 people. Studies have shown that when smaller areas of geography are used to calculate the index of dissimilarity, levels of segregation are actually higher. Other limitations with the index are that it cannot gauge how concentrated or centralized the populations of interest are. Nevertheless, because of its ease of interpretation and its detection of evenness, the index of dissimilarity remains a core measure used in the residential segregation literature.

Samantha Friedman

See also Segregation, Residential

Further Readings

Iceland, John, Daniel H. Weinberg, and Erika Steinmetz. 2002. *Racial and Ethnic Residential Segregation in the United States: 1980–2000.* U.S. Census Bureau, Census Special Report, CENSR-3. Washington, DC: U.S. Government Printing Office.

Massey, Douglas S. and Nancy A. Denton. 1988. "The Dimensions of Residential Segregation." *Social Forces* 67:281–315.

INEQUALITY

The study of inequality lies at the heart of the sociology of social problems. No matter what the social problem might be, different forms of inequality influence the generation of the problem, the consequences of the problem for diverse groups, the societal reaction to the problem, and the solutions and social policies intended to address the problem. In each of these dimensions, social problems correlate with inequality. Analyzing the relationship between various forms of inequality and social problems is central to sociological theory and empirical research.

Among some of the strongest forms of inequality influencing social problems are social class, race, and gender. And, while these are some of the most significant influences on social problems, they are also problems in and of themselves. No understanding of social problems makes sense without attention to race, class, and gender. But race, class, and gender are not the only correlates of social inequality. Also influencing social problems are social factors such as age, national origin, sexual orientation, ethnicity, and family status, among others. Exactly how these different social factors of inequality relate to social problems and how they interrelate are the basis for much social problems theory and empirical research.

Inequality and the Generation of Social Problems

One way to think about how inequality relates to social problems is to ask how social problems are generated. Social stratification based on race, class, and gender forms the structural context from which social problems are created. Social inequality, structured into society, blocks opportunities for some groups, generating the conditions from which social problems emerge. The sociological literature offers countless examples of the consequences of blocked opportunity.

Research shows, for example, a strong correlation between unemployment and multiple social problems, including crime, violence, divorce, and substance abuse, to name a few. As one example, an extraordinarily large difference exists in the homicide rate of black Americans, Latinos, and whites—explained as the result of social structural conditions of both the class and race status of poor, minority men. Were non-Latino whites subjected to the same social structural conditions of inequality as are racial/ethnic minorities, white homicide rates would likely be equal to those of racial/ethnic minorities. Various measures of risk, including death by homicide, firearms, and automobile accidents, are also strongly influenced by gender. This is the result, most argue, of greater

risk-taking behavior among men. The interactive mix of gender, race, and class can be a lethal combination.

Race, gender, and class also affect the likelihood of experiencing social problems other than crime and violence. For example, low-income and minority communities will more likely be sites for hazardous waste facilities and toxic dumping, not only degrading the neighborhood environment but also placing residents at greater risk for poor health. Although many such communities have organized an environmental justice movement to protest dumping in their neighborhoods, the relative lack of political power in low-income and minority communities makes environmental racism a persistent social problem.

Social problems stemming from structural inequality are also prevalent in education and work. Rates of educational attainment are higher among white Americans than among either African Americans or Latinos/as. School dropout rates, too, significantly relate to both race and income status. Hispanic students have, by far, the highest dropout rate, followed by African American students, but income matters too: Students from low-income families have twice the dropout rate of those from middle-income families and four times the dropout rate of those from high-income families. Family disadvantage also strongly relates to racial variations in math and reading comprehension for schoolchildren, and the higher the family income is, the higher are student test scores and rates of educational attainment.

At the root of educational attainment problems lie inequalities among schools themselves. Inner-city schools with large concentrations of minority and poor students suffer from inadequate facilities, poor funding, and understaffing. Furthering the problem of inequality in schooling is the resegregation of schools that is currently under way. Since 1980, segregation in U.S. schools has dramatically increased, resulting in increasing educational isolation of black and Latino/a students. School segregation partially follows from residential segregation but also results from the diminution of state-sponsored plans to challenge racial segregation in education.

Segregation is not just a matter of race, however. As inequality grows in the United States, schools are also becoming more stratified by social class. Residential and school segregation separate people not only by race but also by class. This creates disparities in school quality *across* neighborhoods and *within* schools. From ability groupings within schools to across-school differences in curricular offerings and facilities, social class, along with race, produces inequality across *and* within schools. Added to this is the gender inequality that continues to characterize education. Although much progress has been made in reducing educational disparities between girls and boys, a gender gap persists in what students learn and the work girls and boys are prepared to do.

Structured inequality is also present in the social problems associated with work. Where, how, and whether people work is fundamentally a matter of race, class, and gender. Much research shows that gender and race are good predictors of earning differentials; they also strongly influence occupational distribution. Indeed, the greater the concentration of women and minorities in an occupation, the more degraded is the pay. Gender and race affect not only the economic status of women and people of color but also the social and psychological consequences of persistent race and gender discrimination in the workplace.

In sum, extensive evidence shows the influence of social inequality on the generation of social problems, but are there actually more social problems among disadvantaged groups? This is the subject of debate. One answer is that social inequality produces an underclass of people who turn to crime for lack of other options. Blocked opportunity, in this argument, produces social problems—more likely among the poor and minority groups. Another answer is that, because social problems occur within disadvantaged strata of society, they are more subject to surveillance and, thus, more visible than are social problems that occur within the middle and upper classes. This area of research points to the hidden nature of social problems within more privileged communities, as well as to the increased rates of policing and other forms of surveillance, such as via social service agencies, that make social problems more likely to be detected among the poor and disadvantaged. Recognizing that identifying is part of how they are generated underscores the importance of understanding not just where problems occur but also how they are created through perceptions and judgments made in society.

Inequality and Societal Reactions

Inequality also strongly influences societal responses to social problems. Research consistently shows that victims of social problems are treated differently within various social institutions. This is especially apparent in studies of the criminal justice system, although this is not the only institutional site for seeing the influence of inequality on social problems. Yet, a multitude of studies show that the race of the accused produces differential rates of arrest, prosecution, and sentencing. Studies of rape, for example, show that not only are black perpetrators more likely to be arrested, prosecuted, and sentenced, but the rape itself is more likely to be reported when the perpetrator in black, regardless of the victim's race. There is also an interactive effect between the race of the victim and the race of the alleged perpetrator in how justice—or perhaps better stated, injustice—is administered. Studies of the death penalty, as just one example, find strong evidence of racial discrimination in death penalty verdicts. And race of the victim, as well as race of the defendant, is an influence, with the death penalty more likely to result when the victim is a white woman. Throughout the criminal justice system, racial minorities experience disproportionate punitive treatment. They are more likely than whites to be arrested and convicted, and they are given longer sentences than whites, even when the crime is the same.

Empirical evidence of societal reactions to social problems is also evident in the influence of social class. Corporate crime, for example, if measured in terms of dollar value, is far more severe than street crime, but corporate criminals are not punished as harshly as street criminals. Furthermore, corporate crime is also less likely to be detected, and when corporate criminals are punished, they receive more lenient punishments. Gender matters, too: Together with race, gender is predictive of whether a defendant secures pretrial release.

The societal response to social problems can also be seen in the context of how clients are treated in other social institutions. The simple fact is that authorities, generally speaking, tend to treat people differently, depending on factors like class, race, and gender. Social stereotypes, even when unintentionally expressed, guide people's judgments about one another in various realms of life. Thus, employers tend to typify black women as single mothers—regardless of the employees' actual parental or marital status; drug offenders who most closely resemble stereotypes of dangerous drug users receive substantially more punitive sentences than those who do not conform to the stereotype; teachers' perceptions of students' race and ethnic status influence their judgments about the students' likely academic success; and racial prejudice underlies public attitudes about punishment for crime with those likely to support the most punitive policies holding the racial prejudice. In each case, social judgments not only influence how people are perceived but also produce consequences for how people are treated.

This is the essential insight of labeling theory, especially when considered in the context of structural inequality. Labeling theory is the idea that, once given a "marker" (or "label"), the so-labeled identity tends to stick and others perceive that person accordingly, regardless of the person's actual social behavior. The person so labeled may even adopt the so-designated identity, thus becoming what others perceive him or her to be. Labeling theory has been extensively applied in the study of deviant behavior, explaining how, once people are labeled as deviant, whether or not they engage in deviant behavior, they are treated as such.

Although used primarily in studies of social deviance and crime, labeling theory is also useful in thinking about other social problems. In schools, for example, who is perceived as "at risk," and what are the consequences of this perception? Race, gender, and class strongly influence such judgments, with young black men especially vulnerable to such attributions.

Where do these social judgments originate? Although surely the mass media are not the only source of such learned assumptions, clearly media depictions of various groups and various social problems strongly influence social stereotypes. How the news portrays social problems, for example, can influence public understanding of social problems. On the one hand, the media, for example, tend to depict violence as if it were random, with anyone having an equal chance of being victimized—an assumption that directly contradicts sociological evidence of the patterned character of violence. At the same time, however, the media also portray social problems via strong class, race, and gender stereotypes. News reports on the state of the economy disproportionately discuss economic events as they affect economic elites and investors, much less often reporting on problems that affect the general workforce. The media's depiction of welfare also shows an increased tendency to identify African American women with images of dependency. And, although media depictions of women have improved in some regard in recent years, women are still highly sexualized and degraded in popular culture. Exposure to sexualized imagery of women has an effect on men's and women's sexual relationships, making relationships more adversarial and making young people more accepting of interpersonal violence.

In summary, although inequality has a strong influence on the generation of the likelihood of social problems, social problems may be more evenly distributed across the population than is commonly perceived, but societal judgments influence the perception and detection of social problems. Because disadvantaged groups are more likely to be overseen by official agencies and are more likely stereotyped in the dominant culture, the appearance is created that they are more prone to social problems.

Inequality and Its Consequences

Another way to think about the influence of inequality on social problems is to examine the consequences of social problems for different groups. This can be seen at different levels—for individuals, for families and communities, and for society as a whole.

At the individual level, experiencing one social problem can lead to others. For example, studies find that having contact with the criminal justice system has a significant effect on one's lifetime earnings, thus exacerbating the initial effect of the problem of criminal labeling. Likewise, experiencing mental illness can decrease an individual's annual income by several thousand dollars. Sexual abuse not only is a problem in and of itself but is also a factor in high rates of school dropout, substance abuse, later sexual violence, prostitution, and even violent offending. However, the consequences of social problems are not always so devastating; social networks can facilitate coping with social problems. At the same time, disruption of one's support networks—influenced in turn by the strength of the network—can lead to further social and psychological distress.

The ripple effect of social problems occurs not just among individuals but also in families and communities. Among college students, for example, studies find that African American students from racially segregated neighborhoods experience higher levels of family stress than do other students—largely because of the social problems found in their home communities.

Finally, social problems have consequences for society as a whole, as is illustrated by considering the costs of maintaining people in prison versus the cost of investing in education. The government, including federal, state, and local direct costs, is currently spending over $185 billion per year on correctional facilities—a 423 percent increase since 1982. This amounts to $209 per person per year in the United States. And, while educational funding in total is still higher than spending levels for correctional facilities, many argue that the increase in incarceration witnessed in recent years comes at the expense of support for education, especially at the state level. Every social problem a society faces has costly consequences—measured in both economic and social terms. The total cost of teen pregnancy to society is estimated at $9.6 billion per year, measured by summing the costs of public assistance, child health and welfare, incarceration, and lost tax revenues.

There are costs other than economic ones that cannot be measured in quantitative terms. Rising rates of fear in society, high rates of imprisonment, more gated communities (prisons for the lower class, gated housing for elites), and, potentially, greater violence all amount to societal level consequences. Furthermore, economic inequality threatens the very stability of societies and leads to more coercive social control. Cross-national research findings, for instance, show a tendency for expansion of state-based social control when there is internal economic inequality in a given society.

Inequality and Solutions

The strong correlation between inequality and social problems begs the question of what needs to be done to solve some of the nation's most difficult problems. Many analysts are now documenting the increasing inequality characterizing the nation in the early 21st century. Should inequality grow, it is predictable that social problems will increase.

Some policies for change may only exacerbate the problems of social inequality. In education, for example, new programs, such as vouchers, charter schools, and school choice, that are intended to improve educational quality, may only increase racial and class segregation in schooling. Welfare reform, legislated to encourage work and reduce the alleged dependency of women on welfare, has unintended consequences that reproduce inequality. Welfare rolls have been reduced, but poverty has increased; more women formerly on welfare have become employed but in low-wage jobs that have not improved their economic status. And without state support, many have also lost the related benefits—such as subsidized housing, food stamps, child care, and health care—that would otherwise serve them. Thus, while welfare "dependency" may be perceived as less of a problem, homelessness and the impoverishment of women and their children may be worse than ever.

Social changes addressing social problems can come from the "bottom up" through community organizing and grassroots mobilization. Change can also come from the "top down," through state-based action, legal and policy reform, or the application of social services. Either way, thinking about the impact of change on different social groups is a fundamental part of addressing social problem reform. Comprehensive social change engages fundamental questions of national values and the collective commitment to serving all of a nation's people. Where is the balance between values of individual freedom and collective social justice? How can a nation maintain individual freedom to pursue economic success while also supporting a social contract to support the nation's citizenry? Although such value-laden questions are not typically those asked by sociologists researching social problems, they are nonetheless an important component of thinking about the connection between social problems and inequality. It is unlikely that this connection will be severed, but reducing its impact can become more of a national priority.

Margaret L. Andersen

See also Culture of Poverty; Educational Equity; Environmental Racism; Equal Protection; Health Care, Access; Hypersegregation; Income Disparity; Justice; Poverty; Racism; Relative Deprivation; School Segregation; Segregation, Residential; Sentencing Disparities; Sexism; Stratification, Age; Stratification, Gender; Stratification, Race; Stratification, Social; Underclass Debate; Welfare

Further Readings

Andersen, Margaret L. 2008. *Thinking about Women: Sociological Perspectives on Sex and Gender.* 8th ed. Boston: Allyn & Bacon.

Ferguson, Ann Arnett. 2001. *Bad Boys: Public Schools and the Making of Black Masculinity.* Ann Arbor, MI: University of Michigan Press.

Fleury-Steiner, Benjamin Doy. 2004. *Jurors' Stories of Death: How America's Death Penalty Invests in Inequality.* Ann Arbor, MI: University of Michigan Press.

Hays, Sharon. 2004. *Flat Broke with Children: Women in the Age of Welfare Reform.* Berkeley, CA: University of California Press.

Kennelly, Ivy. 1999. "'That Single-Mother Element': How White Employers Typify Black Women." *Gender & Society* 13(April):168–92.

Kozol, Jonathan. 1992. *Savage Inequalities: Children in America's Schools.* New York: Harper.

———. 2006. *The Shame of the Nation: The Restoration of Apartheid Schooling in America.* New York: Three Rivers.

Lewis, Amanda. 2003. *Race in the Schoolyard: Negotiating the Color Line in Classrooms and Communities.* New Brunswick, NJ: Rutgers University Press.

Pellow, David. 2002. *Garbage Wars: The Struggle for Environmental Justice in Chicago.* Cambridge, MA: MIT Press.

Reiman, Jeffrey. 2006. *The Rich Get Richer and the Poor Get Prison.* 8th ed. Boston: Allyn & Bacon.

INFANT MORTALITY

Infant mortality is the death of an infant less than 1 year old. It is commonly described by the infant mortality rate (IMR), which is calculated by dividing the number of newborns dying at under a year of age by the number of live births during the year within a population. Analysts can use such data to compare the health and well-being of people across and within countries. The health status of infants in a society is a gauge of the overall health of the population and is an important predictor of the next generation's health. The significance of infant mortality to public health and epidemiology is that the rate can determine how successful a population is in preventive health measures for pregnant women, the access to and quality of prenatal care, and rate of immunization in a community.

Historically, infant mortality was responsible for the deaths of a significant percentage of children born around the world, and the death of an infant before his or her first birthday was a common occurrence. However, since the 20th century, improvements in basic health care, sanitation, and living conditions have led to a significant decline of IMRs in the West.

Infant Mortality in the United States

Major causes of U.S. infant mortality include congenital abnormalities, preterm/low birth weight, pregnancy-related problems, respiratory distress syndrome, and sudden infant death syndrome (SIDS). The dramatic decrease in the U.S. IMR during the 20th century primarily reflected fewer babies dying from pneumonia and influenza, prematurity, and low birth weight as a result of better, more available technology and medicine. However, among developed countries, the United States has the second worst newborn mortality rate. The poor IMR in the United States is due to substantial disparities in race/ethnicity, education, income, and health within the population. Overall, not all U.S. racial and ethnic groups have benefited equally from the long-term downward trend in infant mortality.

In the United States, prematurity/low birth weight (less than 5.5 pounds at birth) is one of the major determinants of infant mortality and has been the leading cause of death for black infants for more than a decade. In New York City, for example, infants born to black non-Hispanic mothers have an IMR more than twice the rate of those born to white non-Hispanic mothers. This difference is especially stark in communities with a high percentage of black residents. The factors that contribute to these disparities are difficult to isolate as they interact with each other, but some areas studied include the overall health of the mother, socioeconomic status, and social stressors. The stress of marginalization associated with racism has been investigated as a cause of poorer health among minorities. It is probable that these stressors can have an effect on women before conception as well as during pregnancy, which may contribute to poor birth outcomes. There are also disparities between whites and other ethnic groups. For example, compared with non-Hispanic whites, SIDS deaths among American Indian and Alaska Natives are 2.3 times greater. U.S. efforts to decrease infant mortality across ethnic groups focus not only on the individual behaviors of women but also on the communities in which they live, their economic standing, and their social status, since many factors can affect pregnant women and the health of their babies.

Infant Mortality in Developing Countries

Each year about 2 million babies worldwide die within their first 24 hours, and over 7 million babies born in sub-Saharan Africa, Asia, Latin America, and the Middle East do not live to their first birthday. Their deaths most commonly result from pneumonia and dehydration caused by diarrhea. In developing nations, IMRs correlate inversely with a nation's per capita income, and in countries where people make less money the IMR is significantly higher. The relationship between poverty and infant mortality is closely related because the structural conditions of poverty such as poor sanitation, lack of primary health care, malnutrition, and lack of access to clean water can be detrimental to newborns, particularly vulnerable ones.

Social factors within developing countries also have an effect on infant mortality and the ability of newborns to survive their first year. The age at which women have children can affect birth outcomes, with adolescents and women over 40 years old more at risk for giving birth to low birth weight babies. The spacing between births is another factor that can affect birth outcomes. Babies born less than 2 years apart are at greater risk of being born with a vulnerable condition, particularly when they are born to mothers who are malnourished or in a weakened physical state. Influencing interval length between births is access to, and use of, modern contraception methods to control the timing between pregnancies. High IMRs also correlate with high fertility rates, as many families attempt to balance infant deaths by having more babies to ensure the survival of some children to eventually help support the family. Unfortunately, poor parents are often unable to devote enough resources, for such things as education, to each child within a large family, making it difficult to rise out of poverty. Both reducing the IMR within developing countries through improved health conditions and shifting social norms regarding women and childbirth can have a dramatic effect on improving the quality of life of the society.

Martine Hackett

See also Birth Rate; Contraception; Fertility; Health Care, Access; Life Expectancy; Mortality Rate; Poverty; Total Fertility Rate

Further Readings

Mullings, Leith and Alaka Wali. 2001. *Stress and Resilience: The Social Context of Reproduction in Central Harlem.* New York: Kluwer Academic/Plenum.
Save the Children. 2006. "State of the World's Mothers 2006: Saving the Lives of Mothers and Newborns." Westport, CT: Save the Children. Retrieved December 27, 2007 (http://www.savethechildren.org/publications/SOWM_2006_final.pdf?stationpub=ggstc&ArticleID=&NewsID).
Singh, G. K. and S. M. Yu. 1995. "Infant Mortality in the United States: Trends, Differentials, and Projections, 1950 through 2010." *American Journal of Public Health* 85:957–64.

INFLATION

Simply defined, inflation is a persistent increase in the average price level of goods, commodities, and services. Typically measured as an annual percentage rate of change on an index number, in the United States, the inflation rate finds common expression using the consumer price index (CPI), a time-series measure of a weighted average of prices of a specified set of goods and services. Other key indices track producer prices, wholesale prices, and commodity prices. Currently, the base period for the CPI is the average prices in the 1982–84 period. Since 1950, the average annual inflation rate in the United States, as measured by the CPI, has typically fluctuated between 1 percent and 4 percent. However, the country experienced a much higher average annual inflation rate of 7.09 percent for the 1970–79 period, with a peak in 1974 of 11.1 percent, as a result of the Vietnam War and the price increases caused by the 1973 oil embargo by members of the Organization of Petroleum Exporting Countries (OPEC).

While it is generally acknowledged that economies are likely to function more efficiently if the rate of inflation is low, little consensus exists about the causes of inflation. The two basic categories of inflation in the economic literature are demand-pull inflation and cost-push inflation. Demand-pull inflation comes from increases in aggregate demand, whereas cost-push inflation results from decreases in aggregate supply. In modern economies, however, inflation is not a simple phenomenon of rising prices but is greatly affected by the supply of money. With the advent of fiat money, governments can have a significant impact on the rate of inflation through the manipulation of the money supply and the subsequent impact on the value of money.

An inevitable by-product of inflation is income redistribution, as the burden of increasing prices is not shared equally across all socioeconomic classes. In general, inflation tends to have a regressive impact due to the disproportionate loss of purchasing power, particularly among lower income groups and those on fixed incomes. Another aspect of income redistribution involves the "inflation tax," caused by the government financing current expenditures through the printing of money. The resulting increase in the money supply has the effect of causing a decrease in the value of cash-based assets.

The sociological literature on inflation is relatively sparse, although there have been a handful of prominent contributions. For instance, an early contribution adopted a social conflict perspective in arguing that the inflationary period of the 1970s was largely a result of an intensification of distributional conflicts between labor and employers. In contrast, a more recent contribution emphasized the growth of the use of monetary policies by governments as a way of understanding the dynamics of inflation. The recent resurgence in economic sociology holds promise for future sociological analyses of inflation and its effects.

Jonathon Mote

See also Budget Deficits, U.S.; Mixed Economy

Further Readings

Aldous, Joan, Rodney Ganey, Scott Trees, and Lawrence C. Marsh. 1991. "Families and Inflation: Who Was Hurt in the Last High-Inflation Period?" *Journal of Marriage and the Family* 55:123–34.

Goldthorpe, John H. 1978. "The Current Inflation: Towards a Sociological Account." In *The Political Economy of Inflation,* edited by F. Hirsch and J. H. Goldthorpe. Cambridge, MA: Harvard University Press.

Smith, Michael R. 1992. *Power, Norms and Inflation: A Skeptical Treatment.* New York: Aldine de Gruyter.

INNER CITY

Social problems related to industrialization, immigration, criminality, and poverty were initially perceived as problems of the city in its entirety and were later associated more with the inner city. With the rapid post–World War II expansion of a distinctive suburban realm, the concept of "inner city" achieved wide currency. The identification of the inner city with social problems is a primarily North American phenomenon, even if exported to other settings such as Great Britain. The inner city was perceived as the converse of the suburbs. Thus suburbs were clean, safe, modern, and mainstream middle class, but the inner city supposedly was dirty, dangerous, outdated, poor, and inhabited by minorities. Indeed, the inner city most often served as a backdrop for film noir.

Clearly, depicting the inner city as a homogeneous entity overtaken by social problems was a gross oversimplification. In most metropolitan regions, the inner city was a complex entity, containing both poor areas and elite enclaves. Still, on the whole, the 1950s, 1960s, and 1970s were not kind to the inner city. As suburban growth proceeded apace, many inner-city districts lost their middle-class populations and thus underwent a steep filtering-down process. Accelerating socioeconomic decline was a reduction in employment as manufacturing relocated to the suburbs, thus severing the symbiotic relationship previously existing between working-class neighborhoods and close-by sources of employment.

As the condition of their housing deteriorated and perception increased about their poor adaptability to a modern, car-oriented lifestyle, many inner-city neighborhoods became a refuge for residents denied access to other parts of the metropolitan region because of low income and racial segregation. This is when the inner city became synonymous in the media and popular imagination with social pathology. Not without justification, the inner city was portrayed as overridden with poverty, crime, addiction, school abandonment, and teenage pregnancies. As social status declined, so did the housing stock, sometimes to the ultimate abandonment stage. In some cases, as in Detroit and Newark, the inner city still bears the scars of the 1960s riots. Analysts associate inner-city living conditions with the transgenerational reproduction of an "underclass."

Inner-city problems became a target for public policy, such as the urban renewal program, first launched by the 1949 Housing Act, whose purpose was to replace "slums" with public housing and commercial development. But relocation problems and difficult living conditions in public housing projects prompted a revision of policies. The Model Cities program of the 1960s attempted to correct some of the problems of urban renewal by making more room for public participation. Also victimizing the inner city was its location between downtown and the suburbs, which caused it to be sliced by expressways. Whereas land uses in the suburbs adapted to the presence of expressways, in the inner city these highways generally involved a destruction of the built environment and attendant displacement of residents.

Two books contributed to reversed thinking about the inner city. The Herbert Gans 1962 study of Boston's West End revealed the existence of rich social networks in a neighborhood awaiting renewal. Most influential perhaps was Jane Jacobs, who in 1961 wrote a strong defense of the traditional inner city against the then rising popularity of urban renewal. In *The Death and Life of Great American Cities,* she celebrated the role that the original inner-city landscape, particularly the commercial street, played in fostering intense social interaction. She contrasted the high level of activity she observed along her Greenwich Village street with the desolation and high criminality experienced in areas changed by urban renewal. The message of these two works was clear: The social environment of traditional inner-city neighborhoods was generally superior to that provided by urban renewal projects.

In subsequent decades, favorable views on the inner city spread to well-educated young professionals preferring a central area to suburban living. Fueling the resulting gentrification phenomenon was the appeal of historical architecture, the diversity and street life of core area neighborhoods, and proximity to work for dual-income families. Successions of ever richer and risk-aversive households drove gentrification: first bohemians and struggling artists, then young, upwardly mobile professionals ("yuppies"), and, last, wealthy lawyers, doctors, and executives.

Although a clear cause of homelessness (e.g., the conversion of a rooming house containing 20 low-income tenants into an impeccably restored home for a single wealthy couple), the view that gentrification itself is responsible for the replacement of the working class by richer professionals is an oversimplification. First, such a transition stems in part from the shrinkage of the traditional middle class accompanied by the rise of professional and managerial categories. Second, many well-educated newcomers to core area neighborhoods were in fact marginal gentrifiers, sharing the values, tastes, education, and some professional attributes of mainstream gentrifiers, but without a stable financial and professional situation.

Gentrification typically affected former working-class neighborhoods with the most distinctive architecture and best accessibility to amenities and employment, bypassing the ones severely deteriorated

and crime-ridden. In large prosperous metropolitan regions, however, the entire inner city is now subject to gentrification or condominium redevelopment, another source of social change.

The inner city evolved into a place of extremes, a mirror of the economic polarization of recent decades. It is not unusual to find expensive condos juxtaposed with parks harboring large homeless populations. Conflicts flare easily in such environments, for example, when marginal residents are displaced to prevent their interference with economic development strategies targeted at the middle class and tourists.

From an urban planning perspective, interest in the inner city has recently been stimulated by the smart growth movement, which relies in part on core area revitalization and intensification to counter sprawl and growing automobile dependence.

Pierre Filion

See also Gentrification; Social Change; Urban Decline; Urban Renewal; Urban Underclass; White Flight

Further Readings

Anderson, Martin. 1964. *The Federal Bulldozer: A Critical Analysis of Urban Renewal, 1949–1962.* Cambridge, MA: MIT Press.

Gans, Herbert. 1962. *The Urban Villagers.* New York: Free Press.

Husock, Howard. 2003. *America's Trillion-Dollar Mistake: The Failure of American Housing Policy.* Chicago: Ivan R. Dee.

Jacobs, Jane. 1961. *The Death and Life of Great American Cities.* New York: Random House.

Ley, David. 1996. *The New Middle Class and the Remaking of the Central City.* Oxford, England: Oxford University Press.

Rose, Damaris. 1984. "Rethinking Gentrification: Beyond the Uneven Development of Marxist Urban Theory." *Environment and Planning D: Society and Space* 2(1):47–74.

Wilson, William J. 1987. *The Truly Disadvantaged: The Inner City, the Underclass, and Public Policy.* Chicago: University of Chicago Press.

INNER-RING SUBURB

Inner-ring suburbs, or what some call "first" suburbs, are communities that developed just outside of central cities during the period following World War II. Initially these suburbs were bedroom communities for mostly affluent, white residents who commuted back and forth, often by streetcar, from work in the urban core to their home life in a safe, low-density neighborhood. Levittowns are examples of such communities.

Studying the characteristics of inner-ring suburbs is not a straightforward process. U.S. Census Bureau data are limited in the definition of suburbs as the residual portion of metropolitan areas that lies outside of central cities. Given this amorphous category, it is hard to distinguish between inner- and outer-ring suburbs. Case studies of specific metropolitan areas, particularly those that are more historical in nature, more clearly distinguish between inner- and outer-ring suburbs.

However, until recently, few studies identified differences among suburbs on a national level. The best strategy, established by researchers at the Brookings Institution, goes back to the 1950 decennial census and identifies counties that were part of the metropolitan United States at that time, which were adjacent to, or included, the top 100 cities. The county or the portion of the county that did not contain the central city was designated as an inner-ring, or first, suburb. In total, 64 counties were identified using this technique, including Nassau, New York; Arlington, Virginia; and Middlesex, Massachusetts.

Using this methodology, researchers have learned much about the character of inner-ring suburbs, relative to newer, or outer-ring, suburbs and central cities. One of the most striking features of inner-ring suburbs is that they housed nearly one fifth of the U.S. population in 2000, while central cities and newer suburbs housed 12.9 and 14.3 percent of the U.S. population, respectively. Equally important is the fact that the nature of the population in inner-ring suburbs is racially and ethnically diverse. In 2000, one third of the population in these areas comprised racial/ethnic minorities, surpassing the proportional representation at the national level (30 percent). Moreover, 29 percent of the U.S. foreign-born population lived in inner-ring suburbs, compared with 28 percent living in central cities. Finally, inner-ring suburbs have maintained a higher socioeconomic status. For example, in 2000, 31 percent of the adult population in these areas had a college education, compared with 26 percent and 28 percent in central cities and outer-ring suburbs, respectively. Likewise, average housing values in 2000 were the highest in inner-ring suburbs.

Whether the future of inner-ring suburbs is as bright as their past, however, remains to be seen. Poverty rates have been growing in these areas, particularly during the 1990s. More alarming is the fact that their poor neighborhoods have grown in recent decades, while there has been a general reduction of such neighborhoods in central cities. With trends in urban sprawl continuing, the future for inner-ring suburbs appears to be a challenging one.

Samantha Friedman

See also Urbanization; Urban Sprawl

Further Readings

Puentes, Robert and David Warren. 2006. *One-Fifth of America: A Comprehensive Guide to America's First Suburbs.* Washington, DC: Brookings Institution Press.

INNOCENCE PROJECT

The Innocence Project is a nonprofit legal clinic that originally focused only on cases where postconviction DNA testing of evidence could demonstrate an individual's innocence. The Innocence Project was started by Barry Scheck and Peter Neufeld in 1992 at the Benjamin N. Cardozo School of Law, where students worked (and still do) on cases involving a defendant's innocence under supervision of a team of attorneys and clinic staff. Focusing invariably on indigent defendants, the Innocence Project typically enters into a case as a last resort, after an individual has exhausted all other legal avenues for relief.

As DNA technology became more accessible, other innocence projects began in law schools across the United States. By the end of 2006, innocence projects were operating at 40 law schools in every region of the United States. Increasingly, such projects broadened the scope of their investigation from only cases involving DNA testing to a wide array of cases involving other important indicators of a defendant's innocence, including faulty eyewitness testimony and police or prosecutorial misconduct. The projects have been remarkably successful in proving innocence. Indeed, by August 2006, at least 183 people had been exonerated by postconviction DNA testing, and literally hundreds more had been exonerated based on other types of evidence.

Although the empirical literature on wrongful convictions has grown exponentially in the wake of the innocence project movement of the past 15 years, social scientists began investigating the issue as early as 1932. Edwin Borchard's classic, *Convicting the Innocent: Sixty-Five Errors of Criminal Justice,* provides fascinating documentation of wrongful convictions stemming from prosecutorial and police misconduct, ineffective counsel, racial discrimination, mistaken identification in eyewitness testimony, and perjury of witnesses. Throughout the 1950s and 1960s, other studies of wrongful convictions, such as E. S. Gardner's *The Court of Last Resort* of 1952, Frank and Frank's *Not Guilty* of 1957, and Edward D. Radin's classic *The Innocents* of 1964 documented similar findings.

The high-profile exonerations of 13 death row prisoners in Illinois in 2000 led to the creation of more innocence projects and more available funding for empirical analysis of wrongful convictions. Recent research on wrongful convictions provided new and important insight into this phenomenon. Sophisticated quantitative analyses of wrongful convictions discovered that the quality of appellate defense was an important and statistically significant predictor of whether or not a defendant was wrongfully convicted of a capital crime.

In the policy arena, innocence projects have recently made a significant impact on the development of national legislation—most notably the passage of the Innocence Protection Act of 2004 (IPA). Relying chiefly on the testimony of Barry Scheck and other leaders in the innocence project movement, the IPA provides rules and procedures for federal inmates applying for DNA testing. Specifically, IPA creates a Post-Conviction DNA Testing Grant Program, authorizes grants to states for improving their capital prosecution and capital defender programs, and provides funding to assist families of murder victims.

Benjamin Fleury-Steiner

See also Capital Punishment; Prison

Further Readings

Harmon, Talia. 2001. "Predictors of Miscarriages of Justice in Capital Cases." *Justice Quarterly* 18:949–68.

The Innocence Project. (http://www.innocenceproject.org/).

Institutional Ethnography

Institutional ethnography is an alternative sociology that examines social relations and social institutions from the standpoint of the experiences of particular, active subjects. It is distinct from other sociological modes of investigation in that it is not under the direction or conceptual control of any sociological theory; rather, inquiry begins in and remains in the social world in which we live.

The aims of institutional ethnography investigations are twofold. The first is to discover how it is that day in and day out we put together our social world, including how our local everyday activities are linked to and coordinated by social relations that are not entirely visible from any one location. Thus, institutional ethnography research expands people's knowledge of their everyday worlds beyond that which they develop through their routine participation. The second aim is to build knowledge of institutional processes in general and to develop new ways of discovering ruling relations. This work involves an examination of studies done in varied institutional settings and drawing out those relations and social processes commonly found across institutions. Throughout institutional ethnography investigations, however, the focus is on the material world: what people are doing, with whom they are doing it, and the conditions under which their activities are carried out.

Canadian sociologist and founder of institutional ethnography Dorothy E. Smith described institutional ethnography in the 1970s as an articulation of the women's movement in North America. She identified two different modes of consciousness active in her life of running a household and being a mother and her life as a scholar in the university. The life in the home was one of particularities and real people, whereas the life of the university was abstract and the social relations were extra-local. Yet, through her involvement in the women's movement, Smith learned to take her own experience as a woman as the basis for how she could know the world. She also realized, as did many others involved in the women's movement, that the academic disciplines were written almost exclusively by men and from their viewpoint. Furthermore, the disciplines—sociology in Smith's case—claimed objectivity while excluding women, their knowledge, and their concerns from the scholarly discourse. Smith concluded that it was necessary to remake sociology from the ground up. This alternative sociology would be a "sociology *for* women," one which would discover the social relations which shaped women's everyday experiences.

In 1986, the term *institutional ethnography* first appeared in print in Smith's article "Resources for Feminist Research." Indeed, the conceptual design of institutional ethnography was to aid women in understanding the social organization of their lives. Yet, it soon became evident that the social relations shaping the experiences of women shaped those of men as well, and in the 1990s institutional ethnography evolved as a "sociology for people." A network of institutional ethnographers (many of whom were students of Smith at the Ontario Institute for Studies in Education) formed, and they initiated research from the standpoint of people with AIDS, teachers, social workers, nurses, nursing home residents, and others.

The topics of institutional ethnography research are generally some issues or problems that people experience in their everyday lives, but the starting point (or point of departure) for the investigation is people's actual experiences. This research is a two-step process. In the first step research begins with one's own experience or with that of another actor, but in either case special attention focuses on what people actually do and on what they say about their activities. That is, the researchers attend to "work" and work "knowledges." In institutional ethnography the term *work* expands beyond the sphere of paid labor to include any intended activity taking time and effort. "Work knowledges" refers to what people know of their work and how this work is coordinated with the work of others. Through the exploration of work and work knowledges, researchers learn of the local social organization and of the actors' knowledge of this organization. Furthermore, people's work and talk of work provide clues to the investigators regarding how local organization connects to the coordinating work of others. In the second step the researchers take up the clues, as evidence of local participation in the institutional practices, and trace this evidence—found in the form of discourse, spoken and textual—to the extra-local social relations.

Institutional ethnography research commonly examines texts, especially those replicable and standardized, since they coordinate people's activities in local settings. They mediate social relations, coordinating the doings of people translocally. Texts, as taken up in local settings, enter actions and organize actions at multiple sites. While one party in the text is fixed, the reader is not. While attending to a text, the reader is active in interpreting and acting upon the text; that is, a text–reader conversation forms. In the text–reader conversation, the reader "activates" the text by taking it up and incorporating it into the local setting, thus hooking the local into the institutional. By activating the text,

the reader becomes an agent of the text. This is not to imply that the text completely controls the reader. The reader may resist or disagree with the textual discourse, but through its activation, the text becomes unavoidable. Furthermore, in many work processes, one textual step follows another textual step, each dependent upon the prior step and the anticipated next step, and so on. Thus, filled-out forms and generated reports transform particular events into generalized forms that are critical in coordinating the work of others. Such regulation through texts is widespread in modern, literate societies, and it is a foundational consideration in institutional ethnographic investigations.

Institutional Ethnography of "Social Problems"

In sociology, "social problems" emerge as social objects through the ongoing research and theoretical activity of sociologists, and their existence then becomes taken for granted within the discipline. However, as both the discipline and the historical contexts evolve, a reconstruction of these social problems often follows. Smith, however, noted a difficulty with this objectification of social problems and suggested that social problems be viewed as a form of social organization operating within public text-mediated discourse, a complex of social relations within relations of ruling. As this social organization enters the local and particular actualities, experiences connect with, and translate into, standardized and generalized forms. This is a political process by which a particular experience becomes known as a social problem and other troubles align with it as cases of the social problem. Thus, "social problems" serve as a mechanism by which particular interests acquire objective status. The discourse of social problems provides a statement of general interest which may be contradicted if investigations of so-called social problems begin with experience in the local setting, rather than with interpretations provided by sociological discourse. For example, what appears as a problem of "illiteracy" or of "single-parent families" in the discourse may be found to be a shortcoming of capitalist practices in the local setting.

Paul C. Luken

See also Ethnomethodology; Feminism; Feminist Theory; Social Constructionist Theory; Standpoint Theory

Further Readings

Campbell, Marie. 2004. *Mapping Social Relations: A Primer in Doing Institutional Ethnography.* Lanham, MD: AltaMira.

Smith, Dorothy E. 1989. *The Everyday World as Problematic: A Feminist Sociology.* Boston: Northeastern University Press.

———. 1993. "'Literacy' and Business: 'Social Problems' as Social Organization." Pp. 327–46 in *Reconsidering Social Constructionism: Debates in Social Problems Theory,* edited by J. A. Holstein and G. Miller. New York: Aldine de Gruyter.

———. 1993. *Text, Facts, and Femininity: Exploring the Relations of Ruling.* New York: Routledge.

———. 1999. *Writing the Social: Critique, Theory, and Investigations.* Toronto, ON: University of Toronto Press.

———. 2005. *Institutional Ethnography: A Sociology for People.* New York: AltaMira.

———, ed. 2006. *Institutional Ethnography as Practice.* Lanham, MD: Rowman & Littlefield.

INTERGENERATIONAL MOBILITY

Intergenerational mobility refers to the movement of individuals and groups away from the station of their parents or other forebears. Intergenerational movements across socioeconomic class boundaries are the hallmark of open societies and a central concern among social scientists.

Open societies, sometimes referred to as class societies, are those in which intergenerational mobility is possible. In such circumstances it is common to find adult children fairing better than their parents—upward mobility—on an assortment of socioeconomic indicators. Conversely, we can reasonably expect to find some adult children fairing worse than their parents—downward mobility—though this has less often been the case in more developed and developing societies. Closed societies, often referred to as caste societies, are those in which the socioeconomic statuses of parents are entirely predictive of those of their adult children, with little possibility for any social mobility. The prevalence and character of intergenerational mobility may gauge the extent of meritocratic or democratic practice in a given society, but measuring intergenerational mobility is not straightforward.

Children may outperform or underperform their parents on several different dimensions. Some of the most widely recognized studies of intergenerational mobility compare occupational statuses of adults with those of their parents. Because occupational status changes relatively infrequently, it may be appropriate to compare parents and children at a single point in time. However, because income and wealth tend to increase as individuals advance toward retirement age, there is a crucial temporal dimension that must be considered in any attempt to assess intergenerational mobility.

The most accurate assessments of intergenerational mobility examine the achievements of two or more generations viewed at the same or a similar place in the life course. For example, it may be misleading to compare 50-year-old parents with their 25-year-old children since the former group is, on average, well established whereas their adult children are "just getting started" and may be in transient class locations. Using such a comparison, we might conclude that children are fairing worse than their parents and thus must have experienced downward mobility. A comparison of the same group of adult children with their parents 25 years earlier, when the parents themselves were 25 years old, would likely lead to different, more accurate, conclusions regarding the extent and character of intergenerational mobility.

However it is measured, upward intergenerational mobility was a pronounced feature of the 20th-century American experience. Immigration, urbanization, industrialization, and education are a few of the factors that facilitated this trend by introducing children of relatively humble origins—children of immigrants, children of farmers, lower- and working-class children, and racial minority children—into an opportunity structure that, while not free of discrimination, was more open than at any time in the past. In the early years of the 21st century, declining educational funding and quality, export of entry-level jobs, declining influence of labor unions, a minimum wage not keeping up with inflation, and regressive taxation have made significant (upward) intergenerational mobility more difficult. This is particularly true for lower- and working-class parents and children who are disproportionately racial and ethnic minorities.

Amon Emeka

See also Social Mobility; Stratification, Social

Further Readings

Hout, Michael. 2004. "Social Mobility and Inequality: A Review and an Agenda." Ch. 26 in *Social Consequences of Growing Inequality,* edited by K. Neckerman. New York: Russell Sage.

INTERLOCKING DIRECTORATES

Applied to a pair or small group of organizations, *interlocking directorates* are instances of persons serving on the board of directors of multiple organizations, constituting an overlap in membership among the boards of those organizations. Applied to a population of organizations, the term *interlocking directorates* refers to a condition in which there are sufficient board member overlaps among the organizations that a path can be traced between any two organizations in the set, either directly or via a series of board overlaps between intermediary organizations. This condition typifies many interorganizational environments. Often the organizations of interest are large corporations, in which instances of interlocking directorates are also known as *corporate interlocks.*

Organizational theories suggest interlocking directorates may serve organizations in a variety of ways. They provide a channel of communication between organizations, which can then facilitate interorganizational coordination, be a vector for the diffusion of innovations, and enable values and practices to become normative across organizations. Director interlocks may also provide a competitive advantage in surviving in an uncertain environment, by providing information about that environment and acting as agents of the organization. Resource dependence theory specifically sees interlocking directorates as a device for gaining access to needed resources, expertise, price advantages, or lower transaction costs, a view supported by the tendency of firms to have representatives of suppliers, large customers, and experts in law and finance on their boards.

Critics of capitalism see interlocking directorates variously as means by which individual capitalists centralize power and exercise control of corporations in which they have an ownership stake, as a device for capitalist class cohesion and collective control over organizational resources and thus the economy and politics, or as a mechanism of bank control whereby commercial lending institutions ensure the safety of and return on their capital loans to industry while exercising control over the economy.

Interlocking directorates have been viewed as a social problem since the anti-trust movement, circa 1900, because their existence calls into question the independence of corporate governance, they aid in suppressing competition, and they contribute to monopoly or oligopoly control of sectors of the economy, thus upsetting market pricing and possibly retarding product development. As a means by which a power elite may have control of economic and political resources, interlocking directorates are also relevant to the study of social inequalities, the distribution of resources in society, and the understanding of the impact of formal organizations on a variety of social problems.

Conversely, interlocking directorates can aid in addressing social problems by providing channels of resource mobilization, as shown by the tendency of philanthropic donations to follow interlocks between corporate and charity organizations, or providing a mechanism for coordinating service organizations. Interlocking directorates as a strategy for negotiating a competitive and uncertain environment and coordinating with other organizations could also be viewed as a solution to social problems from the perspective of an organization.

As a type of social network, interlocking directorates are often studied using the methodological tools of social network analysis.

Blyden Potts

See also Class; Inequality; Monopolies; Oligopoly; Power Elite; Resource Mobilization

Further Readings

Mizruchi, Mark S. 1996. "What Do Interlocks Do? An Analysis, Critique, and Assessment of Research on Interlocking Directorates." *Annual Review of Sociology* 22:271–98.

INTERMARRIAGE

Intermarriage is the marriage between spouses of different races or different ethnicities and is therefore either inter-racial or interethnic. Marriage between a white and a black is an inter-racial marriage, while a marriage between a Japanese and a Chinese is an interethnic marriage. The difference between race and ethnicity, however, is not always clear. Interethnic marriages have a much longer history than do inter-racial marriages in the United States. Even in early colonial times, European immigrants of different nationalities and religions intermarried. Inter-racial marriages, on the other hand, have faced higher social stigma and legal restrictions that did not end until after the mid-20th century.

In scholarly writings, intermarriage can also refer to a union between spouses of different social characteristics. For example, a marriage between an educated person and an uneducated person might be called an educational intermarriage, regardless of the couple's race or ethnicity. References to such intermarriages, however, are rather limited.

Similar to intramarriages, intermarriages occur for reasons such as romantic attractions and status matching between partners, but intermarriages are associated with higher probabilities of divorce than intramarriages, due to the greater social barriers the intermarried couples often have to face. Studies of marital happiness also yielded evidence that intermarried couples tend to report lower levels of marital satisfaction.

U.S. intermarriages have steadily increased in the past few decades, growing from 0.7 percent of all marriages in 1970 to 5.4 percent in 2000, while the actual number of such marriages rose by tenfold in the same period. The Census Bureau reports that the most common type of intermarriage occurs between whites and Asians.

Why do people marry out of their racial or ethnic groups? Sociological theories on intermarriage basically fall into two categories: availability and choice. Availability of potential marriage partners speaks to the structural constraints that either promote or limit intermarriages. The most important structural constraints are the number of racial or ethnic groups in the marriage market and the relative sizes and internal sex ratios of these groups. More groups potentially lead to more intermarriages, whereas group sizes inversely affect intermarriage rates. Because intermarriage involves spouses from two groups, the same number of such marriages dictates different rates between large groups and small groups, with the latter inevitably carrying higher rates. Imbalanced sex ratios of the marriageable population within a group, on the other hand, will "force" the extra men or women to outmarry. Many immigrant groups in the United States initially experienced severe sex ratio imbalances as a result of gender-specific immigration. For these groups, intermarriage rates often differed by gender.

The second category of theories that explain intermarriage focuses on choices for mates, mostly status exchange between couples. The increased intermarriages in the United States in recent decades coincided with higher educational achievements of many minorities and their participation in the labor force with whites of comparable socioeconomic status. Both the educational institutions and the workplace provide opportunities for inter-racial and interethnic interactions between people of similar statuses, thus promoting intermarriages. Rising intermarriages, in turn, reduce stigma against intergroup relations and make intermarriages a more accepted choice. Besides similar socioeconomic status, cultural preference is another consideration of mate selection, with people choosing mates with similar traditions, religions, and other cultural practices. This tendency explains selective intermarriage within large ethnic circles, such as pan-Asian, pan-Hispanic, and pan–Pacific Islanders. For example, Asians of different nationalities tend to intermarry more often than they marry non-Asians.

Choice is, of course, not independent of availability, and the two interact to affect a racial group's inter-racial or interethnic marriage rates. High concentration of a minority group may provide higher availability of within-group mates, in addition to promoting close-knit cultural settings that strengthen ingroup solidarity that might work against intergroup relations. Asian Americans, for example, are highly concentrated on the West Coast, especially in California, where Asian intermarriage rates are lower than in other states, after controlling for social status.

Choice by gender and race also seems to occur in the inter-racial marriage market. White–black intermarriages are more likely between white women and black men, while white–Asian intermarriages tend to be between white men and Asian women, although the reverse patterns have slowly increased in recent decades.

Intermarriage serves as an indicator of a minority group, especially an immigrant group, integrating or assimilating into the mainstream society, especially through intermarriage with whites. Outmarriage rates by themselves, however, may not indicate how likely a group will be to outmarry, because group size affects these rates. Through the use of complicated statistical models, sociologists can measure tendencies of endogamy (ingroup marriage) and exogamy (out-group marriage) by controlling for group size and other factors. Such studies often find that whites are less endogamous than most minorities. That is, minorities actually have a stronger tendency to keep their members in within-group marriages.

Xuanning Fu

See also Assimilation; Cultural Capital; Cultural Values; Race; Segmented Assimilation

Further Readings

Heaton, Tim B. and Stan T. Albrecht. 1996. "The Changing Pattern of Interracial Marriage." *Social Biology* 43:203–17.

Kalmijn, Matthijs. 1998. "Intermarriage and Homogamy: Causes, Patterns, and Trends." *Annual Review of Sociology* 24:395–421.

Lee, Sharon M. and Barry Edmonston. 2005. "New Marriages, New Families: U.S. Racial and Hispanic Intermarriage." *Population Bulletin* 60:2.

Qian, Zhenchao and Daniel T. Lichter. 2001. "Measuring Marital Assimilation: Intermarriage among Natives and Immigrants." *Social Science Research* 30(June):289–312.

INTERNAL COLONIALISM

The concepts of "internal colonies" and "internal colonization" embrace expansive interdisciplinary efforts to explain economic, class, cultural, and racial domination and subordination of groups and geographies within the boundaries of a single society. *Internal colonies* refer to geographic sites that are often spatially controlled, dominated, and destabilized cultural lifeworlds and to underdeveloped and exploited regions, communities, and groups. Internal colonies exist even when dominant and subordinated groups intermingle and geographies are blurred. *Internal colonization* refers to the historical and contemporary processes of maintaining domination and subordination. These explorations examine the incorporation and cross-fertilization of class, racial, and sexual domination in a country's internal colonies; the role of the state, market, and dominant civic organizations in disciplining the colonial order; the presence of political subjugation; the function of legal and extra-legal forms of domination and violence; and the significance of ideology and culture.

Studies of internal colonies and internal colonization overlay a broad swath of groups and countries from blacks and Chicanos/as in the United States to Northern Ireland as an underdeveloped English internal colony. Studies utilize the concepts to investigate realities as disparate as the underdevelopment of poor children in public schools to environmental racism.

The concepts have a contentious history. Lenin, Marx, and Gramsci referred to internal colonies in their characterizations of peripheral underdeveloped areas in European countries. W. E. B. Du Bois, Robert Blauner, and other U.S. scholars employed a similar framework in looking at the underdevelopment of blacks.

Despite the promise of the initial conceptual developments, antipathy to Marxist analyses, particularly in the United States, limited the full integration of the concepts of internal colonies into the social sciences, public administration, and development studies. Even though some U.S. analysts at the turn of the 20th century encouraged the study of American colonization and empire, official exhortations and academic texts minimized the country's colonizing history of Native Americans, Mexicans, blacks, Puerto Ricans, and Filipinos/as under the rubric of "American exceptionalism." Furthermore, the cold war erected a particularly inhibiting barrier to the integration of the concepts. The United States promoted capitalist modernization as an alternative to socialism, promising newly independent countries that lessons learned from the history of Western industrialization translated into concrete, positive prescriptions for modern industrial development. Few American analysts, notably those shaping and writing the dominant theories and texts on race relations, attempted to show that the underdeveloped "ghettos"—Appalachia and similar peripheral areas in the United States—were not modernized by industrialization. U.S. diplomats also squashed efforts by blacks to present their case of internal underdevelopment to the United Nations.

The concepts reemerged in the 1960s and the 1970s, influenced by a confluence of events and studies, including the global anti-colonial struggles and the civil rights movement, especially the Black Power movement; new theories of colonial hegemony; renewed global interpretations of the core, periphery, and semiperiphery represented by dependency theories; world-systems theory and labor market segmentation; new historical interpretations of colonialism and imperialism; and the emergence of postcolonial studies.

Walter Stafford

See also Black Power Movement; Chicano Movement; Conflict Perspective; Hegemony; Inner City; World-Systems Analysis

Further Readings

Hechter, Michael. 1999. *Internal Colonialism: The Celtic Fringe in British National Development.* New Brunswick, NJ: Transaction.

INVASION-SUCCESSION

Ernest W. Burgess and other Chicago School sociologists developed the concept of "invasion-succession" in the 1920s to describe land use in the expanding U.S. industrial cities. Borrowing ecological concepts from natural science, Burgess saw the city's land use as a mosaic resulting from market forces plus the cultural preferences of distinct groups of residents. Enlarged by migration, cities expanded outward from the central intersection of their rail, water, and trolley routes. Profitable enterprises—banks, law firms, department stores—and individuals with an interest in a central location were able to command commercial space in the business district or housing in adjacent "gold coast" apartments. Factories relying on ports and railroads dominated nearby areas. Their need for workers attracted migrants from the rural South as well as displaced farmers and laborers from overseas. Forced by poverty to take the cheapest housing, newcomers congregated in densely packed tenements in and near the factory zones. Speculators facilitated this clustering by building insubstantial rental flats and subdividing older housing that was abandoned as the wealthy moved on. Residents able to pool family wages were sometimes able to purchase buildings in these areas, creating temporary stability and facilitating ethnic homogeneity.

In-migrants, often lacking English, created ethnic enclaves in these zones of first settlement to reproduce familiar cultures. They supported churches and synagogues, religious schools, ethnic shops and restaurants, athletic teams, newspapers, and night life. The congruence between enclaves and political wards allowed residents to elect officials who delivered jobs, contracts, and services. The concentration of enclave populations supported an ethnic small business class and preserved familiar ways of life in otherwise alien cities.

These neighborhoods, however, also experienced disequilibrium. Where central business districts expanded into these zones, office buildings replaced tenements. When residents adjusted to urban life and took advantage of expanding economies, they increased their incomes and sought better housing elsewhere. Many in the native-born generation sought greater independence from ethnic oversight by moving to less-homogeneous areas of second settlement. At the same time, a succession of new groups arrived. Initially, Irish wards became dominated by Jews or Italians. Some of these, in turn, became African American neighborhoods. The transition could be peaceful or conflictive, depending on its speed and the state of competition for the cheapest housing. The fact that the wider society invidiously sorted groups by race and ethnicity at the border, at work, and in politics heightened ethnic tensions while the need to share political and religious institutions promoted accommodating shifts in resources.

In the 1960s, manufacturing began a sharp decline in U.S. cities. Using the power of eminent domain and federal subsidies for "slum clearance," cities sought renewal by demolishing the many ethnic neighborhoods remaining on the edge of their central business districts. Often office towers and convention centers took their place as economies shifted to a service base. While luxury apartment towers lured many white-collar professionals from the suburbs to the urban core, others sought out and renovated what remained of older substantial housing and converted obsolete industrial lofts into spacious living quarters. Artists replaced garment workers and were themselves replaced by attorneys; tenements that continued to house the oldest and least mobile Italians or Ukrainians were converted to upscale housing by speculators and expanding universities. This gentrification, initiated by professionals who saw themselves as "pioneers in the urban wilderness," was quickly seized upon by city governments. They delineated historical districts, zoned streets for pedestrian use, moved cultural facilities downtown, and encouraged developers to create "festival marketplaces" for well-off residents and tourists. In many cases, a restaurant veneer of an ethnic enclave was all that remained. Government worked hand in hand with the postindustrial economy in this invasion-succession dynamic, enhancing the overall economy of cities but at the price of reducing the stock of affordable housing and ignoring manufacturing employment.

Charles R. Simpson

See also Urban Decline; Urban Infrastructure; Urbanization; Urban Renewal; Urban Sprawl

Further Readings

Burgess, Ernest W. 1925. "The Growth of the City: An Introduction to a Research Project." Pp. 47–62 in *The City,* edited by R. E. Park and E. W. Burgess. Chicago: University of Chicago Press.

Gans, Herbert J. [1962] 1982. *The Urban Villagers: Group and Class in the Life of Italian Americans.* New York: Free Press.

Smith, Neil. 1996. *The New Urban Frontier: Gentrification and the Revanchist City.* London: Routledge.

IQ TESTING

Intelligence quotient (IQ) testing is scientifically controversial and has a varied history. Most IQ tests consist of verbal and performance test items that result in a score with a mean of 100 and standard deviation of 15. As such, the majority of the population (84 percent) lies in a range of 85 to 115 on most IQ tests. Of the numerous discussions of the 20th-century development of intelligence measures, most conclude with one or more of the following precepts:

1. Current cognitive ability measures, traditionally called "IQ tests," now use broader definitions of intelligence factors and less age/development focus, so instead of the descriptor "IQ," "cognitive" or "ability" or "intelligence" or "intellectual aptitude" is more commonly used.

2. Although part of cognitive ability is inherited, debate continues as to the exact proportion and influence of genetics versus environment.

3. IQ or cognitive ability tests are strong predictors of academic achievement and social success within groups, but score variability due to education and opportunity makes individual predictions possible but not definitive.

4. IQ tests effectively screen for cognitive strengths and weaknesses deserving special education opportunities, including programs for the retarded or gifted. Discrepancies between IQ scores and specific areas of achievement are often used to diagnosis learning disabilities.

Despite demonstrated uses of cognitive ability measures (IQ tests) in schools and employment, a number of scholarly works debate social consequences, ethnic discrimination, and biological determinism. Certainly scholars differ on the use or potential misuse of IQ tests; some even hold that intelligence is social in origin.

Recent research examines recognized phenomena not yet completely explained. These include the notion of multiple intelligences, the longitudinal increase in IQ over the past century, and emotional intelligence as a corollary of cognitive intelligence. All of these lines of scholarship start with traditional IQ testing as a historical or psychometric basis for a springboard to new theories and measures.

Regardless, the widespread use of IQ tests continues and will likely be a topic of research and discussions for the foreseeable future. Started in 1946, an international organization (MENSA) open only to the top 2 percent of IQ-tested people now has more than 100,000 members, suggesting that IQ testing has a popularly desirable outcome for high scorers. No doubt the theories and measures of factors underlying the popular notion of intelligence will continue to foster research and debate.

William S. Lang

See also Basic Skills Testing; Minimum Competency Test

Further Readings

Chabris, Christopher F. et al. 1998. "Does IQ Matter?" *Commentary* 106(5):13–23. Retrieved December 27, 2007 (http://www.wjh.harvard.edu/~cfc/Chabris1998b.html).

Neisser, Ulric et al. 1995. *Intelligence: Knowns and Unknowns.* Report of a Task Force Established by the Board of Scientific Affairs of the American Psychological Association. Washington, DC: Science Directorate. Retrieved December 27, 2007 (http://www.michna.com/intelligence.htm).

Islam and Modernity

The evolution of religion and its relationship to the rest of society was a major topic of early sociological theory. One of its earliest and most persistent propositions—reaffirmed by many contemporary theorists of the sociology of religion—is that religion, like any other institution, is a dynamic entity and that its functional differentiation is a fundamental part of social processes. In this theoretical framework, religious institutional arrangements are thought to be evolving according to the perceived needs of the sociohistorical time period. As religion impacts the larger society, it too is impacted by the dominant patterns of society. Moreover, the various institutional arrangements either support or are in competition with one another. However, the topic of Islam and modernity, as it has evolved in the modern era, is a complex one largely due to shifting and multidimensional interpretations of both Islam and the concept of modernity.

The word *Islam,* which means "surrender," is related to the Arabic word *salaam,* or "peace." Islam as a religion means "submission to the will of God." It stands in a long line of Abrahimic religious traditions that share an uncompromising monotheism. The foundation of Islamic values and practices is the Koran and Hadith, which are composed of the teachings and the deeds of the Prophet Muhammad. For Muslims, the Koran is the Book of God (Allah) revealed to Muhammad by means of the angel Gabriel. In a very deep sense, Islam is the Koran and the Koran is Islam. Today Islam is the religion of one fifth of the world's population (1.2 billion), and, as the second largest religion, it exists not only in the Middle East but also in Africa, South Asia, East Asia, Europe, and the United States.

Modernity is a term used to describe the condition of being "modern." Since the term *modern* is used to describe a wide range of periods, modernity must be taken in context. In the field of sociology, many of the defining characteristics of modernity—such as specialization, rationalization, secularization, and universalism—stem from the relatively small communities to the more large-scale societies. In this context, social changes which are common to many different levels of social integration are not limited to the Western European societies. In other words, modernization is a general, abstract process, also found in non-Western societies, including Islamic society.

The Evolution of Islam

For more than 1,400 years, Islam has been in a constant state of evolution, going through many phases in its development, including the formation of nation-states in the Muslim world. However, Islam has not yet evolved to a point where there is a separation of religion and state, as found in the history of Western civilization. Historically, Islam developed both as a faith and as a political order. While Islam provided the basic framework of meaning and direction for political, social, and cultural life, it has continually adapted to the cultural, political, and social realities of various regions.

Thus, throughout history, Islam manifested itself in different cultures and societies, creating in each case a unique expression of Islamic culture. This evolutionary process gave rise to an Islamic civilization that is multiracial and multicultural.

Islam also inspired a rich civilization in which Muslim scholars made important advances in sciences such as mathematics, algebra (itself an Arabic word), astronomy, and medicine. Muslim scholars have long been recognized for their contributions to the preservation of classical learning during the Dark Ages. It was through Muslim thinkers' translations of the Greek works of Plato, Aristotle, and other classical thinkers that these works reached Europe and contributed to the first flowerings of the Renaissance. Most Islamic thinkers maintain that the initial encounter between Islam and the West during Islam's early years of expansion represented a dynamic and fruitful interaction. According to many historians, this was because Islam possessed ample power to absorb and assimilate intercultural elements. Some historians even maintain that despite the fact that the history of Christianity and Islam has been marked by mutual hostility and confrontation, medieval Islam was a religion of remarkable tolerance for its time, allowing Jews and Christians the right to practice their religions. Thus, in its prime time, during the period that Islam was a dominant and expanding civilization, it exhibited a great amount of tolerance.

However, the "Golden Age" of Islam was short-lived and lasted only a few centuries. By the 12th century, a decline in the political and intellectual development of the Islamic world had set in. Most Islamic thinkers agree that the impediment to change was not Islam itself as a religion but rather the emergence of religiopolitical structure in the Islamic world. Other historians believe that this decline was due to the reinterpretation of Islam by powerful conservative religious leaders.

Islam in Modern Times

The history of Islam in modern times is essentially the history of the Western impact on Muslim societies. The modern era in Islam's history can be said to begin around 1800 CE, which marks the time when Napoleon Bonaparte and his forces were in Egypt. Following that, the European powers colonized one Islamic country after another. Thus, the rise of modern Europe coincided with European colonial rule, a humiliating experience for Muslims conscious of their proud past. After World War I, the European invasion of the Islamic world intensified as a result of more political and economic dominance.

Cultural and political confrontations with Europe caused Muslims to become defensive and more hostile toward Western political and cultural influences. In the shadow of European colonialism, Muslim thinkers and intellectuals developed conflicting strategies to reconcile traditional Islamic values with modernity. Their responses to modernity provoked a great deal of controversy, particularly among Muslim thinkers and *Ulema* (religious leaders). Secularists, while overemphasizing external factors such as colonialism and imperialism as the cause of the rapid decline of the Islamic world, advocated the restriction of religion to private affairs and its exclusion from public life. Meanwhile, the conservative sectors led by religious leaders conceived of Islam not only as a religion that allowed for no change but also as a total way of life. These religious leaders also became increasingly suspicious of independent reasoning or personal reinterpretation (*Ijtihad*). Ijtihad is an inherent tradition in Islam and serves as a juristic tool that allows for independent reasoning to articulate Islamic law on the issues where textual sources are silent. The conservatives did not favor "opening the door of Ijtihad," whereas the Islamic reformists argued that Ijtihad equipped Muslims to meet the challenge of social change by the reinterpretation of Islam. In other words, to the reformists, Ijtihad was a tool to reconcile Islamic values with modernity.

Like most religious traditions, Islam has had, and continues to have, multiple interpretations and applications throughout its history and even more so today. As a result, there are a variety of Islamic movements, which display the many faces and forms of Islam. However, the phenomenon of interpretation and reinterpretation in Islam is complicated by the fact that no organized hierarchy or centralized religious authority exists in Islam. Religious authority in Islam is distributed among numerous Ulema and jurists whose authority stems from the willingness of the faithful to accept their decrees (*fatva*).

The concept of Islam and modernity as presently conceived can be best explained by focusing on the developments that have occurred in the past 4 decades in the Muslim world. Since the late 1960s, Islamic revivalism has increasingly come to dominate religious and political discourse in much of the Muslim world. Muslim thinkers and political activists in Iran and other Islamic societies have responded to Western-style modernity in a variety of ways. However, since the Iranian Revolution of 1979, there has been a sharpened distinction between two general approaches or orientations toward modernization: the traditionalists and the reformists. The key difference between traditionalists and reformists is their understanding and interpretations of the Koran, Islamic history, and prophet traditions. (It must be noted that this categorization is somewhat arbitrary and that individuals and groups may overlap from one orientation to another.)

Traditionalists define Islam in a narrow and restrictive sense. They maintain that Islamic traditions are fixed and fully articulated in the past. Therefore, any change is regarded as a departure from what they call the "straight path" of Islam. The traditionalists emphasize the total self-sufficiency and comprehensiveness of Islam, and when they speak of Islamization, they mean a reinstituting of the *Shariah,* or traditional Islamic law. The traditionalists reject modernity, which they perceive to mean Western secularism and popular sovereignty. They believe Islam is the very antithesis of secular Western democracy. However, whereas modernity as a general process is rejected, selective modernization in the areas of science and technology is not. The basic tenet of traditionalists is a demand for a return to "pure" Islam, if not the "original" Islam. This orientation has its roots in the fiercely independent traditionalist interpretation of Islam by the Wahhabists in modern Saudi Arabia.

The reformists' view is in sharp contrast to views held by the traditionalists, particularly the conservative Ulema, who have historically preoccupied themselves with the literal interpretation of the Koran. The reformists believe that Islamic principles and values can be applied to meet modernity. Whatever the differences in orientation and agenda, reformists believe that Islam is compatible with the core values of modernity, such as individual freedom and democratic values. Leading reformists have argued that there is no inherent contradiction between Islam and democracy. They view the traditionalists' view on Islam and politics as too rigid and not workable for the realities of modern life. Moreover, the reformists maintain that Islam itself is evolving as a religion and that the will and beliefs of the majority must shape the Islamic state. However, the reformists do not think of modernity in terms of a total break from the past or historical Islamic culture. To reformists, modernity implies not only new and better technologies and improved standards of living but also a political culture in which Islamic values are cherished and individual rights are protected.

Today, a combination of mass education, mass communication, and political awareness is dramatically transforming the Muslim-majority world. While the conflict between the traditionalists and reformists persists, the reformists have expanded the ongoing debate of modernity and Islam to include democratic issues such as pluralism, women's rights, and human rights. However, the central proposal of the reformists continues to be a demand for the reopening of the door of Ijtihad (modern Islamic interpretation), to allow for the adaptation of Islamic laws to the realities of modern life.

Despite setbacks in recent years, particularly the politicization of Islam by extremist groups (radical Islamists), there is compelling evidence that the reformist movement is growing. Recent developments in Iran, Turkey, Malaysia, Indonesia, and Egypt offer an even more striking indication of Muslim interest in modernity, democracy, and civic pluralism. The quest for modernity and democracy among Muslims today is one of the most prominent and transformative issues of our time. Today, an increasing number of Muslim thinkers in these countries have concluded that no contradiction between Islam and modernity exists if conceived as the emergence of new kinds of public space and a greater sense of autonomy for both men and women. However, the political realities of most Islamic societies cannot be overlooked, as most Islamic countries still remain largely nondemocratic and authoritarian. At the present time, we are still watching a process of experimentation and changes unfold.

Maboud Ansari

See also Religion and Conflict; Religion and Politics; Religious Extremism; Religious Prejudice

Further Readings

Armstrong, Karen. 2002. *Islam: A Short History.* New York: Modern Library.

Esposito, John L. 2004. *Islam: The Straight Path.* 3rd ed. New York: Oxford University Press.

Glasse, Cyril. 2003. *The New Encyclopedia of Islam.* Lanham, MD: AltaMira.

Murata, Sachiko and William Chittick. 1994. *The Vision of Islam.* New York: Cragon.

Rahman, Fazlur. 2002. *Islam.* Chicago: University of Chicago Press.

Index